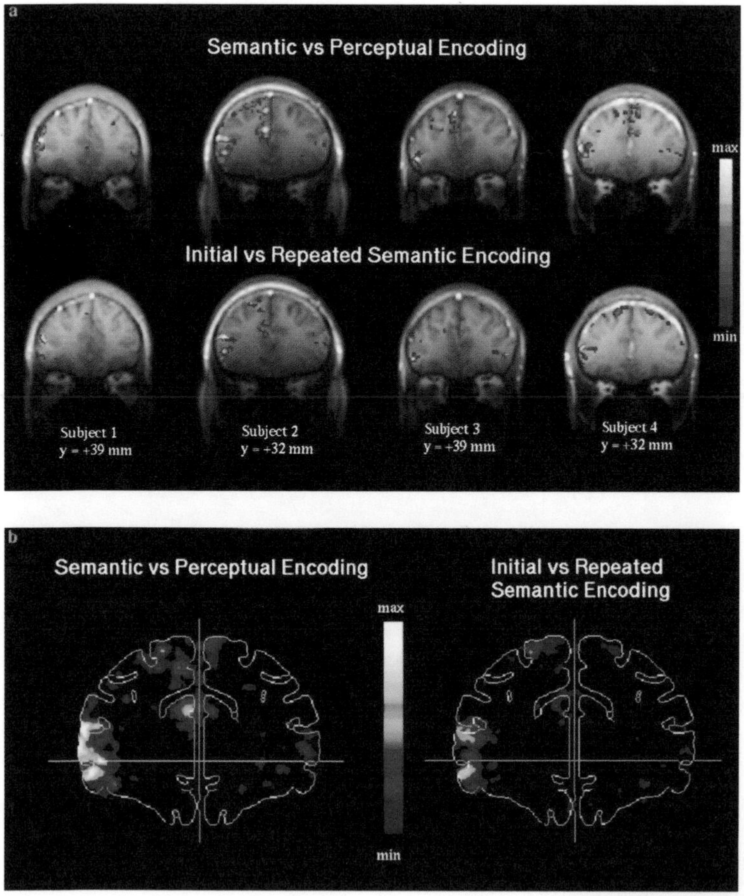

Functional activation maps. The left side of each image corresponds to the left side of the brain. In (a), greater activation is observed during semantic versus perceptual encoding (upper row) and during initial versus repeated semantic encoding (lower row). From "Functional Magnetic Resonance Imaging of Semantic Memory" by J.D.E. Gabrieli, et al, in *Psychological Science*, 7, 278–283, (1996).

In (b), the left image shows increased activation during semantic versus perceptual encoding in the left inferior prefrontal cortex and left cingulate cortex; the right image shows higher activation for initial versus repeated semantic encoding in the left inferior prefrontal cortex. From "Functional Magnetic Resonance Imaging of Semantic Memory" by J.D.E. Gabrieli, et al, in *Psychological Science*, 7, 278–283, (1996).

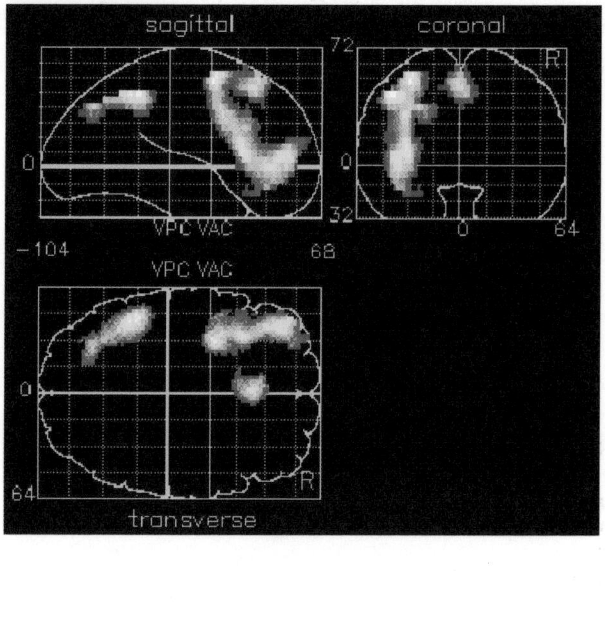

Brain regions activated in the analogy-literal comparison (white, higher activation; yellow, intermediate activation; red, lower activation). From "Toward Neuroanatomical Models of Analogy: A Positron Emission Tomography Study of Analogical Mapping" by Charles M. Wharton, et al, in *Cognitive Psychology*, 40, 173–197, (2000).

Why Do You Need this New Edition?

If you're wondering why you should buy this new edition of *Cognition*, here are 9 really good reasons!

1. Themes of **embodied cognition** and **emotion** woven throughout the text. This will provide you with a better handle on how these issues relate to your everyday experience, as well as to other psychology courses you may be taking.
2. Many new **Prove It!** sections—a very popular feature in this book—that allow you to put what you've been learning to the test. These are ideal if you are currently in, or will be taking, a class on experimental design and methodology, as these sections will provide you with ideas to get some studies going.
3. New and expanded coverage of issues relating to the **neuroscience** of memory and cognition. This will be particularly helpful for those students anticipating careers in health care as well as those developing their understanding of psychology.
4. Brand new sections on **trans-saccadic memory** and **Gestalt grouping principles** (Chapter 3). Both concepts expand ideas about how we build up a coherent and complete mental picture of the world from the fragmentary and jumbled pieces we are given.
5. New and expanded sections on the role of **inhibition** in attention (Chapter 4), as well as improved coverage on how the way you **automatically** do things by force of habit may lead you astray from your intentions.
6. Expanded sections on different types of **working memory** and **visual spatial cognition** (Chapter 5). This text includes a new section discussing how having a better memory may not always work to your advantage. Sometimes we outthink ourselves.
7. Entirely new sections on different types of **categorization** (Chapter 7). These will help you understand how people deconstruct and understand the world that they live in.
8. New and expanded sections on language understanding and conversation (Chapter 10). These place psycholinguistic studies more into your everyday world.
9. Expanded chapters on reasoning and problem solving (Chapters 11 & 12). These chapters discuss everyday rules of thumb and the analogies people use to deal with problems that the world presents.

Fifth Edition

COGNITION

Mark H. Ashcraft

University of Nevada, Las Vegas

Gabriel A. Radvansky

University of Notre Dame

Prentice Hall

Boston Columbus Indianapolis New York San Francisco Upper Saddle River
Amsterdam Cape Town Dubai London Madrid Milan Munich Paris Montreal Toronto
Delhi Mexico City Sao Paulo Sydney Hong Kong Seoul Singapore Taipei Tokyo

Editorial Director: Leah Jewell
Editor in Chief: Susan Hartman
Executive Editor: Jeff Marshall
Editorial Project Manager: LeeAnn Doherty
Editorial Assistant: Amy Trudell
Director of Marketing: Brandy Dawson
Marketing Manager: Nicole Kunzmann
Production Editor: Pat Torelli
Manufacturing Manager: JoAnne Sweeney
Cover Designer: Kristina Mose-Libon
Manager, Cover Visual Research & Permissions: Karen Sanatar
Cover Art: *www.shutterstock.com*
Full-Service Project Management: Preparé, Inc.
Composition: Preparé, Inc.
Printer/Binder: Edwards Brothers, Inc.
Cover Printer/ Printed Endpapers: Edwards Brothers, Inc.
Text Font: 10/12 Minion

Credits and acknowledgments borrowed from other sources and reproduced, with permission, in this textbook appear beginning on page 561.

Library of Congress Cataloging-in-Publication Data

Ashcraft, Mark H.
Cognition / Mark H. Ashcraft, Gabriel A. Radvansky.—5th ed.
p. cm.
Rev. ed. of: Human memory and cognition. c2006.
Includes bibliographical references and index.
ISBN 0-13-605046-8 (alk. paper)
1. Memory. 2. Cognition. I. Radvansky, Gabriel A. II. Ashcraft, Mark H. Human memory and cognition. III. Title.
BF371.A68 2010
153—dc22 2009012948

10 9 8 7 6 5 4 3 2 1

Prentice Hall
is an imprint of
PEARSON

www.pearsonhighered.com
ISBN 10: 0-13-605046-8
ISBN 13: 978-0-13-605046-9

BRIEF CONTENTS

CONTENTS

PREFACE

TO THE STUDENT

The psychology of human memory and cognition is fascinating, dealing with questions and ideas that are inherently interesting; how we think, reason, remember, and use language, to name just a few. When cognitive psychologists talk research at conventions, they are agitated, intense, and full of energy. In contrast to this enthusiasm, however, undergraduate texts often portray the field as dull, too concerned with the minutiae of experimental method and technical jargon and not concerned enough with the interesting issues. Without slighting the empirical foundation of the field, we have tried to capture some of the excitement of the area. All professors want their students to understand the material, of course, but we also want you to appreciate cognitive psychology as one of the most interesting and memorable topics of your student career. Several features of the book are designed to accomplish this:

- To engage your interest and understanding, examples of the main points are sprinkled throughout the text. Each of the chapters has a box that asks you to "Prove It," the box giving you a demonstration project that can be done quickly to illustrate the points being made.
- Mastering the terminology of a new field can be difficult. To help you with the jargon, critical terms are boldfaced in the text and defined immediately in italicized print. Each chapter's terms are listed at the end of the chapter, and the entire collection of terms and definitions appears in the Glossary at the end of the book. Try studying for exams by playing a Jeopardy!-like game with the glossary; one person reads a definition, the other names the defined term.
- Each major section of a chapter ends with a brief Section Summary. This, along with the listing of glossary terms at the end of each chapter, should help you check your understanding and memory as you study. Note that some people find it helpful to read the Section Summaries first as a preview of the section's content.
- We use a more colloquial style than is customary in the field (or in texts in general), using the first person, posing direct questions to you, inserting parenthetical commentary, and so on. Our students have told us that these features make the book more enjoyable to read; one said, "It's interesting—not like a textbook," which we take as a compliment. Some professors may expect a more formal, detached style, of course. We would rather have you read and remember the material than have you cope with a book selected because of a careful pedantic style. Besides, you will have plenty of time to deal with boring books in graduate school.

TO THE INSTRUCTOR

Like the first four editions, this one is directed primarily toward undergraduates at the junior and senior level, who are probably taking their first basic course in memory and cognition. They have also been used successfully in introductory graduate surveys, especially when first-year students need a more thorough background in memory and cognition. There is much continuity between the fourth edition of Cognition and this one: The foundation areas in cognition are still covered thoroughly, as you'll see in the Contents.

But this revision has several new features that you'll want to note:

- There continue to be tremendous increases in the study of memory and cognition with the technologies and perspectives of cognitive neuroscience. This was reflected in prior editions, and this emphasis continues to grow in the fifth edition. These discussions of neuroscience are integrated within the individual chapter topics. A major section of Chapter 2 provides background information on neurons and the brain, so that even students without formal coursework on the biological basis of cognition will be prepared for the neuroscience evidence they'll encounter throughout the book.
- There has been a thorough updating of the book, adding and expanding on important topics and developments that are central to the field, such as embodied cognition research, new research on working memory and individual differences, extensive coverage of research on autobiographical memory, new strides in online investigations of comprehension and reading, and new perspectives on heuristics in decision making. As always, there has also been some careful pruning of topics and streamlining of presentation to make room for the new material.
- As in the first four editions, we have tried to strike a balance between basic core material and cutting-edge topics. As cognitive psychology continues to evolve, it is important to maintain some continuity with older topics and evidence. Students need to understand how we got here, and instructors cannot be expected to start from scratch each time they teach the course. We've preserved the overall outline and organization of the book, while updating the sections to reflect newer material.
- An Instructor's Manual and Test Item File also are available on the Instructor's Resource Center on pearsonhighered.com or by contacting your local Pearson sales representative.

We hope that the balance between classic research and current topics, the style we have adopted, and the standard organization we have used will make the text easy to teach from and easy for students to read and remember. More important, we hope that you will find our portrayal of the field of cognitive psychology useful. As always, we are delighted to receive the comments and suggestions of those who use this book, instructors and students alike. You can contact Mark Ashcraft by writing in care of the Psychology Department, University of Nevada Las Vegas, 4505 S. Maryland Pkwy, Box 455030, Las Vegas, NV 89154-5030, or by e-mailing him at mark.ashcraft@unlv.edu. You can contact Gabe Radvansky by writing in care of the Department of Psychology, University of Notre Dame, Notre Dame, IN 46556, or by e-mailing him at gradvans@nd.edu.

ACKNOWLEDGMENTS

The list of students, colleagues, and publishing professionals who have helped shape this project continues to grow.

For editorial support and assistance, we thank Jeff Marshall, Executive Editor; LeeAnn Doherty, Associate Editor; Amy Trudell, Editorial Assistant; and Nicole Kunzmann, Marketing Manager.

Professional colleagues who have assisted across the years include R. Reed Hunt, John Jonides, Michael Masson, James S. Nairne, Marjorie Reed, Gregory B. Simpson, Richard Griggs, Richard Jackson Harris, Donald Homa, Paul Whitney, Tom Carr, Frances Friedrich, Dave Geary, Mike McCloskey, Morton Gernsbacher, Art Graesser, Keith Holyoak, George Kellas, Mark Marschark, Randy Engle, Fred Smith, Pamela Ansburg, Jeremy Miller, J.L. Nicol, Jennie Euler, Bob Slevc, and Joe Magliano.

And, in addition to our undergraduate classes, who have tested many of the ideas and demonstrations in the book, we'd like to thank a few special students who have helped in a variety of ways, from reading and critiquing to duplicating and checking references: Mike Faust, David Fleck, Elizabeth Kirk, David Copeland, Don Seyler, Tom Wagner, Paul Korzenko, and Jeremy Krause. We're very grateful to all.

Mark H. Ashcraft
Gabriel A. Radvansky

CHAPTER

1

Cognitive Psychology

An Introduction

What a piece of work is man. How noble in reason! How infinite in faculty! In form and moving how express and admirable! In action how like an angel! In apprehension, how like a god! (Act 2, scene 2)[1]

SHAKESPEARE'S *Hamlet*

One difficulty in the psychological sciences lies in the familiarity of the phenomena with which they deal. A certain intellectual effort is required to see how such phenomena can pose serious problems or call for intricate explanatory theories. One is inclined to take them for granted as necessary or somehow "natural."

CHOMSKY, 1968, p. 24

[1]Unlike Shakespeare, modern writers have been sensitized to the sexist bias implied by the use of *man, he,* and so on in a generic sense. We have attempted to avoid such usage whenever possible, or to alternate between *he* and *she* on a section-by-section basis.

This book is about human memory and cognition, and specifically about the scientific study of human memory and cognition. Let's start with a quick definition of terms and return later for the more formal definitions. For the moment, consider memory and cognition to be the mental events and knowledge we use when we recognize an object, remember a name, have an idea, understand a sentence, or solve a problem. In this book, we consider a broad range of subjects, from basic perception through complex decision making, from seemingly simple mental acts such as recognizing a letter of the alphabet to very complicated acts such as participating in a conversation. We will ask questions such as: How do we read for meaning? How do we memorize facts? What does it mean to forget something? How do we know that we don't know something? The unifying theme behind all this is one of the most fascinating and important questions of all time: How do people think?

Note that we are interested in an empirical, scientific approach to human memory and thought. This places us in the branch of modern psychology called cognitive psychology. The discipline of psychology has largely accepted the empirical, scientific approach to the study of mind and behavior. Thus one of the central features of modern cognitive psychology is its allegiance to objective, empirical methods of investigation. We are experimentalists, and this is the approach you will read about in this book. However, while we do present a lot of studies, we also try to make connections with your everyday experiences and how these experiences may be relevant to the issues being discussed.

Within the boundaries of objective scientific methods, cognitive psychology is asking an enormous range of fascinating questions. Since the beginnings of modern cognitive psychology about 50 years ago, there has been an explosion of interest in cognition and in the cognitive approach to human behavior and thought both in and outside of psychology proper. These questions that were on the back burner for too long—such as "How do we read?" or "How do we use language?"—are now active areas of research. The pent-up interest in these questions, unleashed during the cognitive revolution of the late 1950s, has yielded tremendous progress. Furthermore, we now acknowledge, seek, and sometimes participate in the important contributions of disciplines such as linguistics, computer science, and the neurosciences. This interdisciplinary approach, this joining of diverse forces, is called **cognitive science**, *the scientific study of thought, language, the brain—in short, the scientific study of the mind.*

The most basic aim of this book is to tell you what has been discovered about human memory and cognitive processes and to share the conclusions and insights about the particularly human activity called thought. Human memory—your memory, with its collection of mental processes—is the most highly sophisticated, flexible, and efficient computer available today. How does it work? As amazing as electronic computers are, their capabilities are primitive compared with what you do routinely in even a single minute's worth of thinking. The need to understand ourselves is basic, and this includes an understanding of how our minds work.

Another aim of this book is to describe how cognitive psychology has made these discoveries. You'll understand and better appreciate the information in this book if you also understand how research is done, how new knowledge is acquired in the scientific pursuit of cognition. Few of you will become cognitive scientists yourselves, but presumably most of you have decided to major in psychology or a related field. Because the cognitive approach has come to influence many areas in modern psychology—indeed, the evidence suggests that cognitive psychology is at the core and remains "the most prominent school" of thought in modern psychology (Robins, Gosling, & Craik, 1999)—your mastery of psychology as a whole will be enhanced by an understanding of cognitive psychology.

A final aim of this book is to illustrate the pervasiveness of cognitive psychology and its impact on other fields outside psychology proper. As you read a moment ago, cognitive science is a multidisciplinary field. This fusion and cross pollination of disciplines and ideas represents the conviction that researchers in linguistics, artificial intelligence, the neurosciences, economics, and even anthropology can contribute important ideas to psychology and vice versa. Psychology has a long tradition of influencing educational practice, and the potential for cognitive psychology to continue these contributions is both obvious and important. Even fields as diverse as medicine, law, and business are incorporating findings from cognitive psychology—for example, a cognitive psychologist named Kahneman won the Nobel Prize in Economics in 2003 for his work on decision making (see Chapter 11 for a full account of Kahneman's work, and Kahneman, 2003b, for a first-person description of the collaborative work that led to the Nobel). But it should not be surprising that cognitive psychology is relevant to so many other fields. After all, what human activity doesn't involve thought?

THINKING ABOUT THINKING

Let's begin to develop an intuitive feel for our topic by considering some examples, coming back later to improve our quick definitions of the terms *memory* and *cognition*. For all three examples that follow, you should read the question and come up with the answer, but more importantly you should try to be as aware as possible of the thoughts that cross your mind as you consider the question. The first question is easy:

1. *How many hands did Aristotle have?*

For such a ridiculously easy question, of course we are not particularly interested in the correct answer, "two." We are quite interested, however, in the thoughts you had as you considered the question. Most students report a train of thoughts something like this: "Dumb question, of course he had two hands. Wait a minute—why would a professor ask such an obvious question? Maybe Aristotle had only one hand. Nah, I would have heard of it if he had had only one hand—he must have had two."

A bit of informal cognitive analysis will uncover some of the different thoughts you have while arriving at your answer. Keep track of the analysis with the list in Table 1-1; as you read the later questions, refer to Table 1-1 to see which processes and steps apply to all the questions and what new ones should be added. Bear in mind that Table 1-1 merely illustrates the intuitive analysis; it is no substitute for the full description of these processes and steps found later in the book. ▲

First, although you were no doubt unaware of it, a large group of perceptual processes were brought into play to deal with the written words of the question. Highly overlearned visual processes focused your eyes on the printed line, then moved your focus across the line bit by bit, registering the printed material into some kind of

TABLE 1-1 Summary of the Intuitive Cognitive Analysis

Processes	Topic and Chapter
Sensory and perceptual	
Focus eyes on print	Visual perception, sensory memory: Chapter 3
Encode and recognize printed material	Pattern recognition, reading: Chapters 3 and 10
Memory and retrieval	
Look up and identify words in memory	Memory retrieval: Chapters 5–8
Retrieve word meanings	
Comprehension	
Combine word meanings to yield sentence meaning	Semantic retrieval, comprehension: Chapters 7–10
Evaluate sentence meaning, consider alternative meanings	Comprehension: Chapters 9 and 10
Judgment and decision	
Retrieve answer to question	Semantic retrieval: Chapters 8 and 9
Determine reasonableness of question	Comprehension, conversation: Chapters 9 and 10
Judge speaker's intent and knowledge	Decision making and reasoning: Chapter 11
Computational (Question 2)	
Retrieve fact knowledge	Semantic retrieval: Chapter 7
Retrieve knowledge of how to divide and execute procedure	Procedural knowledge: Chapters 6, 11, and 12

memory system. Smoothly and rapidly, another set of processes looked up the encoded material in memory and identified the letters and words. Of course, few if any readers of a college text pay conscious attention to the nuts and bolts of perceiving and identifying words unless the vocabulary is unfamiliar or the printing is faint. Yet your lack of awareness of these stages does not mean they didn't happen; ask any first-grade teacher about the difficulties children have in learning to identify letters and their sounds and putting these components together into words.

We have encountered two important lessons already. First, mental processes can occur with little conscious awareness. This is especially true of processes that have received a great deal of practice, such as reading skills. Second, even though these processes can operate very quickly, they are quite complex, involving difficult motor, perceptual, and mental acts. Their complexity makes it even more amazing how efficient, rapid, and seemingly automatic they are.

As you identified the individual words in the first question, you were also accessing or looking up the meanings of those words and then fitting those meanings together to understand the question. Surely you weren't consciously aware of looking up the meaning of the word *hands* in a mental dictionary. But just as surely, you did search for and find that entry in memory, stored together with all your other general knowledge about the human body. A few students insist that they wondered whether the question might be referring to a different Aristotle—maybe Aristotle Onassis—because a question about the philosopher Aristotle's hands seems so odd.

Now we are getting to the meat of the process. With little effort, we retrieve the information from memory that the word *Aristotle* refers to a human being, a historical figure from the distant past. Many people know little about Aristotle beyond the fact that he was a Greek philosopher. Yet this seems to be enough, combined with what we know to be true of people in general, to determine that he was probably just like everyone else: He had two hands. Those who consider Aristotle Onassis seem to reach the same stage as well. Even though they may know a few facts about this more contemporary person (Greek shipping magnate, married Jacqueline Kennedy), they probably find no specific information in memory about the number of hands he had, so they make the default assumption that it was two. Think of how differently you would have understood the question if it had been "How many hands does Aristotle have?" Tipped off by the present tense, would you have searched your memory for a still-living person named Aristotle? Would you have explicitly asked yourself whether Aristotle Onassis was dead, or would you have tried to find some unusual, maybe metaphorical way of interpreting the question?

At a final (for now) stage, people report a set of thoughts and judgments that involve the reasonableness of the question, similar in many respects to the interpretations of remarks in a conversation. In general, people do not ask obvious questions, at least not of other adults. If they do, however, it is often for another reason—a trick question, maybe, or sarcasm. Consequently, students report that for a time they decided that maybe the question wasn't so obvious after all. In other words, there was a return to memory to see whether there was some special knowledge about Aristotle that pertains to his hands. The next step is truly fascinating. The majority of students claim to have thought to themselves, "No, I would have known about it if he had had only one hand," and they decide that indeed it was an obvious question after all.

This lack-of-knowledge reasoning process is a fascinating topic because so much of our everyday reasoning is done without benefit of complete knowledge. In an interesting variation, we have asked students, "How many hands did Beethoven have?" Knowing of Beethoven's musical fame typically leads to the following inference: "Because he was a musician, he probably played the piano, and he could not possibly have been very successful at it with only one hand; therefore he must have had two." An occasional student goes even further with the intriguing answer, "Two, but he did go deaf before he died."

Now *that's* interesting! Someone found a connection between the disability implied by the question "How many hands?" and a related shred of evidence in memory, Beethoven's deafness. Such an answer shows how people can also consider implications, inferences, and other unstated connections as they reason and make decisions: It shows what a great deal of knowledge can be considered even for a simple question. The answer also illustrates the role of prior knowledge in such reasoning, where the richer body of information about Beethoven can lead to a more specific inference than was possible for the Aristotle question.

Although this informal analysis does not exhaust the discussion of cognitive processes in reading, memory retrieval, or comprehension, it does orient you to some of the important features of cognitive psychology and its subject matter. Let's continue with the other questions to see what else is in store for you in this book.

IN DEPTH

Interpreting Graphs

If you're good at interpreting data presented in graphs, do not bother with the rest of this box; just study the figures. Some students struggle with graphed material, not understanding what is being shown as well as their professors think. Because you will encounter a lot of graphed data in this book, you need to understand what you are looking at and what it means. Take a moment to go through these simple graphs to see how they are put together and what to pay attention to when you interpret the data.

The figure in this box is a simple graph of response time data, the time it takes to respond to an item. We almost always abbreviate response time as RT, and it is usually measured in milliseconds (ms), thousandths of a second (because thought occurs so fast). In the figure, the label on the *y*-axis says "Vocal RT"; in other words, these people were making vocal responses (speaking), and the researchers measured the time between the onset of a simple multiplication problem and the vocal response. The numbers on the *y*-axis show you the range of RTs that were observed. The dependent variable is always the measure of performance we collect in the experiment—here it is vocal RT—and it always goes on the *y*-axis.

The *x*-axis in the left panel is labeled "Multiplication problems," and we've plotted just two problems, 2 × 3 and 6 × 9. It is customary to show a more general variable than this on the *x*-axis, as shown in the right panel. There you see a point for a whole set of small multiplication problems, from 2 × 3 up to 4 × 5; a set of medium-size problems such as 2 × 7 and 8 × 3; and a set of large problems, such as 6 × 8 and 9 × 7. So the *x*-axis label in the right panel says "Size of problem." A general rule for the proportions of a graph is that the length of the *x*-axis is slightly shorter than the height of the *y*-axis; a 3 to 4 (or maybe a 4 to 5) ratio is about right, so that if the height of the *y*-axis is 4 inches, the *x*-axis should be about 3 inches long. Notice that the *y*-axis is now in whole seconds, to save some space and preserve the graph's proportions.

Now the data. The points we plot in the graph are almost always the mean or average of the dependent variable, RT in this case. Both panels show two curves or lines each, one for college students, the other for fourth-grade students; Campbell and Graham (1985) tested

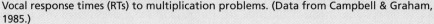

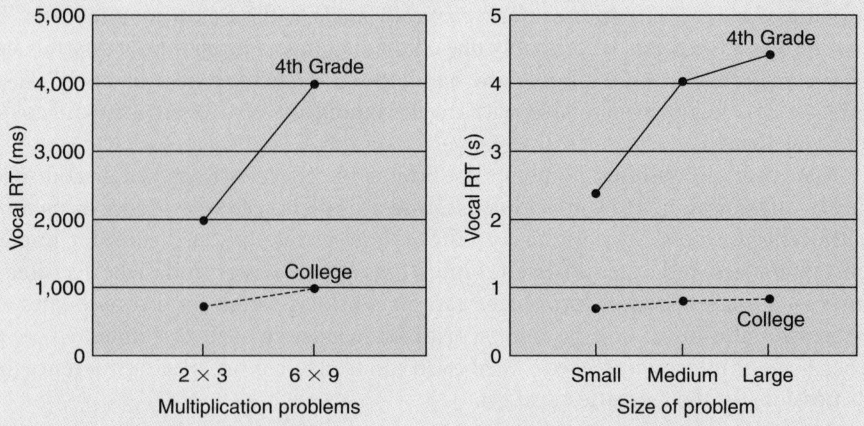

Vocal response times (RTs) to multiplication problems. (Data from Campbell & Graham, 1985.)

fourth-graders and college students on the simple multiplication problems. Notice first that the curves for fourth-graders are much higher. If you read the values from the *y*-axis in the left panel, the average fourth-grader took 1,940 milliseconds to answer "6" to the problem 2 × 3, compared to 737 milliseconds for the average college student. In the right panel, the average fourth-grader took about 2,400 milliseconds to respond to small problems, 4,100 to medium, and 4,550 to large. Compare this much greater increase in RT as the problems get larger with the pattern for college students: There was still an increase, but only from 730 milliseconds to almost 900 milliseconds.

Why did Campbell and Graham find slower performance for fourth-graders? No doubt because college students have had far more practice in doing simple multiplication problems than have fourth-graders. In other words, college students know multiplication better, have the facts stored more strongly in long-term memory, and so can access and retrieve the facts more rapidly. It is a perfectly sensible, cognitive effect that the strength of information in memory influences the speed of your retrieval. And it is easily grasped by looking at and understanding the graphed results. (You will read about this experiment again in Chapter 2, including a variety of interpretations for the other major result in the figures, that RT was longer for the larger problems.)

2. *What is 723 divided by 6?*

This question relies on a different kind of knowledge than the Aristotle question: the knowledge of arithmetic that you learned in grade school. Just as was true as you read the words in the first question, many of your mental processes happened more or less automatically for the division problem: identifying the digits, accessing your knowledge of arithmetic procedures, and so on. Yet you were probably consciously aware of the problem-solving steps in doing long division: Divide 6 into 7, subtract 6 from 7 to get the first remainder, bring down the 2, then divide 12 by 6, and so on. These steps are mentioned at the bottom of Table 1-1, "Computational," which would include your knowledge of how to do long division. Cognitive psychology is no less interested in your mental processing of arithmetic problems or in the knowledge you acquired in school than in the informal reasoning processes you used for Question 1. In other words, the fact that you were explicitly taught how to divide does not make your mental processes less interesting. If anything, it may make them more interesting because we might be able to find parallels between teaching methods and people's mental processes (see Chapter 12 for some further information on the cognitive psychology of arithmetic and math).

The third question is in many ways more typical of cognitive psychology's interests and research than the first two. For reasons that will become more convincing throughout the book, a great deal of research in cognitive psychology has timed people as they make simple yes-or-no decisions about questions such as the following:

3. *Does a robin have wings?*

Most adults find themselves unable to say much of anything about their train of thoughts when answering this question. Indeed, many people insist, "I just knew the answer was yes." (In honesty, many people also question the sanity of an investigator who asks such seemingly trivial questions.) One purpose of the informal analysis for

Question 1 was to illustrate just how much of our cognitive processing can occur below the level of awareness, or automatically. As you probably realize by now, cognitive psychology does not find the notion that "I just knew it" to be particularly useful, however certain you are that no other thoughts occurred to you. Clearly, you had to read the words, find their meanings in memory, check the relevant facts, and make your decision in a similar fashion to the previous examples. Each of these steps (and there are many more steps involved here) is a *bona fide* mental act, the very substance of cognitive psychology. Furthermore, each step takes some amount of time to be completed. A question such as Question 3 takes adults about one second to answer; the question "Does a robin have feet?" takes a little longer, around 1.2 or 1.3 seconds. Even such small time differences can give us a wealth of information about mental processing and human memory.

What seems strikingly different for Question 3 is that almost none of the mental processes required much awareness or conscious activity; the question seems to have been processed automatically. Because such automatic processes are so pervasive in mental activity, we are particularly interested in understanding them.

Section Summary

- Cognitive psychology is the scientific study of human mental processes. This includes perceiving, remembering, using language, reasoning, and solving problems.
- Intuitive analysis of examples such as "How many hands did Aristotle have?" and "Does a robin have wings?" indicates that many mental processes occur automatically (very rapidly and below the level of conscious awareness).

MEMORY AND COGNITION DEFINED

Now that you have an idea of the topics we are concerned with in cognitive psychology, we need to state more formal definitions of the terms *memory* and *cognition*. It will also be useful to spend a moment discussing the topics you will and will not find covered in this text. Most of us have a reasonably good idea of what the term *memory* means, something like "being able to remember or recall some information." As defined in Webster's *New World Dictionary* (1980), memory consists of "the power, act, or process of recalling to mind facts previously learned or past experiences." Note that both of these definitions are hopelessly circular; memory is "being able to remember" or "the process of recalling to mind." Although this circularity is unfortunate, the definitions do point to several critical ideas (note that the circularity is almost built into the words, all of which came from related Indo-European bases meaning "to think" and "to remember").

First, the event or information being recalled from memory is one from the past. In other words, we *remember* things from the past but *experience* things in the present. Quite literally, any past event that is currently recalled is evidence of memory; it could be a childhood memory from years ago or something that only happened moments ago. Second, the term *memory* refers to a process, a mental act in which stored information is recovered for some current use. This recovery or retrieval of what has been placed in memory specifies the process of interest, "getting out" something that was previously "put in." Note that the term *retrieval* here includes both varieties of remembering: the conscious, intentional recalling to mind implied in Webster's definition and the more automatic (or even unaware) kind of retrieval discussed in the examples earlier.

Finally, the term *memory* also refers to a place, a location where all the events, information, and knowledge of a lifetime are stored. This sense of the word is especially evident in the models and theories of cognition that rely on divisions such as short-term and long-term memory. Although it is obviously true that there is some physical location in your brain where facts and processes are stored, this "location" sense of the word was often taken rather metaphorically; regardless of *where* it happens, there is some memory system that holds information for later retrieval. But especially now, with the advent of modern imaging devices such as positron emission tomography (PET) and magnetic resonance imaging (MRI), neuroscience is making progress in exploring functions and processes as they occur—or occasionally are disrupted—in the brain and identifying regions and areas responsible for those functions and processes. Chapter 2 introduces you to some of this new methodology and orientation, preparing you to read about recent advances in our knowledge of brain-cognition relationships throughout this book.

A formal definition of the term *memory* captures the essential ingredients of the preceding discussion. Consider **memory** to mean *the mental processes of acquiring and retaining information for later retrieval and the mental storage system that enables these processes.* Operationally, memory is demonstrated whenever the processes of retention and retrieval influence your behavior or performance in some way, even if you are unaware of the influence. Furthermore, we understand this definition to include retention not just across hours, weeks, or years, but even across very brief spans of time, in any situation in which the original stimulus event is no longer present. Note also that memory refers to three different kinds of mental activities in this definition: initial acquisition of information (usually called learning or encoding), subsequent retention of the information, and then retrieval of the information (Melton, 1963). Because all three activities are logically necessary to demonstrate that remembering has taken place, we include them in our broader definition of the term *memory* as well.

The term *cognition* is much richer in its connotations and is an umbrella term for all higher mental processes. One dictionary defines it as "the mental process or faculty of knowing, including aspects such as awareness, perception, reasoning, and judgment" (*The American Heritage College Dictionary*, 1997). In Neisser's (1967) landmark book, *Cognitive Psychology*, he claimed that cognition "refers to all the processes by which the sensory input is transformed, reduced, elaborated, stored, recovered, and used . . . [including] such terms as sensation, perception, imagery, retention, recall, problem solving, and thinking" (p. 4). For the present, we use a definition that is somewhat easier to remember but just as broad: **Cognition** is *the collection of mental processes and activities used in perceiving, remembering, thinking, and understanding, as well as the act of using those processes.*

Whereas our definition of the term *memory* is fairly specific, the definition of cognition is still somewhat slippery. A term such as *thinking* in a scientific definition begs for clarification or at least a catalog of examples. You might decide that dreaming is a perfectly valid act of cognition, according to the definition, and it is. However, you would then be puzzled that cognitive psychology largely ignores dreaming (but see Mandler, 1984, and Antrobus, 1991, for example), in part because it is so hard to study the content of dreams accurately. So, why do we include some topics but ignore others?

One purpose of the examples in the previous section is to suggest that cognitive psychology is largely, though not exclusively, interested in what might be considered everyday, ordinary mental processes. The processes by which we read and understand, for instance, are entirely commonplace—not simple, by any means, but certainly routine. On the other hand, we should not amend the definition to include only "normal" mental activities. It is true that cognitive psychology generally does not directly deal with the psychologically "abnormal," such as the varieties of thought disturbance associated with schizophrenia (although a cognitive approach to these problems is certainly possible). The problem with excluding the "nonnormal" processes is that the unusual or rare may also be tossed out, impoverishing our science in the process. Rather than change the definition, we assume that cognition usually refers to the customary, commonplace mental activities that most people engage in as they interact with the world around them. As you will see, this still casts a rather broad net as we fish for topics to investigate and interpretations to explain our results.

Nonetheless, there are still omissions, sometimes glaring and sometimes not. To the distress of some (e.g., Neisser, 1976), most of our research deals with the sense modalities of vision and hearing rather than other sensory ways of knowing the world, and it focuses very heavily on language; as Keil (1991, p. 287) quipped, "Minds talk a lot . . . they see a little, but they don't feel much else." More disturbing, possibly, is our reliance on seemingly sterile experimental techniques and methods (this is Neisser's more substantive criticism), techniques that ask simple questions and may therefore yield overly simple views about the operation of cognitive systems. In Neisser's term, much of our cognitive research lacks **ecological validity**, or *generalizability to the real-world situations in which people think and act.* As a simple example, imagine how different your reading and comprehension processes might be if you were shown this paragraph one word at a time, each word for only a fraction of a second. The method would prevent you from slowing down when your comprehension lagged, from returning your gaze to a previous word or sentence you may have misinterpreted, and so on. And yet this method has been used to investigate reading and comprehension.

Although Neisser's criticism was sensible, it was possibly premature. We find great complexity in cognitive processing, even when artificially simple tasks are performed. At our current level of sophistication, we might be overwhelmed if our tasks were permitted to be more complex or if we tried to investigate the full range of a behavior in all its detail and nuance. In other words, in the early stage of investigation it is reasonable for scientists to take an approach called **reductionism**, *attempting to understand complex events by breaking them down into their components.* After all, an artificially simple situation can sometimes reveal rather than obscure a process, and sometimes we gain insight by preventing a process from occurring in its regular fashion (see Mook, 1983, for a fine discussion of the entire issue of ecological validity). Of course, it is also reasonable to expect that scientists eventually will put the pieces back together again and deal with the larger event as a whole. In fact, recent developments seem to hold just that sort of promise.

Section Summary

- Memory is composed of the mental processes of acquiring and retaining information for later use (encoding), the mental retention system (storage), and then using that information (retrieval).
- Cognition is the complex collection of mental processes and activities used in perceiving, remembering, and thinking and the act of using those processes.

AN INTRODUCTORY HISTORY OF COGNITIVE PSYCHOLOGY

You have now encountered cognitive psychology by example and by definition, so we next turn to its history and development. This treatment should give you a better appreciation of what cognitive psychology is and how it became so. Figure 1-1 summarizes

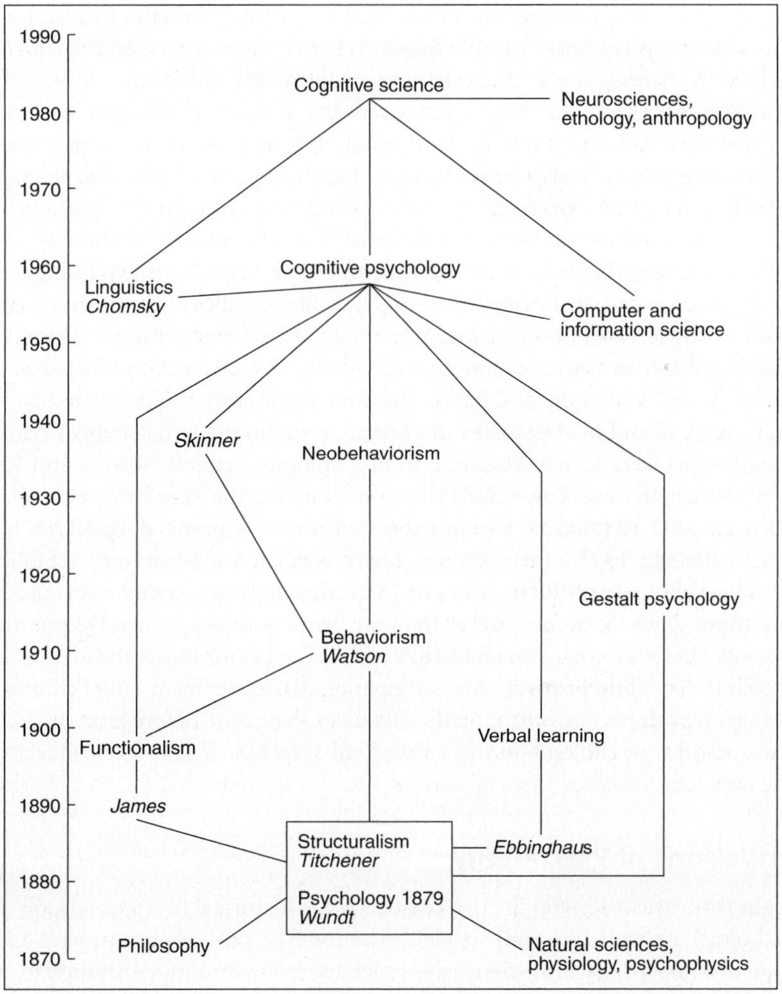

FIGURE 1-1

the main patterns of influence that produced cognitive psychology and cognitive science, with approximate dates shown along the side. As you read, study the figure to decide which pathways indicate positive influences and where ideas and questions from an earlier movement continued to inspire the approach that followed. Think also about the pathways that indicate negative influences, where a later approach specifically rejected elements of its predecessor.

To a remarkable extent, the scientific study of human memory and cognition is quite new. Although elements of our explanations, and certainly many of our experimental tasks, appeared even in the earliest years of psychology, the bulk of the work theorizing has been created since the 1950s. And yet, as is true of most topics in psychology, interest in human memory and cognitive processes is as old as recorded history. Aristotle, born in 384 BC, considered the basic principles of human memory and proposed a theory of memory in his treatise *De Memoria* (*Concerning Memory;* Hothersall, 1984). Even a casual reading of ancient works such as Homer's *The Iliad* or *The Odyssey* reveals that people have always wondered about how the mind works and how to improve its functioning (as told in Plato's *Phaedrus*, Socrates fretted that the invention of written language would weaken reliance on memory and understanding, just as modern parents worry that calculators will weaken children's mastery of math). Philosophers of every age have considered the nature of thought and memory. Descartes even decided that the ultimate proof of human existence is our awareness of our own thought: *Cogito ergo sum,* "I think, therefore I am" (Descartes, 1637, p. 52, in Hothersall, 1984, p. 28). Given this preoccupation with thought and mind in Western culture, it is no wonder that Ebbinghaus' (1908, p. 1) comment, "Psychology has a long past but only a short history," is so widely repeated in histories of psychology.

The critical events at the beginning of psychology's "short history" occurred in the mid- to late 1800s. It was as if the important intellectual and cultural influences of the day converged most strongly on one man, Wilhelm Wundt, and on one place, Leipzig, Germany. In 1879, Wundt established the first laboratory for psychological experiments, at the University of Leipzig. Of course, several notable individuals had already begun what was later seen as research on psychological topics: Weber's and Fechner's work in psychophysics, Helmholtz's discoveries about the speed of neural impulses, and Broca's and Wernicke's identification of brain regions devoted to language processes (Banich, 1997), for instance. There was even a laboratory established by American psychologist William James in 1875, although apparently it was used largely for classroom demonstrations rather than for genuine experiments. Despite these developments, there is a consensus that 1879 marks the beginning of the formal academic, empirical discipline of psychology, a separate discipline from either philosophy or physiology. Wundt built his work on the advances that came before him, developments that gave rise to psychology and psychological research. It is to these developments that we now turn.

Anticipations of Psychology

We begin with Aristotle, who for two reasons is the historical first we typically point to in psychology. Aristotle generally is viewed as the first philosopher to have advocated an empirically based, natural science approach to understanding. Although he was certainly not the only great thinker to have insisted on *observation as the basis for all science,* he was the first to express this fundamentally important idea—the position known as **empiricism**. Second, Aristotle's inquiry into the nature of thought and mind by his own natural science method led him to a reasonably objective explanation of how learning and memory take place. This explanation could not be considered a theory of memory by modern standards, nor should we expect it to be. On the other hand, the basic principle Aristotle identified, that of associations, has figured prominently in many psychological theories of the past century.

Equally important to psychology as a whole was *Aristotle's insistence that the mind is a "blank slate" at birth*, a ***tabula rasa***, or clean sheet of paper (Watson, 1968). This notion claims that the experiences of the individual are of paramount importance because experience, rather than inborn factors, "writes" a record onto the blank paper. It is possible that no other issue has so preoccupied philosophers of all ages, an issue we call the "nature versus nurture" or "heredity versus environment" debate. In cognitive psychology, we encounter the controversy in several places, most notably when we discuss theories of language (see Chapters 2 and 9).

There have been many fits and starts in the study of memory over the years since Aristotle. For example, St. Augustine, in Chapter X of his *Confessions*, presents a surprisingly modern account of memory. Most other anticipations of psychology date from the Renaissance and later periods and consist largely of developments in scientific methods and approaches. By the mid-1800s, positions such as Descartes's rational approach had been discarded in favor of observational or empirical methods. By the time psychology appeared, the general procedures of scientific inquiry had been developed and, for the most part, were accepted by all scientific disciplines and areas. There was widespread agreement on the need for science to be based on objective procedures and on methods such as careful quantification and definition and empirical observation. Given the notable progress made in scientific fields such as physics, biology, and medicine by the mid-1800s, it is not surprising that the early psychologists thought the time was ripe for a true science of the mind.

Early Psychology

Four early psychologists are of particular interest in our study of cognitive psychology. They are Wilhelm Wundt, Edward Titchener, Hermann von Ebbinghaus, and William James.

WILHELM WUNDT To a large extent, the early psychologists were students of Wilhelm Wundt (1832–1920); this was especially true of the early American psychologists (Benjamin, Durkin, Link, Vestal, & Acord, 1992). Beginning in 1875, when he moved to the University of Leipzig, Wundt directed more than 200 doctoral theses on psychological topics (Leahey, 2000). Such important psychologists as William James, Hugo Munsterberg, Charles Spearman, James McKeen Cattell, and Edward Titchener studied with Wundt, even if they did not receive their degrees with him, primarily investigating topics that Wundt felt were appropriate to a new science of the mind. Wundt continually updated his book *Principles of Physiological Psychology*, reporting new results obtained in his laboratory, and he also founded the first psychology journal,

Wilhelm Wundt

Philosophical Studies (neither of these titles seems to match modern connotations of the terms). His influence was far reaching because his was the first truly psychological system. In fact, Leahey (1992b) credited Wundt with starting the only true scientific revolution in psychology.

Unfortunately, Wundt's interests in the last 20 years of his career went largely unrecognized until recently. His work on language, according to Leahey (2000), foreshadowed some modern insights to a remarkable degree but was largely ignored in his own time. And his work on child psychology and other applied topics (his term was *Volkerpsychologie,* or psychology of the people) was rejected; the influential Titchener, for instance, believed that these topics did not belong in psychology. American psychologists, never enthusiastic about contributions from Europe, may have found an additional excuse for their narrow and biased attitudes when Wundt became an enthusiastic German nationalist during World War I (Benjamin et al., 1992).

In terms of psychology, Wundt believed strongly that the proper topic of study for psychology was "conscious processes and immediate experience"; today, we would place these topics somewhere near the areas of sensation, perception, and attention. To study such processes in a scientific manner, in addition to the extensive use of response time measures, Wundt devised the method of *Selbst-Beobachtung.* Translated literally as "self-observation," this generally is known in English as **introspection**, *a method in which one looks carefully inward, reporting on inner sensations and experiences.* By all accounts, Wundt intended this to be a careful, reliable, and, above all else, scientific method. For instance, Hothersall (1984, pp. 88–89) noted, "Wundt's introspection was a rigidly controlled, arduous, experimental procedure. . . . To yield valid introspections Wundt insisted that certain rules be enforced: the observer had to be 'master of the situation,' in a state of 'strained attention.' . . . All observations were to be repeated many times; and finally, experimental conditions were to be varied systematically to allow a general description of mental contents." The observers in these experiments needed a great deal of training so that they would report only the elements of experience that were immediate and conscious. Reports in which memory intruded—Wundt's term was *mediate* or *mediated experience*—were to be excluded.

EDWARD TITCHENER For American psychology in Wundt's tradition, the most important figure was Edward Titchener, an Englishman who came to Cornell University in 1892 to direct its psychology laboratory. Titchener's work with Wundt had convinced him that psychology's knowledge was obtainable only with the introspection. As his career at Cornell progressed, Titchener became more dogmatic in his convictions and his definition of psychology. Topics like mental illness, educational applications, and social psychology (including Wundt's broader interests) were "impure" because they could not be studied with introspection. Like Wundt, Titchener insisted on careful control and rigorous training for his introspectors, who were required to avoid what he called "the stimulus error" of describing the physical stimulus rather than the mental experience of that stimulus. Moreover, "certain introspections were defined as correct, and certain others as in error, with the final authority being Titchener himself" (Hothersall, 1984, p. 105). By these means, Titchener studied *the structure of the conscious mind, the sensations, images, and feelings that were the very elements of the mind's structure.* He called this **structuralism**, the first major movement or school of psychological thought (see Figure 1-1).

Such an exclusive system was destined for difficulties. In particular, it seems (not just in retrospect) downright unscientific that a person, Titchener, would be the ultimate authority to validate the observations, instead of relying on more conventional methods (e.g., replication of results by other investigators). As other researchers applied the introspective methods in their own laboratories, differences and contradictory results began to crop up. For instance, a controversy developed over "imageless thought" (see Leahey, 2000, for example). Researchers of the Würzburg School found evidence of imageless thought in their studies. When Titchener found no such evidence in his own studies, he claimed that the Würzburg researchers' findings were wrong, merely the product of sloppy methods and poorly trained observers. (In a similar dispute over sensory and motor reaction times, Titchener's methodological criticism was that the participants had been untrained observers. He would surely have disapproved of modern insistence on naive volunteers from Intro Psych.) These disputes, along with other developments, hastened the decline of Titchener's once-powerful structuralism.

HERMANN VON EBBINGHAUS In contrast to the structuralism of Wundt and Titchener, there was the theoretically modest but eventually more influential work of Hermann von Ebbinghaus (see Chapter 6). Ebbinghaus was a contemporary of Wundt in Germany, although he never studied with Wundt in person. In fact, Ebbinghaus' achievements in memory and forgetting are all the more impressive because he worked outside the establishment of the time. Watson (1968) noted that Ebbinghaus was familiar with Wundt's writings but, if anything, viewed Wundt's pessimism about studying higher mental processes as a challenge rather than a deterrent to pursuing that work. Historical accounts suggest that Ebbinghaus read Wundt's book, decided that a study of the mind by objective methods *was* possible, and set about the task of figuring out how to do it.

Hermann von Ebbinghaus

Lacking a formal laboratory and serving in a nonpsychological academic position with no similar-minded colleagues, Ebbinghaus was forced to rely on his own resources to study memory, even to the extent that he alone served as a subject in his research. Ebbinghaus' goal was to study memory, using thoroughly objective methods. He reasoned that for this goal to be accomplished, he needed to use materials that had no preexisting associations. Thus the first step in his method involved constructing stimulus lists of *nonsense syllables,* consonant–vowel–consonant (CVC) trigrams that, by definition, had *no* meaning whatsoever. Ebbinghaus would learn a list (e.g., of 16 items) to an arbitrary criterion of mastery (e.g., two perfect recitations), then set the list aside. On a later occasion, he would relearn the same list, noting how many fewer trials he needed to relearn the list to the same criterion. His measure of learning in these studies was the "savings score," the number (or proportion) of trials that had been saved in memory between the first and second sessions. By this method, Ebbinghaus examined forgetting as a function of time that intervened between the two learning sessions, degree of learning or overlearning, and even the effect of nonsense versus meaningful material (he compared forgetting curves for nonsense syllables and meaningful poetry).

Ebbinghaus' methods and results, described in his 1885 book, were acclaimed widely as the very model of scientific inquiry into the processes of memory; for instance, Titchener praised Ebbinghaus' work as the most significant progress in studying associations since Aristotle (1919; cited in Hall, 1971). It is difficult to point to another psychologist of his day, aside from Freud, whose specific contributions or methods continue to be used. It is certainly true that the field of verbal learning, throughout the 20th century, owed a great deal to Ebbinghaus; after all, he was the first to invent a reasonably scientific, enduring method to study memory and mental processes. The Ebbinghaus tradition, depicted in Figure 1-1, is one of the strongest of all the influences on cognitive psychology. Perhaps no other influence in the figure is as positive as this century-old tradition begun by Ebbinghaus.

William James

WILLIAM JAMES American philosopher and psychologist William James, a contemporary of Wundt, Titchener, and Ebbinghaus, provided at Harvard an alternative to Titchener's rigid system. His approach to psychology was strongly influenced by the writings of Darwin, and was a kind of **functionalism** in which *the functions of consciousness, rather than its structure, were of interest.* Thus James asked questions such as "How does the mind function?" and "How does it adapt to new circumstances?"

James's informal analyses led to some useful observations on a variety of topics. To note one of interest to us, he proposed that memory consists of two parts: an immediately available memory of which we are currently aware and a larger memory, usually hidden or passive, that is the repository for past experience. The notion of memory being divided into several parts, based on their different functions, is popular today. Indeed, the first serious models of human information processing, in the 1950s and 1960s, included the two kinds of memory James discussed in 1890.

Probably because of his personal distaste for experimentation and his far-reaching interests, James seems not to have espoused the Ebbinghaus methods of studying memory, although he apparently had high regard for that work. Titchener dismissed James as a "half hearted" researcher (Boring, 1950), and—worse yet—interested in topics Titchener found inappropriate. Ultimately, however, James's far-reaching thoughts and proposals were far more influential to psychology than any of Titchener's work (see Miller's introduction to the 1983 edition of James's classic 1890 book *Principles of Psychology*).

Given other developments at the time, however, James's influence on the psychology of human memory and cognition was delayed, for it was John B. Watson, in 1913, who stridently solidified the new direction American psychology was taking, a direction that specifically rejected both the structuralist and functionalist approaches as well as many of their concerns. This new direction was behaviorism.

Behaviorism and Neobehaviorism

It is a mistake to suggest that all American psychology from 1910 through the 1950s was completely behaviorist. During this time, the fields of clinical, educational, and social psychology, to name a few, continued in their own development, pursuing their own agendas. In a sense, other branches of psychology developed parallel to behaviorism; they were contemporary fields with little contact or mutual influence. Furthermore, Leahey (2000) noted that there were significant changes within behaviorism itself, changes that eventually smoothed the transition to cognitive psychology; Leahey called it "mediated neobehaviorism," meaning that there were some unobservable, mediating variables included in neobehaviorism's theorizing. Nonetheless, experimental psychology traditionally has been the discipline of researchers concerned with learning, memory, perception, thought, and related topics. These psychologists, mostly in academic settings, were responsible for the birth and rearing of behaviorism and for its eventual dominance in American experimental psychology.

Everyone who has taken introductory psychology knows of John B. Watson, the early behaviorist who offered, "Give me a dozen healthy infants, well-formed, and my own specified world to bring them up in and I'll guarantee to take any one at random and train him to become any type of specialist I might select—doctor, lawyer, artist, merchant, chief and, yes, even beggarman and thief, regardless of the talents, penchants, tendencies, abilities, vocations, and race of his ancestors" (Watson, 1924, p. 104). Although Watson admitted in his very next sentence that he was exaggerating, he made it clear that he viewed experience as the primary factor in determining even the largest aspects of one's behavior. Rarely in the history of science has anyone taken so extreme a position on the nature versus nurture issue as Watson. (Histories of psychology note that this extreme position of "environmentalism" was not typical of his early, scholarly works but only of his later writings.)

Watson's firm belief, stated unequivocally in his 1913 "manifesto," was that observable, quantifiable behavior was the proper topic of psychology, not the fuzzy and unscientific concepts of thought, mind, and consciousness. He viewed attempts to understand the "unobservables" of mind and thought as inherently and hopelessly unscientific, and pointed to the unresolved debates in structuralism as evidence. Thus psychology was redefined as *the scientific study of observable behavior,* the program of **behaviorism**. There was no room here for hidden mental processes because behavioral laws were supposed to relate observable behavior to objective, observable stimulus conditions within the environment. To Watson, being a doctor was a matter of learning appropriate "doctor behaviors." No appeal to the mind, to innate abilities, or to mental activities was necessary, and no important limitations on the learning process were acknowledged.

Why did such a radical redefinition of psychology's interests have such broad appeal, gain so many adherents, and become so dominant? There is no doubt that part of the enthusiasm for a psychology of behavior was a result of the work that Pavlov and others were doing on conditioning and learning. Here was a definite, scientific approach that was going somewhere, in contrast to the seemingly endless debates in structuralism. (Strangely, Watson seems to have been unaware of Ebbinghaus' careful, empirical studies of learning and memory, work that even the dogmatic Titchener saw as valuable.) Furthermore, the measurement and quantification that accompanied behaviorism mirrored the already successful sciences such as physics. By modeling psychology on their methods and quantification, psychology might also gain acceptance as a true science as well (Leahey, 2000, calls this mentality "physics envy").

Beginning in the late 1890s, the new behaviorism attracted many practitioners and adherents (Leahey, 2000). In a very real sense, Watson's 1913 article was not a rallying cry but a final statement of behaviorist triumph. However, not all psychologists were eager to climb on this bandwagon. Naturally, some took an early wait-and-see attitude. For instance, Titchener's loyal student Edwin G. Boring, whose definitive book, *History of Experimental Psychology*, appeared in 1929, condescended in his preface that behaviorism was "as yet undignified by the least trace of antiquity." However, in his 1950 edition, Boring admitted that "for a while in the 1920s it seemed as if all America had gone behaviorist" (p. 645, although this admission is contained in a chapter somewhat pejoratively called "Behavioristics"). And other research traditions, especially the verbal learning tradition begun by Ebbinghaus, continued along as well. But these traditions were "second-class citizens" as behaviorism's emphasis on observable stimuli and responses came to dominate American experimental psychology. Two of behaviorism's greatest legacies to modern psychology were its emphasis on methodological rigor in its experiments and the reliance on observables, methodological traditions continued to this day.

This period of behaviorism and then neobehaviorism was one of inactivity for cognitive psychology. For instance, the word most commonly used to describe Watson is *antimentalistic*. Any concept or idea that smacked of mentalism, such as consciousness, memory, or mind, was to be excluded from psychology. This restriction in the scope of psychology, in hindsight, seems almost a willful blindness to the existence of obviously important phenomena. And it certainly produced some curious and convoluted explanations. For instance, because of the need to explain such ostensibly mental activities as thought and language in nonmentalistic terms, Watson developed the notion of implicit behavior. Implicit or covert behavior was said to be a reduced, inner version of the normally observable behavior that psychology investigated. Thus "thought" to Watson was "nothing more than subvocal talking or muscular habits learned in overt speech which become inaudible as we grow up" (Watson, 1968, p. 427).

Although a few psychologists continued to pursue cognitive topics—Bartlett of Great Britain is a notable example—the most visible part of American experimental psychology focused on observable, learned behaviors, especially in animals (but see Dewsbury, 2000, for the rich history of research on animal cognition during the behaviorist period). Even the decidedly cognitive approach of Tolman, whose article "Cognitive Maps in Rats and Men" (1948), a molar (as opposed to molecular) approach to behaviorism, is still worth reading, included much of the behaviorist tradition: concern with the learning of new behaviors, animal studies, and interpretation based closely on the observable stimuli in an experimental situation. Gestalt psychology, which emigrated to the United States in the 1930s (Mandler & Mandler, 1969), always maintained an interest in human perception, thought, and problem solving but never captured the loyalties of many American experimentalists (although we look back now at some of their research with greater respect).

Thus the behaviorist view continued to dominate American experimental psychology until the 1940s, when B. F. Skinner emerged as one of its most vocal, even extreme, advocates. Much in keeping with Watson's earlier sentiments, Skinner also argued that mental events such as thinking have no place in the science of psychology—not that they are not real, necessarily, but that they are unobservable and hence unnecessary to a scientific explanation of behavior.

Dissatisfaction with Behaviorism: The Winds of Change

As we saw earlier, it is difficult, if not impossible, to determine precisely when historical change takes place, when a movement or trend gains sufficient recognition to be proclaimed a *fait accompli.* 1879 saw the founding of academic, empirical psychology, yet we point to important research, and even to books with "psychology" in their titles, that predate 1879. Watson's 1913 article has been called the manifesto that instituted behaviorism, yet it is more properly viewed as the culmination of two decades of gradually shifting allegiances.

It is even more difficult to pinpoint historical change when it is recent. Many psychologists look kindly on the idea that there was a cognitive revolution in the mid- to late 1950s, an abrupt change in research activities, interests, and scientific beliefs on the part of experimentalists, a definitive break from the previously dominant behaviorism (Baars, 1986). However, several psychologists disagree; see Leahey (1992a, p. 458), who suspected that such talk was largely a kind of "radical chic" more appropriate to the 1960s. Regardless of the debate, it is indisputably true that the experimental psychology of today is quite different from that of the 1940s and 1950s. Psychology seemed to "lose its mind" during behaviorism's day in the sense that memory, thought, and other mental activities were largely ignored. Conversely, our psychology of today has "come back to its senses"—and to its memory and mental activities as well.

Because of the nature and scope of these changes, many psychologists regard the current cognitive approach as a revolution, a revolution in which behaviorism was rejected because of its lack of progress on—or even interest in—important questions. It was replaced with cognitive psychology and the information-processing approach. Lachman et al. (1979) provided an especially compelling account of the cognitive revolution from the standpoint of Kuhn's (1962) classic work on the history of science. However, some historians claim that the cognitive revolution was not a true scientific revolution at all but merely "rapid, evolutionary change" (see Leahey, 1992b, for this lively counterargument). In either case, the years from 1945 through 1960 were a period of crisis for American neobehaviorism and of rapid reform in the thinking and research of experimental psychologists. The serious challenges to neobehaviorism came both from within its own ranks and from outside, prodding psychologists toward the new direction to be taken.

CHALLENGES AND CHANGES: THE 1940S AND 1950S To neobehaviorism, the ultimate importance of learning—the acquisition of new behaviors by means of conditioning—was the central article of faith; learning *was* psychology. Although some behaviorists paid lip service to the notion of instincts, species-specific behaviors, and other nonlearned sorts of behavior, none of the important theories of learning gave serious consideration to these ideas. Speaking anthropomorphically, we find that the animal subjects often thumbed their noses at such theoretical purity and behaved according to their own laws. Researchers began finding significant instances in which conditioned behaviors, supposedly under the control of reinforced learning, began to change in the direction of instinctive behavior. For instance, "the Brelands found instances in which animals did not perform as they should. In 1961, they reported their difficulties in a paper whose title, 'The Misbehavior of Organisms,' puns on Skinner's first book, *The Behavior of Organisms.* For example, they tried to teach pigs to carry wooden coins and deposit them in a piggy bank (how cute!). Although they could teach behaviors, the Brelands found that the behavior degenerated in pig after pig. The animals would eventually pick up the coin, drop it on the ground and root it . . . [as if] 'trapped by strong instinctive behaviors' that overwhelm learned behaviors" (Leahey, 2000, p. 501). Garcia's work (Garcia, McGowan, & Green, 1972) on conditioned nausea led to similar conclusions. Rather than associating the current environment with beginning to feel sick, rats correctly associated the nausea with the fluid they'd drunk an hour earlier, a sensible instinctive outcome that contradicted behaviorism's laws.

For behaviorism, committed to the *tabula rasa* position that exalts learned behaviors, these were serious difficulties. No ready explanation by means of the principles of reinforced learning was available to account for instinctive drift or for the fact that the immediately present stimulus was less important than the fluid that actually induced nausea. Incorporating instincts into the theories would have been a blunt admission that the laws of conditioning and learning were not general, that they were modified by other overpowering, central factors. To make matters worse, Skinner asserted that a theory of behavior was not even necessary, finding theory building to be a distraction from the main business of gathering data. Such a position seemed to undermine the intense efforts that had been exerted in developing and testing theoretical positions such as Hull's (1943) and Tolman's (1948). What an unpleasant time to have been a behaviorist, beset by significant nonlearned behaviors, unresolvable theoretical disputes, and a position that asserted that theorizing was a waste of time!

WORLD WAR II Lachman et al. (1979) made an additional point about this growing dissatisfaction within the ranks of the neobehaviorists. They noted that many academic psychologists were involved with the U.S. war effort during World War II, in one capacity or another. Psychologists accustomed to studying animal learning in the laboratory were "put to work on the practical problems of making war . . . trying to understand problems of perception, judgment, thinking, and decision making" (p. 56). Many of these problems arose because of soldiers' difficulties with sophisticated technical devices: skilled pilots who crashed their aircraft, radar and sonar operators who failed to detect or misidentified enemy blips, and so on.

Lachman et al. (1979) were very direct in their description of this situation:

> *Where could psychologists turn for concepts and methods to help them solve such problems? Certainly not to the academic laboratories of the day. The behavior of animals in mazes and Skinner boxes shed little light on the performance of airplane pilots and sonar operators. The kind of learning studied with nonsense syllables contributed little to psychologists trying to teach people how to operate complex machines accurately. In fact, learning was not the central problem during the war. Most problems arose after the tasks had already been learned, when normally skillful performance broke down. The focus was on performance rather than learning; and this left academic psychologists poorly prepared.* (pp. 56–57)

As Bruner, Goodnow, and Austin (1956) put it, the "impeccable peripheralism" of stimulus–response (S–R) behaviorism became painfully obvious in the face of such practical concerns.

To deal with these practical concerns, wartime psychologists were forced to conceive of human behavior differently. The concepts of attention and vigilance, for instance, were important to an understanding of sonar operators' performance; experiments on the practical and then theoretical aspects of vigilance began (see especially Broadbent, 1958, Chapter 6, and Wickens, 1984, on the emergence of human factors as a distinct area of psychology). Decision making was a necessary part of this performance, too, and from these considerations came such developments as signal detection theory. These wartime psychologists rubbed shoulders with professionals from different fields—those in communications engineering, for instance, from whom new outlooks and perspectives on human behavior were gained. They had seen firsthand how empty the behaviorist toolbox was and how other approaches held promise for their own work. Thus these psychologists returned to their laboratories after the war determined to broaden their own research interests and those of psychology as well.

VERBAL LEARNING **Verbal learning** was *the branch of experimental psychology that dealt with humans as they learned verbal material, composed of letters, nonsense syllables, or sometimes words.* Earlier, the groundbreaking research of Hermann von Ebbinghaus was mentioned, in which objective methods for studying human memory were invented and used. This work started the verbal learning tradition within experimental psychology (see Chapter 6), which derives its name from the behaviorist context in which it found itself. Verbal learning was defined as the use of verbal materials in various learning paradigms. Even casual examination of published articles during the 1920s and 1930s reveals a fairly large body of verbal learning research, with reasonably well-established methods and procedures. Tasks such as serial learning, paired-associate learning, and to an extent free recall were the accepted methods of investigation, using Ebbinghaus-inspired nonsense syllables.

Verbal learners held many beliefs similar to the behaviorists. For example, verbal learners agreed on the need to use objective methods; although an occasional allusion to introspections was made, this was usually in the sense that they "confirmed" the conclusions drawn from more objective measures. There also was widespread acceptance of the central role of learning, conceived as a process of forming new associations, much like the learning of new associations by a rat in a Skinner box. From this perspective, a theoretical framework was built that proposed a number of concepts that are widely accepted today. For example, a great deal of verbal learning was oriented around providing accounts of interference among related but competing items that had been learned in the experiment. They were "behavior*alists*," in Leahey's (1992b) description, committed to the methods of observing behavior but not bound to the "empty organism" view of radical behaviorism.

Lachman et al. argued that this more moderate view in verbal learning circles made it easy for psychologists to accept the new cognitive psychology of the 1950s and 1960s: There were many indications in their results that an adequate psychology of human learning and memory needed more than just observable behaviors. For instance, the presence of meaningfulness in almost any "nonsense" syllable had been acknowledged early on; Glaze (1928) titled his paper "The Association Value of Nonsense Syllables" (and apparently did so with a straight face). At first, such irksome associations were controlled for in the experiments, to avoid contamination of the results. Later, it became apparent that the memory processes that yielded those associations were more interesting to study than to control. Hall (1971) called this the "new look" in verbal learning, with its greater emphasis on memory rather than on learning processes.

In this tradition, Bousfield (1953; Bousfield & Sedgewick, 1944) reported that, under free recall instructions, words that were associated with one another (e.g., *car* and *truck*) tended to cluster together in recall, even though they had been arranged randomly in the stimulus list. In this research, there was clearly the implication that existing memory associations led to the reorganization of the words during recall. Such obvious evidence of processes occurring between the stimulus and the response—in other words, mental processes—led verbal learning to propose a variety of mental operations such as rehearsal, organization, storage, and retrieval.

Another outstanding achievement of the verbal learning tradition was the derivation and refinement of laboratory tasks for learning and memory that remain useful today. In acceptance of the need for objective procedures and methods, the verbal learners borrowed from Ebbinghaus' example of careful attention to rigorous methodology. From this they developed tasks that seem to measure the outcomes of mental processes in valid and useful ways. Some of these tasks were more closely associated with behaviorism than others, such as the paired-associate learning task.

Because these tasks lent themselves to tests of S–R associations in seemingly direct ways, they became somewhat overused. (Some have noted the popularity of the paired-associate task and the verbal learners' tendency to study performance on the task rather than the principles of human memory revealed by the task. One of our professors likened this situation to "an archaeologist who studies his shovel.") Nonetheless, verbal learning gave cognitive psychology an objective, reliable methodology for studying mental processes; research that was built upon later (e.g., Stroop, 1935); and a set of inferred processes such as storage and retrieval to investigate. Therefore, the influence of verbal learning on cognitive psychology, as shown in Figure 1-1, was almost entirely positive.

LINGUISTICS The changes in verbal learning from its early work to around 1960 seem to have been a gradual evolutionary shifting of interests and interpretations that blended almost seamlessly into cognitive psychology. In sharp contrast, 1959 saw the publication of an explicit, defiant challenge to behaviorism. Watson's 1913 article has been called a behaviorist manifesto, crystallizing the view against introspective methods and those who practiced them. To an equal degree, Noam Chomsky's 1959 article was a cognitive manifesto, an utter rejection of purely behaviorist explanation of the most human of all behaviors: language.

A bit of background is needed to appreciate the significance of Chomsky's article (see Leahey's Chapter 14, titled "Years of Turmoil," for an amplified version of this story). In 1957, B. F. Skinner published a book titled *Verbal Behavior*, a treatment of human language from the radical behaviorist standpoint of reinforcement, stimulus–response associations, extinction, and so on. His central point was that the psychology of learning, that is, the conditioning of new behavior by means of reinforcement, provided a useful and scientific account of human language. In oversimplified terms, Skinner's basic notion was that human language, "verbal behavior," followed the same laws of learning that had been discovered in the animal learning laboratory: A reinforced response is expected to increase in frequency, a nonreinforced response should extinguish, a response conditioned to a certain stimulus should be emitted to the same stimulus in the future, and so on. In principle then, human language, obviously a learned behavior, could be explained by the same sort of mechanism, with knowledge of the current reinforcement contingencies and past reinforcement history of the individual.

Noam Chomsky, a linguist at the Massachusetts Institute of Technology, reviewed Skinner's book in the journal *Language* in 1959. The very first sentence of his review notes that many linguists and philosophers of language "expressed the hope that their studies might ultimately be embedded in a framework provided by behaviorist psychology" and therefore were interested in Skinner's formulation. Chomsky alluded to Skinner's optimism that the problem of verbal behavior would yield to behavioral analysis because the reinforcement principles discovered in the animal laboratory "are now fairly well understood . . . [and] can be extended to human behavior without serious modification" (Skinner, 1957, cited in Chomsky, 1959, p. 26).

But by the third page of his review, Chomsky stated that "the insights that have been achieved in the laboratories of the reinforcement theorist, though quite genuine, can be applied to complex human behavior only in the most gross and superficial way.

Noam Chomsky

. . . The magnitude of the failure of [Skinner's] attempt to account for verbal behavior serves as a kind of measure of the importance of the factors *omitted* from consideration" (p. 28, emphasis added). The fighting words continued. Chomsky asserted that if the critical terms *stimulus, response, reinforcement,* and so on are used in their technical, animal laboratory sense, then "the book covers almost no aspect of linguistic behavior" (p. 31) of interest. His central theme was that Skinner's account used the technical terms in a nontechnical, metaphorical way, which "creates the illusion of a rigorous scientific theory [but] is no more scientific than the traditional approaches to this subject matter, and rarely as clear and careful" (pp. 30–31).

To illustrate his criticism, Chomsky noted the careful operational definitions that Skinner provided in the animal learning laboratory, such as for the term *reinforcement.* But unlike the distinct and observable pellet of food in the Skinner box, Skinner claimed that reinforcement for human verbal behavior could even be administered by the person exhibiting the behavior, that is, self-reinforcement. In some cases, Skinner continued, reinforcement could be delayed for indefinite periods or never be delivered at all, as in the case of a writer who anticipates that her work may gain her fame for centuries to come. When an explicit and immediate reinforcer in the laboratory, along with its effect on behavior, is generalized to include nonexplicit and nonimmediate (and even nonexistent) reinforcers in the real world, it truly does seem, as Chomsky argued, that Skinner had brought along the vocabulary of a scientific explanation but left the substance behind. As Chomsky bluntly put it, "A mere terminological revision, in which a term borrowed from the laboratory is used with the full vagueness of the ordinary vocabulary, is of no conceivable interest" (p. 38). The explanation was merely dogmatic, not at all scientific.

Chomsky's own position on language, emphasizing the novelty of human language and the internal rules for language use, is discussed in Chapter 9; there, the influence of linguistics on cognitive psychology (Figure 1-1) is described in some detail. For now, the essential message involves the impact of Chomsky's review on experimental psychology (not to mention the impact on linguistics itself; see Wasow, 1989). As Lachman et al. (1979) note, this dispute could not easily be dismissed. Language *was* an important behavior—and a learned one at that—to be understood by psychology. A dominant approach that offered no help in understanding this was useless, not to mention embarrassing.

To a significant number of people, Chomsky's arguments summarized the dissatisfactions with behaviorism that had become so apparent. For these people, the irrelevance of behaviorism to the study of language, and, by extension, the study of any significant human behavior, was now painfully obvious. In combination with the other developments, the wartime fling with mental processes, the expansion of the catalog of such processes by verbal learning, and the disarray within behaviorism itself, it was clear that the new direction for psychology, growing in influence throughout the 1950s, would take hold.

Section Summary

- The modern history of cognitive psychology began in 1879 with Wundt and the beginnings of experimental psychology as a science.
- The behaviorist movement rejected the use of introspections and substituted the study of observable behavior.
- Modern cognitive psychology, which dates from approximately 1960, rejected much of the behaviorist position but accepted its methodological rigor. Many diverse viewpoints, assumptions, and methods converged to help form cognitive psychology, including those from verbal learning, linguistics, and computer science. This was at least a rapid, evolutionary change in interests, if not a true scientific revolution.

COGNITIVE PSYCHOLOGY AND INFORMATION PROCESSING

The New Direction

If we had to pick a date that marks the beginning of cognitive psychology, we might pick 1960. This is not to say that significant developments in the study of cognition were not present before this date, for they were. This is also not to say that most experimental psychologists who studied humans became cognitive psychologists that year, for they did not. As with any major change, it takes a while for the new approach to catch on, for people to learn the new rules, to feel free to speak the new language, and, indeed, to decide that the new direction is worth following (some decided it was not worth following; see Skinner, 1984, 1990, for example). Several significant events clustered around 1960, however, events we look back on from our period of hindsight as having been significant departures from the mainstream that came before. Just as 1879 is considered the formal beginning of psychology and 1913 the beginning of behaviorism, so 1960 seems to approximate the beginning of cognitive psychology in its modern form.[2]

Let's pick up the threads of what came before this date, to see what the new cognitive psychology and information processing approaches were all about. One of the most significant threads was Chomsky's 1959 review; such a forceful argument against a purely behaviorist position could not be—and was not—ignored. Chomsky argued that the truly interesting part of human language, indeed the very key to understanding it, was exactly what Skinner had omitted from his book: mental processes and cognitive structures. Chomsky also argued that language users follow rules when they

[2]Gardner (1985, p. 28) stated, "There has been nearly unanimous agreement among the surviving principals that cognitive science was officially recognized around 1956. The psychologist George A. Miller ... has even fixed the date, 11 September 1956." Miller recalled a conference from September 10 to 12, 1956, at MIT, attended by leading researchers in communication and psychology. On the second day of the conference, there were papers by Newell and Simon on the "Logic Theory Machine," by Chomsky on his theory of grammar and linguistic transformations, and by Miller himself on the capacity limitations of short-term memory. Others whom Gardner cited suggest that, at a minimum, the five-year period 1955 to 1960 was the critical time during which cognitive psychology emerged as a distinct and new approach. By analogy to psychology's selection of 1879 as the starting date for the whole discipline, 1960 is special in Gardner's analysis: In that year, Jerome Bruner and George Miller founded the Center for Cognitive Studies at Harvard University.

generate language, rules that are stored in memory, cognitive structures operated on by mental processes. The so-called empty organism psychology of stimulus–response connections was empty in the sense that behaviorists did not deal with properties of the organism that come between the physical stimulus and the behavioral response. In Chomsky's view, it was exactly there, *in* the organism, that the key to understanding language would be found.

To a large extent, researchers in verbal learning and other fields were making the same claim. As noted, Bousfield (1953) found that people cluster or group words together on the basis of the associations among them. Memory and a tendency to reorganize on the part of the person clearly were involved in this performance. Where were these associations? Where was this memory? And where was this tendency to reorganize? They were in the person, of course, in human memory and mental processes. A particularly clear statement of the involvement of a person's mental processes appeared in Tulving's 1962 article, "Subjective Organization in Free Recall of 'Unrelated' Words." Even when the words to be learned were unrelated, people still reorganized them, a strategy for recall that was clearly coming from within.

During the 1950s, there were reports on human attention, first from British researchers such as Cherry and Broadbent, that were thematically related to the wartime concern with attention and vigilance. Again, fascinating attention and perceptual processes were being isolated and investigated, processes whose unseen, mental nature could not be denied and yet whose existence could not be denied either. A classic paper in this area, Sperling's monograph on visual sensory memory, appeared in 1960. (MacLeod, 1992, noted that there was a marked increase around 1960 in citations to the rediscovered Stroop [1935] task.)

Possibly the single most startling development of this period, certainly in terms of its impact on society, was the invention of the modern digital computer. Initial work had begun in the 1930s and 1940s on what we now call computer science, although philosophers had conceived of such a machine in general terms long before the technology existed to build one (e.g., Haugeland, 1985). At some point during the 1950s, a few psychologists realized the possible relevance of computing to issues in psychology. It dawned on psychology, in a sense, that in some interesting and possibly useful ways, computers behave much like people (not surprising, according to Norman, 1986, p. 534, because "the architecture of the modern digital computer . . . was heavily influenced by people's naive view of how the mind operated"). They take in information, do something with it internally, then eventually produce some observable product. The product gives clues to what went on during the internal phase. The various operations performed by the computer were not unknowable merely because they occurred internally. They were under the direct control of the computer program, the instructions given to the machine to tell it what operations to perform.

The realization that human mental activity might be understood by analogy to the seemingly intelligent (or at least intelligent-acting) machine was a significant breakthrough. The computer provided an existence proof for the idea that unobservable processes could be reliably studied and understood. Especially important was the notion of symbols and their internal manipulation. That is, the computer is a symbol-manipulating machine; its operation involves interpreting the symbols fed to it in the computer program, then performing the operations that those symbols specify. The insight that the human mind might also be fruitfully considered as a symbol-manipulating system usually is attributed to Allen Newell and Herbert Simon. According to Lachman et al. (1979), their conference in 1958 had a tremendous impact on those who attended, for at this conference Newell and Simon presented an explicit analogy between information processing in the computer and information processing in humans. This important work, probably as much as anything Simon did in the field of economics, was the basis for the Nobel Prize awarded to him in 1978 (see Leahey, 2003, for a full account of Simon's contributions).

Among the many indirect results of this conference was the 1960 publication of a book by Miller, Galanter, and Pribram called *Plans and the Structure of Behavior.* The book suggested that human problem solving could be understood as a kind of planning in which mental strategies or plans guide behavior toward its eventual goal. Why was this book viewed as a scientific contribution, involving as it did such mentalistic ideas as plans, goals, and strategies? Because the mentalistic plans, goals, and strategies were not just unobservable, hypothetical ideas. Instead, they were ideas that in principle could be exactly specified, in a program running on a lawful, physical device: the computer. (We will have much more to say about computers and computer models of cognition throughout the book.)

The Assumptions of Cognitive Psychology

We turn finally to three assumptions that pervade cognitive psychology: that mental processes exist, that they can be studied scientifically, and that people are active information processors.

MENTAL PROCESSES EXIST Surely by now you have figured out the single most defining feature of cognitive psychology: a scientific interest in human mental activity and processes. Whereas the behaviorists intentionally avoided any theorizing about the higher mental processes, these processes are exactly what cognitive psychology investigates. Our most basic assumption in cognitive psychology is that mental processes exist, that they are absolutely key to a complete, useful psychology.

MENTAL PROCESSES CAN BE STUDIED SCIENTIFICALLY Not only do mental processes exist, but their very reality means that they are an appropriate topic for scientific inquiry. That is, we believe that an objective, scientific study of mental processes can be accomplished and is exactly the province of the science of psychology. In science, saying that a phenomenon or effect exists in physical reality is basically the same as saying that it can be studied by the objective, quantifiable methods of scientific practice. By saying that mental processes exist, we are also claiming that they are lawful, systematic events and that they can be studied.

We are very mindful of the checkered history of investigations into the higher mental processes. We fault the structuralists, such as Wundt and Titchener, not for their interests but for their methods. Our biggest lesson from the behaviorist era, and also from the example set by verbal learning, was about scientific methods and procedures. Unlike the structuralists, cognitive psychology relies on measures of behavior that are as objective and reliable as possible. That is, we attempt to unravel the complex questions of mental activity with tasks and measures of behavior that are quantifiable, open to scientific scrutiny, easily replicated by other investigators, and faithful to the scientific empirical tradition. As best we can, we avoid measures that are colored by subjective bias or influence, as the old introspectionism was.

ACTIVE INFORMATION PROCESSORS A third basic assumption, implied by the first two, is the idea that humans are active participants in the act of cognition. Miller (cited in Pylyshyn, 1984) called us *informavores,* beings that actively obtain and process information (in fact, Miller was referring to all information-processing systems by that term, even the kind built with silicon chips). The behaviorist, in contrast, viewed the subject as a largely passive creature, one who waited around for a stimulus to occur, then responded to it in ways determined by previous conditioning and current stimulus conditions.

Cognitive psychology rejects this behaviorist outlook. We believe that humans actively process the stimuli around them, selecting some parts of that environment for further processing, relating those selected parts to information already stored in memory, and then doing something as a result of processing. And if no external stimulation is present, we occupy ourselves with internal, mental stimulation. (To prove the point, try this: Stop reading for a moment and try to keep your mind completely inactive and blank for a full minute—no thoughts, recollections, or even daydreams.)

We believe that people do not passively respond on the basis of simple conditioning or reinforcement. Instead, people respond actively on the basis of their mental processing of events and information. And, as you saw in the examples at the beginning of the chapter, an enormous amount of mental activity can underlie even very simple question answering. All this mental processing is evidence of the active nature of people and their cognitive processes.

These three features form the core of cognitive psychology: our assumptions that human mental activities exist, that those activities can be studied scientifically, and that the person doing the relevant mental activities is an active information processor. These ideas have a *metatheoretical* status in cognitive psychology. That is, they are above and beyond any particular theory of cognitive processes; they are so central to our discipline that they are assumed to be true. It is the various implications drawn from them that are tested in our experiments.

Section Summary

- The three most basic assumptions of cognitive psychology are that mental processes exist, they can be studied scientifically, and humans are active information processors.

Key Terms

behaviorism (p. *17*)
cognition (p. *9*)
cognitive science (p. *2*)
ecological validity (p. *10*)
empiricism (p. *13*)
functionalism (p. *16*)
introspection (p. *14*)
memory (p. *9*)
reductionism (p. *10*)
structuralism (p. *15*)
tabula rasa (p. *13*)
verbal learning (p. *21*)

CHAPTER

2

The Cognitive Science Approach

The basic reason for studying cognitive processes has become as clear as the reason for studying anything else: because they are there. . . . Cognitive processes surely exist, so it can hardly be unscientific to study them.

NEISSER, 1967, p. 5

There is no evidence that the human LTM [long-term memory] is fillable in a lifetime, or that there is a limit on the number of distinguishable symbols it can store. Hence, we assume that the IPS [Information Processing System] has a potentially infinite vocabulary of symbols, and an essentially infinite capacity for symbol structures.

NEWELL & SIMON, 1972, pp. 19–20, 792

A basic tenet of cognitive psychology was the computer analogy for the mind: the mind is to the brain as software is to hardware in a computer. . . . The problem with the computer analogy is that hardware and software are independent only for very special types of computational systems. . . systems that have been engineered. . . to make [them] independent. . . . The brain was "designed" by very different pressures. . . . As cognitive psychologists finally began to learn about neuropsychology, it became apparent that cognitive functions break down in characteristic and highly informative ways after brain damage.

FEINBERG & FARAH, 1997, p. 15

This chapter, like the first, is largely introductory. In Chapter 1 you got a general idea of what cognitive psychology is all about, and you read a bit of its history. The purpose was to make cognitive psychology a living, breathing thing for you—not some obscure, academic quest that only PhDs can be interested in but a dynamic and vibrant approach to questions of human memory and thought. We tried to give you some of the flavor of the field and a sense of the excitement cognitive psychologists feel for their topic by describing some of the shouting matches that gave birth to cognitive psychology. A student 40 or 50 years ago, fired with curiosity about how memory works, would have been sent off to study retroactive interference, paired-associate learning, and serial position curves. The same student today is sent off to study human reasoning, language comprehension, memory disruptions in stroke victims, and so forth. This is certainly a more rewarding set of questions to study; there *has* been progress (Simon, 1992).

GUIDING PRINCIPLES

Nonetheless, it is also true that these newer questions and interests often are difficult to pin down in a scientific fashion. The practitioners of a science need more than just the questions to decide what experiments ought to be done and how they ought to do them. In particular, scientists need a framework to guide them, a set of assumptions that tells them where to start, what to look for, what to beware of. This general framework sometimes is called a **metatheory**, where *meta* means above or beyond. A metatheory is this *set of assumptions and guiding principles,* a kind of Michelin guide that helps us find our way through unknown territory.

To a large extent, cognitive psychology's Michelin guide or metatheory for many years was the **information-processing approach**. This broadly defined approach described cognition as *the coordinated operation of active mental processes within a multicomponent memory system*. The human information-processing system that was described was a general model of human memory and cognition. Originally, the term *information processing* had a rather narrow connotation, one that emphasized a one-by-one sequence of mental operations in which one operation was assumed to end before another could begin. You will read about this strict approach and how it generated some important discoveries and ideas. You will also read about its drawbacks and limitations and how these led to the broader, less restrictive approaches of contemporary cognitive science. We'll talk a bit about the cognitive science approach and how some of the themes you will encounter in a moment fit into that approach.

A big part of that new cognitive science approach—the new look of cognitive science—is its multidisciplinary nature, the way it has opened up to ideas and discoveries from other research views. This is most dramatically illustrated by the influential role now played by neuroscience. 15 or 20 years ago, a cognitive psychologist could get along reasonably well—do important research, teach useful classes—with little knowledge of the human brain structure and functioning. But now a wealth of new information is available about cognition and the brain—how cognitive processes are implemented in the brain, how brain damage in selected regions affects our mental processes, and how this evidence tells us a great deal about normal cognition. This evidence is especially dependent on several high-tech methods of brain imaging, methods originally developed for medical use. We will spend some time talking about the anatomy and functioning of the brain to prepare you to appreciate this important new evidence.

THEMES

As we work through the various approaches, we will start to see themes that appear repeatedly across topics. Some of these themes have been important from the beginning of modern cognitive psychology or even the beginning of psychology in 1879; attention is an excellent example here. Others appeared later, augmenting and elaborating some of the early cognitive models you will study; the distinction between implicit and explicit memory is a good example. Finally, some have only recently been appreciated as relevant and useful and are still working their way through our research methods and approaches; the neuroscience contributions are the best example. You won't find sections throughout this book labeled with the themes. Instead, the themes crop up across several areas of cognitive science, in several different contexts. If you can read a chapter and identify and discuss the themes that pertain to it, then you probably have a good understanding of the material. As a preview, see Table 2-1 for a list and brief description of seven particularly important themes that we'll encounter throughout the book. ▲

MEASURING INFORMATION PROCESSES

Getting Started

Gernsbacher told of an illustration she encountered in a cognitive psychology course (which we in turn paraphrase here); call it "the factory question." You are looking at a factory from a distant hill. You can't see into the factory, and you can't go inside either. Your task is to figure out what happens in the factory, what the factory does, and how it does it (Robertson & Gernsbacher, 1999).

TABLE 2-1 Seven Themes of Cognition

Attention	This is an all-important but poorly understood mental process. It is limited in quantity, essential to most processing, but only partially under our control. Is it a mechanism? A limited pool of mental resources? If attention controls mental processing, what controls attention? Why do some processes occur automatically, whereas others require conscious attentive processing?
Data-driven versus conceptually driven processing	Some processing relies heavily on the information we get from the environment (data-driven or bottom-up processing). Other processes rely heavily on our existing knowledge (conceptually driven or top-down processing). Conceptually driven processing can be so powerful that we often make errors, from mistakes in perception up through mistakes in reasoning. But could we function without it?
Representation	How is information represented in memory? Can the different kinds of knowledge we have in memory all be formatted in the same mental code, or are there separate codes for the different types of knowledge?
Implicit versus explicit memory	We have direct and explicit awareness of certain types of memories; you remember the experience of buying this textbook, for example. But some memories or memory processes are implicit; they are there but not necessarily with conscious awareness. This raises all sorts of interesting issues about the unconscious and its role in cognition; for instance, can an unconscious process affect your behavior and thinking?
Metacognition	This is awareness of our own cognitive system and knowledge and insight into its workings. It is the awareness that prompts us to write reminders to ourselves to avoid forgetting something. But is this awareness and knowledge completely accurate? Does it sometimes mislead us?
Brain	Far more than the cognitive psychology of the past, brain–cognition relationships and questions concern us now. How and where a fact is stored in the brain are very different questions from how and where the fact is stored in memory, with radically different answers appropriate to each question. And yet neuroscience and cognitive sciences are becoming more and more mutually relevant and influential. Will all of psychology eventually evolve into biology and neuroscience?
Embodiment	An emerging awareness in cognitive psychology is that the way we think about and represent information reflects the fact that we need to interact with the world—it's called "embodied cognition." How do we capture the world in our mental life? How do the ways that our bodies interact with the world influence our thinking? How do we incorporate and take into account physical realities in how we think about and process information?

One approach to the question is to watch what comes into the factory, to try to figure out what happens inside; if wood is delivered, then the factory might make furniture but probably doesn't manufacture cars. Another is to watch what comes out; if it's boxes of cereal, you are in a better position to guess what happens in the factory than if the output is small metal things. Better than either of these methods is to watch both what comes in and what goes out, trying to make some kind of connection between the two.

More active, probing methods of answering the question might work, too. For example, consider what might happen to the factory's output if you disrupted the arriving supplies in some way, say by slowing down their delivery. Would fewer outputs be produced in this situation? Would the factory's output be of lower quality? Or would the factory stop producing outputs altogether? What would happen if you doubled the inputs per unit of time? If the outputs didn't double, too, then you might decide there was some internal limitation in the factory in terms of rate of production.

Cognitive psychology is faced with the same kind of problem you face in the factory example; indeed, this is the same problem we have always faced when wondering about how the mind works. Another way of casting the problem of cognitive psychology is that it is trying to reverse engineer the brain in much the same way that engineers reverse engineer devices that they can't get into. Putting it simply, we want to know: What happens in there? What happens in the mind—or in the brain, if you prefer—when we perceive, remember, reason, and solve problems? How can we peer into the mind to get a glimpse of the mental processes that operate so invisibly? What methods can we use, analogous to what you might do to answer the factory question, to obtain some scientific evidence on mental processes?

Time and Accuracy Measures

The question of how we peer into the mind to investigate mental processes boils down to a question of measurement: How do we measure mental processes in a scientifically acceptable way? Are there aspects of these otherwise unseen, unobservable mental events that *are* observable, that *can* be measured? You read in Chapter 1 about Wundt's method of introspection. What methods did the newly reborn cognitive psychology of the 1950s and 1960s use to overcome the problems Wundt and his followers encountered?

Of the four general types of measures used by cognitive science, two have been particularly common ways of obtaining the scientific evidence we seek, the *time* it takes to perform some task and the *accuracy* of that performance. Because these measures, both dating back to the 1800s, are so pervasive, it is important to discuss them here at the outset. (The other two types, verbal reports and neuropsychological evidence, are discussed later in the chapter.)

RESPONSE TIME Many research programs in cognitive psychology place a heavy reliance on measures such as **response time (RT)**, *a measure of the time elapsed between some stimulus and the person's response to the stimulus* (RT is typically measured in milliseconds, abbreviated *ms;* a millisecond is a thousandth of a second). Why is a time-based measure so important, especially when the actual time differences can be so small, say, on the order of 40 to 50 ms? (By the way, the term "reaction time" is equivalent to "response time.")

Consider the following reasons. It has been known for a long time that individual differences among people often can be revealed by RT measures. In 1868 Dutch physiologist Donders (1868/1969) pointed out that the measure is potentially much more informative than this, in a proposal for studying the "Speed of Mental Processes" by means of RT. A moment's reflection reveals why cognitive psychology uses response time measures so frequently: *Mental events take time.* That's an important statement—

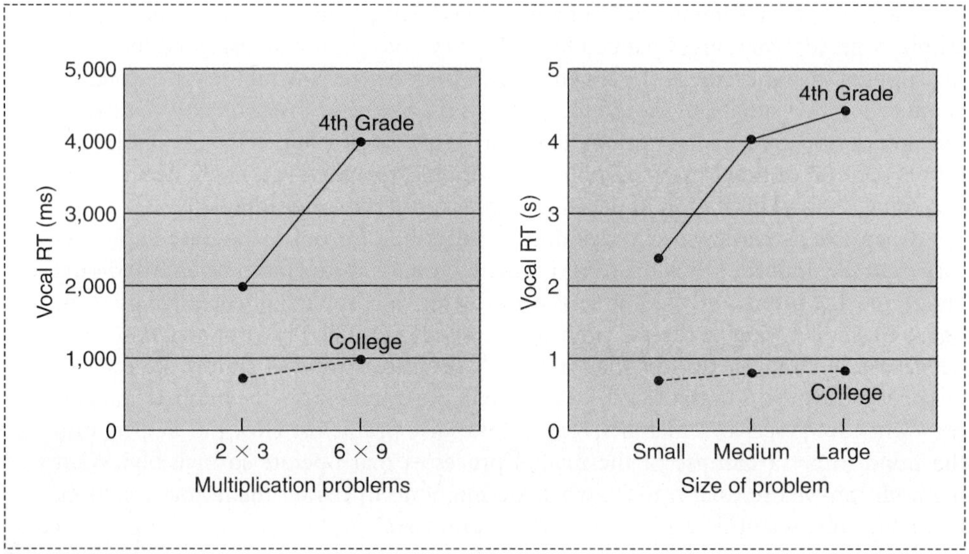

FIGURE 2-1
Vocal response times (RTs) to multiplication problems. Data from Campbell & Graham (1985).

the mental processes and events we want to understand occur in real time and can be studied by measuring how long they take. Given this, it is no surprise that a preferred method of "peering into the head" is to examine how long a certain set of mental processes takes to be completed. As Donders and many others have observed, careful comparisons of people's RTs to different stimuli can often give a strong clue to the mental processes going on internally.

Here's an example of the kind of reasoning that can flow from measuring RTs. An area of research known as mathematical cognition investigates how we store mathematical knowledge in memory and how that knowledge is applied in various tasks. Consider two simple arithmetic problems, such as $2 \times 3 = ?$ and $6 \times 9 = ?$ The left panel of Figure 2-1 shows the time it took a sample of fourth-graders and a sample of college adults to solve these problems (Campbell & Graham, 1985). The figure shows two important effects: an obvious age difference in which young children were slower than adults and an effect related to the problems, longer RT for 6×9 than for 2×3. The right panel of the figure shows comparable functions for the entire range of multiplication problems, from small problems such as 2×3 to medium (e.g., 7×3) and large (e.g., 6×9) problems. For both age groups, the curves increase as the size of the problems increases, commonly known as the problem size effect (e.g., Stazyk, Ashcraft, & Hamann, 1982).

Think of the basic assumption again: Mental processes take time. The implication here is that greater elapsed time is evidence that some process or subprocess took longer in one case than in the other. What could account for that? Most adults would agree that 6×9 is harder than 2×3, but that by itself is not a very useful observation; of course a harder decision will take longer to make. But why would 6×9 be harder? After all, we learned our multiplication facts in grade school. Haven't we had sufficient experience since then to equalize all the basic facts, to make them pretty much the same in difficulty? Apparently not.

So what might account for the increase in RT? It is unlikely that it takes longer to perceive the numbers in a larger problem—and also unlikely that it takes longer to start articulating the answer once you have figured it out. On the other hand, another possibility is that smaller problems have some kind of advantage in memory, perhaps something to do with knowing them better or being more certain about their answers. This might even result from an advantage dating back to grade school that somehow persisted into adulthood, such as the fact that arithmetic problems with smaller numbers (from 2 to 4) occur much more frequently in grade school textbooks than large ones (Ashcraft & Christy, 1995; Clapp, 1924). Another possibility is that smaller problems are easier to figure out or compute in a variety of ways. Aside from simply remembering that 2 × 3 is 6, you could also count up by 2s or 3s easily and rapidly. But counting up by 6s or 9s would take much longer and be much more error prone (LeFevre et al., 1996).

The point here is not to explain exactly why one kind of problem takes longer to solve than another (see Ashcraft, 1995, or Geary, 1994). Instead, the point is to show how much more focused and interesting our questions about mental processing can be when we use time-based measures. (For a different but very powerful use of time measurements, see the section of Chapter 10 on reading and research that simply records how long your eyes gaze at the individual words on the page.)

ACCURACY All of cognitive psychology's research is not based solely on RT measures. Often we are interested in some measure of people's accuracy, broadly defined. Sometimes we simply note which words a person recalled correctly and which were omitted. The earliest use of accuracy as a measure of mental processes was the seminal work by Ebbinghaus, published in 1885. As you will read in Chapter 6, Ebbinghaus compared correct recall of information in a second learning session with recall of the same material during original learning as a way of measuring how much material had been saved in memory.

◆ Figure 2-2 shows a classic serial position curve, a graph showing the percentage of items correctly recalled, plotted on the *x*-axis against each item's original position in the list. In this particular experiment (Glanzer & Cunitz, 1966), the items in the list were shown one at a time, and participants had to wait either 0, 10, or 30 s before they were allowed to recall the items. Making it even more difficult, the delay interval was filled with counting backward by 3s (see Chapter 5 for details). In this situation, it is clear that the participants' memory of the items was influenced by its initial position in the list—recall was much higher for early items than for those in the middle of the list. And notice the big effect that delaying recall with backward counting had at the late positions.

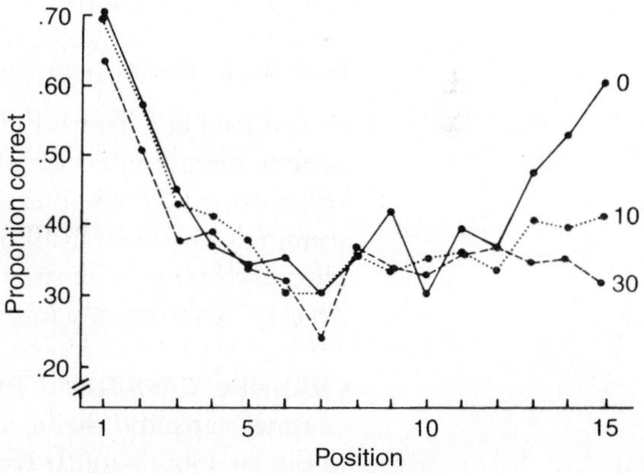

◆ **FIGURE 2-2**
Serial position curves, showing the decrease in accuracy at the end of the list when 0, 10, or 30 s of backward counting intervenes between study and recall.

Clearly, we cannot conclude that early list positions *always* had an advantage over late list positions—look how accurately the very last items were recalled when there was no delay interval. Instead, the bowed shape of the curve tells us something more complex and diagnostic about memory: Maybe recalling the items from the end of the list depends on a different kind of memory than recalling the early words, and maybe that memory that can be disrupted by activity-filled delays.

More modern variations on simple list-learning tasks look not only at percentage correct on a list, but also at the incorrect responses, such as looking at any recalled words that were not on the studied list (these are called *intrusions*). Did the person remember a related word such as *apple* rather than the exact word that was studied, *pear?* Was an item recalled because it resembles the target stimulus in some other way, such as remembering *G* instead of *D* when a string of letters was studied? Of course, this approach is similar to the Piagetian tradition of examining children's errors in reasoning, such as failure to conserve quantity or number, to examine their cognitive processes.

In more complex situations, the term *accuracy* takes on even richer connotations. For instance, if we ask people to read and paraphrase a paragraph, we do not score the paraphrase according to verbatim criteria (although the lack of verbatim memory is interesting in its own right). Instead, we score the paraphrase based on its meaning, on how well it preserves the ideas and relationships of the original. Preserving the gist, the overall idea, is something our memories do rather well according to most of the research findings (e.g., Neisser, 1981). Remembering exact, verbatim wording, on the other hand, is something we seldom do well at all, perhaps because we often don't need to remember this level of detail. Although accuracy and inaccuracy in paraphrases can be a bit harder to pin down than simple recall of lists, they can be especially informative about memory processes (see Chapter 8).

Guiding Analogies

As you read in Chapter 1, a growing number of psychologists in the 1940s and 1950s became disenchanted with behaviorism. It simply seemed too narrow and exclusionary to cope with complex human behavior and performance. During this time, the seemingly unrelated fields of communications engineering and computer science supplied psychology with some intriguing ideas and useful analogies that were central to developing the human information-processing approach.

CHANNEL CAPACITY To highlight just one, psychologists found the issue of **channel capacity** useful, a concept borrowed from communications engineering (a similar, more popular term would be *bandwidth*). In the design of a telephone communication system, for instance, one of the built-in limitations is that *any channel—any physical device that transmits messages or information—has a limited capacity*. In simple terms, one telephone wire can carry just so many messages at the same time and loses information if the capacity is exceeded. Naturally, communications engineers tried to design equipment and techniques to get around these built-in limitations, thereby increasing the overall capacity of a channel.

At some point, psychologists noticed that, in several important ways, humans could be thought of as limited-capacity channels, too. After all, there does seem to be a limit on how many things you can do, or think about, at a time. Maybe we are like transmitters of information, with a built-in limitation in the amount of information we can handle simultaneously. This insight lent a fresh perspective to human experimental psychology. Suddenly it made sense to ask questions such as: How many sources of information can humans pay attention to at one time? What information is lost if we overload the human system? Where is the limitation, and can we overcome it? We discuss some of this research and thinking in several chapters, especially those dealing with perception, attention, and short-term memory. For now, it's enough to say that this pollination of ideas from communications engineering helped the budding cognitive psychology determine its new approaches and directions.

THE COMPUTER ANALOGY Even more influential than the "message" that psychology received from communications engineering was the "input" from computer science. Although the limited-capacity channel idea is important (actually, in its current form, the idea of limited attention is extremely important, as you'll see in Chapters 4 and 5), it is just one part of the general information-processing approach to human performance. Computer science, on the other hand, developed a machine that in many ways seemed to reflect the very essence of the human mental system. This machine, in its own way, seemed to do many of the things that humans do, things that cognitive psychologists very much wanted to understand. Because those things are unseen when both computers and humans do them, there was good reason for drawing *the computer analogy* to human cognition. Basically, this analogy said that human information processing may be similar to the steps and operations in a computer program, similar to the flow of information from input to output when a computer processes information. If this is true, then thinking about how a computer accomplishes various tasks might give us some useful insights into how humans process information.

There is at least one more reason for our reliance on computers and the computer analogy. Some of the more ambitious theories in cognitive science are written as computer programs. Indeed, one theorist with a computer-based model of cognition is so enthusiastic that the computer code of his basic theory is available on a website (for an introduction to this theoretical approach, go to ***http://act.psy.cmu.edu*** or see Anderson & Lebiere, 1998). Researchers are encouraged to download the code and modify and adapt it to their own particular research topics.

One important feature of formal computer models involves explicitness. The formalities of computer programming force the theorist to be very precise and explicit in devising the pieces of a psychological theory; a vague concept might go unnoticed in a verbal theory, but vagueness just won't work in computer code. Interestingly, the enormous capacity of modern computers is also a factor in this approach; in fact, some theories require such a huge number of computations that they could not exist without high-speed computers to do the processing. A prime example of this is the connectionist modeling approach discussed at the end of this chapter.

Section Summary

- Information processing was the dominant metatheory, the dominant approach, in cognitive psychology until the mid-1970s.

- Measuring information processes, the mental processes of cognition, has relied heavily on time and accuracy measures. Differences in response time (RT) can yield interpretations about the speed or difficulty of mental processes, leading to inferences about cognitive processes and events. Accuracy of performance, whether it measures correct recall of a list or accurate paraphrasing of text, also offers evidence about underlying mental processes.
- Although channel capacity was an early, useful analogy in studying information processing, a more influential analogy was later drawn between humans and computers, that human mental processing might be analogous to the sequence of steps and operations in a computer program. Computers still provide an important tool for theorizing about cognitive processes.

THE INFORMATION–PROCESSING APPROACH

Enough of computers for a while—it's time to explore the human information-processing system more carefully. We will examine both the original, narrowly defined strict information-processing approach and the current, broader approach. We will present the standard theory of human information processing, a general description of the human information-processing system, the major outlines of which are still widely accepted. When we get to the section on process models, however, we will discuss the strict information-processing approach and how research was conducted within this framework. Process models were an important adjunct to the standard theory but turned out to be too dependent on some assumptions that proved to be unwarranted. So, as the story unfolds, you will read about more recent developments, ideas that didn't fit into the strict approach very well, ideas that led to the current, broader cognitive approach.

The Standard Theory

■ Figure 2-3 illustrates the standard theory of human information processing, often called the modal model, as it existed in the early 1970s. It is adapted from one of the first such models to receive widespread acceptance, the Atkinson and Shiffrin (1968,

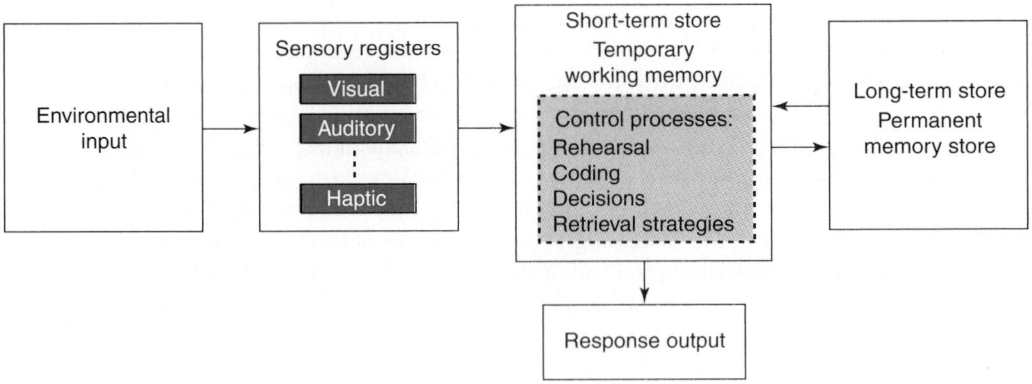

■ **FIGURE 2-3**
Information flow through the memory system in the Atkinson and Shiffrin (1968, 1971) model, the original standard theory in the information-processing approach.

1971) model of human memory. Note first that the basics of the system included three memory components: **sensory memory**, **short-term memory**, and **long-term memory**. At the input end, environmental stimuli flow into the processing system, with each sense modality having its own sensory register or memory. Some of this encoded information is selected and forwarded to short-term memory, a temporary working memory system with several **control processes** at its disposal. The short-term store could both transmit information to and retrieve information from long-term memory. It was also the component of the system responsible for response output, for communicating with the outside world in some observable fashion. If consciousness is anywhere in the memory system, it is here.

Let's use the multiplication example described earlier to trace the flow of processing through Figure 2-3. You read "$2 \times 3 = ?$" and encode the visual stimulus into a visual sensory register; **encoding** is *the act of taking in information and converting it to a usable mental form*. Because you are paying attention, the encoded stimulus is passed almost immediately to the short-term store, or short-term memory (STM). This STM is a working memory system where the information you are consciously aware of is held for further mental processing. For the multiplication example, the system determines that it needs to search long-term memory (LTM) for the answer to the problem. One of the control processes in working memory initiates this search, while others maintain the problem until processing is completed. After the relevant memory search has occurred, LTM "sends" the answer, 6, to STM, where the final response can be prepared and sent to the appropriate device, say, the speech mechanism.

At each step in this sequence, processing consumes some amount of time. By comparing these times and applying some basic reasoning, we can start getting an idea of the underlying mental processing. Thus, as you saw in Figure 2-1, a problem such as 2×3 takes college adults about 700 ms to answer, compared to slightly more than 1,000 ms average for the problem 6×9 (values are taken from Campbell & Graham, 1985). The additional 300 ms might plausibly be due, as argued above, to the long-term memory retrieval stage, say, because of differences in how easily the problems can be located in LTM.

A Process Model

Although the general Atkinson and Shiffrin model provided a useful summary function, we often needed something simpler and more focused to develop explanations of results. A common theoretical technique was to conceptualize performance in terms of a process model, a small-scale model that delineated the specific mental steps involved in a task and made testable predictions. Formally, a **process model** is *a hypothesis about the specific mental processes that take place when a particular task is performed.*

A PROCESS MODEL FOR THE LEXICAL DECISION TASK Let's pick a task that is typical of research in cognitive psychology to explore the use of process models and to see some of the limitations that paved the way for a more flexible, broadly defined information-processing approach. The task we are interested in here is **lexical decision**, sometimes called the "word/nonword task," *a timed task in which people decide whether letter strings are or are not English words* (see Meyer, Schvaneveldt, & Ruddy, 1975; this task and representative results are discussed further in Chapter 7). In this task we show a series of letter strings. On each trial the participant must look at this and decide

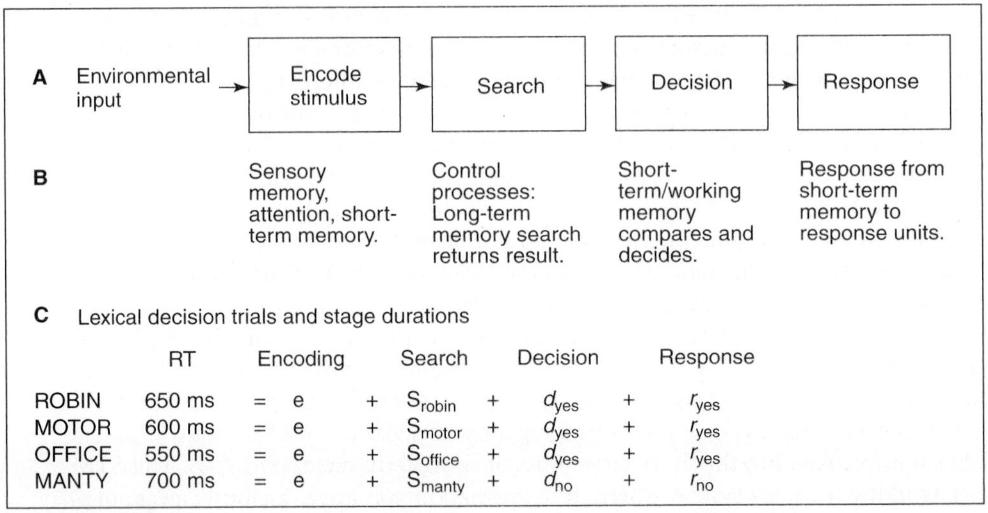

★ **FIGURE 2-4**
A. A general process model, adapted from Sternberg (1969). **B.** A list of the memory components and processes that operate during the separate stages of the process model. **C.** A process analysis of the lexical decision task, where RT to each letter string is the sum of the durations of the separate stages. Note that for the three word trials, the only systematic difference arises from the search stage; encoding, decision, and response times should be the same for all three word trials, according to the logic of process models and the assumptions of sequential and independent stages of processing.

whether they form a word; that is, "Is this letter string in your 'lexicon,' your mental dictionary?" On any given trial, the letter string might either be a true word, such as MOTOR, or it might be a nonword (usually called a pseudoword), such as MANTY. People are asked to respond rapidly but accurately, and the response time to each letter string is the main performance measure. (Note that the pseudowords are wordlike in their appearance, spelling patterns, pronounceability, and so on, so that people won't judge all the stimuli on such tangential factors.)

Logically, what sequence of processes or events must happen in this task? In the ★ process model shown in Figure 2-4, the first stage of processing involves *encoding* the stimulus, taking in the visually presented letter string and transferring it to the holding mechanism of short-term or working memory. Now that the stimulus is in the mental system, working memory calls long-term memory, asking whether the stimulus is stored there. Some kind of *search* through long-term memory takes place, either finding the letter string or not. In either event, the outcome of the search is returned to working memory and forms the basis for the person's *decision,* either "yes, it's a word," or "no, it's not." If the decision is yes, then one set of motor *responses* is prepared and executed, say, pressing the button on the left; the alternative set of responses is prepared and executed for pressing the other button.

LEXICAL DECISIONS AND THE WORD FREQUENCY EFFECT Say that our results revealed a relationship between RT and the frequency or commonness of the words (this is not just a hypothetical result; word frequency is almost always an important influence on RT in the lexical decision task). For instance, we might have tested words at low, medium, and high levels of frequency in the language; ROBIN occurs quite infrequently, only twice per (approximately) million words, MOTOR is of moderate frequency, occurring 56 times per million, and OFFICE is of high frequency, occurring 255 times per million (all word frequencies from Kucera & Francis, 1967; for comparison purposes, the most frequent printed word in English is THE, occurring 69,971 times). *It takes significantly longer to judge words of lower frequency than it does to judge high-frequency words* (Allen & Madden, 1990; Whaley, 1978). This is the **word frequency effect**. Other variables are also known to affect the latencies or times, but the word frequency effect is enough here to develop our example of a process model and interpretation.

For the sake of argument, say that our low-frequency words such as ROBIN took an average of 650 ms, our medium-frequency words such as MOTOR took an average of 600 ms, and our high-frequency words such as OFFICE averaged 550 ms. What does the process model in Figure 2-4 tell us about such a result? Logically, we would not expect that encoding the various words would be influenced by the frequency effect; otherwise we would have to make the improbable assumption that high-frequency words are easier to see. Because this is unlikely, we instead assume that the encoding stage is unaffected by word frequency. The normal time needed for encoding, whatever that might be, should be the same for low-, medium-, and high-frequency words (and for pseudowords, too). So encoding time should be a constant.

Likewise, all three of these cases will yield a successful search, so the same message is being sent to the decision stage: "Yes, it's a word." Therefore, we would not expect any time differences in the decision stage for the low-, medium-, or high-frequency word trials because they would all require the same decision (yes). And finally, "yes" responses should all take the same amount of time for the response stage; it should not take any longer to press the "yes" key for ROBIN or MOTOR than for OFFICE, because all three words prompt the same response. Thus encoding, decision, and response stage times should all be constants, regardless of word frequency.

The only stage left is the search stage. And, on reflection, this stage of processing seems likely to be influenced by word frequency. For instance, it could easily be that words used more frequently in our language might be stored more strongly in memory, or maybe even stored repeatedly in memory (e.g., Logan, 1988); either possibility could yield shorter search times. Alternatively, the more common words in our language might be encountered earlier, on the average, when we search through the mental lexicon. This would also produce shorter latencies to higher-frequency words. On these grounds, then, we might tentatively conclude that word frequency has an effect on the search stage because word frequency is somehow embedded into people's long-term memory record for the words of their language. Any factor that affects the long-term memory search should influence the search stage of processing and should produce a time or accuracy difference because of the altered operation of that stage. Using the numbers supplied earlier, it seems that the search process takes an extra 50 ms for each change from high to medium to low word frequency.

The Strict Information Processing Approach

It is not appropriate now to develop a full-blown theory of long-term memory storage as a function of word frequency. Instead, you need to appreciate the nature of the process analysis that we just performed. Only when you understand this kind of analysis, and the assumptions embedded in this approach, will you be able to understand the important criticisms of a strict information-processing approach and see where the current approach has relaxed or discarded some of the strong assumptions.

The first was the assumption of **sequential stages of processing**. It was generally assumed that there is *a sequence of stages or processes,* such as those depicted in Figure 2-4, *that occur on every trial, a set of stages that completely account for mental processing in the task.* Importantly, the order of the stages was believed to be fixed, on the grounds that each stage provides a result that is necessary for the operation of the next one. More to the point, this assumption of sequential stages usually implied that one and only one stage can be performed at any one time. In other words, sequential processing not only means that the sequence of stages is fixed, but also implies strict one-after-another operation.

The influence of the computer analogy is especially clear here. Modern computers have achieved high speeds of operation, but most are still serial processors: They still perform operations one by one, in a sequential order. And yet there is no *a priori* reason to expect that humans are limited to one-by-one processing in all situations. Thus, this is where critics of the strict information-processing approach tended to cluster, at the assumption of sequential, one-at-a-time stages of processing.

The second assumption, really an extension of the first, was that the stages were **independent and nonoverlapping**. That is, *any single stage was assumed to finish its operation completely before the next stage in the sequence could begin, and the duration of any single stage had no bearing or influence on the other stages.* Thus, at the beginning of a trial, the encoding process starts, completes its operations, and passes its result along to the next stage in sequence, the search stage. Then and only then could the search stage begin, followed after its completion by the decision and response stages. With these assumptions, the total time for any trial could be interpreted as the sum of the durations for each independent stage; because mental processes take time and because each stage is a separate mental process, the total time for a trial could be viewed as the sum of the times for all the individual stages. (Think back to the factory example; how long it takes to assemble and install a car's engine should have no influence on how long it takes to install the car's seats.)

In our earlier example, then, the 50 ms differences between ROBIN, MOTOR, and OFFICE would be attributed to the search stage. In other words, because encoding, decision, and response all take constant amounts of time, only the search stage is left to account for the time differences attributable to the three levels of word frequency. The memory search for these words, then, is presumably slowed down when the words are of lower frequency.

Some Difficulties

What prompted cognitive psychology to move away from this strict information-processing approach and the simplicity of process models? Let's focus on three of the difficulties as a way of summarizing the field's maturation toward the updated, current cognitive approach.

PARALLEL PROCESSING As research within the strict information-processing approach was done, new evidence accumulated that began to cast doubt on the assumptions of serial, nonoverlapping stages of processing. Instead of finding evidence that this or that mental process operated in a simple, one-by-one fashion, studies began documenting just the opposite: evidence that multiple mental processes can operate *simultaneously,* in **parallel.**

An excellent example (partly because it is intuitive, even if you are only moderately skilled at keyboarding) involves typing. Salthouse (1984) performed an in-depth examination of how skilled typists type and how performance changes across age. His data argued for a four-process model; the input stage encoded the to-be-typed material, a parsing stage broke large reading units (words) into separate characters, a translation stage transformed the characters into finger movements, and an execution stage triggered the keystrokes. Most significantly, all his evidence indicated that these multiple stages were operating simultaneously, in parallel: While one letter is being typed, another is being translated into a finger movement, and the input stage is encoding upcoming letters, even as many as eight characters in advance of the one being typed.

The point for now is that a strict process model explanation that insists on sequential, serial processing cannot easily account for performance that comes from parallel functioning of mental stages. Yet Salthouse's evidence was for parallel processing. Even the age effect he found argued for the importance of parallel processing; older typists counteracted the tendency toward slower finger movements by increasing their "look ahead" span at the upcoming letters. (The evidence of parallel processing has become even more convincing now as we consider evidence from the neurosciences. See Townsend & Wenger, 2004, for a thorough discussion of the serial versus parallel processing issue.)

CONTEXT EFFECTS A second difficulty for simple process models and the strict information-processing approach arose when investigators took the effects of context into account. A simple example of this is the speed-up in deciding that MOTOR is a word if you have already processed MOTOR recently; at a minimum, the process model would have to be expanded so that words presented on other test trials could influence performance on the current trial (see the discussion of "repetition priming" in Chapters 6 and 7).

A more compelling demonstration of the effect of context comes from work on lexical ambiguity, the fact that many words have more than one meaning. As an example, Simpson (1981) had participants perform a modified lexical decision task, judging letter strings such as *DUKE* or *MONEY* (or *MANTY* or *ZOOPLE*) after they had read a context sentence. When the letter string and sentence were related—for instance, "The vampire was disguised as a handsome count," followed by DUKE—the lexical decision on DUKE was faster than normal. The reason involved priming (again, see Chapters 6 and 7), the notion that concepts and words in memory become activated in memory and hence easier to process. In this case, because the context sentence primed or activated the royalty sense of the word *count*, the lexical decision response to DUKE was speeded up.

Why was this kind of result a difficulty for the process model approach? This was a problem because there was no mechanism in simple process models to account for the priming effect, the speeding up of the lexical decision by context or some outside event (the sentence was "outside" of the timed trial). Look again at Figure 2-4; is there any component that allows a context sentence to influence the speed of the processes? No, you would need a meaning-based component that would keep track of recently activated meanings, a component that would speed up the search process when meanings matched but not when the meanings were unrelated. (A similar component would also have to be added to account for some of Salthouse's results on typing, such as the finding that familiar passages can be typed more rapidly than novel ones.)

OTHER LIMITATIONS A final kind of limitation with the strict information-processing approach, with its emphasis on process models, involved other, often slower kinds of mental processing that cognitive psychology was interested in. As you probably noticed, process models were particularly applicable to RT results, to predicting latencies in different stimulus conditions (e.g., low-, medium-, and high-frequency words). Unfortunately, they tended to be less useful for accuracy-based investigations of cognitive processes; percentage correct on a list of words or the nature of one's errors in recall simply did not fit in with the sequential processing character of the process model approach.

In a similar vein, many of the cognitive processes we are interested in are slower and more complex than those investigated with process models. As you will learn in the last two chapters of this book, investigations of decision making and problem solving often involve processing that takes *much* longer than most RT tasks; for example, some cryptarithmetic problems (substitute digits for letters in the problem SEND + MORE; see Chapter 12) routinely take 15 to 20 minutes! Process models are virtually useless in such situations. Instead, a far more meaningful measurement of these mental processes would involve a verbal report or **verbal protocol** procedure, in which participants are asked to *verbalize their thoughts as they solve the problems.* In fact, this is the third type of measure in cognitive research that was mentioned earlier; it is less widely used than time and accuracy, but important nonetheless (see Nisbett & Wilson, 1977 and Ericsson & Simon, 1980 for different views on the usefulness of verbal protocols). Putting it simply, nothing in the process model approach could accommodate results from verbal protocol methods.

In short, the strict information-processing approach became too confining because of its embedded assumptions about sequential processing and because it tended to slight or even ignore certain kinds of data. Cognitive psychology needed a more broadly based approach to do justice to the range of mental processes that needed to be studied.

Section Summary

- The strict information-processing approach suggested that mental processing could be understood as a sequence of independent processing stages, such as the sensory, short-term, and long-term memory stages in the standard theory of Atkinson and Shiffrin.

- Process models, in particular, tended to be appropriate for fairly simple, rapid tasks that were usually measured by response times, such as the lexical decision task.
- Although the strict information-processing approach was responsible for many important developments and insights, evidence of parallel processing and context effects started to show some of its limitations; for example, research on skilled typing shows a high degree of **parallel processing**. Another difficulty was that slower, more complex mental processes, such as those in the study of decision making and problem solving, were not easily studied within the strict approach.

THE MODERN COGNITIVE APPROACH: COGNITIVE SCIENCE

The information-processing approach just described was a dominant way of doing business in cognitive psychology until the mid-1970s. Much of the research even today resembles research done under that approach—we still use RT measures, for instance. But its difficulties ultimately led to a broadened, less restrictive approach, now called **cognitive science**. In general, cognitive science is *the study of thought, using all available scientific techniques and including all relevant scientific disciplines for exploring and investigating cognition*. By expanding the range of methods and evidence we use, cognitive science takes a multidisciplinary approach to the study of cognition.

What follows is a two-part description of this approach. First, we focus briefly on some of the more traditional methods and techniques that still contribute to cognitive science and offer an update of the standard model you studied earlier. We then discuss at some length the background material you need to understand the biggest change in the field, material on the anatomy and functioning of the human brain. It is no longer possible to know cognitive psychology without knowing about the brain and about the evidence neuropsychology is contributing. To help you integrate this newer evidence into your understanding, this book presents important evidence from the neurosciences throughout rather than segregating it into its own separate chapter.

Updating the Standard Theory

Figure 2-5 shows a seemingly minor revision of the Atkinson and Shiffrin (1971) standard model, a revision in which the three memory components have been arranged in a triangle. Closer examination of the figure shows several other changes: The arrows between components are now bidirectional, each component can now affect each other component, and an attentional mechanism of some sort is shown as having an explicit influence throughout (the triangular, interactive scheme here was inspired by Neisser's 1976 notion of the "perceptual cycle"). ▲

PARALLEL PROCESSING How do these changes fix what was wrong with the standard model of the late 1960s and early 1970s? Recall that the first difficulty with process models was the difficulty of parallel processing. Basically, in contrast to the rigidly serial, sequential nature of the standard model, evidence accumulated that different mental components could operate simultaneously, in parallel. Arranging the components in a triangle rather than in a horizontal row helps get away from the "one after the other" flavor of the standard model.

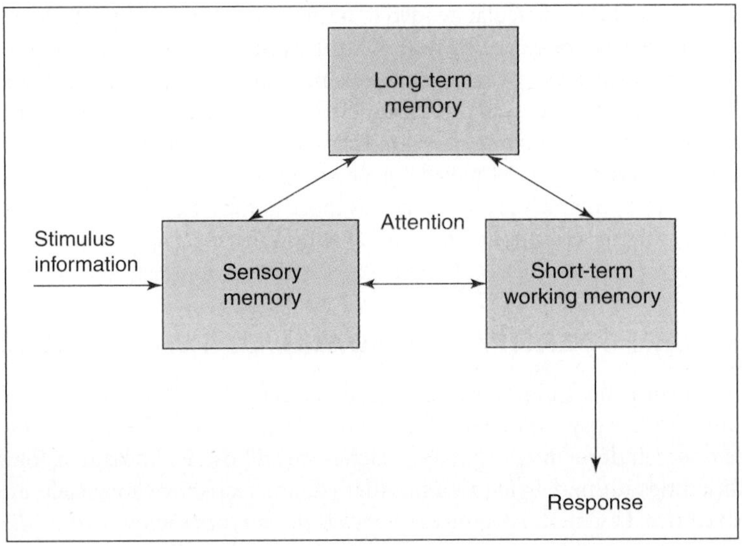

▲ **FIGURE 2-5**
A revised information-processing model, showing how components can continually interact with each other and how attention influences all three components. Adapted from Neisser (1976).

It also helps move us away from the simple computer analogy that formerly was so central to the information-processing approach, the analogy that sold us on serial processing. Computers were—and, for the most part, still are—serial processors, but people definitely are not. Furthermore, the computer analogy told us that one could understand the software of a system without having to worry about the hardware: You could study how the program worked, how it processed information, without understanding the switches and wiring of the physical machine that did the computing. The analogy therefore suggested that cognition could be understood with little reference to the brain, to the physical organ in which cognition takes place.

An enormously important lesson we have learned from neuroscience is that this simple idea—that there is little need to understand the brain—is simply wrong. In a compelling and clear fashion, the brain shows countless ways in which different cognitive components and processes—modules, if you like (Barrett & Kurzban, 2006; Fodor, 1983)—are continually operating simultaneously, in parallel. There is even some neurological evidence that different regions of the brain are more specialized for different processing tasks, such as encoding, responding, memory retrieval and controlling the stream of thought (Anderson, Qin, Jung, & Carter, 2007).

CONTEXT A second change, the bidirectional arrows, liberalizes the standard model even more, helping to account for context and other effects. As you can see in the revised model, information that is active in long-term memory, for example, can easily have an effect *right now* on sensory memory, the input stage for external stimuli. Here is a simple example:

> As you read a sentence or paragraph, you begin to develop a feel for its meaning. Often you understand well enough that you can then skim through the rest of the material, possibly reading so rapidly that lower-level processes such as proofreading and noticing typograpical errors may not function as accurately as they usually do. *Did you see the mistake?*

What? Mistake? If you fell for it, you failed to notice the missing *h* in the word *typographical*, possibly because you were skimming but probably because the word *typographical* was expected, predictable based on meaning. You may have even "seen" the missing *h* in a sense. Why? Because your understanding of the passage, its meaningfulness to you, may have been strong enough that the missing *h* was supplied by your long-term memory.

We call such effects **top-down**, or **conceptually driven processing**, *when existing context or knowledge has an influence on earlier or simpler forms of mental processes*. It's one of the recurring themes in cognition (look again at Table 2-1). For another example, adapted from Reed (1992), read the following sentence:

FINISHED FILES ARE THE RESULT OF YEARS OF SCIENTIFIC STUDY COMBINED WITH THE EXPERIENCE OF MANY YEARS.

Now, read it a second time, counting the number of times the letter F occurs.

If you counted fewer than six, try again—and again, if necessary. Why is this difficult? Because you know that function words such as *of* carry very little meaning, your perceptual, input processes are prompted to pay attention only to the content words. Ignoring function words, and consequently failing to see the letter *F* in a word such as OF, is a clear-cut example of conceptually driven processing (for an explanation of the "missing letter effect," see Greenberg, Healy, Koriat, & Kreiner, 2004).

Fixing the Narrowness

The final difficulty mentioned earlier concerned the narrowness of the strict information-processing approach, particularly its emphasis on RT measures of simple, fairly rapid mental processes. To a greater degree than was true before, cognitive science is now open to results based on a variety of research techniques, the verbal protocol technique prominent among them. To be sure, there are still detractors of verbal protocols, and studying the parameters of the method remains an important task (see Ericsson & Simon, 1993, for an update on how to do it). But the method is still useful, capable of revealing important observations about cognition. Furthermore, broadening cognitive psychology to include such techniques is very much in the spirit of other broadenings, in particular opening up to the evidence obtained from the neurosciences.

The early approach did serve its purpose. It gave us some important insights, helped illuminate some of its own shortcomings, and ultimately guided us to more informative ways of doing science.

Section Summary

- The strict information-processing approach to cognition was replaced with a broader, more inclusive approach now known as cognitive science. This approach describes cognition as the coordinated, often parallel operation of mental processes within a multicomponent memory system. The approach is deliberately multidisciplinary, accepting evidence from all the sciences interested in cognition.

NEUROCOGNITION: THE BRAIN AND COGNITION TOGETHER

We start with a stunning story of cognitive disruption to motivate our interest in neurocognition. Tulving (1989) described a patient known as K. C., a young man who sustained brain damage in a motorcycle accident. Some nine years after the accident, he still showed pervasive disruption of long-term memory. The fascinating thing about his memory impairment was that it was selective: K. C. remains perfectly competent at language, his intelligence is normal, and he is able to converse on a number of topics. But when he is asked about an experience from his own past, he doesn't remember; in Tulving's words, "he cannot remember, in the sense of bringing back to conscious awareness, a single thing that he has ever done or experienced in the past" (p. 362). For example, even though he remembers how to play chess, he does not remember ever having played it before. He knows his family had a vacation house on a lake, but he doesn't have any recollections of being there. K. C.'s brain damage seemed to destroy his ability to access what we'll call episodic memory, his own autobiographical knowledge, while leaving his general knowledge system—his semantic memory—intact. This pattern is called a **dissociation**, *a disruption in one component of mental functioning but no impairment of another*. Can these two forms of long-term memory, episodic and semantic memory, be the same, given K. C.'s dissociation between the two? Probably not. So we now ask a more general question: How must the cognitive system be organized for disruptions such as these to take place?

The area of investigation we are introducing here is sometimes called *cognitive neuropsychology*. As important as the evidence from brain damage is, we also need other kinds of evidence, for example information about the neurochemical and neurobiological activities that support normal learning and thought or about the changes in the brain that accompany aging. We are therefore interested in contributions from all the various neurosciences—neurochemistry, neurobiology, neuroanatomy, and so on—as they relate to human cognition.

Understanding cognitive handicaps is an obvious goal; no one can dispute the importance of rehabilitation and retraining for patients with brain damage. But our interest in cognitive science goes a step further. We want to understand *normal* cognition from the standpoint of the human brain. That is, we want to learn about normal cognition through whatever means available. Toward this goal, more and more investigators are examining the behavioral and cognitive effects of brain damage (e.g., McCloskey, 1992), using those observations to develop and refine theories of normal cognition (Martin, 2000). As you will see throughout this book, sometimes the great misfortune of brain damage leads to a clearer understanding of normal processes.

Likewise, cognitive science is now putting to good use the new, high-tech brain imaging capabilities we have adopted from medicine. We can now use brain images based on positron emission tomography (PET) scans and magnetic resonance imaging (MRI) to localize regions of activity during different kinds of cognitive processing, testing not just brain-damaged individuals but normal, intact ones as well (see Poldrack & Wagner, 2004, and Sarter, Berntson, & Cacioppo, 1996, for thoughtful discussions about neuroimaging evidence and cognition).

We first cover a bit of neural functioning here, then look at some major anatomical features of the brain. We then conclude by talking about several methods of study-

IN DEPTH

Dissociations and Double Dissociations

The concept of dissociation—the opposite of association—is important, so we should spend a little more time on it.

Consider two mental processes that "go together" in some cognitive task, called process A and process B. By looking at these processes as they may be disrupted in brain damage, we can determine how separable the processes are.

Complete separability is a double dissociation. Evidence of a double dissociation requires at least two patients, with "opposite" or reciprocal deficits. For example,

- Patient X has a brain lesion that has disrupted process A. His performance on tasks that use process B is intact, not disrupted at all.
- Patient Y has a lesion that has damaged process B, but tasks that use process A are normal, not disrupted by the damage.

Think of a double dissociation as illustrated in the simple diagram below and refer back to it later in the book as you read about processes that are dissociated. If these circles depicted actual brain regions, such as those used in language processes (Chapter 9), then damage to either one of them could easily leave the other one unaffected.

- In a simple dissociation, process A could be damaged while process B remains intact, yet no other known patient has the reciprocal pattern. For example, semantic retrieval (retrieving the meaning of a concept) could be intact while lexical retrieval (finding the name for the concept) could be disrupted; this is called anomia (see Chapter 7). In this situation lexical retrieval is dissociated from semantic retrieval, but it is probably impossible to observe the opposite pattern; how can you name a concept if you can't retrieve the concept in the first place?
- In a full or complete association (lack of dissociation), disruption of one of the processes always accompanies disruption in the other process. This pattern implies that processes A and B rely on the same region or brain mechanism, such as recognizing objects and recognizing pictures of those objects (see Chapter 3).

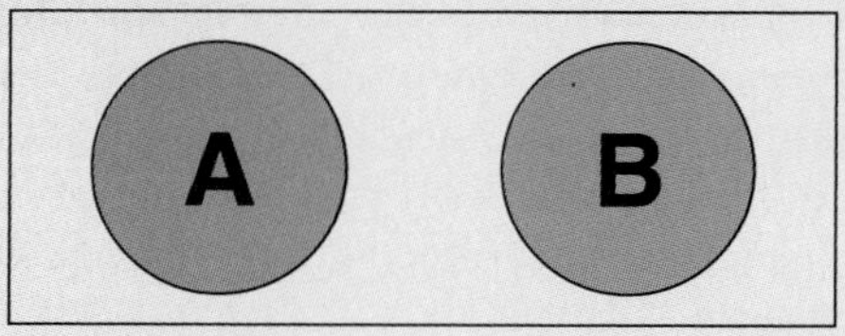

ing brain and cognition, including a computer-based modeling approach inspired by neuroscience. Just as the cognitive influence on neuroscience has been a rejuvenating one, in the opinions of several researchers (e.g., Moscovitch, 1979; Seron, 1982), the cross-fertilization for cognition has been crucial and will only become more so with time. Of course, we can focus only on a few highlights; as Crick and Asanuma (1986, p. 333) said of their own chapter, "It is clearly impossible to describe most of what is known, even though this represents [only] a tiny fraction of what one would like to know."

Basic Neurology

At birth, the human brain weighs approximately 400 g (about 14 oz). It grows to an average of 1,450 g in adults, slightly more than 3 lbs, and is roughly the size of a ripe grapefruit. The basic building block of the brain, indeed of the entire nervous system, is the **neuron**, *a cell that is specialized for receiving and transmitting a neural impulse.* Neurons are the components that form nerve tracts throughout the body and in all brain structures. How many neurons are there in the brain? Available estimates vary tremendously. Kolb and Whishaw (1996) suggest a grand total of 180 billion cells of all types in the brain, including not only neurons, but nonneural cells, too (e.g., connective and circulatory tissue). Some 80 billion of these cells, in Kolb and Whishaw's estimate, are "directly engaged in information processing" and cognition (p. 39). To put that figure in perspective, consider that the Milky Way Galaxy has about 100 billion stars.

● **NEURONS** Figure 2-6A illustrates an idealized or prototypical neuron. The details of structure vary, but each neuron within the nervous system has the same general features. At one end of the neuron, many small branchlike fingers called *dendrites* gather a neural impulse into the neuron itself. In somewhat more familiar terms, the dendrites are the *input* structures of the neuron, taking in the message that is being passed along in a particular neural tract.

The central portion of each neuron is the cell body, or *soma,* where the biological activity of the cell is regulated. Extending from the cell body is a longish extension or tube, the *axon,* which ends in another set of branchlike structures called *axon terminals* or sometimes *terminal arborizations;* the latter term derives from the treelike form of these structures. The axon terminals are the *output* end of the neuron, the place where the neural impulse ends within the neuron itself. Obviously, this is the location where an influence on the next neuron in the pathway must take place.

Figure 2-6B is a diagram of the elements of the nervous system that are activated during a simple reflex, such as jerking your arm away when you accidentally touch a hot stove. *Receptor cells* react to the physical stimulus and trigger a pattern of firing down *sensory neurons.* These neuron tracts pass the message along into the spinal cord. For a simple reflex, the message loops quickly through the spinal cord and goes back out to the arm muscles through a tract of *motor neurons* that terminate at *effector cells,* which connect directly to the muscle fibers and cause the muscles to pull your arm away.

As the reflex triggers the quick return of a message out to the muscles, it simultaneously routes a message up the spinal cord and into the brain. Thus the second route involves only the central nervous system, the spinal cord, and brain. There is only one kind of neuron in the central nervous system, called an *interneuron* or *association neuron.* Because we are concerned only with the brain here, we are interested only in the interneurons of the central nervous system. For simplicity, we'll just refer to them as neurons here.

SYNAPSES There may be relatively few or many axon terminals emanating from a single neuron. In either case these terminals are adjacent to dendrites from other

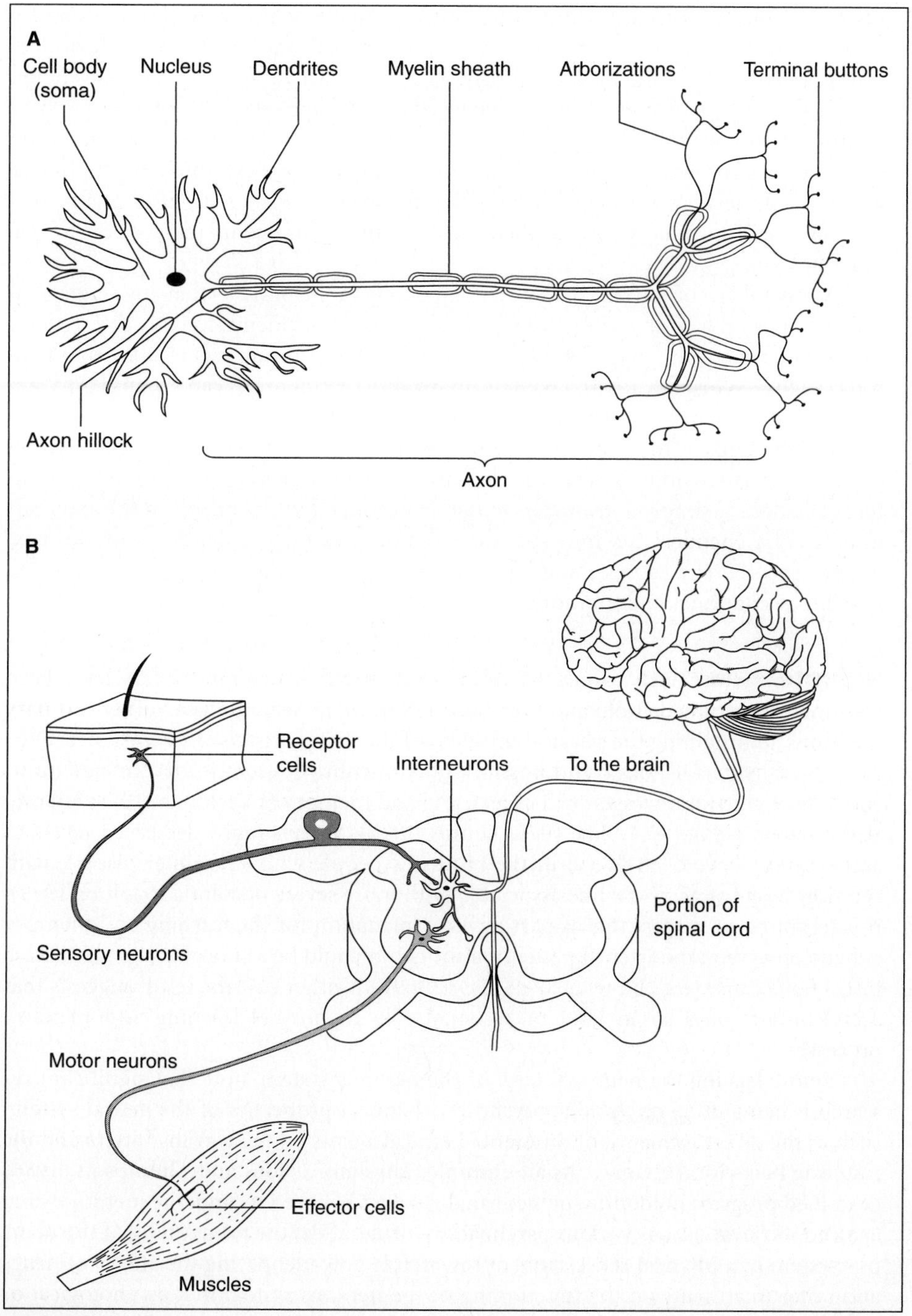

● **FIGURE 2-6**
An illustration of the various structures of the neuron. Note that the lower diagram illustrates a sensory–motor reflex arc.

neurons. Thus an impulse within a neuron terminates at the axon terminals and is taken up by the dendrites of the next neurons in the pathway, the neurons whose dendrites are adjacent to the axon terminals. The *region where the axon terminals of one neuron and the dendrites of another come together* is the **synapse**. For the most part, the neurons do not actually touch one another (some regions of the brain contradict this rule). Instead, the synapses in the human nervous system are extremely small physical gaps or clefts between the neurons. Note that the word *synapse* is also used as a verb: A neuron is said to synapse on another, meaning that it passes its message on to that other neuron.

A general law of the nervous system, especially in the brain, is that any single neuron synapses on a large number of other neurons. The evidence for this *divergence* is that a typical neuron synapses on anywhere from 100 to as many as 15,000 other neurons (Kolb & Whishaw, 1996). Likewise, many different neurons can synapse on a single destination neuron, a principle known as *convergence.*

For the bulk of the nervous system, the bridge across the synaptic cleft involves chemical activity within the synaptic cleft itself. A neuron releases a chemical transmitter substance, or simply a *neurotransmitter,* from small *buttons* or *sacs* in the axon terminals. This chemical fits into specific receptor sites on the dendrites of the next neuron and thereby causes some effect on that next neuron. Two general effects are possible, excitation and inhibition.

NEUROTRANSMITTERS Some 60 or more different neurotransmitters have been identified and studied (Kolb and Whishaw, 1996). Many seem to have rather ordinary functions, maintaining the physical integrity of the living organism, for instance. Others, especially acetylcholine and possibly norepinephrine, seem to have major influences on cognitive processes such as learning and memory (Drachman, 1978; Sitaran, Weingartner, Caine, & Gillin, 1978; Squire, 1987). Interestingly, decreased levels of acetylcholine have been found in the brains of people with Alzheimer disease, with very low levels of acetylcholine associated with more severe dementia (Samuel, 1999). It is tempting to suggest this as part of the explanation for the learning and memory deficits observed among such patients, although it could be a side effect of the disease instead of a cause (e.g., Banich, 2004; Riley, 1989). In either case the result suggests that acetylcholine plays some kind of essential role in normal learning and memory processes.

Before leaving the neuronal level of the nervous system, note that significant research is being done on various psycho-biochemical properties of the neural system, such as the direct influence of different chemical agents on neurotransmitters and the resulting behavioral changes. As an example, Abraham (2006) and Thompson (1986) described progress in identifying neuronal changes believed to underlie memory storage and retrieval. Just as various psychoactive drugs affect the functioning of the nervous system in a physical sense, current research is now identifying the effects of drugs and other treatments on the functioning of the nervous system in a psychological or cognitive sense (e.g., the effect of alcohol intoxication; Nelson, McSpadden, Fromme, & Marlatt, 1986).

Brain Anatomy

Ignoring many levels of intermediate neural functioning and complexity, we now take a tremendous leap from the level of single neurons to the level of the entire brain, the awesomely complex "biological computer." To account for all human behavior, including bodily functions that occur involuntarily (e.g., digestion), would entail an extensive discussion of both the central and the peripheral nervous systems. But to explore neurocognition, we can limit ourselves to just the central nervous system, the brain and spinal cord. In fact, our discussion even omits much of the central nervous system, save for the neocortex (or cerebral cortex), which sits at the top of the human brain, and a few other nearby structures.

In Figure 2-7 the physically lower brain structures are collectively called the old brain or brain stem. This portion of the brain is older in terms of evolution, for the most part governing basic, primitive functions (e.g., digestion, heartbeat, and breathing). The old brain structures are present in all mammals. ◆

Figure 2-8 shows the **neocortex**, or **cerebral cortex**, *the top layer of the brain, responsible for higher-level mental processes.* The neocortex is a wrinkled, convoluted structure that nearly surrounds the old brain. According to Kolb and Whishaw (1996), the two halves or hemispheres cover about 2500 cm2 and are from about 1.5 to 3 mm thick, about as thick as the cover of this textbook. The wrinkling comes about by trying to get such a large surface area in a small space. It would be like trying to get a piece ■

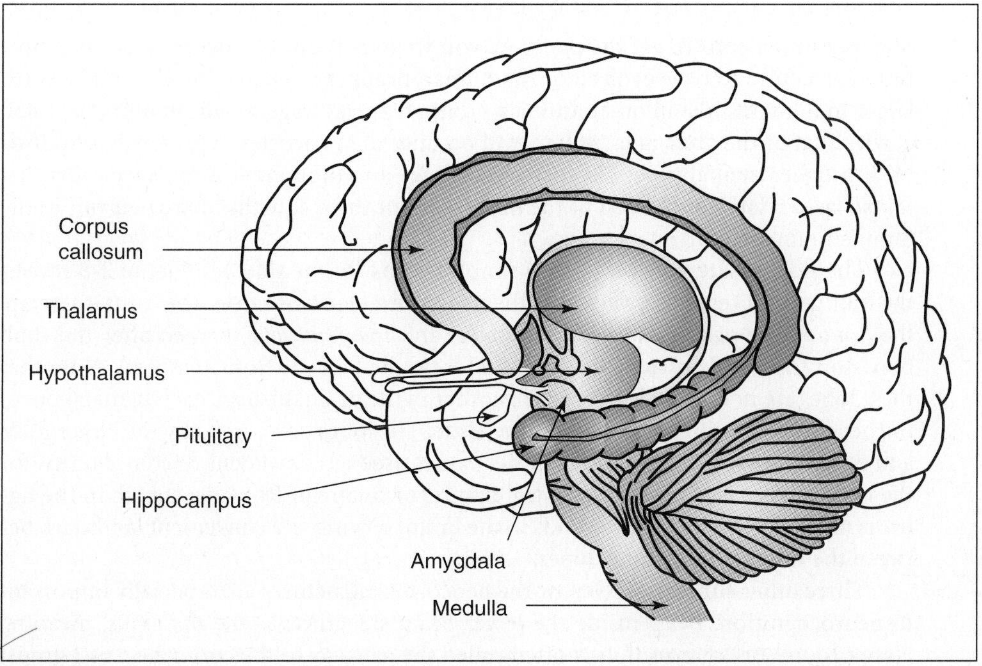

◆ **FIGURE 2-7**
Lower brain structures.

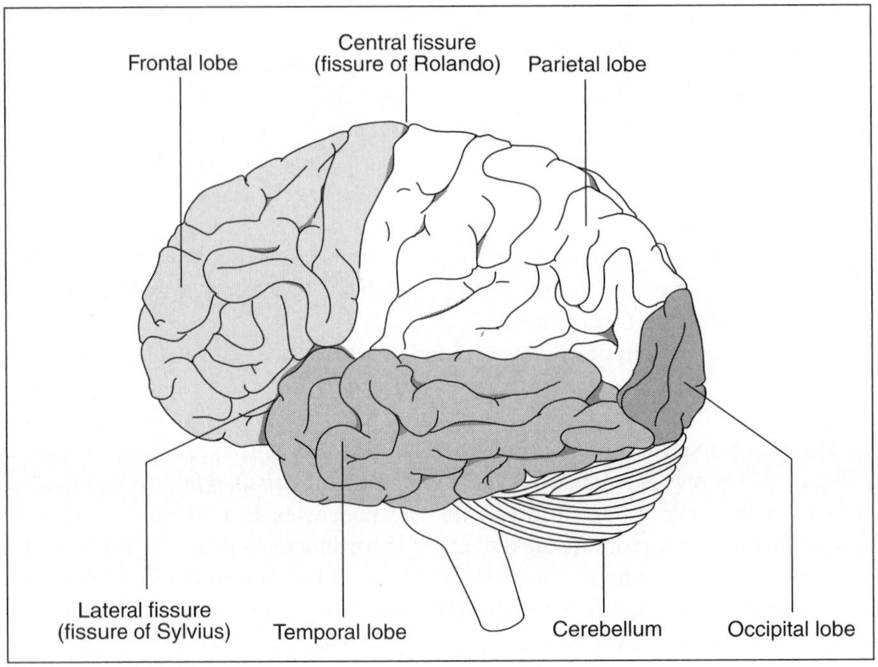

FIGURE 2-8
The four lobes of the neocortex.

of paper into a cup. To get the paper in, you wrinkle it up. The neocortex is the most recent structure to have evolved in the human brain (*neo* means "new") and is much larger in humans than in other animals; compare the average weight in humans, 1,450 g, with that of the great apes, 400 g. And because the neocortex is primarily responsible for higher mental processes such as language and thought, it is not surprising that it is so large relative to the rest of the brain—about three-fourths of the neurons in the human brain are in the neocortex.

The side, or lateral, view (*lateral* simply means "to the side") in Figure 2-8 reveals the four general regions, or *lobes,* of the neocortex; clockwise from the front, these are the *frontal lobe, parietal lobe, occipital lobe,* and *temporal lobe,* named after the skull bones on top of them (e.g., the temporal lobes lie beneath your temples). Note that these lobes are not separate from one another in the brain. Instead, each hemisphere of the neocortex is a single sheet of neural tissue. The lobes are formed by the larger folds and convolutions of the cortex, with the names used as convenient reference terms for the regions. As an example, the central fissure, or fissure of Rolando, shown in the figure is merely one of the deeper folds in the brain, serving as a convenient landmark between the frontal and parietal lobes.

Three other subcortical (below the neocortex) structures are especially important to neurocognition. Deep inside the lower brain structures is the *thalamus,* meaning "inner room" or "chamber." It is often called the gateway to the cortex because almost all messages entering the cortex come through the thalamus (a portion of the olfactory sense of smell is one of the very few exceptions). In other words, the thalamus is the major relay station from the sensory systems of the body into the neocortex.

Just above the thalamus is a broad band of nerve fibers called the *corpus callosum.* As described later, the corpus callosum ("callous body") is the primary bridge across which messages pass between the left and right halves—the hemispheres—of the neocortex.

The third structure is the *hippocampus,* from the Latin word for "sea horse," referring to its curved shape. The hippocampus lies immediately interior to the temporal lobes, that is, underneath the temporal lobes but in the same horizontal plane. Research on the effects of hippocampal damage is described later in the book (especially in Chapter 6), including one of the best known case histories in neuropsychology, that of patient H. M.

Principles of Functioning

Two important principles of functioning in the neocortex are described here, necessary background knowledge for understanding the effects of brain function on cognitive processes. These principles involve the ideas of contralaterality and hemispheric specialization.

CONTRALATERALITY When viewed from the top, the neocortex is divided into two mirror-image halves, the left and right cerebral hemispheres. This follows a general law of anatomy, that with the exception of internal organs such as the heart, the body is basically bilaterally symmetrical. What is somewhat surprising, however, is that *the receptive and control centers for one side of the body are in the opposite hemisphere of the brain.* This is **contralaterality** (*contra* means "against" or "opposite"). In other words, for evolutionary reasons that will probably remain obscure, the right hemisphere of the brain receives its input from the left side of the body and also controls the left side. Likewise, the left hemisphere receives input from and controls output to the right side of the body. As an example, people who have a stroke in the left hemisphere will often have some paralysis in the right half of the body. There are a few exceptions, such as the olfactory nerves, in which there are ipsilateral (same side) connections.

HEMISPHERIC SPECIALIZATION The second issue concerning lateralization involves different specializations within the two cerebral hemispheres. Despite their mirror-image appearance, the two hemispheres do not mirror one another's abilities. Instead, each hemisphere tends to specialize in different abilities and tends to process different kinds of information. This is the full principle of **cerebral lateralization** and specialization: *Different functions or actions within the brain tend to rely more heavily on one hemisphere or the other or tend to be performed differently in the two hemispheres.* This is not to say that a process or function can happen *only* in one particular hemisphere. It merely says that there is often a tendency, sometimes strong, for one or the other hemisphere to be especially dominant in different processes or functions.

The most obvious evidence of lateralization in humans is the overwhelming incidence of right-handedness across all cultures and apparently throughout the known history of human evolution (Corballis, 1989). Accompanying this tendency toward right-handedness is a particularly strong left-hemispheric specialization in humans for language. That is, for the majority of people, language ability is especially lateralized in the left hemisphere; countless studies have demonstrated this general tendency (see Provins, 1997, for a review of the handedness–speech relationship).

In contrast, the right hemisphere seems to be somewhat more specialized for nonverbal, spatial, and more perceptual information processing (see Banich, 2004, and Moscovitch, 1979, for reviews of such left–right hemisphere characterizations). For instance, the evidence suggests that face recognition (Ellis, 1983) and mental rotation (Deutsch, Bourbon, Papanicolaou, & Eisenberg, 1988), both requiring spatial and perceptual processing, are especially dependent on the right cerebral hemisphere. Table 2-2 provides a summary of data on cerebral lateralization. ★

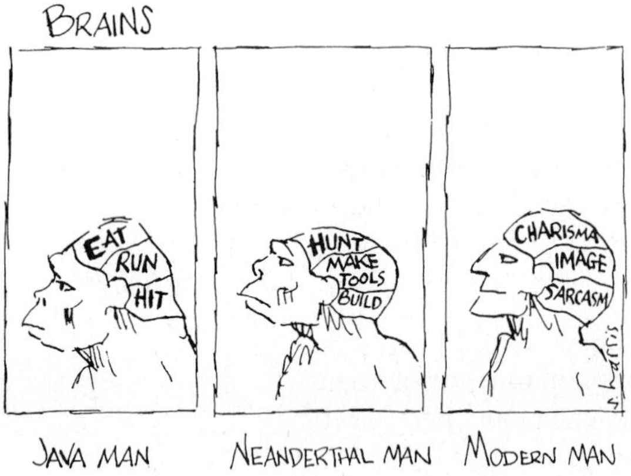

Many people have heard of these "left brain versus right brain" issues, often from the popular press. Such treatments are notorious for exaggerating and oversimplifying laterality and specialization. For instance, in these descriptions the left hemisphere ends up with the rational, logical, and symbolic abilities—the boring ones—whereas the right hemisphere gets the holistic, creative, and intuitive processes—the sexy ones! Corballis (1989, p. 501) noted that the right hemisphere achieves "a certain cult status" in some such treatments.

But even ignoring that oversimplification, it is far too easy to misunderstand the principles of lateralization and specialization, too easy to say "process X happens in *this* hemisphere, process Y in *that* one." Even the simplest act of cognition, say naming a picture, involves multiple components, distributed widely across both hemispheres, and complex coordination of the components. Disruption of any one of those could disrupt picture naming. Thus several different patients, each with dramatically different localized brain damage, could show an inability to name a picture, each for a different reason relating to different lateralized processes.

★ **TABLE 2-2 Summary of Data on Cerebral Lateralization**

Function	Left Hemisphere	Right Hemisphere
Visual system	Letters, words	Complex geometric patterns, faces
Auditory system	Language-related sounds	Nonlanguage environmental sounds, music
Somatosensory system	?	Tactile recognition of complex patterns, Braille
Movement	Complex voluntary movement	Movements in spatial patterns
Memory	Verbal memory	Nonverbal memory
Language	Speech	Prosody
	Reading	Narrative
	Writing	Inference
	Arithmetic	
Spatial processes		Geometry, sense of direction, mental rotation of shapes

Note: These functions of the respective hemispheres are mediated predominantly by one hemisphere in right-handed people.

Nonetheless, there is a striking division of labor in the neocortex, in which the left cerebral hemisphere is specialized for language. This is almost always true; it characterizes up to 85% or 90% of the population. The percentages are this high, however, only if you are a right-handed male with no family history of left-handedness and if you write with your hand in a normal rather than inverted position (Friedman & Polson, 1981). If you are female, if you are left-handed, if you write with an inverted hand position, and so on, then the "left hemisphere language rule" is not quite as strong. In such groups, the majority of people have the customary pattern, but the percentages are not as high; for example, Bryden's (1982) review indicated that 79% of women have language lateralized to the left hemisphere. Thus directing language input to the left cerebral hemisphere is optimal and efficient for many people, but not for all. (For simplicity, however, we rely on the convenient fiction that language is processed in the left hemisphere for most people; see Banich, 2004, for useful discussions.)

Split-Brain Research and Lateralization

Despite the exaggerated claims you often read, there has been a good deal of careful work on the topic of lateralization and specialization of different regions in the two hemispheres. Among the best known is the research on split-brain patients.

Before about 1960, evidence of hemispheric specialization was rather indirect; neurologists and researchers simply noted the location and kind of head injury that was sustained and the kind of behavioral or cognitive deficit that was observed after the injury. Sperry (e.g., 1964; Gazzaniga & Sperry, 1967), however, put the facts of anatomy together with a surgical procedure for severe epilepsy. In this operation, the corpus callosum is completely severed to restrict the epileptic seizure to just one of the cerebral hemispheres. For patients who had this radical surgery, a remarkably informative test could be administered, one that could reveal the different abilities and actions of the two hemispheres. That is, from the standpoint of brain functioning, when a patient's corpus callosum is surgically cut, the two hemispheres cannot communicate internally with each other—information in one hemisphere cannot cross over to the other. Sperry's technique was to test such people by directing sensory information to one side or the other of the body (e.g., by placing a pencil in the left or right hand of such a patient or presenting a visual stimulus to the left or right visual field), then observing their behavior.

For example, if a patient had a pencil placed in the left hand (the patients were prevented from seeing the objects and their hands, of course), the neural impulse went to the right hemisphere but then could not cross over into the left hemisphere. The patients usually were able to demonstrate how to use the object when the sensation was sent to the right hemisphere—for example, they could make the appropriate hand movements as if they were writing with the pencil. But they usually could not name the object unless it was placed in the right hand. This is exactly what would be expected from someone whose knowledge of language is localized in the left hemisphere but whose perceptual, nonverbal knowledge is localized in the right hemisphere. Similar effects were obtained with purely visual stimuli as well, that is, when the left half of a picture was projected to the right hemisphere and vice versa. A caveat to this work is that these patients all had long-term, severe epilepsy, and this condition may have altered the organization of their mental abilities, although some of the basic separation of abilities revealed is likely to be accurate. (Incidentally, Sperry earned the Nobel Prize for medicine in 1981 for his research; the award was made jointly to him and to Hubel and Wiesel, whose research on specialized feature detectors in the visual cortex is described in Chapter 3.)

Although the principle of laterality has been a mainstay of neurological research for a long time, recent evidence suggests that lateralization usually is not as absolute as was previously believed (e.g., in the area of language and speech; see Chapter 9). For such reasons, current researchers usually subscribe to the less extreme version of this principle. For instance, we say that different functions tend to occur more or less efficiently in one hemisphere or the other, or they tend to occur somewhat differently in one side or the other (Banich, 2004; Friedman & Polson, 1981; Moscovitch, 1979), or that the two hemispheres contribute different components to an ability or process (see Gardner, 1985; Gazzaniga, 1995; and the entire February 1998 issue of *Current Directions in Psychological Science,* vol. 7, for useful discussions of this issue).

Methods of Investigation

The methods for investigating the structure and functioning of the brain fall into two broad categories, those involving medically based techniques and those based on behavioral assessments.

LESIONS Needless to say, the investigation techniques used by Sperry, deliberate lesioning of the brain, are limited in their usefulness for revealing the secrets of cognitive processing. Only two kinds of subjects—laboratory animals and patients with medical conditions requiring brain surgery—can be used. A long-standing tradition, however, reports case studies of people or groups of people who by disease or accident have experienced damage or lesions to the brain. Much of the evidence described throughout the book comes from victims of strokes, diseases, aneurysms, head injuries, and other accidental circumstances. In all cases, the site and extent of the brain lesion are important guides to the kind of disruption in behavior that is observed and vice versa (a clear description of the lesion method is found in Damasio & Damasio, 1997).

DIRECT STIMULATION A variety of other techniques have also been used to study localization of function in the brain. In particular, consider the method of direct stimulation, pioneered by Penfield, the famous Canadian neurosurgeon. In Penfield's technique, the patient in brain surgery remained conscious during the surgery, with only a local anesthetic used to prevent pain in the scalp. The surgeon then applied minute electrical charges to the exposed brain, thus triggering very small regions. The patient was then asked to answer questions or report out loud the thoughts and memories that entered awareness. By comparing the patient's reports with the different regions that ▲ are stimulated, a map of cerebral functioning can be developed (Figure 2-9).

Generally, the patients in Penfield's procedure reported ideas or episodes that had a dreamlike quality. Although they occasionally reported seemingly distinct memories, it was seldom possible to check on the accuracy of these reports. Their dreamlike nature suggests that they were heavily influenced by reconstructive processes; that is, they may not have been genuine memories. On the other hand, by stimulating different regions

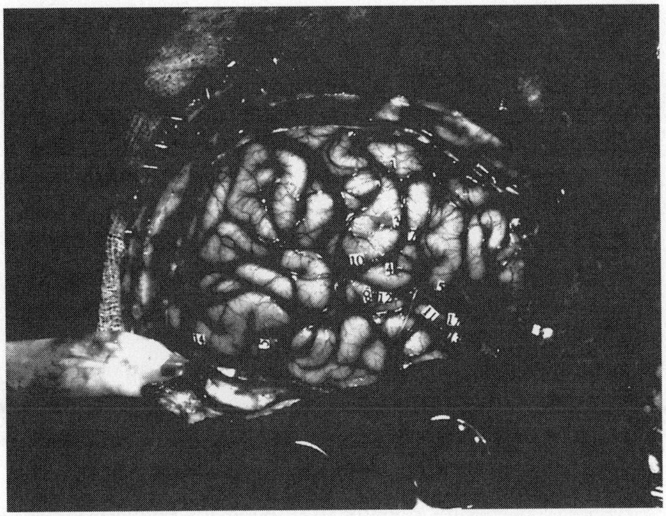

▲ **FIGURE 2-9**
The exposed cortex of one of Penfield's patients. Numbers indicate the areas of the brain Penfield stimulated with the electric probe. When area 13 was stimulated, the patient recalled a circus scene. Stimulating other areas also evoked specific memories. From Penfield (1958).

of the exposed brain, a great deal was discovered about the localization of different functions, kinds of knowledge, and so on, in different parts of the neocortex (e.g., Ojemann, 1982; Ojemann & Creutzfeldt, 1987; Penfield & Jasper, 1954; Penfield & Milner, 1958; for an update on such methods, see Gordon, Hart, Boatman, & Lesser, 1997).

Although such research often yields fascinating evidence, it has some clear difficulties. For one, it is restricted to clinical settings (i.e., patients needing brain surgery). Second, there is the caveat again that at least some evidence that the organization of a patient's brain function may differ substantially from the normal pattern (e.g., in epileptic patients; Kolb & Whishaw, 1996), thus limiting the generalizability of such results.

NEUROIMAGING TECHNOLOGY Much work is now being done with the recent developments in the medical technology of brain imaging (e.g., Toga & Mazziotta, 1996; see Posner, 1997, for a concise introduction). Imaging techniques such as the **computed tomography** (CT) scan and **magnetic resonance imaging** (MRI) can give surprisingly clear pictures of the structure of a living brain, as shown in Figure 2-10. More exciting are techniques that yield images of the *functioning* of the brain, such as the **positron emission tomography** (PET) scan or **functional MRI** (fMRI) techniques (see the several color plates inside the cover of this book). In this technique the image shows regions of the brain with heightened neural activity, with different colors reflecting high or low levels of blood flow, oxygen uptake, and the like. The logic is very straightforward: If a region becomes active because of mental processing, the metabolic rate of that region increases, so increases in oxygenated blood flow are seen (for an excellent and thorough introduction to the fMRI technique, see Huettel, Song, & McCarthy, 2004).

An advantage to these techniques, at least from the perspective of cognitive science, is that they show the brain in action rather than just the physical structures. Such scans are called *functional* because they show the brain as it is functioning, as it performs some mental task. A second advantage is that they can be applied with (apparently) minimal risk to normal people.

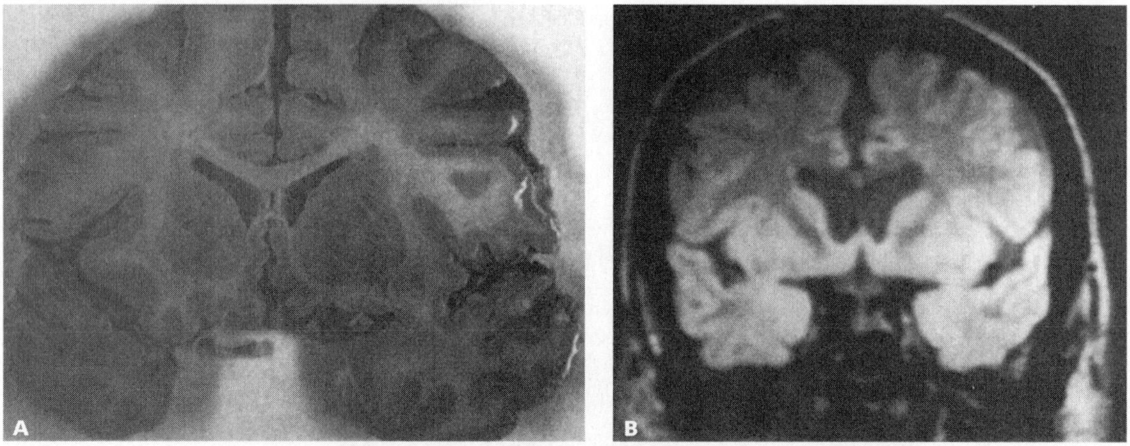

FIGURE 2-10
The clarity of a magnetic resonance imaging view (**B.**) of the brain as compared with a photograph of a dissected brain (**A.**). The position of the coronal section is shown in the photo.

The set of color pictures from Tulving's (1989) article on the dissociation between episodic and semantic memory (color plate #3) relied on a similar procedure, computer-assisted detection of blood flow patterns in a patient injected with an irradiated substance that binds to oxygen in the blood. Note, however, that imaging techniques that measure blood flow have a time lag drawback; the increase in metabolic activity can lag anywhere from several hundred milliseconds to several seconds after the cognitive activity.

Data from neuroimaging studies can be used not only to verify and expand theories of cognition, but can also be used to help solve more applied and clinical problems. Take the example of dyslexia. Recent work has shown that people with dyslexia show different patterns of neural processing as revealed by various neuroimaging technologies (Shaywitz, Mody, & Shaywitz, 2006). For example, some people have a genetically based form of dyslexia in which there are problems in the occipital-temporal region (where the occipital and temporal lobes meet) of the left hemisphere (which is strongly associated with language processing). Specifically, there appears to be a disruption of processing in this region of the brain that makes it difficult to accurately assemble sets of letters into words. In comparison, another group of dyslexics show very adequate processing in the left occipital-temporal region. Their dyslexia, instead, seems environmentally based, related to poorer educational support and other factors, and shows a stronger connection to the right hemisphere prefrontal region, which is associated with memory retrieval. In essence, rather than mentally sounding words out, they treat words more as wholes, attempting to retrieve word meanings directly. As a result, less frequent and new words become much more difficult to process, and dyslexics of this type show very different and persistent difficulties with reading.

ELECTROENCEPHALOGRAMS AND EVENT-RELATED POTENTIALS Other techniques measure the brain's electrical activity online, immediately. Traditionally, brain wave patterns were studied rather crudely with electroencephalogram (EEG) recordings. In this technique, electrodes are placed on the person's scalp, and the device records the patterns of brain waves. More recently, researchers have focused on **event-related potentials (ERPs)**, *the momentary changes in electrical activity of the brain when a particular stimulus is presented to a person* (e.g., Donchin, 1981; Rugg & Coles, 1995).

As an example, read the following sentence (adapted from Banich, 2004, based on Kutas & Hillyard, 1980): "Running out the door, Patty grabbed her jacket, her baseball glove, her cap, a softball, and a skyscraper."

Of course you noticed that *skyscraper* does not fit the context of the sentence; it's called a semantic anomaly. What is fascinating is that the ERP recording of your brain wave activities would show a marked change about 400 ms after you read *skyscraper:* an electrically negative wave called N4 or N400. The N4 would be present, though smaller, if the last word in the sentence had been *lamp* and at baseline if the last word were *bat.*

Osterhout and Holcomb (1992) found this N4 effect for semantic anomalies and also a similar effect when the grammar or syntax of the sentence violated normal language rules. They showed their participants control sentences along with sentences that contained grammatical or syntactic anomalies:

(Control) John told the man to leave.

(Anomalous) John hoped the man to leave.

With this manipulation of syntactic anomaly, Osterhout and Holcomb found a pronounced P6 or P600 effect, an electrically positive change in activity, roughly 600 ms after reading the word *to* (the word that signals the syntactic violation). Figure 2-11 shows their ◆

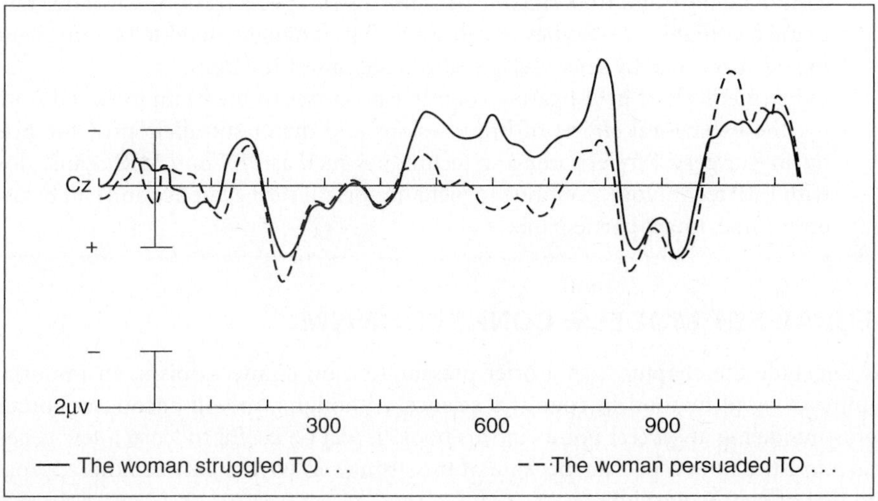

◆ **FIGURE 2-11**
Mean ERPs to syntactically acceptable sentences (solid curve) and syntactically anomalous sentences (dotted curve). The P600 component, shown as a dip in the dotted curve, shows the effect of detecting the syntactic anomaly. Note that in this figure, positive changes go downward.

Reprinted with permission from "Introduction and Overview" by E. D. Bigler, R. A. Yeo, and F. Turkheimer, in *Neuropsychological Function and Brain Imaging* (p. 10), edited by E. D. Bigler, R. A. Yeo, and E. Turkheimer, 1989, New York, Plenum Press.

result. Clearly, our language comprehension system reacts differently—and very quickly—when we encounter unusual or incorrect sentences.

ERP technology is especially good at telling *when* mental mechanisms operate in an online task, but assessments of *where* this process occurs is much trickier and not very precise. By carefully controlling surrounding conditions and measuring the elapsed time since a stimulus was presented, we can begin to see how the electrical activity of the brain changes moment by moment when the person is processing a stimulus.

Section Summary

- Aside from time and accuracy measures and more modern methods based on verbal reports, cognitive science specifically includes a variety of measures from neuroscience, in particular brain imaging data.
- In addition to the basic functioning of neurons, a thorough understanding of modern cognitive science must include an understanding of brain anatomy and two important principles of brain function and architecture: the principle of contralaterality and the principle of hemispheric specialization. The latter refers to the fact that specific types of processes (e.g., language) tend to be represented in and controlled by separate, lateralized regions of the brain.
- Other methods of investigating cognitive processes in the brain included studying the behavioral effects of brain lesions and direct stimulation of the brain during surgery. Modern imaging techniques such as PET and MRI scans, along with ERP technology, continue to yield important new evidence and can be used on normal, intact participants.

NEURAL NET MODELS: CONNECTIONISM

We conclude the chapter with a brief presentation on connectionism, an important computer-based method in cognitive science. Although you will encounter connectionist modeling at several points in this book, it will be useful to learn a few general characteristics now, especially because of the strong similarities between this approach and that of neurocognition.

Connectionist models are often called **neural net models** or **parallel distributed processing (PDP) models**; for our purposes the three terms are treated as synonymous. They refer to *a computer-based technique for modeling complex systems.* A fundamental principle in connectionist models is that the simple nodes or units that make up the system are interconnected. Knowledge, all the way from the simplest to the most complex, is represented in these models as simple interconnected units. The connections between units can either be excitatory or inhibitory; that is, the connections can have positive or negative weights. The basic units receive positive and negative activation from other units; and, depending on these patterns, they in turn transmit activation to yet other units. Furthermore, the interconnectedness of these basic units usually is described as "massive" because there is no particular restriction on the number of interconnections any unit can have. That is, in principle, any bit of knowledge or information can be connected or related to an almost limitless number of other units.

Figure 2-12 illustrates an early connectionist model by McClelland and Rumelhart (1981), a model that dealt with word recognition. The bottom row of nodes or units represents simple features, simple patterns such as a horizontal line and a vertical line, each connected to letters at the next higher level, which in turn are connected to words at the top level. For simplicity, look at the feature on the far left, the horizontal line. The connection directly up from that to the capital letter *A* would be a positive, excitatory connection because the letter *A* has two horizontal lines. The connection from this feature up to the letter *N*, however, would be a negative, inhibitory one: If the feature detection system detects a horizontal line, this works against recognition of the letter *N*. In the same fashion, the capital *A* would have a positive connection up to the word ABLE because *A* is in the first position there, but it would have a negative, inhibitory connection to TRAP because TRAP does not begin with the letter *A*.

Referring to such models by the term *parallel distributed processing* highlights a different facet of the brain and the computer system. Mental processes operate in a thoroughly parallel fashion and are widely distributed across the brain; likewise, processing in a PDP model is thoroughly parallel and distributed across multiple levels of knowledge. As an example, even as the feature detectors at the bottom of the model are

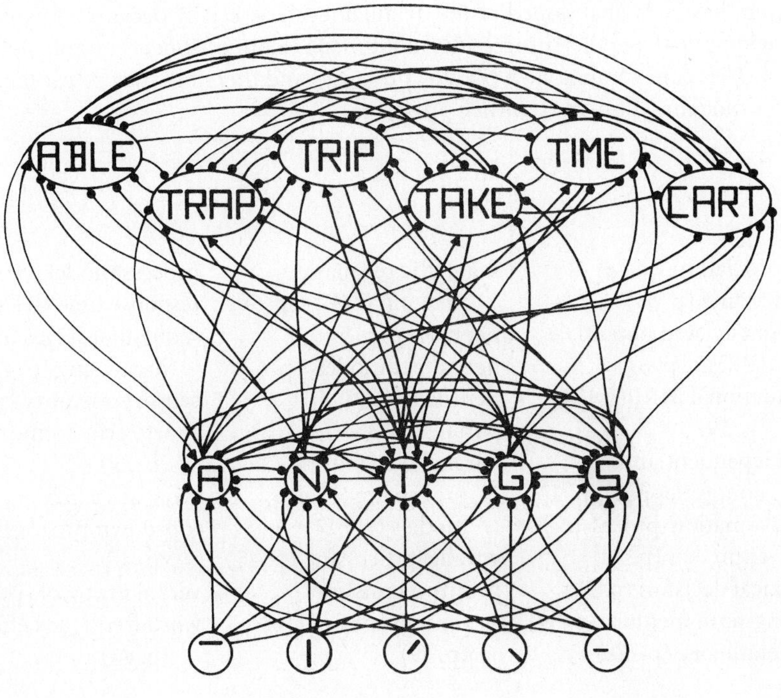

FIGURE 2-12
An illustration of part of McClelland and Rumelhart's (1981) PDP model of feature, letter, and word recognition. From "An Interactive Activation Model of Context Effects in Letter Perception: Part 1. An Account of Basic Findings" by J. L. McClelland and D. E. Rumelhart, 1981, *Psychological Review, 88*, p. 30. Copyright 1981 by the American Psychological Association. Reprinted by permission.

being matched to an incoming stimulus, word units at the top of the model may already be activated. Thus, activation from higher levels may influence processing at lower levels, even as the lower levels effect activation at higher levels.

Consider how the system would recognize the word TRAP in the sentence "After the bear attacked the visiting tourists, hunters went into the forest to set a trap." Even as the feature and letter detector units would be working on the *T*, then the *R*, and so forth, word units at the top would have already received activation based on the meaning and context of the sentence; with bears attacking tourists and hunters going into the forest, the word TRAP is highly predictable from the context, but CART would not be (just as "bat" was predictable but "skyscraper" wasn't in the example given earlier). Given this context, TRAP would be more easily recognized, perhaps because the features within the letters would have been activated by the context already. In this fashion, the comprehension and word recognition systems would be operating in parallel with the feature and letter detection systems, each making continuing, simultaneous contributions to each other and to overall mental processing.

The similarity of the connectionist scheme to the functioning of the brain is obvious and vitally important—it is widely believed that connectionist models operate on the same, or at least very similar, basic principles as the brain (McClelland, Rumelhart, & Hinton, 1986). In other words, the connectionist framework may give us an excellent way of modeling and simulating cognitive processes (for a recent example, see Monaghan & Pollmann, 2003).

Section Summary

- The notion that human cognition is analogous to processing in a computer system has been abandoned at the detailed level, especially because of evidence of widespread parallel processing in humans. Connectionist (neural net, PDP) models can simulate such parallel processes and therefore may be excellent ways of modeling human cognitive processes.

Key Terms

cerebral cortex (p. *53*)
cerebral lateralization (p. *55*)
channel capacity (p. *36*)
cognitive science (p. *45*)
computed tomography (CT) (p. *59*)
conceptually driven processing (p. *47*)
connectionist models (p. *62*)
contralaterality (p. *55*)
control processes (p. *39*)
dissociation (p. *48*)
encoding (p. *39*)
event-related potentials (ERPs) (p. *61*)
functional MRI (fMRI) (p. *59*)
independent and nonoverlapping (p. *42*)
information-processing approach (p. *30*)
lexical decision (p. *39*)
long-term memory (p. *39*)
metatheory (p. *30*)
magnetic resonance imaging (MRI) (p. *59*)
neocortex (p. *53*)
neural net models (p. *62*)
neuron (p. *50*)
parallel (p. *43*)
parallel distributed processing (PDP) models (p. *62*)
parallel processing (p. *45*)
positron emission tomography (PET) (p. *59*)
process model (p. *39*)
response time (RT) (p. *33*)
sequential stages of processing (p. *42*)
sensory memory (p. *39*)
short-term memory (p. *39*)
synapse (p. *52*)
top-down processing (p. *47*)
verbal protocol (p. *44*)
word frequency effect (p. *41*)

CHAPTER

3

Perception and Pattern Recognition

Even psychologists who ought to know better have acted as if they believed (1) that the person's visual experience directly mirrors the stimulus pattern; (2) that his visual experience begins when the pattern is first exposed and terminates when it is turned off; (3) that his experience, itself a passive—if fractional—copy of the stimulus, is in turn mirrored by his verbal report.

NEISSER, 1967, p. 16

Where an object fails to be recognized by sight, it often happens that the patient will recognize and name it as soon as he touches it with his hand. This shows in an interesting way how numerous the associative paths are which all end by running out of the brain through the channel of speech. The hand-path is open, though the eye-path be closed.

JAMES, 1890, p. 61

It's a wonder we can see anything at all, or hear anything, for that matter. The structure of the eye is so implausible, even backward, and the ear so indirect, so incredibly unlikely, that our impressive sensory powers are all the more amazing. We can see the flame of a single candle, on a dark night, from a distance of 20 miles, we can hear a watch ticking 20 feet away in a large, quiet room, and (some of you please note!), we can smell a single drop of perfume diffused into the entire volume of a six-room apartment (Galanter, 1962). And this sensitivity is far exceeded by the complexity of mental processing once perception begins. Because we "understand" what we have seen so quickly, with so little effort, "we can be deceived into thinking that vision should therefore be fairly simple to perform" (Hildreth & Ullman, 1989) and likewise for hearing and the other senses. As you will realize over and over in this chapter (and throughout this book), the fact that a process is rapid and happens out of your awareness does not mean it is simple or simple to investigate. Indeed, if anything, just the opposite is probably true.

This chapter presents a basic study of perception and pattern recognition, in both vision and hearing. We focus especially on the mechanisms and properties of the visual and auditory sensory registers because they are at the most prominent intersections between the environment and human cognition (other animals make prominent use of other senses, such as the sense of smell in dogs). Several theories of perception and pattern recognition are covered, including an elaboration of the connectionist model you were presented in Chapter 2. And in the final section of the chapter, we consider brain-related disruptions in perception and pattern recognition, like those James was discussing in his quotation earlier. We will see what deficits in recognition tell us about the normal processes we take for granted.

VISUAL PERCEPTION

▲ Figure 3-1 illustrates the basic sensory equipment of human vision. Light waves enter the eye, are focused and inverted by the lens, and are projected onto the **retina**. The retina is composed of three layers of neurons: *rods and cones, bipolar cells, and ganglion cells* (see Figure 3-1B). The rods and cones form the back layer of neurons and are the ones stimulated by light, beginning the process of vision. Patterns of neural firing from the rods and cones are passed on to a second layer, the bipolar cells, which collect the messages and move them along to a third layer, the ganglion cells. The axons of the ganglion cells converge at the rear of the eye, forming the bundle of fibers that is the optic nerve. This signal exits the eye and continues through various structures, eventually projecting to the visual cortex of the occipital lobe, in the lower rear portion of the brain.

A brief explanation is in order about how the eyes transmit visual information to the brain. The contralaterality principle in vision is not as simple as "left eye to right hemisphere." Instead, each eye transmits to the occipital lobes of *both* hemispheres. Importantly, each half of the retina gathers information from the contralateral visual
● field. As shown in Figure 3-2, where you are looking is your *fixation point*. The left half of the retina in each eye receives images from the right visual field (the house), and the right half of each retina receives images from the left visual field (the tree). Thus, the right visual field—the solid lines in the figure—projects to the left half of the retina in both eyes, and this information is then transmitted to the left hemisphere. Similarly,

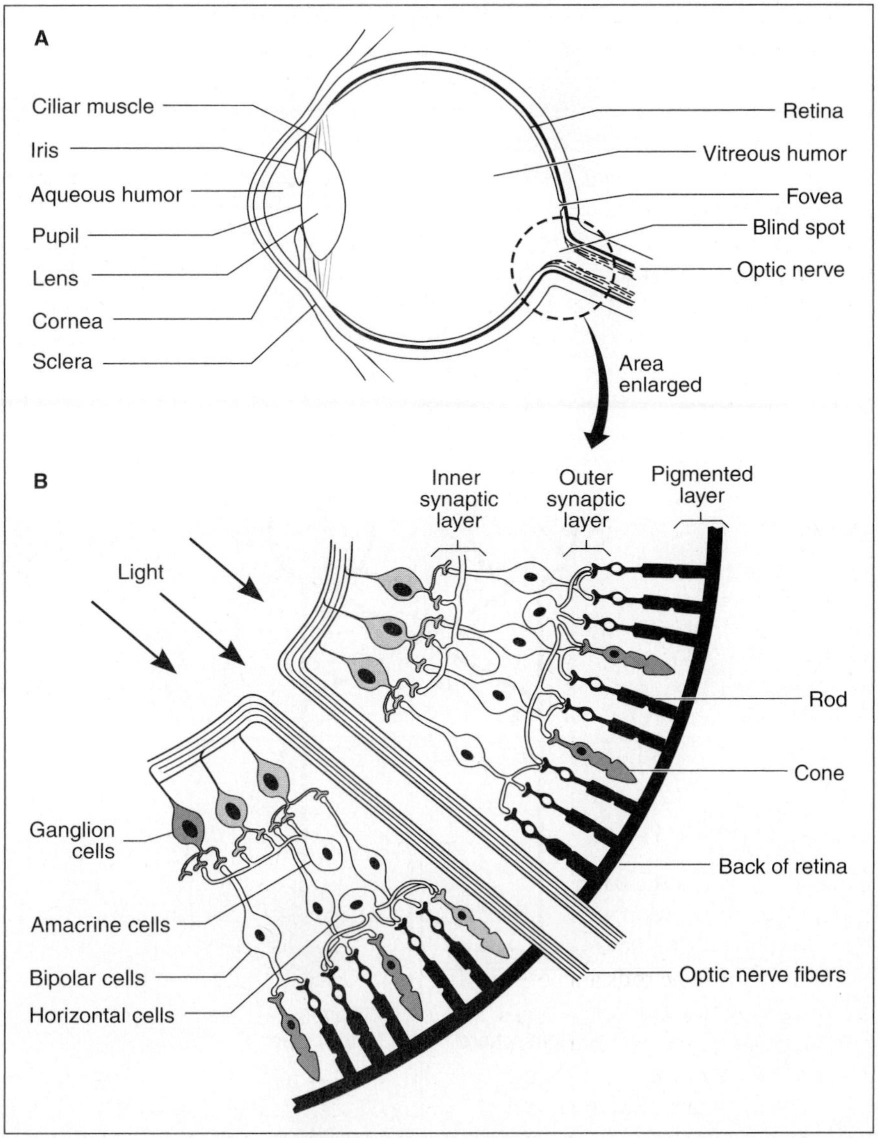

▲ **FIGURE 3-1**
A. The structure of human eye, foveal pit, the optic nerve and other structures.
B. The retina, rods and cones, and ganglion cells. From Hothersall, 1985.

stimuli in the left visual field—the dotted lines—project to the right half of both retinas, and are then sent to the right hemisphere.

Of special interest in this quick physiology lesson is the idea of *compression*, a transformation that analyzes and summarizes visual input. In essence, the message that finally reaches the visual cortex represents an already processed and summarized record of the original stimulus (Haber & Hershenson, 1973). There are approximately 120 million rods on each retina and about 7 million cones. Most of the cones lie in the *small area* known as the **fovea**, *which provides us with our most accurate, precise vision*. At least some of the cones in the fovea have their own "private" bipolar cells for relaying impulses: *One*

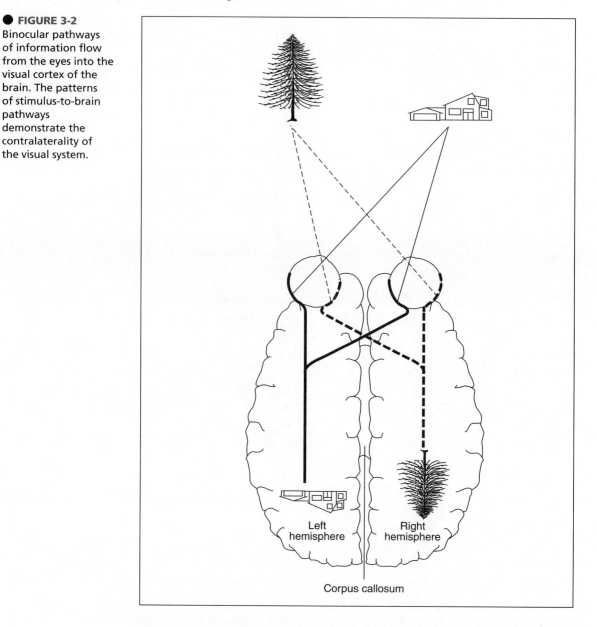

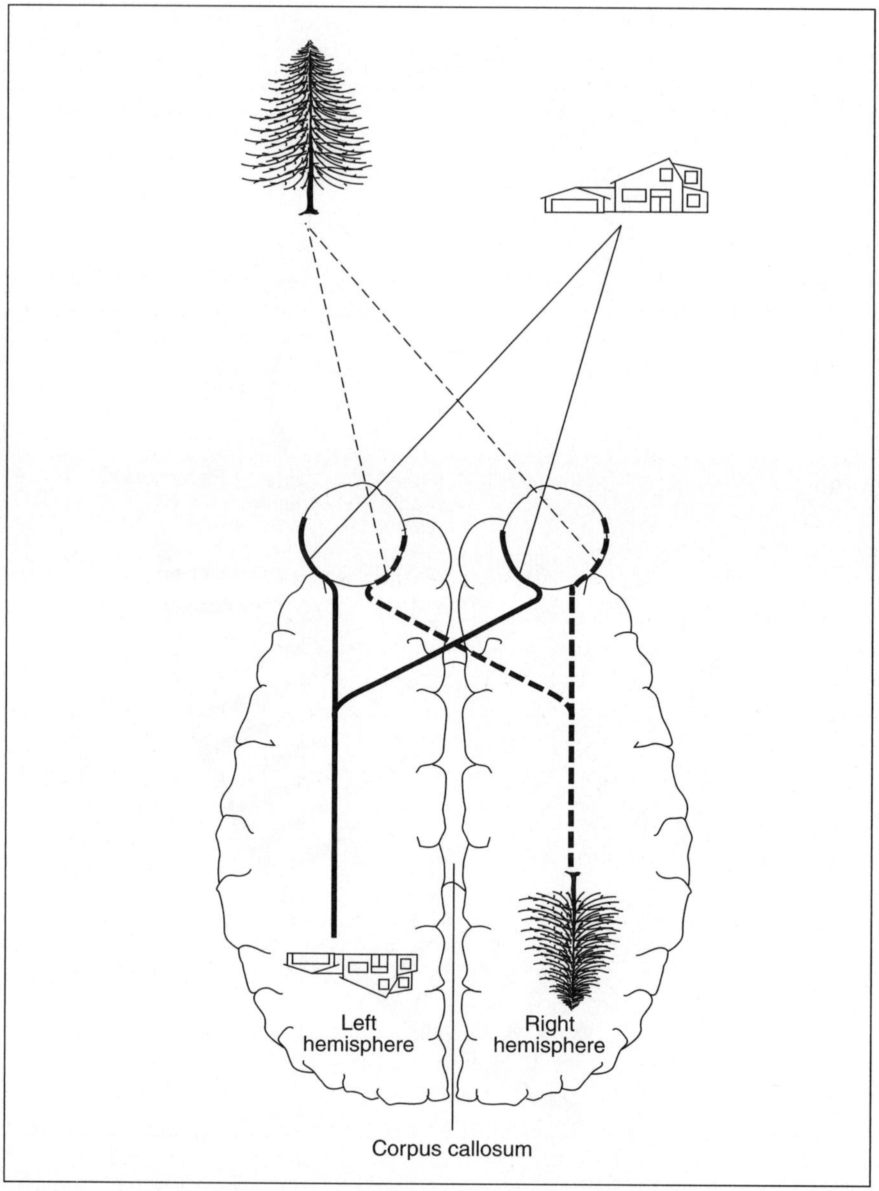

● FIGURE 3-2 Binocular pathways of information flow from the eyes into the visual cortex of the brain. The patterns of stimulus-to-brain pathways demonstrate the contralaterality of the visual system.

cone connects with *one* bipolar cell (technically, a cone *synapses* onto a bipolar cell). In contrast, in peripheral vision, about 20 degrees from the fovea, tens or even hundreds of rods converge on a single bipolar cell. Such convergence clearly results in a loss of information because a bipolar cell cannot "know" which of its many rods triggered it.

Finally, only about 1 million ganglion cells combine to form the optic nerve. So, essentially, vision is compressed from 120 million bits of information down to one million. Thus even the relatively "raw" messages reaching the brain, not yet processed by the cognitive system, have been reduced and summarized to an enormous degree.

Despite this compression, human vision is still amazingly sensitive and acute. Like all good summaries, the visual system preserves the most useful information, the edges, contours, and any kind of change, and omits the less useful, steady-state information.

We have been talking about **sensation**, the *reception of stimulation from the environment and the initial encoding of that stimulation into the nervous system.* Our primary interest is what happens next, what we *do* with this encoded information from the optic nerve. In other words, we want to understand **perception**, *the process of interpreting and understanding sensory information.* As such, we need to explore the stages of visual perception and information processing. We begin with how the eye gathers information from the environment, and then turn to the memory system that retains that information, visual sensory memory.

Gathering Visual Information

Let's eliminate one belief, an apparently common misunderstanding about vision, right away. Winer, Cottrell, Gregg, Fournier, and Bica (2002) asked college students a seemingly simple question, "How does vision work?", using several variations in the task (some tasks involved computer displays, some asked participants to draw a picture or answer a verbal question). In *every* variation, Winer et al. found a substantial percentage of college students exhibited "extramission," the belief that that vision involves some kind of ray or wave going out from the eyes to the object being perceived (think of the rays emanating from Superman's eyes). For instance, "when adults were asked to draw whether something comes into or goes out of the eyes when a person sees a balloon, 69% placed outward-pointing arrows in their drawings" (p. 419). Another 33% gave extramission responses even when asked about looking at a shining light bulb, where the correct answer should be obvious (the bulb emits light, which comes into the eyes). To the extent that this is truly a common misunderstanding or (mistaken) belief, we should correct it here—vision is *not* the result of some force or ray or "thing" coming out from our eyes *toward* the thing we're looking at. Instead, vision is triggered when the reflection of light from an object hits our eyes. (As discussed in the next chapter, the participants in the study by Winer et al. were probably indicating that the "thing" coming out of the eyes, the "Superman ray," is attention.)

A more subtle misbelief deserves a bit more explanation. It is easy to believe, naively, that we take in visual information in a smooth and continuous fashion whenever our eyes are open. After all, our visual experience is of a connected, coherent visual scene that we can scan and examine at will. This is also largely an illusion, however, one that you can easily disconfirm by a simple observation. Watch someone's eyes as he or she reads. You will see that your friend's eyes do not sweep smoothly across a line of print. Instead, they jerk across the line, bit by bit, with pauses between the successive movements.

Here are the facts. The *eye sweeps from one point to another in fast movements* called **saccades** (French for "jerk," pronounced "*suh-KAHD*"), movements that are interrupted by *pauses* called **fixations** (Figure 3-3). The saccade itself is quite rapid, but also quite variable; some researchers claim that saccades take anywhere from 25 ms to about 100 ms, whereas in reading tasks, estimates are in the 150 to 175 ms range (Rayner, 1998). And it takes up to 200 ms to plan and trigger the movement (Haber & Hershenson, 1973). During the saccade, there is suppression of the normal visual

PROVE IT

Yogi Berra supposedly once said something to the effect that "you can observe a lot just by watching." Very little of the evidence you're reading about in this chapter, however, can be observed easily without specialized apparatus; for instance, you need a tachistoscope to present visual stimuli in a highly controlled, precise fashion. But you can make some important and revealing observations just by watching someone's eyes (this also relates to material you will read in Chapter 9).

Get very close to a friend's face and watch as he or she reads a passage of text silently and as he or she looks at a photo or drawing, maybe something as complex as the photo in Figure 3-3. At a minimum, what you'll see—the fast, jerky saccades of the eye movements—will disprove your intuitions that the eyes move smoothly and regularly across a line of print or systematically around a photograph or picture.

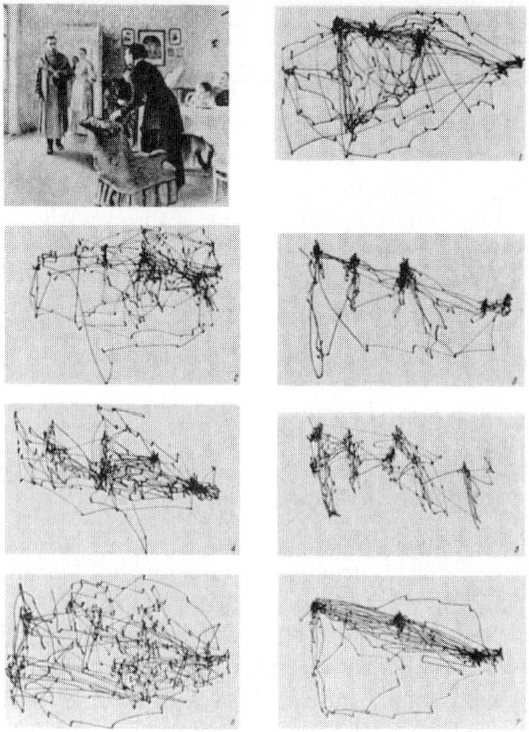

◆ **FIGURE 3-3**
Saccade and fixation paths of a participant looking at the photograph in the upper left. The traces show fixations and paths when the participant merely viewed the photograph (Trace 1), had to estimate the economic status of the family in the photograph (Trace 2), judged the ages of the family members (Trace 3), guessed what the family had been doing before the visitor arrived (Trace 4), had to remember their clothing (Trace 5), had to remember the locations of the family members and objects (Trace 6), estimated how long the visitor had been away from the family (Trace 7). From Yarbus (1967); adapted from Solso (1995).

processes, even those that do not involve the current visual scene. In essence, some types of thinking stop when we are moving our eyes. For example, if given a task involving rotating mental images, people cease rotating the images during a saccade (Irwin & Brockmole, 2004).

In short, for the most part we take in visual information only during a fixation (and as explained later, probably only during the first brief moments of fixation). It is almost as if we are blind during the actual sweeping saccade movement (if the eye did encode information during the saccade, we'd see a smear). As a quick demonstration of this, try to watch your own eyes make saccades while looking in a mirror. You can't do it. You can only acutely see the part of the visual field you are looking directly at. In confirmation of this, several investigations document what is called **change blindness**, our *failure to notice changes in visual stimuli (e.g., photographs) when those changes occur during a saccade* (e.g., Hollingworth, 2003; Simons & Ambinder, 2005).

Assume something in the range of 250 to 300 ms for an entire fixation–saccade cycle. At that rate, there is enough time for about three or four complete visual cycles per second. Each cycle registers a distinct and separate visual scene, although only a radical shift in gaze would make one cycle's input completely different from the previous one.

A final important detail concerns the triggering of saccades themselves and more generally the engagement of visual attention. As Allport (1989) noted, there is a competition-like situation in visual attention. On the one hand, attention must be interruptible. That is, we need to be prepared to react quickly to the unexpected, as when sudden movement alerts us to a possibly dangerous situation (a car running a red light as you drive through the intersection). While you are deliberately focusing your visual attention on one stimulus, the visual system must be able to react to other visual inputs, those outside the focus of visual attention, to at least some degree (e.g., Theeuwes, Kramer, Hahn, & Irwin, 1998). As you will read later, much of this low-level processing appears to occur in parallel with other visual processing and involves detection of simple visual features (Treisman & Gelade, 1980).

On the other hand, visual attention should not be *too* interruptible. We cannot constantly be switching from one input to another—from the words in this sentence to your desk lamp to the scene outside your window to the color of the wall. If attention switched that frequently and erratically, visual (and mental) continuity would be destroyed. Balancing these competing tendencies is an ongoing process of monitoring; we evaluate the importance of current activity, of maintaining visual attention, relative to the importance or urgency of stimuli outside the current attentional focus.

It seems clear that more research needs to be done on this monitoring or interruption process, to determine how it works or fails to work. That is, several researchers have demonstrated that *we sometimes fail to see an object we are looking at directly, even a highly visible one, because our attention is directed elsewhere* (Mack, 2003); this is the phenomenon of **inattentional blindness**, blindness due, in some sense, to our lack of attention to an object. In a particularly dramatic demonstration of this effect, Haines (1991) tested experienced pilots in flight simulators. A few of them proceeded to land the simulator, paying close attention to the gauges and dials on the instrument panel but failing to notice that another airplane was blocking the runway (see Mack & Rock, 1998, for a full account). That's a fairly dramatic example, to be sure, but indicative of our mental processing, nonetheless. Likewise, additional research needs to flesh out what is known about cognitive processing during saccades, in particular which cognitive processes are disrupted—and which are not—when we deliberately move our eyes (Irwin & Brockmole, 2004).

Visual Sensory Memory

We turn now to visual sensory memory. Because this memory system has such a short duration, generally we have few useful intuitions about its operation. Unusual circumstances, however, can give us some clues. Thus we begin with such a circumstance.

Everyone has seen a flash of lightning during a thunderstorm. Think about that for a moment, then make a guess as to the duration of the light we see in an otherwise darkened backyard (or other visual scene) when a bolt of lightning strikes. Most people guess that the flash of light lasts a little more than a half second or so, maybe closer to a whole second sometimes. If your estimate was in this neighborhood, then it is reasonable—but not as an estimate of the physical duration of the lightning. The bolt of lightning is actually three or four separate bolts. Each bolt lasts about 1 millisecond (ms), and there is a separation of about 50 ms between bolts. Thus the entire lightning strike lasts no more than about 2/10 of a second, or 200 ms, and is composed of several individual flashes (Trigg & Lerner, 1981).

Given that it was so off, what was reasonable about your estimate? It was your *perception* of a flash of light extended in time. This phenomenon is called **visual persistence**, the *apparent persistence of a visual stimulus beyond its physical duration*. This usually includes the subjective feeling that you can look around the scene and that the scene fades away rather than being "switched off." In Loftus and Irwin's (1998) words, "Two empirical facts are clear. . . . First, something that *looks like* the physical stimulus continues to be present for a brief time following stimulus offset. Second, *information can be acquired from the stimulus* for a brief period following stimulus offset in much the same way as it can be acquired while the stimulus is physically present" (p. 136).

Our perception of lightning is a mental event that reflects visual persistence.

In terms of physiology, the neural activity on the retina that is caused by the lightning flash does not outlast the flash itself. The eye does not continue to send "lightning" messages after the flash is over (unless a retinal afterimage is involved). Your perception of the lightning is a mental event that reflects visual persistence in that you perceive a lighted scene that then fades away. Because any persistence of information beyond its physical duration defines the term *memory*, the processes of visual perception (as opposed to sensation) must begin with a memory system, some sort of *temporary visual buffer that holds visual information for brief periods of time*. This memory is called **visual sensory memory**; Neisser's (1967) term **iconic memory** is equivalent.

AMOUNT AND DURATION OF STORAGE The classic cognitive research on the characteristics and processes of visual sensory memory was reported by Sperling and his coworkers (1960; Averbach & Sperling, 1961). Sperling presented a visual stimulus for a carefully controlled period of time, usually on the order of milliseconds, to study "the information available in brief visual presentations," the title of his important paper in 1960.

A typical iconic memory experiment by Sperling presented arrays of letters and digits to people for very brief durations. In all cases, the task was to report what could be remembered from the display. For example, people were shown a series of trials, each with a 3 × 4 array of letters (three rows, four letters per row). The array was shown for 50 ms and was followed by a blank postexposure field. Finally, a signal was given to report the letters. See Figure 3-4 for a schematic diagram of a typical trial. ■

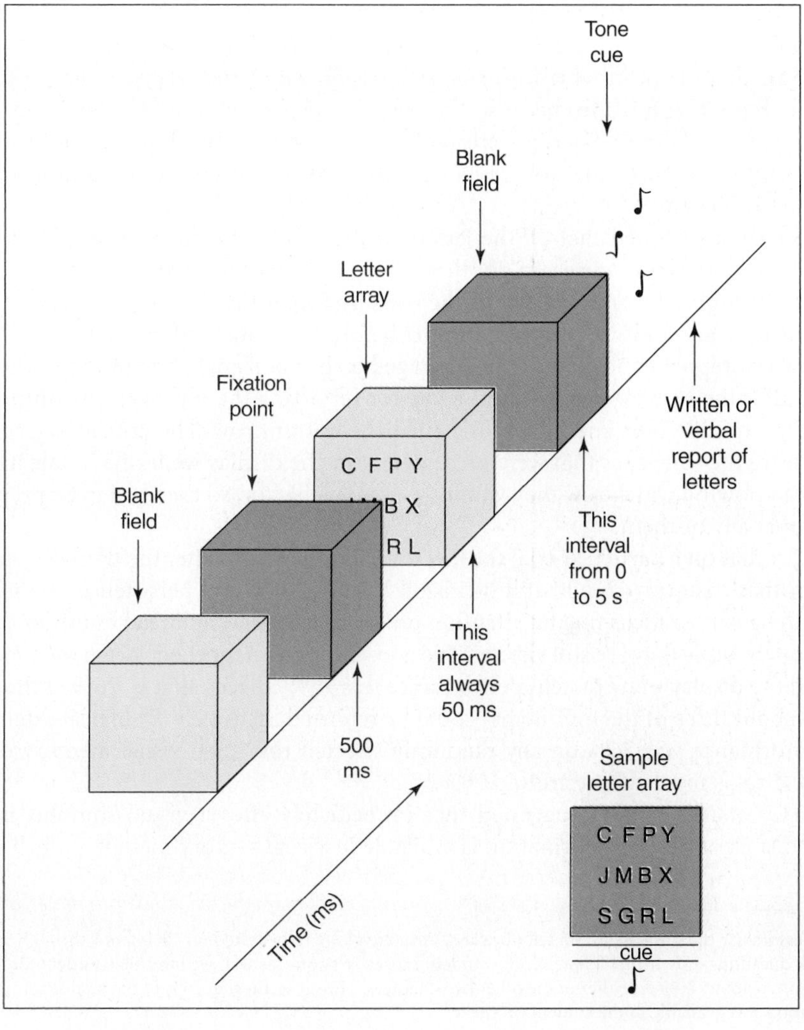

FIGURE 3-4 A schematic diagram of a typical trial in Sperling's (1960) experiments. After a fixation point appears for 500 ms, the letter array is displayed. The visual field after the display is blank. The tone cue can occur at the same time as the postfield, or it can be delayed up to 5 s. Data from Sperling, 1960.

Sperling found that people generally reported no more than four or five items correctly in this kind of test. When fewer than five items were shown, performance was essentially perfect; when more than five were shown, people averaged about 4.5 letters correct. For a display of 12 letters, there was 37% accuracy. Furthermore, he found that this level of accuracy remained essentially the same for exposures as long as 500 ms and even as short as 5 ms (Sperling, 1963). It seemed that an average of 4.5 items correct reflected a default strategy. That is, people said they could not possibly remember all 12 letters, because the display seemed to fade from view too rapidly; even though they had seen the entire display, it disappeared too quickly. Consequently, they apparently decided before the trial began that they would concentrate on just one or two of the rows, trying to maximize their performance on at least a part of the display. Their level of performance, about 4 or 5 items, was what would be expected based on the **span of apprehension**, *the number of individual items recallable after any short display* (also known as the *span of attention* or the *span of immediate memory;* see Chapters 4 and 5).

What distinguished Sperling's research from the many studies that preceded it was the ingenious condition he developed to contrast with these results. The condition just described, in which *people are to report any letters they can*, is called the **whole report condition** because the whole display was to be reported. The contrasting condition Sperling created is called the **partial report condition**, *in which only one of the rows was to be reported.* The logic behind this condition was absolutely elegant.

Sperling reasoned that *all* the letters of the display might be available initially but then might fade more rapidly than they could be reported. If so, then people should be highly accurate on any of the rows the experimenter might choose at random if they are told which row to report before too much fading took place. So in the partial report condition, he prearranged a special signal: A high tone, sounded right after the display went off, was a cue for reporting the top row, a medium tone cued the middle row, and a low tone cued the bottom row. The crucial ingredients here were the tone cues that were presented after the display went off. People had no way of knowing which row they would be responsible for, so they had to be prepared to report any of them.

Say that on a particular trial the low tone sounded right after the display went off. Given that the array should still be visible because of visual persistence, the person should be able to focus mental attention on the bottom row and read out those letters accurately while they are still visible. This is exactly what happened. When the tone followed the display immediately, performance was 76% correct; that is, 76% of the cued row (about three of the four items) could be reported accurately. By logical extension, if performance was 76% on any randomly selected row, then visual memory of the *entire* display must also be around 76%.[1]

This startling result suggested that immediately after a visual stimulus is displayed, a great deal of information is available in visual sensory memory, much more

---

[1] Professors use the same logic. We tell our class, "You are going to be tested on Chapters 1 through 3," then we ask questions only from Chapter 2. If a student scores 76% on this test, we infer that student also could have gotten about 76% on either of the other two chapters. Thus it seems that 76% of the total amount of information was available to the student on the test.

than could be reported aloud. On the other hand, we would not expect this much of the display to remain visible and reportable for very long. After all, the whole report condition almost never exceeded four or five items, averaging 37% of the whole display. As expected, performance in the partial report group began to decline as the information in iconic memory began to fade. As the blank postfield interval got longer—more and more time passed until the tone—performance dwindled further. With a 1 s delay, partial report performance was 36%, almost exactly what the whole report condition achieved (Sperling, 1960).

Similar results, from a study that showed 18 letters in the displays, are shown in Figure 3-5 in the curve for light prefields and postfields. In Sperling's words, "The explanation for these results is that the visual image of the stimulus persists for a short time after the stimulus has been turned off, and that the people can utilize this rapidly fading image. In fact, naive participants typically believe that the physical stimulus fades out slowly" (1963, p. 22). This was our naive impression of the flash of lightning as well. As the fading continues, however, less and less of the original display is still visible in iconic memory, until by 1 s the only reportable items are the few that were transferred into the more durable short-term memory store. ★

So, the results indicated that at least 17 of the 18 letters were available in the initial **icon** (an image in iconic memory often are called the icon, *the visual image that resides in iconic memory*). This study (Averbach & Sperling, 1961) also varied the

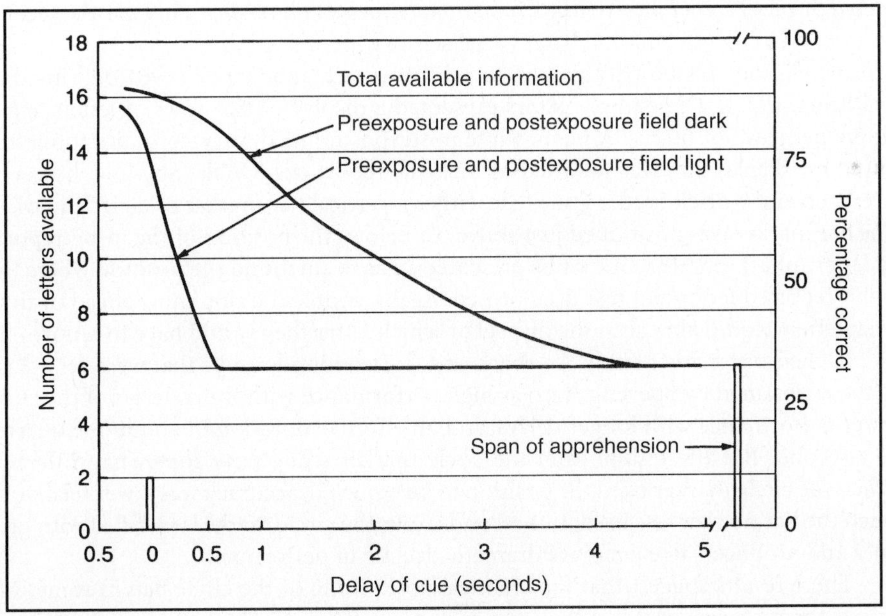

★ **FIGURE 3-5**
One person's results on the number of letters available for report, as revealed by the partial report condition. The number of reportable letters drops sharply within 0.25 s when the postexposure field is light; the information persists much longer when the postexposure field is dark. The vertical bars on the *x*-axis show the number of letters reported under the whole report. From Averbach & Sperling, 1961.

visual characteristics of the stimulus to demonstrate the particularly visual (as opposed to mental) nature of the icon and iconic memory storage. Dark preexposure and postexposure fields lengthened the useful readout period of iconic information when compared with light preexposure and postexposure fields (just as a lightning bolt is more visible in a nighttime storm than a daytime storm because of the contrast with the background). More than 50% of the letters were still available after a 2 s cue delay when dark fields were used (see Figure 3-5). In contrast, accuracy dropped to 50% with light fields after only a quarter of a second. As would be expected of a visually based memory, the light and dark contrast of the stimulus display itself also affected the results, with better iconic visibility for sharper contrasts.

ERASURE AND INTERFERENCE A related series of experiments by Sperling and others explored the loss of information from iconic memory more carefully. The original research suggested that forgetting was *a passive process like fading* or **decay**; that is, the mere passage of time degraded the icon, making it illegible after a short interval. This must certainly be true because care was taken to prevent subsequent stimuli from entering the visual store (the blank postexposure fields). But, of course, in normal vision, no such blank field follows the visual input to our eyes: We look around continuously, shifting visual gaze from one stimulus to another all the time. What happens to iconic memory when a second stimulus is presented to the person, when one visual scene is immediately followed by another? The answer, in short, was **interference**, *forgetting caused by the effects of intervening stimulation or mental processing*. This was the second reason for losing information from visual sensory memory.

A well-known study of this was done by Averbach and Coriell (1961; reprinted in Coltheart, 1973). These investigators presented a display of two rows of letters, eight letters per row, for 50 ms. A blank white postexposure field, varying in duration, followed the display and was followed by a partial report cue. Unlike Sperling, however, Averbach and Coriell used a visual cue, either a vertical bar marker or a circle marker. The bar marker was positioned just above (or below) the position of the to-be-reported letter, and the circle marker was presented so as to surround the position where the to-be-reported letter had just disappeared. Again, people did not know ahead of time what letters would appear in the display or which letter they would have to report.

In their bar marker study, Averbach and Coriell found results that were very close to those obtained by Sperling, such as high performance with short delays of the cues, lower performance with longer delays, and an effective duration of about one quarter of a second. But the results from the circle marker study were somewhat different. When the circle marker cued the position to be reported, accuracy was lower relative to when the bar marker was used. In a second study, the circle marker was filled with grid lines and produced an even more dramatic decline in performance.

These results suggest that the identical positioning of the circle had in some way erased the memory trace for the letter in that position. Note what an unusual event this is: "*A later visual stimulus can drastically affect the perception of an earlier one*" (Averbach & Coriell, cited in Coltheart, 1973, p. 16, emphasis added). This is called **backward masking**. The masking stimulus, if it occurs soon enough after the letter display, interferes with the perception of the earlier stimulus presented at the same position. In some backward masking studies, people claim that they saw *only* the mask, even though their other performance indicates that the sensory system did indeed register the first stimulus (data on this go back as far as Werner, 1935; see Kahneman, 1968, for a review). In general, *when the contents of visual sensory memory are degraded by subsequent visual stimuli*, the loss of the original information is called **erasure**, a specific kind of interference.

Because the visual world is not being continuously sampled by iconic memory, cognition must make inferences about what goes on in between. As an illustration of this, when you are watching a movie or television, you are seeing a series of still pictures presented in rapid fashion, one after the other. The pictures change faster than your iconic memory can decay, replacing one another. Your brain fills in any jumps in position, producing the illusion of motion. This mental perceptual inference of illusory motion is called **beta movement** (Wertheimer, 1912). It is one of the principles derived by the Gestalt psychologists to account for the organization of the perceptual world (more about Gestalt perceptual principles later).

Another, related perceptual illusion occurs when you see lights moving or flowing around on a movie marquee or chasing Christmas lights. This is something called the **phi phenomenon** (Wertheimer, 1912). Essentially, when iconic memory receives visual images in relatively close proximity in space and time, it will infer a virtual movement.[2] So, in essence, beta movement occurs when making inferences from one picture to the next, as in a movie, but phi movement involves illusory tracking of an object in space.

The Early Parts of a Fixation

The evidence collected by Sperling, Averbach and Coriell, and many others led cognitive psychology to propose that iconic memory was the initial step in visual information processing. The phenomenon of visual persistence, as revealed in the quarter-second duration of information, was replicated many times. This convinced cognitive psychology that iconic memory existed and that it was the important first phase in visual perception (Neisser, 1967). Theories of visual perception therefore included iconic storage as an integral part of visual perception.

But newer evidence is showing even more fascinating results. A study by Rayner, Inhoff, Morrison, Slowiaczek, and Bertera (1981) serves as a good example. These researchers examined performance during a reading task (see Chapter 10 for more research on the process of reading), using an eye-tracker for precise timing measurements. After people had fixated a word for a mere 50 ms, the word was replaced with an irrelevant stimulus, which remained in view for another 175 ms to fill up the rest of the fixation time. Surprisingly, this did not affect reading at all—participants often did not notice that the word had even changed. In Coltheart's (1983) words, "Continuous. . . sampling of the text throughout a fixation does not occur. Once the

---

[2] The Phi phenomenon was important in the establishment of automated railroad crossings. Back in the day, important railroad crossings had a railroad employee who would swing a lantern to warn vehicles that they were approaching a crossing. The automated crossings were designed with two lights that would blink at the appropriate rate to produce the Phi phenomenon and produce the perception of a swinging lamp. However, when the first automated crossings were built, they got the timing off—it just looked like two lights alternating on and off. Nevertheless, the railroad companies stuck with that timing.

text has been fixated for 50 ms or so, its presence during the remainder of the fixation is *irrelevant* and makes *no* contribution to reading" (p. 18, emphasis added).

This is important—this is very important, so you should stop and think about it for a moment. Despite what it feels like, as you read these words on this page, you are not viewing these words continuously, with your eyes sweeping smoothly across the page. You are seeing them in extremely brief bursts, extracting information quickly and then devoting mental energy to processing them further, unaware of your "down time" during the fixation and of your blindness during the following saccade.

Several investigators have also collected evidence on what might be called "dynamic icons," that is, iconic images that contain movement (see Finke & Freyd, 1985; Irwin, 1991, 1992; Loftus & Hanna, 1989). Treisman, Russell, and Green (1975) presented a brief (100 ms) display of six moving dots and asked people to report the direction of movement. Partial report performance was superior to whole report performance, and accuracy under partial report declined across time. In short, the moving images of the dots were decaying just as the static letter grid had in Sperling's procedures.

In other words, visual perception is not a process of flipping through successive snapshots, with three or four snapshots per second. Instead, it may be more accurately described as a process of focusing on the visually attended elements of successive fixations, where each fixation encodes a dynamic segment of the visual environment.

In fact, integration across brief intervals of time can occur even *without* eye movements. The evidence presented by Loftus and Irwin (1998) shows that temporal integration—perceiving two separate events as if they had occurred at the same time—happens seamlessly when visual events occur within about 20 ms of each other. Equally interesting, it seems to happen without any conscious awareness that two separate events have occurred. Events separated by 40 ms or more, or separate events that themselves last for 40 ms or more, tend not to be integrated as completely. With these longer durations, in other words, people can more easily detect that two separate events happened rather than just one.

A Summary for Visual Sensory Memory

How do all these different results make sense: the wholesale input of visual stimulation; the persistence, decay, erasure, and integration of information; and the concept of visual attention?

Consider the following: Under normal viewing conditions, one moment's visual input replaces the previous visual input by means of erasure or "writing over." Under unusual circumstances, such as with single brief glimpses, even the shortest stimulus displays will seem to last about 250 or 300 ms because of visual persistence, the duration of a normal iconic memory. With a blank postexposure field, which artificially prevents any subsequent stimulus, the perceptual fading of the icon is even visible.

The continuous stream of successive glimpses in normal vision, however, serves as an eraser under more normal viewing conditions. Under those normal circumstances, we are not aware of any fading. Note here that the rapid extraction of information during the first few milliseconds of exposure appears to be critical to the perception of continuous vision. Indeed, it may be that the first 50 ms or so are all we need to encode visual information. During the remaining time, we *attend* to the information—pay attention to it—and begin to replace that icon with new information from the next fixation.

The entire sequence of encoding visual information—selecting part of it for further processing, planning subsequent eye movements, and so on—is very active and rapid. The visual continuity we experience, our feeling that we see continuously, without breaks, pauses, or blank intervals, is due to the constant updating of visual sensory memory and to our focus on attended information. As we attend to a visual stimulus, we seem to be examining the readout from iconic memory. In the meantime, a new visual scene is being registered in sensory memory. Our mental processes then pick up the thread of visual information in the newly registered scene, providing a smooth transition from one attended display to the next.

Focal attention was Neisser's (1967) term for this *mental process of visual attention*, such as the mental redirection of attention when the partial report cue is presented. It seems that focal attention, or simply *visual attention*, might be the bridge between successive scenes registered by visual sensory memory. This bridging prevents us from sensing the blank space of time occupied by the eye's saccades by directing focal attention to elements of the icon. Although we *sense* a great deal of visual information, what we *perceive* is the part of a visual scene selected for focal, visual attention. To exaggerate a bit, what you are perceiving right now is not the printed page in front of you. Instead, you are perceiving the processed and attended portions of the displays that were registered in sensory memory, your iconic trace, as processed by visual attention.

Trans-saccadic Memory

In order to build up a complete understanding of the visual world, we need to move our eyes, head, and body, gathering in visual information across each successive fixation. How do we put all of these fixations together? This is done using a type of iconic memory known as **trans-saccadic memory** (e.g., Irwin, 1996), *the memory system that is used across a series of eye movements.* An important question regarding this issue is how iconic memory tracks information about the world to figure out how to put together information from different fixations. It does not appear that we use retinal coordinates (where the images fall on the eyes) to integrate information across eye movements, nor do we seem to use spatial coordinates (where things are in space) to accomplish this (Irwin, Yantis, & Jonides, 1983).

Instead, trans-saccadic memory appears to work by using what are called *object files* (Kahneman, Triesman, & Gibbs, 1992). Object files are representations of individual objects that iconic memory uses to track what is going on in the world. Evidence for their use in trans-saccadic memory comes from studies in which people are asked to detect changes in objects after a saccadic eye movement (Henderson & Anes, 1994). For example, one type of change detection would be detecting if a letter changed to a plus sign in a display. In general, people are fairly accurate at detecting changes in objects they focused on in a display. Importantly, this does not occur for all objects in the visual scene, but only for those to which a person is actively attending. Our brain assumes that everything else is more or less stable, which is why we may miss those changes.

Section Summary

- The eye sweeps across the visual field in short, jerky movements called saccades, taking in information during brief fixations. The information encoded in these fixations is stored in visual sensory memory for no more than about 250 ms. This iconic image, which may include movement, fades rapidly or can be erased by subsequent visual stimulation. Much more information is stored in visual sensory memory than can be reported immediately. Information that is reported has been transferred to short-term memory by the process of focal attention.
- Recent work suggests that we do not continuously extract information from the visual scene around us but instead extract most of the information we need within the first 50 ms of fixation. Thus, visual sensory memory is a fast-acting, rapidly adapting system ideally suited for processing information in real time in a continuously dynamic world.
- To build up a complete mental representation of the world, we use trans-saccadic memory. This integration does not appear to use retinal or spatial coordinates to map information from different eye fixations together. Instead, iconic memory appears to track the various entities in the world using object files of what they are doing, and how they might be changing. However, this also requires that a person is actively attending to those objects.

PATTERN RECOGNITION

We turn now to one of the most intriguing and debated topics in visual perception, the identification of visual patterns. The role of visual sensory memory is to encode the visual information into the memory system, so that pattern recognition can take place.

As you will see in the following sections, pattern recognition does not occur instantly, although it does happen automatically and spontaneously. Instead, perceptual pattern recognition is, in many ways, a problem solving process, although much of the mental work occurs subconsciously and very rapidly. Essentially, what is occurring in perception is that a person needs to identify the nature of the two- or three-dimensional objects based on the proximal images reaching the retina. Often these images are compromised in some way, such as being occluded by another object, being against a complex visual background, and so on. There are a number of ways that vision parses the visual image to extract information about the objects that are actually present, and there are a number of principles that it follows in doing this.

Gestalt Grouping Principles

Perhaps the best-known and established of these are the Gestalt grouping principles. These were principles of perceptual organization laid out by the Gestalt psychologists (see Chapter 1) in the early to mid 20th century. What these principles do is identify those characteristics of perception in which ambiguities in a stimulus are resolved to help determine which entities are present. The most basic of these principles is the *figure-ground* principle. This is the idea that when viewing an image, part of the image will be treated as the figure or foreground (the object identified), which is segregated from the visual information upon which this object is set (the background). Classic examples illustrating the determination of figure-ground are so-called reversible figures, such as the one shown in Figure 3-6A in which a person shifts back and forth between what is the foregrounded object, and what is the background. At one moment it might be two faces, whereas in the next it might be a vase. ▲

Several of the Gestalt grouping principles are aimed at providing a more complete percept from incoming image information that may be fragmentary or incomplete. In many ways, they follow the principle of *closure*, in which a person "closes up" an image that has gaps or parts missing, perhaps because they are being occluded (blocked) by some other object. There are a number of ways in which closure is applied, based on various stimulus characteristics. An example of closure can be observed in Figure 4-1 (page 114). Although it looks like just a collection of blobs, they can be joined using the principle of closure to give the impression of a dog (a Dalmation).

Additional Gestalt principles included the principle of *proximity*, in which elements that are near one another tend to be grouped together in perception. This is

▲ **FIGURE 3-6**
A. An illustration of the Gestalt figure-ground perceptual grouping principle.

▲ **FIGURE 3-6** (cont.)
B. An illustration of the Gestalt perceptual grouping principle of closure.

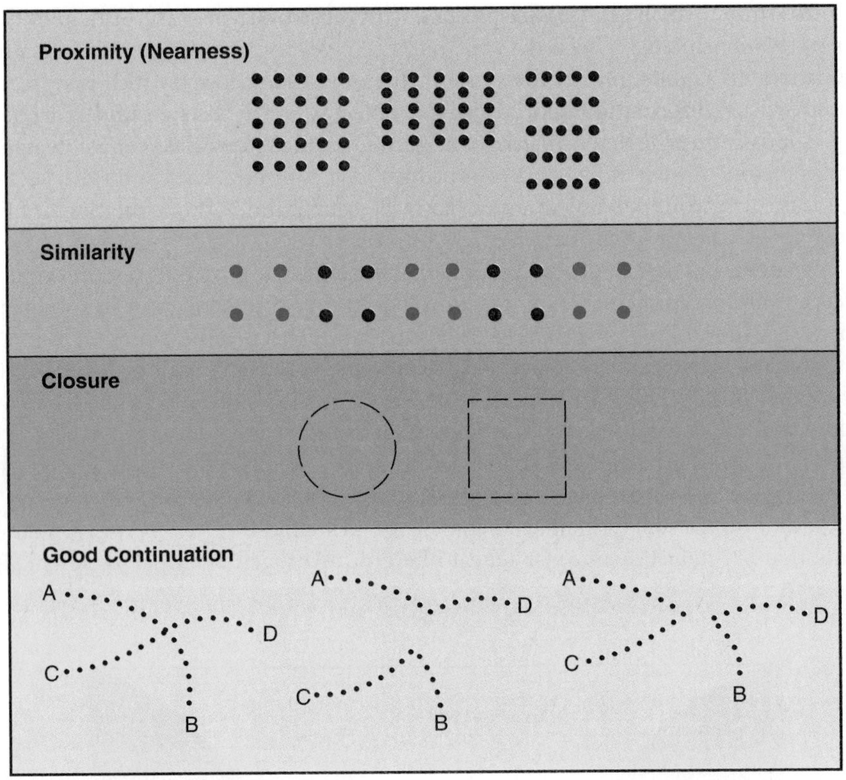

B.

shown in Figure 3-6B. Because of this principle, you see a flight of geese as forming a V. Another principle is *similarity*, in which elements that are visually similar in some way, such as having a similar color or texture, tend to be grouped together. This is shown in Figure 3-6B. An example of the use of similarity in perception is when you tend to see the individual dots on a television or computer screen as being part of the same object if they have a similar color or visual texture.

Finally, some of these grouping principles take into account some form of trajectory. In some cases, the trajectory is the edge of an object. Essentially, the principle of *good continuation* assumes that when there is an edge that is occluded or interrupted, people will assume that it continues along in a regular fashion. In the example shown in Figure 3-6B people tend to perceptually organize this as a single straight line passing through a second oscillating line. They tend not to parse this image as a line that starts out straight, then oscillates, then goes straight again, or some other way. Finally, a related principle is that of *common fate*, which states that entities that move together are perceptually grouped together. For example, when an animal moves in the forest it is easier to spot, even if it is in some branches, than if it remains motionless. This is because the movement allows the perceptual system to group those various points together because they are moving together.

Although we can use the Gestalt grouping principles to some degree in the process of pattern recognition, we need to go deeper to understand how a visual stimulus can be recognized as a familiar pattern. How does your cognitive system manage to input a visual stimulus such as *G* or *tree* and end up recognizing them as familiar, meaningful symbols? How do we recognize patterns of handwriting, or different printed fonts, despite incredible variability? The following sections present some ideas about how pattern recognition occurs by looking at the case of pattern recognition for written language.

The Template Approach

As Neisser (1967) pointed out, pattern recognition would be a simplified problem, though still thorny, if all the equivalent patterns we saw were identical. That is, if there were one and only one way for the capital letter *G* to appear, then the mental process that determines that it is a *G* would be easier to investigate. But, the visual environment is not so conveniently organized. An enormous variety of visual patterns, in countless combinations of orientation and size, will all be categorized as the capital letter *G*, and likewise for all other letters, figures, shapes, and so on.

Perhaps this categorization is done by means of **templates**, *stored models of all categorizable patterns*. When the computer at your bank reads your checking account number, it is performing a template matching process, trying to make physical identity matches between the numbers on your check and its stored templates for the digits 0 through 9. When the computer recognizes a pattern, it has matched it to one of its stored digit or letter templates.

Although the template approach has simplicity and economy on its side, and we do have preferred viewing angles for many objects (called the *canonical view*), it has little else to recommend it. As an explanation of human pattern recognition, it is seriously flawed for a variety of reasons. We have already covered the primary reason, the enormous variability in the patterns that we can recognize. Other reasons exist, too; for example, how long would it take you to learn the infinite number of possible patterns (for all of the objects in the world, the different orientations they can be in, the various distances they can be from you, etc.) that you can recognize or to search through them in memory? Would you have room left in memory for anything else?

Visual Feature Detection

A distinct improvement over the template approach is the notion of **feature analysis** or **feature detection**. A feature is a *very simple pattern, a fragment or component that can appear in combination with other features* across a wide variety of stimulus patterns. A good example of such a visual feature might be a single straight, horizontal line, which appears in capital letters *A*, *G*, *H*, *L*, and so on; others would be vertical or diagonal lines, curves, and so forth. In Chapter 2 you read a brief introduction to a connectionist model of word recognition (refer back to Figure 2-12); the lowest level of representation in that model was exactly this, the feature level.

In general, feature theories claim that we recognize patterns by first identifying the building-block features. Rather than matching an entire templatelike pattern for capital *G*, we first identify the elemental features that are present in the *G*. When "circle opening right" and "horizontal straight" segments are detected, the features match with those stored in memory for capital *G*.

The feature approach has been popular enough that several investigators have proposed rather elaborate theories of feature-based pattern recognition and have carefully worked out the "catalog" of features in written or printed letters (e.g., Gibson, 1965). We'll discuss one such model in some detail because it is a particularly clear example of feature detection models. Understanding Pandemonium will also help you understand the reasons behind interactive, connectionist approaches.

PANDEMONIUM Selfridge (1959), an early advocate of feature detection, described a model of pattern recognition he called **Pandemonium**; an illustration of the model is shown in Figure 3-7. In Selfridge's imaginative description, Pandemonium reigns in the process of pattern recognition because of the mental mechanisms that process a visual stimulus. These mechanisms were *demons* in Selfridge's model, little mental demons who shout out loud as they attempt to identify patterns.

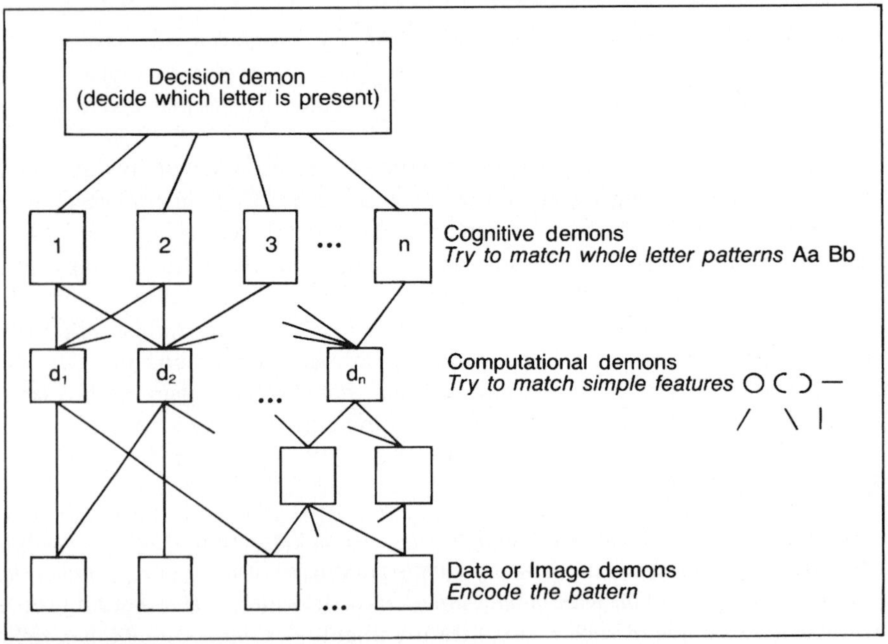

FIGURE 3-7
Selfridge's (1959) Pandemonium model. The image demons encode the visual pattern. The feature demons try to match the simple features present in the pattern. Cognitive demons represent the combination of features that are present in different letters of the alphabet; each tries to match the several computational demons that match the stimulus input. Finally, the decision demon identifies the pattern by selecting the loudest cognitive demon, the one whose features most nearly match the pattern being presented. Adapted from Selfridge, 1959.

As the figure shows, a pattern is encoded by a set of *data demons*. Next, the *computational demons* begin to act. These computational demons are the feature analyzers in Selfridge's model; each one has a single, simple feature it is trying to match in the stimulus pattern. For instance, one demon might be trying to match a simple horizontal line, another would try to match a vertical line, another a curve opening to the right, and so on. When a computational demon matches a stimulus feature, it begins to shout excitedly.

At the next level up, listening to all this shouting is a set of *cognitive demons*. The cognitive demons represent the different letters of the alphabet, one for each letter. Each one is listening for a particular combination of demons to shout: For instance, the *G*-demon is listening for the "open curve" and the "horizontal bar" feature analyzers or demons to shout. Any evidence from the computational demons that suggests a match with the stimulus causes the cognitive demon to begin shouting as well: Based on the feature analysis evidence, it thinks that *it* is the matching pattern. Several of the cognitive demons will be shouting at once because several letters usually share some features (e.g., *C* and *G*). Thus the one who shouts the loudest is the one whose pattern is most nearly matched by the input stimulus. The loudest cognitive demon is finally heard by the *decision demon*, the highest-level demon in the model. This demon has the final say in recognizing and categorizing the pattern.

THREE IMPORTANT IDEAS Aside from the vividness of the model's description of scores of shouting demons producing a noisy Pandemonium, Selfridge's model incorporated several ideas that are important to the issue of pattern recognition. First, at base, it was a feature detection model. The features that were detected and reported by the demons were elementary, simple features—components that in different combinations represent the letters of the alphabet being recognized (Selfridge's model was not limited to letters, but the process is more easily described using letters as examples).

There are now several related lines of evidence for feature detection in visual pattern recognition (e.g., Pritchard, 1961). Especially convincing are the neurophysiological studies showing that specialized visual cortex cells exist for various simple visual features and patterns. The most widely known evidence of this kind comes from research pioneered by Hubel and Wiesel (1962). Using sophisticated electrode implant procedures, these researchers found neurons in cats' brains that respond only to vertical lines, other neurons that respond only to diagonals, and so on. On the assumption that the human brain is not radically different from a cat's at the level of neuronal functioning, this suggests that feature detection may even have a physiological status in the nervous system (for similar evidence in monkeys, see Maunsell & Newsome, 1987). Furthermore, it means that psychological theories of pattern recognition must be compatible with this neurological evidence.

A second important notion in Selfridge's model was the idea of parallel processing; the computational demons all work at the same time, each one trying to match its own feature while all the others are doing the same thing. With this aspect of his model, Selfridge was pointing out that feature detection or analysis is probably a simultaneous or parallel process instead of a serial, "one-after-the-other" process. This seems to be a very reasonable position, even if we use printed text as our only

Identifying a pattern with minimal cues. Pablo Picasso, "Citando al toro con la capa" (Plate Six from the book La Tauromapuia o arte de torear by Jose del Gado alias Pepe Ilo [Barcellona: Gustavo Gili/Ediciones la cometa, 1959], 1957, Sugar lift aquatint.) Fine Arts Museum of San Francisco, Bruno and Sadie Adriani Collection, 1971.28.107.

evidence. That is, the number of individual feature tests needed to recognize all the letters in a single line of print must be quite large. Given the speed with which adults can read a single line, we would have to assume an impossibly fast rate of feature detection if the process is occurring serially. Neisser, Novick, and Lazar (1963) found evidence consistent with the proposal of parallel processing of features when their participants could scan for the presence of 10 different letters just as quickly as they could scan for 1.

The third important idea captured by the Pandemonium model was that perception is, in a very real sense, a problem solving process. The world presents the visual system with bits and pieces of features and relations. The visual system must put these together in such a way as to accurately identify the objects that are out there in the world. Often the system gets this correct. However, occasionally errors will occur, as with visual illusions, or when you mistakenly identify one object as something else, such as when you are driving and swerve to avoid hitting a chipmunk, only to discover a moment later that it is only a dead leaf.

Beyond Features: Conceptually Driven Pattern Recognition

Even Selfridge knew that Pandemonium was missing an important ingredient. Basically, Pandemonium was a completely bottom-up processing system, that is, a completely **data-driven processing system** in which *processing is driven by the stimulus pattern, the incoming data.* In Pandemonium, the patterns to be recognized came in to the image demons at the bottom, then were processed higher and higher until the top-level demon finally recognized the pattern. And yet, Selfridge presented examples like those shown in Figure 3-8, illustrations of the way context can influence pattern recognition. How adequate is the bottom-up, feature detection approach as an explanation of visual pattern recognition? Did you "see" the words *THE* and *CAT* despite the unusual middle letters? Do you "see" the letter *B* and the number *13* in the bottom half of the figure, even though these two are identical? So what was the missing ingredient?

◆ **FIGURE 3-8**
Top-down effects in pattern recognition. **A.** The effect of context on letter recognition (adapted from Selfridge, 1959). **B.** The effect of context on pattern recognition. The *B* and the *13* are identical. From Coren & Ward, 1989.

To pick up on the theme introduced in Chapter 2, the missing ingredient was *context*, a mechanism that would allow context and a person's expectations to influence the recognition of patterns. Such effects are called top-down processing, or **conceptually driven processing effects**, in which *context and higher-level knowledge influence lower-level processes* (remember "typograpical"?). In Figure 3-8 your knowledge of English words and spelling patterns leads you to perceive the middle letters as different, and looking at a line of numbers sets up an expectation for seeing *13* rather than *B*. Let's examine some experimental evidence that supports the feature theory approach but also makes the case for conceptually driven processing.

In Neisser's (1964) classic research on visual search, people saw pages of characters, 50 lines of printed letters, with four to six letters per line. Their task was to scan the page as rapidly as possible to find the one occurrence of a prespecified letter (in other tasks, Neisser asked people to find the line *without* a certain character). As an illustration of the task, do the visual searches presented in Figure 3-9, timing yourself as you find the targets. Notice how hard it is to find a line *without* a specified letter and to find a letter that is physically similar to the distractor letters in the display.

Finding the *K* in the angular-letter column is difficult because the features that define *K* are also sprinkled liberally throughout the angular letters. Likewise, finding the *Z* in the third column is easier than finding it in the fourth. Because the third column contains mostly rounded-feature letters, most of the detectable features in the display can be ignored; the pattern recognition system can shut off the curve-detecting features when it is searching for the *Z* in this kind of display (see Duncan & Humphreys, 1989, for careful consideration of visual search when the similarity of targets and nontargets varies).

There's the shortcoming: We have to "shut off" some feature detectors to explain fast search for *K* in the round-letter condition (analogously, in Duncan and Humphreys's [1989] approach, variations in the nontarget letters influenced the speed of search for targets). But where did the instruction to shut off those detectors come from? Not from the feature detectors themselves, of course. Feature detectors do only one thing—they detect visual features. Instead, this instruction came from some place "higher up," something that "realizes" you can ignore the dissimilar letter shapes. This is the contribution of your existing knowledge to the lower-level process of feature detection—it's conceptually driven processing.

FIGURE 3-9
Neisser's (1964) search lists. In list A, the target is the letter *K*; in list B, the target is the line without the letter *Q*; in lists C and D, the target is the letter *Z*.

A. Search for *K*	B. Search for line without *Q*	C. Search for *Z*	D. Search for *Z*
EHYP	ZVMLBQ	ODUGQR	IVMXEW
SWIQ	HSQJMF	QCDUGO	EWVMIX
UFCJ	ZTJVQR	CQOGRD	EXWMVI
WBYH	RDQTFM	QUGCDR	IXEMWV
OGTX	TQVRSX	URDGQO	VXWEMI
GWVX	MSVRQX	GRUQDO	MXVEWI
TWLN	ZHQBTL	DUZGRO	XVWMEI
XJBU	ZJTQXL	UCGROD	MWXVIE
UDXI	LHQVXM	DQRCGU	VIMEXW
HSFP	FVQHMS	QDOCGU	EXVWIM
XSCQ	MTSDQL	CGUROQ	VWMIEX
SDJU	TZDFQB	OCDURQ	VMWIEX
PODC	QLHBMZ	UOCGQD	XVWMEI
ZVBP	QMXBJD	RGQCOU	WXVEMI
PEVZ	RVZHSQ	GRUDQO	XMEWIV
SLRA	STFMQZ	GODUCQ	MXIVEW
JCEN	RVXSQM	QCURDO	VEWMIX
ZLRD	MQBJFT	DUCOQG	EMVXWI
XBOD	MVZXLQ	CGRDQU	IVWMEX
PHMU	RTBXQH	UDRCOQ	IEVMWX
ZHFK	BLQSZX	GQCORU	WVZMXE
PNJW	QSVFDJ	GOQUCD	XEMIWV
CQXT	FLDVZT	GDQUOC	WXIMEV
GHNR	BQHMDX	URDCGO	EMWIVX
IXYD	BMFDQH	GODROC	IVEMXW
QSVB	QHLJZT		
GUCH	TQSHRL		
OWBN	BMQHZJ		
BVQN	RTBJZQ		
FOAS	FQDLXH		
ITZN	XJHSVQ		
VYLD	MZRJDQ		
LRYZ	XVQRMB		
IJXE	QMXLSD		
RBOE	DSZHQR		
DVUS	FJQSMV		
BIAJ	RSBMDQ		
ESGF	LBMQFX		
QGZI	FDMVQJ		
ZWNE	HQZTXB		
QBVC	VBQSRF		
VARP	QHSVDZ		
LRPA	HVQBFL		
SGHL	HSRQZV		
MVRJ	DQVXFB		
GADB	RXJQSM		
PCME	MQZFVD		
ZODW	ZJLRTQ		
HDBR	SHMVTQ		
BVDZ	QXFBRJ		

To be sure, pattern recognition starts by processing the incoming pattern, a bottom-up process; no one doubts that the cognitive system is triggered by the physical data or pattern and that it identifies patterns on the basis of stimulus features. Nonetheless, this bottom-up emphasis slights the contribution made by the cognitive system. It misses the effect of **context**, the influence of *surrounding information and your own knowledge*. We often identify a pattern that is *not* in the original stimulus at all, such as the word *the* in the last clause. You misread that sentence, didn't you? And now you know where the missing *the* came from: It came from you, from your knowledge of language. Top-level conceptual knowledge, already stored in memory, augments or assists lower-level processes such as pattern recognition.

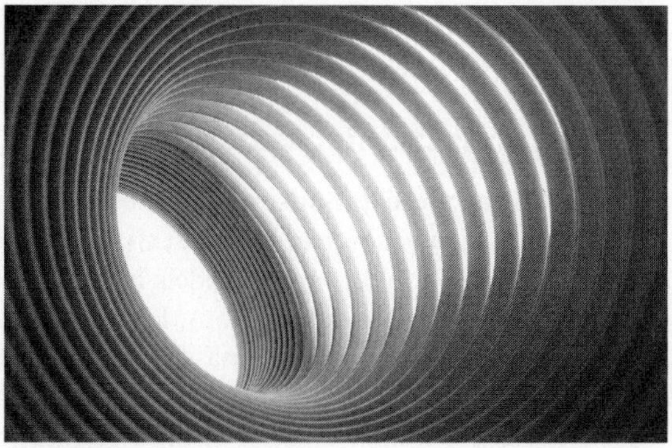

Without context.

Here's another set of sentences that illustrate the point about top-down processing (sentences from Morris & Harris, 2002).

When she spilled the ink there was ink all over.
She ran her best time yet in the rice last week.
I broke a wine class in my class yesterday.

Morris and Harris investigated several interesting context or top-down processing effects using such sentences. In the first sentence, the word *ink* is repeated. When the sentence is presented word-by-word at a rapid rate (this is called the *RSVP method,* for *Rapid Serial Visual Presentation*), a rather surprising result is obtained, called *repetition blindness.* In particular, people often fail to report the second occurrence of *ink*—even though it's shown the second time, people report having seen "When she spilled the ink there was all over" (see also Kanwisher, 1987, 1991). **Repetition blindness** therefore is *the tendency to not perceive a pattern, whether a word, a picture, or any other visual stimulus, when it is quickly repeated.* The basic explanation of repetition blindness is that cognition has just identified the stimulus, so it "expects" *not* to see the same thing again.

The other interesting effect noted by Morris and Harris was a misreading effect, a tendency to read a word that *should* be in the sentence, based on context, rather than the one that actually appears, e.g., *race* instead of *rice*, and *glass* instead of *class* in the other two sentences. Morris and Harris found that repetition blindness and misreading combined their effects. For example, in "ink–ink" trials, a strong repetition blindness effect occurred—the second "ink" was reported less than 50% of the time, compared to a control sentence like, "When she dropped the box there was ink all over," where "ink" was reported over 80% of the time. The percentages were very similar in the "class–class" sentences—but only when the first "class" was read correctly. When the biasing context led participants to read "wine glass," however, there was no repetition blindness at all—reports of "class" were correct on about 70% of the trials. Thus even in situations ("class–class") that should produce repetition blindness, the critical variable was what word ("glass") the person had actually understood—in other words, what was in the person's mental context for the sentence.

Conceptually driven *and* data-driven processes are combined in most pattern recognition situations, not to mention more complex cognitive processes such as comprehension of language. And an excellent way to model this, to explore how this combination works, is within the connectionist model introduced in Chapter 2. Think

With context.

of this model as Pandemonium Plus, a bottom-up model like Selfridge's with an added top-down processing effect.

Connectionist Modeling

Connectionist modeling is a theoretical and computational approach to some of the most challenging issues in cognitive science. Connectionist models involve a *massive* number of mathematical computations. Essentially, each unit in a connectionist layer may be massively connected with as many or all of the units in the next layer of the model. The impact of each experience on each of these connections would need to be computed. A connectionist or parallel distributed processing model often is implemented as a computer model, with a set of formulae that perform computations on the model's basic units. Even if the number of units is fairly small, the number of separate computations in a single run of the model is staggeringly large because of massive numbers of connections among the units.

To flesh out the word recognition model (McClelland & Rumelhart, 1981; Rumelhart & McClelland, 1986), we'll use a model that recognizes four-letter words, such as *TREE*. We start with some of the basics of connectionist modeling, including some of the special vocabulary. Table 3-1 provides a list of basic terms and assumptions, with some explanations to help you. Consult Table 3-1 and Figure 3-10 frequently as you read the next section.

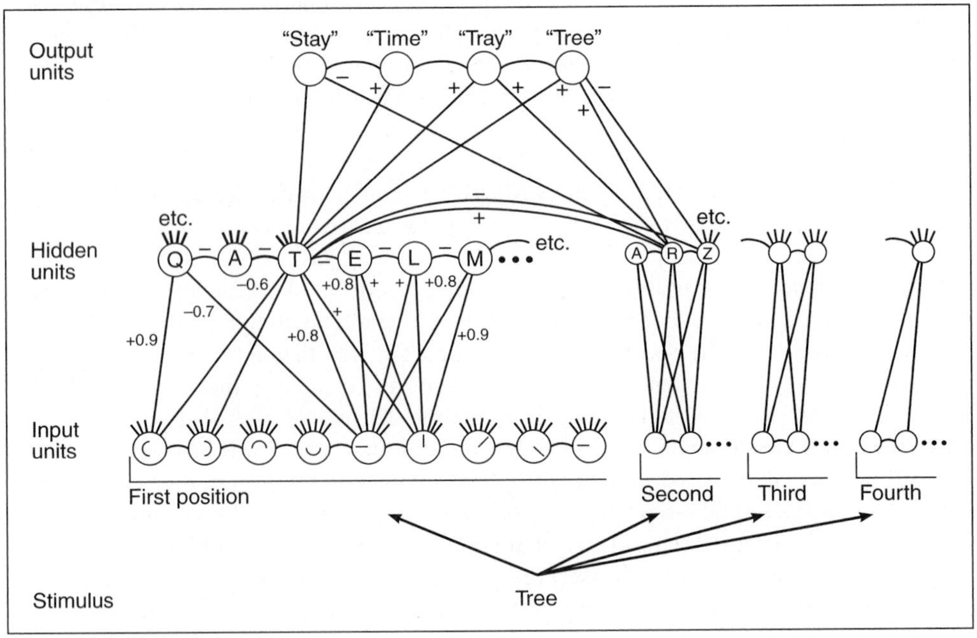

▲ FIGURE 3-10
A portion of the PDP network for recognizing four-letter words. The bulk of the illustration involves identifying the first letter of the word.

★ **TABLE 3-1 A Primer of Connectionist Terminology and Assumptions**

Basic Statement of PDP Principles

- Complex mental operations are the combined effects of the massively parallel processing that characterizes the network. The processing is distributed across all levels of the network (hence the term *parallel distributed processing*).
- The network is composed of (usually) three levels of units: the input level, hidden level, and output level. The internal "hidden" layer is invisible to an outsider. Units in each of these levels are interconnected (hence the term *connectionism*). The connections are either positively or negatively weighted.
- Positive connection weights pass excitation, or excitatory activation, to the connected unit; negatively weighted connections pass inhibition, or inhibitory activation. A unit transmits its activation to connected units if it has received enough positive activation to reach threshold. The analog here is excitatory and inhibitory neurotransmitters, which play a similar role in the nervous system.
- Connection weights are assigned as a function of training, in which feedback as to correctness or incorrectness leads to a mathematical adjustment of weights. When a network is given this procedure and the weights have stabilized, the network is said to have been trained up. Back propagation is the most commonly used training method, although others exist.
- The obvious similarities between PDP models and the neurological structures and activities in the brain are usually quite intentional; connections sometimes are called synapses, excitation and inhibition are parallel to those processes in the neocortex, and the entire approach is commonly known as *neural net modeling*.

Lexicon of Other Connectionist Terms

Back propagation	The most commonly used training procedure, in which the weight-adjusting phase proceeds from the output units back in to the other layers, each unit propagating a series of computations.
Delta rule	The mathematical rule for adjusting weights during training, where delta (Δ) stands for "change."
Distributed representation	The representation for a letter, word, concept, and so on is said to be distributed because the knowledge is spread widely across the units and their weights.
Local minima	Occasionally in the training procedure the system seems to have found the most stable baseline values for the weights, the global minimum; think of the global minimum as the deepest "valley." But the system may just be trapped in a local minimum or valley.
Massively parallel processing	Almost all units in the system have some role in each step of processing, and all units operate simultaneously.

INPUT UNITS Let's build the simple connectionist framework illustrated in Figure 3-10 piece by piece. In this structure there are three levels of units. First, at the bottom, are the *input units*. These are extremely basic, elementary "cells" in the structure, which receive the inputs from the environment. Our example is visual word recognition, so our input units are simple visual detectors. That is, we have a set of nine input units, each of which responds to the different basic visual features of the letters of the alphabet. To build on what you already understand, consider the input units to have exactly the same function as the data and computational demons in the Pandemonium model shown in Figure 3-7. Our input units here encode and respond to simple visual features in letters of the alphabet. Thus the input unit level in this illustration is the feature-detector level.

HIDDEN UNITS How do these input units work? When a stimulus is presented to the input device, one or more of the input units matches the features in the stimulus. When this happens, each unit that matches activates a set of connected units in the middle level of the structure, the *hidden unit* level; *hidden* here simply means that this level is completely internal, always one step removed from either input or output. In our diagram the hidden units correspond to the letter level. Note that the activation is sent across the pathways or connections that link the units together; *these* are the connections in connectionism.

The connections always have a weight attached to them, a weight that represents the relationship between the linked units. Some of the weights are positive, and some are negative. For example, in Figure 3-10 the horizontal straight bar feature has positive weights connecting it to the letters *T*, *E*, and *L* because those letters all contain that feature (to minimize confusion in looking at the figure, many of the connections have not been drawn fully, and only a few numerical weights are given). Conversely, the weights between the horizontal straight bar feature and the letters *C*, *O*, *Q*, and so on are negative. Likewise, all the curved features at the input level have positive weights to curved letters and negative weights to angular letters.

Hidden units that receive enough positive activation, called *excitation*, govern the outcome of processing (think of shouting demons). Units receiving negative activation, or *inhibition*, end up having little control over the outcome. Eventually, after all the weights have been factored into the computational formulae, activations at the output level come into play.

OUTPUT UNITS Where is this getting us? Imagine that you were trying to build a machine (program a computer) that could identify visually presented words, such as the four-letter words we are considering here. What you see in Figure 3-10 is primarily the connectionist network for the first position in the four-letter words. Three more sets of connections, shown in reduced form at the right of the figure, essentially duplicate the same connections again, once for each position in the four-letter word. Given these additional positions, we can now talk about the *output units*, the units that report the system's response to the question "What is this word?"

For simplicity, only a handful of four-letter words are shown at the level of output units in the figure. Note, however, that three of the word-level units are consistent with the letter detection performed on *T* in the first position; that is, three of the words begin with a *T*. Now think about the fuller representation of such a model, a model that identifies four-letter words. Each of the four input unit segments will perform as described earlier, forwarding both positive and negative activation to the hidden units, these in turn forwarding positive and negative activations to the output units. At the end of the run of the model, presumably one of the several output units will have received enough positive activation to exceed its threshold. When this happens, that unit responds by answering the question, "What is this word?"

One more complexity is needed now, the one that gets top-down effects into the model. Reflect for a moment on how likely the spelling pattern *TZ* is at the beginning of English words. Not very likely, is it? On the other hand, *TA*, *TE*, *TI*, and similar consonant–vowel pairs are quite likely, as are a few consonant–consonant pairs such as *TH* and *TR*. These likelihoods are also represented in the network; to distinguish them visually from the other connections, they are shown with curve-shaped connections. The overall effect of these letter-to-letter weights is that the activations in the system can make up for missing features at the perceptual level.

Figure 3-11, taken from Rumelhart and McClelland's (1986) work, shows the final levels of activation for three possible words, given the partially obscured stimulus pattern shown at the bottom. The illustration shows an important feature of connectionist models: Enough knowledge is represented in the system, by means of the weights for letter-to-letter sequences, that the model identifies the word *work* even when the last letter could also be an *R*.

Why is this so important? It is important because it is a concrete illustration of the general theme of top-down or conceptually driven processing. If you saw the partially obscured pattern in Figure 3-11, you would identify the word as *work*, based on your knowledge that *worr* is not a word in English. Your higher-level knowledge of English words would be assisting your perceptual process here in service of identifying the word. This is exactly what's happening in the connectionist

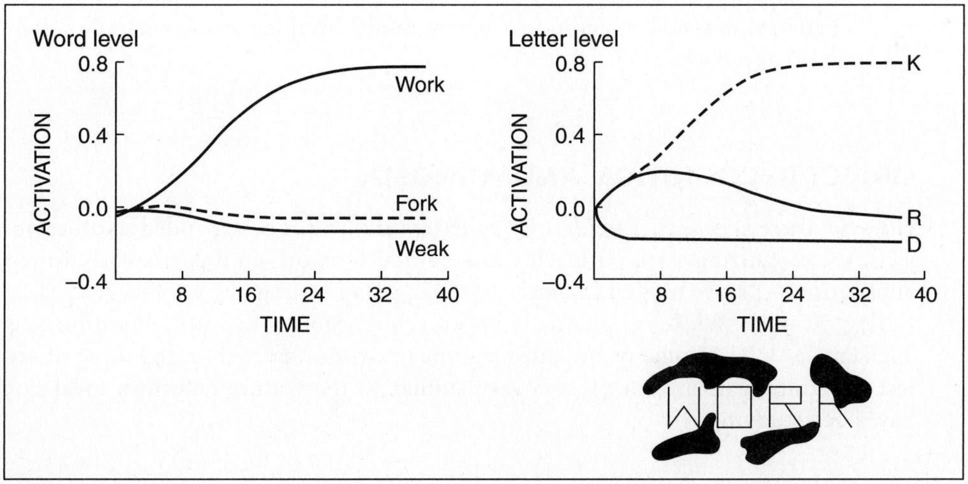

● **FIGURE 3-11**
A possible display that might be presented to the connectionist model of word recognition and the resulting activations of selected letter and word units. The letter units are for the letters indicated in the fourth position of a four-letter display. Adapted from Rumelhart & McClelland, 1986.

model; higher-level knowledge, coded as simple weighted connections in the massive network, is participating in the lower-level task of identifying letters.[3]

Such connectionist models satisfy the difficulty you read about earlier: the need for top-down processing in Pandemonium. In Figure 3-10 the top-down effect is especially prominent in the curved connections, which represent mutual excitation and inhibition of units. But the approach has far more important consequences than merely providing a way to repair Pandemonium. As you will read at several points in this book, connectionist accounts of a whole range of cognitive operations can provide new insights into ways of modeling and understanding human cognition. Indeed, connectionist models are finding applications in a stunningly large number of fields (e.g., see Corder, 2004, on a neural net application to landing a crippled airliner).

Section Summary

- Recognition of visual patterns follows principles of organization that have been known for quite some time. The most familiar of these are the Gestalt grouping principles. These include figure-ground segregation, closure, proximity, similarity, good continuation, and common fate.
- Recognition of visual patterns is not a process of matching stored templates to a visual stimulus. Feature detection provides a much more convincing account of visual recognition, where the features being detected are elementary patterns that can be combined to form letters and other visual stimuli.
- A feature detection account of pattern recognition, such as Pandemonium, must be augmented by conceptually driven processes to account for the known effects of context in visual recognition. Current models of this sort include the connectionist approach.

OBJECT RECOGNITION AND AGNOSIA

How can these approaches to identifying letters and words be expanded to other objects, to recognizing a tree, a briefcase, a human face, or—in a particularly timely application—a knife hidden in a carry-on bag going through airport security (McCarley, Kramer, Wickens, Vidoni, & Boot, 2004; Smith, Redford, Washburn, & Taglialatela, 2005)? Some of the most significant work reported on the topic of object recognition involves a process very similar to the feature detection ideas you have been studying.

[3] The handwritten census forms for the year 2000 U.S. Census were read by what is basically a connectionist system. The software identified letters and words both by analyzing features and by knowing what kinds of letter and spelling patterns were likely to be found on different questions. For instance, the system knew that "McN" is a likely spelling pattern in a person's last name but is unlikely as a spelling pattern in a person's job name or profession.

Recognition by Components

The basic idea proposed in Biederman's (1987, 1990) recognition by components (RBC) theory is that we recognize objects by breaking them down into their components, then looking up this combination of components in memory to see which object matches the combination. In this model, the human recognition system has a small number of *basic "primitives," simple three-dimensional geometric forms* like those shown in Figure 3-12. These forms are called **geons**, a combined form of *geometric ions* (remember *ions* from chemistry?). Recognizing a briefcase, for example, involves analyzing the object into its two geons, the rectangular box (geon 2 in the figure) and the curved cylinder (geon 5). By itself, detecting the rectangular box geon would match the memory representation for "brick" or "box." When that component and the curved cylinder on top are detected, the combination would match what is stored in memory for "briefcase" or "suitcase."

Biederman (1987) argued that mental representations of all three-dimensional objects in the world are composed of geons, much as written language is composed of letters, combined and recombined in different fashions. Thus, when we recognize objects, we break them down (parse is the technical term) into their components and note where the components join together. This pattern is then matched to information stored in memory to yield recognition.

Two aspects of these patterns are particularly important. First, we find the edges of objects. This enables us to determine which edges maintain the same relationships to one another regardless of viewing orientation; however you look at a brick, the three long edges that are visible remain parallel to one another.

Second, we scan regions of the pattern where the lines intersect (vertices), usually places where deep concave angles are formed. Look at the deep concave angles on the briefcase object in Figure 3-12, where the curved component joins the rectangle.

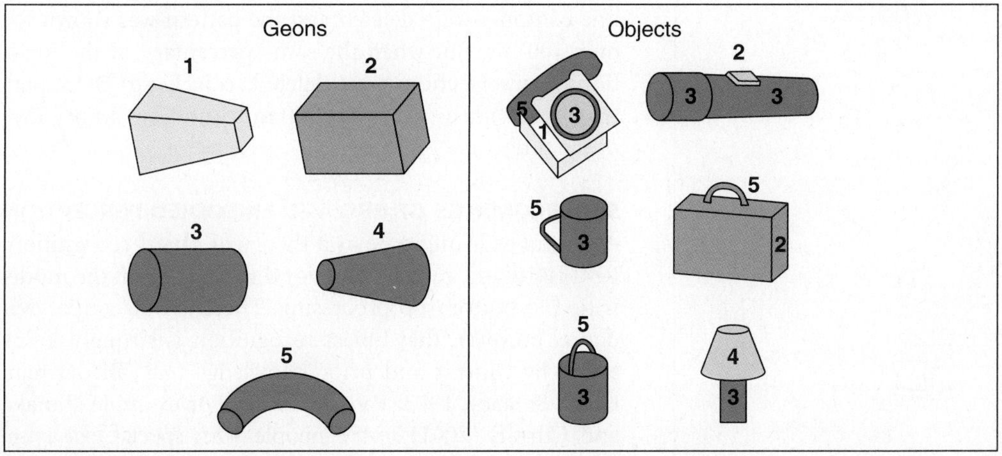

◆ **FIGURE 3-12**
Geons (components) and the objects they make. From Biederman, 1990.

Examining the edges and the areas of intersection enables us to determine which basic components are present in the pattern: rectangular solid joined on the upper surface by a curved segment. This description of the object is then compared with stored descriptions in memory, something like "Briefcase: rectangular solid joined on the upper surface by a curved segment." When we find a match between the identified components and the stored representation, we have recognized the pattern.

EVIDENCE FOR RBC In his investigations of the RBC model, Biederman discovered several important facts about object recognition. For one, the emphasis on the importance of vertices turns out to be critical. If a pattern is degraded, it matters a great deal *where* it was degraded. If segments of the smooth, continuous edges are missing, it is relatively easy to fill in the missing parts from memory and so recognize the pattern. Alternatively, if the parts that are missing are in important locations where the vertices are missing, recognition is much more difficult.

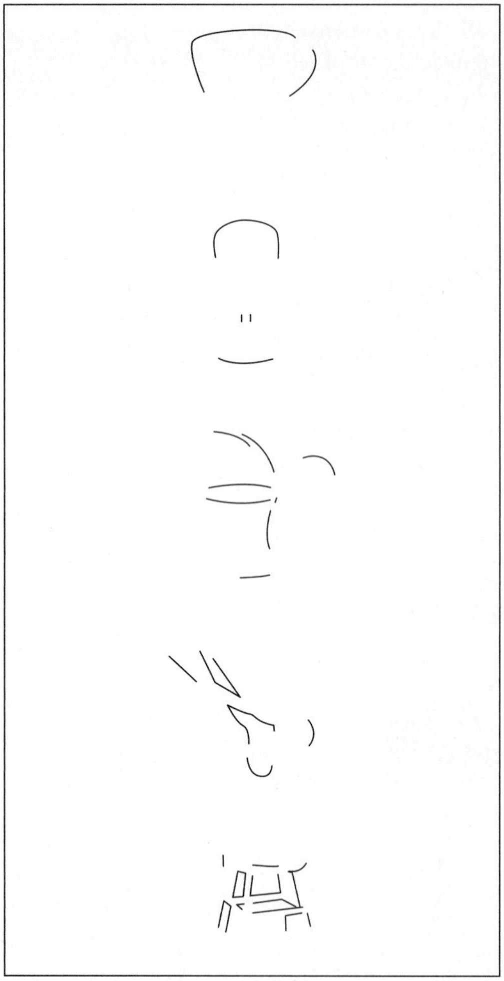

■ **FIGURE 3-13**
Nonrecoverable objects. From Biederman, 1987.

Figure 3-13 shows several "nonrecoverable" drawings, that is drawings for which people either cannot recover from the deletions or take much longer before recognizing the object. Look at these carefully now and try to figure out what the objects are. It is so difficult because the vertices have been deleted. Now look at Figure 3-14. Here you see recoverable versions of the drawings that were degraded to the same degree as the images in Figure 3-13. However, in this case, the parts of the continuous edges have been deleted but the vertices remain visible. Here it is relatively easy to identify the original objects (you *can* identify them, can't you?). In Biederman's data (Biederman & Blickle, 1985), participants never made more than 30% errors in identifying recoverable patterns, even when 65% of the continuous line contours were deleted and the pattern was shown for only 100 ms. But when the same percentage of the junctions or intersections were deleted, as in Figure 3-13, participants made errors in the 100 ms condition almost 55% of the time.

SHORTCOMINGS OF RBC AND EMBODIED PERCEPTION As useful as it might be as a theory of object recognition, RBC is still incomplete. A major difficulty is that the model is tied to bottom-up processing. There is now ample evidence, however, that object recognition is strongly influenced by context and prior knowledge (e.g., Biederman, Glass, & Stacy, 1973; Palmer, 1975). For example, Tanaka and Curran (2001) tested people with special expertise, "bird experts" and "dog experts," people who averaged more than 20 years of experience in local bird and dog organizations. These people showed neurological evidence of enhanced, early recognition in their areas of expertise, compared to how they recognized objects outside of those areas (e.g., plants).

Indeed, Dell'acqua and Job (1998) claimed that object recognition is automatic, given that judgments of a perceptual feature (is this picture elongated horizontally or vertically?) were strongly affected by the identity of the object. There is also evidence that retrieval of an object's identity (at least in terms of the category it belongs to) occurs as fast as identification that there is even something there, i.e., that a stimulus is being presented (Grill-Spector & Kanwisher, 2005; but see Bowers & Jones, 2008). (In a sense, this is similar to results in the lexical decision task you read about in Chapter 2, how a word's meaning influences performance even though the task does not require accessing word meaning.)

Second, the model suggests that perceiving components is the first major step in object recognition, suggesting that the whole is perceived by first identifying the components. There are data, however, that show that people can perceive the overall shape and pattern of an object as rapidly and accurately as they perceive the components (e.g., Cave & Kosslyn, 1989)—and of course there's the data from Dell'acqua and Job, claiming that the whole object is recognized automatically based on stored knowledge about it (see Bukach, Bub, Masson, & Lindsay, 2004, for a similar claim, and L. Smith, 2003, on how children demonstrate this knowledge-enhanced recognition by 25 months of age). All of these contradict the features-first aspect of the model.

Third, our perception of objects can be influenced by our expectations of how we will interact with those objects. That is, embodied cognition can influence perception. For example, the ease with which objects are identified can be influenced by the actions people would take to use those objects (Desmarais, Dixon & Roy, 2007). That is, over and above the visual features that compose the objects' shape, people also use their knowledge of what the object is, and how they would interact with it, to help them identify what it is. As an example, people view hills as being steeper and distances walked as being longer if they are wearing a heavy backpack, and perceive balconies as being higher if they have a fear of heights (Proffitt, 2006). Moreover, emotions can meaningfully influence perception. For instance, people generally recognize objects faster if they are emotionally meaningful (such as identifying briefly flashed words like "death" and "love") than if they are not (Zeelenberg, Wagenmakers, & Rotteveel, 2006).

Finally, neuropsychological evidence shows that object recognition is a joint effort between two mental processes and two different regions of the brain, one responsible for features and components—"bits and pieces," as it were—and another for overall shape and global patterns—the *Gestalt*, or overall form. Interestingly, most of this neuropsychological evidence comes from studying people who, because of some kind of brain damage, have lost the fundamental ability we have been discussing here, the ability to look at something and rapidly recognize what it is.

Agnosia

You've been reading about perception and pattern recognition, studying how mental mechanisms such as feature detection and top-down processing are responsible for our ability to recognize objects and entities around us. But we have not questioned *that*

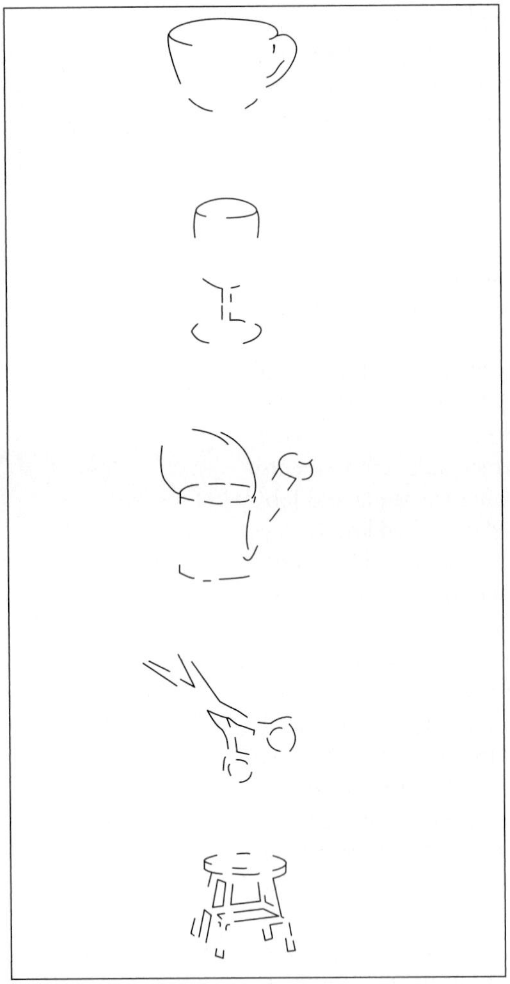

★ **FIGURE 3-14**
Recoverable objects. From Biederman, 1987.

it happens, never thought that there might be problems in actually recognizing a simple, ordinary object. It is amazing to learn that a person can lose the ability to recognize objects, the ability to glance at something and immediately know what it is. There's an object, say a cup sitting on the kitchen counter or a briefcase sitting on the floor. We encode the stimulus, the set of features or geons, into the visual system. It is then an automatic, seemingly instantaneous step from encoding to identification: You see the thing, and you immediately *know* that it's a cup—right?

Wrong. What you'll read about now is a cognitive deficit, caused by brain damage, in which people can no longer perform the seemingly instantaneous mental steps of pattern recognition. There are certainly types of brain damage that can disrupt the recognition of printed language, letters and words, and you will read about some of this in Chapter 10, after the section on reading. But for now, we look at a different kind of disruption of recognition, when the recognition of objects—real-world *things*—is disrupted. We're talking about **agnosia**, defined as *a failure or deficit in recognizing objects*, either because the pattern of features cannot be synthesized into a whole or because the person cannot then connect the whole pattern to meaning (from the prefix *a*, meaning "not," and the Greek root *gnostic*, meaning "to know"; Freud is the one who first applied this name to the disorder).

When this disruption affects a person's recognition of faces, sometimes while leaving object recognition intact, it is called **prosopagnosia**, *a disruption of face recognition.* The fact that there are separate conditions for the inability to recognize objects and faces is important because it shows that perceptual recognition is a very complex system in which different brain systems are responsible for different qualities of information. The perceptual system is not necessarily a one-size-fits-all system, but is configured from a number of different specialty systems that typically work in seamless harmony.

Bear in mind that when we talk about agnosia and agnosics (patients with agnosia), we are not talking about people whose basic sensory systems are damaged. It is clear when an agnosic patient is tested that the person can see, can detect visual stimuli; this is not blindness. Instead, it is a cognitive, mental loss; the agnosic can input the basic visual stimulus but cannot do anything with that encoded information.

Probably the most famous case of agnosia—and prosopagnosia too—is the title story in *The Man Who Mistook His Wife for a Hat* (Sacks, 1970), about an elderly music professor (called Dr. P.) who had lost his ability to recognize objects and faces. At the end of a session with his doctor, he reached over and grasped his wife's head as if reaching to pick up his hat. In another meeting with the doctor, he was able to describe the components or elementary features of an object yet was unable to identify the object he was looking at:

> *"About six inches in length," he commented. "A convoluted red form with a linear green attachment."*
> *"Yes," I said encouragingly, "and what do you think it is, Dr. P.?"*
> *"Not easy to say."...*
> *"Smell it," I suggested.*
> *"Beautiful!" he exclaimed. "An early rose. What a heavenly smell!"*
>
> (Sacks, 1970, pp. 13–14)

He mistook the grandfather clock in the hall for a person and started with outstretched hand to greet it. Although he could describe the parts of an object (there were five "out-pouchings," and so forth) he could not identify a glove that the doctor held in front of him. Dr. P. had a serious and pervasive visual agnosia, a profound loss in the ability to visually recognize things.

Although agnosia is not necessarily limited to vision—there can be auditory agnosias, for example—it is true that an agnosia is modality specific. That is, a person with visual agnosia has disrupted recognition of objects presented visually but no necessary involvement of hearing, touch, or other sensory systems (Dr. P. recognized the rose by smelling it). Likewise, there are subtypes of visual agnosia, each with a somewhat different type of deficit, each stemming from different regions of the brain.

The first form of visual agnosia is called **apperceptive agnosia**, *a basic disruption in perceiving patterns*. That is, although the ability to process rudimentary visual features, say color or brightness, is not disrupted, "the ability to coalesce this basic visual information into a percept, an entity, or a whole is lost" (Banich, 2004, p. 195). Figure 3-15 shows that the region usually associated with apperceptive agnosia is in the right hemisphere, in the parietal lobe (the top right illustration). If the agnosia is severe, the person has almost no ability to discriminate between objects, for instance between a square and a rectangle, and is unable to copy or match simple shapes. In less severe cases, there can still be difficulties with patterns like those in Figure 3-14, the patterns that you probably had little or no difficulty identifying (Warrington & James, 1988). They somehow cannot fill in the missing contours to perceive the whole form or pattern.

In **associative agnosia**, a second major type of agnosia, the person does seem able to construct a mental percept; he or she can combine the perceived features into a whole pattern. The disruption is that the person still *cannot associate the pattern with meaning*, still cannot link the perceived whole with stored knowledge about its identity. For example, a person tested by Ratcliff and Newcombe (1982) copied a drawing of a ship's anchor quite well and was able to give an accurate verbal definition of an anchor. The patient could not, however, identify the drawing he copied, nor could he draw an anchor from memory. In Gazzaniga, Ivry, and Mangun (1998, pp. 164–165), a

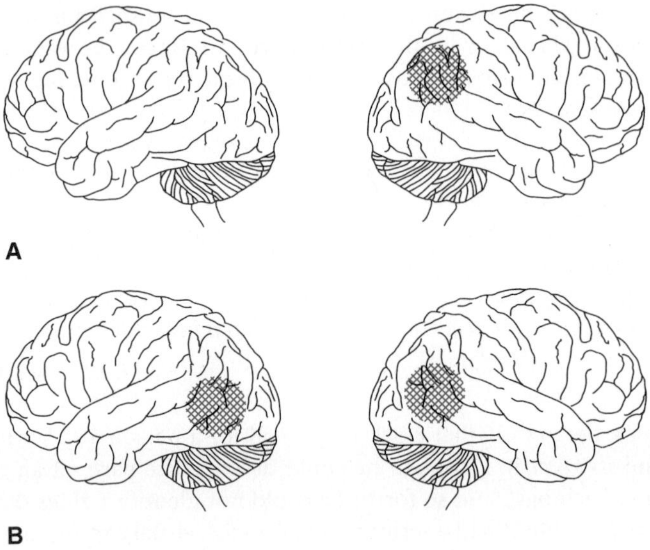

▲ **FIGURE 3-15**
A. The left and right hemispheres of the brain, showing that apperceptive agnosia usually is limited to posterior (rear) regions of the right hemisphere parietal lobe (the cross-hatched region).
B. Both left and right hemispheres have cross-hatched regions at the junction of the temporal and occipital lobes, the region usually damaged in associative agnosia.
From Banich (1997).

patient known as P. T. with associative agnosia was shown a drawing of a combination lock. He perceived the overall round shape and the number markings around the edge but could only guess that the object was a telephone or a clock. Finally, with much prompting, he identified the lock, but only because he noticed that he had been twirling his fingers around, as if pantomiming how to open a combination lock.

Implications for Cognitive Science

What do these neurological disruptions mean for our understanding of normal perception and pattern recognition? How does evidence like this advance our understanding of cognition?

Start with the deficits known as apperceptive agnosia, where the *a* prefix to *perceptive* denotes some kind of perceptual failure. Here we have a serious disruption in a very early stage of perceptual processing, possibly even the first step after a stimulus is encoded into the visual system. It is a disorder of feature detection, a malfunction in the process of extracting features from visual stimuli. Biederman's (1990) geons, for instance, are not being identified or at least not processed much beyond noticing small segments or junction points. Furthermore, it may be important that apperceptive agnosia seems to result from damage in the right hemisphere, in the parietal region; there is growing evidence that the right hemisphere is more involved in global processing, to include forming global patterns, and that the left hemisphere plays more of a role in local processing (i.e., processing small components and features). If so, then it seems reasonable to talk about a disrupted mechanism for forming a *Gestalt* from the features, where this disrupted mechanism would correspond to the symptoms of apperceptive agnosia.

Associative agnosia is a deeper dysfunction: The *Gestalt* or pattern has been formed but seems to have lost the associative pathway to the meaning and name of the object. As shown in Figure 3-15, the damaged regions in associative agnosia tend to be lower, more toward the temporal lobe, and in both hemispheres. This pathway, from the vision centers in the occipital lobe forward and down toward the temporal lobe, is commonly called the *"what" pathway*, the pathway that is activated when you look at something to decide *what* it is. The temporal lobes are particularly associated with areas related to language and word meaning. And connecting from a perceived pattern to its meaning and name is the impairment in associative agnosia.

In conclusion, the varieties of agnosia tell us at least three important things about the perception and identification of patterns and objects. First, detecting the features in a visual stimulus is a separate (and later) process from the sensory steps that encode a stimulus into cognition. The basic features—whether horizontal lines in a capital *A*, geons, or something else—must be extracted from already encoded sensory information. Second, detecting the visual features is critical in constructing a perceived pattern, a percept. If the stimulus features cannot be extracted, then the person cannot "get" the *Gestalt*, cannot form an overall pattern or percept. Finally, there is a separate step involved in hooking up the pattern with its meaning and name, involving the visual association from the pattern to the knowledge stored about it in memory. This is different from knowing the meaning and name of an object in verbal form. Indeed, given that P.T. only later realized what his pantomime meant, it seems likely that the visual association path can be isolated from all of the other ways of knowing about objects and patterns.

In short, simple, "immediate" recognition of objects—the cup, the briefcase—is neither simple nor immediate. The disruptions known as agnosia, whether caused by difficulties in feature detection or in associating patterns with meaning, provide additional evidence of the complexity of perception and pattern recognition.

Section Summary

- The recognition by components theory claims that we recognize objects by extracting or detecting three-dimensional components, geons, from encoded visual stimuli, then access memory to determine what real-world objects contain those components. The most informative parts of objects tend to be parts where the components join together; people have more difficulty recognizing objects when the intersections are degraded visually than when long, connecting segments are degraded.
- Studies of patients with visual agnosia demonstrate the complexity of perception and pattern recognition. Patients with apperceptive agnosia sometimes are unable to detect even elementary features from stimuli and therefore have difficulty in perceiving a whole pattern or *Gestalt*. Those with associative agnosia can perceive the whole but still cannot associate the pattern with stored knowledge to identify the object.

AUDITORY PERCEPTION

Auditory stimuli consist of sound waves moving the air. The human auditory mechanism that responds to these stimuli is an awkward combination of components, a Rube Goldberg–type mechanism that translates the sound waves into a neural message. (Google *Rube Goldberg* if you don't know about the contraptions he drew.) First, the sound waves are funneled into the ear, causing the tympanic membrane, or eardrum, to vibrate. This in turn causes the bones of the middle ear to move, which then sets in motion the fluid in the ear's inner cavity. The moving fluid then moves the tiny hair cells along the basilar membrane, generating the neural message, which is sent along the auditory nerve into the cerebral cortex (e.g., Forgus & Melamed, 1976). Thus from the unpromising elements of funnels, moving bones and fluid, and the like (Figure 3-16) arises our *sense of hearing* or **audition**.

Interestingly, both ears project auditory sensations to both hemispheres of the brain, although the majority of the input obeys the principle of contralaterality. The primary auditory cortex, normally shown as a region in the superior (upper) medial (midway back) temporal lobe, actually extends somewhat further rearward in the brain, into the parietal lobe (Kolb & Whishaw, 1996; in Figure 2-8 in the last chapter, follow the Sylvian fissure to the rear of the temporal lobe to get an idea). Auditory input to the brain is sent primarily to this auditory cortex, although at least four other nearby zones and several secondary areas are also affected.

The sensitivity of our sense of hearing is of particular interest because it defines our auditory world. A pure tone, such as that generated by a tuning fork, is a traveling sound wave with a regular frequency, a smooth pattern of up-and-down cycles per unit of time. Generally, humans are sensitive to patterns as low as 20 cps (cycles per second) and as high as 20,000 cps, although the upper limits decline with age, which is why old fogies (like the authors of this book) cannot hear very high pitches. Most of the sound patterns we are interested in, such as those generated by spoken speech or music, are of great complexity, combining dozens of different frequencies that vary widely in intensity or loudness. In terms of the sound wave patterns, these different frequencies are superimposed and can be summarized in a spectrum (see examples under "Phonology" in Chapter 9).

In one sense, human hearing is not particularly impressive: Dogs, for instance, are sensitive to much higher frequencies than we are. In quite a different sense, our hearing is almost unbelievably complex. For instance, we can discriminate accurately between highly similar sounds even from birth: The slight difference between the sounds "pah" and "bah" is noticed by newborn infants (Eimas, 1975). And most impressive of all, we routinely convert the continuous stream of sounds known as speech into a comprehended message with little or no apparent effort, at a rate of about two or three words per second. How does this auditory system work? How does it coordinate with our knowledge of language to yield recognition and comprehension so rapidly?

Auditory Sensory Memory

The term **auditory sensory memory** is used interchangeably with Neisser's (1967) term **echoic memory**. Both terms refer to a *brief memory system that receives auditory stimuli and preserves them for some amount of time.* Neisser's argument on the existence

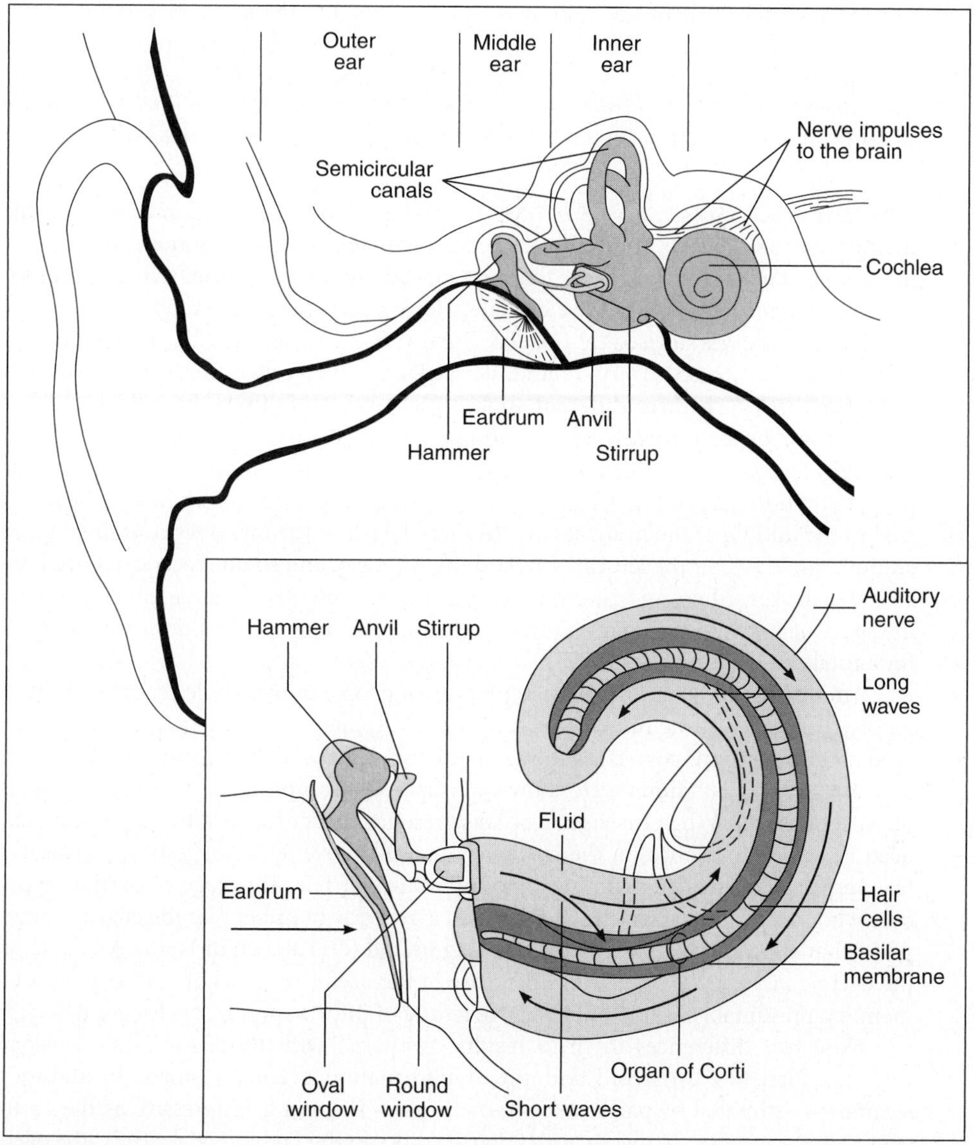

● **FIGURE 3-16**
Gross structure of the human ear and a close-up of the middle and inner ear structures. From Price, 1987.

of echoic memory is still airtight: "Perhaps the most fundamental fact about hearing is that sound is an intrinsically temporal event. Auditory information is always spread out in time; no single millisecond contains enough information to be very useful. If information were discarded as soon as it arrived, hearing would be all but impossible. Therefore, we must assume that some 'buffer,' some medium for temporary storage, is available in the auditory cognitive system" (1967, pp. 199–200).

On the other side of the coin, it is equally clear that the memory system cannot (and should not) preserve the raw echoic memory trace forever. As was the case in iconic memory, only confusion would result if all auditory traces were held indefinitely. Thus the function of echoic memory is to encode sensory stimulation into the memory system and hold it just long enough for the rest of the mental system to gain access to it.

AMOUNT AND DURATION OF STORAGE What is the effective duration of echoic memory? To answer this question, we need a task that is the auditory analogue of Sperling's work. That is, we need a task that presents auditory stimuli briefly, in different locations, and in such a way that we can cue selected parts for partial report.

Such a task was devised by Darwin, Turvey, and Crowder (1972; see also Moray, Bates, & Barnett, 1965). Darwin et al. devised what they called the three-eared man procedure, in which three different spoken messages came from three distinct locations. People heard recorded letters and digits through stereo headphones, with one message played to the left ear, one message to the right ear, and the final message was played into both ears. Of course, the message played into both ears seemed to be localized in the middle of the head, at the "third ear." Each of the messages contained three stimuli, say, *T 7 C* on the left ear, *4 B 9* on the right ear, and so on. Each sequence lasted 1 s on the recording, and all three sequences were presented simultaneously. Thus in the space of 1 s, three different sequences of letter and digit combinations were played, for a total of nine separate stimuli.

After the auditory messages were presented, people in the whole report condition reported as many of the nine items as they could remember. Their performance averaged about four items correct, as shown in the top-right panel of Figure 3-17. People in the partial report condition were shown a visual cue, prompting recall of the left, right, or center message. When the visual cue was presented immediately after the stimuli had been heard, performance on the cued ear was well above 50%, suggesting that nearly five items out of the original nine were still available. The advantage of partial report over whole report was maintained even with a 4 s delay in presenting the cue, although performance did decline during that waiting period (also shown in Figure 3-17). Thus the decline in accuracy suggested a decrease in the useful contents of auditory sensory memory, presumably because of a passive fading of information across longer delays.

Note two differences in these results compared with those for visual sensory memory. First, the estimated amount of information originally stored in auditory memory—estimated by partial report, of course—was not as impressive as the 75 to 90% values found for iconic memory. Participants in the Darwin et al. study exceeded the level of about five items available out of the presented nine only on the third-position items, those presented last in the sequences (shown in the larger graph of the figure). Second, there is the distinct possibility that sensory traces reside in auditory memory for a longer time if they represent simpler information. In general, the 4 s duration found by Darwin et al. (1972) is longer than most estimates, probably because of the simplicity of the stimuli they used (most of the studies described later used coherent spoken language). In contrast, the 4 s estimate is much shorter than the 10 s storage found by Eriksen and Johnson (1964), but Eriksen and Johnson's participants merely had to detect a simple tone while performing an attention-capturing task (they read novels for two hours; see also Watkins & Watkins, 1980).

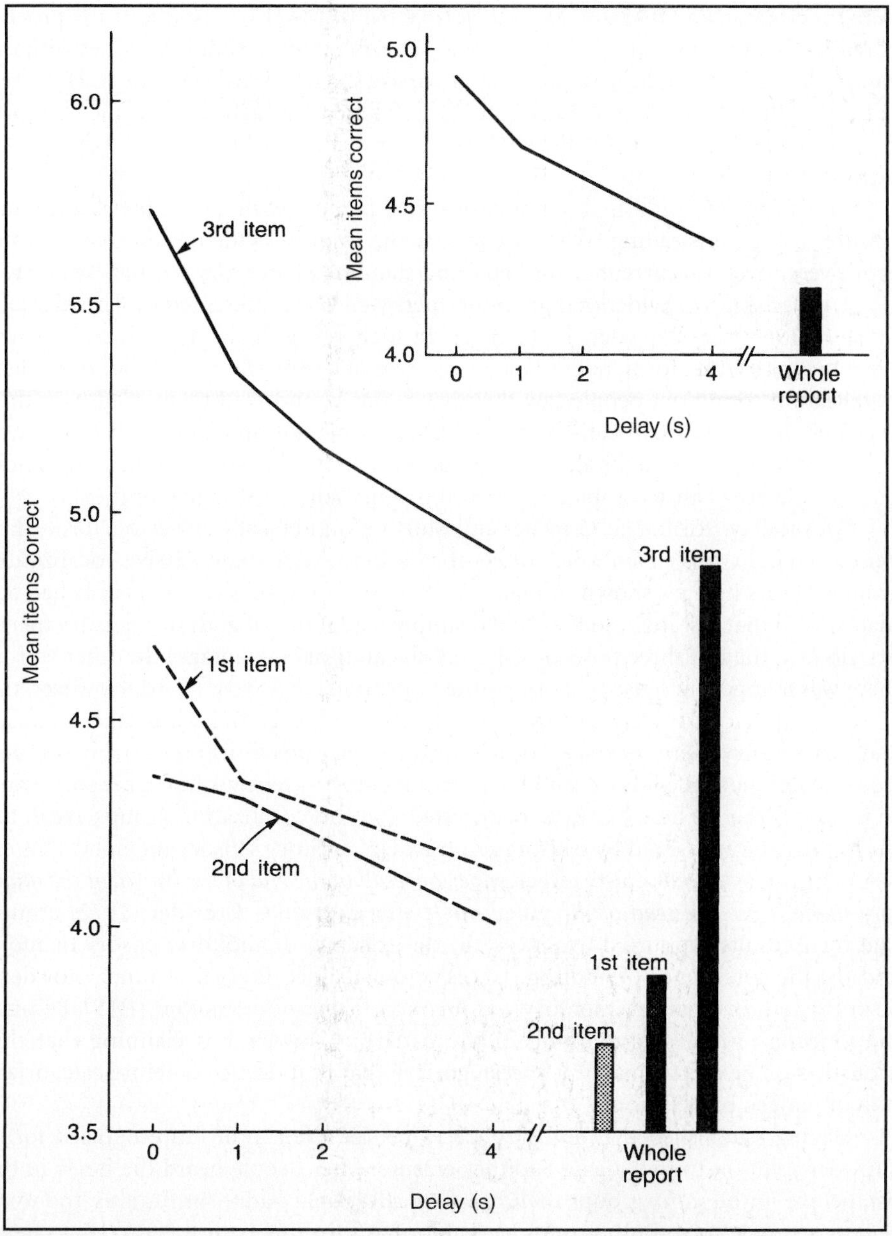

◆ **FIGURE 3-17**
Partial report results in the "three-eared man" procedure. The average number of items recalled correctly is shown for the first, second, and third items in the three lists, across varying delays in the presentation of the partial report cue. The insert shows overall performance, along with the vertical bar that shows whole-report accuracy. From Darwin et al., 1972.

PERSISTENCE AND ERASURE OF AUDITORY INFORMATION Without the process of redirected attention, the auditory trace in sensory memory simply vanishes with the passage of time, the auditory equivalent of passive fading in iconic memory. However, remember that there is also evidence of another kind of forgetting in iconic memory, due to erasure by subsequent stimuli. Is there any evidence of this in auditory sensory memory?

In a word, yes, although a straightforward parallel with iconic persistence and erasure may be misleading. We will consider the original evidence, then discuss the controversy over the current status and understanding of auditory sensory memory.

The best-known evidence on auditory persistence was presented by Crowder and Morton (1969; also Crowder, 1970, 1972). In their research, a list of nine digits was presented in written form, at the fairly rapid rate of two items per second. In a Silent Vocalization condition, people saw the nine numbers and read them silently as they appeared. In the Active Vocalization condition, people not only saw the list, but were also asked to name the digits aloud as they appeared. In the Passive Vocalization condition, people heard an accompanying recording that named the digits for them.

For recall performance, Crowder and Morton found hardly any errors for the last item when there was an auditory trace—that is, in the Active and Passive Vocalization groups. Errors here, as shown in Figure 3-18, were below 10%. These people had actually heard that last item, so they could simply read it out of auditory sensory memory (in fact, the last three positions showed the auditory advantage). In other words, there was a lingering sensory trace for the last sounds that were heard. However, the Silent group had many errors for the last items, around 50%, because there was no auditory sensory memory trace. (Recall for the earlier positions presumably resulted from a combination of short- and long-term memory—rehearsal of some sort—and so is not of interest here.) Crowder suggested that the Vocalization groups' recall for the last items was assisted by still-present traces in auditory sensory memory. This effect is known as the **modality effect**, *superior recall of the end of the list when the auditory mode is used instead of the visual mode of presentation.* Crowder (1972) argued that these results supported two ideas, (a) the existence of auditory sensory memory and (b) the persistence of auditory traces across a short interval of time. Crowder's term for auditory sensory memory was *precategorical acoustic storage (PAS)*. Because *categorization* implies recognition of the pattern, Crowder was claiming that this acoustic storage mechanism was *pre*categorical; that is, it occurred before categorization or pattern recognition.

Having established that auditory traces persist, even in an unrecognized form, Crowder went on to investigate auditory erasure. After people heard the items in the list, people in the *suffix* groups then heard an additional auditory stimulus: the word *zero* or a simple tone. Both groups were told that this final item was merely a cue to begin recalling the list. In reality, of course, the auditory *suffix* was intended to erase or interfere with the lingering auditory trace for the last items in the list. As predicted, the verbal suffix group showed a higher error rate on the last items. However, the tone-suffix group had very few errors. The auditory suffix had indeed degraded or erased the auditory trace for the last digits in the list when the suffix was similar to the list. ■ Figure 3-18 summarizes this program of research.

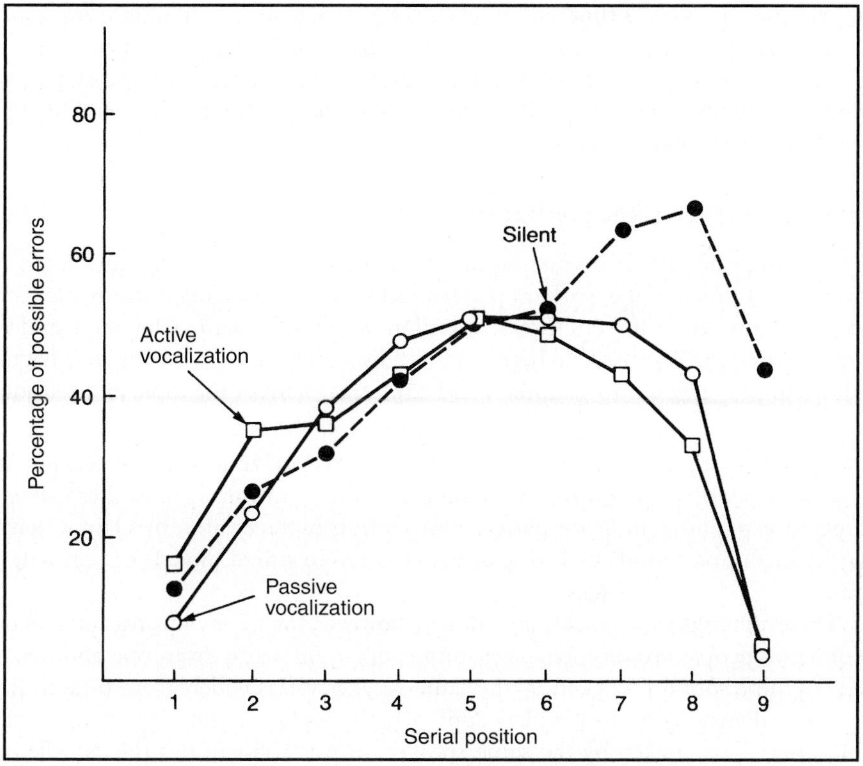

FIGURE 3-18 The number of errors in recall as a function of position in the list of items to be recalled. Note that the two vocalization groups show almost no errors on the last item, compared with the silent group, which had no auditory trace of the list.

This memory interference effect is called the **suffix effect**, *inferior recall of the end of the list in the presence of an additional, meaningful, non-list auditory stimulus.* This is similar to the erasure effect in vision in that it varies depending on speech versus nonspeech suffixes, physical differences, and so on (see also Conrad, 1960; Greene & Crowder, 1984, 1986).

In general, the more the suffix is like the information on the list, the greater the suffix effect (Ayers, Jonides, Reitman, Egan, & Howard, 1979). What the person thinks the suffix is also influences the outcome. In a study by Neath, Surprenant, and Crowder (1993), people heard a "baa" sound at the end of a list of words; if they were told that the sound was made by a person, there was a larger suffix effect than if they were told it was made by a sheep.

In summary, auditory sensory memory is similar to visual sensory memory at a general level, but the details of storage duration and amounts are different. Both systems register sensory information and hold it for a brief period of time: 250 to 500 ms in vision but 2,000 to 4,000 ms in audition. This duration for auditory sensory memory, however, may vary with the complexity of stored information. Generally, more information is encoded than can be reported; however, capacity in auditory sensory memory may be proportionately lower than that of visual sensory memory, although this issue is not easy to pin down. The items held in both sensory systems are prone to loss over short periods of time, either by fading or by erasure, when interfering auditory stimuli are processed. Finally, if attention is redirected during the critical interval, information can be sent to short-term memory, preventing it from being lost. Just as in vision, our auditory world usually is one of continuous stimulation, not bursts of sound followed by empty intervals.

Auditory Pattern Recognition

We will postpone further discussion of auditory pattern recognition until later. The reason is that much of the work on pattern recognition in hearing is more interesting in the context of two different topics: attention, which we cover in Chapter 4, and language, covered in Chapter 9. So here is a brief discussion, with just enough intriguing findings to propel you into Chapter 4 and a full treatment of the topic of attention.

TEMPLATES Attempts to understand how we recognize sounds, especially language, have paralleled the work on visual pattern recognition. That is, there were attempts at explaining auditory pattern recognition by templates, by claims that we identify incoming sounds by trying to match them to stored models or templates in memory.

These attempts were quickly abandoned, however, for an obvious reason: Not only do different people produce language sounds quite differently from one another, but even the same sound produced by the same speaker varies widely from time to time. Even more damaging to the template approach, the "same" sound varies from word to word, even when spoken by the same speaker. In psycholinguistics this is called the **problem of invariance**; the problem is that *the sounds of speech are not invariant from one time to the next.* Instead, any particular sound changes physically depending on what sound preceded it in a word and what sounds are going to follow it.

FEATURE DETECTION Parallel to the work in vision, feature detection models of auditory pattern recognition were more successful than template models. But for the most part, research on feature detection leads to the same conclusion in audition as it did in vision: loads of evidence that *context*—in other words conceptually driven processing—plays a decisive role.

CONCEPTUALLY DRIVEN PROCESSING Let's take two classic examples of research showing the effects of context, of conceptually driven processing effects. In the first, Pollack and Pickett (1964) recorded the idle conversations of volunteers who were waiting to be in a research project. The recordings were then played to other volunteers to see whether they could identify the words, which, of course, they could. But in the more interesting condition, individual words were spliced out and presented in isolation. Here, only about half of all the words could be identified. Removing words from their normal context made it extremely difficult to recognize the patterns. By inference, then, context plays an important role in spoken word identification.

In the second example, Warren and Warren (1970) presented speech to people and asked them to report what they had heard. The recordings were engineered so that

PROVE IT

The influence of top-down processing on perception is very powerful, and we typically do not notice it. In cognitive psychology we can manipulate whether people use top-down knowledge or not by giving some people knowledge they can later use, and others not. However, there are cases in our everyday lives when the influence of knowledge becomes very clear, such as when we listen to songs.

While the lyrics of many songs are clear from the first time you hear them, there are also songs in which it takes some time to figure out just what the singer is singing. Everyone has had this experience when listening to a song for the first time. However, after you read the lyrics in the liner notes, it can be amazing how clear the words seem when you hear the song the next time. You can demonstrate this with some of your friends by playing songs to each other that you know are difficult to get the first time around, and then having a second listen after reading the lyrics. What happens here is that your prior knowledge (top-down processing) can now help organize the incoming auditory perceptual stream, allowing you to correctly parse the lyrics.

We don't always have a lyric sheet to help us figure out what a singer is singing, and we are left with other knowledge we have to figure the words out. While we usually get this right, we can get it wrong, sometimes with hilarious results. There is a web site of mis-heard lyrics (sometimes called "mondegreens") that chronicles the failures of top-down processing on auditory perception (***www.kissthisguy.com***). One example is the person who thought that Jimi Hendricks, in the song Purple Haze, was singing "'scuze me while I kiss this guy" rather than the actual lyrics, "'scuze me while I kiss the sky." Another involved the Beatles' line "the girl with kaleidoscope eyes," mis-heard as "the girl with colitis goes by."

one specific *language sound* (the technical term is **phoneme**) was removed from a single word. Participants heard the altered sentences shown in Table 3-2, where an asterisk indicates the sound that was removed. The word they recognized is shown at the right of each sentence. For instance, even though they heard "*eel," hearing the rest of the sentence, "on the axle," was sufficient for them to perceive the word *wheel.* In fact, most never even noticed anything strange at all about what they heard; it all sounded completely natural. It's a simple but powerful demonstration: Perception and identification of speech are heavily dependent on context, on top-down processing. It's also a nice reminder of the difference between sensation and perception, the physical, sensory nature of sensation but the overwhelmingly cognitive nature of perception. ★

★ **TABLE 3-2 Warren and Warren's (1970) Sentences and Participants' Responses**

Participant Reports	Participant Hears
It was found that the *eel was on the axle.	wheel
It was found that the *eel was on the shoe.	heel
It was found that the *eel was on the orange.	peel
It was found that the *eel was on the table.	meal

Note: The asterisks represent deleted sounds.

Section Summary

- Auditory stimulation is stored briefly in auditory sensory memory, for periods up to 4 s or so for language-based information. Although auditory sensory memory lasts longer than visual sensory memory, its capacity may not be as large as visual sensory memory.
- Generally, the last items in a list presented auditorially are recalled better than items presented visually (the modality effect); furthermore, an auditory suffix added to the end of the list degrades performance on the last list items, demonstrating erasure from auditory sensory memory.
- Theories of auditory pattern recognition resemble those in vision; that is, they involve feature detection plus a substantial role for top-down processing.

Key Terms

agnosia (p. *98*)
apperceptive agnosia (p. *99*)
associative agnosia (p. *99*)
audition (p. *102*)
auditory sensory memory (p. *102*)
backward masking (p. *76*)
beta movement (p. *77*)
change blindness (p. *71*)
conceptually driven processing effects (p. *87*)
connectionist modeling (p. *90*)
context (p. *88*)
data-driven processing system (p. *86*)
decay (p. *76*)
echoic memory (p. *102*)
erasure (p. *77*)
feature analysis (p. *83*)
feature detection (p. *83*)
fixation (p. *69*)
focal attention (p. *79*)
fovea (p. *67*)
geons (p. *95*)
icon (p. *75*)
iconic memory (p. *72*)
inattentional blindness (p. *71*)
interference (p. *76*)
modality effect (p. *106*)
Pandemonium (p. *84*)
partial report condition (p. *74*)
perception (p. *69*)
phi phenomenon (p. *77*)
phoneme (p. *109*)
problem of invariance (p. *108*)
prosopagnosia (p. *98*)
repetition blindness (p. *89*)
retina (p. *66*)
saccades (p. *69*)
sensation (p. *69*)
span of apprehension (p. *74*)
suffix effect (p. *107*)
templates (p. *83*)
Trans-saccadic memory (p. *79*)
visual persistence (p. *72*)
visual sensory memory (p. *72*)
whole report condition (p. *74*)

CHAPTER

4

Attention

Everyone knows what attention is. It is the taking possession by the mind, in clear and vivid form, of one out of what seem several simultaneously possible objects or trains of thought. Focalization, concentration, of consciousness are of its essence. It implies withdrawal from some things in order to deal effectively with others.

JAMES, 1890, PP. 381–382

As he did every morning after waking, Bill went into the bathroom to begin his morning ritual. After squeezing toothpaste onto his toothbrush, he looked into the mirror and began to brush his teeth. Although he brushed the teeth on the right side of his mouth quite vigorously, for the most part he ignored those on the left side. . . . He shaved all the stubble from the right side of his face impeccably but did a spotty job on the left side. . . . [After eating at a diner,] when Bill asked for the check, the waitress placed it on the left side of the table. After a few minutes, he waved the waitress over and complained, saying "I asked for my tab 5 minutes ago. What is taking so long?"

BANICH, 1997, P. 235

Attention, one of cognitive psychology's most important topics and one of our oldest puzzles, in Neisser's (1976) description is "psychology's most elusive target." What does it mean to pay attention to something? To direct your attention to something? To be unable to pay attention because of boredom, lack of interest, or fatigue? What sorts of things, whether external stimuli or internal thoughts, grab or capture our attention? How much control do we have over our attention? Is it always a matter of concentration and determination when you pay attention to something? Or are some things easy to attend to, and if so why? (Cognitive science says "attend to," meaning "pay attention," even though the dictionary claims that to be an archaic usage.) We have to work at paying attention to some things (most topics in a faculty meeting, for example). But for other topics, it seems effortless: A good spy novel rivets my attention, just as a great cognition lecture rivets yours (!).

MULTIPLE MEANINGS OF ATTENTION

Attention is one of the most pervasive topics in cognitive psychology and one of the thorniest, possibly because we mean so many different things by the term. We use the term *attention* to describe a huge range of phenomena, from the basic idea of arousal and alertness all the way up to consciousness and awareness. Some attention processes are extremely rapid, so that we are aware only of their outcomes, if that, and others are slow enough that we seem to be aware of them—and able to control them—throughout. In some cases, attention is reflexive. Even when we deliberately concentrate on something, that concentration can be disrupted and redirected by an unexpected, attention-grabbing event, such as the sudden loud noise in the otherwise quiet library. In other cases, we are frustrated that our deliberate attempts to focus on some task are so easily disrupted by another train of thought; you try very hard to pay attention to a lecture, only to find yourself daydreaming about last weekend's party.

▲ Table 4-1 presents a list of six different connotations of the term *attention*. For organizational purposes, this chapter is structured around that list to impose some coherence on the field, to help you see the forest and prevent your getting lost in the trees (the final type of attention in the table is nearly synonymous with short-term or working memory, so it is not discussed until the next chapter). Although other organizational schemes are possible, this approach should help you develop an understanding

TABLE 4-1 Six Meanings of Attention

Input Attention	Controlled Attention
Alertness or arousal	Selective attention
Orienting reflex or response	Mental resources and conscious processing
Spotlight attention and search	Supervisory attentional system

of the topic of attention and see how some topics flow into others. The list will also help avoid some confusion that arises when the term *attention* is used for processes or mechanisms more precisely described by another term, such as *arousal.*

At every turn, we confront four interrelated ideas. *First,* we are constantly presented with more information than we can attend to. *Second,* there are serious limits in how much we can attend to at once. *Third,* we can respond to some information and perform some tasks with little if any attention. And *fourth,* with sufficient practice and knowledge, some tasks become less and less demanding of our attention.

BASICS OF ATTENTION

Let's start by giving two general metaphors for *attention*, both of which apply throughout the list in Table 4-1.

ATTENTION AS A MENTAL PROCESS **Attention** can be thought of as *the mental process of concentrating effort on a stimulus or a mental event.* By this we mean that attention is an activity that occurs within cognition, a process. This process focuses a mental resource—effort—on either an external stimulus or an internal thought. When it refers to an external stimulus, attention is the mental mechanism by which we actively process information in the sensory registers pertaining to that entity. In fact, the operation of iconic memory and spatial visual attention use the same underlying neural substrates, such as a shared frontal-parietal network (Ruff, Kristkjánsson, & Driver, 2007). When you examine a picture like that in Figure 4-1, you focus your mental energies on an external stimulus, the splotches and patches of black and white in a puzzling photograph. If you have never seen this before, you struggle to identify it, to recognize the pattern in it; you are reduced to heavy reliance on data-driven processing. Your focus in the attempt to identify the pattern was *attention.* Sustained attention then led, after some time, to identifying the Dalmatian.

In principle, the focusing of your attention on a visual stimulus is no different than when you focus attention on a word, idea, or concept. For example, your professor says something unexpected (e.g., describing an idea as "green"), and you puzzle over the remark, trying to find a way to interpret it that makes sense (can an idea that promotes conservation and ecology be described as "green"? See also Chapter 9). It is this concentration of attention we are illustrating here, attention focused on and driving the mental event of remembering, searching for information stored in memory, and attempting to comprehend.

FIGURE 4-1
First identification of the pattern relies almost exclusively on data-driven processing, whereas later identification relies heavily on conceptually driven processing.

ATTENTION AS A LIMITED MENTAL RESOURCE Now consider attention as a mental resource, a kind of mental fuel. In this sense, attention is *the limited mental energy or resource that powers cognition.* It is a mental commodity, the stuff that gets used when we pay attention. According to this metaphor, attention is the all-important mental resource necessary to run cognition, to make it operate.

A fundamentally important idea here is that of limitations: Attention is limited, finite. We usually state this by talking about the limited capacity of attention. Countless experiments, to say nothing of everyday experiences, reveal the limits of our attention, the capacity to attend to stimuli, to remember events that just happened, to remember things we are supposed to do. In short, there is a limit to how many different things we can attend to and do all at once.

It does not take long to think of everyday situations that reveal these limitations. You can easily drive down an uncrowded highway in daylight while carrying on a conversation. You can easily listen to the news on the radio under normal driving conditions. In the middle of a heavy rainstorm, however, you can't talk to the person sitting in the passenger seat; in rush hour traffic, you can't (or shouldn't try to) do business on the cell phone. Under such demanding circumstances, the radio and the conversation are annoyances or irritating—even dangerous—distractions, and you have to turn down the volume and turn off the phone.

BASIC INPUT ATTENTIONAL PROCESSES

We'll start with a section on the more basic types of attention listed in Table 4-1, those occurring early in the stream of processing. These are the processes that seem either reflexive or automatic, are low-level in terms of informational content, and occur rapidly. They are especially involved in *the basic processes of getting sensory information into the cognitive system,* so they can generally be called forms of **input attention**.

Alertness and Arousal

It almost seems axiomatic to say that part of what we mean by *attention* involves the basic capacity to respond to the environment. This most basic sense refers to alertness and arousal as a necessary state of the nervous system: The nervous system must be awake, responsive, and able to interact with the environment. At the physiological level, arousal is at least partly a function of the reticular activating system (RAS), a lower brain stem system in charge of, among other things, basic arousal and consciousness (Kolb & Whishaw, 1996). It seems intuitive that the nervous system must be aroused in order to pay attention. You cannot attend to stimuli while you are unconscious, although certain stimuli can impinge on us and rouse us to a conscious state (e.g., alarm clocks, smoke detectors, or other loud noises).

While consciousness is important, to some degree there also needs to be an element of alertness. That is, we need to monitor the environment for new, interesting, and/or important events. Sometimes this can be difficult, especially when this alertness needs to be strung out over long period of time during which nothing much happens. The *maintenance of attention for infrequent events over long periods of time* is known as **vigilance** or **sustained attention**. The study of vigilance began during World War II with British radar operators (Mackworth, 1948). However, vigilance is important in so many other domains, including air traffic control, sonar detection, and nuclear power plant operations (Warm, 1984). Even quality inspections in a factory involve some degree of vigilance as workers constantly monitor for important but relatively infrequent flaws in products (Wiener, 1984).

There are a number of fundamental phenomena that have been observed in vigilance research over the years (see See, Howe, Warm, & Dember, 1995, for a review). For instance, there is a decline in performance as time in the task wears on, showing that people have difficulty maintaining their attention on a single task over long periods of time. This decline takes about 20-35 minutes to complete. Interestingly, the problems that occur with a decline in vigilance do not appear to involve people not noticing the signal in the task they are doing, but instead are due to problems in making the decision to respond that they have detected something, a shift in response bias. Vigilance is also affected by the neurological and physiological state of the person, such as a whether people are too hot or cold, their level of arousal, or if they have been taking drugs (Warm, 1984). Finally, there are also a number of aspects of the task that can influence how effective people are, such as how long the signal is (longer is better), how often there is a signal (more frequent is better), and how busy the background is (less busy is better) (Warm & Jerison, 1984).

Although nobody disputes that arousal and alertness are a necessary precondition for most cognitive processes, this view may overemphasize a kind of thinking known as **explicit processing**. Explicit processes are those *involving consciousness processing, conscious awareness that a task is being performed, and usually conscious awareness of the outcome of that performance.* The opposite is known as **implicit processing**, *processing with no necessary involvement of conscious awareness* (Schacter, 1989, 1996). As you will see, the distinction between implicit and explicit is often in terms of memory performance, especially long-term memory. When you are asked to learn a list of words and then name them back, that's an *explicit memory* task: You are consciously aware of being tested and aware that you are remembering words you just studied. By contrast, you can also demonstrate memory for information *without* awareness, which is *implicit memory*. For example, you can reread a text more rapidly than you read it the first time, even if you have no recollection of ever reading it before (Masson, 1984).

There is some evidence showing that some important mental processing can be done with only minimal attention. Much of this is discussed later, especially in sections on long-term memory. For now, consider a study by Bonebakker et al. (1996; see Andrade, 1995, for a review of learning under anesthesia) in which they presented recorded lists of words to surgery patients, one list just before and another during surgery, and then tested memory up to 24 hours later. Despite the fact that all the patients were given general anesthesia, and so were unconscious during the surgery itself, they nonetheless showed memory for words they heard. Keep in mind, however, that they were only remembering 6-9% more words compared to a control condition of new words. They certainly did not learn any complex ideas. So, you do need to pay attention to learn well. It's just that small amounts of learning can sometimes occur unconsciously.

A powerful part of the study was that performance was based on an implicit memory task, the *word stem completion task*. Patients were given word stems and told to complete them with the first word that occurred to them. To ensure that the task was measuring implicit memory, patients were further asked to exclude any words they explicitly remembered hearing, such as the words they remembered hearing before receiving anesthesia. For example, say that they heard *BOARD* before surgery and *LIGHT* during surgery. When tested 24 hours after surgery, the patients completed the word stems (e.g., *LI_ _ _*) with words they had heard during surgery *(LIGHT)* more frequently than they did with presurgery words *(BO_ _ _)* or with control words that had never been presented. In other words, they remembered hearing *BOARD* and excluded it on the word stem task. Because they did not explicitly remember *LIGHT,* they finished *LI_ _ _* with *GHT,* presumably because their memory of *LIGHT* was implicit. The results demonstrated that the patients had implicit memory of the words they had heard while under the anesthesia.

So that you understand this procedure, and because we will encounter it several times in later chapters, here is a more focused version of the task. Imagine that you saw a list of words including *SCHOOL* and *SHELF.* Relying on explicit memory, you would probably complete the stem *SCH_ _ _* with *SCHOOL*. But if I asked you to exclude words you explicitly remembered, you would find another way of completing that stem, say *SCHEME*; likewise, you might exclude *SHELF* and write *SHELL*. By chance, you might complete the stem *CRA_ _ _* with *CRADLE* or *CRAYON,* neither of which you saw before. Here is the implicit part. Try it yourself. Complete the following word stems with the first word that comes to your mind: *PAP_ _*; *GRE_ _*. *PAPER* is a pretty common completion for the first one, probably because paper is a fairly common word (it has not appeared in this chapter yet). But if you completed the second as *GREEN* without explicitly remembering that you read about "green ideas" earlier, then that probably was an implicit memory effect.

Orienting Reflex and Attention Capture

Now consider another kind of attention, the kind caused by a reflexive response in the nervous system. In a quiet room, an unexpected noise grabs your attention away from what you were doing and may involve a reflexive turning of your head toward the source of the sound. In vision, of course, you move your eyes and head toward the unexpected stimulus, the flash of light or sudden movement in your peripheral vision. This is the **orienting reflex**, *the reflexive redirection of attention that orients you toward the unexpected stimulus.* This response is found at all levels of the animal kingdom and is present very early in life. Although a host of physiological changes accompany the orienting reflex, including changes in heart rate and respiration (Bridgeman, 1988), we focus on its more mental aspects. The cognitive manifestation of all of this is a redirection of attention toward something, even if the eyes and body do not actually move toward the source. As such, we refer to this process as **attention capture**, which is *the spontaneous redirection of attention to stimuli in the world based on physical characteristics.*

Current thinking suggests that the orienting reflex is a location-finding response of the nervous system. That is, an unexpected stimulus, a noise or a flash of light, triggers the reflex so that you can locate the stimulus, find where it is in space. This enables you to protect yourself against danger, in the reflexive, survival sense; after all, what if the unexpected movement is from a rock thrown at you or some other threat (e.g., Ohman, Flykt, & Esteves, 2001)? Note that this system also allows you to monitor for more positive survival stimuli, such as noticing a baby's face (Brosch, Sander, Pourtois, & Scherer, 2008). Given that the response helps you locate the stimulus, it is not surprising that some of the neural pathways involved correspond to the *"where" pathway* (a companion to the "what" pathway involved in object recognition). Briefly, the "where" pathway projects from the visual cortex to upper (superior) rearward (dorsal) regions of the parietal lobe in the brain; in fact, the "where" pathway is called the dorsal pathway (and the *"what" pathway* is also called the ventral pathway).

Cowan (1995) noted that the kinds of stimuli that trigger the orienting reflex boil down to two categories: (a) stimuli that are significant for the organism (the rock thrown toward your head) and (b) stimuli that are novel. What is significant to you often has some relation to emotions. Because emotion and attention use some of the same neural components, such as the amygdala, portions of the frontal lobes, and the anterior cingulate cortex, emotion can affect the direction of attention (Vuilleumeir, 2005). For example, people are more likely to direct their attention to emotionally arousing stimuli, such as seeing a snake in the grass. Attention can also influence how you feel about things. For example, people develop negative emotion toward things that they try to ignore (Fenske & Raymond, 2006).

Note also that attention is not only directed by objects and entities in the environment, but we can also have our attention directed buy social cues. Perhaps the biggest cue is noticing where other people are looking (Kingstone, Smilek, Ristic, Friesen, & Eastwood, 2003). In fact, there has been some suggestion that our face and eyes have evolved in such a way to communicate this sort of attention directing information (Emery, 2000). Even our language can influence how we direct attention. For example, a study by Estes, Verges, and Barsalou (2008) showed that attention can be directed based on the meanings of words activated in long-term memory. In this study people saw a cue word in the middle of the screen, which was soon followed by either an X or an O at either the top or the bottom of a computer screen. The task was to indicate which of these two letters was seen by pressing one of two buttons. They found that people were faster to respond to a letter probe if the meaning of the cue word signified a direction consistent with the location of the letter. So, if the cue word was *hat*, people would respond to the letters faster if they were on the top of the screen rather than the bottom. Similarly, if the word was *boot*, the opposite was true.

We also orient toward novel things when something *different* occurs: the unexpected sound in the quiet library, sudden and unexpected movement (Abrams & Christ, 2003; Franconeri & Simons, 2003), the abrupt onset of a new object (Davoli, Suszko, & Abrams, 2007; Yantis & Jonides, 1984), a change in the color of an object (Lu & Zhou, 2005), the change in pitch in a professor's voice during a lecture, maybe the word *different* in italics in a textbook paragraph. Orienting focuses the organism so it can devote deliberate attention to the stimulus if warranted; Cowan (1995) called these voluntary attentive processes. In this sense, orienting is a preparatory response, one that prepares the system for further voluntary processing. In visual attention, fMRI neurological scanning has shown that the attention capture process itself seems to involve retinotopic (specific places on the retina in your eye) portions of the occipital lobe, the part of the brain dedicated to vision. This is in contrast to more controlled aspects of attention that involve portions of the dorsal parietal and frontal cortex, further down the stream of neural activity in the brain (Serences et al., 2005).

If the stimulus that triggered the orienting reflex occurs over and over again, it is no longer novel or different; now it has become part of the normal, unchanging background. The process of **habituation** begins to take over, *a gradual reduction of the orienting response back to baseline.* For example, if the unexpected noise in the quiet library is the ventilation fan coming on, you first notice it but then grow accustomed to it. You have oriented to the stimulus, and then that response has habituated, to the point that you will probably orient again when the fan *stops* running. When the constant noise stops, *that* is a change that triggers the orienting response.

Spotlight Attention and Visual Search

The last sense of *attention* to be considered among the input attentional processes is a kind of visual attention. It is related to perceptual space, that is, the spatial arrangement of stimuli in your visual field and the way you search that space for information. It is a different process than the orienting response in that there is no necessary movement of the eyes or head, although there is a strong correlation with eye movements (researchers often exploit this relationship to have a general idea of where attention has been directed using eye-tracking devices). Instead, there is a mental shift of attentional focus, as if a spotlight beam were focused on a region of visual space, enabling you to pick up information in that space more easily (think of the "Superman beam" mentioned in the previous chapter, e.g., Bahr, 2003; Winer et al., 2002).

A large amount of work on this kind of visual attention has been reported, including some work that has found distinct regions of the brain that seem to be involved in focused, visual attention.

◆ **THE SPOTLIGHT OF VISUAL ATTENTION** Consider Figure 4-2, which depicts three different kinds of displays in Posner's spatial cuing task (Posner, Nissen, & Ogden, 1978; Posner, Snyder, & Davidson, 1980). People in this task are first asked to fixate the centered plus sign on the visual display, are then shown a directional cue, and finally see a simple target (the thing they are supposed to respond to). The task was to press a button when people detect the target. For 80% of the cued trials, the arrow pointed to the direction where the target actually did appear 1 s later. On the remaining 20% of

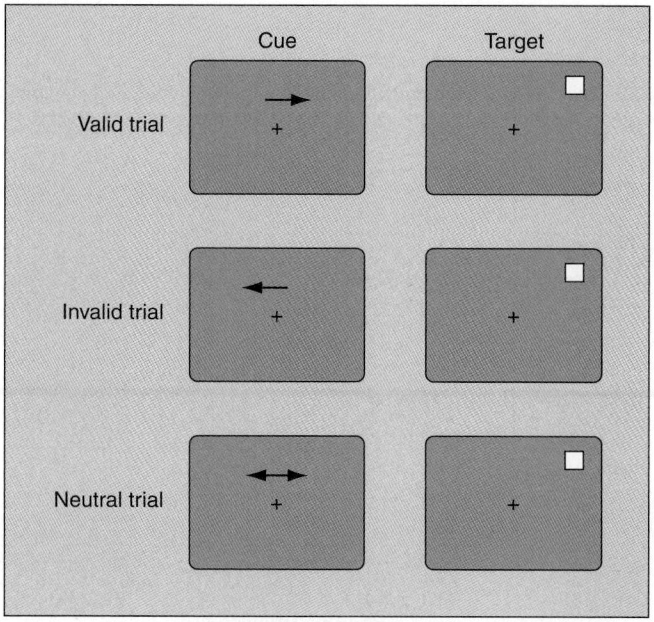

◆ **FIGURE 4-2**
In Posner's spatial cuing task, the person fixates on the plus sign in the center of the screen, then sees an arrow pointing left or right or a two-headed arrow. For the targets shown in the figure, with a target appearing on the right, the right-pointing arrow is a valid cue, the left-pointing arrow an invalid cue, and the two-headed arrow a neutral cue. In this experiment, one-headed arrow cues were valid on 80% of the trials.

the cued trials, however, the cue was invalid: It pointed to the wrong side. Neutral trials provided an uninformative cue, a two-headed arrow indicating that the target would appear equally often on the left or right. Throughout the task, people were required to maintain fixation on the plus sign. That is, they could shift only their *mental* attention to the space where they thought the target might appear but were not permitted to move their eyes.

The results, shown in Figure 4-3, were very clear. When people shifted attention to the correct area (the Valid 80% point in the figure), response time (RT) to detect the target was significantly faster than the neutral, uncued condition. This speedup is known as a **benefit** or **facilitation**, *a faster-than-baseline response resulting from the useful advance information.* When the target appeared in the unexpected location, however, there was a significant **cost**, *a response slower than baseline because of the misleading cue.* Interestingly, further analysis suggested that the cost of having directed attention to the wrong place resulted from a three-part process, (a) disengaging attention from its current focus, (b) moving the attentional spotlight to the target's true location, then (c) engaging attention at that new location.

Posner et al. (1980) concluded from this and related experiments that the attentional focus being switched was a cognitive phenomenon; it was not tied to physical eye movements but instead to an internal mechanism. They suggested that "attention can be likened to a spotlight that enhances the efficiency of detection of events within its beam" (p. 172). So **spotlight attention** is *the mental attention-focusing mechanism that prepares you to encode stimulus information.* Furthermore, Posner et al. suggested that this shift in attention is essentially the same as the redirection of attention in the orienting reflex, with one big difference: It is voluntary. Therefore, it can happen before a stimulus occurs and can be triggered by cognitive factors such as expectations.

FIGURE 4-3 Consider the response time (RT) points in the neutral condition to be baseline performance on detecting targets. When a valid cue was presented, there was a reduction in RT for targets in both the left and right visual fields ("Valid 80%"). When the cue was invalid, there was a slow-down in detecting the target in both visual fields ("Invalid 20%"). From Posner, Snyder, & Davidson (1980).

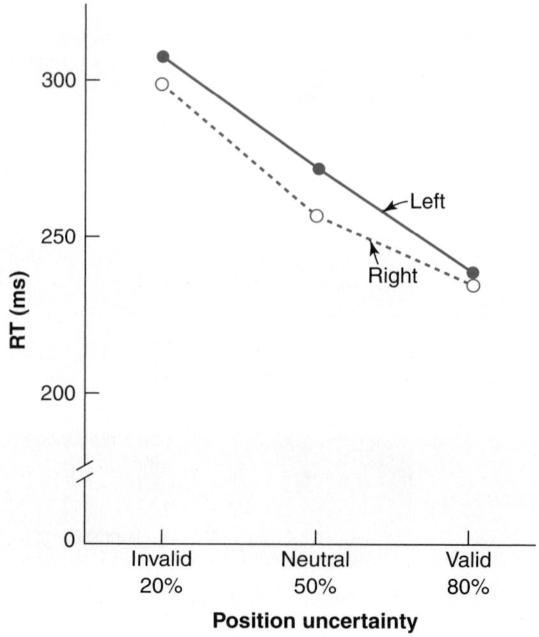

As Cave and Bichot (1999) pointed out, countless studies of visual attention, many of them inspired by Posner's work, have adopted the spotlight metaphor. Much of that work has explored the characteristics and limits of visual attention, attempting to evaluate how useful the metaphor is. The evidence suggests that the mental spotlight does not sweep, enhancing the intermediate locations along the way, but instead it jumps (much as the saccade does). On the other hand, there is also supportive evidence for the similarity between a real spotlight and spotlight attention. For example, it appears that the size of the spotlight beam can be altered, depending on circumstances (see Cave & Bichot, 1999, for an extensive review).

★ **VISUAL SEARCH** Look at Figure 4-4, and do these quick demonstrations. In the first panel, search for either a letter *T* or a boldfaced letter; in the other two panels, search for a boldfaced *T*. As you performed these visual searches, you surely noticed that searching for *T* in the first panel was stunningly simple; it hardly seemed like a search, did it? Instead, didn't the *T* just "pop out" at you? In contrast, searching for *T* in the middle panel probably was a slow process, and finding it in the last panel probably took even longer. A classic, everyday example of difficult visual search can be found in the "Where's Waldo" children's books.

A series of studies by Treisman and her associates (Treisman, 1982, 1988, 1991; Treisman & Gelade, 1980) examined visual search. Typically, people were told to search a visual display for either of two simple features (e.g., letter *S* or a blue letter) or a conjunction of two features (e.g., a green *T*). The search for a simple feature was called a *feature search*: Participants responded "yes" when they detected the presence of either of the specified features, either a letter *S* or a blue letter. In the *conjunction search* condition, they had to search for the combination of two features, *T* and the color green.

★ **FIGURE 4-4**
In the left panel, search either for a capital *T* or a boldfaced letter. In the other two panels, search for a boldfaced capital *T*.

In the searches you did, the first were feature searches, and the last panel illustrated a conjunction search (the target had to be both boldfaced and a *T*).

In the typical result (Treisman & Gelade, 1980, Experiment 1), people could search rapidly for an item identified by the presence of a unique feature. It made little or no difference whether they searched through a small or a large display; for instance, people were able to search through as few as 5 patterns or as many as 30 in about the same amount of time, approximately 500 ms. The target object just seemed to "pop out" of the display. Because there was no increase in RT across the display sizes, Treisman and Gelade concluded that visual search for a dimension such as shape or color occurs in parallel across the entire region of visual attention. Such a search must be largely automatic and must represent very early visual processing. In the results, shown in Figure 4-5, this is the flat, low function of the graph. ▲

PROVE IT

The Visual Search Task

Here we have a fairly simple task to do with your friends and a stopwatch that illustrates the difference between feature and conjunction searches in visual attention. Using two different colors of marker pens, make up a few sheets of paper, or some 4 X 6 index cards, on which you draw letters in two distinct colors, say red and green. For simplicity's sake, let's restrict ourselves to Xs and Ts. In all cases, we'll have your participants search for a *green T*.

For the *feature* search trials, you will have a number of red Xs and Ts all over the paper. On the "yes" sheets, you'll put a green T in one spot on the paper; on the "no" sheets, you'll just have red Xs and Ts. Make a separate sheet, one for "yes" trials and one for "no" trials, with 4 Xs and Ts, then do the same for 6 Xs and Ts, then 8, 10, and 12 (don't forget to go back and put the green T in for your "yes" trials). For the *conjunction* trials, in addition to the green T for the "yes" sheets, you'll put green Xs and red Ts on the sheets; as before, you'll also have "no" sheets that only have green Xs and red Ts.

Tell your participants that the task is to find the green T as fast as possible. When they find the green T, have them raise their right hand. However, if they don't think the green T is there, have them raise their left hand. Time people (the second hand/display on your watch is fine) each time. The standard result is that the feature search items should show a fairly constant retrieval rate regardless of the number of distractors. This is because the target letter should pop out under these circumstances. In comparison, for the conjunction search items should be an average increase in response time as the number of distractors increases.

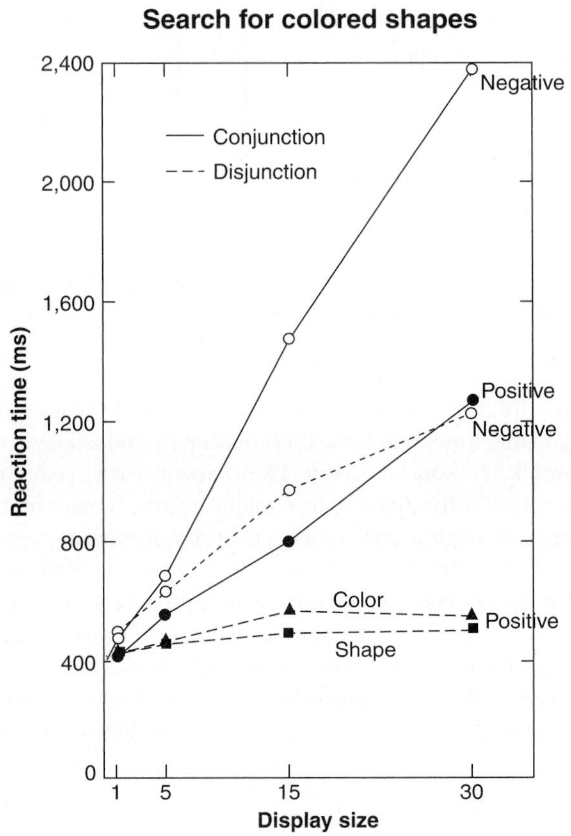

▲ **FIGURE 4-5** Search times when targets were of a specified color or shape. The dashed lines are for the disjunction search conditions (e.g., search for either a capital *T* or a boldfaced letter). The solid lines show search times for the conjunction condition (e.g., search for a boldfaced *T*). The important result is that disjunctive search times did not increase as the display size grew larger, but the conjunction search times did.

But when people had to do a conjunction search, such as a green *T*, they took more time, up to 2,400 ms, as more and more distractors filled the display (distractors for both conditions were brown *T*s and green *X*s). Such conjunction search seems a more serial, one-by-one process and a far more conscious, deliberate act. This is the steeply increasing function in Figure 4-5.

Because a visual search can be complex, people need a way to keep track of what they have already checked and what they have not. A big problem would occur if a person kept checking the same, useless items over and over again, and never checking others. To help people from returning to inappropriate locations there is a special attention process. This is called **inhibition of return** (Klein, 2000; Posner & Cohen, 1984) in which *recently checked locations are mentally marked by attention as places that the search process would not return to.* This process appears to be guided by the operations of the superior colliculus and the parietal lobe (Klein, 2000; Vivas, Humphreys, & Fuentes, 2006), consistent with the idea that inhibition of return is an important visual process (involving the superior colliculus) as well as knowledge of where things are in space, the "where" neural pathway (involving the parietal lobe).

In some sense, the locations are inhibited from or kept out of the search pattern. These items were highly activated in cognition because they were attended to, and what inhibition of return does is turn this activation down. So, only those locations that are likely to still have the item you're looking for continue to be searched. A consequence of this is that people are slower to respond to events (such as a change in brightness) in locations that have recently been searched, and inhibited, relative to other locations. Imagine searching for a friend at the airport as many people are arriving from a number of different flights. What you do is visually search through the faces as they come out of security. It would not be helpful if you kept scanning the same faces over and over again. What inhibition of return does is keep you from returning to them, having your visual search move on to other faces, hopefully allowing you to find your friend faster.

Contrasting Input and Controlled Attention

Treisman's two conditions provide clear evidence of both a very quick, automatic attentional process—essentially the capture of attention due to "pop-out"—and a much slower, more deliberate attention, the type used for the conjunction search. In line with Johnston, McCann, and Remington's (1995) suggestion, we use the term *input attention* for the fast, automatic process of attention, the type of process we have been talking about in this section. The slower one, the terms of Johnston et al., is *controlled attention,* to which we turn in a moment. It is important to discuss these as separate aspects of attention as research has suggested that these two forms of attention operate with some degree of independence (Berger, Henik, & Rafal, 2005).

Consider the early, rapid stages of feature detection as relying on spotlight attention (Posner & Cohen, 1984). The spotlight is directed toward a visual display and "enhances the detection of events within its 'beam'" (Kanwisher & Driver, 1992). It provides the encoding route into the visual system. It is this attentional focus mechanism that provides early, extremely rapid feature detection for the ensuing process of pattern recognition. It is especially visual; for instance, it has been called posterior attention because the earliest stages of visual perception occur in the posterior region of the brain, in the occipital lobe, as illustrated in Figure 4-6 (see also the inside front cover illustration of neural activity in ● the occipital lobe when a visual stimulus is presented), as well as the involvement of the superior colliculus (Berger et al., 2005).

The spotlight attention we are talking about—and we presume there is also an equivalent attention mechanism for other senses—appears to be rapid, automatic, and perceptual. It is thereby distinguished from the slower, controlled or conscious attention process that matches the more ordinary connotation of the term *attention*. The "regular" kind is the conscious attention that we have loosely equated with awareness. Based on some neurophysiological evidence, we might even call this frontal or anterior attention because activity in the frontal regions of the brain seems to accompany elements of conscious awareness, such as awareness of the meaning of a word (Posner et al., 1992).

Conscious or controlled attention prepares us to respond in a deliberate way to the environment. It is slower, operates in a more serial fashion, and is especially influenced by conceptually driven processes. Spotlight attention, however, is a basic, rapid attentional mechanism that seems to operate in parallel across the visual field, in a highly automatic fashion. It is especially data driven, funneling aspects of the environment into the cognitive system. Conscious attention then enables us to respond to that environment.

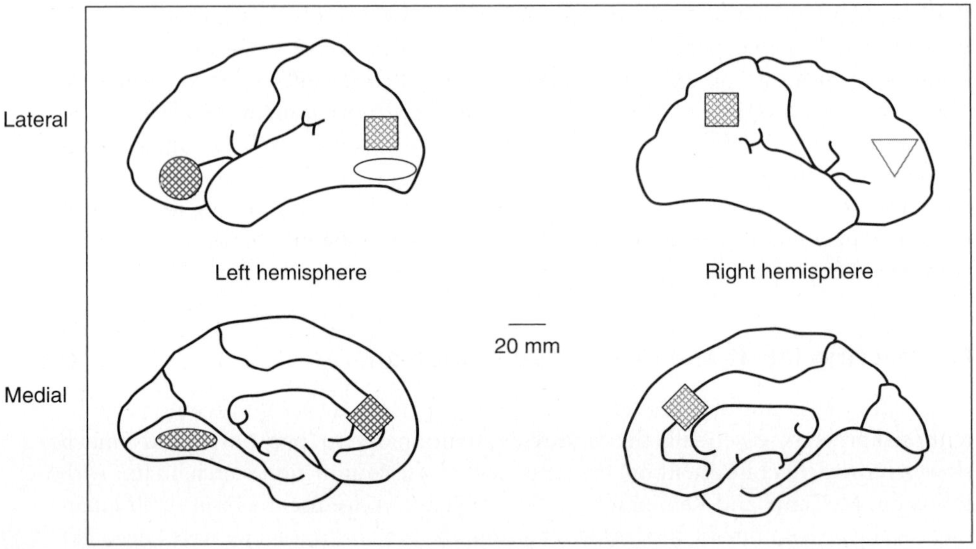

FIGURE 4-6
The top two drawings show lateral (side) views of the left and right hemispheres of the brain, and the bottom two show medial views, as if the hemispheres had been split down the center from front to back, showing inner portions of the cortex. The geometric shapes refer to different regions of the brain that are involved in attention; squares denote regions involved in the attentional network, the triangle denotes a region related to vigilance, and the diamond denotes a part of the anterior attentional network; the circle and oval denote word processing regions for semantic associates and visual word forms, respectively. From Solso (1998).

Hemineglect: An Attention Deficit

In many cases, cognitive science has gained insight into a cognitive process when there has been some disruption to the system, as often happens in the case of brain damage. The study of attention is no exception to this. Go back to the beginning of the chapter and reread the quotation from Banich (1997) about Bill. Bill suffers from *hemineglect*, a syndrome that leads to such behavior as brushing only the teeth on his right, washing only his right arm, and shaving only the right side of his face. To many people, this phenomenon is almost too bizarre to believe, maybe because the processes of mental attention have always been so closely tied to perception and voluntary movement and so automatic that we think they are indivisible parts of the same process. Look at yourself in a mirror, then look at the left side of your face—no problem, you merely move your eyes, shift your direction of gaze, and look at it. If I ask you to stare straight ahead and then attend to something in your left field of vision, say the letter *X* on a computer screen, your normal response is to shift your eyes toward the left and focus on the target. You simply look at the *X* and pay attention to it. You can even shift your mental attention to the left without moving your eyes.

The syndrome known as **hemineglect** (or hemi-inattention) is a disruption in the ability to refocus your attention to one side of your face or the other, to the *X* on the left of the computer screen. It is a *disruption or decreased ability to attend to something* *in the (often) left field of vision. Hemi* means "half," and *neglect* means "to ignore" or "to fail to perceive." Thus hemineglect is a disorder of attention in which one half of the perceptual world is neglected to some degree and cannot be attended to as completely or accurately as normal. Some form of hemineglect is often observed in stroke victims, even if it is in a more limited and temporary form. Very often, the neglect is of the left visual field, for stimuli to the left of the current fixation, the current focus of attention. And because of the principle of contralaterality, it is not surprising that the brain damage leading to hemineglect is often in the right hemisphere, in particular, certain regions of the right parietal lobe (see Intriligator & Cavanagh, 2001, for evidence that localizes selective attention in the parietal lobe).

Here are the facts (see Banich, 1997, or Rafal, 1997, for complete treatments): A patient with hemineglect cannot voluntarily direct attention to half of the perceptual world, whether the to-be-perceived stimulus is visual, auditory, or any other type of sensation. In some cases, the neglect is nearly total, as if half of the perceptual world has simply vanished, is simply not there in any normal sense of the word. In other cases, the neglect is partial, so for such people it is more accurate to say that they are *less able* to redirect their attention than are normal people. In either case, there is a disruption in the ability to control attention. Note that this is not a case of sensory damage like blindness or deafness. The patient with hemineglect receives input from both sides of the body and can make voluntary muscle movements on both sides. And in careful testing situations, such patients can also respond to stimuli in the neglected field. But somehow, the deliberate devotion of controlled attention to one side is deficient.

Bisiach and Luzatti (1978) present a compelling description of hemineglect. The afflicted individuals were from Milan, Italy, with which they were quite familiar prior to their brain damage. This study focused on the main piazza in town, a broad open square with buildings and shops along the sides and a large cathedral at one end. These patients were asked to imagine themselves standing at one end of the piazza, facing the cathedral, and to describe what they could see. They uniformly described only the buildings and shops on the right side of the piazza. When asked to imagine themselves standing on the steps of the cathedral, facing back the opposite way, they once again described what was on their right side. From this second view, of course, what they described was exactly what they had omitted from their earlier descriptions. Likewise, they now omitted what they had described earlier.

Critically important here is the observation that these reports, based on memory, were exactly the kind of reports patients with hemineglect give when actually viewing a scene; if these patients had been taken to the piazza, they probably would have seen and described it the same way as they did from memory. (For a similar account, see "Eyes Right!" in Sacks, 1970; the patient there eats the right half of everything on her dinner plate, then complains about not getting enough food.) Figure 4-7 shows some drawings made by patients with hemineglect. Here, patients were asked to copy drawings or to draw from memory, but the nature of their drawings was no different in either case. These drawings show a dramatic neglect for the left-hand sides of objects: a flower with no petals on the left, a clock face with no numbers on the left. In the standard line bisection task ("draw a slash through the middle of a horizontal line"), hemineglect patients position the slash too far to the right, as if bisecting only the right

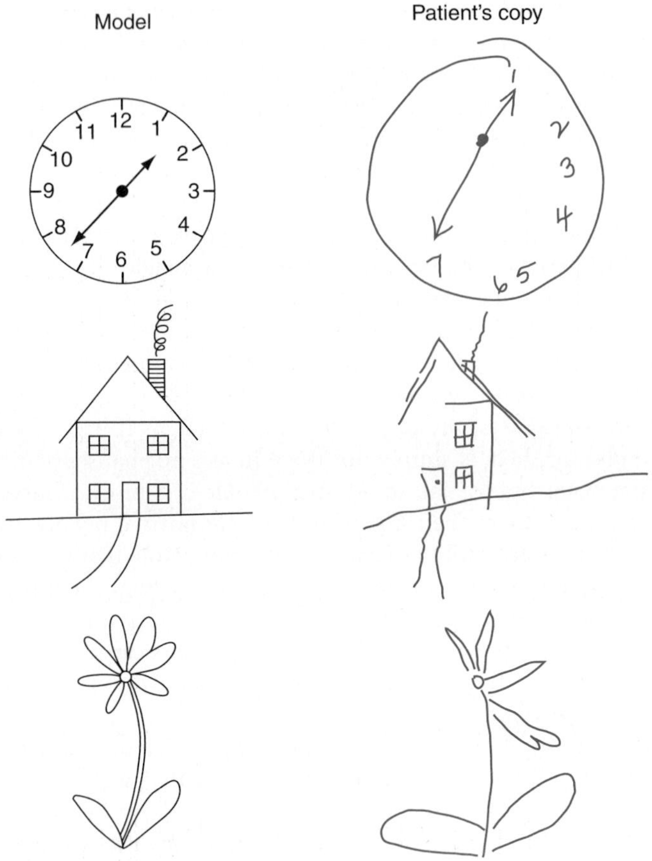

◆ **FIGURE 4-7** Drawings copied by a patient with contralateral neglect. From F. E. Bloom and A. Lazerson. *Brain, Mind, and Behavior,* 2nd ed. New York: W. H. Freeman and Co., p. 300. Copyright © 1988. Reprinted with permission of W. H. Freeman and Co.

half of the entire horizontal line. The illustrations in Figure 4-8 show a similarly revealing result. Here, the patient was asked to look at the top drawing in that panel and then draw the black part. Then the patient was asked to look at and draw the white part of the figure. In both cases, the patient was able to focus on whichever part was called for but could pay attention only to the right half of that part. Because the right half of the white part does not have a jagged edge, neither did the patient's drawing, and because the right half of the black part does have a jagged edge, the patient's drawing did as well.

A careful analysis of the disruptions seen in patients with hemineglect has recently been provided by Duncan et al. (1999) in the context of the Theory of Visual Attention (Bundesen, 1990). Duncan et al. noted that several important advances in understanding hemineglect have been made, especially when the patients are tested with some standardized cognitive tasks such as Posner's spatial cuing task, which you read about earlier. For example, it turns out that patients with hemineglect often can attend to stimuli in the neglected field but only if nothing else is displayed that might attract their attention. That is, they can detect a simple stimulus in the left visual field (the field contralateral to their brain damage), even if that is the portion of the world they

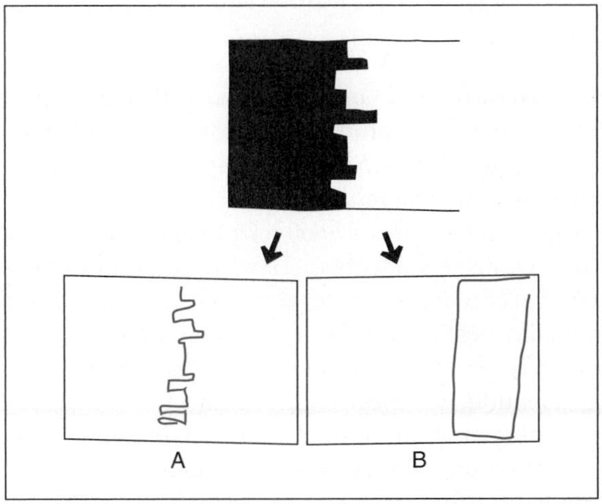

FIGURE 4-8 Object-based neglect is demonstrated by the copying performance of a patient with left hemispatial neglect. **A.** When asked to copy the black object, the patient did well because the jagged contour is on the right side of the black object. **B.** When asked to copy the white object, the patient was unable to copy the jagged contour because it is on the left side of the object being attended. From Marshall & Halligan (1994).

normally neglect. The ability to detect the same stimulus is dramatically reduced if a stimulus in the right visual field (ipsilateral to their brain damage) is presented at the same time (see Danziger, Kingstone, & Rafal, 1998, for evidence of an orienting response in the neglected field).

This tendency to ignore the contralateral field when a competing stimulus is presented in the ipsilateral field is called *extinction*. It appears to be caused by something like attention capture. When a right-side (ipsilateral) stimulus is presented, it captures the person's attention and prevents attention from being devoted to the left (contralateral). In a sense then, hemineglect patients may neglect one side only because there is usually something on the other side that captures their attention. In a very real sense, Bill might have been able to focus on shaving the left side of his face if he had not been able to see his right side.

In a curious way, hemineglect seems to disrupt both input and controlled attention. First, input attention is devoted largely or exclusively to a stimulus in the "good" or preserved field, the ipsilateral field (the term *ipsilesional* is also used, meaning "same side as the brain lesion"). The stimulus in this field captures the patient's input attention. But then it appears that hemineglect patients cannot disengage attention from that ipsilateral stimulus. Because attention toward the right cannot be disengaged, they cannot shift their attention voluntarily to the left. Thus, capture of attention on one side has disrupted a shift of controlled attention toward the other side.

In their analysis, Duncan et al. (1999) noted that their patients with hemineglect showed standard deficits in attention to the contralateral side but also some rather strong bilateral deficits related to attentional capacity; in other words, there were accuracy deficits on the neglected side but capacity difficulties on both sides. Interestingly, there was little evidence that the conceptually driven aspects of their attention were affected. It may be some time before such results and their implications for the normal processes of attention are fully understood. But even now, it is clear that such fractionation of performance—some abilities preserved, some disrupted—will be important in our further understanding of attention (for a neural net modeling approach to hemineglect, see Monaghan & Shillcock, 2004).

Section Summary

- Attention is a pervasive and complex topic, with meanings and connotations ranging from alertness and arousal up through the notions of automatic and conscious processing. Attention can be thought of as a mental process or mechanism or as a limited mental resource.
- Three basic senses of the term *attention* refer to alertness and arousal, the orienting reflex, and the spotlight of attention. These correspond to input attention, a fast process involved in encoding environmental stimuli into the mental system. Interestingly, in vision, the mental spotlight of attention can be shifted without any movement of the eyes, confirming the mental rather than perceptual nature of attention.
- A disorder of attention, hemineglect, shows how it can be affected by brain damage, thus informing us about normal attention. In hemineglect, a patient is unable to direct attention voluntarily to one side of space, so he or she neglects stimuli presented on that side. The evidence suggests that this arises from an inability to disengage attention from a stimulus on the nonneglected side, hence disrupting the process of shifting attention to the opposite side.

CONTROLLED, VOLUNTARY ATTENTION

We turn now to several senses of the term *attention* that point to the controlled, voluntary nature of attention. **Controlled attention**, in contrast to what you've just been studying, refers to *a deliberate, voluntary allocation of mental effort or concentration. You* decide to pay attention to this stimulus and ignore others, and paying attention this way may be effortful. The study of controlled attention began with research done in the 1950s and 1960s.

Dangerously divided attention.

In a classroom situation, students must constantly filter out the unimportant from the important details. This is an example of selective attention in auditory perception.

Cognitive psychology has always been intrigued by the observation that at any moment scores of different sensory messages are impinging on us. We can neither attend to all of them (we would be overwhelmed instantly), nor can we afford for our attention to be captured by one, then another, then another of the multiple sensory inputs (we would lose all coherence, all continuity). Therefore, it makes sense to ask questions about **selective attention**, *the ability to attend to one source of information while ignoring or excluding other ongoing stimuli around us.* How do we do this? How do you screen out the surrounding noises to focus on just one? How can you listen covertly to the person on your right, who is gossiping about someone you know, while overtly pretending to listen to a conversational partner on your left? (And how did you notice in the first place that the person on your right was gossiping?) Somewhat the converse of selective attention is the topic of divided attention: How do we divide or share our attentional capacity across more than one source of information at a time, and how much information are we picking up from the several sources?

A classic example of how these questions involve real world problems is the issue of whether we can really talk on a cell phone and drive at the same time, dividing our attention between two demanding tasks (Spence & Read, 2003; Strayer & Johnston, 2001). In short, the general answer is, "No, we really can't." Talking on the cell phone can lead to inattention blindness in which people fail to attend to or process information about traffic, even if they are looking directly at it. This is equally true for both hand-held and hands-free cell phone conversations, but not true for listening to the radio or books on tape/CD (Strayer & Drews, 2007). This is likely because you are actively involved in cell phone conversations, but not in what is going on over the radio. In these studies, people drive a simulator while having their eye movements monitored (so the experimenter knows what they are looking at and for how long). Under these circumstances, people who are engaged in phone conversations are less likely to recognize road signs or other important traffic events, even when they look directly at them. This is even revealed in EEG recordings of driver's brains, not just what they consciously report. What is happening is that when you are actively involved and interacting in a conversation, your limited capacity attention is drawn away from your immediate environment, and as a consequence, your driving suffers and becomes more dangerous. At a more general level, the question becomes: When do we start reaching the limits of our attentional capacity?

Selective Attention and the Cocktail Party Effect

When there are many stimuli or events around you, you may try to focus on just one. The ones you are trying to ignore are distractions that must be excluded. *The mental process of eliminating those distractions* is called **filtering** or **selecting.** Some aspect of attention seems to filter out unwanted, extraneous sources of information so we can select the one source we want to attend.

The process of selective attention seems straightforward in vision: You move your eyes, thereby selecting what you attend to. As you just saw, however, attention is separate from eye movements: You can shift your attention even without eye movements. But in hearing, attention has no outward, behavioral component analogous to eye movements, so cognitive psychology has always realized that selective attention in hearing was thoroughly cognitive. This accounts for the heavy investment in filter theories of auditory perception. If we cannot avoid hearing something, we then must select among the stimuli by some mental process, filtering out the unimportant and attending to the important.

DUAL TASK OR DUAL MESSAGE PROCEDURES A general characteristic of many attention experiments involves the procedure of *overload.* In brief, we can overload the sensory system by presenting more information than it can handle at once and then test accuracy for some part of the information. This has usually involved a **dual task procedure**. *Two tasks are presented such that one task captures attention as completely as possible.* Because attentional resources are so consumed by the primary task, there are few if any resources left over for conscious attention to the other tasks. By varying the characteristics or content of the messages, we can make the listener's job easier or harder. For instance, paying attention to a message spoken in one ear while trying to ignore the other ear's message is more difficult when both messages are spoken by the same person.

Going a step further, when we examine performance to the attended task, we can ask about the accuracy with which the message is perceived and about the degree of interference caused by the second message. We can also look at accuracy for information that was not in the primary message, the unattended message in the other ear. If there is any evidence of remembering the unattended message, or even some of its features, we can discuss how unattended information is processed and registered in memory.

THE SHADOWING EXPERIMENTS Some of the earliest cognitive research on auditory selective attention was performed by E. Colin Cherry (1953; Cherry & Taylor, 1954). Cherry was interested in the phenomena of speech recognition and attention. Cherry characterized his research procedures, and for that matter the question he was asking, as the cocktail party problem (although you can think of it as a dorm party problem):

How do we pay attention to and recognize what one person is saying when we are surrounded by other spoken messages? To simulate this real-world situation in the laboratory, Cherry (see also Broadbent, 1952) devised the workhorse task of auditory perception research, the **shadowing task**. In this task, Cherry recorded spoken messages of different sorts, then played them to a person who was wearing headphones. The task was to "shadow" the message coming into the right ear, that is, *to repeat the message out loud as soon as it was heard.* In most of the experiments, people were also told to ignore the other message, the one coming to the left ear. (It makes no difference which ear is shadowed and which is ignored. For simplicity, assume that the right ear always receives the to-be-shadowed attended message and the left ear receives the unattended message.)

Although this sounds simple, it takes a surprising amount of attention and concentration to shadow a message accurately. People were quite accurate in producing "shadows," although they spoke in a monotone, with little intonational stress, and lagged behind the message by a second or so. Interestingly, people seem unaware of the strangeness of their spoken shadows and usually cannot remember much of the content of the shadowed message once the task is over.

This task consumed enough attention to leave little, if any, for other purposes. In a typical session, the recording began with a continuous coherent message presented to the right (attended) ear and another coherent message to the left (unattended ear). Once the person began to shadow, the message in the left ear was changed. After some amount of time, people were interrupted and asked what, if anything, they could report about the unattended message.

They could report accurately on a variety of physical characteristics, such as if it changed from human speech to a tone. They also usually detected a change from a male to a female voice. However, when the unattended message was changed to reversed speech, only a few people noticed "something queer about it." Changes from English to a different language generally went unnoticed, and, overall, people were unable to identify words or phrases of the unattended message. In a dramatic confirmation of this last result, Moray (1959) found that even a word presented 35 times in the unattended message was never recalled (see also Wood & Cowan, 1995b).

Selection Models

It appears that a physical difference between the messages permits people to distinguish between them, and eases the job of selectively attending to the target task (Johnston & Heinz, 1978). Investigators routinely call this *early selection*. This refers to one of the earliest phases of perception, an acoustic analysis based on physical features of the message. The evidence is that people can select a message based on sensory information, such as loudness, location of the sound source, pitch, and so on (Egan, Carterette, & Thwing, 1954; Spieth, Curtis, & Webster, 1954; Wood & Cowan, 1995a).

EARLY SELECTION THEORY This evidence, indicating that people could somehow tune their attention to one message and ignore the other, prompted Donald Broadbent (1958) to propose an early filter theory of attention. In Broadbent's view, attention acts

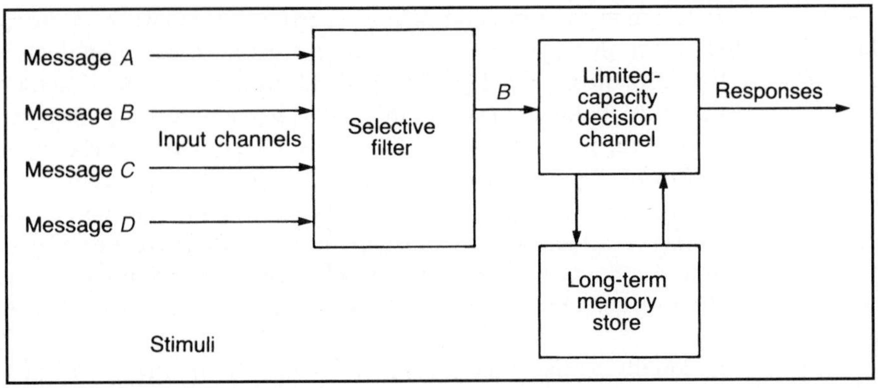

★ **FIGURE 4-9** Broadbent's filter theory of selective attention. Four messages are presented, yet only one is selected and passed to the limited-capacity decision mechanism. Adapted from Broadbent (1958).

★ as a selective filter, as shown in Figure 4-9. Regardless of how many competing channels or messages are coming in, the filter can be tuned, or switched, to any one of them, based on characteristics such as loudness or pitch. Note that only one message can pass through the filter at a time. In other words, despite the many incoming signals, only one message can be sent along through the filter into the "limited-capacity decision channel," (essentially short-term memory). Only the information on the attended, "passed along" message affects performance, in Broadbent's view, because only it gets past the filtering mechanism.

It was soon realized that the filter idea had serious problems. For one, intuition tells us that we often notice information from a message we are not attending, as when you hear your name spoken in a crowded, noisy place. Moray (1959) found evidence for this: Although people did not recall a word presented 35 times to the unattended ear, a third of the people heard their own name spoken (see Wood & Cowan, 1995b, for a recent replication of this effect). Not everyone detects their name equally easily; some people detect it more often than others. Conway, Cowan, and Bunting (2001) found that people who have less cognitive capacity (a.k.a. working memory; that is, they can hold fewer items in mind at one time, see Chapter 5) were more likely to detect their name. In other words, people who were less able to focus on a task, such as remembering a list of letters, appear to be more prone to distraction, and are more likely to process and detect information that they are supposed to ignore, such as information on an unattended channel in this task.

More generally, these findings have implications about the nature of the attention filter. If Broadbent's early filter theory were correct, then only the attended and passed-along information should be available for further processing, where attention is directed by physical cues. Yet clear evidence is available that unattended information can somehow slip past the filter (but see Lachter, Forster, & Ruthruff, 2004, who argue that some small amount of attention had been devoted to the "unattended" stimuli).

LATE SELECTION THEORY Treisman (1960, 1964) did a series of studies to explore this slippage more closely. She used the standard shadowing task but varied the nature of the unattended message across a more subtle range of differences. She first replicated Cherry's findings that selective attention was easy when physical differences existed.

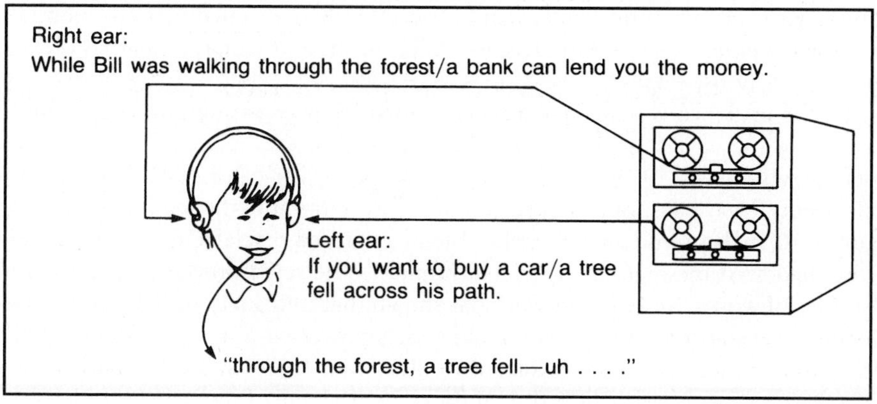

▲ **FIGURE 4-10**
The shadowing task. Two messages are played simultaneously into different ears; then, at the slash, the ear-of-arrival is switched for the two messages. Adapted from Lindsay & Norman (1977).

Then she turned to the situation in which physical differences were absent; both the attended and unattended messages were recorded by the same speaker. Because the same pitch, intonation, stress, and so on were in both messages, early selection should not be possible. Yet she found that people could shadow quite accurately. The basis for the selection was *message content,* what the message was *about* rather than what it sounded like. In this situation, the grammatical and semantic features are the basis for selection (*semantic* refers to meaning). Because attentional selection occurs after all the initial processing of the message is done, this has been called *late selection.* It is certainly later in the stream of processing than early selection based on sensory features yet before the moment of having to respond aloud with the shadowed speech.

To show the power of late selection, Treisman did a study now considered a classic (1960); the setup is depicted in Figure 4-10. Treisman arranged the recording so that the coherent message being shadowed was unexpectedly shifted to the unattended channel. Quite literally, the sentence that was being said switched from the right to the left ear. Despite a high degree of practice and concentration needed, people routinely switched to the unattended message, although they did not continue to shadow the "wrong" ear for very long. Clearly, there must be some processing of the unattended message, unlike the prediction from Broadbent's theory. Semantic elements of the unattended channel must be receiving some analysis or there would be no basis for preferring it when the sentences switched ears. ▲

Based on such results, Treisman rejected the "early selection" notion. Instead, she claimed that all incoming messages receive some amount of low-level analysis, including an analysis of the physical characteristics. When the unattended messages yield no useful or important information, they are attenuated, in Treisman's terms; they are reduced not in their volume or physical characteristics but in their informational importance to ongoing processing. In the process of shadowing, we arrive at an identification of the words and phrases on the attended message.

Treisman (1965) felt that it was during this process of semantic analysis that we make our selection among messages, selection at a "late" stage. This places selective attention well within the cognitive apparatus, of course, and permits attention to be affected by the semantic aspects of the message—that is, a top-down effect. A more extreme view, proposed by Deutsch and Deutsch (1963), claimed that selection takes place only after *all* messages have received full acoustic and semantic analysis (i.e., just before the response stage).

So the evidence is that quite a bit of information is getting into cognition: the meaning of the words on the unattended channel, for example, in Treisman's study (1960; see also Lewis, 1970; Carr, McCauley, Sperber, & Parmelee, 1982, found comparable results for visual stimuli). Intrusion of the word *tree* into the shadow, as shown in Figure 4-10, makes sense only if *tree* has been recognized as related to the forest theme of the shadowed message, an effect that implies some rapid process of accessing the meanings of words. More recent work has shown that information that is not actively attended, and subject to inattention blindness, is processed if it is consistent with our goals and intentions (Koivisto & Revonsuo, 2007; Marsh, Cook, Meeks, Clark-Foos, & Hicks, 2007; Most, Scholl, Clifford, & Simons, 2005). In all of the cases in which unattended information was processed, it was consistent with some enduring or temporal goal a person had, such as hearing their own name, completing the idea conveyed by a sentence, or whatever may be satisfying a person's goals at the time. This is why when you are hungry, images of food are so hard to ignore, even if you are trying to concentrate on something else.

MIND WANDERING Perhaps one of the most obvious and ubiquitous examples of not being able to use our attention the way that we want to is when our minds drift from the task that we are supposed to be focusing on to some other, irrelevant idea. **Mind wandering** is *the situation in which a person's attention and thoughts wander from the current task to some other, inappropriate line of thought.* We all regularly experience mind wandering in our daily lives, such as when we start to daydream during a boring lecture, start thinking about a significant other when sitting at a traffic light, or get to the bottom of a page and realizing that we have no idea what was just read. In these cases we have decoupled our attention from the environment to focus more exclusively on our own internal thoughts, often without an awareness that our mind is wandering, until we catch ourselves (Smallwood, McSpadden, & Schooler, 2007).

As you know, your mind is more likely to wander when you are bored than when you are engaged and absorbed in something. Essentially, when you are really concentrating, all of your attention is completely engaged in the task you are focused on, and it is difficult for distractions to lure it away. However, when your intended primary task is not taking all of your attention, other ideas can break through, and take your attention away (Smallwood & Schooler, 2006). Under these circumstances, your attention will drift from what you are supposed to be thinking about to something else, leaving your memory for what you are supposed to be doing much poorer. The surprising prediction that is made here is that people with *more* working memory capacity are more likely to mind wander. This is because they will be more likely to have capacity available over and above what is required by the current task. These people get distracted by things that are in the environment, but are not part of what they are supposed to be attending. Such a proneness to mind wander impedes cognition, such as the ability to learn things in school (Smallwood, Fishman, & Schooler, 2007).

An important point to note is that your mind does not wander randomly. Instead, you are more likely to disengage from the current task and mind wander by thinking about things that are current concerns for you, or are relevant to your long-term goals. If you think about those cases where your mind wanders, you'll find that you are often daydreaming about things that are important to you in one way or another. Often, there may be something in the environment, such as a person you see, a word that you hear or read, or a smell of perfume, that directs your attention away from what you need to be doing and toward something else.

INHIBITION AND NEGATIVE PRIMING Most of the discussion of attention to this point has focused on what gets attended to and activated in cognition, as well as some filter to keep irrelevant information from entering the stream of processing. At this point, we would like to discuss a cognitive mechanism that has been proposed to keep irrelevant information out that goes beyond the idea that there is a filter that only allows the selected information to be processed further on. This is the cognitive attention mechanism of **inhibition**. What inhibition does is that it *actively suppresses mental representations of salient but irrelevant information so that its activation level is reduced, perhaps below the resting baseline level.* In this section we'll look at how inhibition may be operating to help people select out relevant information.

In order for inhibition to be operating, there needs to be a salient source of interfering and irrelevant information. That is, the irrelevant information needs to be strong and wrong. Under those circumstances, people will use inhibition. A classic demonstration of this was provided in a study by Tipper (1985). In this study, people were presented with a series of pairs of line drawings of objects, with one object presented in green, and the other in red. The task was to name the red object as quickly as possible. The important condition here was those trials on which the green object on the previous trial (called the *prime* trial) was the red object to be named on the next trial (called the *target* trial). What was observed was that people were *slower to respond to the target trials when they were preceded by these to-be-ignored distractor primes compared to control trials where the ignored object on the prime trial was some other object.* This response time slow-down is called **negative priming** (Neill, 1977; Tipper, 1985).

The explanation for this is that when people are looking at the display, in addition to their processing of the red object, there is some activation and processing of the green object as well because people are looking directly at it. That is, the mental representation of the identity of that object becomes activated, and serves as a source of interference in naming the red object. However, because the identity of this object is irrelevant to the task, what attention does is actively inhibit and suppress this information in cognition. So, when the person then needs to use this information on the next trial, because it has been inhibited, it takes longer to activate and use, thereby slowing down a person's response time (however, see Mayr & Buchner, 2006, and Neill, Valdes, & Terry, 1995, for alternative accounts of negative priming that do not involve an active inhibitory mechanism).

The idea that inhibition is an important part of attention has been extended to many other areas of psychology, particularly those dealing with individual differences. For example, in developmental psychology, attentional inhibition is thought to increase with age (Diamond & Gilbert, 1989), making it difficult for young children to maintain focus. In contrast, in older adults there is increased difficulty suppressing irrelevant information (Hasher & Zacks, 1988). Inhibitory problems are also thought be present in schizophrenia (Beech, Powell, McWilliams, & Claridge, 1989), with schizophrenics having trouble keeping unwanted thoughts out of consciousness. Less extreme, people who are depressed also have trouble inhibiting irrelevant information (MacQueen, Tipper, Young, Joffe, & Levitt, 2000), leading them to have trouble with focusing on the task at hand.

Section Summary

- Controlled or conscious attention is slower and more voluntary. Selective attention, the ability to focus on one incoming message while ignoring other incoming stimuli, is a complex ability, one investigated since the beginnings of modern cognitive science. The evidence shows that we can select one message and reject others, based on physical characteristics or on more semantic characteristics. The later the process of selection acts, the more demanding it is of the limited capacity of the attention mechanism.
- When our attention is not fully engaged, our minds can wander off topic. Mind wandering is more likely to occur when there is mental capacity left over and available. Moreover, when we mind wander, the things that we allow our attention to drift to are typically things that we have enduring concerns about, such as things we are anxious or excited about.

ATTENTION AS A MENTAL RESOURCE

An important and far-reaching meaning of the term *attention*—this one may be closer to our everyday meaning—treats attention as mental effort, as a mental resource that fuels cognitive activity. If we selectively attend to one particular message, we are deliberately focusing mental energy on that message, concentrating on it to the exclusion of other messages (clearly what James had in mind in the quotation at the beginning of the chapter). This sense involves the idea that attention is a limited resource, that there is only so much mental fuel to be devoted here or there at any one time (Kahneman, 1973, also suggested that capacity might be somewhat elastic, in that increasing the task load might also increase a person's arousal, thus making additional resources available). Approaches that emphasize this meaning of the term are called resource theories.

A corollary to this idea of limited capacity is that attention, loosely speaking, is the same as consciousness or awareness. After all, if you can be consciously aware of only one thing at a time, doesn't that illustrate the limited capacity of attention? Even on a much smaller scale, when we process very simple stimuli, there is evidence of this limit to attention. If you are asked to respond to a stimulus and then immediately to a second one, your second response is delayed a bit. This is called the **psychological refractory period** by some researchers and the **attentional blink** by others, which is *a brief slow-down in mental processing due to having processed another very recent event* (e.g., Barnard, Scott, Taylor, May, & Knightley, 2004; Pashler & Johnson, 1998), but in both cases the implication is the same—allocating attention to the first stimulus momentarily deprives you of the attention needed for the second. However, consistent with the idea that information is processed at a meaningful level, the attentional blink is attenuated if the stimuli that occurs during what would be the blink are emotionally loaded, such as "whore," compared to emotionally neutral words, such as "veiled" (Anderson, 2005). Thus, emotional relevance and intensity can over-ride other, standard operating procedures (e.g., the normal attentional blink).

A related idea, which you encountered in the previous section, is that this kind of attention is deliberate, willful, intended—*controlled*–attention. *You* decide to pay attention to a signal, or you decide *not* to attend to it. *You* decide to pay attention to the lecture instead of your memory of last night's date, and when you realize your attention has wandered, you willfully redirect it to the lecture, determined *not* to daydream about last night until class is over.

The James quotation at the beginning of this chapter is also interesting because of another insight he had about attention: the idea that we may do more than one thing at a time if the other processes are habitual. When processes are less automatic, however, then attention must oscillate among them if they are done simultaneously, with no consequent gain of time. The key point is the idea of automatic processes; that some mental events can happen without draining the pool of resources: attention. Putting it simply, the germ of James's idea, automaticity, has become central to cognitive psychology's views on attention, pattern recognition, and a host of other topics. And cognitive science has devoted a huge effort to recasting James's ideas about automaticity and attention into more formal, quantifiable concepts.

Automatic and Conscious Processing Theories

In place of the former approach, the limited-capacity attentional mechanism and the need for filtering in selective attention, the current view is that a variety of perceptual and cognitive processes can be executed in an automatic fashion, *with little or no necessary involvement of a conscious, limited-attention mechanism.* Two such theories of **automaticity** have been proposed, one by Posner and Snyder (1975) and one by Shiffrin and Schneider (Schneider & Shiffrin, 1977). These theories differ in some of their details but are similar in their overall message (see also Logan & Etherton, 1994; for discussions that oppose the idea of mental resources, see Navon, 1984, and Pashler, 1994).

AUTOMATIC PROCESSING Posner and Snyder described three necessary characteristics for the "diagnosis" of an automatic process, listed in Table 4-2. First, an automatic process occurs without intention; in other words, you can't prevent it from happening, and once it does start, you can't stop it. A standard and compelling example of this is the

TABLE 4-2 Diagnostic Criteria for Automatic and Conscious Processing

Automatic	Conscious
The process occurs without intention, without a conscious decision.	The process occurs only with intention, with a deliberate decision.
The mental process is not open to conscious awareness or introspection.	The process is open to awareness and introspection.
The process consumes few if any conscious resources; that is, it consumes little if any conscious attention.	The process uses conscious resources; that is, it drains the pool of conscious attentional capacity.
(Informal) The process operates very rapidly, usually within 1 s.	(Informal) The process is slow, taking more than a second or two for completion.

Stroop phenomenon (named after the task described in Stroop, 1935). Words such as *RED GREEN BLUE YELLOW* were presented visually, written in mismatching colors of ink (e.g., *RED* printed in green ink). It was found that when people have to name the ink color, they must ignore the printed words themselves. This leads to tremendous interference, a slowing of the ink color naming, caused by the mismatching information and the contradictory impulses to name the word and the ink color (this is an extremely easy demonstration to do, by the way). Note that this requires that a person be able to automatically read. People who are illiterate in a language would not show a Stroop effect. That said, it is also the case that poor readers tend to show larger Stroop effects than good readers (Protopapas, Archonti, & Skaloumbakas, 2007), perhaps because better readers have greater executive control over their attentional resources.

In Posner and Snyder's terms, accessing the meaning of the written symbol *RED* is automatic: It requires no intention; it happens whether you want it to or not. In the research that demonstrates automatic access to word meaning, the term we use is **priming**. A word *activates* or primes its meaning in memory and, as a consequence, primes or activates meanings closely associated with it. This priming makes related meanings easier to access: Because of priming, they are boosted up, or given an extra advantage or head start (just as well water is pumped more easily when you prime the pump; see Dunbar & MacLeod, 1984, and MacLeod, 1991, for an explanation of Stroop interference based on priming).

Second, an automatic process does not reveal itself to conscious awareness. You cannot describe the mental processes of looking up the word *RED* in memory. Contrast this with the awareness you had when you answered the Aristotle or division questions in Chapter 1.

The third criterion of automaticity is that a fully automatic process consumes few if any resources. Such a process should not interfere with other tasks, certainly not those that rely on conscious resources.[1] As an example, walking is so automatic for

[1] Interference in the Stroop task occurs in part because the two automatic processes, reading the word and detecting the ink color, eventually compete with one another when it is time to make a response. That is, both processes are trying to output their results to the same speech mechanism, but the responses are incompatible ("red," "green"). When we say that an automatic process generally does not interfere with other processes, it is assumed that we are speaking of situations in which the two processes are not competing for the same response mechanism.

PROVE IT
The Stroop Task

An almost fail-safe demonstration of automaticity, in particular the automatic nature of accessing word meaning, involves the Stroop task. With several different colors of marker pens, write a dozen or so color names on a sheet of paper, making sure to use a *different* color of ink than the word signifies (e.g., write *red* in green ink); alternatively, create a deck of 3 × 5 cards, with one word per card. Make a control list of noncolor words (e.g., *hammer, card, wall*), again in colored inks. (And try it yourself right now—name the color of the ink for the words at the top of the color plate, inside the front cover of the book).

Explain to your participant that the task is to name the *ink color* as rapidly as possible. Time the person (the second hand/display on your watch is more than sufficient, or keep track of naming errors, another way to measure the Stroop interference) on each kind of list. The standard result is that the color word list will require substantially longer for ink color naming than the control list. Other useful control lists are simple blotches of color, to check on the speed of naming the colors, and pseudowords ("manty," "zoople," and the like) written in different ink colors.

According to several studies (e.g., Besner & Stolz, 1999; Manwell, Roberts, & Besner, 2004; Vecera, Behrmann, and McGoldrick, 2000), you should be able to eliminate the Stroop effect by getting people to focus on just *part* of the word or to say the first letter position (this might be easier if you used the 3 × 5 card method) or by printing only one letter in color. This work suggests that reading the whole word is a kind of "default" setting for visual attention, which might be changed depending on the task and instructions, and that our selective attention mechanism can select either whole objects (words) or their parts (letters) as the focus.

adults that it simply does not interfere with other processes; you can walk and talk at the same time.

A fourth criterion is informal but nonetheless useful, and is commonly noted as a characteristic of automaticity. Automatic processes tend to be fast; as a rule, a response taking no more than 1 s is heavily automatic. (For evidence of very slow automatic processing, in a person with brain damage, see Wingfield, Goodglass, & Lindfield, 1997.)

CONTROLLED PROCESSING Let's contrast these diagnostic criteria for automaticity with those for conscious or controlled processing (see Table 4-2). First, controlled processes occur only with intention. They are optional and can be deliberately performed or not. Second, conscious processes are open to awareness; we know they are going on, and, within limits, we know what they consist of. Finally, and of greatest importance, conscious processes use *attention.* They consume some of the limited attentional resources we have.

A demanding conscious process should leave few resources available for a second task that also uses conscious processing. Driving during a hard rainstorm consumes too many resources for you to listen simultaneously to the news on the radio. Alternatively, you may stop walking if you are thinking about something that requires an intense amount of thinking. Of course, if the second task can be done fairly automatically, then both tasks may proceed without interference; for example, you can easily walk and carry on a casual conversation at the same time.

INTEGRATION WITH CONCEPTUALLY DRIVEN PROCESSES We can go one step further, integrating this explanation into the idea of conceptually driven processing. Think back to the shadowing research you read about. Attending to one of two incoming messages, and shadowing that message aloud, demands conscious, deliberate attention. Such a process is under direct control, the person is aware of performing the process, and the process consumes most of the available mental resources that can be allocated. Presumably, no other conscious process can be performed simultaneously with the shadowing task without affecting performance in one or the other task (or both). When the messages are acoustically similar, then people must rely on differences of content to keep them separate. But by tracking the meaning of a passage, the person's conceptually driven processes come into play in an obvious way. Just as people "restored" the missing sound in "the *eel was on the axle" (Warren & Warren, 1970), the person in the shadowing task "supplied" information about the message from long-term memory. Once the participant began to understand the content of the shadowed message, then his or her conceptually driven processes assisted by narrowing down the possible alternatives, suggesting what might come next.

Saying that conceptually driven processes "suggest what might come next" is an informal way of referring to the important process of priming. You shadow, "While Bill was walking through the forest." Your semantic analysis primes related information and thereby suggests the likely content of the next clause in the sentence; it is likely to be about trees, and it is unlikely to be about banks and cars. At this instant in time, your "forest" knowledge has been primed or activated in memory. It is ready (indeed, almost *eager*) to be perceived because it is so likely to be contained in the rest of the sentence. Then *tree* occurs on the unattended channel. Because we seem to access the meanings of words in an automatic fashion, the extra boost given to *tree* by the priming process pushes it over into the conscious attention mechanism. Suddenly, you're saying "a tree fell across" rather than sticking with the right-ear message. Automatic priming of long-term memory has exerted a top-down influence on the earliest of your cognitive processes, auditory pattern recognition and attention.

THE ROLE OF PRACTICE AND MEMORY If accessing word meaning is automatic, then you might wonder about some of the shadowing research described earlier in which people were insensitive to the unshadowed message, failing to detect the word presented 35 times, the reversed speech, and so on. If word access is automatic, why didn't these people recognize the words on the unattended channel? A plausible explanation is practice. It seems likely that the inability to be influenced by the unattended message was caused by a relative lack of practice on the shadowing task. As several studies have shown, with greater degrees of practice even a seemingly complex and attention-consuming task becomes easy, or less demanding of attention's full resources. In fact, Logan and Klapp (1991; see also Zbrodoff & Logan, 1986) suggested that the effect of practice is to store the relevant information in memory; that is, that the necessary precondition for automatic processing is memory. Interestingly, once a process or procedure has become automatic, devoting explicit attention to it can even lead to worse performance (e.g., Beilock & Carr, 2001).

One of the compelling strengths of the Shiffrin and Schneider (1977) theory of automatic and conscious processing (actually, they use the term *controlled* instead of *conscious* processing) is the role they award to old-fashioned, repetitive practice. They asked people to detect one or more target stimuli in successively presented displays (e.g., hold targets *2* and *7* in memory, then search for either of them in successively presented displays of stimuli). For some people, the targets were consistent across hundreds of trials, always digits, for instance. This was called Consistent Mapping. For people in the Varied Mapping groups, the targets were varied across trials (e.g., *2* and *7* might be targets on one trial, *3* and *B* on another, *M* and *Z* on yet another).

The role of practice in automaticity.

The essential ingredient here is practice on the stimuli and task. Unlike the Varied Mapping groups, people who received Consistent Mapping had enormous amounts of practice in scanning for the same targets. Across many experiments, people in the Consistent Mapping conditions developed quick automatic detection processes for their unchanging targets, to the point that they could search for any of four targets in about 450 ms, even in the largest display size (four characters shown at once). People in the Varied Mapping conditions, on the other hand, needed longer search times for larger displays. At the large display size, their four-target search time was 1,300 ms (Experiment 2, Schneider & Shiffrin, 1977). These people had not developed automatic detection processes because the stimuli they had to detect kept changing. In short, their search used controlled processing.

Rounding out their evidence on the effect of prolonged practice, Shiffrin and Schneider administered 2,100 detection trials to another group of people, consistently using one set of letters for the targets and a different set for the distractors. After this lengthy procedure, they then reversed the target and distractor sets, forcing people to search for targets that were previously distractors and to ignore distractors that were previously targets. Shiffrin and Schneider suspected that "automatic detection would prove impossible and that the people would be forced to revert to controlled search" (p. 133). This is exactly what happened. As shown in Figure 4-11, panel A, RTs after the reversal took 2,400 trials before they were as rapid as the search times were in the initial testing condition. And as panel B shows, accuracy quickly climbed above 80% in the initial testing condition, but it took 1,800 trials after the reversal of targets and distractors before accuracy reached near 80% again.

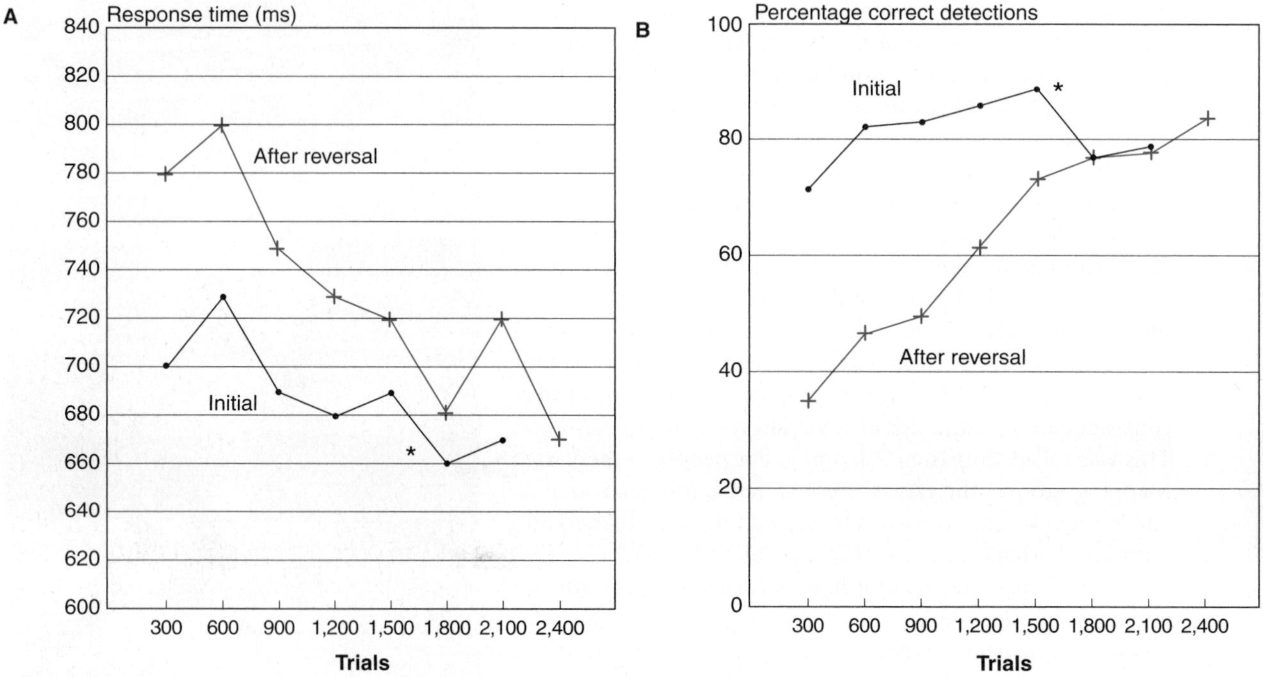

◆ **FIGURE 4-11**
A. Response times from Shiffrin and Schneider's detection task for the initial 2,100 trials of detection and for the 2,400 trials after the target and distractor sets were reversed. **B.** Percentage of correct detections of targets for the same initial and after-reversal conditions. In both, the asterisk denotes the point during the initial condition when the time for stimulus presentation was reduced from 200 ms to 120 ms.

A Synthesis for Attention and Automaticity

Attention, in its usual, everyday sense, is equivalent to conscious mental capacity. We can devote these attentional resources to only one demanding task at a time or to two somewhat less demanding tasks simultaneously, as long as they do not exceed the total capacity available. This devotion of resources means that few, if any, additional resources are available for other demanding tasks. Alternatively, if a second task is performed largely at the automatic level, then it can occur simultaneously with the first because it does not draw from the conscious resource pool (or, to change the metaphor, the automatic process has achieved a high level of skill; see Hirst & Kalmar, 1987). The more automatically a task can be performed, the more resources are available for other tasks.

The route to automaticity, it appears, is practice and memory. With repetition and overlearning comes the ability to perform automatically what formerly needed conscious processing. A particularly dramatic illustration of the power of practice was done by Spelke, Hirst, and Neisser (1976). With extensive practice, two people were able to read stories at normal rates and with high comprehension, while they simultaneously copied words at dictation or even categorized the dictated words according to meaning. Significantly, once practice has yielded automatic performance, it seems especially difficult to undo the practice, to overcome what has now become an automatic and, in a sense, autonomous process (Zbrodoff & Logan, 1986).

The demands on attention and memory in flying a jet airplane are enormous. The pilot must simultaneously pay conscious attention to multiple sources of information while relying on highly practiced, automatic processes and overlearned actions to respond to others.

Disadvantages of Automaticity

We have been talking as if automaticity is always a positive, desirable characteristic, as if anything that reduces the drain on the limited available mental capacity is a good thing. This is not entirely true, however. There are several situations in which achieving automaticity can lead to difficulties (Reason, 1990). You may experience **action slips**, which are u*nintended, often automatic, actions that are inappropriate for the current situation* (Norman, 1981).

Action slips can occur for a number of reasons, each involving a lapse of attention (i.e., and it seems foolish), and you wouldn't have done it if you had been paying more attention. In some cases, the environment has been altered from the way it would normally be, such as pressing a button to open a door that is already (unusually) propped open. Sometimes action slips are brought about by a change that requires people to relearn something they have become accustomed to doing another way. For example, your new car may have some of its controls in a different location from where they were on the older one, so you have to overcome the habit of reaching to the left dashboard to turn on the lights (this is why some controls, e.g., accelerator and brake pedals, do not change position). Often action slips occur when people have started something, but are distracted (Botvinick & Bylsma, 2006), and they lapse into a more automatic pattern of behavior of doing the wrong thing, or forgetting a needed step, such as turning on the coffee machine.

In other cases, people start doing something that they frequently do, but at an inappropriate time. A classic example involves the man whose wife told him to go back to the bedroom and change his tie one evening. When he did not return after a suitable amount of time, she went to the bedroom to find out what was keeping him. When she got there, she found that he had undressed and was in bed. What had happened was that there were a number of stimuli in the environment that triggered a more automatic pattern of action. Specifically, when he normally went to his room at night and took off his tie, this was the beginning of his routine that ended in his going to bed. This automatic pattern of behavior was triggered by these stimuli (it may sound like brain damage, but it's not—we all do something like this at one time or

FIGURE 4-12
Results of Barshi and Healy's experiment, showing the percentage of participants detecting the five embedded errors in proofreading multiplication problems. Problems were presented in fixed or varied order. Data from Barshi & Healy (1993).

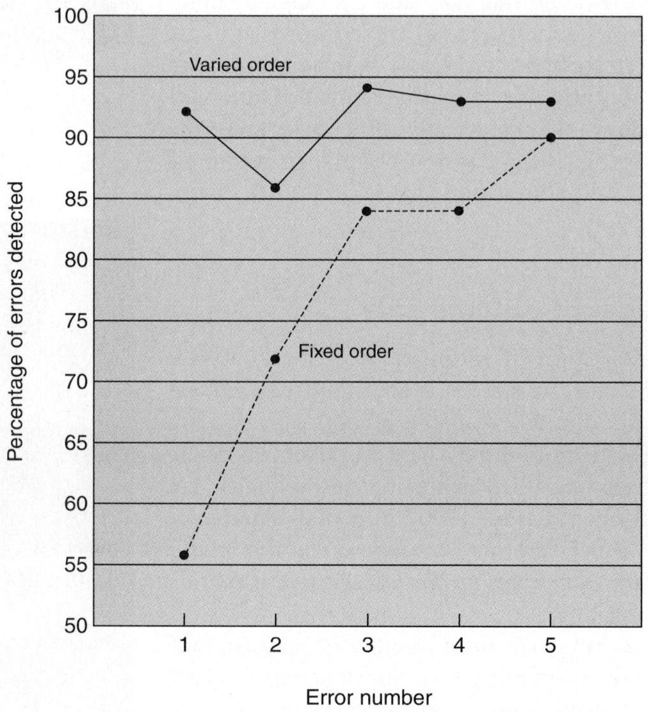

another). A different, more common example is when you find yourself driving to work or school when you meant to go someplace you go to less often.

Sometimes we *should* be consciously aware of information or processes that have become too routine and automatic. Barshi and Healy (1993) provided an excellent example, using a proofreading procedure that mimics how we use checklists. People in their study scanned pages of simple multiplication problems. Five mistakes such as "$7 \times 8 = 56$" were embedded in the pages of problems. People saw the same sets of 10 problems over and over. But in the fixed order condition, the problems were in the same order each time; in the varied order condition, the problems were in a different order each time. Those tested in the fixed order condition missed more of the embedded mistakes than those in the varied order condition; an average of 23% missed in fixed order, but only 9% missed with varied orders. Figure 4-12 shows this result across the five embedded errors. Performance did improve in the fixed order condition as more and more of the mistakes were encountered. But the first multiplication error was detected only about 55% of the time, compared with the more than 90% detection rate for the varied order group.

The fixed order of problems encouraged automatic proofreading, which disrupted accuracy at detecting errors. In fact, it took either an earlier error that *was* detected or a specific alerting signal (their Experiment 3) to overcome the effects of routine, automatic proofreading.

The implications of this kind of result should be clear. Pilots are required to go through checklist procedures, say for landing an airplane, to ensure safety. Yet because the items on the checklist are in a fixed order, repeated use of the list probably leads to a degree of automaticity and probably a tendency to miss errors. This is exactly what happened in March 1983: A plane landed in Casper, Wyoming, without its landing gear down, even though the flight crew had gone through its standard checklist procedure and had "verified" that the wheels were down. In Barshi and Healy's words, this incident "reminded the crew and the rest of the aviation community that the countless repetitions of the same procedure can lead to a dangerous automatization" (1993, p. 496). It's interesting to wonder which is worse, too much automatization of procedures, as exemplified by the Barshi and Healy study, or too much attention paid to the procedures, as in the Haines (1991) study you read about in Chapter 3 (hint: experienced pilots in flight simulators).

Section Summary

- When attention is viewed as a limited mental resource, issues of task complexity become concerned with how automatic or controlled different mental processes are. Automatic processes are rapid, are not dependent on intent, are unavailable to conscious awareness, and place few if any demands on limited attentional resources. Conscious or controlled processes are the opposite, rather slow, requiring intention, open to conscious awareness, and heavily demanding of attentional resources.
- Mental processes become more automatic as a function of practice and overlearning. A disadvantage of automaticity is that it is difficult to reverse the effects of practice in an automated task, and automaticity can lead to errors of inattention, including action slips.

Key Terms

action slips (p. *143*)
attention (p. *113*)
attention capture (p. *117*)
attentional blink (p. *137*)
automaticity (p. *137*)
benefit or facilitation (p. *119*)
controlled attention (p. *128*)
cost (p. *119*)
dual task procedure (p. *130*)
explicit processing (p. *115*)
filtering (p. *130*)
habituation (p. *118*)
hemineglect (p. *124*)
implicit processing (p. *115*)
inhibition (p. *135*)
inhibition of return (p. *122*)
input attention (p. *114*)
mind wandering (p. *134*)
negative priming (p. *135*)
orienting reflex (p. *117*)
priming (p. *138*)
psychological refractory period (p. *137*)
selecting (p. *130*)
selective attention (p. *129*)
shadowing task (p. *131*)
spotlight attention (p. *119*)
sustained attention (p. *115*)
vigilance (p. *115*)

CHAPTER

5

Short-Term Working Memory

Elementary memory makes us aware of . . . the just past. The objects we feel in this directly intuited past differ from properly recollected objects. An object which is recollected, in the proper sense of that term, is one which has been absent from consciousness altogether, and . . . is brought back . . . from a reservoir in which, with countless other objects, it lay buried and lost from view. But an object of primary memory is not thus brought back; it never was lost; its date was never cut off in consciousness from that of the immediately present moment. In fact it comes to us as belonging to the rearward portion of the present space of time, and not to the genuine past.

JAMES, 1890, PP. 643–647

The term capacity, as used in discussions of short-term memory, often conjures up images of a limited number of items or chunks that can be stored (e.g., 7 ± 2). However, my sense is that WM capacity is not about individual differences in how many items can be stored per se *but about differences in the ability to control attention to maintain information in an active, quickly retrievable state.*

ENGLE, 2002, P. 20

Primary memory, elementary memory, immediate memory, short-term memory (STM), short-term store (STS), temporary memory, supervisory attention system (SAS), working memory (WM)—all these terms refer to the same general memory component. It is this aspect of memory where the "immediately present moment," in James's explanation, is held in consciousness. It is the location, so to speak, of the conscious attention system discussed in Chapter 4. It is the means by which active mental effort is expended, whether to remember a phone number or to help in memorizing your own new phone number. This is where comprehension occurs: short-term, working memory. What it is, what it does, and how it does it are the topics of this chapter.

Note that James's term *primary memory* suggests that it is the first memory stage. It's not, of course. A stimulus first encounters sensory memory on its way into the information-processing system. But short-term working memory is the memory we are conscious of, allowing us to offer intuitions and introspections about its functioning. Many but not all of those intuitions and introspections match what has been discovered empirically. However, some mental processes that occur in short-term working memory are not open to consciousness: They are automatic. These processes yield no useful introspections; indeed, people often feel that they do not exist. (This is why short-term working memory is only *roughly* the same as consciousness. Although we are aware of its contents, we are not necessarily aware of the *processes* that occur in it.)

Modern research on short-term working memory came hard on the heels of the selective attention studies of the mid-1950s.[1] George Miller's (1956) classic article, which we discuss shortly, is an excellent example of this upsurge in interest. A common observation, that we can remember only a small number of isolated items presented

[1]There was also some research on short-term memory before the behaviorist period. For instance, Mary W. Calkins, the first woman to serve as president of the American Psychological Association, conducted such work in the 1890s and reported several important effects that were "discovered" in the 1950s and 1960s. See Madigan and O'Hara (1992) for an account of the "truly remarkable legacy" (p. 174) of this pioneering woman.

rapidly, began to take on new significance as psychology groped toward a new approach to human memory. Miller's insightful remarks were followed shortly by the surprising Brown (1958) and Peterson and Peterson (1959) reports. An amazingly simple three-letter stimulus, such as *MHA*, was forgotten almost completely within 15 s if the person's attention was diverted by a distractor task of counting backward by threes. Such reports were convincing evidence that the limited capacity of memory was finally being pinned down and given an appropriate name: short-term memory.

As we proceed we will see shift from the term *short-term memory* to *working memory*. Why do we have two terms? Stated simply, the terms have different connotations. *Short-term memory* is the older of the two and conveys a simpler idea. It is the label we usually use when the focus is on the input and storage of new information. When a rapidly presented series of digits is tested for immediate recall, for example, we generally refer to short-term memory. Likewise, when we focus on the role of rehearsal, we are examining how short-term memory helps the memorization of new information, highlighting the "control processes" (Atkinson & Shiffrin, 1971; look back at Figure 2-4) of the short-term store. Short-term memory is observed whenever short retention is being tested—no more than 15 or 20 s—and when little, if any, transfer of new information to long-term memory is involved.

Working memory, in comparison, is the newer term and has been the focus of substantial research over the past few decades. The term often has the connotation of a mental workbench, a place where mental effort is applied (Baddeley, 1992a, 1992b; Baddeley & Hitch, 1974). Thus, when word meanings are retrieved from long-term memory and put together to understand a sentence, working memory is where this happens. Traditional immediate memory tasks may be a subset of working memory research but usually are only secondary to reasoning, comprehension, or retrieval processes. Indeed, Baddeley proposed that the short-term memory responsible for digit span performance is but a single component of the more elaborate working memory system.

SHORT-TERM MEMORY: A LIMITED-CAPACITY BOTTLENECK

If you hear a string of about 10 single digits, read at a constant and fairly rapid rate, and are asked to reproduce the string in order, generally you cannot recall more than about 7 of them. The same result is obtained with unrelated words (see the "Prove It" projects on page 156 for sample lists and try testing a few willing volunteers). This is roughly the amount you can say aloud in about 2 s (Baddeley, Thomson, & Buchanan, 1975) or the amount you can recall in 4 to 6 s (Dosher & Ma, 1998; see also Cowan et al., 1998). This limit has been recognized for so long, it was included in the earliest intelligence tests (e.g., Binet's 1905 test; see Sattler, 1982). Young children and people of subnormal intelligence generally have a shorter span of apprehension, or memory-span. In the field of intelligence testing, it is almost unthinkable to devise a test *without* a memory-span component. Note that this is a general aspect of short-term memory, and is not something special about spoken words or digits. For example, a similar finding is observed with letters in Amercian Sign Language (ASL) (Wilson & Emmorey, 2006), which clearly is a much more visual and nonspoken/auditory relative to English words and digits.

The Magical Number Seven, Plus or Minus Two

For our purposes, the importance of this limitation is that it reveals something fundamental about human memory. Our immediate memory cannot encode vast quantities of new information and hold it accurately. There is a severe limit to this. Miller stated this limit aptly in the title of his 1956 paper: "The Magical Number Seven, Plus or Minus Two: Some Limits on Our Capacity for Processing Information." We can process large amounts of information in the sensory memories, and we can hold truly vast quantities of information in permanent long-term memory. Yet the intermediary between sensory and long-term memory is troublesome. Short-term memory is the narrow end of the funnel, the four-lane bridge with only one open tollgate; it is the bottleneck in our information-processing system.

OVERCOMING THE BOTTLENECK And so this limitation remains unless what we are trying to remember is richer and more complex than seven digits, or unless the information is grouped in some way, as in the 3–3–4 grouping of a telephone number or the 3–2–4 grouping of a Social Security number. In Miller's terms, a *richer, more complex item* is properly called a **chunk** of information. By chunking items together into groups, we can overcome this limitation and "break (or at least stretch) this informational bottleneck" (Miller, 1956, p. 95).

The following is a simple example of the power of chunking, of forming larger units:

BYGROUPINGITEMSINTOUNITSWEREMEMBERBETTER

No one can remember 40 letters correctly if they are treated as 40 separate, unrelated items. But the effect of chunking is that grouping together the isolated items enables us to retain more information. You can easily remember the eight words because they are familiar ones that combine grammatically to form a coherent thought. You can remember a Social Security number more easily by grouping the digits into the 3–2–4 pattern. And you can remember a telephone number more easily if you group the last four digits into two two-digit numbers (of course the point generalizes beyond U.S. Social Security and phone numbers).

The technical term for this *process of grouping items together, then remembering the newly formed groups* is **recoding**. By recoding, people hear not the isolated dots and dashes of Morse code but whole letters, words, and so on. The principle behind recoding is straightforward: Recoding reduces the number of units held in short-term memory by increasing the richness, the information content, of each unit. Try recoding the longest digit list in the "Prove It" lists, at the end of the chapter, into two-digit numbers (28, 43, and so on). This illustrates the mental effort needed for recoding (in fact, Brooks & Watkins, 1990, suggested that there is already a subgrouping effect in the memory span, with the first half enjoying an advantage over the second half).

Toll booths force a bottleneck in a highway's traffic flow.

Two conditions are important for recoding. First, we can recode if there is sufficient time or resources to apply a recoding scheme. Second, we can recode if the scheme is a well-learned, as the Morse code becomes with practice. In a dramatic demonstration of this, over the period of a few months, one person in a study by Chase and Ericsson (1982) could recall 82 digits in order by applying a highly practiced recoding scheme he invented for himself. But what about situations when an automatic recoding scheme is not available? What is the fate of items in short-term memory? Can we merely hold the usual 7 ± 2 items?

Forgetting from Short-Term Memory

Under some circumstances, we cannot hold even *half* that many items in short-term memory. Research by Brown (1958) and Peterson and Peterson (1959) provided a compelling demonstration of this. The central idea in the Brown and the Peterson and Peterson work was that *forgetting might be caused simply by the passage of time before testing*—in other words, forgetting caused by **decay**. In their experiments, a simple three-letter trigram (e.g., *MHA*) was presented to the people, followed by a three-digit number (e.g., *728*). People were told to attend to the letters, then to begin counting backward by threes from the number they had been given. The counting was done aloud, in rhythm with a metronome clicking twice per second. The essential ingredient here is the distractor task of backward counting. This clearly requires a great deal of attention (if you doubt this, try it yourself, making sure to count twice per second). Furthermore, it surely prevents rehearsal of the three letters because rehearsal uses the same cognitive mechanism as the backward counting. At the end of a variable period of time, the people were asked to report the three-letter item. The results were so unexpected, and the number of researchers eager to replicate them so large, that the task acquired a name it is still known by—the **Brown–Peterson task**.

The surprising result was that memory of the three-letter trigram was only slightly better than 50% after 3 s of counting; accuracy dwindled to about 5% after 18 s ▲ (Figure 5-1). The letters were forgotten so quickly even though short-term memory was not overloaded—a 50% loss after only 3 s (assuming perfect recall with a zero-second delay). On the face of it, this seemed evidence of a simple decay function: With an increasing period of time, less and less information remained in short-term memory.

Later research, especially that by Waugh and Norman (1965), questioned some of the assumptions made in this research. Waugh and Norman thought that the distractor task itself might be a source of interference. Specifically, if the numbers spoken during backward counting interfered with the short-term memory trace, then longer counting intervals would have created more interference. Waugh and Norman's reanalysis of several studies confirmed their suspicion. Especially convincing were the results of their own probe digit task. People heard a list of 16 digits, read at a rate of either 1 or 4 digits per second. The final item in each list was a repeat of an earlier item, and it served as the probe or cue to recall the digit that had followed the probe in the original list. For instance, if the sequence *7 4 6 9* had been presented, then the probe *4* would have cued recall of the *6*.

The important part of their study was the time it took to present the 16 digits. This took 16 s for one group (a long time) but only 4 s (a short time) for the other group. If forgetting were caused by decay (a time-based process), then the groups

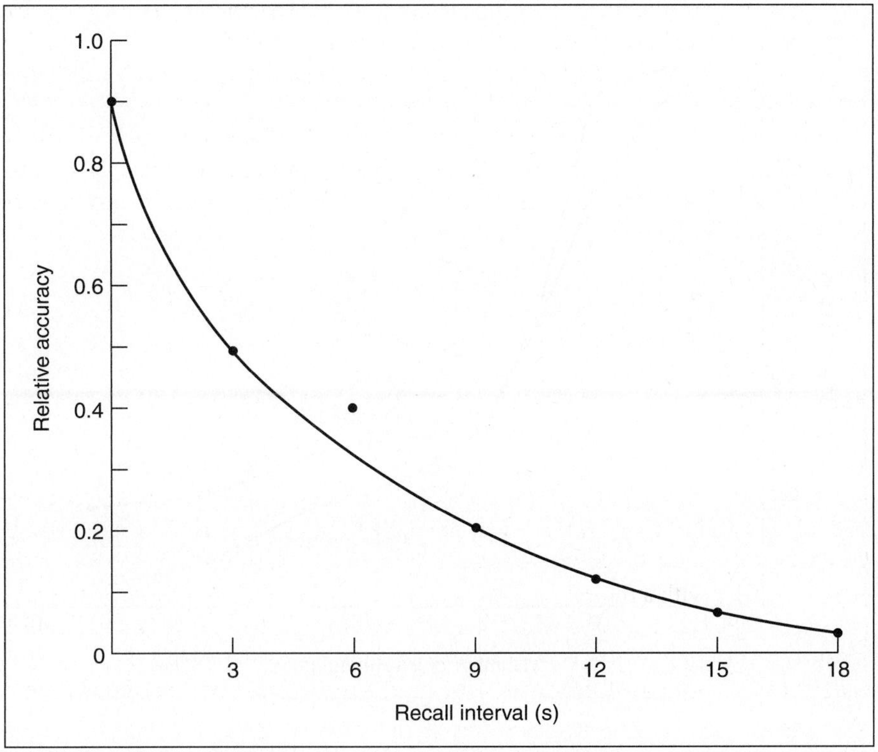

▲ **FIGURE 5-1** Relative accuracy of recall in the Brown–Peterson task across a delay interval from 0 to 18 s. People had to perform backward counting by threes during the interval. From Peterson & Peterson (1959).

should have differed markedly in their recall because so much more time had elapsed in the 16 s group. Yet, as Figure 5-2 shows, the two groups differed little. This result suggests that forgetting was influenced by the number of intervening items between the critical digit and the recall test, not simply the passage of time. In other words, forgetting in short-term memory was caused by interference, not decay (for cross-species evidence of interference, see Wright & Roediger, 2003). ●

PROACTIVE AND RETROACTIVE INTERFERENCE (PI AND RI) Shortly after the Peterson and Peterson report, Keppel and Underwood (1962) reported an effect that also challenged the idea of forgetting from short-term memory being caused by decay. They found that people forgot at a dramatic rate only after they had been tested on several trials. On the first trial, memory for the three-letter trigram was almost perfect. Keppel and Underwood's explanation was that as you experience more and more trials in the Brown–Peterson task, recalling the trigram becomes more difficult because the *previous* trials are generating interference. This form of interference is called **proactive interference (PI)**, *when older material interferes forward in time with your recollection of the current stimulus.* This is the opposite of **retroactive interference (RI)**, in which *newer material interferes backward in time with your recollection of older items.* The loss of information in the Brown–Peterson task, according to Keppel and Underwood, was caused by proactive interference.

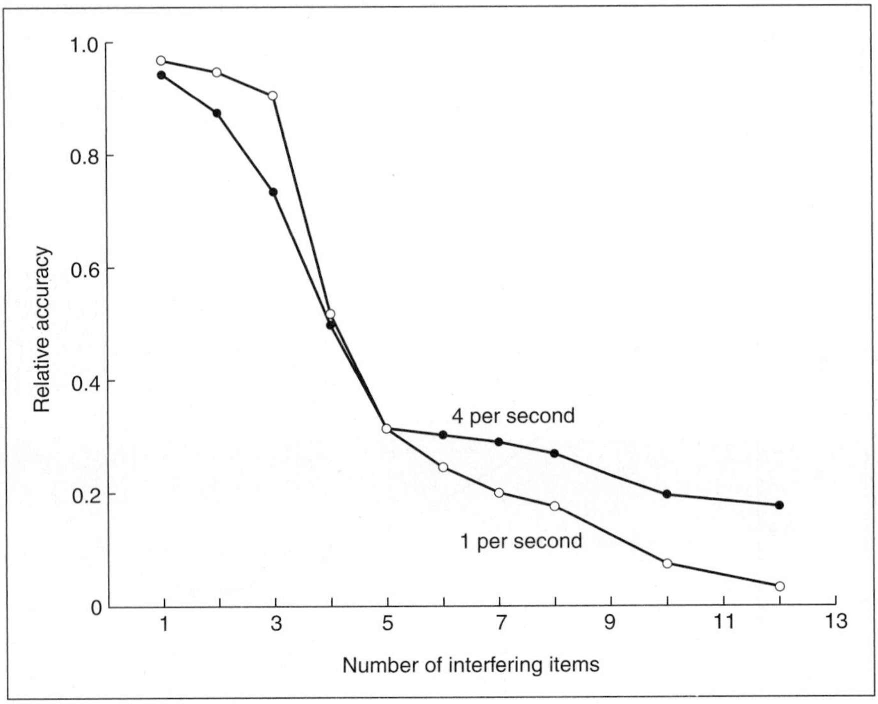

FIGURE 5-2 Relative accuracy in the Waugh and Norman (1965) probe digit experiment as a function of the number of interfering items spoken between the target item and the cue to recall; rate of presentation was either 1 or 4 digits per second.

RELEASE FROM PI An important adaptation of the interference task was done by Wickens (1972; Wickens, Born, & Allen, 1963). He gave people three Brown–Peterson trials, using three words or numbers rather than trigrams. On the first trial, accuracy was near 90%, but it fell to about 40% on Trial 3. At this point Wickens changed to a different kind of item for Trial 4. People who had heard three words per trial were given three numbers, and vice versa. The results were dramatic. When the nature of the items was changed, performance on Trial 4 returned to the 90% level of accuracy (Wickens also included a control group who received the same kind of stimulus on Trial 4 as they had gotten on the first three trials, to make sure their performance continued to fall, which it did). Figure 5-3 illustrates this result.

The interference interpretation is clear. Performance deteriorates because of the buildup of proactive interference. If the to-be-remembered information changes, however, then you are released from the interference. Thus, **release from PI** occurs *when the decline in performance caused by proactive interference is reversed because of a switch in the to-be-remembered stimuli.* Release from PI also occurs when the change is semantic, or meaning-based, in nature. Wickens (1972) also devised lists that switched from one semantic category to another. Release from PI was also observed under these circumstances (see Figure 5-4). However, an important twist here is that the more related the items on the fourth list were to the original category, the less release from PI was experienced. Thus, short-term memory, to some degree, uses semantic information.

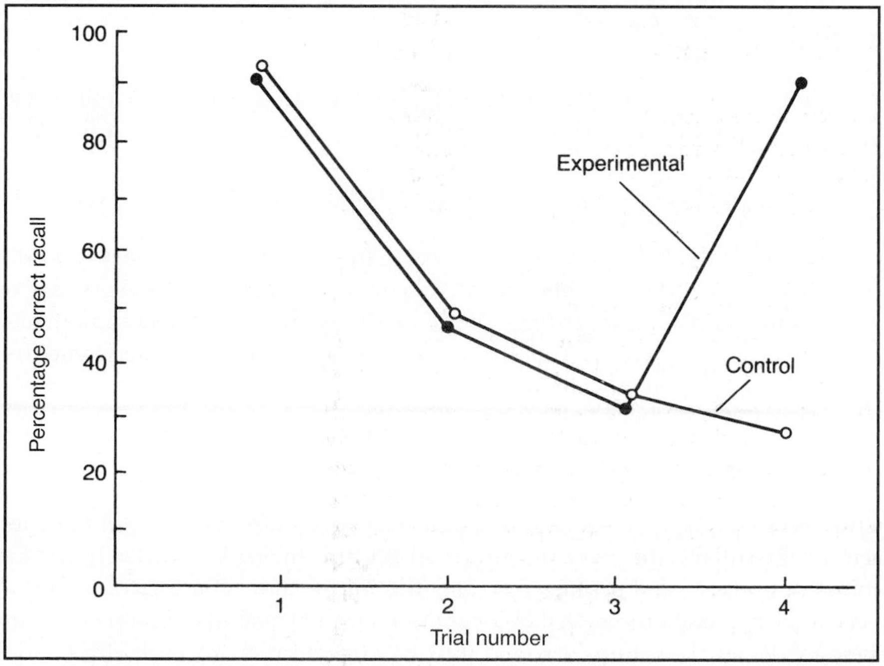

◆ **FIGURE 5-3**
Recall accuracy in a release from PI experiment by Wickens, Born, and Allen (1963). Triads of letters are presented on the first three trials, and proactive interference begins to depress recall accuracy. On Trial 4, the control group gets another triad of letters; the experimental group gets a triad of digits and shows an increase in accuracy, known as release from PI.

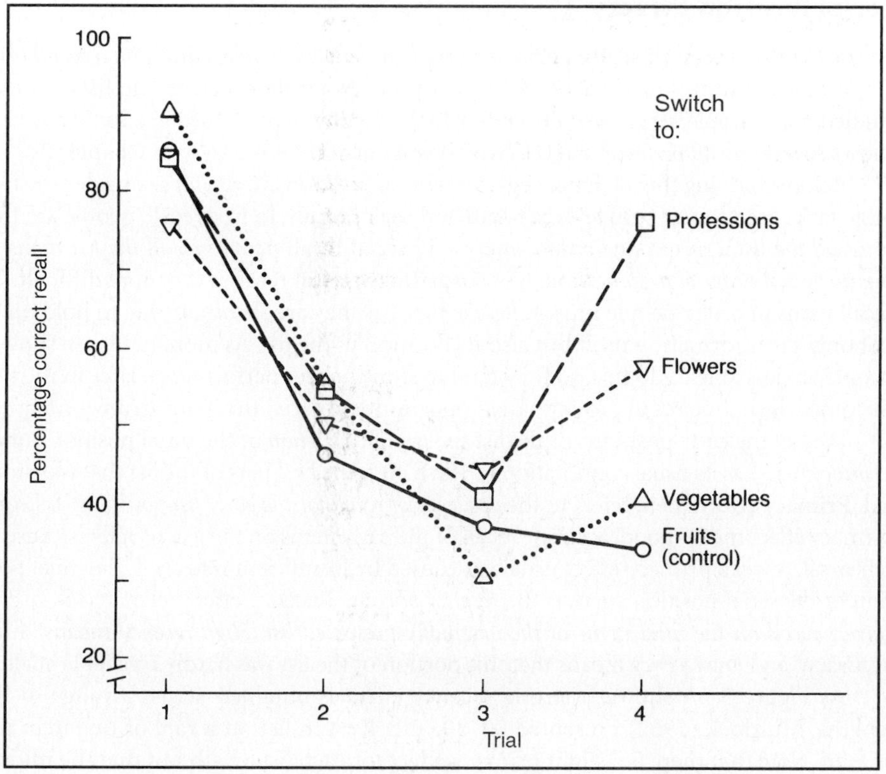

■ **FIGURE 5-4**
Recall accuracy in a release-from-PI experiment by Wickens and Morisano (reported in Wickens, 1972). All participants received word triads from the fruit category on Trial 4. On Trials 1 through 3, different groups received triads from the categories *fruits* (control condition), *vegetables, flowers,* and *professions*.

Section Summary

- Short-term or working memory is an intermediate system between the sensory and long-term memories. Its capacity for holding information is limited, by most accounts, to only 7 ± 2 units of information. The processes of chunking and recoding, grouping more information into a single unit, are ways of overcoming this limit or bottleneck.
- Whereas a decay explanation of forgetting from short-term memory is possible, most of the research implicates interference or competition as the primary reason for short-term forgetting. The research suggests two kinds of interference: retroactive interference from the distractor task and proactive interference from multiple trials on the same kind of material.

SHORT-TERM MEMORY RETRIEVAL

In this section of the chapter we consider the retrieval of information from short-term memory. Essentially, this refers to the actual act of bringing knowledge to the foreground of thinking, and perhaps reporting this information. Our focus is on two aspects of the retrieval process that highlight fundamental qualities of human memory. These are the serial position curve and studies of the retrieval process itself.

Serial Position Effects

To start with, a **serial position curve** is a *graph of item-by-item accuracy on a recall task. Serial position* simply refers to the original position an item had in the list that was ★ studied; for example, *serial position 3* refers to the item presented third in a list. Figure 5-5 shows several serial position curves (which you encountered briefly in Chapter 2).

Before studying the evidence regarding serial position curves, let's consider the two basic tasks used to test people: **free recall** and **serial recall**. In free recall, people are free to *recall the list items in any order,* whereas in serial recall people *recall the list items in their original order of presentation.* Not surprisingly, serial recall is the more difficult. To recall items in order, people must rehearse them as they are shown, trying to hold on to not only the information itself but also its position in the list. As more items are shown, people are less able to do this, so they tend to show poorer performance later in the list. In comparison, free recall provides the opportunity to recall the items in any order.

We call the early positions of the list the *primacy portion* of the serial position curve. *Primacy* here has its usual connotation of "first": It is the first part of the list that was studied. **Primacy effect**, then, refers to the *accuracy of recall for the early list positions.* A strong primacy effect means good, accurate recall of the early items on the list, usually because of rehearsal. A weak primacy effect usually is caused by insufficient rehearsal. The final portion of the serial position curve is the *recency portion.* **Recency effect** refers to *the level of correct recall on the final items of the originally presented list. High recency* means "high accuracy," and *low recency* means that this portion of the list was hardly recallable at all.

As Figure 5-5A shows, a strong recency effect is obtained across a range of list lengths; Murdock (1962) presented 20, 30, and 40 item lists at a rate of one item per second. Note that there is a slight primacy effect for each list length but that the middle portion of the lists showed low recall accuracy. Apparently, the first few items were re-

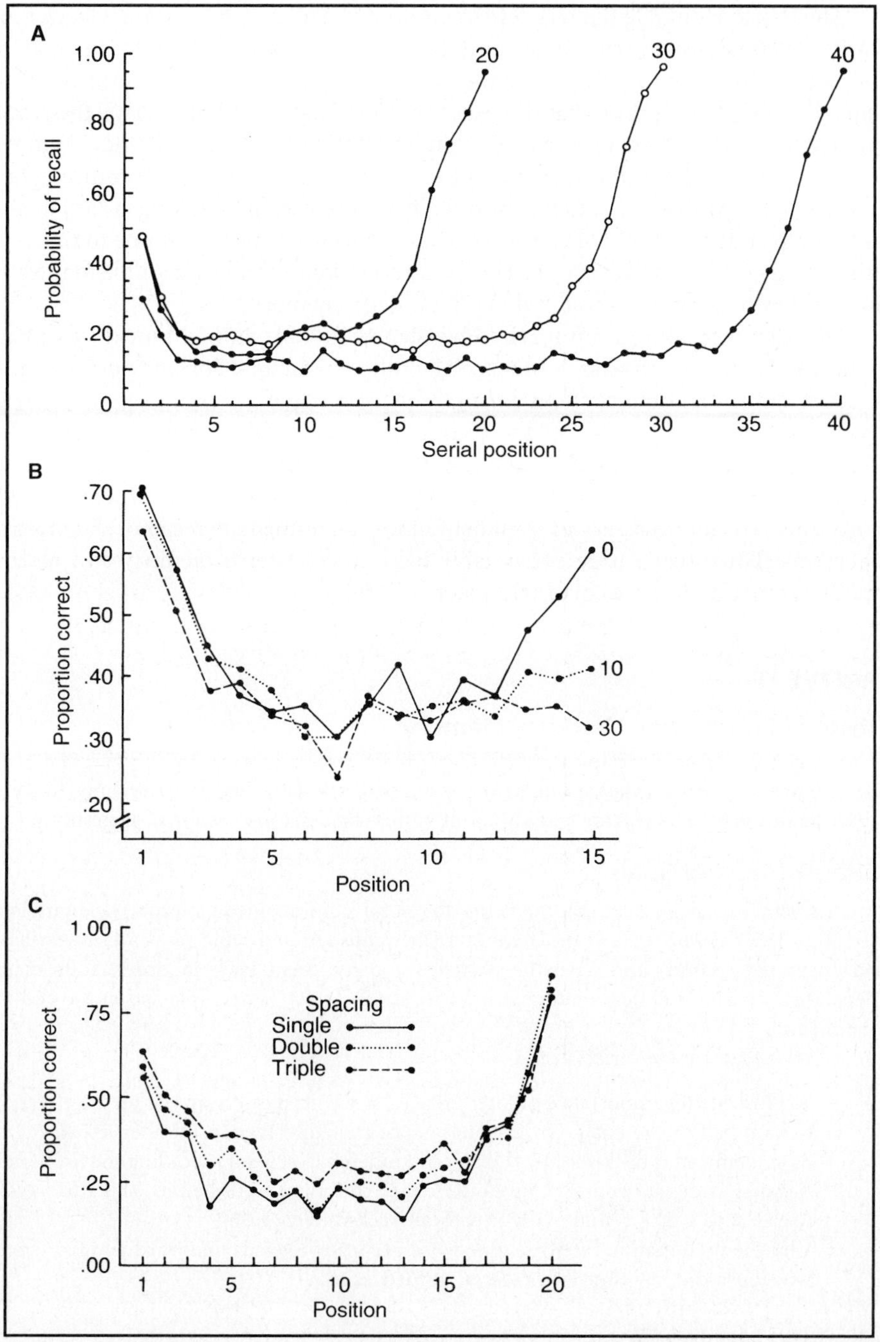

★ **FIGURE 5-5**
A. Serial position curves showing recall accuracy across the original positions in the learned list. Rate of presentation was one item per second.
B. Serial position curves showing the decrease in recency when 10 or 30 s of backward counting is interpolated between study and recall.
C. Three different rates of presentation: single (3 s), double (6 s), and triple (9 s).

hearsed enough to make them recallable from long-term memory, but not enough time was available for rehearsing items in the middle of the list. For all lists, though, the strong recency effect can be attributed to recall from short-term memory.

The way to eliminate the recency effect should be no surprise to you. Glanzer and Cunitz (1966) showed their participants 15-item lists, required them to do an attention-consuming counting task for either 10 or 30 s, then asked people to recall the items. In contrast to a group that was asked for immediate recall (0 s delay), the groups that had to perform the counting task before recall showed very low recency (Figure 5-5B). Alternatively, the primacy portion of the list was unaffected by the counting task. In other words, the early list items must be in a more permanent, long-term memory for them to endure the 30 s of counting. These items seem more immune to the interfering effects of the distractor task. The most recent items were susceptible to interference, so they must have been stored in a short-term memory.

Other manipulations, summarized by Glanzer (1972), showed how the two parts of the serial position curve are influenced by different factors. For our purposes, note that providing more time per item during study (spacing of 3 versus 6 versus 9 s, in the figure) had almost no effect on the recency effect but did alter the primacy effect (Figure 5-5C; from Glanzer & Cunitz, 1966). Additional time for rehearsal enabled people to store the early items more strongly in long-term memory. Moreover, additional time was not necessary or even helpful for the immediate recall of the most recent items. These items were presumably held in short-term memory and recalled rapidly before interference could take place.

PROVE IT

Tests of Short-Term, Working Memory

Several tests of short-term, working memory can be given with very little difficulty, to confirm the various effects you are reading about in this chapter. Here are some suggestions.

Simple Memory Span

Make several lists, being sure that the items do not form unintended patterns; use digits, letters, or unrelated words. Read the items at a fairly constant and rapid rate (no slower than one item per second) and have the participant name them back in order. Your main dependent variable will be the number or percentage correct. See sample lists at the end of the chapter.

Try a few of these variations:

- To illustrate the importance of interference, have your participants do an interference task on half of the trials. On an interference trial, give them a number like 437 and have them count backward by threes, out loud, for 15 s, before recalling the list items.
- Keeping list length constant, give different retention intervals before asking for recall (e.g., 5 s, 10 s, 20 s), either with or without backward counting.
- Vary the presentation rate (e.g., one word per second versus one word per 3 s) to see how the additional time for rehearsal influences recall.

Working Memory Span

Follow the examples given in the text to construct a working memory span test, e.g., from one to six unrelated sentences, each followed by an unrelated word, where the participant must process the sentence and then, at the end of the set, recall the unrelated words that appeared. Span size will be the number of words recalled correctly, assuming that the sentences were comprehended.

Short-Term Memory Scanning: The Sternberg Task

We turn now to a different question: How do we access or retrieve the information stored in short-term memory? This is the short-term memory equivalent of a question that seems sensible to our introspections: How do we retrieve information from long-term memory? Such a question is particularly interesting when retrieval, whether from short- or long-term memory, is extremely rapid and out of conscious awareness (e.g., does a robin have feathers?). The focus of this section is simply how the rapid process of retrieval happens in short-term memory. To answer this question, we turn to another memory task: recognition.

All students are familiar with a common version of a recognition task: multiple choice tests. In this format you select the one correct alternative, and reject the others as being incorrect. From the standpoint of cognition, you have said "Yes" to the correct alternative, indicating, "Yes, I recognize that as the information I studied for the test." Similarly, deciding that an alternative is wrong is the same as deciding, "No, that choice is new. I haven't studied it before." Clearly, making these decisions requires you to access stored knowledge then compare the alternatives to that knowledge. When one of the alternatives matches your knowledge, then you can respond, "Yes, that's the correct alternative." The important angle in cognitive science is that we can time people as they make their "yes/no" recognition decisions and try to infer the underlying mental processes used in the task on the basis of how long they took. It was this procedure Saul Sternberg used in addressing the question of how we access information in short-term memory.

Sternberg (1966, 1969, 1975) began his work by noting that the use of response time (RT) tasks to infer mental processes had a venerable history, dating back at least to Donders's work in the 1800s. Donders had proposed a subtractive method for determining the time necessary for simple mental events. For example, if your primary task involves processes A, B, and C, you devise a comparison task that has only processes A and C in it. After giving both tasks, you subtract the A + C time from the A + B + C time. The difference should be a measure of the duration of process B because it is the process that was subtracted from the primary task.

Sternberg pointed out a major difficulty with Donders's subtractive method. It is virtually impossible to make sure that the comparison task, the A + C task, contains *exactly* the same A and C processes as they occur in the primary task. There is always the possibility that the A and C components may be inadvertently altered when you eliminate process B. If so, then subtracting one from the other can't be justified. Sternberg's solution was a genuine innovation. Rather than trying to eliminate one process from the primary task, he arranged it so that the critical process would have to *repeat* some number of times during a single trial. Across an entire study there would be many trials on which process B had occurred only once, many on which it occurred two times, three times, and so forth. He then examined the RTs for these successive conditions, and inferred the nature of process B by determining how much time was *added* to people's responses for each repetition of process B. This, along with some statistical reasoning that accompanied it, is referred to as the *additive factors* method.

THE STERNBERG TASK The task Sternberg devised was a short-term memory scanning task, now simply called a Sternberg task. People first were given a short list of letters, one at a time, at the rate of one per second. This group of letters was called the memory set. People then saw a single letter, the probe item, and responded "yes"

TABLE 5-1 Sample Sternberg Task

Trial	Memory set items	Probe items	Correct response
1	R	R	Yes
2	LG	L	Yes
3	SN	N	Yes
4	BKVJ	M	No
5	LSCY	C	Yes

or "no" depending on whether the probe was in the memory set. So, for example, if you stored the set *l r d c* in short-term memory and then saw the letter *d*, you would respond "yes." If the probe item were *m*, however, you would respond "no."

In a typical experiment, people were given several hundred trials, each consisting of these two parts, memory set then probe item, as shown in Table 5-1. Memory sets were from one to six letters long (digits were used in some experiments), well within the span of short-term memory, and were changed on every trial. Probes changed on every trial, too, and were selected so that the correct response was "yes" on half the trials and "no" on the other half. More importantly, across the hundreds of trials, when the probe item matched one of the letters in the memory set, it matched each position in the set equally frequently. This is illustrated by Trials 2 and 3 in Table 5-1. Take a moment to try several of these trials, covering the probe item until you have stored the memory set in short-term memory, then covering the memory set and uncovering the probe, then making your "yes/no" judgment. (For a better demonstration, have someone read the memory sets and probe items to you out loud.)

Figure 5-6 illustrates the **process model** that Sternberg (1969) proposed for this task, simply *a flowchart of the four separate mental processes that occurred during the timed portion of every trial.* At the point marked "Timer starts running here," the person begins to encode the probe. Once this is finished, the search or scan through short-term memory could begin. That is, the mentally encoded probe could be compared with the items in memory to see whether there was a match. A simple "yes" or "no" decision could then be made, after which the person could make the physical response that stopped the timer, a button press.

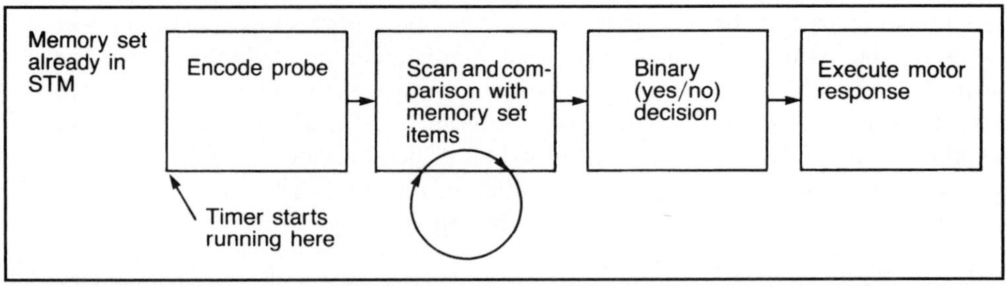

FIGURE 5-6
The four-stage process model for short-term memory scanning. Adapted from Sternberg (1969).

In Sternberg's task, it was the search process, the scan through the contents of short-term memory, that was of particular interest. Notice—this is critical—that it was *this* process that was repeated different numbers of times, depending on how many items were in the memory set. That is, when two items were stored in short-term memory, the scan process would have to occur twice, once for the item in position 1, once for the item in position 2. If five items were stored, likewise, the probe would be compared with each of the five. Thus, by manipulating the size of the memory set, Sternberg influenced the number of cycles through the search process. And by examining the slope of the RT results, he could determine how much additional time was necessary for each cycle through that process.

STERNBERG'S RESULTS Figure 5-7 shows Sternberg's (1969) results. There was a linear increase in RT as the memory set got larger and larger, and this increase was nearly the same for both "yes" and "no" trials. The equation at the top of the figure shows that the *y*-intercept of this RT function was 397.2 ms. Hypothetically, if there

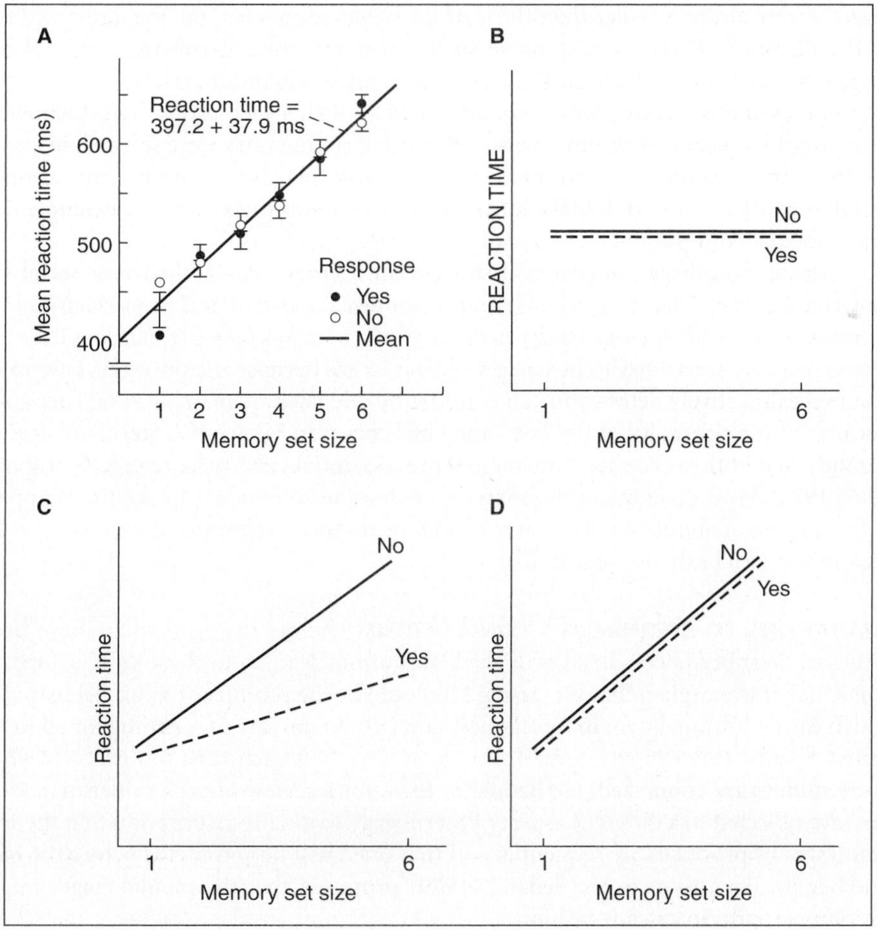

◆ **FIGURE 5-7**
Reaction time in the short-term memory scanning task, for "yes" (shaded circles) and "no" (unshaded circles) responses. Reaction time increases linearly at a rate of 37.9 ms per additional item in the memory set.

had been zero items held in short-term memory, the *y*-intercept would be the combined time for the encoding, decision, and response stages, the stages that occur only once per trial (refer back to Figure 5-6). More importantly, the slope of the equation was 37.9 ms; for each additional item in the memory set, the mental scanning process took an additional 37.9 ms. Putting it slightly differently, the results indicated that the search rate through short-term memory is approximately 38 ms per item—*very* fast.

What kind of mental search would produce these results? Sternberg considered three possibilities. The most intuitively appealing alternative was called *serial self-terminating search*. In this kind of search, the positions in short-term memory are scanned one by one, and the scan stops when a match is found; this is how you search for a lost object, say your car keys. The idea is that, on the average, the slope of the RT trials for "yes" responses should be smaller than the slope for "no" responses. On the "no" trials, all positions have to be searched before you can decide that the probe was not in the memory set. But on "yes" trials, people would encounter matches at all positions in the memory set, sometimes early, sometimes late, with equal frequencies at all positions. This would yield a pattern similar to that of the visual search task you read about in Chapter 4; in Figure 4-5, the slopes of the positive curves ("yes, I found the target") were always smaller than those of the negative curves ("no, the target was not in the display"). However reasonable such a search seems, Sternberg's data did not match the prediction—he found the same slope for both kinds of trials.

The second possibility was a *parallel search*, in which each position in the memory set would be scanned simultaneously. If short-term memory were scanned in parallel then there should be no increase in RT—if all the positions are scanned simultaneously, it should not take longer to scan six items than three, for example. But again, the data did not match this prediction.

Instead, Sternberg inferred that short-term memory is searched in a **serial exhaustive** fashion. That is, *the memory set is scanned one item at a time (serial), and the entire set is scanned on every trial, whether or not a match is found (exhaustive)*. Notice that exhaustive search has to be correct for "no" trials because the positions have to be scanned exhaustively before you can confidently and accurately make a "no" decision. Because of the similarity of the "yes" and "no" curves in Figure 5-7, Sternberg argued strongly that both reflect the same mental process, serial exhaustive search (Sternberg, 1969; 1975). How quickly can the contents of short-term memory be scanned? Apparently at a rate of about 38 ms per item. And how do we search short-term memory? By means of a serial exhaustive search.

LIMITATIONS TO STERNBERG'S CONCLUSIONS Across the years, there have been critics of Sternberg's conclusions or the assumptions leading to those conclusions. In particular, it was argued that increasing RTs could be the product of a parallel search in which each additional item to be scanned slows down the rate of scanning for all items (much as a battery can run several motors at once, but each runs more slowly when more motors are connected; see Baddeley, 1976, for a review of such criticisms). Others have objected to a different aspect of Sternberg's work: the assumption that the several stages or processes are sequential and that one must be completed before the next one begins. For instance, McClelland (1979) proposed that the mental stages might overlap partially, in cascade fashion.

Still, Sternberg's work pushed the field forward toward more useful ways of studying cognition, such as phenomena related to cognitive aging (e.g., Oberauer, 2001; Oberauer, Wendland, & Kliegl, 2003). Most research based on RT tasks (e.g., Treisman's visual search task and many long-term memory tasks) owes credit, even if only indirectly, to Sternberg's ground-breaking and insightful work.

Section Summary

- Serial position curves reveal the operation of two kinds of memory performance. Early positions in a to-be-recalled list are sensitive to deliberate rehearsal that transfers information into long-term memory, whereas later positions tend to be recalled with high accuracy in the free recall task; this latter effect is called the recency effect and is due to the strategy of recalling the most recent items first. Asking people to perform a distractor task before recall usually eliminates the recency effect because the distractor task prevents them from maintaining the most recent items in short-term memory.
- Sternberg's paradigm, short-term memory scanning, provided a way to investigate how we search through short-term memory. Sternberg's results indicated that this search is a serial exhaustive process occurring at a rate of about 38 ms per item to be searched. The Sternberg task illustrates how the short-term memory search processes of different kinds of people (children, adults, people under drug influences) might be investigated and how other kinds of memory search processes might be studied (e.g., long-term memory).

WORKING MEMORY

Working memory, in many ways, can be viewed as an augmentation of the short-term memory concept. By the mid-1970s, all sorts of roles and functions were being attributed to short-term memory in tasks involving problem solving, comprehension, reasoning, and the like. Yet, as Baddeley pointed out, remarkably little research had actually demonstrated those kinds of roles and functions in STM (Baddeley, 1976; Baddeley & Hitch, 1974; Baddeley & Lieberman, 1980). For example, pay attention to how you solve the following problem:

$$\frac{(4 + 5) \times 2}{3 + (12/4)}$$

How can a simple "7 ± 2" system capture the problem-solving and keeping-track processes here? Didn't you compute part of the expression, hold that intermediate answer in memory while computing the next part, then hold the updated intermediate value, and so forth? Likewise, sentence comprehension can sometimes tax short-term memory almost palpably; for instance:

I know that you are not unaware of my inability to speak German.

Can you feel the burden on your controlled processing when you have to figure out—almost translate—the meaning of a sentence piece by piece, then put the pieces together? ("not unaware" equals "aware," "inability to speak German" means "cannot speak German," and so on). But notions such as the burden or load on short-term memory, or switching between processing and remembering, are not addressed by simple approaches that emphasize 7 ± 2 "slots."

Going beyond intuitive examples, Baddeley and Hitch (1974) documented their position on the need for an elaborated short-term memory by describing a dramatic case study, originally reported by Warrington and Shallice (1969; also Shallice & Warrington, 1970; Warrington & Weiskrantz, 1970). These authors described a patient "who by all normal standards, has a grossly defective STS. He has a digit span of *only two items,* and shows grossly impaired performance on the Peterson short-term forgetting task. If STS does indeed function as a central working memory, then one would expect this patient to exhibit grossly defective learning, memory, and comprehension. No such evidence of general impairment is found either in this case or in subsequent cases of a similar type" (Baddeley & Hitch, 1974, pp. 48–49, emphasis added; also Baddeley & Wilson, 1988; Vallar & Baddeley, 1984). In a similar vein, McCarthy and Warrington (1984) reported on a patient who could repeat back only a one-item short-term memory list of unrelated words—a memory span of only one word!—but could nonetheless report back six- and seven-word sentences with about 85% accuracy. Despite the fact that both types of lists relied on short-term memory, performance on one type was seriously affected by the brain damage, and the other was only minimally affected.

How can working memory and short-term memory be the same thing, Baddeley and Hitch reasoned, when a patient with grossly defective STM performance exhibits no memory deficiencies in other tasks attributed to STM? If unrelated words and the words in sentences are both processed by the same short-term memory system, then how can performance be so good on sentences and so poor on unrelated words? To anticipate their conclusions, the problem lies with the theory of an undifferentiated STM. In Baddeley's view, traditionally defined STM is but one component of a larger, more elaborate system, **working memory**.

The Components of Working Memory

A description of Baddeley's working memory system provides a useful context for the studies described later; (see Baddeley & Hitch, 1974; Salame & Baddeley, 1982; Baddeley, 2000a). Note first that Baddeley's original working memory theory had three major components. The main part of the system is the *central executive* (or sometimes *executive control*), assisted by two auxiliary systems: the *phonological loop* and the *visuo-spatial sketch pad*. Both of these, in Baddeley's view, had specific sets of responsibilities, assisting the central executive by doing some of the lower-level processing involved in a task. Thus, in the arithmetic problem mentioned earlier, the central executive would be responsible for retrieving values from memory (4 + 5, 9 × 2) and applying the rules of arithmetic; whereas a subsystem, the phonological loop, would then hold the intermediate value 18 in a rehearsal-like buffer until it was needed again. Recently, a third auxiliary system, the *episodic buffer* has been added to the model (Baddeley, 2000a). This portion of working memory is a buffer used to integrate information already in working memory with information retrieved from long-term memory. It is the part of working memory where different types of information are bound together to form a complete memory, such as storing together the sound of someone's voice with an image of his/her face.

The division of working memory components is supported by neurological evidence. Smith and Jonides (1999; also Smith, 2000) have reviewed a number of studies that used various brain imaging techniques to identify regions of heightened activity in various working memory tasks. In general, the thinking is that those brain regions that are involved in perception are also recruited by working memory for the storage of information, regions toward the posterior (back) of the brain, and that the rehearsal and processing of information is controlled by those aspects of the brain involved in motor control and attention (Jonides, Lacey, & Nee, 2005). Figure 5-8 shows a diagram of the left hemisphere of the brain, with important areas for verbal storage and executive processes labeled. For the Sternberg task, the scanning evidence showed strong activations in a left hemisphere parietal region, noted at the numbered area 40 in the figure (following the standard Brodmann's area map), and three frontal sites, Broca's area (number 44), and the left supplementary motor area (SMA) and premotor area (number 6).

As you will read in Chapter 9, Broca's area is important in the articulation of language, so finding that it was activated here was not surprising. Alternatively, tasks that emphasize executive control, such as switching from one task to another, tend to show strong activity in Brodmann's area 46, the dorsolateral prefrontal cortex. This area has been isolated so frequently in tests of executive control that it's commonly referred to by the abbreviation DLPFC, and is viewed as absolutely central to an understanding of

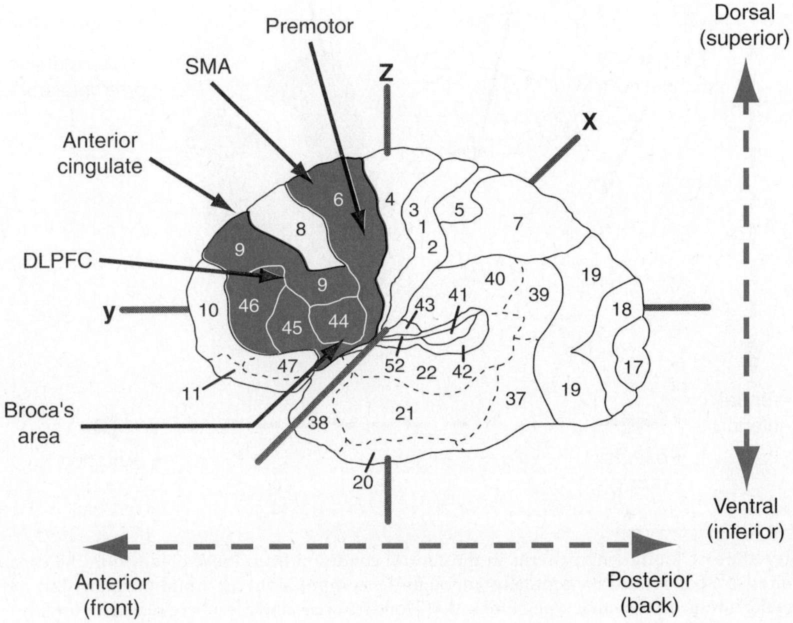

FIGURE 5-8 The left hemisphere regions of the frontal lobe of the brain that are especially important in verbal working memory tasks: the premotor and supplementary motor area (SMA), Brodmann area 6; the anterior cingulate and the dorsolateral prefrontal cortex (DLPFC), Brodmann area 9; and Broca's area, Brodmann area 44. From Smith & Jonides (1999).

executive attention (Kane & Engle, 2002; for an argument that task switching does not involve executive control, see Logan, 2003). The neurological basis for executive control is also supported by recent work showing that executive functions in cognition may have a significant genetic basis (Friedman, Miyake, Young, DeFries, Corley, & Hewitt, 2008).

Other studies have shown specific brain regions involved in visual working memory. In one (Jonides et al., 1993), people were shown a pattern of three random dots; the dots were then removed for 3 s, and a circle outline appeared; the task was to decide whether the circle surrounded a position where one of the dots had appeared earlier. In the control condition, the dots remained visible while the circle was shown, thus eliminating the need for remembering the locations. Positron emission tomography (PET) scans were taken, and the control pattern of activations was subtracted from those in the full task. Because the tasks differed only in the need to remember the dot positions, the difference presumably showed the regions of the brain that were responsible for remembering the spatial locations.

▲ Three right hemisphere regions, noted in Figure 5-9, showed heightened activity, so they presumably were the regions especially involved in spatial working memory. They were a portion of the occipital cortex, a posterior parietal lobe region, and the premotor and DLPFC region of the frontal lobe. In related work, when the task required spatial information for responding, it was the premotor region that was more active; when the task required object rather than spatial location information, the DLPFC was more active (Jonides et al., 1993; see also Miyake et al., 2000, for a review of various executive functions attributed to working memory).[2]

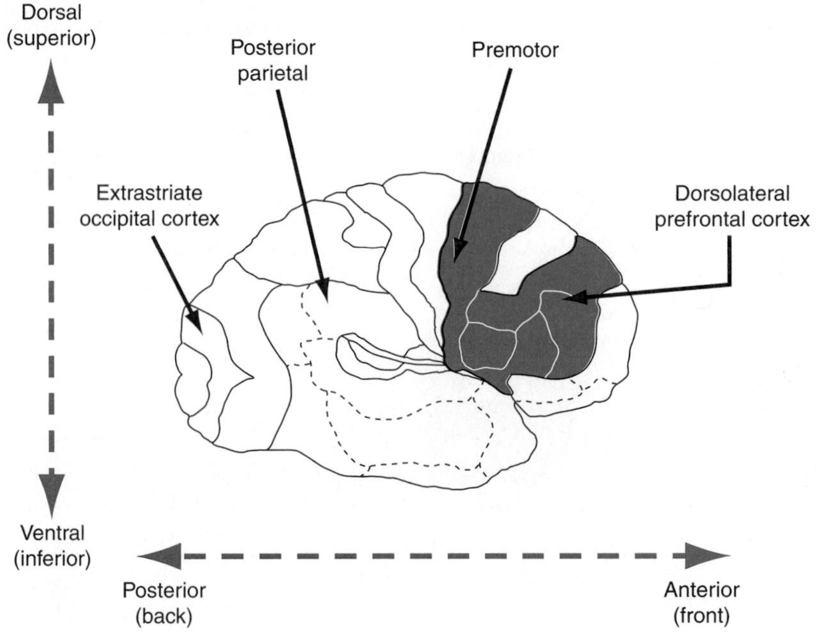

▲ FIGURE 5-9 The right hemisphere regions of the brain that are especially important in visual and spatial working memory tasks: the extrastriate occipital cortex; the posterior parietal lobe, the premotor area, and the dorsolateral prefrontal cortex (DLPFC). From Smith (2000).

[2] The procedure of subtracting patterns in the control condition from those obtained in the experimental condition is straightforward conceptually, although the computations are mind boggling. But notice that conceptually it rests on the same type of logic that Donders used (and Sternberg rejected), finding a control task that contains all of the experimental tasks' components except the one of interest. It will be surprising if this method does not come under attack again, in its newer application to brain imaging.

The Central Executive

The *central executive* is the heart of working memory. Think of a large corporation in which the chief executive or executive director is in charge of the difficult tasks such as planning, initiating activities, and making decisions. Likewise in the working memory system, the **central executive** is in charge of *planning future actions, initiating retrieval and decision processes as necessary,* and *integrating information coming into the system.* To continue with the arithmetic example, the central executive triggers the retrieval of facts such as "4 + 5 = 9" and invokes the problem-solving rules such as "how to multiply and divide." Furthermore, the central executive also "realizes" that the intermediate value 18 must be held momentarily while further processing occurs. Accordingly, it activates the phonological loop, sending it the value 18 to rehearse for a few moments until that value is needed again by the executive.

Each of the subsystems has its own pool of attentional resources, but the pools are very limited. Give any of the subsystems an undemanding task and it can proceed without disrupting activities occurring elsewhere in working memory. However, if a subsystem is given a particularly difficult task, then it either falters or it must drain additional resources from the central executive. Moreover, the central executive has its own pool of resources that can be depleted if it is overtaxed. For example, people who do something that places a heavy strain on the central executive, such as ignoring distracting information as it scrolls across the bottom of a television screen or exaggerating their emotional expressions, have greater difficulty with central executive processing immediately thereafter (Schmeichel, 2007).

The Phonological Loop

The **phonological loop** is *the speech- and sound-related component responsible for rehearsal of verbal information and phonological processing.* As Figure 5-8 shows, this component recycles information for immediate recall, including articulating the information in auditory rehearsal (see Baddeley, 2000b; Jones, Macken, & Nicholls, 2004; and Mueller, Seymour, Kieras, & Meyer, 2003, for a debate on the articulatory versus phonological basis of this subsystem).

There are two components of the phonological loop, the phonological store and the articulatory loop. The **phonological store** is essentially *a passive store component of the phonological loop.* This is the part that holds on to verbal information. However, information in the phonological store will be forgotten unless it is actively rehearsed and refreshed. Thus, rehearsal is the role of the **articulatory loop**, *the part of the phonological loop involved in the active refreshing of information in the phonological store.* One way of thinking about these two components of the phonological loop is that the phonological store is like your inner ear—you can hear yourself talk to yourself, or imagine hearing music. Similarly, the articulatory loop is like your inner voice, when you mentally say things to yourself.

Researchers have found a number of reliable effects that provide some insight into how the phonological loop works. We'll cover three of them here. These are the word length effect, the articulatory suppression effect, and the phonological similarity effect. The **word length effect** is *the finding that the longer the words are that people need to* *remember, the fewer they can remember* (Baddeley, Thompson, & Buchanan, 1975). For example, people can remember fewer multisyllable words, like "bribery" and "clarify," than single syllable words, like "Braille" and "cleanse," even though they have the same number of letters. Similarly, people can remember more short duration words, like "wicket" and "bishop," than long duration words, like "friday" and "harpoon." This is because words are slowly degrading in the phonological store, and need to be refreshed by the articulatory loop. Shorter words take less time to rehearse, and so a person can refresh these items faster in the store. However, because the longer words take more time to rehearse, it is more likely that people will lose other items in the phonological store, resulting in poorer memory for the set as a whole (Cowan, Baddeley, Elliot, & Norris, 2003).

This is further supported by a study in which Welsh participants, whose working memory was tested in Welsh, had lower working memory spans, presumably because of the longer (hence slower to articulate) words. The same people had higher working memory spans when they were tested in English. (See Baddeley, 1992a, and Ellis & Hennelly, 1980, for details.)

The **articulatory suppression effect** is *the finding that people have poorer memory for a set of words if they are asked to say something while they are trying to remember* (Murray, 1967). This does not have to be anything complicated, but can be something simple, like repeating the word "the" over and over again. What is happening here is that the act of speaking during the retention period consumes resources in the articulatory loop. As a result, words in the phonological store cannot be refreshed, and are lost. A related phenomenon is the irrelevant speech effect (Colle & Welsh, 1976). It is hard to keep information in the phonological loop when there is irrelevant speech in the environment. This irrelevant speech intrudes on the phonological loop, consuming resources, and causing you to forget verbal information. This is why it is so difficult to read (and then remember what you read) when you are in a room with other people talking. So, try to study somewhere quiet.

Finally, the **phonological similarity effect** is *the finding that memory is poorer when people need to remember a set of words that are phonologically similar, compared to a set of words that are phonologically dissimilar* (Baddeley, 1966; Conrad & Hull, 1964). For example, it would be harder to remember the set "boat," "bowl," "bone," and "bore," compared to trying to remember the set "stick," "pear," "friend," and "cake." This happens because words that sound similar can become confused in the phonological store. One thing that happens is that, because the words sound similar, it is hard to keep track of what was rehearsed and what wasn't. As a consequence, some words may not get rehearsed, and so are forgotten (Li, Schweickert, & Gandour, 2000). In addition, as bits and pieces of them become forgotten or lost, people need to reconstruct them. As a result, people are more likely to make a mistake by misremembering a word that sounded like it should have been in the set, but wasn't—for example, recalling the word "bold" in the first set described earlier. In general, when people misremember words in working memory, they tend to be words that sound similar, rather than having a similar meaning. This suggests that this aspect of working memory relies primarily on phonological information, rather than semantic information.

While we have spent a great deal of time covering phonological aspects of the phonological loop, there is some evidence that there is a broader language-based aspect of this part of working memory, rather than a necessarily sound-oriented one. In his clever study, Shand (1982) tested people who were congenitally deaf and skilled at American Sign Language (ASL). They were given five-item lists for serial recall, presented as either written English words or ASL signs. One list contained English words that were phonologically similar *(SHOE, THROUGH, NEW)* though not similar in terms of the ASL signs. Another list contained words that were cherologically similar in ASL, that is, similar in the hand movements necessary for forming the sign (e.g., wrist rotation in the vicinity of the signer's face), although they did not rhyme in English. Recall memory showed confusions based on the cherological relatedness. In other words, the deaf people were recoding the written words into an ASL-based code and holding *that* in working memory. Their errors naturally reflected the physical movements of that code rather than verbal or auditory features of the words.

The Visuo-Spatial Sketch Pad

The **visuo-spatial sketch pad** is *a system specialized for visual and spatial information*, holding or maintaining that kind of information in a short-duration buffer. If you must generate and hold a visual image for further processing, it's the visuo-spatial sketch pad system at work.

The operation of the visuo-spatial sketch pad can be illustrated by considering a study by Brooks (1968). People were asked to hold a visual image in working memory, a large block capital *F*, then scan that image clockwise, beginning at the lower left corner. In one condition, people said "yes" aloud if the corner they reached while scanning was at the extreme top or bottom of the figure and "no" otherwise; this was the "image plus verbal" condition. The other condition was an "image plus visual" search condition: While people scanned the mental image, they also had to search through a printed page, locating the column that listed the "yes" or "no" decisions in the correct order. Thus, two different secondary tasks were combined with the primary task of image scanning; all the tasks used the visuo-spatial sketch pad of working memory. The result was that making verbal responses—saying "yes" or "no"—was easy and yielded few errors. However, visual scanning of printed columns was much more difficult and yielded substantial errors. This is because scanning the response columns forced the visuo-spatial sketch pad to divide its resources between two tasks. As a consequence, performance suffered.

A number of effects have been observed that illustrate basic qualities of the visuo-spatial sketch pad. One of the overarching principles of this aspect of working memory is the influence of embodied cognition. As you will see, processing in the visuo-spatial sketch pad acts as if a person were actively interacting with objects in the world. It is not an abstract code, but a dynamic system that allows a person to predict what would happen next if he or she were actually involved in a situation. We will discuss three diagnostic phenomena here: mental rotation, boundary extension, and representational momentum.

The most dramatic evidence for the visuo-spatial sketch pad of working memory comes from work on mental rotation (Cooper & Shepard, 1973; Shepard &

PROVE IT

Articulatory Suppression

One of the mainstays of research on the phonological loop is the articulatory suppression task. As described above, for this task people are asked to repeat words aloud over and over again while trying to remember another set of verbal/linguistic information. The basic idea is that the repeated talking consumes the resources of the articulatory loop, making it difficult for people to maintain other information. On the face if it, the articulatory suppression task sounds very easy, and that it should not be too difficult. However, actually doing it is a humbling experience of how limited your working memory capacity is, and our ability to do more than one thing at a time when the same part of working memory needs to be used.

To illustrate the powerful influence of articulatory suppression, below are two lists of 10 words each. Copy then down onto a set of note cards. These are just examples, and you can make more lists if you want. Then find a few people to be your participants. Have them read each list of cards by allowing them to see each one for 1 second before moving on to the next. When the end of the list is reached, the person should write down as many words as can be remembered. For one list, have the people simply read the words. However, for the other list, the articulatory suppression list, have them say the word "the" over and over again (the, the, the, . . .) while reading the words, and have them keep saying "the the the" until the end of the list is reached. What you should find is that your participants' performance is worse under articulatory suppression than when they can read in peace and quiet.

Across	Figure
Result	Action
Center	Mother
Reason	Became
Effect	Making
Period	Really
Behind	Either
Having	Office
Cannot	Common
Future	Moment

Metzler, 1971). **Mental rotation** involves people *mentally turning, spinning, or rotating objects in the visuo-spatial sketch pad of working memory*. In one study, people were shown drawings of pairs of three-dimensional objects and they had to judge whether they were the same shape. The critical factor was the degree to which the second drawing was "rotated" from the orientation of the first drawing. To make accurate judgments, people had to do some mental transformation on one of the objects, mentally rotating it into the same orientation as the other so they could judge it "same" or "different." Figure 5-10 displays several such pairs of drawings and the basic findings of the study.

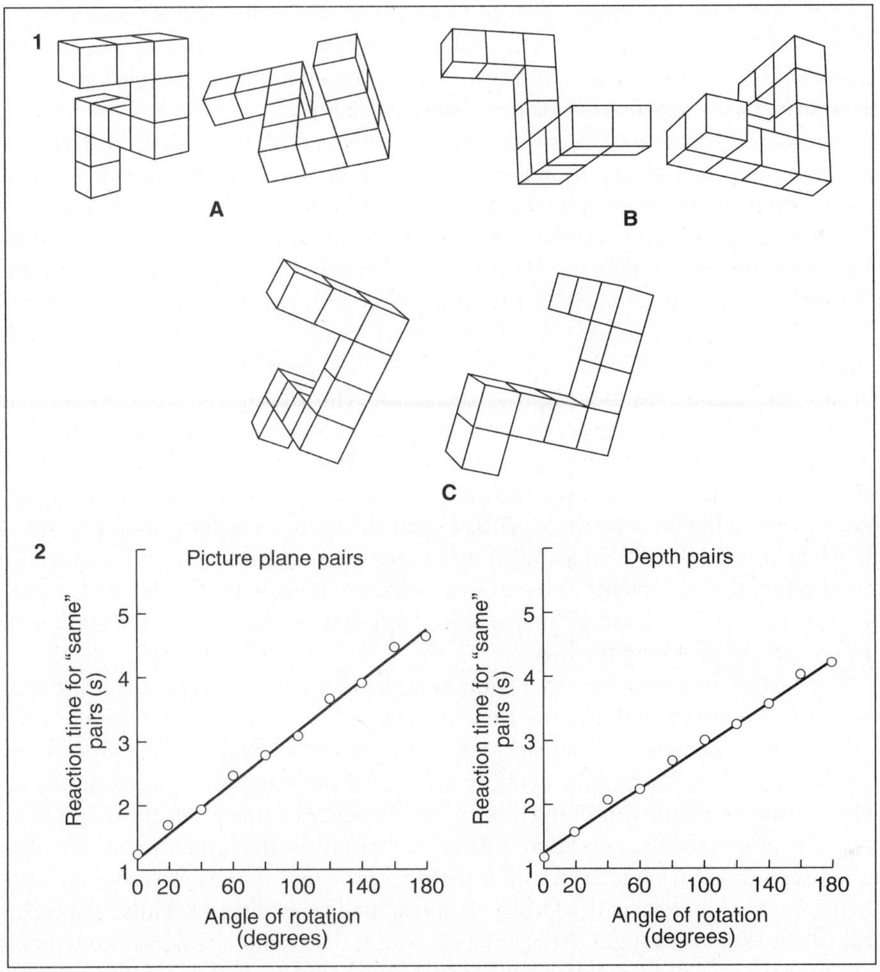

FIGURE 5-10
1. Three pairs of drawings are shown. For each, rotate the second drawing and decide whether it is the same figure as the first drawing. The *A* pair differs by an 80-degree rotation in the picture plane, and the *B* pair differs by 80 degrees in depth; the patterns in *C* do not match. **2.** The RTs to judge "same" are shown as a function of the degrees of rotation necessary to bring the second pattern into the same orientation as the first. Reaction time is a linear function of the degree of rotation.

The overall result was that people took longer to make their judgments as the angular rotation increased. In other words, a figure that needed to be rotated 120 degrees took longer to judge than one needing only 60 degrees of rotation, much as what would be found if a person were to manually turn the objects. In fact, performance can be enhanced if people are given tactile feedback (by holding an object in their hands) when the object is the same shape and moves in the same way (Wraga, Swaby, & Flynn, 2008), consistent with an embodied cognition interpretation of this mental rotation.

In the Cooper and Shepard (1973) report, people were shown the first figure and were told how much rotation to expect in the second figure. This advance information on the degree of rotation permitted people to do the mental rotation ahead of time. Interestingly, the mental processes seem much the same if you ask people to retrieve an image from long-term memory then hold it in working memory while performing mental rotation on that image. That is, researchers have found regular time-based effects of rotation, and activation in the visual (parietal) lobes, when people are asked to retrieve an image from long-term memory and rotate it mentally in working memory (Just, Carpenter, Maguire, Diwadkar, & McMains, 2001).

Another illustration of the properties of the visuo-spatial sketch pad is **boundary extension**, in which *people tend to misremember more of a scene than was actually viewed, as if the boundaries of an image were extended further out* (Intraub & Richardson, 1989). In studies of boundary extension, people might see a series of still pictures. Later, their memory is tested for what was seen in the pictures. This can be done by either having people draw what they remember, or identify the image they saw earlier. What is typically found is that people tend to misremember having viewed the picture from further back than was the case. That is, people misremember information from beyond the bounds of the actual picture (for example, if a person saw a picture of a stuffed animal on a set of steps, he or she will misremember more steps than were actually seen). What is going on here is that visuo-spatial working memory adds knowledge of what is beyond the picture boundary, based on previous world knowledge of what is likely to be there. This is then stored in long-term memory. This is why when you think back to a show you've seen on television or at the movies, you tend to remember the events as if you were actually there, with no edge to the world. You don't typically remember the image as it appears on the screen (or even remember sitting there watching the show.)

The last of the visuo-spatial phenomena considered here (and there are many more) is **representational momentum**, which is *the phenomenon of misremembering the movement of an object further along its path of travel than where it actually was when it was last seen* (Hubbard, 1995; 2005). In a typical representational momentum study, people see an object moving along a computer screen. At some point the object disappears. The task is for the person to indicate the point on the screen where the object was last seen. What is typically found is that there is a bias to misremember the object as being further along its path of travel than it actually was (Freyd & Finke, 1984; Hubbard, 1990). What is thought to be going on here is that visuo-spatial working memory is simulating the movement as if it were actually happening in the world, predicting where that object will be next. This prediction then enters into the decision process and people place the object further along its path.

Representational momentum can be influenced by other embodied aspects of the situation as well. For example, there is also a bias to remember objects as being further down than they actually were, as if they were being drawn down by gravity (Hubbard, 1990). There is also evidence that visuo-spatial working memory takes into account friction (Hubbard, 1990), centripetal, and impetus forces (Hubbard, 1996), even if physics has shown these ideas to be wrong, as in the case of impetus. Finally, if an object is moving in an oscillating motion, back and forth like a pendulum, and it disappears just before it is about to swing back, people will misremember it as having started its backswing (Verfaille & Y'dewalle, 1991).

Overall, it should be clear to you that there is a lot of active mental processing in the visuo-spatial sketch pad. This part of working memory is really doing a lot of work, even if you are not consciously aware of much of it. Moreover, this work is oriented around trying to capture physical aspects of the world (accurately or not) and help you predict what objects will do next, so that you can better interact with them, such as intercepting or avoiding them, with a minimum of conscious cognitive mental effort.

The Episodic Buffer

As we mentioned earlier, the **episodic buffer** is *the portion of working memory where information from different modalities and sources are bound together to form new episodic memories* (Baddeley, 2000a). In other words, this is the part of working memory where the all-important chunking process occurs, but it also includes perceptual processes, such as the integration of color with shape in visual memory (Allen, Baddeley, & Hitch, 2006). Because this portion of working memory has been incorporated into the working memory model fairly recently, we will have less to say about it relative to the other parts.

One study that may clarify the workings of the episodic buffer was done by Copeland & Radvansky (2001). In this study, people were given a working memory span test (these sorts of tests are described in detail later). For this study, people read a series of sentences and had to remember the last word of the sentences in a given set. What was manipulated was the phonetic similarity of the words in a set. Sometimes the words were phonologically similar, and other times not. The phonological similarity effect described in the phonological loop section above would predict that working memory performance would be worse for the phonologically similar items. However, because the words were presented at the end of meaningful sentences, rather than alone, people could use their semantic understanding of the sentences and bind this with their memory for the words. The result was that, under these circumstances, memory for the phonologically similar words was better than the dissimilar words, much as you would find with poetry or song lyrics.

Another study by Jefferies, Lambdon, Ralph, and Baddeley (2004) illustrates the capacity needed for integrating information in the episodic buffer. In their study, people were given lists of words, lists of unrelated sentences, and lists of sentences that formed a coherent story. People were asked to learn these lists either alone or under a more demanding dual task situation (see below) that involved pressing buttons on a keyboard when an asterisk appeared in a corresponding box on the computer screen. They found that working memory resources were especially important for remembering the lists of words and the lists of unrelated sentences; when working memory resources were consumed by the dual task, memory for the words and unrelated sentences was compromised relative to memory for the story sentences. In other words, the working memory capacity needed to chunk the information for words and unrelated sentences was being consumed by the secondary task. But for the related sentences, because the meaningful interrelations among them were easily derived, memory performance was relatively unaffected by the dual task. The ease of integrating the sentences into a coherent story reduced the demand for working memory resources.

Section Summary

- Working memory, a broader conceptualization of our short-term memory, consists of a central executive system and three major subsystems. The most commonly investigated subsystem is the phonological loop, responsible for verbal and auditory information. The other major slave system is the visuo-spatial sketch pad, which maintains more holistic visual and spatial information. Finally, the third component is the relatively more recent episodic buffer, a system that integrates or binds information from different parts of working memory and/or long-term memory.
- The various components of working memory are thought to operate relatively independently of one another, perhaps by using different neural substrates, although there can be some overlap for especially demanding tasks.
- There are capacity limits in the system. Dual task methods can be used to study strains on individual components of the system, or on the overall capacity of working memory. For example, the subsystems may drain extra needed capacity from the central executive in situations of high working memory demands.

ASSESSING WORKING MEMORY

In general, there are two primary ways of assessing working memory. These are the dual task method and measures of working memory span. In the first case, performance within an individual is examined by having the person perform a secondary task, one that will consume working memory resources at the same time as some primary task; this is the dual task method, often used to see how disruptive the secondary task will be. In comparison, in the approach that uses working memory span tests, we obtain a measure of a person's working memory capacity. Across a range of individuals and abilities, we compare the span scores to people's performance, to see what relationships emerge. Let's consider each of these methods in turn.

Dual Task Method

For the dual task method, one of the tasks done by a person is identified as the primary one that we are most interested in. The other is designated as a secondary task that is done simultaneously with the first. Both tasks must rely to some significant degree on working memory. In general, we are interested in how the two tasks can be done together and whether there is any competition or interference between them. Any two tasks that are done simultaneously may show complete independence, complete dependence, or some intermediate level of dependency. If neither task influences the other, then we infer that they rely on separate mental mechanisms or resources. If one task always disrupts the other, then they presumably use the same mental resources.

Finally, if the two tasks interfere with each other in some circumstances but not others, then there is evidence for a partial sharing of mental resources. Usually such interference is found when the difficulty of the tasks reaches some critical point at which the combination of the two becomes too demanding. Researchers manipulate the difficulty of the two tasks just as you would adjust the volume controls on a stereo, changing the left and right knobs independently until the combination hits some ideal setting. In the research, we vary the difficulty of each task separately—we crank up the "difficulty knobs" on the two tasks, so to speak—and observe the critical point at which performance starts to suffer.

An important aspect of working memory that the dual task method highlights is that information that is processed in one component may not interfere with processing in another part of the system. For example, information that uses central executive resources will be relatively unaffected by processing that consumes resources in one of the subsystems. In one experiment (Baddeley & Hitch, 1974, Experiment 3) people were asked to do a reasoning task. They were shown a stimulus such as *AB* and were timed as they read and responded "yes" or "no" to sentences about it. A simple sentence here would be "*A* precedes *B*," an active affirmative sentence. An equivalent meaning is expressed by "*B* is preceded by *A*," but it's more difficult to verify because of the passive construction. There were also negative sentences, such as "*B* does not precede *A*," and "*A* is not preceded by *B*" (as well as false sentences, e.g., "*B* precedes *A*"). The sentence difficulty was a way of manipulating how much the central executive was needed.

While doing the reasoning task, people also had to perform one of three secondary tasks: (a) articulatory suppression, (b) repeating the numbers 1 through 6, or (c) repeating a random sequence of digits (the sequence was changed on every trial). Note how the amount of articulation in the three tasks was about the same (a speaking rate of four to five words per second was enforced), but the demands on the central executive steadily increased. There was also a control condition in which there was no concurrent articulation.

◆ Figure 5-11 shows the reasoning times for these four conditions. The control condition showed that even when reasoning was done alone, it took more time to respond to the difficult sentences. Adding articulatory suppression or repeated counting added a bit more time to the reasoning task but did not change the pattern of reasoning times to any great degree; the curves for "the the the" and "one two three . . ." in the figure have roughly the same slope as the control group's pattern. This is because these tasks do not strongly consume working memory resources, However, the random digit condition yielded a different pattern. As the sentences grew increasingly difficult, the added burden of reciting the random sequence of digits took its toll. In fact, for the most difficult sentences in the reasoning task, correct judgments took nearly 6 s when random digits had to be recycled through memory at the same time, compared with only 3 s in the control condition. This was the pattern Baddeley predicted. When the secondary task is very difficult, the articulatory loop must drain or borrow some

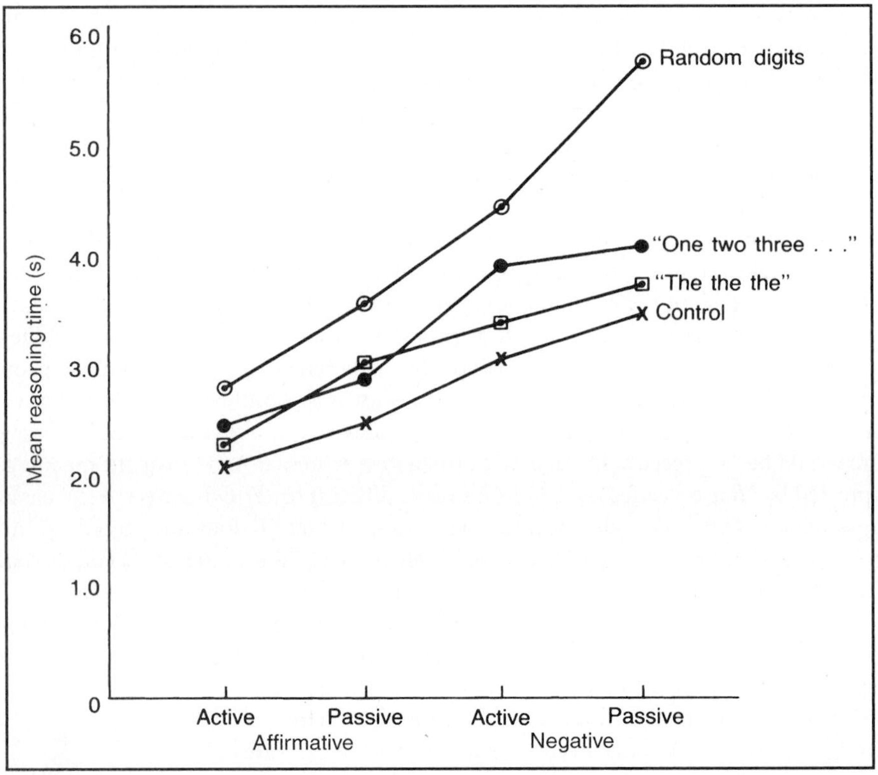

◆ **FIGURE 5-11** Average reasoning time is shown as a function of two variables: the grammatical form of the reasoning problem and the type of articulatory suppression task that was performed simultaneously with reasoning. In the random digits condition, a randomly ordered set of six digits had to be repeated out loud during reasoning; in the other two suppression tasks, either "the the the" or "one two three four five six" had to be repeated out loud during reasoning.

of the central executive's resources. This means that the central executive has to slow down or sacrifice accuracy.

This dual task interference is not only seen with abstract tasks such as verbal reasoning. It has also been shown that dividing attention during driving, such as talking on a cell phone, disrupts the ability to make important judgments, such as when to brake. In general, dual task processing leads to significantly and meaningfully slower braking (Levy, Pashler, & Boer, 2006). In other words, when you tax working memory resources, the ability of the central exective to effectively process information is compromised.

Similar research has also been reported comparing the visuo-spatial sketch pad and the phonological loop. As one example Logie, Zucco, and Baddeley (1990; but see Morey & Cowan, 2004, for a contrasting view) selected two different primary tasks: a visual memory span task and a letter span task. These were paired with two secondary tasks, one involving mental addition and the other visual imagery. In the visual memory span task, people saw a grid of squares on the computer screen, with a random half of them filled in. After a moment, the grid disappeared and was followed by an altered grid pattern where one of the previously filled squares was now empty. People had to point to the square that was changed, using their memory of the earlier pattern as recorded by the visuo-spatial sketch pad. In contrast, the letter memory span task, the other primary task, should have used the phonological loop.

For the secondary tasks, Logie et al. used a mental addition task thought to be irrelevant to the visuo-spatial system and an imaging task thought to be irrelevant to the phonological loop. The results are shown in Figure 5-12. First, look at the left half of the graph, which reports the results of the visual span (grid pattern) task. Each person performed the span task alone, to determine baseline, then along with the secondary tasks. The graph shows the percentage *drop* in dual task performance as compared to baseline. For instance, visual span performance dropped about 15% when the addition task was paired with it; so, dual task performance was at 85% of the single-task baseline. In other words, doing mental addition disrupted visual memory to only a modest degree. But when the secondary task involved visual imagery, as shown by the second bar in the graph, visual memory span dropped about 55%. This is a large interference effect, suggesting that the visuo-spatial sketch pad was stretched beyond its limits.

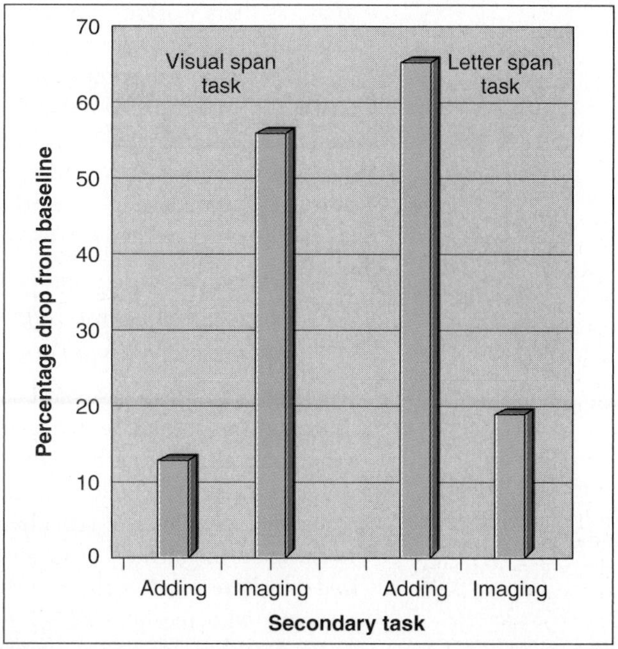

FIGURE 5-12
Results from Logie, Zucco, and Baddeley's (1990) experiment on the visuo-spatial sketch pad. Two secondary tasks, adding and imaging, were combined with two primary tasks, a visual span or a letter span task. The results are shown in terms of the percentage drop in performance measured from baseline; the larger the drop, the more disruption there was from the secondary task.

The right half of the figure shows performance on the letter span task. Here, the outcome was reversed; mental addition was very disruptive to the letter span task, leading to a 65% decline, whereas the imaging task depressed letter span scores only a modest 20%. Thus, only minor declines in performance were observed when the secondary task used a different part of working memory. But substantial declines occurred when the primary and secondary tasks used the same pool of resources (see Baddeley & Lieberman, 1980, for some of the original research on the visuo-spatial sketch pad). Recent work suggests that the impact dual tasks such as these are having is on the encoding aspect of a task, rather than the retention of information in working memory per se (Cowan & Morey, 2007).

Working Memory Span

A different means of investigating working memory (and still compatible with the evidence you have been studying) is an individual differences approach. As in any area of psychology, when we speak of individual differences, we're talking about characteristics of individuals—anything from height to intelligence—that differ from one person to the next and can be measured and related to other factors.

Since about 1980, a growing body of evidence has accumulated that there are genuine individual differences in working memory capabilities, and that these differences are related to various cognitive processes. In this research, people are first given a test to assess their working memory spans. They are then divided into groups, say into high-span and low-span groups. These groups are then given standard cognitive tasks. The intent is to interpret group differences as a function of working memory span. Consider a program of research by Engle and his coworkers (Engle, 2001; Rosen & Engle, 1997; see Engle, 2002, for an excellent introduction). First, people are given a working memory span task: The task requires simultaneous mental processing and storage of information in working memory. For example, a person might see the following sentences and words, one at a time (from Engle, 2001):

> *For many years, my family and friends have been working on the farm. SPOT*
> *Because the room was stuffy, Bob went outside for some fresh air. TRAIL*
> *We were fifty miles out at sea before we lost sight of the land. BAND*

People read the first sentence aloud, then said the capitalized word aloud; then they read the second sentence and word, then the third. At that point, people were asked to recall the three capitalized words, demonstrating that they had stored them in working memory. A follow-up question about one of the sentences was also asked to make sure people had actually comprehended the sentences (e.g., "Who has been working on the farm?"). Scores on this span task are based on the number of capitalized words recalled, assuming that the questions are also answered correctly. Thus, someone who recalled "*SPOT TRAIL BAND*" and answered the question correctly (and was able to do this at least two out of three times with lists of the same length), but no more, would have a memory span of 3.

In other versions of the test, the sentences might be replaced with arithmetic statements (e.g., "Is $(6 \times 2) - 2 = 10$? BEAR") to be judged true or false, or visual patterns requiring counting (e.g., "count the blue squares in three successive patterns, remembering each of the totals for later recall"). In yet others, people answer brief questions about each sentence before moving on to the next, with the storage part being tested by having people recall the final word in each sentence. All of these are working memory span tasks because they all involve both *processing* and *storage:* Process the sentence for meaning, for instance, and store the word for recall.

Many investigators have used working memory span tasks to measure working memory capacity. The original work that used this method (Daneman & Carpenter, 1980) examined reading comprehension as a function of span. There were significant correlations between working memory span scores and performance on the comprehension tasks. One of the most striking correlations was between span and verbal Scholastic Aptitude Test (SAT) scores; it was .59, whereas simple memory span scores seldom correlated significantly with SATs. (As a reminder, simple memory span tasks, such as remembering a string of digits, test only the storage of items, whereas working memory span tasks involve both storage and processing.) This strong correlation means that there is some important underlying relationship between one's working memory span and the verbal processing measured by the SAT.

The strongest correlation in Daneman and Carpenter's work was a .90 correlation between memory span and performance on a pronoun reference test. Here, people read sentences one by one and at some point confronted a pronoun that referred back to a previous noun. In the hardest condition, the noun had occurred up to six or seven sentences earlier. The results are shown in ★ Figure 5-13. Dramatically, people with the highest working memory span of 5 scored 100% correct on the pronoun test, even in the "seven sentences ago" condition. People with the lowest spans (of 2), got 0% correct in that condition. The implication was that people with higher working memory spans were able to keep more relevant information active in working memory as they comprehended the sentences.

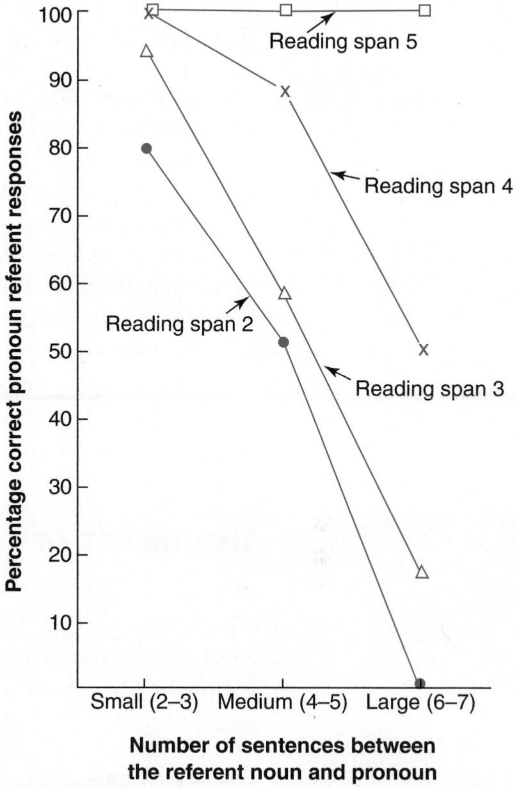

★ **FIGURE 5-13**
The percentage of correct responses to the pronoun reference task when the antecedent noun occurred a small, medium, or large number of sentences before the pronoun, as a function of participants' working memory (reading) span. From Daneman & Carpenter (1980).

Research since this initial report has extended these findings. Basically, if a task relies on a need to control attention, scores on the task correlate strongly with working memory span. In fact, Engle (e.g., 2002) argued that working memory capacity *is* executive attention and offers the equation "WM = STM + controlled attention." i.e., working memory is the combination of traditional short-term memory plus our controlled attention mechanism (Kane & Engle, 2003; for thorough updates, see Daneman & Merikle, 1996; Engle, 2002; and Miyake & Shah, 1999). This involves both the maintenance of information in the short term as well as the ability to access needed information in long-term memory (Unsworth & Engle, 2007).

There is also some evidence that basic working memory abilities can change with practice. For example, there is a general finding that women tend to perform less well than males on visuo-spatial tasks. That is, they are not as effective at using the visuo-spatial sketch pad of working memory. However, with some training, such as 10 hours experience playing action-based video games, the performance of females can reach the levels of males (Feng, Spence, & Pratt, 2007). Overall, this sort of work, along with the research by Chase and Ericsson (1982) described earlier (as well as others, e.g., Verhaegen, Cerella, & Basak, 2004), suggests that people can develop various strategies to more efficiently and effectively use their working memories over and above any base level of capacity they may have.

That said, working memory span scores do not provide insight into all aspects of cognitive abilities. For example, a study by Copeland and Radvansky (2004) gave people a variety of working memory span tasks, and also assessed their performance at more complex levels of comprehension, such as remembering event descriptions, drawing inferences about causes and effects, and detecting inconsistencies in a text. Under those circumstances, there was little evidence of a relation between working memory span and performance for these more complex processes. Thus, while working memory span highlights important cognitive abilities, it is not the complete story. There is individual variation that can be attributed to other factors as well.

Section Summary

- One common method for assessing working memory is to use dual task methodologies. In these tasks, people are asked to simultaneously perform at least two tasks. Researchers then assess how performance on the primary task is affected by the addition of the secondary task, and the theoretical relationship between the two.
- An alternative research strategy is to test participants' working memory span, then examine differences in cognitive performance as a function of their span (e.g., high- versus low-span). This approach has revealed a substantial number of tasks that show a strong relationship between span and performance. The implication is that working memory span assesses an individual's controlled attentional processes, which are significant aspects of one's performance all the way from selective attention tasks up through reading comprehension.

THE IMPACT OF WORKING MEMORY ON COGNITION

As noted earlier, working memory does not exist or operate independently of other aspects of cognition. It is the vital nerve center of a great deal of activity, especially conscious activity. In the next few sections, we discuss some ways that working memory influences processing in a variety of domains, including attention, long-term memory, and reasoning.

Working Memory and Attention

Conway, Cowan, and Bunting (2001) examined working memory span and its relation to the classic cocktail party effect of hearing one's own name while paying attention to some other message. About 65% of the people with low working memory spans detected their name in the dichotic listening task, versus only 20% of those with high spans. The interpretation was that high-span people were selectively attending to the shadowed message much more effectively than the low-span people, so weren't as likely to detect their names on the unshadowed message. In contrast, the low-span people seemed to have difficulty blocking out or inhibiting attention to the distracting information in the unattended message—so they were more likely to hear their own names (see Kane, Brown, McVay, Silvia, Myin-Germeys, & Kwapil, 2007, for evidence that high-span people are better at concentrating more generally, and are less likely to engage in mind wandering).

In a similar demonstration, Kane and Engle (2003) examined performance in the classic Stroop task (remember from the "Prove It" box in Chapter 4?). The task requires you to name the colors of ink in which words are printed, where a word like *GREEN* is sometimes printed in a mismatching color (e.g., *GREEN* in red ink). There was a strong Stroop effect in the results, of course—approximately a 100 ms slowdown on mismatching items. More to the point, there was no difference in the Stroop effect for high- and low-span groups when the words were always printed in a mismatching color (*GREEN* printed in red ink) or when half of the words were presented that way;

everyone remembered the task goal—ignore the word—in these conditions. But when only 20% of the words were in mismatching colors, low-span people made nearly twice as many errors as high-span participants. Because mismatching trials were relatively rare, the low-span people seemed less able to maintain the task goal in working memory. High-span individuals had less difficulty maintaining that goal.

In a more everyday example, Sanchez and Wiley (2006) tested people with different memory spans, giving them texts to read that included illustrations. These illustrations were often irrelevant to the main points of the text, such as having a picture of snow in a passage about ice ages—the snow is related to the topic, but does not provide or support any additional new information. As such, performance would be better if working memory capacity were to focus on the relevant details in the text. Sanchez and Wiley found that people with lower working memory spans were more likely to be "seduced" by the irrelevant details in the pictures. That is, these people had greater difficulty controlling the contents of their current stream of thought, and were more likely to be led astray by attractive, but unhelpful, sources of knowledge. They were more likely to be distracted by irrelevant information.

Working Memory and Long-Term Memory

Long-term memory function can also depend on working memory. Rosen and Engle (1997), for instance, had high- and low-span people perform a verbal fluency task: Generate members of the animal category as rapidly as possible for up to 15 min. High-span people outperformed their low-span counterparts, a difference noticeable even 1 min into the task. Intriguingly, in a second experiment, both span groups were tested in the fluency task alone and in a dual-task setting. While naming animals, people had to simultaneously monitor the digits that showed up, one by one, on the computer monitor and press a key whenever three odd digits appeared in the sequence. This attention-consuming task reduced performance on the animal naming task, but only for the high-span people, as shown in Figure 5-14. Low-span people showed no decrease in their fluency task performance.

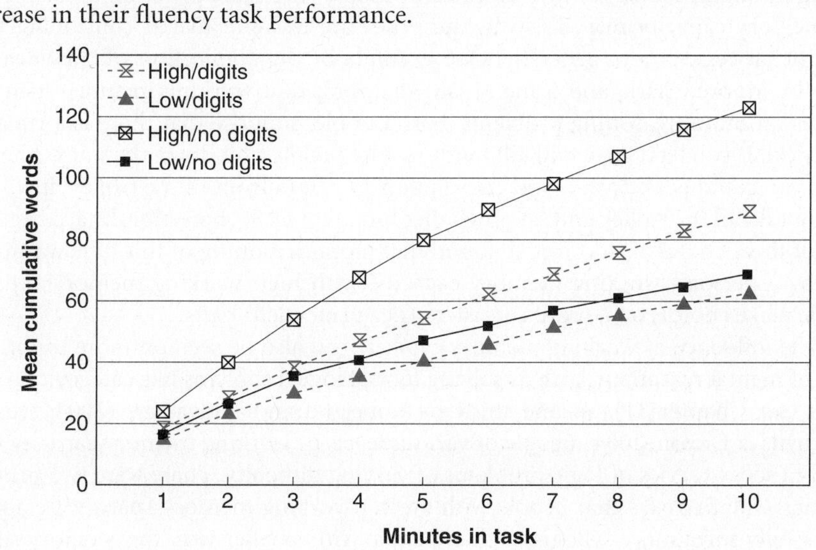

▲ **FIGURE 5-14** The cumulative number of animal names generated by participants of high (open points) or low (filled points) working memory span. Dashed lines indicate performance when participants performed the secondary task of monitoring a stream of digits while generating animal names. From Rosen & Engle (1997).

Rosen and Engle suggested that the normal, automatic long-term memory search for animal names was equivalent in both groups. But high-span people were able to augment this with a conscious, controlled strategic search; in other words, along with regular retrieval, the high-span people could deliberately ferret out additional, hard-to-find animal names using this controlled attentional process. This additional "ferreting" process relied on working memory. As a consequence, the added digit monitoring task used up the working memory resources that had been devoted to the controlled strategic search. This made the high-span group perform more like the low-span group had been performing.

Other studies show the importance of working memory. Kane and Engle (2000), for instance, found that low-span people experience more proactive interference (PI) in the Brown–Peterson task than do high-span people. High-span people presumably used their controlled attentional processes to combat PI, so they showed an increase in PI when they had to perform a simultaneous secondary task that loaded working memory (see Bunting, Conway, & Heitz, 2004; Cantor & Engle, 1993, and Radvansky & Copeland, 2006, for an exploration of the role of working memory span in managing associative interference during retrieval). More generally, low-span people appear to search a wider range of knowledge, making them more prone to having irrelevant information intrude on their retrieval (Unsworth, 2007). In Hambrick and Engle (2002), high-span individuals showed better performance than low-span people on a long-term memory retrieval task, even when both groups were equated for the rather specialized domain knowledge being tested (what a nice experiment to participate in—people listened to simulated radio broadcasts of baseball games).

Working Memory and Reasoning

This idea that working memory involves a controlled attention mechanism can be tied to more general issues of cognitive and behavioral control, such as those needed in reasoning through problems. More specifically, people who score lower on tests of working memory capacity may do so because they are less effective at controlling their thought processes more generally. One example of the application of this idea is a study by Moore, Clark, and Kane (2008) that looked at working memory span and choices on moral reasoning problems. For example, suppose that there is a runaway trolley car. If you let it go, it will kill four unaware people a bit down the track. Alternatively, you could push a very large person next to you in front of the trolley; it will kill him, but derail the trolley and save the other four people. So, how morally acceptable is each of these choices? Moore et al. found that moral reasoning of this type was mediated by a person's working memory capacity, with high working memory capacity people make choices on a more consistent (i.e., principled) basis.

The influence of working memory capacity can also be seen on more traditional sorts of mental reasoning, such as solving formal logic problems like categorical syllogisms (see Chapter 11). In one study by Copeland and Radvansky (2004; see also Markovits & Doyon, 2004) people of various levels of working memory capacity were asked to solve a series of logic problems of varying difficulty. There were two primary findings. The first was that people with greater working memory spans were able to successfully solve more syllogisms than people with smaller working memory spans.

Moreover, working memory span also seemed to be related to the strategies people used to reason, with people with smaller working memory spans using simpler strategies. It may be that having greater working memory capacity allows one to keep more information active in memory, allowing a person to explore different alternatives when trying to reason and draw conclusions.

Sometimes Small Working Memory Spans Are Better

Intuitively, it would seem that people with greater working memory capacity, or those who engage working memory resources more effectively, are more likely to succeed, and generally this is true. However, there are some interesting exceptions that highlight how working memory is used in more complex cognitive tasks. One of these exceptions is illustrated in a study by Beilock and DeCaro (2007). In this study, high- and low-span people were given math problems to solve. Under normal conditions, high-span people tended to perform better. However, participants were then placed in a high-pressure situation; they were told that they were being timed, that their performance would be videotaped so math experts could evaluate their performance, that they would be paid for improving their performance, and so forth. In this high-pressure condition, working memory capacity was consumed with task irrelevant anxiety-induced thoughts, and performance in both the high- and low-span groups was equivalent. Thus, when people have their working memory capacity consumed by irrelevant thoughts, they are more likely to use simpler, less effective, strategies. This shift to simpler strategies tended to equate people by causing the high-span people to solve the problems more like the low-span people, who were using simpler strategies in the first place.

Of particular interest, in a second experiment, people were asked to perform a series of word problems that required a complex series of steps (i.e., $B - A - 2 \times C$). Then under low- or high-pressure conditions, people were given a series of new problems, some of which required a simpler solution (i.e., $A - C$). Beilock and DeCaro (2007) found that the low-span people were actually more likely to use the simpler, correct solution than the high-span participants. The explanation for this is that low-span people are less likely to derive rule-based strategies for solving problems (because they have less capacity to do so) and are more likely to draw from previous similar experiences in memory. Thus, when they are given the problems with the simpler solutions, the low-span people will be less dependent on a complex, rule-based strategy they derived earlier, and so are more likely to use the more appropriate, simpler strategy (for other examples of better performance by people with smaller working memory spans, see Colflesh & Conway, 2007; Cokely, Kelley, & Gilchrist, 2006).

Overview

The general conclusion from all these studies is that *working memory* is a more suitable name for the attention-limited workbench system of memory. Working memory is responsible for the active mental effort of regulating attention, for transferring information into long-term memory by means of rehearsal, and for retrieving information from long-term memory.

Importantly, there is an overall limitation in the mental resources or capacity available to working memory; it is a closed system, with only some fixed quantity of resources to spread around. In other words, when extra resources are drained by the subsystems, they are not replaced by some other component. Instead, the central executive suffers along with insufficient resources for its own work. Naturally, as processes become more automatic, fewer resources are tied down (e.g., working memory is unrelated to counting when there are only two or three things to count but is influenced for larger quantities; Tuholski, Engle, & Baylis, 2001). And, interestingly, there are some studies suggesting that overall capacity can change through strategy or rehearsal training (Turley-Ames & Whitfield, 2003), with corresponding changes in neural activity (Olsen, Westerberg, & Klingberg, 2004).

The "Engle tradition" of research emphasizes the general nature of working memory capacity as a measure of executive attention, and de-emphasizes the multicomponent working memory approach advocated by Baddeley. Part of Engle's reason for this is the generality of the working memory effects—as he notes, working memory span predicts performance on a variety of tasks. It may also be implicated in age-related cognitive decline among older adults (e.g., Salthouse, Atkinson, & Berish, 2003). Of particular importance, working memory span routinely correlates strongly with overall measures of intelligence, especially so-called *fluid intelligence* (the ability to reason and solve novel problems; see also Kane et al., 2004). Common to both the Baddeley and the Engle approaches, however, is a central set of principles. Working memory is intimately related to executive control, to the deliberate allocation of attention to a task, and to the maintenance of efficient, effective cognitive processing and behavior. There is a limitation in the system, however, in the overall amount of attention available at any one time, even for those who have a greater absolute capacity in the first place. And the ability to deliberately focus and allocate attention, and to suppress or inhibit attention to extraneous factors, is key to higher-order cognitive processing.

Section Summary

- Working memory abilities and performance are critical to many tasks assessed by cognitive psychologists. For example, working memory capacity is strongly related to the ability to engage attention. It has also been shown to be strongly related to the efficiency with which simple facts can be retrieved from long-term memory.
- While larger working memory capacity is generally associated with superior cognitive performance, there are cases where circumstances favor smaller working memory capacity. These are typically circumstances where it is better not to devote too much attention to a task.
- Although there is no clear view on exactly what working memory is, as evidenced by the Baddeley multi-component model and the Engle attentional con-

trol view, there are a number of agreed-upon characteristics of what working memory is able to do. These include its limited capacity, the ability to simultaneously handle certain types of noninterfering forms of information, the fact that people differ in their working memory capacities and abilities, and that these individual differences are related to performance on a variety of tasks.

Key Terms

articulatory loop (p. *165*)
articulatory suppression effect (p. *166*)
boundary extension (p. *170*)
Brown–Peterson task (p. *150*)
central executive (p. *165*)
chunk (p. *149*)
decay (p. *150*)
episodic buffer (p. *171*)
free recall (p. *154*)
mental rotation (p. *168*)
phonological loop (p. *165*)
phonological similarity effect (p. *166*)
phonological store (p. *165*)
primacy effect (p. *154*)
proactive interference (PI) (p. *151*)
process model (p. *158*)
recency effect (p. *154*)
recoding (p. *149*)
release from PI (p. *152*)
representational momentum (p. *170*)
retroactive interference (RI) (p. *151*)
serial exhaustive search (p. *160*)
serial position curve (p. *154*)
serial recall (p. *154*)
visuo-spatial sketch pad (p. *167*)
word length effect (p. *165*)
working memory (p. *162*)

Sample Lists for Simple Memory Span Tests

Digits
8 7 0 3 1 4
7 1 5 0 5 4 3 6
2 8 4 3 6 1 2 9 7 5
Words
leaf gift car fish rock
paper seat tire horse film beach forest brush
bag key book wire box wheel banana floor bar pad block radio boy

CHAPTER

6

Learning and Remembering

Memory is the most important function of the brain; without it life would be a blank. Our knowledge is all based on memory. Every thought, every action, our very conception of personal identity, is based on memory. . . . Without memory, all experience would be useless.

EDRIDGE-GREEN, 1900

We must never underestimate one of the most obvious reasons for forgetting, namely, that the information was never stored in memory in the first place.

LOFTUS, 1980, P. 74

This is the first of three chapters specifically devoted to long-term memory, the relatively permanent storage vault for a lifetime's worth of knowledge and experience. Why do we need three chapters? First, as indicated in the Edridge-Green quotation: Long-term memory is fundamental to nearly every mental process, to almost every act of cognition. You cannot understand human cognition unless you understand long-term memory. Second, long-term memory is an enormous area of research with a long (for psychology) history. In fact, the area is so large that it is impossible to do it justice unless some divisions are used. Third, everyone is curious about his or her own memory. Who has not complained, at one time or another, about forgetfulness, about the unreliability of memory? Are these complaints justified? Is there some design flaw in human memory that leads to these problems?

Long-term memory is all about divisions and subdivisions, with various theorists advocating one or another scheme to categorize the varieties of long-term memory. We used to argue over whether long-term memory was a single, indivisible storage system or whether multiple systems were involved (e.g., McKoon & Ratcliff, 1986; Tulving, 1989). Now, it seems, the debates are about *how many* memory components there are (Schacter, 1989; Squire, 1986, 1993; Tulving, 1985, 1993), with evidence from cognitive neuroscience playing a prominent role. Instead of taking a hard line for or against any particular scheme, we simply adopt one of the more useful ones as an organizational device.

Look at Figure 6-1, a taxonomy suggested by Squire (1986, 1993). As the figure shows, an overall distinction can be made between **declarative** or **explicit memory** and **nondeclarative** or **implicit memory**. In this system, declarative or explicit memory is *long-term memory knowledge that can be retrieved and reflected on consciously;* in other words, a by-product of retrieving such knowledge is that we are consciously aware of it. The two kinds of declarative knowledge, episodic and semantic memory, are the topics of this chapter and the next. In contrast, nondeclarative or implicit memory (also "procedural" memory) is *knowledge that can influence thought and behavior without any necessary involvement of conscious awareness.* The key to this distinction is the conscious awareness part—one has it, one doesn't.

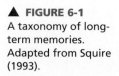

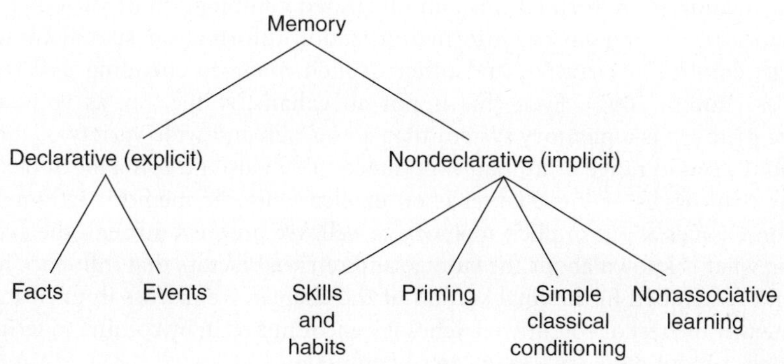

▲ **FIGURE 6-1**
A taxonomy of long-term memories. Adapted from Squire (1993).

A brief example may help clarify this distinction. If we ask you what happened when you passed your driver's test, we're asking you to retrieve knowledge from **episodic memory**, that is, *memory of the personally experienced and remembered events.* When you retrieve that information, you become conscious of it: You're aware of the event, it's in your consciousness, you can talk about it, and so forth. Episodic memory not only enables you to record your personal history in memory, it also supports "time travel," the mental ability to "relive experiences by thinking back to previous situations and happenings . . . and to mentally project oneself into the anticipated future" (Wheeler, Stuss, & Tulving, 1997, p. 331). Alternatively, if we ask you what a driver's license is, we're asking you to retrieve knowledge from **semantic memory**, your *general world knowledge.* You retrieve the concept of a driver's license, and it becomes explicit: The concept is now in your conscious awareness. Notice that just as episodic memory is your mental slide show, semantic memory is your mental encyclopedia, and both involve explicit knowledge that you can become consciously aware of (Tulving, 1972, 1983, 1993).

But there is more going on than rises to the level of conscious awareness. As you are reading this sentence, you are encountering the term *driver's license* again; in fact, that was the fourth time you encountered it. Although you are not conscious of it, you are now faster at reading that term than you were the first time; the speedup in rereading is called repetition priming. This effect happens at the nondeclarative, implicit level. Likewise, if we gave you some word stems an hour from now and asked you to fill in the blanks with the first word that comes to mind, you would be more likely than chance to complete "LIC___" as "LICENSE" because you have encountered the word recently. Importantly, these effects occur even if you do not recall having seen the word *license* in the previous paragraph (but teasing apart the influences of conscious and unconscious contributions to this is no simple matter; see Buchner & Wippich, 2000; Jacoby, 1991; Jacoby, Toth, & Yonelinas, 1993).

An important aspect of episodic memory, as already noted in the last chapter, is that episodic memories are integrated mental representations. Different bits and pieces of information from different parts of our conscious and unconscious mental worlds are woven together to form the fabric of episodic memory. In Chapter 5 we introduced the episodic buffer, the component of working memory that integrated different types of knowledge together to form episodic memories. Although many of the examples given in this chapter may rely on linguistic materials, such as word lists, episodic memories are formed from an integrated combination of various types of information, including sensory information, motor information, spatial knowledge, language, emotions, narrative, and other explicit memory encoding and retrieval processes (Rubin, 2007). Even this is not an exhaustive list. So, as you can see, episodic memory is a memory system that uses a rich and wide variety of information about a broad range of human experience, which also gives it a lot of flexibility.

The main focus of this chapter is on explicit, episodic memory, although we'll cover some issues about implicit memory as well. We progress through the evidence, covering what is known about the storage and retrieval factors that influence how we learn and remember. In the final section of the chapter, we discuss implicit memory the same way the rest of cognitive psychology encountered it: by coming to terms with the evidence about memory loss in cases of amnesia.

PRELIMINARY ISSUES

Let's start on the topic of episodic memory by considering three preliminary issues. First, we will talk about a classic, ancient approach to learning and memory, mnemonic devices. We'll then spend a little time on the first systematic research ever done on human memory, Ebbinghaus's pioneering work, published in 1885. These topics suggest that people have always been aware of some of the workings—and failings—of memory. Today we call such awareness *metamemory* or, more generally, *metacognition*; these terms refer to our understanding of our own memory and cognition. Here's a warning: As you read the three chapters on long-term memory, bear in mind that just as your frustrations about your own memory problems probably are exaggerated, so is your certainty about remembering. It's a genuine paradox; our memories are better than we often give ourselves credit for, and worse than we are often willing to believe or admit.

Mnemonic Devices

The term *mnemonic* (pronounced "*ne-MAHN-ick*") means "to help the memory"; it comes from the same Indo-European base word as *remember, mind*, and *think*. A **mnemonic device** is an *active, strategic learning device or method*, a rehearsal strategy. Formal mnemonic devices use preestablished sets of aids and considerable practice on the to-be-remembered information in connection with the preestablished set. The strengths of mnemonic techniques include the following principles: (1) The material to be remembered is practiced repeatedly, (2) the material is integrated into an existing memory framework, and (3) the device provides a means of retrieving the information. We'll cover two traditional mnemonic devices, and then turn to the issue of inventing new ones as the need arises.

CLASSIC MNEMONICS The first historical mention of mnemonics is in Cicero's *De oratore*, a Latin treatise on rhetoric (the art of public speaking, which in Greek and Roman days meant speaking from memory). The power of mnemonics is tremendous; among other things, mnemonic devices enabled Greek orators to memorize and recite entire epics such as *The Iliad* and *The Odyssey* (see Yates, 1966). Cicero describes a technique based on visual imagery and memorized locations. The mnemonic is called the **method of loci** (*loci* is the plural of *locus*, meaning "a place"; pronounced "*LOW-sigh*").

There are two keys to the method of loci: first, the memorized physical locations; and second, the mental images of the to-be-remembered items, one per location. First, choose a known set of locations that can be recalled easily and in order. You might select a set of 10 or 12 locations you encounter in a walk across campus, or as you arrive home. Now form a mental image of the first thing you want to remember and mentally place that thing into the first location, continuing with the second item in the second location, and so on. Form a good mental image of the item in its place (McDaniel & Einstein, 1986). When it's time to recall the items, all you need to do is mentally stroll through your set of locations, "looking" at the places and "seeing" the items you have placed there. Although there is some evidence that a more bizarre image can be more memorable when used occasionally (Burns, 1996; Einstein & McDaniel, 1987), there is

TABLE 6-1 The Method of Loci

Set of Loci	Word to Be Remembered	Grocery List and Images
Driveway	Grapefruit	Grapefruit instead of rocks along side of driveway
Garage door	Tomatoes	Tomatoes splattered on garage door
Front door of house	Lettuce	Lettuce leaves hanging over door instead of awning
Coat closet	Oatmeal	Oatmeal oozing out the door when I hang up my coat
Fireplace	Milk	Fire got out of control, so spray milk instead of water
Easy chair	Sugar	Throw pillow is a 5 pound bag of sugar
Television	Coffee	Mrs. Olson advertising coffee
Dining-room table	Carrots	Legs of table are made of carrots

also an important role for the distinctiveness of the image (Kroll, Schepeler, & Angin, 1986). Some (e.g., Hirshman, Whelley, & Palij, 1989) suggest that the "surprise response" of encountering something that violates your expectations is part of this distinctiveness effect (wouldn't you be surprised to see a horse up in a tree?). Table 6-1 gives an example of this technique.

Another mnemonic device is the **peg word mnemonic** (Miller, Galanter, & Pribram, 1960), in which *a prememorized set of words serves as a sequence of mental "pegs" onto which the to-be-remembered material can be "hung."* The peg words rely on rhymes with the numbers one through ten, such as "One is a bun, two is a shoe," and so on (Table 6-2). The to-be-learned material is then hung on the pegs, item by item, making sure that the rhyming word and the to-be-remembered item form a mental image. For the list "cup, flag, horse, dollar . . .," create a visual image of a flattened tin cup, dripping with ketchup, inside your hamburger bun; for flag, conjure up a visual image of your running shoes

TABLE 6-2 The Peg Word Mnemonic Device

Numbered Pegs	Word to Be Learned	Image
One is a bun	Cup	Hamburger bun with smashed cup
Two is a shoe	Flag	Running shoes with flag
Three is a tree	Horse	Horse stranded in top of tree
Four is a door	Dollar	Dollar bill tacked to front door
Five is a hive	Brush	Queen bee brushing her hair
Six is sticks	Pan	Boiling a pan full of cinnamon sticks
Seven is Heaven	Clock	St. Peter checking the clock at the gates of Heaven
Eight is a gate	Pen	A picket fence gate with ballpoint pens as pickets
Nine is a vine	Paper	Honeysuckle vine with newspapers instead of blossoms
Ten is a hen	Shirt	A baked hen on the platter wearing a flannel shirt

with little American flags fluttering in the breeze as you run; and so on (go ahead and form images for the rest of the list as an exercise to understand the principles of mnemonic devices). Now at recall, all you have to do is first remember what peg word rhymes with one, then retrieve the bun image you created, looking inside to see a cup. Similarly, what peg word rhymes with *two*, and what image do you find along with *shoe?*

THE THREE MNEMONIC PRINCIPLES Mnemonic effectiveness involves three principles. First, it provides a structure for learning, for acquiring the information. The structure may be elaborate, like a set of 40 loci, or simple, like rhyming peg words. It can even be arbitrary if the material is not particularly extensive. (The mnemonic *HOMES* for the names of the five Great Lakes—Huron, Ontario, Michigan, Erie, and Superior—isn't related to the to-be-remembered material, but it is quite simple.)

Second, using visual images, rhymes, or other kinds of associations and the effort and rehearsal necessary to form them, the mnemonic helps create a durable and distinctive record of the material in memory, one that won't easily be forgotten (what's sticking out of your running shoes?). Therefore, the mnemonic helps safeguard against various kinds of loss in memory (but see Thomas & Wang, 1996, for somewhat less optimistic results concerning the long-term benefits of some mnemonic systems).

Finally, the mnemonic guides you through retrieval by providing effective cues for recalling the information. As we discuss later, this function of the mnemonic device is critically important because much of what we call forgetting seems often to be a case of retrieval difficulty. In fact, it can't be stressed enough how the active use of retrieval cues—and practicing retrieval—are important for successful performance (extended retrieval practice was the key in Chaffin & Imreh's [2002] study of how a concert pianist learned, remembered, and performed a challenging piece).

This three-step sequence may sound familiar to you and will surely become more so throughout this chapter. It is the sequence we talk about every time we consider learning and memory: the *encoding* of new information, its *retention* over time, and *retrieval* of the information (Melton, 1963). Your performance in any situation that involves memory depends on all three steps. Any one of the three might be the faulty process that accounts for poor performance, and all three must be done successfully for good performance. A good mnemonic device, including those you invent for yourself (e.g., Wenger & Payne, 1995), will ensure success at each of the three stages. (Incidentally, don't count on some magic bullet to enhance your memory. Research has found little if any evidence that ginkgo biloba or any other "memory enhancer," including the use of "subliminal learning" tapes, actually has any real effect at all; Gold, Cahill, & Wenk, 2002, 2003; Greenwald, Spangenberg, Pratkanis, & Eskenazi, 1991; McDaniel, Maier, & Einstein, 2002).

The Ebbinghaus Tradition of Memory Research

We turn now to the first systematic research on human learning and memory, done by the first serious human memory investigator, German psychologist Hermann von Ebbinghaus.

As indicated in Chapter 1, the Ebbinghaus tradition began more than 100 years ago, with his publication of *Uber das Gedachtnis* (1885; the English translation, first published in 1913 and reprinted in 1964, is *Memory: A Contribution to Experimental Psychology*). As is commonly known, Ebbinghaus used only himself as a subject in his studies.

In the process of his investigations, he had to invent his own memory task, his own experimental stimuli, and his own set of procedures for testing and data analysis. Few could do as well today. In devising how to analyze his results, he even came close to inventing what we now would call a within-groups *t* test (Ebbinghaus, 1885/1964, footnote 1, p. 67). We tend to think of Ebbinghaus merely as the inventor of the nonsense syllable, the meaningless consonant-vowel-consonant (CVC) trigrams that he used as items in his studies. This is a seriously impoverished view of Ebbinghaus' contributions.

THE EBBINGHAUS RESEARCH To begin with, it is helpful to consider *why* Ebbinghaus felt compelled to invent and use nonsense syllables (or at least, items that varied in meaningfulness; Hoffman, Bringmann, Bamberg, & Klein, 1987). His rationale was that he wanted to study the properties of memory and forgetting, the fundamentals, apart from the influence of prior knowledge. As such, words would complicate his results. If he had used words it would be less clear whether his performance reflected the simple exercise of memory, or the influence of his prior knowledge. Putting it simply, *learning* seems to imply acquiring *new* information. Yet words are not new, so "learning" a list of words in some sense is a misnomer. And a control factor he adopted, to reduce the possible intrusion of mnemonic factors, was the rapid presentation rate of 2.5 items per second (note his accurate metacognition here, that mnemonic and rehearsal processes take time).

The task Ebbinghaus devised, his only experimental task, was the **relearning task**, in which *a list is originally learned, set aside for a period of time, then later relearned to the same criterion of accuracy*. In most cases, this criterion was one perfect recitation of the list, without hesitations. After relearning the list, Ebbinghaus computed the **savings score** as the measure of learning; the savings score was simply *the reduction, if any, in the number of trials (or the time) necessary for relearning, compared to original learning*. Thus, if it took 10 trials to originally learn a list but only 6 for relearning, there was a 40% savings (4 fewer trials on relearning divided by the 10 original trials). By this method, *any* information that was left over in memory from original learning could have an influence, conscious or not (see Nelson, 1978, 1985; Schacter, 1987). Work by MacLeod (1988) indicates that the influence of relearning is on the recall phase; that is, relearning seems to help retrieve information that was stored in memory yet is not recallable.

Figure 6-2 presents Ebbinghaus' forgetting curve, showing the reduction in savings as a function of time until relearning (see Slamecka, 1985, for details on the huge number of learning trials Ebbinghaus subjected himself to in his research; for Figure 6-2, he learned and relearned more than 1,200 lists of nonsense syllables). Ebbinghaus relearned the lists after one of seven intervals: 20 min, 1 hr, 9 hr, 1 day, 2 days, 6 days, or 31 days. As is clear from the figure, the most dramatic forgetting occurs early after original learning. This is followed by a decrease in the rate of forgetting; a full 42% was forgotten at 20 min, 56% at 1 hr, 64% after 9 hr, and so on. These forgetting functions have been reanalyzed, and they follow the same function as obtained in a variety of other memory tests (technically, a negatively accelerating power function; Wixted & Ebbesen, 1991).

Other fundamental results Ebbinghaus obtained were impressive not because they were surprising, but because they were the first empirical demonstrations of them. For example, he investigated the effects of repetitions, studying one list 32

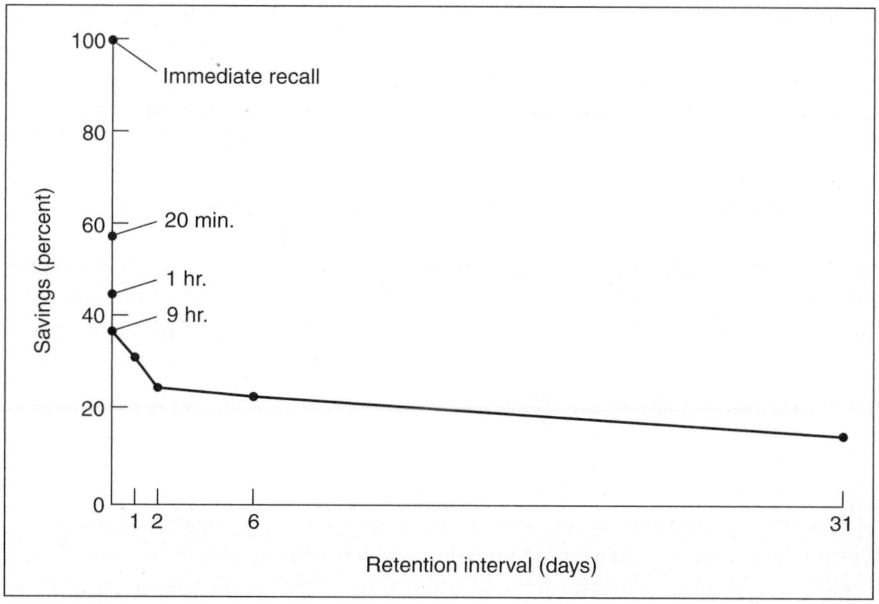

FIGURE 6-2 The classic forgetting curve from Ebbinghaus (1885/1913). The figure shows the reduction in savings across increasing retention intervals (time between original learning and relearning).

times and another 64 times. Upon relearning, the more frequently repeated list showed about twice the savings of the less frequently repeated list; in other words, *overlearning* yields a stronger record in memory. Longer lists took more trials to learn than shorter lists but showed higher savings upon relearning. In essence, although it is harder to learn a long list originally, the longer list is then remembered better, because there was more opportunity to overlearn it (there were more trials in learning before eventual mastery of the whole list). The connection between difficulty of learning and memory has been confirmed repeatedly across the years (e.g., Schneider, Healy, & Bourne, 2002).

Finally, in one study (Chapter 8), Ebbinghaus continued to relearn the same set of lists across a five-day period. The savings scores showed no forgetting at all. As an interesting contrast here, Ebbinghaus also reported his results on relearning passages of poetry (kept at 80 syllables). After the fourth day of learning, the savings was 100%.

EVALUATING THE EBBINGHAUS TRADITION There is no disagreement that Ebbinghaus had a tremendous impact on the field of verbal learning and, later, cognitive psychology. In a set of papers commemorating the 100th anniversary of the 1885 publication, a consensus emerged about the value of his work. On the one hand, Ebbinghaus' contribution represented "a door being opened into the human mind, the realization—contrary to then established wisdom—that it is in fact possible to gain positive knowledge about human memory" (Mandler, 1985, p. 464). Slamecka (1985) simply called him "the founder of our discipline."

On the other hand, he studied the learning of nonsense syllables, deliberately excluding meaning from his studies. Much subsequent research, up through the 1960s (and even the 1970s), continued to use nonsense syllables, even as it became clearer that such results were missing the central point: If people constantly use mediating, mnemonic, and rehearsal strategies to memorize information, then we should be investigating that, not trying to prevent it. A more balanced, temperate view is that in the absence of prior research, Ebbinghaus quite properly simplified the experimental situation so as to get interpretable results (Kintsch, 1985), a research strategy that is no longer necessary. The fault lies less with Ebbinghaus than with his successors, who slavishly stuck to his methods without questioning their intent or usefulness.

THE CURRENT POSITION If we consider the position that is accepted today and contrast it with the model of Ebbinghaus' research, we arrive at the study of episodic long-term memory. Today's view consists of at least three parts. First, people invent meaning, regardless of the experimenter's wishes. Human memory relies heavily on meaning and this should be the focus of our research. Second, we also recognize that the participants in memory experiments are active. They do not recite syllables passively to make an impression on memory, but instead are intent on applying mental resources and strategies to almost every learning situation.

The third part of the current view is that results based on meaningless stimuli are of limited use when we attempt to understand how people learn and remember. This is an issue of ecological validity, saying in essence that traditional laboratory results do not apply to real-world situations. This is too strong a position; much evidence from laboratory tasks does generalize to real-world settings. Still, issues of autobiographical memory, false memories, and thematic influences on memory would not have been studied if we had stuck with relatively impoverished experimental stimuli and list learning paradigms.

Metamemory

Think about these two issues, mnemonics and Ebbinghaus' groundbreaking work, from a larger perspective: They both involve intuitions about memory, what makes remembering easier or harder. This self-awareness about the workings of memory is known as **metamemory**, *knowledge about (meta) one's own memory, how it works, and how it fails to work*. In most researchers' view, metamemory is a part of a broader self-awareness called **metacognition**, *knowledge about one's own cognitive system and its functioning.*

Research on these topics has raised at least two important issues. First is the importance of metacognitive awareness. A number of studies have focused on metacognitive judgments, such as people's "judgments-of-learning" and "feeling-of-knowing" estimates (Leonesio & Nelson, 1990; Nelson, 1988). It is clear that part of a person's behavior in a learning task—at least for a motivated adult—involves self-monitoring, assessing how well one is doing and adjusting study strategies based on that assessment (e.g., Son, 2004). These metacognitions are helpful in guiding people to know when to change their answers on multiple choice exams (Higham & Garrard, 2005). However, metacognitive awareness can occasionally mislead us, leading to either over- or under-confidence that we've learned something (e.g., Koriat, Sheffer, & Ma'ayan, 2002).

The second issue involves self-regulation, what you do with your metacognitive awareness. If you realize you are not doing some task particularly well, what mental processes or procedures do you follow to improve your performance? How do you improve your performance? Some of the research on metacognition gives some insight into some of the difficulties people have. For example, Mazzoni and Cornoldi (1993) report that people often "labor in vain," that is devote more study time to difficult items, and yet do not improve performance much at all (see also Nelson, 1993; Metcalfe, 2002). Alternatively, Thiede (1999; see also Metcalfe & Kornell, 2003) argues that when study time is used in appropriate ways, a positive, sensible relationship between monitoring and self-regulation emerges. This is what Son and Metcalfe (2000) call the *region of proximal learning*, studying information that is just beyond one's current knowledge and saving the more difficult material for later. The problem is that people are often poor judges of what they have and have not learned, and make choices about what to study based on this inaccurate information (Metcalfe & Finn, 2008).

Section Summary

- Long-term memory is a multicomponent system, with a major division between declarative memories and nondeclarative memories. Declarative memory consists of two major parts, episodic and semantic memories; nondeclarative memory includes priming and procedural or motor learning. Declarative memories can be verbalized, but nondeclarative memories cannot; conscious awareness of the memory is unnecessary for implicit memory tasks but always accompanies explicit memory tasks.
- A classic method for improving memory involves mnemonic devices, specialized strategies that ensure adequate storage of the information and provide a systematic method for retrieval. Classic mnemonic devices, such as the method of loci, use a variety of techniques, especially visual imagery, to improve performance; familiarity with the mnemonic method provides a foundation for understanding both storage and retrieval effects in memory performance.
- Ebbinghaus was the first person to do extensive investigations of learning and forgetting. Working on his own, he invented methods for doing such studies. The relearning task revealed a sensitivity to the demands of simple recall tasks; such tasks tap consciously retrievable information but may underestimate the amount of information learned and retained. The classic forgetting curve he obtained, along with his results on practice effects, inspired the tradition of verbal learning and, later, cognitive psychology. Several of his empirical and methodological insights reflect metacognitive awareness.

STORING INFORMATION IN EPISODIC MEMORY

How do people store information in episodic memory? How is new information recorded in long-term memory so that it is preserved until some future time when it is needed? And how can we measure this storage of information? Ebbinghaus' research investigated one kind of storage variable, repetition, and one memory task, relearning. He found that an increase in the number of repetitions led to a stronger memory, a *trace* of the information in memory that could be relearned more quickly. This suggests that frequency is a fundamental variable in learning: Information that is presented more frequently is stored more strongly in memory.

A corollary of this is that people should be good at remembering how frequently something has occurred. Hasher and Zacks (1984) summarize a large body of research on how sensitive people are to the frequency of events. Because people's estimates of relative frequency generally are good, they proposed that frequency information is encoded into memory in an automatic fashion, with no deliberate effort or intent. Although just how automatic this is has been disputed (Greene, 1986; Hanson & Hirst, 1988; Jonides & Jones, 1992), there is no doubt that event frequency has a large impact on long-term memory. (See Anderson & Schooler, 1991, and Schooler & Anderson, 1997, for the intriguing relationship between the need to retrieve information from memory and the frequency or recency of that information in the environment.)

The flip side of frequency is distinctiveness. Isn't it easier to remember an unusual, unexpected, or distinctive event than a more conventional one? There is a long history of studies of this topic, technically called the **isolation effect**, but more commonly known as the **von Restorff effect**, named after the woman who did the first study (von Restorff, 1933). The effect is simply *improved memory for one piece of information that is distinct from the information around it*, such as printing one word in a list in red ink or changing its size (Cooper & Pantle, 1967; Kelley & Nairne, 2001; Schmidt, 2002, showed photos of 15 models, one of which was nude). The isolation effect clearly relies on memory for the list in order for the distinctive item to be noticed as distinctive. In a study by Kishiyama, Yonelinas, and Lazzara (2004) people who were amnesic (as a result of damage to their medial temporal lobes and hippocampus) did not show the von Restorff effect (see Figure 6-3). ★ That is, because they could not remember the other items in the list very well, they could not identify the isolated item as unique, and so it did not stand out in memory. Thus distinctiveness, which normally results in better memory retrieval, was simply not effective for this group of people.

More generally, the isolation effect is probably the metacognitive basis for highlighting passages in your textbook—the distinctiveness of the color compared to the white background of the page makes that passage noticeable, and calls your attention to it. Too much highlighting, of course, renders none of the passages distinctive!

But what about more typical situations, when the world doesn't highlight the material for you to make it either more frequent or distinctive? How do you learn and remember something new, such as a list of words or a list of seven themes in a cognition textbook? We consider three important storage effects here: rehearsal, organization, and imagery. A summary of these will then lead us to the topic of retrieval and a discussion of forgetting.

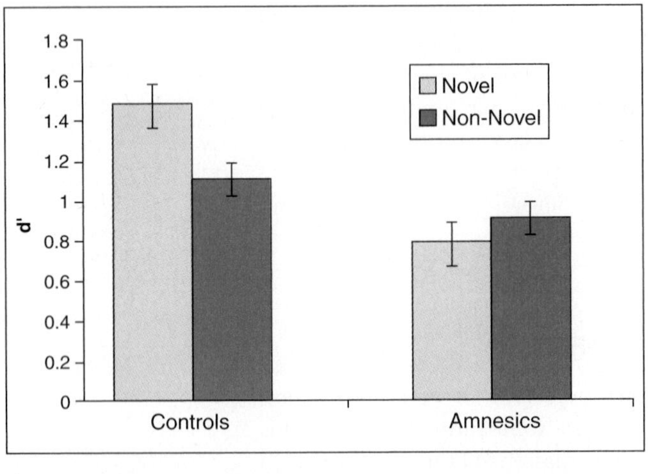

★ **FIGURE 6-3**
Accuracy data from Kishiyama, Yonelinas, and Lazzara (2004) (using the signal detection measure of d') showing memory for a novel distinctive item (the von Restorff effect) for normal controls on the left and amnesics on the right. Notice that performance is better for the novel information for the normal controls, but not for the amnesics.

Rehearsal

Why do we rehearse?

Atkinson and Shiffrin (1968) made a fundamental statement on storage in their model of human memory. In their theory, information in short-term memory may be subjected to **rehearsal**, *a deliberate recycling or practicing of the contents of the short-term store.* They proposed two effects of rehearsal. First, rehearsal maintains information in the short-term store. Second, the longer an item is held in short-term memory, the more likely that it will also be stored in long-term memory. Basically, the idea is that rehearsal "copies" the item into long-term memory, with the strength of the long-term memory trace depending on the amount of rehearsal. In short, rehearsal transfers information into long-term memory (see also Waugh & Norman, 1965).

Frequency of Rehearsal

What evidence is there of this effect of rehearsal? Aside from Ebbinghaus', many experiments have shown that rehearsal leads to better long-term retention. For example, Hellyer (1962) used the Brown–Peterson task, with CVC trigrams, and with an arithmetic task between study and recall. On some trials the trigram had to be spoken aloud one, two, four, or eight times. Figure 6-4 shows the results. The more frequently an item was rehearsed, the better it was retained across the distracting period. However, while repetition and rehearsal do clearly improve memory, more recent work suggests that it is not the repeated study that produces the primary memory benefit, but rather the repeated attempts at trying to remember that help (Karpicke & Roediger, 2007). ▲

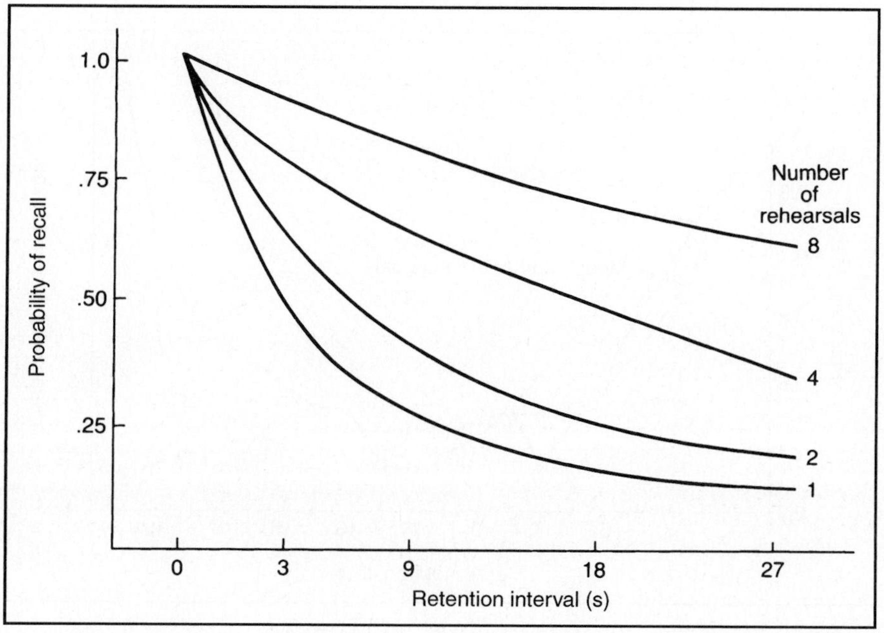

▲ **FIGURE 6-4**
Hellyer's (1962) recall accuracy results as a function of the number of rehearsals afforded the three-letter nonsense syllable and the retention interval.

REHEARSAL AND SERIAL POSITION EFFECTS More evidence on the effects of rehearsal was provided in a series of studies by Rundus (1971; Rundus & Atkinson, 1970). In these experiments, Rundus had people learn 20-item lists of unrelated words, presenting them at a rate of 5 s per word. People were asked to rehearse aloud as they studied the lists, repeating whatever words they cared to during each 5 s presentation. Rundus then tabulated the number of times each of the words was rehearsed and compared this to the likelihood of later recalling the word correctly. Figure 6-5 shows his most telling results. In the early primacy portion of the serial position effect, there was a direct positive relationship between the frequency of rehearsal and the probability of recall. In other words, the primacy effect was entirely dependent on rehearsal. The early items can be rehearsed more frequently and so are recalled better. High recall of the late positions, the recency effect, was viewed as recall from short-term memory, which is why they were recalled so well despite being rehearsed so little.

Although we discussed serial position curves in Chapter 5 with respect to short-term memory, generally serial position curves are observed in long-term memory as well. That is, given an event of a certain type, such as going to the movies, people are likely to remember their first and last experiences better, and not so much those in the middle (e.g., Sehulster, 1989). This even applies to semantic information, such as knowledge of the Presidents of the United States (Roediger & Crowder, 1976). While some people have argued that the cognitive machinery involved in long-term memory is a result of different processes than those observed in short-term memory (Davelaar, Goshen-Gottstein, Ashkenazi, Haarmann, & Usher, 2005), there has also been some effort to suggest that the same principles are driving serial position curves in both the short and long-term memory (e.g., Brown, Neath, & Chater, 2007).

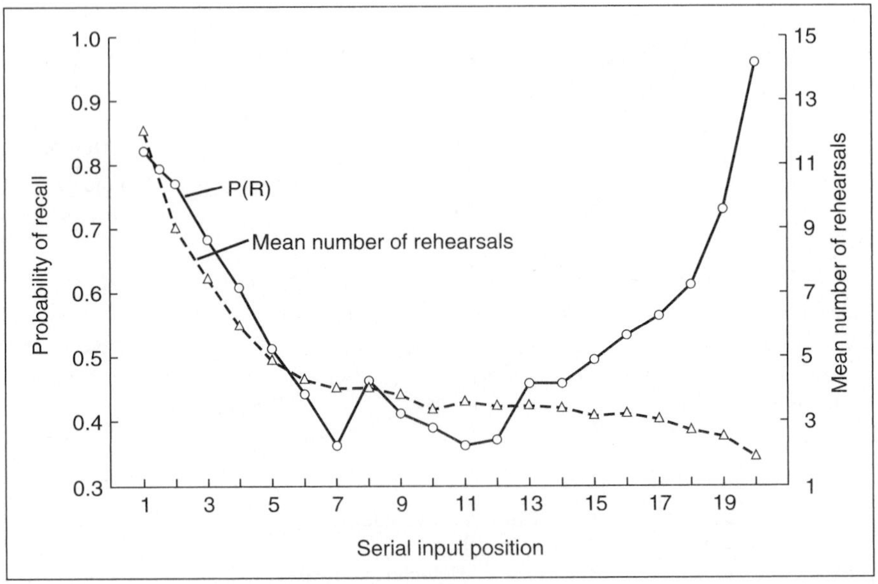

FIGURE 6-5
In the figure, the probability of recall, P(R), is plotted against the left axis, and the number of rehearsals afforded an item during storage is plotted against the right axis. The similar pattern of these two functions across the primacy portion of the list indicates that rehearsal is the factor responsible for primacy effects.

Two Kinds of Rehearsal

A more refined view of rehearsal is the idea that there are two kinds of rehearsal, each with different effects on storage (Craik & Lockhart, 1972). **Maintenance rehearsal** is *low-level, repetitive information recycling.* This is the rehearsal you would use to recycle a phone number to yourself until you dial it. The idea is that once you stop rehearsing, the information leaves no permanent record in memory. In Craik and Lockhart's view, maintenance rehearsal maintains information at a particular level in memory, without storing it permanently. As long as information is subjected to maintenance rehearsal, it can be retrieved. Once the maintenance rehearsal stops, however, it will likely vanish.

Elaborative rehearsal is *a more complex rehearsal that uses the meaning of the information to help store and remember it.* When information is subjected to elaborative rehearsal, according to Craik and Lockhart, the information is stored more deeply in memory, and makes contact with the meaning of the information. As a consequence, material that was rehearsed elaboratively should be more permanently available; in short, it should be remembered better. You might include imagery or mnemonic elaboration in your elaborative rehearsal, you might try to construct sentences from the words in a list you are trying to learn, you might impose some organization or structure on the list, or you might even try to convert nonsense syllables like BEF into more meaningful items like BEEF. Stating it differently, maintenance rehearsal maintains an item at its current level of storage, whereas elaborative rehearsal moves the item more deeply, and stores it more permanently, into memory.

Depth of Processing

Craik and Lockhart (1972) proposed a theory of memory very different from the stage approach of sensory, short-, and long-term memory. They embedded their two kinds of rehearsal into what they called **levels of processing**, or **depth of processing**, framework. The essence of this framework is as follows. Information receives some amount of mental processing. Items receiving only incidental attention are processed at a shallow level (as in hearing the sounds of the words without attending to meaning, as a daydreamer might do during a lecture). Other items are subjected to more intentional and meaningful processing. This deeper processing elaborates the representation of that item in memory, for example, by drawing relationships between already-known information and what is being processed.

Several predictions from the depth of processing framework were tested with a fair degree of initial success. For example, if information is processed shallowly, with only maintenance rehearsal, then the information should not be particularly memorable later; if it is only maintained, then it should not be stored at a deep, meaningful level in long-term memory. This was the kind of result that was obtained. As an example, Craik and Watkins (1973) devised a monitoring task; people heard a long list of words but only had to keep track of the most recent word beginning with, say, a *G*. In a surprise recall test, people showed no recall differences for "*G*-words" held a long time versus those maintained only briefly (see also Craik & Tulving, 1975).

Challenges to Depth of Processing

A useful development associated with the depth of processing approach was a set of tasks often used to test the theory. Basically, people would be given a page filled with words and asked to do some task. For instance, one group might be asked to check off all the words containing the letter *e*, another might be asked to check words that rhyme with *door*, and another to check off the words naming types of animals. Going from letters to rhymes to word meaning meant deeper processing, and better memory later on. These were *incidental learning* conditions, i.e., learning was incidental to the task instructions, not an intended part of the task (there would always be another group, given intentional learning instructions, to use as a comparison). This comparison of intentional and incidental learning is still useful in a variety of settings.

Nonetheless, as research proceeded and difficulties cropped up, enthusiasm for the depth of processing approach began to dim. Much of this was caused by Baddeley's (1978) review paper "The Trouble with Levels." A major point in this review concerned the problem of defining levels independently of retention scores (see Glenberg & Adams, 1978; Glenberg, Smith, & Green, 1977). In essence, no method existed for deciding ahead of time whether a particular kind of rehearsal would prompt shallow or deep processing. Instead, we had to wait and see whether it improved recall. If it did, it must have been elaborative rehearsal; if it did not, it must have been maintenance rehearsal. (So, for example, our intuition is that checking off words with the letter *e* represents superficial, shallow processing—but if learning were strong in that condition, we might be tempted to claim, after the fact, that even scanning words for a particular letter involved elaborative processing.) The circularity of this reasoning should be obvious; higher recall is the evidence that elaborative rehearsal was involved in a task, but the same higher recall is also the evidence that shows that elaborative rehearsal improves recall.

TASK EFFECTS A second point in Baddeley's (1978) review concerned task effects. That is, a genuine difficulty arose with the levels of processing approach when different memory tasks were used. The reason for the difficulty was simply that very different results were obtained using one or another task.

We have known since Ebbinghaus that different memory tasks shed different kinds of light on the variables that affect performance. Ebbinghaus used a relearning task, so that even material that was difficult to retrieve might have a chance of influencing performance. In a similar vein, a substantial difference generally is found between performance on recall and **recognition tasks**. In recognition, people are shown items that were originally studied, known as "old" or target items, as well as items that were not on the studied list, known as "new" or distractor items. They must then decide which items are targets and which are distractors. Recognition accuracy usually is much higher than it is with recall (see Table 6-3 for a list and description of all these tasks). Furthermore, recognition performance is influenced by two different factors, recollection—the actual remembering of the information—and familiarity—the general sense that you've experienced the information before (e.g., Curran, 2000; Yonelinas, 2002). Indeed, studies on false memory that you'll read about in Chapter 8 often ask participants whether they actually "remember" experiencing the event in question or whether they just "know" that it happened. Such procedures acknowledge openly that recognition (and recall, in some settings) can be influenced by both recollection and familiarity.

TABLE 6-3 Standard Memory Tasks and Terminology ◆

Relearning Task

1. Original learning: Learn list items (e.g., list of unrelated words) to some accuracy criterion.
2. Delay after learning the list.
3. Learn the list a second time.

Dependent variables: The main dependent variable is the savings score: how many fewer trials are needed during relearning relative to number of trials for the original learning. If the original learning took 10 trials and relearning took 6, then relearning took 4 fewer trials. S score = 4/10; expressed as a percentage, savings was 40%.

Independent or control variables: Rate of presentation, type of list items, length of list, accuracy criterion.

Paired-Associate Learning Task

1. A list of pairs is shown, one pair at a time. The first member of the pair is called the stimulus, and the second member is the response (e.g., for the pair "ice–brush," "ice" is the stimulus term and "brush" is the correct response).
2. After one study trial, the stimulus terms are shown, one at a time, and the person tries to name the correct response term for that stimulus.
3. Typically, the task involves several successive attempts at learning, each attempt including first a study trial then a test trial; the order of the pairs is changed each time. In the anticipation method, there is just one continuous stream of trials, each consisting of two parts: presenting the stimulus alone, then presenting the stimulus and response together. Across repetitions, people begin to learn the correct pairings.

Dependent variables: Typically the number of study test trials to achieve correct responding to all stimulus terms ("trials to criterion") is the dependent variable.

Independent and control variables: Presentation rate, length of list, the types of items in the stimulus and response term lists, and the types of connections between them. Very commonly, once a list had been mastered, then either the stimulus or response terms would be changed, or the item pairings would be rearranged (e.g., "ice–brush" and "card–floor" in the first list, then "ice–floor" and "card–brush" on the second list).

Recall Task

Serial Recall Task: Learn the list information, then recall the items in their original order of presentation.

Free Recall Task: Learn the list information, then recall the items in any order.

1. Learn list items.
2. Optional delay or distractor task during delay.
3. Recall list items.

Dependent variables: The main dependent variable is the number (or percentage) of list items recalled correctly. If multiple lists are presented, recall accuracy often is scored as a function of the original position of the items in the list. Occasionally, other dependent variables involve order, speed, or organization of recall (e.g., items recalled by category—"apple, pear, banana, orange"—before a different category was recalled in a free recall task).

Independent or control variables: Rate of presentation (usually experimenter paced), type of list items, length of list.

Recognition Task (Episodic)

1. Learn list items.
2. Optional delay or distractor task during delay.
3. Make yes/no decisions to the items in a test list: "Yes," the item was on the original list, or "no," it was not on the original list. This is often called deciding whether the item is "old," that is, on the original list, or if it is "new," not on the original list. Old items are also called targets, and new items are also called distractors or lures.

Dependent variables: In episodic tasks, the dependent variable usually is a measure of accuracy, such as the percentage correct on the test list. Correct decisions on old items can be called hits, and incorrect decisions on new items can be called false alarms.

Independent or control variables: Same as in recall tasks.

Recognition is easier and takes much less effort than recall; indeed, recognition does not seem to require deliberate retrieval at all because the answer is presented to the person, who then only has to make a new versus old decision. Because more information is stored in memory than can be retrieved easily, recognition generally shows greater sensitivity to the influence of stored information (the issue of *how much* easier recognition is than recall is difficult to resolve, however; see research on the attentional demands of recognition by Craik, Govoni, Naveh-Benjamin, & Anderson, 1996, and by Hicks & Marsh, 2000).

The relevance of this to the issue of depth of processing is simply that most of the early research that supported the levels of processing approach used recall tasks. When recognition was used, however, maintenance rehearsal had clear effects on long-term memory. A clever set of studies by Glenberg, Smith, and Green (1977) confirmed this. Glenberg et al. used a standard Brown–Peterson task, asking people to remember a four-digit number as the (supposedly) primary task. During retention intervals that varied in duration, people had to repeat either one or three words aloud as a distractor task (don't confuse the distractor task here with distractor items, items tested in recognition that were not shown originally). Because people were led to believe that digit recall was the important task, they presumably devoted only minimal effort to the word repetitions; that is, they probably used only maintenance rehearsal. After the supposedly "main" part of the task was complete, the people were given a surprise recall task; the results showed the standard effect. But when they were given a surprise recognition task, the amount of time spent rehearsing *did* influence performance; words rehearsed for 18 s were recognized significantly better than those rehearsed for shorter intervals.

In the depth of processing view, shallow processing should always lead to poorer retention than deep, semantic processing. Yet the Glenberg et al. studies disconfirmed this central prediction; mere repetition in short-term memory did affect retention (see Wixted, 1991, for a report on the positive effects of maintenance rehearsal and the metacognitive effects of deciding which type of rehearsal to use). Shallow processing can result in equal or even superior performance. (But in general, elaborate, semantic processing will always help you improve your memory more than shallow, maintenance rehearsal.)

Generation and Enactment

A basic idea overarching the depth of processing account is that the more you do with information, the better it will be remembered. Apart from whether the depth of processing view per se is viable, there are numerous examples of how doing more with information makes it easier to remember later. In this section we'll look at two well-known effects that illustrate the basic principle that hard work has its rewards: the generation effect and the impact of enactment on memory.

The **generation effect** is the finding that *information you generate or create yourself is better remembered compared to information you only heard or read*. This effect was first reported by Slamecka and Graf (1978). In their study, for the *read* condition, people simply read words printed on cards. However, for the *generate* condition people needed to generate the word. This was done by giving a word and the first letter of the word that was to be recalled, with the instruction that the to-be-generated word had to be related to the word that was read. For example a person might see Long-S______ where the word "short" needed to be generated. The results showed that people remembered words better when they were generated as compared to when they were just read.

In their extensive review of work on the generation effect, Bertsch, Pesta, Wiscott, and McDaniel (2007) reported that this very robust finding was more likely to occur with free recall, when people had to generate more of the information themselves, and that the effect grew larger over longer delays. Importantly, the generation effect does not only apply to lists of words, but also to textbook material (e.g., deWinstanley & Bjork, 2004). In short, the generation effect is another example that the more effort you put into mentally processing information, the more likely it will be remembered later, and for a longer time.

Another way to engage in deep encoding is to take advantage of the **enactment effect**, in which there is *improved memory for participant-performed tasks, relative to those that are not.* In such studies, we usually have one group of people actually do some activity, and we compare their performance to groups that either watch someone else doing the activity or groups that simply read about doing the activity. For example, a person might be told to "break the match," "point at the door," or "knock on the table," to watch someone else perform those actions, or to simply listen to the sentences. In general, people remember the items better if they were acted out compared to otherwise (e.g., Engelkamp & Dehn, 2000; Saltz & Donnenwerth-Nolan, 1981). In essence, the additional mental effort needed to engage in the task can be thought of as another form of deep processing because the person needs to spend more effort decoding the sentence, and then figuring out exactly what to do.

The value of the enactment effect can be seen in a more practical application, such as learning the lines of dialogue. Interestingly, there is now evidence that even untrained nonactors (i.e., novice actors) learn dialogue, as in the script of a play, better when the dialogue and stage movements are rehearsed together (Noice & Noice, 2001; see also Freeman & Ellis, 2003, and Shelton & McNamara, 2001, for other multimodality effects on learning). Physical movement, in other words, can be part of an enhanced mnemonic.

One possible explanation for the enactment effect is that this is another dual coding phenomenon, similar to what you read about with regard to mental imagery. That is, people may remember information better because they would have both a verbal and a motor code in memory, causing their performance to be better. However, this does not appear to be the case. Instead, enactment appears to improve memory for specific items by helping people better organize and structure information about the specific actions that they do (Koriat & Pearlman-Avnion, 2003). The idea that people are not engaged in dual coding is supported by the fact that the enactment effect is only observed for memory for individual actions, and there is not substantial memory improvement for learning a sequence of actions (e.g., Steffens, 2007). If the enactment effect were caused by a dual coding of information, then there should be a benefit for sequences of actions as well, but there is not.

Organization in Storage

Another vitally important piece of the storage puzzle involves **organization**, *the structuring or restructuring of information as it is being stored in memory.* Part of the importance of organization is derived from the influence it exerts: Well-organized material can be stored and retrieved with impressive levels of accuracy. The earliest research on organization (or clustering) was done by Bousfield. In his earliest study (Bousfield & Sedgewick, 1944), he asked people to name, for example, as many birds as they could. The result was that people tended to name the birds in subgroups, such as "robin, bluejay, sparrow—chicken, duck, goose—eagle, hawk." To study this further, Bousfield (1953) gave people a 60-item list to be learned for **free recall**, simply *a recall task in which the items can be recalled in any order*. Unlike other work at that time, Bousfield used related words for his lists, 15 words each from the categories *animals, personal names, vegetables*, and *professions*. Although the words were presented in a randomized order, people tended to recall them by category; for instance, "dog, cat, cow, pea, bean, John, Bob." Bousfield's interpretation was that the greater-than-chance grouping of items into clusters "implies the operation of an organizing tendency" (p. 237).

Where did this organizing tendency come from? Not from the words themselves—it would be foolish to say that the words exerted the tendency to organize themselves. No, the tendency was in the *participants*, in their unseen mental activities that went on during learning. Obviously, people noticed at some point that several words were drawn from the same categories. They used the reasonable strategy of grouping the items together on the basis of category (there is a nice metamemory effect here as well). This implies that people were reorganizing the list as it was presented. The consequence of this reorganization was straightforward: The way the material had been stored governed how it was recalled.

The power of organizational schemes for improving information storage in long-term memory was demonstrated convincingly by Bower, Clark, Lesgold, and Winzenz (1969). Four hierarchies of words were presented in the organized condition, arranged

GOOD ADVICE

Improving Your Memory

Baddeley (1978) was one of the critics of the depth of processing viewpoint, concluding that it was valuable only at a rough, intuitive level but not particularly as a scientific theory. Although that may be true, it is hard to beat Craik and Lockhart's insights if you're looking for a way to improve your own memory. Think of maintenance versus elaborative rehearsal as simple recycling in short-term memory versus meaningful study and transfer into long-term memory.

Apply this now to your own learning. When you are introduced to someone, do you merely recycle that name for a few seconds, or do you think about it, use it in conversation, and try to find mnemonic connections to help you remember it? When you read a text, do you merely process the words at a fairly simple level of understanding, or do you actively elaborate when you are reading, searching for connections and relationships that will make the material more memorable? In other words, incorporate the depth of processing ideas into your own metacognition. Try inventing a mnemonic (which will invoke the generation effect), applying elaborative rehearsal principles, or actively doing something with the information, such as drawing a diagram (which will invoke the enactment effect) to something you may need for this course, such as the seven themes of cognition presented in Chapter 2.

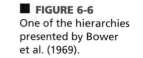

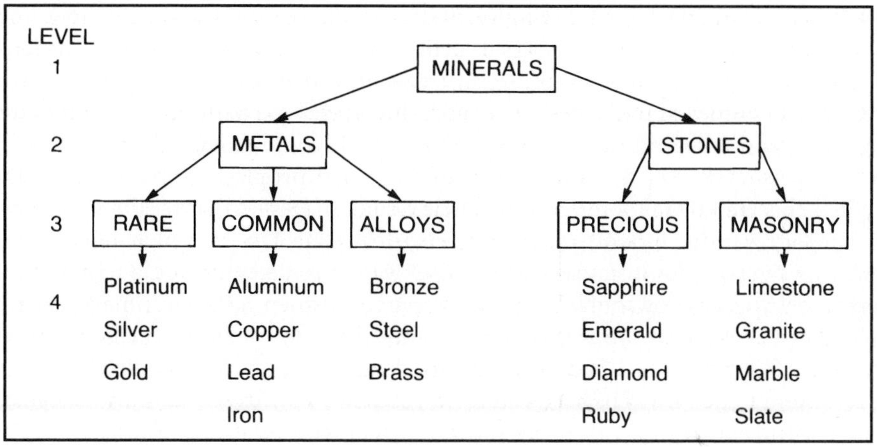

FIGURE 6-6 One of the hierarchies presented by Bower et al. (1969).

as lists with headers (one of the four hierarchies is shown in Figure 6-6); for instance, under *stones* was *precious*, and under that were *sapphire, emerald, diamond*, and *ruby*. The control group was shown words in the same physical arrangements, but the words were randomly assigned to their positions. Participants got four trials to learn all 112 words; their performance is shown in Table 6-4. Presenting the words in the hierarchically organized fashion led to 100% accuracy on Trials 3 and 4, an amazing feat given the number and unfamiliarity of the words. In contrast, the control group managed to recall only 70 words out of 112 by Trial 4, 62% accuracy.

This same organizational principle, if used effectively, can lead to what seem like astounding feats of memory. Individuals with exceptional memories, such as people who memorize *pi* out to insane numbers of digits, are essentially using this sort of basic organizational strategy (e.g., Ericsson, Delaney, Weaver, Mahadevan, 2004), along with other basic memory skills, such as imagery (e.g., Takahashi, Shimizu, Saito, & Tomoyori, 2006). This not only applies to words and numbers, but even to complex sets of information. As Anderson (1985) pointed out, a chapter outline can serve much the same function as the Bower et al. hierarchies, with obvious implications for students' study strategies (*there's* a strong hint).

Another reason for clustering studies was that they demonstrated people's strategies for learning in an obvious and objective fashion. Many studies used a free recall

TABLE 6-4 Average Percentage of Words Recalled over Four Trials as a Function of Organization

Conditions	1	2	3	4
Organized	65%	94.7%	100%	100%
Random	18.3	34.7	47.1	62.5

Adapted from Bower et al., 1969.

task, then examined the effects of different degrees of list organization, different numbers of categories, different numbers of items within categories, and so on. Clustering and organization were then examined in terms of a creative array of dependent variables, such as order of recall, degree of clustering, speed and patterning of pauses during recall, and rehearsal (see reviews by Johnson, 1970; Mandler, 1967, 1972). As an example, Ashcraft, Kellas, and Needham (1975) had people rehearse aloud as they studied clustered or randomized lists. Their results suggested that recalling the words by category was due to reorganization during rehearsal. That is, people tended to rehearse by category; for instance, when "horse" was presented, this would trigger the rehearsal of "dog, cat, cow, horse" together. Apparently, when sufficient time is provided people can reorganize the words as they store them in memory. Furthermore, the number of times a word had been rehearsed during study was predictive of recall order; more frequently rehearsed categories, as well as words within those categories, were recalled earlier than categories and words that received less rehearsal.

SUBJECTIVE ORGANIZATION Don't misunderstand the above section: Organization during rehearsal is *not* limited to lists of words with obvious, known categories. Some of the earliest and most provocative evidence of organization came from a study by Tulving (1962) on the subjective organization of unrelated words—literally, organization imposed by the participant (for an update, see Kahana & Wingfield, 2000).

Tulving used what was called the multitrial free recall task, in which the same list of words is presented repeatedly across several trials, where each trial had a new reordering of the words. His analysis looked at the regularities that developed in the recall orders. For example, a person might recall the words "dog, apple, lawyer, brush" together on several trials. This consistency, despite the experimenter's reordering from trial to trial, suggested that the person had formed a cluster or chunk composed of those four items using some idiosyncratic basis. For example, a person might link the words together in a sentence or story: "The dog brought an apple to the lawyer, who brushed the dog's hair." Regardless of how they were formed, the clusters were used repeatedly during recall, serving subjectively as a kind of organized unit. Tulving called this **subjective organization**, that is, *organization developed by a person for structuring and remembering a list of items without experimenter-supplied categories.* In other words, even "unrelated" words become organized through the mental activity of a person imposing an organization.

Imagery

The last storage variable considered here involves **visual imagery**, *the mental picturing of a stimulus that affects later recall or recognition.* Of course, we have discussed some visual imagery effects already, such as mental rotation, and the imagery-based mnemonic devices. What we focus on now, however, is the effect of visual imagery on the storage of information in long-term memory, the possible boost that imagery gives to material you are trying to learn.

An early contributor to the understanding of how imagery impacts memory was Alan Paivio. Paivio (1971) reviewed scores of studies that illustrated the generally beneficial effects of imagery on memory. These effects are beyond those caused by other variables, such as word- or sentence-based rehearsal, or meaningfulness (Bower, 1970;

Yuille & Paivio, 1967). As one example, Paivio described a **paired-associate learning** study by Schnorr and Atkinson (1969; see Table 6-5) in which items were presented in pairs, the first item designated the stimulus item, the second the response item. The task is to *learn the list so that the correct response item can be reproduced whenever the stimulus item is presented.* Thus, if you saw the pair "elephant–book" during study, you would be tested during recall by seeing the term "elephant" and your correct response would be "book" (the later section on interference describes this task in more detail). Schnorr and Atkinson had people study half of a list by forming a visual image of the two terms together. The other half of the list was studied by rote repetition. On immediate recall, the pairs learned by imagery were recalled at better than 80% accuracy, compared to about 40% for the rote repetition pairs. The superiority of imagery was found even after a one-week retention interval. It is also important to note that the formation of mental images is not an automatic process. It requires attention and effort, which may be part of the reason for the benefit it provides.

Studies such as this one led Paivio to propose the **dual coding hypothesis** (Paivio, 1971), which states that *words that denote concrete objects, as opposed to abstract words, can be encoded into memory twice*, once in terms of their verbal attributes and once in terms of their imaginal attributes. Thus a word like *book* enjoys an advantage in memory—because it can be recorded twice, once as a word and once as a visual image; there are two different ways it can be retrieved from

TABLE 6-5 Lists of Paired Associates

List 1 (*A–B*)	List 2 (*C–D*)	List 3 (*A–B$_r$*)
tall–bone	safe–fable	plan–bone
plan–leaf	bench–idea	mess–hand
nose–fight	pencil–owe	smoke–leaf
park–flea	wait–blouse	pear–kiss
grew–cook	student–duck	rabbit–fight
rabbit–few	window–cat	tall–crowd
pear–rain	house–news	nose–cook
mess–crowd	card–nest	park–few
print–kiss	color–just	grew–flea
smoke–hand	flower–jump	print–rain
List 4 (*A–B′*)	**List 5 (*A–C*)**	**List 6 (*A–D*)**
smoke–arm	tall–bench	smoke–fable
mess–people	plan–pencil	print–idea
rabbit–several	nose–wait	mess–owe
park–ant	park–student	pear–blouse
plan–tree	grew–window	rabbit–news
tall–skeleton	rabbit–house	grew–duck
nose–battle	pear–card	park–cat
grew–chef	mess–color	nose–nest
pear–storm	print–flower	plan–just
print–lips	smoke–safe	tall–jump

memory, one way for each code. A term like *idea*, however, probably has only a verbal code available for it because there is not an obvious image that it evokes. (This is not to say that people cannot create an image to help remember a word like *idea*, such as a light bulb, but merely that the image is much more available and natural for concrete words.)

Emotion and Survival Value

In addition to the various aspects of memory that can be highlighted to improve memory, including depth of encoding, generation, enactment, distinctiveness, organization and imagery, there are two other things that can improve performance. Both of these have to do with characteristics of the information itself. These are emotion and survival value.

People tend to remember emotional information better than neutral information. If you merely think back on your own life, the events that tend to be easier to remember are those associated with more emotional intensity. This has also been demonstrated in laboratory work. For example, people remember emotionally arousing pictures better than neutral ones (Bradley, Greenwald, Petry & Lang, 1992), particularly the details of negative images (Kensinger, Garoff-Eaton, & Schacter, 2006). People also remember emotional utterances better than neutral ones (Armony, Chochol, Fecteau, & Belin, 2007). Work using fMRI scanning, such as that by Dolcos, Labar, and Cabeza (2005) and Kensinger and Corkin (2004), has shown that the superior memory for emotional memories appears to reflect the involvement of the amygdala, and medial temporal lobe structures, such as the hippocampus, with the amygdala-hippocampus network being more important for emotional intensity, and a hippocampal-frontal lobe network being more important for emotional valence (whether the emotion is positive or negative, happy or sad).

So, why does emotion help memory so much? Well, there are probably a number of reasons that, together, help make emotional memories easier to remember. First, emotional events are likely to be things that are important to us. As a consequence, people are likely to devote more attention to processing that information relative to something that is more emotionally neutral. Part of this is driven by the recruitment of the amygdala, which is a critical brain structure for processing emotions. There is also some evidence that emotionally charged memories appear to benefit more by the process of memory consolidation offered by sleep compared to emotionally neutral memories (Hu, Stylos-Allan, & Walker, 2006).

Looking more at behavior, Ritchey and Radvansky (2008) had people view pictures that were emotionally positive, negative, or neutral while performing an *n*-back task. (An *n*-back task is a common assessment of working memory in which the person indicates whether the current item is the same or different from the item *n* positions back in the list. For instance, in a 2-back task using letters, if the current item was B, you'd say "yes" if the letter you saw two items ago was also B.) In the Ritchey and Radvansky study, the comparison item was always 2 items back from the current one. They found that emotional content greatly slowed processing during the *n*-back task, suggesting that emotion information consumes more attention when it is being actively processed in working memory. However, on a recognition memory test 1 week later, people were better at remembering the emotional than the neutral items. So, the additional attention at encoding helped later memory.

Another reason why emotion may help memory is that emotional information is more distinctive. Much of what we encounter in our day-to-day lives does not elicit much in the way of a strong emotional reaction. As such, truly emotional information is more likely to be distinctive, resulting in a kind of a von Restorff effect.

In order for memory to be of value to us, it needs to give us something useful. It should help us survive in the world. The survival motivation is very strong, and may be part of what is behind some of the emotion and memory effects we have been talking about. Obviously, knowledge of what can either increase or decrease our survival is going to be particularly important. Thus, if a person can bring a survival perspective to bear on what they are learning, it can improve performance. This was shown clearly in a study by Nairne, Thompson, and Pandeirada (2007; see also Nairne, Pandeirada, & Thompson, 2008; Weinstein, Bugg, & Roediger, 2008). In this study people were given lists of words. During the first part of the study, people were simply asked to rate the words for pleasantness, relevance to moving to a foreign land, personal relevance, or survival value (e.g., finding food and water or avoiding predators). What they found was that words that were rated high on survival value were much more likely to be remembered later. The survival angle has such a strong impact on memory that it can outperform the effects of other well-known memory enhancing strategies such as imagery, self-reference, and generation (Nairne, Pandeirada, & Thompson, 2008). Thus, if we think about how information relates to our ability to survive, endure, or otherwise be useful, this takes advantage of fundamental motivations we have, and these can be leveraged to improve memory (Wurm, 2007; Wurm & Seaman, 2008).

Context and Encoding Specificity

We conclude this section on storage with a short discussion that also previews several important ideas for the topic of retrieval. What generalizations can we draw from research on rehearsal, organization, and imagery? How are we to understand the phenomenon of storage into episodic memory? The best way to understand storage is to consider it in light of retrieval.

In Tulving and Thompson's (1973) view, an important influence on memory is **encoding specificity**. This phrase means that information is encoded into memory *not* as a set of isolated, individual items. Instead, *each item is encoded into a richer memory representation, one that includes the context an item was in during encoding*. Thus, when you read *cat* in a list of words, you are likely to store not only the word *cat* but also information about the context you read it in. In a classic study of encoding specificity, Godden and Baddeley (1975) had people learn a list of words. Half of these people learned the list on land, and the other learned the list under water (all of these people were scuba divers). They were then given a recall test for the list. The important twist is the context in which they tried to recall the information. Half of the people recalled the items in the same context. However, the other half recalled the information in the other context. The interesting finding, as shown in Figure 6-7, was that memory was better when the encoding and retrieval contexts were the same, relative to when they were different.

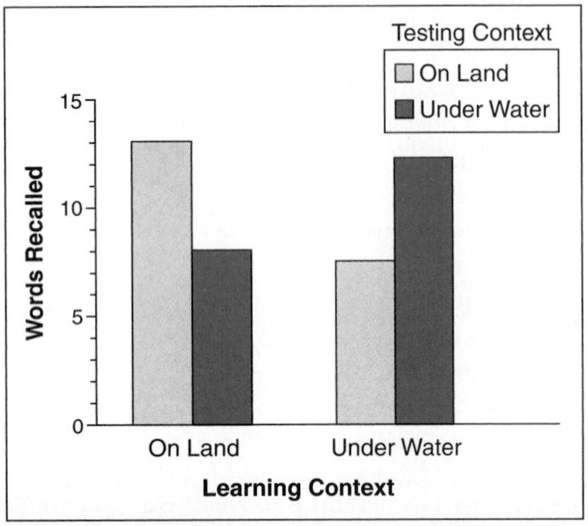

● **FIGURE 6-7**
The classic encoding specificity result reported by Godden and Baddeley (1975), showing better performance when the encoding context matched the retrieval context. That is, memory for things learned on land was better when tested on land as opposed to under water, whereas things learned under water were better remembered when the people were tested under water as opposed to on land.

A more everyday example of encoding specificity is the experience of going to a room in your home to do something, but when you get there, you can't remember why you are there. However when you return to where you started, you suddenly remember. That is, reinstating the original context allowed you to remember. This is also why witnesses may return to the scene of a crime. Being there again reinstates the context, helping them remember details that might otherwise be forgotten.

More generally, when your memory is tested, with free recall for instance, you attempt to retrieve the record or trace left by your original encoding. By encoding the context along with the item, the context helps serve as an excellent **retrieval cue**—*a useful prompt or reminder for the information to be retrieved.* As another example, if you study pictures under a picture rehearsal condition, then picture cues will enhance your performance (Morris, Bransford, & Franks, 1977). If the conditions during the test are quite different—for example, if you are given word fragment cues after pictorial rehearsal—then the likelihood of successful retrieval decreases. The original context cues give you the best access to the information during retrieval, and these cues can be verbal, visual, or something else (Schab, 1990, for instance, has found that odors are effective contextual cues).

The encoding specificity phenomenon can be quite broad ranging. It not only applies to sensory information, such as what things looked like, sounded like, smelled like, and so on, but also to your own internal state. A variant of encoding specificity, called *mood congruent learning,* is the finding that it is easier to remember things if you are in the same emotional state now as you were when you originally learned the information (Bower, 1981). Thus, it is easier to remember happy times when you are happy compared to when you are sad, depressed, angry, or in some other emotional state. Another variant of the encoding specificity effect is *state-dependent learning,* which is the finding that people are more likely to remember things when their physiological state at retrieval matches that at encoding. For example, in one study Goodwin et al. (1969) found that people made fewer errors on a memory test when they recalled information when they were drunk (a particular physiological state) if they had learned that information inebriated, than if they tried to recall it when they were sober!

In summary, storage of information into episodic long-term memory is affected by a number of factors that can lead to a stronger memory trace. Moreover, the congruence between study and test contexts can be vital. Relevant rehearsal, including organizational and imaginal elements, improves performance. Rehearsal that turns out to be irrelevant for the test conditions generally is of little benefit.

Section Summary

- Important variables in storage are rehearsal and organization, regardless of whether the information is verbal or perceptual. Maintenance and elaborative rehearsal have two different functions, the former for mere recycling of information without increasing the likelihood of retrieval, the latter for more semantically based rehearsal, which was claimed to process the information more deeply into memory. Difficulties in this depth of processing framework involve definitions of the two types of rehearsal and specification of the idea of depth. When memory is tested with recognition, the results often disconfirm the hypothesis that maintenance rehearsal merely maintains information and does not make it more memorable; the same is true of implicit memory tasks.
- Generally, the amount of rehearsal is positively related to recall accuracy for the primacy portion of a list. Organization, especially by category but also by subjectively defined chunks or clusters, improves memory because it stores the information securely and provides a useful structure for retrieval. According to encoding specificity, contextual information that was encoded along with the studied information can serve as an effective retrieval cue.
- Memory can be affected by our emotional state. More emotionally intense information is generally easier to remember. Moreover, as with mood congruent learning, it is easier to remember information that matches our current mood as compared to when there is a mismatch.

RETRIEVING EPISODIC INFORMATION

We turn now to the other side of the coin, retrieving information from episodic memory. And as we do, we reencounter the two theories of forgetting that have preoccupied cognitive psychology from the very beginning: decay and interference.

Decay

It's a bit unusual for the name of a theory to imply its content as clearly as does the term *decay*. Nonetheless, that is what decay theory was all about: The older a memory trace is, the more likely that it has been forgotten, just as the print on an old newspaper fades into illegibility. The principle dates back to Thorndike (1914), who called it the law of disuse: Habits, and by extension memories, are strengthened when they are used repeatedly, and those that are not used are weakened through disuse. Thorndike's proposal was a beautiful theoretical hypothesis, easily understood and straightforward in its predictions. Unfortunately, it's wrong, at least as far as long-term memory is concerned.

The difficulty with the decay theory of forgetting is that it says that the passage of time causes forgetting. A definitive attack on decay theory was given by McGeoch (1932), who argued that the *activities* that occur during a period of time are responsible for our forgetting, not time itself. In other words, time doesn't cause forgetting—it's what happens during that time that does. Although some argue that there is still some validity to the decay theory (Schacter, 1999), it is difficult to imagine the experiment that would provide a clean, uncontaminated demonstration of it. As a time interval passes, there can be any number of opportunities for interference, even if caused merely by the momentary thoughts you have while your mind wanders. And the time interval would also give you opportunities for selective remembering and rehearsal of events, which would boost remembering of old information.

Interference

Interference theory and tests of interference effects were a staple in the experimental diet of verbal learners. There were at least two reasons for this. First, the arguments against decay theory and for interference theory were convincing, on both theoretical and empirical grounds. Demonstrations such as the often-cited Jenkins and Dallenbach (1924) study made complete sense within an interference framework: After identical time delays, people who had remained awake after learning recalled less than those who slept afterward (Figure 6-8). The everyday activities encountered by awake people seemed to interfere with their memory. Fewer interfering activities intervened for sleeping people, so their performance was better. (Interestingly, this effect may also depend on the amount of rapid eye movement (REM) sleep you get after learning; see Karni, Tanne, Rubenstein, Askenasy, & Sagi, 1994).

This effect was recently replicated by Drosopoulos, Schulze, Fischer, and Born (2007) who further concluded that the memory benefit from sleep serves as a means of mitigating the effects of interference. However, this benefit of reducing interference was primarily for information that was not strongly encoded (that is, not well learned) to begin with. Although how much interference a person experiences is linked to how related the material is (as seen in Chapter 5), there are other reasons for long-term memory forgetting that are influenced by whether you get some sleep or not.

Specifically, when you create and store new long-term memories, they don't instantly appear in your brain in a well-established form. Instead, there is a period of time during which memories go through an important process known as **consolidation**, *the more permanent establishment of memories in the neural architecture*. Later in this chapter we'll see about the consequences of a dramatic disruption in consolidation that can result in amnesia. For now, it is important to note that the disruption that is seen when people are awake (and not when people sleep) is interference of the memory consolidation process (Wixted, 2005). This occurs by having new information encoded into memory that uses the same neural parts (such as the hippocampus) that were used by the older information. This reuse of neural networks interferes with memories for the older information, thus disrupting the consolidation process and resulting in forgetting.

This interference process would be somewhat like writing messages in clay. Imagine writing a message in a bit of clay, then writing even more messages on the clay. Sometimes you'll write over messages that you had previously written, making the earlier ones harder to recover. This is the type of interference we are talking about. On the other hand, sometimes a message doesn't get written over, and eventually the clay may harden. In this case, the message will consolidate into the clay, making it harder to

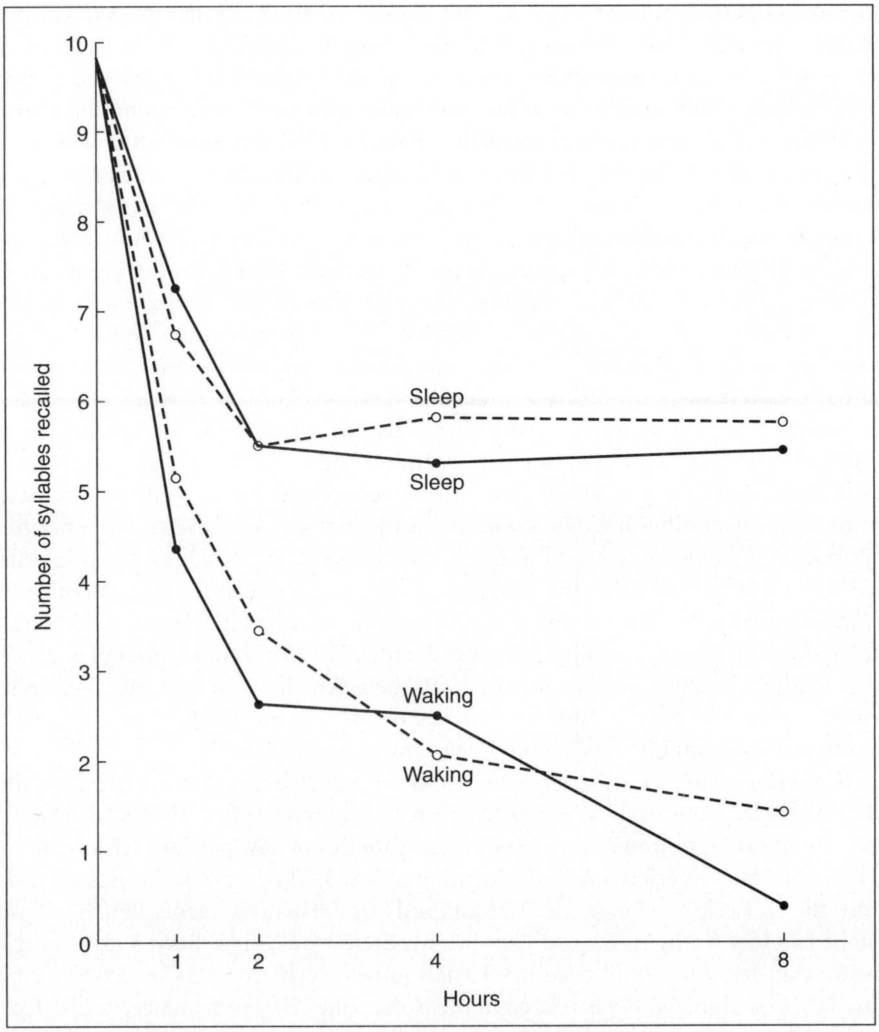

◆ **FIGURE 6-8**
The classic Jenkins and Dallenbach (1924) result, showing higher recall of nonsense syllables for two people who slept after acquisition versus remaining awake after acquisition.

disrupt. Ultimately, these older memories are more robust, and less prone to disruption, a pattern you'll read about later in the section on amnesia.

A second reason for the popularity of interference studies is that interference effects were easily obtained, especially with a task already in wide use, the paired-associate learning task. This task was a natural for studying the components of interference—and, by the way, it conformed to the behaviorist *Zeitgeist* or "spirit of the times" prior to the cognitive revolution. Unlike consolidation-disrupting interference, the interference explored by paired-associate learning tasks was due to what is known as *cue-overload*. In these cases, there are many memories that are related to a specific memory cue, and they compete with one another during retrieval.

PAIRED-ASSOCIATE LEARNING A few moments studying the paired-associate learning task will help you understand interference theory. The basic elements of paired-associate learning are as follows (see also Table 6-3): *A list of stimulus terms is paired, item by item, with a list of response terms. After learning, the stimulus terms should prompt the recall of the proper response terms.* The items were often CVCs, and sometimes words. In the anticipation method, a person first saw a stimulus term alone, tried to name the correct response term that went with it, then saw the stimulus-response pair together. Of course, people had to guess on the first trial because they had not seen any pairs before. After that, the number of correct responses grew across repeated trials, showing (in behaviorist terminology) that the correct responses had become conditioned to the appropriate stimuli. A typical procedure was to bring a person up to some accuracy criterion, one perfect trial, for instance, then present another paired-associate list for learning.

Table 6-5 presents several paired-associate lists to use as a demonstration. Imagine learning List 1 to a criterion of one perfect trial (try it to get a good idea of what the task is like). After that, you would switch to the second half of the study, which would involve learning another list. The similarity of the first and second lists was of critical importance. If you were switched to List 2, you would experience little or no interference because List 2 contains terms that are very dissimilar to List 1's terms. In the lingo of interference theory, this was the *A–B, C–D* condition, where the letters *A* through *D* refer to different lists of stimulus or response terms. This condition represented a baseline condition because there is no similarity between the *A–B* and the *C–D* terms (however, you may have needed fewer trials on the second list because of "general transfer" effects from List 1, warmup or learning to learn).

If you shifted to List 3, there would have been "massive" negative transfer; it would have taken you more trials to reach criterion on the second list. This is because the same stimulus and response terms were used again but in new pairings. Thus your experience on List 1 interfered with the learning of List 3. The term for this is $A–B, A–B_r$, where the subscript *r* stands for "randomized" or "re-paired" items. Finally, if you switched to List 4 (the $A–B, A–B'$ condition), there would have been a great deal of positive transfer; you would need fewer trials to reach criterion on the second list because List 4 (designated B') is related to the earlier one (*B*). For instance, in List 1 you learned "plan–leaf"; in List 4, "plan" went with "tree."

These are all *proactive* transfer and interference effects showing the effects a prior task has on current learning. We discussed proactive interference (PI) and release from ■ PI at some length in Chapter 5. Table 6-6 gives the general experimental design for a proactive interference study as well as for a retroactive interference (RI) study. As a reminder, retroactive interference occurs when a learning experience interferes with recall of an *earlier* experience; the newer memory interferes backward in time ("retro").

Both proactive and retroactive interference have been examined extensively (or excessively, depending on your view), with complex theories built on the results. Although an extensive literature is available, no attempt is made to cover it in depth here (but see standard works such as Postman & Underwood, 1973; Underwood, 1957; Underwood & Schultz, 1960; and Klatzky, 1980, Chapter 11, for a very readable summary). Instead, we summarize a major difficulty encountered in this work, important because it was instrumental in the shift to a cognitive approach to memory.

TABLE 6-6 Designs to Study Two Different Kinds of Interference

	Learn	Learn	Test	Interference Effect
Proactive Interference (PI)				
PI group	*A–B*	*A–C*	*A–C*	*A–B* list interferes with *A–C;* e.g., an *A–B* word intrudes into *A–C*
Control group	—	*A–C*	*A–C*	
Retroactive Interference (RI)				
	Learn	**Learn**	**Test**	**Interference Effect**
RI group	*A–B*	*A–C*	*A–B*	*A–C* list interferes with *A–B;* e.g., an *A–C* word intrudes into *A–B*
Control group	*A–B*	—	*A–B*	

PROBLEMS OF MEANING The behaviorist tradition held that paired-associate learning was essentially a matter of association formation. In other words, the *B* terms in an *A–B* list became associated with their *A* terms, so that presenting a stimulus from the *A* list should elicit the *B* response term. If you then learn a new list, say *A–C*, then the *A–B* associations would have to be unlearned while the new *A–C* connections were being conditioned (e.g., Kintsch, 1970; Underwood & Postman, 1960). The term *unlearned*, of course, is what we call "forgotten." A definitive demonstration that this was *not* generally true was provided by Slamecka (1966). Before having people learn the *A–B* and then the *A–C* list, he had them generate their own associates to the *A* words (e.g., to the *A* word *cat*, you might generate *dog*). According to interference theory, learning the *A–B* list and then *A–C* should have resulted in unlearning the original free associates. But of course it did not: After showing the normal interference effect in learning *A–C*, people had no difficulty recalling their original free associates to the *A* words. What should have been altered by interference, the preexisting associations, were immune to it. In the face of existing associations in memory, laboratory-induced interference seemed downright puny.

The mismatch between interference theory predictions and the (obvious) result suggested that theories based on paired-associate learning and interference were irrelevant to understanding memory. It seemed possible that the paired-associate learning laws were not general, that they applied only to nonsense syllable learning in a paired-associate task. As Jenkins (1974) put it in the title of his article: "Remember that old theory of memory? Well, forget it!"

Retrieval Failure

Since the mid-1960s, a different theory came to dominate cognitive psychology's view of forgetting. Both the decay and interference theories suggested that information in long-term memory can truly be forgotten, that is, lost from memory. This definition of the term **forgetting**, *loss from memory*, was implicit in the mechanisms thought to account for forgetting, such as unlearning. Forgetting is now used without the notion of complete loss from memory, however, to refer to situations in which there is difficulty remembering. For example, one line of research looks at "retrieval-induced forgetting," the temporary forgetting of information because of having recently retrieved related information (e.g., Anderson, Bjork, & Bjork, 2000; MacLeod & Macrae, 2001). Similarly, Anderson (2003) has suggested that forgetting is an active executive control process, designed to override mistaken retrieval of related information ("activated competitors" in Anderson's terms). Note that even here, the unwanted information that is causing interference is still in memory—if it weren't, there'd be no need to override it.

The current view on forgetting makes different claims from interference theory. In essence, there may be no *genuine* forgetting from long-term memory, aside from loss due to organic or physical factors, such as stroke or diseases like Alzheimer's Dementia. Instead, forgetting is often due to retrieval failure or sometimes a process of retrieval inhibition, a deliberate (though only partially successful) attempt to forget (e.g., when you try to forget an unpleasant memory or an incorrect fact; Bjork & Bjork, 2003).

AN EVERYDAY EXAMPLE Everyone is familiar with retrieval failure, although it often parades under a different name. Students claim that they knew the information but that they "blocked" on it during the exam; if this is not just a rationalization, then it is an example of retrieval failure. The more straightforward experience is the classic **tip-of-the-tongue (TOT)** phenomenon.[1] People are in the TOT state when they are *momentarily unable to recall information, often a person's name, that they know is stored in long-term memory*. Interestingly, although you may be unable to retrieve a word or name during a TOT state, you usually have access to partial information about it, such as the sound it starts with, its approximate length, and the stress or emphasis pattern in pronunciation. (Brown & McNeill, 1966, is the classic TOT paper; see also Jones, 1989; Koriat, Levy-Sadot, Edry, & de Marcas, 2003; and Meyer & Bock, 1992. Burke, MacKay, Worthley, and Wade, 1991, provide a list of questions that can be used to trigger the TOT state, if you want to try it as a demonstration.)

But retrieval failure, like the TOT phenomenon, is not limited to lapses in remembering names or unusual words. As Tulving and his associates found, it is a fundamental aspect of memory.

RESEARCH ON RETRIEVAL FAILURE An early demonstration of retrieval failure is a study by Tulving and Pearlstone (1966) in which two groups of people studied the same list of 48 items, four words from each of 12 different categories (e.g., animals, fruits, sports; other people learned shorter lists or lists with fewer items per category, but we focus only on the two most dramatic groups here). The items were preceded by the appropriate category name, such as "crimes—treason, theft; professions—engineer, lawyer," and people were told that they had to remember only the items. Because

[1]TOT is pronounced "*tee-oh-tee*," not like the word *tot*. Furthermore, it is often used as a verb: "The subject TOTed ("*tee-oh-teed*") seven times on the list of 20 names." For another regrettable example of "cognitive verbs," see Chapters 9 and 10, on "garden pathing."

both groups were treated identically until the beginning of recall, it can be assumed that both had learned the same amount of information. At retrieval, one group was asked for standard free recall. The other group was given the names of the categories as retrieval cues, that is, a **cued recall** condition.

The results were both predictable and profound in their implications. The free recall group remembered 40% of the items, whereas the cued recall group named 62%. In short, the free recall group had reported only a portion of what was actually learned. We know they learned more because the cued group had the same learning experience, yet recalled more. As Tulving and Pearlstone (1966, p. 389) put it, "Information about many words must be *available* in the storage . . . even when this information is not *accessible*" (emphasis added) under free recall conditions. One conclusion we can draw confirms intuitions dating back to Ebbinghaus; recall often underestimates how much information was learned. Recognition scores, not to mention savings scores, usually show higher retention.

A more important implication is that unsuccessful retrieval, say in the absence of cues, might be a critical, possibly major, cause of forgetting. On this view, *information stored in long-term memory remains there permanently*, and so is **available**, just as a book on the library shelf is available. Successful performance depends also on **accessibility**, *the degree to which information can be retrieved from memory*. Items that are not accessible are not immediately retrievable, just as the misshelved book in the library is difficult to locate or retrieve. This suggests that information is not lost *from* memory but is lost *in* memory, so to speak. This loss of access persists until an effective retrieval cue is presented that locates the item that cannot be retrieved.

Retrieval Cues

We've already discussed how access can be increased via *encoding specificity* by reinstating the original learning context. More generally, this can be thought of as increasing access by providing effective retrieval cues. So, let's look at retrieval cues more generally. Any cue that was encoded along with the learned information should increase accessibility. This is why the category cues helped people in Tulving and Pearlstone's study recall more than they otherwise would have. Similarly, this is why recognition usually reveals higher performance than recall. In a recognition test, you merely have to pick out which of several alternatives is the correct choice. What better retrieval cue could there be than the very information you are attempting to retrieve?

You haven't really forgotten all seven names. If you need a big hint try searching the Internet for "The Seven Dwarfs".

Subsequent research has demonstrated the power of the retrieval cues in dramatic fashion.

★ ▲ (By far the most convincing demonstration we've ever seen is presented in Tables 6-7 and 6-8, taken from the Bransford & Stein, 1984, book on problem solving; do that demonstration now, before reading further.)

Thomson and Tulving (1970) asked people to learn a list of words for later recall. Some of the words were accompanied by cue words printed in lowercase letters; people were told they need not recall the cue words but that the cues might be helpful in learning. Some of the cue words were high associates of the list items, such as "hot–COLD," and some were low associates, such as "wind–COLD." During recall, people were tested for their memory of the list under one of three conditions: low- or high-associate cues or no cues.

★ **TABLE 6-7**

This demonstration experiment illustrates the importance of retrieval cues. You need a blank sheet of paper and a pencil. Please follow the instructions exactly.

Instructions: Spend 3 to 5 s reading each of the following sentences, and read through the list only once. As soon as you are finished, cover the list and write down as many of the sentences as you can remember (you need not write "can be used" each time). Please begin now.

A brick can be used as a doorstop.
A ladder can be used as a bookshelf.
A wine bottle can be used as a candleholder.
A pan can be used as a drum.
A record can be used to serve potato chips.
A guitar can be used as a canoe paddle.
A leaf can be used as a bookmark.
An orange can be used to play catch.
A newspaper can be used to swat flies.
A TV antenna can be used as a clothes rack.
A sheet can be used as a sail.
A boat can be used as a shelter.
A bathtub can be used as a punch bowl.
A flashlight can be used to hold water.
A rock can be used as a paperweight.
A knife can be used to stir paint.
A pen can be used as an arrow.
A barrel can be used as a chair.
A rug can be used as a bedspread.
A telephone can be used as an alarm clock.
A pair of scissors can be used to cut grass.
A board can be used as a ruler.
A balloon can be used as a pillow.
A shoe can be used to pound nails.
A dime can be used as a screwdriver.
A lampshade can be used as a hat.

Now that you have recalled as many sentences as you can, turn to Table 6-8.

TABLE 6-8 ▲

Do *not* look back at the list of sentences in Table 6-7. Instead, use the following list as retrieval cues and write as many sentences as you can. Be sure to keep track of how many you can write down, so you can compare this with your earlier recall performance. Begin now.

flashlight	lampshade
sheet	shoe
rock	guitar
telephone	scissors
boat	leaf
dime	brick
wine bottle	knife
TV antenna	pen
bathtub	pan
record	board
orange	newspaper
ladder	barrel
rug	balloon

The results were exactly as predicted by encoding specificity. High associates used as retrieval cues benefited recall both when the high associate had been presented during study and when no cue word had been presented. Presumably, when no cue word was presented, people spontaneously retrieved the high associate during input and encoded it along with the list item. In contrast, when low associates had been presented, only low associates functioned as effective retrieval cues. High associates used as retrieval cues were no better than no cues at all. In other words, if you had studied "wind–COLD," receiving "hot" as a cue word for "COLD" was of no value. Retrieval cues thus can even override existing associations during recall. (Note that encoded cues do not cause unlearning of the preexisting association; they simply function as more effective cues during the task.)

Demonstrations of the effectiveness of retrieval cues are common in everyday experience: For instance, you hear a "golden oldie" on the radio, and it reminds you of a particular episode (a special high school dance, with particular classmates, and so forth). This even extends to general context effects: Marian and Neisser's (2000) bilingual participants remembered more experiences from the Russian-speaking period of their lives when they were interviewed in Russian, and more from the English-speaking period when interviewed in English (see also Schrauf & Rubin, 2000); actors remember

"*I forget the name of the product, but the jingle on TV goes something like 'Ya-dee-dum-dee-rah-te-dum-dee-rah-dee-dum.'*"

their lines better when enacting their stage movements from a performance, even three months later (and with intervening acting roles; Noice & Noice, 1999). And here's a customized example of failure to recall a recallable word. Think of all the words you have read in this chapter and the lists you have learned. Limiting yourself to just these words, can you remember a word that is highly associated with "parade"? No? Maybe it will be easier with a more appropriate retrieval cue. Fill in the blank with the following cue: "two-shoe-______."

TESTING IS LEARNING It is pretty clear that when you are listening to a lecture, reading a book, or studying in some other way, you are learning new information. Moreover, when you take a test, such as an essay exam, a fill-in-the-blank, or a multiple choice test, the contents of your memory are being assessed. An interesting point is that you are learning even when you are being tested. Every time you encounter information, whether you are studying it or being tested on it, counts as a learning trial, a fact that has been known for a long time (e.g., Gates, 1917; Roediger & Karpicke, 2006). Essentially, the additional experience that you get from tests actually helps you remember the information better – better even than studying, especially if you need to generate the answers rather than pick them out of a multiple choice list (McDaniel, Roediger, & McDermott, 2007). Still, this testing benefit does apply to recognition (multiple-choice) tests as well (Marsh, Roediger, Bjork, & Bjork, 2007), and to non-verbal material, such as maps (Carpenter & Pashler, 2007). So, an effective tool to help you study and learn the material for this or any other class you may take is for you to take practice tests if they are available. If they are not available, an ideal step to take for your study group would be to make up practice tests for each other, and give each other these tests. It may sound like a lot of work, but your memory for the material will be much better than spending the same amount of time studying by yourself.

ALL THAT GLITTERS IS NOT GOLD There is no question that, for the most part, retrieval cues help memory retrieval. However, there are a few notable exceptions to this. One of these is the **part-set cuing** effect (Slamecka, 1968), which is the finding that *if you cue people with a subset of a list of words, they will have more difficulty recalling the rest of the set than if they had not been cued at all.* In other words, cuing people with part of the information impairs memory compared to doing nothing. For example, if someone asked you to name the seven dwarves (from *Snow White*), you would have a harder time with the last four if you were told the names of three of them, than if you were simply asked to name all seven of them by yourself. One thing that is causing the part-set cuing effect is that when people are provided with part-set cues, these items disrupt the retrieval plan that a person would normally use by imposing a different organization of the material. This inconsistency disrupts retrieval, resulting in a processing cost. Also, some people have suggested that part-set cuing involves the use of an active inhibitory mechanism (Aslan, Bäuml, & Grundgeiger, 2007), much like what would be occurring in retrieval failure. In short, when a person is presented with a part-set cue, this causes an implicit retrieval of those items. At that time, the related memory traces serve as competitors, and are actively inhibited.

PROVE IT
Part Set Cuing

It seems surprising that giving people part of a set of information will make their performance worse as compared to giving them nothing. And yet, this is exactly what the part set cuing effect says will happen.

Make several lists of words. Each list should be 48 words long from 4 categories (e.g. tools, birds, countries, etc.), with 12 words from each category. Then get two groups of your friends. For both groups, read the lists of words to them, with the words in a random order (not grouped by category). Do this at a pace of about 1 word per second. Then after reading the list, have one group try to recall the entire list of 48 words. For the other group, read to them a subset of 24 words (6 from each category), and then have them try to recall the remaining 24.

When scoring their recalls, for both groups, do not count the ones that were read to the second group (the part-set cue group), but only the other 24. This is because what you are trying to test is how well people do on those particular items as a function of whether they got the part-set cues or not. If everything goes well, you should find that the people to whom you read half of the list will have a harder time than the people that simply tried to recall the entire list.

Section Summary

- Decay and interference were once thought to cause forgetting from long-term memory. Although interference is easily demonstrated using proactive or retroactive interference tasks, the evidence now suggests that interference disrupts retrieval. Thus, retrieval failure is not true forgetting because information remains available in long-term memory. Instead, retrieval failure is caused by loss of access to the stored information. Effective retrieval cues provide access to otherwise irretrievable information. Part-set cuing is a rare exception to this rule.
- Tip-of-the-tongue states illustrate that even when information cannot be successfully completly retrieved, partial information may be available. This partial retrieval may be so strong that retrieval seems imminent.
- Taking a test on material not only serves to assess what is and is not in memory, it also provides an opportunity to reinforce what is learned. An effective study practice would be to work in groups making tests of your own and taking practice tests generated by your classmates.

AMNESIA AND IMPLICIT MEMORY

We study cognitive dysfunctions caused by brain damage, such as the agnosias you read about in Chapter 3, to understand cognition and its organization. Sometimes the patterns of disruptions and preserved abilities can tell us a great deal about how cognition works. As you will see, this has been an especially fruitful way to understand long-term memory, by considering what is damaged and what remains intact in cases of amnesia (see Paller, 2004, for an excellent introduction to the neurocognitive approach to memory).

Amnesia is *the loss of memory or memory abilities caused by brain damage or disease.* Amnesia is one of the oldest and most thoroughly investigated mental disruptions caused by brain disorders, as well as one of the more common results of brain injury and damage. Although some amnesias are temporary, due to a blow to the head or even acute emotional or physical stress (e.g., transient global amnesia; Brown, 1998), the amnesias we are interested in here are relatively permanent, caused by enduring changes in the brain.

Many different kinds of amnesias have been studied, and we have space to discuss only a few of these. A few bits of terminology will help you understand the material and alert you to the distinctions in memory that are particularly relevant.

First, the loss of memory in amnesia is always considered in relation to the time of the injury. If a person suffers *loss of memory for events before the brain injury*, this is called a **retrograde amnesia**. Note that *retro-* here has the same connotation as in the discussion of retroactive interference; the loss is backward in time. Interestingly, retrograde amnesia almost always shows a temporal gradient—typically, memories that are more distant in time from the injury are less impaired (e.g., Brown, 2002; see Wixted, 2004, for a useful discussion, and the analogy to writing on clay discussed earlier). This temporal gradient of retrograde amnesia is often referred to as following *Ribot's Law,* which basically states that *the older the memory is, the better it will be preserved.* The other form of amnesia is **anterograde amnesia**, *disruption of memory for events occurring after the brain injury, especially a disruption in acquiring new long-term memories.* A person can often show both forms of amnesia, although the extent of the memory loss usually is different for events before and after the damage—for example, anterograde amnesia often seems more extensive, simply because it disrupts learning from the time of the brain damage on to the present. The cases we'll talk about here are extreme in that the memory disruption seems to be complete: so-called profound or dense amnesia. Most cases of amnesia are not as complete as these.

Second, we are trying to understand the architecture of memory, how the various components are interrelated, whether some components are independent of others, and so on. This is an analysis of dissociations, where the term **dissociation** refers to *a disruption in one component of the cognitive system but no impairment of another.* If two mental processes—call them *A* and *B*—are dissociated, then *A* might be disrupted by brain damage while *B* remains normal; patient K. C., described later, displays this kind of pattern. Sometimes a different patient is discovered who has the reverse pattern: *B* is disrupted by the brain damage, but *A* is intact. When two such complementary patients are found, with *reciprocal patterns of cognitive disruption*, then the abilities *A* and *B* are said to be **doubly dissociated** (see **Dissociation** in the Glossary).

Importantly, a double dissociation implies not only that *A* and *B* are functionally independent, but also that *A* and *B* are implemented in different regions of the brain (a simple example would be seeing and hearing, either of which can be damaged without affecting the other). A simple dissociation is not as strong. If process *A* is damaged while *B* remains normal, it could be that research has not yet found a patient with the reciprocal pattern. Or it could be that process *A* can be selectively damaged without affecting *B* but that damage to process *B* would always disrupt *A*. The opposite of a dissociation is an association, that is, a situation in which *A* and *B* are so completely associated that damage to either process would always disrupt the other (e.g., recognizing objects and recognizing pictures of objects).

Finally, the most useful cases to study are those of focal brain lesions, in which the damage is to a small, restricted area of the brain. Cases such as that of patient K. C. illuminate the underlying mental processes more clearly because many of his mental processes are intact despite the dysfunction caused by the focal lesion. Unfortunately, the widespread damage and neural deterioration of some injuries or diseases, such as Alzheimer's disease, make it difficult to pin down the neurogenerator of the cognitive functions that are disrupted: So many regions are damaged that no single one can be pinpointed as the region responsible for a particular ability.

Dissociation of Episodic and Semantic Memory

PATIENT K. C. We begin with a case history of a patient whose amnesia speaks directly to the topic of this chapter: episodic memory. Tulving (1989) described a detailed study of patient K. C. (you read a brief account of this in Chapter 2), who experienced serious brain injury, especially in the frontal regions, in a motorcycle accident. As a result of this injury, K. C. shows a seemingly complete loss of episodic memory: He is completely amnesic for his own autobiographical knowledge. In Tulving's words, "K. C.'s case is remarkable in that he cannot remember, in the sense of bringing back to conscious awareness, a single thing that he has ever done or experienced in the past. . . . K. C. does not remember any personally experienced events from either before or after his accident" (p. 362). K. C. has profound retrograde and anterograde amnesia. He shows a "massive failure to retrieve" (Tulving, 1989, p. 363), along with failure to store any new personal experiences in long-term memory.

Interestingly, although K. C.'s episodic memory system no longer works, his semantic memory does. In fact, he is adept at answering questions about his past by relying on general, semantic knowledge; when asked about his brother's funeral, he responded that the funeral was very sad, not because he remembers attending the funeral (he did not even remember that he had a brother) but because he knows that funerals are sad events.

K. C.'s pattern of memory disruption, intact semantic memory yet damaged episodic retrieval, is evidence of a dissociation between episodic and semantic memory. This suggests that episodic and semantic memories are separate, distinct systems, enough so that one can be damaged while the other stays intact. In terms of Squire's (1987) taxonomy (look back to Figure 6-1), K. C. has lost one of the two major components of declarative knowledge, his episodic memory.

FUNCTIONAL IMAGING EVIDENCE As Tulving (1989) acknowledged, there are limitations on what can be learned about normal cognition from data from brain damaged patients (but see Caramazza, 1986, and Caramazza & McCloskey, 1988, for a spirited defense of case studies). Patient K. C. may be unique; no other reports describe patients incapable of recalling *any* personal memories (although there are a few cases of near total loss of pretraumatic episodic memory; Rubin & Greenberg, 1998). Because we might worry about the generality of such results—an isolated case such as K. C. could have been atypical before his accident—Tulving presented further support for his conclusions, studies of brain functioning among normal individuals (for an overview, see Nyberg, McIntosh, & Tulving, 1998).

Turn to the color illustrations in the front cover of the book, and you will see a set of photographs. In these pictures (color plate #3), the blood flow to the brain is being measured; you read about this technique in Chapter 2. The logic behind such a procedure is that mental activity, say retrieving a particular memory, involves an increase in neural activity. This increase shows up as an increase in cerebral blood flow to those brain regions being activated. Thus, by injecting a small dose of radioactive material (irradiated gold in Tulving's report) into the bloodstream, the apparatus detects regions of the brain that have higher concentrations of radioactivity on a short time scale (e.g., 12 separate intervals of 0.2 s each across an 80 s period).

What do the photographs show? In the left panel, the person was thinking about a generic memory, the history of astronomy that he had read about many years before. In the right panel, the person was recalling personal memories from a summer nearly 50 years before, that is, a 50-year-old episodic memory. The red areas in the pictures show regions where the blood flow was above the baseline level, and the green regions show where blood flow was lower than average.

Clearly, *different* brain activity resulted for these two types of memories. If the memory of the history of astronomy is a genuine semantic memory, then different regions of the brain are more active when retrieving semantic versus episodic memories. (Similar results were obtained for recent semantic and episodic memories; see also Wood, Taylor, Penney, & Stump, 1980.) If anything, episodic retrieval was accompanied by greater activation in the anterior (front) regions of the brain. This agrees with research on patients with amnesia, showing that the frontal lobes are especially important for time-related aspects of memories (see reviews by Kesner, 1998; Schacter, 1987, 1996; and Wheeler et al., 1997). Semantic retrieval, conversely, seemed more likely to activate more posterior (rear) regions of the brain.

Anterograde Amnesia

The modern story of anterograde amnesia begins with a classic, well-known case history. A popular theoretical stance in 1950 was that memories are represented throughout the cortex, distributed widely rather than concentrated in one specific place or region. This position was clearly articulated by well-known researcher Karl Lashley in his famous 1950 paper "In Search of the Engram." Three years later, an accidental discovery by the neurosurgeon William Scoville "revolutionized the study of the memory process" (Kolb & Whishaw, 1996, p. 357; see this source for the complete story). Scoville performed radical surgery on a patient known as H. M., sectioning (lesioning) H. M.'s hippocampus in both the left and right hemispheres in an attempt to gain control over his severe epileptic seizures. To Scoville's surprise, the outcome of this surgery was pervasive anterograde amnesia; H. M. became unable to learn and recall anything new. Although his memory of events before the surgery remained intact, as did his overall IQ (118, well above average), he completely lost the ability to store new information in long-term memory.

Across the years, H. M. has served as a participant in hundreds of tasks (e.g., Milner, Corkin, & Teuber, 1968), documenting the many facets of his anterograde amnesia. His memory of events prior to the surgery, including his childhood and school days, is quite good, with some gaps. His language comprehension is normal, and his vocabulary is above average. Yet any task that requires him to retain information across a delay shows severe impairment, especially if the delay is filled with an interfering task. These impairments apply equally to nonverbal and verbal materials. For instance, after a 2 min interference task of repeating digits, he was unable to recognize photographs of various faces. He is unable to learn sequences of digits that go beyond the typical short-term memory span of seven items. In a conversation reported by Cohen (in Banich, 1997), he told about some rifles he had (it was a childhood memory). This reminded him of some guns he had also had, so he told about them. Telling about the guns took long enough, however, that he forgot he had already talked about the rifles, so he launched into the rifle story again, which then reminded him of the guns—and so on until his attention was diverted to some other topic.

H. M.'S IMPLICIT MEMORY Interestingly, the evidence also suggests strongly that H. M.'s memory is normal when it comes to procedural learning. That is, he was able to learn a rather difficult motor skill, mirror-drawing; this task requires a person to trace between the lines of a pattern while looking at it and the pencil only in a mirror (Figure 6-9). H. M.'s performance (the bottom portion of the figure) showed a normal learning curve, with very few errors on the third day of practice. Note, though, that on

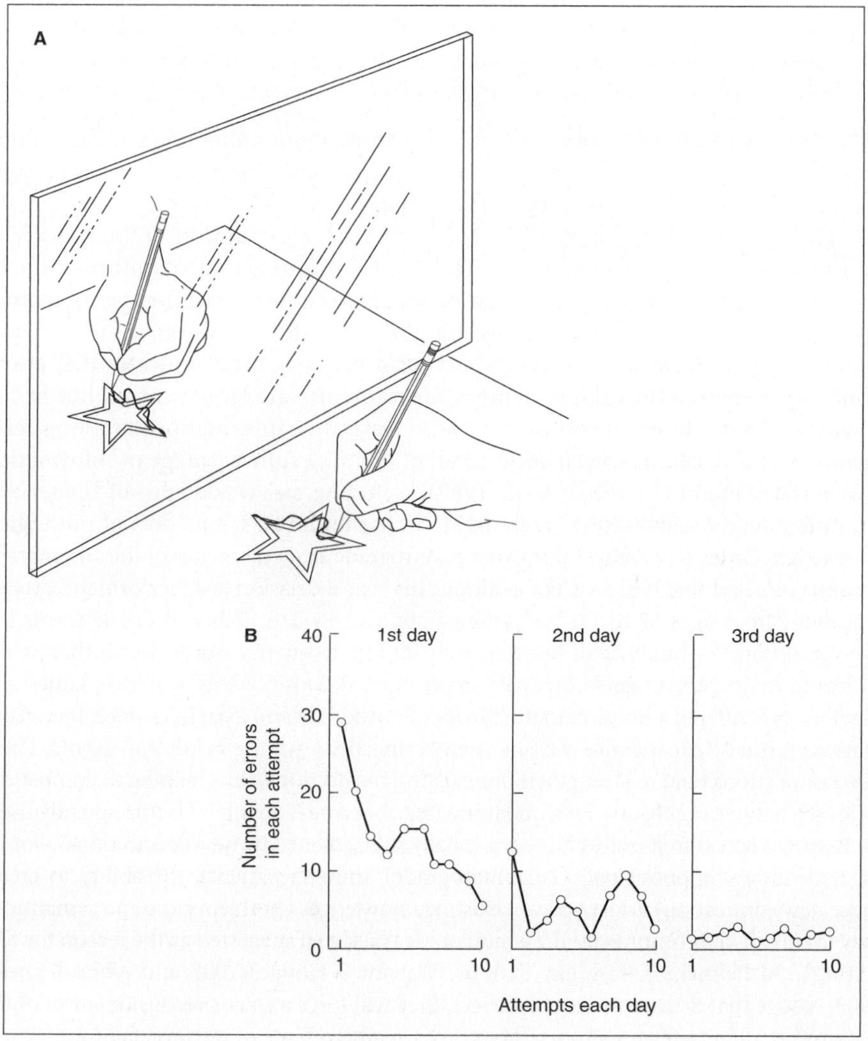

FIGURE 6-9
A. In this test the task is to trace between the two outlines of the star while viewing his or her hand in a mirror. The reversing effect of the mirror makes this a difficult task initially. Crossing a line constitutes an error. **B.** Patient H. M. shows clear improvement in the motor learning star task, an instance of implicit learning and memory. After Blakemore (1977).

days 2 and 3 he did not remember ever having done the task before; he had no explicit memory of ever having done it, despite his perfectly normal pattern of performance based on implicit memory.

Likewise, H. M. has also shown systematic learning and improvement on the Tower of Hanoi problem you will read about in Chapter 12. Although he did not remember particular moves of the problem and spoke of not remembering the task itself, his performance nonetheless improved across repeated days of practice (reported in Kolb & Whishaw, 1996). Such empirical demonstrations confirm what clinicians working with amnesia patients have known or suspected for a long time: Despite profound difficulties in what we normally think of as memory, aspects of the patients' behavior do demonstrate a kind of memory—in other words, implicit memory (see Schacter, 1996, especially his Chapter 6, for an eloquent, first-person narrative). Referring back to Figure 6-1, all of the subtypes underneath "nondeclarative (implicit)" memory—skill learning, priming, and so forth—represent different aspects of implicit memory, that is, different forms and types of performance in which implicit memories can be displayed (Squire, 1993; see Gupta & Cohen, 2002, and Roediger, Marsh, & Lee, 2002, for reviews).

IMPLICATIONS FOR MEMORY What do we know about human memory as a function of H. M.'s disrupted and preserved mental capacities? How much has this person's misfortune told us about memory and cognition?

The most apparent source of H. M.'s amnesia is a disruption in the transfer of information to long-term memory. That is, H. M.'s retrieval of information he learned before surgery is intact, indicating that his long-term memory *per se*, including retrieval, was unaffected. Likewise, his ability to attend to questions and answer them and to perform other simple short-term memory tasks indicates that attentional, awareness, and working memory functions also are largely intact. But he has a widespread disability in transferring new declarative information into long-term memory. This disability affects most or all of H. M.'s explicit storage of information in long-term memory (Milner et al., 1968), including real-world episodic material.

Interestingly, follow-up research on H. M. has found additional loss of presurgical knowledge (James & MacKay, 2001), that is, retrograde amnesia on top of the anterograde amnesia he's had since surgery. For example, his lexical decision task performance, tested repeatedly from ages 57 to 71, has declined appreciably. His ability to define words has likewise declined—but both of these are only for low-frequency words, words that we are all less likely to run across in everyday experience. Because of this evidence, James and MacKay have offered a revision to the theory of retrograde amnesia. In essence, they claim that we normally encode into memory new connections among words and events. These new connections tend to strengthen our existing connections, thus helping to combat deterioration due to aging and infrequent use (e.g., because "squander" is infrequently used, we may lose access to it unless it is occasionally strengthened by new connections). For H. M. and other "hippocampal" (i.e., anterograde) amnesia patients, the ability to create those new connections is lost, so even existing knowledge—both episodic and semantic—may eventually be compromised. (A similar idea has been suggested as the reason for forgetting in Alzheimer's disease; e.g., Simons, Graham, & Hodges, 2002, and White & Ruske, 2002. Notice that if these views are correct, they will force a major reconsideration of the notion that all long-term memory forgetting is really an issue of retrieval failure.)

It is a mistake to conclude from this that H. M.'s memory disruption—say the process of explicit rehearsal—takes place in the hippocampus. Instead, it seems more likely that the hippocampus is a critical pathway for successful transfer to long-term memory, a route through which the process takes place rather than the actual site of that process. In Squire's (1987, p. 180) view, this route or pathway idea is central to understanding how "amnesia appears to reflect neither direct injury to, nor loss of, those brain regions in which information is processed and stored. Instead, amnesia seems best explained by hypothesizing a neural system, which is damaged in amnesia, that *ordinarily* participates in memory storage without being itself a *site* of storage." Other research on patients with similar lesions (e.g., Penfield & Milner, 1958; Zola-Morgan, Squire, & Amalral, 1986) confirms the importance of the hippocampus to this process of storing new information in long-term, explicit memory. In some sense then, the hippocampus is a gateway into long-term memory. In Squire's (1992) view, the hippocampus is essential for declarative or explicit memory (see Eichenbaum & Fortin, 2003, for an excellent introduction to the relationship between the hippocampus and episodic memory, and Barnier, 2002, for an extension of these effects to posthypnotic amnesia).

Implicit and Explicit Memory

To repeat a point made at the beginning of this chapter, the operative word in these definitions is *conscious.* Explicit memories, whether episodic or semantic, come to us with conscious awareness and therefore have an explicit effect on performance, an effect that could be verbalized. For example, name the third letter of the word meaning "unmarried man." The very fact that you can say *c* and name the word *bachelor* attests to the fact that this is an explicit memory and an explicit effect on performance. In contrast, fill in the following word stems: "gre__, lic__, fl__." Even without any involvement of conscious awareness, you may have filled these in with the words "green, license, flag"—or, more appropriately, across some number of students reading this chapter, a larger percentage may have completed those stems that way than would have been expected by chance. The words *green, license*, and *flag* occurred in this chapter; we even made a point, early on, that you were reading *license* more rapidly after encountering it in an earlier paragraph, an effect called repetition priming. Importantly, we all demonstrate such implicit effects as repetition priming, amnesic or not (Graf & Schacter, 1987; Kolers & Roediger, 1984).

One general form of implicit memory is **repetition priming**. In repetition priming, *a previous encounter with information facilitates later performance on the same information, even unconsciously.* Repetition priming has been established in a number of different research tasks, such as word identification and lexical decision (Morton, 1979), word and picture naming (Brown, Neblett, Jones, & Mitchell, 1991), and rereading fluency (Masson, 1984). In all these, a previous encounter with the stimulus yields faster performance on a later task, even though you may not consciously remember having seen it before (see Logan, 1990, for the connection of repetition priming to automaticity).

In a classic demonstration of repetition priming, Jacoby and Dallas (1981) asked people to study a list of familiar words, answering a question about each as they went through the list. Sometimes the question asked about the physical form of the word, as in, "Does it contain the letter *L*?" Sometimes the question asked about the word's sound, as in, "Does it rhyme with *train*?" And sometimes, the question asked about a semantic characteristic of the word, as in, "Is it the center of the nervous system?" This was a direct manipulation of the participants' *depth of processing*, which you studied earlier. Asking about the physical form of the word should induce only shallow processing, according to that framework, leading to poor memory later. Asking about rhymes demands somewhat deeper processing, and asking about semantic characteristics should demand full, elaborative processing on the list words.

At test, explicit memory was assessed by a yes/no recognition task ("Did this word occur in the study phase?"). Here, recognition accuracy was affected by the type of question answered during study. When a question related to the physical form, recognition performance was at chance, 51% (see Figure 6-10). When the question had been asked about the sound of the word, performance improved. And when semantic processing had been elicited, recognition accuracy was high, 95%. What made this a test of explicit memory was that people had to say "yes" or "no" based on whether they had seen the word earlier. As we would expect, more elaborative processing led to better explicit memory performance.

The other test given, the implicit memory test, was a perceptual test. Here, words were shown one at a time for only 35 ms, followed by a row of asterisks as a mask. People merely had to report the word they saw. In other words, the perceptual test did not require the people to remember which words they had seen earlier. They just had to identify the briefly presented words. For perceptual recognition, identification of the words averaged about 80%, regardless of how they had been studied. In comparison, only 65% of control words that had not appeared earlier were identified (i.e., with physical, rhyme, or semantic questions; Figure 6-10). ◆

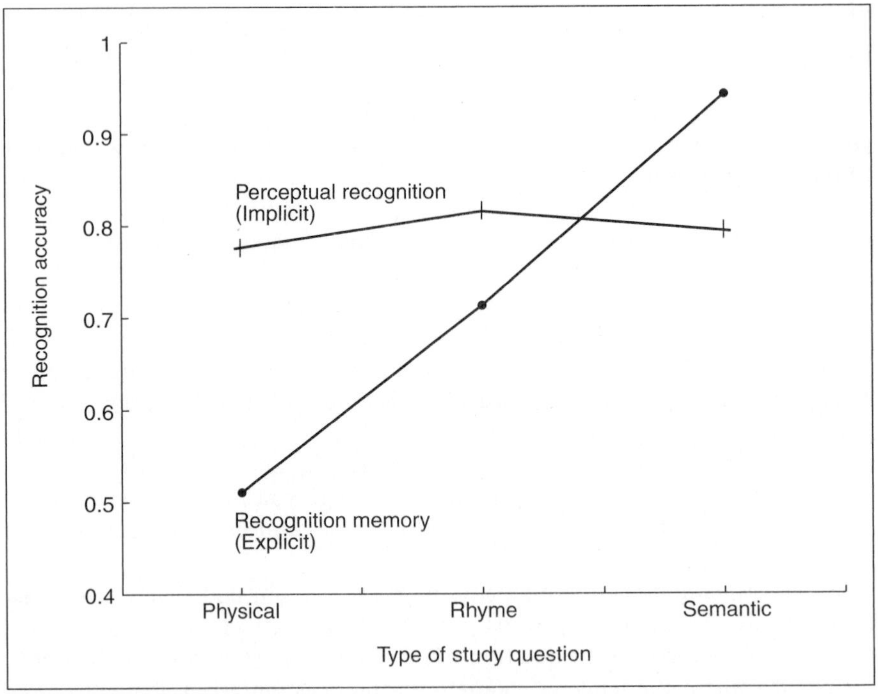

◆ **FIGURE 6-10**
Recognition accuracy for words tested with an explicit or implicit memory task. Words were originally studied with questions asking about physical, rhyme, or semantic characteristics of the words. The figure shows that implicit memory performance was unaffected by the original type of learning.

This is a typical implicit memory result. Even with no conscious recollection of the original event, there is facilitation when the stimulus is repeated. Measures of explicit memory, a recall or recognition task, generally show strong effects of how the information was studied. But measures of implicit memory, say a perceptual or word stem completion task, usually show significant priming regardless of how information was studied (see also Roediger, Stadler, Weldon, & Riegler, 1992; Thapar & Greene, 1994); for work on forgetting and interference in implicit memory, see Goshen-Gottstein & Kempinsky, 2001, and Lustig & Hasher, 2001, and Kinder & Shanks, 2003, for a counter-argument).

Implicit memory can also refer to motor tasks, such as knowing how to ride a bicycle, play a musical instrument, play a sport, and so on. Under these circumstances, implicit memory is more often called *procedural memory*. Like other implicit memories, procedural memories are very durable, and, once acquired, show a very shallow forgetting curve. Remember the saying that once you learn to ride a bike you never forget? This can also be seen in cases of profound amnesia. These individuals may lose a great deal of declarative knowledge, but their procedural knowledge or skills remain largely intact. They can even acquire new skills. For example, H.M.'s performance on the mirror drawing task was an example of procedural memory.

Note that just because a memory is implicit does not mean it has no influence on conscious experience. For example, implicit memory is involved in one idea about what causes the *déjà vu* experience (Brown, 2004). A new place may seem familiar to you, even though you've never been there before, not because of some psychic connection, but because the place is similar enough to other places you've been to. As a result, the new place seems familiar. However, for whatever reason, you are not consciously aware of these other places that you are unconsciously reminded of. The end result is that you have this eerie feeling of familiarity when you enter a place you know you've never been before.

If we had ignored the cognitive neuroscience evidence from patients such as H. M. and K. C.—indeed, if we had stuck slavishly to Ebbinghaus-inspired nonsense syllables—we would have missed the boat. We would have missed the evidence that there is a second, less obvious kind of long-term memory, a kind not dependent on conscious recollection. We would have missed the whole important issue of implicit memory.

Section Summary

- Studies of people with amnesia caused by brain damage have taught us a great deal about the components of long-term memory. Patient K. C. shows total amnesia for episodic information, although his semantic memory is unimpaired, suggesting a dissociation between episodic and semantic memories. Patients like H. M., a person with anterograde amnesia, typically are unable to acquire new explicit memories but show intact implicit learning and memory. The medial temporal area and especially the hippocampus are very important for the formation of new explicit memories, but different brain structures underlie implicit learning.

Key Terms

accessibility (p. *215*)
amnesia (p. *220*)
anterograde amnesia (p. *220*)
available (p. *215*)
consolidation (p. *210*)
cued recall (p. *215*)
declarative memory (p. *185*)
depth of processing (p. *197*)
dissociation (p. *220*)
doubly dissociated (p. *220*)
dual coding hypothesis (p. *205*)
elaborative rehearsal (p. *197*)
enactment effect (p. *201*)
encoding specificity (p. *207*)
episodic memory (p. *186*)
explicit memory (p. *185*)
forgetting (p. *214*)
free recall task (p. *202*)
generation effect (p. *200*)
implicit memory (p. *185*)
isolation effect (p. *194*)
levels of processing (p. *197*)
maintenance rehearsal (p. *197*)
metacognition (p. *192*)
metamemory (p. *192*)
method of loci (p. *187*)
mnemonic device (p. *187*)
nondeclarative memory (p. *185*)
organization (p. *201*)
paired-associate learning (p. *205*)
part-set cuing (p. *218*)
peg word mnemonic (p. *188*)
recognition tasks (p. *198*)
rehearsal (p. *195*)
relearning task (p. *190*)
repetition priming (p. *225*)
retrieval cue (p. *208*)
retrograde amnesia (p. *220*)
savings score (p. *190*)
semantic memory (p. *186*)
serial recall task (p. *199*)
subjective organization (p. *204*)
tip-of-the-tongue (TOT) (p. *214*)
visual imagery (p. *204*)
von Restorff effect (p. *194*)

CHAPTER

7

Knowing

Semantic memory is the memory necessary for the use of language. It is a mental thesaurus, organized knowledge a person possesses about words and other verbal symbols, their meaning and referents, about relations among them, and about rules, formulas, and algorithms for the manipulation of these symbols, concepts, and relations.

TULVING, 1972, P. 386

Human concepts are probably . . . like hooks or nodes in a network from which many different properties hang. The properties hanging from a node are not likely to be all equally accessible; some properties are more important than others, and so may be reached more easily or quickly. . . . Thus, a concept would be a set of interrelationships among other concepts . . . everything is defined in terms of everything else . . . like a dictionary.

COLLINS & QUILLIAN, 1972, PP. 313–314

This chapter is concerned with a different kind of long-term memory from that discussed in Chapter 6. It concerns **semantic memory**, literally "memory for meaning," our *permanent memory store of general world knowledge.* It has been variously described as a thesaurus, a dictionary, and an encyclopedia. Semantic memory is your conceptual knowledge. It is the permanent repository of information you use to comprehend and produce language, to reason, to solve problems, and to make decisions. Episodic memory is a personal, autobiographical store. We typically say "I remember that . . . ." or "I remember when . . . ." when recalling an episodic memory—"I remember a minor traffic accident on the way to work this morning," "I remember when I first saw the Eiffel Tower in Paris." Semantic memory, by contrast, is a generic storehouse of knowledge. We say "I know that . . ." when retrieving a semantic or general memory—"I know that birds have wings, that people can be injured in car accidents, that Paris is in France." In fact, *generic memory* (Hintzman, 1978) might be a better name for this system (although way too boring). That is, whereas your episodic memory differs substantially from mine, our semantic memories are largely similar—not in exact content, depending on our cultural backgrounds, but certainly similar in terms of structure and processes (but see Medin & Atran, 2004, and Nisbett, Peng, Choi, & Norenzayan, 2001, on some cultural differences in cognitive processing). Thus, you have no idea what specific things happened during *my* driver's license test, but we all share a highly similar semantic concept of a driver's license test.

The distinction between episodic and semantic memory is not simply one of convenience but does seem to reflect different kinds of mental processes. This can even been seen neurologically. For example, Prince, Tsukiura, and Cabeza (2007) have shown that episodic memory more heavily depends on some different (but related) brain regions (e.g., hippocampus and anterior prefrontal cortex) as compared to semantic memory (e.g., lateral temporal lobe and posterior prefrontal cortex). This is also evident in the amnesia patients discussed in the last chapter who typically lose personal, episodic memories, but not general semantic memories.

As Tulving (1972) noted, the first use of the term *semantic memory* appears to have been in M. Ross Quillian's doctoral dissertation in 1966. Quillian set himself the task of programming a computer to understand language. The inspiration for this work came not from psychology but from computer science and artificial intelligence (AI). Machine translation, as it was known, had been a long-standing goal in computer science, yet progress toward this goal had been surprisingly slow. The overly confident predictions of the 1950s had failed to take into account a subtle yet important fact: Even the simplest acts of human comprehension require vast amounts of knowledge. Thus for computers to understand, answer questions, or paraphrase, they needed this kind of knowledge base. This was Quillian's goal: to provide that extensive knowledge base, to see whether the AI system could then "understand." The implicit point, of course, would be that humans also need this vast storehouse of knowledge. The study of that vast storehouse is the study of semantic memory.

This chapter covers the basics of semantic memory, the fundamental structures and processes investigated in semantic memory research. This includes topics such as how concepts are stored in memory and how they are retrieved. We consider several approaches to semantic memory and two important ideas introduced earlier in the book: priming and automaticity. That plus a treatment of neuropsychological disorders set the stage for Chapter 8, where the divisions of long-term memory are studied together. There, we delve into the question of how we use the facts and events stored in long-term memory, how our episodic and semantic systems interact, especially as applied to memory for real-world events and episodes, and to topics such as false memories and memory illusions. Throughout both chapters—indeed, throughout the rest of the book—the theme we are most concerned with is the representation of knowledge, in Kintsch's (1974) terms, the representation of meaning in memory, and retrieval of that knowledge.

SEMANTIC MEMORY

A study on leading questions, also discussed in Chapter 8, provides a convenient entry into the topic of semantic memory. Loftus and Palmer (1974) showed people several short traffic safety films that involved car accidents. People were asked to describe each accident after seeing the film and then were asked a series of questions. One of the questions asked for an estimate of the cars' speeds (which people are notoriously poor at estimating). One group of people was asked, "About how fast were the cars going when they hit each other?" The other groups were asked almost the same question, except that the verb *hit* was replaced with either *smashed, collided, bumped*, or *contacted.* As you might expect, people who got the stronger verbs such as *smashed* gave higher estimates of speed. The question led them to a biased answer.

Hold it. *Why* would we expect this effect? Why are we not surprised that people estimated higher speeds when the question said *smashed* instead of *bumped* or *hit*? Our intuitive answer is that *smashed* implies a *more severe* accident than *bumped*. But consider this intuitive answer again. How did those people know that *smashed* implies a more severe accident? It is not enough merely to say that *smashed* implies something more severe. We are asking a more basic question than that. We want to know what is stored in memory that tells you what *smash* and *bump* mean. How is the difference between those two concepts represented in memory, and how do you retrieve those concepts when you encounter those words? How does memory represent the fact that *smashed* implies a severe accident, that moving cars have drivers, that robins have wings, or that bananas, canaries, and daisies are all yellow? In short, what is the structure and content of semantic memory *per se*, and how do we access the knowledge stored in it?

As you just read, one of the earliest systematic attempts to answer such questions (aside from philosophical and linguistic analyses) was Quillian's (1968, 1969) work in artificial intelligence. His model of semantic memory, TLC (for *Teachable Language Comprehender*), was not a genuine psychological model but rather a computer program for understanding language. Very shortly, however, Quillian began a collaboration with Allan Collins, and their psychological model based on TLC was the first serious attempt in cognitive psychology to explain the structure and processes of semantic memory.

The Collins and Quillian (and Loftus) Model

The Collins and Quillian model of semantic memory (1969, 1970, 1972; Collins & Loftus, 1975) was a theory of semantic memory, comprehension, and meaning. At the heart of the model were two fundamental assumptions, one about the *structure* of semantic memory and one about the *process* of retrieving information.

NODES IN A NETWORK Collins and Quillian viewed the concepts in semantic memory as being nodes in a network. In other words, the structure of semantic memory was a **network**, *an interrelated set of concepts or interrelated body of knowledge.* Each concept is represented as a **node**, *a point or location in the semantic space.*

Furthermore, concept nodes are linked by **pathways**, *labeled, directional associations between concepts.* This entire collection—nodes connected via pathways—is the network. Note that in this structure, every concept is related to every other concept, in that some combination of pathways, however indirect and long, can be traced between any two nodes. (By analogy, any two cities are connected by a direct route or an indirect series of highways and roads; Reisberg, 1997.)

SPREADING ACTIVATION The major process that operates on the network is **spreading activation**, *the mental activity of accessing and retrieving information from this network.* Concepts usually are in a quiet, unactivated state, at baseline. For example, as you are reading this sentence, one of the many concepts in your semantic memory that is probably not activated is "ROMANCE." But when you read the word, its mental representation received a boost in activation. "ROMANCE" was no longer quiet and unactivated; it was activated. (Here, words will be italicized, and concept names will be printed in capital letters.)

A key feature of activation is that it spreads throughout the network along the pathways to other concepts to which it is linked, activating the nodes it encounters along the way. In Collins and Quillian's description, the "search continually widens like ▲ a harmless spreading plague" (1972, p. 326). Look at Figure 7-1A, a simple diagram of a few concepts and the pathways among them. Even such a simple network represents a great deal of information. For instance, some of the facts in this network are that "ROBIN" is a member of the category "BIRD," that a "ROBIN" has a "RED BREAST," that a "CANARY" is "YELLOW," and so on. Each of the connections records an elementary fact or **proposition**, *a relation between two concepts.*

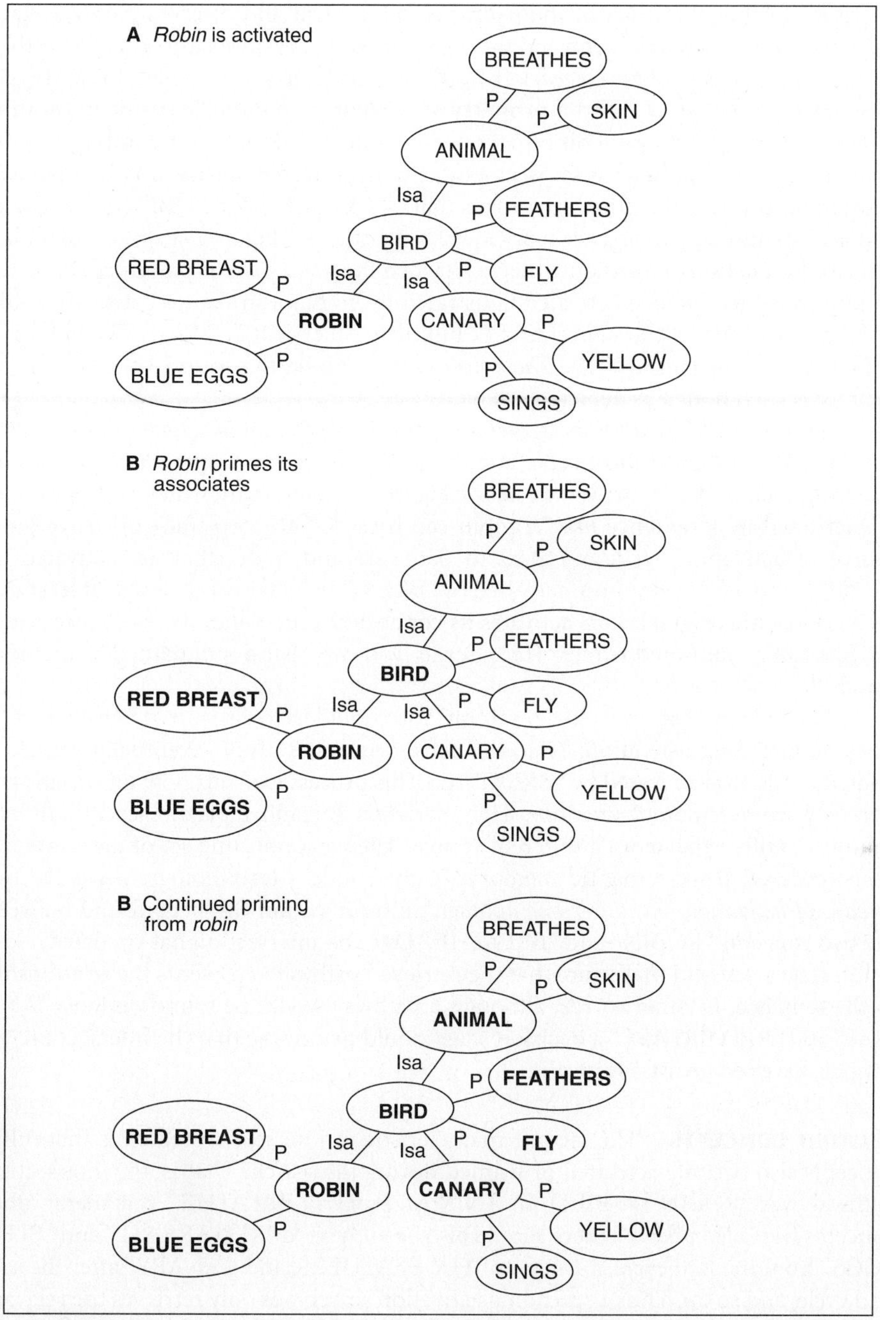

▲ FIGURE 7-1
A portion of the semantic network is illustrated. **A.** The concept "ROBIN" has been activated and is shown in boldface. **B.** The spreading activation from "ROBIN" has activated concepts linked to "ROBIN," such as the boldface "BIRD," "RED BREAST," and "BLUE EGGS." **C.** The continued spread of activation that originated from "ROBIN" is depicted.

Note further that each of the pathways is a labeled and directed pathway. Each pathway specifies a relationship and the direction of that relationship. Thus "ROBIN *is a* BIRD," *is a member of the category* "BIRD," and "BIRD has the *property* FEATHERS." (The latter statement is called a **property statement**. The *isa* relationship, indicating category membership, was a bit of jargon contributed by Rumelhart, Lindsay, & Norman [1972] meaning "is a," as in "is a member of the category.") Direction is important because the reversed direction is not true, that is "*All BIRDS are ROBINS." (Sentences that are intentionally wrong are marked with an asterisk.) Figure 7-1 shows what happens to this portion of a semantic network when the word *robin* is presented. First, the concept node for *robin* is activated, illustrated by boldface in Figure 7-1A. After this, activation spreads to the concepts it is linked to, like "BIRD," "RED BREAST," and "BLUE EGGS" in Figure 7-1B. *Those* concepts continue the spread of activation to their associated nodes, as depicted in Figure 7-1C.

The spread of activation is triggered each time a concept is activated in semantic memory. Thus when *two* concepts are activated, there are *two* spreads of activation, one from each node. As an exercise, study Figure 7-1A and mark which concept nodes are activated by a sentence like "A robin can breathe." To keep track of the original source of activation, write a *1* next to pathways and nodes that are activated by "ROBIN" and a *2* next to those activated by "BREATHE." Take this through at least two cycles: First, the original node activates its connected nodes; and, second, those nodes activate their connected nodes. (In a sense, you are "hand simulating" a memory search.)

What did you discover in that exercise? You should have discovered two characteristics of spreading activation. First, the activation of "ROBIN" eventually primed a node that was *also* activated by "BREATHE." This process explains how information is retrieved from semantic memory. The "harmless spreading plague" eventually encounters another one from a different source. Then a connecting set of pathways has been retrieved from semantic memory. In the model's terminology, *when the two spreads of activation encounter one another*, an **intersection** has been found between the two concepts "ROBIN" and "BREATHE." Once an intersection has occurred, a decision stage occurs to make sure that the retrieved pathway represents the relationship in the sentence. In other words, although a pathway would be found between "ANIMAL" and "RED BREAST," a decision stage would determine that the intersection "all animals have red breasts" is invalid.

RELATED CONCEPTS The second characteristic of intersection search is that other concepts also become activated or primed during the search. That is, the intersection pathway was "ROBIN *isa* BIRD *isa* ANIMAL *property* BREATHE." But many other concepts were also primed; there should also be a *1* next to "RED BREAST" and "BLUE EGGS" from the first cycle, a *1* next to "FLY, FEATHERS, and CANARY" after the second cycle, and so on. Thus a spreading activation search not only retrieves the relevant pathway between two concepts, it also activates related concepts. To be sure, more and more distant concepts, connected by longer pathways, do not receive as much activation as those that are close. Even close, related concepts do not remain activated forever, because activation always decays after some amount of time. Nonetheless, for a short period, nearby related concepts are boosted in their activation levels, making them temporarily more accessible. This priming of related concepts is key to an understanding of semantic processing; we return to it repeatedly throughout the chapter and indeed throughout the book.

Smith's Feature Comparison Model

The semantic network model was not the only major contender as a description of semantic memory. We focus here on a prominent feature comparison model because it offered a clear contrast to the semantic network approach (see Chang, 1986, for a review of major models).

FEATURE LISTS Smith's model (Rips, Shoben, & Smith, 1973; Smith, Rips, & Shoben, 1974) was much simpler than the Collins and Quillian network in its structure, but more elaborate in its assumptions about retrieval. Its most basic structural element was the **feature list**, which assumes that semantic memory is a collection of lists of **semantic features**, *simple, one-element characteristics or properties of the concept.* Thus the concept "ROBIN" would be a list of its features, such as animate, red-breasted, and feathered (Figure 7-2). Furthermore, these feature lists were ordered in terms of *definingness.* That is, the feature lists are ordered in priority, with the most defining features for a concept at the top and the least at the bottom. Thus an essential feature is a **defining feature**, such as *animate* for "BIRD." Conversely, features that are not defining (e.g., "ROBIN" *perches in trees*) would be at the bottom. These lower features are called **characteristic features**, *features that are common but not essential to the meaning of the concept.* Thus characteristic features do not define "ROBIN": Robins may or may not perch in trees. But defining features are essential: If it is a robin, it has to be animate.

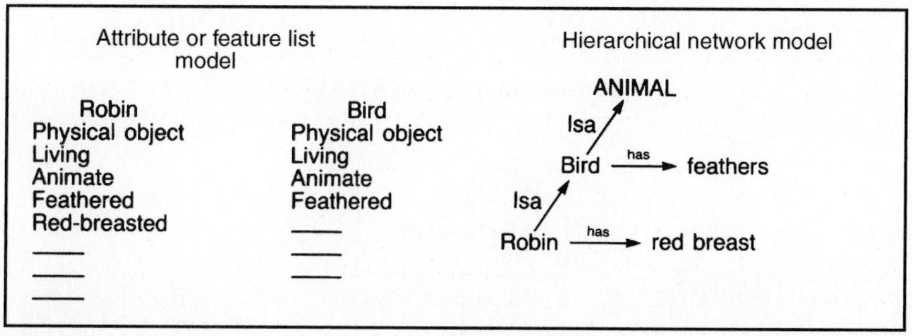

FIGURE 7-2
Information in semantic memory is represented differently in feature list models and in hierarchical network models. In feature list models, a concept is represented as a list of simple semantic features; in hierarchical network models, concepts are represented as nodes that connect to other nodes via pathways. The Smith et al. (1974a,b) model is a feature list model, and the Collins and Quillian (1972) model is a hierarchical network model. Adapted from Smith (1978).

FEATURE COMPARISON The process of retrieval in the Smith model was feature comparison; follow along with the sequence in Figure 7-3 as you read. Suppose you are given the sentence "A robin is a bird" and have to make a true/false judgment. According to the model, you would access the concepts "ROBIN" and "BIRD" in semantic memory and then compare the features on the two lists. This Stage I process involved a rapid, global comparison of features: A randomly selected subset of features on each of the lists is compared to "compute" the similarity between the two concepts. This comparison yields a feature overlap score, an index of the similarity of the two concepts. For illustration, assume that these scores range from 1 to 10.

Of course, for "A robin is a bird," the feature lists should overlap a great deal; there are very few "ROBIN" features that are not also "BIRD" features. The outcome of this process would be a very high overlap score (e.g., 8 or 9), so high that you confidently respond "yes" immediately. Conversely, for "A robin is a bulldozer," there is so little feature overlap (e.g., 1 or 2) that you respond "no" immediately without further processing. Smith et al. call these "fast yes" and "fast no" Stage I responses. When overlap scores are very high or very low, there is no need to continue the search, so a response is made immediately.

What about when the relationship is not quite so obvious? First, consider "A chicken is a bird." Most people's intuition is that chickens are a less representative example of the bird category: They do not perch or make nests in trees, they do not fly, and so on. In such cases, the Stage I comparison would find only an intermediate degree of overlap, and a second comparison is necessary, called a Stage II comparison. Unlike a fast Stage I comparison, a Stage II comparison is careful and slow, and only defining features are used. Thus, because it is true that chickens are birds, there is a match on all the features in this stage, yielding a "slow yes" response. Similarly, for "A bat is a bird," the overlap score is intermediate, which triggers Stage II. Here, however, there are important mismatches: The characteristic features that make bats similar to birds are not considered, and the defining features (mammal, furry, teeth, etc.) mismatch. Thus, the Stage II comparison gives evidence that the sentence is false.

◆ **FIGURE 7-3**
The comparison and decision process in the Smith et al. model, with sample sentences.

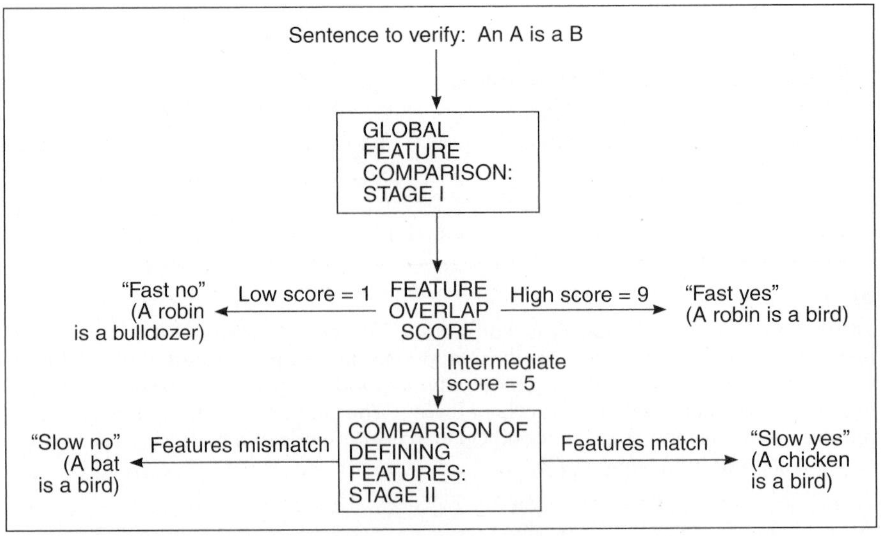

Empirical Tests of Semantic Memory Models

Typical birds?

Many early tests of semantic memory models used the **sentence verification task**, in which *simple sentences are presented for the yes/no decisions*. The items often used the frame "An *S* is a *P*" (e.g., "A robin is a bird" or "A canary is green"), where *S* stood for *subject* (robin, canary), and *P* stood for *predicate* (bird, green). Accuracy for such decisions would not tell us much; people seldom make mistakes about such simple facts. Thus response time (RT) measures were primarily used. Table 7-1 lists the characteristics of such yes/no recognition tasks when they are used in semantic memory settings.

Collins and Quillian (1969) tested a basic prediction from their model: Two concepts that are closer together in the network should take less time to verify than two that are farther apart. Refer again to Figure 7-1 and your "hand simulation." If we assume that this portion of semantic memory is accurately represented in the figure, then several predictions can be made. First, you should be quicker to verify "A robin is a bird" than "A robin is an animal," because it

TABLE 7-1 Recognition Tasks in Semantic Memory

In Table 6-3 the recognition task consisted of two basic steps: The person first learned a set of words on a list and then made yes/no decisions on a test list ("yes" if the test word was on the studied list, "no" if it was not on the studied list). The two important features that make a recognition test are as follows:

People make yes/no or forced-choice decisions.

The decisions are based on information stored in memory.

For semantic memory research, this task has been generalized to include information already stored in long-term memory before the beginning of the experiment.

Generalized recognition task (semantic)

Information to be tested is already in long-term memory, such as knowledge of categories ("A robin is a bird") or words.

People make yes/no decisions to a sequence of test items, presented one at a time. Unlike episodic recognition tasks, here the "yes" response usually means the item is true. For example, in a sentence verification task, people say "yes" to "A robin is a bird," that is, to any sentence that is true. In a lexical decision task, people respond "yes" if the letter string is a word (e.g., "MOTOR") and "no" if it is not (e.g., "MANTY").

Dependent variables: Typically, the major dependent variable is response time (RT), although accuracy is also important. Because the task usually involves yes/no decisions, guessing rate usually is 50%; if accuracy drops to 70% or 80%, then RT is questionable, often because people have traded accuracy for speed (i.e., they are faster than they would have been if they had maintained higher accuracy). Occasionally, people are given a response deadline; that is, they are given a signal after some brief interval, say 300 ms, and must respond immediately after the signal. In such a task, error rate becomes the major dependent variable. Different patterns of brain waves have also been used instead of RT or errors (see the description of Kounios & Holcomb, 1992, in this chapter).

Independent variables: An enormous range of independent variables can be tested; such as the semantic relatedness between concepts in a sentence like "An *S* is/has a *P*"; word length, frequency, concreteness, and the like in a lexical decision task; and the number of times a stimulus (word, picture) is repeated in the sequence of trials and how recently it was repeated (called lag).

★ **FIGURE 7-4**
Reaction time to superordinate (S) sentences and property (P) sentences is shown as a function of levels within the hierarchy. An S2 sentence involves a superordinate connection two levels up the hierarchy; S1 means one level up in the hierarchy; a 0 level sentence had the predicate stored at the same hierarchical level. From Collins and Quillian (1969).

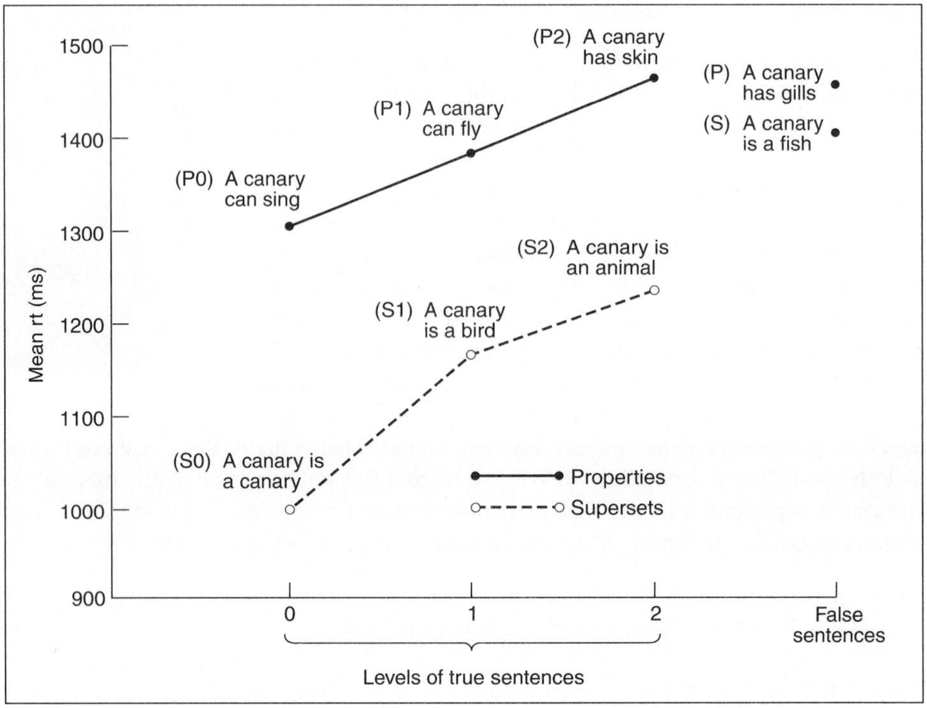

should take less time for activation to spread and intersect when the two concepts are separated by only one pathway rather than two. Likewise, it should take less time to verify that canaries are yellow than that they can fly or breathe, for the same reason.

★ Figure 7-4 shows the results of Collins and Quillian's (1969) study. In the figure, S indicates a superordinate statement, or an *isa* sentence, and P indicates a property statement. Tagged onto the S or P is a digit from 0 to 2, which indicates how many levels in the hierarchy the search proceeded through. As you can see, response time increased as the semantic distance between the two concepts increased.[1] However, subsequent work by researchers, such as Rips et al. (1973) showed that human semantic memory is not structured as nicely as the Collins and Quillian model implies. For example, people verify the statement "A pig is an animal" faster than they verify "A pig is a mammal," although the Collins and Quillian model predicts the opposite result.

Semantic Relatedness

▲ Figure 7-5 illustrates a modified network representation of the *bird* category that incorporates the issue of semantic relatedness. These pathways are of different lengths, reflecting the results that stronger associations are verified faster than weaker ones (this result was clearly anticipated by Collins and Quillian; see the introductory quotation). Finally,

[1]Collins and Quillian tested many more concepts than just canaries and robins, of course, although the tradition in this area of research is to illustrate the models using these words. In a depressing example of literal-mindedness, one of our students once answered an essay question on semantic memory by saying, "Collins and Quillian devised a psychological model to explain what people know about birds.

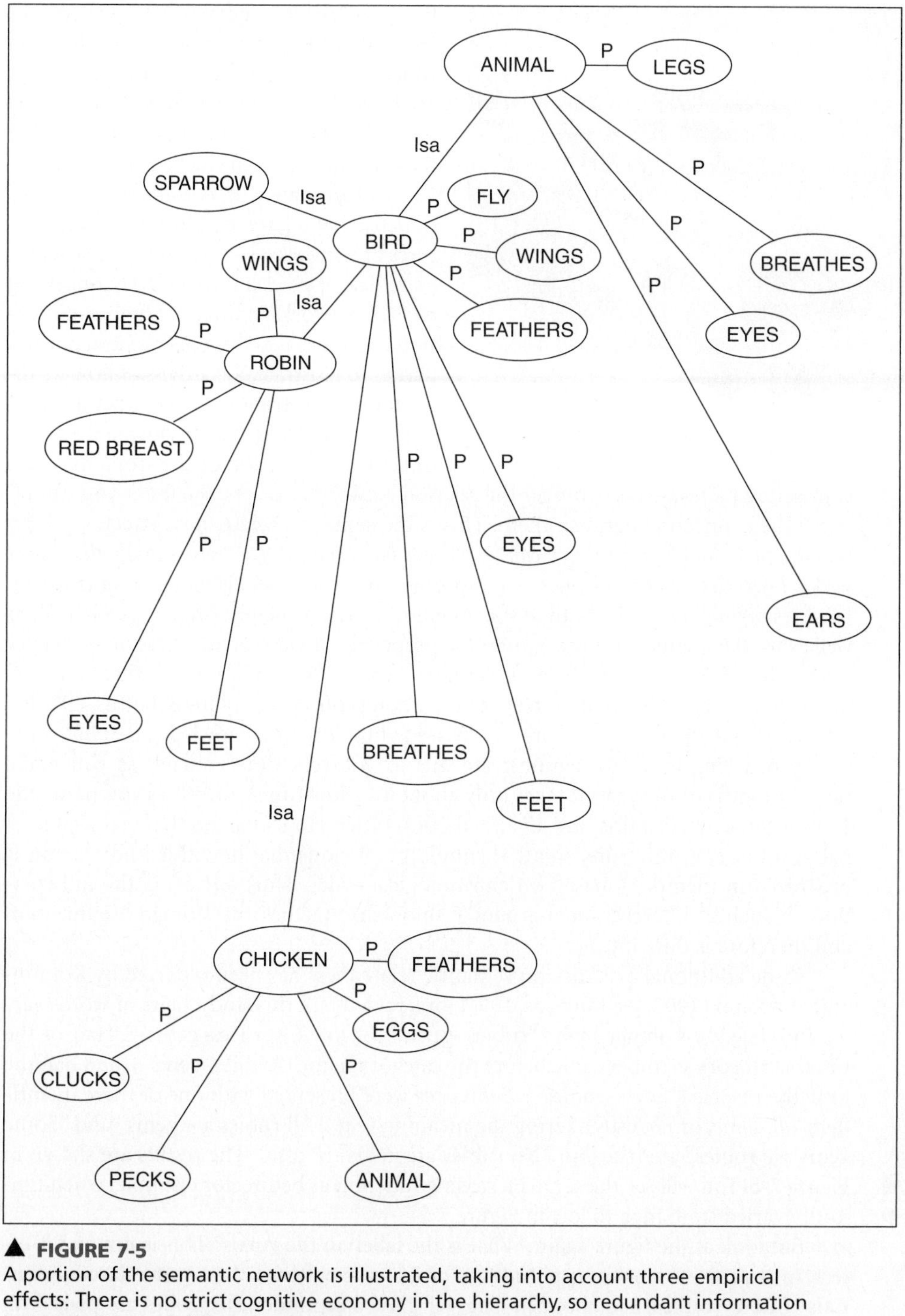

▲ **FIGURE 7-5**
A portion of the semantic network is illustrated, taking into account three empirical effects: There is no strict cognitive economy in the hierarchy, so redundant information is stored at several different concepts; typical members of the category are stored more closely to the category name or prototype member; and properties that are more important are stored more closely to the concept than those of lesser importance.

What a typical car used to look like.

this network illustrates the feature of typicality (elaborated on later in the chapter) in which more typical examples of a concept are linked by shorter pathways. This is why the link between robin and bird is shorter than the link between chicken and bird.

Unfortunately, it is difficult in a two-dimensional figure to illustrate other features of networks. For example, the strict hierarchical approach is incorrect. Conceiving of such networks in three- or higher-dimensional space makes this easier to imagine but harder to illustrate. Regardless of how we diagram the illustrations, the prediction from such a network is that performance varies directly as a function of the strength of the connecting pathway. The stronger the relation between concepts, the faster you can retrieve the connection between them. This is the **semantic relatedness effect**: *Concepts that are more highly interrelated can be retrieved and judged true more rapidly than those with a lower degree of relatedness.* An important ingredient here is that this semantic relatedness principle applies both to statements of category membership ("An *S* is a *P*") as well as to statements that may capture the properties of various members of a category ("An *S* has a *P*"; Ashcraft, 1978; Hampton, 1984). The implication is that semantic memory's structure is based on relatedness among concepts (Collins & Loftus, 1975).

This relatedness can be more clearly seen with semantic knowledge that has some strong ordering to it. To demonstrate this to yourself, time yourself as you name the 12 months of the year; it takes only about 5 s. Now time yourself as you name the 12 months again, but this time in alphabetical order. How long did that take—at least half a minute, if not more, right? It should be obvious that how this information is organized in memory—based on chronological order. Thus retrieving the information in such a different, incongruent fashion mismatches the storage organization and therefore is difficult.

Some additional evidence on semantic relatedness has been reported by Kounios and Holcomb (1992; see Kounios, 1996, for a review). In this study, pairs of words varied in relatedness, either high ("rubies–gems") or low ("spruces–gems"). Half of the time, a category member came before the category name ("rubies–gems"), and half the time the reverse ("gems–rubies"). Sentences were presented with one of three quantifiers, *all, some*, or *no*, thus altering the meaning (e.g., "All rubies are gems" and "Some gems are rubies" are true, but "No rubies are gems" is false). The results are shown in Figure 7-6. You will see the same increasing function as before, for example, when typicality varied from high to low in Figure 7-7.

But look at the figure again. What is the label on the *y*-axis? This is not an RT effect. Instead, these are the amplitudes of brain wave patterns, the **event-related potentials (ERPs)** you learned about in Chapter 2. As a reminder, electrodes are placed on the people's scalps, and the electrical patterns of brain activity are tracked across time, beginning with the onset of an item (the "event" in "event-related potentials"). In other

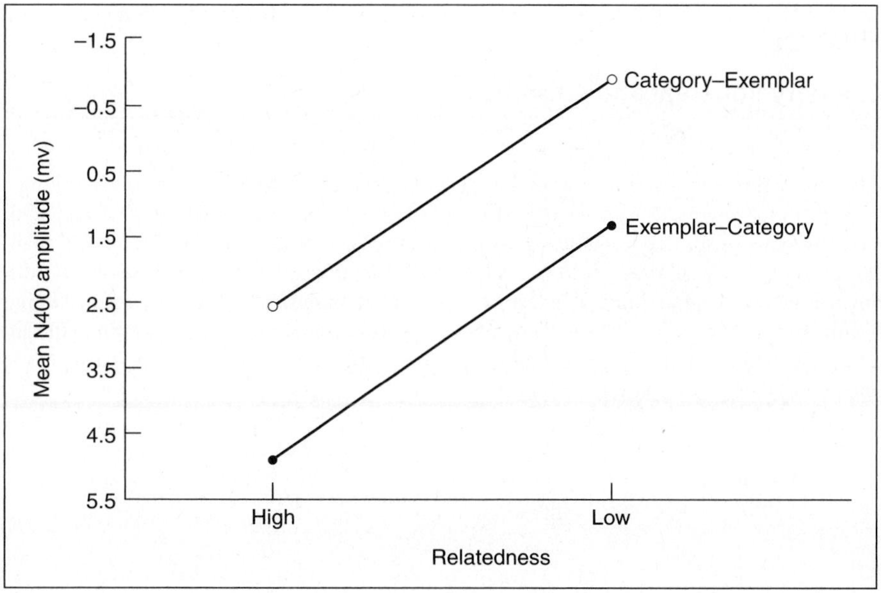

● **FIGURE 7-6**
Mean N400 amplitude recorded from three midline sites as a function of semantic relatedness and prime–target order.

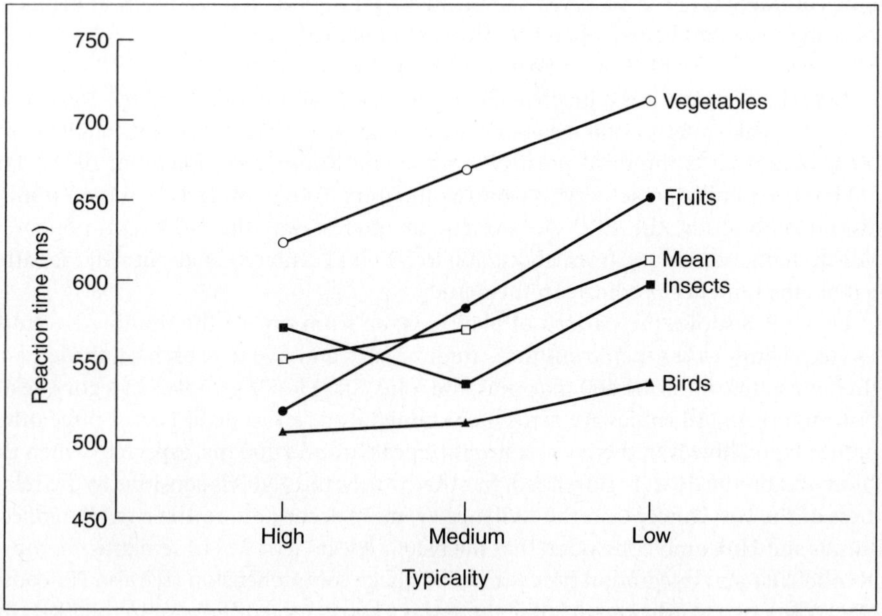

◆ **FIGURE 7-7**
Mean RTs to members of categories that are high, medium, or low in typicality. The RTs are much shorter than in comparable studies because the category names were given at the beginning of a block of trials and did not change within the block. Thus each trial consisted of only the target word, and people judged whether it belonged to the given category name.

words, Kounios and Holcomb replicated the semantic relatedness effect using electrical activity in the brain. As Kounios (1996; Kounios, Kotz, & Holcomb, 2000) explains, ERPs have become a useful measurement of cognition. A major reason for this usefulness is the time-lagged nature just mentioned; present an item, and a certain ERP component occurs within a certain window of time (e.g., within 300 to 500 ms of the

PROVE IT

Category Retrieval and Episodic Influences

To illustrate that semantic memory is organized according to the principle of semantic relatedness, time some participants as they generate lists of words for you (e.g., see how long it takes them to generate 20 words), or give people a fixed amount of time (say, 30 s) and tabulate how many words they generate in that period. You should test several well-known semantic categories, such as trees, flowers, vegetables, fruits, insects, or mammals. Now contrast those results with some different categories, such as red things, things that are soft, or things beginning with the letter *m*. You will see some evidence of semantic relatedness even in the latter examples; for instance, in the *red things* category, people are more likely to name *apple* and *tomato* together than *apple* and *fire engine*.

As an added episodic memory twist, at the end of the category retrieval exercise, have your participants take a new sheet of paper and list as many of the words they generated as they can remember, cautioning them to name *only* words they produced. Do you find more intrusions from the semantic categories?

stimulus). By carefully controlling for muscle movements (including eye blinks), we can be confident that the observed change in electrical potential is a result of cognitive processing that was elicited when the item was presented.

Several different ERPs have been studied. For example, there is an ERP known as the *P300*; the *P* means it is a positive change in electrical potential, and the *300* means the change peaks roughly 300 ms after the item is presented (it is also called a P3 component because it is the third positive component; Kounios & Holcomb, 1992). The P300 has been linked to activity in working memory (Donchin, 1981). In the Kounios and Holcomb study, the ERP component of interest was the N400 component, a *negative* change occurring from about 300 to 500 ms (centered at about 400 ms) after the item, the sentence predicate in their study.

■ Figure 7-8 shows the pattern of N400s, taken from one of the midline electrode sites (recordings were taken from three midline sites and five sites each on the left and right hemispheres). At the 400 ms point, the solid curve for "Exemplar–category, related" stimuli (e.g., "All rubies are gems") continued its negative drift. For all three other sentence types, however, there was a negative peak around 400 ms, especially when the subject and predicate were unrelated. In other words, the N400 is sensitive to the relatedness of the two concepts in the sentence or, more accurately, to their *un*relatedness. Kounios and Holcomb concluded that the N400 reflects retrieval in semantic memory, and coherence and integration processes in language comprehension (see also Holcomb, 1993). When two words were related, there was a substantial difference in the ERP pattern compared to when the words were semantically unrelated.

One semantic-based result addressed in Kounios (1996) makes particularly good sense, given what we know about lateralization in the cerebral hemispheres. Most research suggests that the left hemisphere of the brain is dominant for verbal and language-based tasks, whereas the right hemisphere is dominant for visual and spatial information. Kounios describes a match between ERP results and Paivio's (1990) dual-

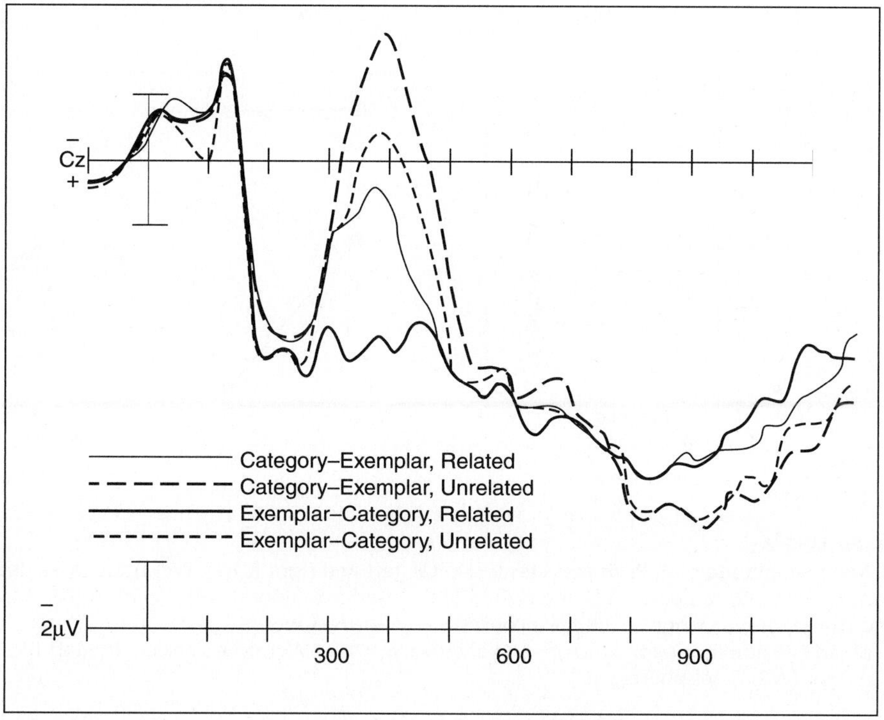

■ **FIGURE 7-8**
The event-related potentials at one midline site (*Cz*) for four types of trials; "Exemplar–category" and "Category–exemplar" refer to the order of the words. The onset of the target is shown by the vertical bar at the beginning of the time lines.

coding theory. Recall the Paivio work you studied in Chapter 6, that concrete words are learned and recalled better than abstract words because they can be represented both verbally and by a mental image (Paivio, 1971). Paivio (1990) suggests that there are two distinct systems for representing knowledge: the verbal system, which contains word meanings; and the concrete system, which contains knowledge based on visual images. His hypothesis was that the word-based knowledge would be located in the left hemisphere and image-based representations in the right. Thus, concrete words enjoy an advantage because they recruit processes in both hemispheres.

Kounios and Holcomb (1994) used a lexical decision task, showing both concrete (e.g., *table*) and abstract (e.g., *justice*) words. In addition to measuring RTs, they also examined ERPs, providing physiological support for Paivio's predictions. As shown in the bottom of Figure 7-9, ERPs for concrete words were equal and high for both hemispheres. In contrast, the amplitude of the ERPs was markedly lower in the right than in the left hemisphere for abstract words, and both of these amplitudes were lower than those for concrete words. ★

The complexity and organization of semantic memory is still just being uncovered. Semantic memory not only takes into account hierarchal and property relations, abstractness, and concreteness, but also considers factors about how we interact with things in the world. There are embodied and emotional influences on semantic memory. For example, Kalénine and Bonthoux (2008) presented people with sets of three pictures (e.g., either a coat, a jacket, and a stove or a coat, a hanger, and a stove), asking them to identify which of two choice pictures went with a first one. Two factors were manipulated in this study. One was the relationship of

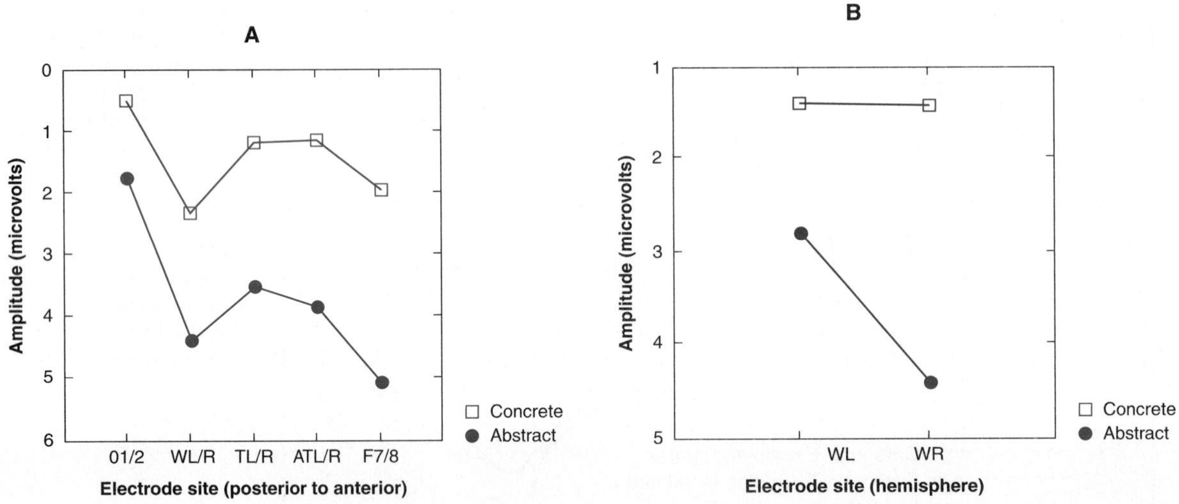

★ **FIGURE 7-9**
A. Mean amplitude of ERPs at five sites (occipital, left and right [01/2]; Wernicke's area, left and right [WL/R], temporal, left and right [TL/R], anterior temporal, left and right [ATL/R], and frontal, left and right [F7/8]), for concrete and abstract words.
B. Mean ERP amplitude for concrete and abstract words at Wernicke's area in the left (WL) and right (WR) hemispheres.

the correct answer to the third picture. These could be objects that were either *conceptually* related (e.g., coat-jacket) or were *functionally* related (e.g., coat-hanger). The other factor was whether the objects could be interacted with and manipulated by people or not (e.g., coat can be but a castle cannot). What they found was that people were faster to respond to conceptually related items for objects that you can't manipulate, but were faster to respond to functionally related items for objects that you can manipulate (e.g., coat-hanger). Thus, the efficiency with which you use your semantic memory depends on both how you are using semantic memory and how you interact with the world.

In terms of the role of emotion in memory, a study by Kissler, Herbert, Peyk, and Junghofer (2007) asked people to read a series of words while ERP recordings were made (they were given a free recall test at the end to make sure they were actually reading). The results showed a difference in cortical processing as a function of the emotional intensity of the words that were read. Specifically, in the occipito-temporal area (around where the occipital and temporal lobes meet), about 250 ms after the presentation of the word, there was an increase in cortical activity for more emotionally intense words relative to emotionally neutral words. Thus, when people access information in semantic memory, any emotional content becomes available as well. Emotion is part of semantic memory.

AMOUNT OF KNOWLEDGE The amount of knowledge we have makes a difference during memory search and retrieval—more knowledge and greater semantic relatedness go together. Several lines of work have provided evidence of the benefits of greater knowledge. For example, Pexman et al. (2003) found that reading times were faster for words having more features—properties, basically—than for words with fewer features. Yates, Locker, and Simpson (2003) found comparable effects in a lexical decision task, contrasting words with large versus "sparse" semantic neighborhoods; a large neighborhood word like *bear* has many associates in memory, compared to a sparse neighborhood word like *suds*.

The influence of amount of knowledge even extends to different settings and tasks. For example, Hambrick (2003) had people learn new information (about basketball), and found that the strongest influence on learning was the amount of domain knowledge they already had—in other words, the more you know about something, the easier it is to learn new related knowledge. Moreover, Westmacott and Moscovitch (2003) found that performance on a variety of tasks (they used recall, recognition, fame judgment, and speeded reading) was enhanced when there was some "autobiographical significance" to the famous names they were shown—for instance, remembering that you had heard Winston Churchill's voice in a radio broadcast was an indicator of autobiographical significance, as opposed to simply knowing that Churchill had been the prime minister of Great Britain during World War II. Presumably, the greater your knowledge of a topic, the more highly integrated and related that knowledge is in memory. This leads to more activation in memory and enhanced retrieval.

PERCEPTUAL SYMBOLS Many of the characterizations of semantic memory that have been discussed to this point were inspired by computer models of memory. However, more recent work suggests that semantic memory may have a more embodied character. That is, our understanding of the world reflects our experience of the world through our senses and our interactions with things. One prominent such view is Barsalou's (1999) theory of **perceptual symbols**, which states that *semantic memory is built up of sensory and motor elements derived from experience.*

One example of the influence of perceptual symbols on semantic memory can be seen in study by Pecher, Zeelenberg, and Barsalou (2003) in which people were given a series of concept-property word pairs, such as "LEAVES-rustling." The task was to indicate whether the property was true of that concept. The critical comparison was the influence of one pair of items on another pair. Suppose that the second pair was "LEAVES-rustling." For *same modality* trials, the first pair would have referred to a property in same modality (hearing in this case). For example, a same modality pair here might be "BLENDER-loud". In comparison, for the *different modality* trials, the property of the object in the first pair involved some other sensory modality, such as "CRANBERRIES-tart," which involves the sense of taste. Pecher et al. found that people were slower to respond to the second pair when it involved a different modality, presumably because people needed to switch the type of semantic processing they were doing. Similar results are observed when the concepts share hand shapes (e.g., for holding something or not; Klatsky, Pellegrino, McCloskey, & Doherty, 1989). Thus, semantic memory appears to capture information in an embodied manner that takes into account our perceptual and motor interactions with the world.

Section Summary

- Semantic memory contains our long-term memory knowledge of the world. Early studies of the structure and processes of semantic memory generated two kinds of models, network approaches and feature list approaches.
- In the Collins and Quillian network model, concepts are represented as nodes in a semantic network, with connecting pathways between concepts. Memory retrieval involved the process of spreading activation: Activation spreads from the originating node to all the nodes connected to it by pathways. Several early studies, using the sentence verification task, supported an early version of this model.
- Smith et al. claim that semantic concepts are lists of semantic features. Verification in their model consists of accessing the feature lists and performing a comparison on the features.
- The important effect documented in this work was semantic relatedness, that concepts that are highly related are more easily processed. It also appears that the amount of knowledge stored in memory affects performance, possibly because more knowledge leads to higher semantic relatedness.
- Neurological measures, such as the N400 component of an ERP, can provide some insight into semantic processing. For example, the N400 is larger when a person encounters information that is semantically unrelated or anomalous.
- In contrast to earlier theories in cognitive psychology, such as theories of semantic networks, recent theories of perceptual symbols assume that semantic memories are created out of our experience with the world. Perceptual experience can play a large role in this sort of semantic memory creation.

PRIMING IN SEMANTIC MEMORY

Four important principles are associated with the idea of spreading activation: Activation spreads, the spreading takes time, activation becomes diffused as it spreads farther from the origin, and the activation decays across time. Researchers have tested these ideas, especially as they related to the principle of semantic relatedness. Researchers wondered exactly how far into the network this activation spreads, and how long-lasting the effect would be. Does more activation spread to highly related concepts? Does it decay faster for less related concepts?

Why all this interest in spreading activation, the mental **priming** of concepts? The reason is straightforward: Priming is a fundamental consequence of retrieval from semantic memory. It is one of the most frequently tested—and discussed (e.g., McNamara, 1992; Ratcliff & McKoon, 1988)—effects in long-term memory. It is key to an understanding of semantic processing; we return to it repeatedly throughout the book, so you need to understand priming, how it affects semantic memory processing, and how it has been studied.

Nuts and Bolts of Priming Tasks

In Chapter 2, priming was defined as the activation of concepts and their meanings. It was part of the automatic process observed in the Stroop task, discussed in Chapter 4 (retrieval cue: name the color of the ink, not the color word itself). Priming can activate all kinds of concepts that express a joint meaning of several concepts together (e.g., Mathis, 2002; Peretz, Radeau, & Arguin, 2004).

Let's introduce some vocabulary for the priming task; Figure 7-10 gives an illustration, and Table 7-2 gives an explanation. To begin with, we have the **prime**, which is *any item that is presented first*, to see whether it influences a later process. The term is also used as a verb, as when we say that an item *primes* later information. Next is the **target**, *the item that follows the prime;* the target *is* that later information. It is the concept we believe may be affected by the prime. So primes precede the targets, and targets are primed (i.e., are influenced by the primes).

When this influence is beneficial, for instance when the target is easier or faster to process, this *positive influence on processing* is called **facilitation**; sometimes we simply call this **benefits**. Facilitation is almost always a shortening of RTs compared with performance in a baseline condition (when the prime and target are unrelated). Occasionally, the influence is negative, as when a prime is antagonistic to the target and so is irrelevant or misleading. When the prime slows down RT performance to the target, the *negative influence on processing* is called **inhibition**; in this case, we also say that there were **costs** associated with the prime.

If we are interested in how long activation takes to dissipate, we need to keep track of the period of time between the prime and the target. Sometimes this time is filled with other items or trials. In this case the **lag** between prime and target, usually the *number of intervening stimuli*, is our index of the separation between prime and target. For example, *lag 2* would simply mean that two trials came between the prime and the target.

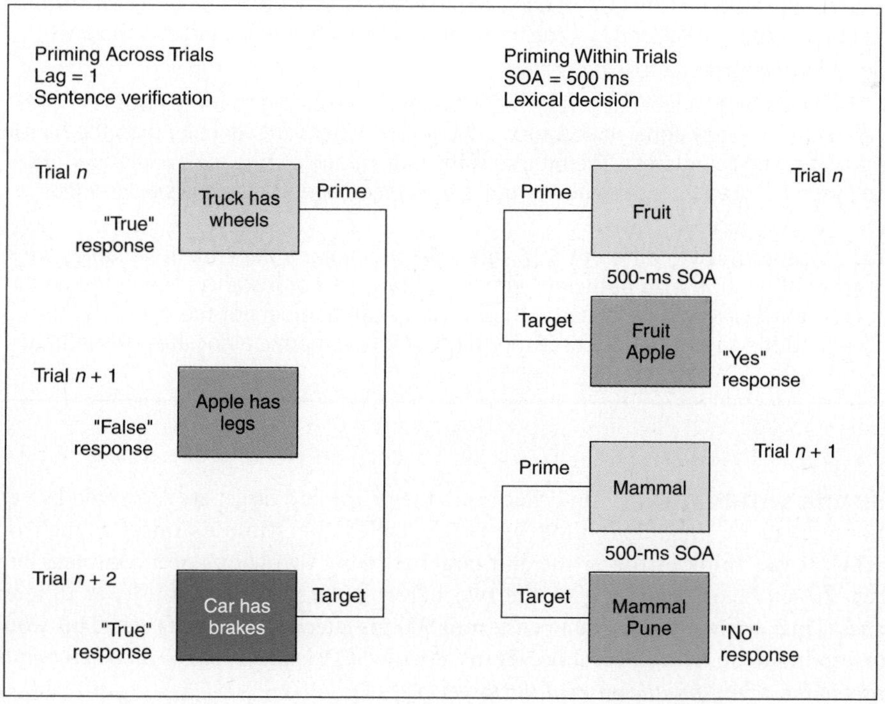

▲ **FIGURE 7-10**
A depiction of two types of priming tasks.

TABLE 7-2 Priming Tasks

Essential Terminology

Prime: The stimulus or part of the stimulus expected to have some effect; the prime can either be related to the target (e.g. "bird–robin"), unrelated to the target (e.g., "truck–robin"), or neutral (e.g., "XXXXX–robin").

Target: The stimulus or part of the stimulus expected to be affected by the prime.

Lag: The spacing between the prime and target in an across-trials priming task; for example, lag 2 means two trials came between the prime and target.

SOA: Stimulus onset asynchrony, the time interval between the prime and the target in a within-trial priming task, usually measured in milliseconds.

Priming across Trials

Almost any generalized recognition task (see Table 7-1) can be adapted to a priming task.

Trials are arranged so that the prime trial and the target trial are separated by a fixed number of unrelated trials, for example, at lag 0 or at lag 2. Care must be taken so that an equal number of related targets are true and false so people will not respond "yes" merely on the basis of trial-to-trial relatedness.

Priming within Trials

Most studies of priming within trials use a lexical decision task or another format in which the complete stimulus can be separated into two parts (e.g., Kounios and Holcomb, 1992, presented sentences such as "Some gems are rubies" in two parts, "Some gems are" as the prime and "rubies" as the target).

Each trial has both a prime and a target. The prime is presented briefly and is followed by the target after some interval of time (SOA).

Three types of primes—related, unrelated, and neutral—usually are presented at all SOAs. In some studies, the prime is followed by a blank or unfilled (short) interval, and in some the prime is masked before the target is shown.

For both types of priming tasks, we have the following:

Dependent variables: The dependent variable generally is reaction time, assuming that the error rates for the different conditions are approximately equal. If accuracy is the major dependent variable, then the hit rate and the false alarm rate are of particular interest. The hit rate is the percentage of true trials responded to correctly (saying "yes" to "yes trials") and the false alarm rate is the percentage of false trials responded to incorrectly (saying "yes" to "no trials").

Independent variables: Aside from using different SOA intervals, the major independent variables are always the types and degrees of relationships between primes and targets. For instance, the prime could be a category name, and the targets would be either high or low typical members of the category; the prime could be a sentence, and the targets would be either high or low semantic associates of the final word in the sentence.

PRIMING WITHIN TRIALS In other cases, the prime and target are separated by various intervals of time. This time interval is called the **stimulus onset asynchrony (SOA)**. If you think of the prime and target as being two halves of a complete item, then the onset or beginning of the two halves occurs asynchronously, at different times. Thus, we might present a prime and 500 ms later present the target. This would correspond to an SOA interval of 500 ms. So, the SOA is *the length of time between the onset of the prime and the onset of the target.*

Empirical Demonstrations of Priming

Let's consider a pair of experiments on word naming, an early report by Freedman and Loftus (1971) and one by Loftus and Loftus (1974) that built on the earlier result. Both were studies of priming within semantic memory.

Freedman and Loftus (1971) were interested in the process of word naming and retrieval and how it was affected by priming. They asked people to name a member of a category that either began with a certain letter or was described by a certain adjective; for example, "name a fruit beginning with *P*," or "name a red flower." On half of the trials, people saw either the letter or the adjective as a prime and the category name as the target. In the other half of the trials, the reverse was used: The category name was the prime, and the letter or adjective was the target.

PRIMING WITHIN TRIALS Freedman and Loftus found that the category name is an effective prime. In their data, performance was faster for trials such as "fruit–*P*" than trials when the letter or adjective served as the prime ("*P*–fruit" or "red–fruit"). This suggested that the category name activated its semantic representation and that this activation spread to the members of the category. When the letter or adjective was then presented, a relevant member of the category such as *plum* or *apple* had already been primed, so it was faster to retrieve from semantic memory. Conversely, letter or adjective primes had very little effect, which is another way of saying that there is no psychologically meaningful category in semantic memory corresponding to "words beginning with *P*" or "red things."

PRIMING ACROSS AND WITHIN TRIALS Loftus and Loftus (1974) used this word naming task again but with two twists. Often during the experiment, a trial such as "fruit–*P*" was followed by another "fruit" trial; the first was the prime, and the second was the target. (Note the double priming manipulation here. Not only was one trial the prime for a target trial, but within each trial there was also a prime and a target, as in "fruit–*P*," just as in the earlier experiment.) Sometimes the target trial followed immediately, at a lag of 0, and sometimes at a lag of 2, when two unrelated trials intervened. The results are shown in Figure 7-11A. ◆

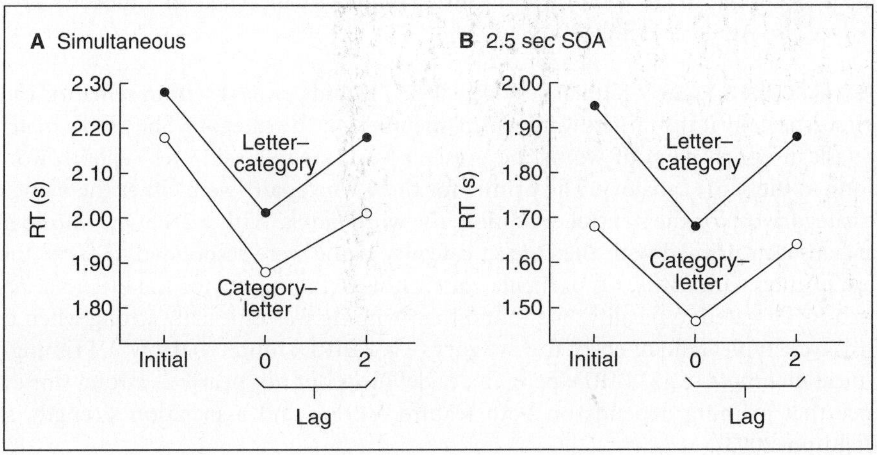

◆ **FIGURE 7-11** Reaction time is shown for simultaneous presentation of the prime and target **A**, and an SOA of 2.5. **B.** In both panels the curves show RT to the prime ("initial") and the targets at lags 0 and 2. From Loftus and Loftus (1974).

Notice three things about the results. First, seeing the category name as a prime (seeing it first) always yielded faster performance than seeing letter primes: The RT for the line with the open circles is at least 100 ms lower at every point. Second, the RTs at lag 0 are much shorter than those for the initial prime trial. In other words, seeing two "fruit" trials in a row reduced the processing time for the second one by at least 300 ms. *That* is priming across trials. And third, notice that the priming effect at lag 2 is not as strong as the effect at lag 0; performance was still faster than baseline but not as fast as in the immediate priming condition. In other words, the priming from the initial trial had dissipated or decayed somewhat at lag 2; there was still a benefit, but it was not as strong.

The second twist in the Loftus and Loftus study is shown in Figure 7-11B. This part of the study was nearly the same as the first part, except that the prime (the category name or letter) appeared by itself for 2.5 s on every trial and was then followed by the target. This was a manipulation of SOA, the time between the two parts of a stimulus. So Figure 7-11A shows what happened with simultaneous presentation, and Figure 7-11B displays the results with a 2.5 s SOA (bear in mind that the values on the *y*-axis are different for the two panels).

What does Figure 7-11B tell us? All of the curves there are lower than the equivalent curves in Figure 7-11A. In other words, when people saw the prime for 2.5 s, they could name a word that fit the letter restriction more rapidly than when they were simultaneous. There was more priming, a greater spread of activation, with the additional time; with more time, more members of the category became activated. Just as interesting, the priming also seemed to have decayed or dissipated across intervening trials because lag 2 responses were slower than lag 1 responses. While most studies look at this decay of the influence of priming over a few seconds, there is evidence that prior exposure can facilitate performance even 17 years later (Mitchell, 2006), although the precise cause of this very, very long-term priming is not well known.

Priming in Other Tasks

Similar outcomes have been reported in many other tasks. For example, priming across trials has been reported using sentence verification (Ashcraft, 1976). A sentence such as "A sparrow has feathers" facilitated another sentence about the same category, such as, "A robin can fly," but only if the target sentence concerned an important property (see also Anaki & Henik, 2003).

THE MATCHING TASK Similarly, Rosch (1975) found priming within semantic categories, especially if the targets were typical members of the category. She used a matching task in which pairs of words are presented and people said "yes" if both words belong to the same category. The primes for these word pairs were either the name of the category or, for the neutral condition, the word *blank*. With a 2 s SOA, word pairs that had been primed with the correct category name were responded to faster than those primed with *blank*. Of particular interest were the results for the other variable Rosch investigated: typicality. She found that priming was especially strong when the words were typical members of the category (e.g., "BIRD; robin, sparrow"). Priming of atypical members (e.g., "BIRD; penguin, eagle") was but not nearly as strong (for evidence that priming depends on both feature overlap and association strength, see Hutchison, 2003).

PRIMING AND THE LEXICAL DECISION TASK As you read in Chapter 2, a workhorse task in cognitive science is **lexical decision**, in which *people judge whether a string of letters is a word* (remember MOTOR and MANTY?); customarily, RT is the primary index of performance. The name of the task comes from the word *lexicon*, meaning a dictionary or a list of words. So in a sense, the lexical decision task asks you whether the string of letters is a genuine entry in your mental lexicon, your mental dictionary.

A huge range of topics has been investigated using lexical decision. The groundbreaking work was reported by Meyer and Schvaneveldt (1971; also Meyer et al., 1975). These investigators presented two letter strings at a time and told people to respond "yes" only if both were words. In addition to trials with unrelated words such as "TRUCK PAPER," they included trials with related words ("yes" trials were matched with an equal number of "no" trials on which at least one of the letter strings was not a word; e.g., "CHAIR ZOOPLE"). The related condition yielded the most dramatic result in this study. Two related words such as "BREAD BUTTER" are judged more quickly as words than two unrelated words such as "NURSE BUTTER." Table 7-3 displays Meyer and Schvaneveldt's results and shows this priming effect clearly. Related words were judged in 855 ms, compared to 940 ms for unassociated words.

One particularly interesting aspect of these results—in fact, of all results with lexical decision—is the following. It is not logically necessary for people to access the meanings of words in this task. Technically, they need only "look up" the words in the mental lexicon. Yet the results repeatedly show the influence of meaning: It is the *meaningful* connection between "BREAD" and "BUTTER" that facilitates this decision, not some lexical connection (you might think because both begin with *B* that there is a lexical basis for the facilitation, but the same benefits are found for word pairs with dissimilar spellings, such as "NURSE DOCTOR"). It seems as if we cannot look up the lexical entry for a word without also accessing its meaning.

Automatic and Controlled Priming

This facilitation in priming appears to be automatic; that is, it happens extremely rapidly and with no deliberate intention (e.g., Smith, Bentin, & Spalek, 2001). When you see a word, you access its meaning automatically, even though you are not required to by the task, although semantic activation later may be redirected by conscious, deliberate efforts.

TABLE 7-3 Priming in the Lexical Decision Task

Type of Stimulus Pair					
Top String	**Bottom String**	**Correct Response**	**Sample Stimuli**	**Mean RT(ms)**	**Mean % Errors**
Word	Related word	Yes	Nurse–doctor	855	6.3
Word	Unrelated word	Yes	Bread–doctor	940	8.7
Word	Nonword	No	Book–marb	1,087	27.6
Nonword	Word	No	Valt–butter	904	7.8
Nonword	Nonword	No	Cabe–manty	884	2.6

Source: From Meyer and Schvaneveldt (1971).

Here's an example. Neely (1976, 1977; Neely, Keefe, & Ross, 1989) selected word pairs so that one of the members was the primary associate to the other at least 40% of the time (based on free association norms). These related pairs were contrasted with unrelated word pairs and also with a condition in which the neutral letter *X* was paired with a word. For all trials, people had to judge whether the target string, the second member of each pair, was an English word (lexical decision). As Figure 7-12 shows, the processes of making lexical decisions were facilitated when the prime was a related, associated word. Benefits of priming grew from 17 ms at the shortest SOA to 56 ms with a 2,000 ms (2 s) SOA. And inhibition was observed for the unrelated word pairs; there was a nearly constant 16 ms cost of receiving an unrelated word as a prime. The SOA is important here because we would expect conscious processes to take longer. But responding more quickly is evidence of automatic processing.

In Neely's (1977) second study, people saw a letter string on each trial and had to make a lexical decision. Each letter string was preceded by a neutral prime (baseline condition), or by a category name prime that was either related or unrelated to the target. Table 7-4 summarizes the experiment and shows sample stimuli. Because the results are a bit complicated, we'll take them in stages.

First, Neely found standard semantic priming. For prime–target trials such as "BIRD–robin," there was facilitation, as shown in the left panel of Figure 7-13 (notice that any point above the dashed line at 0 ms indicates facilitation, and any point below indicates inhibition). Because he found this speedup even at very short SOAs, the conclusion is that normal semantic priming is automatic: The spread of activation

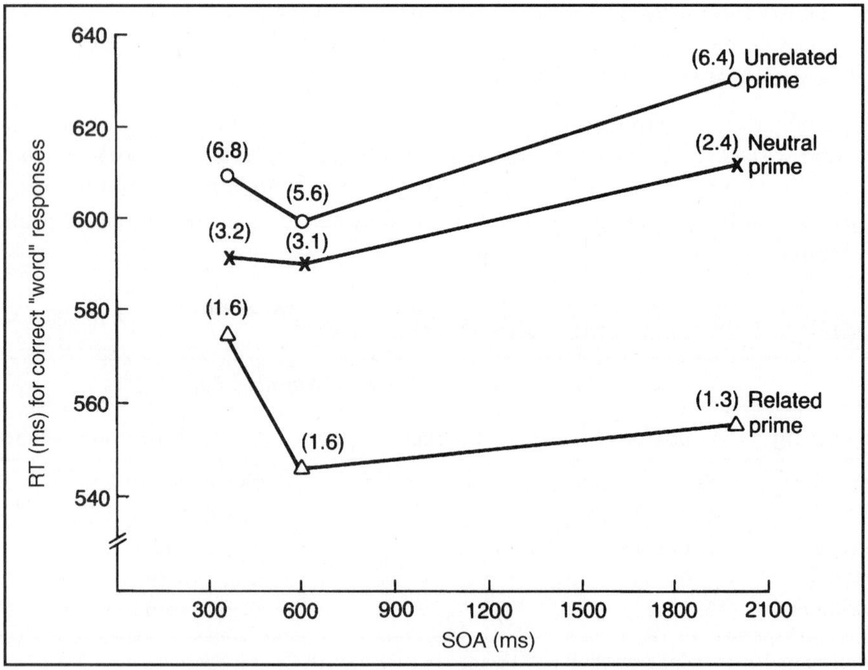

★ **FIGURE 7-12** Reaction time to lexical decision targets is shown across SOA intervals for unrelated, neutral, and related prime conditions. The numbers in parentheses are the error rates in each condition. From Neely (1976).

TABLE 7-4 Conditions and Stimuli for Neely's (1977) Study

Condition	Sample Stimulus[a]
No Category Shift Expected	
No shift	BIRD–robin
Shift	BIRD–arm
Category Shift Expected from "Building" to "Body Part"; from "Body" to "Part of a Building"	
No shift	BODY–heart, BUILDING–window
Shift to expected category	BODY–door, BUILDING–leg
Shift to unexpected category	BODY–sparrow

[a]Prime is in capital letters.

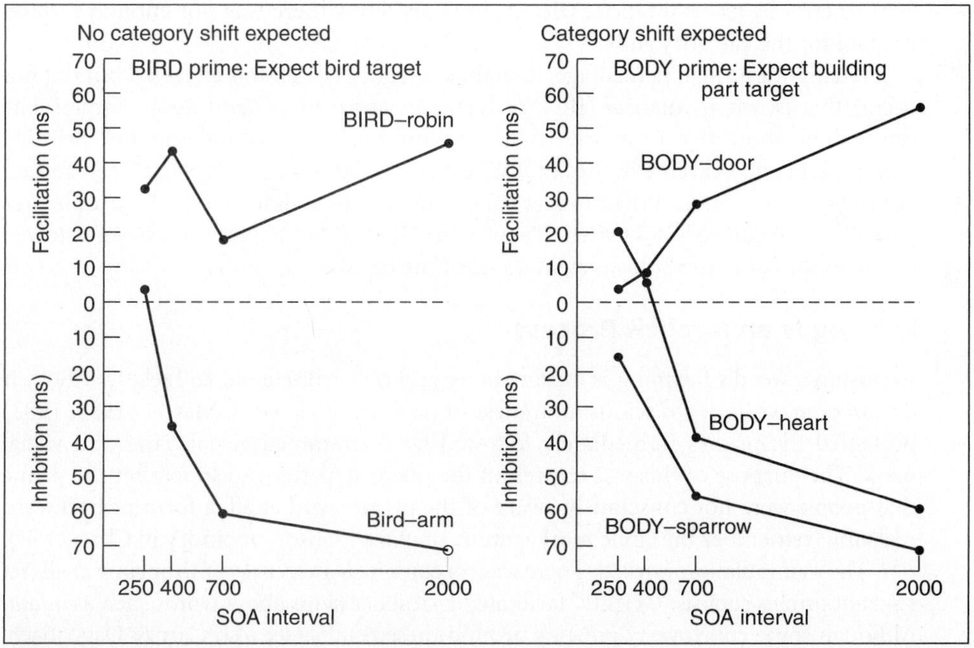

FIGURE 7-13
Reaction time to lexical decision targets. In the left half, people saw a prime and did not expect a shift in category; sample stimuli are "BIRD–robin" for a relevant prime and "BIRD–arm" for an irrelevant prime. In the right half, people expected the target to come from the building category if they saw "BODY" as a prime and from the body part category if they saw "BUILDING" as a prime. When the shift in category occurred as expected, RT was facilitated at longer SOAs. When the expected shift did not occur, there was facilitation at the short SOA when the prime was relevant ("BODY–heart"). Inhibition occurred when the shift was completely unexpected ("BODY–sparrow"). From Neely (1977).

happens very rapidly. Notice also that this curve showed more facilitation as the SOA got longer. This suggests that with more and more time to prepare, priming grew stronger because of the additional effect of conscious factors.

Second, he found inhibition, a slowing down of RT, when the prime was unrelated to the target. If you had seen "BIRD" as a prime, you were then slower to decide that *arm* was a word. Not surprisingly, this inhibition effect grew stronger across longer and longer SOAs: Again, the conscious preparation for a member of the *bird* category worked against you when you saw *arm* as the target.

The truly impressive (and complicated) part of Neely's study comes next. He told people that when they saw one particular prime, such as the category name "BODY," they should expect to see a target from a *different* category, such as a part of a building (e.g., *door*). Likewise, if they saw "BUILDING" as a prime, they should expect to see a body part, such as *arm,* as the target. What happened then? When the switch from one category ("BODY") to a different one (*door*) happened, there was priming only at the long SOAs, as shown in the top right of Figure 7-13. This makes perfectly good sense; you see "BODY," and it takes you a bit of time to remember that you should see an item from the building category next. When you are given that bit of time, you are ready for *door, window*, and so forth. But notice that at the shortest SOA, there was no facilitation. Clearly, at short SOAs there was not enough time to prepare for the category shift.

Finally, for a small percentage of trials, a category switch was expected but did not occur; that is, when you saw "BODY" but then saw *arm* or *heart* as the target? The clever thing about this, of course, is that it should tap into normal semantic priming because arm and heart are in the "BODY" category. This was exactly what Neely found, but only at short SOAs. When longer times were given, with longer SOAs, people prepared for the category to switch. Then, when that *didn't* happen, they were slowed down, as shown in the bottom right panel of the figure.

Priming Is an Implicit Process

Accessing a word's meaning is automatic (e.g., Friedrich, Henik, & Tzelgov, 1991). It occurs even without conscious awareness of having seen a word. Marcel (1980; 1983) presented the primes immediately followed by a scrambled visual pattern, a visual mask. The purpose of this was to present the masking pattern so soon after the prime that people were not consciously aware of the prime word at all, a form of backward masking (remember the circle marker study on visual sensory memory in Chapter 3?).

The manipulation worked. There was no conscious awareness of the prime at all. Yet relevant primes such as "CHILD" facilitated lexical decisions about words such as *infant*. Although some controversy grew up around these results (see also Carr & Dagenbach, 1986; Carr et al., 1982; Merikle, 1982), substantial work indicates that the effect is genuine and important (Hirshman & Durante, 1992; McRae & Boisvert, 1998). Semantic priming, in the lexical decision task and other settings, can occur automatically, without conscious identification of the prime. In terminology introduced at the beginning of Chapter 6, we also refer to such effects as implicit, processes that can occur without any necessary involvement of conscious awareness.

For now, think of priming as a two-component process. As you have been reading, a significant degree of priming is obtained under very rapid conditions (e.g., SOAs less than 250 ms). Such a rapid effect suggests that priming can operate automatically, without the need for conscious awareness or recollection. This is the essence of implicit memory. Explicit memory, on the other hand, refers to intentional, deliberate, and conscious mental processing, including recollection and awareness (Schacter, 1989). In Neely's (1977) "expect a switch" conditions, it took extra time for people to switch from "BUILDING" to the conscious expectation of *body part*. But once they did, there was also a priming effect caused by more conscious processing. Because they had to deliberately remember to switch, this was an explicit memory priming effect.

We are still figuring out how all the pieces fit together in the distinction between implicit and explicit memory. There has been some concern over the measurement of implicit processes and ways of separating implicit and explicit processes (Buchner & Wippich, 2000; Cowan & Stadler, 1996; Jacoby, Toth, & Yonelinas, 1993; Palmeri & Flanery, 1999). Likewise, there has been debate—even argument—about unconscious priming, i.e., does genuine priming without conscious processing and attention really exist, can it be demonstrated, couldn't at least some conscious processing have adulterated the results (e.g., Draine & Greenwald, 1998; Greenwald, Abrams, Naccache, & Dehaene, 2003; Greenwald & Draine, 1998; Greenwald, Klinger, & Schuh, 1995; Merikle & Reingold, 1998; and Naccache, Blandin, & Dehaene, 2002)?

But even now there is agreement that priming has a clear implicit basis and that implicit and explicit memories are separate entities, as shown in the Squire (1993) taxonomy in Chapter 6 (Figure 6-1). Indeed, there can be; (implicit) priming effects can be observed in ERPs, patterns from cortical recordings (e.g., Heil Rolke, & Pecchinenda, 2004), and even in cases when the people have lost the (explicit) ability to recall information consciously (i.e., in cases of amnesia, as in Levy, Stark, & Squire, 2004; see Schacter & Badgaiyan, 2001, for a readable introduction to neuroimaging results on priming).

Section Summary

- In the priming task, a prime of some degree of relationship to a target is presented first, and RT to the target is measured. When the prime is relevant, RT to the target usually is speeded up, even at very short time intervals (SOAs). This is generally taken as evidence that semantic priming is an automatic process. When the prime is irrelevant to the target, RT is generally slowed down at longer SOAs. This is usually interpreted as evidence that irrelevant primes generate a conscious expectation that slows down processing when the expectation is misleading. Among the tasks used to examine priming in semantic memory are word naming, sentence verification, and lexical decision tasks.
- Evidence also suggests that priming is an implicit memory process. There is an ongoing debate, however, about whether possible conscious contributions to the priming effects have been completely ruled out.

SCHEMATA AND SCRIPTS

Now that we've laid out some of the basics of semantic memory, let's move on to a more specific and complex way of using general knowledge. We are often called upon to use world knowledge to understand the various events and circumstances that we encounter. We'll start out by looking at memory for a story. Table 7-5 contains a story called "The War of the Ghosts." The story is important not only because of the psychological points it raises, but also for historical reasons: Bartlett (1932) used it in one of the earliest research programs on remembering meaningful material. Do the demonstration in the table now, before reading further.

Now that you have read and recalled the story, spend a moment jotting down some of the thoughts that occurred to you as you read the story and then tried to recall it. For example, if you remembered some specific details, comment on what made those details more memorable to you. Did you get most of the story line correct, or did you have to do some guessing? What was your sense of the story as you read it? You no doubt reflected on how peculiar the story was, with unfamiliar names and characters, vague and hard-to-understand twists of the story line, and unexplainable events. The story is a North Pacific Indian (Eskimo) folktale, so it is not surprising that it differs so much from other stories with which you are familiar.

Once you have exhausted your intuitions, look at Table 7-6 and compare your recalled version with the retellings in the table. Although your version may be closer to the original, because so little time passed between reading and recalling, you should be able to see points of similarity to the tabled retellings.

TABLE 7-5 Bartlett's (1932) "The War of the Ghosts"

Read the following, then attempt to reproduce the story by writing it down from memory.

One night two young men from Egulac went down to the river to hunt seals, and while they were there it became foggy and calm. Then they heard war-cries, and they thought: "Maybe this is a war-party." They escaped to the shore, and hid behind a log. Now canoes came up, and they heard the noise of paddles, and saw one canoe coming up to them. There were five men in the canoe, and they said:

"What do you think? We wish to take you along. We are going up the river to make war on the people."

One of the young men said: "I have no arrows."

"Arrows are in the canoe," they said.

"I will not go along. I might be killed. My relatives do not know where I have gone. But you," he said turning to the other, "may go with them."

So one of the young men went, but the other returned home.

And the warriors went on up the river to a town on the other side of Kalama. The people came down to the water, and they began to fight, and many were killed. But presently the young man heard one of the warriors say: "Quick, let us go home: that Indian has been hit." Now he thought: "Oh, they are ghosts." He did not feel sick, but they said he had been shot.

So the canoes went back to Egulac, and the young man went ashore to his house and made a fire. And he told everybody and said: "Behold I accompanied the ghosts, and we went to fight. Many of our fellows were killed, and many of those who attacked us were killed. They said I was hit, and I did not feel sick."

He told it all, and then he became quiet. When the sun rose he fell down. Something black came out of his mouth. His face became contorted. The people jumped up and cried.

He was dead.

Bartlett's Research

Bartlett (1932), like Ebbinghaus, wanted to study human memory with the methods of experimental psychology. Very much unlike Ebbinghaus, however, he wanted to study memory for *meaningful* material, so he used folktales, ordinary prose, and pictures. His typical method had people study the material for a period of time, then recall it several times, once shortly after study and again at later intervals. By comparing successive recalls, Bartlett examined the progressive changes in what people remembered.

Using these methods, Bartlett obtained evidence that human memory for meaningful material is not especially reproductive, that is, does not reproduce the original passage in any strict sense. Instead, Bartlett characterized this sort of remembering as "an effort after meaning." The modern term for this is **reconstructive memory**, in which *we construct a memory by combining elements from the original material together with existing knowledge.*

TABLE 7-6 Two Retellings of Bartlett's (1932) "The War of the Ghosts"

First recall, attempted about 15 min after hearing the story:

Two young men from Egulac went out to hunt seals. They thought they heard war-cries, and a little later they heard the noise of the paddling of canoes. One of these canoes, in which there were five natives, came forward towards them. One of the natives shouted out: "Come with us: we are going to make war on some natives up the river." The two young men answered: "We have no arrows." "There are arrows in our canoes," came the reply. One of the young men then said: "My folk will not know where I have gone"; but, turning to the other, he said: "But you could go." So the one returned whilst the other joined the natives.

The party went up the river as far as a town opposite Kalama, where they got on land. The natives of that part came down to the river to meet them. There was some severe fighting, and many on both sides were slain. Then one of the natives that had made the expedition up the river shouted: "Let us return: the Indian has fallen." Then they endeavored to persuade the young man to return, telling him that he was sick, but he did not feel as if he were. Then he thought he saw ghosts all round him.

When they returned, the young man told all his friends of what had happened. He described how many had been slain on both sides.

It was nearly dawn when the young man became very ill; and at sunrise a black substance rushed out of his mouth, and the natives said one to another: "He is dead."

Second recall, attempted about 4 months later:

There were two men in a boat, sailing towards an island. When they approached the island, some natives came running towards them, and informed them that there was fighting going on on the island, and invited them to join. One said to the other: "You had better go. I cannot very well, because I have relatives expecting me, and they will not know what has become of me. But you have no one to expect you." So one accompanied the natives, but the other returned.

Here there is a part I can't remember. What I don't know is how the man got to the fight. However, anyhow the man was in the midst of the fighting, and was wounded. The natives endeavored to persuade the man to return, but he assured them that he had not been wounded.

I have an idea that his fighting won the admiration of the natives.

The wounded man ultimately fell unconscious. He was taken from the fighting by the natives.

Then, I think it is, the natives describe what happened, and they seem to have imagined seeing a ghost coming out of his mouth. Really it was kind of materialisation of his breath. I know this phrase was not in the story, but that is the idea I have. Ultimately the man died at dawn the next day.

Two particularly notable aspects of Bartlett's results led him to this conclusion. The first concerns omissions, information people failed to recall. For the most part, Bartlett's participants did not recall many details of the story, either specific names (e.g., Egulac) or specific events in the narrative (e.g., the phrase "His face became contorted"). The level of recall for the main plot and sequence of events was not too bad, but minor events often were omitted. As a result, the retellings are shorter than the original. Of course, people were not asked for *verbatim* (word-for-word) recall, so rephrasing and condensing are to be expected. Nonetheless, there were significant losses of information.

A second aspect of Bartlett's results is more interesting. There was a strong tendency for the successive recalls to normalize and rationalize the events in the story. That is, people added to and altered the stories, by supplying additional material that was not in the original (the island mentioned after four months, for example). These changes often made the story more "normal," conventional, or reasonable. Because the story was strange to Bartlett's participants, his friends and colleagues in Great Britain, it is not surprising that their retellings modernized and demystified the original. For example, note how the ghost theme becomes less prominent in the two retellings in Table 7-6, even though *ghosts* is in the title of the story. What is fascinating about this result is the *source* of this additional material. Where did it come from, if not from the story itself? It came from the people's semantic memories.

Schemata

Bartlett borrowed the idea of a **schema** to explain the source of these adjustments and additions (although he complained about the vagueness of the term). In his view a schema was "an active organisation of past reactions or past experiences" (1932, p. 201), essentially what we have been calling general world knowledge. More generally, a schema is *a stored framework or body of knowledge about some topic.* Bartlett claimed that when we encounter new material, such as the "Ghosts" story, we try to relate the material to something we already know, to existing schemata (the plural of "schema"). If the material does not match an existing schema, then we tend to alter the material to make it fit (similar in spirit to Piaget's *assimilation*). Therefore recall is not a true, exact recall or reproduction of the original material. Instead, it is a reconstruction based on elements from the original story and on our existing schemata.

The use of semantic knowledge, such as schemas to fill in our knowledge with more expected information, can sometimes lead to errors. When related but unusual bits of information are encountered, a person's schema may dominate cognitive processing, leading a person to make errors that, when caught, reveal this powerful influence. Questions such as 19 and 20,

(19) How many animals of each kind did Moses take onto the ark?

(20) What is the nationality of Thomas Edison, inventor of the telephone?

show the less-than-desirable context and cognitive effects that can crop up. Read questions 19 and 20 again, if you didn't notice the semantic illusion (Erickson & Mattson, 1981; Reder & Kusbit, 1991). The reason we fall for the illusion, that we do not immediately notice what is wrong with the sentence, should be clear: It's another illustration of the power of schemas on cognition and conceptually driven processing.

EXTENSIONS OF RECONSTRUCTIVE EFFECTS Subsequent research fleshed out some of the details of this generalization and has added to our understanding of the importance of existing knowledge or schemata. For example, knowledge of the theme or topic of a passage improves people's memory of the passage (Bransford & Johnson, 1972; Dooling & Lachman, 1971). On the other hand, providing a theme, say, by attaching a title to a story, can also distort recall or recognition in the direction of the theme.

A clever—and very early—demonstration of this distortion effect was provided by Sulin and Dooling (1974). One group of people read a paragraph about a fictitious character: "Gerald Martin's seizure of power. Gerald Martin strove to undermine the existing government to satisfy his political ambitions. Many of the people of his country supported his efforts" (p. 256). A second group read the same paragraph, but the name *Adolf Hitler* was substituted for *Gerald Martin.* After a five-minute waiting period, people were shown a list of sentences and had to indicate whether each was exactly the same, nearly the same, or very different from one in the original story.

Pre-experimental knowledge—that is, existing knowledge about Hitler—led to significant distortions in the recognition of sentences. People who read the Hitler paragraph rated sentences as "the same" more frequently when the sentences matched their existing knowledge about Hitler, even though the original passage contained no such information (e.g., "Hitler was obsessed by the desire to conquer the world," p. 259). Furthermore, these *thematic effects,* as they were called, grew stronger in the group that was tested one week after reading the story.

This thematic effect was particularly striking in a second experiment conducted by Sulin and Dooling. One group read an account about Carol Harris ("Carol Harris was a problem child from birth. She was wild, stubborn, and violent"). Only 5% of the people in this group said "yes" one week later when asked if the sentence "She was deaf, dumb, and blind" had been part of the passage. In a contrasting group, the same paragraph was presented, but the name *Helen Keller* was used. Fully 50% of these people said "yes" one week later to the same critical question. The same pattern of results was also obtained by Dooling and Christiaansen (1977), in which people were told that the paragraph about Carol Harris that they had read a week before had in fact been about Helen Keller. Just as before, people responded "yes" to statements that referred to thematically consistent information, as if they were drawing inferences from their existing knowledge rather than remembering the passage on its own terms. Dooling and Christiaansen concluded that thematic effects are prominent during retrieval, at the time of test, because they were observed a full week after exposure to the passage.

In general, the more expertise a person has, the more elaborate and developed their schemata for that type of knowledge. While these schemata can be helpful at encoding, by directing a person's attention to what is and is not relevant, helping organize that knowledge, and so forth, there are also some pitfalls. For example, experts have a greater tendency to classify individual experiences in terms of their extensive schemas. As a result, they are less likely to actually store and remember individual events (Castel, McCabe, Roediger & Heitman, 2007).

PROVE IT
Schematic Distortion

This aim of this "Prove It" section is to give an opportunity to observe how schemata can distort memory for a text that a person reads, and how to overcome that distortion. This demonstration is based on a study reported by Hasher and Griffin (1978). Essentially, what we are looking for here are things that people recall from a text that was read earlier, but which were never actually mentioned in that text, that is, information that would be in a person's schema, but not what he or she actually read. What you should do is get two groups of people. Have them all read the story below. Tell each group that this story is called "The Escaped Convict." After some period of time has elapsed (at least 10 minutes), ask your groups to recall the story. For one group, remind them that the title of the story was "The Escaped Convict." However, for the other group of people, act all flustered and tell them that you screwed up, and that the actual title of the story was "The Deer Hunter."

After people are done, look at what they have recalled from the story. One of the things that you should find is that people in the repeated titled group should recall details about an escaped convict that weren't actually in the story. This illustrates how a schema can distort a person's memory to make it more schema consistent. The other thing that you may find is that people in the title switch group have relatively few intrusions of new information, having to do with either the escaped convict or deer hunter themes. If so, then what you've been able to do is make memory more accurate by discrediting the schema information in semantic memory, and leading people to rely more on their episodic memory of what they actually read.

The Escaped Convict / The Deer Hunter

The man walked carefully through the forest. Several times he looked over his shoulder and scrutinized the woods behind him. He trod carefully trying to avoid snapping twigs and small branches that lay in his path, for he did not want to create excess noise. The chirping of the birds in the trees almost annoyed him, their loud calls serving to distract him. He did not want to confuse those sounds with the type he was listening for.

Source: Hasher & Griffin (1978)

Scripts

Schemata vary in their degree of structure and complexity. While some are quite simple and basic, others are very complex and intricately structured. One specific type of schema captures the order in which things occur. These are called **scripts**, *the large-scale semantic knowledge structures that guide our interpretation and comprehension of ordered daily experience.* These structures are detailed semantic memory concepts. For example, consider the large amount of knowledge you have in memory, that guides your comprehension of even a simple story:

> ***Billy was excited about the invitation to his friend's birthday party. But when he went to his room and shook his piggy bank, it didn't make a sound. "Hmm," he thought to himself, "maybe I can borrow some from Mom."***

SCRIPTS IN MEMORY Think for a moment about the common meaning of the word *script:* the dialogue and actions that are to be performed by the actors and actresses in a play. The script for a play details exactly what is supposed to happen in a stage production. In similar fashion, a mental script is a general knowledge structure about ordinary events and situations. In other words, a script is a mental representation of what is supposed to happen in a particular circumstance. Are you going to a restaurant? Your mental script tells you what to expect, the order of events, who the central characters are, and what you and they are supposed to do. Are you invited to a birthday party, taking an airplane flight, or sitting in a class on human memory and cognition? Your generalized knowledge of what happens in these settings guides your comprehension as the events unfold, and leads to certain expectations.

The overall theory behind scripts is straightforward. People store in memory a generalized representation of events they have experienced, and this representation is invoked, or retrieved, when a new experience matches an old script. One function of a script, in a written or spoken story, is that it provides a kind of shorthand for the whole event; you need not describe every element of the experience but can merely refer to the whole event by invoking the script. More important, the activated script provides a framework or context within which new experiences can be understood and within which a variety of inferences can be drawn to complete your understanding (Abbot, Black, & Smith, 1985; Reiser, Black, & Abelson, 1985; Seifert, Robertson, & Black, 1985).

Let's develop this notion of scripts with a few examples. Consider the following abbreviated stories (taken or adapted from Schank & Abelson, 1977, pp. 38–40):

> *(9) John went to a restaurant. He asked for a hamburger. He paid the check and left.*
>
> *(10) John went to a restaurant. He asked the waiter for a hamburger. He paid the check and left.*
>
> *(11) John went into the restaurant. He ordered a Big Mac. He paid for it and then ate it while driving to work.*

According to Schank and Abelson (1977), our understanding of stories 9 and 10 is guided by our scripted knowledge of a particular situation: going to restaurants. Story 11 is understood by a particular variant or track. Schank and Abelson claim that we record a large number of separate scripts in our memories. The average adult, having experienced many different instances of eating in restaurants, has a generalized script representation of this situation (and scripts for countless other situations, too). Whenever we encounter a story like 9, elements of the story trigger or activate the appropriate script; in a real sense, the script is primed. As a consequence, all subsequent events in the story (or events in a real-world experience) are interpreted with reference to the script that is activated in memory.

Consider a somewhat longer story (from Abelson, 1981):

> *(12) John was feeling very hungry as he entered the restaurant. He settled himself at a table and noticed that the waiter was nearby. Suddenly, however, he realized that he'd forgotten his reading glasses.*

Although this story does not necessarily call up any particular track of the general restaurant script, it does illustrate some of the predictive and interpretive power of script theory. Almost all readers (or listeners) will understand John's problem as "unable to read the menu." It makes little difference that "the menu" or even "a menu" was never mentioned. The restaurant script is activated, which in turn activates the whole set of **frames** (also called slots), *details about specific events within the script.* This prepares you to receive specific information about those frames. When the detail comes along, such as "the waiter," that particular detail is stored in the appropriate frame. If the detail does not come along (e.g., "the menu"), it is inferred from the script knowledge. Your comprehension then proceeds normally after "forgotten his reading glasses" because the unmentioned "thing you read in a restaurant" is supplied by the script.

In script terminology, the menu is a **default value** for the frame, *the common, typical value or concept that occupies the frame.* In the restaurant script, the default value "MENU" is the ordinary way that patrons find out what is available for dinner. Thus unmentioned details in the story are filled in by the default values. This means that a storyteller does not need to mention everything. We merely assume that the listener will supply any missing details from the stored script. Thus two plausible continuations of 12, one assuming the default value and one not, might be

(12a) Rather than go to his car to get his glasses, John asked the waiter to tell him what kinds of sandwiches they had.

(12b) But then the waiter told him that he wouldn't need his glasses because tonight's dinner was a buffet.

★ **PREDICTIONS** Figure 7-14 presents a generic restaurant script, based on Schank and Abelson's (1977) work, as an indication of the generalized knowledge represented in scripts. If you have such a conventional restaurant script, this enables you to under-

★ **FIGURE 7-14** A depiction of a standard restaurant script. Adapted from Schank and Abelson (1977).

```
Script: Restaurant        Roles: Customer
 Track: –                        Waiter
Props: Tables                    Cook
       Menu                      Cashier
       Food                      Owner
       Check
       Money

Entry conditions: Cust. is hungry, has money
 Exit conditions: Cust. not hungry, has less money
                  Owner has more money

SCENE 1: Entering → Cust. into restaurant
                    To table
                    Sit down

SCENE 2: Ordering → Menu on table
                          or
                    Asks for menu–waiter brings menu
                    Cust. reads menu
                    Cust. places order
                    Cust. waits for food → cook prepares food

SCENE 3: Eating → Waiter gets food from cook,
                    brings to Cust.
                  Cust. eats food → options
                                    Cust. returns food
                                    Cust. orders more

SCENE 4: Exiting → Waiter brings check
                   Cust. pays cashier, leaves tip for waiter
                   Cust. leaves restaurant
```

stand and predict the various events in the sequence. An individual with different experiences, however, may have some difficulties in understanding what is going on, for example, a small child who has only been to fast food restaurants. Thus comprehension should suffer to the degree that your current experience mismatches your script.

A well-known example of such processing difficulties is presented in the story in Table 7-7 (Bransford, 1979); be sure to make an honest effort to understand the story before you read the explanation in the bottom portion of the table. As this passage shows, a story may activate a script but mismatch the expected events in the script. Depending on the severity of the mismatch, we would predict difficulties in comprehension and recall. On the other hand, if a person lacks a specialized track within the script, we would predict comprehension based on the more general script that is in memory.

A final prediction from script theory is important enough that it must be developed in greater detail. Note from the shorthand and default ideas mentioned earlier that everything need not be mentioned in a story for a person to understand. In fact, as Schank and Abelson (1977, p. 38) put it, "When someone decides to tell a story that references a script, he recognizes that he need not (and because he would otherwise be considered rather boring, should not) mention every detail of his story. He can safely assume that his listener is familiar with the referenced script and will understand the story as long as certain crucial items are mentioned." In other words, the shorthand function of scripts relieves us of mentioning all the slots or frames in the script. We can assume that the reader or listener will *infer* those unmentioned details by means of the stored script.

TABLE 7-7 Restaurant Episode with Explanation

Jim went into the restaurant and asked to be seated in the gallery. He was told that there would be a one-half hour wait. Forty minutes later, the applause for his song indicated that he could proceed with the preparation. Twenty guests had ordered his favorite, a cheese soufflé.

Jim enjoyed the customers in the main dining room. After two hours, he ordered the house specialty—roast pheasant under glass. It was incredible to enjoy such exquisite cuisine and yet still have fifteen dollars. He would surely come back soon.

Assume, therefore, that Jim went to a very special type of restaurant. The owner allows people who can cook at least one special meal to compete for the honor of preparing their specialty for other customers who desire it. Those who wish to compete sit in the gallery rather than the main dining room (although a central stage is accessible to both).

The competition centers on the competitor's entertaining the crowd, by singing, for example, or dancing or playing an instrument. The approval of the crowd is a prerequisite for allowing the person to announce his or her cooking specialty. The rest of the crowd then has the option of ordering it, and the person receives a certain amount of money for each meal prepared. After doing the cooking and serving the meal to the customers, the person can then order from the regular restaurant menu and pay for it out of the money received for cooking. In general, this arrangement benefits the manager as well as the person. The manager obtains relatively inexpensive entertainment, and the person is usually able to make more than enough money to pay for an excellent meal.

From Bransford (1979)

A strong prediction of script theory is that people's recall of a story is influenced not merely by the details that were mentioned, but also by the events and details that were inferred based on scripted knowledge. For example, in the story about Billy and the birthday party, didn't you read "maybe I can borrow some money from Mom"? (Answer: No, you didn't.) Likewise, if we developed a longer restaurant story, you might "recall" that the customer left a tip for the waiter, even though no tip was ever mentioned in the original passage. Where do the "money from Mom" and the "tip" come from? They come from your script, from your long-term semantic and scripted knowledge (in a few moments, you will read about some research by Loftus and Palmer; the broken glass there came from the same place). And, importantly, such "recall" reflects reconstructive memory processes.

Evidence of Scripts

Convincing evidence of these predictions has been collected. Why did Sulin and Dooling's participants "remember" that they had read "She was deaf, dumb, and blind"? Because they were told that the story was about Helen Keller, thus triggering their memory of other information about Helen Keller.

Evidence specific to the script theory approach has been reported by a variety of researchers (Bower, Black, & Turner, 1979; Graesser, 1981; Graesser & Nakamura, 1982; Long, Golding, Graesser, & Clark, 1990; Maki, 1989). The article by Smith and Graesser (1981) is a good representation of such data. Smith and Graesser were investigating the role of typicality or relevance of specific events and actions in people's memory for script-based passages: Do we remember predictable events and actions better than unpredictable ones, or is it the other way around? They presented ten passages to people, each one related to a different scripted activity (e.g., taking the dog to the vet, washing a car, cleaning an apartment), and tested them with a recall or recognition task. Tests were conducted 30 min after people heard the passages, then again after 2 days, 1 week, and 3 weeks.

What made the Smith and Graesser evidence so compelling was the care they took in constructing their passages. Stories mentioned both typical and atypical actions within each script situation; Smith and Graesser collected norms in order to know what is typical and what is not. In their standard analyses of recall and recognition performance, typical information was remembered better than atypical information. These scores, however, were then corrected for guessing because the high accuracy on typical information probably included both events that were genuinely remembered as well as events that were merely reconstructed from the script knowledge.

When the scores were corrected for reconstructed guesses, recall and recognition were higher for atypical events than for typical events. In other words, in a story about taking the dog to the vet, people showed more accurate memory for the unusual, atypical events that occurred (e.g., "While waiting for the vet, Jack dropped his car keys"). Typical events, those anticipated by the script (e.g., "Jack led the dog into the waiting room"), were recalled more poorly once the scores had been corrected for guessing. Thus memory for the stories conformed to the schema-copy-plus-tag hypothesis: You store a copy of the generic script as your main memory for the story and tag onto that generic script the specific, atypical details that occurred (Graesser, 1981; Schutzwohl, 1998).

Hannigan and Reinitz (2001) investigated a somewhat different script effect—in particular, cause and effect. That is, they introduced manipulations into the scripted stories that corresponded either to a cause of an event or to an effect of some event. For example, in a slide sequence that depicted going grocery shopping, some participants saw a woman taking an orange from the bottom of a pile of oranges—but they didn't see the pile of oranges rolling to the floor. In a different condition, participants saw the oranges on the floor, but not the slide showing the woman taking the orange from the pile. In other words, some participants saw the cause (pull an orange from the bottom), and some saw only the effect (oranges on the floor). Their script-guided comprehension of the story, however, made up for causes they didn't see. That is, when they saw the effect, they mistakenly judged new cause scenes (i.e., never seen before) as "old"—if you've seen the oranges on the floor, you're more likely to remember later on that you saw the woman pulling an orange from the bottom of the pile. Keep in mind, of course, that this is an error, at least in the technical sense. But in terms of script knowledge, and what we generally know to be true about cause and effect, remembering the woman pulling an orange from the bottom of the pile is completely understandable—after all, *something* had to cause the oranges to fall to the floor. (See Hannigan & Reinitz, 2003, for evidence that an object from one scripted scene, say a vase of flowers in a restaurant, can easily "migrate" to a different restaurant memory.)

Section Summary

- Through his early work with materials such as "The War of the Ghosts" Bartlett was able to develop a schema theory. From this view, schemata are generalized knowledge structures, and so semantic memories, that people can use as guides for common experiences. Schemata can help organize information to facilitate learning, but can also cause people to misremember information in a more schema-consistent fashion.
- Scripts are large-scale representations of complex events and episodes, such as going to a restaurant or attending a birthday party. Script knowledge can be represented in the same kind of network structure as propositions and is assumed to be accessed by similar processes, such as spreading activation. A story invokes a script by mentioning headers, and these in turn activate the entire script.
- Script theories make a variety of predictions about comprehension and retrieval and provide a useful way to explain how people understand and interact with the real world, including how people can "remember" events because they are consistent with a stored script.

CONCEPTS AND CATEGORIZATION

Let's look at another area of study that addresses the principle of semantic relatedness, namely the structure of concepts and categories in semantic memory. This discussion also sets the stage for several processes to be considered in later chapters. As preparation for this, you might look up the word *bird* or *flower* in your dictionary and note any illustration that accompanies the definition.

Concept Formation

Traditional research on concept formation (e.g., Bourne & Bunderson, 1963) showed people a series of arbitrary patterns and asked them to categorize each one as belonging or not belonging to the concept being tested. In these studies, people were not told what the target concept was ahead of time: They had to develop the concept by guessing and paying attention to the feedback they received. For example, you might be shown geometric figures of circles and squares, some large and some small, some darkened and some light. The relevant concept might be "large darkened circle," which you would acquire slowly by paying attention to the feedback you received as you guessed your way through a set of patterns. We know fairly well what factors influence performance (e.g., the number of dimensions that are relevant and the number that are redundant; see Kintsch, 1970, for a summary). What we will do in this section of the chapter is look at more modern and complex ideas about how our semanic memories abstract and create the categories and concepts that we use everyday.

Theories of Categorization

As you move about the world, doing your day-to-day activities, you interact with a wide range of entities – objects, people, situations, and so forth. In many cases, the particular entities you are dealing with may be novel to you. For example, when walking down the street, you may come across a particular squirrel you've never encountered before. Will it attack you? Is it food? Will it run away? Will this squirrel make a good pet? What does it eat? How does it reproduce and raise its young? Can it vote in an election? You know what it is likely to do, and how you should interact with it, by using your categorical knowledge of what a squirrel is. Categories are convenient aspects of semantic memory that allow us to predict what is likely to happen in new encounters in the world. Essentially, when you are using your categories you are treating individual members as if they were more or less the same (all squirrels are pretty much alike, after all). This allows you to save a lot of time and mental effort. While this is a benefit in most situations, categorization can have a few drawbacks, such as when we overextend our categories, for example using stereotypes (which are a kind of category) to draw conclusions about people we hardly even know.

CLASSIC VIEW OF CATEGORIZATION There are three general classes of theories about categorization that we'll cover. These are the classic view, probabilistic theories, and explanation-based theories. Note that each theory of categorization has some strong points for some of the ways people create and use their categories, and they all also have some weaknesses.

The **classic view of categorization** (e.g., Bruner, Goodnow, & Austin, 1956) takes the position that *people create and use categories based on a system of rules*. That is, if something satisfies a set of rules, then it is a member of a category, whereas if it does not then it isn't. Of critical importance is that the rules identify *necessary* and *sufficient* features for something to be a member of a category. For example, the category BACHELOR can be defined this way: A bachelor is an unmarried adult male. These features are necessary in that if they are not present, the person would not be considered a bachelor. A person who is a married adult male would not qualify, nor would an unmarried male child, or an unmarried adult female (although she could be a bachelorette). These features are also sufficient in that nothing more is needed to identify what a bachelor is. For example, what a person's occupation is, the kind of car they drive, how tall they are, how many legs they have—these are all features that may be present, but they do not contribute to identifying the category beyond the sufficient ones.

The classic view of categorization follows on scientific taxonomies, such as the definition of what makes an animal a member of one species or another. This is the type of classification that allows us to identify a bat as a mammal rather than a bird, a penguin as a bird rather than an amphibian, and a chimpanzee as an ape rather than a monkey. It is quite clear that people can create and use categories that are defined by necessary and sufficient rules. When presented with novel stimuli, people can often readily derive the features that define a category. The more important question is whether this is how our semantic memories derive and use categories. That is, is this a psychologically real way of describing human categorization? There is a great deal of evidence to suggest that it is not. Before turning to other theories of categorization, let's cover some important aspects of human categorization.

CHARACTERISTICS OF HUMAN CATEGORIES So, if semantic memory doesn't typically use necessary and sufficient rules or features to create categories, what are human categories like? One of the clearest things is that the categories in our semantic memories tend to be loose and fuzzy. That is, members of a category vary in how truly they fit the category. This is called *graded membership*. For example, take the category BIRD. The zoological taxonomy of what make a creature a bird is fairly clear. But if you stop to think about it, some birds are better birds than others. Most people would agree that robins, sparrows, hawks, and cardinals are better examples of the BIRD category than say penguins, chickens, ostriches, and flamingos–those just aren't good examples of the category, are they? Thus, there is some variability in the degree to which members belong to a category. We can even say things like "*loosely speaking*, a bat is a bird, although *technically* it is a mammal." The use of these linguistic hedges indicates that even the boundaries of a category are not fixed. As another example, for the category FRUIT, apples, peaches, oranges, and pears are good examples of this category, while coconuts, tomatoes, cucumbers, and walnuts are not such good members. So, loosely speaking, tomatoes are vegetables, but technically, they are fruits. Also, technically coconuts aren't nuts, they're seeds.

The amazing things about graded category membership is that people show evidence of this principle even for categories that are clearly defined by necessary and sufficient rules. In one study by Armstrong, Gleitman, and Gleitman (1983), people showed evidence of graded category membership for the categories EVEN NUMBER and ODD NUMBER. People typically will say that 4 is a better member of the category EVEN NUMBER than 28! Thus, it seems clear that graded category membership is a fundamental principle of the process of human categorization in semantic memory.

There are some other principles of categorization that are related to graded membership. The first of these is the idea that categories have some sort of **central tendency**. This is *the idea that there is some mental core or center to the category where the best members will be found*. This is related to the idea of **typicality effects**, important to the ideas presented in the Smith et al. model of semantic memory discussed earlier. Thus, categories reflect **typicality**, *the degree to which items are viewed as typical, central members of a category*. In general, the time to make category judgments depends on how typical or central the item is in its category. The typicality of various category members is reflected in what is known as category norms, originally developed by Battig and Montague (1969) and more recently updated by Van Overschelde, Rawson, and Dunlosky (2004), in which people listed members of various categories. The norms showed that some items are listed as members of a category more frequently than others, such as listing *robin* more frequently as a member of the bird category (85%) than *chicken* ((9%). (In a rather chilling real-world example of the importance of typicality and frequency, Novick [2003] showed that airplanes increased tremendously in their rated typicality as vehicles for a period of about a month after the September 11, 2001, terrorist attacks on the United States, but dwindled back to baseline about four to five months later.) This important effect is now called the typicality effect: *Typical members of a category can be judged more rapidly than atypical members* (see also Casey, 1992). Figure 7-7 illustrates the effect obtained in the research by Smith et al.

One clever study on typicality was reported by Rips (1975). In this study people read a story about an island inhabited by only eight species of animals: sparrows, robins, eagles, hawks, ducks, geese, ostriches, and bats. One group of people read that a highly contagious disease had been discovered among all the sparrows; another group read that the robins had the disease: another that eagles were affected, and so on. People were then asked to estimate the percentages of the other animals that would also contract the disease. Interestingly, people's estimates yielded strong evidence of typicality. Species that are rated as more typical, such as sparrows, were judged very likely to infect almost all the other species. Atypical members, such as geese, were judged likely to infect only other atypical members—ducks, for instance—and this to a much lesser degree. The underlying issue was typicality. People assumed that if a typical instance had an important property, then that was sufficient to predict that all instances, typical and atypical, would share the property as well. However, if the property was true of an atypical instance, people tended to doubt that it would be shared throughout the category (experts augment this kind of reasoning with domain-specific knowledge; Shafto & Coley, 2003).

The typicality or centrality of a member of a category depends in part on the number of attributes it shares with other members of a category, with more central members having a greater number of these typical features (Rosch, 1978; Rosch & Mervis, 1975). Thus, while different members of a category may or may not have certain features, they all share a **family resemblance**. That is, there is some set of features that many or most of the category members have, although all features may not be present in all members. Think of your own family—various members have different combinations of the features that are found across the different individuals.

Finally, related to the family resemblance principle is the idea that real-world features do not occur independently of one another. Instead, they come in bundles: for example, the things in the real world that have wings often have beaks too. We structure our mental categories in terms of these **correlated attributes**, with typical instances of the category stored centrally, at the core of the concept's meaning, and with atypical instances stored more peripherally. These factors, correlated features and typicality, play a major role in the organization of semantic memory (McRae, de Sa, & Seidenberg, 1997).

So, in short, there appear to be a number of aspects of how humans create and use categories that are inconsistent with the classical view of categorization. That is, the characteristics like typicality, family resemblance, and correlated attributes are inconsistent with the idea that categories would be defined by necessary and sufficient features. So, in the next few sections we'll look at some other ideas about human categorization that are more flexible and allow for people to create categories that have these characteristics.

PROBABILISTIC THEORIES OF CATEGORIZATION Some of the more successful theories that have been developed beyond the classical view are what can be called **probabilistic theories**. These are theories that assume that categories in semantic memory are created by taking into account various probabilities and likelihoods across a person's experience.

One way of deriving categories probabilistically is by using a **prototype**, which is essentially the *central, core instance of a category*. A prototype is an average of all of your experiences with members of a category. Imagine taking many pictures of many types of dogs, and then morphing all of those images together. That average would be a prototype. Note that the prototype is an idealized representation that probably does not correspond to any individual member. For a prototype view, our mental categories are represented with reference to the prototype, with typical members stored close to the prototype and peripheral members stored farther away. Again, when you think of a *dog*, your prototype is unlikely to correspond to a chihuahua but instead would be more like a German shepherd, a golden retriever, or some other more "doggy dog." Similarly for your *bird* category, the prototype would be a rather ordinary, typical, nondescript bird, and the *flower* category would be a generic flower.

While the idea that people are using prototypes for semantic memory categories is appealing, there are some aspects of human categories that are not captured by a prototype, such as category size variability, correlated attributes, and anything else about the category that requires a person to consider the category as a whole. A prototype cannot do this because it is only a single mental representation that captures the average of the category members, not the variation among the members. Another, somewhat different and competing idea about how people use probabilistic information to create and use categories is **exemplar theory**, which assumes that when people think about categories, they are *mentally taking into account each experience, instance or example, of the various encounters that have been experienced with members of that category* (e.g., Medin, Goldstone, & Gentner, 1993; Murphy & Medin, 1985; Nosofsky, 1986; Rips, 1989; Rips & Collins, 1993). Thus, an "exemplar" is, basically, an example—robin is an exemplar of the bird category. Exemplar theory, in contrast to prototype theory, claims that we store exemplars in memory, then make categorization judgments by comparing the object to be classified to the stored exemplars.

Notice that both approaches often make the same or similar predictions—prototype theory predicts that a typical example is judged rapidly because it is highly similar to the prototype, and exemplar theory says it's because the typical example resembles so many of the stored exemplars. Because of this similarity, it is often difficult to distinguish between these two views, although there have been several attempts to do so (e.g., Feldman, 2003; Rehder, 2003). Chin-Parker and Ross (2004) have shown how multiple types of classification schemes are possible, either prototype or exemplar based, depending on how people are mentally oriented and are processing the information. They oriented people to either "diagnostic" features (it has to have this feature to be a member of the category—which sounds a bit like the classic view of categorization) or "prototypical" features (members of the category typically have this feature) in a learning task. The results showed that the categorization could be learned in either way, but people showed sensitivity only to the kind of feature they had used during learning. In other words, if they learned via the diagnostic features, they did not show sensitivity to the prototype, and likewise for the other group, learning via prototypes then showing no sensitivity to diagnostic features (for work on slower reasoning and decision making in this type of task, see Ross & Murphy, 1999, and Yamaguchi & Markman, 2000).

So, in sum, probabilistic theories move beyond the classical view by allowing people to average across their experiences, and with the need to derive hard and fast rules about what is and is not in a category. Whether by using prototypes or averaging across all known examples, this provides our semantic memory with the flexibility to understand and appropriately interact with all kinds of new instances or category members that we encounter in our everyday experiences in the world.

EXPLANATION-BASED THEORIES There is no question that probabilistic theories do a much better job at capturing human categorization than the classic theory. However, there are also a few issues that these theories have trouble with. For one, there is a circularity problem. In prototype and exemplar theories, how does memory know which experiences should be averaged across to form a category without knowing what the category is ahead of time?

Another issue is the high degree of flexibility of semantic memory categories. For example, think of the category "Things to take out of a burning building." Even without learning this information, you can generate a category on the fly, so to speak, that has all of the qualities of more traditional categories, such as birds, tools, or fruits. These **ad hoc categories** are categories a person creates based on situational circumstances, and which have characteristics of regular categories (Barsalou, 1983). Ad hoc categories show graded structure (e.g., a baby is a better member of this category than a television set), have a prototype (e.g., a highly valued, irreplaceable thing that can be damaged by fire), exhibit typicality effects (e.g., the family dog would be highly typical, but a visiting neighbor is something that most people are unlikely to list), and so forth. The categories people form are also influenced by the context a person is in. So, the color gray is more like white in the context of hair color, but more like black in the context of clouds.

These sorts of findings have led to a different type of theory of semantic memory classification called **explanation-based theories**. According to these views, semantic categories are essentially theories of the world we create to explain why things are the way they are. This highlights the important aspect of our categories: that they are structures we impose on the world, structures that may or may not reflect how the world actually is. For example, *shoe* is in the same category as *brick*, but in a different category than *sock*, if your category is "Things to pound a nail with if you don't have a hammer." This is because we have a concept or theory about what makes something good for hammering a nail, and can then apply this to the world around us. People can use their understanding of the causal relations among category members to make inferences about the internal structure and functioning of other members of a category (Rehder & Burnett, 2005).

These sorts of explanation-based theories are also reflected in findings that show the influence of embodied cognition on the use of semantic concepts. A study by Borghi, Glenberg, and Kaschak (2004) clearly makes this point. In this study, people were asked to indicate whether certain words corresponded to parts of an object, such as a car. Importantly, prior to this people read a sentence that encouraged them to take a particular perspective, such as either "You are driving a car" (inside) or "You are washing a car" (outside). The results showed that response times to names of parts were faster when they conformed to the person's perspective. For example, people who were told to imagine they were driving a car responded faster to parts that were in the interior of the car (e.g., speedometer) than the parts on the outside of the car (e.g., trunk), whereas the reverse was true for the other perspective. Thus, this shows that people can take an embodied perspective during semantic memory retrieval, and this can then influence the ease with which they retrieve information.

Related to this is the idea that people treat categories by following the principle of **psychological essentialism** (Medin, 1989), in which they *treat members of a category as if they have the same underlying, perhaps invisible, property or essence.* In some cases, this corresponds to something real, such as the chemical composition of a liquid, the DNA of an animal, or the water content of different cloud formations. Other times, these essences are strictly psychologically imposed. For example, there is no underlying essence that makes an object a member of the category TOOL. Tools vary widely in their shape, size, components, and so forth. Yet, they all seem to have a certain "tool-ness" that we "recognize." The basic point of psychological essentialism is that people are making decisions about how to categorize things not just on how they look or how they use them, but also based on their beliefs, right or wrong, about the various members of a category. This is related to why you may view people who are members of one particular social group as being distinct from another. (e.g., if you think to yourself "there is just something about the girls in my sorority that sets them apart.")

So, in sum, explanation-based theories capture some of the conscious and unconscious problem solving and reasoning that we go through to try to make sense of the world. By using these mini-theories for what makes a category, we don't need to rely on the hard and fast rules of the classic view, and don't have to mentally average or abstract across our experiences in order to derive a category, as with the probabilistic views. Instead, we can bring our power of reasoning to bear on the causal structure of the world—that is, why things are the way they are—to better understand how it can be organized and classified. Overall, these various theories of categorization demonstrate that people have a number of ways of mentally characterizing their world, a number of ways to draw on their old experiences to help them act and think in a way that will increase their success and performance in new situations.

Section Summary

- The classic view of human categorization is that people use necessary and sufficient rules. Although people *can* make classifications in this way, they typically do not in most situations.

- For probabilistic views, categories take into account regularities, such as typicality and correlated attributes, to produce categories with graded structures.
- According to the prototype view, categories are organized based on an averaged representation, the prototype, against which all other members of the category are compared.
- Exemplar theories claim that we store multiple examples or exemplars in memory, then make judgments by comparing an item to the stored exemplars.
- Explanation based theories assume that people are problem solving when they create categories. This is done by developing (largely implicit) theories of what goes into a category. This is why people can create ad hoc categories on the fly, and exhibit psychological essentialism—the intuitive belief that members of a category share an underlying essence.

CONNECTIONISM AND THE BRAIN

Connectionism

A more advanced way to model human memory rather than a semantic network is to use the approach of **connectionism**. You have had small doses of this already, for example when we considered word recognition in Chapter 3. Recall that the computer was trying to recognize the word "WORK" but that the final *K* was obscured. Because of connections between letter-level and word-level nodes, the system ended up identifying the word correctly.

At the most fundamental level, **connectionist models** (also known as **PDP models** and **neural net models**) contain a massive network of interconnected nodes. Depending on the model, the nodes can represent almost any kind of information, from the simple line segments and patterns considered for letter recognition to the more complex features and characteristics we have discussed about semantic memory. What makes connectionist models attractive is that, in principle, any type of knowledge can be represented by the nodes and their weighted, interconnecting pathways.

Examine Figure 7-15, a sample connectionist network for part of the "FURNITURE" category (Martindale, 1991). First, notice that each concept is connected to other nodes by pathways. The difference here is that each pathway has a number next to it, the path weights or weightings mentioned earlier. The weightings are the indicators of how strongly or weakly connected two nodes are; generally, the weighting scale goes from −1.0 to +1.0, with positive numbers indicating pathways that facilitate and negative numbers indicating inhibition. So, for example, the weighting between "FURNITURE" and "CHAIR" is +0.8, indicating that "CHAIR" is an important, central member of the category; "ASHTRAY," however, with its +0.1, is very weakly associated with "FURNITURE."

If we present the category name "FURNITURE" to the model, heavily weighted members such as "CHAIR" and "SOFA" are highly activated, and the system can make decisions about them quite rapidly. This is like the priming experiments you've read about: "FURNITURE" would prime "CHAIR." But "RUG" might actually be slower than baseline if primed by "FURNITURE." To understand this, note first that the weighted connection from "FURNITURE" to "RUG" is weak. Second, because

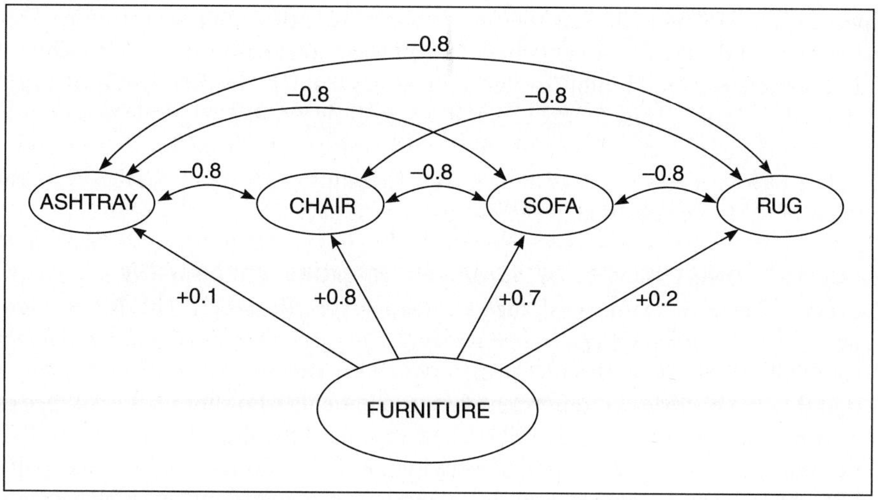

FIGURE 7-15 A small portion of a connectionist network. Note that the nodes at the same level exert an inhibitory influence on each other and receive different amounts of facilitation from the category name. Adapted from Martindale (1991).

"FURNITURE" primes "CHAIR" and "SOFA" a great deal, these nodes tend to inhibit, tend to spread negative activation, to "RUG"; see the weight of –0.8 between "CHAIR" and "RUG." (When neighbors at the same level inhibit one another, this is called lateral inhibition.)

Much effort has gone into creating connectionist models of various cognitive processes (e.g., McClelland & Rumelhart, 1981; Rogers et al., 2004; Seidenberg & McClelland, 1989). And in the area of semantic memory, there is a model of semantic priming (Masson, 1995), and a connectionist model of word meaning (McRae et al., 1997).

The glimpse at connectionism here is rather simplified. In many respects connectionist models make different assumptions from those of older spreading activation models. For instance, activating a node in a network model means activating that particular point in the network, followed by a spread of the activation to surrounding nodes. In a connectionist model, however, a concept is defined as a pattern of activation across units in the network. Priming is explained by the similarity of activation patterns between a prime and a target: The "FURNITURE" concept has a similar pattern of activation to the pattern for "CHAIR," so the one serves as an effective prime for the other.

The Brain

What is exciting about connectionist models is that the approach gives us a tool for understanding the richness of cognition, a working "machine" in a sense that lets us see what happens when multiple layers of knowledge influence even the simplest acts of cognition.

Particularly compelling (Seidenberg, 1993) are four frequently mentioned advantages of connectionist models. First, they are structurally more similar to the network of neurons in the brain. That is, the brain is a massive set of interconnected neurons, just as a connectionist network is a massive set of interconnected units. Second, the individual units are similar to those in the brain. In the nervous system, a neuron either fires or it does not; and, when it does fire, it affects the neurons it synapses on. This aspect of neural firing parallels the fire/no-fire nature of connectionist units. Third, the positive and negative weights between units in connectionist models mimic the action of excitatory and inhibitory neural synapses. Fourth, the best description of the activity of a connectionist model is that it is massively parallel: Multiple processes, including spreads of activation and inhibition, are co-occurring in a connectionist model at various levels, much as there is overwhelming evidence of parallel processing in the brain (McClelland et al., 1986; Rumelhart, 1989).

A CONNECTIONIST MODEL OF SEMANTIC MEMORY IMPAIRMENT A puzzling disorder in semantic memory is called a **category-specific deficit**. This is *a disruption in which the person loses access to one semantic category of words or concepts while not losing others*. Warrington and McCarthy (1983; also Warrington & Shallice, 1984) reported the case histories of four brain-damaged patients who showed this strange dissociation. The patients they described had serious difficulties in identifying living things but little or no difficulty in identifying nonliving things. For instance, patient J. B. R. could identify only 6% of a set of pictures of living things, such as *parrot* and *daffodil*, and could define only 8% of the words that named those living things. But when shown pictures of nonliving things, such as *tent* and *briefcase*, J. B. R. was successful at naming them 90% of the time and defining them 79% of the time.

How could semantic memory be splintered to the extent that a person's access to categories of living things would be disrupted while access to nonliving things would be preserved? Or, more to the point, could semantic memory be organized into just these two very broad categories, living and nonliving things? This may be a bit too convenient; we might wonder, "Why living versus nonliving things? Why not concrete versus abstract, high versus low frequency, or some other distinction?"

Warrington and Shallice (1984) suggested a more plausible explanation. Suppose that the bulk of your knowledge about living things is coded in semantic memory in terms of sensory properties: A parrot is a brightly colored animal that makes a distinctive sound. Likewise, suppose that most of what you know about nonliving things involves their functional properties: A briefcase is for carrying around papers and books. Warrington and Shallice suggested that a possible reason for the dissociation in their patients could be a selective loss or blocking of sensory knowledge. If so, that might explain the patients' impairments in naming and defining living things.

Going a step further, Farah and McClelland (1991) built a connectionist model to evaluate the Warrington and Shallice hypothesis; their work gives us a glimpse at how connectionism and neurocognition can join forces in explaining this kind of memory impairment. In their model semantic memory contained two types of knowledge or features about concepts—visual features (sensory) and functional features—with this knowledge being acquired by visual or verbal input to the semantic system. After constructing and training the model (establishing its memory, in a sense), Farah and McClelland "lesioned" it. That is, they "damaged" the visual units in the semantic memory network by altering the connection weights or disconnecting the visual units from the rest of the network.

The outcome of this procedure was strikingly similar to the patients' dissociations. That is, when the visual units were lesioned, the network showed extremely poor accuracy in associating names and pictures of living things; this is shown in the left

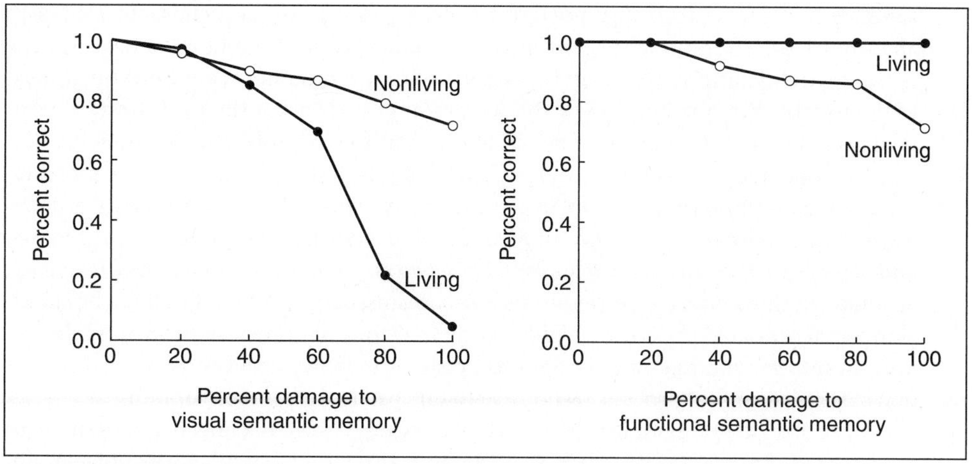

◆ **FIGURE 7-16**
Performance of the basic model, as measured by probability of correctly associating names and pictures for living and nonliving things, after different amounts of damage to visual and functional semantic units.

panel of Figure 7-16, as is the modest decline in accuracy for the *nonliving thing* category. Conversely, when the network's functional units were lesioned rather than the visual units, it was the *nonliving* category that suffered a bit (right panel, Figure 7-16; for updates, see Cree & McRae, 2003, and Rogers et al., 2004). ◆

Does this demonstration prove that impairment of patient J. B. R.'s visual semantic knowledge accounts for the dissociation? No; the model makes the correct prediction, a point in its favor, but such evidence is not a proof that the model is correct. Instead, think of the Farah and McClelland demonstration in this way. Warrington and Shallice asked, in essence, "Is it possible that impairment of sensory knowledge could produce the dissociation between living and nonliving things?" An appropriate answer to this question is: "Yes, it is possible, because just such a dissociation was produced or simulated in a connectionist model." In other words, the model provides a degree of assurance (probably a large degree) that the Warrington and Shallice hypothesis is reasonable and should be pursued further with both the impaired patients and connectionist modeling.

Shelton & Caramazza (1999) reviewed and summarized such case studies and the semantic disruptions that have been documented, and suggested that some refinements must be made to the visual versus functional discrimination suggested by Farah and McClelland. They noted the myriad dissociations described in the literature, including those in which patients' spoken output is disrupted despite intact written output (and vice versa) and those in which only some part (say, animals) of the *living things* category is disrupted. They suggested that the visual versus functional distinction may not be powerful enough to capture all the evidence. In an intriguing proposal, they speculated that a plausible distinction in semantic storage might be one between things that are evolutionarily significant, such as food and animals—both from the *living* category—and nonliving things, objects that have functional but not survival importance. Such a dissociation, if it characterized both anatomical and functional organization of memory, could then be the basis for the semantic dissociations observed in patients with brain damage; we would just need to document that one portion of the *living things* category—the evolutionarily important category—had been damaged to account for patients' naming deficits.

We conclude on this theoretical note, that the suggested distinction in Shelton and Caramazza (1999) represents a form of modularity (Fodor, 1983). **Modularity** is *a theoretical perspective in which different abilities, characteristics, types of cognitive processes, and so forth are theorized to be represented in separate components or modules in memory.* Modules, in this sense, are autonomous mechanisms, designed biologically to be standalone, independent processors, highly specialized for only one task or process. In important respects modules are thought to operate much like reflexes do, specialized for one particular kind of process, responsive to one particular kind of stimulus.

In terms of the evidence you have been studying, it is conceivable that word knowledge—knowledge of which word is the name of a particular concept—might be a separate module from knowledge of the concept itself. On the evidence summarized by Shelton and Caramazza (1999), we might postulate a separate module for written output (an orthographic module) and spoken output (a phonological module). You will read about other dissociated processes and abilities later, especially when we consider language in Chapter 9. For now, bear in mind that the answer to the question "How is memory organized?" might be some combination of connectionist-inspired networks and separate, modularity-inspired components, all of which interact smoothly (except in people with brain damage) to support cognition.

SEMANTIC MEMORY LOSS There are other brain disorders that affect the semantic system and especially the part of semantic memory known as **lexical memory**, *the mental lexicon or dictionary where our word knowledge (as distinct from conceptual knowledge) is stored.* One is *a deficit in word finding*, known as **anomia** (or sometimes **anomic aphasia**). At a superficial level, anomia is similar to a tip-of-the-tongue (TOT) state in which you are unable to name the word even though you are certain you know it. However, there are critical differences. Whereas people in a TOT state generally have partial knowledge about the unrecallable word, such as the number of syllables or the first sound, anomic patients have no such partial knowledge. Instead, there is complete and successful retrieval of the semantic concept followed by inability to find the word that names it (Ashcraft, 1993; for work on everyday forgetting—temporary inhibition—in semantic memory, see Johnson & Anderson, 2004). For example, Kay and Ellis's (1987) anomic patient was unable to name the word *president* but in attempting to find the word blurted out "Government . . . leader . . . John Kennedy was one." Cases such as these suggest that the mental representation of a concept is distinct from the representation of that concept's name, such that the concept itself can be retrieved even though the name may be blocked.

Section Summary

- Priming and spreading activation appear to be central constructs in theories of semantic memory, especially in connectionist approaches. These approaches even furnish persuasive analyses of semantic disruptions caused by brain damage, so-called category-specific deficits. The differences between connectionist and modular approaches to the mind have not been resolved.

Key Terms

ad hoc categories (p. *270*)
anomia (p. *276*)
anomic aphasia (p. *276*)
benefits (p. *247*)
category-specific deficit (p. *274*)
central tendency (p. *267*)
characteristic features (p. *235*)
classic view of categorization (p. *266*)
connectionism (p. *272*)
connectionist models (p. *272*)
correlated attributes (p. *268*)
costs (p. *247*)
default value (p. *262*)
defining feature (p. *235*)
event-related potentials (ERPs) (p. *240*)
exemplar theory (p. *269*)
explanation-based theories (p. *270*)
facilitation (p. *247*)
family resemblance (p. *268*)
feature list (p. *235*)
frames (p. *262*)
inhibition (p. *247*)
intersection (p. *234*)
lag (p. *247*)
lexical decision (p. *251*)
lexical memory (p. *276*)
modularity (p. *276*)
network (p. *232*)
neural net models (p. *272*)
node (p. *232*)
pathways (p. *232*)
PDP models (p. *272*)
perceptual symbols (p. *245*)
prime (p. *247*)
priming (p. *246*)
probabilistic theories (p. *269*)
property statement (p. *234*)
proposition (p. *232*)
prototype (p. *269*)
psychological essentialism (p. *271*)
reconstructive memory (p. *257*)
schema (p. *258*)
scripts (p. *260*)
semantic features (p. *235*)
semantic memory (p. *230*)
semantic relatedness effect (p. *240*)
sentence verification task (p. *237*)
spreading activation (p. *232*)
stimulus onset asynchrony (SOA) (p. *248*)
target (p. *247*)
typicality (p. *268*)
typicality effects (p. *267*)

CHAPTER

8

Using Knowledge in the Real World

The first notion to get rid of is that memory is primarily or literally reduplicative, or reproductive. . . .Remembering is not the re-excitation of innumerable fixed, lifeless and fragmentary traces. It is an imaginative reconstruction, or construction, built out of. . .a whole active mass of organised past reactions or experience, and. . . a little outstanding detail which commonly appears in image or in language form.

BARTLETT, 1932, PP. 204, 213

Sometimes we forget the past and at other times we distort it; some disturbing memories haunt us for years. Yet we also rely on memory to perform an astonishing variety of tasks in our everyday lives. Recalling conversations with friends or recollecting family vacations, remembering appointments and errands we need to run, calling up words that allow us to speak and understand others, remembering food we like and dislike, acquiring knowledge needed for a new job – all depend, in one way or another, on memory.

SCHACTER, 1996, P. 1

Having studied episodic and semantic memory separately in the previous two chapters, we must now put them back together. You read about the evidence of a dissociation between episodic and semantic memories, showing how they are separate in several important respects; after all, patient K. C. seems to have lost his entire episodic memory, suffering brain damage that nonetheless preserved his semantic memory. Be that as it may, we also need to understand the normal, everyday operation of long-term memory, the continual, coordinated, cooperative processes of interaction between the episodic and semantic systems that let us understand and remember our experiences. Thus, this chapter is about these interactions, about using our knowledge in real-world settings.

In Chapter 7, you read of a distinguishing feature of semantic memory research, that we test people on the knowledge they already have, knowledge they bring to the laboratory. Episodic tasks, in contrast, present the to-be-learned material to people, then test their memory of that material. Although most of the research presented in this chapter also presents specific materials to people, there are at least two major differences from standard episodic memory situations. First, the material to be learned is deliberately meaningful. This means we usually will not be presenting lists of words for recall or simple yes/no sentences for semantic verification. Instead, we are interested in people's memory for passages of text they read or hear, memory for natural events that happen to them, and so forth. As you will see, what we remember from our everyday experiences is significantly influenced by semantic knowledge, our knowledge of concepts, relationships, and general information about the world. The term for this effect, when already-known information influences our memory of new events, is conceptually driven processing.

A second difference in this chapter is that there is a far greater emphasis on accuracy of performance rather than the speed (RT) of performing; in fact, in many cases the emphasis is on *inaccuracy*. A stunning aspect of many of the results you will read about is inaccurate, error-prone memory performance, such as eyewitness recollection of the details of an event that are just plain wrong. Schacter (1996) writes eloquently of the "fragile power" of memory, the paradoxical situation in which we are capable of remembering amazing quantities of information yet have a strong tendency to misremember under a variety of circumstances. We focus on the fragile part of this description in this chapter.

THE SEVEN SINS OF MEMORY

In a very approachable work, Schacter (1999) provides some specifics about the fragile nature of memory by enumerating Seven Sins of Memory, seven ways in which our long-term memory lets us down (see Table 8-1). Material about the first three of the Seven Sins was covered in Chapter 6. First, there is a transience to long-term memory, a tendency to lose access to information over time. Although we attributed that to interference and retrieval failure in Chapter 6, Schacter asserts that there may also be genuine forgetting from long-term memory, especially when a memory is not used and hence not rehearsed. Second, we tend to be absent-minded, losing track of information, details, intended activities, and so on. The absent-mindedness can be both for information from the past and also for future activities; when studying *remembering to do something in the future*, we're studying *prospective memory*. In Schacter's view, absent-mindedness is largely a failure of attention during encoding, especially because we may have been relying on automatic processing, thus failing to encode information at a deeper, more elaborate level (for attention-based explanations of prospective memory, see Marsh & Hicks, 1998; R. E. Smith, 2003; Smith &

TABLE 8-1 The Seven Sins of Memory

Sin	Description
Transience	The tendency to lose access to information across time, whether through forgetting, interference, or retrieval failure
Absent-mindedness	Everyday memory failures in remembering information and intended activities, probably caused by insufficient attention or superficial, automatic processing during encoding
Blocking	Temporary retrieval failure or loss of access, such as the tip-of-the-tongue state, in either episodic or semantic memory
Misattribution	Remembering a fact correctly from past experience but attributing it to an incorrect source or context
Suggestibility	The tendency to incorporate information provided by others into your own recollection and memory representation
Bias	The tendency for knowledge, beliefs, and feelings to distort recollection of previous experiences and to affect current and future judgments and memory
Persistence	The tendency to remember facts or events, including traumatic memories, that one would rather forget, that is, failure to forget because of intrusive recollections and rumination

From Schacter (1999).

Bayen, 2004). Third, we sometimes experience blocking, a temporary loss of access to information, say in a stressful situation such as an exam. The most common example of such blocking is the tip-of-the-tongue (TOT) phenomenon.

Schacter describes the first three as sins of omission: Just when you need to remember something, you can't. The next three of the Seven Sins, all of which appear repeatedly throughout this chapter, are better described as sins of commission—situations in which you remember something, but the memory involves an error, maybe an incorrect time or person, maybe a detail you picked up from a different source. In brief, these three sins are misattribution, suggestibility, and bias. As you will learn in this chapter, misattribution consists of remembering something but being mistaken about the correct source of the information. Suggestibility is closely related to this and involves incorporating information supplied by other sources into your own memory of an event. And bias is a version of top-down processing; it involves "the distorting influences of present knowledge, beliefs, and feelings on recollection of previous experiences" (Schacter, 1999, p. 193). (Schacter's final Sin of Memory is persistence, by which he means the intrusive recollection of past events, especially traumatic ones—quite literally, failure to forget. We run into this briefly in the section on repressed and recovered memories. Consult the original Schacter, 1999, article for the accumulating neuroscience evidence on these sins).

FACTS ABOUT THE WORLD

In most or all reconstructive memory studies, we often intentionally lure people into making mistakes. That is, we present meaningful material such as a story or a set of related sentences, then do something that invites mistakes of one sort or another. This is unlike most of the episodic and semantic memory studies you've read about, where people are simply asked to learn and remember material in a straightforward way.

This is not to say that such research on reconstructive memory is unrepresentative, biased, or in some other way unfair or misleading. There are many situations in everyday affairs in which related information lures us into remembering something that was not in the original. Furthermore, it is obviously important to understand how human memory can be influenced by such factors. On the other hand, there is a more general kind of research in which semantic and episodic factors are combined, but the people are not deliberately misled or lured into mistakes. In this other kind of research, we are interested in what people can recall when presented with ordinary connected prose. Put simply, aside from the occasionally distorting or misleading effects that knowledge can exert, what are the more ordinary effects of knowledge as we understand simple sentences, stories, and other forms of connected discourse?

The Nature of Propositions

In this section we discuss the idea that what people remember from meaningful material is the idea or gist of information—in other words, we don't usually remember superficial aspects of a passage, exact words or exact phrasings, but we do remember the basic idea. But psychology needs ways to represent those ideas, needs a scientific way to quantify or graph meaning, to pin down what the vague term *meaning* means. And to do research on content accuracy, we need some way to score recall to see how well people remembered the meaningful content of a sentence.

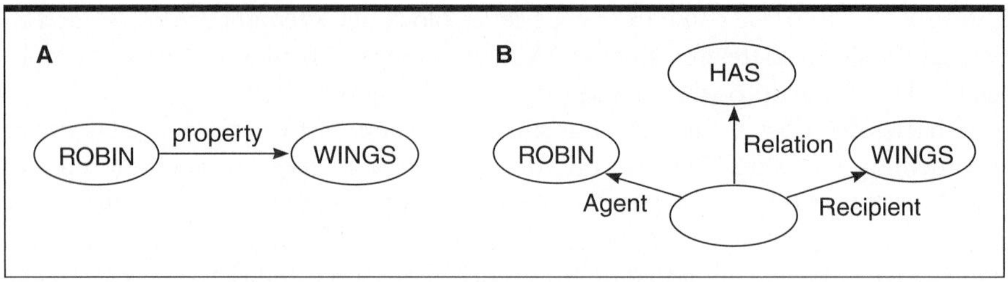

● **FIGURE 8-1**
A simple network representation **A** and propositional representation **B** of "A robin has wings."

The semantic unit that codes meaning is called a **proposition**. A proposition is a representation of meaning that can be stored in and retrieved from memory. A proposition represents the meaning of a single, simple idea, the smallest unit of knowledge about which you can make true/false judgments. Let's begin with this basic unit of meaning by learning the terminology of propositions and learning how they are structured.

THE BASICS In Chapter 7, the term *proposition* was defined as a simple relationship between two concepts, such as, "A robin has wings." Figure 8-1A diagrams this relationship using network nodes and pathways. In Figure 8-1B the sentence is also diagrammed as a proposition. If you compare the two, you will see that the propositional representation is slightly different. First, we place a central concept node in the diagram to represent the overall idea. Then each concept is attached to the node by its own labeled pathway. The differences between the left and right diagrams are largely superficial.

ELABORATED PROPOSITIONS Just as we can account for semantic knowledge in terms of a network structure, propositional theories attempt to account for our mental representation of the meanings of sentences as networks of interconnected propositions. To illustrate, consider a sentence and its propositional representation, as presented in Figure 8-2 (sentence from Anderson & Bower, 1973; notational scheme based on Anderson, 1985). The sentence,

> *(1) The hippie touched the debutante in the park*, is represented here as a set of interrelated concepts, one for each main word in the sentence. Each relationship among the words is specified by the type of pathway that connects the nodes (e.g., agent, recipient or patient, location). Thus sentence 1 is composed of five *relationships or connections of meaning*, five **semantic cases:**
>
> "TOUCH" is the **relation** in the sentence, the *topic or major event* in the sentence.
>
> "HIPPIE" is the **agent** for this event, the *actor or person* who did the touching.
>
> "DEBUTANTE" is the **patient** (or **recipient**) of the event, the *one who received the action* of touching.
>
> "PARK" is the **location** of the event, and the
>
> "PAST" is the **time** at which the touching occurred.

An alternative format for representing propositions involves a *relation*, usually the verb, followed by *an ordered list of concepts*, the **arguments** of the relation (e.g., Kintsch, 1974; see the bottom of Figure 8-2).

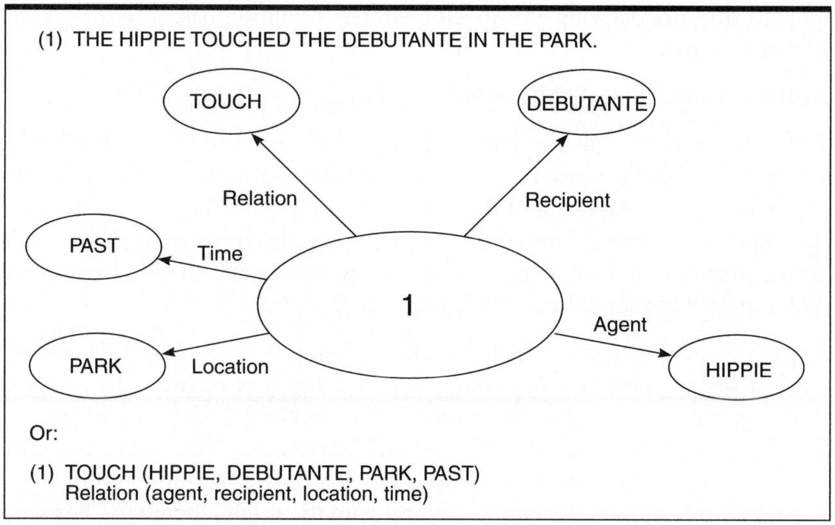

◆ **FIGURE 8-2**
A propositional representation, in "node-plus-pathway" notation and in written form, of the sentence "The hippie touched the debutante in the park." Network notation after Anderson (1980) and Anderson and Bower (1973); written proposition after Kintsch (1974).

Rules for Deriving Propositions

Proposition-based theories are widely seen within cognitive psychology as one way to represent complex meanings. Because meaning is so critical to an understanding of human cognition and because you need to understand this approach, we will spend some time dealing with propositions, learning how to derive them from connected discourse. Table 8-2 presents some sample sentences to use in practicing the rules; the rules themselves are somewhat modified from Anderson's (1980, pp. 106–107) list. ■

TABLE 8-2 Sample Passage from Sachs (1967) Including Multiple-Choice Recognition Test for Critical Sentence ■

Read the passage below at a comfortable pace but without looking back. After you have finished reading, your memory of one of the sentences in the paragraph will be tested.

There is an interesting story about the telescope. In Holland, a man named Lippershey was an eye-glass maker. One day his children were playing with some lenses. They discovered that things seemed very close if two lenses were held about a foot apart. Lippershey began experimenting and his "spyglass" attracted much attention. He sent a letter about it to Galileo, the great Italian scientist. Galileo at once realized the importance of the discovery and set about to build an instrument of his own. He used an old organ pipe with one lens curved out and the other in. On the first clear night he pointed the glass toward the sky. He was amazed to find the empty dark spaces filled with brightly gleaming stars! Night after night Galileo climbed to a high tower, sweeping the sky with his telescope. One night he saw Jupiter, and to his great surprise discovered near it three bright stars, two to the east and one to the west. On the next night, however, all were to the west. A few nights later there were four little stars.

Now, without looking back, decide which of the following sentences occurred in the paragraph.

a. He sent Galileo, the great Italian scientist, a letter about it.
b. Galileo, the great Italian scientist, sent him a letter about it.
c. A letter about it was sent to Galileo, the great Italian scientist.
d. He sent a letter about it to Galileo, the great Italian scientist.

Check to see whether your answer was correct by referring back to the paragraph.

Spend a few minutes deriving a propositional representation based on those rules for the following sentence.

(4) The hungry lion ate Max, who starved it.

★ Figure 8-3 contains corresponding steps to the rules that follow, illustrating the process of constructing a propositional representation of sentence 4. (Network diagrams are far easier to understand than other formats, so we'd encourage you to stick with the "node and pathway" notation.) Any rule preceded by an asterisk is an elaboration or modification of Anderson's scheme (but paraphrases are not starred). All rules should be applied to each sentence being analyzed.

1. Find all relational terms in the sentence. These usually are verbs, sometimes adjectives or relational expressions such as *father of* or occasionally prepositions such as *above* or *on top of*. In sentence 4 the relations are *hungry, eat*, and *starve*.
2. Write a simple sentence or phrase for each relation, and give each one a number. Each sentence will contain only the one relation and its noun arguments. Each sentence will be one of the propositions from the original sentence. For sentence 4, you should get three separate simple sentences:
   (5) The lion was hungry.
   (6) The lion ate Max.
   (7) Max starved the lion.
3. Draw an oval to represent the overall node for each proposition, sentences 5 through 7, and number each to correspond to its simple sentence. Write the relation next to its oval and connect the node to the relation by an arrow labeled *relation*.
4. Add a node to each proposition for each argument, each noun or nounlike word in the proposition (ignore function words such as *the*). Two classes of nouns should be distinguished here. If a noun refers to a specific person or object, such as Max, simply write the noun. If a noun refers only to an instance of a category, such as *lion*, then create a new node and give it an arbitrary name such as *X*. The *X* will stand for this particular instance of the category. Connect the *X* to its class noun with an *isa* arrow. Do not create different nodes for the same noun, but use the same node for both instances; *there should be only one *Max* node, even though *Max* occurs in propositions 6 and 7.
5. Connect all the arguments to the numbered oval with arrows. Label the arrows with an appropriate semantic label, such as *agent, patient/recipient,* or *location*.
6. Rearrange the network to make it neat. *In other words, there is no significance at all to the position of the nodes. The meanings are coded in terms of nodes that are connected and the nature of the pathway or arrow that connects them.

Are Propositions Real?

However elegant the propositional approach is in representing meaning, the ultimate test of their usefulness is empirical. It is fine to have an objective, systematic, and reasonable way of representing meaning, as is provided by propositional-based theories of meaning (e.g., Anderson, 1976; Kintsch, 1974). Yet, if this approach were not supported by research, it would be little more than an intellectual curiosity. Fortunately, research reports have documented the utility of these structures. We discuss a few to give you the flavor of this kind of research.

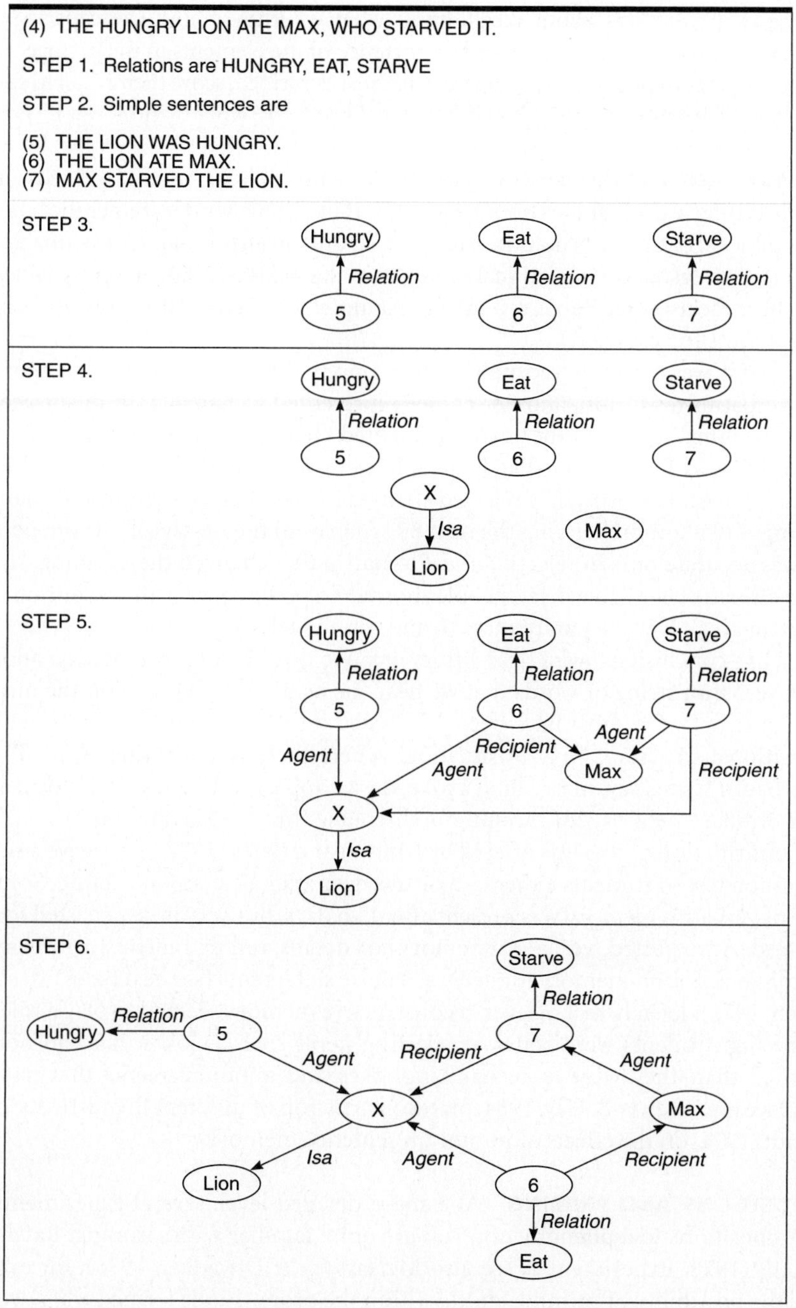

★ **FIGURE 8-3**
Steps in deriving a propositional representation for "The hungry lion ate Max, who starved it." Adapted from Anderson (1980).

The basic idea in all these tests is fairly straightforward. First, choose the samples of connected text that are going to be presented and derive their propositional structure. Then, determine which portions of the structure are more important to an understanding of the passage and which are less important; details of a minor episode, for instance, are relatively unimportant, but the overall outcome of a main episode is very important.

Draw some predictions about recall, given what we know about the capacity of the memory system and the structure and importance of the elements in the passage. Finally, give the passages to people and, using the rules just described, score their recall to see what is and is not remembered, what is and is not distorted, and what is and is not invented.

REMEMBERING PROPOSITIONS Let's begin with a classic study by Sachs (1967). She was testing a general idea about memory, that people tend to remember meaning rather than verbatim information. Her participants heard passages of connected text and were then tested on one critical sentence in the passage 0, 80, or 160 syllables after it had been heard. (See Table 8-2 for an example; why not read it now and confirm Sachs's results for yourself?)

The test was a simple recognition test among four alternatives. One alternative was a verbatim repetition, another choice represented a change both in surface form and in meaning, and the other two represented changes only in surface form. When recognition was tested immediately, people were very good at recognizing the exact repetition; in other words, they rejected changes in superficial structure and changes in meaning. After comprehending the next 80 syllables in the passage, however, performance was accurate only in rejecting the alternative that changed the meaning. In other words, after the 80 syllable delay, people showed no preference for the repetition (*d*, the correct answer) over the paraphrases (*a* and *c* in the table).

Sachs's conclusions were straightforward: We quickly lose information about the actual, verbatim string of words that we hear (or read), but we do retain the meaning. We reconstruct what must have been said based on the meaning that is stored in the propositional structure. Only in situations where there is something "special" about the verbatim string, say, in recalling a joke, do we appear to retain surface form as part of our ordinary memory for meaningful discourse (but see Masson, 1984).

Confirmation of this was offered by Kintsch and Bates (1977), who gave a surprise recognition test to students either two or five days after a classroom lecture. Some evidence of verbatim memory was present after two days, but very little persisted five days afterward. As expected, verbatim memory for details and extraneous comments was better than verbatim memory for general lecture statements (see also Bates, Masling, & Kintsch, 1978). Even here, however, reconstructive memory seemed to play a role in remembering; students were better at rejecting items such as jokes that had not been presented than they were at recognizing jokes and announcements that had been heard (see also Brewer & Hay, 1984, on reconstruction of different linguistic styles, and Schmidt, 1994, on the effects of humor on sentence memory).

PROPOSITIONS AND PRIMING At a more detailed level, several experiments have tied propositions to a phenomenon you are quite familiar with, priming. Ratcliff and McKoon (1978, Experiment 2; see also McNamara & Diwadkar, 1996), for example, tested the possibility of priming effects within the propositions formed when we comprehend sentences. They presented sentences and told people to learn them for a later unspecified memory test. The test sentences were written so that each would contain two propositions, for example,

> Geese crossed the horizon as wind shuffled the clouds.
>
> The chauffeur jammed the clutch when he parked the truck.

After a 20-minute interval filled with an unrelated task, single words were shown in a recognition task and people had to say "yes" if the word had been in one of the learned sentences and "no" otherwise.

The priming manipulation was in the sequencing of the trials during recognition. Sometimes the word on one trial (the prime) was immediately followed on the next trial by a word (the target) from the same sentence, and sometimes the target was from a different sentence. Furthermore, when the prime and target were from the same sentence, they were either from the same proposition or from different propositions. For example, in the "geese" sentence above, the pair *geese–horizon* came from the same proposition, whereas the pair *geese–clouds* came from different propositions.

In the baseline condition, where primes and targets were from different sentences (e.g., *geese–clutch*), mean RT to targets was 847 ms (Experiment 2), as shown in Table 8-3. ▲ This is the *unprimed* condition because the unrelated propositions from different sentences would not be stored together during learning. But when the prime and target words did come from the same sentence, the RT to the target was shorter: 709 ms when they had been in the same proposition and 752 ms when they were in different propositions within the same sentence (again, see Table 8-3 for examples). In other words, a prime–target pair such as *geese–horizon* was 138 ms faster than baseline (847 ms to 709 ms), because of priming within the proposition. A pair such as *geese–clouds* was 95 ms faster than baseline (847 ms to 752 ms), because of priming between the two propositions.

The support for propositional theories should be clear. Words from the same sentence should be represented and stored together in memory. And words from the same phrase or clause should be even more closely related in the stored propositions. Thus even though the words were not related in the strict sense of semantic memory—*horizon* is not a semantic property of *geese*, after all—words stored together in a sentence's proposition still prime one another.

PROPOSITIONS AND INTERFERENCE Taking the idea that people are storing propositions in memory and that these are organized in a network structure, as we have been discussing, we can make some predictions about how this will affect performance. First, as noted earlier, a given concept can have multiple associations with it. That is, a node in a network can have multiple links to multiple concepts. Furthermore, we can assume that there is a limit to people's cognitive resources—that is how much of a network a person

TABLE 8-3 Priming Results from Ratcliff and McKoon (1978) ▲

Condition	RT to Target	Priming Effect
Across sentences	847 ms	None; baseline
Between two propositions in the same sentence	752 ms	95 ms facilitation
Within a single proposition	709 ms	138 ms facilitation
Examples		
Across sentences	geese–clutch	
Between two propositions in the same sentence	geese–clouds	
Within a single proposition	geese–horizon	

can search at once. We've already covered a number of these sorts of mental limits in our discussions of attention and working memory, and we're just extending that logic here. Given these two simple assumptions we can make some predictions about memory.

In a classic study, Anderson (1974) had people memorize a list of sentences about people in locations, such as "The hippie is in the park." The important part of the study was that, across the list, he varied the number of associations with the person and location concepts. That is, a given person in the study list could be described as being in 1, 2, or 3 different locations, and each location could have 1, 2, or 3 different people in it. When we graph a network representation of this type of information, we can see various number of links "fanning" off a given concept node.

Now, Anderson (1974) further assumed that the amount of activation that could spread along the links of the network was limited. As such, the more links there were fanning off a concept node in memory, the more widely the activation was distributed, and the longer that the processing of the activation along any one of those pathways took. The end result is the prediction that the more links there are off a given concept—the more links fanning off a concept node—the slower the retrieval process will be. This, of course, would yield a longer response time, which is exactly what happened in Anderson's (1974) study. After people memorized the list of sentences they were given a recognition test, in which they had to indicate whether the test sentences were studied on the list or not. The **fan effect** that was found was that *when more words associated with a concept, response times were longer.*

The fan effect, clearly, is a retrieval interference effect—the more words associated with a concept, the slower people were to retrieve any one of them. In an interesting extension of this finding, Bunting, Conway, and Heitz (2004; see also Radvansky & Copeland, 2006) looked at the fan effect in terms of the working memory capacity of their participants. They found that people with lower working memory capacity exhibited greater interference—a larger fan effect—than people with a higher working memory capacity. That is, people with less working memory capacity were further disrupted when their capacity was divided up among many words (larger "fans"). They were working with fewer working memory resources to begin with, so a cognitive task that placed a greater burden on them had a more disruptive effect because they had less extra capacity to compensate for that disruption.

Section Summary

- Comprehending and remembering ideas involves constructing propositional representations in which meaningful elements are represented as nodes connected by various pathways (e.g., agent, recipient). Propositions form the base of several important lines of research.
- Considerable evidence has been reported in support of propositions. For example, we tend to remember the gist or general meaning of a passage but not the more superficial aspects like exact wording. We routinely "recognize" a sentence as having occurred before even if the sentence is a paraphrase. And concepts stored in a common proposition during comprehension serve as better primes than those stored in different propositions.
- Network theories of how we store and retrieve propositions have been able to make accurate predictions of future memory performance, such as the fan effect.

SITUATION MODELS AND EMBODIED COGNITION

There is a great deal of evidence that basic idea units can influence memory. However, there is more to life than simple ideas. One of the themes of this text is embodied cognition, the idea that how we think is influenced by how we act or are otherwise involved with the world. One way that embodied cognition manifests itself is the idea that people are creating models (Johnson-Laird, 1983; Zwaan & Radvansky, 1998) of the situations described, and do not just create memories of the simple propositional ideas in sentences. One way of thinking about different types of mental representations and their influence on memory comes from van Dijk and Kintsch's (1983) work on language comprehension.

Levels of Representation

According to van Dijk and Kintsch, there are three levels of representation. These are the surface form, the textbase, and the situation model. The surface form corresponds to a verbatim mental representation of the exact words used, as well as the syntax of the sentences read or heard. At the intermediate level is the textbase. These are the basic idea units actually present in a text you might read. The textbase level would correspond more directly with the propositional representations you read about in the previous section. At the third level is the situation model. This is a representation of the state of affairs described by a text, rather than a representation of the text itself. So, the idea is that not only can you create different kinds of mental representations and memories of what you may be reading, but that you're creating all of them in parallel.

This division of different kinds of mental representation can be seen in terms of how well people remember information at the different levels over time. This is most clearly illustrated in a study by Kintsch, Welsch, Schmalhofer, and Zimny (1987). In this study, people read a text and then took a later memory test. For the test, people were shown individual sentences and indicated whether they had been read before or not. Four types of memory probes were used on the recognition test: (a) verbatim probes, which were exact versions of the sentences that had been read earlier, (b) paraphrases, which captured the same ideas as the ideas in the text, but with a different wording, (c) inferences, which were ideas that were likely to be true, but not actually mentioned in the text, and (d) "wrongs," incorrect probes that were thematically consistent with the passage but were incorrect if one had read and understood the passage. Kintsch et al. (1987) compared performance on these various types of memory probes to assess the strength of the representations at the various levels. For example, by comparing performance on the verbatim probes and paraphrases one can estimate memory for the exact wording. This is because both of these probe types refer to ideas that were actually in the text, but only one uses the exact wording. So, the degree to which memory is better in the verbatim condition compared to the paraphrase condition is a measure of surface form memory.

The results Kintsch et al. (1987) found are shown in Figure 8-4. As can be seen, while memory for all three levels was reasonably good immediately after reading, there are big differences in performance later on depending on what is being assessed. First, for the surface form, verbatim information was lost very quickly from memory and reached chance performance by the end of the four days. Second, memory was better for the textbase level than for the surface form. So, while people may forget the exact words they read before, they are better at remembering the ideas that were presented (cf. the work described by Sachs earlier in the chapter). However, even memory at this level is showing some decline

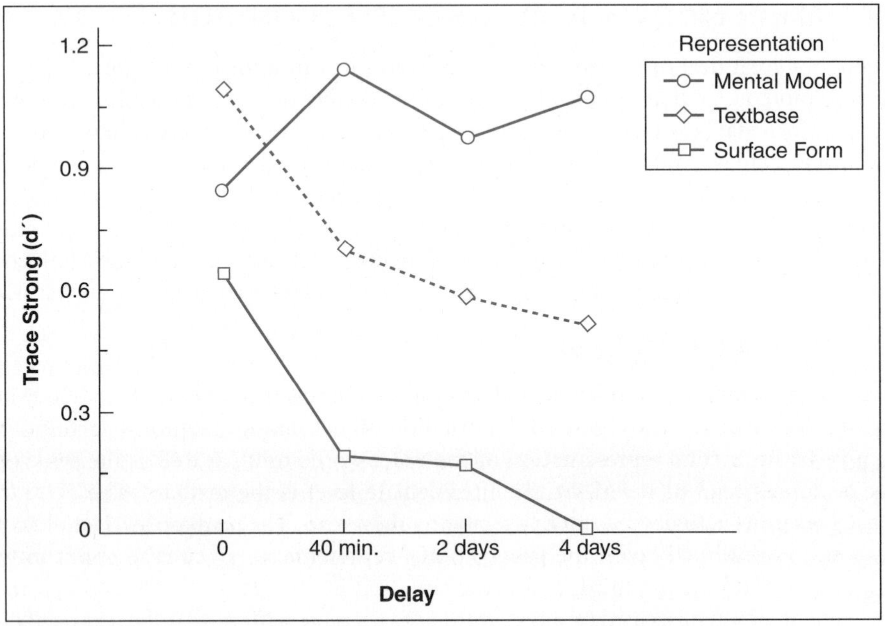

FIGURE 8-4 Retention of knowledge at the surface form, textbase, and situation model levels. Adapted from Kintsch et al. (1987).

over time. But, for the third level, the situation model, performance started out high and then stayed high, with little evidence of forgetting over the four day retention interval. So, there is something psychologically real about looking at mental representations in this way.

A more everyday example of this would be your memory for a newspaper article you might read. Soon after reading the article, your ability to remember verbatim sentences from the article is pretty poor. Furthermore, over time, you start to forget what specific ideas were actually read in the article, and what ideas or inferences you may have created when you were trying to understand it. However, you have a relatively good memory over time for the events described in the article, and this memory stays with you for a much longer period of time.

Remembering Facts

So, now that we've seen that situation models are remembered better over the long term, are there any other benefits? Yes, there are. Think back a few sections to our discussion of the fan effect. As you remember, a fan effect is an increase in retrieval time that accompanies an increase in the number of associations with a concept. However, this can shift around somewhat when we start thinking about how the studied information might be organized into situation models. For example, in one study Radvansky & Zacks (1991) had people memorize sentences about objects in locations, such as the following:

The potted palm is in the hotel.
The potted palm is in the museum.
The potted palm is in the barber shop.
The pay phone is in the library.
The welcome mat is in the library.
The waste basket is in the library.

Under these circumstances, how people think about the situations described by the learned sentences influences the ease with which they remember this information later. In the first three sentences, there is a fan of 3 off the object concept because the potted palm is described as being in three places. According to propositional network theories, the division of the spreading activation during retrieval would cause retrieval to proceed more slowly. Similarly, according to a situation model view, because these three sentences are likely to be interpreted as referring to three different events, people would create a separate situation model for each one. Then during retrieval, these three situation models would each contain a potted palm, and interfere with one another, thereby producing a fan effect.

In comparison, for the last three sentences, there is again a fan of 3, this time off the location concept, because there are three objects in the library. However, in this case, it is not difficult for people to think of these three sentences as referring to a common event. As such, people can integrate this information into a single situation model and store one representation in memory (e.g., one library, with a pay phone, welcome mat, and waste basket in it). Then, during memory retrieval, because everything is stored together in a single situation model, there should be no retrieval interference, and no fan effect. This is exactly what was observed. As you can see in Figure 8-5, Radvansky and Zacks (1991) found a fan effect when there was a single object in multiple locations, but not when there was a single location with multiple objects.

This mental organization is based on how people are thinking about how we interact with the world, and is shown clearly in a study by Radvansky, Spieler, & Zacks (1993) in which students learned sentences about people in small locations that typically contain only a single person, such as witness stand, tire swing, or store dressing room. Here, a situation in which multiple people are in one of these locations is unlikely. But, because people can move from place to place, a person-based organization is plausible—and this is what is observed with a fan effect for a single location being associated with multiple people, but not for a single person being associated with multiple locations.

METAMEMORY

Much of what we have been discussing in this text regarding memory is the ability of a person to remember some sort of content information, such as a word on a list, a picture, a face, a story, and so on. In this section, we take a different tack. Instead of looking at what we remember, we will look at how good we are at assessing how accurate our own memories will be. That is, metamemory concerns your ability to assess when you've learned something, that you need to remember something in the future, and even the basics of what you do and do not know.

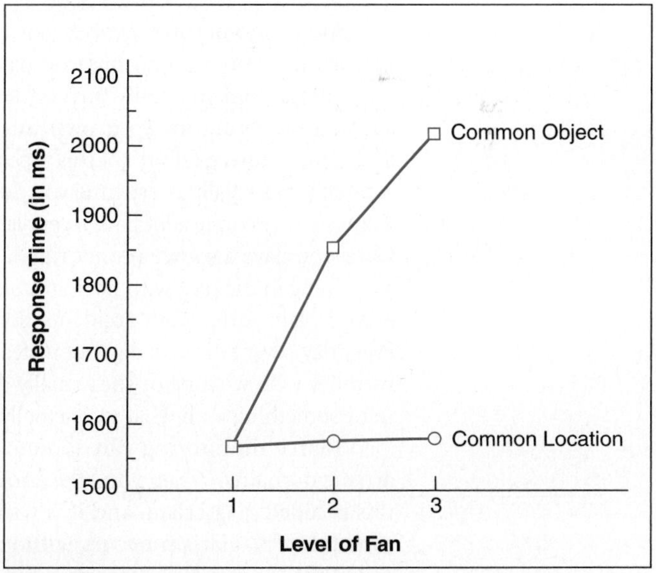

◆ **FIGURE 8-5**
Response times to sentence memory probes as a function of the level of fan (number associated with a sentence concept) Data are divided based on whether the shared concept is a single location with multiple objects or a single object in multiple locations. Derived from Radvansky and Zacks (1991).

Source Monitoring

First, let's consider your ability to remember where information came from. **Source monitoring** (Johnson, Hashtroudi, & Lindsay, 1993) is *the ability to accurately remember the source of a memory, be it something you encountered in the world or something that you imagined.* Failures of source monitoring can sometimes occur in which a person remembers the content of the information, but cannot accurately attribute it to a particular source. Source monitoring is a complex process that involves many parts of the brain. The hippocampus seems to be important for integrating content and source information, the prefrontal cortex is important for searching and using source information, and the temporal lobes are important for remembering content information itself (Senkfor & Van Petten, 1998). In extreme cases, such as schizophrenia, people experiencing hallucinations may be having trouble source monitoring—that is, distinguishing between what is real and what is only imagined (Ditman & Kuperberg, 2005).

An example of source monitoring might be if you have a memory of a fact about a historical figure and it is important to know whether this is a fact that came from a history textbook, or an inaccurate fictionalization that came from a novel. That is, to know how reliable this fact is that you've drawn up from your memory, you need to know where you learned it. If you misremember the source of an idea as being a textbook when it actually came from a movie, then you mistakenly think that fiction is fact, a source monitoring failure. This can be very important, as you will see later in the chapter, in situations such as trying to determine whether something was actually witnessed during an accident or crime. A more everyday example of this sort of source monitoring would be trying to remember which of your friends told you a secret. If you get this wrong, then you could be in big trouble with one (or more) of your friends.

Source monitoring involves not only trying to distinguish between things that may have come to you from various external sources, but also things that you thought of yourself. For example, did you really turn off the oven, or did you just think about it? This type of source monitoring for your own internal thoughts and actions is also very important. Source monitoring failures of this type typically occur for those activities that you engage in routinely. Essentially, every time you do something, you store a memory of that experience. Things you do quite a lot have a very large number of memory traces stored. What happens when you have a source monitoring failure is that you confuse a memory of having done something in the past with having actually done it today, even though you didn't. This may even explain some work accidents; somebody forgot to do some simple task that's done every day, several times a day, but instead just remembered having done it, and confused the memory with what he or she actually did (or didn't do). Confusing the memory of having done something with what you actually did is, of course, the source monitoring error.

Source monitoring can sometimes have serious consequences in academic and artistic domains. When you take another person's ideas and present them as your own, this is called plagiarism, and it is wrong. You should know this well by now. However, sometimes plagiarism occurs without the plagiarist actually consciously trying to do something known to be wrong. This phenomenon is known as **cryptomnesia** (Brown & Murphy, 1989), in which *a person unconsciously plagiarizes something he has heard or read before, but because he has forgotten the source, mistakenly thinks that it is a new idea that he thought of.* Essentially, a person remembers the idea, melody, or whatever, but has forgotten the source of the information. As a consequence, the person thinks that the idea is a novel one, and is not aware of the plagiarism unless it is discovered and pointed out by another person. Factors that increase the likelihood of experiencing cryptomnesia are those that make memory of the original source less likely. For example, if people elaborate on an idea, they are less likely to remember the original source, and are more likely to only remember their own thoughts on the idea (Stark & Perfect, 2008).

Cryptomnesia is more likely to occur when people have their attention and working memory resources directed elsewhere. For example, in one study (Brown & Murphy, 1989), people were asked to sit in a circle, generating members of a category one person after the other (e.g., for the category TOOL, one person might say "hammer," the next "screwdriver," the next "pliers," etc.) without repeating anything that had been said earlier. The results showed that a person was more likely to repeat a previously said item—that is, to plagiarize someone else in the group—if it had just been said, immediately before the person repeated it. This actually makes good sense, from the standpoint of attention and working memory. Imagine yourself in this situation. As your turn is approaching, you start racking your brains for something to say. When the person just before you is talking, you are likely to have some of your attention drawn away from that person, and are focusing more on your own thoughts, trying to come up with something to say. As a consequence of this divided attention, you may store a memory for the word that person said, but are less likely to store the source information as well. Then, because that word was primed by having heard it, you retrieve it from memory, but you are not able to retrieve the source. So you say it, unaware that it had just been mentioned. This effect is even more pronounced in people with smaller working memory capacities, such as older adults (McCabe, Smith, & Parks, 2007).

Prospective Memory

Another interesting aspect of memory in the real world focuses not on dredging up information from the past, but instead looks at knowing how to use your memory to do things in the future. This is called **prospective memory** (Loftus, 1971), *the ability to remember to do something in the future.* This is in contrast to retrospective memory, memory for things that happened in the past.

In general, there are two basic kinds of prospective memory (Einstein & McDaniel, 1990). The first is *time-based prospective memory*. For this kind of prospective memory, a person needs to remember to do something based on the passage of time. This can be after a certain amount of time has passed, such as needing to remember to take the pizza out of the oven in ten minutes, remembering to take your medication at 3:00, or remembering to call your mother on Mother's Day. In general, time-based prospective memory is more difficult because it requires people to keep track of time, which we are generally not very good at.

The other basic kind of prospective memory is *event-based prospective memory*. For this type of prospective memory, a person needs to remember to do something when a certain event occurs, for example giving your roommate a message when you see her, remembering to stop at the hardware store next time you drive by, or remembering how to give CPR when you see someone in distress. In general, event-based prospective memory is easier than time-based prospective memory. This is because a

PROVE IT

Cryptomnesia

For this demonstration you will need at least three volunteers (although you can use more). It is a variation of a study by Brown and Halliday (1991) that can result in people reporting answers that they present as their own, but which, in fact, other people gave. This is cryptomnesia. Have your three volunteers sit in a circle. Tell them that you will first read the name of a category, such as "Countries," "Flowers," "Insects," and so on (prepare a list of 10 or so category names ahead of time). Then, going around in a circle, people will need to name members of that category aloud, without using names that were said previously. What is likely to happen is that at various times people will say things that someone else had already said. Furthermore, these should be more likely to be things that the person just before them in the circle had said as compared to the person just after him or her. To make this a bit more likely, give people a time limit of 5 seconds or so to say their answer. You will need to record what people say, so an audio recording might be better than trying to write things down. You should also limit the number of times you go around the circle before the task becomes very hard. Limiting the number of responses to 25 or so should do this.

After the first part of the task is completed, write down, in random order, the responses people gave. Then ask people to pick out which ones they themselves said. Simply have them circle the ones they remember saying. This can be done an hour after the first part, or a day later, or a week later. If you want to get fancy, you could have several groups of volunteers and see how the amount of time that passed influences your results. What you may find here is people will pick answers that they did not actually say. Again, there are more likely to be things that were said by the person just before them in the circle.

person does not need to monitor the passage of time, but is reminded of the intended action when the relevant event occurs. Under these circumstances, people are either actively monitoring the environment for the event cue, or have previously formed a mental association with that cue and the intended action, so are spontaneously reminded when the reminder presents itself (Einstein & McDaniel, 2005; Marsh, Hicks, & Cook, 2005)—basically, the event cue acts as a retrieval cue. A good strategy, by the way, is to take advantage of your superior event-based memory performance by turning a time-based prospective memory task into an event-based task. For example, set a timer rather than trying to remember to notice the time on a clock yourself, or mark a date on a calendar rather than trying to remember an appointment in your head (of course, you'll still have to remember to look at your calendar).

Knowing What You Know

Strategies like that—turning a time-based prospective memory task into an event-based task—start to resemble a situation that involves **metamemory**, people's knowledge about their own memory system and its functioning. In this section we'll look at three ways that researchers examined what people know, and what they think they know. The first of these should seem familiar to you; it's the assessment that you, as a student, often make when you study. These are called **judgments of learning** (Arbuckle & Cuddy, 1969), in which *a person makes a prediction, after studying some material, whether that information will be remembered on a later memory test (was it learned?)*. This is of obvious importance because of how we use that kind of self-assessment. If your assessment, your judgment of learning, is that some body of knowledge has been learned sufficiently, that suggests to you that it requires less additional study time (say for an upcoming test), whereas if you decide that the information or knowledge has not been learned, it requires more study time.

So, how good are people at judging whether they've learned something? The answer is "it depends." Generally, when a person is asked to make a judgment of learning immediately after studying some material, the estimates of future performance are poor predictors of what will, and will not, be remembered. However, if there is a meaningful delay between studying and being asked to predict future performance, estimates become much better (Dunlosky & Nelson, 1994). This is because the delay allows information to be removed from working memory, and the person has a more accurate estimate of what it will be like to try to retrieve that information from long-term memory later. Otherwise, if the information is currently active in working memory, there is a bias to mistakenly assume that it will be easier to remember it later because it is easy to think about it at the moment.

Another way to assess metamemory is to look at cases where people fail to remember a piece of knowledge or information. When this occurs, the person might be asked to make a **feeling of knowing** judgment (Hart, 1965) in which *an estimate is provided of how likely it is that that item will be recognized on a later memory test.* An everyday example of this might be a situation in which you see someone in a mall that you know, and you start up a conversation even though you can't remember the person's name. A likely reason for the retrieval failure is that you are seeing the person out of the normal context in which you interact with him or her (Grupuso, Lindsay, & Masson, 2007). In this situation, you might provide a high feeling of knowing estimate for the name—you feel that you would recognize the name if you heard it or saw it. In comparison, if the person you were talking to was someone you did not feel that you knew, your feeling of knowing judgment would be low because you would feel that the person's name would not be in your memory. Essentially, a feeling of knowing rating provides some measure of how familiar something is. That is, it is an estimate that there has been an increase in activation of some memories, with some partial knowledge possibly being retrieved, but not enough to recall the needed information (Koriat, 1993; 1995).

An experience that is related to feeling of knowing is the **tip-of-the-tongue state** (Brown & McNeill, 1966), where you feel like the word or name you can't remember is on the verge of being remembered. This is actually the primary difference between a tip-of-the-tongue state and the feeling of knowing state. In feeling of knowing, despite a strong feeling that you could recognize the information later, you cannot say much more about the inaccessible information. In comparison, when a person is in a tip of the tongue state, *there is a feeling that retrieval is imminent* (Brown, 1991). Often a person can provide a great deal of additional information, or partial retrieval, about the word that may be on the tip of the tongue. For example, the person may know what letter the word begins with, how many syllables it has, and even words that rhyme with it, and still not be able to recall it (Hanley & Chapman, 2008). There are a number of ideas about what may be causing the tip-of-the-tongue experience. For example, when people are in this state they tend to recall related words, which then become more active in memory, causing interference and blocking the retrieval of the desired memory. Alternatively, the various, similar memories may be actively inhibiting the needed memory because they are in competition. These ideas would explain why a word that is on the tip of your tongue may suddenly be remembered several minutes later when the retrieval competition has had time to diminish, and the memory can be readily retrieved.

FALSE MEMORIES, EYEWITNESS MEMORY, AND "FORGOTTEN MEMORIES"

Schacter (1996) spoke of the fragile nature of memory and the Seven Sins of Memory, discussing how our memories can fail us in certain situations. And indeed, we've been discussing a variety of situations and effects that show different kinds of memory weaknesses in this chapter – the fan effect, which can lead to retrieval interference, source monitoring failures, cryptomnesia, poor predictions based on judgments of learning, and the like. Is this what Schacter meant when he talked about the "sins" of memory, the weaknesses in our memory systems? What is the weakness that Schacter pinpointed; what situations did he have in mind? A straightforward answer is that memory fails us in exactly those situations that call for absolutely accurate recall, completely correct recollection of real-world events exactly as they happened. The weakness of our memory system seems to be that we are often unable to distinguish between what really happened and what our existing knowledge and comprehension processes might have contributed to recollection. We discuss two research programs that show incorrect or distorted memory, then tackle the difficult issues raised by these results.

In eyewitness memory and testimony, any new information about an event is integrated with relevant existing knowledge. Thus, we are less than accurate when we attempt to retrieve such knowledge because we are often unable to discriminate between new and original information.

False Memories

A simple yet powerful laboratory demonstration of **false memory**, *memory of something that did not happen*, was reported by Roediger and McDermott (1995), based on a demonstration by Deese (1959; see Roediger & McDermott, 2000, for an excellent introduction to this work and the DRM—Deese–Roediger–McDermott—task, as it's often called). Roediger and McDermott had people study 12-item lists made up of words such as *bed, rest, awake*, and *pillow*, words highly associated with the word *sleep*. Importantly, *sleep* was never presented in the list. Instead, it was the *critical lure* word, a word that was highly related to the other words in the list but which never actually appeared. In immediate free recall, 40% of the participants recalled *sleep* from the list and later recognized it with a high degree of confidence. This is a false memory.

In a second study, people studied similar multiple lists, either recalling the list immediately or after a distractor task (arithmetic). Then, everyone was given a recognition task. During free recall, 55% of the participants recalled the lure. The recognition results, shown in Figure 8-6, were even more dramatic. Of course, a few people "recognized" nonstudied words that were unrelated to the study list words (e.g., *thief* for the *sleep* list). More importantly, correct recognition for studied words increased to well above chance for the study/arithmetic lists and even higher for study/recall lists. But false recognition of the critical lure was higher than correct recognition of words actually shown on the list, showing the same pattern of increases across conditions. There was an 81% false alarm rate for critical lures when the lists had been studied and recalled. In other words, falsely remembering the lure during recall strengthened memories of the lure word, leading to a higher false recognition rate. When questioned further, most people claimed to "remember" the critical lure word rather than merely "know" it had been on the list.

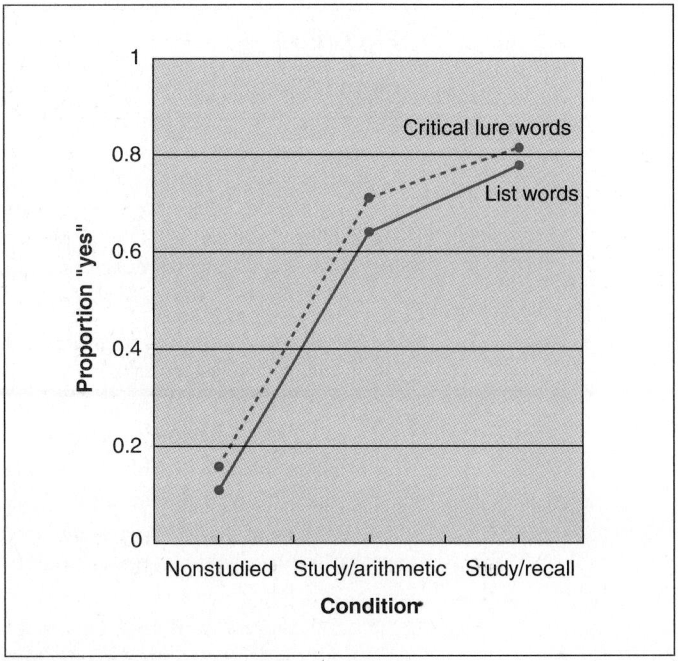

FIGURE 8-6
Roediger and McDermott's (1995) results.

In terms of content accuracy–memory for the ideas—this performance is good, exactly what we would expect; you see a list of words such as *bed, rest, awake*, and *pillow*, and, because the list is "about" sleep, you then recall *sleep*. But in terms of technical accuracy, memory for the exact experience, performance is poor because people came up with the word *sleep* based on their understanding of the list and then could not distinguish between what had really been there and what was supplied from memory. These sorts of meaning-based false memories are formed rather quickly, in as little as 4 seconds (Atkins & Reuter-Lorenz, 2008). It appears that the critical process here is not the automatic spread of activation, such as that observed in lexical decision priming, but the use of the thematic information in the study lists during efforts to remember what had been heard earlier (Meade, Watson, Balota, & Roediger, 2007). Roediger and McDermott's (1995, p. 812) conclusion about this compelling memory illusion summarized the situation aptly:

> *All remembering is constructive in nature. . . .The illusion of remembering events that never happened can occur quite readily. Therefore, as others have also pointed out, the fact that people may say they vividly remember details surrounding an event cannot, by itself, be taken as convincing evidence that the event actually occurred.*

PROVE IT

False Memory

This is a fairly easy demonstration to perform if you have several volunteers and about 15 min. available. It is an adaptation of the Deese (1959), Roediger & McDermott (1995) method, shorter than the original experiment while demonstrating the same effect; see Stadler, Roediger, and McDermott (1999) for additional word lists that can be used. Prepare enough copies of your distractor task (e.g., a page full of simple arithmetic problems) to have one for each volunteer.

1. Tell your volunteers they will hear three lists and afterward will be asked to recall as many of the words as they can; order of recall is not important.
2. Read the three lists to your volunteers at an "easy" speaking rate, about one word per 2 s. Pause only briefly between lists.
3. After finishing the third list, have your volunteers do 2 min. of arithmetic, finishing as many problems as they can.
4. Ask your volunteers to write down as many words as they can remember from the three lists. Give ample time (approximately 3 min.) so they can get as many words as possible.
5. When everyone is done, have them all turn over their sheets of paper and make recognition decisions, one by one, to the 20-word recognition test. For each word, they should say "no" if the word was not on the list and "yes" if it was on the list. When they say "yes," also have them note whether they remember the word specifically or whether they just "know" it was on the list.
6. Look especially for recall of the words *sleep, thief,* and *chair,* because these are the nonpresented, critical lures. On recognition, look for false alarms (saying "yes") to the critical lures in positions 5, 13, and 16.

Word Lists

bed, rest, awake, tired, dream, wake, snooze, blanket, doze, slumber, snore, nap, peace, yawn, drowsy

steal, robber, crook, burglar, money, cop, bad, rob, jail, gun, villain, crime, bank, bandit, criminal

table, sit, legs, seat, couch, desk, recliner, sofa, wood, cushion, swivel, stool, sitting, rocking, bench

Recognition List

1-dream, 2-fork, 3-weather, 4-bracelet, 5-chair, 6-robber, 7-stool, 8-traffic, 9-snooze, 10-couch, 11-radio, 12-jail, 13-sleep, 14-sand, 15-blanket, 16-thief, 17-bed, 18-boy, 19-skin, 20-cushion

Scoring Key

"Yes" words	1, 6, 7, 9, 10, 12, 15, 17, 20
"No" words	2, 3, 4, 8, 11, 14, 18, 19
Critical lures	5, 13, 16

Integration

False memories can also be created by inappropriately combining information from different sources or events, where the combined information becomes linked or fused in memory. To illustrate this, let's look at a classic set of studies by Bransford and Franks (1971, 1972). This set of results will make more sense to you if you begin with the demonstration in Table 8-4. ★

Bransford and Franks (1971) were interested in the general topic of how people acquire and remember ideas, not merely individual sentences but integrated wholes. They asked people to listen to sentences like those in Table 8-4 one by one, and then (after a short distractor task) answer a simple question about each sentence. After going through this procedure for all 24 sentences and taking a five-minute break, people were given another test. During this second test, people had to make yes/no recognition judgments, saying "yes" if they remembered reading the sentence in the original set and "no" otherwise. They also had to indicate, on a ten-point scale, how confident they were about their judgments: Positive ratings (from 1 to 5) meant they were sure they had seen the sentence, negative ratings

TABLE 8-4 Sample Experiment of Bransford and Franks (1971) ★

Instructions: Read each sentence in the table individually. As soon as you have read each one, close your eyes and count to five. Then look at and answer the question that follows each sentence. Begin now.

The girl broke the window on the porch.	Broke what?
The tree in the front yard shaded the man smoking his pipe.	Where?
The hill was steep.	What was?
The sweet jelly was on the kitchen table.	On what?
The tree was tall.	Was what?
The old car climbed the hill.	What did?
The ants in the kitchen ate the jelly.	Where?
The girl who lives next door broke the window on the porch.	Lives where?
The car pulled the trailer.	Did what?
The ants ate the sweet jelly that was on the table.	What did?
The girl lives next door.	Who does?
The tree shaded the man who was smoking his pipe.	What did?
The sweet jelly was on the table.	Where?
The girl who lives next door broke the large window.	Broke what?
The man was smoking his pipe.	Who was?
The old car climbed the steep hill.	The what?
The large window was on the porch.	Where?
The tall tree was in the front yard.	Was what?
The car pulling the trailer climbed the steep hill.	Did what?
The jelly was on the table.	What was?
The tall tree in the front yard shaded the man.	Did what?
The car pulling the trailer climbed the hill.	Which car?
The ants ate the jelly.	Ate what?
The window was large.	What was?

(from –1 to –5) meant they were sure they had not. *Without* looking back at the original sentences, take a moment now to make these judgments about the sentences in Table 8-5; "OLD" means "Yes, I've seen it before" and "NEW" means "No, I didn't see it before."

All 28 sentences in this recognition test are related to the original ideas in the first set of sentences. The clever aspect of the recognition test is that only 4 of the 28 sentences had in fact appeared on the original list; the other 24 are new. As you no doubt noticed, the separate sentences were all derived from four basic idea groupings, such as

TABLE 8-5 Sample Experiment by Bransford and Franks (1971)

Instructions: Check "OLD" or "NEW" for each sentence, then indicate how confident you are on a scale from 1 to 5 (5 is "very high confidence").

	OLD/NEW	Confidence (–5 to +5)
1. The car climbed the hill.	________	________
2. The girl who lives next door broke the window.	________	________
3. The old man who was smoking his pipe climbed the steep hill.	________	________
4. The tree was in the front yard.	________	________
5. The ants ate the sweet jelly that was in the kitchen.	________	________
6. The window was on the porch.	________	________
7. The barking dog jumped on the old car in the front yard.	________	________
8. The tree in the front yard shaded the man.	________	________
9. The ants were in the kitchen.	________	________
10. The old car pulled the trailer.	________	________
11. The tree shaded the man who was smoking his pipe.	________	________
12. The tall tree shaded the man who was smoking his pipe.	________	________
13. The ants ate the jelly on the kitchen table.	________	________
14. The old car, pulling the trailer, climbed the hill.	________	________
15. The girl who lives next door broke the large window on the porch.	________	________
16. The tall tree shaded the man.	________	________
17. The ants in the kitchen ate the jelly.	________	________
18. The car was old.	________	________
19. The girl broke the large window.	________	________
20. The ants ate the sweet jelly that was on the kitchen table.	________	________
21. The ants were on the table in the kitchen.	________	________
22. The old car pulling the trailer climbed the steep hill.	________	________
23. The girl broke the window on the porch.	________	________
24. The scared cat that broke the window on the porch climbed the tree.	________	________
25. The tree shaded the man.	________	________
26. The old car climbed the steep hill.	________	________
27. The girl broke the window.	________	________
28. The man who lives next door broke the large window on the porch.	________	________

STOP. Count the number of sentences judged OLD.

"The ants in the kitchen ate the sweet jelly that was on the table." Each of the complete idea groupings consisted of four separate simple propositions; for example,

The ants were in the kitchen.
The ants ate the jelly.
The jelly was sweet.
The jelly was on the table.

The original set of sentences (Table 8-4) presented six sentences from each idea grouping. Two of the six were called "ones," simple, one-idea propositions such as "The jelly was on the table." Another two sentences were "twos," where two simple propositions were merged, as in "The ants in the kitchen ate the jelly." Finally, the last two were "threes," as in "The ants ate the sweet jelly that was on the table." In Bransford and Franks's first two experiments, only ones, twos, and threes were presented on the original list; in the third experiment, a few fours also appeared during learning, but this made no difference in the results. In all three experiments, the final recognition test (Table 8-5) presented ones, twos, threes, and the overall four for each idea grouping.

So what did they find? Just as your performance probably indicated, people overwhelmingly judged threes and fours as old; in other words, they judged that they had seen them on the study list (just as you probably judged question 20, the four, as old). Furthermore, they were very confident in their ratings, as shown in Figure 8-7 (taken from Experiment 3). That is, people were recognizing the sentences that expressed the overall idea grouping most thoroughly, even when they had not seen exactly those sentences during study. Such responses are called *false alarms*, saying "OLD" when the correct response is "NEW."

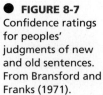

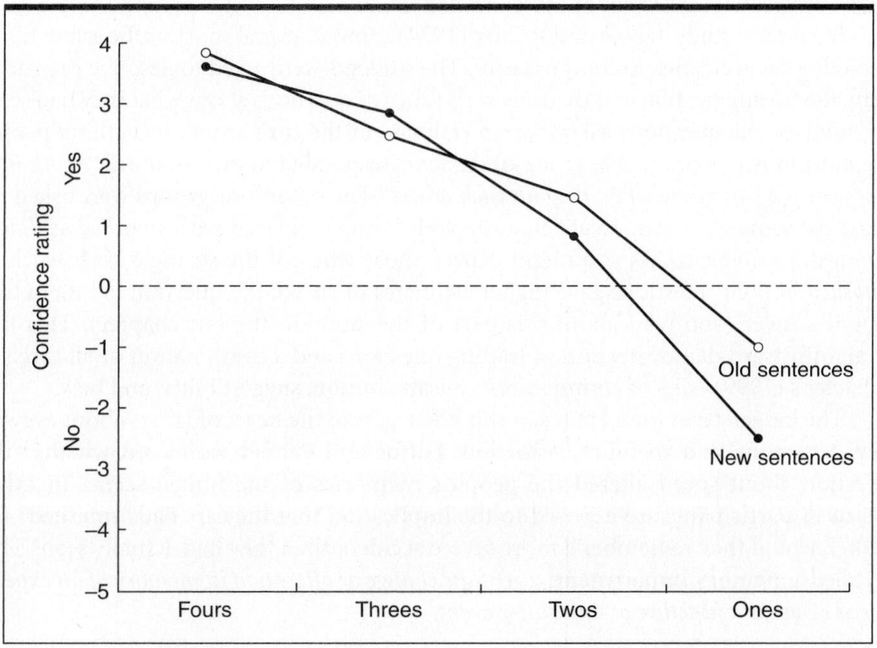

FIGURE 8-7 Confidence ratings for peoples' judgments of new and old sentences. From Bransford and Franks (1971).

Moreover, people were not confident about having seen old sentences (e.g., sentences 11, 17, 23, and 26 in Table 8-5); the only sentences they were sure about were noncase sentences (e.g., sentences 3, 7, 24, and 28 in Table 8-5), in which ideas from different groupings had been combined. Furthermore, they were fairly confident that they had not seen ones, as shown by the strong negative ratings in the figure (between 21 and 23), even though they had seen several sentences that were that short (e.g., sentence 9 in Table 8-5). Because the shorter sentences did not express the whole idea, people believed that they had not seen them before.

These results (Bransford & Franks, 1971, 1972) suggest that people had acquired a more general idea than any of the individual study sentences had expressed. In essence, people were reporting a *composite* memory, one in which related ideas were stored together in memory. All the related ideas were fused together, forming one memory of the whole idea. Therefore, later recognition performance was entirely reasonable: They were matching the combined ideas in the recognition sentences to their composite memory. Rather than verbatim memory, Bransford and Franks found "memory for meaning," memory based on the **integration** of related material.

Leading Questions and Memory Distortions

Another line of research gives us a simple yet powerful demonstration of how inaccurate our memories can be. This is the program of research begun by Elizabeth Loftus and her colleagues on the topic of leading questions and memory distortion (see Loftus, 2003 and 2004, for highly readable introductions to this area). Loftus started by examining the effects of leading questions, that is, questions that tend to suggest to the person what answer is appropriate. She wondered whether there were long-term consequences of leading questions in terms of what people remember about events they have witnessed (you read about this in Chapter 7).

In an early study, Loftus and Palmer (1974) showed several short traffic safety films, depicting car accidents, to college classes. The students were asked to describe each accident after seeing the film and then answer a series of questions about what they had seen.

One of the questions asked for an estimate of the car's speed, something people are notoriously poor at. One group of students responded to the question, "*About how fast were the cars going when they hit each other?*" The other four groups were asked almost the same question, except that the verb *hit* was replaced with *smashed, collided, bumped*, or *contacted*. As you might expect, those who got the stronger verbs such as *smashed* in their questions gave higher estimates of speed; the question led them to a biased answer (you read about this part of the study in the last chapter). This is a straightforward demonstration of leading questions and a combination of all three of Schacter's (1999) "sins of commission": misattribution, suggestibility, and bias.

The longer-term importance of this effect gets to the heart of issues about eyewitness testimony and memory distortion. Loftus and Palmer wondered whether the question about speed altered the people's memories of the filmed scene. In other words, if participants are exposed to the implication that the cars had "smashed" together, would they remember a more severe accident than they had actually seen? This is called a **memory impairment**: *a genuine change or alteration in memory of an experienced event as a function of some later event.*

This is exactly what Loftus and Palmer found in their second experiment. A week after the original film and questions, people were given *another* set of questions about the original film (but they did not see the film again). One of the questions asked, "Did you see any broken glass?" Many of the participants in the "smashed" group said "yes," even though there had been none in the film. In fact, 34% of the "smashed" group said "yes," compared with only 14% of the group who saw *hit* (and 12% of those who had not been asked for a speed estimate). Furthermore, the likelihood of saying "yes" grew stronger as the estimates of speed went up, as shown in Figure 8-8. At each point in the graph, "remembering" broken glass was more common for people who had seen "smashed."

Think about that again. Although they had not seen any broken glass in the film, they remembered broken glass, partly as a function of their own speed estimate and partly as a function of the verb they had been questioned with a week earlier. It seems that what happened *after* the memory was formed altered its nature. The question about "smashed" was not just a leading question; it was a source of misleading information.

The Misinformation Effect

Investigators have developed several tasks to test for the effects of misleading information. In a typical experiment, people see the original event in a film or set of pictures (e.g., pictures depicting a car accident, with one showing a stop sign). Later, they are exposed to additional information, such as a narrative about the accident. Some people receive only neutral information, whereas others are given a bit of misinformation (the narrative mentions "the yield sign," for instance). Finally, there is a memory test, often a yes/no recognition task that asks about the critical piece of information: Was there a stop sign or a yield sign? (See also Zaragoza, McCloskey, & Jamis, 1987, who used a recall task.)

A common result is that *some people incorrectly claim to remember the misinformation*, the yield sign here; this is the **misinformation effect.** Belli (1989), for instance, found that misled people showed more than 20% lower accuracy than did control groups who were not exposed to the misinformation. Furthermore, Loftus, Donders, Hoffman, and Schooler (1989) found that misled groups were faster in their incorrect judgments—picking the yield sign, for example—than in their correct decisions. This suggests a surprising degree of misplaced confidence on the part of the misled people. What is particularly troubling is that misinformation effects

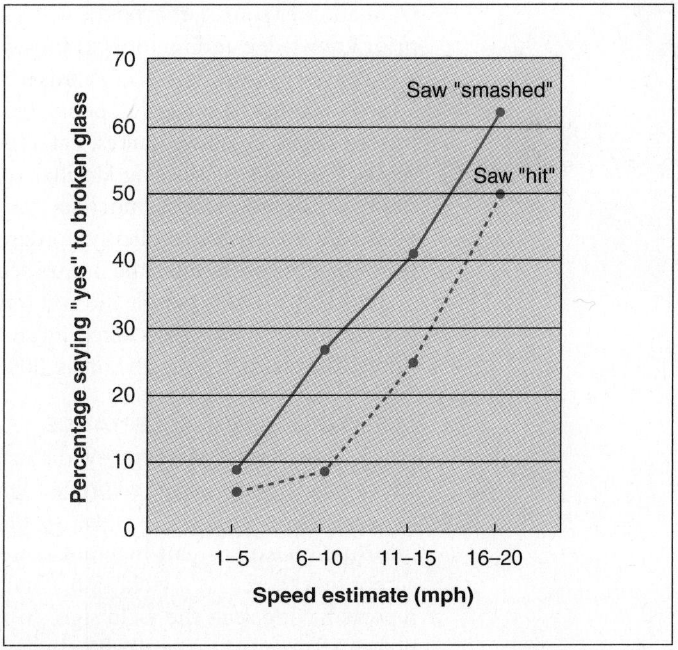

◆ **FIGURE 8-8**
Loftus and Palmer's (1974) results.

can persist even if the information is later corrected. For example, a study by Lewandowsky, Stritzka, Oberauer, and Morales (2005) looked at misinformation about the Iraq War that was reported by the press, and then later retracted. However, people continued to inappropriately remember the misinformation as true. This was particularly true for Americans who had more support for the war, than by Australians or Germans, who had less support. These later groups better remembered that the misinformation was false and had been retracted.

Source Misattribution and Misinformation Acceptance

Several reviews and summaries (Ayers & Reder, 1998; Loftus, 1991; Loftus & Hoffman, 1989; Roediger, 1996) outline the overall message of this research. As Loftus (1991) noted, alteration of the original memory may be only one part of memory distortion. Based on the accumulated evidence there seem to be three important memory distortion effects: source misattribution, misinformation acceptance, and overconfidence in the accuracy of memory.

SOURCE MISATTRIBUTION Sometimes people come to believe that they remember something that never happened. This is called **source misattribution**, *the inability to distinguish whether the original event or some later event was the true source of the information.* In essence, source misattribution suggests a confusion in which we cannot clearly remember the true source of a piece of knowledge (Zaragoza & Lane, 1994). Using the stop sign/yield sign example, source misattribution occurs when we cannot correctly distinguish whether memory of the yield sign came from the original film or from another source, maybe the mistaken narrative that was read later or maybe from prior knowledge and memory (Lindsay, Allen, Chan, & Dahl, 2004).

Another example of source misattribution can be seen in experiments on the false fame effect. In these studies, people read a list of nonfamous names, which increases the familiarity of those names. Later, people are more likely to judge the names as famous, essentially confusing familiarity with fame (Jacoby, Woloshyn, & Kelly, 1989). That is, they have lost memory for the source of the feeling of familiarity (that it had been read on a list of explicitly nonfamous names), so made their decisions solely on the basis of how familiar the names seemed to be. Interestingly, this confusion is particularly likely when people did not remember reading the original list of names, suggesting that the effect occurred at an implicit level (Kelley & Jacoby, 1996; see also Busey, Tunnicliff, Loftus, & Loftus, 2000).

MISINFORMATION ACCEPTANCE According to Loftus (1991), a second, possibly larger component of memory distortion is called **misinformation acceptance**, in which participants *accept additional information as having been part of an earlier experience without actually remembering that information.* For example, a person in a misinformation experiment may not remember seeing a stop sign but is quite willing to accept that there was a yield sign when the narrative mentions it. Later on, the person reports having seen the yield sign. In short, people are willing to accept information presented after the fact and often become certain about these "secondhand" memories. These tendencies probably grow stronger as more time elapses since the event and the original memory become less accessible (Payne, Toglia, & Anastasi, 1994).

IMPLANTED MEMORIES More recent work has adopted yet another method to examine the acceptance of misinformation, by trying to implant memories of events that never happened. Early use of this approach (e.g., Hyman, Husband, & Billings, 1995; Loftus & Hoffman, 1989) involved telling people childhood stories about themselves that their parents had supplied to the researchers, then questioning them about their memory for the episode. Unknown to the person, one of the stories was a fictional, although plausible, event (called a *pseudo-event;* for instance, "when you were six, you knocked over a punch bowl at a wedding reception"). A surprisingly large number of people come to accept the bogus story as true, and claim to "remember" it. For example, none of the participants of Hyman et al. claimed to remember the pseudo-event when they were first told about it, but fully 25% came to "recall" it by their third session of questioning.

More recently, several studies have looked at other means of conveying misinformation or pseudo-events. Wade, Garry, Read, and Lindsay (2002), for example, showed people a photo of themselves as children, riding in a hot-air balloon. There had never been a hot-air balloon ride, however—the photos were digitally altered to include an actual picture of the person as a child. Fully 50% of the (now adult) people later reported memories of the ride in the hot-air balloon.

Note, however, that this procedure may be *too* persuasive—if you saw a picture of yourself riding in a hot-air balloon at age six, wouldn't you just decide that it must have happened, and that your memory was faulty? As a follow-up to this study, and to check on this idea, Lindsay, Hagen, Read, Wade, and Garry (2004) implanted a memory of a pseudo-event with the aid of a more conventional photograph—they got participants' grade school class photos from their families, and showed those photos as "memory cues." The pseudo-event was a prank the person was told he/she and a friend had pulled in grade school, sneaking some Slime (that brightly colored gelatinous toy, made by Mattel) into the teacher's desk. Three childhood stories, two true events and one pseudo-event, were read to everyone, and half of them were also shown their grade-school class picture. People were asked to recall whatever they could about the three stories, then to come back in a week for further testing. They were encouraged to spend some time every day "working at remembering more about that event" during the week.

Figure 8-9 presents only the results for the pseudo-event, tabulating in each condition the percentage of people having no memory of the event, the percentage having images but not memories of the event, and the percentage that reported having genuine memories of the pseudo-event. Look first at the left half of the figure, showing the results from Session 1. Here, well over 50% of the people who merely heard the story said they had no memory of the event, a correct memory, and roughly 15% claimed they *did* remember it, an incorrect memory. Surprisingly, only about 33% of the group who saw the class photo was correct ("no memory") in Session 1, but fully 30% in the photo group were wrong when they claimed they did remember the event.

The most stunning result involved how the photo group changed from Session 1 to 2. There were modest drops in the number of people who (correctly) recalled no memories of the Slime event, but the percentage of people who incorrectly claimed to remember the event climbed from 30% to nearly 70% in the photo group. Apparently, having a photo that "took them back" to grade school years boosted the acceptance of misinformation and seemed to implant the bogus memory more thoroughly and

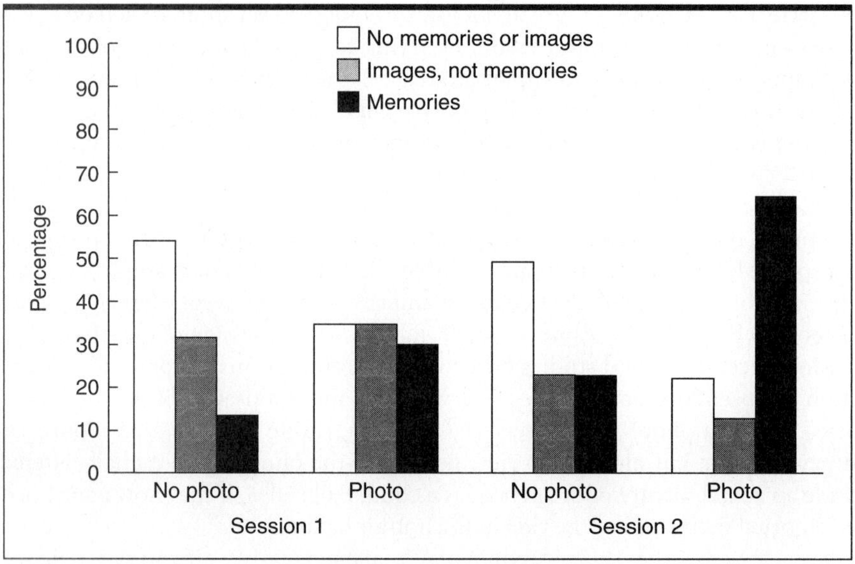

FIGURE 8-9 The percentages of people in the no-photo and photo groups who claimed to have no memories of the pseudo-event, claimed to have images but not memories, and claimed to have genuine memories. The left panel shows performance in the original session, and the right panel shows session 2 results, collected one week later. From Lindsay et al., 2004, p. 152. American Psychological Society.

convincingly. Indeed, the authors reported that after the people were told that the Slime event had in fact never happened, they often expressed surprise (e.g., "You mean that didn't happen to me?").

OVERCONFIDENCE IN MEMORY Despite our feeling that we remember events accurately ("I saw it with my own eyes!"), we often misremember what we have experienced. And, as you've just read, we can be induced to form memories for events that never happened on the basis of suggestion, evidence, or even just related information (e.g., the class photos).

And, as if this weren't bad enough, we often become unjustifiably confident in the accuracy of our own memories (see Wells, Olson, & Charman, 2002, for an overview) and surprisingly unaware of how unreliable memory can be (a classic illustration is ★ shown in Figure 8-10). As you read a moment ago, Roediger and McDermott's (1995) participants not only (falsely) recalled and recognized the critical lure, the majority of them claimed that they genuinely remembered it, claiming to have explicit, "vivid memory" of hearing the word in the list. The ultimate reason for this overconfidence, aside from a basic belief in ourselves, seems to involve two factors. The first is **source memory**, our *memory of the exact source of information.* As several investigators note (e.g., Schacter, 1996), our source memory often is very flawed; we cannot accurately distinguish whether the source of some piece of information was the original event, some later event, or even our own general knowledge of the relevant situation. A second reason may have something to do with **processing fluency**, *the ease with which something is processed or comes to mind*, as if you thought to yourself, "I remembered 'sleep' too easily to have just imagined that it was on the list, so it must have been on the list" (see Kelley & Lindsay, 1993). As Loftus and Hoffman (1989, p. 103) put it, both memory psychologists and the courts should find it interesting that such memories can arise through the process of suggestion or exposure to misinformation and become "as real and as vivid as a memory that arose from. . .actual perception."

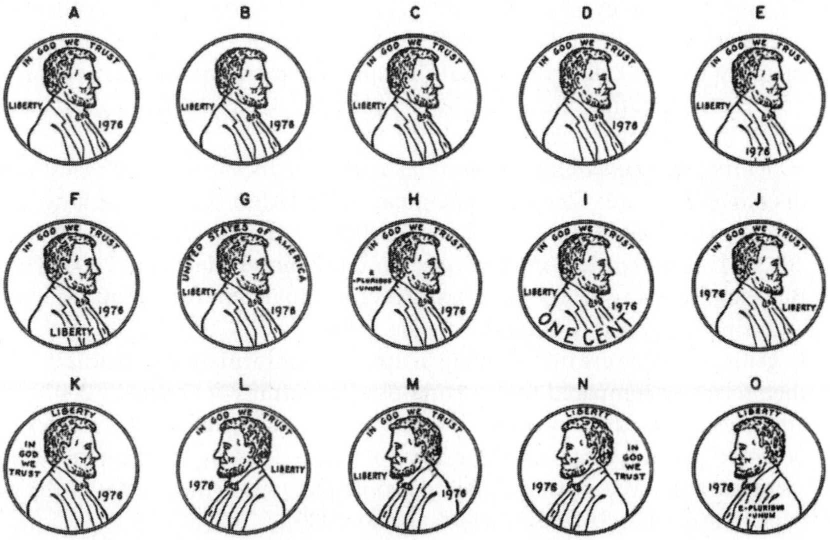

★ **FIGURE 8-10**
Which penny drawing is accurate? From Nickerson and Adams (1979).

Stronger Memory Distortion Effects

But can something as simple as this in the laboratory explain real-world inaccuracies in memory? Probably so. Consider just a sampling of recent experiments on false memories and memory distortions:

- Repeated exposure to misinformation increases memory reports of the misinformation (Mitchell & Zaragoza, 1996) and, at least when the information was read in story format, increases the tendency to believe that the information was known prior to being in the experiment (Marsh, Meade, & Roediger, 2003). There has been some suggestion that the retrieval of misinformation may actually suppress the availability of accurate information, thereby increasing the impact of misinformation (MacLeod & Saunders, 2008).
- Repeated retrieval of misinformation strengthens later recall and confidence about the misinformation (Roediger, Jacoby, & McDermott, 1996; Schreiber & Sergent, 1998), as do repeated attempts to remember (Henkel, 2004), or any efforts that involve the person actually generating information (Lane & Zaragoza, 2007).
- Repeated questioning about an event can enhance recall of certain details and induce forgetting of others, even when no misinformation was present (Shaw, 1996; Shaw, Bjork, & Handal, 1995). Repeated questioning also increases confidence in one's memories, whether they are correct or not (Heaps & Nash, 2001; Shaw, 1996).

- Talking about an event can impair memory for that event. This is called **verbal overshadowing** (e.g., Schooler & Engstler-Schooler, 1990). Somehow your memory for your description can disrupt your memory for what you actually saw. Even providing the name of the category an object belongs to (such as "chair") can impede memory (Lupyan, 2008).
- *Imagining that something happened increases later memory reports that it actually did happen*—a situation called **imagination inflation** (Garry, Manning, Loftus, & Sherman, 1996; Garry & Polaschek, 2000; Hyman & Pentland, 1996; Libby, 2003; Mazzoni & Memon, 2003; Seamon, Philbin, & Harrison, 2006; Thomas, Bulevich, & Loftus, 2003), as can instructions to accept consistent information as having happened (Brainerd & Reyna, 1998).
- In general, people are more willing to accept misinformation as true if it involves themselves as compared to someone else (Desjardins & Scoboria, 2007). These effects can be further magnified by showing people pictures of themselves, either doctored pictures that place the person in a false situation (putting the person in a hot-air balloon), or even showing people pictures of themselves at the age in which the event occurred (Garry & Gerrie, 2005).
- Misinformation effects are often found even when people are told to be careful about mistakes or warned that misleading information might be presented (Belli, Lindsay, Gales, & McCarthy, 1994; Chambers & Zaragoza, 2001; Eakin, Schreiber, & Sergent-Marshall, 2003; Neuschatz, Benoit, & Payne, 2003; Watson, McDermott, & Balota, 2004), which might normally be expected to make people more cautious. Misinformation effects are not limited to situations when memory is explicitly being tested; for example, Dodd and MacLeod (2004) found the effect even when people believed they were merely performing a typical Stroop color naming task.
- There is a social aspect to false memory as well. Suggestions from others can make you more certain that an event happened or that you remember it (e.g., Meade & Roediger, 2002; Zaragoza, Payment, Ackil, Drivdahl, & Beck, 2001). As Roediger, Meade, and Bergman (2001) put it, "False memories are contagious; one person's memory can be infected by another person's errors" (p. 365).
- Misinformation is more likely to disrupt or interfere with memory for correct information when it follows the correct information rather than precedes it, even when people are aware of the misinformation (Brown, Brown, Mosbacher, & Dryden, 2006). That is, misinformation has a greater retroactive interference effect than a proactive interference effect.

It doesn't take much to realize the implications of this work: Memory is pliable. Memories of events can be altered and influenced, both by the knowledge people have when the event happens and by what they encounter afterward. People report that they remember events that did not happen. And in many cases, they become confident about their accuracy for those events.

Repressed and Recovered Memories

There are broad, disturbing implications of these findings, certainly with respect to eyewitness testimony but more broadly to all situations in which people are trying to remember real-world events (Mitchell & Zaragoza, 2001). If we can "remember" things with a high degree of confidence and conviction, even though they never happened, then how seriously should eyewitness testimony be weighed in court proceedings? Juries usually are heavily influenced by eyewitnesses. Is this justified? Should a person be convicted of a crime based solely on someone's memory of a criminal act? The controversy over recovered memories is an obvious and worrisome arena in which our understanding of human memory is critical.

Here is a summary of a recovered memory case. A person "recovers" a memory, possibly a horrible childhood memory of abuse. The absence of that memory for many years is said to indicate that the experience was repressed or intentionally forgotten. Although the recovery sometimes is spontaneous, it can also be an outcome of psychotherapy, in which the individual and therapist have done "memory work" to bring the memory into awareness. Now that the awful memory is "recovered," the person may seek restitution, such as having the remembered perpetrator brought to trial. It goes without saying that there is often no objective way to determine whether the recovered memory is real, no sure way to determine whether the remembered event actually happened. Therefore these cases often simply become one person's word against another's, both people claiming the truth.

The past few years have seen a rise in court cases involving recovered memories, and several people have been convicted of crimes based on someone's recovered memory (Loftus, 1993; Loftus & Ketcham, 1991). Cognitive science has become involved in this controversy for the obvious reason, our understanding of how memory works. As the research has developed, certain aspects of the recovered memory situation have fallen under greater scrutiny.

Of these, two are especially important. First is the notion of **repression**, *intentional forgetting of painful or traumatic experiences* (Freud, 1905/1953). There is little hard, empirical evidence on the nature of this type of forgetting, however, often not even reliable estimates on how often it occurs. And some data suggest that the opposite reaction may occur in cases of trauma: Painfully clear and explicit memory of the trauma (Schacter's seventh sin, persistence). Cognitive science is no closer than clinical psychology in determining whether the evidence weighs more heavily for or against the process of repression (but see Nadel & Jacobs, 1998, on possible neurobiological differences for traumatic memories, and Arrigo & Pezdek, 1997, for a useful perspective on studying repressed memories).

More worrisome is that some therapeutic techniques for helping a client recover a memory are similar to variables shown to increase false memories, including imagery, suggestive questioning, and repetition. In fact, essentially these techniques were used in a case that documents how a completely false, fabricated memory can be "implanted" in a susceptible person (Ofshe, 1992). And as several studies have shown, it is not necessary to go to extreme lengths to implant a memory (Loftus & Coan, 1994; Wade et al., 2002). Indeed, on a minor scale, all you have to do is present a list of words such as *bed, rest, awake*, and *pillow*, and the word *sleep* emerges.

No one doubts that child abuse and other personal traumas occur. And no one questions the need for genuine victims to overcome such tragedy. But it is equally important that cognitive science provide its expertise on issues that hinge so critically on memory. And we should be especially mindful that memories are (sadly) prone to distortion and error, perhaps especially so for genuine victims of abuse (Bremner, Shobe, & Kihlstrom, 2000) as well as those who report recovered memories (Clancy, Schacter, McNally, & Pitman, 2000). The very reconstructive processes that bestow power on long-term memory bring with them a degree of fragility.

This sort of work is especially difficult because there are no reliable indicators of true versus false memories. There are some overall patterns that distinguish true from false memories. For example, overall people show less confidence in false memories than true memories, tend to recall them later, and provide less detail about false than true memories (Frost, 2000; Heaps & Nash, 2001). Moreover, there is some evidence of different physiological processing for true versus false memories. As one example, it has been shown that true memories are more likely to produce distinct patterns of gamma oscillations in certain regions of the brain (Sederberg, Schulze-Bonhage, Madsen, Bromfield, Litt, Brandt, & Kahana, 2007) (EEG recordings show regular oscillations at different frequencies, and gamma oscillations occur in the 28-100 Hz range. You may remember studying these different oscillations when you learned about the different stages of sleep in other psychology classes.)

Section Summary

- Several paradigms give clear evidence of false memories, such as the Roediger and McDermott (1995) list presentation studies and eyewitness memory research by Loftus and others. "Remembering" in such situations is affected by source misattribution, the acceptance of misinformation, and bias. People tend to be overconfident about their memories, regardless of the distortions that might be involved.
- Cases of "forgotten" and "recovered" memories are particularly difficult to assess because of the fragile, reconstructive nature of memories. It is a concern, however, that therapeutic techniques used to assist in "recovering" memory of trauma are so similar to variables like repetition and repeated questioning, variables that increase the false memory effect.

Recognition memory for information acquired across an extended period is remarkably accurate across many years, whereas recall performance begins to decline within months.

AUTOBIOGRAPHICAL MEMORIES

Let's conclude this chapter on a less controversial topic: *the study of one's lifetime collection or narrative of personal memories*, or **autobiographical memory**. In the past few years there has been an increase in the number of studies about autobiographical memory, real-world investigations of memory for more natural experiences and information, and some important theoretical advances on what might be called the self-memory system (Conway & Pleydell-Pearce, 2000). A set of impressive investigations by Bahrick and his colleagues illustrates the nature of real-world memory for personal events.

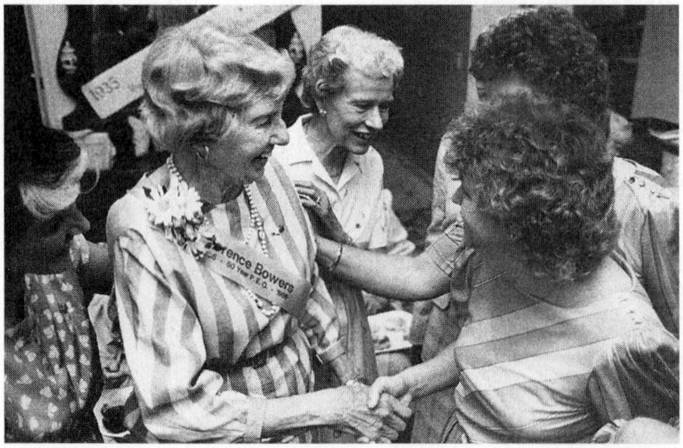

The Bahrick Work

Bahrick, Bahrick, and Wittlinger (1975) reported a fascinating study titled "Fifty Years of Memory for Names and Faces." Nearly 400 people, ranging in age from 17 to 74, were tested for their retention of name and face information about members of their own high school graduating classes. For the youngest people, this represented a retention interval of only two weeks; for the oldest, the retention interval was 57 years. Pictures and names were taken from high school yearbooks and were used in a variety of retention tests. In particular, people were asked for free recall of names and then were given five other tests: name recognition, picture recognition, picture-to-name matching, name-to-picture matching, and cued recall of names using pictures as cues.

Figure 8-11 shows the average performance on these six tests across the retention intervals, that is, time since graduation. The free recall curves on the right show an average of just under 50 names accessible for free recall a mere 3 months after graduation. Because the average size of graduating classes for everyone was 294 (and no one had fewer than 90 in their classes), this level of free recall is quite low: It works out to only about 15% of classmates' names. This number then dwindles further, so that the oldest group, having graduated an average 48 years earlier, recalled only about 18 names, something like 6% recall. Cued recall, with pictures as cues, was largely the same as free recall. ▲

In contrast, however, all four recognition tests showed impressive levels of retention. Simple recognition of names and faces was 90% at the 3-month retention interval. Name recognition did not begin to decline noticeably until about 15 years later, and picture recognition remained in the 80 to 90% range until about 35 years later. And, as Bahrick et al. point out, the decline in the very oldest group may have been influenced by factors related to physical aging, possibly introducing a negative bias for the oldest group.

What leads to such impressive levels of retention, particularly when we compare them with the lower performance of people in laboratory memory studies? As Bahrick

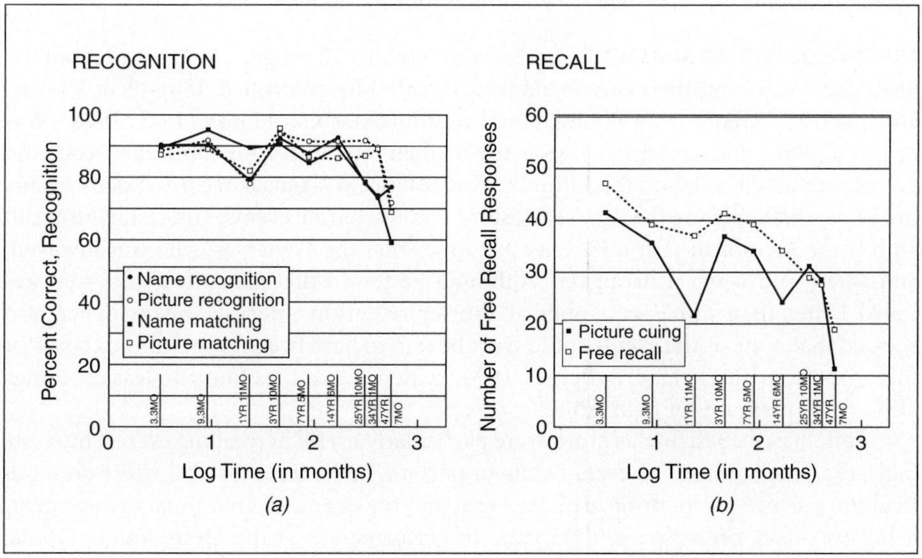

▲ **FIGURE 8-11** Results from the Bahrick et al. (1975) study of memory of faces and names across 50 years. From Bahrick, Bahrick, and Wittlinger (1975).

You know the name
You know the number
007
GOLDENEYE

Do you remember when you saw this? Whom you saw it with? Where you saw it?

et al. note, in the typical situation, people have learned the names and faces of their classmates across a four-year (or longer) period. This situation is called prolonged acquisition. According to the authors, this principle has two important components, overlearning and distributed practice. First, the information tested in the Bahrick et al. study was overlearned to a much higher degree than laboratory studies have examined (even Ebbinghaus didn't test the effects of a four-year learning phase). The result of such overlearning is much-improved retention.

Second, prolonged acquisition represents learning that was distributed across a long period of time, in contrast to typical memory experiments in which learning opportunities are massed together over a short period. This neatly confirmed the standard laboratory finding that distributed practice leads to better retention than massed practice (Underwood, Keppel, & Schulz, 1962). Bahrick's work, including memory of foreign language (1984; Bahrick, Bahrick, Bahrick, & Bahrick, 1993), memory of math learned in school (Bahrick & Hall, 1991), and memory of a city's streets and locations 50 years later (Bahrick, 1983) shows this to be one of the soundest bits of advice cognitive psychology gives to students. Distribute your practice and learning rather than massing it together (a.k.a., cramming). Indeed, the Bahrick results suggest that the laboratory-based effect not only is general to more naturalistic settings, but is magnified when naturalistic, everyday memories are tested (see Burt, 1992, and Burt, Kemp, & Conway, 2001, for similar work on diarists' autobiographical memories).

PSYCHOLOGISTS AS SUBJECTS Several modern-day Ebbinghauses have adopted the procedure of testing their own memories in carefully controlled, long-term studies. One major difference from Ebbinghaus' procedure was that Linton (1975, 1978), Wagenaar (1986), and Sehulster (1989) tested their memories for naturally occurring events, not artificial laboratory stimuli. For instance, Wagenaar recorded daily events in his own life for more than six years, some 2,400 separate events, and tested his recall with combinations of four different cue types: what the event was, who was involved, and where and when it happened. Although he found that pleasant events were recalled better than unpleasant ones at shorter retention intervals, his evidence also showed that none of the events could truly be said to have been forgotten (but contrast this with the Bahrick, Hall, & Berger, 1996, evidence that bias toward pleasant things affects our memories of high school grades).

Time-based cues, furthermore, were particularly useful in recalling events. Interestingly, the time lag since an event, while important, had a less powerful effect on recall than the salience or importance of the event and the degree of emotional involvement. Sehulster's data, on memory of 25 years of performances at the Metropolitan Opera, showed very similar effects; that is, the importance or intensity of the performance was a predictor of superior recall.

Phenomena of Autobiographical Memory

The research on autobiographical memory has revealed a number of phenomena that characterize memory for our lives. In this section, we present three of them to give you an idea of why it is important to consider autobiographical memory beyond what is known about episodic and semantic memory. More specifically, we will consider infantile amnesia, or why you have trouble remembering events from when you were a young child, the reminiscence bump, and spontaneous memories.

INFANTILE AMNESIA Think about the first thing you can remember. What is your earliest memory? Where were you? What was going on? Who were you with? How old were you? For most people, this memory will be from the ages of 2-4 years old. But, wait a minute! What about all of the things that came before that? Why can't we remember anything earlier than that age? Furthermore, if you think about it, your memory for your childhood is quite spotty, getting better only as you got older. **Infantile amnesia** is *the inability to remember early life events and very poor memory for your life at a very young age.* One of the first people to discuss this phenomenon was Sigmund Freud (1899/1938). He thought that this was a true amnesia in which there was a catastrophic forgetting of early life events. According to him, this was done to protect the ego from threatening psychosexual content. However, there has been little empirical support for this idea across the years, so we won't consider it further.

Instead, it appears more likely that infantile amnesia is not an amnesia at all. That is, it is not a massive forgetting of things that would otherwise be remembered. Instead, this aspect of autobiographical memory reveals how memory is developing. Keep in mind that humans are born neurologically immature and quite helpless. It takes some time for the nervous system to develop to the point that we can have autobiographical memories. Clearly there is some sort of memory system, even before birth. Newborns prefer the sound of their own mother's voice, which they heard *in utero*. Moreover, implicit, procedural learning begins almost immediately as a person learns to do various things such as control their head, arms, and legs, to more complex tasks such as sitting up, using a spoon, and dumping cereal on the floor. Children also are developing semantic memories as they learn what things are, and what they are called. They also have episodic memories in that they are clearly influenced by things such as context. However, young children have a difficult time remembering specific events from their lives, especially as they move away from them.

Infantile amnesia appears to resolve itself as one develops a sense of self and can start organizing information around this self concept (Howe & Courage, 1993). There are even neurological correlates that indicate the use of self-referential memories as opposed to more general knowledge (Magno & Allan, 2007). As we have noted earlier, information that you can relate to yourself is often remembered best. So, in a sense, the offset of infantile amnesia marks the beginning of autobiographical memory. A number of things likely contribute to the development of the self concept. For example, this is also the time when there is a tremendous increase in the child's use of expressive language (K. Nelson, 1993). If you think about your own autobiographical memories, they are heavily influenced by language in terms of their content, their structure, and how you think about them. Also, this period of time is when the hippocampus is maturing, allowing more complex memories to be formed (Nadel & Zola-Morgan, 1984). Finally, at this age, a child has started to develop schemas and scripts that are complex enough to begin making sense of the world in a more adult-like fashion, thereby facilitating memory for individual life experiences (K. Nelson, 1993).

REMINISCENCE BUMP When you talk to people older than the typical college student, you might find that they have a bias to remember events from when they were in college. Why is that? Are they trying to make a social connection with you? Was that the best time of their lives? While we can't answer most of these questions, we can tell you that your observation is correct, and that we can provide some insight into the first question. The **reminiscence bump** is *superior memory than would otherwise be expected for life events around the age of 20, between the ages of 15 and 25.* This is illustrated in Figure 8-12 (Rubin, Rahhal, & Poon, 1998). What this figure shows is the rate of remembering events from a person's life as a function of how old the person was at the time (older adults are used here to make the reminiscence bump clearer). These studies often use what is known as the Galton-Crovitz technique (Crovitz & Shiffman, 1974; Galton, 1879), in which people are presented with lists of words, and asked to respond with the first autobiographical memory that comes to mind. The first thing to notice is that most of the reported memories come from the recent past, and that the further away in time the event is (the older the event is, hence the younger a person was at the time), the less likely it will be recalled. However, note that around the age of 20 there is a tendency to remember more events than would be expected if this were a normal forgetting curve. So, why does this happen?

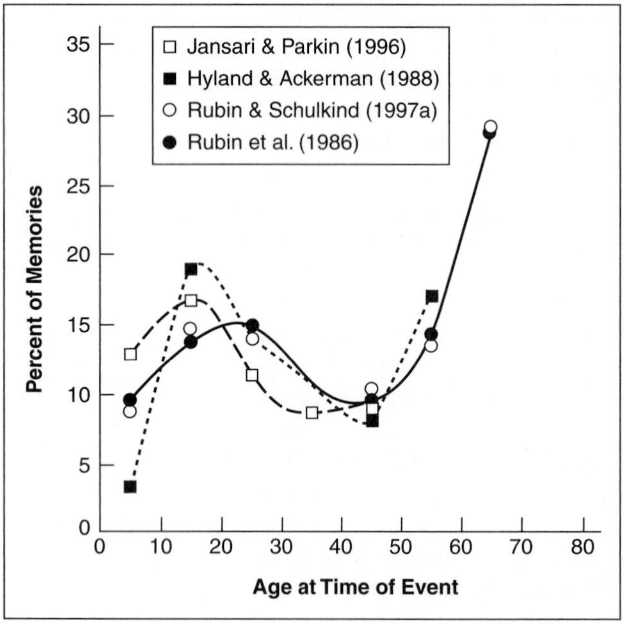

FIGURE 8-12
Illustration of the reminiscence bump (note that data from the most recent decade have been excluded to make the bump clearer). Note that memory performance is better around the age of 20. Adapted from Rubin, Rahhal, and Poon (1998).

There are a number of ideas about what causes the reminiscence bump. One view is that memory tends to be better for things that happen for the first time. For example, it is easier to remember your first kiss than your 27th, although you may have just as much fun during each. This is a period in a person's life when a number of things are happening for the first time—the first time a person lives alone, drives, votes, gets a real job, gets a speeding ticket, pays taxes, and so on. Because there are so many "firsts," it is easier to remember events from this period of your life. This idea is supported by the fact that people who move from one country to another, where another language is spoken, show a reminiscence bump for the time of their immigration, regardless of how old they were at the time (Schrauf & Rubin, 1998). Presumably this move brought on a number of new experiences, a number of "firsts" that made that time in their life more memorable.

Another idea is that we remember so much more from this period of our lives because we expect to. That is, we all carry out cultural life scripts (Berntsen & Rubin, 2004; Rubin & Berntsen, 2003) about when the exciting times in our lives are supposed to be, such as graduating from school, getting married, buying your first home, having your first child, and so on. There is also a "life stories" account that is based on the story of our lives that we create over time and as we develop (Glück & Bluck, 2007). According to this view, part of what is driving the reminiscence bump is the expectation that people are supposed to remember more from these important points in their lives. In fact, when people recall events from their lives, the intensity that they report for those events, particularly positive events (e.g., weddings, birth of children, graduations, etc.), corresponds with the cultural expectation (Collins, Pillemer, Ivcevic & Gooze, 2007). Another source of support for this idea is the fact that people show a reminiscence bump for a character they read about in a novel (Copeland, Radvansky, & Goodwin, 2009). That is, people remember events about a character better when the character was around 20, or when the character went through major life change (such as having her long-time husband die and going out into the working world), as compared to earlier events in the novel (when the character was younger), or chapters that were read more recently (when the character was older). This seems more likely to occur if people are using life scripts about what should be more memorable to actually guide their memory retrieval.

SPONTANEOUS MEMORY Autobiographical memories are recalled into consciousness not only when we actively try to remember, but they also occur spontaneously, without any clear effort to do so. Often these memories refer to single events, rather than general periods of time (Berntsen & Hall, 2004). An example of a spontaneous memory would be remembering a specific event that happened during a specific chemistry class when you were in high school compared to just remembering that you took chemistry in high school. These spontaneous memories are often triggered by some cue—literally a retrieval cue—in the environment. For example, a person may see a highly valued object (an old playtoy) that then has the power to elicit a strong autobiographical memory (Jones & Martin, 2006). In general, emotional intensity is commonly a critical aspect of such triggered autobiographical memories (Talarico, LaBar, & Rubin, 2004).

Perhaps some of the strongest cues for spontaneously bringing about autobiographical recollections are odors. Memories elicited by odors produce a stronger feeling of being back in time (what it was like to experience the event long ago) (Herz & Schooler, 2002; Willander & Larsson, 2006). Moreover, odors elicit stronger emotions in the person experiencing the memory (Herz & Schooler, 2002; Willander & Larsson, 2007).

The Irony of Memory

We conclude on the topic of the irony of memory: the question of how this powerful, flexible system can also be so fragile, so prone to errors.

Distinctiveness or rated memorability is an important determinant of how accurately we remember an event, such as the attack on the World Trade Center.

IS HUMAN MEMORY SO AWFUL? We complain about how poor our memories are, how forgetful we are, how hard it is to learn and remember information. We deal with difficulties of the transience of our memories, our absent-mindedness, the occasionally embarrassing blocking we experience when trying to remember. Are these accurate assessments of our memories (e.g., Roediger & McDermott, 2000)?

Well, they're probably exaggerated. First, as Anderson and Schooler (1991) note, when we complain about memory failures, we neglect the huge stockpile of facts and information that we expect memory to store and to provide immediate access to. We underestimate the complexities, not to mention the sheer volume, of information stored in memory (e.g., some have estimated that the typical adult has at least a half-million–word vocabulary, and it is almost impossible to estimate how many people we have known across the years).

Second, we fall into the trap of equating remembering with recall. When we say we have forgotten something, we probably mean we are unable to recall it right now. But as you have read, recall is only one way of testing memory. Recognition and relearning are far more forgiving in terms of showing that information has indeed been retained in memory. (And third, we focus on the failures of retrieval, without giving credit for the countless times we remember accurately; see also Chapter 11, on our tendency to search for confirming evidence.)

How much cognitive psychology will you remember in a dozen years? Your honest estimate is (probably) "not much at all." If so, then you have seriously underestimated your memory. A study by Conway, Cohen, and Stanhope (1991) examined exactly that: students' memory of the concepts, specific facts, names, and so on from a cognitive psychology course taken up to 12 years earlier. Figure 8-13 shows their results. Recall of

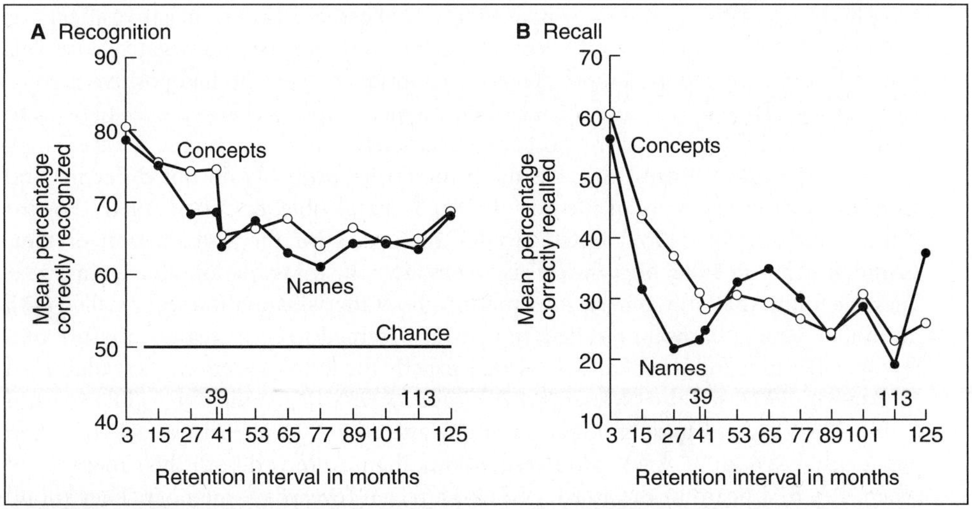

◆ **FIGURE 8-13**
A. Mean percentages of correctly recognized names and concepts across retention intervals. **B.** Mean percentages of correctly recalled names and concepts across retention intervals. From Conway, Cohen, and Stanhope (1991).

material dwindled quite a bit across the 12 years, from 60% to 25% for concepts, for example. But recognition for the same material dropped only a bit, from 80% to around 65 to 70%. Correct recognition for all categories of information remained significantly above chance across all 12 years. Your honest estimate—your metacognitive awareness of having information in storage—can be quite inaccurate.

FLASHBULB MEMORIES On the other hand, we often seem to have—or believe we have—extremely accurate and very detailed memories of particular events, especially when the events were surprising or highly unusual. For example, Winograd and Killinger (1983) examined the flashbulb memories (Brown & Kulik, 1977) of college students for a significant event, the assassination of President Kennedy in 1963 (note that people were asked to recall their own particular circumstances when they heard news of the event, not whether they remembered the event itself). The data showed an increase in the amount of recallable information as a function of age in 1963, but the evidence also showed that the surprise or shock involved in such events may not be necessary for high levels of retention; people showed high recall for the Nixon resignation and the moon landing of the U.S. astronauts, neither of which was an unexpected, surprise occurrence.

Distinctiveness of the event, however, seems quite important (Dodson & Schacter, 2002; Hunt & Lamb, 2001; Schmidt, 1985). This is reminiscent of the von Restorff effect you encountered earlier. And it is strikingly similar to the "surprise response" discussed in Chapter 6 in connection with the effects of bizarre imagery on mnemonics (Hirshman et al., 1989). However, there is a further need for the person to be emotionally involved in the event. Kensinger and Schacter (2006) reported people's memories of the Red Socks—Yankees World Series games. Not surprisingly, it made a difference if they were Red Socks fans (winners, positive affect), Yankees fans (losers, negative affect), or not a fan of either team (neutral). People who had both positive and negative emotions about the outcome reported more detailed memories. People who had positive memories, however, showed less consistency (their memory reports changed over time), and more overconfidence (they were more inappropriately confident than the Yankees fans).

Several studies suggest that flashbulb memories probably do not differ in kind from more ordinary types of memories (McCloskey, Wible, & Cohen, 1988). For instance, Christianson (1989) tested Swedes' memories for the assassination of their prime minister in 1986, once barely six weeks after the assassination and again a year later. He found that only general information about the assassination was recalled with accuracy. Details that were recalled, in contrast, seemed to be a creative mixture of a few specifics plus more general knowledge, exactly the kind of memory first identified by Bartlett (1932; see also Neisser, 1982; Weaver, 1993). In a similar vein, Talarico and Rubin (2003) tested undergraduates the day after the 9/11 terrorist attack and then again either 1, 6, or 32 weeks afterward, asking them to record both their memory of when they first heard of the attack and also a recent "everyday" memory. They found that both flashbulb and everyday memories declined across time in their consistency, but that the people *believed* that their flashbulb memories remained highly accurate—in other words, flashbulb memories were special "only in their *perceived* accuracy" (p. 455, emphasis added; see also Schmolck, Buffalo, & Squire, 2000, who tested people's recollections of the O. J. Simpson trial).

Conway et al. (1994) performed a similar, extensive study and did find evidence of special memory mechanism. They tested people on their personal recollections at the time of British prime minister Margaret Thatcher's surprise resignation, first just two weeks after the event, then again nearly a year later. More than 86% of their sample from the U.K. had accurate, detailed recollections of the event, including specific personal details (e.g., what they had eaten for breakfast that day). Because fewer than 30% of the non-U.K. participants had such memories, the authors concluded that vivid, accurate flashbulb memories can be formed. Furthermore, you are more likely to form a flashbulb memory if you view the event as especially important to you and if it has an emotional effect on you (see also Libkuman, Nichols-Whitehead, Griffith, & Thomas, 1999, on the role of emotional arousal in remembering). Interestingly, visual imagery and emotions seem to be especially important in the recollection of autobiographical memories (Rubin, Schrauf, & Greenberg, 2003); in those authors' words, "highly relived memories almost always had strong visual images," according to participants' self-reports. And in addition to the visual images, Schmidt (2004) found that the participants' emotionality also influenced the errors made in recalling personal memories of the 9/11 attack (for a list of criteria needed to form a flashbulb memory, see Finkenhauer et al., 1998).

But here's the irony again: Is memory good, even flashbulb-quality good, or is it widely subject to the sins of misattribution, suggestibility, bias, and the rest? The circumstances Conway et al. (1994) isolated as important for forming flashbulb memories—high level of importance, high affective response to the event—should also characterize memories of traumatic events, exactly those that are in dispute in cases of repressed and recovered memories.

Section Summary

- Studies of autobiographical memory, or memory in real-world settings, show the same kinds of effects as laboratory studies but sometimes more strongly. Recognition memory for information acquired across an extended period is remarkably accurate across many years, whereas recall begins to decline within months.
- Distinctiveness, importance of the event to oneself, and the level of one's affective response are all important factors in remembering real-world events, especially those that seem to produce flashbulb memories. The ironies of memory—a powerful, large-capacity system that is nonetheless quite prone to error—have not been completely explained.

Key Terms

agent (p. *282*)
arguments (p. *282*)
autobiographical memory (p. *310*)
cryptomnesia (p. *292*)
false memory (p. *296*)
fan effect (p. *288*)
feeling of knowing (p. *295*)
imagination inflation (p. *308*)
infantile amnesia (p. *313*)
integration (p. *302*)
judgments of learning (p. *295*)
location (p. *282*)
memory impairment (p. *302*)
metamemory (p. *294*)
misinformation acceptance (p. *304*)
misinformation effect (p. *303*)
patient (p. *282*)
processing fluency (p. *306*)
proposition (p. *282*)
prospective memory (p. *293*)
recipient (p. *282*)
relation (p. *282*)
reminiscence bump (p. *314*)
repression (p. *309*)
semantic cases (p. *282*)
source memory (p. *306*)
source monitoring (p. *292*)
source misattribution (p. *304*)
time (p. *282*)
tip-of-the-tongue (TOT) state (p. *295*)
verbal overshadowing (p. *308*)

CHAPTER

9

Language

The beginning of wisdom is learning the names of things.

CONFUCIUS

Language is a system of signs, different from the things signified, but able to suggest them.

JAMES, 1890, P. 980

I personally think we developed language because of our deep inner need to complain.

LILY TOMLIN, "THE SEARCH FOR SIGNS OF INTELLIGENT LIFE IN THE UNIVERSE," TIME, OCTOBER 7, 1985

Language, along with music, is one of the most common and universal features of human society. More than any other aspect of human knowledge, language pervades every facet of our lives, from our most public behavior to our most private thoughts. We might imagine a society that has no interest in biology, or even one with no formal system of numbers and arithmetic. But it is inconceivable that a society would have no language, no means of communication. Every culture, no matter how primitive or isolated, has language; every person, unless deprived by nature or accident, develops skill in the use of language. The reason is obvious: Language gives us power.

This is a chapter on the basics of language, its characteristics, functions, structure, and form. **Linguistics** is *the academic discipline that takes language as its topic,* and a good deal of what you'll read has come to us from that discipline. As you learned in Chapter 1, linguistics had a profound influence on cognitive psychology. It was a major turning point when Chomsky rejected behaviorism's explanation of language; according to Wasow (1989), Chomsky's influence on the field of linguistics was equally dramatic. Because approaches such as Chomsky's seemed likely to yield new insights and understanding, psychology renewed its interest in language in the late 1950s and early 1960s, borrowing heavily from linguistic theory.

And yet, as psychologists began to apply and test linguistic theory, they discovered an important limitation in the purely linguistic approach. Language is a purposeful activity. It's there to *do* something: to communicate, to express thoughts and ideas, even to complain. Linguistics, however, focused on language itself as a formal, almost disembodied system. In such an approach, the *use* of language by humans was seen as less interesting, tangential, or even irrelevant. Upon reflection, this view denied a fundamental interest of psychology—behavior. Thus a new branch of cognitive psychology evolved, called **psycholinguistics**, *the study of language as it is learned and used by people.*

We present only a brief survey of linguistics and psycholinguistics here. This chapter and the next focus on the nature and structure of language and cover two of the three traditional concerns in psycholinguistics, language comprehension and production. The third concern, language acquisition, is beyond the scope of this book.

LINGUISTIC UNIVERSALS AND FUNCTIONS

Defining Language

Webster's (1980) defines *language* as "the expression or communication of thoughts and feelings by means of sounds, and combinations of such sounds, to which meaning is attributed: human speech." That's not a bad start. For example, one particularly critical idea in the definition is that meaning is *attributed* to the sounds rather than residing in or being part of those sounds. As an illustration, the difference in sound between the words *car* and *cars* is the *s* sound, denoting plural in English. As often as not, this is the meaning of a final *s* sound, "more than one of something." But this meaning is not inherent in the *s* sound, any more than the word *chalk* necessarily refers to the white stuff used on blackboards. This is an important idea: Language is based on arbitrary connections between linguistic elements, such as sounds, and the meanings denoted by them.

A language does not have to be spoken to be a true language, as sign language for the deaf and symbolic computer languages show.

The definition is a bit confining, however. For instance, it restricts language to sounds, to human speech. By this rule, writing would not be language, nor would sign language for the deaf. It is true that writing is a recent development, dating back only about 5,000 years, compared to the development of articulate speech, theorized to have occurred some 100,000 years ago (e.g., Corballis, 2004). It is equally true that the development of writing depended critically on the existence of a spoken language. Thus the spoken, auditory form of a language is more basic than the written version; is there any doubt that children would fail to acquire language if they were exposed only to books instead of to speech? Nonetheless, we include written language in our definition for the reason that reading and writing are major forms of communication in modern society.

Let's offer a definition that is more suitable for our purposes. **Language** is *a shared symbolic system for communication.* First, language is symbolic. It consists of units (e.g., sounds that form words) that symbolize or stand for the referent of the word; the referent, the thing referred to by the final *s,* is the meaning *plural.* Second, the symbol system is shared by all users of a language culture. Language users all learned the same set of arbitrary connections between symbols and meaning, and they also share a common rule system that appropriately translates the symbols-to-meaning connections. Third, the system enables communication. The user translates from the thought into a public message, according to the shared rule system. This enables the receiver to retranslate the message back into the underlying thought or meaning.

Language Universals

Hockett (1960a, b; 1966) proposed a list of 13 **linguistic universals,** *features or characteristics that are common to all languages.* To distinguish human language from animal communication, Hockett proposed that only human language contains all 13 features. Several of the universals he identified, such as the vocal–auditory requirement, are not essential characteristics of human language, although they were likely essential to its evolution. Other features are critically important to our analysis here. Hockett's full list ▲ is presented in Table 9-1, along with short explanations. We limit our discussion to four of these, plus two others implied but absent from the list.

SEMANTICITY As you already know, the term *semantic* means "meaning." It is an important point that language exhibits **semanticity**, that *language conveys meaning.* For example, the sounds of human language carry meaning, whereas other sounds that we make, say coughing or clearing our throats, are not part of our language because

TABLE 9-1 Hockett's Linguistic Universals

- **Vocal–auditory channel.** The channel or means of transmission for all linguistic communication is vocal–auditory. Hockett excluded written language by this universal because it is a recent invention and because it is not found in all language cultures.
- **Broadcast transmission and directional reception.** Linguistic transmissions are broadcast, that is, transmitted in all directions from the source, and can be received by any hearer within range; therefore, the transmission is public. By virtue of binaural hearing, the direction or location of the transmission is conveyed by the transmission itself.
- **Transitoriness: rapid fading.** The linguistic transmission is of a transitory nature; it has to be received at exactly the right time, or it will fade (as contrasted with, say, a message transmitted to a recording device, which preserves the information). This implies that the hearer must perform the message preservation task by recording the message on paper or storing information in memory.
- **Interchangeability.** "Any speaker of a human language is capable, in theory, of saying anything he can understand when someone else says it. For language, humans are what engineers call 'transceivers': units freely usable for either transmission or reception" (Hockett, 1960a). In other words, because I can understand a sentence you say to me, I can therefore say that sentence back to you: I can both receive and transmit any message. Contrast this with certain animal systems in which males and females produce different calls or messages that cannot be interchanged.
- **Total feedback.** The human speaker has total auditory feedback for the transmitted message, simultaneous with the listener's reception of the message. This feedback is used for moment-to-moment adjustments to the production of sound.
- **Specialization.** The sounds of language are specialized to convey meaning, that is, linguistic intent, as opposed to nonlanguage sounds. Consider a jogger saying, "I'm exhausted," when the speech act conveys a specific meaning. Contrast this with a jogger panting loudly at the end of a run, when the sounds being produced have no necessary linguistic function (although a hearer might infer that the jogger is exhausted).
- **Semanticity.** Linguistic utterances, whether simple phrases or complete sentences, convey meaning by means of the symbols we use to form the utterance.
- **Arbitrariness.** There is no inherent connection between a symbol and the concept or object to which it refers; there is only an arbitrary connection between sound and meaning. Contrast this with iconic communication systems, such as the bee's waggle dance.
- **Discreteness.** Although sound patterns can vary continuously across several dimensions (e.g., duration of sound, loudness of sound), language uses only a small number of discrete ranges on those dimensions to convey meaning. Thus languages do not rely on continuous variation of vowel duration, for instance, to signal changes in meaning.
- **Displacement.** Linguistic messages are not tied in time or space to the topic of the communication; this implicates an elaborate memory system within the speaker or hearer to recall the past and anticipate the future.
- **Productivity.** Language is novel, consisting of utterances that have never been uttered or comprehended before; new messages, including words, can be coined freely by means of rules and agreement among the members of the language culture.
- **Duality of patterning (duality of structure).** A small set of sounds, or phonemes, can be combined and recombined into an infinitely large set of sentences, or meanings. The sounds have no inherent meaning; the combinations do have meaning.
- **Cultural or traditional transmission.** Language is acquired by exposure to the culture, to the language of the surrounding people. Contrast this with various courtship and mating communications of animals, in which the specific messages are genetically governed.

they do not usually convey meaning in the normal sense of the word. (I'm ignoring here the example of a roomful of students coughing in unison at, say, a professor's boastful remark, to indicate a collective opinion. In this situation the coughing sound is *paralinguistic* and functions much the way rising vocal pitch indicates anger. Then again, it could just be a roomful of coughing students.)

ARBITRARINESS The feature of arbitrariness was encountered in the definition of language. **Arbitrariness** means that *there is no inherent connection between the units (sounds, words) used in a language and their meanings*. To be sure, there are a few exceptions, such as onomatopoeias like *buzz*, *hum*, and *zoom* (but as Pinker, 1994, notes, some units we think of as onomatopoetic, such as a pig's oink, aren't; that sound is "boo-boo" in Japanese). But far more commonly, the language symbol bears no relationship to the thing itself. The word *dog* has no inherent correspondence to the four-legged furry creature, just as the spoken symbol *silence* does not resemble its referent, true silence. Hockett's example drives the point home; *whale* is a small symbol for a very big thing, and *microorganism* is a big symbol for an extremely small thing.

Because there are no built-in connections between symbols and their referents, knowledge of language must involve learning and remembering the arbitrary connections. It is in this sense that we speak of language as being a shared system. We all have learned essentially the same connections, the same set of word-to-referent associations, and stored them in memory as part of our knowledge of language. Thus by convention—by agreement with the language culture—we all know that *dog* refers to one particular kind of physical object. Obviously, we have to know what word goes with what referent because there's no way to look at an object and decide what its name must be.

Two important consequences of the arbitrariness of language deserve special attention, partly because they help to distinguish human language from animal communication and partly because they tell us about the human language user. These two consequences concern flexibility and the principle of naming. Neither of these was listed by Hockett, although they are derived from his point about arbitrariness.

FLEXIBILITY OF SYMBOLS Note that arbitrariness makes language symbolic. *Desk* and *pupitre* are the English and French symbols for a particular object. Were it not for the history of our language, we might call it a *zoople* or a *manty*. A consequence of this symbolic aspect of language is that the system demonstrates tremendous **flexibility**. That is, *because the connection between symbol and meaning is arbitrary, we can change those connections and invent new ones*. We routinely shift our terms for the things around us, however slowly such change takes place.

Contrast this flexibility with the opposite of a symbolic system, called an iconic system. In an iconic system, each unit has a physical resemblance to its referent, just as a map is physically similar to the terrain it depicts. In such a system there is no flexibility because changing the symbol for a referent would make the connection arbitrary.

NAMING A corollary to arbitrariness and flexibility involves **naming** (Glass & Holyoak, 1986). *We assign names to all the objects in our environment, to all the feelings and emotions we experience, to all the ideas and concepts we conceive of*. Obviously,

wherever it is you are sitting right now as you read this book, each object in the room has a name. Of course, in an unfamiliar or unusual place (an airport control tower or a car repair shop) you may not know the name of something, but it never occurs to you that the thing might have no name.

Furthermore, we don't stop by naming just the physical objects around us. We have an elaborate vocabulary by which we refer to unseen characteristics, privately experienced feelings, and other intangibles and abstractions. Terms such as *perception, mental process, spreading activation*, and *knowledge* have no necessary physical referent, nor do words such as *justice, cause, truth, likewise*, and *however* refer to concrete objects. Indeed, we even have words such as *abstractions* and *intangibles* that refer to the *idea* of being abstract. And, going one step further, we generate or invent names for new objects, ideas, and activities, and so forth. Think of the new vocabulary that had to be invented and mastered to describe the various actions and operations for using the Internet and modern technology, for instance. Because we need and want to talk about new things, new ideas, and new concepts, we invent new terms. (See Kaschak & Glenberg, 2000, on how we invent new verbs from already known words; e.g., "to crutch" or "to google.")

DISPLACEMENT One of the most powerful devices our language gives us is *the ability to talk about something other than the present moment*, a feature called **displacement**. By conjugating verbs to form past tense, future tense, and so on, we can communicate about objects, events, and ideas that are not present but are remembered or anticipated. And when we use constructions such as "If I go to the library tomorrow, then I'll be able to . . . .," we demonstrate a particularly powerful aspect of displacement: We can communicate about something that has never happened, and indeed might never happen, while anticipating future consequences of that never-performed action. To illustrate the power and importance of displacement to yourself, try speaking only in the present tense for about five minutes. You'll discover how incredibly limiting it would be if we were "stuck in the present."

PRODUCTIVITY By most accounts, the principle of productivity (also called generativity by some) is an important linguistic universal because it gives language a notable characteristic—novelty. Indeed, the novelty of language, and the productivity that novelty implies, formed the basis of Chomsky's (1959) critique of Skinner's book (see Chapter 1) and the foundation for Chomsky's own theory of language (1957, 1965). It is an absolute article of faith in both linguistics and psycholinguistics that the key to understanding language and language behavior lies in an understanding of novelty, an understanding of the productive nature of language.

Consider the following: Aside from trite phrases, customary greetings, and so on, hardly any of our routine language is standardized or repetitive. Instead, the bulk of what we say is novel. Our utterances are not memorized, are not repeated, but are new. This is the principle of **productivity**, that *language is a productive and inherently novel activity, that we generate utterances rather than repeat them.* We (your textbook authors) lecture on the principle of productivity every time we teach our memory and cognition classes, each time uttering a stream of sounds, a sequence of words and sentences, that is novel, new, literally invented on the spot. Even in somewhat stylized situations, as in telling a joke, the language is largely new. Only if the punchline requires a specific wording, do we try to remember the exact wording of a previously used sentence.

What does this mean? It means that language is a *creative* system, not a repetitive one. We do not recycle sentences. Instead, we create them on the spur of the moment, now in the active voice, now in the passive, with a prepositional phrase sometimes at the beginning, sometimes at the end, and so on. In a very real sense then, applying our productive rules of language to the words in our vocabulary permits us to generate an infinite number of utterances.

How can we understand any and all of the infinite set of sentences? What does it mean for a theory of language that speakers and listeners can generate and comprehend any one of this numberless set? In brief, it means that language users must have some flexible basis for producing or generating novel utterances, for coming up with the different sequences of symbols that can be comprehended. And, likewise, comprehenders must have the same flexible basis to hear the sequence of words and recover from them what the intended meaning is. By most accounts, the basis for such productivity is a set of rules. To anticipate later sections of the chapter, rules form the basis for each level of language we discuss, from our phonological system up through the highest level of analysis, the conceptual and belief systems we hold as we comprehend language.

Animal Communication

The contrast between flexible, productive human language and animal communication is staggering. Animal communication is seen in a wide range of circumstances, from primates to insects. For example, bees communicate the location of honey through a waggle dance (Dyer, 2002; Sherman & Visscher, 2002; von Frisch, 1967). Essentially, they orient themselves within the hive to the relative position of the sun, and then act out a dance that conveys how the flight will progress to get to the source of the nectar. This is even more impressive given that it is fairly dark in a bee hive and the dance is performed on a vertical surface.

Closer to humans, consider the signaling system of vervet monkeys (Marler, 1967). This system consists of several distress and warning calls, alerting an entire troupe to imminent danger. These monkeys produce a guttural "rraup" sound to warn of an eagle, one of the monkey's natural predators; they "chutter" to warn of snakes and "chirp" to warn of leopards. The system thus exhibits semanticity, an important characteristic of language. That is, each signal in the system has a different, specific referent (eagle, snake, and leopard). And furthermore, these seem to be arbitrary connections: "Rraup" doesn't resemble eagles in any physical way.

"Matthews ... we're getting another one of those strange 'aw blah es span yol' sounds."

But as Glass and Holyoak (1986) note, the troupe of monkeys cannot get together and decide to change the meaning of "rraup" from *eagle* to *snake*. The arbitrary connections to meaning are completely inflexible in these systems. (This inflexibility results at least in part from genetic influence; compare this with Hockett's last universal, cultural transmission.) Furthermore, there is a vast difference between naming in human languages and in animal communication. There seem to be no words in the monkey system for other important objects and concepts in their environment, such as "tree" (or even for more emotional or abstract concepts, given Harlow's [1953] famous demonstrations of the security and comfort needs of baby Rhesus monkeys). And as for displacement and productivity, consider the following quotation from Glass and Holyoak (1986, p. 448): "The monkey has no way of saying 'I don't see an eagle,' or 'Thank heavens that wasn't an eagle,' or 'That was some huge eagle I saw yesterday.'"

Although it seems that that there are no true languages among the various animal communication systems, this is not to say that nothing can be learned about language from studying animals. As one illustration of this, work by Hopkins, Russell, and Cantalupo (2007) used MRI imaging with chimpanzees to show that there was a lateralization of function as a consequence of tool use. Moreover, those regions of the brain that were more affected corresponded to Broca's and Wernicke's areas in humans, which correspond to critical areas of human language production and comprehension (as you will see later in the chapter). This suggests that our development of language as a species may be tied, to some extent, to the development of tool use by our ancestors.

In short, beyond a level of arbitrariness, animal communication does not exhibit the characteristics that appear to be universally true of human language. There appear to be no genuine languages in animals, although there may be genuine precursors to human language among various apes. In human cultures, genuine language is the rule. (For a more up-to-date discussion of animal cognition, see Bekoff, Allen, & Burghardt, 2002.)

Levels of Analysis, a Critical Distinction, and the Sapir-Whorf Hypothesis

We conclude this introduction with three points. The first concerns the five levels of analysis for an exploration of language. The second is a traditional distinction between language performance and competence. And finally, we talk briefly about the relationship between language and cognition, specifically the question of how strongly our language influences our thinking, known as the Sapir-Whorf linguistic relativity hypothesis (1956).

LEVELS OF ANALYSIS The traditional view of language from linguistics is that it is the set of all acceptable, well-formed utterances. In this scheme, the set of rules used to generate the utterances is called a **grammar**. In other words, the grammar of a language is *the complete set of rules that will generate all the acceptable utterances and will not generate any unacceptable, ill-formed ones.* According to most linguists (e.g., Chomsky, 1965), such a grammar operates at three levels: Phonology of language deals with the sounds of language; syntax deals with word order and grammaticality; and semantics deals with accessing and combining the separate word meanings into a sensible, meaningful whole.

Miller (1973) proposed that language is organized on five levels (Table 9-2). In addition to the three traditional levels of phonology, syntax, and lexical or semantic knowledge, Miller suggested that a psychological approach to language must include two higher levels as well. He called these the level of conceptual knowledge and the level of beliefs. For organizational purposes, we focus primarily on the first three of the levels in this chapter. The last two levels of analysis are addressed in Chapter 10.

A CRITICAL DISTINCTION Chomsky (1957, 1965) insisted that there is an important distinction to be drawn in any investigation of language, the distinction between **competence** and **performance**. Competence is *the internalized knowledge of language and its rules that fully fluent speakers of a language have.* It is an ideal knowledge, to an

TABLE 9-2 Miller's (1973) Five Levels of Language Analysis

Level	Explanation
1. Phonology	Analysis of the sounds of language as they are articulated and comprehended in speech
2. Syntax	Analysis of word order and grammaticality (e.g., rules for forming past tense and plurals, rules for determining word ordering in phrases and sentences)
3. Lexical or semantic	Analysis of word meaning and the integration of word meanings within phrases and sentences
4. Conceptual	Analysis of phrase and sentence meaning with reference to knowledge in semantic memory
5. Belief	Analysis of sentence and discourse meaning with reference to one's own beliefs and one's beliefs about a speaker's intent and motivations

extent, in that it represents a person's complete knowledge of how to generate and comprehend language. Performance is *the actual language behavior a speaker generates, the string of sounds and words that the speaker utters.*

When we produce language, not only are we revealing our knowledge of language, but also passing that knowledge through the human information-processing system. Therefore, it is not surprising that performance produces errors. Speakers may lose the train of thought as they proceed through a sentence, and so may be forced to stop and begin again. We pause, repeat ourselves, stall by saying "ummm," and so on. All these **dysfluencies**, these *irregularities or errors in otherwise fluent speech*, can be attributed to the language user. Lapses of memory, momentary distractions, intrusions of new thoughts, "hiccups" in the linguistic system—all of these are imperfections in the language user rather than in the user's basic knowledge of the language. These were performance-related aspects that Chomsky was not particularly interested in, as a linguist. Psychology, on the other hand, views them as potentially rich sources of evidence for understanding language and language users.

THE SAPIR-WHORF HYPOTHESIS We tend to think of mental processes, including those related to language, as universal, as being equally true of all languages. Even slight familiarity with another language, however, reveals at least some of our beliefs to be misconceptions.

An organizing issue in studies of cultural influences on language and thought is how one's language affects one's thinking. This topic is commonly called the Sapir-Whorf hypothesis, or more formally the **linguistic relativity hypothesis** by Whorf (1956). This idea comes out of work by Edward Sapir, a linguist and anthropologist and his student Benjamin Whorf. The basic idea was that *the language you know shapes the way you think about events in the world around you.* In its strongest version, the hypothesis claims that language *controls* both thought and perception to a large degree; that is, you cannot think about ideas or concepts that your language does not name. In its weaker version, the hypothesis claims that your language *influences* and shapes your thought, for instance making it merely more difficult, rather than impossible, to think about ideas without having a name for them.

In a series of studies testing the Sapir-Whorf hypothesis, Eleanor Rosch tested members of the Dani tribe in New Guinea on a perceptual and memory test (Rosch-Heider, 1972). She administered both short- and long-term memory tasks, using chips of different colors as the stimuli. She found that the Dani learned and remembered more accurately when the chips were "focal" colors rather than "nonfocal" colors, for example when the learning trial presented a "really red red" as opposed to a "sort of red red." In other words, the central, perceptually salient, "good" red was a better aid to accuracy than the nonfocal "off-red." The compelling aspect of the study that tested the Sapir-Whorf hypothesis involved the language of the Dani people; their language contains only two color terms, one for "dark" and one for "light." Nothing in their language expresses meanings such as "true red" or "off-red," and yet their performance was influenced by the centrality of focal versus nonfocal colors. Thus, this is an example where a person's language could have affected cognitive processes (the language had very few color terms), and yet the perceptual and categorization processes were largely unaffected. Results such as these seemed to be disconfirmation of the strong Sapir-Whorf hypothesis, most researchers agreed.

Current thinking finds some merit in the weaker form of the Sapir-Whorf hypothesis, however, the hypothesis that language does indeed influence our thoughts to some degree (e.g., Boroditsky, 2001, but see Chen, 2007; January & Kako, 2007). Take just one example, involving number. "English speakers have no difficulty expressing the idea that, if there are 49 men and 37 pairs of shoes, some men will have to go without shoes. There are non-literate societies where this would be a difficult situation to describe, because the language may have number terms only for 'one-two-many' (Greenberg, 1978)" (Hunt & Agnoli, 1991, p. 385; see also Roberson, Davies, & Davidoff, 2000; Malt, Sloman, & Gennari, 2003, discuss how one's linguistic and cultural history influence perception and naming). In other words, one person's language and culture would make it very difficult to think and talk about this situation—12 men going barefoot—whereas another person's language and culture supports that kind of thinking and expression.

Section Summary

- Language is our shared system of symbolic communication, unlike naturally occurring animal communication systems. True language involves a set of characteristics, linguistic universals, that emphasize the arbitrary connections between symbols and referents, the meaningfulness of the symbols, and our reliance on rules for generating language.
- Three traditional levels of analysis—phonology, syntax, and semantics—are joined by two others in psycholinguistics, the level of conceptual knowledge and the level of one's beliefs. Linguists focus on an idealized language competence as they study language, but psycholinguists are also concerned with language performance. Therefore the final two levels of analysis take on greater importance as we investigate language users and their behavior.
- To some degree, we can use people's linguistic intuitions, their linguistic competence, to discover what is known about language; language performance, on the other hand, is also affected by memory lapses and the like.
- The Sapir-Whorf linguistic relativity hypothesis made a claim that language controls or determines thought, making it impossible to think of an idea if there was no word for it in the language. The weak version of this hypothesis is generally accepted now; language exerts an influence on thought, by making it more difficult to think of an idea without having a word to name or express it.

PHONOLOGY: THE SOUNDS OF LANGUAGE

In any language interaction, the task of a speaker is to communicate an idea by translating that idea into spoken sounds. The hearer goes in the opposite direction, translating from sound to intended meaning. In essence, a person is transferring the contents of his or her mind to another person (a lot like E.S.P., only in a plausible – spoken!—way). Among the many sources of information available in the spoken message, the most obvious and concrete one is the sound of the language itself, the stream of speech signals that must be decoded. Other sources of information, say the gestures and facial expressions of the speaker, can be eliminated, as in a telephone conversation, with little disruption of the communication; in fact, gestures convey somewhat less information to listeners than you might suspect, though possibly help a speaker more than you'd expect (Alibali, Heath, & Myers, 2001; Krauss, 1998; Ozyurek, 2002; Wagner, Nusbaum, & Goldin-Meadow, 2004). But you can't do without the words and the sounds that form those words. Thus our study of the grammar of language begins at this basic level of **phonology**, *the sounds of language and the rule system for combining them.*

Sounds in Isolation

To state an obvious point, different languages sound different: They are composed of different sets of sounds. *The basic sounds that compose a language* are called **phonemes**. If we were to conduct a survey, we would find around 200 different phonemes across all known spoken languages. No single language uses even half that many, however. English, for instance, contains about 46 phonemes (experts disagree on whether some sounds are separate phonemes or blends of two phonemes; the disagreement centers on diphthong vowel sounds, as in *few*, seemingly a combination of "ee" and "oo"). Hawaiian, on the other hand, uses only about 15 phonemes (Palermo, 1978). Note here that there is little significance to the total tally of phonemes in a language; no language is superior to another because it has more (or fewer) phonemes.

Table 9-3 shows the Glucksberg and Danks (1975) typology of the phonemes of English, based on the characteristics of their pronunciation. For consonants, three variables are relevant: place of articulation, manner of articulation, and voicing. *Place of articulation* is the place in the vocal tract where the disruption of airflow takes place; as shown in Figure 9-1, a bilabial consonant such as /b/ disrupts the airflow at the lips, whereas /h/ disrupts the column of air at the rear of the vocal tract, at the glottis. Second, *manner of articulation* is how the airflow coming up from the lungs is disrupted. If the column of air is completely stopped and then released, it's called a stop consonant, such as the consonant sounds in *bat* and *tub*. A fricative consonant, such as the /f/ in *fine*, involves only a partial blockage of airflow. Finally, *voicing* refers to whether the vocal cords begin to vibrate immediately with the obstruction of airflow (for example, the /b/ in *bat*) or whether the vibration is delayed until after the release of air (the /p/ in *pat*).

Vowels, by contrast, involve no disruption of the airflow. Instead, they differ on two dimensions, placement in the mouth (front, center, or back) and tongue position in the mouth (high, middle, or low). Scan Table 9-3, pronouncing the

TABLE 9-3 English Consonants and Vowels

English Consonants

Manner of Articulation		Bilabial	Labio-dental	Dental	Alveolar	Palatal	Velar	Glottal
Stops	Voiceless	P (*pat*)			t (*tack*)		k (cat)	
	Voiced	b (*bat*)			d (*dig*)		g (*get*)	
Fricatives	Voiceless		f (*fat*)		s (*sat*)	š (iss*h*)		h (*hat*)
	Voiced		v (*vat*)	∂ (*then*)	z (*zap*)	ž (*azure*)		
Affricatives	Voiceless					č (church)		
	Voiced					ǰ (*judge*)		
Nasal		m (*mat*)			n (*nat*)		η (sing)	
Liquids					l (late)	r (rate)		
Glides		w (*win*)				y (*yet*)		

English Vowels

	Front	Center	Back
	i (beet)		u (boot)
High			U (book)
	i (b*i*t)		
		əl (b*i*rd)	o (bode)
Middle	e (baby)	ə (sof*a*)	
	ε (bet)		ɔ (bought)
	æ (bat)	^ (b*u*t)	
Low			
			a (palm)

From Glucksberg and Danks (1975).

sample words, and try to be consciously aware of the characteristics that you (if you're a native or fluent English speaker) know so thoroughly at an unconscious, automatic level.

Let's develop a few more conscious intuitions about phonemes. Stop for a moment and put your hand in front of your mouth. Say the word *pot* and then *spot*. Did you notice a difference between the two /p/ sounds? Most speakers produce a puff of air with the /p/ sound as they say *pot*; we puff very little (if at all) for the /p/ in *spot* if it's spoken normally. Given this, you would have to agree that these two /p/ sounds are different at a purely physical level. And yet you hear them as the same sound in those two words; you treat them as the same sound when you hear and comprehend those ★ words. Figure 9-2 shows actual spectrograph patterns for two families of syllables, the /b/ family on the left and the /d/ family on the right. Note how remarkably different "the same" phoneme can be.

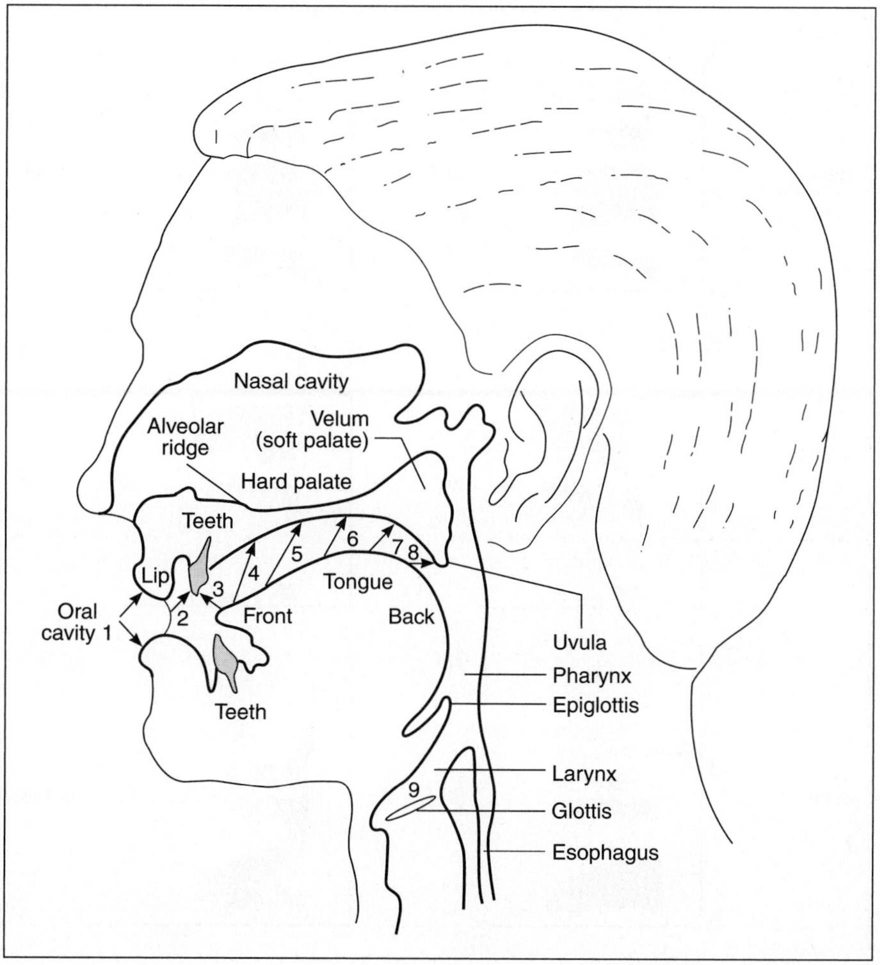

FIGURE 9-1 The vocal tract, illustrating places of articulation: 1, bilabial; 2, labiodental; 3, dental; 4, alveolar; 5, palatoalveolar; 7, velar; 8, uvular; 9, glottal. From Fromkin & Rodman (1974).

For psycholinguistics, the two /p/ sounds, despite their physical differences, are both instances of the same phoneme, the same basic sound group. That is, the fact that these two different sounds are treated as if they were the same in English means that they represent one phoneme. So let's redefine the term phoneme as *the category or group of language sounds that are treated as the same, despite physical differences among the sounds.* In other words, the English word *spot* does not change its meaning when pronounced with the /p/ sound in *pot*.

A classic illustration of phoneme boundaries is shown in Figure 9-3, from a study by Liberman, Harris, Hoffman, and Griffith (1957). When the presented sound crossed a boundary, that is, between stimulus values 3 and 5 and between 9 and 10, identifications of the sound switched rapidly from /b/ to /d/ and then from /d/ to /g/. Variations within the boundaries did not lead to different identifications; despite the variations, all the sounds from values 5 to 8 were identified as /d/. ▲

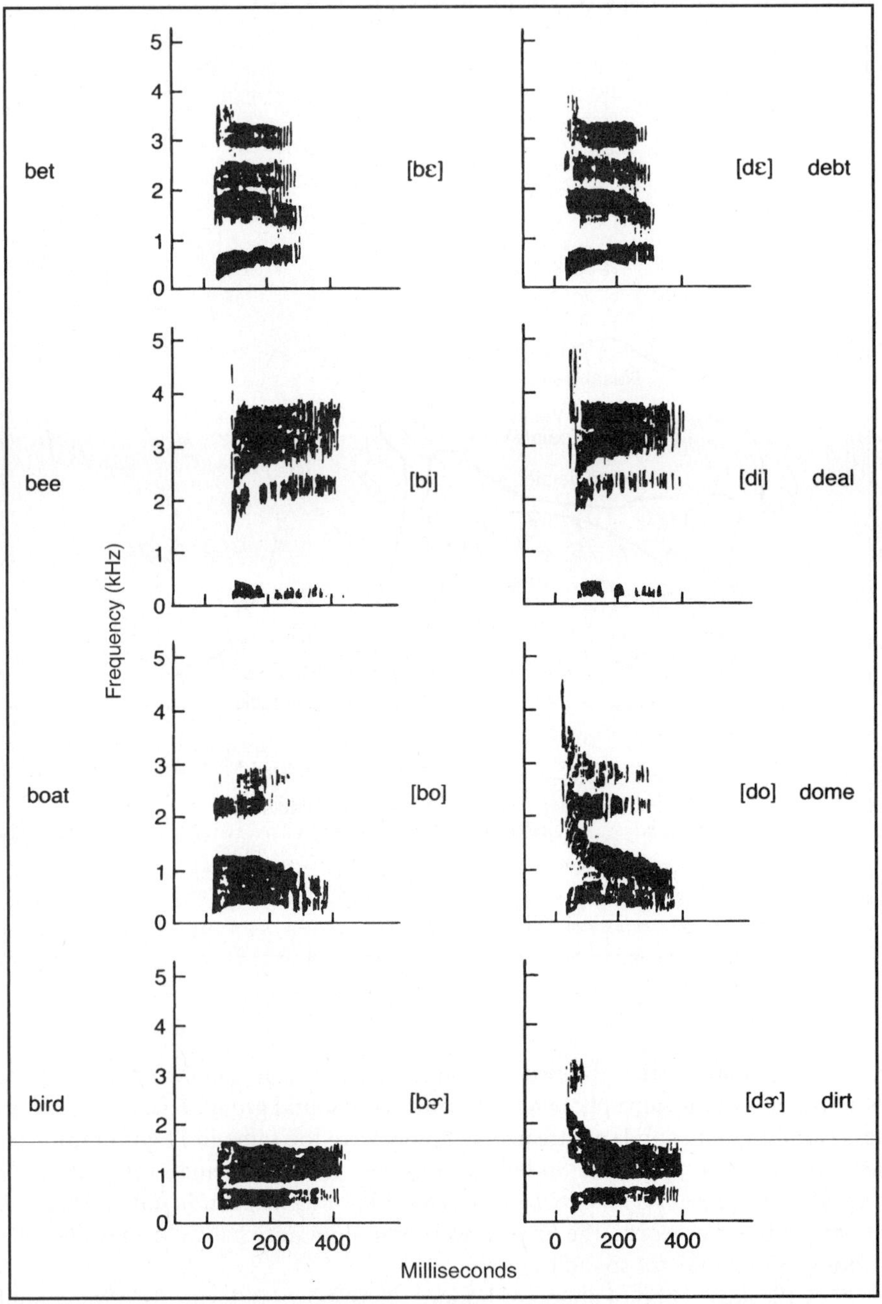

★ **FIGURE 9-2** Spectrographic patterns of two families of syllables, showing the changes across time in the physical sound patterns. Depicted is the problem of invariance for consonants. There are dramatic changes in the initial portions of the patterns, induced by the following vowel, even though the consonant sounds from top to bottom are all classified as the same phoneme. For instance, the /b/ sounds in *bet* and *bird* are physically very different, yet both are perceived as /b/. In contrast, the /b/ and /d/ sounds in *bet* and *debt* are very similar physically but are perceived as different phonemes. From Jusczyk, Smith, & Murphy (1981).

There are two critical ideas here. First *all the sounds falling within a set of boundaries are perceived as the same, despite physical differences among them.* This is called **categorical perception**. Because English speakers discern no real difference between the hard /k/ sounds in *cool* and *keep*, they are perceived categorically, that is, perceived as belonging to

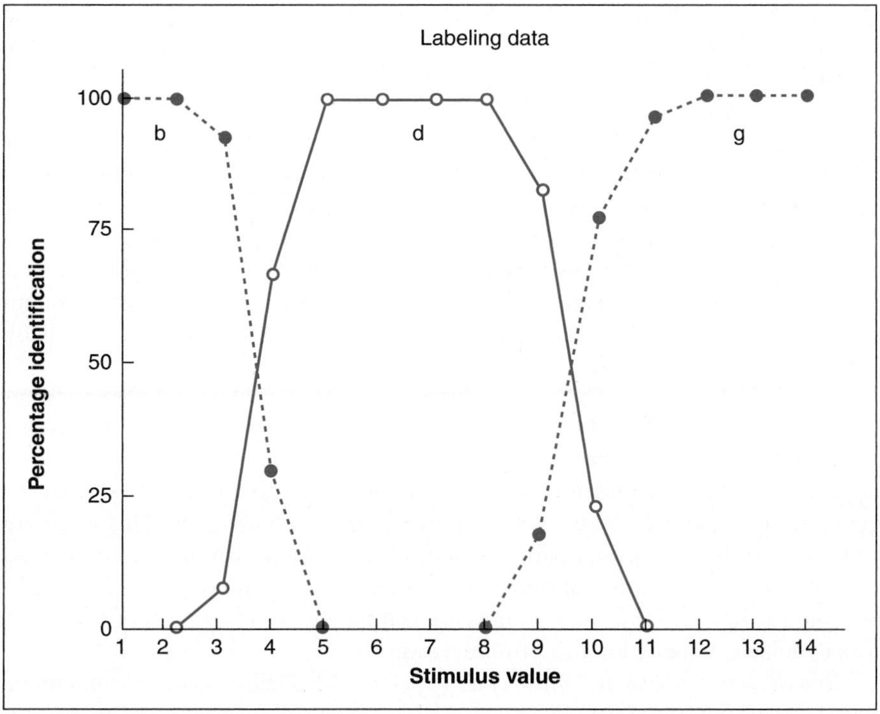

▲ **FIGURE 9-3**
One person's labeling data for synthesized consonants ranging from /b/ to /g/. Note that small changes in the stimulus value (e.g., from values 3 to 4) can result in a complete change in labeling, whereas larger changes (e.g., from values 4 to 8) that do not cross the phoneme boundary do not lead to a change in labeling. From Liberman et al. (1957).

the same category, the /k/ phoneme. Second, different phonemes are the sounds that are perceived as different by speakers of the language. The physical differences between /s/ and /z/ are important in English; changing from one to the other gives you different words, such as *ice* and *eyes*. Thus, the /s/ and /z/ sounds in English are different phonemes.

An interesting side effect of such phonemic differences is that you can be insensitive to differences of other languages if your own language doesn't make that distinction. Spanish does not use the /s/ versus /z/ contrast, so native speakers of Spanish have difficulty distinguishing or pronouncing *ice* and *eyes* in English. Conversely, the hard /k/ sounds at the beginning of *cool* and *keep* are interchangeable in English; they are the same phoneme. But, this difference is phonemic in Arabic; the Arabic words for *heart* and *dog* differ only in their initial sounds, exactly the two different hard /k/ sounds in *cool* and *keep*.

Combining Phonemes into Morphemes

From a stock of about 46 phonemes, English generates all its words, however many thousands that might be. This fact, that a small number of units can be combined so flexibly into so many words, is the linguistic universal of productivity at the level of phonology. So, from a small set of phonemes we can generate a functionally infinite number of words. Recall further that the essential ingredient of productivity is rules. We turn now to the rules of combining phonemes into words.

PHONEME COMBINATIONS Let's work with a simple example here. There are three phonemes in the word *bat*: the voiced stop consonant /b/, the short vowel sound /ae/, and the final voiceless /t/. Substitute the voiceless /p/ for /b/, and you get *pat*. Now rearrange the phonemes in these words, and you'll discover that some of the arrangements don't yield English words, such as **abt*, **tba*, and **atp*. Why? What makes **abt* or **atp* illegal strings in English?

Although it's tempting to say the reason is that syllables like **abt* cannot be pronounced, a moment's reflection suggests that this is false. After all, many such "unpronounceable" strings are pronounced in other languages; for example, the initial *pn-* in the French word for *pneumonia* is pronounced, whereas English makes the *p* silent. Instead, the rule is more specific. English usually does not use a "voiced–voiceless" sequence of two consonants within the same syllable; in fact, it only seldom uses any two-consonant sequence when both are in the same "manner of articulation" category. (Of course, if the two consonants are in different syllables, then the rule doesn't apply.)

PHONEMIC COMPETENCE AND RULES Why does this seem to be an unusual explanation? The reason is that our knowledge of English phonology and pronunciation is not particularly verbalizable. You can look at Table 9-3, try to think of words that combine consonants, and come up with tentative pronunciation rules. This is different from knowing the rules in an easily accessed and expressible fashion. And yet you are a true expert at deciding what phoneme sequences can and cannot be used in English. Your implicit knowledge of how sounds are combined tells you that **abt* is illegal because it violates a rule of English pronunciation.

This *extensive knowledge of the rules of permissible English sound combinations* is your **phonemic competence**. These rules tell you what is and isn't permissible; *bat* is, but **abt* isn't. No one ever explicitly taught you these rules; you abstracted them from your experience as you acquired language. This competence tells you that a string of letters like "pnart" is legal only when the *p* is silent but that "snart" is a legal string—not a word, of course, but a legal combination of sounds. Speakers of the language have this phonemic competence as part of their knowledge of language, an implicit, largely unverbalizable part to be sure, but a part nonetheless.

Speech Perception and Context

We are now ready to approach the question of how people produce and perceive speech. Do we hear a word and segment it in some fashion into its separate phonemes? When we speak, do we string phonemes together, one after another, like stringing beads on a necklace?

CATEGORICAL PERCEPTION AND THE PROBLEM OF INVARIANCE The answer to both questions is "No." Even when the "same" sound is being pronounced, it is not physically identical to other instances of that "same" sound. The sounds *change*—they change from speaker to speaker and from one time to the next within the same speaker. Most prominently, they change or vary from one word to another, depending on what sounds precede and follow.

This *variability in sounds* is the **problem of invariance**. This term is somewhat peculiar because the problem in speech perception is that the sounds *are not* invariant; they change all the time. You saw an illustration of this in Figure 9-2, where the initial /b/ and /d/ sounds looked very different in the spectrographic patterns

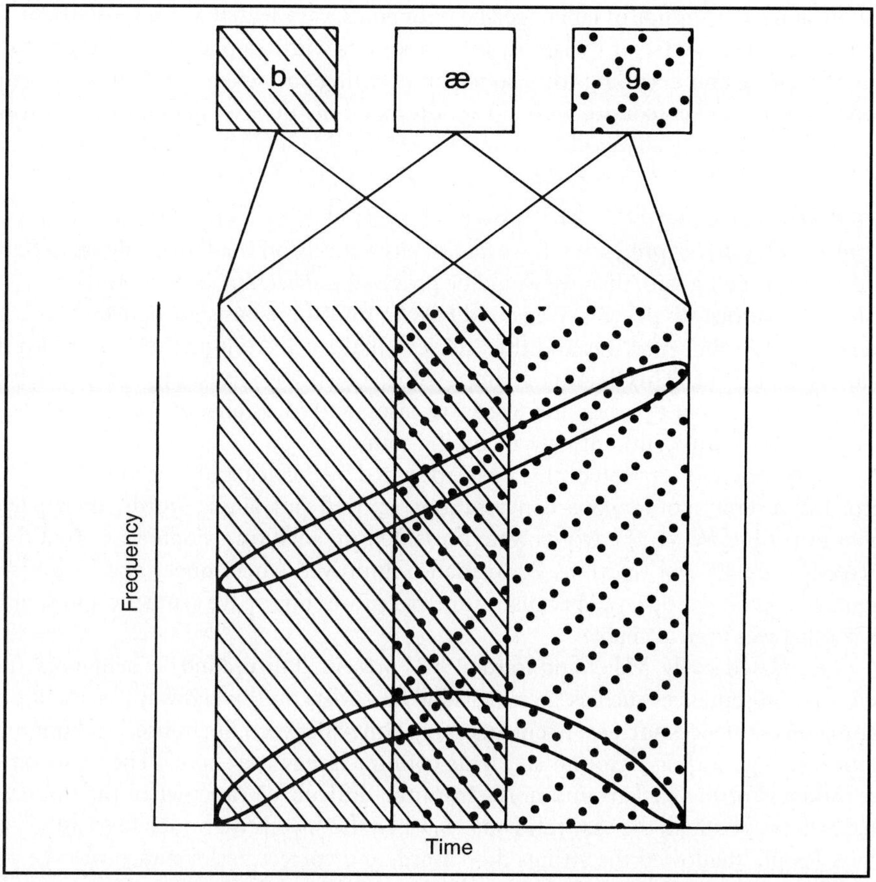

FIGURE 9-4 Coarticulation is illustrated for the three phonemes in the word *bag;* solid diagonals indicate the influence of the /b/ phoneme and dotted diagonals, the influence of /g/. From Liberman (1957).

depending on the vowel that followed. A second illustration of the problem of invariance is in Figure 9-4, which shows the influence of each of the three phonemes in the word *bag*. To pronounce *bag*, do you simply articulate the /b/, then /ae/, then /g/? No! As the figure shows, the /ae/ sound influences both /b /and /g/, the /g/ phoneme (dotted lines) exerts an influence well back into the /b/ sound, and so on.

The technical term for this is **coarticulation**: *More than one sound is articulated at the same time.* As you type the word *the* on a keyboard, your right index finger starts moving toward *h* before your left index finger has struck the *t*. In like fashion, your vocal tract begins to move toward the /ae/ before you have articulated /b/ and toward /g/ before even finishing the /b/. This is another illustration of the problem of invariance: Each phoneme changes the articulation of each other phoneme and does so depending on what the other phonemes are. The problem of invariance is made clearer by considering what we do when we whisper. Whispering changes some of the vocal characteristics of the phonemes. For example, voiced phonemes become voiceless. Yet, we typically have little trouble understanding what is being whispered to us.

In short, the sounds of language, the phonemes, vary widely as we speak them. Yet we tolerate a fair degree of variability for the sounds within a phoneme category, both when listening and decoding from sound to meaning and when speaking, converting meaning into spoken sound. How do we do this; how do we tolerate this variability and still decipher the changeable, almost undependable spoken signal?

THE EFFECT OF CONTEXT The answer is *context.* Putting it another way, the answer is *conceptually driven processing.* If we had to rely entirely on the spoken signal to figure out what was being said, then we would be processing speech in an entirely data-driven fashion, a bottom-up process. We would have to find some basis for figuring out what every sound in the word was and then retrieve that word from memory based on the analysis of sound. This is almost impossible, given the variability of phonemes. Instead, context—in this case the words, phrases, and ideas already identified—leads us to correct identification of new, incoming sounds.

A clever demonstration of this was performed by Pollack and Pickett (1964). They recorded several spontaneous conversations, spliced out single words, then played them to people. When the words were presented in isolation, people identified them correctly only 47% of the time. Performance improved when longer and longer segments of speech were played because more and more supportive syntactic and semantic context was then available.

In a related study, Miller and Isard (1963) presented three kinds of sentences: fully grammatical sentences such as "Accidents kill motorists on the highways," semantically anomalous sentences such as "Accidents carry honey between the house," and ungrammatical strings such as "Around accidents country honey the shoot." They also varied the loudness of the background noise, from the difficult –5 ratio, when the noise was louder than speech, to the easy ratio of +15, when the speech was much louder than the noise. People shadowed the strings they heard, and correct performance was the percentage of their shadowing that was accurate. As shown in Figure 9-5, accuracy improved significantly going from the difficult to easy levels of speech-to-noise ratios. More interestingly, the improvement was especially dramatic for grammatical sentences, as if grammaticality helped counteract the background noise. For instance, at the ratio labeled 0 in the figure, 63% of the grammatical sentences were shadowed accurately, compared with only 3% of the ungrammatical strings. Indeed, even at the easiest ratio of +15, fewer than 60% of the ungrammatical strings could be repeated correctly.

TOP-DOWN AND BOTTOM-UP PROCESSES More recent evidence is largely consistent with these early findings. That is, there is a combination of data-driven and conceptually driven processing in speech recognition, a position now called the integrative or interactive approach (Rapp & Goldrick, 2000). At a general level, this approach claims that a variety of conceptually distinct language processes, from the perception of the sounds up through integration of word meanings, operate simultaneously, each having the possibility of influencing the ongoing activity of other processes. While features of the speech signal are being analyzed perceptually, a listener's other linguistic knowledge is also being called into play at the same time. These higher levels of knowledge and analysis operate in parallel with the phonemic analysis, and help the perceptual mechanism identify the sounds and words (Dell & Newman, 1980; Pitt & Samuel, 1995; Samuel, 2001). Moreover,

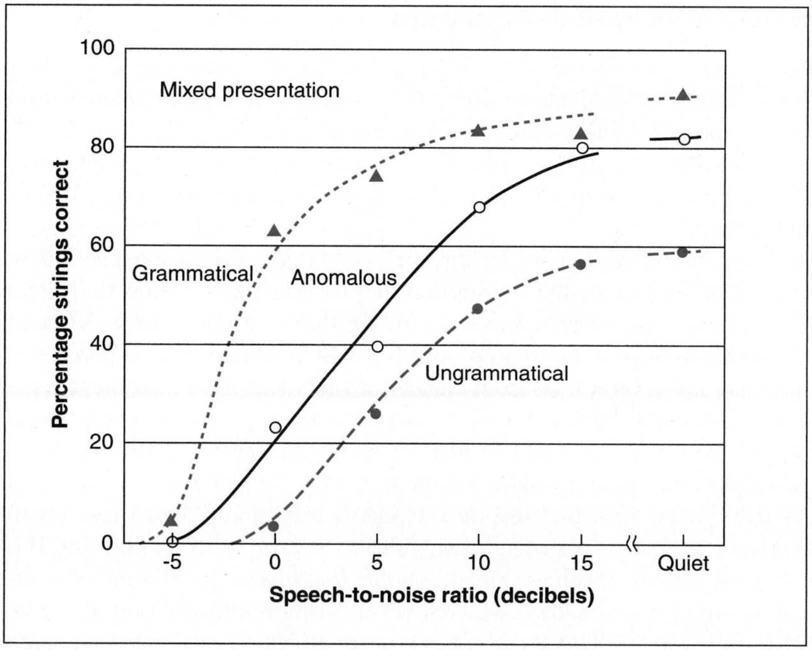

◆ **FIGURE 9-5**
Percentage of strings shadowed correctly. From Miller & Isard (1963).

in order to overcome the relative dearth of invariant information in the speech signal, it appears that language perception relies heavily on characteristic knowledge of the speaker, such as whether the person speaks with a lisp (Kraljik, Samuel, & Brennan, 2008).

As a concrete example, imagine a sentence that begins "The grocery bag was . . ." You are processing the *bag* segment of this speech signal. Having already processed the previous word to at least some level of semantic interpretation, you have developed a useful context for the sentence. To be simple about it, *grocery* limits the number of possibilities that can be mentioned in the sentence (recall in Chapter 3, where people "heard" the missing /p/ in "The *eel was on the orange"; see Table 3-2.) Similar evidence of the role of context was reported by Marslen-Wilson and Welsh (1978) in a task that asked people to detect mispronunciations, and by Dell and Newman (1980) in a task that asked people to monitor spoken speech for the occurrence of a particular phoneme (recall also the demonstrations of context effects in Treisman's shadowing experiments, e.g., 1960, 1964).

Such results are so powerful that any reasonable theory of speech recognition must account for both aspects of performance, the data driven and the conceptually driven. A specific connectionist model that does exactly that was proposed by McClelland and Elman (1986). In their TRACE model, information is continually being passed among the several levels of analysis in a spreading activation fashion. Lexical or semantic knowledge, if activated, can alter the ongoing analysis at the perceptual level by "telling" it what words are likely to appear next; the model's predictions of what words are likely to appear are based on semantic knowledge. At the same time, phonemic information is passed to higher levels, altering the patterns of activation there (see Dell, 1986, for a spreading activation network theory of sentence production, and Tyler, Voice, & Moss, 2000, for a useful review).

Embodiment in Speech Perception

The perception of speech is critical for language. Intuitively this may seem like an odd place for aspects of embodied cognition to show up. However, speech perception is actually where one of the first embodied theories of cognition came from (although it was not labeled as such at the time). This is the **motor theory of speech perception** (see, e.g., Liberman, Cooper, Shankweiler, & Studdert-Kennedy, 1967; Liberman & Mattingly, 1985).

According to the motor theory of speech perception, people perceive language, at least in part, by comparing the sounds that they are hearing with how they themselves would move their own vocal apparatus to make those sounds. That is, we create embodied representations of how those sounds might be said to help us perceive spoken speech. There are several lines of evidence for this idea (for an excellent review, see Galantucci, Fowler, & Turvey, 2006). As some examples, people find it much easier to understand synthesized speech if it takes issues of coarticulation into account, rather than simply presenting a string of phonemes. Also, the parts of the cortex that are more active during speech perception overlap substantially with those involved in speech production. This is similar to the idea of mirror neurons that fire when primates observe actions of others. Finally, people find it easier to comprehend speech if they can see the person talking, which gives them more information about how the sounds are being made. This theory does not explain all aspects of speech perception, such as how people who could never speak can understand spoken language. However, it does illustrate how the structure of our bodies, and how we use them in the environment (in this case moving around the air with our vocal apparatus), influences cognition.

A Final Puzzle

As if the preceding sections weren't enough to convince you of the need for conceptually driven processing, consider one final feature of the stream of spoken speech. Despite coarticulation, categorical perception, and the problem of invariance, we naively believe that words are somehow separate from each other in the spoken signal, that there is a physical pause or gap between spoken words, just as there is a blank space between printed words.

This is not true. Our intuition is entirely wrong. Analysis of the speech signal shows that there is almost no consistent relationship between pauses and the ends of words. If anything, the pauses we produce while speaking are longer *within* words than between words. As evidence of this, see Figure 9-6, a spectrograph recording of a spoken sentence. Inspection of the patterns in correspondence to the words listed at the bottom illustrates the point: The pauses in the spectrograph bear no particular relationship to the ends of words. There must be other kinds of information that the human information processor uses to decode the spoken language signal.

How can our intuitions about our own language, that words are articulated as separate units, be so wrong? (Note that our intuitions about foreign languages—they sound like a continuous stream of speech—are more accurate.) How do we segment the speech stream and come to know what the words and phrases are? Part of the

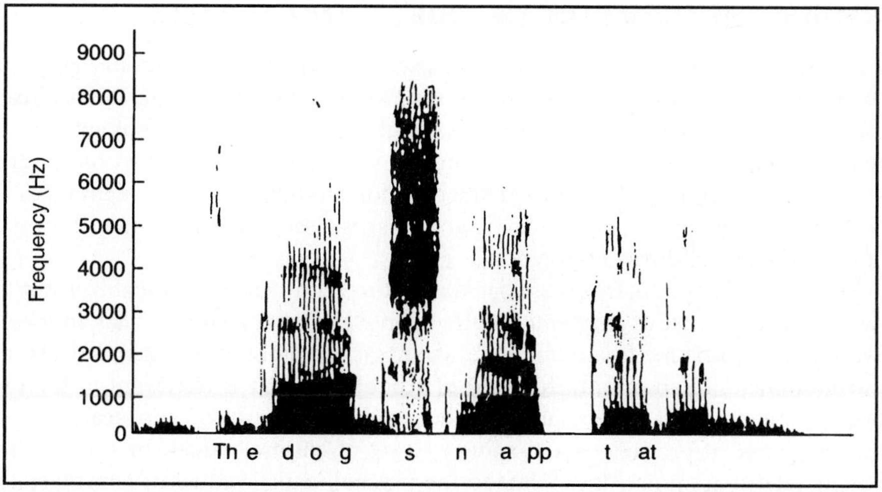

FIGURE 9-6
A spectrogram from the sentence "John said that the dog snapped at him," taken from fluent spoken speech. Note that the pauses or breaks do not occur regularly at the ends of words; if anything, they occur more frequently *within* the individual words (e.g., between the /s/ and /n/ sounds, between the /p/ and /t/ sounds; compare with the end of *the* and the beginning of *dog*). From Foss & Hakes (1978).

answer is our knowledge of words in the language and the fact that some phoneme combinations simply cannot or do not form words (Norris, McQueen, Cutler, & Butterfield, 1997). Another part of the answer to these questions is syntax, the second level of language analysis and the topic we address next.

Section Summary

- Phonology is the study of the sounds of language. Spoken words consist of phonemes, the smallest units of sound that speakers of a language can distinguish. Surprisingly, a range of physically different sounds are classified as the same phoneme; we tolerate a fair degree of variation in the sounds we categorize as "the same," called categorical perception.
- Categorical perception is particularly important in the study of speech recognition because the phonemes in a word exhibit coarticulation, overlapping effects among successive phonemes, such that an initial sound is influenced by the sounds that follow and the later sounds are influenced by what came before.
- Speech recognition relies heavily on conceptually driven processes. This includes our knowledge of the sentence and word context, our estimates of how we would produce the sounds ourselves, and our knowledge of what the words in our language are.

SYNTAX: THE ORDERING OF WORDS AND PHRASES

At the second level of analysis we have **syntax**, *the arrangement of words as elements in a sentence to show their relationship to one another; or sentence structure*. We've already studied how sounds combine to form meaningful words. At this level of analysis, we are interested in how the words are sequenced to form meaningful strings, the study of syntax. Just as with phonology, where the rules for combining sounds might be called a phonological grammar, our syntactic grammar is a set of rules for ordering words into acceptable, well-formed sentences.

If you have a connotation associated with the word *syntax*, it probably is not the psycholinguistic sense of *grammar* but the "school grammar" sense instead. In school, if you said "He ain't my friend no more," your teacher might have responded, "Watch your grammar." To an extent, this kind of school grammar is irrelevant to the psycholinguistic study of syntax. Your teacher was being *prescriptive* by teaching you what is proper or prestigious according to a set of cultural values. In another way, though, school grammar does relate to the psycholinguistic study of language; language is for expressing ideas, and anything that clarifies this expression, even arbitrary rules about "ain't" and double negatives, improves communication. (And finally, your teacher was sensitive to another level of language: People do judge others on the quality of their speech.)

WORD ORDER Unlike the school grammar idea, the psycholinguistic study of syntax is *descriptive*; that is, it takes as its goal a description of the rules of how words are arranged to form sentences. Let's take a simple example, one that taps into your syntactic competence. Which is better, sentence 3 or 4?

(3) *Beth asked the man about his headaches.*

(4) **About the Beth headaches man asked his.*

Your "school grammar" taught you that every sentence must have a subject and a verb. According to that rule, sentence 4 is just as much a sentence as 3. Your syntactic competence, on the other hand, tells you that sentence 4 is ill-formed, unacceptable. You can even specify some of the rules that are being violated; for example, definite articles such as *the* do not usually precede a person's name, and two nouns usually don't follow one another in the same phrase or clause.

The point here is that the meaning of a sentence is far more than the meanings of the words. The "far more" here is the arrangement or sequencing of the words. We're speaking of syntactic word order rules for English (Gershkoff-Stowe & Goldin-Medow, 2002, argue that word order is more than just syntax, and that it reflects a more general property of human thought). More than some languages (e.g., Latin), English relies heavily on word order. Consider "red fire engine" versus "fire engine red" (or even "red engine fire"). Despite the fact that *red* and *fire engine* can be nouns, our word order knowledge tells us that the first word in these phrases is to be treated as an adjective, modifying the following noun. Thus by varying word order alone, "red fire engine" is a fire engine of the usual color, and "fire engine red" is a particular shade of red.

PHRASE ORDER There's more to it than just word order, however. We also rely on the ordering of larger units such as phrases or clauses to convey meaning. Consider the following sentences:

(5) Bill told the men to deliver the piano on Monday.

(6) Bill told the men on Monday to deliver the piano.

In these examples, the positioning of the phrase "on Monday" helps us determine the intended meaning, whether the piano was to be delivered on Monday or whether Bill had told the men something on Monday. Thus, the sequence of words and phrases contains clues to meaning, clues that speakers use to express meaning and clues that listeners use to decipher meaning.

NUMBER AGREEMENT Yet another part of syntax involves the adjustments we make depending on other words in the sentence. In particular, parts of every sentence are a subject and a verb. It's required, furthermore, that the subject and verb agree in number—if the subject of the sentence is singular, you must use a singular verb, as in "The car has a flat tire" (obviously, pronouns have to be coordinated in terms of number, too). As Bock (1995, p. 56) noted, agreement helps listeners know what the topic of a sentence is going to be about. For example, consider "The mother of the girls who was . . ." versus "The mother of the girls who were . . ." You're pretty sure that the first sentence is going to be about the mother, and the second one about the girls just because of the number agreement of "was" versus "were." So number agreement, like word and phrase order, is a clue to meaning, part of the spoken and written language that we rely on when we comprehend. (See Bock, Eberhard, & Cutting, 2004, Bock & Miller, 1991, and Hartsuiker, Anton-Mendez, & van Zee, 2001, for experimental work on number agreement errors, e.g., when you make the verb agree in number with the nearest noun rather than the subject noun, as in "*The difficulty with all of these issues are that . . .").

In general, we need to understand what these syntactic clues are and how they are used. We need to explore the sets of syntactic rules that have been proposed to understand the influence of syntactic factors on comprehension. We begin by looking at the underlying syntactic structure of sentences, taking a piece-by-piece approach to Chomsky's important work.

Chomsky's Transformational Grammar

At a general level, Chomsky intended to "describe the universal aspects of syntactic knowledge" (Whitney, 1998), that is, to capture the syntactic structures of language. He noted that language has a hierarchical phrase structure: The words do not simply occur one after the other, each with equal status. Instead, they come in groupings, such as "on Monday," "the men," and "deliver the piano." Furthermore, these groupings can be altered, either by moving them from one spot to another in the structure or by modifying them to express different meanings (e.g., by changing the statement into a question). These two ideas—words come in phrase structure groupings, and the groupings can be modified or transformed—correspond to the two major syntactic rule systems in Chomsky's theory, as shown in Figure 9-7. ★

★ **FIGURE 9-7** A depiction of Chomsky's "transformational grammar." From Whitney (1998).

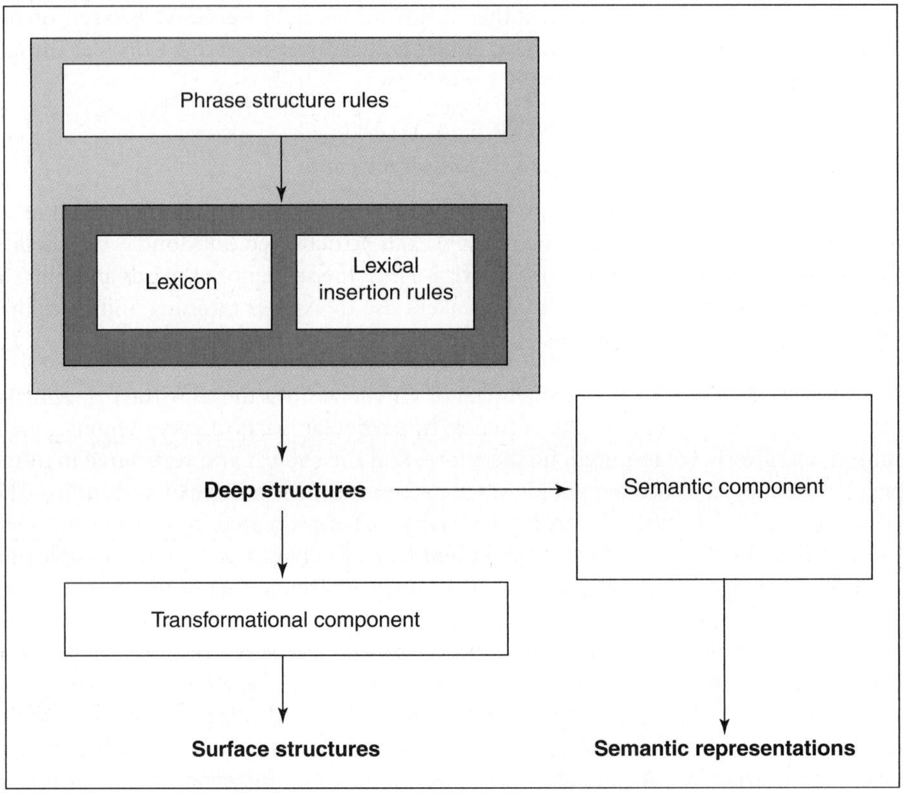

PHRASE STRUCTURE GRAMMAR Let's start by discussing phrase structure grammar, the rules (grammar) that generate the overall structure or form of sentences. An important point in Chomsky's system is that the **phrase structure** grammar accounts for *the constituents of the sentence, the word groupings and phrases that make up the whole utterance, and the relationships among those constituents.* To illustrate the nature of a phrase structure grammar, consider a well-known example sentence from Lachman et al. (1979):

(7) The patio resembles a junkyard.

In a phrase structure grammar, the entire sentence is symbolized by an *S*. In this grammar, the sentence *S* can be broken down into two major components, a noun phrase *(NP)* and a verb phrase *(VP)*. Thus the first line of the grammar illustrated in ▲ Figure 9-8A shows $S \rightarrow NP + VP$, to be read, "The sentence can be rewritten as a noun phrase plus a verb phrase." In the second rule, the *NP* can be rewritten as a determiner *(D)*, an article such as *the* or *a*, plus a noun *(N)*: $NP \rightarrow D + N$; in other words, a noun phrase can be rewritten as a determiner and a noun. In rule 3 we see the structure of a verb phrase; a *VP* is rewritten as a verb (*V*) plus an *NP*: $VP \rightarrow V + NP$.

As Figure 9-8B shows, six rewrite rules are necessary for generating the sentence. A different but equivalent depiction of the grammar is shown in Figure 9-8C, in which a tree diagram shows the most general components at the top and the specific words at

A. Rewrite rules

1. S(entence)	→ NP (noun phrase)	+ VP (verb phrase)
2. NP	→ D(eterminer)	+ N(oun)
3. VP	→ V(erb)	+ NP
4. N	→ patio, junkyard, ...	etc.
5. V	→ resembles, ...	etc.
6. D	→ the, a, ...	etc.

B. Sentence generation by rule (derivational history)

S → NP + VP	(by Rule 1)
S → D + N + VP	(by Rule 2)
S → D + N + V + NP	(by Rule 3)
S → D + N + V + D + N	(by Rule 2)
S → the + N + V + D + N	(by Rule 6)
S → the + patio + V + D + N	(by Rule 4)
S → the + patio + resembles + D + N	(by Rule 5)
S → the + patio + resembles + a + N	(by Rule 6)
S → the + patio + resembles + a + junkyard	(by Rule 4)

C. Tree diagram

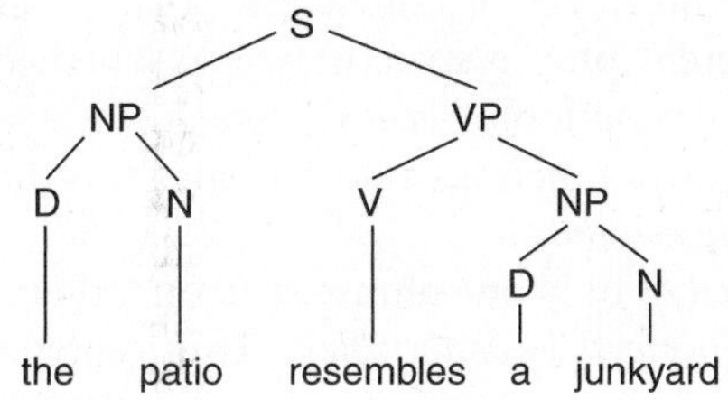

D. Bracket equivalent of tree diagram

{(The patio) (resembles (a junkyard))}

▲ **FIGURE 9-8**
A depiction of a phrase structure grammar: **A.** The rewrite rules of the grammar; **B.** Sentence generation by the rules; **C.** A tree diagram or hierarchical representation; **D.** A "bracket equivalent" diagram of the sentence. From Lachman et al. (1979).

the bottom. An advantage of the tree diagram is that it reveals the hierarchical structure of the sentence as well as the internal structure and interrelations. Finally, a bracket equivalent is shown in Figure 9-8D.

THE INADEQUACY OF PHRASE STRUCTURE GRAMMAR ALONE Chomsky's theory relied heavily on a phrase structure approach because it captures an important aspect of language—its productivity. That is, this kind of grammar is generative; by means of such phrase structure rules, an entire family of sentences can be generated. Furthermore, the phrase structure grammar is joined with two other components, the lexical entries (the words we insert into a sentence) and the lexical insertion rules (the rules for putting the words into their slots). These components, as shown in Figure 9-8, generated the first representation of the sentence in the theory, the **deep structure** representation. In Chomsky's view the deep structure is *an abstract syntactic representation of the sentence* being constructed, with only bare-bones lexical entries (words).

The deep structure is critical for two reasons. First, it is the representation that is passed along to the transformational "fix-it" rules to yield the surface structure of the sentence; we deal with those in a moment. Second, the deep structure is also submitted to a semantic component, the component that "computes" meaning. This takes the deep structure and produces a semantic representation of the sentence, a representation that reflects the underlying meaning of the sentence being constructed. Notice that, because of the separate treatment of the semantic component, a sentence's true meaning might not be reflected accurately in the **surface structure**; a surface structure might be **ambiguous**, or *have more than one meaning*. For instance, consider two classic (overworked?) examples of ambiguous sentences:

(8) Visiting relatives can be a nuisance.

(9) The shooting of the hunters was terrible.

A moment's reflection reveals the ambiguities. The first sentence could mean "Going to visit one's relatives can be a nuisance" or "Having one's relatives come to visit can be a nuisance"; sentence 9 could be referring to lousy hunters or to wounded hunters. These alternative meanings are revealed when we **parse** the sentences, when we *divide the sentences into phrases and groupings*, much the way the phrase structure grammar does. The two meanings of sentence 8—that is, the two deep structures—correspond to two different phrase structures. For sentence 8, the ambiguity boils down to the grammatical function of *visiting*, whether it is used as an adjective or a verb. These two grammatical functions translate into two different phrase structures (*verb+noun* versus *adjective+noun*).

Sentence 9, however, has only one phrase structure; there is only one way to parse it: {[*the shooting of the hunters*] [*was terrible*]}. Thus sentence 9 is ambiguous at the level of surface structure. Because phrase structure rules can generate such ambiguous sentences, Chomsky felt that this illustrated a limitation of the pure phrase structure approach: There must be something missing in the grammar. If it were complete, it wouldn't generate ambiguous sentences.

A second difficulty Chomsky pointed out involves examples such as the following:

(10a) Pierre bought a fine French wine.

(10b) A fine French wine was bought by Pierre.

According to phrase structure rules, there is almost no structural similarity at all between these two sentences; they have radically different surface structures. And yet they mean nearly the same thing. People's intuitions, that active and passive paraphrases are more or less identical at the level of meaning, are not captured by the phrase structure approach. According to the phrase structure grammar, sentences 10a and 10b are different.

TRANSFORMATIONAL RULES Chomsky's solution to such problems was to postulate a second component to the grammar, a set of **transformational rules** that handle the many specific surface forms that can express an underlying idea. These transformational rules *convert the deep structure into a surface structure, a sentence ready to be spoken*. By applying different transformations, we can form an active declarative sentence, a passive voice sentence, a question, a negative, a future or past tense, and so on. With still other transformations, phrases can exchange places, and words can be inserted and deleted. In this view, sentences 10a and 10b differ only in their surface structures; one deep structure (the core meaning) is transformed in two different fashions.

Thus the sentences have different *transformational histories* in that different transformational rules are applied to the deep structure, one set including the active voice, one the passive voice. Likewise, for a simple deep structure idea such as {(boy kisses girl)}, the transformational grammar could generate any of the following, depending on which particular grammatical transformations were selected:

(11a) The boy kissed the girl.

(11b) The girl was kissed by the boy.

(11c) Was the girl kissed by the boy?

More elaborate rules are also applied by this transformational component, including rules that allow us to combine ideas, such as the idea that {(boy kisses girl)} and the idea that {(girl is pretty)}:

(12a) The boy kissed the pretty girl.

(12b) The boy kissed the girl who was pretty.

(12c) The girl whom the boy kissed was pretty.

(12d) Will the girl who is pretty be kissed by the boy?

Thus one surface structure for the {(girl) (is) (pretty)} idea is merely "the pretty girl"; an equivalent structure, in terms of meaning, is "the girl who is pretty." On the other hand, sentences 12c and 12d are the most difficult to comprehend, largely because of the passive voice and the embedded relative "who" clauses.

Limitations of Transformational Grammar

A great deal of early psycholinguistic research was devoted to structural aspects of language. For example, there was a lot of focus on testing the derivational complexity hypothesis. This hypothesis suggests that the difficulty of comprehending a sentence is directly related to the number of grammatical transformations applied. In other words, if a deep structure has two transformations applied to it, it is more difficult to comprehend than if only one transformation is applied. Early results tended to support the theory (e.g., Palermo, 1978). However, over time, psychology became dissatisfied with this linguistically motivated approach. Work by Fodor and Garrett (1966) was especially instrumental in dimming the enthusiasm. They noted that much of the support for the derivational complexity hypothesis failed to control potentially important factors. For instance, a derivationally more complex sentence generally has more words in it than a simpler one (contrast sentences 12a and 12c).

Moreover, there was a metatheoretical point of view. To oversimplify a bit, as Figure 9-7 shows, the major components were said to be the syntactic rules for generating first a deep then a surface structure. Aspects of meaning were literally off to the side, tangential to the thrust of the theory. In a very real sense, this illustration depicts the difficulty psychology had with linguistic theory: It seemed that meaning was secondary to syntax. It's almost as if the theory, as it was applied to language *use*, suggested that we first make up our minds what phrase constituents we're going to use and only then decide what we're going to talk about. The emphasis on syntax clearly slighted the importance of semantics. For psychologists concerned with how we use

© 1981 United Feature Syndicate, Inc.
THE CAT SAW A MOUSE.
"IF YOU DON'T MIND MY ASKING, ABOUT HOW MUCH DOES A SENTENCE-DIAGRAMMER PULL DOWN A YEAR?"
THAVES/MAY 10-13

With the permission of Bob Thaves.

language to express meaning, this seemed to be heading in the wrong direction.

Note that this is an oversimplified view, making it sound as if Chomsky encouraged linguists to avoid meaning. It was not that extreme. In fact, Chomsky repeatedly emphasized the joint importance of both syntax and semantics. He pointed out that even a perfectly grammatical, syntactically acceptable sentence may have no genuine meaning and be semantically anomalous. His most famous example is "Colorless green ideas sleep furiously." It's clear that the sentence is grammatically acceptable—consider a sentence with completely parallel syntax, such as "Tired young children sleep soundly." But, Chomsky's sentence has no meaning in any ordinary sense.

Still, Chomsky's work never dealt satisfactorily with meaning, in the view of psychologists. And trying to apply his theory to the actual use of language—that is, turning his competence-based theory into a performance theory of language production and comprehension—only made it more apparent that a different approach was necessary.

We turn to the major focus of this research, the semantic level of analysis, in a moment. But first, we must conclude this section on syntax with the current psycholinguistic view of syntax.

The Cognitive Role of Syntax

From a psychological perspective, what is the purpose of syntax? Why follow a set of syntactic rules? Essentially, we use syntax to help figure out meaning. If an infinite number of sentences are possible in a language, then the one sentence being said to us right now could be about *anything*. Syntax helps listeners extract meaning and helps speakers convey it.

Bock's (1982) article on a cognitive psychology of syntax discusses several important issues that psycholinguistics must explain. She notes that the syntactic burden falls more heavily on the speaker than the listener. That is, when you have to produce a sentence rather than comprehend it, you must create a surface structure, a string of words and phrases to communicate your idea as well as possible. Thus syntax becomes a feature of language that is particularly related to the speaker's mental effort.

AUTOMATIC PROCESSING Two points Bock raises should illustrate some current directions in the psycholinguistic study of syntax. First, consider the issues of automatic and conscious processes as they apply to language production. As we know, automatic processes are the product of a high degree of practice or overlearning. Bock noted that several aspects of syntactic structure are consistent with the notion of automaticity. For instance, children rely heavily on regular word orders, even if the native language they are learning has irregular word order. The purpose is that by relying over and over on the same syntactic frames, they can be generated and used more automatically. Similarly, adults tend to use only a few syntactic structures with regularity, suggesting that they can be called into service rapidly and automatically.

Interestingly, the syntax you use can be strongly influenced by a previous sentence, quite literally syntactic priming (Bock, 1986; West & Stanovich, 1986). Bock's later work (Bock & Griffin, 2000) found evidence that a particular syntactic construction can prime later ones up to lag 10 (i.e., with ten intervening sentences), even in written language (Branigan, Pickering, & Cleland, 1999; Branigan, Pickering, Steward, & McLean, 2000).

PLANNING In Bock's second point, she reviewed evidence of an important interaction between syntax and meaning. In general, we tailor the syntax of our sentences to the accessibility of the lexical or semantic information being conveyed. This is known as the **given-new strategy** (Clark & Clark, 1977). Phrases that contain more accessible information, or given information, tend to occur earlier in sentences. This is information that is either well-known or recently discussed in a discourse (and so more available). In comparison, less accessible, newer concepts tend to come later, possibly to give ourselves extra time for retrieval (but see Clifton & Frazier, 2004, for an alternative account). Ferreira and Swets (2002) demonstrated this in a clever experiment, by asking people to state the answer to easy and hard addition problems, in sentence frames like "The answer is __." They found that people delayed nearly half a second more before they started talking when the problem was hard (e.g., 23 + 68) than when it was easy (e.g., 21 + 22). Clearly speech production is sensitive to variables that involve memory retrieval.

Our planning and execution of speech is also sensitive to grammatical complexity and presumably to the possibility that a listener (or a speaker, for that matter) might lose track of information if too much time passes. As an example, Stallings, MacDonald, and O'Seaghdha (1998) showed a particular kind of syntactic adjustment used for complex noun phrases, "heavy NPs" in their words ("heavy" because they're long). Specifically, we tend to shift heavy NPs to the end of a sentence, and insert other material in between the subject and NP, but not when the noun phrase is short. Consider the simple sentence "The boy found the textbook in his car." The noun phrase (the textbook) is short, so doesn't need to be shifted. But, if there's more to say about the textbook, you might say "The boy found in his car the textbook that had been lost for so long," shifting the textbook phrase to the end and putting "in his car" in the middle. But you probably wouldn't shift the short noun phrase to the end, as in "The boy found in his car the textbook." Moving "the textbook" to the end isn't needed here because the listener's working memory isn't being over-taxed. But the heavy NP "the textbook that had been lost for so long" is sufficiently long that working memory might lose essential information, the connections between the boy, the car, and finding the book, if the phrase separated those ideas by too many intervening ideas. More generally, as syntactic complexity increases, this increasingly taxes working memory (e.g., Fedorenko, Gibson, & Rohde, 2006).

These effects tell us something interesting about the cognitive mechanisms that create sentences. Earlier theories of sentence planning, such as Fromkin's (1971; see Table 9-4), described planning as a sequential process: First you identify the meaning to be conveyed, then you select the syntactic frame, and so on. Recent research, however, shows how interactive and flexible the planning process is (Ferreira, 1996; Griffin & Bock, 2000). Difficulties in one component, for instance word retrieval, can prompt a return to an earlier planning component, say to rework the syntax (Ferreira & Firato, 2002), or can prompt you to delay the sentence. By selecting an alternative syntax, the speaker buys more time for retrieving the intended word (see also Kempen & Hoehkamp, 1987). Needless to say, such a highly interactive system runs counter to strictly hierarchical or sequential approaches to syntax, such as Chomsky's.

In general, we begin our utterances when the first part of the sentence has been planned but before the syntax and semantics of the final portion have been worked out (see Bachoud-Levi, Dupoux, Cohen, & Mehler, 1998, and Griffin, 2003, for comparable effects). The time it takes to begin speaking (e.g., Bock, Irwin, Davidson, & Levelt, 2003) and hesitations in our spoken speech are clues to the nature of planning and memory retrieval, as are the effects of momentary changes in priming, lexical access, and working memory load (Bock & Miller, 1991; Lindsley, 1975). In fact, several reports detail how the false starts, hesitations, and restarts in speaking often reflect both the complexity of the intended sentence and a genuine online planning process that unfolds as the sentence is developed (Clark & Wasow, 1998; Ferreira, 1996; Ferreira & Dell, 2000; see Bock, 1996, for a review of methods of studying language production).

More recent work by Bock and colleagues has taken Chomsky to task even further. In a connectionist model of language processing, Chang, Dell, and Bock (2006) have challenged Chomsky's idea that language has a strong genetic component, as compared to the strong learning stance taken by the behaviorists. That is, Chomsky suggested that although you may need to learn you own language, all humans have a strong genetic bias to learn some language, and that aspects of **transformational grammar** were somehow part of that genetic process. The Chang et al. model assumes, in contrast, that language processing has a strongly learned component, similar to other memory processes. Part of how the model learns a language is by comparing its

TABLE 9-4 Fromkin's (1971) Model for the Planning and Production of Speech

Stage	Process
1	Identify meaning; generate the meaning to be expressed.
2	Select syntactic structure; construct a syntactic outline of the sentence, specifying word slots.
3	Generate intonation contour; assign stress values to different word slots.
4	Insert content words; retrieve appropriate nouns, verbs, adjectives, and so on from the lexicon and insert into word slots.
5	Add function words and affixes; fill out the syntax with function words (articles, prepositions, etc.), prefixes, suffixes.
6	Specify phonetic segments; express the sentence in terms of phonetic segments according to phonological (pronunciation) rules.

predictions for what will be said next to what is actually said, and then adjusting the connection weights based on any discrepancy (see also Griffiths, Steyvers & Tenebaum, 2007 for a predictive model of word meaning in the context of sentences).

Another interesting aspect of the Chang et al. connectionist model is the idea that language may operate in a parallel fashion to vision. That is, there are two routes in visual processing, one for processing *what* something is, and one for processing *where* it is (Ungerleider & Haxby, 1994), with the *what* system taking the ventral visual pathway toward the temporal lobe, and the *where* system taking the dorsal pathway toward the parietal lobe. An idea in the Chang et al. model is that there is a network for processing the meaning aspect of language, and a separate system for the sequencing of the words. Together, these two systems converge to predict what type of word will come next, allowing the system to learn and adjust to new input, such as new words, or new ways of using words (e.g., I *googled* you the other day and was surprised by how many hits there were).

Section Summary

- Syntax involves the ordering of words and phrases in sentence structure and features such as active versus passive voice. Chomsky's theory of language was a heavily syntactic scheme with two sets of syntactic rules. Phrase structure rules were used to generate a deep structure representation of a sentence, and then transformational rules converted the deep structure into the surface structure, the string of words that makes up the sentence.
- There are a variety of syntactic clues to the meaning of a sentence, so an understanding of syntax is necessary to psycholinguists. On the other hand, psycholinguistics has developed its own theories of language, at least in part because of linguists' relative neglect of semantic and performance characteristics.
- Studies of how we plan and execute sentences reveal a highly interactive set of processes, rather than a strictly sequential sequence. We pause, delay, and rearrange sentences as a function of planning and memory-related factors like accessibility and working memory load.

LEXICAL AND SEMANTIC FACTORS: THE MEANING IN LANGUAGE

We now turn to lexical and semantic factors. This is the level of meaning in language. In particular, we refer to retrieval from the **mental lexicon**, *the mental dictionary of words and their meanings.* After rapid perceptual and pattern recognition processes, the encoded word provides access to the word's entry in the lexicon and also to the semantic representation of the concept. The evidence you've read about throughout this book, such as results from the Stroop and the lexical decision tasks, attests to the close relationship between a word and its meaning and the seemingly automatic accessing of one from the other. Recall in the Stroop task that seeing the word *red* printed in green ink triggers an interference process with naming the ink color, clear evidence that *red* was processed to the level of meaning (MacLeod, 1992). Likewise, the lexical decision

PROVE IT
Speech Errors

Fascinating work by Fromkin (1971), Garrett (1975), and others (e.g., Ferreira & Humphreys, 2001; for work on error monitoring, see Hartsuiker & Kolk, 2001) has tabulated and made sense of speech errors that occur when we substitute or change sounds, syllables, words, and so on. Speech errors are not random but are quite lawful. For instance, when we make an exchange error, the exchange is between elements at the same linguistic level; initial sounds exchange places with other initial sounds, syllables with syllables, words with words (e.g., "to cake a bake"). If a prefix switches places, its new location will be in front of another word, not at the end.

Collect a sample of speech errors, say, from radio news broadcasters or your professors' lectures, then analyze them in terms of the linguistic level of the elements involved and the types of errors such as (intended phrase in parentheses):

Shift	She decide to hits it. (decides to hit it)
Exchange	Your model renosed. (your nose remodeled)
Perseveration	He pulled a pantrum. (tantrum)
Blend	To explain clarefully. (clearly/carefully)

task does not require that you access the word's meaning but only that you identify a letter string as a genuine word. Nonetheless, identifying *doctor* as a word primes your decision to *nurse* (e.g., Table 7-3).

Morphemes

A **morpheme** is *the smallest unit of language that has meaning*. To return to the example early in the chapter, the word *cars* is composed of two morphemes: *Car* refers to a concept and a physical object, and *-s* is a meaningful suffix, denoting "more than one of." Likewise, the word *unhappiness* is composed of three morphemes: *happy* as the base concept, the prefix *un-* meaning "not," and the suffix *-ness* meaning "state or quality of being." In general, morphemes that can stand on their own and serve as words are called free morphemes, such as *happy*, *car*, and *legal*, whereas morphemes that need to be linked onto a free morpheme are called bound morphemes, such as *un-*, *-ness*, and *-s*. While the concept of a morpheme is important, it should also be noted that there is some debate as to whether the meaning of a more common word such as *unhappiness* may be stored directly in memory or "computed" from the three morphemes (see Carroll, 1986; Whitney, 1998).

The Lexical Representation

Think about the word *chase* as an example of how free morphemes might be represented in the mental lexicon. The lexical representation of *chase* must specify its meaning, indicate that *chase* means "to run after or pursue, in hopes of catching." Like other semantic concepts, *chase* can be represented in reference to related information, like *run*, *pursue*, the idea of *speed*. Given this, along with what you know about situations in the real world from schemas and scripts, you can easily understand a sentence like

(13) The policeman chased the burglar through the park.

From a more psycholinguistic perspective, however, you know more about *chase* than just its basic meaning. For one thing, you know it's a verb, specifying a kind of physical action. Related to that, you have a clear idea of how *chase* can be used in sentences, the kinds of things that can do the chasing, and the kinds of things that can be chased (e.g., McKoon & Macfarland, 2002). Imagine, then, that your lexical representation of *chase* also includes this additional knowledge; *chase* requires some animate thing or being to do the chasing, some other kind of thing to be chased, and possibly a location where the chasing takes place. Using the terms we discussed in the last chapter for propositions, this additional information could be listed as follows:

	Relation	(agent patient optional location)
	Chase	(Animate being thing or being location)
(13)	Chase	(Policeman burglar park)

Our policeman sentence fits this scheme perfectly.

POLYSEMY: ONE WORD, MULTIPLE MEANINGS While our understand of words like *chase* is very clear, it's not too long before you run into cases of **polysemy**, the fact that *many words in a language may have multiple meanings*. The task of the language processing system is to figure out which meaning is the intended one. While a word may be polysemus, not all meanings are equal. Generally, there is one meaning that is the primary meaning that people typically would think of first when they heard the word, or would likely be listed first in a dictionary. This is called the *dominant* meaning of a word. Other meanings of a word then would be called the *subordinate* meanings. So, take a simple word like *run*. The dominant meaning has something to do with using your legs to move fast. However, there are all kinds of subordinate meanings, such as having a run in your stockings, a movie having a run at the theater, having your nose run, to cut and run (retreat), to run your engine, watching paint colors run, and so on. The way you distinguish which particular meaning to use from the mental lexicon would depend on the context a word is in.

POLYSEMY AND PRIMING Let's consider two examples of how context can resolve polysemy to determine the intended meaning. As one example, the word *count* is ambiguous by itself. Putting the word in a sentence may not help: "We had trouble keeping track of the count." Most of us agree that the sentence does not help much; you still can't tell the intended meaning. What's missing is context, some conceptual framework to guide the interpretation of the polysemus word. With an adequate context, you can determine which sense of the word *count* is intended in these two different contexts:

My dog wasn't included in the final count.

The vampire was disguised as a handsome count.

These sentences, taken from Simpson's (1981, 1984) work on polysemy (you read about this briefly in Chapter 2), point out the importance of context: Context can help determine the intended meaning. With neutral contexts, such as the "We had trouble" sentence, word meanings are activated as a simple function of their dominance: The number sense of *count* is dominant, so that meaning is more activated. But a context that biases the interpretation one way or the other results in a stronger activation for the biased meaning: With *vampire* you activated the meaning of *count* related to nobility and Count Dracula (see also Balota & Paul, 1996; Klein & Murphy, 2002; Piercey & Joordens, 2000; but cf. Binder, 2003; Binder & Rayner, 1998).

The resolution of lexical ambiguity that is found with polysemus words is important for successful comprehension. If you don't get the intended meaning of a word, then you won't get the intended message. It appears that ambiguity resolution works, in part, in a two-stage process. When people encounter an ambiguous word, what they do is activate all of the meanings, at least to some degree. Then in the second stage, they deactivate the inappropriate ones, based on the information from the rest of the discourse context. However, not everyone does this equally well. Work by Gernsbacher and Faust (1991) shows that good readers suppress inappropriate meanings faster. In comparison, poor readers maintained multiple meanings for a much longer period of time, which may be contributing to the problems they are having.

CONTEXT AND ERPS Let's consider a second example, an offshoot of the Kounios and Holcomb work with ERPs that you read about earlier. In one study, Holcomb, Kounios, Anderson, and West (1999; see also Sereno, Brewer, & O'Donnell, 2003) recorded ERPs in a simple sentence comprehension task. People saw sentences one word at a time and were asked to respond after seeing the last word, with "yes" if the sentence made sense and "no" if it did not. The experimental sentences varied along two dimensions, whether the last word was concrete or abstract and whether it was congruent with the sentence meaning or anomalous (i.e., made no sense). As an example, "Armed robbery implies that the thief used a weapon" was a concrete–congruent sentence; substituting *rose* for *weapon* made it concrete but anomalous. Likewise, "Lisa argued that this had not been the case in one single instance" was an abstract–congruent sentence, and substituting *fun* for *instance* made it abstract–anomalous.

◆ Figure 9-9 shows some of the ERP patterns obtained. In the left panel, you see the "normal" ERP patterns for the congruent, sensible sentences; the three profiles, from top to bottom, came from the three midline electrode sites shown in the schematic drawing (frontal, central, and parietal). In the right panel are the ERP patterns when the sentences ended in an anomalous word. Notice first in the left panel that the solid and dotted functions, for concrete and abstract sentences, tracked each other very closely: Whatever neural mechanisms operated during comprehension, they generated similar ERP patterns. But now make a left-to-right comparison of the patterns, seeing the differences in the right panel when the sentences ended in a nonsensical, anomalous word (*rose* in the armed robbery sentence, for example). Here there were marked changes in the ERP profiles. At the central location, for example, there was a steadily downward trend (in the positive direction, in terms of electrical potentials) for sensible sentences but a dramatic reversal of direction for anomalous words.

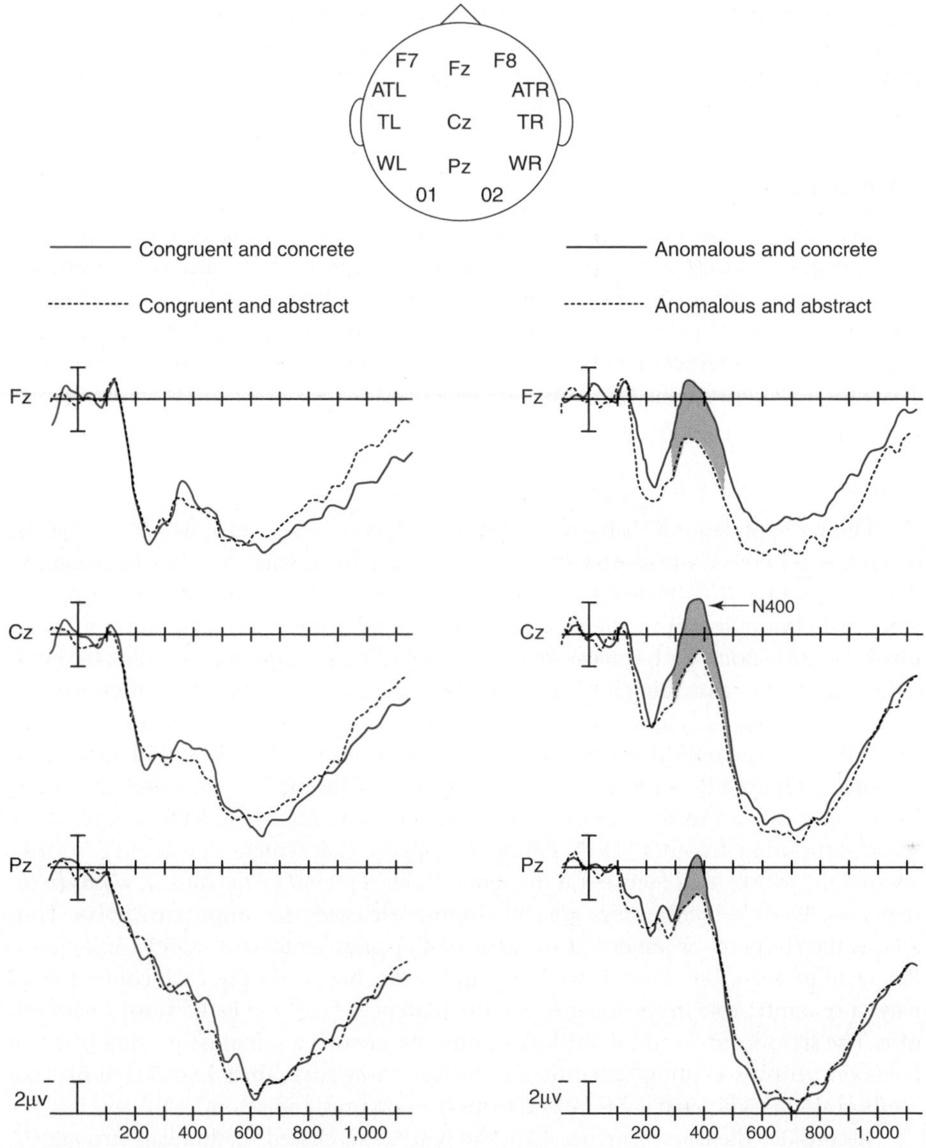

◆ **FIGURE 9-9**
ERP profiles at three midline sites (frontal [F_Z], central [C_Z], parietal [P_Z]) for sentences ending with a congruent (left panel) or contextually anomalous (right panel) word. Adapted from Figures 3 and 4 in Holcomb et al. (1999).

In short, the neural mechanisms involved in comprehension generated dramatically different patterns when an anomalous word was encountered. The mismatch between the context, the already-processed meaning of the sentence, and the final word yielded not only an overt response (the response indicating "no, that sentence makes no sense"), but also a neural response, signifying the brain-related activity that detected the anomalous ending of the sentence. (Don't get confused about directions here. The functions underneath the gridline are electrically positive, so deflection upward in these graphs is a deflection toward the negative, a deflection going in a negative direction; this is what the *N* in *N400* signifies, a "negative going" pattern.) Even at the level of neural functioning then, there is a rapid response to nonsensical ideas that follow sensible context, a kind of "something's wrong here" response that the brain makes some 400 ms after the nonsensical event.

Case Grammar

In this section we consider issues of how the language processing system knows what role a word or concept is playing in a sentence. This approach is called **case grammar**. The ideas came originally from Fillmore (1968). The basic idea is that *the semantic analysis of sentences involves figuring out what semantic role is being played by each word or concept in the sentence and computing sentence meaning based on those semantic roles.* Two sample sentences illustrate this:

(14) The key will open the door.

(15) The janitor will open the door with the key.

Fillmore pointed out that syntactic aspects of sentences—which words serve as the subject, direct object, and so on—often are irrelevant to sentence meaning. For example, in sentences 14 and 15 the word *key* plays different grammatical roles; subject of the sentence in 14 but object of the preposition in 15. For Fillmore, focusing on this difference misses a critical point for language. Regardless of its different grammatical roles, the key is doing exactly the same thing in both cases, playing the same semantic role of *instrument.* A purely syntactic analysis misses this, but a semantic analysis captures it perfectly.

Fillmore's theoretical position was called case grammar. He, along with many others since, proposed that a sentence is best understood "as made up of a verb and a collection of nouns in various 'cases' in the deep structure sense" (p. 375), that is, in the sense of meaning. In other words, Fillmore proposed that sentence processing involves a semantic parsing that focuses on the semantic *roles played by the content words in the sentences.* These semantic roles are called **semantic cases**, or simply **case roles**. Thus *door* is the recipient or patient of the action of *open* in sentences 14 and 15; *janitor* is the agent of *open; key* is the instrument; and so on. Stated simply, each content word plays a semantic role in the meaning of the sentence. That role is the word's *semantic case.* The significant—indeed, critical—point about such a semantic parsing is that it relies on people's existing semantic and lexical knowledge, their knowledge of what kinds of things will open, who can perform the opening, and so on.

Reconsider the *chase* sentence 13, "The policeman chased the burglar through the park," and three variations, thinking of the content words in terms of their semantic roles:

(16) The mouse chased the cat through the house.

(17) His insecurities chased him even in his sleep.

*(18) *The book chased the flower.*

Your lexical and semantic knowledge of *chase* is that some animate being does the chasing, the agent case. Some other thing is the recipient of the chasing, the patient, but that thing need not be animate, just capable of moving rapidly (e.g., you can chase a piece of paper being blown by the wind). On this analysis, it is clear that sentence 13 conforms to the normal situation stored in memory, so it is easy to comprehend. Sentence 16, however, mismatches the typical state of affairs between mice and cats. Nonetheless, either of these creatures can serve as the required animate agent of the relation *chase*, so sentence 16 is sensible. Because of other semantic knowledge, you know that sentence 17 violates the literal meaning of *chase* but could still have a nonliteral, metaphorical meaning. But your semantic case analysis provides the reason sentence 18 is unacceptable. A book is inanimate, so it mismatches the required animate agent role for *chase; book* cannot play the role of agent for *chase*. Likewise, *flower* seems to violate the movable restriction on the patient case for *chase*.

Work by Bresnan (1978; Bresnan & Kaplan, 1982) and Jackendoff (1992) has amplified and extended work on case grammars. For example, in Jackendoff's theory of a cognitive grammar (1992; see Figure 9-10), the goal is to build a conceptual structure, an understanding of the sentence. We use language and language rules to get from the spoken or written sentence to a meaningful mental structure or understanding. Each lexical entry includes the meaning of the word and, for verbs, a list of the arguments or semantic cases that go along with it. Thus, the lexical entry *chase* would state that *chase*

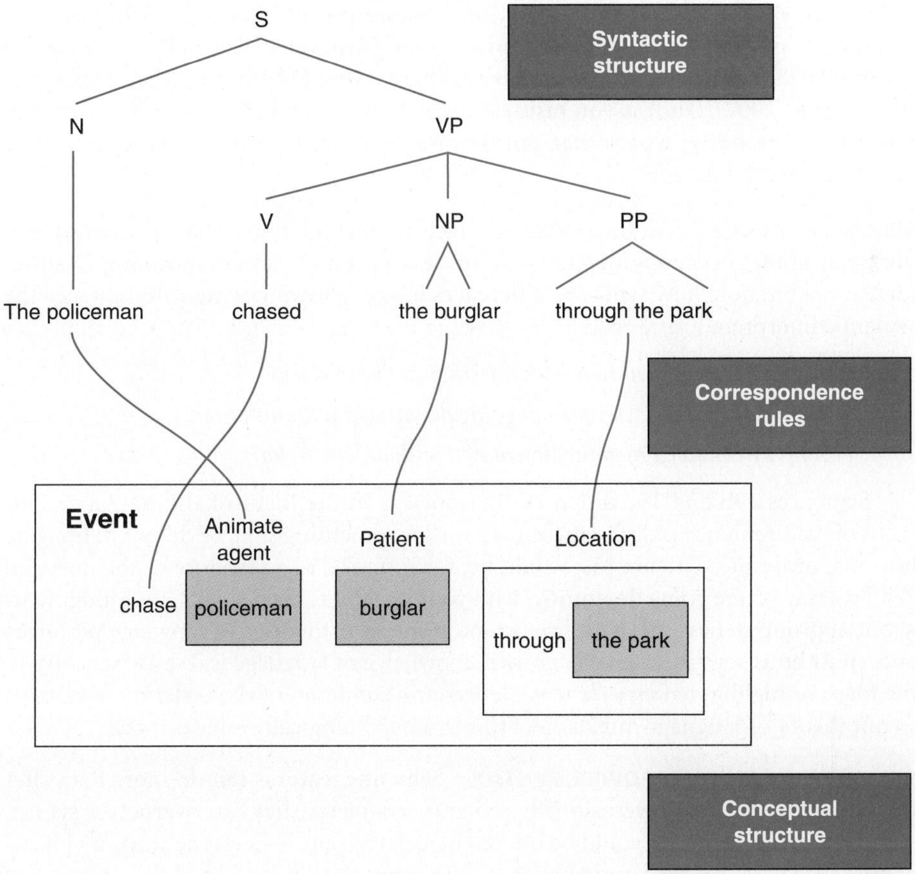

FIGURE 9-10 In Jackendoff's (1992) conceptual semantics approach, comprehension of meaning is the process of arriving at a conceptual structure for the sentence. To accomplish this, we use both the syntactic structure of the sentence and a set of correspondence rules; the correspondence rules translate from syntactic roles (e.g., noun and verb) into semantic roles (agent, patient, and so forth). Adapted from Whitney (1998).

requires an animate agent, some recipient or patient, and so on. Likewise, for *give*, the case arguments would state that an animate agent and recipient are needed for the *give* relation, and some *object* is the thing being given (for an excellent summary of these positions, see Whitney, 1998).

Accordingly, when we perceive words, we look up the concepts in the lexicon. This look-up process accesses not only the word's meaning, but also its syntactic and semantic case roles and any other restrictions. Each word in the sentence is processed as it is encountered with content words being assigned to their semantic roles. If all goes well, the sentence conveys an exact, specified meaning that is captured accurately by the analysis of the cognitive grammar.

Interaction of Syntax and Semantics

Note that semantic factors do not stand alone in language, just as syntactic factors are not independent of semantics. Syntax is more than just word and phrase order rules; it's a clue to how to understand sentences. For example, O'Seaghdha's (1997) evidence shows separable effects of syntactic assignment and semantic integration of word meanings, with syntactic processes occurring before semantic integration. His results, based on RTs, are largely consistent with those in other studies (e.g., Peterson, Burgess, Dell, & Eberhard, 2001, on how we process idioms), including ERP studies of syntactic and semantic processing (Ainsworth-Darnell, Shulman, & Boland, 1998; Friederici, Hahne, and Mecklinger, 1996; Osterhout, Allen, McLaughlin, & Inoue, 2002). And, as you just read, syntax in speech production is sensitive to a word's accessibility; words that can be easily retrieved right now tend to appear earlier in a sentence.

SEMANTIC FOCUS Likewise, semantic factors refer to more than just word and phrase meanings because different syntactic devices can be clues to meaning. To anticipate just a bit, note how syntactic differences in the following sentences influence the semantic interpretation:

(19a) I'm going downtown with my sister at four o'clock.

(19b) It's at four o'clock that I'm going downtown with my sister.

(19c) It's my sister I'm going downtown with at four o'clock.

Sentences 19b and 19c differ subtly from 19a in the focus of the utterance. The focus of each sentence is different, so each means something slightly different. Imagine how inappropriate sentence 19c would be, for instance, as a response to the question "Did you say you're going downtown with your sister at three o'clock?" Our judgments about appropriateness make an important point: Our theories of language performance must be as sophisticated as our own knowledge of language is. We are sensitive to the focus or highlighted aspects of sentences and subtleties of the ordering of clauses, so our theory of language must reflect this in a psychologically relevant way.

SEMANTICS CAN OVERPOWER SYNTAX Semantic features can do more than alter the syntax of sentences. Occasionally semantic characteristics can overpower syntax. Although many examples could be offered here, let's focus on a classic study by Fillenbaum (1974). As you read, note how current terminology would label this an effect of top-down processing.

Fillenbaum presented several kinds of sentences and asked people to write paraphrases that preserved the original meaning. Ordinary "threat" sentences such as "Don't print that or I'll sue you" were then reordered into "perverse" threats, such as "Don't print that or I won't sue you." Regular "conjunctive" sentences such as "John got off the bus and went into the store" were then changed into "disordered" sentences, such as "John went into the store and got off the bus." When Fillenbaum scored paraphrases of reordered sentences, he found remarkably high percentages of changes, as shown in Figure 9-11. More than 50% of people "normalized" the perverse threatening sentences, making them conform to the more typical state of affairs, and more than 60% normalized the "disordered" conjunctive sentences. He then asked people to reread their paraphrases to see whether there was even a "shred of difference" from the originals. More than half the time, people saw no discrepancies. Apparently, their general knowledge was influential enough that it overpowered the syntactic and lexical aspects of the sentences. (Try these examples: "Nice we're having weather, isn't it?" and "Ignorance is no excuse for the law.") ★

In short, sometimes we comprehend not what we hear or read, but what we *expect* to hear or read. This should sound familiar to you, that our existing knowledge exerts an influence on mental processing (Whittlesea, 2004, includes your own subjective experience as a factor too). Chapters 7 and 8 dealt extensively with world knowledge, exactly the kind of knowledge Fillenbaum's participants were consulting when they misinterpreted the perverse sentences. This is the same phenomenon Bartlett (1932), Loftus and Palmer (1974), and others have identified, too, though not in the context of experiments on language use *per se*. Given these similarities between semantic and psycholinguistic ideas, you won't be surprised to find out that the current psycholinguistic view on semantic analysis of language is familiar. In short, the psycholinguistic approach to lexical and semantic factors in language relies on conceptually driven processing.

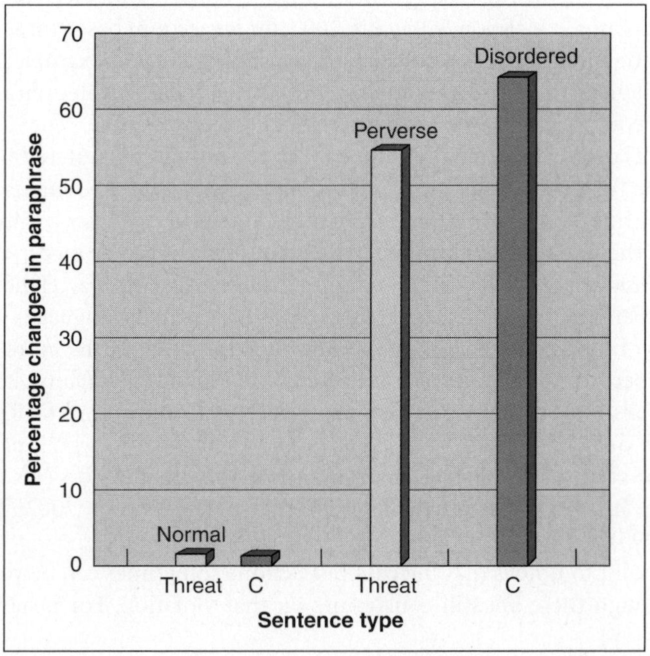

★ **FIGURE 9-11** Fillenbaum's (1974) results. Two kinds of normal sentences were shown, threats and conjunctives (labeled C) such as "John got off the bus and went into the store." Threats were then altered to be "perverse," and conjunctives were disordered (e.g., threat C, "John dressed and had a bath"). From Fillenbaum (1974).

Evidence for the Semantic Grammar Approaches

A major prediction of semantic grammar theory can be stated in two parts. First, we assume that comprehenders begin to analyze the sentence immediately, as soon as the words are encountered. Second, this analysis is a process of assigning each word to a particular semantic case role, with each assignment contributing its part to overall sentence comprehension. As an example, read sentence 20:

(20) *After the musician had bowed the piano was quickly taken off the stage.*

Your analysis of this sentence proceeds easily and without disruption; it's a fairly straightforward sentence. Now read sentence 21:

(21) *After the musician had played the piano was quickly taken off the stage.*

What's different about sentence 21? The verb *played* suggests that the *piano* is the semantic recipient of *play*. When you read *played*, your semantic role assignment for piano was *recipient*. But then you read *was quickly* and realized you had made a mistake in interpretation. Sentences such as 21 are called **garden path sentences**; *the early part of the sentence sets you up so that the later phrases in the sentence don't make sense given the way you assigned case roles in the first part.* Figuratively speaking, the sentence leads you down the garden path; when you realize your mistake, you have to retrace your steps back up the path to reassign earlier words to different cases. Additional examples (from Singer, 1990) of this effect are shown in sentences 22 and 23:

(22) *The groundsman chased the girl waving a stick in her hand.*

(23) *The old train the young.*

Many research reports have studied how people comprehend garden path sentences as a way of evaluating case grammar theory (Frazier & Rayner, 1982; Mitchell & Holmes, 1985; but see McKoon & Ratcliff, 2007, for an account based on semantic plausibility). For the most part, the results have been supportive. For example, when people read such sentences, their eyes tend to fixate much longer on the later phrases, signaling their error in comprehension (e.g., on "was quickly taken off" in sentence 21). As shown ▲ in Figure 9-12, people spent 40 to 50 ms longer when they encountered their error (at point D in the figure; D stands for the disambiguating part of the sentence that reveals the earlier misinterpretation). This is a recovery time effect; it takes additional time to recover from the initial role assignment when that turns out to be incorrect (see Christianson, Hollingworth, Halliwell, & Ferreira, 2001; and Ferreira, Henderson, Anes, Weeks, & McFarlane, 1996, for comparable results with spoken language). Interestingly, the more committed you are to an initial interpretation, that is, the more you "dig in," the harder it becomes to change your interpretation (Tabor & Hutchins, 2004).

There is also important work, also using the eye fixations and fMRI, on how we *parse*—figure out—the syntax of a sentence and the degree to which parsing can be overridden or at least affected by semantic context and other factors (see Clifton et al., 2003; Mason, Just, Keller, & Carpenter, 2003; Rayner & Clifton, 2002; Tanenhaus & Trueswell, 1995).

A final point to note is that the case restrictions sometimes can be violated intentionally, although there are still constraints on that violation. For instance, consider

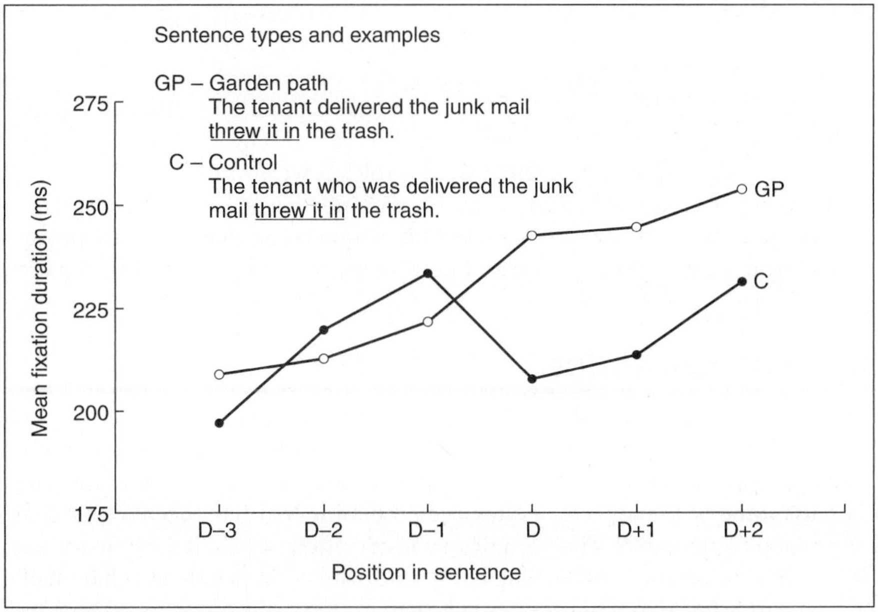

▲ FIGURE 9-12
A depiction of the effect of garden path sentences on reading time. The curves show eye fixations on phrases before and after D, the point in the sentence where the ambiguity is noticed and disambiguated. The top curve shows the data from garden path sentences; eye fixation time grows noticeably longer for these curves at D, when the ambiguity is noticed (the D phrase is underlined in the sample sentences). The bottom curve shows data from the control sentences and no increase in reading time at point D. Data from Rayner, Carlson, & Frazier (1983).

sentence 17 again: "His insecurities chased him even in his sleep." Such a sentence is understood as a technical but permissible violation of the animate restriction for the agent role of *chase*. In a metaphorical sense, we can "compute" how insecurities might behave like an animate agent; thoughts can behave as if they were animate and can take on the properties of pursuing relentlessly, catching, and so on. A particularly fascinating aspect of language involves such figurative uses of words and how case grammar accommodates such usage (see Glucksberg & Keysar, 1990; Keysar, Shen, Glucksberg, & Horton, 2000; Tourangeau & Rips, 1991).

Section Summary

- Semantic factors in language can sometimes override syntactic and phonological effects. The study of semantics breaks words down into morphemes, the smallest meaningful units in language; *cars* contains the free morpheme *car* and the bound morpheme *-s* signifying a "plural."

- Speech errors that people make can be used to help reveal the processes by which language is produced. These speech errors follow regularities that are likely to be produced by otherwise consistent and stable cognitive processes.
- As the study of language comprehension has matured, the dominant approach to semantics claims that we perform a semantic parsing of sentences, assigning words to their appropriate semantic case roles as we hear or read.
- Garden path sentences, where later phrases indicate an error in interpretation, have provided rich information about how syntax and semantics are processed online during comprehension and how we recover from comprehension errors.

BRAIN AND LANGUAGE

While we have covered a number of ways that cognition is related to underlying cortical structure and function, perhaps one of the most fruitful areas of research on the brain-cognition relation is work on language processing. In this section of the chapter we discuss some of the aspects of language processing that have been found to have strong neural components. This includes a consideration of people with intact brains, as well as of how language processing has been disrupted in people who have had the misfortune to suffer some sort of brain damage.

Language in the Intact Brain

With the advent of modern imaging methods, we have begun to learn an extraordinary amount about how the brain processes language from neurologically intact people. Consider a representative study, looking at people's sensitivity to the syntactic structure of sentences. Osterhout and Holcomb (1992) presented sentences to people and recorded the changes in their brain wave patterns (ERPs) as they comprehended. In particular, they examined ERP patterns for sentences that violated syntactic or semantic expectations, comparing these with the patterns obtained with control sentences. When sentences ended in a semantically anomalous fashion ("John buttered his bread with socks"), a significant N400 ERP pattern was observed, much as reported in Kounios and Holcomb's (1992) study of semantic relatedness (see Figure 9-9). But when the sentence ended in a syntactically anomalous fashion ("John hoped the man to leave"), a strong P600 pattern occurred (a positive electrical potential) 600 ms after the anomalous word "to" was seen; see Figure 9-13. This confirms the important and seemingly separate role of syntactic processing during language comprehension.

A wealth of new evidence illustrates the importance to cognitive science of such imaging and neuropsychological techniques and strongly suggests that the upcoming wave of research on language processing will feature techniques such as imaging and ERP methods very prominently. Here are four brief examples.

LEARNING LANGUAGE McCandliss, Posner, and Givon (1997) taught people a new, miniature artificial language and recorded ERPs during learning. Early in training, words in the new language showed ERP patterns typical of nonsense material. But, after five weeks of training, the ERP patterns looked like those obtained with English words. Furthermore, left hemisphere frontal areas reacted to semantic aspects of the language, whereas posterior areas were sensitive to the visual characteristics of the words, the orthography.

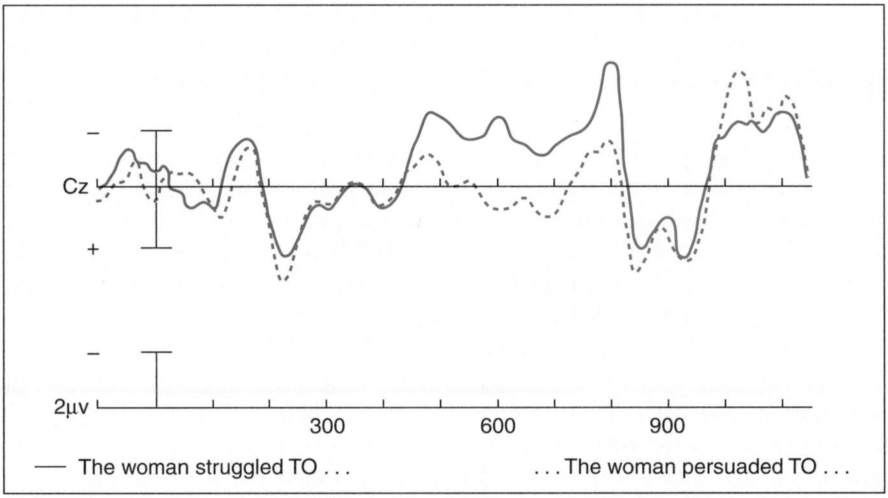

FIGURE 9-13 Mean ERPs to syntactically acceptable sentences (solid curve) and syntactically anomalous sentences (dotted curve). The P600 component, illustrated as a downward dip in the dotted curve, shows the effect of detecting the syntactic anomaly. Note that, in this figure, positive changes go in the downward direction.

SYNTACTIC PROCESSING Rosler, Pechmann, Streb, Roder, and Hennighausen (1998) did an ambitious study on syntactic processing, using ERPs. Sentences were presented word by word; to make sure people were comprehending, they had to answer a question about the sentence 5 s after they saw the last word. The sentences were all grammatical, but some of them differed from normal, canonical word order. The ERP patterns demonstrated a variety of effects; for example, the patterns differed appreciably when the sentences violated canonical word order and when elements in the sentence cued people that an unusual word order would follow. The especially compelling aspect of these results is that the ERP patterns tapped into purely mental processes that are not revealed by outward, behavioral measures such as RT or accuracy.

RIGHT HEMISPHERE LANGUAGE Although the left hemisphere is typically credited with being the primary source of language processing, the right hemisphere has important work to do as well. A general characterization of the role of the right hemisphere in the cortex is that it serves to process information in a more wholistic way, rather than in the more analytic manner characteristic of the left hemisphere. In other words, the right hemisphere is more adept at processing information in a coarse-grained fashion, whereas the left hemisphere is more adept at processing information at a fine-grained level (Beeman, 1998). One role of the right hemisphere is in making more distant, remote semantic connections between words. For example, the connection between *tiger* and *stripe* is relatively direct and close, but the connection between *tiger* and *beach* is more remote, and requires some creativity to see a connection. An illustration of this differential operation of the left and right hemispheres was shown in a study by Coulson, Federmeier, Van Petten, and Kutas (2005). In this study, ERP patterns were recorded in the left and right hemispheres as people read sentences. What they found was that the left hemisphere was more involved in integrating lexical information with sentence level information, such as whether a word is sensible in the context of a given sentence (e.g., responses to the word *tire* after reading the sentence "They were truly stuck, since she didn't have a spare"), but not so much the lexical relations of the words to each other. In comparison, the right hemisphere was more involved in this sort of word to word associative processing (e.g., the fact that *spare* and *tire* are more associated than *spare* and *pencil*).

INDIVIDUAL DIFFERENCES Reichle, Carpenter, and Just (2000) used functional magnetic resonance imaging (fMRI) to look at brain activity while people verified sentence–picture stimuli (e.g., "The star is above the plus," followed by a picture that did or did not match the sentence). When people were asked to use a verbal strategy to make their decisions, brain regions associated with language processing (especially Broca's area) were active; when people were instructed to use a visual imagery strategy, regions in the parietal lobe were active, the same regions that are active when visual–spatial reasoning tasks are given. Interestingly, the language area activity was somewhat lower when high-verbal people were tested and likewise for visual areas in people high in visual–spatial abilities, as if high verbal or spatial ability reduced the amount of brain work needed to perform the task.

Aphasia

A large literature exists on brain-related disorders of language, based on people who through the misfortune of illness or brain injury have lost the ability to use language. Formal studies of such disorders date back to the mid-1800s, although records dating back to 3500 B.C. mention language loss caused by brain injury (see McCarthy & Warrington, 1990). Table 9-5 provides a list and short explanation of these disruptions and some others you've already encountered.

TABLE 9-5 Brain-Related Disruptions of Language and Cognition

Disorder	Disruption of
Language Related	
Broca's aphasia	Speech production, syntactic features
Wernicke's aphasia	Comprehension, semantic features
Conduction aphasia	Repetition of words and sentences
Anomia (anomic aphasia)	Word finding, either lexical or semantic
Pure word deafness	Perceptual or semantic processing of auditory word comprehension
Alexia	Reading, recognition of printed letters or words
Agraphia	Writing
Other Symbolic Related	
Acalculia	Mathematical abilities, retrieval or rule-based procedures
Perception, Movement Related	
Agnosia	Visual object recognition
Prosopagnosia	(Visual) face recognition
Apraxia	Voluntary action or skilled motor movement

The disruption of language caused by a brain-related disorder is called **aphasia.** Aphasia is always the product of some physical injury to the brain sustained either in an accident or a blow to the head or in diseases and medical syndromes such as stroke. A major goal in neurology is to understand the aphasic syndromes more completely so that people who suffer from aphasia may be helped more effectively. From the standpoint of cognitive neuroscience, the language disruptions of aphasic patients can also help us understand language and its neurological basis.

Although there are many different kinds of aphasias, with great variety in their effects and severity, three basic forms are the most common: *Broca's aphasia*, *Wernicke's aphasia*, and *conduction aphasia.*

BROCA'S APHASIA As described by Kertesz (1982), **Broca's aphasia** is characterized by *severe difficulties in producing speech;* it is also called expressive or production aphasia. Patients with Broca's aphasia show speech that is hesitant, effortful, and phonemically distorted. Aside from stock phrases such as "I don't know," such patients generally respond to questions with only one-word answers. If words are strung together, there are few if any grammatical markers present in the utterance, bound morphemes such as *-ing*, *-ed*, and *-ly*. In less severe cases, the aphasia may be limited to more complex aspects of language production, such as the production of verb inflections (Faroqi-Shah & Thompson, 2007). Interestingly, such patients typically show less impairment of comprehension for both spoken and written language.

This syndrome was first described by French neurosurgeon Pierre Broca in the 1860s, who also identified the damaged area responsible for the disorder. The site of the brain damage, an area toward the rear of the left frontal lobe, is therefore called Broca's area. As shown in Figure 9-14 (see also the color plate illustrations), Broca's area lies adjacent to a major motor control center in the brain. ■

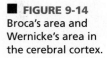

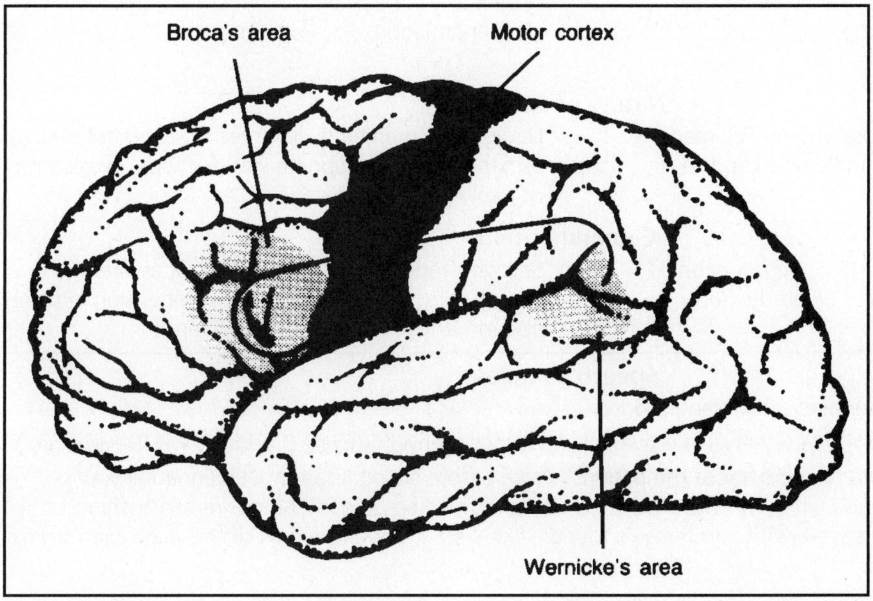

■ **FIGURE 9-14** Broca's area and Wernicke's area in the cerebral cortex.

WERNICKE'S APHASIA Loosely speaking, the impairments in **Wernicke's aphasia** are ★ the opposite of those in Broca's aphasia; see Table 9-6 for a listing of the typical impairments in both aphasias, including speech samples. In patients affected by Wernicke's aphasia, *comprehension is impaired, as are repetition, naming, reading, and writing, but the syntactic aspects of speech are preserved*; it is sometimes called receptive or comprehension aphasia. In this syndrome "copious unintelligible jargon is produced" (Kertesz, 1982, p. 30), either with unrecognizable content words; recognizable but often inappropriate semantic substitutions; or neologisms, invented nonsense words. In Kertesz's description of a woman with Wernicke's aphasia, the nature of the disorder is very apparent:

> She speaks in sentences and uses appropriate pauses and inflectional markers separating lexical items . . .without articulatory errors or hesitations. . . . In an extraordinary fashion, neologisms of variable length and phonemic complexity replace substantive words, mostly nouns and verbs. She talks as if she spoke without mistakes. . .There is a rather curious cool and calm manner about her speech as if she did not realize her deficit . . .a very characteristic feature of this disturbance. (pp. 41–42)

German investigator Carl Wernicke identified this disorder, and the left-hemisphere region that is damaged, in 1874. This region is thus known as Wernicke's area, also illustrated in Figure 9-14. Note that the area, toward the rear of the left temporal

★ **TABLE 9-6 Classic Impairments in Broca's and Wernicke's Aphasias**

Broca's Aphasia	Wernicke's Aphasia
Quality of Speech	
Severely impaired; marked by extreme effort to generate speech, hesitant utterances, short (one-word) responses.	Little if any impairment; fluent speech productions, clear articulation, no hesitations.
Nature of Speech	
Agrammatical; marked by loss of syntactic markers and inflections and use of simple noun and verb categories.	Neologistic; marked by invented words (neologisms) or semantically inappropriate substitutions; long strings of neologistic jargon.
Comprehension	
Unimpaired compared with speech production. Word-finding difficulty caused by production difficulties.	Severely impaired; marked by lack of awareness that speech is incomprehensible; comprehension impaired also in nonverbal tasks (e.g., pointing).

Speech Samples

Broca's aphasia. Experimenter asks the patient's address.

"Oh dear. Um. Aah. O! O dear. Very-there-were-ave. avedeversher avenyer." (Correct address was Devonshire.)

Wernicke's aphasia. Experimenter asks about the patient's work before hospitalization. "I wanna tell you this happened when happened when he rent. His-his kell come down here and is—he got ren something. It happened. In these ropliers were with him for hi-is friend—like was. And he roden all of these arranjen from the pedis on from iss pescid."

lobe, is adjacent to the auditory cortex, in the left temporal lobe, a very different area, with very different abilities, than the Broca's area in the frontal lobe. Note that this demonstrates a double dissociation, a basic distinction at the level of brain organization between syntax and semantics (see Breedin & Saffran, 1999, for a case study showing loss of semantic knowledge but preserved syntactic performance).

CONDUCTION APHASIA Much less common than Broca's and Wernicke's aphasias, **conduction aphasia** is a more narrow disruption of language ability. Both Broca's and Wernicke's areas seem to be intact in conduction aphasia, and people with conduction aphasia can understand and produce speech quite well. Their language impairment is that they are *unable to repeat what they have just heard*. In intuitive terms, the intact comprehension and production systems seem to have lost their normal connection or linkage. And indeed, the site of the brain lesion in conduction aphasia appears to be the primary pathway between Broca's and Wernicke's areas, called the *arcuate fasciculus* (Geschwind, 1970). Quite literally, the pathway between the comprehension and production areas is no longer able to conduct the linguistic message.

ANOMIA Another type of aphasia deserves brief mention here because it relates to the separation of the semantic and lexical systems discussed earlier. **Anomia** or **anomic aphasia** is a disruption of word finding, an *impairment in the normal ability to retrieve a semantic concept and say its name*; you encountered this briefly back in Chapter 7. In anomia, some aspect of the normally automatic semantic or lexical components of retrieval has been damaged. Although moderate word-finding difficulty can result from damage almost anywhere in the left hemisphere, full-fledged anomia seems to involve damage especially in the left temporal lobe (Coughlan & Warrington, 1978; see McCarthy & Warrington, 1990, for details). Although there is a similarity between anomia and the tip-of-the-tongue (TOT) phenomenon, the similarity is superficial. Several researchers (e.g., Geschwind, 1967; Goodglass, Kaplan, Weintraub, & Ackerman, 1976) have found no evidence among anomic patients of the partial knowledge that characterizes a TOT state. Evidence also indicates that anomia can involve retrieval blockage only for the lexical component of retrieval, leaving semantic retrieval of the concept intact (e.g., the patient described in Chapter 7; Kay & Ellis, 1987). This, along with other cases (e.g., Ashcraft, 1993), suggest preserved semantic retrieval but a blockage in finding the lexical representation that corresponds to the already retrieved semantic concept.

OTHER APHASIAS As Table 9-5 shows, a variety of highly specific aphasias are also possible. Although most of these are quite rare, they nonetheless give evidence of the separability of several aspects of language performance. For instance, in *alexia* (or dyslexia), there is a disruption of reading without any necessary disruption of spoken language or aural comprehension. In *agraphia*, conversely, the patient is unable to write. Amazingly, a few reports describe patients with alexia but without agraphia—in other words, patients who can write but cannot read what they have just written (Benson & Geschwind, 1969). In *pure word deafness*, a patient cannot comprehend spoken language, although he or she is still able to read and produce written and spoken language.

There is documentation for even more specific forms of aphasia than those, for instance difficulties in retrieval of verbs in written but not spoken language (Berndt & Haendiges, 2000) and difficulties in naming just visual stimuli, without either generalized visual agnosia or generalized anomia (Sitton, Mozer, & Farah, 2000).

RIGHT HEMISPHERE DAMAGE Despite the fact that most of the aphasias discussed here involve processing in the left hemisphere of the cortex, there is also evidence of the right hemisphere's contribution to language comprehension and production (see Beeman & Chiarello, 1998, for a useful overview of the complementary right- and left-hemisphere language processes).

Work by Beeman (1993; 1998) suggests that a problem right hemisphere damaged people have is an inability to activate an appropriately diverse set of information from long-term memory from which inferences can be derived. In one study, after reading a text, people were given a lexical decision task. Some of the words in the task were related to inferences that needed to be drawn for comprehension. For example, if the person had read in the text "Then he went into the bathroom and discovered that he had left the bathtub water running. He had forgotten about it while watching the news. The mess took him a long time to mop up," then the critical lexical decision probe word might be "overflow." This is an inference because the tub overflowing was actually not mentioned in the text. The results showed that normal controls responded 49 ms faster relative to neutral control words. However, the right hemisphere damaged patients responded 148 ms more *slowly* to these words.

Generalizing from Cases of Brain Damage

Although it is a mistake to believe that our eventual understanding of language will be reducible to a catalog of biological and neurological processes (e.g., Mehler, Morton, & Jusczyk, 1984), knowledge of the neurological aspects of language is useful for something beyond the rehabilitation and treatment of aphasia. What do studies of such abnormal brain processes tell us about normal cerebral functioning and language?

Well, for one, the different patterns of behavioral impairments in Broca's and Wernicke's aphasias, stemming from different physical structures in the brain, implies that these two physical structures are responsible for different aspects of linguistic skill. Furthermore, these selective impairments reinforce the notion that syntax and semantics are two separable but interactive aspects of normal language (e.g., O'Seaghdha, 1997; Osterhout & Holcomb, 1992). That is, the double dissociations indicate that different, independent modules govern comprehension and speech production. Other dissociations indicate yet more independent modules of processing, such as separate modules corresponding to reading and writing.

An intriguing inference from such studies is that the specialized regions signal an innate, biological basis for language; that is, the human nervous system is specifically adapted to learn and use language, as opposed to simply being able to do so. Several theorists have gone so far as to discuss possible evolutionary mechanisms responsible for lateralization, hemispheric specialization, the dissociation of syntax and semantics revealed by Broca's and Wernicke's aphasias, and even cognition in general (Corballis, 1989; Geary, 1992; Lewontin, 1990). These are fascinating lines of reasoning on the nature of language and cognition as represented in the brain.

Section Summary

- Extensive evidence from studies with brain-damaged people and more modern work using imaging and ERP methods reveals several functional and anatomical dissociations in language ability.
- The syntactic and articulatory aspects of language seem centered in Broca's area, in the left frontal lobe, whereas comprehension aspects are focused more on Wernicke's area, in the posterior left hemisphere junction of the temporal and parietal lobes.
- The study of these and other deficits, such as anomia and right hemispheric damage, converges with evidence from imaging and ERP studies to illustrate how various aspects of language performance act as separable, distinct components within the overall broad ability to produce and comprehend language.

Key Terms

ambiguous (p. *346*)
anomia (p. *367*)
anomic aphasia (p. *367*)
aphasia (p. *365*)
arbitrariness (p. *324*)
Broca's aphasia (p. *365*)
case grammar (p. *356*)
case roles (p. *356*)
categorical perception (p. *334*)
coarticulation (p. *337*)
competence (p. *328*)
conduction aphasia (p. *367*)
deep structure (p. *345*)
displacement (p. *325*)
dysfluency (p. *329*)
flexibility (p. *324*)
garden path sentences (p. *360*)
given-new strategy (p. *349*)
grammar (p. *328*)
language (p. *322*)
linguistic relativity hypothesis (p. *329*)
linguistic universals (p. *322*)
linguistics (p. *321*)
mental lexicon (p. *351*)
morpheme (p. *352*)
motor theory of speech perception (p. *340*)
naming (p. *324*)
parse (p. *346*)
performance (p. *328*)
phonemes (p. *331*)
phonemic competence (p. *336*)
phonology (p. *331*)
phrase structure (p. *344*)
polysemy (p. *353*)
problem of invariance (p. *336*)
productivity (p. *326*)
psycholinguistics (p. *321*)
semantic cases (p. *356*)
semanticity (p. *322*)
surface structure (p. *346*)
syntax (p. *342*)
transformational grammar (p. *350*)
transformational rules (p. *346*)
Wernicke's aphasia (p. *366*)

CHAPTER

10

Comprehension: Written and Spoken Language

Language simply does not work in isolation. . . . Understanding what one has heard is a complex process that. . .cannot be reasonably isolated into [separate] linguistic and memory components but must be a combined effort of both.

SCHANK, 1972, PP. 626–628

A language machine that does not interact smoothly with a person's practical knowledge will say little or nothing of importance about the central problems of cognitive psychology.

MILLER, 1977, P. 401

There's more to language than just the words.

JEAN REDPATH, ON A PRAIRIE HOME COMPANION, MAY 4, 1985

Comprehension—even the title of this chapter must be explained a bit, if only because much of Chapter 9 dealt with language comprehension, too. What does the word *comprehension* mean here that it didn't imply in Chapter 9? Basically, the expanded meaning here includes not only the fundamental language processes we studied in Chapter 9, but also the additional processes we use when comprehending realistic samples of language, say a passage in a book or a connected, coherent conversation, or even a perceived event. How do we comprehend? What do we *do* when we read, understand, and remember connected sentences? By taking a larger unit of analysis than isolated sentences, we confront a host of questions and issues that are central to communication and to cognitive psychology. And by confronting Miller's (1973) highest two levels of analysis, conceptual knowledge and beliefs, we address the important issues Miller (1977) describes as the "distant bridge that may someday need to be crossed." In short, it's time to cross the bridge.

GETTING STARTED: AN OVERVIEW

Conceptual and Rule Knowledge

You read about the first three levels of language analysis—the phonological, syntactic, and lexical and semantic levels—in Chapter 9. Let's start digging into comprehension by discussing Miller's (1977) fourth and fifth levels, the conceptual and belief levels. Here's the sentence Miller uses to illustrate these:

(1) Mary and John saw the mountains while they were flying to California.

If this sentence were spoken aloud, your comprehension would begin with phonological processes, translating the stream of sounds into words. Your syntactic knowledge would parse the sentence into phrases and would assist the semantic level of analysis as you determined the case roles for each important word: Mary and John are the agents of *see*, the word *mountains* is assigned the patient or recipient role, *they* is the agent of *fly* in the second main clause, and so on.

So far so good. But this sentence is more challenging than that. It's ambiguous, has more than one meaning. There's the obvious one, that Mary and John looked out the plane window and saw mountains during a flight to California. But there's also the possibility that *they* refers to the mountains. *They* merely denotes something plural, after all, so syntactically, the *they* could refer to the mountains.

Those of you who noticed this ambiguity probably rejected it immediately for the obvious reason: Mountains don't fly. We're getting close to the point Miller is making. Knowing that mountains don't fly is part of your semantic, **conceptual knowledge**. It is not a part of your simpler lexical knowledge about the word *mountains*. Look in as many dictionaries as you'd like, and you won't find "mountains don't fly" in any of them. Accordingly, your comprehension of sentence 1 must also have included a conceptual level of analysis, in which you compared your interpretation with your semantic knowledge.

Miller also argues that **beliefs** are important to understanding comprehension. I could tell you "No, I'm not saying that Mary and John were flying to California.

FRANK & ERNEST reprinted by permission of NEA, Inc. With permission of Bob Thaves.

I'm saying that it was the *mountains* that were flying." Although you can understand that I might think mountains can fly, you wouldn't change your mind about the issue; your belief in your own knowledge and your feeling that I'm lying or playing some kind of trick (or just plain crazy) are an important part of comprehension. A purely linguistic analysis of language misses this occasionally critical aspect of comprehension as well: Think how prominent your beliefs are, and how critical they are to comprehension and memory, when you hear advertisements or speeches in political campaigns.

Rules form yet another part of the knowledge that must be taken into account. In Chapter 9 we discussed tacit rule knowledge at the phonological and syntactic levels, and the distinctly semantic knowledge of case rules. These are all used to understand a sentence. But additional rules are operating when we deal with more complex passages of text or with connected conversation. Some rules have the flavor of strategies; for example, we tend to interpret sentence 2 as focusing on Tina, largely because she is mentioned first in the sentence (Gernsbacher, 1990):

(2) Tina gathered the kindling as Lisa set up the tent.

Several lines of evidence speak to this idea, that we provide a focus to our sentences by using mechanisms such as first mention and certain kinds of reference (e.g., "There was this guy who. . ." instead of "A guy. . .").

Other rules have to do with reference, building bridges between words referring to the same thing. For example, after reading sentence 2, how do you know that the phrase "After she got the fire started" would refer to Tina? Still more rules parade under the name **pragmatics** and refer to a variety of extralinguistic factors in a sentence. As an example, indirect speech acts such as "Do you have the time?" or "Can you open the window?" mean something different from what a literal reading would suggest. And finally, high-level rules operate in conversational interactions, rules that specify how the participants in a conversation structure their remarks and how they understand the remarks of others. As always, simply because you can't state the rule or were never explicitly taught the rule doesn't mean that it isn't there. On the contrary, it simply means that the rules are part of your implicit, tacit knowledge.

The difficulty of language comprehension when working memory is overloaded.

Comprehension Research

Much of the traditional evidence about comprehension relied on people's linguistic intuitions, their (leisurely) judgments about the acceptability of sentences, or simple measures of recall and accuracy. The Sachs (1967) study you read about in Chapter 8 was a classic example of early comprehension research, with a straightforward conclusion. Recall that as people were reading a passage, they were interrupted and tested on a target sentence, either 0, 80, or 160 syllables after the end of the target. Their recognition of the sentence was very accurate at the immediate interval. But beyond that, they were accurate only at rejecting the choice that changed the sentence meaning. That is, people could not accurately discriminate between the true target sentence and the paraphrases: If the choice preserved the original meaning, then people mistakenly "recognized" it. Clearly, these results showed that memory for meaningful passages does not retain verbatim sentences for very long but does retain meaning quite well.

Online Comprehension Tasks

As work on comprehension developed, researchers needed *a task that measures comprehension as it happens*, or an **online comprehension** task. Online comprehension tasks involve the same approach you've been reading about throughout this book: Find a dynamic, time- or action-based task that yields measurements of the underlying mental processes as they occur. Contrast performance in a variety of conditions, pitting factors against each other to see how they affect comprehension speed or difficulty. Then draw conclusions about the underlying mental processes, based on the performance measures.

WRITTEN LANGUAGE Perhaps the most direct assessment of cognition during comprehension involves reading times. These can be gathered by using eye movement data, or having people control the presentation by pressing a button to advance to the next word, clause, or sentence. Reading times for these individual components can then be analyzed, and inferences about online comprehension can be drawn. In general, aspects of comprehension that a person is prepared for are read more quickly, whereas those aspects that require a large involvement of mental resources will result in longer reading times.

▲ **TABLE 10-1 Sample Stimuli and Test Words for Online Comprehension Tasks**

Task	Sentence	Yes	Related	Unrelated	No
Was this word in the sentence?	Ken really liked the boxer.	Ken			Bill
Naming	Ken really liked the boxer.		Dog/fight	Plate	
Lexical decision	Ken really liked the boxer.		Dog/fight	Plate	Lamt

In one commonly used method, a text appears on a computer screen and is immediately followed by a probe word. Sometimes a person must make a "yes" or "no" response to the word, indicating whether it was in the just-read sentence. Sometimes the person must simply name the word or perform a lexical decision task on it. Look at ▲ Table 10-1 to see some sample stimuli and test words for these tasks.

Naturally, performance on these tasks would be timed, and the times would lead us to inferences about the nature and operation of cognition. For example, if the ambiguous word *boxer* activates both the dog and the fighter meanings, then we might expect RT to dog and fight to be about the same, and both of these faster than to the neutral word *plate*. But if *boxer* is interpreted only in one of its two senses, then dog would be faster than fight (or the other way around, depending on which meaning is dominant).

Another way of assessing online comprehension that can be very useful, in addition to measures such as reading times and probe tasks, is the think-aloud verbal protocol method (e.g., Magliano, Trabasso, & Graesser, 1999). In this method, people are asked to verbalize their thoughts as they read a passage of text. The verbal protocols can then be analyzed later to assess what conscious thoughts people were having as they read. For example, how do they link up a current portion of text with events that occurred earlier, were they making predictions about what would happen next, did they notice an inconsistency in the text, and so on? The data generated from think aloud protocols can provide insight into what aspects of a text might be fruitful candidates for further research. For example, this information can be used to focus investigation of which aspects of a text will yield interesting reading time data, or what kind of information to test for using a probe task.

Finally, as in many other areas of cognitive psychology, there has been an increase in the use of neural imaging measures to aid our investigations. For online comprehension, these measures often require the temporal resolution necessary to capture understanding across relatively brief periods of time, as would be done with ERP and fMRI recordings. Using these methods, we can reveal aspects of comprehension that might be difficult to uncover otherwise.

Metacomprehension

Just because you read a passage, and have some understanding of what you've read, doesn't mean you've actually learned something, or will remember it later. Yet, we need to constantly use our **metacomprehension** abilities (e.g., Dunlosky & Lipko, 2007) to *monitor how well we are understanding and will remember information later*. Metacomprehension is important for comprehension and memory because it can influence how much we may study information later, and just what information we devote our time to.

A popular measure of metacomprehension is **judgments of learning** (JOLs) (Arbuckle & Cuddy, 1969). These are *estimates people are asked to make of how well they feel they have learned some material they have just read* (recall that we talked about judgments of learning in Chapter 9 too). Research on JOLs typically compares people's estimates of how well they have learned information with how they actually perform. Unfortunately, in many cases, the relationship between JOLs and actual performance is quite low—in other words, people are typically not very good at estimating whether they've learned something or not. As a consequence, when you plan your later studying and review, say for an upcoming exam, you may not spend the time you need on some material because you think you know it better than you really do. Your test performance would be better if you could better monitor what you have and have not learned.

In addition to the difficulty people having judging whether they have learned something, people also have metacomprehension problems when it comes to choosing how to plan or distribute their study time. Here's an example: Although you learned in Chapter 8 that memory is worse when people study using massed practice (cramming), rather than distributed practice, many people are unaware that massed practice is a poor learning strategy. Another metacomprehension error that people make is to spend their study time focusing on very difficult material. The problem with this is that it is an inefficient comprehension and learning strategy (Nelson & Leonesio, 1988). This **labor-in-vain effect** occurs when *people spend large amounts of time trying to learn information that is too far beyond their current level of knowledge, but end up with little to no new learning.*

A better comprehension strategy is to spend time learning information that falls within the **region of proximal learning** (e.g., Metcalfe, 2002). This is *information that is just beyond a person's current level of understanding.* So, what we have here is a bit like the Goldilocks and the Three Bears story. Obviously it is a waste of time to study information that one knows well (this material is too soft). Also, as the labor-in-vain effect shows, trying to study information that is far too difficult will not help performance either (this material is too hard). However, learning that occurs in the region of proximal learning is just beyond what a person currently knows, so he or she can draw on his or her existing knowledge to use as a scaffolding to integrate the new information into (this material is just right).

In general, most classroom settings are already set up to take advantage of the region of proximal learning, provided you've had the prerequisites, and you keep up with the material in the class. In addition to this, what are some other ways to improve your metacomprehension estimates? Here are three (cf. Dunlosky & Lipko, 2007; Griffin, Wiley, & Thiede, 2008). First, before making a judgment about whether you've learned something or not, wait a few minutes (Dunlosky & Nelson, 1994). Often, when people are making judgments of learning, they are assessing whether they can retrieve the information from long-term memory into working memory. But when you make these judgments right after reading material, there is still a lot of information *in* working memory, and so you are overconfident in your ability to remember the information later when you need it (did you remember this from the last chapter?). Second, rereading the material can also be very helpful. Reading the material prior to lecture, then going to lecture can give you the same benefit, and will save you time and effort later. Finally, generating summaries, or even lists of key words, can boost the accuracy of your JOLs. In this way you will help reveal to yourself what you do and do not know.

Comprehension as Mental Structure Building

A convenient way to organize thinking about comprehension is to use Gernsbacher's (1990) **structure-building** framework as a touchstone. The theory is summarized in Table 10-2. The basic theme is that comprehension is a process of building mental structures. Laying a foundation, mapping information onto the structure, and shifting to new structures are the three principal components.

LAYING A FOUNDATION As we read we begin to build a mental structure that stores the meaning of the sentence in memory. A foundation is initiated as the sentence begins, and typically is built around the first mentioned character or idea. This is equivalent to saying that sentence 6 is about Dave and studying:

(6) Dave was studying hard for his statistics midterm.

MAPPING INFORMATION As more elements appear in the sentence, they are added to the structure, by the process called **mapping**. Mapping here simply means that additional word and concept meanings are added to the "DAVE" structure, elaborating that structure by specifying Dave's activities. For instance, the prepositional phrase "for his statistics midterm" is processed. Because the concept "MIDTERM" is a coherent idea in the context of studying, these words or memory nodes are added to the structure. Inferences that you draw as you read would be added to the structure. For instance, when your conceptual knowledge about "MIDTERM" was activated, you drew the inference that Dave probably was enrolled in a statistics course.

SHIFTING TO A NEW STRUCTURE We continue trying to map incoming words to the current structure on the assumption that those words belong to the structure under construction right now. But at some point, a different idea is encountered that signals a change in focus or topic shift. As an example, consider this continuation of the Dave story:

(7) Because the professor had a reputation for giving difficult exams, the students knew they'd have to be well prepared.

When you read "Because the professor," a coherence process detects the change in topic or focus. One clue is the word *because* or other connectives (e.g., *later*, *although*,

TABLE 10-2 Summary of Gernsbacher's Structure-Building Framework

Process	Explanation
1. Laying a foundation	Initiate a structure for representing clause or sentence meaning.
2. Mapping information	Map or store congruent information into the current structure.
3. Shifting	Initiate a new structure to represent a new or different idea.
Control Mechanisms	**Function**
1. Enhancement	Increase the activation of coherent, related information.
2. Suppression	Dampen the activation of information no longer relevant to current structure.

meanwhile). Another clue involves the introduction of a new character and the inferences you need to draw to figure out who the professor is; you inferred that Dave must be enrolled in a statistics class; and, because midterms are exams given in college classes that are taught by professors, the professor must be the one who teaches that statistics class. At such moments, you close off or finish the "Dave structure" and begin a new one, one about the professor. Although the "Dave structure" still retains its prominence in memory, you are now working on a new current structure, mapping the incoming ideas (e.g., reputation, difficult exams) onto it. And at the end of that phrase, you will have constructed two related but separate structures, one for each meaning (the phrase beginning "the students" will trigger yet another structure to be built, yielding three substructures).

ENHANCEMENT AND SUPPRESSION Finally, two control mechanisms link up with the process of spreading activation. Let's add one more sentence to the Dave story:

> *(6) Dave was studying hard for his statistics midterm.*
>
> *(7) Because the professor had a reputation for giving difficult exams, the students knew they'd have to be well prepared.*
>
> *(8) Dave wanted an A on that test.*

As noted earlier, reading sentence 7 results in a new substructure and a change in focus. Still, the new substructure is related to the first one. That is, two prominent ideas in sentence 7 map onto the ideas from sentence 6; *exams* refers with a different name to the same concept as *midterms*, and the *professor* maps onto the statistics course implied by sentence 6. Such mappings reflect the activation of related memory concepts, especially those mapped into the foundation of the first structure (Millis & Just, 1994). This activation combines with the activation from *midterm* and *statistics course* because of their semantic relatedness. This is the process of **enhancement**, that the many related *concepts are now boosted or enhanced in their level of activation*. This enhancement process is the spreading activation process in semantic memory. It is the degree of enhancement and activation among concepts that predicts which ones will be remembered better or responded to more rapidly. And the more frequently the same set of concepts is enhanced across a sentence, the more coherent the passage is.

Note, however, that the enhancement of some concepts implies that others will lose activation. That is, while sentence 7 enhances the activation of concepts related to "*PROFESSOR*," "*EXAM*," and so on, there is also **suppression** of concepts that are now out of the main discourse focus. In other words, *activated concepts that become unrelated to the focus decrease in activation* by the process of suppression. Figure 10-1 is an illustration of these competing tendencies. Note that as the professor clause is being processed (ideas 3 and 4), the activation level for "DAVE" is suppressed because it's no longer the main discourse focus. Then, as the story unfolds further (ideas 5 to 7), the concept "DAVE" regains its enhancement, and the "PROFESSOR" dwindles. Thus the original Dave structure from sentence 6 receives renewed enhancement when you read in sentence 8 that Dave wanted an *A* on the test (O'Brien, Albrecht, Hakala, & Rizzella, 1995; for an extension of enhancement and suppression to the topic of metaphor comprehension, see Gernsbacher, Keysar, Robertson, & Werner, 2001, and Kintsch, 2000). And, in the meantime, less important concepts become suppressed (or less activated in comparison to central concepts; e.g., McNamara & McDaniel, 2004).

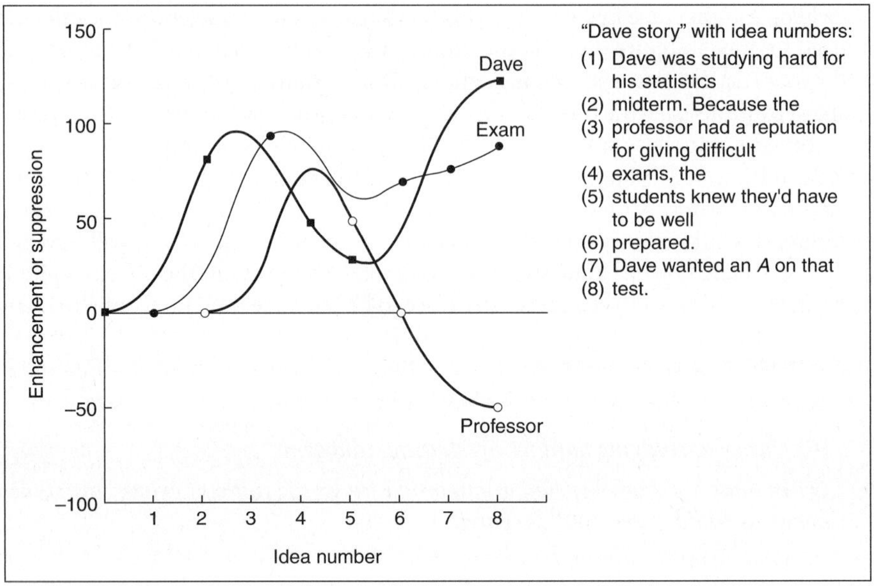
150
100
50
0
−50
−100
Enhancement or suppression
1 2 3 4 5 6 7 8
Idea number
Dave
Exam
Professor
"Dave story" with idea numbers:
(1) Dave was studying hard for his statistics
(2) midterm. Because the
(3) professor had a reputation for giving difficult
(4) exams, the
(5) students knew they'd have to be well
(6) prepared.
(7) Dave wanted an *A* on that
(8) test.

◆ **FIGURE 10-1** Hypothetical activation curves for the concepts *Dave*, *exam*, and *professor* from the "Dave story" in the text. As concepts are introduced or mentioned again (*Dave*, *exam*), their activation becomes enhanced. When the focus shifts, old concepts (*professor*) become suppressed; that is, their activation dwindles.

Levels of Comprehension

As you read earlier, comprehension is a truly complex process, involving a number of different levels. One of the ways of characterizing these different levels was already discussed in Chapter 8, namely van Dijk and Kintsch's (1983) levels of representation theory. As a reminder, at one level is the **surface form**. This is our verbatim mental representation of the exact words and syntax used in a passage of text. At an intermediate level is the **propositional textbase**, which captures the basic idea units present in a text. Finally, there is the level of the *situation model* (Johnson-Laird, 1983; Van Dijk & Kintsch, 1983; Zwaan & Radvansky, 1998), which is *a mental representation that serves as a simulation of a real or possible world as described by a text.*

As you read, try to keep in mind and understand how comprehension may depend on these different levels. For example, research on order of mention in establishing discourse reference will depend on the surface form. Work on bridging inferences requires processing at the textbase level. And finally, work showing how people monitor various aspects of experience involves the situation model.

Section Summary

- A variety of online tasks have been devised to investigate comprehension, such as tasks involving reading times, interruption during reading with memory probe tasks, the use of think-aloud protocols, and neuroimaging evidence.
- Successful comprehension is best achieved when people can self-monitor what they are and are not learning, through judgments of learning. However, these judgments are often poor estimates of how much has actually been learned.

Estimates can be improved by delaying these judgments, rereading, and providing summaries of the material.

- Comprehension involves processing at many levels, including the surface form, textbase, and situation model levels. Evidence of processing at each of these levels can be derived across many different aspects of understanding.

READING

For years, the standard methodology for studying reading had people read a passage of text, then take a memory test, such as a multiple choice or recall test. Such tasks certainly have face validity; they test memory for the text, because much of our reading is for the purpose of learning and remembering what we read.

But this methodology suffers from the fact that it doesn't gather online measures of comprehension, only what people remember of their experience of reading (not that this isn't important, there's just more to what's going on). In Figure 10-1 you saw a graph showing the hypothetical activation levels for concepts in a set of sentences. We would like to know *directly* how concepts vary in their activation levels across a passage because that would tell us a great deal about online reading comprehension. A multiple choice test is far too blunt to give us such answers.

Gaze Duration

At the end of Chapter 9, you saw a figure of eye gaze fixation times, where those times went up when the ambiguity of a sentence became apparent (see Figure 9-12). *This* reveals mental processing at the level of eye gazes, levels of activation, and so on. And this is a methodology you'll read about in this section.

In reading research that assesses gaze duration, the equipment used is called an **eye tracker**, a camera- and computer-based apparatus that records eye movements and the exact words that are fixated in successive eye fixations or gazes; one is depicted in the accompanying photo. In this system, continuous recording of at least one of the eyes, while keeping track of head position, enables the system to determine exactly what you're looking at on the computer screen. As such, the machine records the duration of the eyes' gaze as they scan across lines of text (this system has other purposes in addition to reading, such as evaluating the usefulness of web pages). In one version of this task, people simply see a passage of text on the screen, and the eye tracker apparatus records the eye movements and durations as the words in the passage are read. In another version of this task, people are shown text on a computer screen in a moving

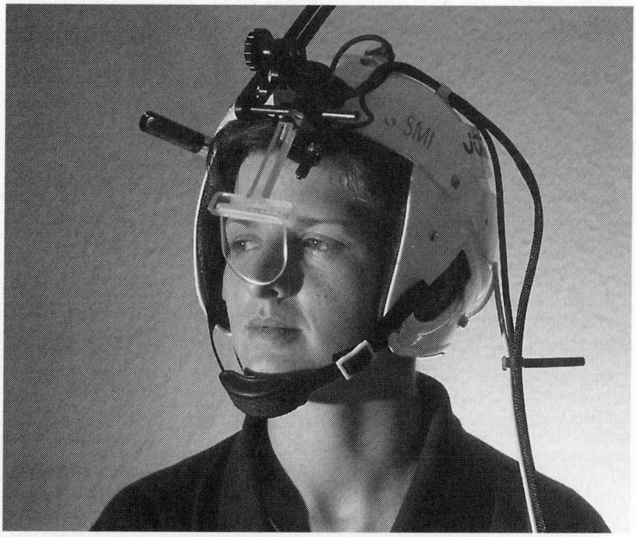

One, monitors the position of the eyes and head as a person scans a computer screen or the environment.

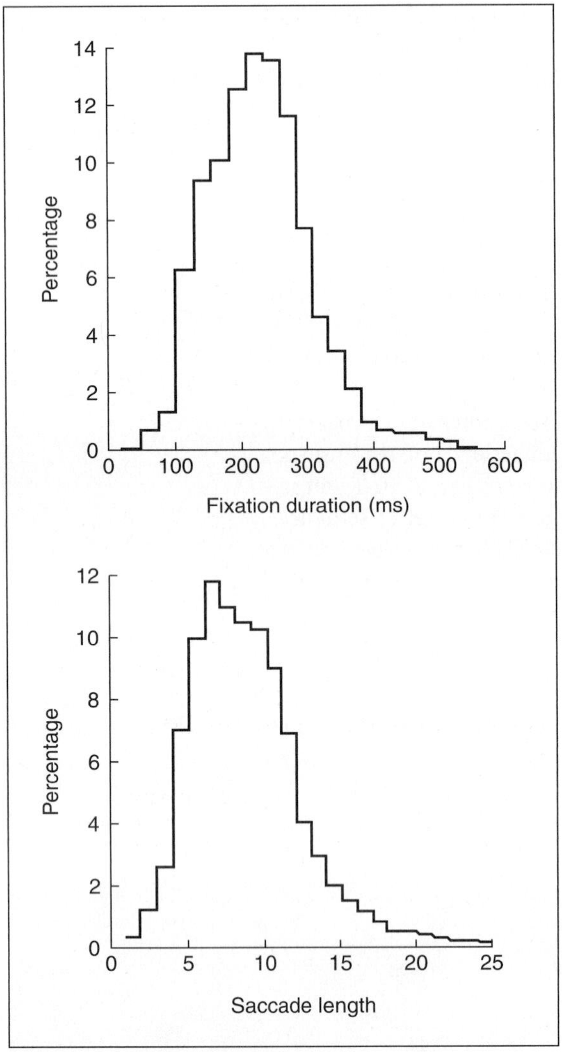

■ **FIGURE 10-2**
Frequency distributions for fixation durations (top) in ms, and saccade length (bottom) in number of character spaces. From Rayner (1998).

window methodology: A word appears briefly at the appropriate location for the current eye fixation, and as the eyes shift to the next fixation point, the first word is concealed as the next one appears.

In both of these tasks, the researcher knows which word is being processed on a moment-by-moment basis and *how long the eyes dwell on each word*, so **gaze duration** is a prime measure of what's going on when people read (see Kambe, Duffy, Clifton, & Rayner, 2003, and Rayner, 1998, for thorough discussions of alternatives). Just as RT measures gave us a window through which to study mental processes, time-based eye movement data provide a window on the process of comprehension and reading.

As you recall from Chapter 3, the eyes move in rapid sweeps—*saccades*—and then stop to focus on a word—**fixations**. Fixations in reading (English) last about 200 to 250 ms, and the average saccade size is from seven to nine letter spaces, although as Figure 10-2 ■ shows, there is considerable variability in these measures (Rayner, 1998). Eye tracking gives us gaze durations on a word-by-word basis, as shown in Figure 10-3. ★ Notice in the left panel of the figure, a good reader moves fairly rapidly through the text (fixation durations in ms are in the circles above the words) and in a forward direction, at least on this passage. In contrast, the poor reader shown in the right panel moves more slowly through the text and makes many regressive eye movements, i.e., returns to an already fixated word. Even at this level of detail, we can draw two conclusions. First, poor readers spend more time going back to reread what they've already processed, and can spend considerably more time on some words than good readers do (e.g., 2,065 ms versus 267 ms on "topography"). Second, even good readers spend variable amounts of time on different words, for example as little as 100 ms on "such" but 566 ms on "a knowledge." This second point is important because characteristics of the words and passages themselves exert a tremendous influence on how we read.

Two assumptions that have guided much of the work using eye movements were the immediacy assumption and the eye-mind assumption (Just & Carpenter, 1980, 1987, 1992). The **immediacy assumption** states that *readers try to interpret each content word of a text as that word is encountered in the passage.* In other words, we do not wait until we take in a group of words, say in a phrase, before we start to process them. Instead, we begin interpreting and comprehending immediately, as soon as we encounter a word in the text. The **eye–mind assumption** is the idea that *the pattern of eye movements directly reflects the complexity of the underlying cognitive processes.*

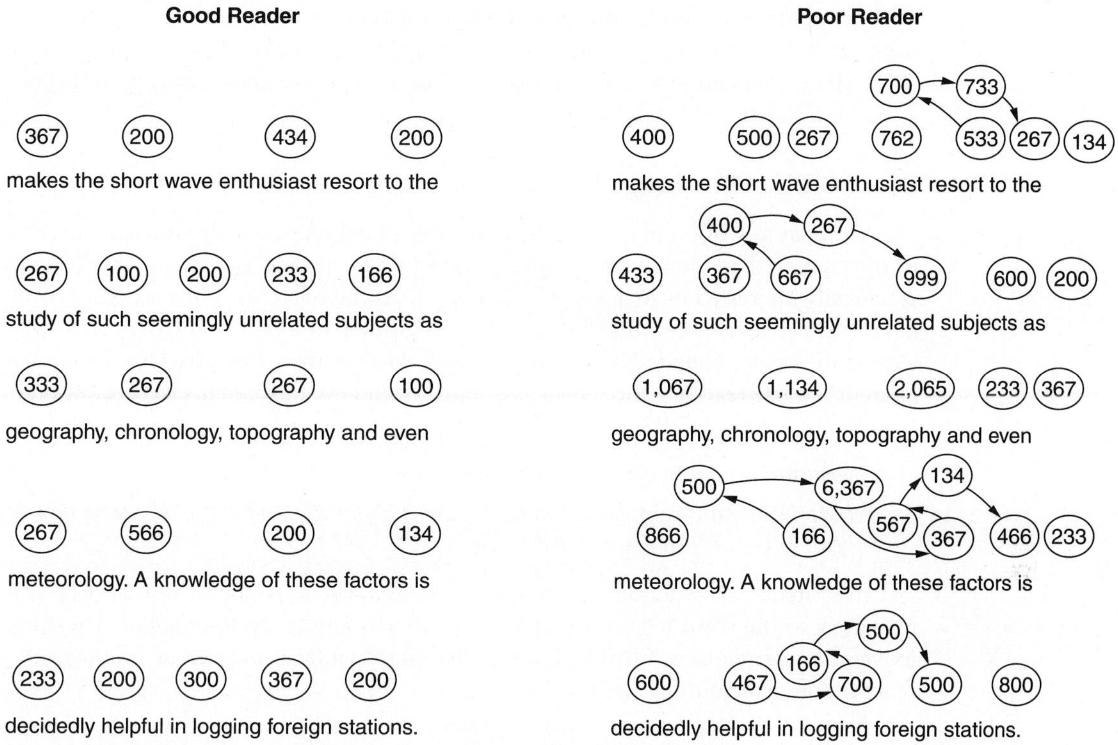

★ **FIGURE 10-3**
The pattern of fixations of a good (left panel) and poor (right panel) reader, showing where the fixations occurred in the sentences and the duration of the fixations (in the circles above the fixation points, measured in ms). Arrows indicate regressive eye movements to earlier words; otherwise the fixations went from left to right. From Just, M.A., & Carpenter, P.A. (1987), *The psychology of reading and language comprehension*. Boston: Allyn & Bacon. Figure 2.1 (p. 27). Credited source Buswell, G. T. (1937). *How adults read*. Chicago: Chicago University Press, Plates II and IV, pp. 6, 7.

While these assumptions allowed a great deal of work to be done in research on reading, and they come close to characterizing the relationship between eye movements and cognition, they do have some limitations. There are limits and constraints on the degree to which eye movements reflect underlying cognition. For example, eye gazes often take in more than one word, depending on the length of the words, the size of the text fonts, and the span of the perceptual beam. So, there is not always a direct one-to-one relationship between an eye fixation and the words being processed. Moreover, eye gazes reflect not only the processing of the current word, but can also reflect the continued processing of previous words, and some anticipatory processing of upcoming words (Kliegl, Nuthmann, & Engbert, 2006). Despite these limits, eye gaze recordings are still a powerful and valuable measure in the reading researcher's toolbox.

Outside of reading, eye gaze can be used to understand other aspects of comprehension, such as the understanding of spoken language. For example, if you listen to and follow a set of directions, say to pick up and move an object from one place to another, your eye movements track the spoken instructions very closely—as you hear,

"Put the apple in the box," your eyes fixate immediately on those objects in the visual scene (Spivey, Tanenhaus, Eberhard, & Sedivy, 2002; see Crosby, Monin, & Richardson, 2008, for an application of eye tracking methods to a question of social cognition, conversational rules, and racism).

Basic Online Reading Effects

An early example of online reading research examined regressive eye movements, that is, movements back to a portion of text that had been read earlier. Just (1976) was specifically interested in such eye movements when the referents in the sentence could not be immediately determined: If an initial assignment of a character to a case role was wrong, then what happened? Was there a regressive eye movement back to the correct referent? People read sentences such as 17 and 18, and eye movements were monitored:

> *(17) The tenant complained to his landlord about the leaky roof. The next day, he went to the attic to get his luggage.*
>
> *(18) The tenant complained to his landlord about the leaky roof. The next day, he went to the attic to repair the damage.*

In sentence 17, when *luggage* was encountered, eye movements bounced up immediately to the word *tenant*. In sentence 18 they bounced up to *landlord*. These eye movements provided evidence of the underlying mental processes of finding antecedents and determining case roles.

Another study provides a demonstration of the detail afforded by eye-trackers. ▲ Look at Figure 10-4, taken from Just and Carpenter (1987; see also Just & Carpenter, 1980). You see two sentences taken from a larger passage. Above the words are two numbers. The top number indicates the order in which people fixated on the elements in the sentence; 1 to 9 in the first sentence and 1 to 21 in the second. The number below is the gaze duration (in ms). So, as an example, the initial word in sentence 1, *Flywheels*, was fixated for 1,566 ms, slightly more than a second and a half. The next word, *are*, was fixated only 267 ms. The fourth word, *of*, wasn't fixated at all by this per-

1 2 3 4 5 6 7 8 9
1566 267 400 83 267 617 767 450 450
Flywheels are one of the oldest mechanical devices known to man.

1 2 3 4 5 6 7
400 616 517 684 250 317 617
Every internal- combustion engine contains a small

8 9 10 11 12 13
1116 367 467 483 450 383
flywheel that converts the jerky motion of the pistons into the

14 15 16 17 18 19 20 21
284 383 317 283 533 50 366 566
smooth flow of energy that powers the drive shaft.

▲ FIGURE 10-4 Eye fixations of a college student reading a scientific passage. Gazes within each sentence are sequentially numbered above the fixated words with the durations (in ms) indicated below the sequence number. From Just and Carpenter (1980).

son, so neither a gaze number nor time is presented there (this is why the "FINISHED FILES" example in Chapter 2 worked: You didn't fixate the function word *of*; see Koriat & Greenberg, 1996). In fact, you can raerragne the lteters in wodrs, usch as is odne in this snentence, and, people have little trouble extracting the meaning. There is some disruption to reading, but not as much as if different letters are substituted for correct letters (Rayner, White, Johnson, and Liversedge, 2006). This suggests that reading does not *require* a strict adherence to the printed form.

In the Just and Carpenter study, these passages were technical writing, in which a new concept, such as a flywheel, is introduced, defined, and explained (indeed, students rated themselves as "entirely unfamiliar" with the topic prior to reading). The average reading rate was about 225 words per minute, slower than for simpler material, such as newspaper stories or novels.

At a general level, note that every content word was fixated. According to Just and Carpenter, this is the norm for all kinds of text. In fact, about 85% of the content words are fixated. Short function words, however, like *the* or *of* often tend not to be fixated; Rayner and Duffy (1988) estimate that function words are fixated only about 35% of the time. Readers also tend to skip some content words if the passage is very simple for them (say, a children's story given to an adult), if they are skimming or speed reading, or if a word is very predictable, based on other constraints in the sentence (Rayner & Well, 1996).

As noted already, gaze durations are quite variable. Recall in Chapter 3 that the duration of a saccade was about 100 ms, followed by a fixation that lasts around 200 to 250 ms. These estimates come from situations in which the viewer is merely gazing out upon a scene, for instance. In reading studies, however, people don't move their eyes as far as in scene perception, averaging 2° of angle versus 5° in scene perception. Hence, saccades during reading are shorter—Rayner (1998) suggests that reading saccades take about 30 ms, versus 40 to 50 ms in scene perception. Although word fixations may be brief, readers often make repeated fixations on the *same* word. In some studies, successive fixations are summed together for data analysis; alternatively, investigators report the first-pass fixations, and sometimes total fixation duration as well. Irwin (1998; also Rayner, 1998), suggests that mental processing continues during saccades, suggesting that we should add saccade time to gaze durations.

A Model of Reading

A real strength of online reading measures is that they provide evidence at *two* levels of comprehension. First, there is evidence of processing at more microscopic, word-level processes at the surface form level. These are crucial to an understanding of reading, and a good deal of evidence at this level exists. For instance, several studies attest to the early use of syntactic features of a sentence when we comprehend not just major syntactic characteristics such as phrase boundaries but even characteristics such as subject–verb agreement (Pearlmutter, Garnsey, & Bock, 1999) and pronoun gender (McDonald & MacWhinney, 1995). Reichle et al. (1998) provide an account of such word-level processes with their E-Z Reader models of eye movement control in reading.

Reading time measures can also be used to examine larger, macroscopic processes, such as comprehension processes at the textbase and situation model levels. We'll hold off a discussion of situation model processing until the next section. At the textbase level, Table 10-3 presents the Just and Carpenter (1980) analysis of the "flywheel" passage in a sector-by-sector fashion—roughly speaking, an idea unit. To the left of each line is a category label; each sector was categorized as to its role in the overall paragraph structure. To the right are two columns of numbers—observed gaze durations for a group of people and estimated durations—based on the "*READER*" model's predictions. For example, the 1,921 ms observed for sector 1 is the sum of the separate gaze

TABLE 10-3 Sector-by-Sector Analysis of "Flywheel" Passage

		Gaze Duration (ms)	
Category	**Sector**	**Observed**	**Estimated**
Topic	Flywheels are one of the oldest mechanical devices	1,921	1,999
Topic	known to man.	478	680
Expansion	Every internal-combustion engine contains a small flywheel	2,316	2,398
Expansion	that converts the jerky motion of the pistons into the smooth flow of energy	2,477	2,807
Expansion	that powers the drive shaft.	1,056	1,264
Cause	The greater the mass of a flywheel and the faster it spins,	2,143	2,304
Consequence	the more energy can be stored in it.	1,270	1,536
Subtopic	But its maximum spinning speed is limited by the strength of the material	2,400	2,553
Subtopic	it is made from.	615	780
Expansion	If it spins too fast for its mass,	1,414	1,502
Expansion	any flywheel will fly apart.	1,200	1,304
Definition	One type of flywheel consists of round sandwiches of fiberglass and rubber	2,746	3,064
Expansion	providing the maximum possible storage of energy	1,799	1,870
Expansion	when the wheel is confined in a small space	1,522	1,448
Detail	as in an automobile.	769	718
Definition	Another type, the "superflywheel," consists of a series of rimless spokes.	2,938	2,830
Expansion	This flywheel stores the maximum energy	1,416	1,596
Detail	when space is unlimited.	1,289	1,252

Just and Carpenter (1980).

durations for that sector (averaged across people). Note also that different kinds of sectors take different amounts of time; for instance, definition sectors have more difficult words in them and are longer than other sector types, so they show longer gaze durations. Even a casual examination of the observed and predicted scores shows that the model does a good job of predicting reading times.

So, in general, an analysis of reading times needs to take into account a number of surface form and textbase factors that are tied to the text itself. For example, reading time is strongly influenced by word length, with words that are composed of more letters or syllables taking longer to read than shorter words. Also, word frequency plays a vital role, with infrequent words resulting in longer reading times as the reader needs to engage in extra mental effort to retrieve this lexical information from memory. Serial position is also an important factor. The further along a person is in a passage, the more of a foundation there is from which to build mental structures, thereby making comprehension easier and faster. Finally, when new arguments are introduced into a passage, this can also increase reading time, because the reader must set up new mental structures to accommodate the new ideas. A more complete listing of factors is shown in Table 10-4.

MODEL ARCHITECTURE AND PROCESSES Figure 10-5 illustrates the architecture and processes of the Just and Carpenter (1980, 1987, 1992) model. Note that several elements are already familiar. For instance, working memory is the location where different types of knowledge—visual, lexical, syntactic, semantic, and so forth—are combined. Not surprisingly, the evidence confirms the importance of working memory in reading comprehension (e.g., Kaakinen, Hyona, & Keenan, 2003). Long-term memory contains a wide variety of knowledge types, semantic knowledge, and knowledge of discourse structure, essentially the kind of information that tells us how passages of text are structured. Additionally, both scheme of domain information, which we've called schemata and scripts, and a person's episodic information are also included. Each of these types of knowledge can match the current contents of working memory and update or alter those contents. In simple terms, what you know combines with what you've already read and understood, and together these permit comprehension of what you are reading now.

Finally, in longer passages, such as the "flywheel" text, two additional processes are observed. Wrap-up is an integrative process that occurs at the end of a sentence or clause. During wrap-up, readers tie up any loose ends; for instance, any remaining inconsistencies or uncertainties about reference are resolved here.

TABLE 10-4 Variables that Affect Reading Times

Variables that Increase Reading Times:

Surface form effects: sweep of the eyes to start a new line, sentence wrap-up, number of syllables, low frequency or new word, unusual spelling patterns

Textbase effects: integration of information (after clauses, sentences, sectors, etc.), topic word, new argument, other error recovery, reference and inference processes, difficulty of passage/topic

Variables that Decrease Reading Times:

Surface form effects: familiar word, higher word frequency, repetition of infrequent word

Textbase effects: appropriate title, supportive context, semantic-based expectation (if confirmed)

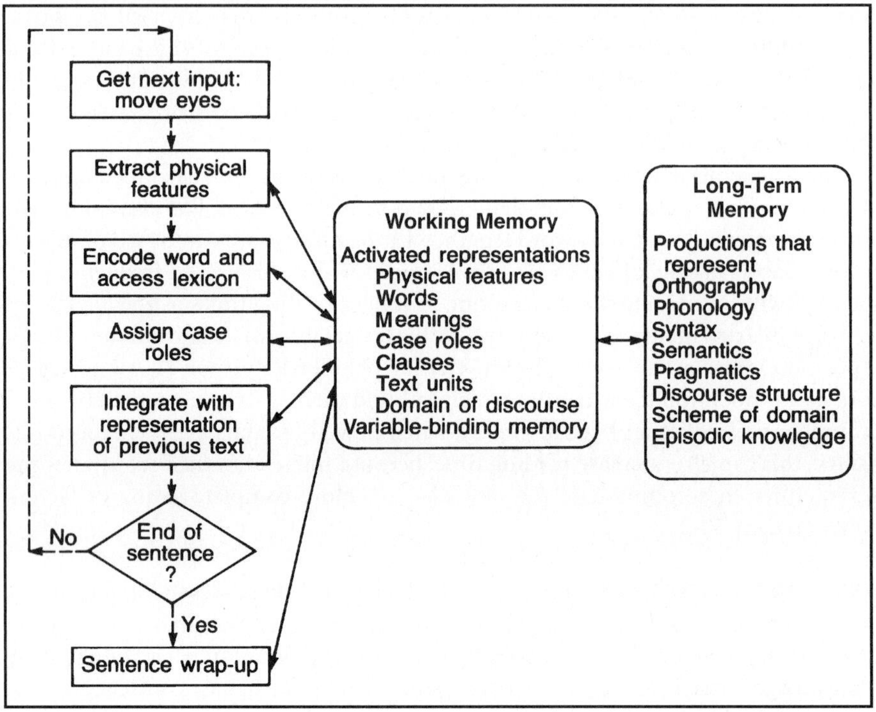

FIGURE 10-5 The Just and Carpenter (1980) model, showing the major structures and processes that operate during reading. Solid lines represent the pathways of information flow; the dashed line shows the typical sequence of processing.

AN OVERVIEW Table 10-4 summarizes surface form and textbase factors that can influence reading times. It also illustrates that online studies have made significant headway in understanding the complex processes of reading. Careful inspection of the table and the gaze durations in Figure 10-4 and Table 10-3 shows several correspondences between text characteristics and gaze durations. For instance, the word *flywheels*, at the beginning of the passage, has a lengthy gaze for several reasons: It is at the beginning of a line, it is a rare word, and it is a topic word in the discourse structure. Note that the second occurrence of *flywheel* has a shorter duration, partly because it is a repetition of a word held in working memory. In Table 10-3, contrast sector 9, "it is made from," with sector 18, "when space is unlimited." Although each has four words, sector 9 has a gaze duration of 615 ms, compared with the 1,289 ms on sector 18. Part of this difference results from the frequency of the words in sector 9 and the fact that this sector conveys less information. Sector 18, conversely, contains a word with four syllables, the last word in a sentence, and the last word in a paragraph.

Other Influences on Reading

An in-depth description of the experiments that support the various models of reading is not possible here—there are simply too many of them to be listed in the space available. Reading comprehension research has become an active area of investigation. Here is just a brief list of some work attesting to the importance of factors listed in Table 10-4:

- The effects of word frequency, syntactic structure, and context (Altmann, Garnham, & Dennis, 1992; Inhoff, 1984; Juhasz & Rayner, 2003; Schilling, Rayner, & Chumbley, 1998)

- The effects of sentence context on word identification (Paul et al., 1992; Schustack, Ehrlich, & Rayner, 1987; Simpson, Casteel, Peterson, & Burgess, 1989), including ERP work showing how rapidly we resolve anaphoric references (van Berkum, Brown, & Hagoort, 1999)
- The effects of ambiguity (Frazier & Rayner, 1990; Rayner & Frazier, 1989) and figurative language (Frisson & Pickering, 1999)
- The effects of topic, plausibility, and thematic structure on reading (O'Brien & Myers, 1987; Pickering & Traxler, 1998; Rayner, Warren, Juhasz, & Liversedge, 2004; Speer & Clifton, 1998; Taraban & McClelland, 1988), especially the relatedness of successive paragraphs and the presence of an informative introductory paragraph (Lorch, Lorch, & Matthews, 1985) or title (Wiley & Rayner, 2000)
- The effects of scripted knowledge on word recognition and comprehension (Sharkey & Mitchell, 1985)
- The effects of discourse structure on the understanding of reference (Malt, 1985; Murphy, 1985) and the resolution of ambiguity (Vu, Kellas, Metcalf, & Herman, 2000)

Additionally, even phonology plays an important role in reading comprehension, such as research showing that phonological information is activated as rapidly as semantic knowledge in silent reading (Lee, Rayner, & Pollatsek, 1999; Rayner, Pollatsek, & Binder, 1998), especially for readers of lower skill levels who rely more on print-to-sound-to-meaning processes than a direct print-to-meaning route (Jared, Levy, & Rayner, 1999).

Furthermore, reading comprehension is affected by linguistic effects in the text as well as by characteristics of the reader. We have already discussed a number of ways that people differ in their language ability, such as the resolution of polysemy, the size of their working memory capacity, and the decoding of words into their meanings.

Section Summary

- Tremendous progress has been made in understanding the mental processes of reading, largely by using the online measures of comprehension, such as reading times and gaze durations.
- Modern models of reading make predictions about reading comprehension based on a variety of factors; for instance, word frequency and recency in the passage influence surface form and textbase processing, respectively.
- Online measures of language comprehension provide a unique window into human cognition. Using these sorts of measures, we can gain moment-to-moment insights into not only the effectiveness of processing, as with reading times, but also into the very contents of people's minds, as with memory probe tasks.

REFERENCE, SITUATION MODELS, AND EVENTS

While the cognitive mechanisms and processes involved in comprehension at the surface form and textbase levels are critically important, they are not the only goals of comprehension. For example, a person who has successfully comprehended something that's been read has not only derived an adequate representation of the text itself. This person also has a fairly clear understanding of the circumstances that are being described—the reference of the text. In this section, we'll address this process of reference, the creation of the mental representations of the described state of affairs, the situation model, and explore how research on comprehension has moved on beyond language to capture event comprehension more generally.

Reference

Reference involves finding the connections between elements in a passage of text, finding the words that refer to other concepts in the sentence. In sentence 6 from earlier, "Dave was studying hard for his statistics midterm," the word *his* refers back to *Dave*. In this situation *Dave* is the **antecedent** of *his*, because *Dave* comes before the pronoun. And *the act of using a pronoun or possessive later on* is called **anaphoric reference**. So, **reference** is the *linguistic process of alluding to a concept by using another name*. Most commonly we use pronouns or synonyms to refer to the antecedent, although there are other types of reference. For example, using a person's name would be a form of identity reference in that it refers back to a previous instance of using their name.

To begin with, reference is as common in language as any other feature we can identify. Part of reference is that it tends to reduce redundancy and repetition. Contrast a normal passage such as 9a with 9b to see how boring and repetitive language would be without synonyms, pronouns, and so on.

> *(9a) Mike went to the pool to swim some laps. After his workout, he went to his psychology class. The professor asked him to summarize the chapter that he'd assigned the class to read.*
>
> *(9b) Mike went to the pool to swim some laps. After Mike swam some laps, Mike went to Mike's psychology class. The professor of Mike's psychology class asked Mike to summarize the chapter that Mike's psychology professor had assigned Mike's psychology class to read.*

This repetition of identity reference can actually be detrimental to comprehension. Research in reference and comprehension has shown what is known as the **repeated name penalty**, *an increase in reading times when a direct reference is used again (e.g., the person's name) compared to when a pronoun is used* (e.g., Almor, 1999; Gordon & Chan, 1995; Gordon & Scearce, 1995). That said, when we produce language, if there is more than one character being discussed or present in a situation, people are less likely to use indirect references, such as pronouns, and are more likely to use a direct reference, such as a person's name (Arnold & Griffin, 2007). This may be more acceptable under these circumstances because there may be some ambiguity as to whom the reference refers.

SIMPLE REFERENCE In naturally occurring discourse, different kinds of reference ★ can occur; Clark's (1977) useful list is shown in Table 10-5. Consider three simple forms of reference:

> *(10) I saw a convertible yesterday. The convertible was red.*
>
> *(11) I saw a convertible yesterday. The car was red.*
>
> *(12) I saw a convertible yesterday. It was red.*

TABLE 10-5 Types of Reference and Implication ★

Direct Reference

Identity. Michelle bought a computer. The computer was on sale.
Synonym. Michelle bought a computer. The machine was on sale.
Pronoun. Michelle bought a computer. It was on sale for 20% off.
Set membership. I talked to two people today. Michelle said she had just bought a computer.
Epithet. Michelle bought a computer. The stupid thing doesn't work.

Indirect Reference by Association

Necessary parts. Eric bought a used car. The tires were badly worn.
Probable parts. Eric bought a used car. The radio doesn't work.
Inducible parts. Eric bought a used car. The salesperson gave him a good price.

Indirect Reference by Characterization

Necessary roles. I taught my class yesterday. The time I started was 1:30.
Optional roles. I taught my class yesterday. The chalk tray was empty.

Other

Reasons. Rick asked a question in class. He hoped to impress the professor.
Causes. Rick answered a question in class. The professor had called on him.
Consequences. Rick asked a question in class. The professor was impressed.
Concurrences. Rick asked a question in class. Vicki tried to impress the professor too.

In sentence 10 the reference is so direct that it seems to require no inference on the part of the listener whatsoever; this is identity reference, using the definite article *the* to refer back to a previously introduced concept, *a convertible*. Likewise, synonym reference requires that you consider whether the second word is an adequate synonym for the first, as in sentence 11; can a convertible also be referred to as "the car"? Pronoun reference requires similar reference and inference steps. In sentence 12 *it* can refer only to the word *convertible*, because the only concept in the earlier phrase that can be equated with *it* is "*CONVERTIBLE.*" That is, in English, the word *it* must refer to an ungendered concept, just as *he* must refer to a male, and so forth. Contrast this with languages in which nouns have gender and pronouns must agree with the gender of the noun; translated literally from French, we get, "Here is the Eiffel Tower. She is beautiful."

An important aspect of reference, beyond the need to match gender and number, is that there is some evidence that the order in which antecedents are encountered influences the likelihood that they will be linked to later reference, consistent with Gernsbacher's structure building framework. Two major effects of this type are: the **advantage of first mention** and the **advantage of clause recency**. In the advantage of first mention, *characters and ideas that were mentioned first in a sentence, at the beginning of an episode, retain a special significance*. For example, in a study by Gernsbacher and Hargreaves (1988), a name probe appeared on the computer screen after a person finished reading the last word of a sentence. The task was to respond, as rapidly as possible, "yes" if the name probe had been in the sentence and "no" if it had not. Thus,

▲ **FIGURE 10-6** Mean reaction time to names that had appeared in the studied sentences when the name was the first- or second-mentioned participant and when the name played the agent or patient case role in the sentence. Data from Gernsbacher and Hargreaves (1988). From Gernsbacher (1990).

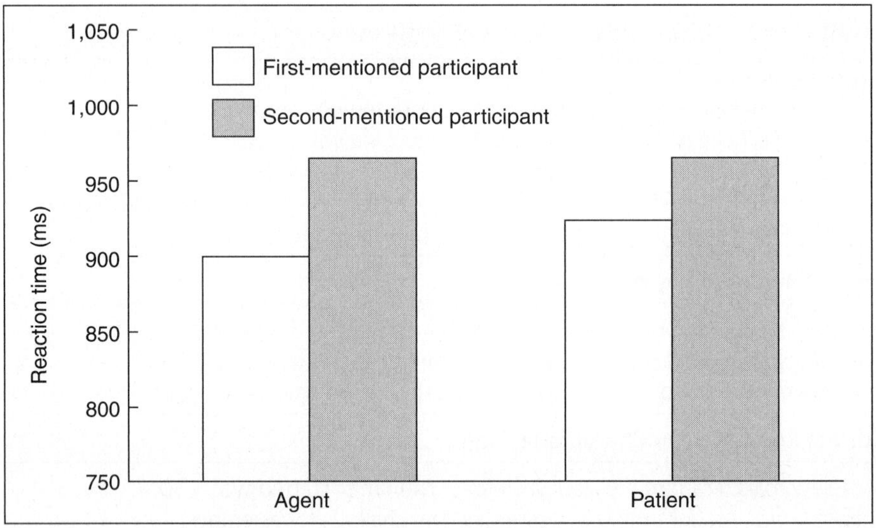

after reading a sentence such as "Tina gathered the kindling as Lisa set up the tent," you'd be shown *Tina*, *Lisa*, or some other name (to control for guessing). As Figure 10-6 shows, when the probe was the first-mentioned agent, it took people about 900 ms to say "yes," compared with more than 950 ms for responding to the second-mentioned agent. Thus, there was a 50 ms advantage of first mention.

There is also a period of time, at the end of the sentence, when the most recent character named has an advantage—this is the *advantage of clause recency*. Again, with the sentence "Tina gathered the kindling as Lisa set up the tent," if you are probed immediately after it, Lisa will have a slight advantage due to recency, but this advantage is short-lived. Immediate probes (no delay) showed a recency advantage of about 50 to 60 ms; but, if the probe was delayed 150 ms, the recency advantage was equal to the first-mention advantage—and after that, there was only evidence of the first-mention effect (Gernsbacher, Hargreaves, & Beeman, 1989). The recency effect goes away very shortly after reading, but the advantage of first mention persists.

Thus, beyond a very transitory recency effect, characters who appeared early in the story, who are in the main discourse focus, retain an advantage in performance; they remain accessible (McKoon, Ratcliff, Ward, & Sproat, 1993). Furthermore, it makes no difference if the first-mentioned character was the agent or patient in the structure, as shown in Figure 10-6; whether the sentence was in the active or passive voice; or whether the character was the syntactic subject of the sentence. The effect even generalizes to Spanish, which has greater flexibility than English in its word order rules (Carreiras, Gernsbacher, & Villa, 1995).

The advantage of first mention is more pronounced when that first character is mentioned by a proper name like Tina; McDonald and Shaibe (2002) found no advantage of first mention when the first-mentioned character was unnamed; e.g., in "The butler helped Calvin at the wedding reception," the butler had no special advantage, although Calvin did. Interestingly, we are not only sensitive to discourse focus when we read and comprehend (Birch & Garnsey, 1995; Birch & Rayner, 1997; Morris & Folk,

TABLE 10-6 Sample Sentences with Indefinite and Definite Articles

Indefinite	Definite
A grandmother sat at a table.	The grandmother sat at the table.
A child played in a backyard.	The child played in the backyard.
Some rain began to pour down.	The rain began to pour down.
An elderly woman led some others outside.	The elderly woman led the others outside.

1998), but we also manipulate the structure of the sentences we produce to highlight discourse focus (Ferreira, 1994). Overall, we use simple heuristics in language comprehension, e.g., that the first-mentioned character is the agent in the sentence, even though such heuristics can sometimes lead to errors in interpretation (see Ferreira, 2003, on the idea of processing heuristics in language comprehension that leads to "good enough" comprehension).

In further work, it has been found that even the article (e.g., *a* or *the*) used can influence reference. Definite articles, such as *the*, convey given information and make sentences seem more coherent and sensible as compared to when indefinite articles, such as *a*, *an*, and *some*, are used (Robertson et al., 2000; see Table 10-6 for sample sentences), and are remembered better later (Haviland & Clark, 1974). For Gernsbacher (1997), *the* is a cue for discourse coherence, enabling us to map information more efficiently and accurately. In one study (Robertson et al., 2000), people read sentences, followed by a recognition test (to make sure people actually tried to comprehend the sentences). Overall, sentences using *the* showed greater evidence of coherence than those with the indefinite *a*, *an*, and *some*. Importantly, people in this study were tested using functional magnetic resonance imaging (fMRI), and the levels of activity of different brain regions were measured. As Figure 10-7 shows, sentences that used the definite article showed greater activation than those with indefinite articles. Moreover,

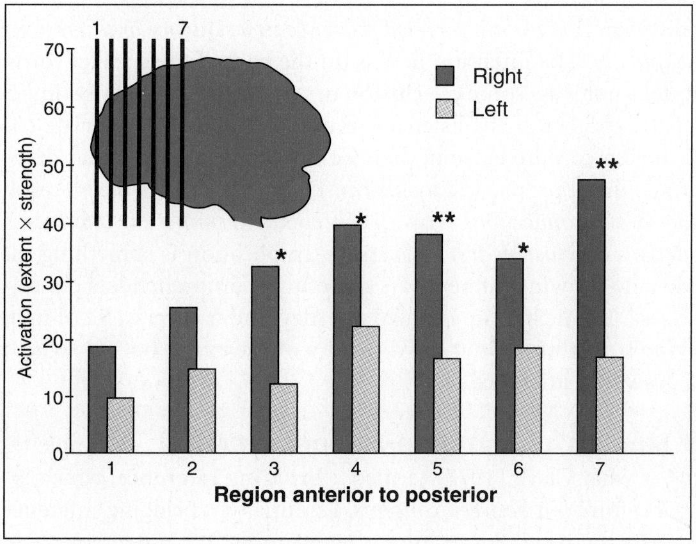

◆ **FIGURE 10-7** Activation levels for sentences presented with definite versus indefinite articles (levels in the figure are difference scores, showing how much greater the activations for definite than indefinite article sentences were), for seven left and right hemisphere locations in the brain. From Robertson et al. (2000).

these activations were greater in the right hemisphere than the left, whereas more commonly it's the left hemisphere that's implicated in language processing (e.g., Polk & Farah, 2002), as you recall from Chapter 9. Thus, these results, together with the other evidence, show that the right hemisphere may be particularly involved in establishing coherence in language comprehension.

Situation Models

In constructing and using a situation model, a person combines information that is available from the text itself, along with prior semantic and episodic knowledge, to create a mental simulation of the events being described. This mental representation is a **situation model** (Johnson-Laird, 1983; Van Dijk & Kintsch, 1983; Zwaan & Radvansky, 1998). A situation model is *a mental representation that serves as a simulation of a real or possible world as described by a text.* Essentially, the important idea is that comprehension is a search after meaning (Graesser, Singer, & Trabasso, 1994). While comprehension does use some passive activation of semantic and episodic memories (e.g., McKoon & Ratcliff, 1992), we also actively build situation models that elaborate on the causal structure of the event a person is trying to understand. In this section we cover two basic processes in the use of situation models in comprehension. The first is the use of inferences to elaborate on the information provided by the text, and the second is the updating of the situation model as shifts in the structure of the situation are encountered.

Instead of specifying everything, we rely on people to know the meanings of our words, to know about syntactic devices that structure our discourse, and to share our general conceptual knowledge of the world (e.g., to know that swimming laps can be a workout, that professors assign chapters for their students to read). In fact, as you'll read in the last section of this chapter, if you *do* specify everything exactly, you're breaking an important conversational rule, and people will be unhappy with you. Let's turn to the processes that comprehenders use to flesh out some missing information: implication and inference.

In **implication** there is *an intended reference in a sentence or utterance, but it is not mentioned explicitly*. The intention here is on the part of the speaker (or writer), who implies but does not state some conclusion or connection; in a sense, implication is in the mind of the speaker. If the listener (reader) draws the appropriate conclusion or connection during comprehension, then we say that the listener has drawn an inference, has drawn the appropriate conclusion. Thus, **inference** is *the process by which the comprehender draws connections between concepts, determines the referents of words and ideas, and derives conclusions from a message.* Implication is something that language producers do, and drawing inferences is something comprehenders do. If your professor says in class, "The next exam is on Wednesday, and it covers a lot of material," he or she is implying something about the difficulty of the exam, but is leaving it up to the students to draw that inference.

INFERENCE MAKING AND SITUATION MODEL CREATION A simple type of inference making is what Clark (1977) termed a **bridging inference**, which is *a process of constructing a connection between concepts.* Essentially, a bridging inference binds two units of language together. For example, determining that a reference like the epithet

PROVE IT

People spontaneously draw inferences as they comprehend language. These inferences are then incorporated into the situation models that were created of what was being heard or read. As a result, people frequently misremember information as having been heard or read, when in fact it was not. For this Prove It section, there is a list of sentences below. Along with each sentence is an inference that people are likely to make (in parentheses). What you should do is read these sentences to a group of volunteers. Then, after all of the sentences have been read, give your volunteers some sort of distractor task, such as having them solve math problems for 3-5 minutes. When the distractor period is over, now have your volunteers try to recall the sentences. What you should find is that people will likely report the inferences that they made while they were comprehending. That is, they will "recall" more information than you actually read to them. These inferences—false memories, in a real sense—are now part of their memory.

1. The housewife spoke to the manager about the increased meat prices (complained)
2. The paratrooper leaped out of the door (jump out of a plane/helicopter)
3. The cute girl told her mother she wanted a drink. (asked)
4. The weatherman told the people of the approaching tornado (warned)
5. The karate champion hit the cement block (broke)
6. The absent-minded professor didn't have his car keys (lost or forgot)
7. The safecracker put the match to the fuse (lit)
8. The hungry python caught the mouse (ate)
9. The man dropped the delicate glass pitcher (broke)
10. The clumsy chemist had acid on his coat (spilled)
11. The barnacle clung to the sides (ship)
12. Dennis sat in Santa's chair and asked for an elephant (lap)

Source: Adapted from Harris and Monaco (1978)

the stupid thing refers to the same entity as *a computer* is a bridging inference – it builds a connection between these two forms of reference, indicating that they refer to the same discourse entity. In bridging inference, the language producer uses reference to indicate the intended kinds of implications. For their part, comprehenders interpret the statement in the same fashion, computing the references and drawing the inferences needed. When the implication and inferences are intended, we call them **authorized**. Alternatively, unintended implications and inferences are called **unauthorized**, as when I say, "Your hair looks pretty today," and you respond, "So you think it was ugly yesterday?" (see also McKoon & Ratcliff, 1986).

The examples in Table 10-5 make it clear that the bridges we need to build for comprehension vary in their complexity, from simple and direct to difficult and remote. Even on intuitive grounds, consider how the following sentences differ in the ease of comprehension:

(13) Marge went into her office. It was very dirty.

(14) Marge went into her office. The floor was very dirty.

(15) Marge went into her office. The African violet had bloomed.

Whereas sentence 13 is a simple case of pronoun reference, sentence 14 refers back to *office* with the word *floor*. Because an office necessarily has a floor, it is clear that the implication in sentence 14 is that it was Marge's office floor that was dirty; in other words, Marge's office is indeed the antecedent. One of the properties you retrieve from your semantic memory is that an office has a floor. Thus, if you comprehend that the office floor was dirty, you must have drawn this inference. But it's an even longer chain of inference to draw the inference in sentence 15 that Marge happens to have an African violet in her office; a floor is necessary, but an African violet isn't. Overall, the integration of this semantic knowledge with the information in the text is part and parcel of creating a situation model.

Think back to our discussion of semantic memory and the typicality of category instances and properties. It seems likely that the structure of concepts in semantic memory activation would influence the ease with which information is inferred during situation model construction (e.g., Cook & Myers, 2004). So, more predictable pieces of information would be processed faster (McKoon & Ratcliff, 1989; O'Brien, Plewes, & Albrecht, 1990); Marge's office necessarily has a floor as well as a desk, a chair, some shelves, and so on. It's conceivable that it has some plants, but that is optional enough that sentence 15 would take more time to comprehend.

Further evidence that people are drawing on their semantic knowledge, and that this knowledge has an embodied character, was in a study by Zwaan, Stanfield, and Yaxley (2002). People read short descriptions of situations, and then were presented pictures of objects. Their task was to indicate whether the pictured object had been in the description they read. The critical manipulation was whether the picture either matched or mismatched the perceptual characteristics of the object in the description. For example, the critical sentence could be either *The ranger saw the eagle in the sky* or *The ranger saw the eagle in its nest* followed by a picture of either an eagle with its wings outstretched or perched (see Figure 10-8). Zwaan et al. found that people responded faster when the picture matched the described state. That is, even though they saw an eagle in both pictures, the eagle with its wings outstretched "matched" the "eagle in the sky" description better, so people responded faster in that condition. Thus, people seemed to be activating perceptual qualities of objects during the comprehension process itself.

People are also aware of what the intended consequence is of someone saying something. *The intended consequence of an utterance* is called a **speech act** (Searle, 1969). For example, if you were to ask your roommate to turn down the stereo, the *speech* itself is the set of words you say, but the *speech act* is your intention, getting your roommate to let you study for an upcoming exam. Not only do people spontaneously derive the implied speech acts of what other people say, but they may misremember what was said in terms of the speech act itself. For example, in a study by Holtgraves (2008), people read a series of short vignettes, some of which conveyed speech acts. For example, suppose people read the following story: "Gloria showed up at the office wearing a new coat. When her coworker Heather saw it she said to her, "Gloria, I like your new coat." The last sentence here conveys the speech act of complimenting Gloria. What Holtgraves found was that people were more likely to mistakenly remember that they had read "I'd like to compliment you on your new coat," an utterance that actually describes the speech act. However, a different group of participants read a different version of the story, in which the last two sentences were: "When her coworker Heather saw it, she said to *her friend Stacy*: "I like *her* new coat." In this condition, people

FIGURE 10-8 Examples of pictures of an eagle in flight or on a perch.

were less likely to misremember having read "I'd like to compliment her on her new coat." Because there was no actual complimenting speech act to Gloria in the second version, people did not store this information in memory, so did not make the memory error.

It should be noted that we do not automatically and spontaneously draw all possible inferences while we read. While some inferences are directly and typically drawn, such as simple and straightforward references, others are more complex and may not be drawn, and possibly shouldn't be drawn. If we did, our cognitive resources would be quickly overwhelmed (Singer, Graesser, & Trabasso, 1994). For example, when you read a sentence like 13 or 14, you are likely not to draw an inference that Marge decided to clean her office, although if the next sentence in the story said that, you'd certainly understand it. Most of the inferences people make are *backward* inferences. That is people are trying to understand what has already been described in the text, and how it all goes together. *Forward* inferences – that is, trying to predict what will happen next — are made under much rarer circumstances (Millis & Graesser, 1994).

It should also be noted that while in some cases we do not draw inferences that we could, we may also draw inferences that we might rather not. For example, there is some work showing that people may draw inferences based on stereotypes, such as gender stereotypes (Duffy & Kier, 2004; Murray, Klin, & Myers, 1993; Garnham, Oakhill, & Reynolds, 2002).

INDIVIDUAL DIFFERENCES Interestingly, there is now accumulating evidence that reference and inference processes depend significantly on individual characteristics of the reader, particularly on the reader's skill. For instance, Long and De Ley (2000) found that less skilled readers resolve ambiguous pronouns just as well as more skilled readers, but they do so only when they are integrating meanings together; the more skilled readers resolve the pronouns earlier, probably when they first encounter a pronoun.

Several studies have also examined inferences as a function of the limited capacity of working memory (e.g., Fletcher & Bloom, 1988). One such study, by Singer, Andrusiak, Reisdorf, and Black (1992), went one step further than this, explaining individual differences in bridging as a function of working memory capacity and vocabulary knowledge. The gist of this work is that the greater your working memory capacity and vocabulary size, the greater is the likelihood that information necessary for an inference will still be in working memory and can be used (see also Long, Oppy, & Seely, 1997; Miyake, Just, & Carpenter, 1994).

Evidence for individual differences in comprehension has also revealed itself in neurological measures. One example of this is a study by Virtue, van den Broek, and Linderholm (2006). In this study people read sentences that had causal constraints that were either weak (e.g., *As he arrived at the bus stop, he saw his bus was already 5 blocks away.*) or strong (*As he arrived at the bus stop, he saw his bus was just pulling away.*). During reading, the researchers presented lexical decision probes that corresponded to likely inferences that the readers might make (e.g., *run* in this case). Importantly, this presentation was done to the left and right hemispheres by presenting the words on either the right or left half (respectively) of the computer screen. The data showed that the right hemisphere was more involved in generating remote associations (that is, associated concepts that are not directly and closely semantically related to the concepts in the sentences). Moreover, people with high working memory capacity activated fewer remote associations than low-span people. Essentially, people with a high working memory span were more focused in the amount of knowledge they activated during comprehension.

UPDATING Situations that we experience or read about are often in a state of flux. Things are always changing, and the situations may differ from one moment to the next. Thus, the cognitive processes involved in comprehension must be able to shift the current understanding to adapt to these on-going changes. There are thought to be a number of **updating** processes that *alter a person's situation model in the face of information about how the situation has changed.* So, we mentally keep track of the various changes that occur in the events that we are comprehending.

There are a large number of studies that have looked at the updating of situation models. To provide a framework for understanding how these changes can occur, we'll use Rolf Zwaan's Event Indexing Model (Zwaan, Langston, & Graesser, 1995; Zwaan, Magliano, & Graesser, 1995; Zwaan & Radvansky, 1998). According to this theory, people actively monitor multiple event dimensions during reading to assess whether there has been a meaningful change along any of them.

There were five dimensions proposed in the original version of the theory: space, time, entity, intentionality (goals), and causality. The idea is that when there is a disruption along any one of these dimensions, people need to update their situation models, and this updating process takes time. For example, a break along the space and time dimensions could happen if a story protagonist moves to a new location, or there is a jump in time (e.g., a week later. . .). At this point, people would need to update their situation models to take this change into account. Similarly if a new character is introduced into a story, the person would need to update the entity dimension of the situation model; if a character has a new goal, the intentionality dimension would be updated; and if something happened in the story that did not have a prior explanation (e.g., "suddenly, a gunshot rang out. . ."), then the causal dimension would need to be updated. Further research has shown that people seem to monitor more than just these five dimensions. For example, people also track emotional information (e.g., Komeda & Kusumi, 2006).

To give you a better idea of what goes on in situation model updating, let's look at a classic paradigm that explores updating along the spatial dimension. In a seminal paper by Morrow, Greenspan, and Bower (1987), people memorized a diagram of a research lab, where each room had four objects in it (see Figure 10-9). They then read ★

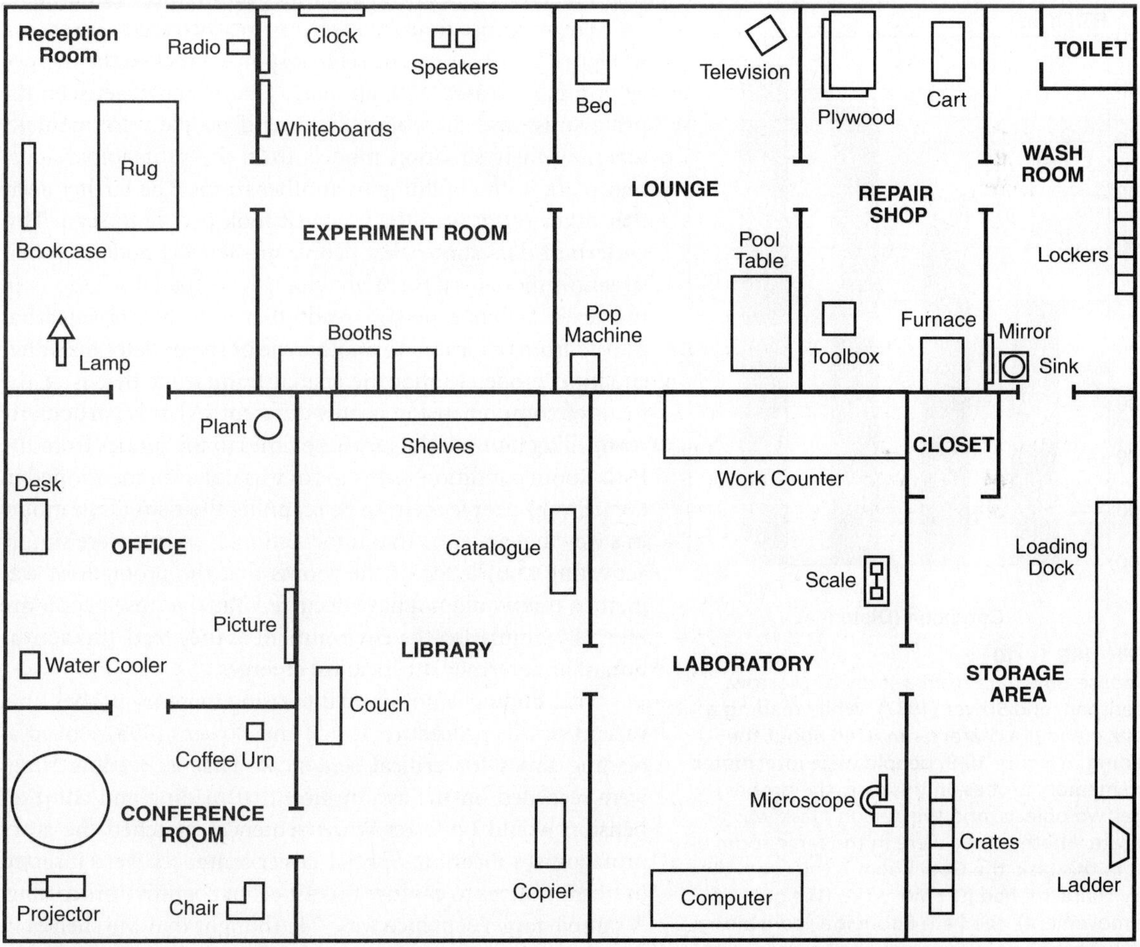

★ **FIGURE 10-9**
Example of the map of the research center memorized by people in Morrow, Greenspan, and Bower's (1987) study of spatial updating during language comprehension.

narratives about people moving about in that space. During reading, people were occasionally probed with pairs of object names, such as *sink-furnace*. The task was to indicate whether the two objects were in the same room or not (in this case, they were not). The critical factor was the distance on the map between the story protagonist's current location, and the location of the probe objects. Moreover, these memory probes came after motion sentences in which the person moved from one room to another, such as "He walked from the laboratory into the wash room." Based on this, four conditions were defined. The Goal Room was the room that the person just moved to; the wash room in this case. The Path Room was the (unmentioned) room that the person walked through to get to the Goal Room; the storage room here. The Source Room was the room the person was in just prior to moving to the Goal Room; the laboratory here. Finally, there was an Other Room condition, which corresponded to probes from any other room in the building.

The response time results from one such study are shown in Figure 10-10. As can be seen, response times to the memory probes increased with an increase in distance between the protagonist and the objects. It is as if people were mentally scanning their situation models from the protagonist's current place in the building to another room. The farther away that other room was, the longer it took people to scan. This pattern of data shows that people are actively updating their situation models as there are changes in spatial locations in the texts. When a person reads that a story character has moved from one room to another, he or she updates his or her situation model so that the spatial framework that is at the focus of comprehension is now different. What is particularly compelling here are the response times to the probes from the Path Room condition—this room was not even mentioned in the text, yet people seem to be scanning their situation model in a way that activates that information. If people were simply activating knowledge of the rooms that the protagonist was in, then this would not have occurred. But, because people are mentally simulating the environment as they read, this activation of an intermediate location emerges.

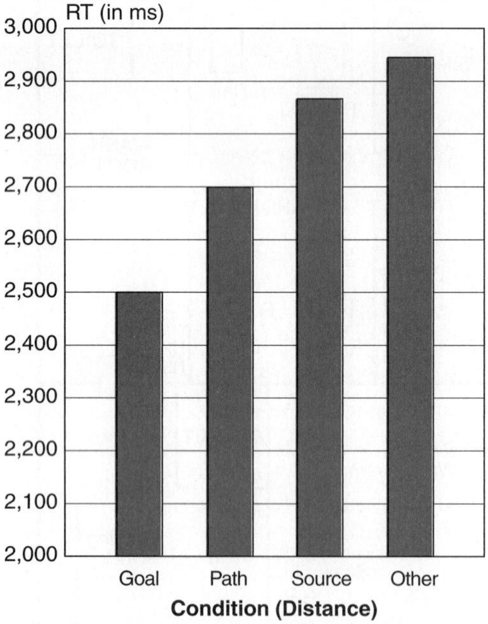

▲ **FIGURE 10-10**
Response time data from a study by Morrow, Greenspan, and Bower (1987). While reading a passage about a character moving about the building in Figure 10-9, people were interrupted with memory probes. In this case, the probes were two objects, and the person's task was to indicate whether they were in the same room or not. In this task, the Goal Room is the room the story character had just moved to (the goal of the movement), the Path Room is a room along the character's path of travel, the Source Room is the room that the movement started from (the source from which the movement began), and the Other room is just some other room in the building.

This finding is not limited to using memory probes. In a variant of this procedure, Rinck and Bower (1995) looked at reading times for critical sentences. That is, reading times were recorded on the assumption that reading and comprehension would be faster when sentences matched the story protagonist's location. Special target sentences were inserted in the narratives to capture this aspect of cognitive processing. A sample target sentence was, "He thought that the shelves in the library still looked like an awful mess." Similar to the memory probe data, they found that reading times slowed down progressively as the protagonist's current location increased in distance from the objects discussed in the text.

Similar influences of situation model updating can be seen for other situation model dimensions, using either memory probe or reading time methodologies, including shifts in time (Gennari, 2004; Zwaan, 1996), monitoring characteristics of story characters (Albrecht & O'Brien, 1995), the processing of character goal information (Lutz & Radvansky, 1997; Suh & Trabasso, 1993), and so on.

Tracking these changes along various dimensions is part of an attempt to create an analog to the world. Recently, work with fMRI recordings has shown that there are increases in brain activity when event shifts are encountered and people need to update their situation models (Speer, Zacks, & Reynolds, 2007). For example, looking at the dimension of time in a story, memory access to events earlier in a sequence is more difficult if the described intervening events are longer in duration (e.g., a year) than if they are shorter (e.g., a day), even if the event is presented as a flashback (that is later in the text than the intervening events) (Claus & Kelter, 2006).

Moreover, the creation of the situation model needs to take into account constraints of embodiment. For example, in a study by de Vega, Robertson, Glenberg, Kaschak, and Rinck (2004; see also Radvansky, Zwaan, Federico, & Franklin, 1998) people were asked to read a series of passages. Embedded in those passages were critical sentences that described two actions that a character was doing, either at the same time or in sequence. If a person is described as doing two things that require the same parts of the body, such as *While chopping wood with his large axe, he painted the fence white*, reading times were substantially slower, as if readers were trying to figure out how this could be done. However, reading times were faster when either different parts of the body were being used, such as *While whistling a lively folk melody, he painted the fence white*, or were done in sequence, such as *After chopping wood with his large axe, he painted the fence white*. Thus, it is clear that people take into account the limits of our human bodies, and the way actions happen in time, to help them comprehend what they are reading.

Events

ON BEYOND LANGUAGE Our discussion of comprehension up to now has largely focused on language comprehension of either written or spoken language, and this reflects the thrust of research in this area. However, this is not the only type of comprehension that people can engage in. We also comprehend events that we see and are involved in. As an example of the first type, work by Magliano (Magliano, Miller, & Zwaan, 2001; Magliano, Taylor, & Kim, 2005) and Zacks (Zacks, Braver, Sheridan, Donaldson, Snyder, Ollinger, et. al., 2001; Zacks, Speer, Swallow, Braver, & Reynolds, 2007) show that people are actively comprehending events viewed on video or film. For example, in a study by Magliano et al. (2001), rather than having people read written texts, people watched narrative films such as *Star Trek 2: The Wrath of Khan*. As people watched these movies, they were asked to indicate when they thought the situation being depicted by the film changed. What was found was that people made these indications at the same points as when situation model theory suggested that people would need to update their understanding if they were reading a text. For example, people indicated that there was a change in the film if a new character entered a scene, if there was a change in spatial location, if something unexpected happened, and so on.

Recently, there have also been some extensions of the study of comprehension to how people understand interactive events in which they find themselves. The development of virtual reality technologies has been particularly helpful here because the experimenter has a great deal of control in creating environments that a person can interact with, which allows the experimenter to make precise, controlled measurements. An example of this is a study by Tamplin, Radvansky, and Copeland (2008) that was modeled after the Morrow et al. (1987) studies described earlier. In these experiments, people memorized the map of a research center, as had been done in the earlier text comprehension work. Then, rather than reading a story, people navigate through a virtual representation of the environment. As they navigate the environment, their primary task is to respond to memory probes that consist of object names at critical points in the environment, also similar to what had been done in the text comprehension work. However, the pattern of data that was obtained was very different, as shown in Figure 10-11.

As can be seen, rather than having information about objects become less available as one moves further and further away from them, this information is similarly available in memory, except for objects in the Path Room. Response times to probes in this condition were much slower, suggesting that people suppressed this information. So, there seems to be something different about how people comprehend events that they are involved in compared to ones that they just read about. Now why would people want to suppress this knowledge? Why isn't it more available since the person had just been in that room? Well, as the argument goes, when people passed through the Path Room, this information was salient because they were actually in that (virtual) context. However, because this was not their destination, this information was irrelevant. As such, knowledge about objects in the Path Room was interfering knowledge in memory. Similar to several other examples of interference in cognition that you have studied in various chapters in this book, this interference can disrupt cognitive processing. So, what we are seeing here is a similar cognitive process (in this case, retrieval interference) that has been observed with simpler materials (e.g., lists of words) showing up in a more real-to-life situation, with similar consequences (i.e., interfering knowledge hinders memory performance).

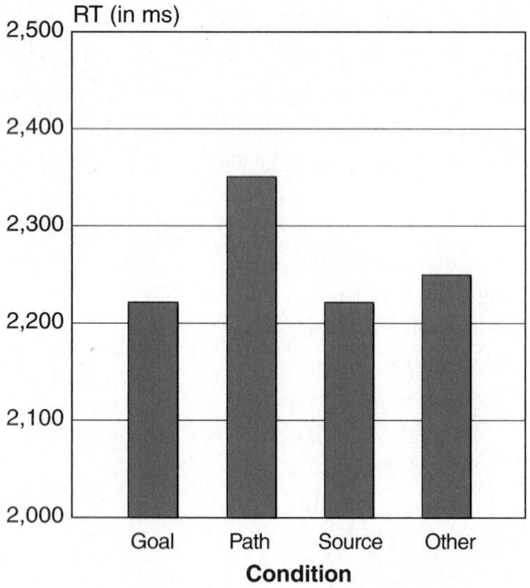

FIGURE 10-11
Response time data from a study by Tamplin, Radvansky, and Copeland (2008). Rather than reading a text, people navigated a virtual environment after memorizing the map of the research center in Figure 10-9. Note the different pattern of data compared to the reading comprehension task illustrated in Figure 10-10.

Section Summary

- Reference in language involves the notion of bridging together and linking different elements of a statement. The source of knowledge that permits speakers to include reference in their messages and listeners to infer the basis for those bridges is not just our knowledge of syntax and word meanings, but the entirety of semantic memory and much top-down processing.

- Situation models are created during comprehension by combining information from the language itself as well as inferences people draw based on their prior semantic and episodic knowledge.
- Evidence also shows the capacity and operation of working memory to be important factors in understanding individual differences in reading comprehension.
- Situation model updating occurs when people detect a meaningful change along any one of a number of event dimensions. This updating process is cognitively effortful, resulting in increases in reading times and brain activity.
- Comprehension occurs not only for language that people hear or read, but also for other aspects of experience, including narrative films, videos, and interactive experiences.

CONVERSATION AND GESTURE

We turn now to the last major section of the chapter, the comprehension of conversation and gesture. We focus on conversation, normal, everyday language interactions, such as an ordinary talk among friends. The issues we consider, however, apply to all kinds of linguistic interactions: how professors lecture and students comprehend, how people converse on the telephone, how an interviewer and a job applicant talk, how we reason and argue with one another (Rips, 1998), and so on. Furthermore, we'll look at how we expand on what we say by moving our hands about, making gestures, and by examining the cognitive role of these gestures.

During a conversation, speakers develop a rhythm as each person takes successive turns speaking. Nonverbal interaction can occur during a turn, such as when a listener nods to indicate attention or agreement.

The Structure of Conversations

Let's examine two characteristics of conversations, the issues of turn taking and social roles, to get started and introduce some of the more cognitive effects we're especially interested in.

TAKING TURNS Conversations are structured by a variety of cognitive and social variables and rules governing the what and how of our contributions. To begin with, we take turns. Typically, there is little overlap between participants' utterances. Generally, two people speak simultaneously only at the change of turns, when one speaker is finishing and the other is beginning. In fact, interchanges in conversation often come in an adjacency pair, a pair of turns that sets the stage for another part of the conversation. For instance, if Ann wants to ask Betty a question, there can be an adjacency pair of utterances in which Ann sets the stage for the actual question:

> Ann: Oh there's one thing I wanted to ask you.
> Betty: mhm
> Ann: in the village, they've got some of those. . .rings. . . . Would you like one?"
> (From Svartik & Quirk, 1980, cited in Clark, 1994)

The neutral "mhm" is both an indication of attention and a signal that Ann can go ahead and ask the question (Duncan, 1972).

The rules we follow for turn taking are straightforward (Sacks, Schegloff, & Jefferson, 1974). First, the current speaker is in charge of selecting the next speaker. This is often done by directing a comment or question toward another participant ("What do you think about that, Fred?"). The second rule is that if the first rule isn't used, then anyone can become the current speaker. Third, if no one else takes the turn, the current speaker may continue but is not obliged to.

Speakers use a variety of signals to indicate whether they are finished with their turn. For example, a long pause at the end of a sentence is a turn-yielding signal, as are a comment directed at another participant, a drop in the pitch or loudness of the utterance, and establishing direct eye contact with another person; the latter is often merely a nonverbal way of selecting the next speaker. If the current speaker is not relinquishing the conversational turn, however, these signals are withheld. Other "failure to yield" signals include trailing off in midsentence without completing the grammatical clause or the thought, withholding such endings as "you know," or even looking away from other participants during a pause (Cook, 1977).

In addition to overt signals of when turn taking may occur, there may be neurological underpinnings as well. Recently, Margaret and Thomas Wilson (Wilson & Wilson, 2005) have suggested that our conversational turn taking may be tied to neurological oscillators that help us keep track of time. The idea is that these oscillators become synchronized to one another on the basis of the rate at which people are producing syllables. These oscillators give us a neurologically based intuition about the pace of the conversation, and when it would be appropriate to step in and take our turn.

SOCIAL ROLES AND SETTINGS The social roles of conversational partners, along with conversational setting, influence the contributions made by participants (Kemper & Thissen, 1981). Formal settings among strangers or mere acquaintances lead to more structured, rule-governed conversations than informal settings among friends (Blom & Gumperz, 1972). Conversations with a "superior"—for instance, your boss or a police officer—are more formal and rule-governed than those with peers (e.g., Brown & Ford, 1961; Edwards & Potter, 1993, and Holtgraves, 1994, discuss the social and interpersonal aspects of such situations).

Cognitive Conversational Characteristics

Conversations are structured by cognitive factors. We focus on three: the conversational rules we follow, the issue of topic maintenance, and the online theories of conversational partners.

CONVERSATIONAL RULES Grice (1975; see also Norman & Rumelhart, 1975) suggested a set of four **conversational rules** or maxims, *rules that govern our conversational interactions with others*, all derived from the **cooperative principle**, *the idea that each participant in a conversation implicitly assumes that all speakers are following the rules and that each contribution to the conversation is a sincere, appropriate contribution.* In a sense, we enter into a contract or pact with our conversational partner, pledging to abide by certain rules and adopt certain conventions to make our conversations manageable and understandable (Brennan & Clark, 1996; Wilkes-Gibbs & Clark, 1992). This includes issues of syntax, where we choose syntactic structures that mention important, discourse focus information early in our sentences (Ferreira & Dell, 2000) or syntactic structures that are less ambiguous (Haywood, Pickering, & Branigan, 2005); intonation and prosody that helps disambiguate an otherwise ambiguous syntactic form (Clifton, Carlson & Frazier, 2006); word choice, as in situations when two conversational partners settle on a mutually acceptable term for referring to some object (Metzing & Brennan, 2003; Shintel & Keysar, 2007); and goes all the way up to the gestures we use to amplify or disambiguate our speech (Goldin-Meadow, 1997; Kelly, Barr, Church, & Lynch, 1999; Ozyurek, 2002). As Table 10-7 shows, the four maxims specify in more detail how to follow the cooperative principle. (Two additional rules have been added to the list for purposes that will become clear in a moment.) ◆

A simple example or two should help you understand the point behind these maxims. When a speaker violates or seems to violate a maxim, the listener assumes there is a reason for this, and may not detect that a violation has occurred (Engelhardt,

TABLE 10-7 Grice's (1975) Conversational Maxims, with Two Additional Rules ◆

The Cooperative Principle

Be sincere, reasonable, and appropriate

- **Relevance:** Make your utterances relevant to the conversation (e.g., stick to the topic; don't state what others aren't interested in).
- **Quantity:** Be as informative as required (e.g., don't overspecify; don't say more or less than you know; don't be too informative).
- **Quality:** Say what is true (e.g., don't mislead; don't lie; don't exaggerate).
- **Manner and tone:** Be clear (e.g., avoid obscurity and ambiguity); be brief; be polite; don't interrupt.

Two Additional Rules

- **Relations with conversational partner:** Infer and respond to partner's knowledge and beliefs (e.g., tailor contributions to partner's level; correct misunderstandings).
- **Rule violations:** Signal or mark intentional violations of rules (e.g., use linguistic or pragmatic markers [stress, gestures]; use blatant violations; signal the reason for the violation). From Grice (1975); see also Norman and Rumelhart (1975).

Bailey, & Ferreira, 2006). That is, the listener still assumes that the speaker was following the overarching cooperative principle so must have intended the remark as something else, maybe sarcasm, maybe a nonliteral meaning (Kumon-Nakamura, Glucksberg, & Brown, 1995). As an example, imagine studying in the library when your friend asks:

(21) Can I borrow a pencil?

This is a straightforward speech act, a simple request you could respond to directly. But if you had just lent a pencil to your friend, and he said,

(22) Can I borrow a pencil with lead in it?

the question means something different. Assuming that your friend was being cooperative, you now have to figure out why he broke the quantity maxim about over-specifying; all pencils have lead in them, and mentioning the lead is a violation of a rule. You infer that it was probably a deliberate violation, where the friend's authorized implication can be expressed as "The pencil you lent me doesn't have any lead in it, so would you please lend me one I *can* use?" In general, people are fairly adept at decoding speech acts, and knowing what a person is trying to achieve by what he or she says. (Holtgraves, 2008).

TOPIC MAINTENANCE We also follow the conversational rules in terms of **topic maintenance**, *making our contributions relevant to the topic and sticking to it.* Topic maintenance depends on two processes, comprehension of the speaker's remark and expansion, contributing something new to the topic.

Schank (1977; see also Litman & Allen, 1987) provides an analysis of topic maintenance and topic shift, including a consideration of what is and is not a permissible response, called simply a move, after one speaker's turn is over. The basic idea here is that the listener comprehends the speaker's comment and stores it in memory. As in reading, the listener must infer what the speaker's main point was or what the discourse focus was. If the speaker, Ben, says,

(23) I bought a new car in Baltimore yesterday,

then Ed, his conversational partner, needs to infer Ben's main point and expand on that in his reply. Thus, sentence (24) is legal because it apparently responds to the speaker's authorized implication, whereas sentence *(25#) is probably not a legal move (denoted by the # sign)*:

(24) Ed: Really? I thought you said you couldn't afford a car.

(25#) Ed: I bought a new shirt yesterday.

Sentence 24 intersects with two main elements for sentence 23, "BUY" and "CAR," so it is probably an acceptable expansion. Sentence 25# intersects with "BUY," but the other common concept seems to be the time case role "*YESTERDAY*," an insufficient basis for most expansions. Thus, in general a participant's responsibility is to infer the speaker's focus and expand on it in an appropriate way. That's the relevance maxim: Sticking to the topic means you have to infer it correctly. Ed seems to have failed to draw the correct inference.

On the other hand, maybe Ed *did* comprehend Ben's statement correctly. If so, then he has deliberately violated the relevance maxim in sentence 25#. But it's such a blatant violation that it suggests some other motive; Ed may be expressing disinterest in what Ben did or may be saying indirectly that he thinks Ben is bragging. And if Ed suspects Ben is telling a lie, then he makes his remark even more blatant, as in 26:

(26) Yeah, and I had lunch with the Queen of England.

ONLINE THEORIES DURING CONVERSATION A final point involves the theories we develop of our conversational partners, something called **theory of mind**. The most obvious one we construct is a **direct theory**. This is the mental model of *what the conversational partner knows and is interested in, what the partner is like.* We tailor our speech so that we're not being too complex or too simplistic, so we're not talking about something of no interest to the listener. Some clear examples of this involve adult–child speech, where a child's smaller vocabulary and knowledge prompt adults to modify and simplify their utterances in a number of ways (DePaulo & Bonvillian, 1978; Snow, 1972; Snow & Ferguson, 1977). But sensitivity to the partner's knowledge and interests is present to some degree in all conversations—although not perfectly, of course. We don't talk to our college classes the way we would to a group of second graders, nor do we launch into conversations with bank tellers about our research. Horton and Gerrig (2002) call this "audience design," i.e., being aware of the need to design your speech to the characteristics of your audience (e.g., Lockridge & Brennan, 2002). Alternatively, if we don't know much about you, we may make an assumption that you know what we know (Nickerson, 2001) and then revise our direct theory as we observe how well you follow our remarks (Clark & Krych, 2004).

Audience design has implications beyond conversations. When we tell stories to people, we modify what we tell them based on who they are and our social relationship to them. This retelling is not the same as recall. We modify the information we report to fit the social situation. In retelling stories, people often engage in exaggerations for some parts, minimize other parts, add information that was not there originally, and leave some bits out altogether, all to suit our audience and the broader message we are trying to convey. This conversational practice may explain, in part, some of the memory errors we make that have a similar nature. That is, our use of cognition, and its evolution, occurred more in the story telling, social environment, not in one that depended critically on verbatim recall (Marsh, 2007).

There is another layer of theories during a conversation, an interpersonal level related to "face management," or public image (Holtgraves, 1994, 1998). Let's call this the **second-order theory**. This second-order theory is *an evaluation of the other participant's direct theory: what you think the other participant believes about you.* Let's develop an example of these

"I want you to know that I'm not nearly the great human being everyone seems to think me to be."

two theories to illustrate their importance. Imagine that you're registering for classes next semester and say to your friend Frank that you've decided to take Psychology of Personality. What would your reaction be if Frank responded to you with these statements?

(27) Why would you want to take that? It's just a bunch of experiments with rats, isn't it?

(28) Yeah, I'm taking Wilson's class next term too. John told me he's going to assign some books he thinks I'll really like.

(29) Maybe you shouldn't take Wilson's class next term. Don't you have to be pretty smart to do all that reading?

In 27 you assume that your friend has made the remark in sincerity, that it was intended to mean what it says. Because you know that research on laboratory animals had little to do with the field of personality, you conclude that your friend knows a lot less about personality theory than you do. In other words, this becomes part of your direct theory, as shown in Table 10-8. For sentence 28, you probably interpret Frank's remark as boastful, intended to show that he's on a first-name basis with the professor. Indeed, Frank has authorized that inference by using a more familiar term of address than is customary (for an analysis of usage of proper names, see Brown & Ford, 1961). You update both your direct theory of Frank and your second-order theory. You update your direct and second-order theories after sentence 29 too, but the nature of the updates is different: You've been insulted by the implication in Frank's response, something like "he thinks I'm not smart enough to take the class."

TABLE 10-8 Examples of Direct and Second-Order Theories

Setting: For all three conversations, Chris's first sentence and direct theory are the same.

Chris: "I think I'll take Personality with Dr. Wilson next term."

Chris's direct theory: Frank is interested in the courses I'm taking.

Conversation 1

Frank replies: "Personality? Ah, that's just a bunch of experiments with rats, isn't it?"

Chris's updated direct theory: Frank doesn't know much about personality research.

Conversation 2

Frank replies: "Yeah, I am too. John told me he's going to assign some books he thinks I'll really like."

Chris's updated direct theory: Frank knows the professor on a first-name basis, and he's bragging about it by calling him John.

Chris's second-order theory: Frank thinks I'll be impressed that he calls the professor John.

Conversation 3

Frank replies: "Hmm, maybe you shouldn't take that class. Don't you have to be pretty smart to do all that reading?"

Chris's updated direct theory: Frank is a jerk; he just insulted me.

Chris's second-order theory: Frank thinks I'm not smart.

Empirical Effects in Conversation

INDIRECT REQUESTS Let's conclude with some evidence about the conversational effects we've been discussing. One of the most commonly investigated aspects of conversation involves **indirect requests**, such as when *we ask someone to do something* ("Close the window"; "Tell me what time it is") *by an indirect and presumably more polite statement* ("It's drafty in here"; "Excuse me, but do you have the correct time?").

An impressive investigation of indirect requests was reported by Clark (1979). The study involved telephone calls to some 950 merchants in the San Francisco area in which the caller asked a question that the merchant normally would be expected to deal with on the phone (e.g., "What time do you close?" "Do you take credit cards?" "How much does something cost?"). The caller would write down a verbatim record of the call immediately after hanging up. A typical conversational interaction was as follows:

(30) *Merchant: "Hello, Scoma's Restaurant."*

Caller: "Hello. Do you accept any credit cards?"

Merchant: "Yes we do; we even accept Carte Blanche."

Of course, the caller's question here was indirect: "Yes" isn't an acceptable answer to "Do you accept any credit cards?" because the authorized implication of the question was, "What credit cards do you take?" Merchants almost always responded to the authorized implication rather than merely to the literal question posed by the caller. Furthermore, they tailored their answers to be as informative as possible while not saying more than is necessary (obeying the second rule, on quantity), as in "We accept *only* Visa and MasterCard," or "We accept *all* major credit cards." Such responses are both informative and brief.

Such research has been extended to include not just indirect requests, but a variety of indirect statements and replies to questions. For instance, Holtgraves (1994) examined comprehension speed for indirect requests as a function of the status of the speaker, whether the speaker was of higher status than the listener (e.g., boss and employee) or whether they were of equal status (two employees). Participants read a

PROVE IT

One of the best student demonstration projects we've ever graded was a test of the politeness ethic in conversational requests. On five randomly selected days, the student sat next to a stranger on the bus, turned, and asked, "Excuse me, but do you have the correct time?" All five strangers answered her. On five other randomly selected days, she said to the stranger, "Tell me what time it is," not in an unpleasant tone, but merely in a direct fashion; none of the strangers answered. Devise other situations in which you violate the politeness ethic or other conversational rules and note people's reactions. If you do it properly, you'll learn about the rules of conversation; but be careful that it doesn't turn into a demonstration project on aggression. Do the same thing again, but this time with a close friend or family member. You'll see how necessary some polite forms are with strangers and how inappropriate they are with people you know well.

short scenario (e.g., getting a conference room ready for a board of directors meeting), which concluded with one of two kinds of indirect statements. Conventional statements were normal indirect requests, such as, "Could you go fill the water glasses?" Negative state remarks were more indirect, merely stating a negative situation and only indirectly implying that the listener should do something (e.g., "The water glasses seem to be empty."). People showed no effects of status when comprehending regular indirect requests; it didn't matter whether it was a peer or the boss who said, "Could you go fill the water glasses?" But comprehension time increased significantly with negative state remarks made by peers. In other words, when the boss says, "The water glasses seem to be empty," we comprehend the conventional indirect request easily. But when a peer says it, we need additional time to comprehend.

INDIRECT REPLIES Holtgraves' (1998) work has also focused on indirect replies, especially the notion of making a "face saving" reply. His participants read a description of a situation, such as:

(31) Nick and Paul are taking the same history class. Students in this class have to give a 20-minute presentation to the class on some topic.

They then read a sentence that gave positive (32) or negative (33) information about Nick's presentation or a sentence that was neutral (34):

(32) Nick gave his presentation and it was excellent. He decides to ask Paul what he thought of it: "What did you think of my presentation?"

(33) Nick gave his presentation and it was truly terrible. He decides to ask Paul what he thought of it: "What did you think of my presentation?"

(34) Nick gave his presentation and then decided to ask Paul what he thought of it: "What did you think of my presentation?"

If you were Paul and faced the prospect of telling Nick that his presentation was awful, wouldn't you look for some face-saving response? This is exactly how people responded when they comprehended Paul's responses. In the excuse condition, Paul says,

(35) It's hard to give a good presentation,

in effect giving Nick a face-saving excuse for his poor performance. Another possible conversational move is to change the topic, to avoid embarrassing Nick, as in

(36) I hope I win the lottery tonight.

Holtgraves (1998) collected several measures of comprehension, including overall comprehension time for the critical sentences 35 and 36. The comprehension times, ★ shown in Figure 10-12 (from Experiment 2), were very clear. When people had heard positive information—the talk was excellent—it took them a long time to comprehend either the excuse (35) or topic change (36) responses. But having heard negative information—the talk was terrible—was nearly the same as having heard nothing about the talk; people comprehended the excuse or topic change responses much more rapidly, and there was no major difference between no information and negative information. People clearly interpreted the violations of the relevance maxim as attempts to save face and avoid embar-

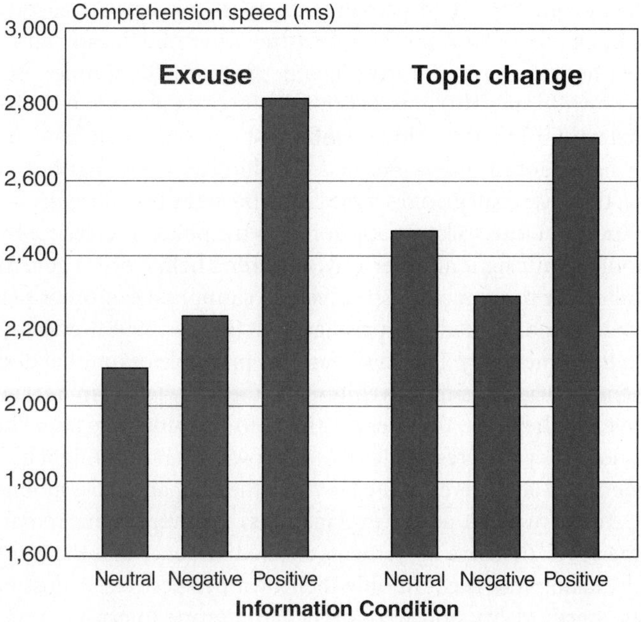

★ **FIGURE 10-12** Comprehension times from Holtgraves' (1998) study. Participants read settings in which either negative information, positive information, or neutral information was offered about a character, followed by a conversational move in which the speaker made an excuse for the character or changed the topic. In both cases it took longer to comprehend the remark when positive information about the character had just been encountered.

rassment. (The Nick and Paul scenario was an "opinion" setting, where Paul is asked to give his opinion. Holtgraves also tested "self-disclosure" scenarios, as when a little boy comes home with his report card and responds with an excuse or a topic change when his mother asks about his grades. The results from the two scenario types were largely the same, so the data in Figure 10-12 are averaged across these two conditions.)

EGOCENTRIC SPEECH One way to think of the evidence on face-saving is in terms of the politeness ethic: Telling someone an unvarnished, difficult truth, or being so honest as to insult someone or hurt his feelings, is usually considered a violation of the politeness ethic (see the rule on manner and tone). On the other hand, when you abruptly change the conversational topic as a face-saving move of your own, a big part of your motive is to influence the other person's second-order theory, as if we think, "I gave a lousy presentation, but I'll make an excuse so he'll think more highly of me." We perhaps give ourselves more credit than is due when we claim that people routinely and easily tailor their conversation to manipulate others—not that it doesn't happen, of course, but that it isn't as simple cognitively as we've been implying.

Work by Keysar (1994; Keysar, Barr, & Horton, 1998) illustrates this cautionary note quite well. A general idea in theories of conversation and pragmatics is called the optimal design principle (Clark, 1992), the idea that speakers "design their utterances so that their addressees have sufficient information to understand them" (Keysar et al., 1998, p. 47). In other words, we tailor our speech to optimize the listener's chances of full understanding, a seemingly noncontroversial idea related to the relevance rule in Table 10-7, along with the rule on relationships with conversational partners (infer your partner's knowledge, interests, and so on).

To test this, Keysar et al. had people read about conversational settings in which one person happens to know something that the other one doesn't and should therefore tailor his or her remarks to inform the other person. The simplest example, drawn from research on children's ability to take someone else's perspective, involves familiar Peanuts characters; Lucy has an old pair of red shoes and a new pair but merely asks Linus to bring her the "red shoes." Because the children knew that Lucy really wanted her new shoes, they were surprised when Linus brought the old pair. In other words, the children expected Linus to know about Lucy's unspoken preference merely because they knew about it. Putting it another way, children's behavior is egocentric: Children seem able to take only their own perspective and cannot take another's (Linus's).

Keysar's work demonstrated a surprising effect, (Keysar, 1998; Keysar et al., 1998) that adults often do the same thing: They disregard the principle of optimal design and speak (and comprehend) as egocentrically as children. Either they fail to appreciate another person's perspective, or they take that perspective into account only after their utterances have been planned. They underestimate how their own utterances might be ambiguous or difficult to understand and overestimate how well they "repair" those ambiguities (Keysar & Henly, 2002). In the research, adults' explanations of conversational remarks, their comprehension times, even their eye movements showed evidence that their initial utterances were egocentric, taking into account only their own perspectives. Adjustments occurred later, almost as afterthoughts, and were particularly prone to errors. In comprehension studies, such adjustments took additional time for people to process.

In Keysar et al.'s view, our first pass at an utterance is egocentric, taking into account just our own perspective, knowledge, and viewpoint. Then, time and mental resources permitting, we monitor or edit our speech plan and adjust it as needed—although probably not enough to suit the listener. Importantly, we would expect this adjustment phase to be error prone, especially under time pressure or other constraints (for instance, working memory limitations), and to miss at least some of the egocentric utterances that are originally planned. The overall message, accordingly, is that our conversational speech is driven in part by our direct and second-order theories but may be more fundamentally driven by a self-centered, egocentric perspective.

Gesture

When we speak, we not only move our lips, tongues, throats and so on, we may also move our arms and hands. This movement, or **gesture**, is *done to facilitate communication to listeners, and excludes sign language and noncommunicative mannerisms, such as touching one's hands to one's face* (McNeill, 1992). That is, the movements we make with our hands in conversation communicate information to people to augment the words we are using. For example, when describing the route you took to get to school, you may make gestures to convey information about turns you made, obstructions you encountered, speeders that you saw, and so on. Although gesture may serve a more holistic function when we use it while speaking, when people gesture in the absence of spoken speech, it takes on more linguistic characteristics, much like sign languages do (Goldin-Meadow, 2006).

Work by researchers such as Bavelas, Gerwing, Sutton, and Prevost (2008) shows that people even gesture when they are talking on the telephone, when they know the person on the other end cannot see them (although they gesture less than when they can see the other person). So, there must be something cognitively important about gesturing that facilitates language production in conversation. It should also be noted that people gesture less when they are speaking into a tape recorder (Bevelas et al., 2008) or when listeners do not appear to be attending to what they are saying (Jacobs & Garnham, 2007), so this impact of gesture has a strong social component, and is not purely psycholinguistic.

Gesture may even help a person learn. Essentially, the gestures a person produces when trying to solve a problem may reveal knowledge that the person has that is in a nascent, implicit stage. In some way, the gestures reveal to the person him- or herself knowledge that is present, but not fully developed in a way that can be used consciously. So, if people are encouraged to gesture, they may make the knowledge conscious faster, and facilitate learning. And, in fact, this is what can happen. In a study by Broaders, Cook, Mitchell, and Goldin-Meadow (2007), third and fourth grade children who were told to gesture while they solved math problems showed an increased ability to develop new strategies and solve those types of math problems faster than children who did not gesture. Moreover, when solving problems together, such as assembling a piece of furniture, these problems are solved more effectively when the person communicating gestures, and the person assembling can use these gestures (Lozano & Tversky, 2006). In essence, gestures communicate embodied information that cognition is able to more directly process than linguistic information (Hostetter & Alibali, 2008).

Section Summary

- Conversations follow a largely implicit set of conversational rules. Some of these involve turn taking and social status and conventions, but many more govern the nature or topic of participants' contributions. Topic shifts involve selecting some part of a person's utterance to form the basis for a new contribution and then adding some new information. Schank's work on topic shift is a particularly important analysis of this process of topic shifting.
- Participants in a conversation develop theories of mind of the other speakers, called direct theories, as well as theories of what the other speakers think of them, called second-order theories. When we converse, we tailor our contributions to these theories and also follow a set of conversational rules, the unspoken contract between conversational partners. When a rule is violated intentionally, usually to make some other point (e.g., sarcasm), we mark our violation so that its apparent illegality as a conversational move is noticed and understood.
- Empirical work on conversational interaction often tests general notions about direct theories, the politeness rule, or indirect requests. Although we sometimes attempt to manipulate another person's direct theory of us, research also shows that the initially planned utterance usually is from a very egocentric perspective, whereas later adjustments may take the other person's perspective into account.
- Gestures made during conversation are a way that simulated spatial and action information can be communicated. Making gestures is part of the social act of conversation, although it may sometimes occur when our partner cannot see us, as when we are talking on the telephone. Gesture even has the ability to serve as a working memory aid and help people solve problems.

Key Terms

advantage of clause recency (p. *389*)
advantage of first mention (p. *389*)
anaphoric reference (p. *388*)
antecedent (p. *388*)
authorized (p. *393*)
beliefs (p. *371*)
bridging inference (p. *392*)
conceptual knowledge (p. *371*)
conversational rules (p. *403*)
cooperative principle (p. *403*)
direct theory (p. *405*)
enhancement (p. *377*)
eye–mind assumption (p. *380*)
eye tracker (p. *379*)
fixations (p. *380*)
gaze duration (p. *380*)
gesture (p. *410*)
immediacy assumption (p. *380*)
implication (p. *392*)
indirect requests (p. *407*)
inference (p. *392*)
judgments of learning (JOLs) (p. *375*)
labor-in-vain effect (p. *375*)
mapping (p. *376*)
metacomprehension (p. *374*)
online comprehension task (p. *373*)
pragmatics (p. *372*)
propositional textbase (p. *378*)
reference (p. *388*)
region of proximal learning (p. *375*)
repeated name penalty (p. *388*)
second-order theory (p. *405*)
situation model (p. *392*)
speech act (p. *394*)
structure building (p. *376*)
suppression (p. *377*)
surface form (p. *378*)
theory of mind (p. *405*)
topic maintenance (p. *404*)
unauthorized (p. *393*)
updating (p. *396*)

CHAPTER 11

Decisions, Judgments, and Reasoning

It does not trouble people much that their heads are full of incomplete, inconsistent, and uncertain information. With little trepidation they go about drawing rather doubtful conclusions from their tangled mass of knowledge, for the most part unaware of the tenuousness of their reasoning. The very tenuousness of the enterprise is bound up with the power it gives people to deal with a language and a world full of ambiguity and uncertainty.

COLLINS, WARNOCK, AIELLO, & MILLER, 1975, P. 383

From the psychologist's point of view, thinking must not be confused with logic because human thinking frequently is not rigorous or correct, does not follow the path of step-by-step deduction—in short, is not usually "logical."

NEWELL & SIMON, 1972, P. 876

This chapter, on decision making and reasoning, and Chapter 12, on problem solving, will round out our study of cognitive psychology. While it's important for you to appreciate the material we've already covered, the picture wouldn't be complete without the slower, more deliberate kinds of thinking that we'll be studying here. How do we reason in logic problems? How do we reason and make decisions under conditions of uncertainty? These are the topics we turn to now.

A general thread that runs through much of the decision-making and reasoning research is that we are often overly influenced by the general world knowledge stored in our memories. The influence of stored information is pervasive; it affects how we perform in the classic forms of reasoning as well as less well-defined judgment and decision-making situations. A second thread is just as pervasive and just as important in decision making: Far more than is logical, we tend to search for evidence that confirms our decisions, beliefs, and hypotheses. In general, we are much less skeptical than we ought to be.

Let's begin by examining two classic kinds of reasoning problems and then switch to a seemingly very simple kind of decision making and reasoning, mental comparisons between concepts or objects. We then proceed to the study of a somewhat different kind of situation, reasoning about the likelihood of events for which relevant information in memory is generally lacking or insufficient. The strategies people use to make these judgments are of particular interest because they reveal a variety of rules of thumb or shortcut methods on which people rely. These methods work well sometimes, but sometimes they lead to distortions and biases in reasoning. Overall, this research provides convincing examples of the uncertainty of human reasoning and the often surprising inaccuracies in our stored knowledge.

FORMAL LOGIC AND REASONING

At some point during their college careers, most students are exposed to the classic forms of reasoning, often in a course on logic. For our purposes, two of these forms, *syllogistic* and *conditional reasoning*, are important (although there are others, such as relational reasoning, e.g., Goodwin & Johnson-Laird, 2005). A general finding is that people are not particularly good at solving such problems correctly when they are presented in an abstract form. Solutions often are better when problems are presented in terms of concrete, real-world concepts. If we generate our own examples, however, solution accuracy depends on how critically or skeptically we generated the examples. In some situations, our world knowledge almost prevents us from seeing the "pure" (i.e., logical) answer to logic problems (e.g., Markovits & Potvin, 2001).

Syllogisms

A **syllogism**, or categorical syllogism, is *a three-statement logical form, with the first two parts stating the premises taken to be true, and the third part stating a conclusion based on those premises.* The goal of syllogistic reasoning is to understand how different premises can be combined to yield logically true conclusions and to understand what combinations of premises lead to invalid or incorrect conclusions.

Often, syllogisms are presented in an abstract form, such as

(1a) All A are B.

All B are C.

Therefore, all A are C.

In this example, the two premises state a certain relation between the abstract elements *A*, *B*, and *C*, basically a class inclusion or subset-superset relation. "*All A are B*" says that the set *A* is a subset of the group *B*, that *A* is included in the set *B*. The third statement is the conclusion. By applying the rules of syllogistic reasoning, it can be determined that the conclusion "*All A are C*" is true in this example; that is, the conclusion follows logically from the premises. Inserting words into the syllogism will verify the truth of the conclusion: for instance,

(1b) All poodles are dogs.

All dogs are animals.

Therefore, all poodles are animals.

One difficulty or confusion that people have is illustrated by the following example:

(1c) All poodles are animals.

All animals are wild.

Therefore, all poodles are wild.

The difficulty here is that the conclusion is logically true; because the conclusion follows from the premises, the syllogism is valid. Of course, it's easy to think of counterexamples, situations in which the conclusion is not true in the real world of poodles; hardly any poodles are wild, after all (Feldman, 1992). Yet the rules of syllogistic reasoning are that the truth of the premises is *separate* from the validity of the syllogistic argument. What matters is that the conclusion does or does not follow from the premises. In the case of example (1c), the conclusion is valid even though the second premise is empirically false. Thus applying syllogistic reasoning to real-world problems is at least a two-step process. First, determine whether the syllogism itself is valid; second, if the syllogism is valid, determine the empirical truth of the premises.

Now consider another example:

(2a) All A are B.*

Some B are C.

Therefore, some A are C.

In formal logic, *some* means "at least one and possibly all," although research shows that some people have trouble understanding this (Schmidt & Thompson, 2008) Try inserting words into this example to see whether the conclusion is correct. For example,

(2b) All polar bears are animals.*

Some animals are white.

Therefore, some polar bears are white.

Despite the fact that words can be substituted that lead to an empirically correct statement, this second syllogism is *false*. Because the two premises do not invariably lead to a correct conclusion, the entire form of the syllogism is invalid (the reason for the asterisk). The incorrectness of the conclusion in (2a) stems from the qualifier *some*. Although the conclusion may be empirically true when you use one or another concrete example, this isn't necessarily the case for *all* examples, as shown by the following:

(2c*) *All polar bears are animals.*
Some animals are brown.
Therefore, some polar bears are brown.

▲ As shown in Figure 11-1, Euler circles can help in determining whether a syllogism is true. For instance, in the first illustration, the "All–All" form shows that it is necessarily true that "All *A* are *C*." The circles, which represent the classes of things known as *A*, *B*, and *C*, are nested such that *A* is a subset of *B* and *B* is a subset of *C*. There is simply no other way to represent the premises in diagrams except by concentric circles (when *A* and *B* are identical, their boundaries overlap completely, and the diagram merely shows one circle labeled both *A* and *B*).

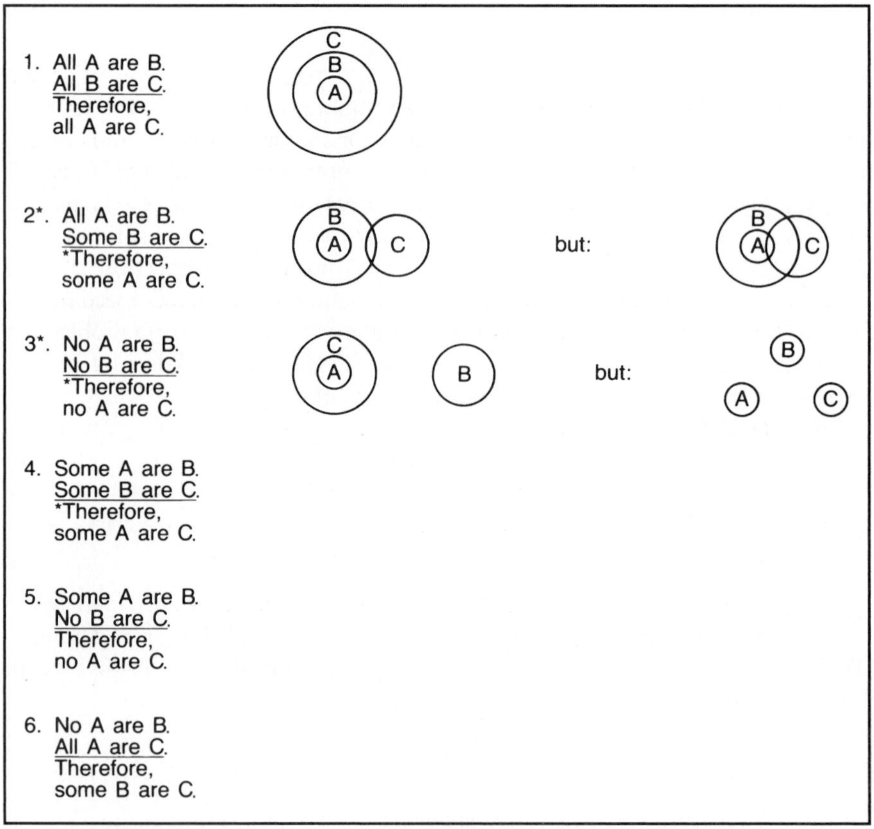

▲ **FIGURE 11-1** Euler circle illustrations for three categorical syllogisms. If a diagram can be constructed that shows the conclusion doesn't hold for all cases, then the conclusion is false. The first diagram in 2* shows why 2* is incorrect; it is not necessarily true that some *A* are *C*. The second diagram in 2* shows that an arrangement can be found that seems to support the argument. Likewise, the first diagram in 3* shows why 3* is incorrect; it is not necessarily true that no *A* are *C*. The second diagram in 3* shows an arrangement that does seem to support the conclusion.

In the second entry in the figure, the *incorrectness* of syllogism 2 is illustrated by the first diagram. In that illustration, a portion of *B* that does not contain *A* is exactly the portion that overlaps with *C*. Thus it isn't necessarily true that some *A* are *C*. The second diagram for this problem, however, illustrates the "Some polar bears are white" conclusion, one that is true of the real world even though the syllogism is not true. (The third syllogism is similar to the second; that is, it's false, but the second diagram seems to show that it's true.)

In general, performance on syllogisms improves when people are shown how to use diagrams or generate specific examples (Helsabeck, 1975). This will work only if you try to find ways to show the syllogism to be false. That is, it is easy to come up with examples or diagrams that mistakenly confirm an incorrect conclusion. Adopting a skeptical attitude about the conclusion and trying to diagram the situation to show how the conclusion is false are more likely to be helpful strategies. As an exercise, try generating diagrams for the final three syllogisms in the figure. As you work, bear in mind that the best strategy is to search for negative evidence. In other words, try to diagram the problem so that the syllogism is shown to be false (see work by Chater & Oaksford, 1999, on a probability-based explanation of such reasoning, and Sloman, 1998, on situations when people fail to draw appropriate category inclusion inferences; e.g., All stereos are electronic equipment, all electronic equipment has parts made of germanium, therefore all stereos have parts made of germanium).

Conditional Reasoning: If *P* Then *Q*

Conditional reasoning is a second kind of logical reasoning. Conditional reasoning problems always contain two parts, a *conditional clause,* a statement that expresses some relationship (*if P then* Q), followed by some *evidence* pertaining to the conditional clause (*p*, for example). **Conditional reasoning** involves *a logical determination of whether the evidence supports, refutes, or is irrelevant to the stated if–then relationship.*

The conditional in these problems is the *if–then* statement. Respectively, the *if* clause and the *then* clause are known as the **antecedent** and the **consequent** of the conditional clause (for clarity, we'll just refer to "the *if*" or "the antecedent," and "the *then*" or "the consequent"). The *if* states the possible cause, and the *then* states the effect of that possible cause. So the conditional *if P then Q* means "if *P* is true, then *Q* is true"; for example, if it rains (*P*) then the streets will be wet (*Q*). So far so good.

After the *if–then,* you are given a second statement, some evidence about the truth or falsity of one of the propositions in the *if–then* relationship. The goal of such reasoning is to take this evidence and decide what follows logically from it. In other words, is the conditional *if–then* statement true or false given this observed evidence, or is the evidence irrelevant to the *if–then*?

The general form of the conditional is *If P, then Q.* The conditional is then followed by the evidence, any one of the four possible outcomes. For "If it rains, the streets will be wet," the four possibilities are

P: In other words, P is true, it's raining.

not P: In other words, P is not true, it's not raining.

Q: In other words, Q is true, the streets are wet.

not Q: In other words, Q is not true, the streets are not wet.

Putting all of this together yields four possibilities:

Conditional	If *P*, then *Q*.	If *P*, then *Q*.	If *P*, then *Q*.	If *P*, then *Q*.
Evidence	*P*.	Not *P*.	*Q*.	Not *Q*.
Conclusion	Therefore, *Q*.	(No conclusion)	(No conclusion)	Not *P*.

According to the conditional *if–then* statement, if some antecedent condition *P* is true, then its consequence (the *consequent*) *Q* is true. If we then obtain evidence showing that *P* is indeed true, it follows logically that *Q* must be true. As an expanded example, consider the following example (adapted from Matlin, 1983), completely worked out for all four possibilities in Table 11-1:

If I am a freshman, then I must register for next semester's classes today.

VALID ARGUMENTS As the table shows, only two of the four possibilities lead to a true conclusion according to the rules of logic. In the first one, when given the evidence that *P* is true, "I am a freshman," then the consequent *Q* must be true, "I do have to register today." This is referred to as *affirming the antecedent*, in other words, saying that the antecedent is true. The classic name for this valid inference is *modus ponens*. Likewise, if the evidence is that *Q* is not true, "I do not have to register today," it must therefore be that *P* is not true, "*I am not a freshman*." This one is called *denying the consequent*, saying that the consequent is not true, is *modus tollens*.

INVALID ARGUMENTS Whereas both of these arguments lead to a correct conclusion, the other two possibilities are not valid. That is, denying the antecedent does not permit the conclusion that the consequent is false; likewise, affirming the consequent does not permit the conclusion that the antecedent is true. Let's continue with the college registration example, "If I am a freshman, then I must register today." If we deny the antecedent by offering the evidence "I am not a freshman,"

TABLE 11-1 Conditional Reasoning

Form	Name	Example
If *P*, then *Q*. Evidence: *P*. Therefore, *Q*.	*Modus ponens:* affirming the antecedent (valid inference)	If I am a freshman, I have to register today. Evidence: I am a freshman. Therefore, I have to register today.
If *P*, then *Q*. Evidence: not *P*. *Therefore, not *Q*.	Denying the antecedent (invalid inference)	If I am a freshman, I have to register today. Evidence: I am not a freshman. *Therefore, I do not have to register today.
If *P*, then *Q*. Evidence: *Q*. *Therefore, *P*.	Affirming the consequent (invalid inference)	If I am a freshman, I have to register today. Evidence: I have to register today. *Therefore, I am a freshman.
If *P*, then *Q*. Evidence: not *Q*. Therefore, not *P*.	*Modus tollens:* denying the consequent (valid inference)	If I am a freshman, I have to register today. Evidence: I do not have to register today. Therefore, I am not a freshman.

this does not lead to the conclusion that "I do not have to register today." It could be that two groups of students must register today; (a) all freshmen and (b) all sophomores in the first half of the alphabet. Thus, just because you're not a freshman doesn't necessarily mean you don't have to register today. Likewise, if we affirm the consequent, we assert that "I must register today." This does not permit the conclusion that "I'm a freshman," however; you might be a sophomore in the first half of the alphabet.

EVIDENCE ON CONDITIONAL REASONING Generally, people are good at inferring the truth of the consequent given evidence that the antecedent is true (affirming the antecedent, *modus ponens*). When given the conditional *if P, then Q* and the evidence that *P* is true, people usually infer correctly that *Q* is true. For instance, Rips and Marcus (1977) found that 100% of their sample drew this correct conclusion. The other valid inference, denying the consequent (*modus tollens*) is more difficult, apparently. Only 57% of Rips and Marcus's participants drew this conclusion (in a simpler version of the problem, 77% concluded correctly that *P* could never be true given the evidence *not Q*). Wason and Johnson-Laird (1972) found similar results in their investigation of conditional reasoning, in which problems were stated in either concrete or abstract form.

Errors in conditional reasoning seem to fall into three broad categories, involving the form of the reasoning problem, the search for evidence, and memory-related phenomena.

FORM ERRORS First, people sometimes draw incorrect conclusions simply by using one of the two invalid forms, either denying the antecedent or affirming the consequent. In fact, they commonly do so when comprehending discourse, according to Rader and Sloutsky (2002). These researchers presented people with short scenarios that contained an *if–then* conditional, then tested their recognition of either words from the stories or ideas in the stories (i.e., was this information in the story?). Table 11-2 gives examples of the stories and their results. Fully 59.2% of the people (incorrectly) "recognized" the affirm-the-consequent conclusion as having been in the story, not much different from the 60.8% who (correctly) recognized the *modus ponens* conclusion. The RT data on recognizing words from the stories showed the same pattern, no difference between "recognizing" the *modus ponens* and affirm-the-consequent conclusions. Apparently, both kinds of conclusions are routinely drawn when we read, even though one of them is logically incorrect (see Bonnefon & Hilton, 2004, for a demonstration of how the desirability of the consequent influences our predictions about the truth of the antecedent).

Another form error is more subtle. People have a tendency to reverse the propositions in the *if* and *then*. They then proceed to evaluate the given evidence against the now-reversed conditional. This kind of error is called an *illicit conversion*. As an example, with a conditional of *If P, then Q* and evidence *Q*, people tend to switch the conditional to **If Q, then P*. They then decide that the evidence *Q* implies that *P* is true. Clearly, this is incorrect because the order of *P* and *Q* in the conditional is meaningful. The *if* often specifies some possible cause, and the *then* specifies a possible effect. Obviously, we cannot draw correct conclusions if we reverse the roles of the cause (*P*) for some outcome and the result (*Q*) of some cause.

TABLE 11-2 Sample Stories and Tests from Rader and Sloutsky (2002).

Participants read four sentences. Sentence 1 was the same for both groups, but Sentence 2 differed between Version *A* and Version *B*. Sentence 3 was the same for both groups, but Sentence 4 differed for the two groups, containing either an inference or no inference. In other words, one-quarter of the participants saw Version A and an Inference, one-quarter saw Version A and No Inference, one-quarter saw Version B and an Inference, and one-quarter saw Version B and No Inference.

1. Frank woke up on his couch after taking a long nap and realized that he didn't know what time it was.
2. (Version A) He thought that if it was cold outside, then it was night.

   OR

   (Version B) He thought that if it was night, then it was cold outside.
3. Still feeling sleepy, Frank arose to open a window.
4. (Inference condition) He discovered that it was cold outside.

   OR

   (No Inference condition) He wondered whether it was cold outside.

Inference Test: Yes/No—Was this information in the story?

The time of day was night.

Argument Form	Percentage saying "yes" to the Inference Test	
	Inference	**No Inference**
***Modus Ponens* (Version A)**		
If it's cold, then it's night. Yes/No—The time of day was night.	60.8%	23.8%
Affirm—the Consequent (Version B)		
If it's night, then it's cold. Yes/No—The time of day was night.	59.2%	20.8%

From: Rader & Sloutsky, 2002, Tables 2 and 4 (pp. 61, 65)

SEARCH ERRORS The second kind of error involves the search for evidence. People often don't search for evidence but instead rely on a first impression or on the first example—the first mental model—that comes to mind (Evans, Handley, Harper, & Johnson-Laird, 1999). Another flaw in the search is called *searching for positive evidence*, also called the **confirmation bias**. Despite the rules of logic, we often seek only the information that confirms a conclusion, information that is consistent with a conclusion we have already drawn or a belief we already have. In fact, knowing an outcome and the conditions that might lead to it causes people to overestimate how likely that outcome is as a result of those prior conditions. That is, because people are more likely to draw backwards causal inferences (as noted in Chapter 10), they mistakenly think that the prior events are more likely to lead to the actual outcome (Koriat, Fiedler, & Bjork, 2006).

As a demonstration, consider the now-classic study of conditional reasoning (reported in Wason & Johnson-Laird, 1972) illustrated at the top of Figure 11-2, the Wason card problem. Four cards are visible to you, as shown in the figure, and each card has a letter on one side and a number on the other. The task is to pick the card or cards you would turn over to gather conclusive evidence on the following rule:

If a card has a vowel on one side, then it has an even number on the other side.

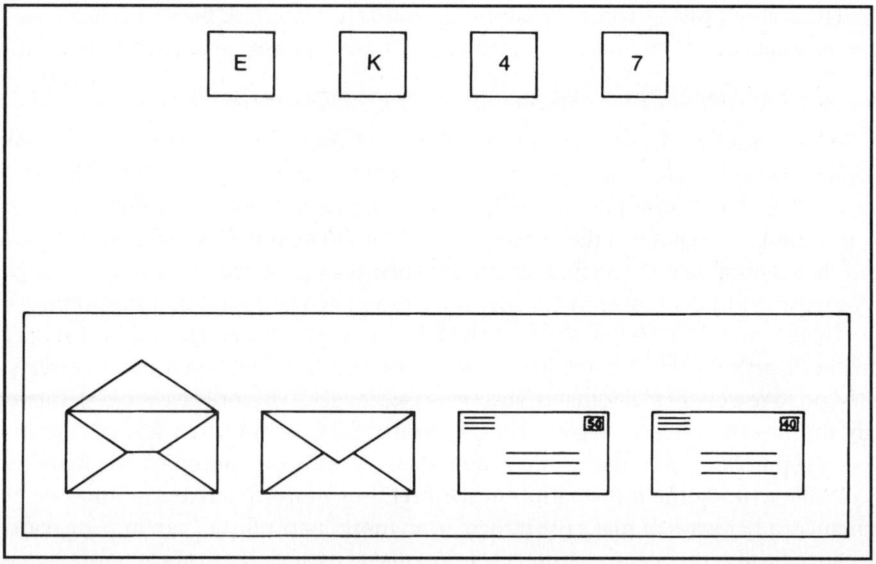

FIGURE 11-2 At the top of the illustration are the four cards in the Wason card problem. Which card or cards would you turn over to obtain conclusive evidence about the following rule: A card with a vowel on it will have an even number on the other side? At the bottom of the illustration are four envelopes. Which envelopes would you turn over to detect postal cheaters, under the rule that an unsealed envelope can be stamped with the less expensive stamp?

Give this statement some thought and decide how you'd test that rule before you continue reading.

Of the people Wason tested, 33% turned over only the *E* card, a correct choice conforming to *modus ponens* (affirming the antecedent). A thorough test of the rule's validity, however, requires that another card be turned over (in other words, the rule might be rephrased "Only if a card has a vowel on one side will it have an even number on the other side"). Only 4% of the people turned over the correct combination to check on this possibility, the *E* card *(modus ponens)* and the 7 card (*modus tollens*). That is, turning over the 7, which might yield negative evidence (*not Q*), was rarely considered. Instead, people preferred turning over the *E* and the 4 card: 46% of the people did this. Note two points. First, turning over the 4 is an instance of the invalid process of affirming the consequent (in other words, the rule doesn't say anything about what will be on the other side of a consonant; it could be an odd or an even number). Second, turning over the *E* represents a search for positive evidence about the rule, the (tentative) "yes" conclusion that *P* is true. Our general tendency is either to stop the search after turning over the *E* (positive evidence) or to continue searching for additional positive evidence (turning over the 4). This pattern of poor performance on this task has spawned a great deal of effort to understand the cognitive processes that give rise to this. Part of this effort includes computerized computational models of human performance (Klauer, Stahl, & Erdfelder, 2007) that reveal that people are not considering the cards one by one when reasoning, but, rather, looking at the configuration of cards before them.

In a different situation, however, Johnson-Laird, Legrenzi, and Legrenzi (1972) found that 21 of 24 people made both of the correct choices. The difference between the two studies had to do with the concreteness of the situation. In the Johnson-Laird et al. study, people were trying to find cheaters on the postal regulations, where unsealed envelopes could be mailed with a less expensive stamp than sealed envelopes.

Think about this situation. What *if–then* rule is being tested? Because either a sealed or an unsealed envelope could be mailed with a more expensive stamp, the rule must be:

If the envelope is sealed, then it must carry the expensive stamp.

When asked to detect cheaters, people turned over not only the sealed envelope (*modus ponens*) but also the envelope stamped with the less expensive stamp, that is, the *modus tollens* choice corresponding to the 7 card. Because the people were not postal workers, it seems clear that it was the concreteness of the situation that oriented the people toward the skeptical attitude mentioned earlier. Their skepticism led them to search actively for negative evidence; in the process, they demonstrated logical conditional reasoning.

There is an unmistakable similarity here to the stages of concrete and formal operations in Piaget's theory of cognitive development, in which children around 12 years of age begin to reason formally, that is, abstractly (see Piaget, 1967, or Flavell, 1963). Interestingly, the present evidence suggests that adults often fail to demonstrate formal or abstract reasoning processes, even though they can reason correctly in more concrete situations.

While making the information in the premises more concrete can improve performance, other ways of make the information more "naturalistic" can impede reasoning. Specifically, people are more likely to make reasoning errors if more intense emotions are involved (Blanchette & Richards, 2004). For example, if people are given the premise "If there is danger, then one feels nervous," they will be more likely to affirm the consequent "there is danger" if told that "Betty feels nervous" as compared to if they are given more emotionally neutral information, such as the letter problem.

PROVE IT

Conditional Reasoning

As you have noticed from reading the chapter, some things can come into play to affect how well people reason, such as whether the problem is naturalistic or abstract. What you can do here is set up a version of the Wason card task, and then come up with some interesting variations. What you will need are four index cards for each version of the task. Set up your task so that each of the four cards corresponds to each of the four response alternatives, namely *Modus Ponens* (Affirming the Antecedent), *Modus Tollens* (Denying the Consequent), Affirming the Consequent, and Denying the Antecedent. You might try having an abstract version, such as the original card layout used by Wason or something similar (e.g., if the card is red on one side, it will be green on the other side), and then some more naturalistic version that you come up with (e.g., the "freshmen registering for class" example from above, or one testing the rule "if a person is drinking alcohol, then he/she is at least 21 years old").

What you should do, after you've made your cards, is lay them down in front of your volunteers, tell them the rule they are verifying, and then have them tell you which card(s) they would choose to turn over.

You might also want to try some variations based on other things you've learned about memory and cognition. For example, what would happen if people were put in a dual task, divided attention situation? What would happen if you made the memory load a verbal load verses a visual/spatial load? Does emotional salience play a role? What if you prime different aspects of a person's semantic memory? The possibilities are endless.

MEMORY-RELATED ERRORS The third category of errors involves limitations in memory. A major proponent of this type of explanation is Johnson-Laird, who suggested that we do reasoning tasks not by some formal logic but by constructing **mental models**, *mental representations of meanings of the terms in reasoning problems* (Johnson-Laird & Byrne, 2002; Johnson-Laird, Byrne, & Schaeken, 1992). It's difficult to flesh out a set of meanings in conditional reasoning problems of the "If *P* then *Q*" variety. But because of our semantic knowledge, it's far easier in concrete, meaningful problems such as:

If it was foggy, then the match was canceled.

It was foggy.

Therefore, the match was canceled.

Furthermore, if additional terms appear in the problem, additional mental models must be derived, two additional ones in the following case:

If it was foggy, then the match was canceled.

The match was not canceled.

Therefore, it was not foggy.

When additional models are needed, the load on working memory mounts and can begin to interfere with reasoning; the same is true when the phrasing of the problem places a greater load on comprehension (e.g., Thompson & Byrne, 2002). And finally, as noted earlier, Evans et al. (1999) point out that if a conclusion matches the first mental model derived from the problem, it is particularly easy to accept the conclusion, leading to fallacies or errors in reasoning.

Hypothesis Testing

Part of the importance of conditional reasoning derives from its connection to scientific hypothesis testing. Consider a typical experimental hypothesis:

If theory A is true, then data resembling X should be obtained in the experiment.

If data resembling *X* are indeed obtained, there is a strong tendency to conclude that theory *A* must be true. That is, if the evidence is that data resembling *X* were obtained, this affirms the consequent. We then feel as if this evidence lets us conclude that *P* is true, that theory *A* is correct. What's wrong with this? It's a simple error of affirming the consequent and concluding mistakenly that this is evidence that the antecedent is true. Note how seductive this error is. Of course, it might be true that theory *A* is correct. But it's also possible that theory *A* is incorrect and that some other (correct) theory would also predict data *X*.

Because of the illogic of affirming the consequent and because we want to test hypotheses, our experiments test a *different* hypothesis than "Theory *A* is correct." As you learned (or will learn) in statistics, we test the null hypothesis in hopes that our evidence will be inconsistent with the predicted null outcome. Note the form of such a test:

If the null hypothesis is true (if P*), then there will be no effect of the variable (then* Q*).*

If we obtain evidence that there *is* an effect of the variable, then we have evidence that the consequent is not true. We can then conclude that the antecedent is not true—in other words, we reject the null hypothesis, deciding that it is false. This is the essence of hypothesis testing, to conclude that the *if* portion (the null hypothesis) is false based on an outcome that denies the consequent of the null hypothesis. Although people make a variety of errors in such situations, especially when the *if–then* relationship becomes more complex (Cummins, Lubart, Alksnis, & Rist, 1991), the typical mistake is simply to search for positive, confirming evidence (Klayman & Ha, 1989). In a similar vein, another strategy is simply to make a judgment as to the relevance or strength of the arguments and base a decision on that (e.g., Medin, Coley, Storms, & Hayes, 2003; Rips, 2001).

Section Summary

- Human reasoning is not especially logical, as shown in formal syllogistic and conditional reasoning problems. In reasoning tasks using syllogisms, conditional reasoning *if–then* problems, and hypothesis testing, people often fail to search for negative evidence. Instead, they often look for positive evidence for a conclusion, called confirmation bias, and are often influenced, both positively and negatively, by semantic knowledge. When a more skeptical attitude is adopted, and when the reasoning involves more concrete concepts, reasoning accuracy tends to improve.

DECISIONS

How do we make decisions? How do we choose among several alternatives, say, on a multiple choice test, or decide which of several options is best? What role does the information stored in memory play in decision making, and how certain are the decisions we make based on that information?

In a sense we've been studying decision making all along in this book, although the decisions often were fairly simple, for example, deciding "yes" or "no" in semantic or lexical decision tasks. At base, decision making can be viewed as a search for evidence, where the ultimate decision depends on some criterion or rule for evaluating the evidence. A search may turn up either positive or negative evidence. How we make decisions as a function of such evidence and how the evidence itself is evaluated are at the heart of decision-making and reasoning.

Let's turn to a very simple setting, in which we compare two objects or symbols, to see how the information stored in memory can influence comparison processes. We'll then turn to more complex decision-making and reasoning situations, again looking for the influence of stored knowledge and the evaluation of that information.

Decisions about Physical Differences

One of the very earliest areas of research in psychology was **psychophysics**; indeed, a great deal of research on psychophysics was conducted well before psychology *per se* came into existence (Fechner, 1860). The topic of interest in psychophysics was the *psycho*logical experience of physical stimulation, that is, *how perceptual experience differs from the physical stimulation being perceived.* In particular, research on psychophysics investigated the relationships between the physical dimensions of stimuli and the subjective, psychological experience of perceiving them.

In general, what was discovered was that the subjective experience of magnitude, regardless of the particular dimension involved (brightness, loudness, or the like), was not identical to the physical magnitude. Instead, there is a psychological dimension of magnitude that forms the basis of our perceptions.

For instance, the perceived brightness of a light is not a linear function of the light's physical brightness. Instead, perceived brightness depends on several factors, such as the absolute level of brightness, the brightness of the background, and the duration of the stimulus. Likewise, the amount by which brightness must be changed in order to perceive the change depends on more than just the amount of physical change in brightness. Perceived change depends critically on the initial level of the light's brightness. A dim light needs only a small boost in brightness for people to detect a difference, whereas a very bright light needs a much larger boost for the change to be noticed. *The amount of change needed for people to detect the change is called a* **just noticeable difference (jnd)** (as in Weber's law; see Haber & Hershenson, 1973, for example). The point is that the size of the jnd increases as the physical stimulus becomes more intense. If only one jnd separates two dim lights, the same physical difference in brightness between two bright lights may not be detectable. Our perceptual mechanism is affected by the psychological dimension of brightness, a different dimension than physical brightness. Thus psychological processing of a stimulus does not accurately mirror the physical stimulus properties. Instead, distortions and alterations of the stimulus are introduced during perception, and these distortions and alterations can be attributed to the human perceiver.

Of particular relevance to our discussion is the **distance** or **discriminability effect**: *The greater the distance or difference between the two stimuli being compared, the faster the decision that they differ* (Woodworth & Schlosberg, 1954). In other words, it's easier to discriminate between two stimuli that are very different (a finger snap versus a gunshot) than between two that are very similar (shots from two different guns). This is not at all a new finding; Moyer and Bayer (1976) cite four separate sources for this effect that were published before 1940.

Decisions about size differences are psychophysical judgments, which are speeded up when stimuli differ by a great amount.

Decisions about Symbolic Differences

More recently, investigators have found that a variety of similar effects in tasks involving **symbolic comparisons**, that is, comparisons not between two physical objects or stimuli but between two mental symbols. The connection with the earlier work is that the distance effect still holds. But because the effect is now based on symbolic rather than physical differences, it is called the **symbolic distance effect**. Just as in psychophysical judgments, the source of the symbolic distance effect is the person making the mental comparison. The big difference is that semantic and other long-term memory knowledge, rather than perceptual information, is influencing decision making. Briefly, the symbolic distance effect is that *we judge differences between symbols more rapidly when they differ considerably on some symbolic dimension, e.g., value.*

★ Consider the stimuli in panels A and B of Figure 11-3. Which dot is higher? Despite the simple nature of this decision, it takes some amount of time to make the decision. To begin with, the time to decide which dot is higher depends on the separation of the dots; the greater the separation, the faster the decision. This is the simple physical distance effect again: Two stimuli can be discriminated more quickly when they differ more (Moyer & Bayer, 1976).

Now consider the bottom two illustrations. For panel C in Figure 11-3, which balloon is higher? For panel D, which yo-yo is lower? It is probably not obvious to you at a conscious level, but when people are asked, "Which balloon is higher?" their judgments

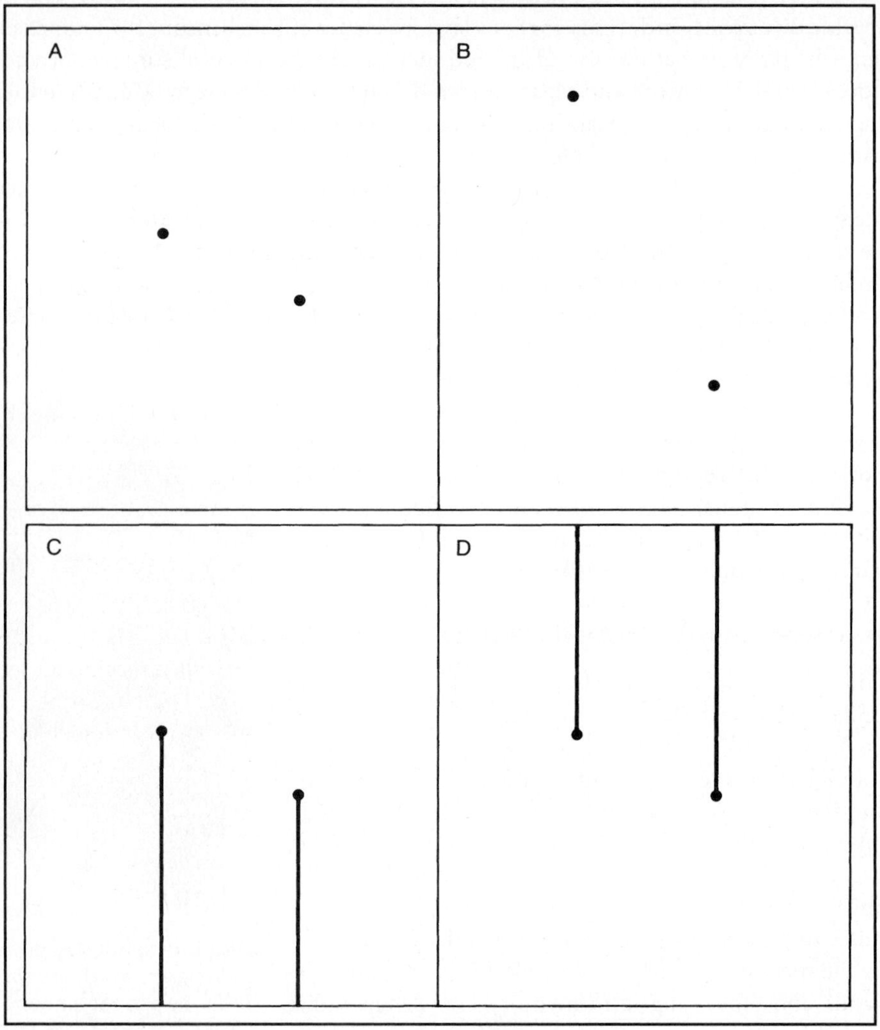

★ FIGURE 11-3 Stimuli used by Banks, Fujii, & Kayra-Stuart (1975) in a study of physical and symbolic comparisons. In the top two panels, people were asked which dot is higher or lower. In the bottom two panels, people were asked which balloon is higher/lower and which yo-yo is higher/lower.

are affected not only by the discriminability of the two heights, but also by the semantic dimension needed for the judgments (Banks, Clark, & Lucy, 1975). In other words, the semantic knowledge that balloons are held at the bottom by strings, float up in the air, and are therefore oriented in terms of highness was a significant influence on the participants' decision times; describing the illustrations as balloons led people to treat the pictures symbolically rather than as mere physically different stimuli. When the same pictured display was accompanied by the question, "Which balloon is lower?" judgments were much slower. And as you would expect, the situation was reversed when people judged stimuli such as those in panel D, the yo-yos. "Which yo-yo is lower?" yielded faster decisions than, "Which yo-yo is higher?" because semantic knowledge about yo-yos is that they hang down from their strings.

The name for this is the **semantic congruity effect** (Banks, 1977; Banks et al., 1975). It states that a person's *decision is faster when the dimension being judged matches or is congruent with the implied semantic dimension in the figure*. In other words, the implied dimension in the balloon illustration is height because balloons float up. When asked to judge "how high" some "high" object is, the judgment is speeded up because "height" is semantically congruent with "high." Likewise, "lowness" is implied in the yo-yo display, so judging which of two "low things" is lower is also a congruent decision. Figure 11-4 displays the general form of the symbolic distance effect and the semantic congruity effect (Banks, 1977). ▲

NUMBER MAGNITUDE Some of the clearest research supporting these idealized curves comes from Banks's work on judgments of numerical magnitude. In this research, people are shown a pair of digits, say, 1 and 2 or 7 and 8. In one condition, the instructions are to pick the smaller of the two values; in another, people are asked to pick the larger value. Of course, in all conditions, the RT to make the judgments is the dependent variable of major interest.

Can you predict what the results of such comparisons are, based on the distance and congruity effects? First, the larger the difference between the digits, the faster the judgments are made. In other words, picking the smaller of the pair 1 and 3 will be faster than picking the smaller of 2 and 3 because 1 and 3 differ from each other more than 2 and 3 do. This is the symbolic distance effect, similar to the physical distance effect but now based purely on the symbolic meanings of the digits and the magnitudes to which they refer; panels B and C in Figure 11-5 show this clearly. Second, judgment time is affected ● by semantic congruity. Picking the smaller of two small digits is faster than picking the larger of two small digits, and the difference is more pronounced when picking the larger instead of the smaller of two large digits; for instance, the 8 and 9 pair in Figure 11-5. When the instructions ask for a judgment of smallness, symbols referring to small quantities are faster; when the instructions ask for a judgment of largeness, symbols referring to large quantities are faster to judge. This is the semantic congruity effect.

A variety of fascinating conclusions are supported by such results. First, when people make mental comparisons of purely symbolic quantities, there is a pronounced semantic distance effect. Just as in psychophysics, the psychological difference is not the same as the physical difference; the mental differences between digits do not perfectly mirror the numerical differences between digits. Banks's research (Banks, et al., 1976) suggests that our mental representation of number and numerical magnitude is a nonlinear one, one in which the psychological distances between larger numbers are

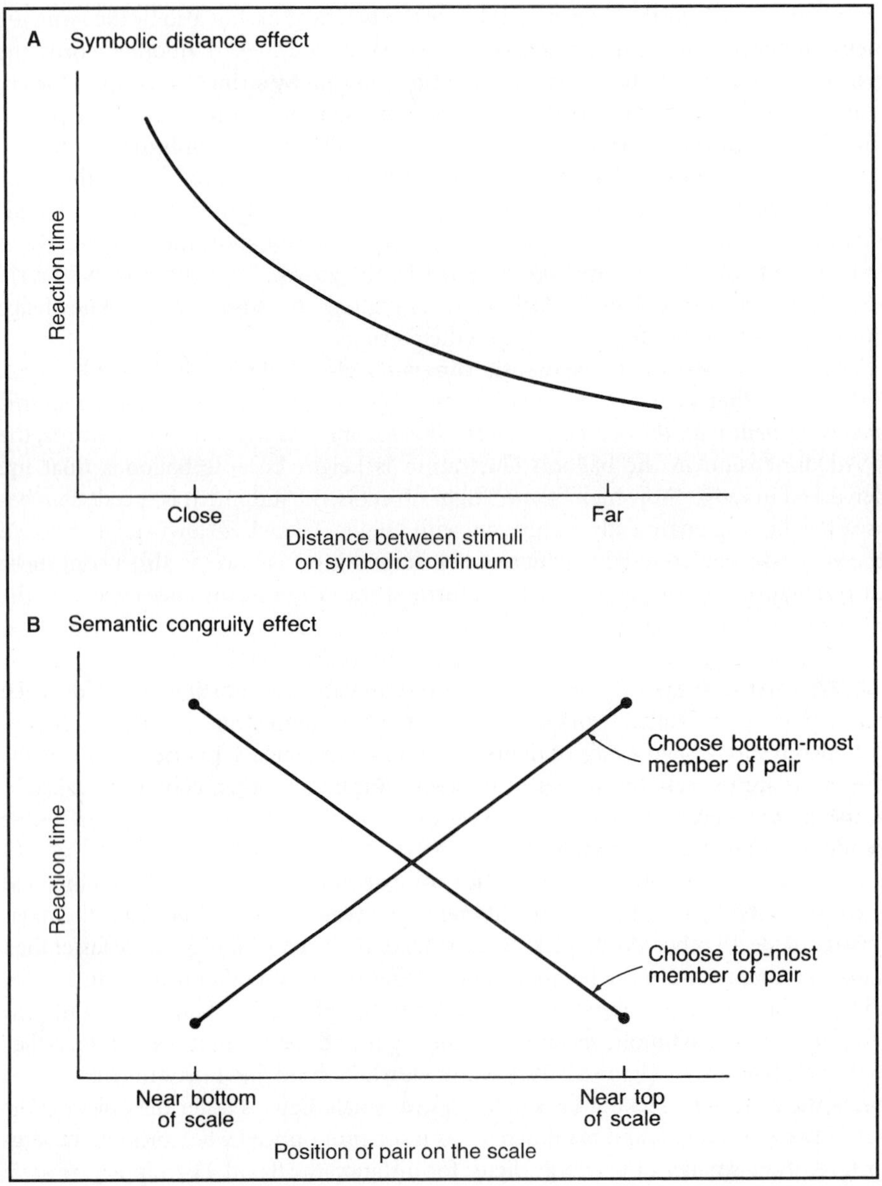

▲ **FIGURE 11-4** Idealized curves: **A.** the symbolic distance effect; **B.** the semantic congruity effect. From Banks (1977).

compressed, relative to the distances between smaller numbers. Thus just as two bright lights are perceived as being more similar than two dim lights, two large numbers are psychologically closer together than two small numbers; 1 and 2 are more different psychologically than 8 and 9 are.

Second, when we judge magnitudes, the dimension of judgment must match the implied semantic dimension for the comparison to be made quickly. A mismatch between the psychological dimension and the one specified by instructions (e.g., "choose

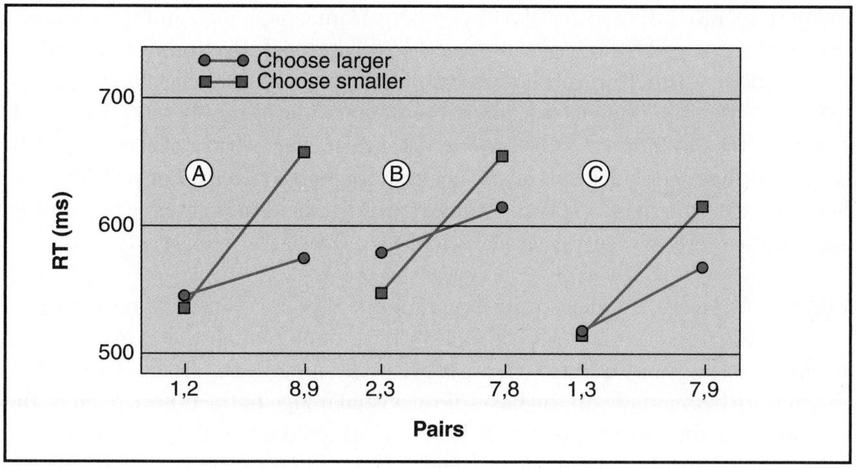

FIGURE 11-5 Response time performance (in ms) on number comparisons. From Banks et al. (1976), Figure 1.

the larger one" when the two things are small) slows down the comparison, even when the same quantities are being compared (see also Marschark & Paivio, 1979; Shoben, Sailor, & Wang, 1989).

At a more global level, the research also attests to another important idea: The particular *form* of a concept's representation in memory exerts an influence on the judgments we make. We are asking people to compare two concepts stored in memory on some dimension of magnitude. By timing their judgments, we can come to understand how those concepts are represented in memory. This kind of task, timed mental comparisons, can be applied widely to all sorts of symbolic concepts, even cases where the underlying magnitude dimension is arbitrary and learned only by trial and error (Tzelgov, Yehene, Kotler, & Alon, 2000).

The influence of embodied cognition can be seen in decision making, even for simple number judgments. In a seminal study, Dehaene, Bossini, and Giraux (1993) had people make judgments about a series of numbers, such as whether they were odd or even. What they found was that *judgments about smaller numbers were made more quickly with the left hand, and judgments about larger numbers were made more quickly with the right hand.* This pattern of performance is known as the **SNARC effect** (for Spatial-Numerical Association of Response Codes). This occurrence of the SNARC effect is consistent with the idea that many people have a mental number line going from left to right with small numbers on the left and larger numbers occurring as one moves to the right (although there are other accounts, e.g., Santens & Gevers, 2008).

This is an embodied effect because most people (two-thirds of people according to Fischer, 2008) typically start counting on their fingers using their left hand. Moreover, left-hand counters show a much stronger SNARC effect than people who start counting with their right hand. This mental arrangement then appears to have a direct influence on how people make decisions and respond based on those decisions. This decision process clearly involves the visuo-spatial sketch pad of working memory more than the phonological loop, as the effect is more disrupted when people are in a visuo-spatial dual task situation as compared to a verbal one (e.g., Herrera, Macizo, & Semenza, 2008). It also appears to be more spatial than visual, as an identical SNARC effect occurs in blind people (Castronovo & Seron, 2007). Note that this effect shows some influence of linguistic relativity (remember the Sapir-Whorf hypothesis from Chapter 9?), in that it is larger for languages that are read left to right as opposed to right to left (Dehaene et al., 1993; Shaki & Fischer, 2008). Furthermore, it does not appear that the basic phenomenon underlying the SNARC effect is unique to our mental representation of numbers. A study by Lidji, Kolinsky, Lochy, and Morais (2007) produced a similar effect with musical pitches. The results showed that people had preference of responding to lower tones with the left and higher tones with the right hand, similar to the arrangement of notes on a piano or guitar string (see also Gevers, Reynvoet, & Fias, 2004, for a day of the week effect).

IMAGERY Which is larger, a squirrel or a rabbit? Which is smaller, a mouse or a dog? Several investigators, notably Moyer (1973), have documented the symbolic distance and semantic congruity effects when people make judgments of this sort. Here, the judgments are being made on the basis of the visual image of the object. That is, the evidence suggests that when people make these larger/smaller judgments about real-world objects, they retrieve mental images of them, then mentally scan the images to determine which one is larger or smaller. Moyer had people estimate the absolute sizes of animals and make timed comparisons between different pairs. His results showed that RT decreased as the differences in size between the animals increased—the symbolic distance effect. Furthermore, the relationship between image size and RT was logarithmic; in other words, the size differences are smaller at the larger end of the scale than at the smaller end, exactly what Banks (1977) found about the mental number line.

A final important aspect of these results relates to mental imagery. As Moyer (1973) and others (Kosslyn & Pomerantz, 1977) argue, results such as these imply strongly that the semantic information being retrieved from memory is perceptual. That is, the retrieved information is in the form of visual images that have been stored in long-term memory, not simply verbal or abstract propositions (see also Anderson, 1983). As confirmation of this, do the following demonstration (inspired by Matlin, 2002): Imagine two clock faces, set at the times listed below. Compare the two clock faces to decide which one's hands make the smaller angle, *A* or *B*.

A	*B*
3:20	7:25
2:15	9:20

In keeping with the symbolic distance effect, your decision times here were probably much faster for the second pair of times. Why? Because 2:15 on a clock face yields a very small angle, but 9:20 yields a large one—and it's easier to discriminate between two things that are very different from each other.

SEMANTIC ORDERINGS Consider some results by Holyoak and Walker (1976). They had people make comparisons along the semantic orderings of time, quality, and temperature; for example, compare "minute versus hour," "average versus poor," "cool versus cold." The instructions said either to choose the longer, better, or warmer or the shorter, worse, or colder of the two concepts in the pair. Just as with the numerical judgment task, performance demonstrated both the symbolic distance and the semantic congruity effects. Judgments were faster when the pair of terms differed a great deal (e.g., perfect versus poor) than when they differed by less (perfect versus excellent). And judgments were faster if the dimension was congruent with the stimulus values; for example, choosing the longer of "century versus decade" was easier than choosing the shorter of those two. And in a study by Friedman (1978), the same kind of symbolic distance and semantic congruity effects were found when the concepts had no physical or quantitative dimension at all; for example, choose the better or worse of pairs such as "lose versus peace" or "hate versus pressure."

The important extension of this is that the distance and congruity effects influenced decisions even when the underlying representations were not quantitative. The implication here is that more abstract orderings must be mentally represented in a similar fashion to number and other quantity-based orderings because they all "behave" in a similar way. Our mental representations of such terms, and in particular the way those terms are ordered, influence our judgments in very much the same way as more quantitative representations do. The nature of the mental representation, furthermore, can introduce distortions that are analogous to those found in perceptual tasks. We make simple comparisons and decisions based on our stored knowledge. The form of that knowledge can distort our judgments to a surprising degree.

Decisions about Geographical Distances

Perhaps not surprisingly, judgments of geographical distance seem to follow the same principles (Baum & Jonides, 1979; Holyoak & Mah, 1982). The point in this research is to have people make distance or location comparisons, then determine what their mental maps are like. In one such study, Holyoak and Mah (1982) tested people at the University of Michigan, asking them to rate the distances between American cities on a 1 to 9 scale. When no particular geographical reference point was given—the neutral condition—people based their judgments on their own local viewpoint. As Figure 11-6 shows, they overestimated distances for nearby Midwestern cities; they rated Kansas City, a fairly nearby city, as much further ◆

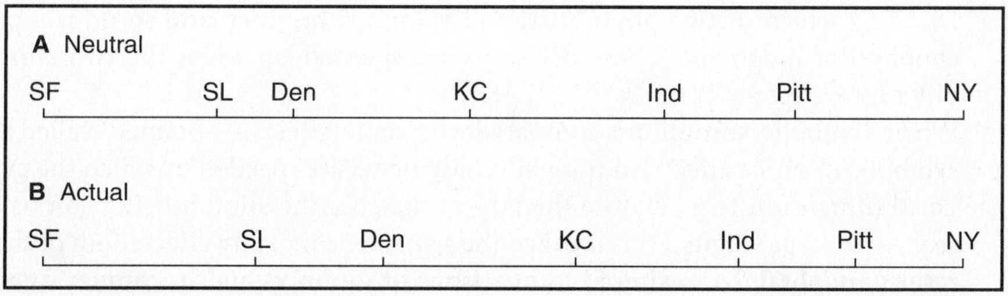

◆ **FIGURE 11-6**
Results of Holyoak and Mah's (1982) study of the relative locations of cities along an east–west line. Estimates in the neutral perspective were made from a person's current location, Ann Arbor, Michigan, roughly halfway between Indianapolis and Pittsburgh on the east–west line. People overestimated the distances to Denver, Kansas City, and Indianapolis, as shown by the actual distances at the bottom.

away than it really is, but Denver and Salt Lake City, more distant cities from Ann Arbor, as much closer together. This is the symbolic distance effect: The farther away the cities were, the closer together they were in the mental representation. They also confirmed a certain egocentrism in adult thought; in a sense, the distorted "New Yorker's view of the world" can be transplanted anywhere (but cf. Friedman, Kerkman, & Brown, 2002, who suggest that one's categories of locations—"that's a northern city," for example—are the important determinant of biased judgments).

In a series of investigations of people's reasoning about geography, Friedman and Brown (2000; Friedman, Brown, & McGaffey, 2002) asked people to estimate the latitude of 34 North American cities (from Edmonton to Miami) and 34 European and North African cities (from Oslo to Cairo). People's estimates fit what they called a *plausible-reasoning process*, where knowledge from a variety of sources is factored into a decision. In particular, people may have some specific knowledge of the location of certain cities. For others, they may only know the city's general region but do not know enough about the region's location. Thus, among other things, the Friedman and Brown studies replicated evidence of the so-called Chicago–Rome illusion, the illusion that Chicago is much farther north than Rome (in fact, they have the same latitude). People maintain the illusion because they view Chicago (correctly) as being in "northern North America," whereas Rome is viewed (also correctly) as southern European or Mediterranean; of course, all of this is based on the misconception that North America and Europe are aligned in latitude (they aren't) and that "northern" and "southern" refer to approximately the same latitudes in both (they don't). Just as is found in reasoning based on magnitude, imagery, and semantic ordering, reasoning about geography is also influenced by conceptual knowledge, by information stored in memory and retrieved to help solve the reasoning problem, however faulty or incomplete that knowledge is (see Friedman & Montello, 2006, for similar results with relative city judgments instead of absolute latitude judgments).

Section Summary

- Deciding which of two physical stimuli is louder, brighter, and so on is a psychophysical judgment. These decisions are speeded up when the two stimuli differ by a great amount.
- When symbolic stimuli are compared, the same effect is obtained, called the symbolic distance effect. Additionally, judgments are speeded up when the evaluated dimension (e.g., choose the larger) matches the stimuli being compared (e.g., two "large" digits); this is called the semantic congruity effect. Both of these results are obtained in simple comparisons of numbers and in comparisons of qualities such as "hot/cold."
- The existence of the SNARC effect when responding to numbers using the left and right hands suggests an embodied component to at least some types of decisions.
- In all symbolic and reasoning situations, including those about geographical location, our mental representation and knowledge influence our judgments.

DECISIONS AND REASONING UNDER UNCERTAINTY

Some of the decisions we've been discussing, such as judging which of two numbers is smaller, are rapid and fairly automatic. Typically we are aware only of the outcome of those processes: We know consciously that we responded "7" to the question "Which is larger, 4 or 7?" If asked why we responded that way, we tend to give intellectualized answers that likely have little if anything to do with the actual mental basis for the decision (Ericsson & Simon, 1993). Furthermore, we are unaware of the exact nature of the mental representation that leads us to the judgment; to be blunt, nobody has conscious awareness of the compressed mental number line, although this is how numerical magnitude is mentally represented from young children up through adults (Banks, 1977; Duncan & McFarland, 1980).

In contrast to such relatively automatic decision making, the bulk of the research on reasoning and decision making investigates processes that are slower and more deliberate. In fact, in many ways the research on such decisions is very similar to the area of problem solving, in which there is a clear connotation of slow, deliberate processing. One aspect of this similarity relates to familiarity: The domains of reasoning and problem solving we investigate are not well known or understood by the person, or they involve material that is not highly familiar. Another similarity involves the idea of uncertainty: There is often no certain answer to the problems or at least no good way of deciding whether a particular type of solution is the correct approach. Despite this, taking a principled and careful look at how people make decisions under uncertainty can provide enormous benefits, and guide further research. For example, there are emerging findings that people who are convicted of crimes and sentenced to jail show principled differences in how they make decisions, and possibly that parts of their brains are working less effectively, thereby leading to these decision making differences (Yechiam, Kanz, Bechara, Stout, Busemeyer, Altmaier & Paulsen, 2008).

And finally, the major conclusions of this kind of research are similar to the conclusions you'll read about in Chapter 12, on problem solving. People make decisions and base their reasoning on a variety of strategies, some good and some not so good. This is also a characteristic of much problem solving. Because of these similarities, investigations of such strategies often are impossible to categorize clearly as reasoning on the one hand or problem solving on the other.

Algorithms and Heuristics

A basic distinction is necessary at the outset to understand the nature of the research you'll be reading about. In many reasoning and problem-solving settings, two general approaches can be taken, an algorithmic approach and a heuristic approach.

An **algorithm** is *a specific rule or solution procedure, often detailed and complex, that is guaranteed to furnish the correct answer if it is followed correctly; for example, a formula.* We are

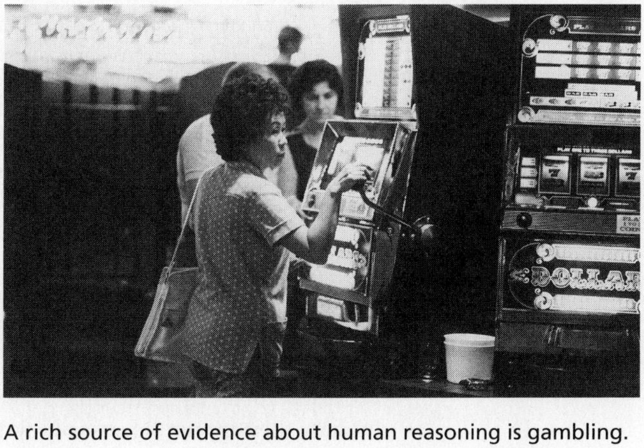

A rich source of evidence about human reasoning is gambling.

familiar with algorithms largely through our schoolwork in arithmetic and mathematics. For example, we all learned an algorithmic approach to complex multiplication, a set of rules for applying operations in certain orders to arrive at the correct answer. If the rules are applied correctly, the algorithm provides the correct answer.

In contrast, a **heuristic** is an informal method or guideline rather than a formal, specified rule. It's a "seat of the pants" *strategy or approach that works under some circumstances*, for some of the time, but *is not guaranteed to yield the correct answer*. (The word *heuristic* comes from the Greek stem meaning "to invent or discover." The same word stem leads to the word *eureka*, the classic exclamation, supposedly uttered by Archimedes in his bathtub, meaning roughly "Aha, I've found it!") Heuristic rules of thumb aren't foolproof or guaranteed—but they're often right.

Answer these questions:

1. *If you toss a fair coin, what is the probability of getting heads?*
2. *If you toss a fair coin, what is the probability of getting heads two times in a row?*

Most people know that the probability of tossing heads is .50—that's a simple 50/50 situation. But you may be hazy about the correct algorithm to apply to the second problem, two heads in a row. It's actually fairly simple and requires two basic probability statements.

First, the chance of getting heads once is 50/50, or stated as a probability, .50.

Second, the probability of any particular sequence of independent events (like coin tosses) is the basic probability of the event (.50) multiplied by itself once for each event in the sequence, that is .50 × .50 for two heads in a row. More formally, the formula is $p(e)^2$, the basic probability of the event $p(e)$ raised to the nth power, where n is the number of events in the sequence. So the answer here is .25 for two heads, $.50^2$ or simply .50 × .50.

People tend to be poor at probability questions. In a survey of an undergraduate class that used those questions, 89% got question 1 correct, but only 42% got the second question right; 37% said that the correct answer was .50, the same as in question one (Ashcraft, 1989). It seemed clear that these people didn't know the formula.

Likewise, people generally don't know the algorithm for answering this kind of question:

3. *If each of 10 people at a business meeting shakes hands (once) with each other person, then how many handshakes are exchanged?*

If you don't know how to compute this, then make an estimate—and then introspect for a moment on how you came up with that estimate. If you guessed, then what guided your guess? The algorithm for this problem is also fairly easy. If N is the number of people, then the number of handshakes is $N \times (N - 1)/2$; for 10 people, that's $10 \times 9/2 = 45$ handshakes. "Without repetitions" simply means that after person *A* shakes *B*'s hand, *B* doesn't then also shake *A*'s hand.

Notice that the algorithm provides a systematic and orderly procedure that is guaranteed to yield the correct result (assuming you do the math correctly). Algorithmic methods, in all these settings, follow the *normative model*, the method or formula provided to us by mathematics and probability. Heuristics, in contrast, seem very human; they are not necessarily systematic or orderly, and they rely heavily on educated guessing. This is referred to as the *descriptive model*, just a description of how the question was answered. A large part of the research on reasoning and decision making looks at how different the normative and descriptive models are, how people diverge from the normative method. Under certain circumstances, or for particular kinds of questions, heuristics seem prone to distortions, inaccuracies, and omissions—the descriptive model diverges from what's normative or "right."

"This CD player costs less than players selling for twice as much."

One reason people use heuristics, rather than algorithms, to make decisions is because heuristics can be used more quickly and easily, which is an advantage when decisions need to be made rapidly. Generally, people will not exert the effort to do more deliberate reasoning when quick and dirty processes will suffice, unless they encounter a difficulty in using their more intuitive judgments (Alter, Oppenheimer, Epley, & Eyre, 2007).

Heuristics, Biases, and Fallacies

By far the most influential work done on decision making and heuristics has been that of Tversky and Kahneman (1973, 1974, 1980; Kahneman, Slovic, & Tversky, 1982; Kahneman & Tversky, 1972, 1973; Shafir & Tversky, 1992). This is one of the areas of cognitive psychology to have a strong and clear influence on other disciplines and fields. Tversky and Kahneman's work on heuristics and fallacies has had an impact in such diverse areas as law, medicine, and business. Most prominently, it has affected the field of economics, and Daniel Kahneman received the Nobel Prize in Economics in 2002 (see Kahneman, 2003a, for a first-person account of that work, and 2003b for his personal history of the collaboration with the late Amos Tversky; see Kahneman & Tversky, 2000, for a compendium of chapters on this approach, and Tetlock & Mellers, 2002, for a review of the book). In a way, it isn't surprising that this topic is of interest to many different fields—after all, think of how many situations and settings involve reasoning and making decisions. The Nobel Prize signifies more than just the relevance of the topic; it signifies noteworthy achievement in tackling and explaining a large and important set of ideas, how humans reason and make decisions.

Kahneman and Tversky's research focused extensively on a set of heuristics and biases that appear to characterize everyday reasoning about uncertain events; an area now called behavioral decision research (Medin & Bazerman, 1999). Their interest was in how people predict the likelihood of future events, how people categorize events, and how various biases and errors in such judgments can be accounted for by an understanding of the reasoning process.

In some of the situations they studied, an algorithm can be applied to arrive at a correct answer. Many of these situations involve probabilistic reasoning, the sort of judgments students often are asked to make in the probability chapter of an undergraduate statistics book. Knowledge of the algorithms doesn't necessarily mean that the person understands them, can use them spontaneously, or can recognize when they should be applied. Indeed, Kahneman and Tversky found that a sample of graduate students in psychology, all of whom had been exposed to the relevant statistical algorithms, did well on simple problems but still relied on a heuristic rather than an algorithm when given more complex situations. However, several studies have shown more positive effects—good transfer and improved reasoning—when some relevant training is given (Agnoli, 1991; Agnoli & Krantz, 1989; Fong & Nisbett, 1991; Lehman, Lempert, & Nisbett, 1988). (Incidentally, reading Tversky and Kahneman's work, such as the 1973 article, often is helpful to students as they *study* probability in a statistics class. See Nisbett, Krantz, Jepson, & Kunda, 1983, on statistical heuristics that people use in everyday reasoning).

Other situations that have been studied involve estimates of likelihood when precise probabilities cannot be assigned or have not been supplied, although elements of statistical and probabilistic reasoning are still appropriate, and situations contrasting verbal and numerical descriptions (for instance, "rain is likely" versus "there's a 70% chance of rain"; Windschitl & Weber, 1999). And finally, some of the settings that have been studied involve very uncertain or even impossible situations, such as asking people to predict the outcome of a hypothetical event. For instance, how would the outcome of World War II have changed if Germany had developed the atomic bomb before the United States?

We begin with the more heavily researched heuristics, the representativeness and availability heuristics, then devote some attention to others. We'll then cover a newer approach that has challenged some of the bedrock assumptions in Kahneman and Tversky's work. As you read, try to develop your own examples of situations that are similar to the stated examples. You'll be surprised at how often we use heuristics in everyday decision making and reasoning. A table at the end of the section will list the heuristics and biases in a convenient summary form.

The Representativeness Heuristic

Back to coin tosses for a moment. If you toss a coin six times in a row, which of the following two outcomes is more likely: HHHTTT or HHTHTT? Most of us would agree—and quite rapidly at that—that the second alternative, with the alternations between heads and tails, is a more likely outcome than the runs of three heads and three tails. But if you stop and think about it, you'll realize that each of these is *exactly* as likely as the other, because each is one of the possible ways six coin tosses can occur (the total number of outcomes is 2^6, that is, 64 sequences of heads and tails).

Part of what fools us is that we think of the alternating pattern HHTHTT as a representative of a whole class of outcomes, in which most of the outcomes have alternations between heads and tails. This is incorrect because the problem asked about the likelihood of exactly the two given sequences, not the general class of sequences. But the mistake we make is an important indicator of how we reason in similar situations (the math for this problem is explained in the Appendix, at the end of this chapter).

According to Kahneman and Tversky (1972), when we judge the likelihood of uncertain events, we do so on the basis of the event's representativeness. The

representativeness heuristic is a judgment rule in which *an estimate of the probability or likelihood of an event is determined by one of two features, how similar the event is to the population of events it came from or whether the event seems similar to the process that produced it.* In other words, we judge whether event *A* belongs to class *B* based on the extent to which *A* is representative of *B*, the degree to which it resembles *B*, or the degree to which it resembles the kind of process that *B* is known to be.

RANDOM PROCESSES In our coin toss example, we know that getting heads or tails is a random process. Given that tossing coins is random, we judge the sequence HHTHTT as more likely than HHHTTT because the sequence HHTHTT resembles the outcome of a random process more than HHHTTT. The thinking here, illogical but understandable, is that a random process ought to look random (e.g., Burns & Corpus, 2004). The sequence of three heads then three tails looks nonrandom and so seems less likely. Likewise, because the likelihood for six tosses is three heads and three tails (in the long run), almost any sequence with three of each will appear more representative than sequences with more of one outcome than the other. (See Pollatsek, Konold, Well, & Lima, 1984, and Nickerson, 2002, for evidence on people's beliefs about random sampling processes, and the ability to produce and perceive randomness.)

REPRESENTATIVENESS OF THE PARENT POPULATION Consider a situation more like Kahneman and Tversky's first criterion, where the event is similar in essential characteristics to its parent population (i.e., to the population of events from which the event of interest is drawn). These authors' example of this situation goes as follows:

> *In a certain town there are two hospitals. In one, about 45 babies are born each day, in the other only about 15. As you know, about 50% of all babies are boys, although on any day, of course, this percentage may be higher or lower. Across one year, the hospitals recorded the number of days on which 60% or more of the babies were male. Which hospital do you think had more such days?*
>
> (After Kahneman & Tversky, 1972, p. 443. Decide on your answer before reading further.)

The majority of people in Kahneman and Tversky's study (28 out of 50) claimed that the number of days with 60% or more male babies would be about the same for the two hospitals. Twelve of the 50 said the larger hospital would have more such days, and only 10 said the smaller hospital would have more days with 60% or more male babies. (Another group was asked about days on which "less than 60%" of the babies were male. These results were similar.) Overall, most people believed that both hospitals would have about the same number of days on which 60% or more (or fewer) of the babies would be male.

Let's explain this. Consider the conclusion that people drew, that both hospitals would have about the same number of "extreme" days. People know that there will be variations around the expected percentage of 50% boy/50% girl and that 60% is somewhat extreme. Because "somewhat extreme" events occasionally happen, a small and a large hospital both having 60% or more male babies is viewed as representative of a larger population. Note the implicit and incorrect assumption here that "extreme" means the same thing for the two hospitals.

In fact, the correct answer is that the smaller hospital will probably have more days on which 60% or more of the babies are male. This is because of an elementary notion in statistics. Extreme or unlikely outcomes are more likely with small sample sizes. That is, with fewer events, the likelihood is greater for variations from the expected proportion. Thus, it is more likely that the small hospital will have more extreme days than the large hospital. The reason is that the 60% proportion is being computed on an average of 15 births instead of 45. Another way of saying this is that, given the fifty-fifty odds, 60% is not as extreme an occurrence out of 15 opportunities as it is out of 45; 60% or more male babies is not as extreme for the small hospital as it is for the large one. (On statistical grounds, this is precisely the same reason that all heads is a more likely outcome for two coin tosses than it is for six coin tosses. See the Appendix at the end of the chapter for the algorithmic and statistical explanations.)

The representativeness heuristic embodies a bias called *insensitivity to sample size* (see Table 11-3 for several of the biases that stem from representativeness). It means that when people reason they fail to take into account the size of the sample or group

TABLE 11-3 Biases in the Representativeness Heuristic

Ignoring base rates (ignoring prior odds) (Adapted from Johnson & Finke, 1985)

Questions:

(a) Why are more graduate students first-born than second-born children?
(b) Why do more hotel fires start on the first ten floors than the second ten floors?
(c) In baseball, are more runners thrown out by pitchers on first base or on second base?

The bias: In all three questions, people tend to ignore base rates. To answer the questions correctly, we should consider:

(a) How many first-born versus second-born people are there?
(b) How many hotels even have a second ten floors?
(c) How many runners on first base versus second base are there?

Base rates and stereotypes

Question:

Frank is a meek and quiet person whose only hobby is playing chess. He was near the top of his college class and majored in philosophy. Is Frank a librarian or a businessman?

The bias: The personality description seems to match a librarian stereotype, whether the stereotype is true or not. Second, we fail to consider base rates, that is, the relative frequencies of the two professions. In other words, there are far more businessmen than librarians, a base rate that tends to be ignored because of the stereotype "match."

Gambler's fallacy

Question:

You've watched a (fair) coin toss come up heads five times in a row. If you bet $10 on the next toss, would you choose heads or tails?

The bias: The gambler's fallacy is that the next toss is more likely to be tails, because "it's time for tails to show up." Of course, the five previous tosses have no bearing at all on the sixth toss, assuming a fair coin. The bias is related to the law of small numbers, in particular, that we expect randomness even on the "local" or short-run outcomes. Thus getting tails after five heads seems more representative of the random process that produces the outcomes, so we mistakenly prefer to bet $10 on tails.

on which the event is based. They seem to believe that both small and large samples should be equally similar to the population they were drawn from. Another way of expressing this is that people believe in the *law of small numbers.* Now the *law of large numbers*—that a large sample is more representative of its population—is true. But people erroneously believe that there is also a law of small numbers, believe that a small sample is just as representative of its parent population as a large sample (see also Bar-Hillel, 1980)—but that isn't the case.

STEREOTYPES Another bias, also resulting from the representativeness heuristic, is of particular importance because it probably affects our reasoning about other people (see Table 11-3 for additional examples and explanations). Kahneman and Tversky (1973) reported evidence on estimations based on personality descriptions. They read various personality descriptions to people, then had them estimate the probability that the described person was a member of one or another profession. They found that people's estimations are influenced by the similarity of a description to a widely held **stereotype**.

Consider first the situation: 100 people are in a room, 70 of them lawyers, 30 of them engineers. Given this situation, answer the following question:

1. *A person named Bill was randomly selected from this roomful of 100 people. What is the likelihood that Bill is a lawyer?*

Simple probability tells us that the chances of selecting a lawyer are .70. People generally reason correctly in a "bare bones" situation. The technical term for these "bare bones," the 70:30 proportion, is *prior odds, prior probabilities,* or simply *base rates.*

Consider two slightly different situations. There are still the same 70 lawyers and 30 engineers. But now you are given a description of two randomly selected people and are asked "What is the likelihood that this person is an engineer?" (adapted from Kahneman & Tversky, 1973, pp. 241-242):

2. *"Dick is a 30-year-old man. He is married with no children. A man of high ability and high motivation, he promises to be quite successful in his field. He is well liked by his colleagues."*
3. *"Jack is a 45-year-old man. He is married and has four children. He is generally conservative, careful, and ambitious. He shows no interest in political and social issues and spends most of his free time on his many hobbies, which include home carpentry, sailing, and mathematical puzzles."*

Here, people did *not* judge the probabilities to be the same as the prior odds. Instead, they assumed that the personality descriptions contained relevant information and adjusted their estimates accordingly. In particular, for both descriptions 2 and 3, people responded that the probability was close to .50, that is, about a fifty-fifty chance that Dick and Jack were engineers.

Description 3 resembles the stereotype many people have of engineers. It mentions such factors as "careful" and "mathematical puzzles." Here, people de-emphasized the prior odds (.30) and based their judgments on the description. Because the description seemed representative of engineers, people adjusted their estimates upward from the .30 level, allowing an influence of the stereotype.

But description 2 was intentionally written to be uninformative about Dick's profession—it offers no relevant information at all. And yet, people still changed their estimates. In fact, people tend to view *any evidence* as a basis for changing and, they hope, improving their prediction (Fischoff & Bar-Hillel, 1984; Griffin & Tversky, 1992).

The correct way to deal with these problems—the normative model—is to assess the usefulness or relevance of the additional information in order to decide how much weight to give it; usefulness is often termed "diagnosticity"—whether it "diagnoses" engineers correctly, in a sense. Then the estimate is adjusted by the appropriate weighting. This is *Bayes's theorem,* which states that estimates should be based on two kinds of information, the base rate of the event and the "likelihood ratio," which is an assessment of the usefulness of the new information. In description 2, the information should have no impact—the description is uninformative; it's not diagnostic. Nonetheless, people still adjusted their estimates.

BELIEFS Our beliefs can also introduce bias, certainly in situations that rely on Bayes's theorem (e.g., Evans, Handley, Over, & Perham, 2002). For instance, it's easy to see how a belief—say in our stereotype about lawyers (or other groups, of course)—could influence your judgments. If the additional evidence is consistent with your beliefs, then you give weight to the evidence and adjust your estimates accordingly; if the additional evidence is inconsistent with your beliefs, you can just ignore it. This is entirely consistent with what you read earlier about confirmation bias—pay attention to the evidence that confirms your beliefs, but pay little attention to evidence that does not support your beliefs.

The effects that beliefs can have on our reasoning are pervasive. For example, Kim and Ahn (2002) showed how clinical psychologists' diagnoses are affected by their own individual "theories" of mental disorders. In particular, if a clinician views symptom *X* as a central cause for disorder *Y,* then hypothetical patients who present symptom *X* are diagnosed as having disorder *Y;* another clinician views symptom *X* as being peripheral, so diagnoses a different disorder. In both cases, the belief guides the diagnosis, rather than the "supposedly" atheoretical symptom lists in the *DSM (Diagnostic and Statistical Manual)* that clinicians are taught to use. Moshinsky and Bar-Hillel (2002) have documented how beliefs can affect even judgments of when different world events happened. They observed that Israeli students often are surprised to learn that an event in U.S. history happened at about the same time as another event in Europe. The source of the surprise is that the United States is representative of the "New" World, so events that happened there are interpreted as being more recent than events in Europe, the "Old" World. In a sense, the United States is more representative of the recent or "not long ago" category. Hence events in the New World were judged as being more recent than those in the Old World.

The Availability Heuristic

What proportion of medical doctors are women? What proportion of U.S. households own a microwave oven, a flat screen TV, or a DVD player? How much safer are you in a commercial airliner than in a private car, or vice versa? Questions such as these ask you to estimate the frequency or probability of real-world events, even though you are unlikely to have more than a few shreds of relevant information stored in memory about those events. Short of doing the fact finding necessary to know the real answers (for the first question, start by phoning the American Medical Association, for example), how do we make such estimates?

The simplest way of making estimates is to try to recall relevant information from memory. Event frequency is a kind of information that is coded in memory (Brown & Siegler, 1992; Hasher & Zacks, 1984), perhaps automatically. So when we try to retrieve examples from memory, their frequency as coded in memory is important. If the retrieval of examples is easy—if examples come to mind easily—we infer that the event must be fairly frequent or common. If retrieval is difficult, then we estimate that it must not be frequent. Interestingly, frequency estimates affect your eventual judgments about the information: If it's repeated often enough, even false statements becomes "truer" (Brown & Nix, 1996).

Frequency is closely related to the second heuristic that Tversky and Kahneman (1973) discussed, the **availability heuristic**. In this heuristic, we estimate the likelihood of events based on how easily examples come to mind. "Ease of retrieval," is what the term *availability* means here.[1] In short, when people have to make estimates of likelihood, their *estimates are influenced by the ease with which relevant examples can be remembered.*

BIASES WITHIN THE AVAILABILITY HEURISTIC Although the availability heuristic often is reliable (indeed, it is often the only way we have of making estimates), some distortions and biases may stem from it. Because our judgments are based on what we can remember easily, any factor that leads to storing information in memory can influence our reasoning. If reasonably accurate and undistorted information is in memory, then the availability heuristic does a good job. But if memory contains information that is inaccurate, incomplete, or influenced by factors other than objective frequency, there may be biases and distortions in our reasoning. As a simple example, if your friend's Volvo needs repeated trips to the mechanic, you may develop a biased view that Volvos are unreliable. If your only source of knowledge is the friend's opinion, the availability heuristic has biased your judgment. More generally, our biases result from other kinds of knowledge stored in memory.

GENERAL WORLD KNOWLEDGE As an illustration of the availability heuristic, estimate the ratio of the number of Chevrolets sold to the number of Cadillacs sold. According to the availability heuristic, you base your estimate on whatever frequency-based knowledge you may have. If you have no personal reason to notice one kind of car more than another, your estimate may be a reasonably fair guess. Apart from personal biases, however, your general world knowledge tells you that Cadillacs are more expensive, and Chevrolets are less expensive. Given such economic factors, you might estimate that fewer Cadillacs are sold than Chevrolets. Alternatively, the cost might cause you to adjust your initial guess, altering your estimate by the additional information that Cadillacs may be less common than your initial guess because of their cost; this is called the *anchoring and adjusting heuristic* (Carlson, 1990). Most people estimated that Chevrolets are about 10 or 15 times more numerous than Cadillacs. According to General Motors data, however, the ratio was almost exactly 5:1.

---

[1]In Chapter 6 "availability" meant whether some information was stored in memory or not, and "accessibility" referred to whether the information could be retrieved or not. Clearly, "availability" in the Kahneman and Tversky sense is referring to "accessibility" in the memory retrieval sense. Kahneman (2003a) has acknowledged that his original choice of terms was confusing in this sense and now refers to this as the accessibility heuristic. We continue to use the original term, however, to be consistent with the 30-year history of its usage in the decision-making literature.

FAMILIARITY BIASES Another example shows clearly how the availability bias is related to ease of recall. Tversky and Kahneman constructed lists of names, 39 names per list, with 19 women's and 20 men's names per list. One group of people heard the lists and then had to recall as many names as they could remember. Another group heard the lists, then estimated whether the list contained more names of men or women. In two of the four lists that were tested, the women's names were famous (e.g., Elizabeth Taylor), and the men's names were not; in the other two lists, the men's names were famous (e.g., Richard Nixon), and the women's names were not. In the recall groups, people remembered an average of 12 of the 19 famous names but only 8 of the 20 less famous names. This shows that familiar or famous names were more easily recalled.

The important connection between ease of recall and estimation bias came from the groups that had to estimate the proportion of male versus female names. Here too, the fame of the names influenced the judgments. People who heard the "famous female" lists estimated that there had been more women's names, and those who heard the "famous male" lists said there had been more men's names. Thus in this study, there was clear evidence, first, that the famous names were more easily recalled and, second, that this greater availability for recall influenced the estimates of frequency. So the **familiarity bias** is just that, *judging events as more frequent or important because they are more familiar in memory.*

SALIENCE AND VIVIDNESS BIASES Examples of the availability heuristic in everyday life are not difficult to imagine. Consider people's feelings about traveling by airplane. Statistically, one is far safer traveling by commercial airliner than by private car (by one estimate, some 25 times safer, based on normalized passenger-miles traveled). People who have no particularly relevant information in memory, that is, those whose only information comes from casual attention to news media and the like, judge that one is much safer when traveling by car (e.g., Hertwig, Barron, Weber, & Erev, 2004).

This bias can be attributed to the factor of **salience or vividness**. The news accounts of an airline accident are more vivid and given more attention than accounts of passenger car accidents. And even though airplane crashes are rare, the number of victims involved often is dramatic enough that the event makes a much stronger impression. So when you estimate air versus car safety, the vividness of the recalled information tends to bias your judgment. In a revealing demonstration, Gigerenzer (2004) examined U.S. highway traffic fatality data for the three months following the 9/11 terrorist attack, on the hypothesis that people's "dread fear" of flying after the attack might have led them to drive instead. As predicted, traffic fatalities were higher in those months than they had been for those months during the previous five years. (Ironically and sadly, approximately 350 additional lives were lost due to increased driving during that three-month period.)

The Simulation Heuristic

A variation on the availability heuristic is the **simulation heuristic**. In this heuristic people make a prediction of future events, or are asked to imagine a different outcome of an event or action. The term *simulation* here comes from computer simulation. In a computer simulation, certain starting values are entered, and the simulation then proceeds to forecast or predict some outcome. In similar fashion, the simulation heuristic involves *a mental construction or imagining of outcomes, a forecasting of how some event will turn out or how it might have turned out under another set of circumstances.*

The ease with which these outcomes can be imagined is the basis for the simulation heuristic. To the extent that a sequence of events can easily be imagined, the events are available. Alternatively, if it is difficult to construct a plausible scenario, the hypothetical outcome would be viewed as unlikely or might not even be constructed or imagined at all. In short, the ease of imagining an outcome is the operative factor in the simulation heuristic.

An example of this heuristic was given earlier, when you were asked to imagine possible outcomes if Germany had developed the atomic bomb before the United States. Given the role the atomic bomb played in ending World War II, people would give that far more weight than if they were asked about the development of some other device, say a long-range bomber or submarine.

Alternatively, imagining a different outcome may be difficult. This should also affect how the simulation heuristic guides our thinking. Consider an example by Kahneman and Tversky (1982, p. 203):

> *Mr. Crane and Mr. Tees were scheduled to leave the airport on different flights, at the same time. They traveled from town in the same limousine, were caught in a traffic jam, and arrived at the airport 30 minutes after the scheduled departure time of their flights. Mr. Crane is told that his flight left on time. Mr. Tees is told that his flight was delayed, and just left five minutes ago. Who is more upset, Mr. Crane or Mr. Tees?*

As you would expect, most everyone decides that Mr. Tees is more upset; in Kahneman and Tversky's study, 96% of the people made this judgment. The unusual aspect of this is that from an objective standpoint, Mr. Crane and Mr. Tees are in identical positions: Both missed their planes, and because of the traffic jam, both *expected* to miss their planes. The reason Mr. Tees might be more upset is that it was more "possible," in some sense, for him to have caught his flight. That is, it's easier to imagine an outcome in which the limousine arrives a few minutes earlier than it is to imagine one in which it arrives a half hour earlier. As such, we feel that the traveler who "nearly caught his flight" will be more upset.

The Undoing Heuristic: Counterfactual Reasoning

A more complete example of the simulation heuristic, including Kahneman and Tversky's (1982) data, is shown in Table 11-4. This illustrates a version of the simulation heuristic, the undoing of an outcome by changing what led up to it. This is called **counterfactual reasoning**, *when a line of reasoning deliberately contradicts the facts in a "what if" kind of way* (e.g., "what would have happened if Germany had developed the bomb first?"; see Mandel & Lehman, 1996; Roese, 1997, 1999; Spellman & Mandel, 1999). This is the process of judging that some event "nearly happened," "could have occurred," "might have happened if only," and so on. Read the story now and decide how you would complete the "if only" phrase before continuing. ★

★ **TABLE 11-4 Stories for the Simulation Heuristic**

	Route Version
1.	Mr. Jones was 47 years old, the father of three, and a successful banking executive. His wife had been ill at home for several months.
2a.	On the day of the accident, Mr. Jones left his office at the regular time. He sometimes left early to take care of home chores at his wife's request, but this was not necessary on that day. Mr. Jones did not drive home by his regular route. The day was exceptionally clear, and Mr. Jones told his friends at the office that he would drive along the shore to enjoy the view.
3.	The accident occurred at a major intersection. The light turned amber as Mr. Jones approached. Witnesses noted that he braked hard to stop at the crossing, although he could easily have gone through. His family recognized this as a common occurrence in Mr. Jones's driving. As he began to cross after the light changed, a light truck charged into the intersection at top speed and rammed Mr. Jones's car from the left. Mr. Jones was killed instantly.
4a.	It was later ascertained that the truck was driven by a teenage boy, who was under the influence of drugs.
5.	As commonly happens in such situations, the Jones family and their friends often thought and often said, "If only. . .," during the days that followed the accident. How did they continue this thought? Please write one or more likely completions.
	Time Version (substitute 2b for 2a)
2b.	On the day of the accident, Mr. Jones left the office earlier than usual to attend to some household chores at his wife's request. He drove home along his regular route. Mr. Jones occasionally chose to drive along the shore, to enjoy the view on exceptionally clear days, but that day was just average.
	"Boy" Focus Version (substitute 4b for 4a)
4b.	It was later ascertained that the truck was driven by a teenage boy named Tom Searler. Tom's father had just found him at home under the influence of drugs. This was a common occurrence, as Tom used drugs heavily. There had been a quarrel, during which Tom grabbed the keys that were lying on the living room table and drove off blindly. He was severely injured in the accident.

Percentage of People Responding to the "If Only" Stem in the Five Different Response Categories

"If Only" Completion Focuses On:	Route Version	Time Version
Route	51%	13%
Time	3%	26%
Crossing	22%	31%
Boy	20%	29%
Other	4%	1%
	n = 65	*n* = 62

From: Kahneman & Tversky (1982).

The results are shown at the bottom of Table 11-4. A surprisingly large number of people—51%—chose to change the unusual event in the Mr. Jones story, that he took a different route home than normal; in the participants' responses, they basically said, "If only he had taken his normal route home, the accident could have been avoided." This is called a **downhill change**, when *we alter an unusual story element, substituting a more typical or normal element in its place*. In general, such changes focus on an unusual event. The change substitutes something more ordinary and thus "normalizes" the story. Other kinds of changes, for instance inserting an unusual event (after he left work, Mr. Jones had a flat tire), were rarely supplied. (By the way, the term "downhill" came from an analogy with cross-country skiing, where the easiest thing to do is ski downhill.)

More recent studies have confirmed this tendency to alter or undo unusual events but not the more common, usual events. That is, while any change to the Mr. Jones story might have undone the accident, people confine themselves largely to downhill or "normalizing" changes. We are biased toward that kind of change for at least three reasons. First, downhill changes are more easily imagined—the ease of retrieval factor again (e.g., Koehler & Macchi, 2004). Second, downhill changes seem more plausible; it's more plausible that Mr. Jones left on time than it is that he left early and then had a flat tire. And third, we have a tendency to judge unusual events as being the cause for an unanticipated outcome (e.g., Roese, 1997; see Reyna, 2004, and Trabasso & Bartolone, 2003, for gist- or comprehension-based explanations of reasoning).

Other factors have also been implicated in counterfactual reasoning. Byrne and McEleney (2000) have suggested that people focus on actions, not failures to act, when they undo events. They had people read a story about Joe and Paul. Joe got an offer to trade his stock in Company *B* for stock in Company *A*, which he did, although he ultimately lost money on Company *A*. Paul got a comparable offer, to trade his stock in Company *A*, but he decided not to take the offer. Staying with Company *A*, he ultimately lost the same amount of money as Joe, even though they both started with the same amount.

Despite the equal loss by both characters, however, 87.5% of the people claimed that Joe, the one who acted, would feel worse about his decision ("If only I hadn't traded my stock"); only 12.5% felt it would be Paul who felt worse. In a companion article, McCloy and Byrne (2000) developed a scenario in which a character is late for an appointment, because of either controllable or uncontrollable factors—the character stopped to buy a hamburger or was delayed because a tree had fallen in the street. The people undid the controllable factors far more frequently, although they distinguished among delaying factors in terms of interpersonal and social norms of how acceptable or polite the factor was; stopping to visit his parents on the way to the appointment was viewed less negatively than stopping for the hamburger.

BLAMING THE VICTIM A puzzle in the Mr. Jones story—and often in other counterfactual reasoning scenarios—was that people seldom focused on the actual cause of the accident, the teenage boy. That is, they seldom altered anything concerning the boy's behavior, even though it was his actions, not Mr. Jones's, that caused the accident. Kahneman and Tversky speculate that this tendency is caused by a focus rule: We tend to maintain properties of the main object or focus of the story unless a different focus is provided. In support of this, when people read a version of the story that focused more on the boy, they were more likely to undo the boy's actions as a way of preventing the accident.

But undoing Mr. Jones's behavior—having him take his normal route home—essentially claims that Mr. Jones was responsible for the accident, because it was his behavior that people altered. It's a case of "blaming the victim," isn't it?—a situation in which the victim rather than the individual who caused the accident is held responsible. This may be especially common when there is an unusual event in the story that could have been altered via a downhill change. For instance, in Goldinger, Kleider, Azuma, and Beike's (2003) clear examples:

> *Paul normally leaves work at 5:30 and drives directly home. One day, while following this routine, Paul is broadsided by a driver who violated a stop sign and receives serious injuries.* (p. 81)

When people consider how much compensation Paul should receive for his injuries and how much punishment is appropriate for the other driver, they examine Paul's behavior closely. In this scenario, however, Paul tends not to be blamed for the accident. But if the scenario is changed to:

> *Paul, feeling restless at work, leaves early to see a movie. . . .Paul is broadsided by a driver. . . .*

and so forth, then we tend to view him as somehow less deserving of compensation. And in an echo of the social norms result of McCloy and Byrne (2000), Goldinger et al. pointed out the following: If *Paul receives an emergency call to return home*, and then is broadsided, "the accident now appears exceptionally tragic, and compensation awarded to him increases" (p. 81). This kind of reversal, observed by Miller and McFarland (1986), depends on how free Paul was to choose what to do and how socially acceptable his choices were.

HINDSIGHT Note, that the simulation heuristic provides a nice explanation of the **hindsight bias** (Fischoff, 1975), *the after-the-fact judgment that some event was very likely to happen or was very predictable, even though it wasn't predicted to happen beforehand*. This is the "I knew it all along" effect. In thinking about the now-finished event, the scenario under which that event could have happened is easy to imagine—after all, it just happened (Sanna & Schwartz, 2006). The connection between the initial situation and the final outcome is very available after the fact, and this availability makes other possible connections seem less plausible than they otherwise would (e.g., Hell, Gigerenzer, Gauggel, Mall, & Muller, 1988, and Hoch & Loewenstein, 1989). The hindsight bias can even distort our perceptual memories. For example, Gray, Beilock, and Carr (2007) report that batters misremember how well they thought they would hit a baseball when they have been hitting well as compared to when they have struggled. That is, the current success with batting causes the player to experience the hindsight bias by misremembering the batting as being better than it actually was.

Interestingly, the hindsight bias even influences our memory for events. People routinely "remember" their original position to be more consistent with their final decision than it really was (Erdfelder & Buchner, 1998; Holyoak & Simon, 1999) and even reconstruct story elements so that they are more consistent with the final outcome. As a demonstration of this, Carli (1999) had two groups of people read a story (about Pam and Peter in Experiment 1, and Barbara and Jack in Experiment 2) either with no ending (control group), a happy ending (Jack proposes marriage to Barbara), or a tragic ending (Peter/Jack rapes Pam/Barbara). The stories had information that was consistent with both scenarios; e.g., "Barbara met many men at parties" and "Pam wanted a family very much"). After finishing the stories, people were questioned about the story events. The groups that heard either one of the stories with an ending agreed far more than the control group that they would have predicted that ending all along—but of course the endings were completely different. And as a follow-up in a later memory test, both groups mistakenly "remembered" information that had not been in the story but was consistent with the ending they had read. (See Harley, Carlsen, & Loftus, 2004, and Mather, Shafir, & Johnson, 2000, for an extension of the hindsight bias to identifying pictures, important for eyewitness testimony situations, and remembering blind dates, respectively.)

APPLICATIONS OF THE SIMULATION HEURISTIC In many ways the simulation heuristic may come closer to what people mean by such terms as thinking and contemplating than anything else we've covered so far. That is, it is easy to recognize less dramatic examples of undoing and other kinds of forecasting or simulating in our everyday thinking, and the influence of factors such as salience and hindsight bias. For example:

> *If I stop for a cup of coffee, I might miss my bus.*
>
> *If I hadn't been so busy yesterday, I would have remembered to go to the ATM for money.*
>
> *In looking back, I guess I could have predicted that waiting until senior year to take statistics was a bad idea.*

Presumably, such thinking often is the reason we decide to do one thing versus another; we think through the possible outcomes of different actions, then base our decision on the most favorable of the forecasted outcomes. Thus the mental simulation process, taking certain input conditions then forecasting possible outcomes, could be an important way to understand cognitive processes related to planning. A general warning is important to bear in mind, based on studies of how people generate possible outcomes of future events (e.g., Hoch, 1984, 1985). If you begin planning by thinking only of the desirable, favorable outcomes, you tend to blind yourself to possible undesirable outcomes—people generated fewer possible negative outcomes if they began by thinking of positive ones. By starting with positives, you also become more confident that the plan you select will have a positive outcome. In other words, overly optimistic predictions at the outset bias our ability to imagine negative outcomes and inflate our view of the likelihood of a positive outcome. ("Hey, what could go wrong if I wait until next week to start my term paper?"; see Petrusic & Baranski, 2003, on how confidence affects decision making.)

Adaptive Thinking and "Fast, Frugal" Heuristics

Another way of thinking about heuristics is an approach referred to as *adaptive thinking*. The biggest proponent of this adaptive thinking view is Gigerenzer (e.g., 1996). In Gigerenzer's view it is a mistake to assume that the correct answer to any decision-making problem must be the normative answer supplied by classic probability theory (e.g., Bayesian probability). Instead, it's important to assess how well people's heuristics actually do in guiding behavior. That is, people use heuristics not just because of memory limitations, incomplete algorithm knowledge, and so forth. They also use them because they work, because they're adaptive in the sense of leading to successful behavior.[2] That is, people use heuristics because they are tractable and robust (Gigerenzer, 2008). Saying that they are *tractable* means that people can mentally keep track of everything they need to use the heuristic, in contrast to algorithms that require people to track an (often) much larger amount of information. Saying that they are *robust* means that they provide reasonable answers under a wide range of circumstances.

Gigerenzer (2008) provides a couple of compelling illustrations of the value of heuristics in everyday reasoning. He notes that the 1990 Nobel Prize winner in economics, Harry Markowitz, derived an algorithm for maximizing the allocation of funds into various financial assets. However, even Markowitz did not use this principle for his own retirement savings, but instead used a simple 1/*N* heuristic (where *N* is the number of possible funds that the investments could go into). According to this heuristic, your retirement funds are equally distributed across the number of available funds. Pretty simple, huh? This is the heuristic used by about half of the people in the real world. Although this strategy is sneered at by many financial wizards, when pitted against 12 different optimal return strategies, the 1/*N* heuristic beat them all. Bravo, heuristics!

The other example Gigerenzer (2008) gives has to do with organ donation. He notes that organ donation is only 28% in the United States, but 99% in France. His explanation has to do with a *go-with-the-default* heuristic. In the United States, the default is not to have your organs donated if you die. That is, people in the U.S. need to make an effort to be an organ donor (so that other people may live), for example by filling out a form or having the option checked on a driver's license. In the absence of this, the default is "not an organ donor." In contrast, the default in France is to be an organ donor.

Part of the appeal of Gigerenzer's approach is that it is "positive," i.e., doesn't emphasize errors or deviations from some norm, but searches for the usefulness of heuristics. A second appealing feature is that the "fast and frugal" heuristics are simple, based on "one-reason decision making" in Gigerenzer's (1996) terms, supported by a growing body of empirical support. And third, the approach seems more open to input from general cognitive principles. For example, it acknowledges and takes into account memory limitations, incomplete knowledge, time limitations, and so forth, as well as the general cognitive processes you've been studying.

This approach has generated a number of heuristics that differ in some ways from those outlined by Kahneman and Tversky and others. A listing of heuristics provided ▲ by Gigerenzer (2008) is given in Table 11-5. We'll look at some of them in more detail in the following sections—namely *satisficing*, *recognition*, and *take-the-best*—to better

[2]This is "adaptive" in an evolutionary sense, an explicit argument in Gigerenzer's approach. If a biological factor is adaptive, in evolutionary terms, it leads to greater success of the individual, hence greater spread of the feature into succeeding generations. In similar fashion, an adaptive heuristic will be successful, so it will be used more widely. Gigerenzer also advocates devoting more attention to the reasoning processes that are used, as opposed to the heavy focus on how answers deviate from the normative model.

TABLE 11-5 Fast and Frugal Heuristics

Heuristic	Description
Recognition	If one of two alternatives is recognized, go with it.
Fluency	If one of two alternatives is recognized faster than the other, go with it.
Take the Best	Given two alternatives, go with the one that is preferred by (a) search through cues in order of validity, (b) stop the search as soon as a cue discriminates, (c) choosing the one this cue favors.
Tallying	Count the number of favoring cues and go with the option that satisfies the most.
Satisficing	Take the first choice that exceeds your aspiration level.
1/*N* (equality)	Allocate resources equally to each of *N* alternatives.
Default	If there is a default, do nothing about it.
Tit-for-Tat	Cooperate at first and then imitate your partner's last behavior.
Imitate the Majority	Look at a majority of people in your peer group, and imitate their behavior.
Imitate the Successful	Look for the most successful person and imitate his or her behavior.

Adapted from Gigerenzer (2008)

illustrate this approach. It should also be noted that while these heuristics can be useful, people can sometimes become overly dependent on one, such as persisting with one when it has become clear that it is no longer optimal, and that a switch in strategies would be better (Bröder & Schiffer, 2006).

SATISFICING HEURISTIC An important heuristic from the adaptive thinking perspective has been on the scene for some time, Simon's (1979) **satisficing** heuristic. This principle states that *we settle for finding a satisfactory way to make a decision by taking the first solution that satisfies some criterion we may have*—it's the "good enough" heuristic. For example, if you are looking for a place to eat dinner while travelling, rather than checking out every single eatery in town, you simply pick the first one that satisfies your criterion, such as "cheap fast food place." People can use this heuristic to make reasonably optimal decisions. You could check out all of the restaurants, but you will likely get hungrier during your search.

THE RECOGNITION HEURISTIC One of Gigerenzer's simplest heuristics is the **recognition heuristic**, where you *base a decision on whether you recognize the thing to be judged.* For instance, if I ask you, "Which city is larger, Kansas City or Junction City?" you might choose Kansas City because you've never heard of the alternative. Of course, it is illogical in some sense to base a decision on ignorance or missing knowledge—"I've never heard of it, so it must be smaller" doesn't come across as a sound, ironclad basis for deciding. On the other hand, to the extent that we notice things and store information in memory about them, the fact that we don't know about something could be informative. This is Gigerenzer's point—when having heard of something correlates with the decision criterion, here the population of the city, then *not*

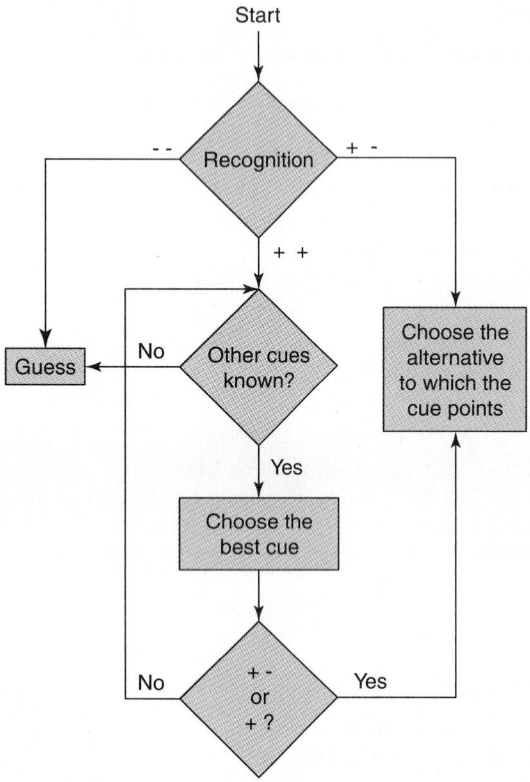

FIGURE 11-7
Flow chart of the "take the best" heuristic. Processing starts with a comparison of two objects, *A* and *B*. If neither is recognized (– –), guess. If one is recognized and one is not (+ –), choose the recognized alternative. If both are recognized (+ +), search for a cue that might discriminate. If one cue is positive and the other is negative or null (+ –) and (+ ?), choose the alternative with the positive cue. If both are positive or both are negative, return to search for another cue. From Goldstein & Gigerenzer (2002).

having heard of something is useful. As Goldstein and Gigerenzer (2002) report, about two-thirds of the Americans surveyed decided (correctly) that San Diego is larger than San Antonio. But all of the Germans they surveyed made the same correct decision, both the ones who had heard of San Antonio and those who hadn't.

"TAKE THE BEST" HEURISTIC Another heuristic is the **"take the best" heuristic** (Gigerenzer & Goldstein, 1996), *where you decide between alternatives based on the first useful information you find.* Essentially, you search the alternatives for some characteristic—Gigerenzer calls this a "cue"—that is relevant and that you might know about, and check to see if one option or the other has a positive value for that cue. For example, if I ask which is larger, Kansas City or Oklahoma City, simple recognition won't work, because you've probably heard of both. You then try to retrieve a cue that will help you decide, a cue that correlates with city populations—maybe something like, "Does the city have a major league sports team?" If you now realize that Kansas City does but Oklahoma City doesn't, you decide Kansas City is larger based on that bit of positive evidence. Of course if I asked you about two cities that both had sports teams, then you'd have to search for yet another cue and continue doing so until one of the cities differed—or until you finally ran out of cues and merely guessed. Figure 11-7 shows a flow diagram of the "take the best" heuristic. The heuristic is simple—you search for some evidence favoring one over the other alternative, and you make your decision as soon as you find such evidence.

The Ongoing Debate

Gigerenzer and Goldstein (1996; also Gigerenzer, 1996, and Goldstein & Gigerenzer, 2002) present considerable modeling and survey data to show how these heuristics can do a very accurate job of making decisions. And other supportive work has begun to appear as well (for instance Burns, 2004, in a challenge to the well-known Gilovich, Vallone, & Tversky, 1985, paper on the "hot hand" in basketball). A final example, quite famous to cognitive psychologists, will illustrate. Take a moment now to read the question in Table 11-6 and do the rankings of the alternatives about Linda, one of the most famous characters in the study of decision making.

LINDA AND THE CONJUNCTION FALLACY Tversky and Kahneman (1983) had people read the Linda question and then complete the rankings of the eight alternatives. They found—as does everyone else—that people endorse the compound

TABLE 11-6 The Linda Problem

Linda is 31 years old, single, outspoken, and very bright. She majored in philosophy. As a student, she was deeply concerned with issues of discrimination and social justice and also participated in antinuclear demonstrations.

Now rank the following options in terms of the probability of their describing Linda. Give a ranking of 1 to the most likely option and a ranking of 8 to the least likely option.

_____ Linda is a teacher at an elementary school.
_____ Linda works in a bookstore and takes yoga classes.
_____ Linda is active in the feminist movement.
_____ Linda is a psychiatric social worker.
_____ Linda is a member of the League of Women Voters.
_____ Linda is a bank teller.
_____ Linda is an insurance salesperson.
_____ Linda is a bank teller and is active in the feminist movement.

Adapted from Tversky & Kahneman (1983).

alternative "bank teller and active in the feminist movement" as more likely than either "bank teller" or "active in the feminist movement." Such a judgment, from purely probabilistic standpoints, is odd. In particular, it illustrates the **conjunction fallacy**, *the mistaken belief that a compound outcome of two characteristics is more likely than either one of the characteristics by itself.* According to strict probability, this is impossible—making up some numbers to illustrate, if the chances are .20 that Linda is a bank teller, and .30 that she is active in the feminist movement, then the conjunction of those two characteristics should never be larger than .20. In fact, in stripped down form, the probability ought to be .06; that is,

> *In a room with 100 people, 20 are bank tellers, 80 are something else. Furthermore, 30 of the people are feminists, and 70 are not. What is the probability of randomly selecting someone who is both a bank teller and a feminist?*

And yet people routinely say that the compound "bank teller and feminist" is more likely (has a higher rank) than the simpler probability that she's a bank teller. Considerable significance has attached to this fallacy in Kahneman and Tversky's work—it comes close to epitomizing the errors, the departures from the normative model, found in human reasoning.

OTHER EXPLANATIONS Considering humans from a broader perspective than simply "lousy probabilists," however, reveals other reasonable interpretations of these rankings and judgments. Indeed, Moldoveanu and Langer (2002) supply a whole variety of explanations to justify this choice. For instance, many people treat the statement "Linda is a bank teller and is active in the feminist movement" not as a conjunction of two characteristics but as a conditional probability—in other words, as if it said, "*Given* that Linda is a bank teller, what is the likelihood that she is active in the feminist movement?" The probabilities for a conditional probability are very different than those for a conjunction.

A second reason, commonly expressed by people, involves the idea of how consistent personality tends to be—in other words, that whatever job a person may end up in, there still should be some consistency in the person's personality, something like "once an activist, always an activist." Such a comment also exemplifies an idea you studied in the last chapter, on conversational rules and the cooperative principle. If you were supposed to judge the Linda problem solely on the basis of the probabilities of being a bank teller and being active in the feminist movement, then there is no communicative need to supply all of the background information on the character—in other words, "Why did you tell me about Linda's activism as a college student if I was supposed to ignore it?" The fact that personality information *was* supplied communicates to people that it is important and should be factored into the answer. So people rather naturally take that into account and come up with a plausible scenario—"OK, maybe she ended up as a bank teller, but she can still be a social activist by being active in the feminist movement." In short, they may be developing a personality-based model of Linda.

The adaptive thinking approach does have its detractors. For instance, Newell and Shanks (2004) have questioned whether the simple recognition heuristic is as powerful as Goldstein and Gigerenzer (2002) claimed, showing how recognition is discounted when other cues of higher validity are presented. Similarly, Newell and Shanks (2003) showed that the "take the best" heuristic is used especially when the mental "cost" (e.g., in terms of time) of information is high. When the cost is low, however, for instance when it takes very little time to retrieve additional information, people seem to rely on that heuristic less frequently. Nonetheless, the comparison of the two approaches is telling. The traditional approach, inspired by Kahneman and Tversky, focuses on how different people's descriptive models are from the normatively correct, probabilistic algorithms. The adaptive thinking approach, in contrast, focuses on people's limitations—in terms of insufficient time, mental capacity, and knowledge—and explores how well our heuristics deal with reality despite those limitations. (Table 11-7 presents a review list of the heuristics, biases, and fallacies discussed so far.)

TABLE 11-7 Review List of Heuristics, Biases, and Fallacies

Heuristic	Biases and Fallacies
Representativeness	Insensitivity to sample size Belief in the law of small numbers Stereotype bias, belief bias, confirmation bias
Availability	Familiarity bias, salience, and vividness bias
Anchoring and adjustment	Order bias
Simulation	Overly optimistic predictions inflate our confidence and prevent thinking of possible negative outcomes
Undoing/counterfactual reasoning	Bias to undo unusual event, bias to focus on action, bias to focus on controllable events, hindsight bias Blaming the victim
Recognition	Familiarity bias
"Take the best"	Reliance on ignorance or lack of knowledge

More recently, there have been some attempts to address how reasoning and decision making take into account people's understanding of the causal structures of situations when making decisions (e.g., Garcia-Retamero, Wallin, & Dieckmann, 2007; Kim, Yopchick, & Kwaadsteniet, 2008; Kynski & Tenebaum, 2007), as opposed to the more statistical approach of Kaneman and Tversky, and the Gigerenzer's adaptive thinking approach. For example (see Kynski & Tenebaum, 2007), using standard base rate information, there is the finding that people who use sunscreen are more likely to develop skin cancer than those who do not, which runs counter to most people's intuitive judgments. This is because most people who don't use sunscreen are not out in the sun to begin with. It is important to note that using sunscreen does not cause skin cancer, rather sunbathing does. When the problem is recast with this additional information, we see that among those people who sunbathe (a smaller group), those who use sunscreen are less likely to get skin cancer. Thus, when people are provided with the appropriate causal structure, their decisions processes can be very good.

This approach can also explain why people make some of the errors that they do. For example, Figure 11-8 illustrates the causal model that many people have of personality and career choice, and how it relates to the lawyer-engineer problem. When statistical principles are applied to this model, then the results are similar to the estimates provided by people. That is, people take into account the causes that produce various outcomes, as well as their combined influence, then make their decisions.

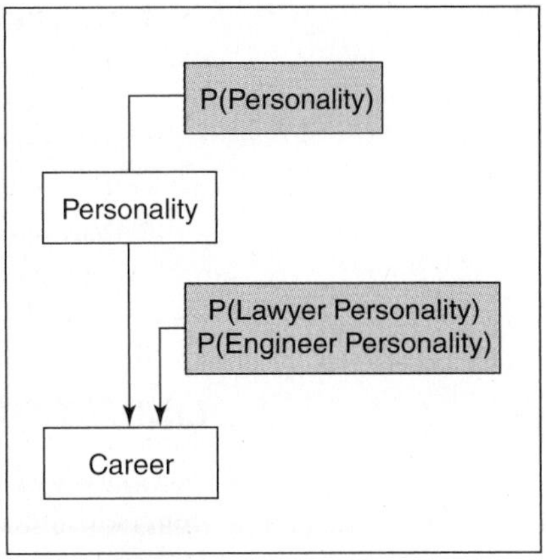

★ **FIGURE 11-8**
Causal model used by Kynski and Tenebaum (2007) to illustrate the concept that people use ideas of causal information and relations to help them make decisions. In this case, people are assuming that there is a causal relationship between a person's personality and his or her career choice.

Section Summary

- Algorithms are systematic rules and procedures that generate correct answers to problems, whereas heuristics are quick, informal rules that are often useful but are not guaranteed to yield the correct solution. Kahneman and Tversky investigated three important heuristics used in circumstances when people reason about uncertain events.
- The representativeness heuristic guides people to judge outcomes as likely if they seem representative of the type of event being evaluated; for instance, a random-looking sequence of coin tosses is judged more representative of coin toss outcomes almost regardless of the true probabilities involved. Included among the reasoning effects predicted by this heuristic are various stereotyping results.
- In the availability heuristic, people judge the likelihood of events by how easily they can remember examples or instances. These judgments therefore can be biased by any other factor that affects memory, such as salience or vividness.
- In the simulation heuristic, people forecast or predict how some outcome could have been different. These forecasts are influenced by how easily the alternative outcomes can be imagined. Interestingly, when people complete "if only" statements, the changes they include tend to normalize the original situation by removing an unusual event and substituting a more common one. Such normalizations can be affected by the *focus* of the situation.

- Work on "fast and frugal" heuristics reveals that simple one-reason decision-making heuristics often do a very good job. These heuristics come from the adaptive thinking approach to decision making, the source of a current debate about the basis for reasoning under uncertainty.
- Recent work on causal reasoning suggests that people use more normative reasoning than has otherwise been suspected if it is assumed that people have a reasonably correct causal model of the situation they are trying to make decisions about.

LIMITATIONS IN REASONING

A central fact in studies of decision making and reasoning bears repeating. We use heuristics because of limitations. There are limitations in our knowledge, both of relevant facts and also relevant algorithms. You had to estimate the latitudes of Chicago and Rome because you (probably) didn't know them; you simply didn't have those facts stored in memory. Likewise, you probably estimated the number of handshakes in the earlier question because you didn't know the relevant algorithm. And there are also limitations in the reasoner that are important, sometimes as ordinary as unwillingness to make the effort needed, but sometimes more central than that.

"Oh, just put me down as undecided."

Limited Domain Knowledge

Everyday examples of how limited knowledge affects decision making and reasoning are abundant. Kempton (1986), for example, looked at reasoning based on analogies, particularly how we develop analogies based on known events and situations to reason about unknown or poorly understood domains. Focusing on a mechanical device, Kempton studied people's understanding of home heating, particularly their understanding of a furnace thermostat. The results indicated that some people's (incorrect) mental model is that a thermostat works like a water faucet: Turn it up higher to get a faster flow of heat. Likewise, many people's behavior suggests that they believe that the call button on an elevator works like a doorbell: If the elevator doesn't arrive reasonably soon, press the button again (there can also be an element of superstitious belief here too, or possibly quasi-magical thinking, as when someone blows on a pair of dice before throwing them; see Shafir & Tversky, 1992).

It should be obvious that our mental models—our cognitive representations of the reasoning or decision-making situation—can vary from true and complete knowledge (expertise, in other words) all the way down to no knowledge or information at all, ignorance. (People's awareness that they do not know something is actually quite interesting itself; see Gentner & Collins, 1981, and Glucksberg & McCloskey, 1981.) The most interesting situation to study is when knowledge is incomplete or inaccurate. Indeed, the fact that we are so concerned with how people estimate under uncertainty, and with their errors in reasoning, implies that complete and certain knowledge usually is not available to people. This focus on errors in reasoning and decision making is reminiscent of the Piagetian tradition of analyzing children's errors. It also represents a tendency in cognitive psychology, to study accuracy or inaccuracy in performance as a way of understanding mental processing.

A MENTAL MODEL OF THE PHYSICAL WORLD: NAIVE PHYSICS Some of the most intriguing research has been in the area of **naive physics,** *people's conceptions of the physical world, in particular, their understanding of the principles of motion.* Figure 11-9 presents several of the problems. The remaining section will be more meaningful to you if you spend a few moments working through the problems before reading further. ▲

By asking people to complete such diagrams and then explain their answers, McCloskey (1983) provided convincing examples of the misconceptions people often have. For instance, in one of his studies (McCloskey, Caramazza, & Green, 1980; see also Freyd & Jones, 1994), 51% of the people believed that a marble would follow a curved path after leaving the tube depicted in Figure 11-9A. Likewise, some 30% responded that the ball in Figure 11-9B would continue on a curved path after the string broke, often adding that this curved path eventually would straighten out. In the airplane question (Figure 11-9C), only 40% gave the correct answer; the most common incorrect answer (36% of the people) was that the ball would fall straight down. Figure 11-10 shows both the correct and incorrect answers people gave to these problems, along with the percentage of people who gave the answers. ●

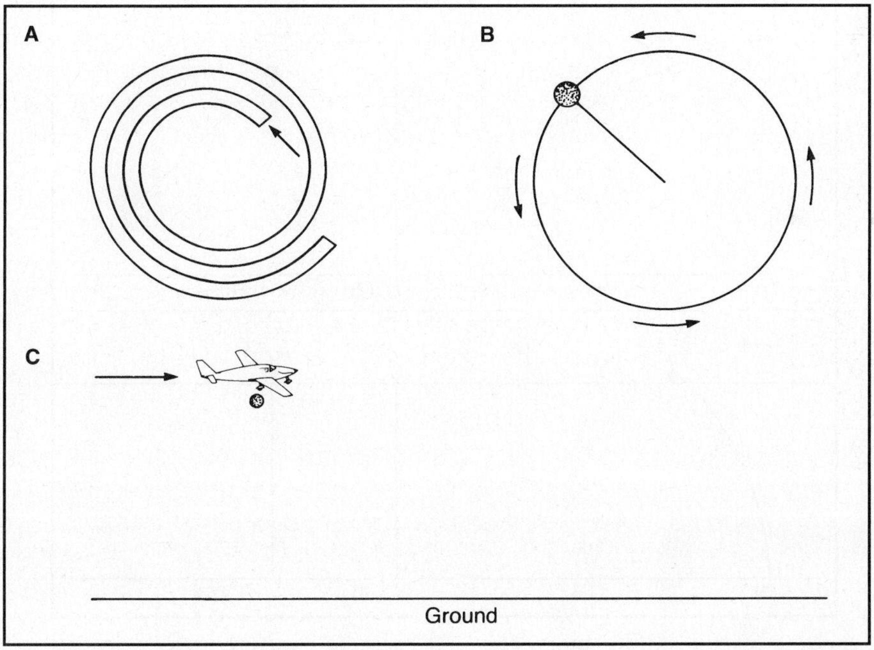

▲ **FIGURE 11-9** Stimuli used by McCloskey.
A. Imagine that the curved tube is on a table top, and a ball or marble is tossed in (see arrow). Draw the path of the ball when it exits the tube. For **B,** imagine that the ball is being twirled around and that the string breaks. Draw the path the ball will take once the string breaks.
C. Imagine an airplane is traveling at a constant speed, and a ball is dropped from the airplane. Draw the path of the ball is it falls to the ground.

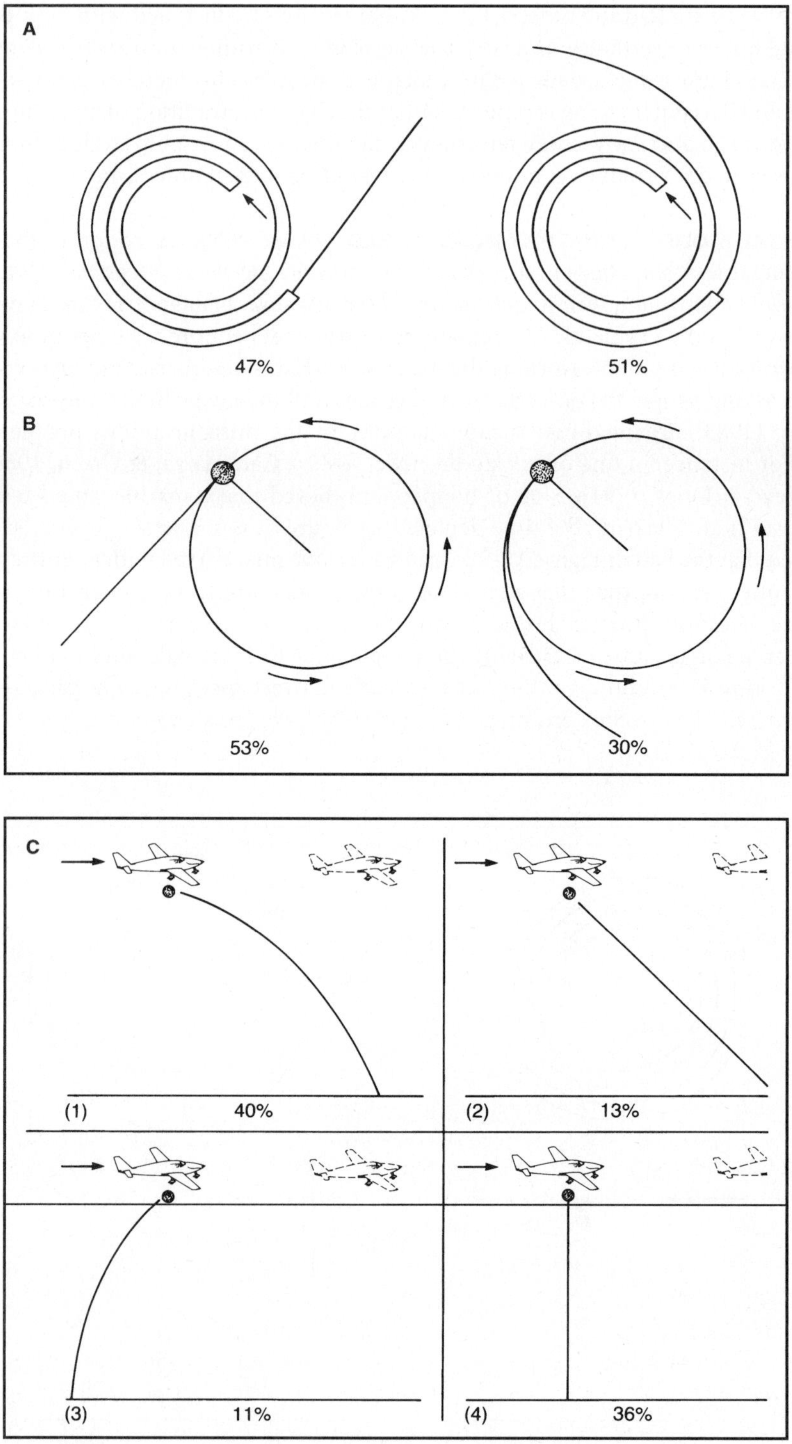

FIGURE 11-10 Stimuli and responses to McCloskey's problems in Figure 11-9, with the percentages of people making that response.

One compelling aspect of McCloskey's results involves the domain of knowledge that was being tested, the motion of physical objects. This is not a rarefied, unusual kind of knowledge. As McCloskey notes, we have countless opportunities in our everyday experience to witness the behavior of objects in motion and to derive an understanding of the principles of motion. Anyone who has ever thrown a ball has had such opportunities. And yet the mental model we derive from that experience is flawed, although there is evidence that the cognitive model we develop is rather different from the perceptual–motor model that actually governs throwing a ball (Krist, Fieberg, & Wilkening, 1993; Schwartz & Black, 1999).

A second compelling aspect to the research concerns the nature of the mental model itself. As analyzed by McCloskey, people's erroneous understanding of bodies in motion is amazingly similar to the so-called impetus theory, which states that setting an object in motion puts some impetus or "movement force" into the object, with the impetus slowly dissipating across time (e.g., Catrambone, Jones, Jonides, & Seifert, 1995; see Cooke & Breedin, 1994, and Hubbard, 1996, on the notion of impetus). For instance, in the tube problem in Figure 11-9A, one person said: "The momentum from the curve [of the tube] gives it [the ball] the arc. . . . The force that the ball picks up from the curve eventually dissipates and it will follow a normal straight line" (McCloskey, 1983, p. 309).

The punchline here is that the impetus theory was the accepted explanation of motion during the 13th and 14th centuries, a view that was abandoned by physics when Newton's laws of gravity and motion were advanced some 300 years ago. The correct mental model, basically, is that a body in motion continues in a straight line unless some other force, such as gravity, is applied. If some other force is applied, then that force combines with the continuing straight line movement. Thus when the ball leaves the tube, or when the string breaks, the ball moves in a straight line; no "curved force" continues to act on it because no such thing as "impetus" has been given to it. Likewise, the horizontal movement of the ball dropped from the airplane continues until the ball hits the ground. This movement is augmented by a downward movement caused by gravity; the ball accelerates vertically as it continues its previous horizontal motion. (If you demonstrated a naive belief in impetus, you might take some consolation in the fact that, across recorded history, people have believed in impetus theory longer than they have in Newton's laws.)

EXPERIENCE AND KNOWLEDGE Only a little research addresses the nature of our experience and the kind of information we derive from it. In some of the naive physics problems, especially the plane problem, an optical illusion seems partly responsible for the "straight down belief" (McCloskey, 1983; Rohrer, 2003). Beyond that, some inattentiveness on the reasoner's part or perhaps difficulty in profiting from real-world feedback may also account for some of the inaccuracy. To be sure, some of the difficulties we experience involve the difficulty of the problems themselves (Proffitt, Kaiser, & Whelan, 1990). For example, Medin and Edelson (1988) found that, depending on the structure and complexity of the problem, people may use base rate information appropriately, may use it inappropriately, or may ignore it entirely. We do know that instruction and training influence reasoning. Taking a physics class improves your knowledge of the rules of motion, but it doesn't completely eliminate the misbeliefs (Donley & Ashcraft, 1992; Kozhevnikov & Hegarty, 2001). Likewise, instruction in statistics, probability, and

PROVE IT

Naive Physics

Having people complete the diagrams on the naive physics beliefs is an almost failsafe project. Be sure you interview your participants on their reasons for drawing the pathways they draw (be sure you understand the correct pathways before you try explaining the principles behind them). And come up with some new diagrams or problems to test other aspects of people's intuitive understanding of motion and gravity, for instance the puzzling "water-level" problem (when a glass of fluid is tilted sideways, people—even those with presumed expertise—draw the line representing the water as perpendicular to the glass, rather than parallel to the horizon; e.g., Hecht & Proffitt, 1995; Vasta & Liben, 1996).

It would be interesting to know how other groups of people respond. For example, in Donley and Ashcraft's (1992) article, the professors in the physics department performed essentially perfectly, whereas professors in other departments were no more accurate than students in the undergraduate physics sequence. It's not clear whether children would perform less accurately than adults; after all, adults do pretty badly. On the other hand, perhaps children will report more interesting reasons for their beliefs. Some adults complete the cliff-and-ball problem below with a "straight out, then straight down" pathway, a pathway called the Road Runner effect, from the cartoon character. It would be interesting to know whether children (or adults) appeal to that in justifying their answers.

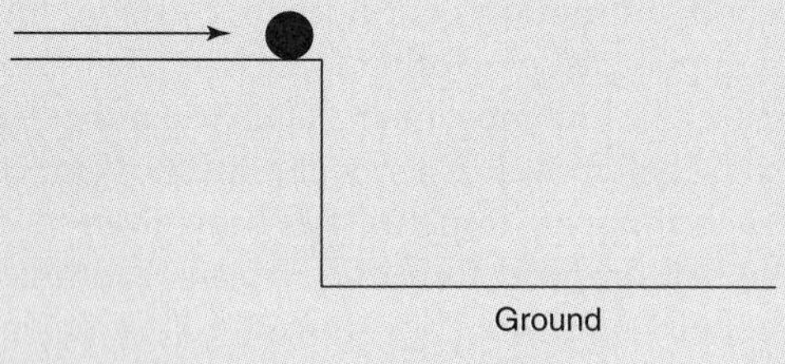

The ball is rolling toward a cliff. Draw the path of the ball as it goes over the edge.

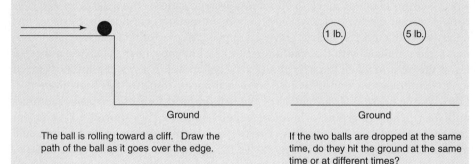

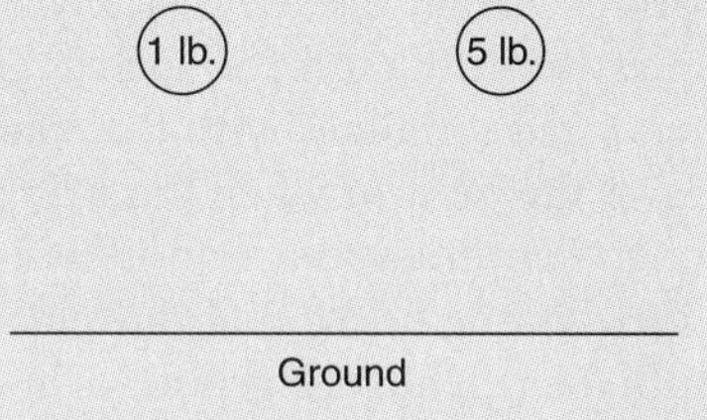

If the two balls are dropped at the same time, do they hit the ground at the same time or at different times?

hypothesis testing improves your ability to reason accurately in those domains (Agnoli & Krantz, 1989; Fong & Nisbett, 1991; Lehman et al., 1988). In short, acquiring a fuller knowledge of the domain is an important part of making more accurate decisions.

The types of reasoning errors we've been encountering here not only apply to physics and statistics problems, but even extend to everyday objects. Lawson (2006) gave people partial drawings of bicycles, such as those shown in Figure 11-11, and asked people to select the drawing from a set of options that correctly depict the proper position of the bicycle frame, pedals, and chain. What she found was that, although bicycles are very familiar objects to most people, an average of 39% errors were made in these selections. Performance was better for expert cyclists, although even they made 15% errors. So, what we can learn from this is that even when people have a great deal of familiarity with a common object, they may still have trouble reasoning about the structure of that object and how it works.

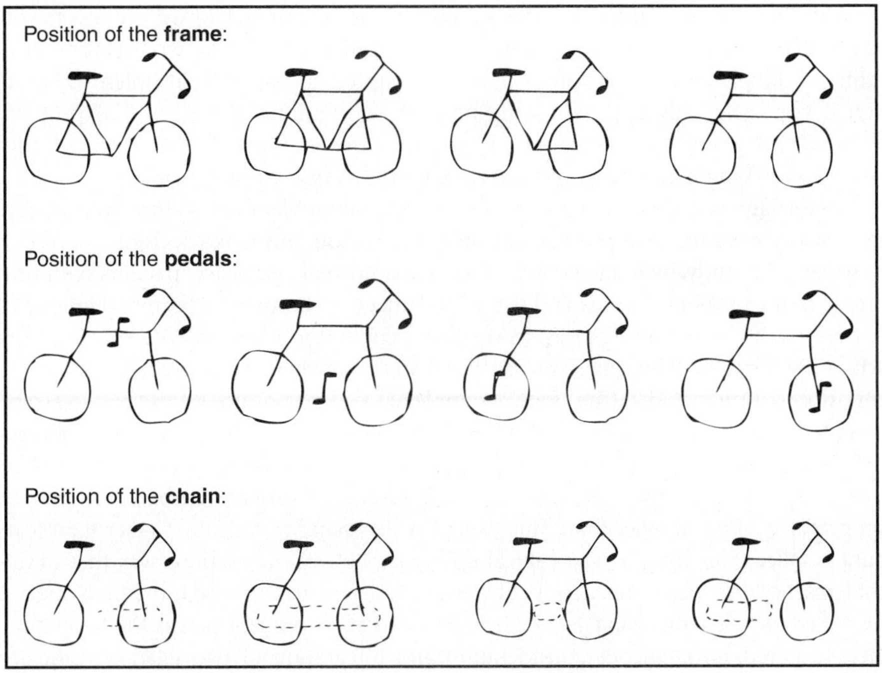

◆ **FIGURE 11-11**
Response choices for a study by Lawson (2006) in which people needed to select the correct location of a bicycle's frame, pedals, and chain.

Limitations in Processing Resources

Likewise, several studies attest to the role of processing resources in adequate decision making and problem solving. Cherniak (1984; see also Tversky & Kahneman, 1983) has studied the *prototypicality heuristic*, a strategy in which we generate examples to reason out an answer rather than follow the correct, logical procedures of deductive reasoning. The heuristic is useful in the sense that it reduces people's errors when they are working under time constraints. But it depends on a limitation, possibly of working memory, possibly of time in which to perform the task, or possibly in the willingness to do the slow, effortful work of following the algorithmic procedure. As an example, what is the answer to the following?

$$8 \times 7 \times 6 \times 5 \times 4 \times 3 \times 2 \times 1$$

Be honest—even though you know how to multiply, you didn't really multiply out all those values, did you? You probably estimated; you used a heuristic. One way we know this is by comparing your estimate to a different problem,

$$1 \times 2 \times 3 \times 4 \times 5 \times 6 \times 7 \times 8$$

In Tversky and Kahneman's (1983) data, people's estimates for the first problem averaged 2,250; but, for the second problem, estimates averaged 512. Heuristic processing was clearly involved, because the estimates depended on whether the arithmetically identical sequences began with a large or small number and because both estimates were wildly inaccurate: The correct answer to 8! is 40,320.

Although it's tempting to say the limitation was in your lack of willingness to solve the problem (a nice way of saying laziness), note that a full solution would take considerable working memory resources if you attempted to solve the problem mentally. Even if you were only approximating in your calculations, a sequence of problem-solving and keeping-track steps would tax working memory. Surely such a limited system as working memory would interfere with this type of processing.

An intriguing study demonstrates an entirely compatible result — that limited working memory resources compromise the ability to reason and make decisions in difficult situations. The study, by Waltz et al. (1999), tested normal people, six patients with brain damage in the prefrontal cortex and five with damage to the anterior temporal lobes. People were given two reasoning tasks. In the first, people read transitive inference problems such as "Beth is taller than Tina. Tina is taller than Amy," where anywhere from two to four propositions were included (the "Beth" example has two propositions), and had to arrange the sentences in order of height (so the "Beth" sentence would be at the top). Problems presented in this order were at Level 1 complexity, and performance was contrasted with Level 2 complexity, in which the propositions were in scrambled order (e.g., for a four-proposition problem, "Beth is taller than Tina. Sally is taller than Laura. Tina is taller than Joyce. Laura is taller than Beth."). The critical difference between conditions was that Level 1 problems, because they were in correct transitive order, never required more than one relation ("Beth is taller than Tina") to be held in mind at one time, whereas the Level 2 sentences required simultaneous consideration and integration of two relations (and that happened two to four times per trial, depending on how many propositions were shown).

In the other half of the experiment, people solved a set of matrix problems from the Raven's Standard Progressive Matrices test (Raven, 1941). Figure 11-12 illustrates three such problems. The problem in Figure 11-12A was a "nonrelational" Level 0 problem; the correct answer merely involved finding the matching pattern among the six choices at the bottom. Figure 11-12B shows a one-relation, Level 1 problem (technically, the relation is "reflect the pattern across the *x*-axis," that is, flip the pattern from bottom to top; the answer

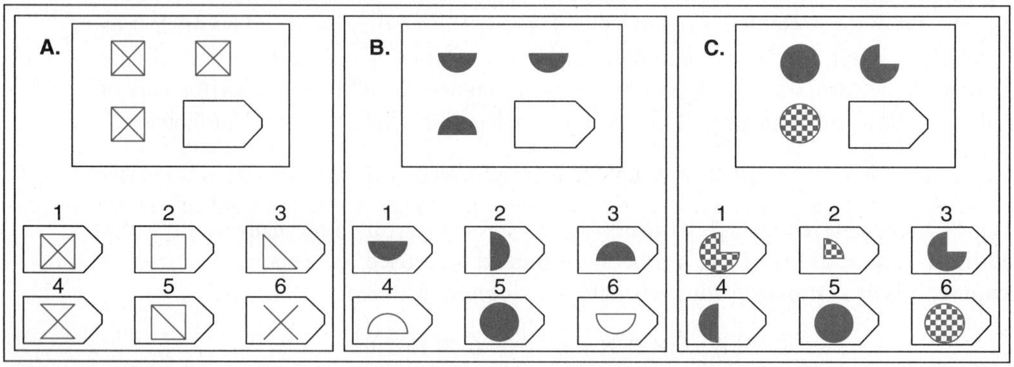

FIGURE 11-12
Examples of reasoning problems taken from the Raven Standard Progressive Matrices test. The task asks people to pick the one correct choice out of six possibilities at the bottom to complete the pattern at the top. **A.** Level 0 problem (nonrelational). **B.** Level 1 problem (one-relation problem). **C.** Level 2 problem (two-relation problem). Correct answers are choice 1 in A, choice 3 in B, and choice 1 in C. Figure 2 from Waltz et al. (1999).

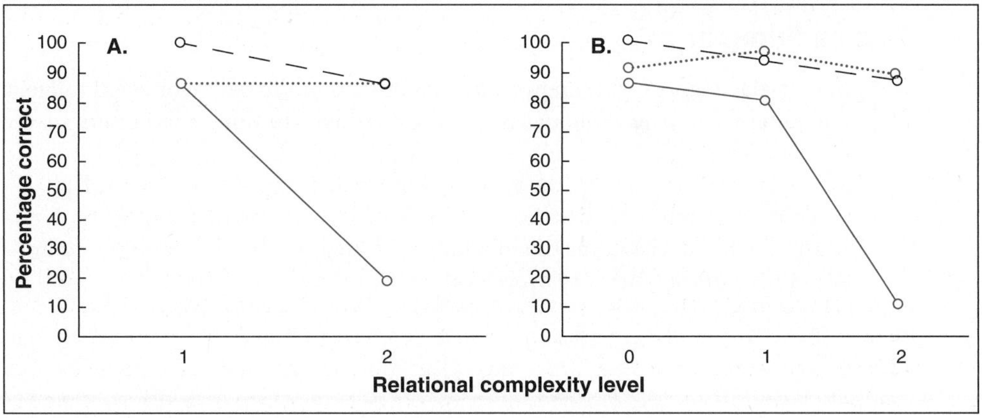

★ **FIGURE 11-13**
Percentage correct in the transitive inference (**A**) and Raven's Matrices (**B**) problems, as a function of relational complexity (Levels 0, 1, and 2), for normals (dashed lines), temporal lobe patients (dotted lines), and prefrontal lobe patients (solid lines).

is choice 3), and Figure 11-12C, a two-relation, Level 2 problem (the two relations are from solid to checked, and remove the upper-right quarter; the correct answer is choice 1).

Waltz et al.'s results for transitive inference are shown in the left half of Figure 11-13. ★ Normal control participants (dashed line) showed only a modest decline in the Level 2 condition and did only slightly better than the patients with temporal lobe damage (the dotted line). But patients with frontal lobe damage (solid line) dropped from more than 80% correct on Level 1 problems to around 20% correct on Level 2 problems, seemingly unable to consider and integrate multiple propositions at the same time. And in the right half of the results, it's clear that the frontal lobe patients were unable to maintain two relational changes at the same time, their performance dropping from about 80% down to around 10% at Level 2. The temporal lobe patients were again very close in performance to the normal controls. Despite this very poor performance by the prefrontal patients, their accuracy on memory tests (for instance, "Which of these names did you read about, Amy or Susan?") was very high, about 96% correct, actually about 10% higher than the normal controls. Here, consistent with material in Chapter 6, it was the temporal lobe patients whose declarative memory for the tasks was poor; their name recognition performance was at 56%, not appreciably different from chance. Thus declarative memory for the tasks was damaged selectively for the temporal lobe patients, but reasoning performance was selectively damaged for the prefrontal patients (see also Wagar & Thagard, 2004).

The results are compatible with the idea that the frontal lobes are important for reasoning and in particular for maintaining relational information in working memory while the reasoning task is being done. The connection between the dorsolateral prefrontal cortex (DLPFC) and executive control in working memory was discussed in Chapter 5. The Waltz et al. results extend that research: "In other words, relational integration may be the 'work' done by working memory. We thus view our results as being consistent with the idea that the DLPFC, which was severely damaged in all our prefrontal patients, is critical for working memory" (1999, p. 123; see also Hinson, Jameson, & Whitney, 2003).

Section Summary

- In everyday reasoning, we rely on mental models of the device or event to make our judgments. These mental models sometimes are quite inaccurate. In the best-known research, people's mental models of physical motion lead them to incorrect predictions (e.g., the trajectory of a ball dropped from an airplane).
- Ongoing research is focused on the kinds of limitations that lead to incorrect reasoning and decision making, including limited domain knowledge and limitations in working memory processes.

Key Terms

algorithm (p. *433*)
antecedent (p. *417*)
availability heuristic (p. *441*)
conditional reasoning (p. *417*)
confirmation bias (p. *420*)
conjunction fallacy (p. *451*)
consequent (p. *417*)
counterfactual reasoning (p. *443*)
discriminability effect (p. *425*)
distance (p. *425*)
downhill change (p. *445*)
familiarity bias (p. *442*)
heuristic (p. *434*)
hindsight bias (p. *446*)
just noticeable difference (jnd) (p. *425*)
mental models (p. *423*)
naive physics (p. 455)
psychophysics (p. *424*)
recognition heuristic (p. *449*)
representativeness heuristic (p. *437*)
salience or vividness (p. *442*)
satisficing (p. *449*)
semantic congruity effect (p. *427*)
simulation heuristic (p. *442*)
SNARC effect (p. *429*)
stereotype (p. *439*)
syllogism (p. *414*)
symbolic comparisons (p. *425*)
symbolic distance effect (p. *425*)
"take the best" heuristic (p. *450*)

APPENDIX: ALGORITHMS FOR COIN TOSSES AND HOSPITAL BIRTHS

Coin Tosses

To begin with the obvious, the probability of a head on one coin toss is .50. Flipping a coin twice and keeping track of the possible sequences yields a .25 probability for each of the four possibilities HH, HT, TH, TT. In general, when the simple event has a probability of .50, the number of possibilities for a sequence of *n* events is 2 raised to the *n*th power. Thus the number of distinct sequences for six coin tosses is 2^6, a total of 64 possibilities.

Two of the 64 possibilities are pure sequences, HHHHHH and TTTTTT. Two more are double sequences, HHHTTT and TTTHHH. All the remaining 60 possibilities involve either or both of the following characteristics: more of one outcome (e.g., heads) than the other and at least one alternation between the two outcomes at a position *other than* halfway through the sequence. Thus the probability of a pure sequence is 2/64, as is the probability of a double sequence. Getting any one of the other 60 possibilities has a likelihood of 1/64. But getting a "randomlike" outcome, that is, any outcome other than straight or double, has a probability of 60/64.

Hospital Births

Many statistics texts contain tables of the binomial distribution, the best way to understand the hospital births example. Because most of these tables go up only to a sample size of 20, we'll use a revised hospital example, comparing hospitals with three versus nine births per day (note that the 1:3 ratio is the same as the original example, 15:45). The probabilities for the original example are more extreme than these, but they'll be in the same direction.

Just as with coin tosses, we are dealing with an event whose basic probability is .50, the likelihood that a newborn infant is male (ignoring the fact that male births are actually slightly more common than 50%). What is the probability that, in three births, all three will be boys? According to the binomial tables (Table 11-A), this probability is .1250. This is the probability that on any randomly selected day, the three-birth hospital will have all boys, $p = .1250$. Across the 365 days in a year, we expect an average of 45.625 such days ($365 \times .1250$).

The temptation now is to consider the likelihood of exactly three boys in the nine-birth hospital. But this is not the relevant comparison. The relevant comparison to the all boys probability in the three-birth hospital would be all boys in the nine-birth hospital. This puts the comparison on the same footing as the original problem, 60% as the "extreme" cutoff.

The probability of exactly nine boys out of nine births is .0020, two chances in a thousand. For a whole year, we expect only 0.73 such days ($365 \times .0020$). Now it should be clearer. The criterion of "extreme," all boys, is much more likely in the smaller sample than in the larger one, $p = .1250$ versus .0020. Multiplied out, the prediction is 45 days for the small hospital and .70 days for the large one.

By extension, and using the appropriate binomial values, the 15-birth hospital should have about 111 days per year with 60% or more boys, contrasted with 42 such days per year for the 45-birth hospital.

TABLE 11-A Binomial Probabilities for Exact Number of Relevant Outcomes, Where the Simple Probability of the Outcome is .50

$n = 3$		$n = 9$		$n = 15$		$n = 45$	
Exact Number of Relevant Outcomes:							
0	.1250	0	.0020	9	.1527	27	.0488
1	.3750	1	.0176	10	.0916	28	.0314
2	.3750	2	.0703	11	.0417	29	.0184
3	.1250	3	.1641	12	.0139	30	.0098
		4	.2461	13	.0032	31	.0047
		5	.2461	14	.0005	32	.0021
		6	.1641	15	.0000	33	.0008
		7	.0703	etc.		34	.0003
		8	.0176	.		35	.0001
		9	.0020	.		36	.0000
						.	
						.	

CHAPTER

12

Problem Solving

It seems that all cognitive activities are fundamentally problem solving in nature. The basic argument . . . is that human cognition is always purposeful, directed to achieving goals and to removing obstacles to those goals.

ANDERSON, 1985, PP. 199–200

The Newell and Simon approach to problem-solving did not produce a flurry of related experiments by other cognitive psychologists, and problem solving never became a central research area in information-processing cognition. . . . Newell and Simon's conceptual work, however, formed a cornerstone of the information-processing approach.

LACHMAN ET AL., 1979, P. 99

A favorite example of "problem solving in action" is the following true story. When I (M.H.A.) was a graduate student, I attended a departmental colloquium at which a candidate for a faculty position was to present his research. As he started his talk, he realized that his first slide was projected too low on the screen. A flurry of activity around the projector ensued, one professor asking out loud, "Does anyone have a book or something?" Someone volunteered a book, the professor tried it, but it was too thick; the slide image was now too high. "No, this one's too big. Anyone got a thinner one?" he continued. After several more seconds of hurried searching for something thinner, another professor finally exclaimed, "Well, for Pete's sake, I don't believe this!" He marched over to the projector, grabbed the book, opened it halfway, and put it under the projector. He looked around the lecture hall and shook his head, saying, "I can't believe it. A roomful of PhDs, and no one knows how to open a book!"

This chapter examines the slow and deliberate cognitive processing called problem solving. Just as with decision making and reasoning, problem solving studies a person who is confronted with a difficult, time-consuming task: A problem has been presented, the solution to the problem is not immediately obvious, and the person often is uncertain what to do next. We are interested in all aspects of the person's activities, from initial understanding of the problem, the steps that lead to a final solution, and, in some cases, the way a person decides that a problem has been solved. Our interest in these questions needs no further justification or explanation than this: We confront countless problems in our daily lives, problems that are important for us to figure out and solve. We rely on our wits in these situations. We attempt to solve the problem by mentally analyzing the situation, devising a plan of action, then carrying out that plan. Therefore, the mental processing involved in problem solving is, by definition, part of cognitive psychology.

Let's start with a simple "recreational" problem (Anderson, 1993). It will take you a minute or two at most to solve it, even if you lose patience with brain teasers very quickly; VanLehn's (1989) nine-year-old child seemed to understand it completely in about 20 seconds and solved it out loud in about two minutes:

> *Three men want to cross a river. They find a boat, but it is a very small boat. It will only hold 200 pounds. The men are named Large, Medium, and Small. Large weighs 200 pounds, Medium weighs 120 pounds, and Small weighs 80 pounds. How can they all get across? They might have to make several trips in the boat. (VanLehn, 1989, p. 532)*

Why should we be interested in such recreational problems? The answer is straightforward. As is typical of all scientific disciplines, cognitive science studies the simple before the complex, searches simpler settings to find basic principles that generalize to more difficult settings. After all, not all the everyday problems we confront are tremendously complex; figuring out how to prop up a slide projector is not of earthshaking significance (well, it probably was to the fellow interviewing for the job). In either case, the reasoning is that we often see large-scale issues and important processes more clearly when they are embedded in simple situations. Indeed, one aspect of problem solving you'll read about, functional fixedness, provides an account of why a roomful of PhDs didn't think about opening the book to make it thinner. Needless to say, functional fixedness was discovered with a simple, recreational problem.

THE STATUS OF THE PROBLEM-SOLVING AREA

Some view problem solving as an odd topic in cognitive psychology. In Bruner's (1973) view problem solving was an important goal to be pursued by psychology, one of the many that had been excluded by behaviorists. Because the overriding concern during the birth of cognitive psychology in the 1950s was to reintroduce the significant mental activities that had been ignored by behaviorism, Bruner's remarks fell on receptive ears.

And yet, the early research in problem solving, exemplified by Newell and Simon's work on chess, cryptarithmetic problems, and logic theorems, did not spawn the same kind of research tradition as, say, Tulving's work on retrieval cues or Collins and Quillian's work on semantic memory. A major reason for this—possibly *the* reason—was methodology. That is, studying significant problem solving requires us to examine a lengthy sample of behavior, often up to 20 or 30 min of activity. This means that the typical measures of RT and accuracy are irrelevant to experiments on problem solving. Instead, the major kind of data in problem solving is the **verbal protocol**, *the transcription and analysis of the participants' verbalizations as they solve the problem.*

Without a doubt, the use of verbal protocols influenced many opinions about problem solving, especially given the similarities between verbal protocols and the discredited method of introspectionism. In fact, the status of verbal reports as data is still a topic of some debate; see Dunlosky and Hertzog (2001); Ericsson and Simon (1980, 1993); Fleck and Weisberg (2004); and Russo, Johnson, and Stephens (1989) for a range of views. This aspect of problem-solving research, along with issues of experimental design, control of variables, and so on, placed it outside the strict information-processing tradition of stage models, flowcharts, and the like. The irony here, of course, is that Newell and Simon's approach—that humans can be conceived of as processors of information—was the very foundation of the information-processing approach. (See Lachman et al., 1979, Chapter 4, for a full account of these influences.)

There are still lingering signs of the division between the information processors and the problem solvers in contemporary cognitive psychology. But in most respects, it has either broken down or become irrelevant. Each group has made discoveries that have been important for the other tradition. For instance, the idea of heuristics, originally derived from problem solving, is applicable and important to a thorough understanding of reasoning, as you read in Chapter 11. Likewise, theories of language comprehension are critical to an understanding of important problem-solving activities (Kintsch & Greeno, 1985). Thus problem solving deserves a prominent place in mainstream cognitive psychology.

Let's begin with a description of the classic problem-solving research of the Gestalt psychologists. As you read in Chapter 1, the Gestalt movement coexisted with behaviorism early in the 20th century but never achieved the central status that behaviorism did. In retrospect, however, it was an important influence on cognitive psychology.

By the way, possibly more than in any material you've read so far, it's important in this chapter for you to spend some time working through the examples and problems. Hints usually accompany the problems, and the solutions are presented in the text or, for numbered problems, at the end of the chapter. Many of the insights of the problem-solving literature pertain to conscious, strategic activities you'll discover on your own as you work through the sample problems. Furthermore, simply by working the examples, you'll probably improve your own problem-solving skills.

GESTALT PSYCHOLOGY AND PROBLEM SOLVING

Gestalt is a German word that translates poorly into English; the one-word translations "whole," "shape," and "field" fail miserably at indicating what the term actually means. Roughly speaking, a **Gestalt** is *a whole pattern, a form, or a configuration*. It is a cohesive grouping, a perspective from which the entire field can be seen. A variety of translations have been used at one point or another (*holism* is probably the best; note, however, holistic psychology, whatever that is, is certainly not the same as Gestalt psychology). No single translation ever caught on, which prompted Boring (1950) to remark that Gestalt psychology "suffered from its name." Consequently, we use the German term *Gestalt* itself, rather than an inadequate translation. Chapter 4 covered perceptual patterns that demonstrate various Gestalt principles (e.g., closure, good continuation). They show that humans tend to perceive and deal with integrated, cohesive wholes. Thus it was the Gestalt psychology movement that advanced the idea that "the whole is different from the sum of its parts."

Early Gestalt Research

The connection between *Gestalt* psychologists and interest in problem solving is best explained by anecdote (see Boring, 1950, pp. 595–597). In 1913 Wolfgang Kohler, a German psychologist, went to the Spanish island of Tenerife to study "the psychology of anthropoid apes" (Boring, 1950, p. 596). Trapped there by the outbreak of World War I, Kohler experimented with visual discrimination among several animal species. In the course of this research, he began to apply Gestalt principles to animal perception. His ultimate conclusion was that animals do not perceive individual elements in a stimulus, but that they perceive relations among stimuli. Furthermore, "Kohler also observed that the perception of relations is a mark of intelligence, and he called the sudden perception of useful or proper relations *insight*" (Boring, 1950, p. 596).

Still stranded on the island, Kohler continued to examine "insight learning." He presented problems to chimpanzees and searched for evidence of genuine problem solving in their behavior. By far the most famous of his subjects was a chimpanzee named Sultan (Kohler, 1927). In a simple demonstration, Sultan was able to use a long pole to reach through the bars of his cage and get a bunch of bananas. Kohler made the situation more difficult by giving Sultan two shorter poles, neither of which was long enough to reach the bananas. After failing to get the bananas, and sulking in his cage for a while, Sultan (as the story goes) suddenly went over to the poles and put one inside the end of the other, thus creating one pole that was long enough to reach the bananas.

Grande builds a three-box structure to reach the bananas, while Sultan watches from the ground. *Insight*, sometimes referred to as an "Ah-ha" experience, was the term Kohler used for the sudden perception of useful relations among objects during problem solving.

Kohler found this to be an apt demonstration of insight, a sudden solution to a problem by means of an insightful discovery. In another situation, Sultan discovered how to stand on a box to reach a banana that was otherwise too high to reach. In yet another, he discovered how to get a banana that was just out of reach through the cage bars: He walked *away* from the banana, out a distant door, and around the cage. All these problem solutions seemed to illustrate Sultan's perception of relations and the importance of insight in problem solving.

Difficulties in Problem Solving

Other Gestalt psychologists, most notably Duncker and Luchins, pursued the research tradition with humans. Two major contributions of this later work are essentially the two sides of the problem-solving coin. One involved a set of negative effects related to rigidity or difficulty in problem solving; the other, insight and creativity during problem solving.

FUNCTIONAL FIXEDNESS Two articles on functional fixedness, one by Maier (1931) and one by Duncker (1945), identify and define this particular difficulty that arises during problem solving. **Functional fixedness** is *a tendency to use objects and concepts in the problem environment in only their customary and usual way*. Maier (1931), for instance, had people work on the two-string problem. Two strings are suspended from the ceiling, and the goal is to tie them together. The problem is that the strings are too far apart for a person to hold one, reach the other, then tie them together. Also available are several other objects, including a chair, some paper, and a pair of pliers. Even standing on the chair does not get the person close enough to the two strings.

In Maier's results only 39% of the people came up with the correct solution during a 10-minute period. The solution (if you haven't tried solving the problem, do so now) involves using an object in the room in a novel fashion. A correct solution is to tie the pliers to one string, swing it like a pendulum, then catch it while holding the other string. Thus the functional fixedness in this situation was failing to think of the pliers in any but their customary function; people were fixed on the normal use for pliers and failed to appreciate how they could be used as a weight for a pendulum.

▲ A similar demonstration is shown in Figure 12-1, the candle problem from Duncker (1945). The task is to find a way to mount the candle on a wall using just the objects illustrated. Can you solve the problem? If you haven't come up with a solution after a minute or two, here's a hint: Can you think of another use for a box besides using it as a container? In other words, the notion of functional fixedness is that we generally think only of the customary uses for objects, whereas successful problem solving often involves finding novel uses for objects. By thinking of the box as a platform or means of support, you can then solve the problem (empty the box, thumbtack it to the door or wall, then mount the candle in it).

It's probably not surprising that problem solvers experience functional fixedness. After all, we comprehend the problem situation by means of our world knowledge, along with whatever procedural knowledge we have that might be relevant. When you find "PLIERS" in semantic memory, surely the most accessible properties involve the normal use for pliers. Far down on your list would be characteristics related to the weight of the

▲ **FIGURE 12-1** The candle problem used by Duncker. Using only the pictured objects, figure out how to mount the candle to the wall.

pliers or aspects of their shape that would enable you to tie a string to them. Likewise, "BOX" probably is stored in semantic memory in terms of "container" meanings—that a box can hold things, that you put things into a box—and not in terms of "platform or support" meanings (see Greenspan, 1986, for evidence on retrieval of central and peripheral properties). Simply from the standpoint of routine retrieval from memory, then, we can understand why people often experience functional fixedness.

NEGATIVE SET A related difficulty in problem solving is **negative set** (or simply *set effects*). This refers to *a bias or tendency to solve problems in a particular way, using a single specific approach, even when a different approach might be more productive.* The term *set* is a rough translation of the original German term *Einstellung,* which means something like "approach" or "orientation"; the (awful) phrase "mind-set" probably is the closest expression we have to the term in English.

The classic demonstration of set effects comes from the water jug problems, studied by Luchins (1942). In these problems, you are given three jugs, each of a different capacity, and are asked to measure out a quantity of water using just the three jugs. As a simple illustration, consider the first problem in Table 12-1. You need to measure out 28 cups of water and can use containers that hold 5, 40, and 18 cups (jugs *A, B,* and *C*). The solution is to fill *A* twice, then fill *C* once, each time pouring the contents into a destination jug. This approach is an addition solution because you add the quantities together. For the second problem, a subtraction solution is appropriate: Fill *B* (127), subtract jug *C* from it twice (–3, –3), then subtract jug *A* (–21), yielding 100.

TABLE 12-1 Water Jug Problems

Problem	Capacity of Jug *A*	Capacity of Jug *B*	Capacity of Jug *C*	Desired Quantity
1	5 cups	40 cups	18 cups	28 cups
2	21 cups	127 cups	3 cups	100 cups

Luchins's Water Jug Problems

Problem	Capacity of Jug *A*	Capacity of Jug *B*	Capacity of Jug *C*	Desired Quantity
1	21	127	3	100
2	14	163	25	99
3	18	43	10	5
4	9	42	6	21
5	20	59	4	31
6	23	49	3	20
7	15	39	3	18
8	28	76	3	25
9	18	48	4	22
10	14	36	8	6

Note. All volumes are in cups.

Luchins's (1942) demonstration of negative set involved sequencing the problems so that people developed a particular set or approach for measuring out the quantities. The second group of problems in Table 12-1 illustrates such a sequence. Go ahead and work the problems now before you read any further.

If you were like most people, your experience on problems 1 through 7 led you to develop a particular approach or set: specifically, $B - 2C - A$: Fill jug *B*, subtract *C* from it twice, then subtract *A* from it to yield the necessary amount (subtracting *A* can be done before subtracting 2*C*, of course). People with such a set or *Einstellung* generally failed to notice the far simpler solution possible for problems 6 and 10, simply $A - C$. That is, about 80% of the people who saw all 10 problems used the lengthy $B - 2C - A$ method for these problems. Compare this with the control participants, who saw only problems 6 through 10: Only 1% of people used the longer method. Clearly, the control people had not developed a set for using the lengthy method, so they were better able to find the simpler solution.

Consider problem 8 now. Only 5% of Luchins's control people failed to solve problem 8. This was a remarkable because 64% of the "negative set" people, those who saw all 10 problems, failed to solve it correctly. These people had such a bias to use the method they had already developed that they were unable to generate a method that would solve problem 8 ($B - 2C - A$ does not work on this problem). Greeno's (1978) description here is useful: By repeatedly solving the first seven problems with the same formula, people learned an integrated algorithm. This algorithm was strong enough to bias their later solution attempts and prevent them from seeing the simple solution, $28 - 3 = 25$. Consistent with this idea—that if people develop a routine way of solving problems then they are more likely to experience Einstellung—there is evidence that experts at a task are more prone to this than others (Bilalic, McLeod, & Gobet, 2008) because they are more likely to have developed a set of routines for solving certain kinds of problems. Moreover, if more varied initial problems are given, then people can more easily generalize their solution to a variety of other problems (e.g., Chen & Mo, 2004).

Several problems that often yield such negative set effects are presented in Table 12-2; hints to help overcome negative set, if you experience it, are at the bottom of the table. These problems lack the precision of Luchins's demonstration, of course: We cannot

TABLE 12-2 Sample Negative Set Problems

Buddhist Monk

One morning, exactly at sunrise, a Buddhist monk began to climb a tall mountain. The narrow path, no more than a foot or two wide, spiraled around the mountain to a glittering temple at the summit. The monk ascended the path at varying rates of speed, stopping many times along the way to rest and to eat the dried fruit he carried with him. He reached the temple shortly before sunset. After several days of fasting and meditation, he began his journey back along the same path, starting at sunrise and again walking at variable speeds with many pauses along the way. His average descending speed was, of course, greater than his average climbing speed.

Show that there is a spot along the path that the monk will occupy on both trips at precisely the same time of day.

Drinking Glasses

Six drinking glasses are lined up in a row. The first three are full of water, the last three are empty. By handling and moving only one glass, change the arrangement so that no full glass is next to another full one, and no empty glass is next to another empty one.

Six Pennies

Show how to move only two pennies in the left diagram to yield the pattern at the right.

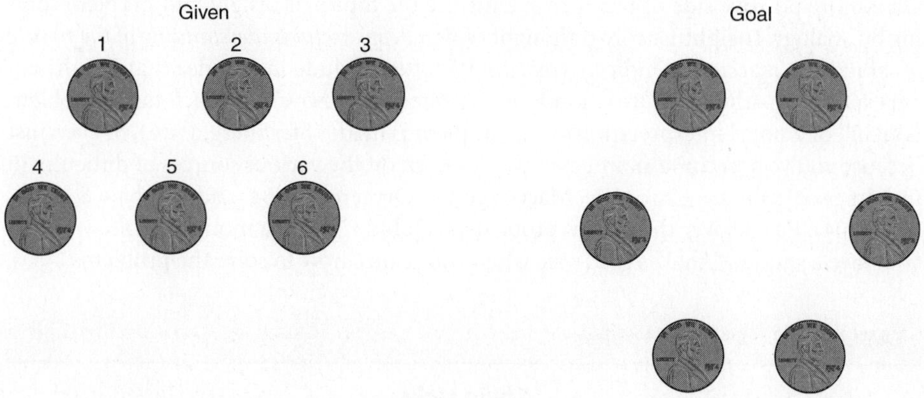

Hints

Buddhist Monk. Although the problem seems to ask for a quantitative solution, think of a way of representing the problem using visual imagery.

Drinking Glasses. How else can you handle a glass of water besides moving it to another location?

Six Pennies. From a different perspective, some of the pennies might already be in position.

point to the exact equation or method that is the negative set in these problems but only to the general approach or incorrect representation people often adopt. On the other hand, the problems are useful in that they seem to resemble real-world problems more closely than the rather arbitrary water jugs do.

As the slide projector problem in the introduction suggests, functional fixedness and negative set probably are common occurrences. Possibly because we eventually find an adequate solution to our everyday problems despite the negative set or without overcoming our functional fixedness (e.g., eventually locating a thinner book), we are less aware of these difficulties in our problem-solving behavior. The classic demonstrations, however, illustrate dramatically how rigid such behavior can be and how barriers to successful problem solving can arise.

Section Summary

- Newell and Simon's insights on the role of computer simulation in an understanding of human information processing were central to the development of cognitive psychology in the late 1950s. Their research methods were different from those developed in verbal learning, so the area of problem solving has only recently become a mainstream topic within cognitive psychology.
- The early Gestalt psychologists studied problem solving and discovered two major barriers to successful performance: functional fixedness and negative set.

INSIGHT AND ANALOGY

Insight

On a more positive side of problem solving are the topics of insight and problem solving by analogy. **Insight** usually is thought of as *a deep, useful understanding of the nature of something, especially a difficult problem.* We often include in the idea that insight occurs suddenly—the "Aha!" reaction—possibly because a novel approach to the problem is taken, or a novel interpretation of the problem is made (Sternberg, 1996), or even just because you've overcome an impasse (for research on the various sources of difficulty in insight problems, see Chronicle, MacGregor, & Ormerod, 2004, and Kershaw & Ohlsson, 2004). Puzzle over the insight problems in Table 12-3 for a moment to see whether you have a sudden "Aha!" experience when you realize how to solve the problems.

TABLE 12-3 Insight Problems

Chain Links
A woman has four pieces of chain. Each piece is made up of three links. She wants to join the pieces into a single closed ring of chain. To open a link costs 2 cents and to close a link costs 3 cents. She has only 15 cents. How does she do it?
Four Trees
A landscape gardener is given instructions to plant four special trees so that each one is exactly the same distance from each of the others. How would you arrange the trees?

TABLE 12-3 (Continued)

Prisoner's Escape

A prisoner was attempting to escape from a tower. He found in his cell a rope which was half long enough to permit him to reach the ground safely. He divided the rope in half and tied the two parts together and escaped. How could he have done this?

Bronze Coin

A stranger approached a museum curator and offered him an ancient bronze coin. The coin had an authentic appearance and was marked with the date 544 B.C. The curator had happily made acquisitions from suspicious sources before, but this time he promptly called the police and had the stranger arrested. Why?

Nine Dots

Connect the nine dots with four connected straight lines without lifting your pencil from the page as you draw.

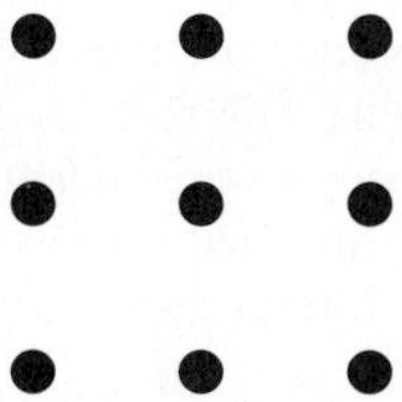

Bowling Pins

The ten bowling pins below are pointing toward the top of the page. Move any three of them to make the arrangement point down toward the bottom of the page.

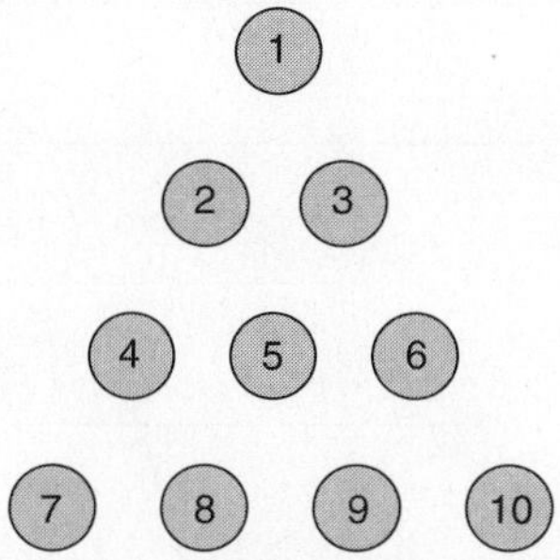

Hints

Chain links. You don't have to open a link on each piece of chain.

Four trees. We don't always plant trees on flat lawns.

Prisoner's escape. Is there only one way to divide a rope in half?

Bronze coin. Imagine that you lived in 544 B.C. What did it say on your coins?

Nine dots. How long a line does the problem permit you to draw?

Bowling pins. Pins 1, 2, 3, and 5 form a diamond at the top of the drawing. Consider where the diamond might be for the arrangement that points down.

Adapted from Metcalfe (1986) and Metcalfe & Wiebe (1987).

Sometimes, the necessary insight for solving a problem comes from an analogy: An already-solved problem is similar to a current one, so the old solution can be adapted to the new situation. The historical example of this is the story of Archimedes, the Greek scientist who had to determine whether the king's crown was solid gold or whether some silver had been mixed with the gold. Archimedes knew the weights of both gold and silver per unit of volume but could not imagine how to measure the volume of the crown. As the anecdote goes, he stepped into his bath one day and noticed how the water level rose as he sank into the water. He then realized the solution to his problem. The volume of the crown could be determined by immersing it in water and measuring how much water it displaced. Excited by his insight, he then jumped from the bath and ran naked through the streets, shouting "Eureka! I have found it!"

Metcalfe and Wiebe (1987; also Metcalfe, 1986) studied how people solved such problems and compared that with how they solved algebra and other routine problems. They found two interesting results. First, people were rather accurate in predicting whether they'd be successful in solving routine problems but not in predicting success with the insight problems. Second, solutions to the insight problems seemed to ★ come suddenly, almost without warning. This result is shown in Figure 12-2. That is, as they worked through the problems, people were interrupted and asked to indicate how "warm" they were, that is, how close they felt they were to finding the solution. For routine algebra problems, "warmth" ratings grew steadily as people worked through

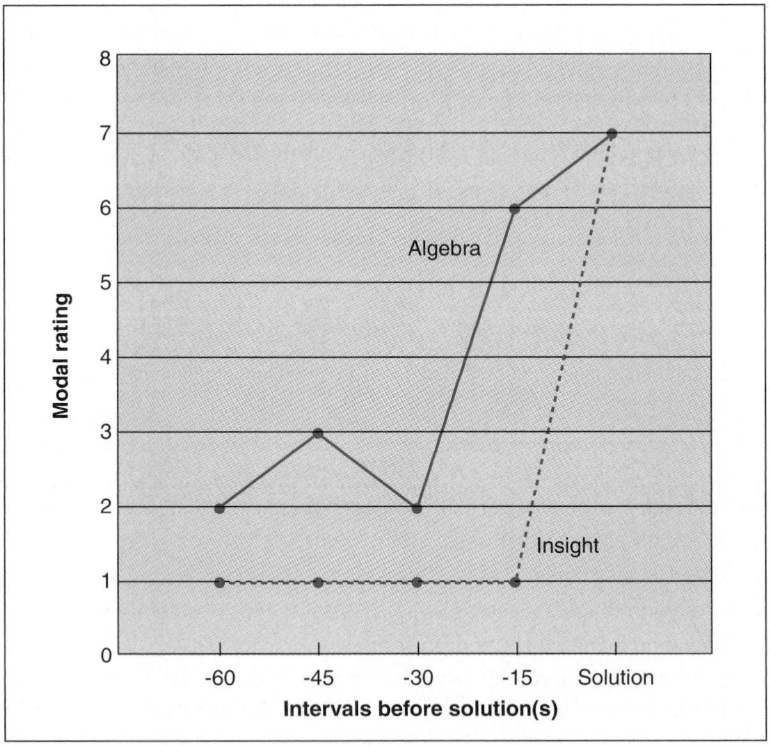

★ FIGURE 12-2 Modal (most frequent) warmth rating in the four time periods leading up to a problem solution. Data from Metcalfe & Wiebe (1987).

"I heard von Schleflin yell 'Eureka,' and then kerblam!"

the problems, reflecting their feeling of getting closer and closer to the solution. But there was little or no such increase for the insight problems even 15 s before the solution was found.

Although these results support the idea that insight arrives suddenly, some people are unconvinced. Classic insight problems can be thought of in simpler terms, say overcoming functional fixedness or negative set (as in prisoner's escape and nine-dot), taking a different perspective (bronze coin), and the like (Smith, 1995). A neuroimaging study by Kounios, Frymiare, Bowden, Fleck, Subramaniam, Parrish, and Jung-Beeman (2006) provides some support for this idea. Using both EEG and fMRI recordings, they found increased cortical activity centered on the frontal lobes (particularly the anterior cingulate cortex) when people produced insight solutions as compared to normal problem solving. Kounios et al.'s theory is that this part of the frontal lobe suppresses the irrelevant information (an attentional process, see Chapter 4) that tends to dominate a person's thinking up to that point. When these dominant thoughts become suppressed, this allows more weakly activated ideas, such as those remote associations drawn by the right hemisphere, to come to the fore, possibly providing the solution to a problem. In other words, part of a person's thought processes were working on the problem along with the steps that were being worked on at the forefront of consciousness (which were going nowhere). When these dead-end thoughts are moved aside, alternative solutions can then present themselves.

This release from irrelevant modes of thinking, seen in the neuroimaging data, can be extended to a process called *incubation*. With incubation, when people have difficulty solving a problem, they may stop working on it for a while. Then at some point, the solution or key to a solution may present itself to them. While this can work at times, it appears that incubation is most useful when people have originally been provided with misleading information, either by others or themselves, that steers them away from the correct solution. What happens during incubation is that the representations for these misleading ideas lose strength, so that later on the more successful alternatives can present themselves (Vul & Pashler, 2007).

In some circumstances, *insight* may mean that we've drawn a critical inference that leads to a solution; for example, there's more than one way to divide a rope in half (Wickelgren, 1974). Weisberg (1995) reports that some people solve insight problems like those in the table without any of the sudden restructuring or understanding that supposedly accompanies insight.

Other evidence, however, suggests that verbalization can interfere with insight, can disrupt "nonreportable processes that are critical to achieving insight solutions" (Schooler, Ohlsson, & Brooks, 1993, p. 166). Furthermore, being unable to report the restructuring that accompanies insight, or the actual insight itself, may be more common in insight situations than we realize. For instance, Siegler and Stern (1998; see also Siegler, 2000) reported a study of second graders solving arithmetic problems then reporting verbally on their solutions. There was the regular computational, noninsightful way to solve the problems, which the second graders followed, but also a shortcut way that represented an insight (e.g., for a problem like 18 + 24 – 24, simply state 18). Almost 90% of the sample discovered the insight for solving such problems, as shown by the dramatic decrease in their solution times from around 12 s for the computational method to a mean of 2.7 s with the shortcut. But they were unaware of their discovery when questioned about how they solved the problems. Within another five trials, however, 80% of the children's verbal reports indicated that they were aware of their discovery.

Analogy

In general, an **analogy** is *a relationship between two similar situations, problems, or concepts*. Understanding an analogy means putting the two situations into some kind of alignment so that the similarities and differences are made apparent (Gentner & Markman, 1997). Take a simple example, the analogy "MERCHANT : SELL :: CUSTOMER : _____." Here, you must figure out the structure for the first pair of terms and then project or *map* that structure onto the second part of the analogy. Because "SELL" is the critical activity of "MERCHANT," the critical activity relationship is then mapped onto "CUSTOMER," and retrieval from memory yields "BUY."

Researchers argue that analogies provide excellent, widely applicable methods for solving problems. That is, if you're confronted with a difficult problem, a useful heuristic is to find a similar or related situation and build an analogy from it to the current problem. According to these authors, such reasoning and problem solving may help us understand a huge variety of situations, such as how students should be taught in school, how people adopt professional role models, and how we empathize with others (Holyoak & Thagard, 1997; Kolodner, 1997). And it's long been held that important scientific ideas, breakthroughs, and explanations have often depended on finding analogies, for instance that neurotransmitters fit into the receptor sites of a neuron much the way a key fits into a lock (see Gentner & Markman, 1997, for a description of reasoning by analogy in Kepler's discovery of the laws of planetary motion). Curiously, analogical problem solving is better when people receive the information by hearing about it rather than reading it (Markman, Taylor, & Gentner, 2007), perhaps reflecting the more natural use of spoken over written language.

ANALOGY PROBLEMS To gain some feeling for analogies, read the parade story at ▲ the top of Table 12-4, a story used by Gick and Holyoak (1980). Try to solve the problem now, before reading the solution at the bottom of the table.

Gick and Holyoak had people read the parade problem, a somewhat different army fortress story, or no story at all. They then asked them to read and solve a second ● problem, the classic Duncker (1945) radiation problem, shown in Table 12-5 (which you should read and try to solve now).

TABLE 12-4 The Parade Problem

A small country was controlled by a dictator. The dictator ruled the country from a strong fortress. The fortress was situated in the middle of the country, surrounded by farms and villages. Many roads radiated outward from the fortress like spokes on a wheel. To celebrate the anniversary of his rise to power, the dictator ordered his general to conduct a full-scale military parade. On the morning of the anniversary, the general's troops were gathered at the head of one of the roads leading to the fortress, ready to march. However, a lieutenant brought the general a disturbing report. The dictator was demanding that this parade had to be more impressive than any previous parade. He wanted his army to be seen and heard at the same time in every region of the country. Furthermore, the dictator was threatening that if the parade was not sufficiently impressive, he was going to strip the general of his medals and reduce him to the rank of private. But it seemed impossible to have a parade that could be seen throughout the whole country.

The Solution

The general, however, knew just what to do. He divided his army up into small groups and dispatched each group to the head of a different road. When all was ready he gave the signal, and each group marched down a different road. Each group continued down its road to the fortress, so that the entire army finally arrived together at the fortress at the same time. In this way, the general was able to have the parade seen and heard through the entire country at once, and thus please the dictator.

The radiation problem is interesting for a variety of reasons, including the fact that it is rather ill defined and thus comparable to many problems in the real world. Duncker's participants produced two general approaches that led to dead ends: Trying to avoid contact between the rays and nearby tissue and trying to change the sensitivity of surrounding tissue to the effects of the rays. But the third approach, reducing the intensity of the rays, was more productive, especially if an analogy from some other, better understood situation was available.

Gick and Holyoak (1980) used this problem to study analogy. In fact, we've just simulated one of their experiments here by having you read the parade story first and then the radiation problem. In case you didn't notice, there are strong similarities between the problems, suggesting that the parade story can be used to develop an analogy for the radiation problem.

Gick and Holyoak found that only 49% of people who first solved the parade problem realized it could be used as an analogy for the radiation problem. A different initial story, in which armies are attacking a fortress, provided a stronger hint about the radiation problem. Fully 76% of these participants used the attack analogy in solving the radiation problem. In contrast, only 8% of the control group, which merely attempted to solve the radiation problem, came up with the dispersion solution (i.e., multiple pathways) described at the bottom of Table 12-5.

When Gick and Holyoak provided a strong hint, telling people that the attack solution might be helpful as they worked on the radiation problem, 92% of them used

TABLE 12-5 Radiation and Attack Dispersion Problems

Radiation Problem

Suppose you are a doctor faced with a patient who has a malignant tumor in his stomach. It is impossible to operate on the patient, but unless the tumor is destroyed the patient will die. There is a kind of ray that can be used to destroy the tumor. If the rays reach the tumor all at once at a sufficiently high intensity, the tumor will be destroyed. Unfortunately, at this intensity the healthy tissue that the rays pass through on the way to the tumor will also be destroyed. At lower intensities the rays are harmless to healthy tissue, but they will not affect the tumor either. What type of procedure might be used to destroy the tumor with the rays without destroying the healthy tissue?

Attack Dispersion Story

A small country was controlled by a dictator. The dictator ruled the country from a strong fortress. The fortress was situated in the middle of the country, surrounded by farms and villages. Many roads radiated outward from the fortress like spokes on a wheel. A general arose who raised a large army and vowed to capture the fortress and free the country of the dictator. The general knew that if his entire army could attack the fortress at once it could be captured. The general's troops were gathered at the head of one of the roads leading to the fortress, ready to attack. However, a spy brought the general a disturbing report. The ruthless dictator had planted mines on each of the roads. The mines were set so that small bodies of men could pass over them safely because the dictator needed to be able to move troops and workers to and from the fortress. However, any large force would detonate the mines. Not only would this blow up the road and render it impassable, but the dictator would then destroy many villages in retaliation. It therefore seemed impossible to mount a full-scale direct attack on the fortress.

Solution to the Radiation Problem

The ray can be divided into several low-intensity rays, no one of which will destroy the healthy tissue. If these several rays are positioned at different locations around the body and focused on the tumor, their effect will combine, thus being strong enough to destroy the tumor.

Solution to the Attack Dispersion Story

The general, however, knew just what to do. He divided his army up into small groups and dispatched each group to the head of a different road. When all was ready he gave the signal, and each group marched down a different road. Each group continued down its road to the fortress, so that the entire army finally arrived together at the fortress at the same time. In this way, the general was able to capture the fortress and thus overthrow the dictator.

the analogy, and most found it "very helpful." In contrast, only 20% of the people in the no-hint group produced the dispersion solution, even though they too had read the attack dispersion story. In short, only 20% spontaneously noticed and used the analogous relationship between the problems. Table 12-6 summarizes Gick and Holyoak's results.

TABLE 12-6 Summary of Gick and Holyoak's (1980) Results

Study 1 (Experiment II originally; after Gick & Holyoak, Table 10)

People in groups *A* and *B* are given a general hint that their solution to one of the earlier stories may be useful in solving the radiation problem.

Group	Order of Stories	Percentage of People Who Used the Analogy on the Radiation Problem
Group *A*	Parade, radiation	49%
Group *B*	Attack dispersion, radiation	76%
Group *C*	No story, radiation	8%

Study 2 (Experiment IV originally)

People in group *A* are given the general hint (as above). People in group *B* are given no hint whatsoever.

Group	Order of Stories	Percentage of People Who Used the Analogy on the Radiation Problem
Group *A* (hint)	Attack dispersion, radiation	92%
Group *B* (no hint)	Attack dispersion, radiation	20%

MULTICONSTRAINT THEORY Holyoak and Thagard (1997) proposed a theory of analogical reasoning and problem solving, based on such results. The theory, called the multiconstraint theory, predicts how people use analogies in problem solving and what factors govern the analogies people construct. In particular, the theory says that people are constrained by three factors when they try to use or develop analogies.

The first factor is problem similarity. There must be a reasonable degree of similarity between the already understood situation, the *source* domain, and the current problem being solved, the *target* domain. In the parade story, for example, the fortress and troops can be seen as similar to the tumor and the rays. Similarity between source and target has been shown to be important in several studies. Chen, Mo, and Honomichl (2004), for example, found that similarities from well-known folk tales to new problems were especially important for finding problem solutions, even if participants did not report remembering the folk tale. On the other hand, Novick (1988) found that novices focus especially on similarities, even when they are only superficial, which can interfere with performance.

The second factor is problem structure. People must establish a parallel structure between the source and target problems so they can map elements from the source to comparable elements in the target. Figuring out these correspondences or mappings is important because it corresponds to working out the relationships of the analogy. In the parade–radiation analogy, you have to map troops onto rays so that the important relationship of different converging roads can serve as the basis for the solution. The most prominent mappings from parade to radiation are shown

FIGURE 12-3 Prominent mappings between the attack and radiation problems.

Mappings		
Attack	→	Radiation
Central fortress	→	Tumor
Attacking troops	→	Rays
Small groups of men	→	Weaker rays
Multiple roads	→	Multiple pathways
Destroy villages	→	Damage healthy tissue

in Figure 12-3. It turns out that mapping the relations is rather demanding; for instance, in a dual-task setting, Waltz, Lau, Grewal, and Holyoak (2000) found that holding on to a working memory load seriously reduced the ability to find correct mappings between two problems. Also, Bassok, Pedigo, and Oskarsson (2008) found that the semantic memory can interfere with drawing analogies. For example, when people are doing addition-based word problems, making the analogy between the word problem and addition was easier when items are semantically similar, such as *tulips* and *daisies* (which are separate things that can easily be added together), but not when there is an inconsistency, such as *records* and *songs*. In this case, the knowledge that songs are parts of records implies a hierarchical, part-whole relationship, so it is more difficult to make the additional analogy where is it easier to think of things that can be treated on more equal footing.

The third factor that constrains people is the purpose of the analogy. The person's goals, and the goal stated in the problem, are important. This is deeper than merely the general purpose of trying to solve the problem. Notice that the goals in the attack and radiation stories match, whereas the goals do not match for parade and radiation (parade involves sending troops *out* from the central fortress, for display purposes, but radiation involves sending rays *in* toward the tumor). This mismatch may have been responsible for the low use of parade as a source for the analogy to radiation. Likewise, Spellman and Holyoak (1996) report a study in which college students drew analogies between two soap opera plots. When different purposes or goals were given in the instructions, the students developed different analogies; that is, their problem solving by analogy was sensitive to purposes and overall goals. A study by Kurtz and Loewenstein (2007) reported that people are more likely to draw on analogies from previous problems when they are comparing two other problems than if they are working on a single problem alone. This suggests that the processing goals and tactics, in this case direct comparison, in use can influence whether people actually use analogies or not.

A final point to note is that most of the work on analogy, like many studies of problem solving, has focused on the conscious, explicit use of analogies. However, there is some evidence to suggest that people may use analogies in a more unconscious, implicit manner as well. In a study by Day and Gentner (2007) people were given pairs of texts to read. When the events described by the second text were analogous to those described in the first (in terms of their relational structure), people read the second text faster. That is, people were able to use their unconscious knowledge of the event structure from the first test to help them understand the second text. When asked, people showed no awareness of this relationship between the two texts. So, in some sense, by having people read the first text, the relational structure of the event was primed, and this made the processing of the second text easier.

Neurocognition in Analogy and Insight

Some exciting work has been reported on the cognitive neuropsychology of analogical reasoning and insight. In an impressive report, Wharton et al. (2000) identified brain regions that are associated with the mapping process in analogical reasoning. In their study, people saw a source picture of geometric shapes, followed by a target picture. They had to judge whether the target picture was an analog pattern—whether it had the same system of relations as the source picture. In the control condition, they judged whether the target was literally the same as the source. See Figure 12-4 for sample stimuli. In the top stimulus, the correct target preserves both the spatial relations in the source (a shape in all four quadrants) and the object relations (the patterned figures on the main diagonal are the same shape, and the shapes on the minor diagonal are different). Response times to analogy trials were in the 1,400 to 1,500 ms range and approximately 900 to 1,000 ms in the literal condition; accuracy was at or above 90% in both kinds of trials.

But the stunning result came from positron emission tomography (PET) scan images taken. Wharton et al. found significant activation in the medial frontal cortex, left prefrontal cortex, and left inferior parietal cortex; these patterns are shown in the final picture on the color plate page. The coronal and transverse views show the smallish medial region of the frontal lobe and the widespread left hemisphere activation clearly. And the sagittal view shows the large involvement of the parietal region especially clearly. (The coronal view is a vertical slice, as if from ear to ear, viewed from the front; transverse is a view looking down from the top; sagittal is a side view, with the front of the brain shown on the left.)

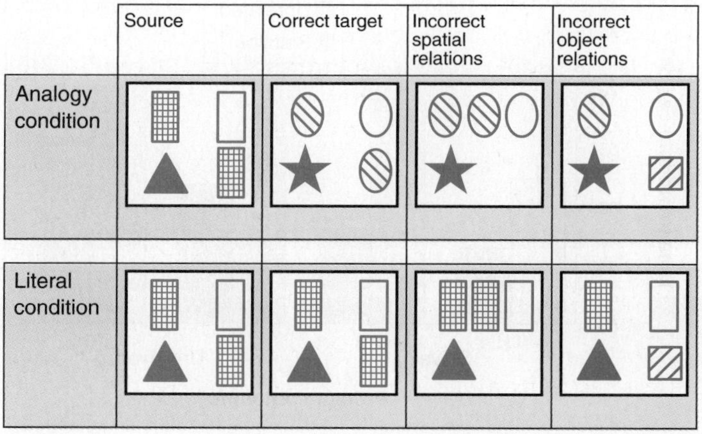

★ **FIGURE 12-4**
A depiction of analogy condition and literal condition trials. The first column shows the source stimuli, the second shows the correct choice, and the third and fourth show incorrect choices for the stated reasons. From Wharton et al. (2000), Figure 2, p. 179.

In contrast, Bowden and Beeman (1998; Beeman & Bowden, 2000) found a significant role for *right* hemisphere processing in solving insight problems. Before reading further, try this demonstration:

What one word can form a compound word or phrase with each of the following? Palm Shoe House

What one word can form a compound word or phrase with each of the following? Pie Luck Belly?

People were given such word triples—called "compound remote associates"—and had to think of a fourth word that combines with each of the three initial words to yield a familiar word pair. On many trials, people fail to find an immediate solution and end up spending considerable time working on the problem. They also report that when they finally solve the problems, the solution came to them as an insight—an "Aha!" type of solution.

In the Bowden and Beeman (1998) study, people saw the problems and then after 15 s were asked to name a new word that appeared on the screen (if they solved the problem before the 15 s was up, they were given the word immediately). When the target word was unrelated to the three words seen before (e.g., "planet"), there was the typical effect, that targets presented to the right visual field, hence the left hemisphere of the brain, were named faster than those presented to the left visual field–right hemisphere. But when the target was the word that solved the insight problem (*tree* in the first problem, *pot* in the second one), there was a significant ▲ priming effect. As shown in Figure 12-5, naming time was significantly shorter for the solution words than for the unrelated words. And the priming effect—the drop-off from "unrelated" to "solution"—was greater for targets presented to the right hemisphere than to the left (in other words, presented to the left visual field so going first to the right hemisphere).

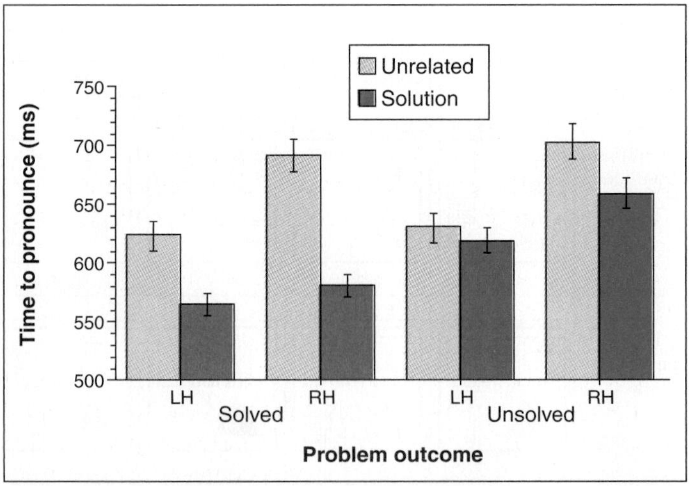

▲ **FIGURE 12-5** Mean naming time (time to pronounce) the target word for solved and unsolved trials. Bars labeled LH refer to target words presented to the right visual field, left hemisphere of the brain; RH means left visual field, right hemisphere. The figure shows priming effects for solution words, especially in the right hemisphere. From Bowden and Beeman (1998).

Putting it differently, semantic priming in the right hemisphere was more prominent than in the left hemisphere for these problems: People were faster to name *pot* when it was presented to the right hemisphere, presumably because it had been primed by the initial three words. The same effect was found in a replication (Bowden & Jung-Beeman, 2003) that used a lexical decision task instead of word naming. As the authors noted, these results fit nicely with other results concerning the role in language comprehension that the right hemisphere plays (you read about this in Chapter 10), especially the part having to do with drawing inferences (Bowden, Beeman, & Gernsbacher, 1995).

Section Summary

- Insight is a deep understanding of a situation or problem, often thought to occur suddenly and without warning. Although there is some debate on the nature of insight, insights may be discovered and used unconsciously and only later be available to consciousness.
- Reasoning by analogy is a complex kind of problem solving in which relationships in one situation are mapped onto another. People are better at developing analogies if given a useful source problem and an explicit hint that the problem might be used in solving a target problem. Holyoak and Thagard's multiconstraint theory of analogical problem solving claims that we work under three constraints as we develop analogies, constraints related to: the similarity of the source and target domains, the structure of the problems, and our purposes or goals in developing the analogies.
- Some new evidence suggests a particularly important role for the left frontal and parietal lobes in solving problems by analogy and a right hemisphere role in insight problems involving semantic priming.

BASICS OF PROBLEM SOLVING

Compared to the Gestalt tradition of research, modern cognitive psychology adopted a more reductionistic approach to the study of problem solving. For instance, Newell and Simon's analysis of a cryptarithmetic problem (1972, Chapter 6) consists of a microscopic analysis and interpretation of every statement made by one person as he solved a problem, all 2,186 words and 20 or so minutes of problem-solving activity. We cycle back here to an elementary question to profit from the greater degree of precision offered by modern cognitive psychology's examination of problem solving. The question, simply enough, is, "What is a problem?"

In Newell and Simon's (1972) description, "A person is confronted with a *problem* when he wants something and does not know immediately what series of actions he can perform to get it" (p. 72). The "something" can be renamed for more general use as a **goal**, *the desired end-point or solution of the problem-solving activity*. Problem solving consists of goal-directed activity, moving from some initial configuration or state through a series of intermediate steps until finally the overall goal has been reached: an adequate or correct solution. The difficulty is determining which intermediate states are on a correct pathway ("Will step *A* get me to step *B* or not?") and in devising operations or moves that achieve those intermediate states ("How do I get to step *B* from here?").

Characteristics of Problem Solving

Let's start by listing several characteristics that define what is and is not a genuine instance of problem solving. Anderson (1980, 1985), for example, lists the following:

- ***Goal directedness.*** The overall behavior or activity we're examining is directed toward achieving some goal or purpose. As such, we exclude daydreaming, for instance; it's mental, but it's not goal directed. Alternatively, if you've locked your keys in your car, both physical and mental activity is going on. The goal-directed nature of those activities, your repeated attempts to get into the locked car, makes this an instance of true problem solving.
- ***Sequence of operations.*** An activity must involve a sequence of operations or steps to qualify as problem solving. In other words, a simple retrieval from memory, say, remembering that 2×3 is 6, is not an instance of problem solving because it does not entail a slow, discernible sequence of separate operations. Alternatively, doing a long division problem and solving the locked car problem definitely involves a sequence of mental operations, so these are instances of problem solving.
- ***Cognitive operations.*** Solving the problem—achieving a solution to the overall goal—involves the application of various cognitive operations. Various operators can be applied to different problems, where each operator is a distinct cognitive act, a permissible step or move in the problem space. For long division, retrieving an answer would be an operator, as would be subtracting or multiplying two numbers at some other stage in problem solution. Often, the cognitive operations have a behavioral counterpart, some physical act that completes the mental operation, such as writing down a number during long division.
- ***Subgoal decomposition.*** As implied by the third characteristic, each step in the sequence of operations is itself a kind of goal, a **subgoal**. A subgoal is *an intermediate goal along the route to eventual solution of the problem.* Subgoals represent the decomposition, or breaking apart, of the overall goal into separate components. In many instances, subgoals themselves must be further decomposed into smaller subgoals. Thus solving a problem involves breaking the overall goal into subgoals, then pursuing the subgoals, and *their* subgoals, one after another until the final solution is achieved. This yields a hierarchical or nested structure to the problem-solving attempt.

An intuitive illustration of such a nested solution structure is presented in Figure 12-6, a possible solution route to the locked car problem. Note that during the solution, the first two plans led to barriers or blocks, thus requiring that another plan be devised (much like the radiation problem). The problem solver finally decided on another plan, breaking a window to get into the locked car. This decision is followed by a sequence of related acts: the search for some heavy object that will break a window, the decision as to which window to break, and so forth. Each of these decisions is a subgoal nested within the larger subgoal of breaking into the car, itself a subgoal in the overall solution structure.

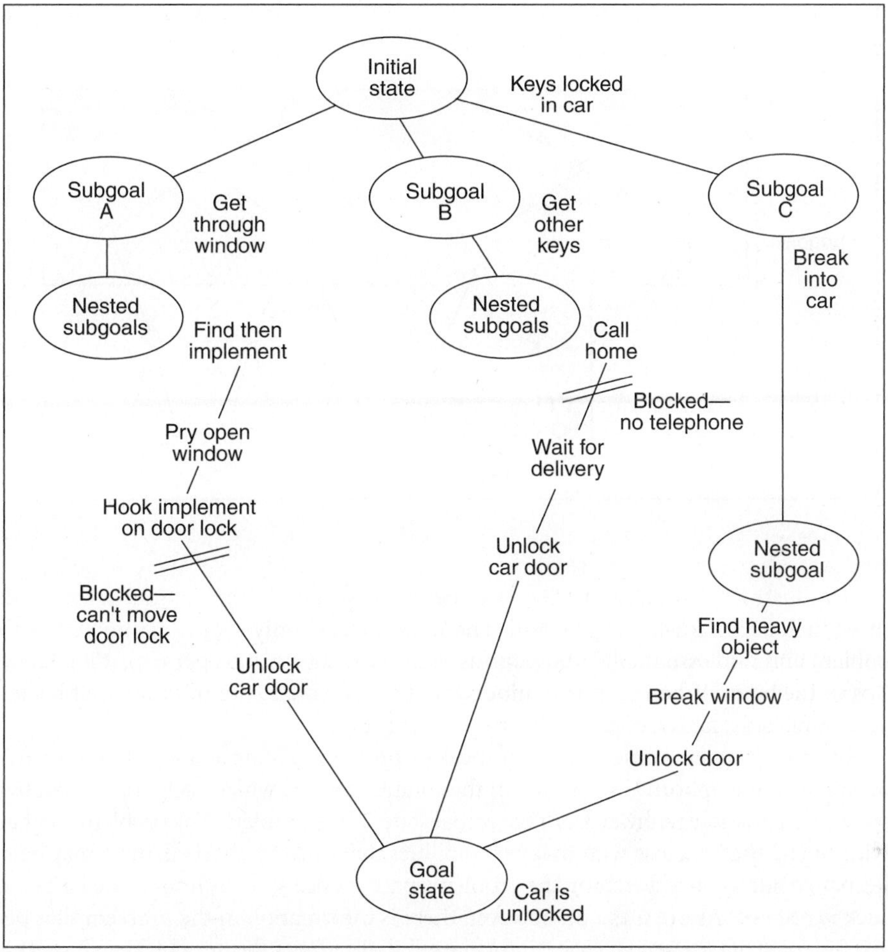

● **FIGURE 12-6**
A representation of part of the problem space for getting into a locked car. Note the barriers encountered under plans *A* and *B*.

A Vocabulary of Problem Solving

These four characteristics define what qualifies as problem solving. Many important ideas are embedded in these four points, however. Let's reexamine some of these points, looking now toward an expanded vocabulary of problem solving, a set of terms we use to describe and understand how people solve problems.

THE PROBLEM SPACE The term *problem space* is critical in analyzing problem solving. Anderson (1985) defines it as the various states or conditions that are possible in the problem. More concretely, the **problem space** includes *the initial, intermediate, and goal states of the problem. It also includes the problem solver's knowledge at each of these steps,* both knowledge that is currently being applied and knowledge that could be retrieved from memory and applied. Any external devices, objects, or resources that are available can also be included in the description of the problem space. Thus a difficult arithmetic problem that must be completed mentally has a somewhat different problem space than the same problem as completed with pencil and paper.

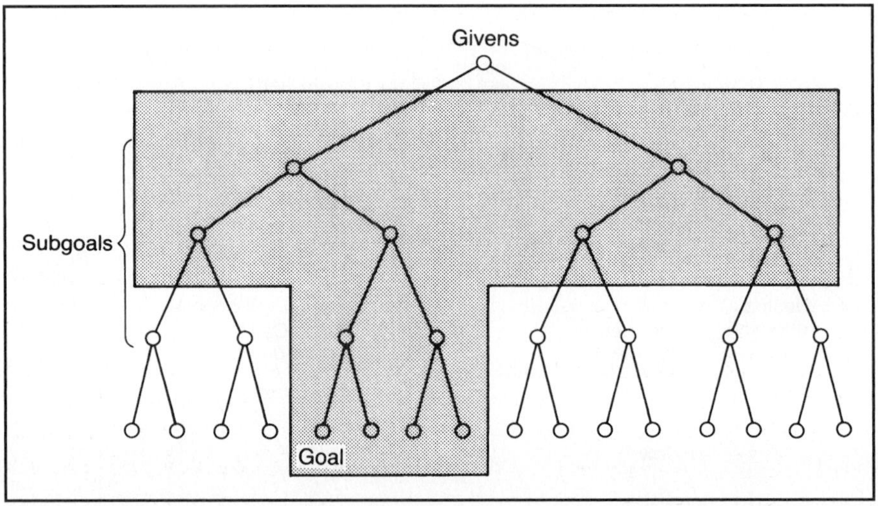

◆ **FIGURE 12-7**
A general diagram of a problem space, with various branches of the space illustrated. Often a hint or an inference can prune the search tree, restricting the search to just one portion; this idea is represented by the shaded area of the figure. Note that, in most problems, the problem space tree is much larger, so the beneficial effect of pruning is far greater. Adapted from Wickelgren (1974).

To illustrate, VanLehn (1989) describes a 60-year-old man's initial error in the "three men and a rowboat" problem. The man focused only on the arithmetic of the problem and said essentially "400 pounds of people, 200 pounds per trip, it'll take two trips of the boat." When he was reminded that the rowboat couldn't row itself back to the original side, he adopted a different problem space.

In some problem contexts, we can speak of problem solving as a search of the problem space or, metaphorically, a search of the solution tree, in which each branch and twig represents a possible pathway from the initial state of the problem. For problems that are "wide open," that is, those with many possibilities that must be checked, there may be no alternative but to start searching the problem space, node by node, until some barrier or block is reached. As often as not, however, there is information in the problem that permits us to restrict the search space, information that reduces the relevant search space to a manageable size. Metaphorically, this information permits us to *prune* the search tree.

◆ A general depiction of this situation is in Figure 12-7. The initial state of the problem is the top node, and the goal state is some terminal node at the bottom. For "wide open" problems, each branch may need to be searched until a dead end is encountered. For other problems, information may be inferred that permits a restriction in the branches that are searched (the shaded area of the figure). Clearly, if the search space can be restricted by pruning off the dead-end branches, then problem-solving efficiency is increased.

THE OPERATORS **Operators** are *the set of legal operations or moves that can be performed during problem solution.* The term *legal* means permissible in the rules of the problem. For example, an illegal operator in the six-penny problem of Table 12-2 would be to move more than two pennies. In "three men and a rowboat," an illegal operator is having the men swim across the river or loading the boat with too heavy a load.

For transformation problems (Greeno, 1978), applying an operator transforms the problem into a new or revised state from which further work can be done. In general, a legal operator moves you from one node to the next along some connecting pathway in the search space. For instance, in solving algebraic equations, one transformation operator is "move the unknowns to the left." Thus for the equation $2X + 7 = X + 10$, applying the operator would move the single X to the left of the equal sign by subtracting X from both sides of the equation.

Often, constraints within the problem prevent us from applying certain operators. In a vague way, the destruction of healthy tissue was such a constraint in the radiation problem. That constraint prevented the simple solution of applying the ray directly, where direct application would be a simple operator. In algebra, by contrast, constraints are imposed by the rules of algebra; for example, you can't subtract X from one side of the equation without subtracting it from the other side too.

THE GOAL The goal is the ultimate destination, goal state, or solution to the problem. For recreational problems in particular, the goal is typically stated explicitly in the problem. Given that recreational problems usually present *an explicit and complete specification of the initial and goal states,* we call them **well-defined problems.** Solutions involve progressing through the legal intermediate states, by means of known operators, until the goal is reached. In contrast, in **ill-defined problems**, *the states, operators, or both may be only vaguely specified.* For instance, the Buddhist monk problem in Table 12-2 states a vague goal ("Show that there is a spot. . ."). Likewise, problems with more real-world character often are distressingly vague in their specification of the goal ("write a term paper that will earn you an *A*," "write a computer program that does *X* in as economical and elegant a fashion as possible," and so on).

AN EXAMPLE: DONALD + GERALD Let's consider a well-known recreational problem now, to pin down some of these terms and ideas. The problem is a cryptarithmetic problem, in which letters of the alphabet have been substituted for the digits in an addition problem. Your task is to reverse the substitutions, to figure out which digits go with which letters to yield a correct addition problem. The restriction is that the digits and letters must be in one-to-one correspondence (only one digit per letter and vice versa). Plan on spending 15 minutes or so on the problem, about the amount of time it takes people on their first attempt. Make notes on paper as you work so you can go back later to retrace and analyze your attempt to solve the problem. (Incidentally, this is the cryptarithmetic problem Newell and Simon's single person worked on.)

$$\begin{array}{r} DONALD \\ +\ GERALD \\ \hline ROBERT \end{array} \qquad (Hint{:}\ D = 5)$$

Now that you've worked on the problem and have found (or come close to) the solution, we can use the insights you developed to fill in our definitions of terms. To begin with, the initial state of the problem consists of the statement of the problem, including the rules, restrictions, and hint you are given. These, along with your own knowledge of arithmetic (and pencil and paper), are your problem-solving tools for this problem. Each conceivable assignment of letters to digits makes up the problem space, and each substitution operator you might apply constitutes a branch or pathway on the search tree (a substitution operator here is an operator that substitutes a digit

Professor Herbert A. Simon

for a letter). Like the shaded area of Figure 12-7, the hint $D = 5$ prunes the search tree by a tremendous amount. Without the hint, you can only start working on the problem by trying arbitrary assignments, then working until an error shows up, then returning to an earlier node and reassigning the letters to different digits. (Even without the hint, however, there is only one solution to this problem.)

You no doubt started working on the problem by replacing the *D*s in the 1s column with 5s, then immediately replacing the *T* with a 0. You also probably wrote a 1 above the 10s column, for the carry operation from 5 + 5. A quick scan of the problem revealed one more *D* that could be rewritten. Note that the position you were in at this point, with three *D*s and a *T* converted to digits, is a distinct step in the solution, an intermediate state in the problem, a node in the problem space. Furthermore, each substitution you made reflected the application of an operator, a cognitive operation that transforms the problem to a different intermediate state.

As you continued to work the problem, you were forced to infer information as a way of making progress. For instance, in working on the 10s column, $L + L +$ the carried 1, you can infer that *R* is an odd number because any number added to itself and augmented by 1 yields an odd number. Likewise, you can infer from the $D + G$ column that *R* must be in the range 5 to 9 and that $5 + G$ can't produce a carried 1. Putting these together, *R* must be a large odd number, and *G* must be 4 or less. Each of these separate inferences, each mental conclusion you draw, is also an instance of a cognitive operation, a simple mental process or operator that composes a step in the problem-solving sequence. Each of these, furthermore, accomplishes progress toward the immediate subgoal, find out about *L*.

Greeno (1978) calls this process a constructive search. Rather than blindly assigning digits and trying them out, people usually draw inferences from the other columns and use those to limit the possible values the letters can take. This approach is typical in arrangement problems, the third of Greeno's (1978) categories, in which some combination of the given components must be found that satisfies the constraints in the problem. In other kinds of arrangement problems, say anagrams, a constructive search heuristic would be to look for spelling patterns and form candidate words from those familiar units. The opposite approach, sometimes known as generate and test, merely uses some scheme to generate all possible arrangements, then tests those one by one to determine whether the problem solution has been found.

A related aspect of problem solving here (it can be postponed, but your solution will be more organized if it's done now) is quite general and almost constitutes good advice rather than an essential feature of performance. Some mechanism or system for keeping track of the information you know about the letters is needed, if only to prevent you from forgetting inferences you've already drawn. Indeed, such an external memory aid can go a long way toward making your problem solving more efficient. In some instances it may even help you generalize from one problem variant to another (as in the next example, the Tower of Hanoi problem). Table 12-7 presents a compressed verbal protocol of the solution to the DONALD problem, which you might want to compare with your own solution pathway. The table also shows intermediate

TABLE 12-7

Intermediate State	Known Values	Reasons and Statements from Protocol
1 5ONAL5 GERAL5 ROBERØ	Ø123456789 T D R is odd	Because D is 5, then T = Ø, and carry a 1 to the next column. So the first column is 5 + something = odd because L + L + 1 = R will make R odd
	G is less than 5 R is odd and greater than 5	R must be bigger than 5 because less than 5 would yield a two-digit sum in the D + G column and there would be an extra column in the answer. G is less than 5.
1 1 5ONAL5 G9RA15 ROB9RØ	Ø123456789 T D E G is less than 5 R is odd, greater than 5	O + E is next. If E were Ø, it would be fine, but T is already Ø. So this column must have a carry brought to it. This means that E must be 9, so that the O + 9 + the carried 1 = O.
1 11 5ONAL5 G9RAL5 ROB9RØ		If E = 9, then A + A must have a carry brought to it, so then the A + A + the carried 1 = 9. 4 would work for A and so would 9, but 9 is already taken.
1 11 5ON4L5 G9R4L5 ROB9RØ	Ø123456789 T AD E R is odd, greater than 5 G is less than 5 L is greater than 5	So A has to be 4. So L + L + the carried 1 has to produce a carry, so L is greater than 5. 5 and 9 are taken.
1 11 5ON4L5 G974L5 7OB97Ø	Ø123456789 T AD R E G is less than 5, L is greater than 5	So the odd R must be 7. Because L + L yields a carry, L isn't 3.
11 11 5ON485 G97485 7OB97Ø	Ø123456789 T AD RLE N is greater than or equal to 3 G is less than 5	L must be 8 because 8 + 8 + 1 = 17. That only leaves O, N, G, and B. Because O + 9 needs a carry, N + 7 has to yield a carry. So N has to be at least 3.
11 11 5ON485 197485 7OB97Ø	Ø123456789 TG AD RLE N is greater than or equal to 3	So G looks like 1. That leaves O, N, and B, for 2, 3, and 6. N can't be 3 because B can't be the Ø in 3 + 7 = 1Ø. And it can't be 2 because 2 + 7 = 9 and the 9 is taken.
11 11 5O6485 197485 7O397Ø	Ø123456789 TGBADNRLE	That leaves N to be 6, so that makes B = 3.
11 11 526485 197485 72397Ø	Ø123456789 TGOBADNRLE	So O has to be 2. Check the addition.

A sample solution of the DONALD problem, showing intermediate states, known values, and an edited protocol. (Zero is drawn with the slash, Ø, to distinguish it from the letter O.)

★ **TABLE 12-8 Additional Cryptarithmetic Problems**

6.	CROSS + ROADS DANGER	7.	LETS + WAVE LATER	8.	SEND + MORE MONEY
Hint: $R = 6$					

★ steps and a notational system for keeping track of known values. Table 12-8 presents more cryptarithmetic problems that you might want to solve.

Section Summary

- We are solving a problem when our behavior is goal directed and involves a sequence of cognitive steps or stages. The sequence involves separate cognitive operations, where each goal or subgoal can be decomposed into separate, smaller subgoals. The overall problem, including our knowledge, is called the problem space, within which we apply operators, draw inferences, and conduct a constructive search for moves that bring us closer to the goal.

MEANS–END ANALYSIS: A FUNDAMENTAL HEURISTIC

Several problem-solving heuristics have been discovered and investigated. You've already read about the analogy approach, and the final section of the chapter illustrates several others. But in terms of overall significance, no other heuristic comes close to means–end analysis. This heuristic formed the basis for Newell and Simon's groundbreaking work (1972), including their very first presentation of the information-processing framework in 1956 (on the "day cognitive psychology was born"; see footnote 2 in Chapter 1). Because it shaped the entire area and the theories devised to account for problem solving, it deserves special attention.

The Basics of Means–End Analysis

Means–end analysis is the best-known problem-solving heuristic. In this approach, *the problem is solved by repeatedly determining the difference between the current state and the goal or subgoal state, then finding and applying an operator that reduces this difference.* Means–end analysis nearly always implies the use of subgoals because achieving the goal state usually involves the intermediate steps of achieving several subgoals along the way.

The basic notions of a means–end analysis can be summarized in a sequence of five steps:

1. Set up a goal or subgoal.
2. Look for a difference between the current state and the goal or subgoal state.
3. Look for an operator that will reduce or eliminate this difference. One such operator is the setting of a new subgoal.
4. Apply the operator.
5. Apply steps 2 through 4 repeatedly until all subgoals and the final goal are achieved.

TABLE 12-9 The Missionary–cannibal Problem

Three missionaries and three cannibals are on one side of a river and need to cross to the other side. The only means of crossing is a boat, and the boat can hold only two people at a time. Devise a set of moves that will transport all six people across the river, bearing in mind the following constraint: The number of cannibals can never exceed the number of missionaries in any location, for the obvious reason. Remember that someone will have to row the boat back across each time.

Hint: At one point in your solution, you will have to send more people back to the original side than you just sent over to the destination.

At an intuitive level, means–end analysis and subgoals are familiar to us and represent "normal" problem solving. If you have to write a term paper for class, you break the overall goal down into a series of subgoals: Select a topic, find relevant material, read and understand the material, and so forth. Each of these may contain its own subgoals.

The Tower of Hanoi

The most thoroughly investigated recreational problems are the missionary–cannibal problem in Table 12-9 (it's also known as the Hobbits–Orcs problem) and the Tower of Hanoi problem in Figure 12-8. These problems show clearly the strengths and limitations of the means–end approach.

THE THREE-DISK VERSION Work on the Tower of Hanoi problem carefully, using the three-disk version in the figure. Try to keep track of your solution so you'll understand how it demonstrates the usefulness of a means–end analysis. So that you'll be familiar with the problem and be able to reflect on your solution, do it several times again after you've solved it. See whether you can become skilled at solving the three-disk problem by remembering your solution and being able to generate it repeatedly. (By the way, an excellent heuristic for this problem is to solve it physically; draw the pegs on a piece of paper and move three coins of different sizes around to find the solution.)

Having done that, consider your solution in terms of subgoals and means–end analysis. Your goal, as stated in the problem, is to move the *ABC* stack of disks from peg 1 to peg 3. Applying the means–end analysis, your first step sets up this goal. The second

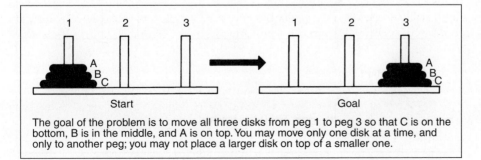

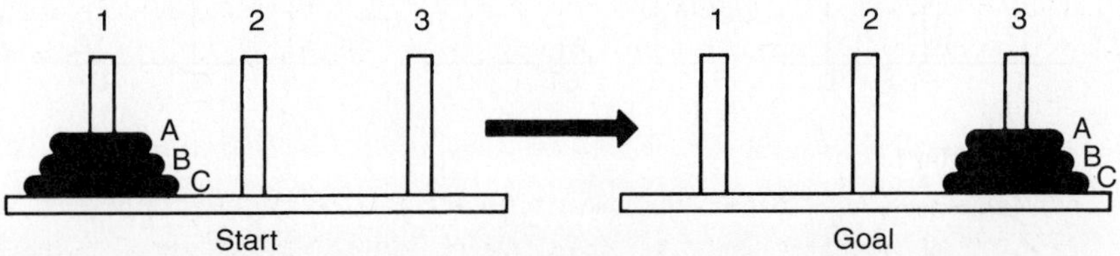

The goal of the problem is to move all three disks from peg 1 to peg 3 so that C is on the bottom, B is in the middle, and A is on top. You may move only one disk at a time, and only to another peg; you may not place a larger disk on top of a smaller one.

FIGURE 12-8 The Tower of Hanoi problem.

step in the analysis reveals a difficulty: There is a difference between your current state and the goal, simply the difference between the starting and ending configurations. You look for a method or operator that will reduce this difference and then apply that operator. As you no doubt learned from your solution, your first major subgoal is "Clear off disk *C*." This entails getting *B* off *C*, which entails another subgoal, getting *A* off *B*.

The next step involves a simple operator that satisfies the most immediate subgoal, "Move *A* to 3," which permits satisfying the next subgoal, "getting *B* off *C*." So the next operator is "move *B* to 2"; it can't go on top of *A* (rule violation), and it can't stay on top of *C* because that prevents achieving a subgoal. Now peg 3 can be cleared by moving *A* to 2. This allows the major subgoal to be accomplished, putting *C* on 3.

From here, it's easy to see the final route to solution: "unpack" *A* from 2, putting it temporarily on 1, move *B* to 3, then move *A* to 3. The seven moves that solve the problem are shown in Figure 12-9. ◆

THE FOUR-DISK VERSION After you've done the problem several times, solving it becomes easy. You come to see how each disk must move to get *C* on 3, then *B*, and finally *A*. Spend some time now on the same problem but use four disks instead of three. Don't work on this version blindly, however. Think of it as a variation on the three-disk problem, where parts of the new solution are "old." As a hint, try renaming the pegs as the source peg, the stack peg, and the destination peg. Furthermore, think

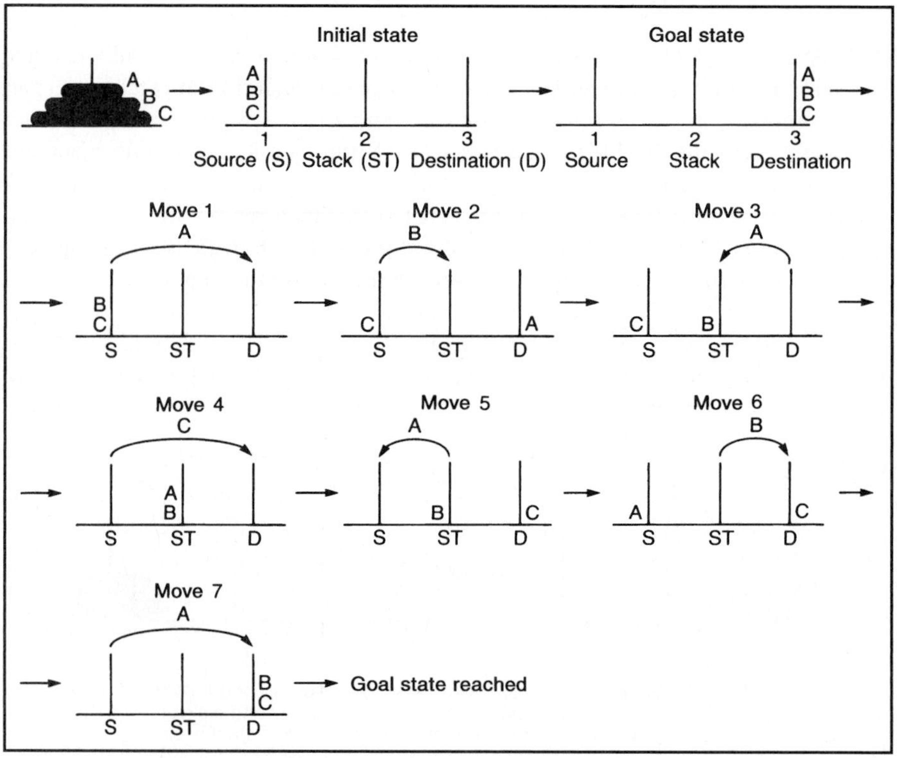

◆ **FIGURE 12-9**
The seven-step solution for the Tower of Hanoi problem. Note that the pegs have been renamed as "Source," "Stack," and "Destination." Moving the three disks takes seven moves. Consider these seven moves as one unit, called "moving a pyramid of three disks."

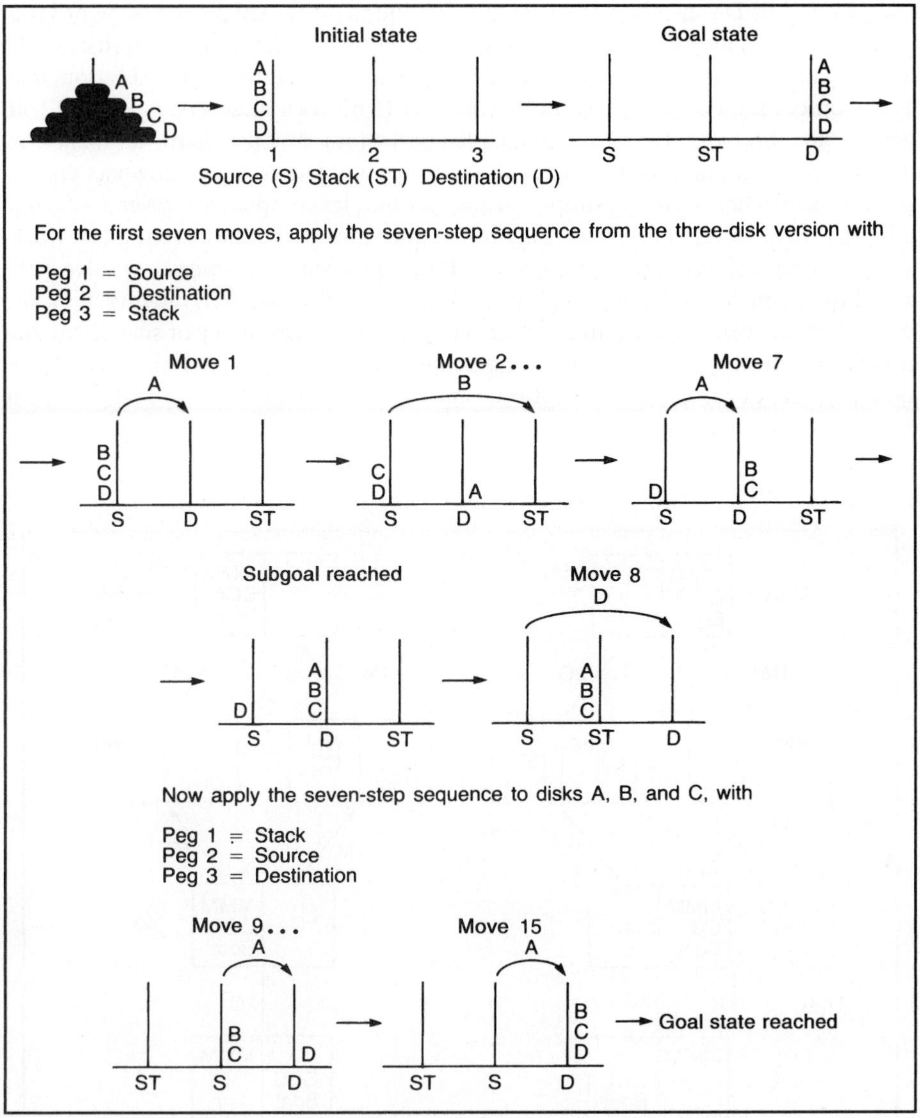

FIGURE 12-10 The four-disk Tower of Hanoi problem, with solution. The variation from the three-disk version is that the pegs must switch roles. In the beginning the subgoal is to move a pyramid of three disks so that *D* can move to peg 3. After that, the subgoal again is to move a three-disk pyramid. In both the first and second halves, the pegs must switch roles for the problem to be solved.

of the seven moves not as seven discrete steps but as a single chunk, "moving a pyramid of three disks," which should help you see the relationships between the problems more clearly (Simon, 1975). According to Catrambone (1996), almost any label attached to a sequence of moves probably will help you remember the sequence better.

What did you discover as you solved the four-disk problem? Most people come to realize that the four-disk problem has two three-disk problems embedded in it, separated by the bridging move of *D* to 3. That is, to free *D* so it can move to peg 3 you must first move the top three disks out of the way, moving a "pyramid of three disks," getting *D* to peg 3 on the eighth move. Then the *ABC* pyramid has to move again to get them on top of *D*—another seven moves. Moving the disks entails the same order of moves as in the simpler problem, although the pegs take on different functions: For the four-disk problem, peg 2 serves as the destination for the first half of the solution, then ★ as the source for the last half. The entire scheme of 15 moves is illustrated in Figure 12-11. Because the three-disk solution is embedded in the four-disk problem—and, likewise, the four-disk solution is embedded in the five-disk problem—this is known as a recursive problem, where *recursive* simply means that simpler components are embedded in the more difficult versions. (According to legend, a group of Buddhist monks is working on the 64-disk version of the Tower of Hanoi problem, and when they solve it the world will come to an end, although what the causal link is between moving disks and the end of the world is never made clear. This implies a "conspiracy of silence" on our part because by recursive extension, "the 64-disk problem is really just the 63-disk version with an extra disk at the bottom, and the 63-disk problem is really just the 62-disk problem, and so on.").

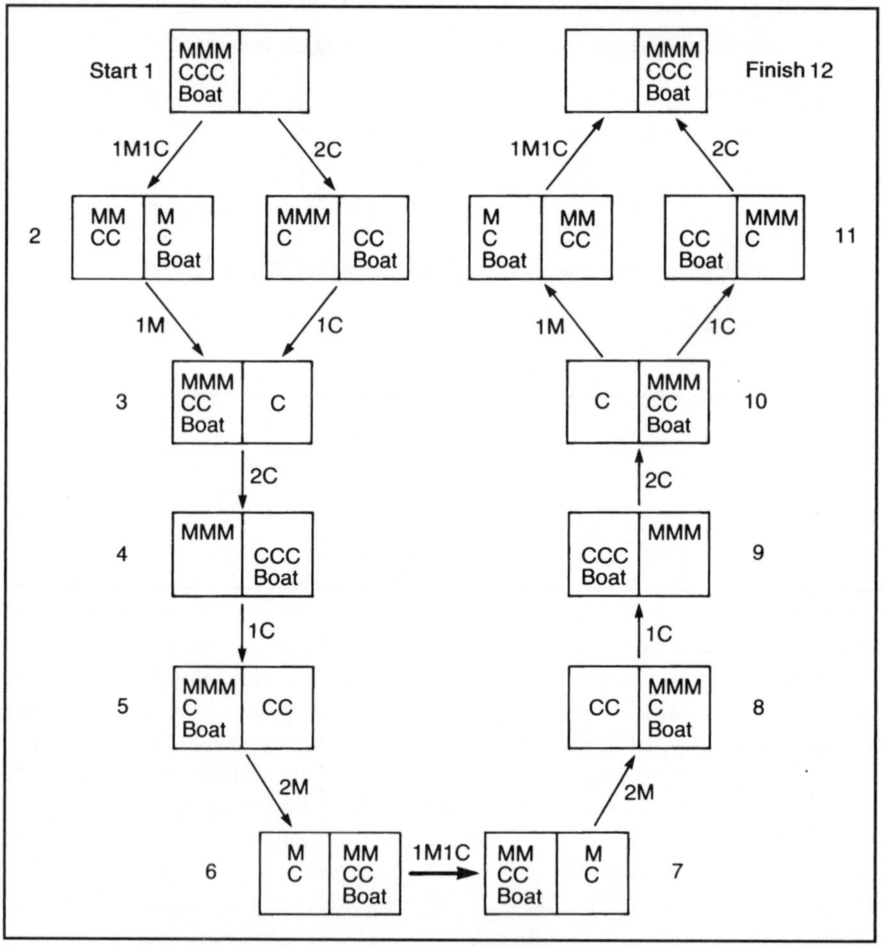

★ FIGURE 12-11 An illustration of the steps needed to solve the missionary–cannibal problem. The left half of each box is the "start side" of the river, and the right half is the "destination side." The numbers and letters next to the arrows represent who is traveling on the boat. From Glass & Holyoak (1986).

General Problem Solver

Means–end analysis was an early focus of research on problem solving, largely because of early work by Newell, Shaw, and Simon (1958; Ernst & Newell, 1969; Newell & Simon, 1972). Their computer simulation was called **general problem solver (GPS)**. This program was *the first genuine computer simulation of problem-solving behavior.* It was a general-purpose, problem-solving program, not limited to just one kind of problem but widely applicable to a large class of problems in which means–end analysis was appropriate. Newell and Simon ran their simulation on various logical proofs, on the missionary–cannibal problem, on the Tower of Hanoi, and on many other problems to demonstrate its generality. (Notice the critical analogy here. Newell and Simon drew an analogy between the way computer programs solve problems and the way humans do: Human mental processes are of a symbolic nature, so the computer's manipulation of symbols is a fruitful analogy to those processes. This was a stunningly provocative and useful analogy for the science of cognition.)

PRODUCTION SYSTEMS An important characteristic of GPS was its formulation as a production system model, essentially the first such model proposed in psychology. A **production** is a pair of statements, called either *a condition–action pair* or *an if–then pair*. In such a scheme, if the production's conditions are satisfied, the action part of the pair takes place. In the GPS application to the Tower of Hanoi, three sample productions might be

1. *If the destination peg is clear and the largest disk is free, then move the largest disk to the destination peg.*
2. *If the largest disk is not free, then set up a subgoal to free it.*
3. *If a subgoal to free the largest disk is set up and a smaller disk is on it, then move the smaller disk to the stack peg.*

Such an analysis suggests a very "planful" solution on the part of GPS: Setting up a goal and subgoals that will achieve the goal sounds exactly like what we would call planning. And indeed, such planning characterizes both people's and GPS's solutions to problems, not just the Tower of Hanoi but all kinds of transformation problems. GPS had what amounted to a planning mechanism, a mechanism that abstracted the essential features of situations and goals then devised a plan that would produce a problem-solving sequence of moves. Provided with such a mechanism and the particular representational system necessary to encode the problem and the legal operators, GPS yielded an output that resembles the solution pathways taken by human problem solvers.

LIMITATIONS OF GPS Later investigators working with the general principles of GPS found some cases when the model did not do a good job of characterizing human problem solving. Consider now the missionary–cannibal problem in Table 12-9; the solution pathway is presented in Figure 12-11. The problem is difficult, most people find, at step 6, where the only legal move is to return one missionary and one cannibal back to the original side of the river. Having just brought two missionaries over, this return trip seems to be moving away from the overall goal. That is, returning one missionary and one cannibal seems to be incorrect because it appears to

PROVE IT

The Hanoi Tower

The problems you've been solving throughout the chapter can be used without change to demonstrate the principles of problem solving. Here are some interesting contrasts and effects you might want to test.

Compare either the time or number of moves people make in learning and mastering the Tower of Hanoi problem when the pegs are labeled *1*, *2*, and *3* and when they are labeled *source*, *stack*, and *destination*. Try drawing the pegs in a triangular pattern rather than in a left-to-right display to see whether that makes the "stack" peg idea more salient. Compare how long it takes to master the problem when your participants learn to do it by moving three coins around on paper and when they keep track of their moves mentally.

increase the distance to the goal: It's the only return trip that moves two characters back to the original side. Despite the fact that this is the only available move (other than returning the same two missionaries who just came over), people have difficulty in selecting this move (Thomas, 1974).

GPS did not have this difficulty because sending one missionary and one cannibal back was consistent with its immediate subgoal. On the other hand, at step 10, GPS is trying to fulfill its subgoal of getting the last cannibal to the destination side and seemingly can't let go of this subgoal. People, however, realize that this subgoal should be abandoned: Anyone can row back over to bring the last cannibal across and in the process finish the problem (Greeno, 1974). GPS was simply too rigid in its application of the means–end heuristic, however: It tried to bring the last cannibal across and then send the boat back again.

BEYOND GPS Newell and Simon's GPS model, and models based on it, often provided a good description of human problem-solving performance (Atwood & Polson, 1976) and provided a set of predictions against which new experimental results could be compared (Greeno, 1974). Despite some limitations (Hayes & Simon, 1974), the model demonstrated the importance of means–end analysis for an understanding of human problem solving.

Section Summary

- The best-known heuristic for problem solving is means–end analysis, in which the problem solver cycles between determining the difference between the current and goal states and applying legal operators to reduce that difference. The importance of subgoals is revealed most clearly in problems such as the Tower of Hanoi.
- Newell and Simon's general problem solver (GPS) was the earliest cognitive theory of problem solving, implemented as a computer simulation. Studying GPS and comparing its performance with human problem solving showed the importance of means–end analysis.

IMPROVING YOUR PROBLEM SOLVING

Sprinkled through the chapter have been hints and suggestions about how to improve your problem solving. Some of these were based on empirical research and some on intuitions that people have had about problem-solving. Let's close the chapter by pulling these hints and suggestions together and offering a few new ones. Table 12-10 ▲ provides a list of these suggestions.

Increase Your Domain Knowledge

In thinking about what makes problems difficult, Simon suggests that the likeliest factor is **domain knowledge**, what one knows about the topic. Not surprisingly, a person who has only limited knowledge or familiarity with a topic is less able to solve problems efficiently in that domain (but see Wiley, 1998, on some disadvantages of too much domain knowledge). In contrast, extensive domain knowledge leads to expertise, a fascinating topic in its own right (see Ericsson & Charness, 1994, and Medin, Lynch, Coley, & Atran, 1997, for example).

Much of the research supporting this comes from Simon's work on the game of chess (Chase & Simon, 1973; Gobet & Simon, 1996; see also Reeves & Weisberg, 1993). In several studies of chess masters, an important but not surprising result was obtained: Chess masters need only a glimpse of the arrangement of chess pieces to remember the arrangement, far beyond what novices or players of moderate skill can do. This advantage holds, however, only when the pieces are in legal locations (i.e., sensible within the context of a real game of chess). When the locations of the pieces are random, then there is no advantage for the skilled players. In more recent work, this advantage of expertise in remembering legal board positions is attributed to experts' more skilled perceptual encoding of the board, literally more efficient eye movements and fixations while looking at the board (Reingold, Charness, Pomplun, & Stampe, 2001).

Automate Some Components of the Problem-Solving Solution

A second connection also exists between the question, "What makes problems difficult?" and the topics you've already studied. Kotovsky, Hayes, and Simon (1985) tested adults on various forms of the Tower of Hanoi problem and also on problem isomorphs,

TABLE 12-10 Suggestions for Improving Problem Solving ▲

Increase your domain knowledge.
Automate some components of the problem-solving solution.
Follow a systematic plan.
Draw inferences.
Develop subgoals.
Work backward.
Search for contradictions.
Search for relations between problems.
Find a different problem representation.
Stay calm.
If all else fails, try practice.

problems with the same form but different details. Their results showed that a heavy working memory load was a serious impediment to successful problem solving: If the person had to hold three or four nested subgoals in working memory all at once, performance deteriorated.

Thus, a solution to this memory-load problem was to automate the rules that govern moves, just as you were supposed to master and automate the seven-step sequence in the Tower of Hanoi. This frees working memory to be used for higher-level subgoals (Carlson, Khoo, Yaure, & Schneider, 1990). This is the same reasoning you encountered early in the book, where automatic processing uses few if any of the limited conscious resources of working memory.

Follow a Systematic Plan

Especially in long, multistep problems, it's important to follow a systematic plan (Bransford & Stein, 1993; Polya, 1957). Although this seems straight-forward, research shows that people do not always generate plans when solving problems, although doing so can dramatically improve performance (Delany, Ericsson, & Knowles, 2004). A plan will help you keep track of what you've done or tried and also keep you focused on the overall goal or subgoals you're working on. For example, on DONALD + GERALD, you need to devise a way to keep track of which digits you've used, which letters remain, and what you know about them. If nothing else, developing and following a systematic plan will help you avoid redoing what you've already done. Keep in mind that people often make errors when planning how long a task will take, but can plan their time better if they break the task down into the problem subgoals, estimate the time needed for each of those, and then add those times together (Forsyth & Burt, 2008).

Draw Inferences

Wickelgren's (1974) advice is to draw inferences from the givens, the terms, and the expressions in a problem before working on the problem itself. If you do this appropriately, it can often save you from wasting time on blind alleys, as in the two trains problem in Table 12-11. It can also help you abandon a misleading representation of the problem and find one that's more suitable to solving the problem (Simon, 1995). Here's a hint: Don't think about how far the bird is flying; think of how far the trains will travel and how long that will take.

Beware unwarranted inferences, the kinds of restrictions we place on ourselves that may lead to dead ends. For instance, for the nine dot problem in Table 12-3, an unwarranted inference is that you must stay within the boundaries of the nine dots.

Develop Subgoals

Wickelgren also recommends a subgoal heuristic for problem solving, that is, breaking a large problem into separate subgoals. This is the heart of the means–end approach. There is a different slant to the subgoal approach, however, that bears mention here. Sometimes in our real-world problem solving, there is only a vaguely specified goal and, as often as not, even more vaguely specified subgoals. How do you know when you've achieved a subgoal, say when the subgoal is "find enough articles on a particular topic to write a term paper that will earn an *A*"?

TABLE 12-11 Two Trains and Fifteen Pennies Problems

Two Trains
Two train stations are 50 miles apart. At 2 P.M. one Saturday afternoon, the trains start toward each other, one from each station. Just as the trains pull out of the stations, a bird springs into the air in front of the first train and flies ahead to the front of the second train. When the bird reaches the second train it turns back and flies toward the first train. The bird continues to do this until the trains meet. If both trains travel at the rate of 25 miles per hour and the bird flies at 100 miles per hour, how many miles will the bird fly before the trains meet?
Fifteen Pennies
Fifteen pennies are placed on a table in front of two players. Players must remove at least one but not more than five pennies on each turn. The players alternate turns of removing pennies until the last penny is removed. The player who removes the last penny from the table is the winner. Is there a method of play that will guarantee victory?
Hints
Fifteen pennies. What do you want to force your opponent to do to leave you with the winning move? What will the table look like when your opponent makes that move?

Simon's (1979) *satisficing* heuristic is important here; recall from Chapter 11 that satisficing is a heuristic in which we find a solution to a goal or subgoal that is satisfactory although not necessarily the best possible one. For some problems, the term paper problem included, an initial satisfactory solution to subgoals may give you additional insight for further refinement of your solution. For instance, as you begin to write your rough draft, you realize there are gaps in your information. What seems originally to be a satisfactory solution to the subgoal of finding references turns out to be insufficient, so you can recycle back to that subgoal to improve your solution. You might only discover this deficiency by going ahead and working on that next subgoal, the rough draft.

Work Backward

Another heuristic is working backward, in which a well-specified goal may permit a tracing of the solution pathway in reverse order, thus working back to the givens. The fifteen pennies problem in Table 12-11 is an illustration, a problem that is best solved by working backward. Many math and algebra proofs can also be worked backward or in a combination of forward and backward methods.

Search for Contradictions

In problems that ask "Is it possible to. . .?" or "Is there a way that. . .?" you should search for contradictions in the givens or goal state. Wickelgren uses the following illustration: Is there an integer x that satisfies the equation $x^2 + 1 = 0$? A simple algebraic operation, subtracting 1 from both sides, yields $x^2 = -1$, which contradicts the known property that any squared number is positive. This heuristic can also be helpful in multiple-choice exams. That is, maybe some of the alternatives contradict some idea

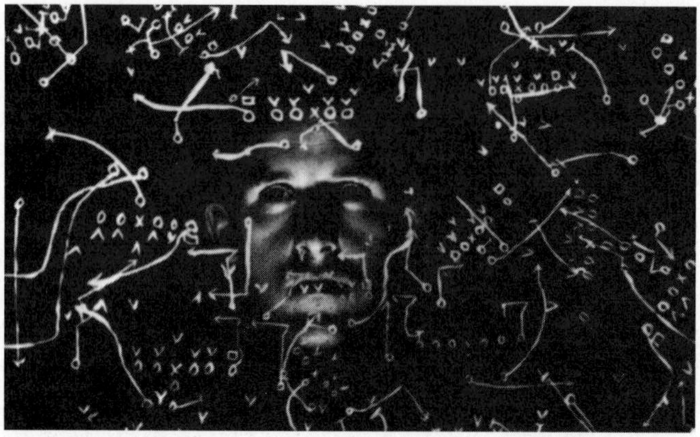

Drawing a diagram to represent a problem helps to improve problem-solving abilities.

or fact in the question or some fact you learned in the course. Either will enable you to rule those choices out immediately.

Search for Relations among Problems

In searching for relations among problems, you actively consider how the current problem may resemble one you've already solved or know about. The four- and more-disk Tower of Hanoi problems are examples of this, as are situations in which you search for an analogy (Bassok & Holyoak, 1989; Ross, 1987). Don't become impatient. Bowden (1985) found that people often found and used information from related problems, but only if sufficient time was allowed for them to do so. Try it on the problem in Figure 12-12.

Find a Different Problem Representation

Another heuristic involves the more general issue of the problem representation, or how you choose to represent and think about the problem you're working on. Often, when you get stuck on a problem, it is useful to go back to the beginning and reformulate or reconceptualize it. For instance, as you discovered in the Buddhist monk problem, a quantitative representation of the situation is unproductive. Return to the beginning and try to think of other ways to think about the situation, such as a visual imagery approach, especially a mental movie that includes action. In the Buddhist

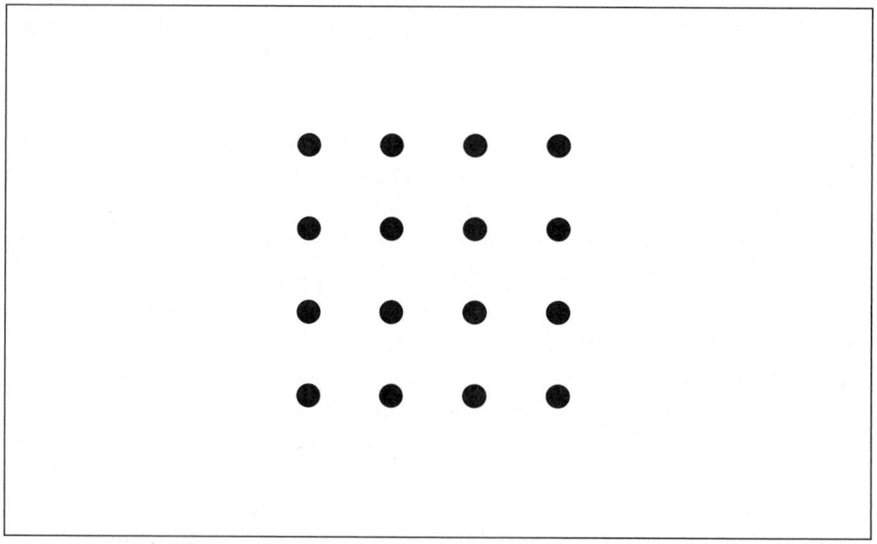

◆ **FIGURE 12-12** Without lifting your pencil, join all 16 dots with six straight lines.

monk problem, superimposing two such mental movies permits you to see him walking up and down at the same time, thus yielding the solution. Likewise, animated diagrams, with arrows moving in toward a point of convergence, helped participants solve the radiation problem in Pedone, Hummel, and Holyoak's (2001) study, as compared to either static diagrams or a series of diagrams showing intermediate points in problem solution (see also Reed & Hoffman, 2004).

Becoming an effective problem solver requires practice to strengthen certain knowledge, as these chess players exhibit.

For other kinds of problems, try a numerical representation, including working the problem out with some examples, or a physical representation, using objects, scratch paper, and so forth. Simon (1995) makes a compelling point that one representation of a problem may highlight a particular feature of a problem while masking or obscuring a different, possibly important feature. According to Ahlum-Heath and DiVesta (1986), verbalizing your thinking also helps in the initial stages of problem solving (but see Schooler et al., 1993).

Earlier, it was suggested that you might master the Tower of Hanoi problem more easily if you took three coins of different sizes. This is more than just good advice. Recall from Chapter 6 where you read about patient H. M., who suffers profound anterograde amnesia. H. M. seems unable to form new explicit long-term memories but apparently is quite normal when implicit learning is tested. The major result you read about was the mirror tracing study: H. M. showed normal learning curves on this task, despite not remembering the task from day to day. Interestingly, H. M. has also been tested on the Tower of Hanoi task, and he learns this task as well as anyone (although he has no explicit memory of ever solving the problem before). The important ingredient here seems to be the motor aspect of the tower problem: Learning a set of motor responses, even a complex sequence, relies on implicit memory. Thus, working the Tower of Hanoi manually by moving real disks or coins around should enable you to learn how to solve the problem from both an explicit and an implicit basis.

Stay Calm

Another point to keep in mind is that problem solving performance can decline if you are anxious. Essentially, when people experience anxiety, they tend to crowd their working memory with irrelevant thoughts about whatever it is they are anxious about. For example, people who are math anxious (i.e., they avoid doing math problems, taking math classes, exploring careers that use a lot of math) do more poorly on math problems because their working memory capacity is consumed by off-topic irrelevant thoughts that stem from their anxiety about doing math (Ashcraft & Krause, 2007; see Beilock, Rydell & McConnell, 2007, for similar findings from stereotype threat). These thoughts take away from the limited capacity you have to devote to the problem, and your performance suffers.

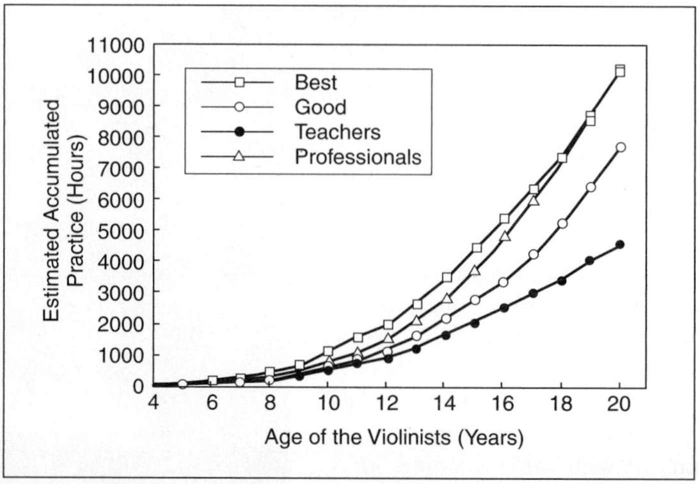

FIGURE 12-13 Illustration of the relationship between amount of practice over the course of years and the level of expertise (from Ericsson, Krampe, and Tesch-Römer, 1993).

If All Else Fails, Try Practice

Finally, for problems we encounter in classroom settings, from algebra or physics problems up through such vague problems as writing a term paper and studying effectively for an exam, a final heuristic should help. It's well known in psychology; even Ebbinghaus recommended it. If you want to be good at problem solving, *practice* problem solving. Practice within a particular knowledge domain strengthens that knowledge, pushes the problem-solving components closer to an automatic basis, and gives you a deeper understanding of the domain. Although it isn't flashy, practice is a major component of skilled problem solving and of gaining expertise in any area (Ericsson & Charness, 1994).

In Ericsson and Charness's (1994) review, people routinely believe that stunning talent and amazing accomplishments result from inherited, genetic, or "interior" explanations, when the explanation usually is dedicated, regular, long-term practice. This relationship between practice and performance level is seen in an analysis of practice and expertise data by Ericsson, Krampe, and Tesch-Römer (1993) shown in Figure 12-13. As can be clearly seen, the people who had higher levels of expertise also were the ones who engaged in more practice. So, clearly, practice is important to becoming an expert. However, it is unclear whether there is also some innate characteristic such as motivation, interest, or talent that could also be driving those people to practice more. Regardless, if you want to become highly skilled at something, your elementary school clarinet teacher was right—you really do need to practice.

Section Summary

- The set of recommendations for improving your problem solving includes increasing your knowledge of the domain, automaticity of components in problem solving, developing and following a plan, and not becoming anxious. Several special-purpose heuristics are also listed, including the mundane yet important advice about practice.

Key Terms

analogy (p. *476*)
domain knowledge (p. *497*)
functional fixedness (p. *468*)
general problem solver (GPS) (p. *495*)
Gestalt (p. *467*)
goal (p. *483*)
ill-defined problems (p. *487*)
insight (p. *472*)
means–end analysis (p. *490*)
negative set (p. *469*)
operators (p. *486*)
problem space (p. *485*)
production (p. *495*)
subgoal (p. *484*)
verbal protocol (p. *466*)
well-defined problems (p. *487*)

Answers to Chapter 12 Problems

Three Men and a Rowboat Medium and Small row themselves across the river, then either one of them rows back to the start side. Large rows himself across to the destination side. The man who stayed on the destination side now rows back to the start side, and both of the lighter men row to the destination.

Buddhist Monk Rather than thinking in terms of one monk, let a different monk walk down from the top on the same day as the other walks up. Looking at it this way, isn't it obvious that the two will meet during their journey? Thus, his walking on separate days is irrelevant to the goal, "Show that there is a spot. . . ."

Six Glasses Numbering the glasses from left to right, pour the contents of glass 2 into glass 5.

Six Pennies Coins 1, 2, 4, and 6 are already in place, so move coins 3 and 5.

Chains and Links Open all three links on one chain; that's 6 cents. Put one opened link at the end of each other piece, then join the pieces by looping a closed link into an opened one. Closing the three links costs 9 cents, for a total of 15 cents.

Four Trees Dead-end approaches try to arrange the trees on a flat, two-dimensional lawn. Instead, think in three dimensions. Put three trees around the base of a hill and the fourth one at the top of the hill. The arrangement is that of an equilateral, three-sided pyramid.

Prisoner's Escape Divide the rope in half by cutting with the length rather than across the length, similar to unbraiding the rope. Tie the two thinner pieces together and lower yourself to the ground.

Bronze Coin In 544 B.C., no one knew what might happen 544 years later, so coins could not have had B.C. stamped on them. The dealer is a crook.

Nine Dots

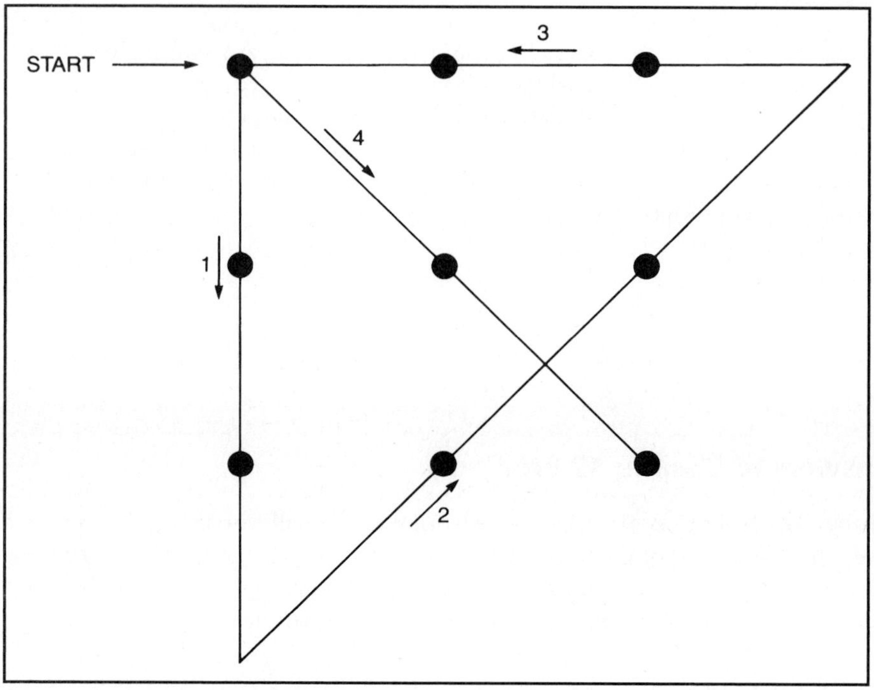

Ten Bowling Pins

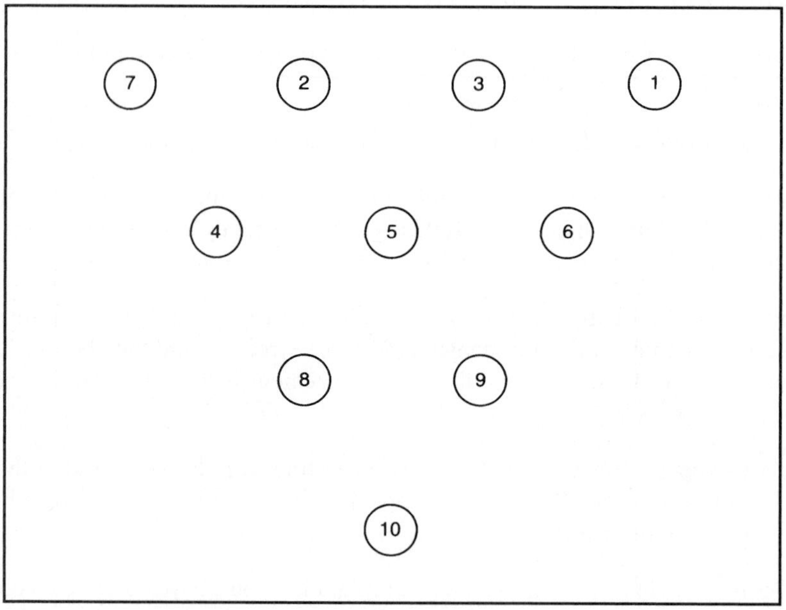

Cryptarithmetic

6. *Cross + Roads*	7. *Lets + Wave*	8. *Send + More*
96,233	*1,567*	*9,567*
+ 62,513	*+ 9,085*	*+ 1,085*
158,746	*10,652*	*10,652*

Two Trains

The trains are 50 miles apart and travel at 25 miles per hour. The trains will meet halfway between the cities in exactly 1 hour. The bird flies at 100 miles per hour, so it will fly 100 miles.

Fifteen Pennies

On your last move you must remove the final penny or pennies. There must be from one to five pennies on the table for you to be the winner. By working backward from this goal, on your next-to-last turn, you must force your opponent to leave you at least one penny on the table. So leave your opponent six pennies when you finish your next-to-last turn. To guarantee victory, make sure that your opponent leaves you from one to five pennies, so remove only as many pennies as you must to leave your opponent with six pennies on the table.

Sixteen Dots

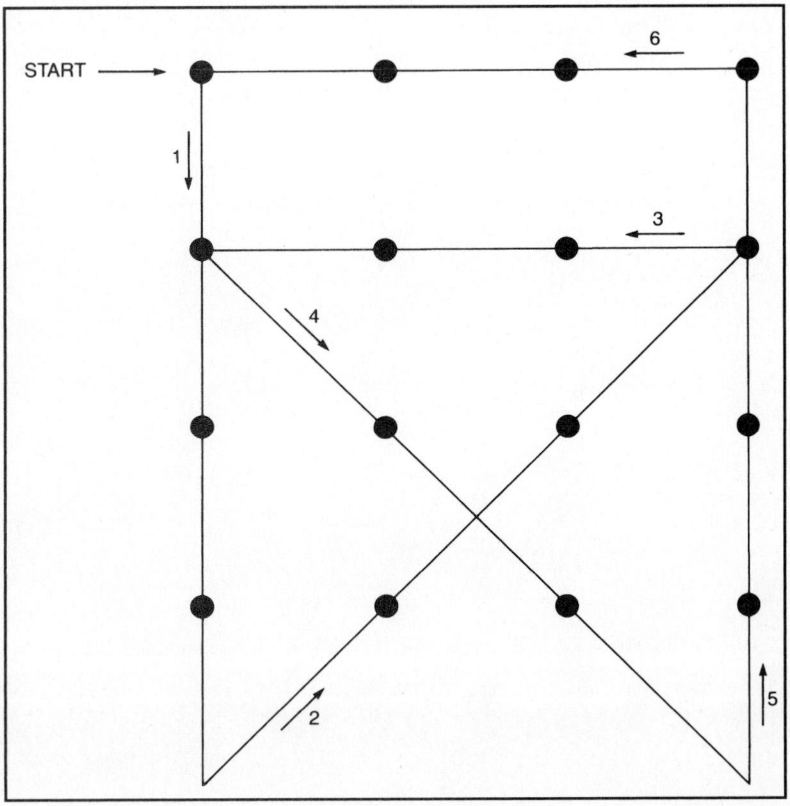

GLOSSARY

Accessibility The degree to which information can be retrieved from memory. A memory is said to be accessible if it is retrievable; memories that are not currently retrievable are said to have become inaccessible (Ch. 6).

Action slips Unintended, often automatic, actions that are inappropriate for the current situation (Ch. 4).

Actor See *agent*.

Ad hoc categories Categories that people can generate on the fly that have all of the qualities of more traditional categories, but which are based on situational circumstances (Ch. 7).

Advantage of clause recency The speedup of RT to information in the most recently processed clause (Ch. 10).

Advantage of first mention The speedup of RT to information mentioned first in the sentence (Ch. 10).

Agent (**also** *actor*) In the case grammar approach, the person who performs some action in a sentence is the agent, such as Bill in "Bill hit the ball with the bat." See also *case grammar* (Ch. 8).

Agnosia A disruption in the ability to recognize objects (Ch. 3).

Agraphia A disruption in the ability to write, caused by a brain disorder or injury (Ch. 9).

Alexia A disruption in the ability to read or recognize printed letters or words, caused by a brain disorder or injury (Ch. 9).

Algorithm A specific rule or solution procedure that is certain to yield the correct answer if followed correctly (contrast with *heuristic*) (Ch. 11).

Ambiguous Having more than one meaning, said both of words (e.g., "bank") and sentences (e.g., "They are eating apples") (Ch. 9).

Amnesia Memory loss caused by brain damage or injury. Retrograde amnesia is loss of memory for information before the damage, anterograde amnesia is loss of memory for information after the damage (Ch. 6).

Analogy A relationship between two similar systems, problems, and so on; a heuristic in which a problem is solved by finding an analogy to a similar problem (Ch. 12).

Anaphoric reference The act of using a pronoun or possessive (or synonym) to refer back to a previously mentioned concept (Ch. 10).

Anomia A disruption of word finding or retrieval, caused by a brain disorder or injury (Chs. 7, 9).

Anomic aphasia See *anomia.*

Antecedent (in conditional reasoning) The *if* clause in standard conditional reasoning *(if–then)* tasks. In the statement "If it rains, then the picnic will be canceled," the antecedent is "If it rains" (Ch. 11).

Antecedent (in language) The concept to which a later word refers; for example, *he* refers to the antecedent *Bill* in "Bill said he was tired" (Ch. 10).

Anterograde amnesia Disruption in memory for events following the brain damage, usually a disruption in the storage of new information after brain damage (Ch. 6).

Aphasia A loss of some or all of previously intact language skills, caused by brain disorder or damage (Ch. 9).

Apperceptive agnosia A form of agnosia in which individual features cannot be integrated into a whole percept or pattern; a basic disruption in perceiving patterns (Ch. 3).

Arbitrariness One of Hockett's (1960) linguistic universals, that the connections between linguistic units (sounds, words) and the concepts or meanings referred to by those units are entirely arbitrary; for example, it is arbitrary that we refer to a table by the linguistic unit *table* (Ch. 9).

Argument In a proposition the arguments are the ordered concepts that specify the meaning of the proposition. The arguments of the relation "HIT" in the sentence "Bill hit the ball yesterday" are "BILL" as the agent, "BALL" as the object, and "YESTERDAY" as the time. See also *case grammar* (Ch. 8).

Articulatory loop The part of the phonological loop involved in the active refreshing of information in the phonological store (Ch. 5).

Articulatory suppression effect The finding that people have poorer memory for a set of words if they are asked to say something while they are trying to remember (Ch. 5).

Associative agnosia A form of agnosia in which the individual can combine perceived features into a whole pattern but cannot associate the pattern with meaning, cannot link the perceived whole with stored knowledge about its identity (Ch. 3).

Attend The verb form of attention, meaning "to pay attention to" (Chs. 3, 4).

Attention The mental energy or resource necessary for completing mental processes, believed to be limited in quantity and under the control of some executive control mechanism (Ch. 4).

Attention capture The spontaneous redirection of attention to stimuli in the world based on physical characteristics (Ch. 4).

Attentional blink A brief slow-down in mental processing due to having processed another very recent event (Ch. 4).

Audition The sense of hearing (Ch. 3).

Auditory sensory memory (also *echoic memory*) The sensory memory system that encodes incoming auditory information and holds it briefly for further mental processing (Ch. 3).

Authorized Intended or correct. An implication of a speaker's statement is said to be authorized if the speaker intended the implication to be drawn; if the listener draws the intended inference, the inference is said to be authorized (contrast with *unauthorized*) (Ch. 10).

Autobiographical memory Memories of specific, personally experienced real-world information, such as of one's activities upon learning of the *Challenger* space shuttle disaster; the study of those memories (Ch. 8).

Automatic, automaticity Occurring without conscious awareness or intention and consuming little if any of the available mental resources (Ch. 4).

Available (in memory research) Present in the memory system. Information is said to be available if it is currently stored in memory (contrast with *accessibility*) (Ch. 6).

Availability heuristic A decision-making heuristic in which we judge the frequency or probability of some event on the basis of how easily examples or instances can be recalled or remembered; thus the basis of this heuristic is ease of retrieval (Ch. 11).

Axon The long, extended portion of a neuron (Ch. 2).

Axon terminals The branchlike ending of the axon in the neuron, containing neurotransmitters (Ch. 2).

Backward masking See *masking.*

Behaviorism The movement or school of psychology in which the organism's observable behavior was the primary topic of interest, and the learning of new stimulus–response associations, whether by classical conditioning or by reinforcement principles, was deemed the most important kind of behavior to study (Ch. 1).

Beliefs The fifth level of analysis of language, according to Miller, in which the listener's attitudes and beliefs about the speaker influence what is comprehended and remembered (Ch. 10).

Benefit See *facilitation.*

Beta movement Illusory movement that occurs when two or more pictures are viewed in rapid succession, as in a movie (Ch. 3).

Bottom-up processing See *data-driven processing.*

Boundary extension The finding that people tend to misremember more of a scene than was actually viewed, as if the boundaries of an image were extended further out (Ch. 5).

Bridging inference Clark's (1977) term for the mental processes of reference, implication, and inference during language comprehension. Metaphorically, a bridge must be drawn from *he* back to *Gary* to comprehend the sentence "Gary pretended he wasn't interested" (Ch. 10).

Broca's aphasia A form of aphasia characterized by severe difficulties in producing spoken speech; that is, the speech is hesitant, effortful, and distorted phonemically (contrast with *Wernicke's aphasia*). The aphasia is caused by damage in Broca's area, a region of the cortex next to a major motor control center (Ch. 9).

Brown–Peterson Task A short-term memory task showing forgetting caused by proactive interference (Ch. 5).

Case grammar An approach in psycholinguistics in which the meaning of a sentence is determined by analyzing the semantic roles or cases played by different words, such as which word names the overall relationship and which names the agent or patient of the action. Other cases include time, location, and manner (Ch. 9).

Case role (also *semantic case*) One of the various semantic roles or functions of different words in a sentence; see also *case grammar* (Ch. 9).

Categorical perception The perception of similar language sounds as being the same phoneme, despite the minor physical differences among them; for example, the classification of the initial sounds of cool and keep as both being the /k/(hard *c*) phoneme, even though these initial sounds differ physically (Ch. 9).

Category-specific deficit A disruption in which a person loses access to one semantic category of words or concepts while not losing others (Ch. 7).

Central executive In Baddeley's working memory system, the mechanism responsible for assessing the attentional needs of the different subsystems and furnishing attentional resources to those subsystems. Any executive or monitoring component of the memory system that is responsible for sequencing activities, keeping track of processes already completed, and diverting attention from one activity to another can be called an executive controller (Ch. 5).

Central tendency The idea that there is some mental core or center to the category where the best members will be found (Ch 7).

Cerebral cortex See *neocortex.*

Cerebral hemispheres (left and right) The two major structures in the neocortex. In most people the left cerebral hemisphere is especially responsible for language and other symbolic processing, and the right for nonverbal, perceptual processing (Ch. 2).

Cerebral lateralization The principle that different functions or actions within the brain tend to be localized in one or the other hemisphere. For instance, motor control of the left side of the body is lateralized in the right hemisphere of the brain (Ch. 2).

Change blindness The failure to notice changes in visual stimuli (e.g., photographs) when those changes occur during a saccade (Ch. 3).

Channel capacity An early analogy for the limited capacity of the human information-processing system (Ch. 2).

Characteristic feature In the Smith et al. (1974a) model of semantic memory, characteristic features are the features and properties of a concept that are common but are not essential to the meaning of the concept; for example, "eats worms" may be characteristic of "BIRD," but the feature is not essential to the central meaning of the concept (contrast with *defining feature*) (Ch. 7).

Chunk A unit or grouping of information held in short-term memory (Ch. 5).

Classic view of categorization The view that takes the position that people create and use categories based on a system of rules that define necessary and sufficient features (Ch. 7).

Clustering The grouping together of related items during recall (e.g., recalling the words apple, pear, banana, orange together in a cluster, regardless of their order of presentation); see also *organization* (Ch. 6).

Coarticulation The simultaneous or overlapping articulation of two or more of the phonemes in a word (Ch. 9).

Cognition The collection of mental processes and activities used in perceiving, remembering, thinking, and understanding, and the act of using those processes (Ch. 1).

Cognitive science A new term designating the study of cognition from the multiple standpoints of psychology, linguistics, computer science, and neuroscience (Chs. 1, 2).

Competence In linguistics the internalized knowledge of language and its rules that fully fluent speakers of a language possess, uncontaminated by flaws in performance (contrast with *performance*) (Ch. 9).

Conceptual knowledge The fourth level of analysis of language in Miller's scheme, roughly equivalent to semantic memory (Ch. 10).

Conceptually driven processing (also *top-down processing*). Mental processing is said to be conceptually driven when it is guided and assisted by the knowledge already stored in memory (contrast with *data-driven processing*) (Chs. 2, 3).

Conditional reasoning The form of reasoning in which the logical consequences of an if–then statement and some evidence are determined; for example, given "If it rains, then the picnic will be canceled," the phrase "It is raining" determines whether the picnic is canceled (Ch. 11).

Conduction aphasia A disruption of language in which the person is unable to repeat what has just been heard (Ch. 9).

Confirmation bias In reasoning, the tendency to search for evidence that confirms a conclusion (Ch. 11).

Conjunction fallacy The mistaken belief that a compound outcome of two characteristics can be more likely than either one of the characteristics by itself (Ch. 11).

Connectionism See *connectionist.*

Connectionist (also *connectionism, neural net modeling, PDP modeling*) The terms refer to a recent development in cognitive theory, based on the notions that the several levels of knowledge necessary for performance can be represented as massive, interconnected networks; that performance consists of a high level of parallel processing among the several levels of knowledge; and that the basic building block of these interconnected networks is the simple connection between nodes stored in memory. For instance, perception of spoken speech involves several levels of knowledge, including knowledge of phonology, lexical information, syntax, and semantics. Processing at each level continually interacts with and influences processing at the other levels, in parallel. The connections in connectionist modeling are the network pathways both within and among the levels of knowledge (Ch. 2, 3, 7).

Conscious attention Awareness; a slower attentional mechanism especially influenced by top-down processing (Ch. 4).

Conscious processing Mental processing that is intentional, involves conscious awareness, and consumes mental resources (contrast with *automatic, automaticity*) (Ch. 4).

Consequent In conditional reasoning, the consequent is the *then* statement; in "If it rains, then the picnic will be canceled," the consequent is "then the picnic will be canceled" (Ch. 11).

Consolidation The more permanent establishment of memories in the neural architecture (Ch. 6).

Context The surrounding situation and its effect on cognition, including the concepts and ideas activated during comprehension (Ch. 3).

Contralaterality The principle that control of one side of the body is localized in the opposite-side cerebral hemisphere. The fact that the left hand, for instance, is largely under the control of the right cerebral hemisphere illustrates the principle of contralaterality (Ch. 2).

Control Processes The part of the standard (Atkinson & Shiffrin) model of memory responsible for the active manipulation of information in short-term memory (Ch. 2).

Controlled attention The deliberate, voluntary allocation of mental effort or concentration (Ch. 4).

Conversational rules The rules, largely tacit, that govern our participation in and contributions to conversations (Ch. 10).

Cooperative principle The most basic conversational postulate, stating that participants cooperate by sharing information in an honest, sincere, and appropriate fashion (Ch. 10).

Corpus callosum The fiber of neurons that connects the left and right cerebral hemispheres (Ch. 2).

Correlated attributes Features that tend to co-occur in various members of a category (Ch. 7).

Cost A response slower than baseline because of the misleading cue (Chs. 4, 7).

Counterfactual reasoning A line of reasoning that deliberately contradicts the facts in a "what if" kind of way; in the simulation heuristic, the changing of details or events in a story to alter the (unfortunate or undesirable) outcome; also *undoing* (Ch. 11).

Cryptomnesia When a person unconsciously plagiarizes something heard or read and because he or she has forgotten the source mistakenly thinks that it is an original idea (Ch. 8).

Cued recall A form of recall in which the person is presented with part of the information as a cue to retrieve the rest of the information (Ch. 6).

Data-driven processing. (also *bottom-up processing***)**

When mental processing of a stimulus is guided largely or exclusively by the features and elements in the pattern itself, this processing is described as being data-driven (contrast with *conceptually driven processing*) (Ch. 3).

Decay Simple loss of information across time, presumably caused by a fading process, especially in sensory memory; also, an older theory of forgetting from long-term memory (Chs. 3, 5).

Declarative memory Long-term memory knowledge that can be retrieved then reflected on consciously; see also *explicit memory* (Ch. 6).

Deep structure In linguistics and psycholinguistics, the deep structure of a sentence is the meaning of the sentence; a deep structure is presumably the most basic and abstract level of representation of a sentence or idea (contrast with *surface structure*) (Ch. 9).

Default value The common or ordinary value of some variable. In script theory, default value refers to an aspect of a story or scene that conforms to the typical or ordinary state of affairs; for instance, "MENU" is the default value that fills the slot in a script in which customers find out what can be ordered in a restaurant (Ch. 7).

Defining feature In Smith et al.'s (1974a) theory of semantic memory, a defining feature is a property or feature of a concept that is essential to the meaning of that concept; for instance, bearing live young is a defining feature of the concept "MAMMAL" (contrast with *characteristic feature*) (Ch. 7).

Dendrites The branching, input structures of the neuron (Ch. 2).

Depth of processing See *levels of processing.*

Direct theory In conversation a direct theory is a person's appraisal of or informal theory about the other participant in the conversation, including information about that other person's knowledge, sophistication, and personal motives (contrast with *second-order theory*) (Ch. 10).

Discriminability effect The greater the distance or difference between the two stimuli being compared, the faster the decision that they differ (Ch. 11).

Displacement One of Hockett's (1960) linguistic universals, referring to the fact that language permits us to talk about times other than the immediate present; language thus permits us to displace ourselves in time, by talking about the past, future, and so on (Ch. 9).

Dissociation Pattern of abilities and performance, especially among brain-damaged patients, revealing that one cognitive process can be disrupted while another remains intact. In a double dissociation, two patients show opposite patterns of disruption and preserved function, further evidence that the cognitive processes are functionally and anatomically separate (Chs. 2, 6).

Distance effect (also *discriminability effect*) An effect, seen particularly in response time, in which two distant or highly discriminable stimuli are more easily judged than two nearby or less discriminable stimuli; for instance, judgments are faster to "poor versus excellent" than to "good versus excellent" (Ch. 11).

Domain knowledge A general term referring to one's knowledge of a specific domain or topic, especially in problem solving (Ch. 12).

Doubly dissociated Two mental processes are said to be doubly dissociated when a deficit in one of them, say due to brain damage, does not necessarily produce a deficit in the other process, and vice versa; for instance, a deficit in language comprehension due to brain damage (in Wernicke's area) does not necessarily produce a deficit in language production (in Broca's area), and vice versa (Chs. 2, 6).

Downhill change In the simulation heuristic, an unusual or unexpected aspect of a story or situation that is changed to be more normal or customary. If a story character left work early and was involved in a car accident, a likely downhill change would be to normalize the unusual characteristic and substitute a more customary aspect, such as leaving work on time (Ch. 11).

Dual coding hypothesis According to Paivio (1971), concrete words can be encoded into memory twice, once as verbal symbols and once as image-based symbols, thus increasing the likelihood that they will be recalled or remembered (Ch. 6).

Dual task procedure A method in which two tasks are performed simultaneously, such that the attentional and processing demands of one or both tasks can be assessed and varied. Dual task methodology is commonly used in studies of attention and attention-dependent mental processing (Ch. 4).

Dysfluency Error, flaw, or irregularity in spoken speech (Ch. 9).

Echoic memory See *auditory sensory memory.*

Ecological validity The hotly debated principle that research must resemble the situations and task demands that are characteristic of the real world rather than rely on artificial laboratory settings and tasks so that results will generalize to the real world, that is, will have ecological validity (Ch. 1).

Elaborative rehearsal In the levels of processing framework, elaborative rehearsal involves any rehearsal activity that processes a stimulus into the deeper, more meaningful levels of memory; any rehearsal that involves meaning, images, and other complex information from long-term memory (contrast with *maintenance rehearsal*) (Ch. 6).

Empiricism The philosophical position, originally from Aristotle, that advances observation and observation-derived data as the basis for all science (Ch. 1).

Enactment effect The finding of improved memory for participant-performed tasks, relative to those that are not acted out (Ch. 6).

Encoding To input or take into memory, to convert to a usable mental form, to store into memory. We are said to encode auditory information into sensory memory; if that information is transferred to short-term memory, then it is said to have been encoded into STM (Ch. 2).

Encoding specificity Tulving's hypothesis that the specific nature of an item's encoding, including all the context that it was encoded in, determines how effectively the item can be retrieved (Ch. 6).

Enhancement In Gernsbacher's theory, the boosting of concepts' levels of activation during comprehension (Ch. 10).

Episodic buffer The portion of working memory where information from different modalities and sources are bound together to form new episodic memories (Ch. 5).

Episodic memory Tulving's term for the portion of long-term memory in which personally experienced information is stored (contrast with *semantic memory*) (Ch. 6).

Erasure The masking or loss of information caused by subsequent presentation of another stimulus; usually in sensory memory (see also *masking*) (Ch. 3).

Event-related potentials (ERPs) Minute changes in electrical potentials in the brain, measured by EEG recording devices and related specifically to the presentation of a particular stimulus; the research technique used for determining neural correlates of cognitive activity (Chs. 2, 7).

Executive control See *central executive.*

Exemplar theory A theoretical view of categorization that assumes that when people think about categories, they are mentally taking into account each experience, instance, or example of the various encounters that have been experienced with members of that category (Ch. 7).

Explanation-based theories Theoretical views of semantic categories that assume that people create mental categories as theories of the world to explain why things are the way they are (Ch. 7).

Explicit memory Long-term memory retrieval or performance that entails deliberate recollection or awareness (Ch. 6).

Explicit processing Involving conscious processing, conscious awareness that a task is being performed, and usually conscious awareness of the outcome of that performance (Ch. 4).

Eye-gaze duration See *gaze duration.*

Eye-mind assumption The assumption that the eye normally remains fixated on a word as long as that word is being actively processed during reading (Ch. 10).

Eye tracker A device used to record eye movements and fixations (Ch. 10).

Eyewitness memory Study of memory for personally experienced episodes with an emphasis on the accuracy or inaccuracy of the report as it relates to misinformation encountered since the original event (Ch. 8).

Facilitation (see also *benefit*) Any positive or advantageous effect on processing, usually because of prior presentation of related information; in RT research, a speedup of RT due to related information (Chs. 4, 7).

False alarm (also *false positive*) An error in a recognition task in which a response of "yes" is made to a new stimulus; any "yes" response in recognition when a "no" response is correct (Ch. 8).

False memory Memory for something that didn't happen (Ch. 8).

Familiarity bias In reasoning, the bias in the availability heuristic in which personal familiarity influences estimates of frequency, probability, and so on; judging events as more frequent or important just because they are more familiar in memory (Ch. 11).

Family resemblance The idea that there is some set of features that is shared by many or most of a category's members, although all features may not be present in all members (Ch. 7).

Fan effect An increase in response time for an increased number of associations with a concept on a study list (Ch. 8).

Feature analysis See *feature detection.*

Feature detection (also *feature analysis*) A theoretical approach, most commonly in pattern recognition, in which stimuli (patterns) are identified by breaking them up into their constituent features (Ch. 3).

Feature list See *semantic features.*

Feeling of knowing An estimate of how likely it is that an item will be recognized on a later memory test (Ch. 8).

Filtering (also *selecting*) Especially in auditory perception, unwanted, unattended messages are filtered or screened out so that only the attended message is encoded into the central processing mechanism (e.g., Broadbent's filter theory) (Ch. 4).

Fixation In visual perception the pause during which the eye is almost stationary and is taking in visual information; also, the visual point on which the eyes focus during the fixation pause (see also *gaze duration*) (Chs. 3, 10).

Flashbulb memories Memories of specific, emotionally salient events, reported subjectively to be as detailed and accurate as a photograph but now considered possibly to be more similar to normal, highly accurate memories (Ch. 8).

Flexibility The characteristic that enables the meaning of a language symbol to be changed and enables new symbols to be added to the language (Ch. 9).

Focal attention Neisser's (1967) term for mental attention directed toward, for example, the contents of visual sensory memory and therefore responsible for transferring that information into short-term memory (Ch. 3).

Forgetting Colloquially, losing information previously stored in memory. More technically, the term usually implies that the stored information is no longer in memory, that it is no longer available in the memory system (Ch. 6).

Fovea The highly sensitive region of the retina responsible for precise, focused vision, composed largely of cones (Ch. 3).

Frame In script theory a slot or event in a stored script. In the restaurant script, for instance, there are frames for "How the customer gets the food" and "Who prepares the food" (Ch. 7).

Free recall The memory task in which the list items may be recalled in any order, regardless of their order of presentation (contrast with *serial recall*) (Chs. 5, 6).

Functional fixedness In problem solving, an inability to think of or consider any but the customary uses for objects and tools (Ch. 12).

Functional MRI (fMRI) A use of MRI technology that provides online evidence about dynamic (functional) processes in the brain (Ch. 2).

Functionalism The movement in psychology, closely associated with James, in which the functions of various mental and physical capacities were studied (contrast with structuralism) (Ch. 1).

Garden path sentence A sentence in which an early word or phrase tends to be misinterpreted and thus must be reinterpreted after the mistake is noticed; for example, "After the musician played the piano was moved off the stage" (Ch. 9).

Gaze duration How long the eyes fixate on a specific word during reading, the principal measure of online comprehension during reading (Ch. 10).

General problem solver (GPS) The first serious computer-based model of problem solving, by Newell, Shaw, and Simon (1958) (Ch. 12).

Generation effect The finding that information you generate or create yourself is better remembered compared to information you only heard or read (Ch. 6).

Generativity See *productivity*.

Geons In Biederman's recognition by components model, the basic primitives, the simple three-dimensional geometric forms in the human recognition system (Ch. 3).

Gestalt A German term adopted into psychological terminology referring to an entire pattern, form, or configuration. The term always carries the connotation that decomposing a pattern into its components in some way loses the essential wholeness of the cohesive pattern (Ch. 12).

Gesture The movement of the hands and arms done to facilitate communication to listeners. This excludes sign language and non-communicative mannerisms, such as touching one's hands to one's face (Ch. 10).

Given-new strategy The idea that words and phrases that contain more accessible information (more active in memory), or given information, tend to occur earlier in sentences, whereas new information in a sentence tends to come later. (Ch. 9).

Goal In problem solving, the end-point or solution to the problem, the ending state toward which the problem-solving attempt is directed (Ch. 12).

Grammar In linguistics and psycholinguistics, a set of rules for forming the words or sentences in a language; optimally, the complete set of rules that characterizes a language, such that the rules generate only acceptable or legal sentences and do not generate any sentences that are unacceptable (Ch. 9).

Habituation A gradual reduction of the orienting response back to baseline (Ch. 4).

Hemineglect A disorder of attention in which half of the perceptual world, often the left, is neglected to some degree, or cannot be attended to (Ch. 4).

Hemispheric specialization The principle that each cerebral hemisphere has specialized functions and abilities (Ch. 2).

Heuristic An informal "rule of thumb" method for solving problems, not necessarily guaranteed to solve the problem correctly but usually much faster or more tractable than the correct algorithm (Ch. 11).

Hindsight bias In reasoning, the bias or attitude that some completed event was very likely to have had just that outcome (Ch. 11).

Hippocampus An internal brain structure, just internal to the temporal lobes, strongly implicated in the storing of new information into long-term memory (Ch. 2).

Icon The contents of iconic (visual sensory) memory; the brief-duration visual image or record of a visual stimulus held in visual sensory memory (Ch. 3).

Iconic memory See *visual sensory memory.*

Ill-defined problem A problem in which the initial, intermediate, or final goal state is poorly or vaguely defined or a problem in which the legal operators (moves) are not well specified (Ch. 12).

Imagination inflation An increase in false memory for an event when the event has been imagined to have happened (Ch. 8).

Immediacy assumption The assumption that readers try to interpret each content word of a text as that word is encountered during reading (Ch. 10).

Implication An unstated connection or conclusion that was nonetheless intended by a speaker (Ch. 10).

Implicit memory Long-term memory performance affected by prior experience with no necessary awareness of the influence (Ch. 6).

Implicit processing Processing in which there is no necessary involvement of conscious awareness (Ch. 4).

Inattentional blindness We sometimes fail to see an object we are looking at directly, even a highly visible one, because our attention is directed elsewhere (Ch. 3).

Independent and nonoverlapping stages The assumption in the strict information processing approach that the stages of processing are independent of one another in their functioning, and that they do not overlap in time. In other words, a stage begins its operations only when a previous stage has finished, and those operations are not changed by previous or subsequent stages (Ch. 2).

Indirect request A question or statement that is not intended to be taken literally but instead is a polite way of expressing the intended meaning; for example, "Do you have the time?" is an indirect way of asking "What time is it?" (Ch. 10).

Infantile amnesia The inability to remember early life events and very poor memory for your life at a very young age (Ch. 8).

Inference Drawing a conclusion based on some statement, as in conversation or reading (Ch. 10).

Inferred or intended topic The idea inferred by the listener or intended by the speaker to be the conversational topic (Ch. 10).

Information-processing approach Broadly defined, the approach that describes cognition as the coordinated operation of active mental processes within a multicomponent memory system. As it was originally used, the term referred to mental processing as a sequence of mental operations, each operation taking in information, manipulating or changing it in some fashion, then forwarding the result to the next stage for further processing. Today the term is taken to refer more generally to the fact that humans encode and process information (Ch. 2).

Inhibition An active suppression of mental representations of salient but irrelevant information so that the activation level is reduced, perhaps below the resting baseline level (Chs. 4, 7).

Inhibition of return A process in which recently checked locations are mentally marked by attention as places that the search process would not return to (Ch. 4).

Input attention The basic processes of getting sensory information into the cognitive system (Ch. 4).

Insight Said to be an essential step in creativity and problem solving, though little if any research supports this notion empirically (Ch. 12).

Integration When memories from different experiences are combined they are integrated into a common memory trace. After this occurs, it is often difficult for the person to identify individual experiences (Ch. 8).

Interference An explanation for "forgetting" of some target information in which related or recent information competes with or causes the loss of the target information (Chs. 3, 6).

Intersection In network models, the connecting pathway between two concepts, the location where activation from two separate nodes meets (Ch. 7).

Introspection The largely abandoned method of investigation in which subjects look inward and describe their mental processes and thoughts; historically, the method of investigation promoted by Titchener (Ch. 1).

Isolation effect See *von Restorff effect.*

Judgments of learning (JOLs) A person makes a prediction, after studying some material, whether that information will be remembered on a later memory test (was it learned?) (Chs. 8, 10).

Just noticeable difference (jnd) In psychophysics the amount by which two stimuli must differ so that the difference can be perceived (Ch. 11).

Labor-in-vain effect An effect that occurs when people spend large amounts of time trying to learn information that is beyond their current level of knowledge, but end up with little to no new learning (Ch. 10).

Lag In studies of mental processing, the number of intervening trials between a prime and a target (Ch. 7).

Language A shared symbolic system for communication (Ch. 9).

Lesion Any damage to brain tissue, regardless of cause (e.g., from an accident, stroke, or surgery) (Ch. 2).

Levels of processing (also *depth of processing*) Craik and Lockhart's (1972) alternative to the standard three-component memory model. Information subjected only to maintenance rehearsal is not being processed more deeply into the meaning-based levels of the memory system and therefore tends not to be recalled or recognized as accurately as information subjected to elaborative rehearsal (Ch. 6).

Lexical decision A simple yes/no task in which subjects are timed as they decide whether the letter string being presented is a word; sometimes called simply the word/nonword task (Chs. 2, 7).

Lexical memory The mental lexicon or dictionary where our word knowledge (as distinct from conceptual knowledge) is stored (Ch. 7).

Lexicon See *mental lexicon.*

Linguistic relativity hypothesis The hypothesis, credited to Whorf, that one's language determines—or at least influences strongly—what one can think about (Ch. 9).

Linguistic universals Features and characteristics that are universally true of all human languages (see also *displacement, productivity*) (Ch. 9).

Linguistics The discipline that studies language as a formal system (Ch. 9).

Location The semantic case or argument in a proposition specifying the place or location of some event (Ch. 8).

Long-term memory (LTM) The portion of the memory system responsible for holding information for more than a period of seconds or minutes; virtually permanent storage of information (Ch. 2).

LTM See *long-term memory.*

Magnetic resonance imaging (MRI) A medical scanning technology that reveals anatomical structure, especially of the brain (see also *functional MRI*) (Ch. 2).

Maintenance rehearsal In the levels of processing approach, rehearsal that merely repeats, recycles, or refreshes information at a particular level via repetition, without processing it to deeper, more meaningful levels of storage (Ch. 6).

Mapping In Gernsbacher's theory, drawing the connections between words and their meanings to the overall meaning of the sentence; in general, the process of determining the connections between two sets of elements, including the relations in analogical problem solving (Ch. 10).

Masking An effect, often in perception experiments, in which a mask or pattern is presented very shortly after a stimulus and disrupts or even prevents the perception of the earlier stimulus (see also *erasure*) (Ch. 3).

Means–end analysis A major heuristic in problem solving, assessing the distance between the current and the goal states, then applying some operator that reduces that distance (Ch. 12).

Memory The mental processes of acquiring and retaining information for later retrieval; the mental storage system that enables these processes (Ch. 1).

Memory impairment A specific interpretation of early eyewitness memory results in which a subsequent piece of information replaces a memory formed earlier, thus impairing memory of the original information (Ch. 8).

Mental lexicon The mental dictionary of long-term memory, that is, the portion of long-term memory in which words and word meanings are stored (Ch. 9).

Mental model The mental representation of a situation or physical device; for example, a person's mental model of the physical motion of bodies or a person's mental model of a thermostat (Ch. 11).

Mental rotation Mental manipulation of a visual short-term memory code that reorients the imaged object in space (Ch. 5).

Metacognition Awareness and monitoring of one's own cognitive state or condition; knowledge about one's own cognitive processes and memory system (Ch. 6).

Metacomprehension The ability to monitor how well we are understanding and will remember information later (Ch. 10).

Metamemory Knowledge about one's own memory system and its functioning (Chs. 6, 8).

Metatheory A general theoretical framework consisting of the assumptions made by practitioners of a science that guide the research activities of those practitioners (Ch. 2).

Method of loci A classic mnemonic device in which the to-be-remembered items are mentally placed, one by one, into a set of prememorized locations, with retrieval consisting of a mental walk through the locations (Ch. 6).

Mind wandering The situation in which a person's attention and thoughts wander from the current task to some other, inappropriate line of thought (Ch. 4).

Misinformation acceptance The tendency to accept information presented after some critical event as being true of the original event itself; for example, accepting then reporting that a yield sign had appeared in an earlier description of a traffic accident (Ch. 8).

Misinformation effect Incorrectly claiming to remember information that was not part of some original experience (Ch. 8).

Mnemonic device Any mental device or strategy that provides a useful rehearsal strategy for storing and remembering difficult material; see *method of loci,* for instance (Ch. 6).

Modality effect In sensory memory research, the advantage in recall of the last few items in a list when those items have been presented orally rather than visually (Ch. 3).

Modularity A theoretical perspective in which different abilities, characteristics, types of cognitive processes, and so forth are theorized to be represented in separate components or modules in memory (Ch. 7).

Morpheme The smallest unit of meaning in language (Ch. 9).

Motor theory of speech perception The idea that people perceive language, at least in part, by comparing the sounds that they are hearing with how they themselves would move their own vocal apparatus to make those sounds (Ch. 9).

MRI See *magnetic resonance imaging.*

Naive physics The study of people's misconceptions about the motion of physical objects, such as a ball rolling off a cliff (Ch. 11).

Naming The characteristic that human languages have names or labels for all the objects and concepts encountered by the speakers of the language (e.g., as opposed to most animal communication systems) (Ch. 9).

Negative priming Slower to respond to the target trails when they were preceded by irrelevant distractor primes compared to control trials where the ignored object on the prime trial was an unrelated item (Ch. 4).

Negative set In problem solving, a tendency to become accustomed to a single approach or way of thinking about a problem, making it difficult to recognize or generate alternative approaches (Ch. 12).

Neocortex (also *cerebral cortex*) The top layer of the brain, newest (*neo-*) in terms of the evolution of the species, divided into left and right hemispheres; the locus of most higher-level mental processes (Ch. 2).

Network A structure for information stored in long-term semantic memory, assumed by several popular models of mental processing. In most network models, concepts are represented as nodes that are interconnected by means of links or pathways; activation is presumed to spread from concept to concept along these connecting pathways (Ch. 7).

Neural net modeling See *connectionist.*

Neurocognition The neurological basis of cognition and the study of the combination of neurological and cognitive factors (Ch. 2).

Neuron A specialized cell that conducts neural information through the nervous system, the basic building block of the nervous system (Ch. 2).

Neurotransmitter The chemical substance released into the synapse between two neurons, responsible for activating or inhibiting the next neuron in sequence (Ch. 2).

Node Especially in network models, a point or location in the long-term memory representation of knowledge; a concept or its representation in memory (Ch. 7).

Nondeclarative memory See *implicit memory* (Ch. 6).

Object See *patient.*

Online comprehension task Task in which measurements of performance are obtained as comprehension takes place; *online* means happening and being measured right now (Ch. 10).

Operator In problem solving, a legal move or operation that can occur during solution of a problem; the set of legal moves within some problem space (e.g., in algebra, one operator is "multiply both sides by the same number") (Ch. 12).

Organization Especially in studies of episodic long-term memory, the tendency to recall related words together, or the tendency to impose some form of grouping or clustering on information being stored in/retrieved from memory; related to chunking or grouping in short-term memory (Ch. 6).

Orienting reflex The reflexive redirection of attention that orients you toward the unexpected stimulus (Ch. 4).

Paired-associate learning A task in which pairs of items, respectively the stimulus and response terms, are to be learned, so that upon presentation of a stimulus, the response term can be recalled; a favorite learning task during the verbal learning period of human experimental psychology (Ch. 6).

Pandemonium Selfridge's early model of letter identification (Ch. 3).

Parallel distributed processing (PDP) See *connectionist.*

Parallel processing Any mental processing in which two or more processes or operations occur simultaneously (Ch. 2).

Parse To divide or separate the words in a sentence into logical or meaningful groupings (Ch. 9).

Part-set cuing The finding that if you cue people with part of a list of words, they will have more difficulty recalling the rest of the set than if they had not been cued at all (Ch 6).

Partial report condition An experimental condition in Sperling's (1960) research in which only a randomly selected portion of the entire stimulus display was to be reported (contrast with *whole report condition*) (Ch. 3).

Pathway In network representations in long-term memory, the connecting link between two concepts or nodes (Ch. 7).

Patient The object or recipient that receives the action in a sentence; one of the semantic cases in a case grammar approach (see also *case grammar*) (Ch. 8).

PDP modeling See *connectionist.*

Peg word mnemonic The mnemonic device in which a prememorized set of peg word connections is used to remember some new information; the peg words typically used are "One is a bun, Two is a shoe," and so on (Ch. 6).

Perception The process of interpreting and understanding sensory information; the act of sensing then interpreting that information (Ch. 3).

Perceptual symbols Symbolic representations used in memory and grounded in sensory and motor elements derived from experience (Ch. 7).

Performance Any observable behavior; in the context of linguistics, any behavior related to language (e.g., speech), influenced not only by linguistic factors, but also by factors related to lapses in attention, memory, and so on (contrast with *competence*) (Ch. 9).

Phi phenomenon Illusory movement that occurs when two images are viewed in rapid succession in different points in space, as in a theater marquee or chasing Christmas lights (Ch. 3).

Phoneme A sound or set of sounds judged to be the same by speakers of a language (e.g., the initial sound in the words cool and keep for speakers of English). Note that because of categorical perception, we tend to judge some physically different sounds as the same and other different sounds as different, that is, belonging to a different phoneme category (Chs. 3, 9).

Phonemic competence One's basic knowledge of the phonology of the language (Ch. 9).

Phonological loop In Baddeley and Hitch's (1974) working memory system, the articulatory loop is the component responsible for recycling verbal material via rehearsal (Ch. 5).

Phonological similarity effect The finding that memory is poorer when people need to remember a set of words that are phonologically similar compared to a set of words that are phonologically dissimiar (Ch. 5).

Phonological store The passive store component of the phonological loop (Ch. 5).

Phonology The study of the sounds of language, including how they are produced and how they are perceived (Ch. 9).

Phrase structure The underlying structure of a sentence in terms of the groupings of words into meaningful phrases, such as "[The young man] [ran quickly]" (Ch. 9).

PI See *proactive interference.*

Polysemy When a word in a language has multiple meanings (Ch. 9).

Pragmatics The aspects of language that are "above and beyond" the words, so-called extralinguistic factors. For instance, part of our pragmatic knowledge of language rules includes the knowledge that the sentence, "Do you happen to know what time it is?" is actually an indirect request rather than a sentence to be taken literally (Ch. 10).

Primacy effect In a recall task the elevation of recall at the early positions of the list (contrast with *recency effect*) (Ch. 5).

Prime The first stimulus in a prime–target pair, intended to exert some influence on the second stimulus (see also *priming*) (Ch. 7).

Priming Mental activation of a concept by some means, or the spread of that activation from one concept to another; also, the activation of some target information by action of a previously presented prime; sometimes loosely synonymous with the notion of accessing information in memory (Chs. 4, 7).

Proactive interference (PI) Interference or difficulty, especially during recall, because of some previous activity, often the stimuli learned on some earlier list; any interference in which material presented at one time interferes with material presented later (Ch. 5).

Probabilistic theories. Theories that assume that categories in semantic memory are created by taking into account various probabilities and likelihoods across a person's experience. Prototype and exemplar theories are both probabilistic theories (Ch. 7).

Problem of invariance In psycholinguistics the problem that spoken sounds are not invariant, that they change depending on what sounds precede and follow in the word (Chs. 3, 9).

Problem space The initial, intermediate, and goal states in a problem, along with the problem solver's knowledge and any external resources that can be used to solve the problem (Ch. 12).

Process model A stage model designed to explain the several mental steps involved in performance of some task, usually implying that the stages occur sequentially and that they operate independently of one another (Chs. 2, 5).

Processing fluency The ease with which something is processed or comes to mind (Ch. 8).

Production, production system A *production* is a simple if–then rule in models of memory processing, stating the conditions *(if)* necessary for some action *(then)* to be taken, whether that action is a physical response or a mental step or operation. A *production system* is a large-scale model of some kind of performance or mental activity based on productions (Ch. 12).

Productivity (also *generativity*) One of Hockett's (1960) linguistic universals, referring to the rule-based nature of language, such that an infinite number of sentences can be generated or produced by applying the rules of the language (Ch. 9).

Property statements Simple statements in which the relationship being expressed is "*X* has the property or feature *Y*" (e.g., "A robin has wings") (Ch. 7).

Proposition A simple idea unit (Chs. 7, 8).

Propositional textbase An intermediate level of representation that captures the basic idea units present in a text (Ch. 10).

Prosopagnosia Disruption in the ability to recognize faces (Ch. 3).

Prospective memory Remembering to do something in the future, e.g., remembering to make a phone call tomorrow (Ch. 8).

Prototype The typical or average member of a category; the central or most representative member of a category. Note that a prototype may not exist for some categories, in which case the category's prototype would be some "average-like" combination of the various members (Ch. 7).

Psycholinguistics The study of language from the perspective of psychology; the study of language behavior and processes (Ch. 9).

Psychological essentialism The idea that people treat members of a category as if they have the same underlying, perhaps invisible, property or essence (Ch. 7).

Psychological refractory period See *attentional blink.*

Psychophysics The study of the relationship between physical stimuli and the perceived characteristics of those stimuli; the study of how perceptual experience differs from the physical stimulation that is being perceived (Ch. 11).

Recall See *free recall* and *serial recall.*

Recency effect In recall performance the elevated recall of the last few items in a list, presumably because the items are stored in and retrieved from short-term memory (contrast with *primacy effect*) (Ch. 5).

Recipient See *patient.*

Recoding Mentally transforming or translating a stimulus into another code or format; grouping items into larger units, as when recoding a written word into an acoustic–articulatory code (Ch. 5).

Recognition heuristic A heuristic in which you base a decision on whether you recognize the thing to be judged (Ch. 11).

Recognition task Any yes/no task in which subjects are asked to judge whether they have seen the stimulus before; more generally, any task asking for a simple yes/no (alternatively, true/false, same/different) response, often including a reaction time measurement (Ch. 6).

Reconstructive memory The tendency in recall or recognition to include ideas or elements that were inferred or related to the original stimulus but were not part of the original stimulus itself (Ch. 7).

Reductionism The scientific approach in which a complex event or behavior is broken down into its constituents; the individual constituents are then studied individually (Ch. 1).

Reference In language the allusion to or indirect mention of an element from elsewhere in the sentence or passage, as by using a pronoun or synonym (Ch. 10).

Region of proximal learning Information that is just beyond a person's current level of understanding (Ch. 10).

Rehearsal The mental repetition or practicing of some to-be-learned material (Ch. 6).

Relation In case grammar the central idea or relationship being asserted in a sentence or phrase. For instance, in "Bill hit the ball with the bat," the central relation is "HIT" (see also *case grammar*) (Ch. 8).

Relearning task An experimental task in which some material is learned, set aside for a period of time, then relearned to the same criterion in hopes that the relearning will take less time or effort to achieve the same level of accuracy; the task used by Ebbinghaus in his research on memory (Ch. 6).

Release from proactive interference (release from PI) The sudden reduction in proactive interference when the material to be learned is changed in some fashion, such as improved recall on a list of plant names after several trials involving animal names. The initial decline was caused by proactive interference, and the improvement on the last trial is caused by release from PI (Ch. 5).

Reminiscence bump Superior memory than would otherwise be expected for life events around the age of 20, between the ages of 15 and 25 (Ch. 8).

Repeated name penalty An increase in reading times when a direct reference is used again (e.g., the person's name) compared to when a pronoun is used (Ch. 10).

Repetition blindness The tendency to not perceive a pattern, whether a word, a picture, or any other visual stimulus, when it is quickly repeated (Ch. 3).

Repetition priming A priming effect caused by the exact repetition of a stimulus; often used in implicit memory tests (Chs. 6, 10).

Representation A general term referring to the way information is stored in memory. The term always carries the connotation that we are interested in the format or organization of the information as it is stored (is the information stored in a semantic representation? a sound-based representation?) (Ch. 2).

Representation of knowledge See *representation.*

Representational momentum The phenomenon of misremembering the movement of an object further along its path of travel than where it actually was when it was last seen (Ch. 5).

Representativeness heuristic A reasoning heuristic in which we judge the likelihood of some event by deciding how representative that event seems to be of the larger group or population from which it was drawn (Ch. 11).

Repression Intentional forgetting of painful or traumatic experiences, especially in Freudian theory (Ch. 8).

Response time (RT) The elapsed time, usually measured in milliseconds, between some stimulus event and the subject's response to that event; a particularly common measure of performance in cognitive psychology (Chs. 2, 7).

Retina The layer of the eye covered with the rods and cones that initiate the process of visual sensation and perception (Ch. 3).

Retrieval Accessing information stored in memory, whether or not that access involves conscious awareness (Chs. 1, 2).

Retrieval cue Any cue, hint, or piece of information used to prompt retrieval of some target information (Ch. 6).

Retroactive interference (RI) The interference from a recent event or experience that influences memory for an earlier event, such as trying to recall the items from list 1 but instead recalling the items from list 2 (Ch. 5).

Retrograde amnesia Loss of memories that preceded the brain damage (Ch. 6).

Rewrite rules In a phrase structure grammar, the rules that specify the individual components of a phrase; for example, a noun phrase is rewritten as a determiner, an adjective, and a noun, NP $\longrightarrow$ D + N (Ch. 9).

RI See *retroactive interference.*

RT See *response time.*

Saccade The voluntary sweeping of the eyes from one fixation point to another (Ch. 3).

Salience, vividness Sources of bias in the availability heuristic in which a particularly notable or vivid memory influences judgments about the frequency or likelihood of such events (Ch. 11).

Sapir-Whorf linguistic relativity hypothesis See *linguistic relativity hypothesis.*

Satisficing Finding an acceptable or satisfactory solution to a problem, even though the solution may not be optimal (Ch. 11).

Savings score In a relearning task, the score showing how much was saved on second learning compared with original learning. For instance, if original learning took 10 trials and relearning took only 6 trials, then savings would be 40% (10 – 6)/10 (Ch. 6).

Schema (plural, *schemata*) In Bartlett's (1932, p. 201) words, "an active organization of past reactions or past experiences"; a knowledge structure in memory (Ch. 7).

Script Schank's term for a schema, a long-term memory representation of some complex event such as going to a restaurant (Ch. 7).

Second-order theory In conversation the informal theory we develop that expresses our knowledge of what the other participant knows about us, summarized by the phrase "what he/she thinks I know" (contrast with *direct theory*) (Ch. 10).

Selecting See *filtering.*

Selective attention The ability to attend to one source of information while ignoring or excluding other ongoing messages. (Ch. 4).

Semantic case (also *case role*) In a case grammar approach, the particular case played by a word or concept is said to be that word's semantic case (see also *case grammar*) (Chs. 8, 9).

Semantic congruity effect In the mental comparison task, reaction time is speeded or judgments are made easier when the basis for a judgment is congruent or similar to the stimuli being compared; for instance, a congruent condition would be "choose the smaller of second or minute," and an incongruent condition would be "choose the smaller of decade or century" (Ch. 11).

Semantic distance effect See *semantic relatedness effect.*

Semantic features (also *feature list*) Properties or characteristics stored in the mental representation of some concept, presumed by some theories to be accessed and evaluated in the process of making semantic judgments (Ch. 7).

Semantic memory The long-term memory component in which general world knowledge is stored (contrast with *episodic memory*) (Chs. 6, 7).

Semantic relatedness effect In semantic memory tasks, reaction time is speeded up or judgments are made easier when the concepts are closer together in semantic distance, when they are more closely related. Note that the effect is reversed when the comparison is false; that is, RT is longer for the comparison "A whale is a fish" than for "A whale is a bird" (Ch. 7).

Semanticity One of Hockett's (1960) linguistic universals, expressing the fact that the elements of language convey meaning (Ch. 9).

Semantics The study of meaning (Ch. 9).

Sensation The reception of physical stimulation and encoding of it into the nervous system (Ch. 3).

Sensory memory The initial mental storage system for sensory stimuli. There are presumably as many modalities of sensory memory as there are kinds of stimulation that we can sense (Ch. 2).

Sentence verification task A task in which subjects must respond true or false to simple sentences (Ch. 7).

Sequential stages of processing An assumption in most process models that the separate stages of processing occur in a fixed sequence, with no overlap of the stages (Ch. 2).

Serial exhaustive search A search process in which all possible elements are searched one by one before the decision is made, even if the target is found early in the search process (Ch. 5).

Serial position curve The display of accuracy in recall across the original positions in the to-be-learned list, often found to have a bowed shape, indicating lower recall in the middle of the list than in the initial or final positions (Ch. 5).

Serial processing Mental processing in which only one process or operation occurs at a time (Ch. 2).

Serial recall A recall task in which subjects must recall the list items in their original order of presentation (contrast with *free recall*) (Chs. 5, 6).

Shadowing task A task in which subjects hear a spoken message and must repeat the message out loud in a very short time; often used as one of the two tasks in a dual task method (Ch. 4).

Short-term memory (STM) The component of the human memory system that holds information for up to 20 s; the memory component where current and recently attended information is held; sometimes loosely equated with attention and consciousness (Ch. 2).

Simulation heuristic A reasoning heuristic in which we predict a future event or imagine a different outcome to completed events; a forecasting of how some event will turn out or how it might have turned out under another set of circumstances (Ch. 11).

Situation model A memory representation of a real or possible-world situation, for example of a situation described in a passage of text (Ch. 10).

SNARC effect An abbreviation for Spatial-Numerical Association of Response Codes the finding that judgments about smaller numbers were made more quickly with the left hand and judgments about larger numbers were made more quickly with the right hand (Ch. 11).

SOA See *stimulus onset asynchrony.*

Source memory Memory of the exact source of information (Ch. 8).

Source misattribution Inability to distinguish whether an original event or a later event was the true source of information (Ch. 8).

Source monitoring The ability to accurately remember the source of a memory, be it something you encountered in the world directly or learned *indirectly from* another source (Ch. 8).

Span of apprehension (also *span of attention*) The number of simple elements (e.g., digits, letters) that can be heard and immediately reported in their correct order; a standard short-term memory task, common on standardized intelligence tests (Ch. 3).

Speech act The intended consequence of an utterance. That is, what you are trying to accomplish when you say something (Ch. 10).

Split brain Refers to patients in whom the corpus callosum has been severed surgically and the resultant changes in their performance because of the surgery or, more generally, to research showing various specializations of the two cerebral hemispheres (Ch. 2).

Spotlight attention A rapid attentional mechanism operating in parallel and automatically across the visual field, especially for detecting simple visual features (Ch. 4).

Spreading activation The commonly assumed theoretical process by which long-term memory knowledge is accessed and retrieved. Some form of mental excitation or activation is believed to be passed or spread along the pathways that connect concepts in a memory network. When a concept has been activated, it has been retrieved or accessed within the memory representation. The process is loosely analogous to the spread of neural excitation in the brain (Ch. 7).

Stereotypes In reasoning, bias in judgments related to the typical characteristics of a profession, type of person, and so on (Ch. 11).

Sternberg task The short-term memory scanning task devised by Saul Sternberg (Ch. 5).

Stimulus onset asynchrony (SOA) In priming studies, the interval of time separating the prime and the target, usually a few hundred milliseconds (Ch. 7).

STM See *short-term memory.*

Structuralism The approach, most closely identified with Titchener, in which the structure of the conscious mind—that is, the sensations, images, and feelings that are the elements of consciousness—was studied; the first major school of psychological thought, beginning in the late 1800s (contrast with *functionalism*) (Ch. 1).

Structure building The process of comprehension in Gernsbacher's theory, of building a mental representation of the meaning of sentences (Ch. 10).

Subgoal In problem solving, an intermediate goal that must be achieved to reach a final goal (Ch. 12).

Subjective organization The grouping or organizing of items that are to be learned according to some scheme or basis devised by the subject (Ch. 6).

Suffix effect The inferior recall of the end of the list in the presence of an additional, meaningful, non-list auditory stimulus (Ch. 3).

Suppression In Gernsbacher's theory the active process of reducing the activation level of concepts no longer relevant to the meaning of a sentence (Ch. 10).

Surface form. The level of representation in language comprehension that corresponds to a verbatim mental representation of the exact words and syntax used in a passage of text (Ch. 10).

Surface structure In linguistics and psycholinguistics, the actual form of a sentence, whether written or spoken (contrast with *deep structure*); the literal string of words or sounds present in a sentence (Ch. 9).

Sustained attention See *vigilance.*

Syllogism (also *categorical syllogism*) A classic reasoning form composed of two premises and one conclusion in which the logical truth of the conclusion must be derived from the premises (Ch. 11).

Symbolic comparison Mental comparisons of symbols, such as digits, usually in a "choose smaller/larger" task (Ch. 11).

Symbolic distance effect The result, in symbolic comparison tasks, in which two relatively different stimuli (e.g., 1 and 8) are judged more rapidly than two relatively similar stimuli (e.g., 1 and 2) because of greater symbolic distance between 1 and 8. Generally, we judge differences between symbols more rapidly when they differ considerably on some symbolic dimension, e.g., the dimension of magnitude (Ch. 11).

Synapse The junction of two neurons; the small gap between the terminal buttons of one neuron and the dendrites of another; as a verb, to form a junction with another neuron (Ch. 2).

Syntax The arrangement of words as elements in a sentence to show their relationship to one another; grammatical structure; the rules governing the order of words in a sentence (Ch. 9).

Tabula rasa Latin term meaning "blank slate." The term refers to a standard assumption of behaviorists that learning and experience write a record on the "blank slate"; in other words, the assumption that learning, as opposed to innate factors, is the most important factor in determining behavior (Ch. 1).

"Take the best" heuristic A heuristic in which you decide between alternatives based on the first useful information you retrieve about the alternatives (Ch. 11).

Target The second part of a prime–target stimulus (see *priming*); any concept or material that is designated as being of special interest (Ch. 7).

Template A model or pattern. In theories of pattern recognition, a template is the pattern stored in memory against which incoming stimuli are compared to recognize the incoming patterns (Ch. 3).

Theory of mind Theories we develop of our conversational partners (Ch. 10).

Time In propositional or semantic case theories, the semantic case referring to when an event took place; e.g., in the sentence "The car climbed the steep hill," Time = the past (Ch. 8).

Tip-of-the-tongue (TOT) effect Momentary retrieval failure, with the sense of being on the verge of retrieving the target concept (Chs. 6, 8).

Top-down processing See *conceptually driven processing.*

Topic maintenance Making conversational contributions relevant to the topic, sticking to the topic (Ch. 10).

Transformational grammar Chomsky's theory of the structure of language, a combination of a phrase structure grammar and a set of transformational rules (Ch. 9).

Transformational rules In Chomsky's transformational grammar, the syntactic rules that transform an idea (a deep structure sentence) into its surface structure; for instance, rules that form a passive sentence or a negative sentence (Ch. 9).

Trans-saccadic memory The memory system that is used across a series of eye movements to build up a more complete and stable understanding of the visual world (Ch 3).

Typicality In semantic categories the degree to which items are viewed as typical, central members of a category; the central tendency of a category (Ch. 7).

Typicality effect In semantic memory research, the result that typical members of a category tend to be judged more rapidly than atypical members (Ch. 7).

Unauthorized Not intended, especially said of inferences drawn during a conversation (contrast with *authorized*) (Ch. 10).

Unconscious processing Mental processing outside of awareness (Ch. 2).

Undoing See *counterfactual reasoning.*

Unit See *chunk.*

Updating The process of altering a person's situation model in the face of information about how the situation has changed (Ch. 10).

Verbal learning The branch of human experimental psychology, largely replaced by cognitive psychology in the late 1950s and early 1960s, investigating the learning and retention of "verbal," that is, language-based, stimuli; influenced directly by Ebbinghaus' methods and interests (Ch. 1).

Verbal overshadowing The finding that memory of what was actually witnessed can be disrupted if a person provides a description of an event (Ch. 8).

Verbal protocol In studies of problem solving, a word-for-word transcription of what the subject said aloud during the problem-solving attempt (Chs. 2, 12).

Vigilance The maintenance of attention for infrequent events over long periods of time (Ch. 4).

Visual imagery The mental representation of visual information; the skill or ability to remember visual information (Ch. 6).

Visual persistence The perceptual phenomenon in which a visual stimulus still seems to be present even after its termination, usually a few hundred milliseconds to a few seconds (Ch. 3).

Visual sensory memory (also *iconic memory***)** The short-duration memory system specialized for holding visual information, lasting no more than about 250 to 500 ms (Ch. 3).

Visuo-spatial sketch pad The visual and perceptual component of Baddeley's working memory model (Ch. 5).

von Restorff effect In a recall task, the elevated accuracy for an item that was noticeably different during list presentation, for instance, because it was written in a different color of ink (Ch. 6).

Well-defined problem A problem in which the initial and final states and the legal operators are clearly specified (Ch. 12).

Wernicke's aphasia One of two common forms of aphasia in which the language disorder is characterized by a serious disruption of comprehension and the use of invented words as well as semantically inappropriate substitutions (contrast with *Broca's aphasia*). The aphasia is caused by damage in the region of the neocortex called Wernicke's area (Ch. 9).

Whole report condition Especially in Sperling's (1960) research, the condition in which the entire visual display was to be reported (contrast with *partial report condition*) (Ch. 3).

Word frequency effect Finding that frequent words in the language are processed more rapidly than infrequent words (Ch. 2).

Word length effect The finding that the longer the words are that people need to remember, the fewer they can remember (Ch. 5).

Working memory The component, similar to short-term memory, in Baddeley and Hitch's (1974) theory in which verbal rehearsal and other conscious processing takes place; also, the component that contains the executive controller in charge of devoting conscious processing resources to the various other components in the memory system (Ch. 5).

REFERENCES

Abbot, V., Black, J. B., & Smith, E. E. (1985). The representation of scripts in memory. *Journal of Memory and Language, 24,* 179–199.

Abelson, R.P. (1981). Psychological status of the script concept. *American Psychologist, 36,* 715–729.

Abraham, W. C. (2006). Memory maintenance: The changing nature of neural mechanisms. *Current Directions in Psychological Science, 15,* 5–8.

Abrams, R. A., & Christ, S. E. (2003). Motion onset captures attention. *Psychological Science, 14,* 427–432.

Agnoli, F. (1991). Development of judgmental heuristics and logical reasoning: Training counteracts the representativeness heuristic. *Cognitive Development, 6,* 195–217.

Agnoli, F., & Krantz, D. H. (1989). Suppressing natural heuristics by formal instruction: The case of the conjunction fallacy. *Cognitive Psychology, 21,* 515–550.

Ahlum-Heath, M. E., & DiVesta, F. J. (1986). The effect of conscious controlled verbalization of a cognitive strategy on transfer in problem solving. *Memory & Cognition, 14,* 281–285.

Ainsworth-Darnell, K., Shulman, H. G., & Boland, J. E. (1998). Dissociating brain responses to syntactic and semantic anomalies: Evidence from event-related potentials. *Journal of Memory* and Language, 38, 112–130.

Albrecht, J. E. & O'Brien, E. J. (1991). Effects of centrality on retrieval of text-based concepts. *Journal of Experimental Psychology: Learning, Memory, and Cognition, 17,* 932–939.

Alibali, M. W., Heath, D. C., & Myers, H. J. (2001). Effects of visibility between speaker and listener on gesture production: Some gestures are meant to be seen. *Journal of Memory and Language, 44,* 169–188.

Allen, P. A., & Madden, D. J. (1990). Evidence for a parallel input serial analysis (PISA) model of word processing. *Journal of Experimental Psychology: Human Perception and Performance, 16,* 48–64.

Allen, R. J., Baddeley, A. D., & Hitch, G. J. (2006). Is the binding of visual features in working memory resource-demanding? *Journal of Experimental Psychology: General, 135,* 298–313.

Allport, A. (1989). Visual attention. In M. I. Posner (Ed.), *Foundations of cognitive science* (pp. 631–682). Cambridge, MA: Bradford.

Almor, A. (1999). Noun-phrase anaphora and focus: The informational load hypothesis. *Psychological Review, 106,* 748–765.

Alter, A. L., Oppenheimer, D. M., Epley, N., & Eyre, R. N. (2007). Overcoming intuition: Metacognitive difficulty activates analytic reasoning. *Journal of Experimental Psychology: General, 136,* 569–576.

Altmann, G. T. M., Garnham, A., & Dennis, Y. (1992). Avoiding the garden path: Eye movements in context. *Journal of Memory and Language, 31,* 685–712.

American Heritage College Dictionary ***(3rd ed.).*** (1997). Boston: Houghton Mifflin.

Anaki, D., & Henik, A. (2003). Is there a "strength effect" in automatic semantic priming? *Memory & Cognition, 31,* 262–272.

Anderson, A. K. (2005). Affective influences on the attentional dynamics supporting awareness. *Journal of Experimental Psychology: General, 134,* 258–281.

Anderson, J. R. (1974). Retrieval of propositional information from long-term memory. *Cognitive Psychology, 6,* 451–474.

Anderson, J. R. (1976). *Language, memory, and thought.* Hillsdale, NJ: Erlbaum.

Anderson, J. R. (1980). *Cognitive psychology and its implications.* San Francisco: Freeman.

Anderson, J. R. (1983). *The architecture of cognition.* Cambridge, MA: Harvard University Press.

Anderson, J. R. (1985). *Cognitive psychology and its implications* (2nd ed.). New York: Freeman.

Anderson, J. R. (1993). Problem solving and learning. *American Psychologist, 48,* 35–44.

Anderson, J. R., & Bower, G. H. (1973). *Human associative memory.* Washington, DC: Winston & Sons.

Anderson, J. R., & Lebiere, C. (1998). *The atomic components of thought.* Hillsdale, NJ: Erlbaum.

Anderson, J. R., Qin, Y., Jung, K-J., & Carter, C. S. (2007). Information-processing modules and their relative modality specificity. *Cognitive Psychology, 54,* 185–217.

Anderson, J. R., & Schooler, L. J. (1991). Reflections of the environment in memory. *Psychological Science, 2,* 396–408.

Anderson, M. C. (2003). Rethinking interference theory: Executive control and mechanisms of forgetting. *Journal of Memory and Language, 49,* 415–445.

Anderson, M. C., Bjork, E. L., & Bjork, R. A. (2000). Retrieval-induced forgetting: Evidence for a recall-specific mechanism. *Psychonomic Bulletin & Review, 7,* 522–530.

Andrade, J. (1995). Learning during anaesthesia: A review. *British Journal of Psychology, 86,* 479–506.

Antrobus, J. (1991). Dreaming: Cognitive processes during cortical activation and high afferent thresholds. *Psychological Review, 98,* 96–121.

Arbuckle, T. Y., & Cuddy, L. L. (1969). Discrimination of item strength at time of presentation. *Journal of Experimental Psychology, 81,* 126–131.

Armony, J. L., Chochol, C., Fecteau, S., & Belin, P. (2007). Laugh (or cry) and you will be remembered. *Psychological Science, 18,* 1027–1029.

Armstrong, S. L., Gleitman, L. R., & Gleitman, H. (1983). What some concepts might not be. *Cognition, 13,* 263–308.

Arnold, J. E., & Griffin, Z. M. (2007). The effect of additional characters on choice of referring expression: Everyone counts. *Journal of Memory and Language, 56,* 521–536.

Arrigo, J. M., & Pezdek, K. (1997). Lessons from the study of psychogenic amnesia. *Current Directions in Psychological Science, 6,* 148–152.

Ashcraft, M. H. (1976). Priming and property dominance effects in semantic memory. *Memory & Cognition, 4,* 490–500.

Ashcraft, M. H. (1978). Property dominance and typicality effects in property statement verification. *Journal of Verbal Learning and Verbal Behavior, 17*, 155–164.

Ashcraft, M. H. (1989). *Human Memory and Cognition*. Glenview, IL: Scott Foresman.

Ashcraft, M. H. (1993). A personal case history of transient anomia. *Brain and Language, 44*, 47–57.

Ashcraft, M. H. (1995). Cognitive psychology and simple arithmetic: A review and summary of new directions. *Mathematical Cognition, 1*, 3–34.

Ashcraft, M. H., & Christy, K. S. (1995). The frequency of arithmetic facts in elementary texts: Addition and multiplication in grades 1–6. *Journal for Research in Mathematics Education, 26*, 396–421.

Ashcraft, M. H., Kellas, G., & Needham, S. (1975). Rehearsal and retrieval processes in free recall of categorized lists. *Memory & Cognition, 3*, 506–512.

Ashcraft, M. H., & Krause, J. A. (2007). Working memory, math performance, and math anxiety. *Psychonomic Bulletin & Review, 14*, 243–248.

Aslan, A., Bäuml, K., & Grundgeiger, T. (2007). The role of inhibitory processes in part-list cuing. *Journal of Experimental Psychology: Learning, Memory, and Cognition, 33*, 335–341.

Atkins, S. A., & Reuter-Lorenz, P. A. (2008). False working memories? Semantic distortion in a mere 4 seconds. *Memory & Cognition, 36*, 74–81.

Atkinson, R. C., & Shiffrin, R. M. (1968). Human memory: A proposed system and its control processes. In W. K. Spence & J. T. Spence (Eds.), *The psychology of learning and motivation: Advances in research and theory* (Vol. 2, pp. 89–195). New York: Academic Press.

Atkinson, R. C., & Shiffrin, R. M. (1971). The control of short-term memory. *Scientific American, 225*, 82–90.

Atwood, M. E., & Polson, P. (1976). A process model for water jug problems. *Cognitive Psychology, 8*, 191–216.

Averbach, E., & Coriell, A. S. (1961). Short-term memory in vision. *Bell System Technical Journal, 40*, 309–328. (Reprinted in Coltheart, M. (1973). *Readings in cognitive psychology*. Toronto: Holt, Rinehart & Winston of Canada).

Averbach, E., & Sperling, G. (1961). Short term storage and information in vision. In C. Cherry (Ed.), *Information theory* (pp. 196–211). London: Butterworth.

Ayers, M. S., & Reder, L. M. (1998). A theoretical review of the misinformation effect: Predictions from an activation-based memory model. *Psychonomic Bulletin & Review, 5*, 1–21.

Ayers, T. J., Jonides, J., Reitman, J. S., Egan, J. C., & Howard, D. A. (1979). Differing suffix effects for the same physical suffix. *Journal of Experimental Psychology: Human Learning and Memory, 5*, 315–321.

Baars, B. J. (1986). *The cognitive revolution in psychology*. New York: Guilford Press.

Bachoud-Levi, A. C., Dupoux, E., Cohen, L., & Mehler, J. (1998). Where is the length effect? A cross-linguistic study of speech production. *Journal of Memory and Language, 39*, 331–346.

Baddeley, A. D. (1966). Short-term memory for word sequences as a function of acoustic, semantic, and formal similarity. *Quarterly Journal of Experimental Psychology, 18*, 302–309.

Baddeley, A. D. (1976). *The psychology of memory*. New York: Basic Books.

Baddeley, A. D. (1978). The trouble with levels: A reexamination of Craik and Lockhart's framework for memory research. *Psychological Review, 85*, 139–152.

Baddeley, A. D. (1986). *Working memory*. Oxford, U.K.: Oxford University Press.

Baddeley, A. D. (1992a). Is working memory working? The Fifteenth Bartlett Lecture. *Quarterly Journal of Experimental Psychology, 44A*, 1–31.

Baddeley, A. D. (1992b). Working memory. *Science, 255*, 556–559.

Baddeley, A. D. (2000a). The episodic buffer: A new component of working memory? *Trends in Cognitive Sciences, 4*, 417–423.

Baddeley, A. D. (2000b). The phonological loop and the irrelevant speech effect: some comments on Neath (2000). *Psychonomic Bulletin & Review, 7*, 544–549.

Baddeley, A. D., & Hitch, G. (1974). Working memory. In G. H. Bower (Ed.), *The psychology of learning and motivation* (Vol. 8, pp. 47–89). New York: Academic Press.

Baddeley, A. D., & Lieberman, K. (1980). Spatial working memory. In R. Nickerson (Ed.), *Attention and performance VIII*. Hillsdale, NJ: Erlbaum.

Baddeley, A. D., Thomson, N., & Buchanan, M. (1975). Word length and the structure of short-term memory. *Journal of Verbal Learning and Verbal Behavior, 14*, 575–589.

Baddeley, A. D., & Wilson, B. (1988). Comprehension and working memory: A single case neuropsychological study. *Journal of Memory and Language, 27*, 479–498.

Bahr, G. S. (2003). Psychologists' belief in visual emission. *American Psychologist, 58*, 494.

Bahrick, H. P. (1983). The cognitive map of a city: 50 years of learning and memory. In G. H. Bower (Ed.), *The psychology of learning and motivation: Advances in research and theory* (Vol. 17, pp. 125–163). New York: Academic Press.

Bahrick, H. P. (1984). Semantic memory content in permastore: Fifty years of memory for Spanish learned in school. *Journal of Experimental Psychology: General, 113*, 1–29.

Bahrick, H. P., Bahrick, L. E., Bahrick, A. S., & Bahrick, P. E. (1993). Maintenance of foreign language vocabulary and the spacing effect. *Psychological Science, 4*, 316–321.

Bahrick, H. P., Bahrick, P. C., & Wittlinger, R. P. (1975). Fifty years of memories for names and faces: A cross-sectional approach. *Journal of Experimental Psychology: General, 104*, 54–75.

Bahrick, H. P., & Hall, L. K. (1991). Lifetime maintenance of high school mathematics content. *Journal of Experimental Psychology: General, 120*, 20–33.

Bahrick, H. P., Hall, L. K., & Berger, S. A. (1996). Accuracy and distortion in memory for high school grades. *Psychological Science, 7*, 265–271.

Balota, D. A., & Paul, S. T. (1996). Summation of activation: Evidence from multiple primes that converge and diverge within semantic memory. *Journal of Experimental Psychology: Learning, Memory, and Cognition, 22*, 827–845.

Banich, M. T. (1997). *Neuropsychology: The neural bases of mental function*. Boston: Houghton Mifflin.

Banich, M. T. (2004). *Cognitive neuroscience and neuropsychology* (2nd ed.). Boston: Houghton Mifflin Company.

Banks, W. P. (1977). Encoding and processing of symbolic information in comparative judgments. In G. H. Bower (Ed.), *The psychology of learning and motivation* (Vol. 11, pp. 101–159). New York: Academic Press.

Banks, W. P., Clark, H. H., & Lucy, P. (1975). The locus of the semantic congruity effect in comparative judgments. *Journal of Experimental Psychology: Human Perception and Performance, 1,* 35–47.

Banks, W. P., Fujii, M., & Kayra-Stuart, F. (1976). Semantic congruity effects in comparative judgments of magnitude of digits. *Journal of Experimental Psychology: Human Perception and Performance, 2,* 435–447.

Bar-Hillel, M. (1980). What features make samples seem representative? *Journal of Experimental Psychology: Human Perception and Performance, 6,* 578–589.

Barnard, P. J., Scott, S., Taylor, J., May, J., & Knightley, W. (2004). Paying attention to meaning. *Psychological Science, 15,* 179–186.

Barnier, A. J. (2002). Posthypnotic amnesia for autobiographical episodes: A laboratory model for functional amnesia? *Psychological Science, 13,* 232–237.

Barrett, H. C., & Kurzban, R. (2006). Modularity in cognition: Framing the debate. *Psychological Review, 113,* 628–647.

Barsalou, L. W. (1983). Ad hoc categories. *Memory & Cognition, 11,* 211–227.

Barsalou, L.W. (1999). Perceptual symbol systems. *Behavioral and Brain Sciences, 22,* 577–660.

Barshi, I., & Healy, A. F. (1993). Checklist procedures and the cost of automaticity. *Memory & Cognition, 21,* 496–505.

Bartlett, F. C. (1932). *Remembering: A study in experimental and social psychology.* London: Cambridge University Press.

Bassok, M., & Holyoak, K. H. (1989). Interdomain transfer between isomorphic topics in algebra and physics. *Journal of Experimental Psychology: Learning, Memory, and Cognition, 15,* 153–166.

Bassok, M., Pedigo, S. F., & Oskarsson, A. T. (2008). Priming addition facts with semantic relations. *Journal of Experimental Psychology: Learning, Memory, and Cognition, 34,* 343–352.

Bates, E., Masling, M., & Kintsch, W. (1978). Recognition memory for aspects of dialogue. *Journal of Experimental Psychology: Human Learning and Memory, 4,* 187–197.

Battig, W. F., & Montague, W. E. (1969). Category norms for verbal items in 56 categories: A replication and extension of the Connecticut category norms. *Journal of Experimental Psychology Monograph, 80* (3, Pt. 2), 1–46.

Baum, D. R., & Jonides, J. (1979). Cognitive maps: Analysis of comparative judgments of distance. *Memory & Cognition, 7,* 462–468.

Bavelas, J., Gerwing, J., Sutton, C., & Prevost, D. (2008). Gesturing on the telephone: Independent effects of dialogue and visibility. *Journal of Memory and Language, 58,* 495–520.

Beech, A., Powell, T., McWilliams, J., & Claridge, G. (1989). Evidence of reduced cognitive inhibition in schizophrenics. *British Journal of Psychology,* 28, 109–116

Beeman, M. J. (1993). Semantic processing in the right hemisphere may contribute to drawing inferences from discourse. *Brain and Language, 44,* 80–120.

Beeman, M. J. (1998). Coarse semantic coding and discourse comprehension. In M. Beeman & C. Chiarello (Eds.), *Brain right hemisphere language comprehension: perspectives from cognitive neuroscience* (pp. 255–284). Malwah, NJ: Erlbaum.

Beeman, M. J., & Bowden, E. M. (2000). The right hemisphere maintains solution-related activation for yet-to-be-solved problems. *Memory & Cognition, 28,* 1231–1241.

Beeman, M. J., & Chiarello, C. (1998). Complementary right- and left-hemisphere language comprehension. *Current Directions in Psychological Science, 7,* 2–8.

Beilock, S. L., & Carr, T. H. (2001). On the fragility of skilled performance: What governs choking under pressure? *Journal of Experimental Psychology: Learning, Memory, and Cognition, 33,* 983–998.

Beilock, S. L., & DeCaro, M. S. (2007). From poor performance to success under stress: Working memory, strategy selection, and mathematical problem solving under pressure. *Journal of Experimental Psychology, 130,* 701–725.

Beilock, S. L., Rydell, R. J., & McConnell, A. R. (2007). Stereotype threat and working memory: Mechanisms, alleviation, and spillover. *Journal of Experimental Psychology: General, 136,* 256–276.

Bekoff, M., Allen, C., & Burghardt, G. (Eds.) (2002). *The cognitive animal: Empirical and theoretical perspectives on animal cognition.* Cambridge, MA: MIT Press.

Belli, R. F. (1989). Influences of misleading postevent information: Misinformation interference and acceptance. *Journal of Experimental Psychology: General, 118,* 72–85.

Belli, R. F., Lindsay, D. S., Gales, M. S., & McCarthy, T. T. (1994). Memory impairment and source misattribution in postevent misinformation experiments with short retention intervals. *Memory & Cognition, 22,* 40–54.

Benjamin, L. T., Jr., Durkin, M., Link, M., Vestal, M., & Acord, J. (1992). Wundt's American doctoral students. *American Psychologist, 47,* 123–131.

Benson, D. J., & Geschwind, N. (1969). The alexias. In P. Vincken & G. W. Bruyn (Eds.), *Handbook of clinical neurology* (Vol. 4, pp. 112–140). Amsterdam: North-Holland.

Berger, A., Henik, A., & Rafal, R. (2005). Competition between endogenous and exogenous orienting of visual attention. *Journal of Experimental Psychology: General, 134,* 207–221.

Berndt, R. S., & Haendiges, A. N. (2000). Grammatical class in word and sentence production: Evidence from an aphasic patient. *Journal of Memory and Language, 43,* 249–273.

Berntsen, D., & Hall, N. M. (2004). The episodic nature of involuntary autobiographical memories. *Memory & Cognition, 32,* 789–803.

Berntsen, D. & Rubin, D. C. (2004). Cultural life scripts structure recall from autobiographical memory. *Memory & Cognition, 32,* 427–442.

Bertsch, S., Pesta, B. J., Wiscott, R., & McDaniel, M. A. (2007). The generation effect: A meta-analytic review. *Memory & Cognition, 35,* 201–210.

Besner, D., & Stolz, J. A. (1999). What kind of attention modulates the Stroop effect? *Psychonomic Bulletin & Review, 6,* 99–104.

Biederman, I. (1987). Recognition by components: A theory of human image understanding. *Psychological Review, 94,* 115–147.

Biederman, I. (1990). Higher-level vision. In E. N. Osherson, S. M. Kosslyn, & J. M. Hollerbach (Eds.), *An invitation to cognitive science* (Vol. 2, pp. 41–72). Cambridge, MA: MIT Press.

Biederman, I., & Blickle, T. (1985). *The perception of objects with deleted contours.* Unpublished manuscript, State University of New York, Buffalo.

Biederman, I., Glass, A. L., & Stacy, E. W. (1973). Searching for objects in real world scenes. *Journal of Experimental Psychology, 97,* 22–27.

Bigler, E. D., Yeo, R. A., & Turkheimer, F. (1989). Introduction and overview. In E. D. Bigler, R. A. Yeo, & F. Turkheimer (Eds.), *Neuropsychological function and brain imaging* (p. 10). New York: Plenum Press.

Bilalić, M., McLeod, P., & Gobet, F. (2008). Inflexibility of experts – Reality or myth? Quantifying the Einstellung effect in chess masters. *Cognitive Psychology, 56,* 73–102.

Binder, K. S. (2003). Sentential and discourse topic effects on lexical ambiguity processing: An eye movement examination. *Memory & Cognition, 31,* 690–702.

Binder, K. S., & Rayner, K. (1998). Contextual strength does not modulate the subordinate bias effect: Evidence from eye fixations and self-paced reading. *Psychonomic Bulletin & Review, 5,* 271–276.

Birch, S. L., & Garnsey, S. M. (1995). The effect of focus on memory for words in sentences. *Journal of Memory and Language, 34,* 232–267.

Birch, S. L., & Rayner, K. (1997). Linguistic focus affects eye movements during reading. *Memory & Cognition, 25,* 653–660.

Bisiach, E., & Luzzatti, C. (1978). Unilateral neglect of representational space. *Cortex, 14,* 129–133.

Bjork, E. L., & Bjork, R. A. (2003). Intentional forgetting can increase, not decrease, residual influences of to-be-forgotten information. *Journal of Experimental Psychology: Learning, Memory, and Cognition, 29,* 524–531.

Blakemore, C. (1977). *Mechanics of the mind.* Cambridge, U.K.: Cambridge University Press.

Blanchette, I. & Richards, A. (2004). Reasoning about emotional and neutral materials. *Psychological Science, 15,* 745–752.

Blom, J. P., & Gumperz, J. J. (1972). Social meaning in linguistic structure: Code-switching in Norway. In J. J. Gumperz & D. Hymes (Eds.), *Directions in sociolinguistics: The ethnography of communication* (pp. 407–434). New York: Holt.

Bloom, F. E., & Lazerson, A. (1988). *Brain, mind, and behavior.* New York: W. H. Freeman.

Bock, J. K. (1982). Toward a cognitive psychology of syntax: Information processing contributions to sentence formulation. *Psychological Review, 89,* 1–47.

Bock, J. K. (1986). Meaning, sound, and syntax: Lexical priming in sentence production. *Journal of Experimental Psychology: Learning, Memory, and Cognition, 12,* 575–586.

Bock, K. (1995). Producing agreement. *Current Directions in Psychological Science, 4,* 56–61.

Bock, K. (1996). Language production: Methods and methodologies. *Psychonomic Bulletin & Review, 3,* 395–421.

Bock, K., Eberhard, K. M., & Cutting, J. C. (2004). Producing number agreement: How pronouns equal verbs. *Journal of Memory and Language, 51,* 251–278.

Bock, K., & Griffin, Z. M. (2000). The persistence of structural priming: Transient activation or implicit learning? *Journal of Experimental Psychology: General, 129,* 177–192.

Bock, K., Irwin, D. E., Davidson, D. J., & Levelt, W. J. M. (2003). Minding the clock. *Journal of Memory and Language, 48,* 653–685.

Bock, K., & Miller, C. A. (1991). Broken agreement. *Cognitive Psychology, 23,* 45–93.

Bonebakker, A. E., Bonke, B., Klein, J., Wolters, G., Stijnen, T., Passchier, J., & Merikle, P. M. (1996). Information processing during general anesthesia: Evidence for unconscious memory. *Memory & Cognition, 24,* 766–776.

Bonnefon, J. F., & Hilton, D. J. (2004). Consequential conditionals: Invited and suppressed inferences from valued outcomes. *Journal of Experimental Psychology: Learning, Memory, and Cognition, 30,* 28–37.

Borghi, A. M., Glenberg, A. M., & Kaschak, M. P. (2004). Putting words in perspective. *Memory & Cognition, 32,* 863–873.

Boring, E. G. (1929). *A history of experimental psychology.* New York: Century.

Boring, E. G. (1950). *A history of experimental psychology* (2nd ed.). New York: Appleton-Century-Crofts.

Boroditsky, L. (2001). Does language shape thought? Mandarin and English speakers' conceptions of time. *Cognitive Psychology, 43,* 1–22.

Botvinick, M. M., & Bylsma, L. M. (2006). Distraction and action slips in an everyday task: Evidence for a dynamic representation of task context. *Psychonomic Bulletin & Review, 12,* 1011–1017.

Bourne, L. E., Jr., & Bunderson, C. V. (1963). Effects of delay of informative feedback and length of postfeedback interval on concept identification. *Journal of Experimental Psychology, 65,* 1–5.

Bousfield, W. A. (1953). The occurrence of clustering in the recall of randomly arranged associates. *Journal of General Psychology, 49,* 229–240.

Bousfield, W. A., & Sedgewick, C. H. W. (1944). An analysis of sequences of restricted associative responses. *Journal of General Psychology, 30,* 149–165.

Bowden, E. M. (1985). Accessing relevant information during problem solving: Time constraints on search in the problem space. *Memory & Cognition, 13,* 280–286.

Bowden, E. M., & Beeman, M. J. (1998). Getting the right idea: Semantic activation in the right hemisphere may help solve insight problems. *Psychological Science, 9,* 435–440.

Bowden, E. M., Beeman, M., & Gernsbacher, M. A. (1995, March). *Two hemispheres are better than one: Drawing coherence inferences during story comprehension.* Paper presented at the annual meeting of the Cognitive Neuroscience Society, San Francisco.

Bowden, E. M., & Jung-Beeman, M. (2003). Aha! Insight experience correlates with solution activation in the right hemisphere. *Psychonomic Bulletin & Review, 10,* 730–737.

Bower, G. H. (1970). Analysis of a mnemonic device. *American Scientist, 58,* 496–510.

Bower, G. H. (1981). Mood and memory. *American Psychologist, 36,* 129–148.

Bower, G. H., Black, J. B., & Turner, T. J. (1979). Scripts in memory for text. *Cognitive Psychology, 11*, 177–220.

Bower, G. H., Clark, M. C., Lesgold, A. M., & Winzenz, D. (1969). Hierarchical retrieval schemes in recall of categorical word lists. *Journal of Verbal Learning and Verbal Behavior, 8*, 323–343.

Bowers, J. S., & Jones, K. W. (2008). Detecting objects is easier than categorizing them. *Quarterly Journal of Experimental Psychology, 61*, 552–557.

Bradley, M. M., Greenwald, M. K., Petry, M. C., & Lang, P. J. (1992). Remembering pictures: Pleasure and arousal in memory. *Journal of Experimental Psychology: Learning, Memory, and Cognition, 18*, 379–390.

Brainerd, C. J., & Reyna, V. F. (1998). When things that were never experienced are easier to "remember" than things that were. *Psychological Science, 9*, 484–489.

Branigan, H. P., Pickering, M. J., & Cleland, A. A. (1999). Syntactic priming in written production: Evidence for rapid decay. *Psychonomic Bulletin & Review, 6*, 635–640.

Branigan, H. P., Pickering, M. J., Stewart, A. J., & McLean, J. F. (2000). Syntactic priming in spoken production: Linguistic and temporal interference. *Memory & Cognition, 28*, 1297–1302.

Bransford, J. D. (1979). *Human cognition: Learning, understanding and remembering.* Belmont, CA: Wadsworth.

Bransford, J. D., & Franks, J. J. (1971). The abstraction of linguistic ideas. *Cognitive Psychology, 2*, 331–350.

Bransford, J. D., & Franks, J. J. (1972). The abstraction of linguistic ideas: A review. *Cognition: International Journal of Cognitive Psychology, 1*, 211–249.

Bransford, J. D., & Johnson, M. K. (1972). Contextual prerequisites for understanding: Some investigations of comprehension and recall. *Journal of Verbal Learning and Verbal Behavior, 11*, 717–726.

Bransford, J. D., & Stein, B. S. (1984). *The ideal problem solver.* New York: Freeman.

Bransford, J. D., & Stein, B. S. (1993). *The ideal problem solver* (2nd ed.). New York: Freeman.

Breedin, S. D., & Saffran, E. M. (1999). Sentence processing in the face of semantic loss: A case study. *Journal of Experimental Psychology: General, 128*, 547–562.

Bremner, J. D., Shobe, K. K., & Kihlstrom, J. F. (2000). False memories in women with self-reported childhood sexual abuse: An empirical study. *Psychological Science, 11*, 333–337.

Brennan, S. E., & Clark, H. H. (1996). Conceptual pacts and lexical choice in conversation. *Journal of Experimental Psychology: Learning, Memory, and Cognition, 22*, 1482–1493.

Bresnan, J. (1978). A realistic transformational grammar. In J. Bresnan, M. Halle, & G. Miller (Eds.), *Linguistic theory and psychological reality* (pp. 1–59). Cambridge, MA: MIT Press.

Bresnan, J., & Kaplan, R. M. (1982). Introduction: Grammars as mental representations of language. In J. Bresnan (Ed.), *The mental representation of grammatical relations* (pp. xvii–iii). Cambridge, MA: MIT Press.

Brewer, W. F., & Hay, A. E. (1984). Reconstructive recall of linguistic style. *Journal of Verbal Learning and Verbal Behavior, 23*, 237–249.

Bridgeman, B. (1988). *The biology of behavior and mind.* New York: Wiley.

Broadbent, D. E. (1952). Speaking and listening simultaneously. *Journal of Experimental Psychology, 43*, 267–273.

Broadbent, D. E. (1958). *Perception and communication.* London: Pergamon.

Broaders, S. C., Cook, S. W., Mitchell, Z., & Goldin-Meadow, S. (2007). Making children gesture brings out implicit knowledge and leads to learning. *Journal of Experimental Psychology: General, 136*, 539–550.

Bröder, A., & Schiffer, S. (2006). Adaptive flexibility and maladaptive routines in selecting fast and frugal decision strategies. *Journal of Experimental Psychology: Learning, Memory, and Cognition, 32*, 904–918.

Brooks, J. O. III, & Watkins, M. J. (1990). Further evidence of the intricacy of memory span. *Journal of Experimental Psychology: Learning, Memory, and Cognition, 16*, 1134–1141.

Brooks, L. R. (1968). Spatial and verbal components of the act of recall. *Canadian Journal of Experimental Psychology, 22*, 349–368.

Brosch, T., Sander, D., Pourtois, G., & Scherer, K. R. (2008). Beyond fear: Rapid spatial orienting toward positive emotional stimuli. *Psychological Science, 19*, 362–370.

Brown, A. S. (1998). Transient global amnesia. *Psychonomic Bulletin & Review, 5*, 401–427.

Brown, A. S. (1991). A review of the tip-of-the-tongue experience. *Psychological Bulletin, 109*, 204–223.

Brown, A. S. (2002). Consolidation theory and retrograde amnesia in humans. *Psychonomic Bulletin & Review, 9*, 403–425.

Brown, A. S. (2004). The déjà vu illusion. *Current Directions in Psychological Science, 13*, 256–259.

Brown, A. S., Brown, C. M., Mosbacher, J. L., & Dryden, W. E. (2006). Proactive and retroactive effects of negative suggestion. *Journal of Experimental Psychology: Learning, Memory, and Cognition, 32*, 1234–1243.

Brown, A. S., & Halliday, H. E. (1991). Cryptomnesia and source memory difficulties. *American Journal of Psychology, 104*, 475–490.

Brown, A. S., & Murphy, D. R. (1989). Cryptomnesia: Delineating inadvertent plagiarism. *Journal of Experimental Psychology: Learning, Memory, and Cognition, 15*, 432–442.

Brown, A. S., Neblett, D. R., Jones, T. C., & Mitchell, D. B. (1991). Transfer of processing in repetition priming: Some inappropriate findings. *Journal of Experimental Psychology: Learning, Memory, and Cognition, 17*, 514–525.

Brown, A. S., & Nix, L. A. (1996). Turning lies into truths: Referential validation of falsehoods. *Journal of Experimental Psychology: Learning, Memory, and Cognition, 22*, 1088–1100.

Brown, G. D. A., Neath, I., & Chater, N. (2007). A temporal ratio model of memory. *Psychological Review, 114*, 539–576.

Brown, J. A. (1958). Some tests of the decay theory of immediate memory. *Quarterly Journal of Experimental Psychology, 10*, 12–21.

Brown, N. R., & Siegler, R. S. (1992). The role of availability in the estimation of national populations. *Memory & Cognition, 20*, 406–412.

Brown, R., & Ford, M. (1961). Address in American English. *Journal of Abnormal and Social Psychology, 62*, 375–385.

Brown, R., & Kulik, J. (1977). Flashbulb memories. *Cognition, 5*, 73–99.

Brown, R., & McNeill, D. (1966). The "tip-of-the-tongue" phenomenon. *Journal of Verbal Learning and Verbal Behavior, 5,* 325–337.

Bruner, J. S. (1973). In J. Anglin (Ed.), *Beyond the information given: Studies in the psychology of knowing.* New York: Norton.

Bruner, J. S., Goodnow, J. J., & Austin, G. A. (1956). *A study of thinking.* New York: Wiley.

Bryden, M. P. (1982). *Laterality: Functional asymmetry in the intact human brain.* New York: Academic Press.

Buchner, A., & Wippich, W. (2000). On the reliability of implicit and explicit memory measures. *Cognitive Psychology, 40,* 227–259.

Bukach, C. M., Bub, D. N., Masson, M. E. J., & Lindsay, D. S. (2004). Category specificity in normal episodic learning: Applications to object recognition and category-specific agnosia. *Cognitive Psychology, 48,* 1–46.

Bundesen, C. (1990). A theory of visual attention. *Psychological Review, 97,* 523–547.

Bunting, M. F., Conway, A. R. A., & Heitz, R. P. (2004). Individual differences in the fan effect and working memory capacity. *Journal of Memory and Language, 51,* 604–622.

Burke, D. M., MacKay, D. G., Worthley, J. S., & Wade, E. (1991). On the tip of the tongue: What causes word finding failures in young and older adults? *Journal of Memory and Language, 30,* 542–579.

Burns, B. D. (2004). Heuristics as beliefs and as behaviors: The adaptiveness of the "hot hand." *Cognitive Psychology, 48,* 295–331.

Burns, B. D., & Corpus, B. (2004). Randomness and inductions from streaks: "Gambler's fallacy" versus "hot hand." *Psychonomic Bulletin & Review, 11,* 179–184.

Burns, D. J. (1996). The bizarre imagery effect and intention to learn. *Psychonomic Bulletin & Review, 3,* 254–257.

Burt, C. D. B. (1992). Reconstruction of the duration of autobiographical events. *Memory & Cognition, 20,* 124–132.

Burt, C. D. B., Kemp, S., & Conway, M. (2001). What happens if you retest autobiographical memory 10 years on? *Memory & Cognition, 29,* 127–136.

Busey, T. A., Tunnicliff, J., Loftus, G. R., & Loftus, E. F. (2000). Accounts of the confidence–accuracy relation in recognition memory. *Psychonomic Bulletin & Review, 7,* 26–48.

Buswell, G. T. (1937). *How adults read.* Chicago: Chicago University Press.

Byrne, R. M. J., & McEleney, A. (2000). Counterfactual thinking about actions and failures to act. *Journal of Experimental Psychology: Learning, Memory, and Cognition, 26,* 1318–1331.

Campbell, J. I. D., & Graham, D. J. (1985). Mental multiplication skill: Structure, process, and acquisition. *Canadian Journal of Psychology, 39,* 338–366.

Cantor, J., & Engle, R. W. (1993). Working-memory capacity as long-term memory activation: An individual differences approach. *Journal of Experimental Psychology: Learning, Memory, and Cognition, 19,* 1101–1114.

Caramazza, A. (1986). On drawing inferences about the structure of normal cognitive systems from the analysis of patterns of impaired performance: The case for single-patient studies. *Brain and Cognition, 5,* 41–66.

Caramazza, A., & McCloskey, M. (1988). The case for single-patient studies. *Cognitive Neuropsychology, 5,* 517–528.

Carli, L. L. (1999). Cognitive reconstruction, hindsight, and reactions to victims and perpetrators. *Personality and Social Psychology Bulletin, 25,* 966–979.

Carlson, B. W. (1990). Anchoring and adjustment in judgments under risk. *Journal of Experimental Psychology: Learning, Memory, and Cognition, 16,* 665–676.

Carlson, R. A., Khoo, B. H., Yaure, R. G., & Schneider, W. (1990). Acquisition of a problem-solving skill: Levels of organization and use of working memory. *Journal of Experimental Psychology: General, 119,* 193–214.

Carpenter, S. K., & Pashler, H. (2007). Testing beyond words: Using tests to enhance visuospatial map learning. *Psychonomic Bulletin & Review, 14,* 474–478.

Carr, T. H., & Dagenbach, D. (1986). Now you see it, now you don't: Relations between semantic activation and awareness. *Brain and Brain Sciences, 9,* 26–27.

Carr, T. H., McCauley, C., Sperber, R. D., & Parmalee, C. M. (1982). Words, pictures, and priming: On semantic activation, conscious identification, and the automaticity of information processing. *Journal of Experimental Psychology: Human Perception and Performance, 8,* 757–777.

Carreiras, M., Gernsbacher, M. A., & Villa, V. (1995). The advantage of first mention in Spanish. *Psychonomic Bulletin & Review, 2,* 124–129.

Carroll, D. W. (1986). *Psychology of language.* Pacific Grove, CA: Brooks/Cole.

Casey, P. J. (1992). A reexamination of the roles of typicality and category dominance in verifying category membership. *Journal of Experimental Psychology: Learning, Memory, and Cognition, 18,* 823–834.

Castel, A. D., McCabe, D. P., Roediger, H. L., & Heitman, J. L. (2007). The dark side of expertise: Domain-specific memory errors. *Psychological Science, 18,* 3–5.

Castronovo, J., & Seron, X. (2007). Semantic numerical representation in blind subjects: The role of vision in the spatial format of the mental number line. *Quarterly Journal of Experimental Psychology, 60,* 101–119.

Catrambone, R. (1996). Generalizing solution procedures learned from examples. *Journal of Experimental Psychology: Learning, Memory, and Cognition, 22,* 1020–1031.

Catrambone, R., Jones, C. M., Jonides, J., & Seifert, C. (1995). Reasoning about curvilinear motion: Using principles or analogy. *Memory & Cognition, 23,* 368–373.

Cave, K. R., & Bichot, N. P. (1999). Visuospatial attention: Beyond a spotlight model. *Psychonomic Bulletin & Review, 6,* 204–223.

Cave, K. R., & Kosslyn, S. M. (1989). Varieties of size-specific visual selection. *Journal of Experimental Psychology: General, 118,* 148–164.

Chaffin, R., & Imreh, G. (2002). Practicing perfection: Piano performance as expert memory. *Psychological Science, 13,* 342–349.

Chambers, K. L., & Zaragoza, M. S. (2001). Intended and unintended effects of explicit warnings on eyewitness suggestibility: Evidence from source identification tests. *Memory & Cognition, 29,* 1120–1129.

Chang, F., Dell, G. S., & Bock, J. K. (2006). Becoming syntactic. *Psychological Review, 113,* 234–272.

Chang, T. M. (1986). Semantic memory: Facts and models. *Psychological Bulletin, 99,* 199–220.

Chase, W. G., & Ericsson, K. A. (1982). Skill and working memory. In G. H. Bower (Ed.), *The psychology of learning and motivation* (Vol. 16, pp. 1–58). New York: Academic Press.

Chase, W. G., & Simon, H. A. (1973). Perception in chess. *Cognitive Psychology, 4,* 55–81.

Chater, N., & Oaksford, M. (1999). The probability heuristics model of syllogistic reasoning. *Cognitive Psychology, 38,* 191–258.

Chen, Y. (2007). Chinese and English speakers think about time differently? Failure of replicating Boroditsky (2001). *Cognition, 104,* 427–436.

Chen, Z., & Mo, L. (2004). Schema induction in problem solving: A multidimensional analysis. *Journal of Experimental Psychology: Learning, Memory, and Cognition, 30,* 583–600.

Chen, Z., Mo, L., & Honomichl, R. (2004). Having the memory of an elephant: Long–term retrieval and the use of analogues in problem solving. *Journal of Experimental Psychology: General, 133,* 415–433.

Cherniak, C. (1984). Prototypicality and deductive reasoning. *Journal of Verbal Learning and Verbal Behavior, 23,* 625–642.

Cherry, E. C. (1953). Some experiments on the recognition of speech, with one and with two ears. *Journal of the Acoustical Society of America, 25,* 975–979.

Cherry, E. C., & Taylor, W. K. (1954). Some further experiments on the recognition of speech with one and two ears. *Journal of the Acoustical Society of America, 26,* 554–559.

Chin-Parker, S., & Ross, B. H. (2004). Diagnosticity and prototypicality in category learning: A comparison of inference learning and classification learning. *Journal of Experimental Psychology: Learning, Memory, and Cognition, 30,* 216–226.

Chomsky, N. (1957). *Syntactic structures.* The Hague: Mouton.

Chomsky, N. (1959). A review of Skinner's Verbal behavior. *Language, 35,* 26–58.

Chomsky, N. (1965). *Aspects of a theory of syntax.* Cambridge, MA: Harvard University Press.

Chomsky, N. (1968). *Language and mind.* New York: Harcourt Brace Jovanovich.

Christianson, K., Hollingworth, A., Halliwell, J. F., & Ferreira, F. (2001). Thematic roles assigned along the garden path linger. *Cognitive Psychology, 42,* 368–407.

Christianson, S. (1989). Flashbulb memories: Special, but not so special. *Memory & Cognition, 17,* 435–443.

Chronicle, E. P., MacGregor, J. N., & Ormerod, T. C. (2004). What makes an insight problem? The roles of heuristics, goal conception, and solution recoding in knowledge-lean problems. *Journal of Experimental Psychology: Learning, Memory, and Cognition, 30,* 14–27.

Clancy, S. A., Schacter, D. L., McNally, R. J., & Pittman, R. K. (2000). False recognition in women reporting recovered memories of sexual abuse. *Psychological Science, 11,* 26–31.

Clapp, F. L. (1924). *The number combinations: Their relative difficulty and frequency of their appearance in textbooks.* Research Bulletin No. 1. Madison, WI: Bureau of Educational Research.

Clark, H. H. (1977). Bridging. In P. N. Johnson-Laird & P. C. Wason (Eds.), *Thinking: Readings in cognitive science* (pp. 411–420). Cambridge, U.K.: Cambridge University Press.

Clark, H. H. (1979). Responding to indirect speech acts. *Cognitive Psychology, 11,* 430–477.

Clark, H. H. (1992). *Arenas of language use.* Chicago: University of Chicago Press.

Clark, H. H. (1994). Discourse in production. In M. A. Gernsbacher (Ed.), *Handbook of psycholinguistics* (pp. 985–1021). San Diego: Academic Press.

Clark, H. H., & Clark, E. V. (1977). *Psychology and language.* New York: Harcourt Brace Jovanovich.

Clark, H. H., & Krych, M. A. (2004). Speaking while monitoring addressees for understanding. *Journal of Memory and Language, 50,* 62–81.

Clark, H. H., & Wasow, T. (1998). Repeating words in spontaneous speech. *Cognitive Psychology, 37,* 201–242.

Claus, B., & Kelter, S. (2006). Comprehending narratives containing flashbacks: Evidence for temporally organized representations. *Journal of Experimental Psychology: Learning, Memory, and Cognition, 32,* 1031–1044.

Clifton, C., Jr., Carlson, K., & Frazier, L. (2006). Tracking the what and why of speakers' choices: Prosodic boundaries and the length of constituents. *Psychonomic Bulletin & Review, 13,* 854–861.

Clifton, C., & Frazier, L. (2004). Should given information come before new? Yes and no. *Memory & Cognition, 32,* 886–895.

Clifton, C., Jr., Traxler, M. J., Mohamed, M. T., Williams, R. S., Morris, R. K., & Rayner, K. (2003). The use of thematic role information in parsing: Syntactic processing autonomy revisited. *Journal of Memory and Language, 49,* 317–334.

Cokely, E. T., Kelley, C. M., & Gilchrist, A. L. (2006). Sources of individual differences in working memory capacity: Contributions of strategy ro capacity. *Psychonomic Bulletin & Review, 13,* 991–997.

Colflesh, G. J. H., & Conway, A. R. A. (2007). Individual differences in working memory capacity and divided attention in dichotic listening. *Psychonomic Bulletin & Review, 14,* 699–703.

Colle, H. A., & Welsh, A. (1976). Acoustic masking in primary memory. *Journal of Verbal Learning and Verbal Behavior, 15,* 17–32.

Collins, A., Warnock, E. H., Aiello, N., & Miller, M. L. (1975). Reasoning from incomplete knowledge. In D. Bobrow & A. Collins (Eds.), *Representation and understanding: Studies in cognitive science* (pp. 383–415). New York: Academic Press.

Collins, A. M., & Loftus, E. F. (1975). A spreading-activation theory of semantic processing. *Psychological Review, 82,* 407–428.

Collins, A. M., & Quillian, M. R. (1969). Retrieval time from semantic memory. *Journal of Verbal Learning and Verbal Behavior, 8,* 240–247.

Collins, A. M., & Quillian, M. R. (1970). Does category size affect categorization time? *Journal of Verbal Learning and Verbal Behavior, 9,* 432–438.

Collins, A. M., & Quillian, M. R. (1972). How to make a language user. In E. Tulving & W. Donaldson (Eds.), *Organization of memory* (pp. 309–351). New York: Academic Press.

Collins, K. A., Pillemer, D. B., Ivcevic, Z., & Gooze, R. A. (2007). Cultural scripts guide recall of intensely positive life events. *Memory & Cognition, 35,* 651–659.

Coltheart, M. (1973). Readings in cognitive psychology. Toronto: Holt, Rinehart & Winston of Canada.

Coltheart, M. (1983). Ecological necessity of iconic memory. *The Behavioral and Brain Sciences, 6,* 17–18.

Conrad, R. (1960). Very brief delay of immediate recall. *Quarterly Journal of Experimental Psychology, 12,* 45–47.

Conrad, R. & Hull, A. (1964). Information, acoustic confusion, and memory span. *British Journal of Psychology, 55,* 75–84.

Conway, A. R. A., Cowan, N., & Bunting, M. F. (2001). The cocktail party phenomenon revisited: The importance of working memory capacity. *Psychonomic Bulletin & Review, 8,* 331–335.

Conway, M. A., Anderson, S. J., Larsen, S. F., Donnelly, C. M., McDaniel, M. A., McClelland, A. G. R., Rawles, R. E., & Logie, R. H. (1994). The formation of flashbulb memories. *Memory & Cognition, 22,* 326–343.

Conway, M. A., Cohen, G., & Stanhope, N. (1991). On the very long-term retention of knowledge acquired through formal education: Twelve years of cognitive psychology. *Journal of Experimental Psychology: General, 120,* 395–409.

Conway, M. A., & Pleydell-Pearce, C. W. (2000). The construction of autobiographical memories in the self-memory system. *Psychological Review, 107,* 261–288.

Cook, A. E., & Myers, J. L. (2004). Processing discourse roles in scripted narratives: The influences of context and world knowledge. *Journal of Memory and Language, 50,* 268–288.

Cook, M. (1977). Gaze and mutual gaze in social encounters. *American Scientist, 65,* 328–333.

Cooke, N. J., & Breedin, S. D. (1994). Constructing naive theories of motion on the fly. *Memory & Cognition, 22,* 474–493.

Cooper, E. H., & Pantle, A. J. (1967). The total-time hypothesis in verbal learning. *Psychological Bulletin, 68,* 221–234.

Cooper, L. A., & Shepard, R. N. (1973). Chronometric studies of the rotation of mental images. In W. G. Chase (Ed.), *Visual information processing* (pp. 75–176). New York: Academic Press.

Copeland, D. E., & Radvansky, G. A. (2001). Phonological similarity in working memory. *Memory & Cognition, 29,* 774–776.

Copeland, D. E., & Radvansky, G. A. (2004). Working memory and syllogistic reasoning. *Quarterly Journal of Experimental Psychology, 57A,* 1437–1457.

Copeland, D. E., & Radvansky, G. A. (2004). Working memory span and situation model processing. *American Journal of Psychology, 117,* 191–213.

Copeland, D. E., Radvansky, G. A., & Goodwin, K. A. (2009). A novel study: Forgetting curves and the reminiscence bump. *Memory, 17,* 323–336.

Corballis, M.C. (1989). Laterality and human evolution. *Psychological Review, 96,* 492–505.

Corballis, M. C. (2004). The origins of modernity: Was autonomous speech a critical factor? *Psychological Review, 111,* 543–552.

Corder, M. (2004). Crippled but not crashed neural networks can help pilots land damaged planes. *Scientific American, 291,* 94–96.

Coren, S., & Ward, L. M. (1989). *Sensation and perception* (3rd ed.). Fort Worth, TX: Harcourt.

Coughlan, A. K., & Warrington, E. K. (1978). Word comprehension and word retrieval in patients with localised cerebral lesions. *Brain, 101,* 163–185.

Coulson, S., Federmeier, K. D., Van Petten, C., & Kutas, M. (2005). Right hemisphere sensitivity to word- and sentence-level context: Evidence from event-related brain potentials. *Journal of Experimental Psychology: Learning, Memory, and Cognition, 31,* 127–147.

Cowan, N. (1995). *Attention and memory: An integrated framework.* New York: Oxford University Press.

Cowan, N., Baddeley, A. D., Elliot, E. M., & Norris, J. (2003). List composition and the word length effect in immediate recall: A comparison of localist and globalist assumptions. *Psychonomic Bulletin & Review, 10,* 74–79.

Cowan, N., & Morey, C. C. (2007). How can dual-task working memory retention limits be investigated? *Psychological Science, 18,* 686–688.

Cowan, N., & Stadler, M. A. (1996). Estimating unconscious processes: Implications of a general class of models. *Journal of Experimental Psychology: General, 125,* 195–200.

Cowan, N., Wood, N. L., Wood, P. K., Keller, T. A., Nugent, L. D., & Keller, C. V. (1998). Two separate verbal processing rates contributing to short-term memory span. *Journal of Experimental Psychology: General, 127,* 141–160.

Craik, F. I. M., Govoni, R., Naveh-Benjamin, M., & Anderson, N. D. (1996). The effects of divided attention on encoding and retrieval processes in human memory. *Journal of Experimental Psychology: General, 125,* 181–194.

Craik, F. I. M., & Lockhart, R. S. (1972). Levels of processing: A framework for memory research. *Journal of Verbal Learning and Verbal Behavior, 11,* 671–684.

Craik, F. I. M., & Tulving, E. (1975). Depth of processing and the retention of words in episodic memory. *Journal of Experimental Psychology, 104,* 268–294.

Craik, F. I. M., & Watkins, M. J. (1973). The role of rehearsal in short-term memory. *Journal of Verbal Learning and Verbal Behavior, 12,* 599–607.

Cree, G. S., & McRae, K. (2003). Analyzing the factors underlying the structure and computation of the meaning of chipmunk, cherry, chisel, cheese, and cello (and many other such concrete nouns). *Journal of Experimental Psychology: General, 132,* 163–201.

Crick, F. H. C., & Asanuma, C. (1986). Certain aspects of the anatomy and physiology of the cerebral cortex. In D. E. Rumelhart, J. L. McClelland, & PDP Research Group (Eds.), *Parallel distributed processing* (Vol. 2, pp. 333–371). Cambridge, MA: MIT Press.

Crosby, J. R., Monin, B., & Richardson, D. (2008). Where do we look during potentially offensive behavior? *Psychological Science, 19,* 226–228.

Crovitz, H. F., & Shiffman, H. (1974). Frequency of episodic memories as a function of their age. *Bulletin of the Psychonomic Society, 4,* 517–518.

Crowder, R. G. (1970). The role of one's own voice in immediate memory. *Cognitive Psychology, 1,* 157–178.

Crowder, R. G. (1972). Visual and auditory memory. In J. F. Kavanaugh & I. G. Mattingly (Eds.), *Language by ear and by eye: The relationships between speech and reading* (pp. 251–276). Cambridge, MA: MIT Press.

Crowder, R. G., & Morton, J. (1969). Precategorical acoustic storage (PAS). *Perception and Psychophysics, 5,* 365–373.

Cummins, D. D., Lubart, T., Alksnis, O., & Rist, R. (1991). Conditional reasoning and causation. *Memory & Cognition, 19,* 274–282.

Curran, T. (2000). Brain potentials of recollection and familiarity. *Memory & Cognition, 28,* 923–938.

Damasio, H., & Damasio, A. R. (1997). The lesion method in behavioral neurology and neuropsychology. In T. E. Feinberg & M. J. Farah (Eds.), *Behavioral neurology and neuropsychology* (pp. 69–82). New York: McGraw-Hill.

Daneman, M., & Carpenter, P. A. (1980). Individual differences in working memory and reading. *Journal of Verbal Learning and Verbal Behavior, 19,* 450–466.

Daneman, M., & Merikle, P. M. (1996). Working memory and language comprehension: A meta-analysis. *Psychonomic Bulletin & Review, 3,* 422–433.

Danziger, S., Kingstone, A., & Rafal, R. D. (1998). Orienting to extinguished signals in hemispatial neglect. *Psychological Science, 9,* 119–123.

Darwin, C. J., Turvey, M. T., & Crowder, R. G. (1972). An auditory analogue of the Sperling partial report procedure: Evidence for brief auditory storage. *Cognitive Psychology, 3,* 255–267.

Davelaar, E. J., Goshen-Gottstein, Y., Ashkenazi, A., Haarmann, H. J., & Usher, M. (2005). The demise of short-term memory revisited: Empirical and computational investigations of recency effects. *Psychological Review, 112,* 3–42.

Davoli, C. C., Suszko, J. W., & Abrams, R. A. (2007). New objects can capture attention without a unique luminance transient. *Psychonomic Bulletin & Review, 14,* 338–343.

Day, S. B., & Gentner, D. (2007). Nonintentional analogical inference in text comprehension. *Memory & Cognition, 35,* 39–49.

Deese, J. (1959). On the prediction of occurrence of particular verbal intrusions in immediate recall. *Journal of Experimental Psychology, 58,* 17–22.

Dehaene, S., Bossini, S., & Giraux, P. (1993). The mental representation of parity and number magnitude. *Journal of Experimental Psychology: General, 122,* 371–396.

Delany, P. F., Ericsson, K. A., & Knowles, M. E. (2004). Immediate and sustained effects of planning in a problem-solving task. *Journal of Experimental Psychology: Learning, Memory, and Cognition, 30,* 1219–1234.

Dell, G. S. (1986). A spreading-activation theory of retrieval in sentence production. *Psychological Review, 93,* 283–321.

Dell, G. S., & Newman, J. E. (1980). Detecting phonemes in fluent speech. *Journal of Verbal Learning and Verbal Behavior, 20,* 611–629.

Dell'acqua, R., & Job, R. (1998). Is object recognition automatic? *Psychonomic Bulletin & Review, 5,* 496–503.

DePaulo, B. M., & Bonvillian, J. D. (1978). The effect on language development of the special characteristics of speech addressed to children. *Journal of Psycholinguistic Research, 7,* 189–211.

Desjardins, T., & Scoboria, A. (2007). "You and your best friend Suzy put Slime in Ms. Smollett's desk": Producing false memories with self-relevant details. *Psychonomic Bulletin & Review, 14,* 1090–1095.

Desmarais, G., Dixon, M. J., & Roy, E. A. (2007). A role for action knowledge in visual object identification. *Memory & Cognition, 35,* 1712–1723.

Deutsch, G., Bourbon, T., Papanicolaou, A. C., & Eisenberg, H. M. (1988). Visuospatial tasks compared via activation of regional cerebral blood flow. *Neuropsychologia, 26,* 445–452.

Deutsch, J. A., & Deutsch, D. (1963). Attention: Some theoretical considerations. *Psychological Review, 70,* 80–90.

de Vega, M., Robertson, D. A., Glenberg, A. M., Kaschak, M. P., & Rinck, M. (2004). On doing two things at once: Temporal constraints on action in language comprehension. *Memory & Cognition, 32,* 1033–1043

deWinstanley, P. A., & Bjork, E. L. (2004). Processing strategies and the generation effect: Implications for making a better reader. *Memory & Cognition, 32,* 945–955.

Dewsbury, D. A. (2000). Comparative cognition in the 1930s. *Psychonomic Bulletin & Review, 7,* 267–283.

Diamond, A., & Gilbert, J. (1989). Development as progressive inhibitory control of action: Retrieval of a contiguous object. *Cognitive Development, 4,* 223–249.

Ditman, T., & Kuperberg, G. R. (2005). A source-monitoring account of auditory verbal hallucinations in patients with schizophrenia. *Harvard Review of Psychiatry, 13,* 280–299.

Dodd, M. D., & MacLeod, C. M. (2004). False recognition without intentional learning. *Psychonomic Bulletin & Review, 11,* 137–142.

Dodson, C. S., & Schacter, D. L. (2002). When false recognition meets metacognition: The distinctiveness heuristic. *Journal of Memory and Language, 46,* 782–803.

Dolcos, F., Labar, K. S., & Cabeza, R. (2005). Remembering one year later: Role of the amygdala and the medial temporal lobe memory system in retrieving emotional memories. *Proceedings of the National Academy of Sciences, 102,* 2626–2631.

Donchin, E. (1981). Surprise!...Surprise? *Psychophysiology, 18,* 493–513.

Donders, F. C. (1969). *Over de snelheid van psychische processen [Speed of Mental Processes].* Onderzoekingen gedann in het Psysiologish Laboratorium der Utrechtsche Hoogeschool (W. G. Koster, Trans.). In W. G. Koster (Ed.), Attention and performance II. *Acta Psychologica, 30,* 412–431. (Original work published 1868)

Donley, R. D., & Ashcraft, M. H. (1992). The methodology of testing naive beliefs in the physics classroom. *Memory & Cognition, 20,* 381–391.

Dooling, D., & Lachman, R. (1971). Effects of comprehension on retention of prose. *Journal of Experimental Psychology, 88,* 216–222.

Dooling, D. J., & Christiaansen, R. E. (1977). Episodic and semantic aspects of memory for prose. *Journal of Experimental Psychology: Human Learning and Memory, 3,* 428–436.

Dosher, B. A., & Ma, J-J. (1998). Output loss or rehearsal loop? Output-time versus pronunciation-time limits in immediate recall for forgetting-matched materials. *Journal of Experimental Psychology: Learning, Memory, and Cognition, 24,* 316–335.

Drachman, D. A. (1978). Central cholinergic system and memory. In M. A. Lipton, A. D. Mascio, & K. F. Killam (Eds.), *Psychopharmacology: A generation of process.* New York: Raven.

Draine, S. C., & Greenwald, A. G. (1998). Replicable unconscious semantic priming. *Journal of Experimental Psychology: General, 127,* 286–303.

Drosopoulos, S., Schulze, C., Fischer, S., & Born, J. (2007). Sleep's function in the spontaneous recovery and consolidation of memories. *Journal of Experimental Psychology: General, 136,* 169–183.

Duffy, S. A., & Kier, J. A. (2004). Violating stereotypes: Eye movements and comprehension processes when text conflicts with world knowledge. *Memory & Cognition, 32,* 551–559.

Dunbar, K., & MacLeod, C. M. (1984). A horse race of a different color: Stroop interference patterns with transformed words. *Journal of Experimental Psychology: Human Perception and Performance, 10,* 622–639.

Duncan, E. M., & McFarland, C. E., Jr. (1980). Isolating the effects of symbolic distance and semantic congruity in comparative judgments: An additive-factors analysis. *Memory & Cognition, 8,* 612–622.

Duncan, J., Bundesen, C., Olson, A., Humphreys, G., Chavda, S., & Shibuya, H. (1999). Systematic analysis of deficits in visual attention. *Journal of Experimental Psychology: General, 128,* 450–478.

Duncan, J., & Humphreys, G. (1989). Visual search and stimulus similarity. *Psychological Review, 96,* 433–458.

Duncan, S. (1972). Some signals and rules for taking speaking turns in conversations. *Journal of Personality and Social Psychology, 23,* 283–292.

Duncker, K. (1945). On problem solving. *Psychological Monographs, 58* (Whole no. 270).

Dunlosky, J., & Hertzog, C. (2001). Measuring strategy production during associative learning: The relative utility of concurrent versus retrospective reports. *Memory & Cognition, 29,* 247–253.

Dunlosky, J., & Lipko, C. (2007). Metacomprehension: A brief history and how to improve its accuracy. *Current Directions in Psychological Science, 16,* 228–232.

Dunlosky, J., & Nelson, T. O. (1994). Does the sensitivity of judgments of learning (JOLs) to the effects of various activities depend on when the JOLs occur? *Journal of Memory and Language, 33,* 545–565.

Dyer, F. C. (2002). When it pays to waggle. *Nature, 419,* 885–886.

Eakin, D. K., Schreiber, T. A., & Sergent-Marshall, S. (2003). Misinformation effects in eyewitness memory: The presence and absence of memory impairment as a function of warning and misinformation accessibility. *Journal of Experimental Psychology: Learning, Memory, and Cognition, 29,* 813–825.

Ebbinghaus, H. (1885/1913). *Memory: A contribution to experimental psychology* (H. A. Ruger & C. E. Bussenius, Trans.). New York: Columbia University, Teacher's College. (Reprinted 1964, New York: Dover)

Ebbinghaus, H. (1908). *Abriss der Psychologie [Survey of Psychology].* Leipzig: Veit & Comp. (Also cited as 1910)

Edridge-Green, F. W. (1900). *Memory and its cultivation.* New York: Appleton & Co.

Edwards, D., & Potter, J. (1993). Language and causation: A discursive action model of description and attribution. *Psychological Review, 100,* 23–41.

Egan, P., Carterette, E. C., & Thwing, E. J. (1954). Some factors affecting multichannel listening. *Journal of the Acoustic Society of America, 26,* 774–782.

Eichenbaum, H., & Fortin, N. (2003). Episodic memory and the hippocampus: It's about time. *Current Directions in Psychological Science, 12,* 53–57.

Eimas, P. D. (1975). Speech perception in early infancy. In L. B. Cohen & P. Salapatek (Eds.), *Infant perception: From sensation to cognition: Vol. II. Perception of space, speech, and sound* (pp. 193–231). New York: Academic Press.

Einstein, G. O., & McDaniel, M. A. (1987). Distinctiveness and the mnemonic benefits of bizarre imagery. In M. A. McDaniel & M. Pressley (Eds.), *Imagery and related mnemonic processes: Theories, individual differences and applications* (pp. 78–102). New York: Springer-Verlag.

Einstein, G. O., & McDaniel, M. A. (1990). Normal aging and prospective memory. *Journal of Experimental Psychology: Learning, Memory, and Cognition, 16,* 717–726.

Einstein, G. O., & McDaniel, M. A. (2005). Prospective memory: Multiple retrieval processes. *Current Directions, 14,* 286–290.

Ellis, H. D. (1983). The role of the right hemisphere in face perception. In A. W. Young (Ed.), *Functions of the right cerebral hemisphere* (pp. 33–64). New York: Academic Press.

Ellis, N. C., & Hennelly, R. A. (1980). A bilingual word-length effect: Implications for intelligence testing and the relative ease of mental calculation in Welsh and English. *British Journal of Psychology, 71,* 43–52.

Emery, N. J. (2000). The eyes have it: The neuroethology, function and evolution of social gaze. *Neuroscience and Biobehavioral Review, 24,* 581–604.

Engelhardt, P. E., Bailey, K. G. D., & Ferreira, F. (2006). Do speakers and listeners observe the Gricean maxim of quantity? *Journal of Memory and Language, 54,* 554–573.

Engelkamp, J., & Dehn, D. M. (2000). Item and order information in subject-performed tasks and experimenter-performed tasks. *Journal of Experimental Psychology: Learning, Memory, and Cognition, 26,* 671–682.

Engle, R. W. (2001). What is working memory capacity? In H. L. Roediger, J. S. Nairne, I. Neath, & A. M. Suprenant (Eds.), *The nature of remembering: Essays in honor of Robert G. Crowder* (pp. 297–314). Washington, D.C.: American Psychological Association Press.

Engle, R. W. (2002). Working memory capacity as executive attention. *Current Directions in Psychological Science, 11,* 19–23.

Erdfelder, E., & Buchner, A. (1998). Decomposing the hindsight bias: A multinomial processing tree model for separating recollection and reconstruction in hindsight. *Journal of Experimental Psychology: Learning, Memory, and Cognition, 24,* 387–414.

Erickson, T. D., & Mattson, M. E. (1981). From words to meanings: A semantic illusion. *Journal of Verbal Learning and Verbal Behavior, 20,* 540–551.

Ericsson, K. A., & Charness, N. (1994). Expert performance: Its structure and acquisition. *American Psychologist, 49,* 725–747.

Ericsson, K. A., Delaney, P. F., Weaver, G., & Mahadevan, R. (2004). Uncovering the structure of a memorist's superior "basic" memory capacity. *Cognitive Psychology, 49,* 191–237.

Ericsson, K. A., Krampe, R. T., & Tesch-Römer, C. (1993). The role of deliberate practice in the acquisition of expert performance. *Psychological Review, 100,* 363–406.

Ericsson, K. A., & Simon, H. A. (1980). Verbal reports as data. *Psychological Review, 87,* 215–251.

Ericsson, K. A., & Simon, H. A. (1993). *Protocol analysis: Verbal reports as data* (Rev. ed.). Cambridge, MA: MIT Press.

Eriksen, C. W., & Johnson, H. J. (1964). Storage and decay characteristics of nonattended auditory stimuli. *Journal of Experimental Psychology, 68*, 28–36.

Ernst, G. W., & Newell, A. (1969). *GPS: A case study in generality and problem solving*. New York: Academic Press.

Estes, Z., Verges, M., & Barsalou, L. W. (2008). Head up, foot down: object words orient attention to the objects' typical location. *Psychological Science, 19*, 93–97.

Evans, J. St. B. T., Handley, S. J., Harper, C. N. J., & Johnson-Laird, P. H. (1999). Reasoning about necessity and possibility: A test of the mental model theory of deduction. *Journal of Experimental Psychology: Learning, Memory, and Cognition, 25*, 1495–1513.

Evans, J. St. B. T., Handley, S. J., Over, D. E., & Perham, N. (2002). Background beliefs in Bayesian inference. *Memory & Cognition, 30*, 179–190.

Farah, M. J., & McClelland, J. L. (1991). A computational model of semantic memory impairment: Modality specificity and emergent category specificity. *Journal of Experimental Psychology: General, 120*, 339–357.

Faroqi-Shah, Y., & Thompson, C. K. (2007). Verb inflections in agrammatic aphasia: Encoding of tense features. *Journal of Memory and Language, 56*, 129–151.

Fechner, G. (1860). *Elements of psychophysics* (English ed. of Vol. 1; H. E. Adler, Trans., D. H. Howes & E. G. Boring, Eds.). New York: Holt, Rinehart & Winston, 1966.

Fedorenko, E., Gibson, E., & Rohde, D. (2006). The nature of working memory capacity in sentence comprehension: Evidence against domain-specific working memory resources. *Journal of Memory and Language, 54*, 541–553.

Feinberg, T. E., & Farah, M. J. (1997). The development of modern behavioral neurology and neuropsychology. In T. E. Feinberg & M. J. Farah (Eds.), *Behavioral neurology and neuropsychology* (pp. 3–24). New York: McGraw-Hill.

Feldman, D. (1992). *When did wild poodles roam the earth? An Imponderables™ book*. New York: HarperCollins.

Feldman, J. (2003). The simplicity principle in human concept learning. *Current Directions in Psychological Science, 12*, 227–232.

Feng, J., Spence, I., & Pratt, J. (2007). Playing an action video game reduces gender differences in spatial cognition. *Psychological Science, 18*, 850–855.

Fenske, M. J., & Raymond, J. E. (2006). Affective influences of selective attention. *Current Directions in Psychological Science, 15*, 312–316.

Ferreira, F. (1994). Choice of passive voice is affected by verb type and animacy. *Journal of Memory and Language, 33*, 715–736.

Ferreira, F. (2003). The misinterpretation of noncanonical sentences. *Cognitive Psychology, 47*, 164–203.

Ferreira, F., Henderson, J. M., Anes, M. D., Weeks, P. A., Jr., & McFarlane, D. K. (1996). Effects of lexical frequency and syntactic complexity in spoken-language comprehension: Evidence from the auditory moving-window technique. *Journal of Experimental Psychology: Learning, Memory, and Cognition, 22*, 324–335.

Ferreira, F., & Swets, B. (2002). How incremental is language production? Evidence from the production of utterances requiring the computation of arithmetic sums. *Journal of Memory and Language, 46*, 57–84.

Ferreira, V. S. (1996). Is it better to give than to donate? Syntactic flexibility in language production. *Journal of Memory and Language, 35*, 724–755.

Ferreira, V. S., & Dell, G. S. (2000). Effect of ambiguity and lexical availability on syntactic and lexical production. *Cognitive Psychology, 40*, 296–340.

Ferreira, V. S., & Firato, C. E. (2002). Proactive interference effects on sentence production. *Psychonomic Bulletin & Review, 9*, 795–800.

Ferreira, V. S., & Humphreys, K. R. (2001). Syntactic influences on lexical and morphological processing in language production. *Journal of Memory and Language, 44*, 52–80.

Fillenbaum, S. (1974). Pragmatic normalization: Further results for some conjunctive and disjunctive sentences. *Journal of Experimental Psychology, 102*, 574–578.

Fillmore, C. J. (1968). Toward a modern theory of case. In D. A. Reibel & S. A. Schane (Eds.), *Modern studies in English* (pp. 361–375). Englewood Cliffs, NJ: Prentice Hall.

Finke, R. A., & Freyd, J. J. (1985). Transformations of visual memory induced by implied motions of pattern elements. *Journal of Experimental Psychology: Learning, Memory, and Cognition, 11*, 780–794.

Finkenhauer, C., Luminet, O., Gisle, L., El-ahmadi, A., van der Linden, M., & Philipott, P. (1998). Flashbulb memories and the underlying mechanisms of their formation: Toward an emotional-integrative model. *Memory & Cognition, 26*, 516–531.

Fischer, M. H. (2008). Finger counting habits modulate spatial-numerical associations. *Cortex, 44*, 386–392.

Fischhoff, B. (1975). Hindsight does not equal foresight: The effect of outcome knowledge on judgment under uncertainty. *Journal of Experimental Psychology: Human Perception and Performance, 1*, 288–299.

Fischhoff, B., & Bar-Hillel, M. (1984). Diagnosticity and the base-rate effect. *Memory & Cognition, 12*, 402–410.

Flavell, J. H. (1963). *The developmental psychology of Jean Piaget*. New York: Van Nostrand.

Fleck, J. I., & Weisberg, R. W. (2004). The use of verbal protocols as data: An analysis of insight in the candle problem. *Memory & Cognition, 32*, 990–1006.

Fletcher, C. R., & Bloom, C. P. (1988). Causal reasoning in the comprehension of simple narrative texts. *Journal of Memory and Language, 27*, 235–244.

Fodor, J. A. (1983). *The modularity of mind*. Cambridge, MA: MIT Press.

Fodor, J. A., & Garrett, M. (1966). Some reflections on competence and performance. In J. Lyons & R. J. Wales (Eds.), *Psycholinguistic papers* (pp. 135–154). Edinburgh, U.K.: Edinburgh University Press.

Fong, G. T., & Nisbett, R. E. (1991). Immediate and delayed transfer of training effects in statistical reasoning. *Journal of Experimental Psychology: General, 120*, 34–45.

Forgus, R. H., & Melamed, L. E. (1976). *Perception: A cognitive-stage approach*. New York: McGraw-Hill.

Forsyth, D. K., & Burt, C. D. B. (2008). Allocating time to future tasks: The effect of task segmentation on planning fallacy bias. *Memory & Cognition, 36,* 791–798.

Foss, D. J., & Hakes, D. T. (1978). *Psycholinguistics: An introduction to the psychology of language.* Englewood Cliffs, NJ: Prentice Hall.

Franconeri, S.L., & Simons, D. J. (2003). Moving and looming stimuli capture attention. *Perception & Psychophysics, 65,* 999–1010.

Frazier, L., & Rayner, K. (1982). Making and correcting errors during sentence comprehension: Eye movements in the analysis of structurally ambiguous sentences. *Cognitive Psychology, 14,* 178–210.

Frazier, L., & Rayner, K. (1990). Taking on semantic commitments: Processing multiple meanings vs. multiple senses. *Journal of Memory and Language, 29,* 181–200.

Freedman, J. L., & Loftus, E. F. (1971). Retrieval of words from long-term memory. *Journal of Verbal Learning and Verbal Behavior, 10,* 107–115.

Freeman, J. E., & Ellis, J. A. (2003). The representation of delayed intentions: A prospective subject-performed task? *Journal of Experimental Psychology: Learning, Memory, and Cognition, 29,* 976–992.

Freud, S. (1899/1938). Childhood and concealing memories. In A. A. Brill (Ed.), *The Basic Writings of Sigmund Freud.* New York: The Modern Library.

Freud, S. (1953/1905). Three essays on the theory of sexuality. In J. Strachey (Ed.), *The standard edition of the complete psychological works of Sigmund Freud* (Vol. 7, pp. 135–423). London: Hogarth. (Original work published 1905).

Freyd, J. J., & Finke, R. A. (1984). Representational momentum. *Bulletin of the Psychonomic Society, 23,* 443–446.

Freyd, J. J., & Jones, K. T. (1994). Representational momentum for a spiral path. *Journal of Experimental Psychology: Learning, Memory, and Cognition, 20,* 968–976.

Friederici, A. D., Hahne, A., & Mecklinger, A. (1996). Temporal structure of syntactic parsing: Early and late event-related brain potential effects. *Journal of Experimental Psychology: Learning, Memory, and Cognition, 22,* 1219–1248.

Friedman, A. (1978). Memorial comparisons without the "mind's eye." *Journal of Verbal Learning and Verbal Behavior, 17,* 427–444.

Friedman, A., & Brown, N. R. (2000). Reasoning about geography. *Journal of Experimental Psychology: General, 129,* 193–219.

Friedman, A., Brown, N. R., & McGaffey, A. P. (2002). A basis for bias in geographical judgments. *Psychonomic Bulletin & Review, 9,* 151–159.

Friedman, A., Kerkman, D. D., & Brown, N. R. (2002). Spatial location judgments: A cross-national comparison of estimation bias in subjective North American geography. *Psychonomic Bulletin & Review, 9,* 615–623.

Friedman, A., & Montello, D. R. (2006). Global-scale location and distance estimates: Common representations and strategies in absolute and relative judgments. *Journal of Experimental Psychology: Learning, Memory, and Cognition, 32,* 333–346.

Friedman, A., & Polson, M. C. (1981). Hemispheres as independent resource systems: Limited-capacity processing and cerebral specialization. *Journal of Experimental Psychology: Human Perception and Performance, 7,* 1031–1058.

Friedman, N. P., Miyake, A., Young, S. E., DeFries, J. C., Corley, R. P., & Hewitt, J. K. (2008). Individual differences in executive functions are almost entirely genetic in origin. *Journal of Experimental Psychology: General, 137,* 201–225.

Friedrich, F. J., Henik, A., & Tzelgov, J. (1991). Automatic processes in lexical access and spreading activation. *Journal of Experimental Psychology: Human Perception and Performance, 17,* 792–806.

Frisson, S., & Pickering, M. J. (1999). The processing of metonymy: Evidence from eye movements. *Journal of Experimental Psychology: Learning, Memory, and Cognition, 25,* 1366–1383.

Fromkin, V. A. (1971). The non-anomalous nature of anomalous utterances. *Language, 47,* 27–52.

Fromkin, V. A., & Rodman, R. (1974). *An introduction to language.* New York: Holt, Rinehart & Winston.

Frost, P. (2000). The quality of false memory over time: Is memory for misinformation "remembered" or "known"? *Psychonomic Bulletin & Review, 7,* 531–536.

Galanter, E. (1962). Contemporary psychophysics. In R. Brown, E. Galanter, E. H. Hess, & G. Mandler (Eds.), *New directions in psychology* (Vol. 1, pp. 87–156). New York: Holt, Rinehart & Winston.

Galantucci, B., Fowler, C. A., & Turvey, M. T. (2006). The motor theory of speech perception reviewed. *Psychonomic Bulletin & Review, 13,* 361–377.

Galton, F. (1879). Psychometric experiments. *Brain: A Journal of Neurology, II,* 149–162.

Garcia, J., McGowan, B. K., & Green, K. F. (1972). Constraints on conditioning. In M. E. P. Seligman & J. L. Hager (Eds.), *Biological boundaries of learning.* New York: Appleton-Century-Crofts.

Garcia-Retamero, R., Wallin, A., & Dieckmann, A. (2007). Does causal knowledge help us be faster and more frugal in our decisions? *Memory & Cognition, 35,* 1399–1409.

Gardner, H. (1985). *The mind's new science: A history of the cognitive revolution.* New York: Basic Books.

Garnham, A., Oakhill, J., & Reynolds, D. (2002). Are inferences from stereotyped role names to characters' gender made elaboratively? *Memory & Cognition, 30,* 439–446.

Garrett, M. F. (1975). The analysis of sentence production. In G. H. Bower (Ed.), *The psychology of learning and memory* (Vol. 9, pp. 133–177). New York: Academic Press.

Garry, M., & Gerrie, M. P. (2005). When photographs create false memories. *Current Directions in Psychological Science, 14,* 321–325.

Garry, M., Manning, C. G., Loftus, E. F., & Sherman, S. J. (1996). Imagination inflation: Imagining a childhood event inflates confidence that it occurred. *Psychonomic Bulletin & Review, 3,* 208–214.

Garry, M., & Polaschek, D. L. L. (2000). Imagination and Memory. *Current Directions in Psychological Science, 9,* 6–10.

Gates, A. I. (1917). Recitation as a factor in memorizing. *Archives of Psychology, 40,* 104.

Gazzaniga, M. S. (1995). Principles of human brain organization derived from split-brain studies. *Neuron, 14,* 217–228.

Gazzaniga, M. S., Ivry, R. B., & Mangun, G. R. (1998). *Cognitive neuroscience: The biology of the mind.* New York: W. W. Norton.

Gazzaniga, M. S., & Sperry, R. W. (1967). Language after section of the cerebral commissures. *Brain, 90,* 131–148.

Geary, D. C. (1992). Evolution of human cognition: Potential relationship to the ontogenetic development of behavior and cognition. *Evolution and Cognition, 1,* 93–100.

Geary, D. C. (1994). *Children's mathematical development: Research and practical applications.* Washington, DC: American Psychological Association.

Gennari, S. P. (2004). Temporal references and temporal relations in sentence comprehension. *Journal of Experimental Psychology: Learning, Memory, and Cognition, 30,* 877–890.

Gentner, D., & Collins, A. (1981). Studies of inference from lack of knowledge. *Memory & Cognition, 9,* 434–443.

Gentner, D., & Markman, A. B. (1997). Structure mapping in analogy and similarity. *American Psychologist, 52,* 45–56.

Gernsbacher, M. A. (1990). *Language comprehension as structure building.* Hillsdale, NJ: Erlbaum.

Gernsbacher, M. A. (1997). Two decades of structure building. *Discourse Processes, 23,* 265–304.

Gernsbacher, M. A., & Faust, M. E. (1991). The mechanism of suppression: A component of general comprehension skill. *Journal of Experimental Psychology: Learning, Memory, & Cognition, 17,* 245–262.

Gernsbacher, M. A., & Hargreaves, D. (1988). Accessing sentence participants: The advantage of first mention. *Journal of Memory and Language, 27,* 699–717.

Gernsbacher, M. A., Hargreaves, D., & Beeman, M. (1989). Building and accessing clausal representations: The advantage of first mention versus the advantage of clause recency. *Journal of Memory and Language, 28,* 735–755.

Gernsbacher, M. A., Keysar, B., Robertson, R. R. W., & Werner, N. K. (2001). The role of suppression and enhancement in understanding metaphors. *Journal of Memory and Language, 45,* 433–450.

Gershkoff-Stowe, L., & Goldin-Medow, S. (2002). Is there a natural order for expressing semantic relations? *Cognitive Psychology, 45,* 375–412.

Geschwind, N. (1967). The varieties of naming errors. *Cortex, 3,* 97–112.

Geschwind, N. (1970). The organisation of language and the brain. *Science, 170,* 940–944.

Gevers, W., Reynvoet, B., & Fias, W. (2004). The mental representation of ordinal sequences is spatially organised: Evidence from days of the week. *Cortex, 40,* 171–172.

Gibson, E. J. (1965). Learning to read. *Science, 148,* 1066–1072.

Gick, M. L., & Holyoak, K. J. (1980). Analogical problem solving. *Cognitive Psychology, 12,* 306–355.

Gigerenzer, G. (1996). On narrow norms and vague heuristics: A reply to Kahneman and Tversky. *Psychological Review, 103,* 592–596.

Gigerenzer, G. (2004). Dread risk, September 11, and fatal traffic accidents. *Psychological Science, 15,* 286–287.

Gigerenzer, G. (2008). Why heuristics work. *Perspectives in Psychological Science, 3,* 20–29.

Gigerenzer, G., & Goldstein, D. G. (1996). Reasoning the fast and frugal way: Models of bounded rationality. *Psychological Review, 104,* 650–669.

Gilovich, T., Vallone, R., & Tversky, A. (1985). The hot hand in basketball: On the misperception of random sequences. *Cognitive Psychology, 17,* 295–314.

Glanzer, M. (1972). Storage mechanisms in recall. In G. H. Bower & J. T. Spence (Eds.), *The psychology of learning and motivation* (Vol. 5, pp. 129–193). New York: Academic Press.

Glanzer, M., & Cunitz, A. R. (1966). Two storage mechanisms in free recall. *Journal of Verbal Learning and Verbal Behavior, 5,* 351–360.

Glass, A. L., & Holyoak, K. J. (1986). *Cognition* (2nd ed.). New York: Random House.

Glaze, J. A. (1928). The association value of nonsense syllables. *Journal of Genetic Psychology, 35,* 255–269.

Glenberg, A., & Adams, F. (1978). Type I rehearsal and recognition. *Journal of Verbal Learning and Verbal Behavior, 17,* 455–464.

Glenberg, A., Smith, S. M., & Green, C. (1977). Type I rehearsal: Maintenance and more. *Journal of Verbal Learning and Verbal Behavior, 11,* 403–416.

Glück, J., & Bluck, S. (2007). Looking back across the life span: A life story account of the reminiscence bump. *Memory & Cognition, 35,* 1928–1939.

Glucksberg, S., & Danks, J. H. (1975). *Experimental psycholinguistics: An introduction.* Hillsdale, NJ: Erlbaum.

Glucksberg, S., & Keysar, B. (1990). Understanding metaphorical comparisons: Beyond similarity. *Psychological Review, 97,* 3–18.

Glucksberg, S., & McCloskey, M. (1981). Decisions about ignorance: Knowing that you don't know. *Journal of Experimental Psychology: Human Learning and Memory, 7,* 311–325.

Gobet, F., & Simon, H. A. (1996). Recall of random and distorted chess positions: Implications for the theory of expertise. *Memory & Cognition, 24,* 493–503.

Godden, D. B., & Baddeley, A. D. (1975). Context-dependent memory in two natural environments: On land and underwater. *British Journal of Psychology, 66,* 325–331.

Gold, P. E., Cahill, L., & Wenk, G. L. (2002). Ginkgo biloba: A cognitive enhancer? *Psychological Science in the Public Interest, 3,* 2–11.

Gold, P. E., Cahill, L., & Wenk, G. L. (2003). The lowdown on ginkgo biloba. *Scientific American, 288,* 86–92.

Goldin-Meadow, S. (1997). When gestures and words speak differently. *Psychological Science, 6,* 138–143.

Goldin-Meadow, S. (2006). Talking and thinking with our hands. *Current Directions in Psychological Science, 15,* 34–39.

Goldinger, S. D., Kleider, H. M., Azuma, T., & Beike, D. R. (2003). "Blaming the victim" under memory load. *Psychological Science, 14,* 81–85.

Goldstein, D. G., & Gigerenzer, G. (2002). Models of ecological rationality: The recognition heuristic. *Psychological Review, 109,* 75–90.

Goodglass, H., Kaplan, E., Weintraub, S., & Ackerman, N. (1976). The "tip-of-the-tongue" phenomenon in aphasia. *Cortex, 12,* 145–153.

Goodwin, D. W., Powell, B., Bremeer, D., Hoine, H., & Stern, J. (1969). Alcohol and recall: State-dependent effects in man. *Science, 163,* 2358–2360.

Goodwin. G. P., & Johnson-Laird, P. N. (2005). Reasoning about relations. *Psychological Review, 112,* 468–493.

Gordon, B., Hart, J., Jr., Boatman, D., & Lesser, R. P. (1997). Cortical stimulation (interference) during behavior. In T. E. Feinberg & M. J. Farah (Eds.), *Behavioral neurology and neuropsychology* (pp. 667–672). New York: McGraw-Hill.

Gordon, P. C. & Chan, D. (1995). Pronouns, passives, and discourse coherence. *Journal of Memory and Language, 34,* 216–231.

Gordon, P. C. & Scearce, K. A. (1995). Pronominalization and discourse coherence, discourse structure and pronoun interpretation. *Memory & Cognition, 23,* 313–323.

Goshen-Gottstein, Y., & Kempinski, H. (2001). Probing memory with conceptual cues at multiple retention intervals: A comparison of forgetting rates on implicit and explicit tests. *Psychonomic Bulletin & Review, 8,* 139–146.

Graesser, A. C. (1981). Prose comprehension beyond the word. New York: Springer-Verlag.

Graesser, A. C., & Nakamura, G. V. (1982). The impact of a schema on comprehension and memory. In G. H. Bower (Ed.), *The psychology of learning and motivation* (pp. 59–109). New York: Academic Press.

Graesser, A. C., Singer, M., & Trabasso, T. (1994). Constructing inferences during narrative text comprehension. *Psychological Review, 101,* 371–395.

Graf, P., & Schacter, D. L. (1987). Selective effects of interference on implicit and explicit memory for new associations. *Journal of Experimental Psychology: Learning, Memory, and Cognition, 13,* 45–53.

Gray, R., Beilock, S. L., & Carr, T. H. (2007). "As soon as the bat met the ball, I knew it was gone": Outcome prediction, hindsight bias, and the representation and control of action in expert and novice baseball players. *Psychonomic Bulletin & Review, 14,* 669–675

Greenberg, J. H. (1978). Generalizations about numeral systems. In J. H. Greenberg (Ed.), *Universals of human language: Vol. 3. Word structure* (pp. 249–295). Stanford, CA: Stanford University Press.

Greenberg, S. N., Healy, A. F., Koriat, A., & Kreiner, H. (2004). The GO model: A reconsideration of the role of structural units in guiding and organizing text on line. *Psychonomic Bulletin & Review, 11,* 428–433.

Greene, R. L. (1986). Effects of intentionality and strategy on memory for frequency. *Journal of Experimental Psychology: Learning, Memory, and Cognition, 12,* 489–495.

Greene, R. L., & Crowder, R. G. (1984). Modality and suffix effects in the absence of auditory stimulation. *Journal of Verbal Learning and Verbal Behavior, 23,* 371–382.

Greene, R. L., & Crowder, R. G. (1986). Recency effects in delayed recall of mouthed stimuli. *Memory & Cognition, 14,* 355–360.

Greeno, J. G. (1974). Hobbits and orcs: Acquisition of a sequential concept. *Cognitive Psychology, 6,* 270–292.

Greeno, J. G. (1978). Natures of problem-solving abilities. In W. K. Estes (Ed.), *Handbook of learning and cognitive processes: Vol. 5. Human information processing* (pp. 239–270). Hillsdale, NJ: Erlbaum.

Greenspan, S. L. (1986). Semantic flexibility and referential specificity of concrete nouns. *Journal of Memory and Language, 25,* 539–557.

Greenwald, A. G., Abrams, R. L., Naccache, L., & Dehaene, S. (2003). Long-term semantic memory versus contextual memory in unconscious number processing. *Journal of Experimental Psychology: Learning, Memory, and Cognition, 29,* 235–247.

Greenwald, A. G., & Draine, S. C. (1998). Distinguishing unconscious from conscious cognition-reasonable assumptions and replicable findings: Reply to Merikle and Reingold (1998) and Dosher (1998). *Journal of Experimental Psychology: General, 127,* 320–324.

Greenwald, A. G., Klinger, M. R., & Schuh, E. S. (1995). Activation by marginally perceptible ("subliminal") stimuli: Dissociation of unconscious from conscious cognition. *Journal of Experimental Psychology: General, 124,* 22–42.

Greenwald, A. G., Spangenberg, E. R., Pratkanis, A. R., & Eskenazi, J. (1991). Double-blind tests of subliminal self-help audiotapes. *Psychological Science, 2,* 119–122.

Grice, H. P. (1975). Logic and conversation. In P. Cole & J. L. Morgan (Eds.), *Syntax and semantics: Vol. 3. Speech acts* (pp. 41–58). New York: Seminar Press.

Griffin, D., & Tversky, A. (1992). The weighing of evidence and the determinants of confidence. *Cognitive Psychology, 24,* 411–435.

Griffin, T. D., Wiley, J., & Thiede, K.W. (2008). Individual differences, rereading, and self-explanation: concurrent processing and cue validity as constraints on metacomprehension accuracy. *Memory & Cognition, 36,* 93–103.

Griffin, Z. M. (2003). A reversed word length effect in coordinating the preparation and articulation of words in speaking. *Psychonomic Bulletin & Review, 10,* 603–609.

Griffin, Z. M., & Bock, K. (2000). What the eyes say about speaking. *Psychological Science, 11,* 274–279.

Griffiths, T. L., Steyvers, M., & Tenebaum, J. B. (2007). Topics in semantic representation. *Psychological Review, 114,* 211–244.

Grill-Spector, K., & Kanwisher, N. (2005). Visual recognition: As soon as you know it is there, you know what it is. *Psychological Science, 16,* 152–160.

Gruppuso, V., Lindsay, D. S., & Masson, M. E. J. (2007). I'd know that face anywhere! *Psychonomic Bulletin & Review, 14,* 1085–1089.

Gupta, P., & Cohen, N. J. (2002). Theoretical and computational analysis of skill learning, repetition priming, and procedural memory. *Psychological Review, 109,* 401–448.

Haber, R. N., & Hershenson, M. (1973). *The psychology of visual perception.* New York: Holt, Rinehart & Winston.

Haines, R. F. (1991). A breakdown in simultaneous information processing. In G. Obrecht & L. W. Stark (Eds.), *Presbyopia research* (pp. 171–175). New York: Plenum Press.

Hall, J. F. (1971). *Verbal learning and retention.* Philadelphia: Lippincott.

Hambrick, D. Z. (2003). Why are some people more knowledgeable than others? A longitudinal study of knowledge acquisition. *Memory & Cognition, 31,* 902–917.

Hambrick, D. Z., & Engle, R. W. (2002). Effects on domain knowledge, working memory capacity, and age on cognitive performance: An investigation of the knowledge-is-power hypothesis. *Cognitive Psychology, 44,* 339–387.

Hampton, J. A. (1984). The verification of category and property statements. *Memory & Cognition, 12,* 345–354.

Hanley, J. R., & Chapman, E. (2008). Partial knowledge in a tip-of-the-tongue state about two- and three-word proper names. *Psychonomic Bulletin & Review, 15,* 156–160.

Hannigan, S. L., & Reinitz, M. T. (2001). A demonstration and comparison of two types of inference-based memory errors. *Journal of Experimental Psychology: Learning, Memory, and Cognition, 27,* 931–940.

Hannigan, S. L., & Reinitz, M. T. (2003). Migration of objects and inferences across episodes. *Memory & Cognition, 31,* 434–444.

Hanson, C., & Hirst, W. (1988). Frequency encoding of token and type information. *Journal of Experimental Psychology: Learning, Memory, and Cognition, 14,* 289–297.

Harley, E. M., Carlsen, K. A., & Loftus, G. R. (2004). The "saw-it-all-along" effect: Demonstrations of visual hindsight bias. *Journal of Experimental Psychology: Learning, Memory, and Cognition, 30,* 960–968.

Harlow, H. F. (1953). Mice, monkeys, men and motives. *Psychological Review, 60,* 23–32.

Harris, R. J. & Monaco, G. E. (1978). Psychology of pragmatic implication: Information processing between the lines. *Journal of Experimental Psychology, 107,* 1–22.

Hart, J. T. (1965). Memory and the feeling-of-knowing experience. *Journal of Educational Psychology, 56,* 208–216.

Hartsuiker, R. J., Anton-Mendez, I., & van Zee, M. (2001). Object attraction in subject-verb agreement construction. *Journal of Memory and Language, 45,* 546–572.

Hartsuiker, R. J., & Kolk, H. H. J. (2001). Error monitoring in speech production: A computational test of the perceptual loop theory. *Cognitive Psychology, 42,* 113–157.

Hasher, L., & Griffin, M. (1978). Reconstructive and reproductive processes in memory *Journal of Experimental Psychology: Human Learning and Memory, 4,* 318–330.

Hasher, L., & Zacks, R. T. (1984). Automatic processing of fundamental information: The case of frequency of occurrence. *American Psychologist, 39,* 1372–1388.

Hasher, L., & Zacks, R.T. (1988). Working memory, comprehension, and aging: A review and a new view. In G.H. Bower (Ed.), *The psychology of learning and motivation* (Vol. 22, pp. 193–225). New York: Academic Press.

Haugeland, J. (1985). *Artificial intelligence: The very idea.* Cambridge, MA: MIT Press.

Haviland, S. E., & Clark, H. H. (1974). What's new? Acquiring new information as a process in comprehension. *Journal of Verbal Learning and Verbal Behavior, 13,* 512–521.

Hayes, J. R., & Simon, H. A. (1974). Understanding written problem instructions. In L. W. Gregg (Ed.), *Knowledge and cognition* (pp. 167–200). Hillsdale, NJ: Erlbaum.

Haywood, S. L., Pickering, M. J., & Branigan, H. P. (2005). Do speakers avoid ambiguities during dialogue? *Psychological Science, 16,* 362–366.

Heaps, C. M., & Nash, M. (2001). Comparing recollective experience in true and false autobiographical memories. *Journal of Experimental Psychology: Learning, Memory, and Cognition, 27,* 920–930.

Hecht, H., & Proffitt, D. R. (1995). The price of expertise: Effects of experience on the water-level task. *Psychological Science, 6,* 90–95.

Heil, M., Rolke, B., & Pecchinenda, A. (2004). Automatic semantic activation is no myth: Semantic context effects on the N400 in the letter-search task in the absence of response time effects. *Psychological Science, 15,* 852–857.

Hell, W., Gigerenzer, G., Gauggel, S., Mall, M., & Muller, M. (1988). Hindsight bias: An interaction of automatic and motivational factors? *Memory & Cognition, 16,* 533–538.

Hellyer, S. (1962). Frequency of stimulus presentation and short-term decrement in recall. *Journal of Experimental Psychology, 64,* 650.

Helsabeck, F., Jr. (1975). Syllogistic reasoning: Generation of counterexamples. *Journal of Educational Psychology, 67,* 102–108.

Henderson, J. M., & Anes, M. D. (1994). Roles of object-file review and type priming in visual identification within and across eye fixations. *Journal of Experimental Psychology: Human Perception and Performance, 20,* 826–839.

Henderson, J. M., & Hollingsworth, A. (2003). Global transsaccadic change in blindness during scene perception. *Psychological Science, 14,* 493–497.

Henkel, L. A. (2004). Erroneous memories arising from repeated attempts to remember. *Journal of Memory and Language, 50,* 26–46.

Herrera, A., Macizo, P. & Semenza, C. (2008). The role of working memory in the association between number magnitude and space. *Acta Psychologica, 128,* 225–237.

Hertwig, R., Barron, G., Weber, E. U., & Erev, I. (2004). Decision from experience and the effect of rare events in risky choice. *Psychological Science, 15,* 534–539.

Herz, R. S., & Schooler, J. W. (2002). A naturalistic study of autobiographical memories evoked by olfactory and visual cues: Testing the Proustian hypothesis. *American Journal of Psychology, 115,* 21–32.

Hicks, J. L., & Marsh, R. L. (2000). Toward specifying the attentional demands of recognition memory. *Journal of Experimental Psychology: Learning, Memory, and Cognition, 26,* 1483–1498.

Higham, P.A., & Garrard, C. (2005). Not all errors are created equal: Metacognition and changing answers on multiple-choice tests. *Canadian Journal of Experimental Psychology, 59,* 28–34.

Hildreth, E. C., & Ullman, S. (1989). The computational study of vision. In M. I. Posner (Ed.), *Foundations of cognitive science* (pp. 581–630). Cambridge, MA: Bradford.

Hinson, J. M., Jameson, T. L., & Whitney, P. (2003). Impulsive decision making and working memory. *Journal of Experimental Psychology: Learning, Memory, and Cognition, 29,* 298–306.

Hintzman, D. L. (1978). *The psychology of learning and memory.* San Francisco: Freeman.

Hirshman, E., & Durante, R. (1992). Prime identification and semantic priming. *Journal of Experimental Psychology: Learning, Memory, and Cognition, 18,* 255–265.

Hirshman, E., Whelley, M. M., & Palij, M. (1989). An investigation of paradoxical memory effects. *Journal of Memory and Language, 28,* 594–609.

Hirst, W., & Kalmar, D. (1987). Characterizing attentional resources. *Journal of Experimental Psychology: General, 116,* 68–81.

Hoch, S. J. (1984). Availability and interference in predictive judgment. *Journal of Experimental Psychology: Learning, Memory, and Cognition, 10,* 649–662.

Hoch, S. J. (1985). Counterfactual reasoning and accuracy in predicting personal events. *Journal of Experimental Psychology: Learning, Memory, and Cognition, 11,* 719–731.

Hoch, S. J., & Loewenstein, G. F. (1989). Outcome feedback: Hindsight and information. *Journal of Experimental Psychology: Learning, Memory, and Cognition, 15*, 605–619.

Hockett, C. F. (1960a). Logical considerations in the study of animal communication. In W. E. Lanyon & W. N. Tavolga (Eds.), *Animal sounds and communication* (pp. 392–430). Washington, DC: American Institute of Biological Sciences.

Hockett, C. F. (1960b). The origin of speech. *Scientific American, 203*, 89–96.

Hockett, C. F. (1966). The problem of universals in language. In J. H. Greenberg (Ed.), *Universals of language* (2nd ed., pp. 1–29). Cambridge, MA: MIT Press.

Hoffman, R. R., Bringmann, W., Bamberg, M., & Klein, R. (1987). Some historical observations on Ebbinghaus. In D. S. Gorfein & R. R. Hoffman (Eds.), *Memory and learning: The Ebbinghaus Centennial Conference* (pp. 57–75). Hillsdale, NJ: Erlbaum.

Holcomb, P. J. (1993). Semantic priming and stimulus degradation: Implications for the role of the N400 in language processing. *Psychophysiology, 30*, 47–61.

Holcomb, P. J., Kounios, J., Anderson, J. E., & West, W. C. (1999). Dual-coding, context availability, and concreteness effects in sentence comprehension: An electrophysiological investigation. *Journal of Experimental Psychology: Learning, Memory, and Cognition, 25*, 721–742.

Holtgraves, T. (1994). Communication in context: Effects of speaker status on the comprehension of indirect requests. *Journal of Experimental Psychology: Learning, Memory, and Cognition, 20*, 1205–1218.

Holtgraves, T. (1998). Interpreting indirect replies. *Cognitive Psychology, 37*, 1–27.

Holtgraves, T. (2008). Automatic intention recognition in conversation processing. *Journal of Memory and Language, 58*, 627–645.

Holtgraves, T. (2008). Conversation, speech acts, and memory. *Memory & Cognition, 36*, 361–374.

Holyoak, K. J., & Mah, W. A. (1982). Cognitive reference points in judgments of symbolic magnitude. *Cognitive Psychology, 14*, 328–352.

Holyoak, K. J., & Simon, D. (1999). Bidirectional reasoning in decision making by constraint satisfaction. *Journal of Experimental Psychology: General, 128*, 3–31.

Holyoak, K. J., & Thagard, P. (1997). The analogical mind. *American Psychologist, 52*, 35–44.

Holyoak, K. J., & Walker, J. H. (1976). Subjective magnitude information in semantic orderings. *Journal of Verbal Learning and Verbal Behavior, 15*, 287–299.

Hopkins, W. D., Russell, J. L., & Cantalupo, C. (2007). Neuroanatomical correlates of handedness for tool use in chimpanzees (Pan troglodytes): Implication for theories on the evolution of language. *Psychological Science, 18*, 971–977.

Horton, W. S., & Gerrig, R. J. (2002). Speakers' experiences and audience design: Knowing *when* and knowing *how* to adjust utterances to addressees. *Journal of Memory and Language, 47*, 589–606.

Hostetter, A. B., & Alibali, M. (2008). Visible embodiment: Gestures as simulated action. *Psychonomic Bulletin & Review, 15*, 495–514.

Hothersall, D. (1984). *History of psychology*. New York: Random House.

Hothersall, D. (1985). *Psychology*. Columbus: Merrill Publishing.

Howe, M. L., & Courage, M. L (1993). On resolving the enigma of infantile amnesia. *Psychological Bulletin, 113*, 305–326.

Hu, P., Stylos-Allan, M., & Walker, M P. (2006). Sleep facilitates consolidation of emotional declarative memory. *Psychological Science, 17*, 891–898.

Hubbard, T. L. (1990). Cognitive representation of linear motion: Possible direction and gravity effects in judged displacement. *Memory & Cognition, 18*, 299–309.

Hubbard, T. L. (1995). Environmental invariants in the representation of motion: Implied dynamics and representational momentum, gravity, friction, and centripetal force. *Psychonomic Bulletin & Review, 2*, 322–338.

Hubbard, T. L. (1996). Representational momentum, centripetal force, and curvilinear impetus. *Journal of Experimental Psychology: Learning, Memory, and Cognition, 22*, 1049–1060.

Hubbard, T. L. (2005). Representational momentum and related displacements in spatial memory: A review of the findings. *Psychonomic Bulletin & Review, 12*, 822–851.

Hubel, D. H., & Wiesel, T. N. (1962). Receptive fields, binocular interaction, and functional architecture in the cat's visual cortex. *Journal of Physiology, 160*, 106–154.

Huettel, S. A., Song, A. W., & McCarthy, G. (2004). *Functional magnetic resonance imaging*. Sunderland, MA: Sinauer Associates.

Hull, C. L. (1943). *Principles of behavior*. New York: Appleton-Century-Crofts.

Hunt, E., & Agnoli, F. (1991). The Whorfian hypothesis: A cognitive psychology perspective. *Psychological Review, 98*, 377–389.

Hunt, R. R., & Lamb, C. A. (2001). What causes the isolation effect? *Journal of Experimental Psychology: Learning, Memory, and Cognition, 27*, 1359–1366.

Hutchison, K. A. (2003). Is semantic priming due to association strength or feature overlap? A microanalytic review. *Psychonomic Bulletin & Review, 10*, 785–813.

Hyman, I. E., Jr., Husband, T.H., & Billings, F. J. (1995). False memories of childhood experiences. *Applied Cognitive Psychology, 9*, 181–197.

Hyman, I. E., Jr., & Pentland, J. (1996). The role of mental imagery in the creation of false childhood memories. *Journal of Memory and Language, 35*, 101–117.

Inhoff, A. W. (1984). Two stages of word processing during eye fixations in the reading of prose. *Journal of Verbal Learning and Verbal Behavior, 23*, 612–624.

Intraub, H., & Richardson, M. (1989). Wide-angle memories of close-up scenes. *Journal of Experimental Psychology: Learning, Memory, and Cognition, 15*, 179–187.

Intriligator, J., & Cavanagh, P. (2001). The spatial resolution of visual attention. *Cognitive Psychology, 43*, 171–216.

Irwin, D. E. (1991). Information integration across saccadic eye movements. *Cognitive Psychology, 23*, 420–456.

Irwin, D. E. (1992). Memory for position and identity across eye movements. *Journal of Experimental Psychology: Learning, Memory, and Cognition, 18*, 307–317.

Irwin, D. E. (1996). Integrating information across saccadic eye movements. *Current Directions in Psychological Science, 5*, 94–100.

Irwin, D. E. (1998). Lexical processing during saccadic eye movements. *Cognitive Psychology, 36,* 1–27.

Irwin, D. E., & Brockmole, J. R. (2004). Suppressing where but not what: The effect of saccades on dorsal- and ventral-stream visual processing. *Psychological Science, 15,* 467–473.

Irwin, D. E., Yantis, S., & Jonides, J. (1983). Evidence against visual integration across saccadic eye movements. *Perception & Psychophysics, 34,* 49–57.

Jackendoff, R. S. (1992). *Languages of the mind: Essays on mental representation.* Cambridge, MA: MIT Press.

Jacobs, N., & Garnham, A. (2007). The role of conversational hand gestures in a narrative task. *Journal of Memory and Language, 56,* 291–303.

Jacoby, L. L. (1991). A process dissociation framework: Separating automatic from intentional uses of memory. *Journal of Memory and Language, 30,* 513–541.

Jacoby, L. L., & Dallas, M. (1981). On the relationship between autobiographical memory and perceptual learning. *Journal of Experimental Psychology: General, 110,* 306–340.

Jacoby, L. L., Toth, J. P., & Yonelinas, A. P. (1993). Separating conscious and unconscious influences of memory: Measuring recollection. *Journal of Experimental Psychology: General, 122,* 139–154.

Jacoby, L. L., Woloshyn, V., & Kelley, C. (1989). Becoming famous without being recognized: Unconscious influences of memory produced by dividing attention. *Journal of Experimental Psychology: General, 118,* 115–125.

James, L. E., & MacKay, D. G. (2001). H. M., word knowledge, and aging: Support for a new theory and long-term retrograde amnesia. *Psychological Science, 12,* 485–492.

James, W. (1890). *The principles of psychology.* New York: Dover.

James, W. (1983 ed). *The principles of psychology.* Cambridge, MA: Harvard University Press.

January, D., & Kako, E. (2007). Re-evaluating evidence for linguistic relativity: Reply to Boroditsky (2001). *Cognition, 104,* 417–426.

Jared, D., Levy, B. A., & Rayner, K. (1999). The role of phonology in the activation of word meanings during readings: Evidence from proofreading and eye movements. *Journal of Experimental Psychology: General, 128,* 219–264.

Jefferies, E., Lambdon Ralph, M. A., & Baddeley, A. D. (2004). Automatic and controlled processing in sentence recall: The role of long-term and working memory. *Journal of Memory and Language, 51,* 623–643.

Jenkins, J. G., & Dallenbach, K. M. (1924). Obliviscence during sleep and waking. *American Journal of Psychology, 35,* 605–612.

Jenkins, J.J. (1974). Remember that old theory of memory? Well, forget it! *American Psychologist, 29,* 785–795.

Johnson, J. T., & Finke, R. A. (1985). The base-rate fallacy in the context of sequential categories. *Memory & Cognition, 13,* 63–73.

Johnson, M. K., Hashtroudi, S., & Lindsay, S. (1993). Source monitoring. *Psychological Bulletin, 114,* 3–28.

Johnson, N. F. (1970). The role of chunking and organization in the process of recall. In G. H. Bower (Ed.), *The psychology of learning and motivation* (Vol. 4, pp. 172–247). New York: Academic Press.

Johnson, S. K., & Anderson, M. C. (2004). The role of inhibitory control in forgetting semantic knowledge. *Psychological Science, 15,* 448–453.

Johnson-Laird, P. N. (1983). *Mental models: Towards a cognitive science of language, inference and consciousness.* Cambridge, MA: Harvard University Press.

Johnson-Laird, P. N., & Byrne, R. M. J. (2002). Conditionals: A theory of meaning, pragmatics, and inference. *Psychological Review, 109,* 646–678.

Johnson-Laird, P. N., Byrne, R. M. J., & Schaeken, W. (1992). Propositional reasoning by model. *Psychological Review, 99,* 418–439.

Johnson-Laird, P. N., Legrenzi, P., & Legrenzi, M. S. (1972). Reasoning and a sense of reality. *British Journal of Psychology, 63,* 395–400.

Johnston, J. C., McCann, R. S., & Remington, R. W. (1995). Chronometric evidence for two types of attention. *Psychological Science, 6,* 365–369.

Johnston, W. A., & Heinz, S. P. (1978). Flexibility and capacity demands of attention. *Journal of Experimental Psychology: General, 107,* 420–435.

Jones, D. M., Macken, W. J., & Nicholls, A. P. (2004). The phonological store of working memory: Is it phonological and is it a store? *Journal of Experimental Psychology: Learning, Memory, and Cognition, 30,* 656–674.

Jones, G. V. (1989). Back to Woodworth: Role of interlopers in the tip-of-the-tongue phenomenon. *Memory & Cognition, 17,* 69–76.

Jones, G. V., & Martin, M. (2006). Primacy of memory linkage in choice among valued objects. *Memory & Cognition, 34,* 1587–1597.

Jonides, J., & Jones, C. M. (1992). Direct coding for frequency of occurrence. *Journal of Experimental Psychology: Learning, Memory, and Cognition, 18,* 368–378.

Jonides, J., Lacey, S. C., & Nee, D. E. (2005). Processes of working memory in mind and brain. *Current Directions in Psychological Science, 14,* 2–5.

Jonides, J., Smith, E. E., Koeppe, R. A., Awh, E., Minoshima, S., & Mintun, M. A. *Nature, 363,* 623–625.

Juhasz, B. J., & Rayner, K. (2003). Investigating the effects of a set of intercorrelated variables on eye fixation durations in reading. *Journal of Experimental Psychology: Learning, Memory, and Cognition, 29,* 1312–1318.

Jusczyk, P. W., Smith, L. B., & Murphy, C. (1981). The perceptual classification of speech. *Perception and Psychophysics, 1,* 10–23.

Just, M. A. (1976, May). *Research strategies in prose comprehension.* Paper presented at the meetings of the Midwestern Psychological Association, Chicago.

Just, M. A., & Carpenter, P. A. (1980). A theory of reading: From eye fixations to comprehension. *Psychological Review, 87,* 329–354.

Just, M. A., & Carpenter, P. A. (1987). *The psychology of reading and language comprehension.* Boston: Allyn & Bacon.

Just, M. A., & Carpenter, P. A. (1992). A capacity theory of comprehension. *Psychological Review, 99,* 122–149.

Just, M. A., Carpenter, P. A., Maguire, M., Diwadkar, V., & McMains, S. (2001). Mental rotation of objects retrieved from memory: A functional MRI study of spatial processing. *Journal of Experimental Psychology: General, 130,* 493–504.

Kaakinen, J. K., Hyona, J., & Keenan, J. M. (2003). How prior knowledge, WMC, and relevance of information affect eye fixations in expository text. *Journal of Experimental Psychology: Learning, Memory, and Cognition, 29*, 447–457.

Kahana, M. J., & Wingfield, A. (2000). A functional relation between learning and organization in free recall. *Psychonomic Bulletin & Review, 7*, 516–521.

Kahneman, D. (1968). Method, findings and theory in studies of visual masking. *Psychological Bulletin, 70*, 404–426.

Kahneman, D. (1973). *Attention and effort.* Englewood Cliffs, NJ: Prentice Hall.

Kahneman, D. (2003a). A perspective on judgment and choice: Mapping bounded rationality. *American Psychologist, 58*, 697–720.

Kahneman, D. (2003b). Experiences of collaborative research. *American Psychologist, 58*, 723–730.

Kahneman, D., Slovic, P., & Tversky, A. (Eds.). (1982). *Judgment under uncertainty: Heuristics and biases.* Cambridge, U.K.: Cambridge University Press.

Kahneman, D., Triesman, A., & Gibbs, B. J. (1992). The reviewing of object files: Object-specific integration of information. *Cognitive Psychology, 24*, 175–219.

Kahneman, D., & Tversky, A. (1972). Subjective probability: A judgment of representativeness. *Cognitive Psychology, 3*, 430–454.

Kahneman, D., & Tversky, A. (1973). On the psychology of prediction. *Psychological Review, 80*, 237–251.

Kahneman, D., & Tversky, A. (1982). The simulation heuristic. In D. Kahneman, P. Slovic, & A. Tversky (Eds.), *Judgment under uncertainty: Heuristics and biases* (pp. 201–208). Cambridge, U.K.: Cambridge University Press.

Kahneman, D., & Tversky, A. (Eds.) (2000). *Choice, values, and frames.* New York: Cambridge University Press.

Kalénine, S., & Bonthoux, F. (2008). Object manipulability affects children's and adults' conceptual processing. *Psychonomic Bulletin & Review, 15*, 667–672.

Kambe, G., Duffy, S. A., Clifton, C. Jr., & Rayner, K. (2003). An eye-movement-contingent probe paradigm. *Psychonomic Bulletin & Review, 10*, 661–666.

Kane, M. J., Brown, L. H., McVay, J. C., Silvia, P. J., Myin-Germeys, I., & Kwapil, T. R. (2007). For whom the mind wanders, and when. *Psychological Science, 18*, 614–621.

Kane, M. J., & Engle, R. W. (2000). Working memory capacity, proactive interference, and divided attention: Limits on long-term memory retrieval. *Journal of Experimental Psychology: Learning, Memory, and Cognition, 26*, 336–358.

Kane, M. J. & Engle, R. W. (2002). The role of prefrontal cortex in working-memory capacity, executive attention, and general fluid intelligence: An individual-differences perspective. *Psychonomic Bulletin & Review, 9*, 637–671.

Kane, M. J., & Engle, R. W. (2003). Working-memory capacity and the control of attention: The contributions of goal neglect, response competition and task set to Stroop interference. *Journal of Experimental Psychology: General, 132*, 47–70.

Kane, M. J., Hambrick, D. Z., Tuholski, S. W., Wilhelm, O., Payne, T. W., & Engle, R. W. (2004). The generality of working memory capacity: A latent-variable approach to verbal and visuospatial memory span and reasoning. *Journal of Experimental Psychology: General, 133*, 189–217.

Kanwisher, N. (1987). Repetition blindness: Type recognition without token individuation. *Cognition, 27*, 117–143.

Kanwisher, N. (1991). Repetition blindness and illusory conjunctions: Errors in binding visual types with visual tokens. *Journal of Experimental Psychology: Human Perception and Performance, 17*, 404–421.

Kanwisher, N., & Driver, J. (1992). Objects, attributes, and visual attention: Which, what, and where. *Psychological Science, 1*, 26–31.

Karni, A., Tanne, D., Rubenstein, B. S., Askenasy, J. J. M., & Sagi, D. (1994). Dependence on REM sleep of overnight performance of a perceptual skill. *Science, 265*, 679–682.

Karpicke, J. D., & Roediger, H. L. (2007). Repeated during retrieval is the key to long-term retention. *Journal of Memory and Language, 57*, 151–162.

Kaschak, M. P., & Glenberg, A. M. (2000). Constructing meaning: The role of affordances and grammatical constructions in sentence comprehension. *Journal of Memory and Language, 43*, 508–529.

Kay, J., & Ellis, A. (1987). A cognitive neuropsychological case study of anomia: Implications for psychological models of word retrieval. *Brain, 110*, 613–629.

Keil, F. C. (1991). On being more than the sum of the parts: The conceptual coherence of cognitive science. *Psychological Science, 2*, 283–293.

Kelley, C. M., & Jacoby, L. L. (1996). Memory attributions: Remembering, knowing, and feeling of knowing. In L. M. Reder (Ed.), *Implicit memory and metacognition* (pp. 287–308). Hillsdale, NJ: Erlbaum.

Kelley, C. M., & Lindsay, D. S. (1993). Remembering mistaken for knowing: Ease of retrieval as a basis for confidence in answers to general knowledge questions. *Journal of Memory and Language, 32*, 1–24.

Kelley, M. R., & Nairne, J. S. (2001). von Restorff revisited: Isolation, generation, and memory of order. *Journal of Experimental Psychology: Learning, Memory, and Cognition, 27*, 54–66.

Kelly, S. D., Barr, D. J., Church, R. B., & Lynch, K. (1999). Offering a hand to pragmatic understanding: The role of speech and gesture in comprehension and memory. *Journal of Memory and Language, 40*, 577–592.

Kempen, G., & Hoehkamp, E. (1987). An incremental procedural grammar for sentence formulation. *Cognitive Science, 11*, 201–258.

Kemper, S., & Thissen, D. (1981). Memory for the dimensions of requests. *Journal of Verbal Learning and Verbal Behavior, 20*, 552–563.

Kempton, W. (1986). Two theories of home heat control. *Cognitive Science, 10*, 75–90.

Kensinger, E. A., & Corkin, S. (2004). Two routes to emotional memory: Distinct neural processes for valence and arousal. *Proceedings of the National Academy of Sciences, 101*, 3310–3315.

Kensinger, E. A., Garoff-Eaton, R. J., & Schacter, D. L. (2006). Memory for specific visual details can be enhanced by negative arousing content. *Journal of Memory and Language, 54*, 99–112.

Kensinger, E. A., & Schacter, D. L. (2006). When the Red Socks shocked the Yankees: Comparing negative and positive memories. *Psychonomic Bulletin & Review, 13*, 757–763.

Keppel, G., & Underwood, B. J. (1962). Proactive inhibition in short-term retention of single items. *Journal of Verbal Learning and Verbal Behavior, 1*, 153–161.

Kershaw, T. C., & Ohlsson, S. (2004). Multiple causes of difficulty in insight: The case of the nine-dot problem. *Journal of Experimental Psychology: Learning, Memory, and Cognition, 30*, 3–13.

Kertesz, A. (1982). Two case studies: Broca's and Wernicke's aphasia. In M. A. Arbib, D. Caplan, & J. C. Marshall (Eds.), *Neural models of language processes* (pp. 25–44). New York: Academic Press.

Kesner, R. P. (1998). Neural mediation of memory for time: Role of the hippocampus and medial prefrontal cortex. *Psychonomic Bulletin & Review, 5*, 585–596.

Keysar, B. (1994). The illusory transparency of intention: Linguistic perspective taking in text. *Cognitive Psychology, 26*, 165–208.

Keysar, B. (1998). Language users as problem solvers: Just what ambiguity problem do they solve? In S. R. Fussell & R. J. Kreuz (Eds.), *Social and cognitive psychological approaches to interpersonal communication* (pp. 175–200). Hillsdale, NJ: Erlbaum.

Keysar, B., Barr, D. J., & Horton, W. S. (1998). The egocentric basis of language use: Insights from a processing approach. *Current Directions in Psychological Science, 7*, 46–50.

Keysar, B., & Henly, A. S. (2002). Speakers' overestimation of their effectiveness. *Psychological Science, 13*, 207–212.

Keysar, B., Shen, Y., Glucksberg, S., & Horton, W. S. (2000). Conventional language: How metaphorical is it? *Journal of Memory and Language, 43*, 576–593.

Kim, N. S., & Ahn, W. (2002). Clinical psychologists' theory-based representations of mental disorders predict their diagnostic reasoning and memory. *Journal of Experimental Psychology: General, 131*, 451–476.

Kim, N. S., Yopchick, J. E., & de Kwaadsteniet, L. (2008). Causal diversity effects in information seeking. *Psychonomic Bulletin & Review, 15*, 81–88.

Kinder, A., & Shanks, D. R. (2003). Neuropsychological dissociations between priming and recognition: A single-system connectionist account. *Psychological Review, 110*, 728–744.

Kingstone, A., Smilek, D., Ristic, J., Friesen, C.K., & Eastwood, J.D. (2003). Attention, researchers! It is time to take a look at the real world. *Current Directions in Psychological Science, 12*, 176–180.

Kintsch, W. (1970). *Learning, memory, and conceptual processes*. New York: Wiley.

Kintsch, W. (1974). *The representation of meaning in memory*. Hillsdale, NJ: Erlbaum.

Kintsch, W. (1985). Reflections on Ebbinghaus. *Journal of Experimental Psychology: Learning, Memory, and Cognition, 11*, 461–463.

Kintsch, W. (2000). Metaphor comprehension: A computational theory. *Psychonomic Bulletin & Review, 7*, 257–266.

Kintsch, W., & Bates, E. (1977). Recognition memory for statements from a classroom lecture. *Journal of Experimental Psychology: Human Learning and Memory, 3*, 150–159.

Kintsch, W., & Greeno, J. G. (1985). Understanding and solving word arithmetic problems. *Psychological Review, 92*, 109–129.

Kintsch, W., Welsch, D., Schmalhofer, F., & Zimny, S. (1987). Sentence memory: A theoretical analysis. *Journal of Memory and Language, 29*, 133–159.

Kishiyama, M. M., Yonelinas, A. P., & Lazzara, M. M. (2004). The von Restorff effect in amnesia: The contribution of the hippocampal system to novelty-related memory enhancements. *Journal of Cognitive Neuroscience, 16*, 15–23.

Kissler, J., Herbert, C., Peyk, P., & Junghofer, M. (2007). Buzzwords: Early cortical response to emotional words during reading. *Psychological Science, 18*, 475–480.

Klatzky, R. L. (1980). *Human memory: Structures and processes* (2nd ed.). San Francisco: Freeman.

Klatzky, R.L., Pellegrino, J.W., McCloskey, B.P., & Doherty, S. (1989). Can you squeeze a tomato? The role of motor representations in semantic sensibility judgments. *Journal of Memory and Language, 28*, 56–77.

Klauer, K. C., Stahl, C., & Erdfelder, E. (2007). The abstract selection task: New data and an almost comprehensive model. *Journal of Experimental Psychology: Learning, Memory, and Cognition, 33*, 680–703.

Klayman, J., & Ha, Y.-W. (1989). Hypothesis testing in rule discovery: Strategy, structure, and content. *Journal of Experimental Psychology: Learning, Memory, and Cognition, 15*, 596–604.

Klein, D. V., & Murphy, G. L. (2002). Paper has been my ruin: conceptual relations of polysemous senses. *Journal of Memory and Language, 47*, 548–570.

Klein, R. (2000). Inhibition of return. *Trends in Cognitive Sciences, 4*, 138–147.

Kliegl, R., Nuthmann, A., & Engbert, R. (2006). Tracking the mind during reading: The influence of past, present, and future words on fixation durations. *Journal of Experimental Psychology: General, 135*, 12–35.

Koehler, J. J., & Macchi, L. (2004). Thinking about low-probability events: An exemplar-cuing theory. *Psychological Science, 15*, 540–546.

Kohler, W. (1927). *The mentality of apes*. New York: Harcourt, Brace.

Koivisto, M., & Revonsuo, A. (2007). How meaning shapes seeing. *Psychological Science, 18*, 845–849.

Kolb, B., & Whishaw, I. Q. (1996). *Fundamentals of human neuropsychology* (4th ed.). New York: Freeman.

Kolers, P. A., & Roediger, H. L. III (1984). Procedures of mind. *Journal of Verbal Learning and Verbal Behavior, 23*, 425–449.

Kolodner, J. L. (1997). Educational implications of analogy: A view from case-based reasoning. *American Psychologist, 52*, 57–66.

Komeda, H., & Kusumi, T. (2006). The effect of a protagonist's emotional shift on situation model construction. *Memory & Cognition, 34*, 1548–1556.

Koriat, A. (1993). How do we know that we know? The accessibility model of the feeling of knowing. *Psychological Review, 100*, 609–639.

Koriat, A. (1995). Dissociating knowing and the feeling of knowing: Further evidence for the accessibility model. *Journal of Experimental Psychology: General, 124*, 311–333.

Koriat, A., Fiedler, K., & Bjork, R. A. (2006). Inflation of conditional predictions. *Journal of Experimental Psychology: General, 135*, 429–447.

Koriat, A., & Greenberg, S. N. (1996). The enhancement effect in letter detection: Further evidence for the structural model of reading. *Journal of Experimental Psychology: Learning, Memory, and Cognition, 22*, 1184–1195.

Koriat, A., Levy-Sadot, R., Edry, E., & de Marcus, S. (2003). What do we know about what we cannot remember? Accessing the semantic attributes of words that cannot be recalled. *Journal of Experimental Psychology: Learning, Memory, and Cognition, 29,* 1095–1105.

Koriat, A., & Pearlman-Avnion, S. (2003). Memory organization of action events and its relationship to memory performance. *Journal of Experimental Psychology: General, 132,* 435–454.

Koriat, A., Sheffer, L., & Ma'ayan, H. (2002). Comparing objective and subjective learning curves: Judgments of learning exhibit increased underconfidence with practice. *Journal of Experimental Psychology: General, 131,* 147–162.

Kosslyn, S. M., & Pomerantz, J. P. (1977). Imagery, propositions, and the form of internal representations. *Cognitive Psychology, 9,* 52–76.

Kotovsky, K., Hayes, J. R., & Simon, H. A. (1985). Why are some problems hard? Evidence from Tower of Hanoi. *Cognitive Psychology, 17,* 248–294.

Kounios, J. (1996). On the continuity of thought and the representation of knowledge: Electrophysiological and behavioral time-course measures reveal levels of structure in semantic memory. *Psychonomic Bulletin & Review, 3,* 265–286.

Kounios, J., Frymiare, J. L., Bowden, E. M., Fleck, J. I., Subramaniam, K., Parrish, T. B., & Jung-Beeman, M. (2006). The prepared mind: Neural activity prior to problem presentation predicts subsequent solution by sudden insight. *Psychological Science, 17,* 882–890.

Kounios, J., & Holcomb, P. J. (1992). Structure and process in semantic memory: Evidence from event-related brain potentials and reaction times. *Journal of Experimental Psychology: General, 121,* 459–479.

Kounios, J., & Holcomb, P. J. (1994). Concreteness effects in semantic processing: ERP evidence supporting dual-coding theory. *Journal of Experimental Psychology: Learning, Memory, and Cognition, 20,* 804–823.

Kounios, J., Kotz, S. A., & Holcomb, P. J. (2000). On the locus of the semantic satiation effect: Evidence from event-related brain potentials. *Memory & Cognition, 28,* 1366–1377.

Kozhevnikov, M., & Hegarty, M. (2001). Impetus beliefs as default heuristics: Dissociation between explicit and implicit knowledge about motion. *Psychonomic Bulletin & Review, 8,* 439–453.

Kraljik, T., Samuel, A. G., & Brennan, S. E. (2008). First impressions and last resorts: How listeners adjust to speaker variability. *Psychological Science, 19,* 332–338.

Krauss, R. M. (1998). Why do we gesture when we speak? *Current Directions in Psychological Science, 7,* 54–60.

Krist, H., Fieberg, E. L., & Wilkening, F. (1993). Intuitive physics in action and judgment: The development of knowledge about projectile motion. *Journal of Experimental Psychology: Learning, Memory, and Cognition, 19,* 952–966.

Kroll, N. E. A., Schepeler, E. M., & Angin, K. T. (1986). Bizarre imagery: The misremembered mnemonic. *Journal of Experimental Psychology: Learning, Memory, and Cognition, 12,* 42–53.

Kucera, H., & Francis, W. N. (1967). *Computational analysis of present day American English.* Providence, RI: Brown University Press.

Kuhn, T. S. (1962). *The structure of scientific revolutions.* Chicago: University of Chicago Press.

Kumon-Nakamura, S., Glucksberg, S., & Brown, M. (1995). How about another piece of pie? The allusional pretense theory of discourse irony. *Journal of Experimental Psychology: General, 124,* 3–21.

Kurtz, K. J., & Loewenstein, J. (2007). Converging on a new role for analogy in problem solving and retrieval: When two problems are better than one. *Memory & Cognition, 35,* 334–341.

Kutas, M., & Hillyard, S. A. (1980). Reading senseless sentences: Brain potentials reflect semantic incongruity. *Science, 207,* 203–205.

Kynski, T. R., & Tenebaum, J. B. (2007). The role of causality in judgment under uncertainty. *Journal of Experimental Psychology: General, 136,* 430–450.

Lachman, R., Lachman, J. L., & Butterfield, E. C. (1979). *Cognitive psychology and information processing: An introduction.* Hillsdale, NJ: Erlbaum.

Lachter, J., Forster, K. I., & Ruthruff, E. (2004). Forty-five years after Broadbent (1958): Still no identification without attention. *Psychological Review, 111,* 880–913.

Lane, S. M., & Zaragoza, M. S. (2007). A little elaboration goes a long way: The role of generation in eyewitness suggestibility. *Memory & Cognition, 35,* 1255–1266.

Lashley, K. D. (1950). In search of the engram. *Symposia for the Society for Experimental Biology, 4,* 454–482.

Lawson, R. (2006). The science of cycology: Failures to understand how everyday objects work. *Memory & Cognition, 34,* 1667–1675.

Leahey, T. H. (1992a). *A history of psychology: Main currents in psychological thought* (3rd ed.). Englewood Cliffs, NJ: Prentice Hall.

Leahey, T. H. (1992b). The mythical revolutions of American psychology. *American Psychologist, 47,* 308–318.

Leahey, T. H. (2000). *A history of psychology: Main currents in psychological thought* (3rd ed.). Englewood Cliffs, NJ: Prentice Hall.

Leahey, T. H. (2003). Herbert A. Smith Nobel Prize in economic sciences, 1978. *American Psychologist, 58,* 753–755.

Lee, H-W., Rayner, K., & Pollatsek, A. (1999). The time course of phonological, semantic, and orthographic coding in reading: Evidence from the fast-priming technique. *Psychonomic Bulletin & Review, 6,* 624–634.

LeFevre, J., Bisanz, J., Daley, K. E., Buffone, L., Greenham, S. L., & Sadesky, G. S. (1996). Multiple routes to solution of single-digit multiplication problems. *Journal of Experimental Psychology: General, 125,* 284–306.

Lehman, D. R., Lempert, R. O., & Nisbett, R. E. (1988). The effects of graduate training on reasoning. *American Psychologist, 43,* 431–442.

Leonesio, R. J., & Nelson, T. O. (1990). Do different metamemory judgments tap the same underlying aspects of memory? *Journal of Experimental Psychology: Learning, Memory, and Cognition, 16,* 464–470.

Levy, D. A., Stark, C. E. L., & Squire, L. R. (2004). Intact conceptual priming in the absence of declarative memory. *Psychological Science, 15,* 680–686.

Levy, J., Pashler, H., & Boer, E. (2006). Central interference in driving: Is there any stopping the psychological refractory period? *Psychological Science, 17,* 228–235.

Lewandowsky, S., Stritzka, W. G. K., Oberauer, K., & Morales, M. (2005). Memory for fact, fiction, and misinformation. *Psychological Science, 16,* 190–195.

Lewis, J. L. (1970). Semantic processing of unattended messages using dichotic listening. *Journal of Experimental Psychology, 85,* 225–228.

Lewontin, R. C. (1990). The evolution of cognition. In D. N. Osherson & E. E. Smith (Eds.), *Thinking: An invitation to cognitive science* (Vol. 3, pp. 229–246). Cambridge, MA: MIT Press.

Li, X., Schweickert, R., & Gandour, J. (2000). The phonological similarity effect in immediate recall: Positions of shared phonemes. *Memory & Cognition, 28,* 1116–1125.

Libby, L. K. (2003). Imagery perspective and source monitoring in imagination inflation. *Memory & Cognition, 31,* 1072–1081.

Liberman, A. M. (1957). Some results of research on speech perception. *Journal of the Acoustical Society of America, 29,* 117–123.

Liberman, A. M., Cooper, F. S., Shankweiler, D. P., & Studdert-Kennedy, M. (1967). Perception of speech code. *Psychological Review, 74,* 431–461.

Liberman, A. M., Harris, K. S., Hoffman, H. S., & Griffith, B. C. (1957). The discrimination of speech sounds within and across phoneme boundaries. *Journal of Experimental Psychology, 54,* 358–368.

Liberman, A. M., & Mattingly, I. G. (1985). The motor theory of speech perception revised. *Cognition, 21,* 1–36.

Libkuman, T. M., Nichols-Whitehead, P., Griffith, J., & Thomas, R. (1999). Source of arousal and memory for detail. *Memory & Cognition, 27,* 166–190.

Lidji, P., Kolinsky, R., Lochy, A., & Morais, J. (2007). Spatial associations for musical stimuli: A piano in the head? *Journal of Experimental Psychology: Human Perception and Performance, 33,* 1189–1207.

Lindsay, D. S., Allen, B. P., Chan, J. C. K., & Dahl, L. C. (2004). Eyewitness suggestibility and source similarity: Intrusions of details from one event into memory reports of another event. *Journal of Memory and Language, 50,* 96–111.

Lindsay, D. S., Hagen, L., Read, J. D., Wade, K. A., & Garry, M. (2004). True photographs and false memories. *Psychological Science, 15,* 149–154.

Lindsay, P. H., & Norman, D. A. (1977). *Human information processing: An introduction to psychology.* New York: Academic Press.

Lindsley, J. R. (1975). Producing simple utterances: How far ahead do we plan? *Cognitive Psychology, 7,* 1–19.

Linton, M. (1975). Memory for real-world events. In D. A. Norman & D. E. Rumelhart (Eds.), *Explorations in cognition* (pp. 376–404). San Francisco: Freeman.

Linton, M. (1978). Real world memory after six years: An *in vivo* study of very long term memory. In M. M. Gruneberg, P. E. Morris, & R. N. Sykes (Eds.), *Practical aspects of memory* (pp. 69–76). Orlando, FL: Academic Press.

Litman, D. J., & Allen, J. F. (1987). A plan recognition model for subdialogues in conversation. *Cognitive Science, 11,* 163–200.

Lockridge, C. B., & Brennan, S. E. (2002). Addressees' needs influence speakers' early syntactic choices. *Psychonomic Bulletin & Review, 9,* 550–557.

Loftus, E. F. (1971). Memory for intentions: The effect of presence of a cue and interpolated activity. *Psychonomic Science, 23,* 315–316.

Loftus, E. F. (1980). *Memory.* Reading, MA: Addison-Wesley.

Loftus, E. F. (1991). Made in memory: Distortions in recollection after misleading information. In G. H. Bower (Ed.), *The psychology of learning and motivation* (Vol. 27, pp. 187–215). New York: Academic Press.

Loftus, E. F. (1993). The reality of repressed memories. *American Psychologist, 48,* 518–537.

Loftus, E. F. (2003). Make-believe memories. *American Psychologist, 58,* 867–873.

Loftus, E. F. (2004). Memories of things unseen. *Current Directions in Psychological Science, 13,* 145–147.

Loftus, E. F., & Coan, D. (1994). The construction of childhood memories. In D. Peters (Ed.), *The child witness in context: Cognitive, social, and legal perspectives.* New York: Kluwer.

Loftus, E. F., Donders, K., Hoffman, H. G., & Schooler, J. W. (1989). Creating new memories that are quickly accessed and confidently held. *Memory & Cognition, 17,* 607–616.

Loftus, E. F., & Hoffman, H. G. (1989). Misinformation and memory: The creation of new memories. *Journal of Experimental Psychology: General, 118,* 100–104.

Loftus, E. F., & Ketcham, K. (1991). *Witness for the defense.* New York: St. Martin's Press.

Loftus, E. F., & Palmer, J. C. (1974). Reconstruction of automobile destruction: An example of the interaction between language and memory. *Journal of Verbal Learning and Verbal Behavior, 13,* 585–589.

Loftus, G. R., & Hanna, A. M. (1989). The phenomenology of spatial integration: Data and models. *Cognitive Psychology, 21,* 363–397.

Loftus, G. R., & Irwin, D. E. (1998). On the relations among different measures of visible and informational persistence. *Cognitive Psychology, 35,* 135–199.

Loftus, G. R., & Loftus, E. F. (1974). The influence of one memory retrieval on a subsequent memory retrieval. *Memory & Cognition, 2,* 467–471.

Logan, G. D. (1988). Toward an instance theory of automatization. *Psychological Review, 95,* 492–527.

Logan, G. D. (1990). Repetition priming and automaticity: Common underlying mechanisms? *Cognitive Psychology, 22,* 1–35.

Logan, G. D. (2003). Executive control of thought and action: In search of the wild homunculus. *Current Directions in Psychological Science, 12,* 45–48.

Logan, G. D., & Etherton, J. L. (1994). What is learned during automatization? The role of attention in constructing an instance. *Journal of Experimental Psychology: Learning, Memory, and Cognition, 20,* 1022–1050.

Logan, G. D., & Klapp, S. T. (1991). Automatizing alphabet arithmetic: I. Is extended practice necessary to produce automaticity? *Journal of Experimental Psychology: Learning, Memory, and Cognition, 17,* 179–195.

Logie, R. H., Zucco, G., & Baddeley, A. D. (1990). Interference with visual short-term memory. *Acta Psychologica, 75,* 55–74.

Long, D. L., & De Ley, L. (2000). Implicit causality and discourse focus: The interaction of text and reader characteristics in pronoun resolution. *Journal of Memory and Language, 42,* 545–570.

Long, D. L., Golding, J., Graesser, A. C., & Clark, L. F. (1990). Inference generation during story comprehension: A comparison of goals, events, and states. In A. C. Graesser & G. H. Bower (Eds.), *The psychology of learning and motivation* (Vol. 25). New York: Academic Press.

Long, D. L., Oppy, B. J., & Seely, M. R. (1997). Individual differences in readers' sentence- and text-level representations. *Journal of Memory and Language, 36*, 129–145.

Lorch, R. F. Jr., Lorch, E. P., & Matthews, P. D. (1985). On-line processing of the topic structure of a text. *Journal of Memory and Language, 24*, 350–362.

Lozano, S. C., & Tversky, B. (2006). Communicative gestures facilitate problem solving for both communicators and recipients. *Journal of Memory and Language, 55*, 47–63.

Lu, S., & Zhou, K. (2005). Stimulus-driven attentional capture by equiluminent color change. *Psychonomic Bulletin & Review, 12*, 567–572.

Luchins, A. S. (1942). Mechanization in problem solving. *Psychological Monographs, 54* (Whole no. 248).

Lupyan, G. (2008). From chair to "chair": A representational shift account of object labeling effects on memory. *Journal of Experimental Psychology: General, 137*, 348–369.

Lustig, C., & Hasher, L. (2001). Implicit memory is vulnerable to proactive interference. *Psychological Science, 12*, 408–412.

Lutz, M. E, & Radvansky, G. A. (1997). The fate of completed goal information. *Journal of Memory and Language, 36*, 293–310.

Mack, A. (2003). Inattentional blindness: looking without seeing. *Current Directions in Psychological Science, 12*, 180–184.

Mack, A., & Rock, I. (1998). *Inattentional blindness.* Cambridge, MA: MIT Press.

Mackworth, N. H. (1948). The breakdown of vigilance during prolonged visual search. *Quarterly Journal of Experimental Psychology, 1*, 6–21.

MacLeod, C. M. (1988). Forgotten but not gone: Savings for pictures and words in long-term memory. *Journal of Experimental Psychology: Learning, Memory, and Cognition, 14*, 195–212.

MacLeod, C. (1992). The Stroop task: The "gold standard" of attentional measures. *Journal of Experimental Psychology: General, 121*, 12–14.

MacLeod, C. M. (1991). Half a century of research on the Stroop effect: An integrative review. *Psychological Bulletin, 109*, 163–203.

MacLeod, M. D., & Macrae, C. N. (2001). Gone but not forgotten: The transient nature of retrieval-induced forgetting. *Psychological Science, 12*, 148–152.

MacLeod, M. D., & Saunders, J. (2008). Retrieval inhibition and memory distortion. *Current Directions in Psychological Science, 17*, 26–30.

MacQueen, G.M., Tipper, S.P., Young, L.T., Joffe, R.T., & Levitt, A.J. (2000). Impaired distractor inhibition on a selective attention task in unmedicated, depressed subjects. *Psychological Medicine*, 30, 557–564.

Madigan, S., & O'Hara, R. (1992). Short-term memory at the turn of the century: Mary Whiton Calkins's memory research. *American Psychologist, 47*, 170–174.

Magliano, J. P., Miller, J., & Zwaan, R. A. (2001). Indexing space and time in film understanding. *Applied Cognitive Psychology, 15*, 533–545.

Magliano, J. P., Taylor, H. A., & Kim, H. J. (2005). When goals collide: Monitoring the goals of multiple characters. *Memory & Cognition, 33*, 1357–1367.

Magliano, J. P., Trabasso, T., & Graesser, A. C. (1999). Strategic processing during comprehension. *Journal of Educational Psychology, 91*, 615–629.

Magno, E., & Allan, K. (2007). Self-reference during explicit memory retrieval: An event-related potential analysis. *Psychological Science, 18*, 672–677.

Maier, N. R. F. (1931). Reasoning in humans: II. The solution of a problem and its appearance in consciousness. *Journal of Comparative Psychology, 12*, 181–194.

Maki, R. H. (1989). Recognition of added and deleted details in scripts. *Memory & Cognition, 17*, 274–282.

Malt, B. C. (1985). The role of discourse structure in understanding anaphora. *Journal of Memory and Language, 24*, 271–289.

Malt, B. C., Sloman, S. A., & Gennari, S. P. (2003). Universality and language specificity in object naming. *Journal of Memory and Language, 49*, 20–42.

Mandel, D. R., & Lehman, D. R. (1996). Counterfactual thinking and ascriptions of cause and preventability. *Journal of Personality and Social Psychology, 71*, 450–463.

Mandler, G. (1967). Organization and memory. In K. W. Spence & J. T. Spence (Eds.), *The psychology of learning and motivation* (Vol. 1, pp. 327–372). New York: Academic Press.

Mandler, G. (1972). Organization and recognition. In E. Tulving & W. Donaldson (Eds.), *Organization of memory* (pp. 139–166). New York: Academic Press.

Mandler, G. (1984). *Mind and body: Psychology of emotion and stress.* New York: Norton.

Mandler, G. (1985). From association to structure. *Journal of Experimental Psychology: Learning, Memory, and Cognition, 11*, 464–468.

Mandler, J. M., & Mandler, G. (1969). The diaspora of experimental psychology: The Gestaltists and others. In D. Fleming & B. Bailyn (Eds.), *The intellectual migration: Europe and America, 1930–1960* (pp. 371–419). Cambridge, MA: Harvard University Press.

Manwell, L. A., Roberts, M. A., & Besner, D. (2004). Single letter coloring and spatial cuing eliminates a semantic contribution to the Stroop effect. *Psychonomic Bulletin & Review, 11*, 458–462.

Marcel, A. J. (1980). Conscious and preconscious recognition of polysemous words: Locating the selective effects of prior verbal context. In R. S. Nickerson (Ed.), *Attention and performance VIII* (pp. 435–457). Hillsdale, NJ: Erlbaum.

Marcel, A. J. (1983). Conscious and unconscious perception: Experiments on visual masking and word recognition. *Cognitive Psychology, 15*, 197–237.

Marian, V., & Neisser, U. (2000). Language-dependent recall of autobiographical memories. *Journal of Experimental Psychology: General, 129*, 361–368.

Markman, A. B., Taylor, E., & Gentner, D. (2007). Auditory presentation leads to better analogical retrieval than written presentation. *Psychonomic Bulletin & Review, 14*, 1101–1106.

Markovits, H., & Doyon, C. (2004). Information processing and reasoning with premises that are empirically false: Interference, working memory, and processing speed. *Memory & Cognition, 32*, 592–601.

Markovits, H., & Potvin, F. (2001). Suppression of valid inferences and knowledge structures: The curious effect of producing alternative antecedents on reasoning with causal conditionals. *Memory & Cognition, 29,* 736–744.

Marler, P. (1967). Animal communication signals. *Science, 35,* 63–78.

Marschark, M., & Paivio, A. (1979). Semantic congruity and lexical marking in symbolic comparisons: An expectancy hypothesis. *Memory & Cognition, 7,* 175–184.

Marsh, E. J. (2007). Retelling is not the same as recalling. *Current Directions in Psychological Science, 16,* 16–20.

Marsh, E. J., Meade, M. L., Roediger, H. L. III (2003). Learning facts from fiction. *Journal of Memory and Language, 49,* 519–536.

Marsh, E. J. Roediger, H. L., Bjork, R. A., & Bjork, E. L. (2007). The memorial consequences of multiple-choice testing. *Psychonomic Bulletin & Review, 14,* 194–199.

Marsh, R. L., Cook, G. I., Meeks, J. T., Clark-Foos, A., & Hicks, J. L. (2007). Memory for intention-related material presented in a to-be-ignored channel. *Memory & Cognition, 35,* 1197–1204.

Marsh, R. L., & Hicks, J. L. (1998). Event-based prospective memory and executive control of working memory. *Journal of Experimental Psychology, 24,* 336–349.

Marsh, R. L., Hicks, J. L., & Cook, G. I (2005). On the relationship between effort toward an ongoing task and cue detection in event-based prospective memory. *Journal of Experimental Psychology: Learning, Memory, and Cognition, 31,* 68–75.

Marshall, J. C., & Halligan, P. W. (1994). Independent properties of normal hemispheric specialization predict some characteristics of visuo-spatial neglect. *Cortex, 10,* 29–63.

Marslen-Wilson, W. D., & Welsh, A. (1978). Processing interactions and lexical access during word recognition in continuous speech. *Cognitive Psychology, 30,* 509–517.

Martin, R. C. (2000). Contribution from the neuropsychology of language and memory to the development of cognitive theory. *Journal of Memory and Language, 43,* 149–156.

Martindale, C. (1991). *Cognitive psychology: A neural-network approach.* Pacific Grove, CA: Brooks/Cole.

Mason, R. A., Just, M. A., Keller, T. A., & Carpenter, P. A. (2003). Ambiguity in the brain: What brain imaging reveals about the processing of syntactically ambiguous sentences. *Journal of Experimental Psychology: Learning, Memory, and Cognition, 29,* 1319–1338.

Masson, M. E. J. (1984). Memory for the surface structure of sentences: Remembering with and without awareness. *Journal of Verbal Learning and Verbal Behavior, 23,* 579–592.

Masson, M. E. J. (1995). A distributed memory model of semantic priming. *Journal of Experimental Psychology: Learning, Memory, and Cognition, 21,* 3–23.

Mather, M., Shafir, E., & Johnson, M. K. (2000). Misremembrance of options past: Source monitoring and choice. *Psychological Science, 11,* 132–138.

Mathis, K. M. (2002). Semantic interference from objects both in and out of scene context. *Journal of Experimental Psychology: Learning, Memory, and Cognition, 28,* 171–182.

Matlin, M. (1983). *Cognition.* New York: Holt.

Matlin, M. (2002). *Cognition* (5th ed.). New York: John Wiley & Sons.

Maunsell, J. H. R., & Newsome, W. T. (1987). Visual processing in monkey extrastriate cortex. *Annual Review of Neuroscience, 10,* 363–401.

Mayr, S., & Buchner, A. (2006). Evidence for episodic retrieval of inadequate prime responses in auditory negative priming. *Journal of Experimental Psychology: Human Perception and Performance,* 32, 932–943.

Mazzoni, G., & Cornoldi, C. (1993). Strategies in study time allocation: Why is study time sometimes not effective? *Journal of Experimental Psychology: General, 122,* 47–60.

Mazzoni, G., & Memon, A. (2003). Imagination can create false autobiographical memories. *Psychological Science, 14,* 186–188.

McCabe, D. P., Smith, A. D., & Parks, C. M. (2007). The role of working memory capacity in reducing memory errors. *Memory & Cognition, 35,* 231–241.

McCandliss, B. D., Posner, M. I., & Givon, T. (1997). Brain plasticity in learning visual words. *Cognitive Psychology, 33,* 88–110.

McCarley, J. S., Kramer, A. F., Wickens, C. D., Vidoni, E. D., & Boot, W. R. (2004). Visual skills in airport security screening. *Psychological Science, 15,* 302–306.

McCarthy, R. A., & Warrington, E. K. (1984). A two route model of speech production: Evidence from aphasia. *Brain, 107,* 463–485.

McCarthy, R. A., & Warrington, E. K. (1990). *Cognitive neuropsychology: A clinical introduction.* San Diego: Academic Press.

McClelland, J. L. (1979). On the time relations of mental processes: An examination of systems of processes in cascade. *Psychological Review, 86,* 287–330.

McClelland, J. L., & Elman, J. L. (1986). The TRACE model of speech perception. *Cognitive Psychology, 18,* 1–86.

McClelland, J. L., & Rumelhart, D. E. (1981). An interactive activation model of context effects in letter perception: Part 1. An account of basic findings. *Psychological Review, 88,* 375–407.

McClelland, J. L., Rumelhart, D. E., & Hinton, G. E. (1986). The appeal of parallel distributed processing. In D. E. Rumelhart, J. L. McClelland, & PDP Research Group (Eds.), *Parallel distributed processing* (Vol. 1, pp. 3–44). Cambridge, MA: MIT Press.

McCloskey, M. (1983). Naive theories of motion. In D. Gentner & A. L. Stevens (Eds.), *Mental models* (pp. 299–324). Hillsdale, NJ: Erlbaum.

McCloskey, M. (1992). Cognitive mechanisms in numerical processing: Evidence from acquired dyscalculia. *Cognition, 44,* 107–157.

McCloskey, M., Caramazza, A., & Green, B. (1980). Curvilinear motion in the absence of external forces: Naive beliefs about the motion of objects. *Science, 210,* 1139–1141.

McCloskey, M., Wible, C. G., & Cohen, N. J. (1988). Is there a special flashbulb-memory mechanism? *Journal of Experimental Psychology: General, 117,* 171–181.

McCloy, R., & Byrne, R. M. (2000). Counterfactual thinking about controllable events. *Memory & Cognition, 28,* 1071–1078.

McDaniel, M. A., & Einstein, G. O. (1986). Bizarre imagery as an effective memory aid: The importance of distinctiveness. *Journal of Experimental Psychology: Learning, Memory, and Cognition, 12,* 54–65.

McDaniel, M. A., Maier, S. F., & Einstein, G. O. (2002). "Brain-specific" nutrients: A memory cure? *Psychological Science in the Public Interest, 31,* 12–38.

McDaniel, M. A., Roediger, H. L., & McDermott, K. B. (2007). Generalized test-enhanced learning from the laboratory to the classroom. *Psychonomic Bulletin & Review, 14,* 200–206.

McDonald, J. L., & MacWhinney, B. (1995). The time course of anaphor resolution: Effects of implicit verb causality and gender. *Journal of Memory and Language, 34,* 543–566.

McDonald, J. L., & Shaibe, D. M. (2002). The accessibility of characters in single sentences: Proper names, common nouns, and first mention. *Psychonomic Bulletin & Review, 9,* 356–361.

McGeoch, J. A. (1932). Forgetting and the law of disuse. *Psychological Review, 39,* 352–370.

McKoon, G., & Macfarland, T. (2002). Event templates in the lexical representations of verbs. *Cognitive Psychology, 45,* 1–44.

McKoon, G., & Ratcliff, R. (1986). Inferences about predictable events. *Journal of Experimental Psychology: Learning, Memory, and Cognition, 12,* 82–91.

McKoon, G., & Ratcliff, R. (1989). Inferences about contextually defined categories. *Journal of Experimental Psychology: Learning, Memory, and Cognition, 15,* 1134–1146.

McKoon, G., & Ratcliff, R. (1992). Inference during reading. *Psychological Review, 99,* 440–466.

McKoon, G., & Ratcliff, R. (2007). Interactions of meaning and syntax: Implications for models of sentence comprehension. *Journal of Memory and Language, 56,* 270–290.

McKoon, G., Ratcliff, R., Ward, G., & Sproat, R. (1993). Syntactic prominence effects on discourse processes. *Journal of Memory and Language, 32,* 593–607.

McNamara, D. S., & McDaniel, M. A. (2004). Suppressing irrelevant information: Knowledge activation or inhibition? *Journal of Experimental Psychology: Learning, Memory, and Cognition, 30,* 465–482.

McNamara, T. P. (1992). Priming and constraints it places on theories of memory and retrieval. *Psychological Review, 99,* 650–662.

McNamara, T. P., & Diwadkar, V. A. (1996). The context of memory retrieval. *Journal of Memory and Language, 35,* 877–892.

McNeill, D. (1992). *Hand and mind: What gestures reveal about thought.* Chicago: University of Chicago Press.

McRae, K., & Boisvert, S. (1998). Automatic semantic similarity priming. *Journal of Experimental Psychology: Learning, Memory, and Cognition, 24,* 558–572.

McRae, K., de Sa, V. R., & Seidenberg, M. S. (1997). On the nature and scope of featural representations of word meaning. *Journal of Experimental Psychology: General, 126,* 99–130.

Meade, M. L., & Roediger, H. L. III. (2002). Explorations in the social contagion of memory. *Memory & Cognition, 30,* 995–1009.

Meade, M. L., Watson, J. M., Balota, D. A., & Roediger, H. L. (2007). The roles of spreading activation and retrieval mode in producing false recognition in the DRM paradigm. *Journal of Memory and Language, 56,* 305–320.

Medin, D. L. (1989). Concepts and conceptual structure. *American Psychologist, 44,* 1469–1481.

Medin, D. L., & Atran, S. (2004). The native mind: Biological categorization and reasoning in development and across cultures. *Psychological Review, 111,* 960–983.

Medin, D. L., & Bazerman, M. H. (1999). Broadening behavioral decision research: Multiple levels of cognitive processing. *Psychonomic Bulletin & Review, 6,* 533–546.

Medin, D. L., Coley, J. D., Storms, G., & Hayes, B. K. (2003). A relevance theory of induction. *Psychonomic Bulletin & Review, 10,* 517–532.

Medin, D. L., & Edelson, S. M. (1988). Problem structure and the use of base-rate information from experience. *Journal of Experimental Psychology: General, 117,* 68–85.

Medin, D. L., Goldstone, R. L., & Gentner, D. (1993). Respects for similarity. *Psychological Review, 100,* 254–278.

Medin, D. L., Lynch, E. B., Coley, J. D., & Atran, S. (1997). Categorization and reasoning among tree experts: Do all roads lead to Rome? *Cognitive Psychology, 32,* 49–96.

Mehler, J., Morton, J., & Jusczyk, P. W. (1984). On reducing language to biology. *Cognitive Neuropsychology, 1,* 83–116.

Melton, A. W. (1963). Implications of short-term memory for a general theory of memory. *Journal of Verbal Learning and Verbal Behavior, 2,* 1–21.

Merikle, P. M. (1982). Unconscious perception revisited. *Perception & Psychophysics, 31,* 298–301.

Merikle, P. M., & Reingold, E. M. (1998). On demonstrating unconscious perception: Comment on Draine and Greenwald (1998). *Journal of Experimental Psychology: General, 127,* 304–310.

Metcalfe, J. (1986). Feeling of knowing in memory and problem solving. *Journal of Experimental Psychology: Learning, Memory, and Cognition, 12,* 288–294.

Metcalfe, J. (2002). Is study time allocated selectively to a region of proximal learning? *Journal of Experimental Psychology: General, 131,* 349–363.

Metcalfe, J., & Finn, B. (2008). Evidence that judgments of learning are causally related to study choice. *Psychonomic Bulletin & Review, 15,* 174–179.

Metcalfe, J., & Kornell, N. (2003). The dynamics of learning and allocation of study time to a region of proximal learning. *Journal of Experimental Psychology: General, 132,* 530–542.

Metcalfe, J., & Wiebe, D. (1987). Intuition in insight and noninsight problem solving. *Memory & Cognition, 15,* 238–246.

Metzing, C., & Brennan, S. E. (2003). When conceptual pacts are broken: Partner-specific effects on the comprehension of referring expressions. *Journal of Memory and Language, 49,* 201–213.

Meyer, A. S., & Bock, K. (1992). The tip-of-the-tongue phenomenon: Blocking or partial activation? *Memory & Cognition, 20,* 715–726.

Meyer, D. E., & Schvaneveldt, R. W. (1971). Facilitation in recognizing pairs of words: Evidence of a dependence between retrieval operations. *Journal of Experimental Psychology, 90,* 227–234.

Meyer, D. E., Schvaneveldt, R. W., & Ruddy, M. G. (1975). Loci of contextual effects on visual word-recognition. In P. M. A. Rabbitt & S. Dornic (Eds.), *Attention and performance* (Vol. 5, pp. 98–118). London: Academic Press.

Miller, D. T., & McFarland, C. (1986). Counterfactual thinking and victim compensation: A test of norm theory. *Personality and Social Psychology Bulletin, 12,* 513–519.

Miller, G. A. (1956). The magical number seven, plus or minus two: Some limits on our capacity for processing information. *Psychological Review, 63,* 81–97.

Miller, G. A. (1973). Psychology and communication. In G. A. Miller (Ed.), *Communication, language, and meaning: Psychological perspectives* (pp. 3–12). New York: Basic Books.

Miller, G. A. (1977). Practical and lexical knowledge. In P. N. Johnson-Laird & P. C. Wason (Eds.), *Thinking: Readings in cognitive science* (pp. 400–410). Cambridge, U.K.: Cambridge University Press.

Miller, G. A. (1983). Introduction. In James, W. (1983 ed), *The principles of psychology*. Cambridge, MA: Harvard University Press.

Miller, G. A., Galanter, E., & Pribram, K. H. (1960). *Plans and the structure of behavior*. New York: Henry Holt.

Miller, G. A., & Isard, S. (1963). Some perceptual consequences of linguistic rules. *Journal of Verbal Learning and Verbal Behavior, 2*, 217–228.

Millis, K. K., & Graesser, A. C. (1994). The time-course of constructing knowledge-based inferences for scientific texts. *Journal of Memory and Language, 33*, 583–599.

Millis, K. K., & Just, M. A. (1994). The influence of connectives on sentence comprehension. *Journal of Memory and Language, 33*, 128–147.

Milner, B., Corkin, S., & Teuber, H. L. (1968). Further analysis of the hippocampal amnesic syndrome: 14–year follow up study of H. M. *Neuropsychologia, 6*, 215–234.

Mitchell, D. B. (2006). Nonconscious priming after 17 years. *Psychological Science, 17*, 925–929.

Mitchell, D. C., & Holmes, V. M. (1985). The role of specific information about the verb in parsing sentences with local structural ambiguity. *Journal of Memory and Language, 24*, 542–559.

Mitchell, K. J., & Zaragoza, M. S. (1996). Repeated exposure to suggestion and false memory: The role of contextual variability. *Journal of Memory and Language, 35*, 246–260.

Mitchell, K. J., & Zaragoza, M. S. (2001). Contextual overlap and eyewitness suggestibility. *Memory & Cognition, 29*, 616–626.

Miyake, A., Friedman, N. P., Emerson, M. J., Witzki, A. H., Howerter, A., & Wager, T. D. (2000). The unity and diversity of executive functions and their contributions to complex "frontal lobe" tasks: A latent variable analysis. *Cognitive Psychology, 41*, 49–100.

Miyake, A., Just, M. A., & Carpenter, P. A. (1994). Working memory constraints on the resolution of lexical ambiguity: Maintaining multiple interpretations in neutral contexts. *Journal of Memory and Language, 33*, 175–202.

Miyake, A., & Shah, P. (Eds.). (1999). *Models of working memory: Mechanisms of active maintenance and executive control.* New York: Cambridge University Press.

Moldoveanu, M., & Langer, E. (2002). False memories of the future: A critique of the applications of probabilistic reasoning to the study of cognitive processes. *Psychological Review, 109*, 358–375.

Monaghan, P., & Pollmann, S. (2003). Division of labor between the hemispheres for complex but not simple tasks: An implemented connectionist model. *Journal of Experimental Psychology: General, 132*, 379–399.

Monaghan, P., & Shillcock, R. (2004). Hemispheric asymmetries in cognitive modeling: connectionist modeling of unilateral visual neglect. *Psychological Review, 111*, 283–308.

Mook, D. G. (1983). In defense of external invalidity. *American Psychologist, 38*, 379–387.

Moore, A. B., Clark, B. A., & Kane, M. J. (2008). Who shalt not kill? Individual differences in working memory capacity, executive control, and moral judgment. *Psychological Science, 19*, 549–557.

Moray, N. (1959). Attention in dichotic listening: Affective cues and the influence of instructions. *Quarterly Journal of Experimental Psychology, 11*, 56–60.

Moray, N., Bates, A., & Barnett, T. (1965). Experiments on the four-eared man. *Journal of the Acoustical Society of America, 38*, 196–201.

Morey, C. C., & Cowan, N. (2004). When visual and verbal memories compete: Evidence of cross-domain limits in working memory. *Psychonomic Bulletin & Review, 11*, 296–301.

Morris, A. L., & Harris, C. L. (2002). Sentence context, word recognition, and repetition blindness. *Journal of Experimental Psychology: Learning, Memory, and Cognition, 28*, 962–982.

Morris, C. D., Bransford, J. D., & Franks, J. J. (1977). Levels of processing versus transfer appropriate processing. *Journal of Verbal Learning and Verbal Behavior, 16*, 519–533.

Morris, R. K., & Folk, J. R. (1998). Focus as a contextual priming mechanism in reading. *Memory & Cognition, 26*, 1313–1322.

Morrow, D. G., Greenspan, S. L., & Bower, G. H. (1987). Accessibility and situation models in narrative comprehension. *Journal of Memory and Language, 26*, 165–187.

Morton, J. (1979). Facilitation in word recognition: Experiments causing change in the logogen models. In P. A. Kolers, M. E. Wrolstad, & H. Bouma (Eds.), *Processing of visible language* (Vol. 1, pp. 259–268). New York: Plenum.

Moscovitch, M. (1979). Information processing and the cerebral hemispheres. In M. S. Gazzaniga (Ed.), *Handbook of behavioral neurobiology: Vol. 2. Neuropsychology* (pp. 379–446). New York: Plenum.

Moshinsky, A., & Bar-Hillel, M. (2002). Where did 1850 happen first—in America or in Europe? A cognitive account for a historical bias. *Psychological Science, 13*, 20–26.

Most, S. B., Scholl, B. J., Clifford, E. R., & Simons, D. J. (2005). What you see is what you set: Sustained inattentional blindness and the capture of awareness. *Psychological Review, 112*, 217–242.

Moyer, R. S. (1973). Comparing objects in memory: Evidence suggesting an internal psychophysics. *Perception and Psychophysics, 13*, 180–184.

Moyer, R. S., & Bayer, R. H. (1976). Mental comparison and the symbolic distance effect. *Cognitive Psychology, 8*, 228–246.

Mueller, S. T., Seymour, T. L., Kieras, D. E., & Meyer, D. E. (2003). Theoretical implications of articulatory duration, phonological similarity, and phonological complexity in verbal working memory. *Journal of Experimental Psychology: Learning, Memory, and Cognition, 29*, 1353–1380.

Murdock, B. B. Jr. (1962). The serial position effect of free recall. *Journal of Experimental Psychology, 64*, 482–488.

Murphy, G. L. (1985). Processes of understanding anaphora. *Journal of Memory and Language, 24*, 290–303.

Murphy, G. L., & Medin, D. L. (1985). The role of theories in conceptual coherence. *Psychological Review, 92*, 289–316.

Murray, D. J. (1967). The role of speech responses in short-term memory. *Canadian Journal of Psychology, 21*, 263–276.

Murray, J. D., Klin, C. M., & Myers, J. L. (1993). Forward inferences in narrative text. *Journal of Memory and Language, 32*, 464–473.

Naccache, L., Blandin, E., & Dehaene, S. (2002). Unconscious masked priming depends on temporal attention. *Psychological Science, 13,* 416–424.

Nadel, L., & Jacobs, W. J. (1998). Traumatic memory is special. *Current Directions in Psychological Science, 7,* 154–156.

Nadel, L., & Zola-Morgan, S. (1984). Infantile amnesia: A neurobiological perspective. In M. Moscovitch (Ed.), *Infant Memory*. New York: Plenum Press.

Nairne, J. S., Pandeirada, N. S., & Thompson, S. R. (2008). Adaptive memory: The comparative value of survival processing. *Psychological Science, 19,* 176–180.

Nairne, J. S., Thompson, S. R., & Pandeirada, N. S. (2007). Adaptive memory: Survival processing enhances retention. *Journal of Experimental Psychology: Learning, Memory, and Cognition, 33,* 263–273.

Navon, D. (1984). Resources: A theoretical soup stone? *Psychological Review, 91,* 216–234.

Neath, I., Surprenant, A. M., & Crowder, R. G. (1993). The context-dependent stimulus suffix effect. *Journal of Experimental Psychology: Learning, Memory and Cognition, 19,* 698–703.

Neely, J. H. (1976). Semantic priming and retrieval from lexical memory: Evidence for facilitatory and inhibitory processes. *Memory & Cognition, 4,* 648–654.

Neely, J. H. (1977). Semantic priming and retrieval from lexical memory: Roles of inhibitionless spreading activation and limited-capacity attention. *Journal of Experimental Psychology: General, 106,* 226–254.

Neely, J. H., Keefe, D. E. & Ross, K. L. (1989). Semantic priming in the lexical decision task: Roles of prospective prime-generated expectancies and retrospective semantic matching. *Journal of Experimental Psychology: Learning, Memory, and Cognition, 15,* 1003–1019.

Neill, W.T. (1977). Inhibition and facilitation processes in selective attention. *Journal of Experimental Psychology: Human Perception & Performance*, 3, 444–450.

Neill, W.T., Valdes, L.A., & Terry, K.M. (1995). Selective attention and the inhitiory control of cognition. In F.N. Dempster & C.J. Brainerd (Eds.), *New perspectives on interference and inhibition in cognition*. (pp. 207–261), New York: Academic Press.

Neisser, U. (1964). Visual search. *Scientific American, 210,* 94–102.

Neisser, U. (1967). *Cognitive psychology*. New York: Appleton-Century-Crofts.

Neisser, U. (1976). *Cognition and reality*. San Francisco: Freeman.

Neisser, U. (1981). John Dean's memory: A case study. *Cognition, 9,* 1–22.

Neisser, U. (1982). *Memory observed: Remembering in natural contexts.* San Francisco: Freeman.

Neisser, U., Novick, R., & Lazar, R. (1963). Searching for ten targets simultaneously. *Perceptual and Motor Skills, 17,* 955–961.

Nelson, K. (1993). The psychological and social origins of autobiographical memory. *Psychological Science, 4,* 7–14.

Nelson, T. O. (1978). Savings and forgetting from long-term memory. *Journal of Verbal Learning and Verbal Behavior, 10,* 568–576.

Nelson, T. O. (1985). Ebbinghaus's contribution to the measurement of retention: Savings during relearning. *Journal of Experimental Psychology: Learning, Memory, and Cognition, 11,* 472–479.

Nelson, T. O. (1988). Predictive accuracy of the feeling of knowing across different criterion tasks and across different subject populations and individuals. In M. Gruneberg, P. Morris, & R. Sykes (Eds.), *Practical aspects of memory: Current research and issues* (Vol. 1, pp. 190–196). New York: Wiley.

Nelson, T. O. (1993). Judgments of learning and the allocation of study time. *Journal of Experimental Psychology: General, 122,* 269–273.

Nelson, T. O., & Leonesio, R. J. (1988). Allocation of self-paced study time and the "labor-in vain effect." *Journal of Experimental Psychology: Learning, Memory, and Cognition, 14,* 676–686.

Nelson, T. O., McSpadden, M., Fromme, K., & Marlatt, G. A. (1986). Effects of alcohol intoxication on metamemory and on retrieval from long-term memory. *Journal of Experimental Psychology: General, 115,* 247–254.

Neuschatz, J. S., Benoit, G. E., & Payne, D. G. (2003). Effective warnings in the Deese–Roediger–McDermott false-memory paradigm: The role of identifiability. *Journal of Experimental Psychology: Learning, Memory, and Cognition, 29,* 35–41.

Newell, A., Shaw, J. C., & Simon, H. A. (1958). Elements of a theory of human problem solving. *Psychological Review, 65,* 151–166.

Newell, A., & Simon, H. A. (1972). *Human problem solving*. Englewood Cliffs, NJ: Prentice Hall.

Newell, B. R., & Shanks, D. R. (2003). Take the best or look at the rest? Factors influencing "one-reason" decision making. *Journal of Experimental Psychology: Learning, Memory, and Cognition, 29,* 53–65.

Newell, B. R., & Shanks, D. R. (2004). On the role of recognition in decision making. *Journal of Experimental Psychology: Learning, Memory, and Cognition, 30,* 923–935.

Newport, E. L., & Bellugi, W. (1978). Linguistic expression of category levels in a visual–gestural language: A flower is a flower is a flower. In E. Rosch & B. B. Lloyd (Eds.), *Cognition and categorization* (pp. 49–71). Hillsdale, NJ: Erlbaum.

Nickerson, R. S. (2001). The projective way of knowing: A useful heuristic that sometimes misleads. *Current Directions in Psychological Science, 10,* 168–172.

Nickerson, R. S. (2002). The production and perception of randomness. *Psychological Review, 109,* 330–357.

Nickerson, R. S., & Adams, M. J. (1979). Long-term memory for a common object. *Cognitive Psychology, 11,* 287–307.

Nisbett, R. E., Krantz, D. H., Jepson, C., & Kunda, Z. (1983). The use of statistical heuristics in everyday inductive reasoning. *Psychological Review, 90,* 339–363.

Nisbett, R. E., Peng, K., Choi, I., & Norenzayan, A. (2001). Culture and systems of thought: Holistic versus analytic cognition. *Psychological Review, 108,* 291–310.

Nisbett, R. E., & Wilson, T. D. (1977). Telling more than we can know: Verbal reports on mental processes. *Psychological Review, 84,* 231–259.

Noice, H., & Noice, T. (1999). Long-term retention of theatrical roles. *Memory, 7,* 357–382.

Noice, H., & Noice, T. (2001). Learning dialogue with and without movement. *Memory and Cognition, 29,* 820–827.

Norman, D. A. (1981). Categorization of action slips. *Psychological Review, 88,* 1–15.

Norman, D. A. (1986). Reflections on cognition and parallel distributed processing. In J. L. McClelland, D. E. Rumelhart, & PDP Research Group (Eds.), *Parallel distributed processing: Explorations in the microstructure of cognition: Vol. 2. Psychological and biological models* (pp. 531–546). Cambridge, MA: MIT Press.

Norman, D. A., & Rumelhart, D. E. (Eds.). (1975). *Explorations in cognition.* San Francisco: Freeman.

Norris, D., McQueen, J. M., Cutler, A., & Butterfield, S. (1997). The possible-word constraint in the segmentation of continuous speech. *Cognitive Psychology, 34,* 191–243.

Nosofsky, R. M. (1986). Attention, similarity, and the identification-categorization relationship. *Journal of Experimental Psychology: General, 115,* 39–57.

Novick, L. R. (1988). Analogical transfer, problem similarity, and expertise. *Journal of Experimental Psychology: Learning, Memory, and Cognition, 14,* 510–520.

Novick, L. R. (2003). At the forefront of thought: The effect of media exposure on airplane typicality. *Psychonomic Bulletin & Review, 10,* 971–974.

Nyberg, L., McIntosh, A. R., & Tulving, E. (1998). Functional brain imaging of episodic and semantic memory with positron emission tomography. *Journal of Molecular Medicine, 76,* 48–53.

Oberauer, K. (2001). Removing irrelevant information from working memory: A cognitive aging study with the modified Sternberg task. *Journal of Experimental Psychology: Learning, Memory, and Cognition, 27,* 948–957.

Oberauer, K., Wendland, M., & Kliegl, R. (2003). Age differences in working memory: The roles of storage and selective access. *Memory & Cognition, 31,* 563–569.

O'Brien, E. J., Albrecht, J. E., Hakala, C. M., & Rizzella, M. L. (1995). Activation and suppression of antecedents during reinstatement. *Journal of Experimental Psychology: Learning, Memory, and Cognition, 21,* 626–634.

O'Brien, E. J., & Myers, J. L. (1987). The role of causal connections in the retrieval of text. *Memory & Cognition, 15,* 419–427.

O'Brien, E. J., Plewes, P. S., & Albrecht, J. E. (1990). Antecedent retrieval processes. *Journal of Experimental Psychology: Learning, Memory, and Cognition, 16,* 241–249.

Ofshe, R. J. (1992). Inadvertent hypnosis during interrogation: False confession due to dissociative state, misidentified multiple personality, and the satanic cult hypothesis. *International Journal of Clinical and Experimental Hypnosis, 40,* 125–156.

Ohman, A., Flykt, A., & Esteves, F. (2001). Emotion drives attention: Detecting the snake in the grass. *Journal of Experimental Psychology: General, 130,* 466–478.

Ojemann, G. A. (1982). Models of the brain organization for higher integrative functions derived with electrical stimulation techniques. *Human Neurobiology, 1,* 243–250.

Ojemann, G. A., & Creutzfeldt, O. D. (1987). Language in humans and animals: Contribution of brain stimulation and recording. In *Handbook of physiology: The nervous system* (Vol. 5). Bethesda, MD: American Physiological Society.

Olsen, P. J., Westerberg, H., & Klingberg, T. (2004). Increased prefrontal and parietal activity after training of working memory. *Nature Neuroscience, 7,* 75–79.

O'Seaghdha, P. G. (1997). Conjoint and dissociable effects of syntactic and semantic context. *Journal of Experimental Psychology: Learning, Memory, and Cognition, 23,* 807–828.

Osterhout, L., Allen, M. D., McLaughlin, J., & Inoue, K. (2002). Brain potentials elicited by prose-embedded linguistic anomalies. *Memory & Cognition, 30,* 1304–1312.

Osterhout, L., & Holcomb, P. J. (1992). Event-related brain potentials elicited by syntactic anomaly. *Journal of Memory and Language, 31,* 785–806.

Ozyurek, S. (2002). Do speakers design their cospeech gestures for their addressees? The effects of addressee location on representational gestures. *Journal of Memory and Language, 46,* 688–704.

Paivio, A. (1971). *Imagery and verbal processes.* New York: Holt.

Paivio, A. (1990). *Mental representations: A dual coding approach.* New York: Oxford University Press.

Palermo, D. S. (1978). *Psychology of language.* Glenview, IL: Scott, Foresman.

Paller, K. A. (2004). Electrical signals of memory and of the awareness of remembering. *Current Directions in Psychological Science, 13,* 49–55.

Palmer, S. E. (1975). The effects of contextual scenes on the identification of objects. *Memory & Cognition, 3,* 519–526.

Palmeri, T. J., & Flanery, M. A. (1999). Learning about categories in the absence of training: Profound amnesia and the relationship between perceptual categorization and recognition memory. *Psychological Science, 10,* 526–530.

Pashler, H. (1994). Dual-task interference in simple tasks: Data and theory. *Psychological Bulletin, 116,* 220–244.

Pashler, H., & Johnson, J. C. (1998). Attentional limitations in dual-task performance. In H. Pashler (Ed.), *Attention* (pp. 155–189). Hove, U.K.: Psychology Press.

Paul. S. T., Kellas, G. Martin, M., & Clark, M. B. (1992). Influence of contextual features on the activation of ambiguous word meanings. *Journal of Experimental Psychology: Learning, Memory, and Cognition, 18,* 703–717.

Payne, D. G., Toglia, M. P., & Anastasi, J. S. (1994). Recognition performance level and the magnitude of the misinformation effect in eyewitness memory. *Psychonomic Bulletin & Review, 1,* 376–382.

Pearlmutter, N. J., Garnsey, S. M., & Bock, K. (1999). Agreement processes in sentence comprehension. *Journal of Memory and Language, 41,* 427–456.

Pecher, D., Zeelenberg, R., & Barsalou, L. W. (2003). Verifying different modality properties for concepts produces switching costs. *Psychological Science, 14,* 119–124.

Pedone, R., Hummel, J. E., & Holyoak, K. J. (2001). The use of diagrams in analogical problem solving. *Memory & Cognition, 29,* 214–221.

Penfield, W. (1958). *The excitable cortex in conscious man.* Liverpool, UK: Liverpool University Press.

Penfield, W., & Jasper, H. H. (1954). *Epilepsy and the functional anatomy of the human brain.* Boston: Little, Brown.

Penfield, W., & Milner, B. (1958). Memory deficit produced by bilateral lesions in the hippocampal zone. *Archives of Neurology and Psychiatry, 79,* 475–497.

Peretz, I., Radeau, M., & Arguin, M. (2004). Two-way interactions between music and language: Evidence from priming recognition of tune and lyrics in familiar songs. *Memory & Cognition, 32,* 142–152.

Peterson, L. R., & Peterson, M. J. (1959). Short-term retention of individual items. *Journal of Experimental Psychology, 58,* 193–198.

Peterson, R. R., Burgess, C., Dell, G. S., & Eberhard, K. M. (2001). Dissociation between syntactic and semantic processing during idiom comprehension. *Journal of Experimental Psychology: Learning, Memory, and Cognition, 27,* 1223–1237.

Petrusic, W. M., & Baranski, J. V. (2003). Judging confidence influences decision processing in comparative judgments. *Psychonomic Bulletin & Review, 10,* 177–183.

Pexman, P. M., Holyk, G. G., & Monfils, M. (2003). Number-of-features effects and semantic processing. *Memory & Cognition, 31,* 842–855.

Piaget, J. (1967). *Six psychological studies* (A. Tenzer, Trans.). New York: Random House.

Pickering, M. J., & Traxler, M. J. (1998). Plausibility and recovery from garden paths: An eye-tracking study. *Journal of Experimental Psychology: Learning, Memory, and Cognition, 24,* 940–961.

Piercey, C. D., & Joordens, S. (2000). Turning an advantage into a disadvantage: Ambiguity effects in lexical decision versus reading tasks. *Memory & Cognition, 28,* 657–666.

Pinker, S. (1994). *The language instinct: How the mind creates language.* New York: William Morrow & Co.

Pitt, M. A., & Samuel, A. G. (1995). Lexical and sublexical feedback in auditory word recognition. *Cognitive Psychology, 29,* 149–188.

Poldrack, R. A., & Wagner, A. D. (2004). What can neuroimaging tell us about the mind? *Current Directions in Psychological Science, 13,* 177–181.

Polk, T. A., & Farah, M. J. (2002). Functional MRI evidence for an abstract, not perceptual, word-form area. *Journal of Experimental Psychology: General, 131,* 65–72.

Pollack, I., & Pickett, J. M. (1964). Intelligibility of excerpts from fluent speech: Auditory vs. structural context. *Journal of Verbal Learning and Verbal Behavior, 3,* 79–84.

Pollatsek, A., Konold, C. E., Well, A. D., & Lima, S. D. (1984). Beliefs underlying random sampling. *Memory & Cognition, 12,* 395–401.

Polya, G. (1957). *How to solve it.* Garden City, NY: Doubleday/Anchor.

Posner, M. I. (1997). Introduction: Neuroimaging of cognitive processes. *Cognitive Psychology, 33,* 2–4.

Posner, M. I., & Cohen, Y. (1984). Components of visual orienting. In H. Bouma & D. G. Bouwhuis (Eds.), *Attention and performance X* (pp. 531–556). Hillsdale, NJ: Erlbaum.

Posner, M. I., Kiesner, J. Thomas-Thrapp, L., McCandliss, B., Carr, T. H., & Rothbart, M. K. (1992, November). *Brain changes in the acquisition of literacy.* Paper presented at the meetings of the Psychonomic Society, St. Louis.

Posner, M. I., Nissen, M. J., & Ogden, W. C. (1978). Attended and unattended processing modes: The role of set for spatial location. In H. L. Pick & I. J. Saltzman (Eds.), *Modes of perceiving and processing information* (pp. 137–157). Hillsdale, NJ: Erlbaum.

Posner, M. I., & Snyder, C. R. R. (1975). Facilitation and inhibition in the processing of signals. In P. M. A. Rabbitt & S. Dornic (Eds.), *Attention and performance V* (pp. 669–682). New York: Academic Press.

Posner, M. I., Snyder, C. R. R., & Davidson, B. J. (1980). Attention and the detection of signals. *Journal of Experimental Psychology: General, 109,* 160–174.

Postman, L., & Underwood, B. J. (1973). Critical issues in interference theory. *Memory & Cognition, 1,* 19–40.

Price, R.H. (1987). Principles of Psychology. Glenview, IL.: Scott Foresman.

Prince, S. E., Tsukiura, T., & Cabeza, R. (2007). Distinguishing the neural correlates of episodic encoding and semantic retrieval. *Psychological Science, 18,* 144–151.

Pritchard, R. M. (1961). Stabilized images on the retina. *Scientific American, 204,* 72–78.

Proffitt, D. R. (2006). Embodied perception and the economy of action. *Perspectives on Psychological Science, 1,* 110–122.

Proffitt, D. R., Kaiser, M. K., & Whelan, S. M. (1990). Understanding wheel dynamics. *Cognitive Psychology, 22,* 342–373.

Protopapas, A., Archonti, A., & Skaloumbakas, C. (2007). Reading ability is negatively related to Stroop interference. *Cognitive Psychology, 54,* 251–282.

Provins, K. A. (1997). Handedness and speech: A critical reappraisal of the role of genetic and environmental factors in the cerebral lateralization of function. *Psychological Review, 104,* 554–571.

Pylyshyn, Z. W. (1984). *Computation and cognition: Toward a foundation for cognitive science.* Cambridge, MA: Bradford.

Quillian, M. R. (1968). Semantic memory. In M. Minsky (Ed.), *Semantic information processing* (pp. 216–270). Cambridge, MA: MIT Press.

Quillian, M. R. (1969). The teachable language comprehender: A simulation program and theory of language. *Communications of the ACM, 12,* 459–476.

Rader, A. W., & Sloutsky, V. M. (2002). Processing of logically valid and logically invalid conditional inferences in discourse comprehension. *Journal of Experimental Psychology: Learning, Memory, and Cognition, 28,* 59–68.

Radvansky, G. A., & Copeland, D. E. (2006). Memory retrieval and interference: Working memory issues. *Journal of Memory and Language, 55,* 33–46.

Radvansky, G. A., Spieler, D. H., & Zacks, R. T. (1993). Mental model organization. *Journal of Experimental Psychology: Learning, Memory, and Cognition, 19,* 95–114.

Radvansky, G. A., & Zacks, R. T. (1991). Mental models and the fan effect. *Journal of Experimental Psychology: Learning, Memory, and Cognition, 17,* 940–953.

Radvansky, G. A., Zwaan, R. A., Federico, T., & Franklin, N. (1998). Retrieval from temporally organized situation models. *Journal of Experimental Psychology: Learning, Memory, and Cognition, 24,* 1224–1237.

Rafal, R. D. (1997). Hemispatial neglect: Cognitive neuropsychological aspects. In T. E. Feinberg & M. J. Farah (Eds.), *Behavioral neurology and neuropsychology* (pp. 319–336). New York: McGraw-Hill.

Rapp, B., & Goldrick, M. (2000). Discreteness and interactivity in spoken word production. *Psychological Review, 107,* 460–499.

Ratcliff, G., & Newcombe, F. (1982). Object recognition: Some deductions from the clinical evidence. In A. W. Ellis (Ed.), *Normality and pathology in cognitive functions* (p. 162). London: Academic Press.

Ratcliff, R., & McKoon, G. (1978). Priming in item recognition: Evidence for the propositional structure of sentences. *Journal of Verbal Learning and Verbal Behavior, 17,* 403–418.

Ratcliff, R., & McKoon, G. (1988). A retrieval theory of priming in memory. *Psychological Review, 95,* 385–408.

Raven, J. C. (1941). Standardization of progressive matrices, 1938. *British Journal of Medical Psychology, 19,* 137–150.

Rayner, K. (1998). Eye movements in reading and information processing: 20 years of research. *Psychological Bulletin, 124,* 372–422.

Rayner, K., Carlson, M., & Frazier, L. (1983). The interaction of syntax and semantics during sentence processing: Eye movements in the analysis of semantically biased sentences. *Journal of Verbal Learning and Verbal Behavior, 22,* 358–374.

Rayner, K., & Clifton, C. Jr. (2002). Language comprehension. In D. L. Medin (Ed.), *Steven's handbook of experimental psychology* (Vol. X, pp. 261–316). New York: Wiley.

Rayner, K., & Duffy, S. A. (1988). On-line comprehension processes and eye movements in reading. In M. Daneman, G. E. MacKinnon, & T. G. Waller (Eds.), *Reading research: Advances in theory and practice* (pp. 13–66). New York: Academic Press.

Rayner, K., & Frazier, L. (1989). Selection mechanisms in reading lexically ambiguous words. *Journal of Experimental Psychology: Learning, Memory, and Cognition, 15,* 779–790.

Rayner, K., Inhoff, A. W., Morrison, P. E., Slowiaczek, M. L., & Bertera, J. H. (1981). Masking of foveal and parafoveal vision during eye fixations in reading. *Journal of Experimental Psychology: Human Perception and Performance, 7,* 167–179.

Rayner, K., Pollatsek, A., & Binder, K. S. (1998). Phonological codes and eye movements in reading. *Journal of Experimental Psychology: Learning, Memory, and Cognition, 24,* 476–497.

Rayner, K., Warren, T., Juhasz, B. J., & Liversedge, S. P. (2004). The effect of plausibility on eye movements in reading. *Journal of Experimental Psychology: Learning, Memory, and Cognition, 30,* 1290–1301.

Rayner, K., & Well, A. D. (1996). Effects of contextual constraint on eye movements in reading: A further examination. *Psychonomic Bulletin & Review, 3,* 504–509.

Rayner, K., White, S. J., Johnson, R. L., & Liversedge, S. P. (2006). Raeding wrods with jumbled letters: There is a cost. *Psychological Science, 17,* 192–193.

Reason, J. (1990). *Human error.* New York: Cambridge University Press.

Reder, L. M., & Kusbit, G. W. (1991). Locus of the Moses illusion: Imperfect encoding, retrieval, or match? *Journal of Memory and Language, 30,* 385–406.

Reed, S. K. (1992). *Cognition: Theory and applications* (3rd ed.). Pacific Grove, CA: Brooks/Cole.

Reed, S. K., & Hoffman, B. (2004). Use of temporal and spatial information in estimating event completion time. *Memory & Cognition, 32,* 271–282.

Reeves, L. M., & Weisberg, R. W. (1993). Abstract versus concrete information as the basis for transfer in problem solving: Comment on Fong and Nisbett (1991). *Journal of Experimental Psychology: General, 122,* 125–128.

Rehder, B. (2003). A causal-model theory of conceptual representation and categorization. *Journal of Experimental Psychology: Learning, Memory, and Cognition, 29,* 1141–1159.

Rehder, B., & Burnett, R. C. (2005). Feature inference and the causal structure of categories. *Cognitive Psychology, 50,* 264–314.

Reichle, E. D., Carpenter, P. A., & Just, M. A. (2000). The neural bases of strategy and skill in sentence–picture verification. *Cognitive Psychology, 40,* 261–295.

Reichle, E. D., Pollatsek, A., Fisher, D. L., & Rayner, K. (1998). Toward a model of eye movement control in reading. *Psychological Review, 105,* 125–157.

Reingold, E. M., Charness, N., Pomplun, M., & Stampe, D. M. (2001). Visual span in expert chess players: Evidence from eye movements. *Psychological Science, 12,* 48–55.

Reisberg, D. (1997). *Cognition: Exploring the science of the mind.* New York: Norton.

Reiser, B. J., Black, J. B., & Abelson, R. P. (1985). Knowledge structures in the organization and retrieval of autobiographical memories. *Cognitive Psychology, 17,* 89–137.

Reyna, V. F. (2004). How people make decisions that involve risk. *Current directions in Psychological Science, 13,* 60–67.

Riley, K. P. (1989). Psychological interventions in Alzheimer's disease. In G. C. Gilmore, P. J. Whitehouse, & M. R. Wykle (Eds.), *Memory, aging and dementia.* New York: Springer.

Rinck, M., & Bower, G. H. (1995). Anaphora resolution and the focus of attention in situation models. *Journal of Memory and Language, 34,* 110–131.

Rips, L. J. (1975). Inductive judgments about natural categories. *Journal of Verbal Learning and Verbal Behavior, 14,* 665–681.

Rips, L. J. (1989). Similarity, typicality, and categorization. In S. Vosniadou & A. Ortony (Eds.), *Similarity and analogical reasoning* (pp. 21–59). Cambridge, U.K.: Cambridge University Press.

Rips, L. J. (1998). Reasoning and conversation. *Psychological Review, 105,* 411–441.

Rips, L. J. (2001). Two kinds of reasoning. *Psychological Science, 12,* 129–134.

Rips, L. J., & Collins, A. (1993). Categories and resemblance. *Journal of Experimental Psychology: General, 122,* 468–486.

Rips, L. J., & Marcus, S. L. (1977). Supposition and the analysis of conditional sentences. In M. A. Just & P. A. Carpenter (Eds.), *Cognitive processes in comprehension* (pp. 185–220). Hillsdale, NJ: Erlbaum.

Rips, L. J., Shoben, E. J., & Smith, E. E. (1973). Semantic distance and the verification of semantic relations. *Journal of Verbal Learning and Verbal Behavior, 12,* 1–20.

Ritchey, M., & Radvansky. G.A. (2009). The Influence of Emotional Content on Working Memory and Long-Term Memory. *Unpublished manuscript.*

Roberson, D., Davies, I., & Davidoff, J. (2000). Color categories are not universal: Replications and new evidence from a Stone-Age culture. *Journal of Experimental Psychology: General, 129,* 369–398.

Robertson, D. A., & Gernsbacher, M. A. (November, 1999). *fMRI evidence of the general cognitive processes underlying discourse comprehension.* Paper presented at the meetings of the Psychonomic Society, Los Angeles.

Robertson, D. A., Gernsbacher, M. A., Guidotti, S. J., Robertson, R. R. W., Irwin, W., Mock, B. J., & Campana, M. E. (2000). Functional neuroanatomy of the cognitive process of mapping during discourse comprehension. *Psychological Science, 11*, 255–260.

Robins, R. W., Gosling, S. D., & Craik, K. H. (1999). An empirical analysis of trends in psychology. *American Psychologist, 54*, 117–128.

Roediger, H. L. III. (1996). Memory illusions. *Journal of Memory and Language, 35*, 76–100.

Roediger, H. L., & Crowder, R. G. (1976). A serial position effect in recall of United States presidents. *Bulletin of the Psychonomic Society, 8*, 275–278.

Roediger, H. L. III, Jacoby, D., & McDermott, K. B. (1996). Misinformation effects in recall: Creating false memories through repeated retrieval. *Journal of Memory and Language, 35*, 300–318.

Roediger, H. L., & Karpicke, J. D. (2006). The power of resting memory: Basic research and implications for educational practice. *Perspectives on Psychological Science, 1*, 181–210.

Roediger, H. L. III, Marsh, E. J., & Lee, S. C. (2002). Kinds of memory. In D. Medin (Ed.), *Stevens' handbook of experimental psychology, Vol. 2* (3rd ed., pp. 1–42). New York: John Wiley & Sons.

Roediger, H. L. III, & McDermott, K. B. (1995). Creating false memories: Remembering words not presented in lists. *Journal of Experimental Psychology: Learning, Memory, and Cognition, 21*, 803–814.

Roediger, H. L. III, & McDermott, K. B. (2000). Tricks of memory. *Current Directions in Psychological Science, 9*, 123–127.

Roediger, H. L. III, Meade, M. L., & Bergman, E. T. (2001). Social contagion of memory. *Psychonomic Bulletin & Review, 8*, 365–371.

Roediger, H. L. III, Stadler, M. L., Weldon, M. S., & Riegler, G. L. (1992). Direct comparison of two implicit memory tests: Word fragment and word stem completion. *Journal of Experimental Psychology: Learning, Memory, and Cognition, 18*, 1251–1269.

Roese, N. (1999). Counterfactual thinking and decision making. *Psychonomic Bulletin & Review, 6*, 570–578.

Roese, N. J. (1997). Counterfactual thinking. *Psychological Bulletin, 121*, 133–148.

Rogers, T. T., Lambon Ralph, M. A., Gerrard, P., Bozeat, S., McClelland, J. L., Hodges, J. R., & Patterson, K. (2004). Structure and deterioration of semantic memory: A neuropsychological and computational investigation. *Psychological Review, 111*, 205–235.

Rohrer, D. (2003). The natural appearance of unnatural incline speed. *Memory & Cognition, 31*, 816–826.

Rosch, E. H. (1973). On the internal structure of perceptual and semantic categories. In T. E. Moore (Ed.), *Cognitive development and the acquisition of language* (pp. 111–144). New York: Academic Press.

Rosch, E. H. (1975). Cognitive representations of semantic categories. *Journal of Experimental Psychology: General, 104*, 192–233.

Rosch, E. H. (1978). Principles of categorization. In E. H. Rosch & B. B. Lloyd (Eds.), *Cognition and categorization* (pp. 27–48). Hillsdale, NJ: Erlbaum.

Rosch, E. H., & Mervis, C. B. (1975). Family resemblances: Studies in the internal structure of categories. *Cognitive Psychology, 7*, 573–605.

Rosch-Heider, E. (1972). Universals in color naming and memory. *Journal of Experimental Psychology, 93*, 10–21.

Rosen, V. M., & Engle, R. W. (1997). The role of working memory capacity in retrieval. *Journal of Experimental Psychology: General, 126*, 211–227.

Rosler, F., Pechmann, T., Streb, J., Roder, B., & Hennighausen, E. (1998). Parsing of sentences in a language with varying word order: Word-by-word variations of processing demands are revealed by event-related brain potentials. *Journal of Memory and Language, 38*, 150–176.

Ross, B. H. (1987). This is like that: The use of earlier problems and the separation of similarity effects. *Journal of Experimental Psychology: Learning, Memory, and Cognition, 13*, 629–640.

Ross, B. H., & Murphy, G. L. (1999). Food for thought: Cross-classification and category organization in a complex real-world domain. *Cognitive Psychology, 38*, 495–553.

Rubin, D. C. (2007). A basic-systems model of episodic memory. *Perspectives on Psychological Science, 1*, 277–311.

Rubin, D. C., & Berntsen, D. (2003). Life scripts help to maintain autobiographical memories of highly positive, but not highly negative, events. *Memory & Cognition, 31*, 1–14.

Rubin, D. C. & Greenberg, D. L. (1998). Visual memory deficit amnesia: A distinct amnesic presentation and etiology. *Proceedings of the National Academy of Sciences, 95*, 5413–5416.

Rubin, D. C., Rahhal, T. A., & Poon, L. W. (1998). Things learned in early adulthood are remembered best. *Memory & Cognition, 26*, 3–19.

Rubin, D. C., Schrauf, R. W., & Greenberg, D. L. (2003). Belief and recollection of autobiographical memories. *Memory and Cognition, 31*, 887–901.

Ruff, C. C., Kristkjánsson, Á., & Driver, J. (2007). Readout from iconic memory and selective spatial attention involve similar neural processes. *Psychological Science, 18*, 901–909.

Rugg, M. D., & Coles, M. G. H. (Eds.). (1995). *Electrophysiology of mind: Event-related brain potential and cognition*. New York: Oxford University Press.

Rumelhart, D. E. (1989). The architecture of mind: A connectionist approach. In M. I. Posner (Ed.), *Foundations of cognitive science* (pp. 133–159). Cambridge, MA: MIT Press.

Rumelhart, D. E., Lindsay, P. H., & Norman, D. A. (1972). A process model for long-term memory. In E. Tulving & W. Donaldson (Eds.), *Organization of memory* (pp. 197–246). New York: Academic Press.

Rumelhart, D. E., & McClelland, J. L. (1986). *Parallel distributed processing: Explorations in the microstructure of cognition: Vol. 1. Foundations*. Cambridge, MA: Bradford.

Rundus, D. (1971). Analysis of rehearsal processes in free recall. *Journal of Experimental Psychology, 89*, 63–77.

Rundus, D., & Atkinson, R. C. (1970). Rehearsal processes in free recall: A procedure for direct observation. *Journal of Verbal Learning and Verbal Behavior, 9*, 99–105.

Russo, J. E., Johnson, E. J., & Stephens, D. L. (1989). The validity of verbal protocols. *Memory & Cognition, 17*, 759–769.

Sachs, J. S. (1967). Recognition memory for syntactic and semantic aspects of connected discourse. *Perception & Psychophysics, 2*, 437–442.

Sacks, H., Schegloff, E. A., & Jefferson, G. (1974). A simplest systematics for the organization of turntaking for conversation. *Language, 50,* 696–735.

Sacks, O. (1970). *The man who mistook his wife for a hat.* New York: Harper & Row.

Salame, P., & Baddeley, A. D. (1982). Disruption of short-term memory by unattended speech: Implications for the structure of working memory. *Journal of Verbal Learning and Verbal Behavior, 21,* 150–164.

Salthouse, T. A. (1984). Effects of age and skill in typing. *Journal of Experimental Psychology: General, 113,* 345–371.

Salthouse, T. A., Atkinson, T. M., & Berish, D. E. (2003). Executive functioning as a potential mediator of age-related cognitive decline in normal adults. *Journal of Experimental Psychology: General, 132,* 566–594.

Saltz, E., & Donnenwerth-Nolan, S. (1981). Does motoric imagery facilitate memory for sentences? A selective interference test. *Journal of Verbal Learning and Verbal Behavior, 20,* 322–332.

Samuel, A. G. (2001). Knowing a word affects the fundamental perception of the sounds within it. *Psychological Science, 12,* 348–351.

Samuel, D. (1999). *Memory: How we use it, lose it and can improve it.* New York: New York University Press.

Sanchez, C. A., & Wiley, J. (2006). An examination of the seductive details effect in terms of working memory capacity. *Memory & Cognition, 34,* 344–355.

Sanna, L. J., & Schwartz, N. (2006). Human judgment: The case of the hindsight bias and its debiasing. *Current Directions in Psychological Science, 15,* 172–176.

Santens, S., & Gevers, W. (2008). The SNARC effect does not imply a mental number line. *Cognition, 108,* 263–270.

Sarter, M., Berntson, G. G., & Cacioppo, J. T. (1996). Brain imaging and cognitive neuroscience: Toward strong inference in attributing function to structure. *American Psychologist, 51,* 13–21.

Sattler, J. M. (1982). *Assessment of children's intellectual and special abilities* (2nd ed.). Boston: Allyn & Bacon.

Schab, F. R. (1990). Odors and the remembrance of things past. *Journal of Experimental Psychology: Learning, Memory, and Cognition, 16,* 648–655.

Schacter, D. L. (1987). Implicit memory: History and current status. *Journal of Experimental Psychology: Learning, Memory, and Cognition, 13,* 501–518.

Schacter, D. L. (1989). Memory. In M. I. Posner (Ed.), *Foundations of cognitive science* (pp. 683–725). Cambridge, MA: MIT Press.

Schacter, D. L. (1996). *Searching for memory.* New York: Basic Books.

Schacter, D. L. (1999). The seven sins of memory: Insights from psychology and cognitive neuroscience. *American Psychologist, 54,* 182–203.

Schacter, D. L., & Badgiayan, R. D. (2001). Neuroimaging of priming: New perspectives on implicit and explicit memory. *Current Directions in Psychological Science, 10,* 1–4.

Schank, R. C. (1972). Conceptual dependency: A theory of natural language understanding. *Cognitive Psychology, 3,* 552–631.

Schank, R. C. (1977). Rules and topics in conversation. *Cognitive Science, 1,* 421–441.

Schank, R. C., & Abelson, R. P. (1977). *Scripts, plans, goals and understanding.* Hillsdale, NJ: Erlbaum.

Schilling, H. E. H., Rayner, K., & Chumbley, J. I. (1998). Comparing naming, lexical decision, and eye fixation times: Word frequency effects and individual differences. *Memory & Cognition, 26,* 1270–1281.

Schmeichel, B. J. (2007). Attention control, memory updating, and emotion regularity temporarily reduce the capacity for executive control. *Journal of Experimental Psychology: General, 136,* 241–255.

Schmidt, J. R., & Thompson, V. A. (2008). "At least one" problem with "some" formal reasoning paradigms. *Memory & Cognition, 36,* 217–229.

Schmidt, S. R. (1985). Encoding and retrieval processes in the memory for conceptually distinctive events. *Journal of Experimental Psychology: Learning, Memory, and Cognition, 11,* 565–578.

Schmidt, S. R. (1994). Effects of humor on sentence memory. *Journal of Experimental Psychology: Learning, Memory, and Cognition, 20,* 953–967.

Schmidt, S. R. (2002). Outstanding memories: The positive and negative effects of nudes on memory. *Journal of Experimental Psychology: Learning, Memory, and Cognition, 28,* 353–361.

Schmidt, S. R. (2004). Autobiographical memories for the September 11th attacks: Reconstructive errors and emotional impairment of memory. *Memory & Cognition, 32,* 443–454.

Schmolck, H., Buffalo, E. A., & Squire, L. R. (2000). Memory distortions develop over time: Recollections of the O. J. Simpson trial verdict after 15 and 32 months. *Psychological Science, 11,* 39–45.

Schneider, V. I., Healy, A. F., & Bourne, L. E., Jr. (2002). What is learned under difficult conditions is hard to forget: Contextual interference effects in foreign vocabulary acquisition, retention, and transfer. *Journal of Memory and Language, 46,* 419–440.

Schneider, W., & Shiffrin. R. M. (1977). Controlled and automatic human information processing: I. Detection, search, and attention. *Psychological Review, 84,* 1–66.

Schnorr, J. A., & Atkinson, R. C. (1969). Repetition versus imagery instructions in the short- and long-term retention of paired associates. *Psychonomic Science, 15,* 183–184.

Schooler, J. W., & Engstler-Schooler, T. Y. (1990). Verbal overshadowing of visual memories: Some things are better left unsaid. *Cognitive Psychology, 22,* 36–71.

Schooler, J. W., Ohlsson, S., & Brooks, K. (1993). Thoughts beyond words: When language overshadows insight. *Journal of Experimental Psychology: General, 122,* 166–183.

Schooler, L. J., & Anderson, J. R. (1997). The role of process in the rational analysis of memory. *Cognitive Psychology, 32,* 219–250.

Schrauf, R. W., & Rubin, D. C. (1998). Bilingual autobiographical memory in older adult immigrants: A test of cognitive explanations of the reminiscence bump and the linguistic encoding of memories. *Journal of Memory and Language, 39,* 437–457.

Schrauf, R. W., & Rubin, D. C. (2000). Internal languages of retrieval: The bilingual encoding of memories for the personal past. *Memory & Cognition, 28,* 616–623.

Schreiber, T. A., & Sergent, S. D. (1998). The role of commitment in producing misinformation effects in eyewitness memory. *Psychonomic Bulletin & Review, 5,* 443–448.

Schustack, M. W., Ehrlich, S. F., & Rayner, K. (1987). Local and global sources of contextual facilitation in reading. *Journal of Memory and Language, 26,* 322–340.

Schutzwohl, A. (1998). Surprise and schema strength. *Journal of Experimental Psychology: Learning, Memory, and Cognition, 24,* 1182–1199.

Schwartz, D. L., & Black, T. (1999). Inferences through imagined actions: Knowing by simulated doing. *Journal of Experimental Psychology: Learning, Memory, and Cognition, 25,* 116–136.

Seamon, J. G., Philbin, M. M., & Harrison, L. G. (2006). Do you remember proposing marriage to the Pepsi machine? False recollections from a campus walk. *Psychonomic Bulletin & Review, 13,* 752–756.

Searle, J. R. (1969). *Speech acts.* Cambridge, England: Cambridge University Press.

Sederberg, P. B., Schulze-Bonhage, A., Madsen, J. R., Bromfield, E. B., Litt, B., Brandt, A., & Kahana, M. J. (2007). Gamma oscillations distinguish true from false memories. *Psychological Science, 18,* 927–932.

See, J. E., Howe, S. R., Warm, J. S., & Dember, W. N. (1995). Meta-analysis of the sensitivity decrement in vigilance. *Psychological Bulletin, 2,* 230–249.

Sehulster, J. R. (1989). Content and temporal structure of autobiographical knowledge: Remembering twenty-five seasons at the Metropolitan Opera. *Memory & Cognition, 17,* 590–606.

Seidenberg, M. S. (1993). Connectionist models and cognitive theory. *Psychological Science, 4,* 228–235.

Seidenberg, M. S., & McClelland, J. L. (1989). A distributed, developmental model of word recognition and naming. *Psychological Review, 96,* 523–568.

Seifert, C. M., Robertson, S. P., & Black, J. B. (1985). Types of inferences generated during reading. *Journal of Memory and Language, 24,* 405–422.

Selfridge, O. G. (1959). Pandemonium: A paradigm for learning. In *The mechanisation of thought processes.* London: H. M. Stationery Office.

Senkfor, A. J., & Van Petten, C. (1998). Who said what? An event-related potential investigation of source and item memory. *Journal of Experimental Psychology: Learning, Memory, and Cognition, 24,* 1005–1025.

Serences, J. T., Shomstein, S., Leber, A. B., Golay, X., Egeth, H. E., & Yantis, S. (2005). Coordination of voluntary and stimulus-driven attentional control in human cortex. *Psychological Science, 16,* 114–122.

Sereno, S. C., Brewer, C. C., & O'Donnell, P. J. (2003). Context effects in word recognition: Evidence for early interactive processing. *Psychological Science, 14,* 328–333.

Seron, X. (1982). Introduction: Toward a cognitive neuropsychology. *International Journal of Psychology, 17,* 149–156.

Shafir, E., & Tversky, A. (1992). Thinking through uncertainty: Nonconsequential reasoning and choice. *Cognitive Psychology, 24,* 449–474.

Shafto, P., & Coley, J. D. (2003). Development of categorization and reasoning in the natural world: Novices to experts, naïve similarity to ecological knowledge. *Journal of Experimental Psychology: Learning, Memory, and Cognition, 29,* 641–649.

Shaki, S., & Fischer, M. H. (2008). Reading space into numbers—A cross-linguistic comparison of the SNARC effect. *Cognition, 108,* 590–599.

Shallice, T., & Warrington, E. K. (1970). Independent functioning of the verbal memory stores: A neuropsychological study. *Quarterly Journal of Experimental Psychology, 22,* 261–273.

Shand, M. A. (1982). Sign-based short-term coding of American Sign Language signs and printed English words by congenitally deaf signers. *Cognitive Psychology, 14,* 1–12.

Sharkey, N. E., & Mitchell, D. C. (1985). Word recognition in a functional context: The use of scripts in reading. *Journal of Memory and Language, 24,* 253–270.

Shaw, J. S. III. (1996). Increases in eyewitness confidence resulting from postevent questioning. *Journal of Experimental Psychology: Applied, 2,* 126–146.

Shaw, J. S. III, Bjork, R. A., & Handal, A. (1995). Retrieval-induced forgetting in an eyewitness–memory paradigm. *Psychonomic Bulletin & Review, 2,* 249–253.

Shaywitz, S. E., Mody, M., & Shaywitz, B. A. (2006). Neural mechanisms in dyslexia. *Current Directions in Psychological Science, 15,* 278–281.

Shelton, A. L., & McNamara, T. P. (2001). Visual memories from nonvisual experiences. *Psychological Science, 12,* 343–347.

Shelton, J. R., & Caramazza, A. (1999). Deficits in lexical and semantic processing: Implications for models of normal language. *Psychonomic Bulletin & Review, 6,* 5–27.

Shepard, R. N., & Metzler, J. (1971). Mental rotation of three-dimensional objects. *Science, 171,* 701–703.

Sherman, G., & Visscher, P. K. (2002). Honeybee colonies achieve fitness through dancing. *Nature, 419,* 920–922.

Shiffrin, R. M., & Schneider, W. (1977). Controlled and automatic human information processing: II. Perceptual learning, automatic attending, and a general theory. *Psychological Review, 84,* 127–190.

Shintel, H., & Keysar, B. (2007). You said it before and you'll say it again: Expectations and consistency in communication. *Journal of Experimental Psychology: Learning, Memory, and Cognition, 33,* 357–369.

Shoben, E. J., Sailor, K. M., & Wang, M.-Y. (1989). The role of expectancy in comparative judgments. *Memory & Cognition, 17,* 18–26.

Siegler, R. S. (2000). Unconscious insights. *Current Directions in Psychological Science, 9,* 79–83.

Siegler, R. S., & Stern, E. (1998). A microgenetic analysis of conscious and unconscious strategy discoveries. *Journal of Experimental Psychology: General, 127,* 377–397.

Simon, H. A. (1975). The functional equivalence of problem solving skills. *Cognitive Psychology, 7,* 268–288.

Simon, H. A. (1979). *Models of thought.* New Haven: Yale University Press.

Simon, H. A. (1992). What is an "explanation" of behavior? *Psychological Science, 3,* 150–161.

Simon, H. A. (May, 1995). *Thinking in words, pictures, equations, numbers: How do we do it and what does it matter?* Invited address presented at the meeting of the Midwestern Psychological Association, Chicago.

Simons, D. J., & Ambinder, M. S. (2005). Change blindness: Theory and consequences. *Current Directions in Psychological Science, 14,* 44–48.

Simons, J. S., Graham, K. S., & Hodges, J. R. (2002). Perceptual and semantic contributions to episodic memory: Evidence from semantic dementia and Alzheimer's disease. *Journal of Memory and Language, 47,* 197–213.

Simpson, G. B. (1981). Meaning dominance and semantic context in the processing of lexical ambiguity. *Journal of Verbal Learning and Verbal Behavior, 20,* 120–136.

Simpson, G. B. (1984). Lexical ambiguity and its role in models of word recognition. *Psychological Bulletin, 96,* 316–340.

Simpson, G. B., Casteel, M. A., Peterson, R. R., & Burgess, C. (1989). Lexical and sentence context effects in word recognition. *Journal of Experimental Psychology: Learning, Memory, and Cognition, 15,* 88–97.

Singer, M. (1990). *Psychology of language: An introduction to sentence and discourse processes.* Hillsdale, NJ: Erlbaum.

Singer, M., Andrusiak, P., Reisdorf, P., & Black, N. L. (1992). Individual differences in bridging inference processes. *Memory & Cognition, 20,* 539–548.

Singer, M., Graesser, A. C., & Trabasso, T. (1994). Minimal or global inference during reading. *Journal of Memory and Language, 33,* 421–441.

Sitaran, N., Weingartner, H., Caine, E. D., & Gillin, J. C. (1978). Choline: Selective enhancement of serial learning and encoding of low imagery words in man. *Life Sciences, 22,* 1555–1560.

Sitton, M., Mozer, M. C., & Farah, M. J. (2000). Superadditive effects of multiple lesions in a connectionist architecture: Implications for the neuropsychology of optic aphasia. *Psychological Review, 107,* 709–734.

Skinner, B. F. (1957). *Verbal behavior.* New York: Appleton-Century-Crofts.

Skinner, B. F. (1984). The shame of American education. *American Psychologist, 39,* 947–954.

Skinner, B. F. (1990). Can psychology be a science of mind? *American Psychologist, 45,* 1206–1210.

Slamecka, N. J. (1966). Differentiation versus unlearning of verbal associations. *Journal of Experimental Psychology, 71,* 822–828.

Slamecka, N. J. (1968). An examination of trace storage in free recall. *Journal of Experimental Psychology, 4,* 504–513.

Slamecka, N. J. (1985). Ebbinghaus: Some associations. *Journal of Experimental Psychology: Learning, Memory, and Cognition, 11,* 414–435.

Slamecka, N. J., & Graf, P. (1978). The generation effect: delineation of a phenomenon. *Journal of Experimental Psychology: Human Learning and Memory, 4,* 592–604.

Sloman, S. A. (1998). Categorical inference is not a tree: The myth of inheritance hierarchies. *Cognitive Psychology, 35,* 1–33.

Smallwood, J., Fishman, D. J., & Schooler, J. W. (2007). Counting the cost of an absent mind: Mind wandering as an unrecognized influence on educational performance. *Psychonomic Bulletin & Review, 14,* 230–236.

Smallwood, J., McSpadden, M., & Schooler, J. W. (2007). The lights are on but no one's home: Meta-awareness and the decoupling of attention when the mind wanders. *Psychonomic Bulletin & Review, 14,* 527–533.

Smallwood, J. & Schooler, J. W. (2006). The restless mind. *Psychological Bulletin, 132,* 946–958.

Smith, D. A., & Graesser, A. C. (1981). Memory for actions in scripted activities as a function of typicality, retention interval, and retrieval task. *Memory & Cognition, 9,* 550–559.

Smith, E. E. (1978). Theories of semantic memory. In W. K. Estes (Ed.), *Handbook of learning and cognitive processes* (Vol. 6, pp. 1–56). Hillsdale, NJ: Erlbaum.

Smith, E. E. (2000). Neural bases of human working memory. *Current Directions in Psychological Science, 9,* 45–49.

Smith, E. E., & Jonides, J. (1999). Storage and executive processes in the frontal lobes. *Science, 283,* 1657–1661.

Smith, E. E., Rips, L. J., & Shoben, E. J. (1974). Semantic memory and psychological semantics. In G. H. Bower (Ed.), *The psychology of learning and motivation* (Vol. 8, pp. 1–45). New York: Academic Press.

Smith, J. D., Redford, J. S., Washburn, D. A., & Taglialatela, L. A. (2005). Specific-token effects in screening tasks: Possible implications for aviation security. *Journal of Experimental Psychology: Learning, Memory, and Cognition, 31,* 1171–1185.

Smith, L. (2003). Learning to recognize objects. *Psychological Science, 14,* 244–250.

Smith, M. C., Bentin, S., & Spalek, T. M. (2001). Attention of semantic activation during visual word recognition. *Journal of Experimental Psychology: Learning, Memory, and Cognition, 27,* 1289–1298.

Smith, R. E. (2003). The cost of remembering to remember in event-based prospective memory: Investigating the capacity demands of delayed intention performance. *Journal of Experimental Psychology: Learning, Memory, and Cognition, 29,* 347–361.

Smith, R. E., & Bayen, U. J. (2004). A multinomial model of event-based prospective memory. *Journal of Experimental Psychology: Learning, Memory, and Cognition, 30,* 756–777.

Smith, S. M. (1995). Getting into and out of mental ruts: A theory of fixation, incubation, and insight. In R. J. Sternberg & J. E. Davidson (Eds.), *The nature of insight* (pp. 229–251). Cambridge, MA: MIT Press.

Snow, C. (1972). Mother's speech to children learning language. *Child Development, 43,* 549–565.

Snow, C., & Ferguson, C. (Eds.). (1977). *Talking to children: Language input and acquisition.* Cambridge, U.K.: Cambridge University Press.

Solso, R. L. (1995). Cognitive psychology (4/e). Boston: Allyn and Bacon.

Solso, R. L. (1998). *Cognitive psychology* (5th ed.). Boston: Allyn & Bacon.

Son, L. K. (2004). Spacing one's study: Evidence for a metacognitive control strategy. *Journal of Experimental Psychology: Learning, Memory, and Cognition, 30,* 601–604.

Son, L. K., & Metcalfe, J. (2000). Metacognitive and control strategies in study-time allocation. *Journal of Experimental Psychology: Learning, Memory, and Cognition, 26,* 204–221.

Speer, N. K., Zacks, J. M., & Reynolds, J. R. (2007). Human brain activity time-locaed to narrative event boundaries. *Psychological Science, 18,* 449–455.

Speer, S. R., & Clifton, C., Jr. (1998). Plausibility and argument structure in sentence comprehension. *Memory & Cognition, 26,* 965–978.

Spelke, E., Hirst, W., & Neisser, U. (1976). Skills of divided attention. *Cognition, 4,* 215–230.

Spellman, B. A., & Holyoak, K. J. (1996). Pragmatics in analogical mapping. *Cognitive Psychology, 31,* 307–346.

Spellman, B. A., & Mandel, D. R. (1999). When possibility informs reality: Counterfactual thinking as a cue to causality. *Current Directions in Psychological Science, 8,* 120–123.

Spence, C., & Read, L. (2003). Speech shadowing while driving: On the difficulty of splitting attention between eye and ear. *Psychological Science, 14,* 251–256.

Sperling, G. (1960). The information available in brief visual presentations. *Psychological Monographs, 74* (Whole No. 48).

Sperling, G. (1963). A model for visual memory tasks. *Human Factors, 5,* 9–31.

Sperry, R. W. (1964). The great cerebral commissure. *Scientific American, 210,* 42–52.

Spieth, W., Curtis, J. F., & Webster, J. C. (1954). Responding to one of two simultaneous messages. *Journal of the Acoustical Society of America, 26,* 391–396.

Spivey, M. J., Tanenhaus, M. K., Eberhard, K. M., & Sedivy, J. C. (2002). Eye movements and spoken language comprehension: Effects of visual context on syntactic ambiguity resolution. *Cognitive Psychology, 45,* 447–481.

Squire, L. R. (1986). Mechanisms of memory. *Science, 232* (4578), 1612–1619.

Squire, L. R. (1987). *Memory and brain.* New York: Oxford University Press.

Squire, L. R. (1992). Memory and the hippocampus: A synthesis from findings with rats, monkeys, and humans. *Psychological Review, 99,* 195–231.

Squire, L. R. (1993). The organization of declarative and nondeclarative memory. In T. Ono, L. R. Squire, M. E. Raichle, D. I. Perrett, & M. Fukuda (Eds.), *Brain mechanisms of perception and memory: From neuron to behavior* (pp. 219–227). New York: Oxford University Press.

Stadler, M. A., Roediger, H. L. III., & McDermott, K. B. (1999). Norms for word lists that create false memories. *Memory & Cognition, 27,* 494–500.

Stallings, L. M., MacDonald, M. C., & O'Seaghdha, P. G. (1998). Phrasal ordering constraints in sentence production: Phrase length and verb disposition in heavy-NP shift. *Journal of Memory and Language, 39,* 392–417.

Stark, L., & Perfect, T. J. (2008). The effects of repeated idea elaboration on unconscious plagiarism. *Memory & Cognition, 36,* 65–73.

Stazyk, E. H., Ashcraft, M. H., & Hamann, M. S. (1982). A network approach to simple multiplication. *Journal of Experimental Psychology: Learning, Memory, and Cognition, 17,* 355–376.

Steffens, M. C. (2007). Memory for goal-directed sequences of actions: Is doing better than seeing? *Psychonomic Bulletin & Review, 14,* 1194–1198.

Sternberg, R. J. (1996). *Cognitive psychology.* Fort Worth, TX: Harcourt Brace.

Sternberg, S. (1966). High-speed scanning in human memory. *Science, 153,* 652–654.

Sternberg, S. (1969). The discovery of processing stages: Extensions of Donder's method. In W. G. Koster (Ed.), *Attention and performance II. Acta Psychologica, 30,* 276–315.

Sternberg, S. (1975). Memory scanning: New findings and current controversies. *Quarterly Journal of Experimental Psychology, 27,* 1–32.

Strayer, D. L., & Drews, F. A. (2007). Cell-phone-induced driver distraction. *Current Directions in Psychological Science, 16,* 128–131.

Strayer, D. L., & Johnston, W. A. (2001). Driven to distraction: Dual-task studies of stimulated driving and conversing on a cellular phone. *Psychological Science, 12,* 462–466.

Stroop, J. R. (1935). Studies of interference in serial verbal reactions. *Journal of Experimental Psychology, 18,* 643–662.

Suh, S. Y., & Trabasso, T. (1993). Inferences during reading: Converging evidence from discourse analysis, talk-aloud protocols, and recognition priming. *Journal of Memory and Language, 32,* 279–300.

Sulin, R. A., & Dooling, D. J. (1974). Intrusion of a thematic idea in retention of prose. *Journal of Experimental Psychology, 103,* 255–262.

Tabor, W., & Hutchins, S. (2004). Evidence for self-organized sentence processing: Digging-in effects. *Journal of Experimental Psychology: Learning, Memory, and Cognition, 30,* 431–450.

Takahashi, M., Shimizu, H., Saito, S., & Tomoyori, H. (2006). One percent ability and ninety-nine percent perspiration: A study of a Japanese memorist. *Journal of Experimental Psychology: Learning, Memory, and Cognition, 32,* 1195–1200.

Talarico, J. M., LaBar, K. S., & Rubin, D. C. (2004). Emotional intensity predicts autobiographical memory experience. *Memory & Cognition, 32,* 1118–1132.

Talarico, J. M., & Rubin, D. C. (2003). Confidence, not consistency, characterizes flashbulb memories. *Psychological Science, 14,* 455–461.

Tamplin, A. K., Radvansky. G.A., & Copeland, D. E. (2008). Moving Through Space: Spatial Updating in Virtual Environments. *Unpublished manuscript.*

Tanaka, J. T., & Curran, T. (2001). A neural basis for expert object recognition. *Psychological Science, 12,* 43–47.

Tanenhaus, M. K., & Trueswell, J. C. (1995). Sentence comprehension. In J. Miller & P. Eiman (Eds.), Handbook of perception and cognition: Speech, language, and communication (2nd ed., Vol 11, pp. 217–262). San Diego: Academic Press.

Taraban, R., & McClelland, J. L. (1988). Constituent attachment and thematic role assignment in sentence processing: Influences of content-based expectations. *Journal of Memory and Language, 27,* 597–632.

Tetlock, P. E., & Mellers, B. A. (2002). The great rationality debate. *Psychological Science, 13,* 94–99.

Thapar, A., & Greene, R. L. (1994). Effects of level of processing on implicit and explicit tasks. *Journal of Experimental Psychology: Learning, Memory, and Cognition, 20,* 671–679.

Theeuwes, J., Kramer, A. F., Hahn, S., & Irwin, D. E. (1998). Our eyes do not always go where we want them to go: Capture of the eyes by new objects. *Psychological Science, 9,* 379–385.

Thiede, K. W. (1999). The importance of monitoring and self-regulation during multitrial learning. *Psychonomic Bulletin & Review, 6,* 662–667.

Thomas, A. K, Bulevich, J. B., & Loftus, E. F. (2003). Exploring the role of repetition and sensory elaboration in the imagination inflation effect. *Memory & Cognition, 31,* 630–640.

Thomas, J. C., Jr. (1974). An analysis of behavior in the hobbits–orcs problem. *Cognitive Psychology, 6,* 257–269.

Thomas, M. H., & Wang, A. Y. (1996). Learning by the keyword mnemonic: Looking for long-term benefits. *Journal of Experimental Psychology: Applied, 2,* 330–342.

Thompson, R. F. (1986). The neurobiology of learning and memory. *Science, 233,* 941–947.

Thompson, V. A., & Byrne, R. M. J. (2002). Reasoning counterfactually: Making inferences about things that didn't happen. *Journal of Experimental Psychology: Learning, Memory, and Cognition, 28,* 1154–1170.

Thomson, D. M., & Tulving, E. (1970). Associative encoding and retrieval: Weak and strong cues. *Journal of Experimental Psychology, 86,* 255–262.

Thorndike, E. L. (1914). *The psychology of learning.* New York: Teachers College.

Tipper, S.P. (1985). The negative priming effect: Inhibitory priming with to be ignored objects. *The Quarterly Journal of Experimental Psychology,* 37A, 571–590.

Titchener, E. B. (1919). *A text-book of psychology.* New York: Macmillan.

Toga, A. W., & Mazziotta, J. C. (Eds.). (1996). *Brain mapping: The methods.* New York: Academic Press.

Tolman, E. C. (1948). Cognitive maps in rats and men. *Psychological Review, 55,* 189–208.

Tourangeau, R., & Rips, L. (1991). Interpreting and evaluating metaphors. *Journal of Memory and Language, 30,* 452–472.

Townsend, J. T., & Wenger, M. J. (2004). The serial-parallel dilemma: A case study in a linkage of theory and method. *Psychonomic Bulletin & Review, 11,* 391–418.

Trabasso, T., & Bartolone, J. (2003). Story understanding and counterfactual reasoning. *Journal of Experimental Psychology: Learning, Memory, and Cognition, 29,* 904–923.

Treisman, A. M. (1960). Contextual cues in selective listening. *Quarterly Journal of Experimental Psychology, 12,* 242–248.

Treisman, A. M. (1964). Monitoring and storage of irrelevant messages in selective attention. *Journal of Verbal Learning and Verbal Behavior, 3,* 449–459.

Treisman, A. M. (1965). The effects of redundancy and familiarity on translating and repeating back a foreign and a native language. *British Journal of Psychology, 56,* 369–379.

Treisman, A. (1982). Perceptual grouping and attention in visual search for features and for objects. *Journal of Experimental Psychology: Human Perception and Performance, 8,* 194–214.

Treisman, A. (1988). Features and objects: The Fourteenth Bartlett Memorial Lecture. *Quarterly Journal of Experimental Psychology, 40A,* 201–237.

Treisman, A. (1991). Search, similarity, and integration of features between and within dimensions. *Journal of Experimental Psychology: Human Perception and Performance, 17,* 652–676.

Treisman, A., & Gelade, G. (1980). A feature integration theory of attention. *Cognitive Psychology, 12,* 97–136.

Treisman, A. M., Russell, R., & Green, J. (1975). Brief visual storage of shape and movement. In P. M. A. Rabbitt & S. Dornic (Eds.), *Attention and performance* (Vol. 5, pp. 699–721). New York: Academic Press.

Trigg, G. L., & Lerner, R. J. (Eds.). (1981). *Encyclopedia of physics.* Reading, MA: Addison-Wesley.

Tuholski, S. W., Engle, R. W., & Baylis, G. C. (2001). Individual differences in working memory capacity and enumeration. *Memory & Cognition, 29,* 484–492.

Tulving, E. (1962). Subjective organization in free recall of "unrelated" words. *Psychological Review, 69,* 344–354.

Tulving, E. (1972). Episodic and semantic memory. In E. Tulving & W. Donaldson (Eds.), *Organization of memory* (pp. 381–403). New York: Academic Press.

Tulving, E. (1983). *Elements of episodic memory.* Oxford, U.K.: Clarendon.

Tulving, E. (1985). How many memory systems are there? *American Psychologist, 40,* 385–398.

Tulving, E. (1989). Remembering and knowing the past. *American Scientist, 77,* 361–367.

Tulving, E. (1993). What is episodic memory? *Current Directions in Psychological Science, 2,* 67–70.

Tulving, E., & Pearlstone, Z. (1966). Availability versus accessibility of information in memory for words. *Journal of Verbal Learning and Verbal Behavior, 5,* 381–391.

Tulving, E., & Thompson, D. M. (1973). Encoding specificity and retrieval processes in episodic memory. *Psychological Review, 80,* 352–373.

Turley-Ames, K. J., & Whitfield, M. M. (2003). Strategy training and working memory task performance. *Journal of Memory and Language, 49,* 446–468.

Tversky, A., & Kahneman, D. (1973). Availability: A heuristic for judging frequency and probability. *Cognitive Psychology, 5,* 207–232.

Tversky, A., & Kahneman, D. (1974). Judgment under uncertainty: Heuristics and biases. *Science, 185,* 1124–1131.

Tversky, A., & Kahneman, D. (1980). Causal schemas in judgments under uncertainty. In M. Fishbein (Ed.), *Progress in social psychology* (Vol. 1, pp. 49–72). Hillsdale, NJ: Erlbaum.

Tversky, A., & Kahneman, D. (1983). Extensional versus intuitive reasoning: The conjunction fallacy in probability judgment. *Psychological Review, 90,* 293–315.

Tyler, L. K., Voice, J. K., & Moss, H. E. (2000). The interaction of meaning and sound in spoken word recognition. *Psychonomic Bulletin & Review, 7,* 320–326.

Tzelgov, J., Yehene, V., Kotler, L., & Alon, A. (2000). Automatic comparisons of artificial digits never compared: Learning linear ordering relations. *Journal of Experimental Psychology: Learning, Memory, and Cognition, 26,* 103–120.

Underwood, B. J. (1957). Interference and forgetting. *Psychological Review, 64,* 49–60.

Underwood, B. J., Keppel, G., & Schulz, R. W. (1962). Studies of distributed practice: XXII. Some conditions which enhance retention. *Journal of Experimental Psychology, 64,* 112–129.

Underwood, B. J., & Postman, L. (1960). Extraexperimental sources of interference in forgetting. *Psychological Review, 67,* 73–95.

Underwood, B. J., & Schulz, R. W. (1960). *Meaningfulness and verbal learning*. Philadelphia: Lippincott.

Ungerleider, L. G., & Haxby, J. V. (1994). "What" versus "where" in the human brain. *Current Opinion in Neurobiology, 4,* 157–165.

Unsworth, N. (2007). Individual differences in working memory capacity and episodic retrieval: The dynamics of delayed and continuous distractor free recall. *Journal of Experimental Psychology: Learning, Memory, and Cognition, 33,* 1020–1034.

Unsworth, N., & Engle, R. W. (2007). The nature of individual differences in working memory capacity: Active maintenance in primary memory and controlled search from secondary memory. *Psychological Review, 114,* 104–132.

Vallar, G., & Baddeley, A. D. (1984). Fractionation of working memory: Neuropsychological evidence for a phonological short-term store. *Journal of Verbal Learning and Verbal Behavior, 23,* 151–161.

Van Berkum, J. J. A., Brown, C. M., & Hagoort, P. (1999). Early referential context effects in sentence processing: Evidence from event-related brain potentials. *Journal of Memory and Language, 41,* 147–182.

Van Dijk, T. A., & Kintsch, W. (1983). *Strategies in discourse comprehension*. New York: Academic Press.

VanLehn, K. (1989). Problem solving and cognitive skill acquisition. In M. I. Posner (Ed.), *Foundations of cognitive science* (pp. 527–579). Cambridge, MA: MIT Press.

Van Overschelde, J. P., Rawson, K. A., & Dunlosky, J. (2004). Category norms: An updated and expanded version of the Battig and Montague (1969) norms. *Journal of Memory and Language, 50,* 289–335.

Vasta, R., & Liben, L. S. (1996). The water-level task: An intriguing puzzle. *Current Directions in Psychological Science, 5,* 171–177.

Vecera, S. P., Behrmann, M., & McGoldrick, J. (2000). Selective attention to the parts of an object. *Psychonomic Bulletin & Review, 7,* 301–308.

Verfaille, K., & Y'dewalle, G. (1991). Representational momentum and event course anticipation in the perception of implied motions. *Journal of Experimental Psychology: Learning, Memory, and Cognition, 17,* 302–313.

Verhaegen, P., Cerella, J., & Basak, C. (2004). A working memory workout: How to expand the focus of serial attention from one to four items in 10 hours or less. *Journal of Experimental Psychology: Learning, Memory, and Cognition, 30,* 1322–1337.

Virtue, S., van den Broek, P., & Linderholm, T. (2006). Hemispehric processing of inferences: the effects of textual constraint and working memory capacity. *Memory & Cognition, 34,* 1341–1354.

Vivas, A. B., Humphreys, G. W., & Fuentes, L. J. (2006). Abnormal inhibition of return: A review and new data on patients with parietal lobe damage. *Cognitive Neuropsychology, 23,* 1049–1064.

von Frisch, K. (1967). *The dance language and orientation of honeybees*. Cambridge, MA.: Harvard University Press.

von Restorff, H. (1933). Uber die wirkung von bereichsbildungen im spurenfeld [On the effect of spheres formations in the trace field]. *Psychologische Forschung, 18,* 299–342.

Vu, H., Kellas, G., Metcalf, K., & Herman, R. (2000). The influence of global discourse on lexical ambiguity resolution. *Memory & Cognition, 28,* 236–252.

Vuilleumeir, P. (2005). How brains beware: Neural mechanisms of emotional attention. *Trends in Cognitive Sciences, 9,* 585–594.

Vul, E., & Pashler, H. (2007). Incubation benefits only after people have been misdirected. *Memory & Cognition, 35,* 701–710.

Wade, K. A., Garry, M., Read, J. D., & Lindsay, S. (2002). A picture is worth a thousand lies: Using false photographs to create false childhood memories. *Psychonomic Bulletin & Review, 9,* 597–603.

Wagar, B. M., & Thagard, P. (2004). Spiking Phineas Gage: A neurocomputational theory of cognitive-affective integration in decision making. *Psychological Review, 111,* 67–79.

Wagenaar, W. A. (1986). My memory: A study of autobiographical memory over six years. *Cognitive Psychology, 18,* 225–252.

Wagner, S. M., Nusbaum, H., & Goldin-Meadow, S. (2004). Probing the mental representation of gesture: Is handwaving spatial? *Journal of Memory and Language, 50,* 395–407.

Waltz, J. A., Knowlton, B. J., Holyoak, K. J., Boone, K. B., Mishkin, F. S., Santos, M. M., Thomas, C. R., & Miller, B. L. (1999). A system for relational reasoning in human prefrontal cortex. *Psychological Science, 10,* 119–125.

Waltz, J. A., Lau, A., Grewal, S. K., & Holyoak, K. J. (2000). The role of working memory in analogical mapping. *Memory & Cognition, 28,* 1205–1212.

Warm, J. S. (1984). An introduction to vigilance. In J. S. Warm (ed.), *sustained attention in human performance* (pp. 1–14). Chinchester, UK: Wiley.

Warm, J. S., & Jerison, H. J. (1984). The psychophysics of vigilance. In J. S. Warm (ed.), *Sustained attention in human performance* (pp. 15–60). Chinchester, UK: Wiley.

Warren, R. M., & Warren, R. P. (1970). Auditory illusions and confusions. *Scientific American, 223,* 30–36.

Warrington, E. K., & James, M. (1988). Visual apperceptive agnosia: A clinico-anatomical study of three cases. *Cortex, 24,* 13–32.

Warrington, E. K., & McCarthy, R. (1983). Category specific access dysphasia. *Brain, 106,* 859–878.

Warrington, E. K., & Shallice, T. (1969). The selective impairment of auditory verbal short-term memory. *Brain, 92,* 885–896.

Warrington, E. K., & Shallice, T. (1984). Category specific semantic impairments. *Brain, 107,* 829–854.

Warrington, E. K., & Weiskrantz, L. (1970). The amnesic syndrome: Consolidation or retrieval? *Nature, 228,* 628–630.

Wason, P. C., & Johnson-Laird, P. N. (1972). *Psychology of reasoning: Structure and content*. Cambridge, MA: Harvard University Press.

Wasow, T. (1989). Grammatical theory. In M. I. Posner (Ed.), *Foundations of cognitive science* (pp. 161–205). Cambridge, MA: MIT Press.

Watkins, O. C., & Watkins, M. J. (1980). The modality effect and echoic persistence. *Journal of Experimental Psychology: General, 109,* 251–278.

Watson, J. B. (1913). Psychology as the behaviorist sees it. *Psychological Review, 20,* 158–177.

Watson, J. B. (1924). *Behaviorism*. New York: Norton.

Watson, J. M., McDermott, K. B., & Balota, D. A. (2004). Attempting to avoid false memories in the Deese–Roediger–McDermott paradigm: Assessing the combined influence of practice and warnings in young and old adults. *Memory & Cognition, 32,* 135–141.

Watson, R. I. (1968). *The great psychologists from Aristotle to Freud*. New York: Lippincott.

Waugh, N. C., & Norman, D. A. (1965). Primary memory. *Psychological Review, 72,* 89–104.

Weaver, C. A. III. (1993). Do you need a "flash" to form a flashbulb memory? *Journal of Experimental Psychology: General, 122,* 39–46.

Webster's New Universal Unabridged Dictionary (1983, 2/e). Cleveland, OH: Dorset & Baber.

Webster's New World Dictionary of the American Language. (1980). 2nd college edition. Cleveland: William Collins.

Weinstein, Y., Bugg, J. M., & Roediger, H. L. (2008). Can the survival recall advantage be explained by basic memory processes? *Memory & Cognition, 36,* 913–919.

Weisberg, R. (1995). Prolegomena to theories of insight in problem solving: A taxonomy of problems. In R. J. Sternberg & J. E. Davidson (Eds.), *The nature of insight* (pp. 157–196). Cambridge, MA: MIT Press.

Wells, G. L., Olson, E. A., & Charman, S. D. (2002). The confidence of eyewitnesses in their identifications from lineups. *Current Directions in Psychological Science, 11,* 151–154.

Wenger, M. J., & Payne, D. G. (1995). On the acquisition of mnemonic skill: Application of skilled memory theory. *Journal of Experimental Psychology: Applied, 1,* 194–215.

Werner, H. (1935). Studies on contour. *American Journal of Psychology, 47,* 40–64.

Wertheimer, M. (1912). Experimentelle studien über das sehen von bewegung (trans. Experimental studies on the seeing of motion). *Zeitschrift für Psychologie und Physiologie der Sinnesorgane, 61,* 161–265.

West, R. F., & Stanovich, K. E. (1986). Robust effects of syntactic structure on visual word processing. *Memory & Cognition, 14,* 104–112.

Westmacott, R., & Moscovitch, M. (2003). The contribution of autobiographical significance to semantic memory. *Memory & Cognition, 31,* 761–774.

Whaley, C. P. (1978). Word–nonword classification time. *Journal of Verbal Learning and Verbal Behavior, 17,* 143–154.

Wharton, C. M., Grafman, J., Flitman, S. S., Hansen, E. K., Brauner, J., Marks, A., & Honda, M. (2000). Toward neuroanatomical models of analogy: A positron emission tomography study of analogical mapping. *Cognitive Psychology, 40,* 173–197.

Wheeler, M. A., Stuss, D. T., & Tulving, E. (1997). Toward a theory of episodic memory: The frontal lobes and autonoetic consciousness. *Psychological Bulletin, 121,* 331–354.

White, K. G., & Ruske, A. C. (2002). Memory deficits in Alzheimer's disease: The encoding hypothesis and cholinergic function. *Psychonomic Bulletin & Review, 9,* 426–437.

Whitney, P. (1998). *The psychology of language.* Boston: Houghton Mifflin.

Whittlesea, B. W. A. (2004). The perception of integrality: Remembering through the validation of expectation. *Journal of Experimental Psychology: Learning, Memory, and Cognition, 30,* 891–908.

Whorf, B. L. (1956). Science and linguistics. In J. B. Carroll (Ed.), *Language, thought, and reality: Selected writings of Benjamin Lee Whorf* (pp. 207–219). Cambridge, MA: MIT Press.

Wickelgren, W. A. (1974). *How to solve problems.* San Francisco: Freeman.

Wickens, C. D. (1984). *Engineering psychology and human performance.* Columbus, OH: Charles E. Merrill.

Wickens, D. D. (1972). Characteristics of word encoding. In A. W. Melton & E. Martin (Eds.), *Coding processes in human memory* (pp. 191–215). New York: Winston.

Wickens, D. D., Born, D. G., & Allen, C. K. (1963). Proactive inhibition and item similarity in short-term memory. *Journal of Verbal Learning and Verbal Behavior, 2,* 440–445.

Wiener, E. L. (1984). Vigilance and inspection. In J. S. Warm (ed.), *Sustained attention in human performance* (pp. 207–246). Chinchester, UK: Wiley.

Wiley, J. (1998). Expertise as mental set: The effects of domain knowledge in creative problem solving. *Memory & Cognition, 26,* 716–730.

Wiley, J., & Rayner, K. (2000). Effects of titles on the processing of text and lexically ambiguous words: Evidence from eye movements. *Memory & Cognition, 28,* 1011–1021.

Willander, J., & Larsson, M. (2006). Smell your way back to childhood. *Psychonomic Bulletin & Review, 13,* 240–244.

Willander, J., & Larsson, M. (2007). Olfaction and emotion: The case of autobiographical memory. *Memory & Cognition, 35,* 1659–1663.

Wilkes-Gibbs, D., & Clark, H. H. (1992). Coordinating beliefs in conversation. *Journal of Memory and Language, 31,* 183–194.

Wilson, M., & Emmorey, K. (2006). Comparing sign language and speech reveals a universal limit on short-term memory capacity. *Psychological Science, 17,* 682–683.

Wilson, M., & Wilson, T. P. (2005). An oscillator model of the timing of turn-taking. *Psychonomic Bulletin & Review, 12,* 957–968.

Windschitl, P. D., & Weber, E. U. (1999). The interpretation of "likely" depends on the context, but "70%" is 70%—right? The influence of associative processes on perceived certainty. *Journal of Experimental Psychology: Learning, Memory, and Cognition, 25,* 1514–1533.

Winer, G. A., Cottrell, J. E., Gregg, V., Fournier, J. S., & Bica, L. A. (2002). Fundamentally misunderstanding visual perception adults' belief in visual emissions. *American Psychologist, 57,* 417–424.

Wingfield, A., Goodglass, H., & Lindfield, K. C. (1997). Separating speed from automaticity in a patient with focal brain atrophy. *Psychological Science, 8,* 247–249.

Winograd, E., & Killinger, W. A., Jr. (1983). Relating age at encoding in early childhood to adult recall: Development of flashbulb memories. *Journal of Experimental Psychology: General, 112,* 413–422.

Wixted, J. T. (1991). Conditions and consequences of maintenance rehearsal. *Journal of Experimental Psychology: Learning, Memory, and Cognition, 17,* 963–973.

Wixted, J. T. (2004). On common ground: Jost's (1897) law of forgetting and Ribot's (1881) law of retrograde amnesia. *Psychological Review, 111,* 864–879.

Wixted, J. T. (2005). A theory about why we forget what we once knew. *Current Directions in Psychological Science, 14,* 6–9.

Wixted, J. T., & Ebbesen, E. B. (1991). On the form of forgetting. *Psychological Science, 2,* 409–415.

Wood, F., Taylor, B., Penney, R., & Stump, B. (1980). Regional cerebral blood flow response to recognition memory versus semantic classification tasks. *Brain and Language, 9,* 113–122.

Wood, N. L., & Cowan, N. (1995a). The cocktail party phenomenon revisited: Attention and memory in the classic selective listening procedure of Cherry (1953). *Journal of Experimental Psychology: General, 124*, 243–262.

Wood, N., & Cowan, N. (1995b). The cocktail party phenomenon revisited: How frequent are attention shifts to one's name in an irrelevant auditory channel? *Journal of Experimental Psychology: Learning, Memory, and Cognition, 21*, 255–260.

Woodworth, R. S., & Schlosberg, H. (1954). *Experimental psychology* (Rev. ed.). New York: Holt, Rinehart & Winston.

Wraga, M., Swaby, M., & Flynn, C. M. (2008). Passive tactile feedback facilitates mental rotation of handheld objects. *Memory & Cognition, 36*, 271–281.

Wright, A. A., & Roediger, H. L. III. (2003). Interference processes in monkey auditory list memory. *Psychonomic Bulletin & Review, 10*, 696–702.

Wurm, L. H. (2007). Danger and usefulness: An alternative framework for understanding rapid evaluation effects in perception. *Psychonomic Bulletin & Review, 14*, 1218–1225.

Wurm, L. H., & Seaman, S. R. (2008). Semantic effects in naming and perceptual identification but not in delayed naming: Implications for models and tasks. *Journal of Experimental Psychology: Learning, Memory, and Cognition, 34*, 381–398.

Yamauchi, T., & Markman, A. B. (2000). Inference using categories. *Journal of Experimental Psychology: Learning, Memory, and Cognition, 26*, 776–795.

Yantis, S., & Jonides, J. (1984). Abrupt visual onsets and selective attention: Evidence from visual search. *Journal of Experimental Psychology: Human Perception and Performance, 10*, 601–621.

Yarbus, A. L. (1967). Eye movements and vision. (trans., B. Haigh). New York: Plenum.

Yates, F. A. (1966). *The art of memory*. Chicago: University of Chicago Press.

Yates, M., Locker, L., Jr., & Simpson, G. B. (2003). Semantic and phonological influences on the processing of words and pseudohomophones. *Memory & Cognition, 31*, 856–866.

Yechiam, E., Kanz, J. E., Bechara, A., Stout, J. C., Busemeyer, J. R., Altmaier, E. M., & Paulsen, J. S. (2008). Neurocognitive deficits related to poor decision making in people behind bars. *Psychonomic Bulletin & Review, 15*, 44–51.

Yonelinas, A. P. (2002). The nature of recollection and familiarity: A review of 30 years of research. *Journal of Memory and Language, 46*, 441–517.

Yuille, J. C., & Paivio, A. (1967). Latency of imaginal and verbal mediators as a function of stimulus and response concreteness-imagery. *Journal of Experimental Psychology, 75*, 540–544.

Zacks, J. M., Braver, T. S., Sheridan, M. A., Donaldson, D. I., Snyder, A. Z., Ollinger, J. M., et al. (2001). Human brain activity time-locked to perceptual event boundaries. *Nature Neuroscience, 4*, 651–655.

Zacks, J. M., Speer, N. K., Swallow, K. M., Braver, T. S., & Reynolds, J. R. (2007). Event perception: A mind/brain perspective. *Psychological Bulletin, 133*, 273–293.

Zaragoza, M. S., & Lane, S. M. (1994). Source misattributions and the suggestibility of eyewitness memory. *Journal of Experimental Psychology: Learning, Memory, and Cognition, 20*, 934–945.

Zaragoza, M. S., McCloskey, M., & Jamis, M. (1987). Misleading postevent information and recall of the original event: Further evidence against the memory impairment hypothesis. *Journal of Experimental Psychology: Learning, Memory, and Cognition, 13*, 36–44.

Zaragoza, M. S., Payment, K. E., Ackil, J. K., Drivdahl, S. B., & Beck, M. (2001). Interviewing witnesses: Forced confabulation and confirmatory feedback increase false memories. *Psychological Science, 12*, 473–477.

Zbrodoff, N. J., & Logan, G. D. (1986). On the autonomy of mental processes: A case study of arithmetic. *Journal of Experimental Psychology: General, 115*, 118–130.

Zeelenberg, R., Wagenmakers, E., & Rotteveel, M. (2006). The impact of emotion on perception: Bias or enhanced processing? *Psychological Science, 17*, 287–291.

Zola-Morgan, S., Squire, L., & Amalral, D. G. (1986). Human amnesia and the medial temporal region: Enduring memory impairment following a bilateral lesion limited to field CA1 of the hippocampus. *Journal of Neuroscience, 6*, 2950–2967.

Zwaan, R. A. (1996). Processing narrative time shifts. *Journal of Experimental Psychology: Learning, Memory, and Cognition, 22*, 1196–1207.

Zwaan, R. A., Langston, M. C., & Graesser, A. C. (1995). The construction of situation models in narrative comprehension: An event-indexing model. *Psychological Science, 6*, 292–297.

Zwaan, R. A., Magliano, J. P., & Graesser, A. C. (1995). Dimensions of situation model construction in narrative comprehension. *Journal of Experimental Psychology: Learning, Memory, and Cognition, 21*, 386–397.

Zwaan, R. A., & Radvansky, G. A. (1998). Situation models in language comprehension and memory. *Psychological Bulletin, 123*, 162–185.

Zwaan, R. A., Stanfield, R. A., & Yaxley, R. H. (2002). Language comprehenders mentally represent the shapes of objects. *Psychological Science, 13*, 168–171.

PHOTO CREDITS

Chapter 1 p. 14: Bettmann/Corbis; p. 15: Bettmann/Corbis; p. 16: The Harvard University Houghton Library Reading Room; p. 20: Gerard Fritz/Stock Connection; p. 24: MIT Press Journals;

Chapter 3 p. 72: Thomas Ives; p. 81: Fine Arts Museums of San Francisco; p. 89: Fundamental Photographs, NYC; p. 89: Fundamental Photographs, NYC;

Chapter 4 p. 128: Getty Images; p. 129: Getty Images; p. 141: Bettmann/Corbis; p. 143: The Image Works;

Chapter 5 p. 149: Photodisc/Getty Images; p. 173: Stock Boston;

Chapter 6 p. 195: Michael Malyszko/Getty Images; p. 215: Photofest;

Chapter 7 p. 237: George Houlton/Photo Researchers, Inc.; p. 240: AP Photo;

Chapter 8 p. 296: Lon C. Diehl/PhotoEdit, Inc.; p. 307: Photo Researchers, Inc.; p. 310: Photolibrary.com; p. 312: Liaison/Getty Images; p. 316: Masatomo Kuriya/Bettmann/Corbis;

Chapter 9 p. 322: Arthur Harvey/Miami Herald Publishing Co.;

Chapter 10 p. 373: Yellow Dog Productions/Image Bank/Getty Images; p. 379: Markus Matzel/DAS FOTOARCHIV/Peter Arnold, Inc.; p. 401: Digital Vision/Getty Images;

Chapter 11 p. 425: ImageState Media Partners Limited; p. 433: Laimute Druskis/Pearson Education/PH College;

Chapter 12 p. 467: Routledge and Kegan Paul Ltd; p. 488: Estate of Herbert A. Simon; p. 500: Myron Davis/Stockbyte/Getty Images; p. 501: Joel Gordon Photography.

Endsheets Left page Middle: Dr. Marcus E. Raichle; Right page top/Middle: John Gabrielli; Right Page Bottom: With permission from Elsevier Ltd./RightsLink. Copyright Clearance Center, Inc.

TEXT CREDITS

Chapter 1 Entry for "cognition" from AMERICAN HERITAGE DICTIONARY OF THE ENGLISH LANGUAGE 4th edition. Copyright © 2000 by Houghton Mifflin Company. Reproduced by permission of Houghton Mifflin Company. **Chapter 1** Definitions of "memory and language" from WEBSTER'S NEW WORLD COLLEGE DICTIONARY 4th edition ed. by Michael E. Agnes. Copyright © 2008 by Wiley Publishing Inc., Cleveland, OH. Reprinted by permission of John Wiley & Sons, Inc.

Illustration and Table Credits

Figure 2-1 Data from Campbell & Graham (1985). **Figure 2-2** From "Serial Position Curves" by M. Glanzer and A. R. Cunitz in Journal of Verbal Learning and Verbal Behavior, 5 (1966) pp. 354-358. Copyright © 1966. Reprinted by permission of Elsevier. **Figure 2-3** From "The Control of Short-Term Memory" by R. C. Atkinson and R. M. Shiffrin, Scientific American, 225, pp. 82-90. Copyright © 1971. Reprinted by permission of the publisher. **Figure 2-11** Figure, p. 10 in "Introduction and Overview", NEUROPSYCHOLOGICAL FUNCTION AND BRAIN IMAGING ed. by E. D. Bigler, R. A. Yeo, and F. Turkheimer. Copyright © 1989. Reprinted by permission of Springer Science & Business Media. **Figure 2-12** From p. 380 in "An Interactive Activation Model of Context Effects in Letter Perception: Part I. An Account of Basic Findings" by J. McClelland and D. E. Rumelhart, *Psychological Review, 88* (1981). Copyright © 1981 by the American Psychological Association. **Table 2-2** Adaptation of table 9.6, p. 205 from FUNDAMENTALS OF HUMAN NEUROPSYCHOLOGY by Bryan Kolb and Ian W. Whishaw. Copyright © 1980, 1985, 1990, 1996 by W. H. Freeman and Company. Used with permission. **Figure 3-5** From "Short-Term Storage of Information in Vision" by E. Averbach and G. Sperling (eds.), INFORMATION THEORY (pp. 196-211). Copyright © 1960. Published by Butterworth, London. **Figure 3-6b** Fig. 3.17, p. 118 from PSYCHOLOGY 2nd edition by Saundra K. Ciccarelli and J. Noland White. Copyright © 2009, 2006 by Pearson Education, One Lake Street, Upper Saddle River, NJ 07458. Reprinted by permission of the publisher. **Figure 3-7** From "Pandemonium: A Paradigm for Learning" by O. G. Selfridge in Teddington Symposium, MECHANIZATION OF THOUGHT PROCESSES, p. 517 . Copyrigh © 1959 by National Physical Laboratory, Teddington, ENGLAND. Reprinted by permission. **Figure 3-8** Adapted from SENSATION & PERCEPTION 3rd ed. by Stanley Coren and Lawrence Ward, copyright © 1989 by Harcourt, Inc. AND "Pandemonium: A Paradigm for Learning" in THE MECHANISATION OF THOUGHT PROCESSES by O. G. Selfridge. Copyright © 1959, H. M. Stationery Office, London. **Figure 3-9** Illustrations, pp. 96 & 97 , from "Visual Search" by Ulric Neisser, *Scientific American*, June 1964. Copyright © 1964 by Scientific American, Inc. All rights reserved. **Figure 3-12** From "Higher-Level Vision" by I. Biederman, et al. (eds.) AN INVITATION TO COGNITIVE SCIENCE, 2, pp. 41-72. Copyright © 1990 by MIT Press, Cambridge, MA. Reprinted by permission. **Figures 3-13, 3-14** From *Computer Vision & Image Understanding* formerly *Computer Vision, Graphics & Image Processing*, Vol. 32, pp. 29-73 by I. Biederman. Copyright © 1985. Reprinted by permission of Elsevier. **Figure 3-15** Figure 5.8 from NEUROPSYCHOLOGY: The Neural Bases of Mental Function by Marie T. Banich. Copyright © 1997 by Wadsworth, a part of Cengage Learning, Inc. All rights reserved. Reproduced with permission. Text/images may not be modified or reproduced in any way without prior written permission of the publisher. *www.cengage.com/permissions*. **Figure 3-16** From PRINCIPLES OF PSYCHOLOGY by R. H. Price.

Copyright © 1987 by Scott, Foresman and Company. Reprinted by permission. **Figure 3-17** From p. 259 in "An Auditory Analogue of the Sperling Partial Report Procedure: Evidence for Brief Auditory Storage" by C. J. Darwin, M. T. Turvey, and R. G. Crowder, *Cognitive Psychology, 3* (1972). Copyright © 1972. Reprinted by permission of Elsevier. **Figure 3-18** From p. 166 in "The Role of One's Own Voice in Immediate Memory" by R. C. Crowder, *Cognitive Psychology, 1* (1970). Copyright © 1970. Reprinted by permission of Elsevier. **Figure 4-3** From p. 163 in "Attention and the Detection of Signals" by Posner, Snyder and Davidson. *Journal of Experimental Psychology: General, 109* (1980) pp. 160-174. Copyright © 1980 by American Psychological Association. **Figure 4-5** From "A Feature Integration Theory of Attention" by A. Treisman and G. Gelade, *Cognitive Psychology, 12* (1980) pp. 97-136. Copyright © 1980. Reprinted by permission of Elsevier. **Figure 4-6** From COGNITIVE PSYCHOLOGY 5th ed. by Robert L. Solso. Copyright © 1998 by Pearson Education. Reprinted by permission of the publisher. **Figure 4-7** Figure 9-16, p. 300 from BRAIN, MIND AND BEHAVIOR by Floyd Bloom, Charles A. Nelson, and Arlyne Lazerson. Copyright © 1985, 1988 by Educational Broadcasting Corporation. Used with permission of W. H. Freeman and Company. **Figure 4-8** "From "Left in the Dark: The Neglect of Theory" by J. C. Marshall and P. W. Halligan, *Neuropsychological Rehabilitation, 4*, 161-167. Copyright © 1994. Reprinted by permission of ITPS, England. **Figure 4-10** From HUMAN INFORMATION PROCESSING 2nd edition by Peter H. Lindsay and Donald A. Norman. Copyright © 1977. Reprinted with permission of Wadsworth, a part of Cengage Learning, Inc. Reproduced by permission. *www.cengage.com/permissions*. **Figure 4-12** From "Checklist Procedures and the Cost of Automaticity" by I. Barshi and A. F. Healy, *Memory & Cognition, 21*, pp. 496-505. Copyright © 1993 by The Psychonomic Society. Reprinted by permission. **Figure 5-2** From "Primary Memory" by N. C. Waugh and D. A. Norman, *Psychological Review, 72* (1965). Copyright © 1965 by American Psychological Association. **Figure 5-4** Reported in Wickens, D. D. 1972. Characteristics word encoding. In CODING PROCESSES IN HUMAN MEMORY ed. by A. W. Melton and E. Martin, pp. 191-215. Washington, DC: Winston/Wiley. **Figure 5-8** Fig. 2 from "Storage and Executive Processes in the Frontal Lobes" by E. E. Smith and J. Jonides, *Science, 283* (1999) pp. 1657-1661. Copyright © 1999 by AAAS. Reprinted by permission of AAAS. **Figure 5-9** Fig. 1, p. 47 from "Neural Bases of Human Working Memory" by E. E. Smith, *Current Directions in Psychological Science, 9* (2000). Copyright © 2000. Reprinted by permission of Blackwell Publishing Ltd. **Figure 5-10** Figs. 1 & 2, p. 702 from "Mental Rotation of Three-Dimensional Objects" by Shepard and Metzler, *Science, 171* (1971) pp.701-703. Copyright © 1971 by AAAS. Reprinted by permission of AAAS. **Figure 5-11** From p. 56 in "Working Memory" by A. D. Baddeley and G. Hitch, *The Psychology of Learning and Motivation, 8* (1974). Copyright © 1974. Reprinted by permission of Elsevier. **Figure 5-13** From "Individual Differences in Working Memory and Reading" by M. Daneman and P. A. Carpenter, *Journal of Verbal Learning and Verbal Behavior, 19* (1980) pp. 450-466. Copyright © 1980. Reprinted by permission of Elsevier. **Figure 5-14** From "The Role of Working Memory Capacity in Retrieval" by V. M. Rosen and R. W. Engle, *Journal of Experimental Psychology: General, 126* (1997) pp. 211-227. Copyright © 1997 by American Psychological Association. **Figure 6-1** Fig. 3 from "The Medial Temporal Lobe Memory System" by L. Squire and S. Zola-Morgan, *Science, 253* (1991 pp. 1380-1386. Copyright © 1991 by AAAS. Reprinted by permission of AAAS. **Figure 6-3** Fig. 3, p. 18 from "The von Restorff Effect in Amnesia: The Contribution of the Hippocampal System to Novelty-Related Memory Enhancements" by M. M. Kishiyama, A. P. Yonelinas and M. M. Lazzara, *Journal of Cognitive Neuroscience, 16*: 1 (January-February, 2004) pp.15-23. Copyright © 2004 by the Massachusetts Institute of Technology. Reprinted by permission of MIT Press Journals. **Figure 6-5** From p. 66 , "Analysis of Rehearsal Processes in Free Recall" by D. Rundus, *Journal of Experimental Psychology, 89* (1971). Copyright © 1971 by American Psychological Association. **Figure 6-6** From "Hierarchal Retrieval Schemes in Recall of Categorized Word Lists" by G. H. Bower, M. C. Clark, A. M. Lesgold, and D. Winzenz., *Journal of Verbal Learning and Verbal Behavior, 8*, 326 (1969). Copyright © 1969. Reprinted with permission of Elsevier. **Figure 6-7** Derived from data in Godden, D. B. & Baddeley, A. D. (1975). "Context-Dependent Memory in Two Natural Environments: On Land and Underwater". *British Journal of Psychology, 66*, 325-331. **Figure 6-8** Figure from "Obliviscence during Sleep and Waking" by Jenkins & Dallenbach, *American Journal of Psychology, 35* (1924), pp. 605-612. Copyright 1924 by the Board of Trustees of the University of Illinois. Used with permission of the author and the University of Illinois Press. **Table 6-4** From "Hierarchal Retrieval Schemes in Recall of Categorized Word Lists" by G. H. Bower, M. C. Clark, A. M. Lesgold, and D. Winzenz., *Journal of Verbal Learning and Verbal Behavior, 8*, 326 (1969). Copyright © 1969. Reprinted with permission of Elsevier. **Tables 6-7, 6-8** From pp. 142-143 of THE IDEAL PROBLEM SOLVER by John D. Bransford and Barry Stein. Copyright © 1984, 1993 by W. H. Freeman and Company. Used with permission. **Figure 7-2** From "Theories of Semantic Behavior" by E. E. Smith in W. K. Estes (ed.) HANDBOOK OF LEARNING AND COGNITIVE PROCESSES, Vol. 6. Copyright © 1978 by Lawrence Erlbaum Associates, Inc. Reprinted by permission. **Figure 7-4** From "Retrieval Time for Semantic Memory" by A. Collins and M. R. Quillian, *Journal of Verbal Learning and Verbal Behavior, 8* (1969) pp. 240-247. Copyright © 1969. Reprinted by permission of Elsevier. **Figure 7-6** From p. 468 in "Structure and Process in Semantic Memory" by J. Kounios and P. J. Holcomb, *Journal of Experimental Psychology: General, 121* (1992). Copyright © 1992 by American Psychological Association. **Figure 7-7** From p. 235 in "Structure and Process in Semantic Memory" by E. E. Smith, E. J. Shoben and L. J. Rips, *Psychological Review, 81* (1974). Copyright © 1974 by American Psychological Association. **Figure 7-8** From p. 469 in "Structure and Process in Semantic Memory" by J. Kounios and P. J. Holcomb, *Journal of Experimental Psychology: General, 121* (1992). Copyright © 1992 by American Psychological Association. **Figure 7-9a&b** From "Concreteness Effects in Semantic Processing: ERP Evidence Supporting Dual-Coding Theory" by J. Kounios and P. J. Holcomb, *Journal of Experimental Psychology: Learning, Memory and Cognition, 20* (1994) pp. 804-823. Copyright © 1994 by American Psychological Association. **Figure 7-11** From "The Influence of One Memory Retrieval on a Subsequent Memory Retrieval" by G. R. Loftus and E. F. Loftus, *Memory & Cognition, 2* (1974) pp. 467-471. Copyright © 1974. Reprinted by permission of The Psychonomic Society. **Figure 7-12** From "Semantic Priming and Retrieval from Lexical Memory: Evidence for Facilitatory and Inhibitory Processes" by J. H. Neely, *Memory & Cognition, 4* (1976) pp. 648-654. Copyright © 1976. Reprinted by permission of The Psychonomic Society. **Figure 7-13** From p. 233 in "Semantic Priming and Retrieval from Lexical Memory: Roles of Inhibitionless Spreading Activation and Limited

Capacity Attention" by J. H. Neely, *Journal of Experimental Psychology: General, 106* (1977), pp. 226-254. Copyright © 1977 by American Psychological Association. **Figure 7-14** Adapted SCRIPTS, PLANS GOALS AND UNDERSTANDING by R. C. Schank and R. P. Abelson. Copyright © 1977. Reprinted by permission of Lawrence Erlbaum Associates, Inc. **Figure 7-15** Adapted from COGNITIVE PSYCHOLOGY: A Neural-Network Approach 1st edition by C. Martindale. Copyright © 1991 by Wadsworth, a part of Cengage Learning, Inc. Reproduced by permission. *www.cengage.com/permissions*. **Figure 7-16** From p. 345 in "A Computational Model of Semantic Memory Impairment: Modality Specificity and Emergent Category Specificity" by M. J. Farah and J. L. McClelland, *Journal of Experimental Psychology: General, 120* (1991). Copyright © 1991 by American Psychological Association. **Table 7-3** From p. 229 in "Facilitation in Recognizing Pairs of Words: Evidence of a Dependence between Retrieval Operations" by D. E. Meyer and R. W. Schvaneveldt, *Journal of Experimental Psychology, 90* (1971). Copyright © 1971 by American Psychological Association. **Table 7-4** From p. 233 in "Semantic Priming and Retrieval from Lexical Memory: Roles of Inhibitionless Spreading Activation and Limited Capacity Attention" by J. H. Neely, *Journal of Experimental Psychology: General, 106* (1977) pp. 226-254. Copyright © 1977 by American Psychological Association. **Figure 8-2** Derived from Anderson (1980) and Anderson and Bower (1973); written proposition after Kintsch (1974). **Figure 8-3** Adapted from COGNITIVE PSYCHOLOGY AND ITS IMPLICATIONS by John R. Anderson. Copyright © 1980, 1985, 1995, 2000 by Worth Publishers and W. H. Freeman and Company. Used with permission. **Figure 8-4** From "Sentence Memory: A Theoretical Analysis" by W. Kintsch, D. Welsch, F. Schmalhofer and S. Zimny in *Journal of Memory and Language, 29* (1987), 133-159. Copyright © 1987. Reprinted by permission of Elsevier. **Figure 8-5** Derived from Radvansky, Spieler and Zacks (1993). **Figure 8-6** From "Creating False Memories: Remembering Words no Presented in Lists" by H. L. Roediger, III and K. B. McDermott in *Journal of Experimental Psychology: Learning, Memory, and Cognition, 21* (1995) 803-814. Copyright © 1995 by American Psychological Association. **Figure 8-7** From p. 346 in "The Abstraction of Linguistic Ideas" by J. D. Bransford and J. J. Franks, *Cognitive Psychology, 2* (1971). Copyright © 1971. Reprinted by permission of Elsevier. **Figure 8-8** From "Reconstruction of Automobile Destruction: An Example of the Interaction Between Language and Memory" by E. R. Loftus and J. C. Palmer, *Journal of Verbal Language and Verbal Behavior, 13* (1974), pp. 585-589. Copyright © 1974. Reprinted by permission of Elsevier. **Figure 8-9** From p. 152 in "True Photos and False Memories" by D. S. Lindsay, L. Hagen, J. D. Read, K. A. Wade and M. Garry in *Psychological Science, 15* (2004), 149-154. Copyright © 2004. Reprinted by permission of Blackwell Publishing Ltd. **Figure 8-10** From "Long-Term Memory for a Common Object" by R. S. Nickerson and M. J. Adams, *Cognitive Psychology, 11* (1979) 297. Copyright © 1979. Reprinted by permission of Elsevier. **Figure 8-11** From p. 66 in "Fifty Years of Memory for Names and Places" by H. P. Bahrick, *Journal of Experimental Psychology, 104* (1975). Copyright © 1975 by American Psychological Association. **Figure 8-12** Adaptation of Figure 1, p. 4 from "Things Learned in Early Adulthood are Remembered Best" by D. C. Rubin, T. A. Rahhal, and L. W. Poon, *Memory & Cognition, 34* (1998) 3-19. Copyright © 1998. Reprinted by permission of The Psychonomic Society. **Figure 8-13** Figs. 1 & 2, p. 401 in "On the Very Long-Term Retention of Knowledge Acquired Through Formal Education: Twelve Years of Cognitive Psychology" by M. A. Conway, G. Cohen, and N. Stanhope, *Journal of Experimental Psychology: General,,120* (1991) pp. 395-409. Copyright © 1991 by American Psychological Association. **Table 8-3** From p. 414 in "Priming in Item Recognition: Evidence for the Propositional Structure of Sentences" by R. Ratcliff and G. McKoon, *Journal of Verbal Learning and Verbal Behavior, 17*(1978). Copyright © 1978. Reprinted by permission of Elsevier. **Tables 8-4, 8-5** From p. 791 in "Remember That Old Theory of Memory? Well, Forget It!" by J. J. Jenkins, *American Psychologist, 29* (1974). Copyright © 1974 by American Psychological Association. **Figure 9-1** Figure, "The Vocal Tract, Illustrating Places of Articulation" from AN INTRODUCTION TO LANGUAGE 7th ed. by V. Fromkin, R. Rodman, and N. Hyams. Copyright © 2003 by Heinle/Arts & Sciences, a part of Cengage Learning, Inc. Reprinted by permission. *www.cengage.com/permissions*. **Figure 9-2** From "The Perceptual Classification of Speech" by P. W. Jusczyk, L. B. Smith, and C. Murphy, *Perception and Psychophysics, 1* (1981) 10-23. Copyright © 1981 by The Psychonomic Society. Reprinted by permission of The Psychonomic Society. **Figure 9-3** From "The Discrimination of Speech Sounds Within and Across Phoneme Boundaries" by A. M. Liberman, K. S. Harris, H. S. Hoffman, and B. C. Griffith in *Journal of Experimental Psychology, 54* (1957) 358-368. Copyright © 1957 by American Psychological Association. **Figure 9-4** Single illustration, "The three phonemes in the word bag" from "Some Results of Research on Speech Perception" by A. M. Liberman, *Journal of the Acoustical Society of America, 29* (1957) pp. 117-123. Copyright © 1957 by Acoustical Society of America. Reprinted by permission of the publisher. **Figure 9-5** From "Some Perceptual Consequences of Linguistic Rules"by G. A. Miller and S. Isard, *Journal of Verbal Learning and Verbal Behavior, 2* (1963) 583-599. Copyright © 1963. Reprinted by permission of Elsevier, Inc. **Figure 9-7** From Whitney (1998). **Figure 9-9** Adapted from figures 3 & 4 in "Dual-Coding, Context Availability, and Concreteness Effects in Sentence Comprehension: An Electrophysiological Investigation" by P. J. Holcomb, J. Kounios, J. E. Anderson and W. C. West, *Journal of Experimental Psychology: Learning, Memory and Cognition, 25* (1999) 721-742. Copyright © 1999 by American Psychological Association. **Figure 9-10** Adapted in Whitney (1998). **Figure 9-11** From "Pragmatic Normalization: Further Results for Some Conjunctive and Disjunctive Sentences", *Journal of Experimental Psychology, 102* (1974) 574-578. Copyright © 1974 by American Psychological Association. **Figure 9-12** From "The Interaction of Syntax and Semantics During Sentence Processing: Eye Movements in the Analysis of Semantically-Biased Sentences" by K. Rayner, M. Carlson, and L. Frazier, *Journal of Verbal Learning and Verbal Behavior, 22* (1983), pp. 358-374. Copyright © 1983. Reprinted by permission of Elsevier. **Table 9-1** From "Logical Considerations in the Study of Animal Communication" by C. F. Hockett in ANIMAL SOUNDS AND COMMUNICATION (pp. 392-430) ed. by W. E. Lanyon and W. N. Tavolga. Copyright © 1960. Reprinted by permission of American Institute of Biological Sciences. **Table 9-3** From EXPERIMENTAL PSYCHOLINGUISTICS: An Introduction by S. Glucksberg and J. H. Danks. Copyright © 1975 by Lawrence Erlbaum Associates, Inc. Reprinted by permission. **Table 9-4** Table 8-2, p. 257 from PSYCHOLOGY OF LANGUAGE 1st ed. by D. W. Carroll. Copyright © 1986 by Wadsworth, a part of Cengage Learning, Inc. Reproduced by permission. *www.cengage.com/permissions*. **Table 9-5** From COGNITIVE NEUROPSYCHOLOGY: A Clinical Introduction by R. A. McCarthy and E. K. Warrington. Copyright © 1990. Reprinted by permission of Elsevier. **Table 9-6** From "Neural Models of Language Processes" by A. Kertesz in NEURAL MODELS OF LANGUAGE PROCESSES ed. by M. A. Arbib, D. Caplan and J. C. Marshall, pp. 25-44. Copyright © 1982. Reprinted by permission of Elsevier. **Figures 10-2** Figure from p. 376 in "Eye Movements in Reading and Information Processing: 20 Years of Research" by K. Rayner, *Psychological Bulletin, 124* (1998) pp. 372-422. Copyright © 1998 by American Psychological Association. **Figure 10-3** Plates III and IV, pp. 6, 7 from HOW ADULTS READ by G. T. Buswell. Copyright 1937. Reprinted by permission of The University of Chicago Press. **Figures 10-4, 10-5** From "A Theory of Reading: From Eye Fixations to Comprehension" by M. A. Just and P. A. Carpenter, *Psychological Review, 87* (1980). Copyright © 1980 by American Psychological Association. **Figure 10-6** Data from p. 703 in "Accessing Sentence Participants: The Advantage of First Mention" by M. A. Gernsbacher and D. Hargreaves, *Journal of Memory and Language, 27* (1988). Copyright © 1988. Reprinted by permission of Elsevier. **Figure 10-7** Fig. 2 from "Functional Neuroanatomy of the Cognitive Processes of Mapping During Discourse Comprehension" by D. A. Robertson, *Psychological Science, 11* (2000) pp. 255-260. Copyright © 2000. Reprinted by permission of Blackwell Publishing Ltd. **Figure 10-9** From "Accessibility and Situation Models in Narrative Comprehension" by D. G. Morrow, S. L. Greenspan, and G. H. Bower, *Journal of Memory and Language, 26* (1987) pp. 165-187. Copyright © 1987 by Elsevier Publishing Company. Reprinted by permission. **Figure 10-10** Based on data reported in Morrow, Greenspan, and Bower (1987). **Figure 10-12** From "Interpreting Indirect Replies" by T. Holtgraves, *Cognitive Psychology, 37* (1998) 1-27. **Table 10-3** From p. 331 in "A Theory of Reading: From Eye Fixations to Comprehension" by M. A. Just and P. A. Carpenter, *Psychological Review, 87* (1980). Copyright © 1980 by American Psychological Association. **Table 10-5** Adapted from Figure 8.2, p. 180 in COGNITIVE PSYCHOLOGY: A Neural-Network Approach 1st edition by C. Martindale. Copyright © 1991 by Wadsworth, a part of Cengage Learning, Inc. Reproduced by permission. *www.cengage.com/permissions*. **Figure 11-2** From COGNITIVE PSYCHOLOGY AND ITS IMPLICATIONS by John R. Anderson. Copyright © 1980, 1985, 1995, 2000 by Worth Publishers and W. H. Freeman and Company. Used with permission. **Figure 11-3** From "The Locus of the Semantic Congruity Effect in Comparative Judgments" by W. P. Banks, H. H. Clark and P. Lucy, Journal of Experimental Psychology: *Human Perception and Performance, 104* (1975). Copyright © 1975 by American Psychological Association. **Figure 11-4** From p. 106 in "Encoding and Processing of Symbolic Information in Comparative Judgments" by W. P. Banks in *Psychology of Learning and Motivation, 11* (1977). Copyright © 1977. Reprinted by permission of Elsevier. **Figure 11-5** Fig. 1 from "Semantic Congruity Effects in Comparative Judgments of Magnitude Digits" by W. P. Banks, M. Fujii, and F. Kayra-Stuart, *Journal of Experimental Psychology: Human Perception and Performance, 2* (1976) pp. 435-447. Copyright © 1976 by American Psychological Association. **Figure 11-6** From p. 334 in "Cognitive Reference Points in Judgments of Symbolic Magnitude" by K. J. Holyoak and W. A. Mah, *Cognitive Psychology, 14* (1982). Copyright © 1982. Reprinted by permission of Elsevier. **Figure 11-7** Fig. 2, p. 653 from "Reasoning the Fast and Frugal Way: Models Bounded Rationality" by G. Gigerenzer and D. G. Goldstein, *Psychological Review, 103* (1996) pp. 650-669. Copyright © 1996 by American Psychological Association. **Figure 11-8** Figure 9, p. 443 from "The Role of Causality under Judgment under Uncertainty" by T. R. Kynski and J. B. Tenebaum, *Journal of Experimental Psychology: General, 136* (2007) pp. 430-450. Copyright © 2007 by American Psychological Association. **Figures 11-9, 11-10** From "Naive Theories of Motion" by M. McCloskey in D. Gentner and A. L. Stevens (eds.) MENTAL MODELS. Copyright © 1983 by Lawrence Erlbaum Associates, Inc. Redrawn/reprinted with permission. **Figure 11-11** Figure 2, p. 1669 from "The Science of Cycology: Failures to Understand How Everyday Objects Work" by R. Lawson, *Memory* & Cognition, 34 (2006) pp. 1667-1675. Copyright © 2006 by The Psychonomic Society. Reprinted by permission of The Psychonomic Society. **Figures 11-12, 11-13** From "A System for Relational Reasoning in Human Prefrontal Cortex" by J. A. Waltz, B. J. Knowlton, K. J. Holyoak, K. B. Boone, F. S. Mishkin, M. M. Santos, C. R. Thomas and B. L. Miller, *Psychological Science, 10* (1999) pp. 119-125. Copyright © 1999. Reprinted by permission of Blackwell Publishing Ltd. **Table 11-1** From "Conditional Reasoning" from COGNITIVE PSYCHOLOGY: Memory, Language and Thought 2nd ed. by Dr. Darlene Howard. Copyright © 1993. Published by Macmillan Publishing Company. Reprinted by permission of the Author. **Table 11-2** Tables 2 and 4, pp. 61, 65 from "Processing of Logically Valid and Logically Invalid Conditional Inferences in Discourse Comprehension" by A. W. Rader and V. M. Sloutsky, *Journal of Experimental Psychology: Learning, Memory and Cognition, 28* (2002) pp. 59-68. Copyright © 2002 by American Psychological Association. **Table 11-4** From "The Simulation Heuristic"by D. Kahneman and A. Tversky in JUDGMENT UNDER UNCERTAINTY: Heuristics and Biases by D. Kahnema, Slov & Tversky (eds.), pp. 201-208. Copyright © 1982. Reprinted by permission of Cambridge University Press. **Figure 12-2** From "Intuition in Insight and Noninsight Problem Solving" by J. Metcalfe and D. Wiebe, *Memory & Cognition, 15* (1987) pp. 238-246. Copyright © 1987 by The Psychonomic Society. Reprinted by permission of The Psychonomic Society. **Figure 12-4** Fig. 2, p. 179 from "Toward Neuroanatomical Models of Analogy: A Positron Emission Tomography Study of Analogical Mapping" by C. M. Wharton, J. Grafman, S. S. Flitman, E. K. Hansen, J. Brauner, A. Marks, and M. Honda, *Cognitive Psychology, 40* (2000) pp. 173-197. Copyright © 2000. Reprinted by permission of Elsevier. **Figure 12-5** From "Getting the Right Idea: Semantic Activation in the Right Hemisphere May Help Solve Insight Problems" by E. M. Bowden and M. J. Beeman, *Psychological Science, 9* (1998) pp. 435-440. Copyright © 1998. Reprinted by permission of Blackwell Publishing Ltd. **Figure 12-7** Fig. 6-1, p. 93 from HOW TO SOLVE PROBLEMS by Wayne Wickelgren. Copyright © 1974 by W. H. Freeman and Company. Used with permission. **Figure 12-11** From COGNITION by A. L. Glass and K. J. Holyoak. Copyright © 1986 by McGraw-Hill, Inc. Reprinted by permission of the authors. **Figure 12-13** Figure 9, p. 379 from "The Role of Deliberate Practice in the Acquisition of Expert Performance" by K. A. Ericsson, R. T. Krampe, and C. Tesch-Römer, *Psychological Review, 100* (1998), pp. 363-406. Copyright © 1998 by American Psychological Association. **Table 12-3** First two examples are from p. 294 in "Feeling of Knowing in Memory and Problem Solving" by J. Metcalfe, *Journal of Experimental Psychology: Learning, Memory, and Cognition, 12* (1986). Copyright © 1986 by American Psychological Association.

NAME INDEX

S

SUBJECT INDEX